Bond's Franchise Guide

2005 Edition

16th Annual Edition

Robert E. Bond
Publisher

Joan Lee
Editor

Source Book Publications
Serving the Franchising Industry
1814 Franklin Street, Suite 820, Oakland, CA 94612
510.839.5471

ISBN 1-887137-39-4

DISCLAIMER

Bond's Franchise Guide is based on data submitted by the franchisors themselves. Every effort has been made to obtain up-to-date, reliable information. As the information returned has not been independently verified, we assume no responsibility for errors or omissions and reserve the right to include or eliminate listings and otherwise edit and present the data based on our discretion and judgment as to what is useful to the readers of this directory. Inclusion in the publication does not imply endorsement by the editors or the publisher. Errors brought to the attention of the publisher and verified to the satisfaction of the publisher will be corrected in future editions. The publisher specifically disclaims all warranties, including the implied warranties of merchantability and fitness for a specific purpose.

Bond's Franchise Guide was previously published as *The Source Book of Franchise Opportunities. The Source Book of Franchise Opportunities* went through 7 Editions before the name was changed in 1995 to *Bond's Franchise Guide.*

This publication is designed to provide its readers with accurate and authoritative information with regard to the subject matter covered. It is sold with the understanding that neither the author nor the publisher is engaged in rendering legal, accounting or other professional services. If legal advice or other expert assistance is required, the services of a competent professional person should be sought.

From a Declaration of Principles jointly adopted by a Committee of the American Bar Association and a Committee of Publishers.

Cover Design by Joyce Coffland, Artistic Concepts, Oakland, CA.

ISBN 1-887137-39-4

Printed in the United States of America.
10 9 8 7 6 5 4 3 2 1

BOND'S FRANCHISE GUIDE is available at special discounts for bulk purchase. Special editions or book excerpts can also be created to specifications. For details, contact **Source Book Publications**, 1814 Franklin Street, Suite 820, Oakland, CA 94612. Phone: (510) 839-5471; Fax: (510) 839-2104.

Preface

At its best, purchasing a franchise is a time-tested, paint-by-the-numbers method of starting a new business. It avoids many of the myriad pitfalls normally encountered by someone starting anew and vastly improves the odds of success. It represents an exceptional blend of operating independence with a proven system that includes a detailed blueprint on starting and managing the business, as well as the all-important on-going support.

But purchasing a franchise is clearly not a foolproof investment that somehow guarantees the investor financial independence.

At its worst, if the evaluation and investment decision is sloppy or haphazard, franchising can be a nightmare. You can lose your original investment plus any assets used to personally secure your debt, not to mention your marriage and your self-confidence.

Your ultimate success as a franchisee will be determined by two factors:

1. The homework you do at the front-end to ensure that you are selecting the optimal franchise for your particular needs, experience and financial resources.

2. Your commitment to work hard and play by the rules once you have signed a binding, long-term franchise agreement. A franchise system is only as good as you make it. In most cases, this involves working 60+ hours per week until you can justify delegating some of the day-to-day responsibilities. It also requires being a team player within the system — not acting as an entrepreneur who does his or her own thing without regard for the system as a whole.

The motivation for writing this annual directory has always been to assist in the evaluation phase of the equation: to provide accurate, in-depth data on the many legitimate companies actively selling franchises. The book is written for the sophisticated businessperson seriously interested in the process of selecting an optimal franchise opportunity: someone willing to commit the time and resources necessary to find the best franchise for his or her particular needs; someone with the wisdom to know that the franchise selection process is exceedingly difficult and filled with potholes; someone keenly aware of the risks — including missed opportunities — of going through the process in a half-hearted way.

We hope we can facilitate the evaluation process by ensuring that the potential franchisee is exposed to the range of options open to him or her and that he or she goes about the selection process in a logical and systematic manner.

ꕥ

Over 1,000 in-depth franchisor profiles are listed on the following pages. These profiles are the result of the detailed three-page questionnaire noted in Appendix A.

No doubt you will be familiar with a large number of the listings. Many are household names. That, incidentally, is one of the primary benefits of franchising. Most people would agree that Blimpie Subs has a better ring to it than Subs-4-U. Apart from the proven systems and procedures, you are buying a recognized name and the reputation that the name enjoys in the marketplace.

ꕥ

After you have decided which of the 45 industry groups hold the most interest, contact all of the companies listed and request a marketing brochure. Thoroughly read their literature and pick out the companies that interest you and that represent a natural fit with your talents and financial resources. You should be able to narrow your choices down to a manageable list of six or eight franchises that fit these criteria. Initiate an in-depth analysis of and dialogue with each of these franchisors. Concurrently, develop a thorough knowledge of the business and/or services that you are considering. Seek the advice of professionals, even if you are experienced in various elements of the evaluation process. Don't leave any stone unturned.

ꕥ

Remember, this is not a game! You are quite literally betting the ranch on your ability to pick a well-managed, market-oriented franchise. You want one that will take advantage of your unique talents and experience and not take advantage of you in the process! Don't take short-cuts. Listen to what the franchisor and your advisors tell you. Don't think you are so clever or independent that you can't benefit from the advice of outside professionals. Don't assume that the franchisor's guidelines regarding the amount of investment, experience, temperament, etc., somehow don't apply to you. Don't accept any promises or "understandings" from the franchisor that are not committed in writing to the franchise agreement. Spend the extra money to talk to and/or meet with other franchisees in the system. The additional front-end investment you make, both in time and money, will pay off handsomely if it saves you from making a marginal, or poor, investment decision. This is one of the few times in business when second chances are rare. Make the extra effort to do it right the first time.

ꕥ

Good luck and Godspeed.

Table of Contents

Section Three — Appendix

Section Four — Index

30 Minute Overview

There are three stages to the franchise selection process: the investigation, the evaluation and the negotiation stages. This book is intended to assist the reader in the first two stages by providing a framework for developing reasonable financial guidelines upon which to make a well-researched and properly documented investment decision.

Understand at the outset that the entire franchise selection process should take many months and can involve a great deal of frustration. I suggest that you set up a realistic timeline for signing a franchise agreement and that you stick to that schedule. There will be a lot of pressure on you to prematurely complete the selection and negotiation phases. Resist the temptation. The penalties are too severe for a seat-of-the-pants attitude. A decision of this magnitude clearly deserves careful consideration.

Before starting the selection process, briefly review the areas covered below.

Franchise Industry Structure

The franchising industry is made up of two distinct types of franchises. The first, and by far the larger, includes product and trade name franchising. Included in this group are automotive and truck dealers, soft drink bottlers and gasoline service stations. For the most part, these are essentially distributorships.

The second group encompasses business format franchisors. This book only includes information on this latter category.

Layman's Definition of Franchising

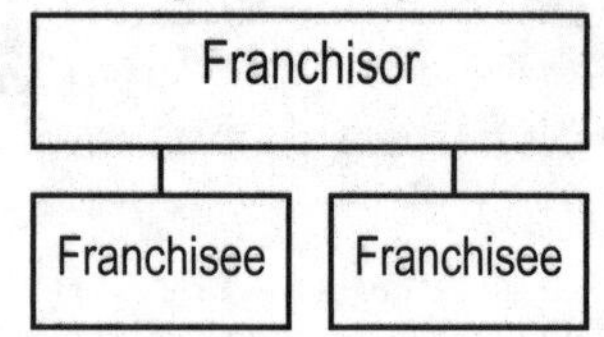

Classic Business Format Model

Business format franchising is a method of market expansion by which one business entity expands the distribution of its products and/or services through independent, third-party operators. Franchising occurs when the operator of a concept or system (the franchisor) grants an independent businessperson (the franchisee) the right to duplicate its entire business format at a particular location and for a specified period, under terms and conditions set forth in the contract (franchise agreement). The franchisee has full access to all of the trademarks, logos, marketing techniques, controls, and systems that have made the franchisor successful. In effect, the franchisee acts as a surrogate for a company-owned store in the distribution of the franchisor's goods and/or services. It is important to keep in mind that the franchisor and the franchisee are separate legal entities.

In return for a front-end franchise fee — which usually ranges from $15,000–35,000 — the franchisor is obligated to "set up" the franchisee in business. This generally includes assistance in selecting a location, negotiating a lease, obtaining financing, building and equipping a site and providing the necessary training, operating manuals and start-up assistance. Once the training is completed and the store is open, the new franchisee should have a carbon copy of other units in the system and enjoy the same benefits they do, whether they are company-owned or not.

Business format franchising is unique because it is a long-term relationship characterized by an on-going, mutually beneficial partnership. On-going services include research and development, marketing strategies, advertising campaigns, group buying, periodic field visits, training updates, and whatever else is required to make the franchisee competitive and profitable. In effect, the franchisor acts as the franchisee's "back office" support organization. To reimburse the franchisor for this support, the franchisee pays the franchisor an on-going royalty fee, generally 4–8 % of gross sales. In many cases, franchisees also contribute an advertising fee to reimburse the franchisor for expenses incurred in maintaining a national or regional advertising campaign.

To work to maximum advantage, both the franchisor and the franchisees should share common objectives and goals. Both parties must accept the premise that their fortunes are mutually intertwined and that they are each better off working in a co-operative effort rather than toward self-serving goals. Unlike the parent/child relationship that has dominated franchising over the past 30 years, franchising is now becoming a true relationship of partners.

The Players

Franchisors

Source Book Publications routinely tracks approximately 2,400 U.S. and Canadian franchisors. We believe this represents the number of legitimate, active franchisors in North America at any point in time. Profiles for more than 1,000 of these franchisors are found in this book, which is published annually by Source Book Publications. Additional copies of this 500+ page directory, considered the definitive directory in the field, are available for $29.95 plus $7.00 for shipping and handling ($42.75 + $9.50 in Canada). Call (510) 839-5471 or fax (510) 839-2104 to place a credit card order, or send a check to Source Book Publications, 1814 Franklin St., Suite 820, Oakland, CA 94612. There is an order form at the end of Chapter 3.

While you may already have your sights on a particular franchise opportunity, it would be short-sighted not to find out as much as you can about both the direct and indirect competition. You might discover that other franchises have similar products or services, but offer superior training and support, a reduced royalty fee or vastly superior financing options. I strongly encourage you to thoroughly utilize *Bond's Franchise Guide* or one of the other franchise directories to fully explore the options open to you.

The Regulatory Agencies

The offer and sale of franchises are regulated at both the federal and state levels. Federal requirements cover all 50 states. In addition, certain states have adopted their own requirements.

In 1979, after many years of debate, the Federal Trade Commission (FTC) implemented Rule 436. This Rule requires that franchisors provide prospective franchisees with a disclosure statement (called an offering circular) containing specific information about a company's franchise offering. The Rule has two objectives: to ensure that potential franchisees have sufficient background information to make an educated investment decision and to provide them with adequate time to do so.

Certain "registration states" require additional safeguards to protect potential franchisees. Their requirements are generally more stringent than the FTC's requirements. These states include California, Florida, Hawaii, Illinois, Indiana, Maryland, Michigan, Minnesota, New York, North Dakota, Oregon, Rhode Island, South Dakota, Virginia, Washington and Wisconsin. Separate registration is also required in the province of Alberta.

For the most part, these registration states require a disclosure format known as the Uniform Franchise Offering Circular (UFOC). The state requirements are generally more demanding than the federal requirements. As a matter of convenience, most franchisors have adopted the UFOC format. This format requires that the franchisor provides a prospective franchisee with the required information at their first face-to-face meeting or at least 10 business days prior to the signing of the franchise agreement, whichever is earlier. Required information includes:

1. The franchisor and any predecessors.
2. Identity and business experience of persons affiliated with the franchisor.
3. Litigation.
4. Bankruptcy.
5. Franchisee's initial fee or other initial payments.
6. Other fees.
7. Franchisee's initial investment.
8. Obligations of franchisee to purchase or lease from designated sources.
9. Obligations of franchisee to purchase or lease in accordance with specifications or from approved suppliers.
10. Financing arrangements.
11. Obligations of the franchisor; other supervision, assistance or services.
12. Exclusive area or territory.
13. Trademarks, service marks, trade names, logotypes and commercial symbols.
14. Patents and copyrights.
15. Obligations of the participant in the actual operation of the franchise business.
16. Restrictions on goods and services offered by franchisee.
17. Renewal, termination, repurchase, modification and assignment of the franchise agreement and related information.
18. Arrangements with public figures.
19. Actual, average, projected or forecasted franchise sales, profits or earnings.
20. Information regarding franchises of the franchisor.
21. Financial statements.
22. Contracts.
23. Acknowledgment of receipt by respective franchisee.

If you live in a registration state, make sure that the franchisor you are evaluating is, in fact, registered to sell franchises there. If not, and the franchisor has no near-term plans to register in your state, you should consider other options.

Keep in mind that neither the FTC nor any of the states has reviewed the offering circular to determine whether the information submitted is true and accurate or not. They merely require that the franchisor make representations based upon a prescribed format. If the information provided is false, franchisors are subject to civil penalties. You should also be aware of the reality that neither the FTC nor the individual states have the staff or budget necessary to pursue a lengthy battle over possible misrepresentations. If you run into problems, your only real option is to retain an attorney and battle a franchisor who may have an in-house legal staff and a bottomless war chest. While you might win the battle, you would most likely lose the war.

It is up to you to read and thoroughly understand all elements of the offering circular and to take full advantage of the documentation that is available to you. Know exactly what you can expect from the franchisor and what your own obligations are. Under what circumstances can the relationship be unilaterally terminated by the franchisor? What is your protected territory? What are the terms of a renewal? Can you expand within your territory? While there is no question that the UFOC is tedious reading, it, nevertheless, provides invaluable information. The penalties for not doing your homework are severe. You will have no one to blame but yourself. Hedge your bet by having a professional also review the UFOC.

The Trade Associations

The **International Franchise Association** (IFA) was established in 1960 as a non-profit trade association to promote franchising as a responsible method of doing business. The IFA currently represents over 750 franchisors in the U.S. and around the world. It is recognized as the leading spokesperson for the industry. For most of its 30+ years, the IFA has represented the interests of franchisors only. In recent years, however, it has initiated an aggressive campaign to recruit franchisees into its membership and to represent their interests as well. The IFA's offices are located at 1350 New York Avenue, NW, Suite 900, Washington, DC 20005. (202) 628-8000; FAX (202) 628-0812.

The **Canadian Franchise Association** (CFA), which has some 250+ members, is the Canadian equivalent of the IFA. Information on the CFA can be obtained by writing the group at 5045 Orbit Drive, Suite 401, Building 9, Mississauga, ON L4W 4Y4, Canada. (905) 625-2896; FAX (905) 625-9076.

What Makes a Winning Franchise

Virtually every writer on the subject of franchising has his or her own idea of what determines a winning franchise. I believe there are five primary factors.

1. A product or service with clear advantages over the competition. These advantages may include brand recognition, a unique, proprietary product or service, or 30 years of proven experience.

2. A standardized franchise system that has been time-tested. A company that has operated numerous units, both company-owned and franchised, has usually worked out most of the bugs in the system. By the time a system has 30 or more operating units, it should be thoroughly tested.

3. Exceptional franchisor support. This includes not only the initial training program, but the on-going support (research & development, refresher training, [800] help-lines, field representatives who provide on-site training, annual meetings, advertising and promotion, central purchasing, etc.).

4. The financial wherewithal and management experience to carry out any announced growth plans without short-changing its franchisees. Sufficient depth of management is often lacking in younger, high-growth franchises.

5. A strong mutuality of interest between franchisor and franchisees. Unless both parties realize that their relationship is one of long-term partners, the system will probably never achieve its full potential. A few telephone calls to existing and former franchisees can easily determine whether the necessary rapport between franchisor and franchisees exists.

The Negotiation Process

Once you have narrowed your options down to your two or three top choices, you now have to negotiate the best deal you can with the franchisor. In most cases, the franchisor will tell you that the franchise agreement cannot be changed. Think twice before you accept the statement that the contract is non-negotiable. Notwithstanding the legal requirement that all of a franchisor's agreements be substantially the same at any point in time, there are usually a number of variables that are flexible. If the franchisor truly wants you as a franchisee, it may be willing to make concessions not available to the next applicant.

Will the franchisor take a short-term note for all or part of the franchise fee? Can you expand from your initial unit after you have proven yourself? If so, can the franchise fee on a second unit be eliminated or reduced? Can you get a right of first refusal on adjacent territories? Can the term of the agreement be extended from 10 to 15 years? Can you include a franchise cancellation right if the training and/or initial support don't meet your expectations or the franchisor's promises? The list goes on ad infinitum.

To successfully negotiate, you must have a thorough knowledge of the industry, the franchise agreement you are negotiating (and agreements of competitive franchise opportunities) and access to experienced professional advice. This can be a lawyer, an accountant or a franchise consultant. Above all else, he or she should have proven experience in negotiating franchise agreements. Franchising is a unique method of doing business. Don't pay

BOND'S FRANCHISE GUIDE
ANNUAL FRANCHISING INDUSTRY OVERVIEW
(As of 12/31/2004)

Exhibit 1

CATEGORY	# of Fran-chisors	Fran-chised Units	Company-Owned Units	Total Operating Units	See Chapter
Automotive Products & Services	151	24,530	2,438	26,968	4
Auto / Truck / Trailer Rental	27	3,984	607	4,591	5
Building & Remodeling / Furniture / Appliance Repair	122	24,475	226	24,701	6
Business: Financial Services	48	13,286	6,950	20,236	7
Business: Advertising & Promotion	26	1,373	70	1,443	8
Business: Internet / Telecommunications / Misc.	71	8,247	863	9,110	9
Child Development / Education / Products	85	6,849	820	7,669	10
Education / Personal Development / Training	53	3,820	858	4,678	11
Employment & Personnel	65	4,848	3,228	8,076	12
Food: Donuts / Cookies / Bagels	61	12,586	1,077	13,663	13
Food: Coffee	35	1,785	469	2,254	14
Food: Ice Cream / Yogurt	55	18,142	1,157	19,299	15
Food: Quick Service / Take-out	390	132,824	28,581	161,405	16
Food: Restaurant / Family-Style	171	18,753	9,020	27,773	17
Food: Specialty Foods	105	7,650	780	8,430	18
Hairstyling Salons	34	7,173	2,494	9,667	19
Health / Fitness / Beauty	115	19,169	2,087	21,256	20
Laundry & Dry Cleaning	19	2,221	30	2,251	21
Lawn and Garden	23	3,478	98	3,576	22
Lodging	68	27,727	3,484	31,211	23
Maid Service & Home Cleaning	22	3,803	181	3,984	24
Maintenance / Cleaning / Sanitation	131	45,503	1,242	46,745	25
Medical / Optical / Dental Products & Services	17	1,551	300	1,851	26
Packaging & Mailing	21	10,043	29	10,072	27
Printing & Graphics	16	3,379	60	3,439	28
Publications	28	1,251	65	1,316	29
Real Estate Inspection Services	21	3,016	364	3,380	30
Real Estate Services	59	23,794	1,461	25,255	31
Recreation & Entertainment	38	2,184	135	2,319	32
Rental Services	9	2,233	804	3,037	33
Retail: Art, Art Supplies & Framing	12	816	27	843	34
Retail: Athletic Wear / Sporting Goods	17	1,821	44	1,865	35
Retail: Clothing / Shoes / Accessories	11	150	111	261	36
Retail: Convenience Stores / Supermarkets / Drugs	23	28,622	5,867	34,489	37
Retail: Home Furnishings	43	3,131	229	3,360	38
Retail: Home Improvement & Hardware	13	11,061	293	11,356	39
Retail: Pet Products & Services	29	1,567	372	1,939	40

CATEGORY	# of Fran-chisors	Fran-chised Units	Company-Owned Units	Total Operating Units	See Chapter
Retail: Photographic Products & Services	16	700	34	734	41
Retail: Specialty	101	7,369	3,508	10,877	42
Retail: Video / Audio / Electronics	25	4,301	9,834	14,135	43
Retail: Miscellaneous	16	1,555	124	1,679	44
Security & Safety Systems	19	1,017	105	1,122	45
Signs	13	2,098	6	2,104	46
Travel	18	5,104	427	5,531	47
Miscellaneous	128	7,707	558	8,265	48
Industry Total	**2,570**	**516,696**	**91,517**	**608,215**	
% of Total		**85.0%**	**15.0%**	**100.0%**	

Exhibit 2

Relative Size - By Number of Total Operating Units:	#	%	**Cum. %**
> 5,000 Total Operating Units	23	0.9%	0.9%
1,000 - 4,999 Total Operating Units	73	2.8%	3.7%
500 - 999 Total Operating Units	88	3.4%	7.1%
250 - 499 Total Operating Units	179	7.0%	14.1%
100 - 249 Total Operating Units	362	14.1%	28.2%
50 - 99 Total Operating Units	320	12.5%	40.7%
25 - 49 Total Operating Units	324	12.6%	53.3%
15 - 24 Total Operating Units	214	8.3%	61.6%
Less Than 15 Total Operating Units	987	38.4%	100.0%
Total	**2,570**	**100.0%**	

Exhibit 3

Country of Origin:	#	%
United States	2,301	89.5%
Canada	269	10.5%
Total	**2,570**	**100.0%**

All of the data in Exhibits 1 - 3 are proprietary and should not be used or quoted without specifically acknowledging Bond's Franchise Guide *as the source.*

BOND'S FRANCHISE GUIDE
ANNUAL FRANCHISING INDUSTRY OVERVIEW
(As of 12/31/2004)

Exhibit 4

CATEGORY	Average Franchise Fee	Average Total Investment	Average Royalty Fee	# Survey Partici-pants	% of Industry Represent.
Automotive Products & Services	23.2K	186.6K	5.3%	76	50.3%
Auto / Truck / Trailer Rental	21.6K	226.0K	9.0%	17	63.0%
Building & Remodeling / Furniture / Appliance Repair	22.8K	202.0K	5.5%	53	43.4%
Business: Financial Services	25.0K	83.7K	9.5%	17	35.4%
Business: Advertising & Promotion	21.3K	57.7K	2.6%	9	34.6%
Business: Internet / Telecommunications / Misc.	23.8K	79.5K	17.9%	27	38.0%
Child Development / Education / Products	26.4K	282.3K	16.6%	36	42.4%
Education / Personal Development / Training	35.3K	137.7K	7.7%	24	45.3%
Employment & Personnel	24.6K	102.3K	9.2%	34	52.3%
Food: Donuts / Cookies / Bagels	25.7K	229.5K	5.1%	29	47.5%
Food: Coffee	23.9K	253.6K	6.0%	15	42.9%
Food: Ice Cream / Yogurt	25.8K	189.7K	4.5%	26	47.3%
Food: Quick Service / Take-out	22.3K	377.0K	4.9%	156	40.0%
Food: Restaurant / Family-Style	32.2K	1021.2K	4.4%	67	39.2%
Food: Specialty Foods	24.8K	265.6K	4.8%	36	34.3%
Hairstyling Salons	28.6K	134.8K	5.3%	13	38.2%
Health / Fitness / Beauty	20.1K	188.6K	6.1%	32	27.8%
Laundry & Dry Cleaning	23.0K	273.9K	4.5%	10	52.6%
Lawn and Garden	26.4K	87.2K	6.6%	14	60.9%
Lodging	28.3K	3592.0K	4.4%	25	36.8%
Maid Service & Home Cleaning	13.5K	55.6K	4.9%	14	63.6%
Maintenance / Cleaning / Sanitation	20.8K	66.9K	8.7%	74	56.5%
Medical / Optical / Dental Products & Services	30.3K	167.8K	5.4%	6	35.3%
Packaging & Mailing	28.2K	135.4K	5.5%	13	61.9%
Printing & Graphics	26.9K	255.7K	6.3%	12	75.0%
Publications	12.6K	26.3K	5.8%	7	25.0%
Real Estate Inspection Services	20.3K	32.5K	7.0%	13	61.9%
Real Estate Services	14.2K	104.0K	5.8%	23	39.0%
Recreation & Entertainment	20.9K	429.2K	9.1%	11	28.9%
Rental Services	16.1K	250.5K	3.7%	6	66.7%
Retail: Art, Art Supplies & Framing	30.9K	127.8K	5.4%	8	66.7%
Retail: Athletic Wear / Sporting Goods	29.9K	257.4K	3.8%	13	76.5%
Retail: Clothing / Shoes / Accessories	26.5K	244.8K	3.7%	3	27.3%
Retail: Convenience Stores / Supermarkets / Drugs	27.5K	354.5K	4.3%	8	34.8%
Retail: Home Furnishings	24.0K	149.1K	4.4%	21	48.8%
Retail: Home Improvement & Hardware	30.2K	344.1K	4.7%	5	38.5%
Retail: Pet Products & Services	23.0K	143.3K	5.0%	10	34.5%

CATEGORY	Average Franchise Fee	Average Total Investment	Average Royalty Fee	# Survey Partici-pants	% of Industry Represent.
Retail: Photographic Products & Services	21.8K	121.9K	3.7%	7	43.8%
Retail: Specialty	26.5K	188.7K	4.8%	41	40.6%
Retail: Video / Audio / Electronics	21.8K	108.5K	4.1%	6	24.0%
Retail: Miscellaneous	23.5K	138.9K	4.1%	9	56.3%
Security & Safety Systems	24.8K	212.9K	6.8%	4	21.1%
Signs	21.8K	115.1K	5.3%	9	69.2%
Travel	17.3K	60.5K	1.6%	7	38.9%
Miscellaneous	36.4K	175.6K	6.3%	34	26.6%
Total Participants				**1,080**	

Exhibit 5

CATEGORY	Average Franchise Fee	Average Total Investment	Average Royalty Fee	# Survey Partici-pants	% of Industry Represent.
Categories with Lowest Average Franchise Fee:					
Publications	12.6K	26.3K	5.8%	7	25.0%
Maid Service & Home Cleaning	13.5K	55.6K	4.9%	14	63.6%
Real Estate Services	14.2K	104.0K	5.8%	23	39.0%
Categories with Lowest Average Total Investment:					
Publications	12.6K	26.3K	5.8%	7	25.0%
Real Estate Inspection Services	20.3K	32.5K	7.0%	13	61.9%
Maid Service & Home Cleaning	13.5K	55.6K	4.9%	14	63.6%
Categories with Lowest Average Royalty Fee:					
Travel	17.3K	60.5K	1.6%	7	38.9%
Business: Advertising & Promotion	21.3K	57.7K	2.6%	9	34.6%
Retail: Clothing / Shoes / Accessories	26.5K	244.8K	3.7%	3	27.3%

All of the data in Exhibits 4 - 5 are proprietary and should not be used or quoted without specifically acknowledging Bond's Franchise Guide *as the source.*

someone $100+ per hour to learn the industry. Make him or her demonstrate that he or she has been through the process several times before. Negotiating a long-term agreement of this type is extremely tricky and fraught with pitfalls. The risks are extremely high. Don't think that you can handle the negotiations yourself, or that you can't afford outside counsel. In point of fact, you can't afford not to employ an experienced professional advisor.

The 4 R's of Franchising

At a young age we're taught that the three R's of reading, 'riting, and 'rithmetic are critical to our scholastic success. Success in franchising depends on four R's — realism, research, reserves and resolve.

Realism

At the outset of your investigation, be realistic about your strengths, weaknesses, goals and capabilities. I strongly recommend you take the time necessary to do a personal audit — possibly with the help of outside professionals — before investing your life's savings in a franchise.

Franchising is not a money machine. It involves hard work, dedication, set-backs and long hours. Be realistic about the nature of the business you are buying. What traits will ultimately determine your success? Do you have them? If it is a service-oriented business, will you be able to keep smiling when you know the client is a fool? If it is a fast-food business, will you be able to properly manage a minimum-wage staff? How well will you handle the uncertainties that will invariably arise? Can you make day-to-day decisions based on imperfect information? Can you count on the support of your spouse after you have gone through all of your working capital reserves and the future looks increasingly cloudy?

Be equally realistic about your franchise selection process. Have you thoroughly evaluated all of the alternatives? Have you talked with everyone you can, leaving no stone unturned? Have you carefully and realistically assessed the advantages and disadvantages of the system offered, the unique demographics of your territory, near-term market trends and the financial projections? The selection process is tiring. It is easy to convince yourself that the franchise opportunity in your hand is really the best one for you before you've done all your homework. The penalties for such slothfulness, however, are extreme.

Research

There is no substitute for exhaustive research!

Bond's Franchise Guide contains over 1,000 franchise listings, broken into 45 distinct business categories. This represents a substantial number of options from which to choose. Other directories also cover the industry in varying degrees of thoroughness and accuracy. Spend the time required to come up with an optimal selection. At a minimum, you will probably be in the business for five years. More likely, you will be in it for 10 years or more. Given the long-term commitment, allow yourself the necessary time to ensure you won't regret your decision. Research is a tedious, boring process, but doing it carefully and thoroughly can greatly reduce your risk and exposure. The benefits are immeasurable.

First, determine which industry groups hold your interest. Don't arbitrarily limit yourself to a particular industry in which you have first-hand experience. Next, request information from all of the companies that participate in those industries. The incremental cost of mailing (or calling) an additional 15 or 20 companies for information is insignificant in the big picture. Based on personal experience, you may feel you already know the best franchise. Step back. Assume there is a competing franchise out there with a comparable product or service, comparable management, etc., but which charges a royalty fee of sales that is 2% lower than your intuitive choice. Over a 10-year period, that could add up to a great deal of money. It certainly justifies your requesting initial information.

A thorough analysis of the literature you receive should allow you to reduce the list of prime candidates to six or eight companies. Aggressively evaluate each firm. Talking with current and former franchisees is the single best source of information you can get. Where possible, visit franchise sites. My experience is that franchisees tend to be candid in their level of satisfaction with the franchisor. However, since they don't know you, they may be less candid about their sales, expenses and income. *"How Much Can I Make?"* is another book by Source Book Publications that should assist in filling this void. Published annually, it details historical sales, expense and/or profit data on actual franchise operations, as provided by the franchisors themselves. The earnings claims statements for more than 100 companies are included, representing the food-service, retail, and service-based industries. For even further information, go to the library and get studies that forecast industry growth, market saturation, industry problems, technical break-throughs, etc.

Reserves

Like any new business, franchising is replete with uncertainty, uneven cash flows and unforeseen problems. It is an imperfect world that might not bear any relation to the clean pro formas you prepared to justify getting into the business. Any one of these unforeseen contingencies could cause a severe drain on your cash reserves. At the same time, you will have fixed and/or contractual payments that must be met on a current basis regardless of sales: rent, employee salaries, insurance, etc.

Adequate back-up reserves may be in the form of savings, commitments from relatives, bank loans, etc. Just make certain that the funds are available when, and if, you need them. To be absolutely safe, I suggest that you double the level of reserves recommended by the franchisor.

Keep in mind that the most common cause of business failure is inadequate working capital. Plan properly so you don't become a statistic.

Resolve

Let's assume for the time being that you have demonstrated exceptional levels of realism, thoroughly researched your options and lined up ample capital reserves. You have picked an optimal franchise that takes full advantage of your strengths. You are in business and bringing in enough money to achieve a positive cash flow. The future looks bright. Now the fourth R — resolve — comes into play. Remember why you chose franchising in the first place: to take full advantage of a system that had been time-tested in the marketplace. Remember also what makes franchising work so well: that the franchisor and franchisees maximize their respective success by working within the system for the common good. Invariably, two obstacles arise.

The first is the physical pain associated with writing that monthly royalty check. Annual sales of $250,000 and a 6% royalty fee result in a monthly royalty check of $1,250 that must be sent to the franchisor. Every month. As a franchisee, you may look for any justification to reduce this sizable monthly outflow. Resist the temptation. Accept the fact that royalty fees are simply another cost of doing business. They are also a legal obligation that you willingly agreed to pay when you signed the franchise agreement. In effect, they are the dues you agreed to pay to belong to the club.

Although there may be an incentive, don't look for loopholes in the contract that might allow you to sue the franchisor or get out of the relationship. Don't report lower sales than actual in an effort to reduce royalties. If you have received the support that you were promised, continue to play by the rules. Honor your commitment. Let the franchisor enjoy the rewards it has earned from your success.

The second obstacle is the desire to change the system. You need to honor your commitment to be a "franchisee" and to live within the franchise system. What makes franchising successful as far as your customers are concerned is uniformity and consistency of appearance, product/service quality and corporate image. The most damaging thing an individual franchisee can do is suddenly and unilaterally introduce changes into a proven system. While these modifications may work in one market, they only serve to diminish the value of the system as a whole. Imagine what would happen to the national perception of your franchise if every franchisee had the latitude to make unilateral changes in his or her operations. Accordingly, any ideas you have on improving the system should be submitted directly to the franchisor for its evaluation. Accept the franchisor's decision on whether or not to pursue an idea.

If you suspect that you have a penchant for being an entrepreneur, for unrestrained experimenting and tinkering, you are probably not cut out to be a good franchisee. Seriously consider this question before you get into a relationship, instead of waiting until you are locked into an untenable situation.

Summary

I hope that I have been clear in suggesting that the selection of an optimal franchise is both time and energy-consuming. Done properly, the process may take six to nine months and involve the expenditure of several thousand dollars. The difference between a hasty, gut-feel investigation and an exhaustive, well-thought-out investigation may mean the difference between finding a poorly-conceived, or even fraudulent, franchise and an exceptional one.

There is a strong correlation between the efforts put into the investigative process and the ultimate degree of success you enjoy as a franchisee. The process is to investigate, evaluate and negotiate. Don't try to bypass any one of these elements.

How to Use the Data

Chapter 2

The appendix includes the original questionnaire sent to some 2,200+ U.S. and Canadian franchisors. Franchisors who did not respond to the original mailing received a follow-up package roughly one month later. The end result was that roughly 40% of the contacted franchisors returned a completed questionnaire.

The data returned has been condensed into the profiles shown on the following pages. In some cases, an answer has been abbreviated to conserve room and to make the profiles more directly comparable. All of the data is displayed with the objective of providing as much background as possible. In those cases where no answer was provided to a particular question within the questionnaire, an "NR" is used to signify "No Response."

Please take a few minutes to acquaint yourself with the composition of the sample profile. Supplementary comments have been added where some interpretation of the franchisor's response is required.

Keep in mind that all of the profile data is based on questionnaires returned by the franchisors themselves, with no effort to verify its accuracy independently. There is no doubt that franchisors had some latitude to exaggerate their response in order to make themselves appear bigger, more mature and/or more franchisee-oriented than they really are. I am confident that some small percentage did just that. The vast majority, however, would see any such deception as dishonest, counter-productive and a general waste of everyone's time.

BLIMPIE SUBS AND SALADS has been selected to illustrate how this book uses the collected data.

Blimpie SUBS & SALADS

Top 100

BLIMPIE SUBS AND SALADS
180 Interstate North Pkwy., SE, # 500
Atlanta, GA 30339
Tel: (800) 447-6256 + 3 (770) 984-2707

Fax: (770) 933-6109
E-Mail: jarcher@blimpie.com
Web Site: www.blimpie.com
Ms. J. Archer, VP Franchise Development

International submarine sandwich chain, serving fresh-sliced, high-quality meats and cheeses on fresh-baked bread. Also offering an assortment of fresh-made salads and other quality products.

BACKGROUND:	IFA MEMBER
Established:	1964; 1st Franchised: 1977
Franchised Units:	1,390
Company-Owned Units:	20
Total Units:	1,410
Dist.:	US-1,349; CAN-0; O'seas-61
North America:	50 States, 4 Provinces
Density:	209 in FL, 193 in GA
Projected New Units (12 Months):	NR
Qualifications:	4, 3, 2, 2, 2, 5
Registered:	CA,FL,HI,IL,IN,MI,MN,NY,ND, OR,RI,SD,WA,WI
FINANCIAL/TERMS:	
Cash Investment:	$25-100K
Total Investment:	$75-250K
Minimum Net Worth:	$100K
Fees:	Franchise — $10-18K
	Royalty — 6%; Ad. — 4%
Earnings Claim Statement:	No
Term of Contract (Years):	20/5
Avg. # Of Employees:	4 FT, 8 PT
Passive Ownership:	Discouraged
Encourage Conversions:	Yes
Area Develop. Agreements:	Yes
Sub-Franchising Contracts:	Yes
Expand In Territory:	Yes
Space Needs:	1,200 SF; FS, SF, SC, RM
SUPPORT & TRAINING:	
Financial Assistance Provided:	Yes(I)
Site Selection Assistance:	Yes
Lease Negotiation Assistance:	Yes
Co-Operative Advertising:	Yes
Franchisee Assoc./Member:	Yes/Yes
Size Of Corporate Staff:	109
On-Going Support:	B,C,D,E,F,G,H,I
Training:	80 Hours in Atlanta, GA; 120 Hours in Local Franchise.
SPECIFIC EXPANSION PLANS:	
US:	All United States
Canada:	All Canada
Overseas:	All except Anti-American Countries

Bond's Top 100 Franchises

As the pre-eminent publisher of books on franchising, Source Book Publications is constantly asked, "What are the best franchises?" Given that there are over 2,400 active North American franchise systems, there clearly is no simple answer. This is especially true given the individual needs, experience and financial wherewithal of a widely divergent pool of prospective franchisees.

To at least partially answer the question, our staff has broken the franchising industry into three major segments — food-service, retail and service-based franchises. Within each group a rigorous, in-depth analysis was performed on literally hundreds of proven franchise systems to arrive at what we feel are the top 100 franchises in each of these segments. Companies were evaluated on the basis of historical performance, brand identification, market dynamics, franchisee satisfaction, the level of initial training and on-going support, financial stability and other key factors.

The end result of this evaluation process is *Bond's Top 100 Franchises*. Each of the companies identified in *Bond's Top 100 Franchises* is also identified in this book, as denoted by a Top 100 icon.

To ensure that we provide the most current information on the dynamics of the industry and its key players, the publication of *Bond's Top 100 Franchises* is an annual effort. Inclusion as a Top 100 company is based solely on merit. There is absolutely no favoritism shown toward any particular franchise. Since we do not permit advertising in our publications, there is also no correlation between the Top 100 selection process and advertising revenues.

Address/Contact

1. **Company name, address, telephone and fax numbers.**

Comment: All of the data published in this book were current at the time the completed questionnaire was received or upon subsequent verification by phone. Over a 12-month period between annual publications, 10–15% of the addresses and/or telephone numbers become obsolete for various reasons. If you are unable to contact a franchisor at the address/telephone number listed, please call Source Book Publications at (510) 839-5471 or fax us at (510) 839-2104 and we will provide you with the current address and telephone number.

2. **(800) 447-6256 + 3; (770) 984-2707.** In many cases, you may find that you cannot access the (800) number from your area. Do not conclude that the company has gone out of business. Simply call the local number.

Comment: An (800) number serves two important functions. The first is to provide an efficient, no-cost way for potential franchisees to contact the franchisor. Making the prospective franchisee foot the bill artificially limits the number of people who might otherwise make the initial contact. The second function is to demonstrate to existing franchisees that the franchisor is doing everything it can to efficiently respond to problems in the field as they occur. Many companies have a restricted (800) line for their franchisees that the general public cannot access. Since you will undoubtedly be talking with the franchisor's staff on a periodic basis, determine whether an (800) line is available to franchisees.

3. **Contact.** You should honor the wishes of the franchisor and address all initial correspondence to the contact listed. It would be counterproductive to try to reach the president directly if the designated contact is the director of franchising.

Comment: The president is the designated contact in approximately half of the company profiles in this book. The reason for this varies among franchisors. The president is the best spokesperson for his or her operation, and no doubt it flatters the franchisee to talk directly with the president, or perhaps there is no one else around. Regardless of the justification, it is important to determine if the operation is a one-man show in which the president does everything or if the president merely feels that having an open line to potential franchisees is the best way for him or her to sense the "pulse" of the company and the market. Convinced that the president can only do so many things well, I would want assurances that, by taking all incoming calls, he or she is not neglecting the day-to-day responsibilities of managing the business.

Description of Business

4. **Description of Business:** The questionnaire provides franchisors with adequate room to differentiate their franchise from the competition. In a minor number of cases, some editing was required.

Comment: In instances where franchisors show no initiative or imagination in describing their operations, you must decide whether this is symptomatic of the company or simply a reflection on the individual who responded to the questionnaire.

Background

5. **IFA.** There are two primary affinity groups associated with the franchising industry — the International Franchise Association (IFA) and the Canadian Franchise Association (CFA). Both the IFA and the CFA are described in Chapter One.

6. **Established: 1964.** Blimpie was founded in 1964, and, accordingly, has 40 years of experience in its primary business. It should be intuitively obvious that a firm that has been in existence for over 40 years has a greater likelihood of being around five years from now than a firm that was founded only last year.

7. **1st Franchised: 1977.** 1977 was the year that Blimpie's first franchised unit(s) were established.

Comment: Over ten years of continuous operation, both as an operator and as a franchisor, is compelling evidence that a firm has staying power. The number of years a franchisor has been in business is one of the key variables to consider in choosing a franchise. This is not to say that a new franchise should not receive your full attention. Every company has to start from scratch. Ultimately, a prospective franchisee has to be convinced that the franchise has 1) been in operation long enough, or 2) its key management personnel have adequate industry experience to have worked out the bugs normally associated with a new business. In most cases, this experience can only be gained through on-the-job training. Don't be the guinea pig that provides the franchisor with the experience it needs to develop a smoothly running operation.

8. **Franchised Units: 1,390.** As of 1/31/05, Blimpies had 1,390 franchisee-owned and operated units.

9. **Company-Owned Units: 20.** As of 1/31/05, Blimpie had 20 company-owned or operated unit.

Comment: A younger franchise should prove that its concept has worked successfully in several company-owned units before it markets its "system" to an inexperienced franchisee. Without company-owned prototype stores, the new franchisee may well end up being the "testing kitchen" for the franchise concept itself.

If a franchise concept is truly exceptional, why doesn't the franchisor commit some of its resources to take advantage of the investment opportunity? Clearly, a financial decision on the part of the franchisor, the absence of company-owned units should not be a negative in and of itself. This is especially true of proven franchises, which may have previously sold their company-owned operations to franchisees.

Try to determine if there is a noticeable trend in the percentage of company-owned units. If the franchisor is buying back units from franchisees, it may be doing so to preclude litigation. Some firms also "churn" their operating units with some regularity. If the sales pitch is compelling, but the follow-through is not competitive, a franchisor may sell a unit to a new franchisee, wait for him or her to fail, buy it back for $0.60 cents on the dollar, and then sell that same unit to the next unsuspecting franchisee. Each time the unit is resold, the franchisor collects a franchise fee, plus the negotiated discount from the previous franchisee.

Alternatively, an increasing or high percentage of company-owned units may well mean the company is convinced of the long-term profitability of such an approach. The key is to determine whether a franchisor is building new units from scratch or buying them from failing and/or unhappy franchisees.

10. **Total Units: 1,410.** As of 1/31/05, Blimpie had a total of 1,410 operating units.

Comment: Like a franchisor's longevity, its experience in operating multiple units offers considerable comfort. Those franchisors with over 15–25 operating units have proven that their system works and have probably encountered and overcome most of the problems that plague a new operation. Alternatively, the management of franchises with less than 15 operating units may have gained considerable industry experience before joining the current franchise. It is up to the franchisor to convince you that it is providing you with as risk-free an operation as possible. You don't want to be providing a company with its basic experience in the business.

11. **Distribution: US-1,349; CAN-0; O'seas-61.** As of 1/31/05, Blimpie had 1,349 operating units in the U.S., 0 in Canada and 61 Overseas.

12. **Distribution: North America: 50 States, 4 Provinces.** As of 1/31/05, Blimpie had operations in 50 states and 4 provinces in Canada.

Comment: It should go without saying that the wider the geographic distribution, the greater the franchisor's level of success. For the most part, such distribution can only come from a large number of operating units. If, however, the franchisor has operations in 15 states, but only 18 total operating units, it is unlikely that it can efficiently service these accounts because of geographic constraints. Other things being equal, a prospective franchisee would vastly prefer a franchisor with 15 units in New York to one with 15 units scattered throughout the U.S., Canada and overseas.

13. **Distribution: Density: FL, GA.** The franchisor was asked "what three states/provinces have the largest number of operating units." As of 1/31/05, Blimpie had the largest number of units in Florida and Georgia.

Comment: For smaller, regional franchises, geographic distribution could be a key variable in deciding whether to buy. If the franchisor has a concentration of units in your immediate geographic area, it is likely you will be well-served.

For those far removed geographically from the franchisor's current areas of operation, however, there can be problems. It is both time consuming and expensive to support a franchisee 2,000 miles away from company headquarters. To the extent that a franchisor can visit four franchisees in one area on one trip, there is no problem. If, however, your operation is the only one west of the Mississippi, you may not receive the on-site assistance you would like. Don't be a missionary who has to rely on his or her own devices to survive. Don't accept a franchisor's idle promises of support. If on-site assistance is important to your ultimate success, get assurances in writing that the necessary support will be forthcoming. Remember, you are buying into a system, and the availability of day-to-day support is one of the key ingredients of any successful franchise system.

14. **Projected New Units (12 Months): NR.** Blimpie did not provide a projected number of new units for the next 12 months.

Comment: In business, growth has become a highly visible symbol of success. Rapid growth is generally perceived as preferable to slower, more controlled growth. I maintain, however, that the opposite is frequently the case. For a company of Blimpie's size, adding 30 new units over a 12-month period is both reasonable and achievable. It is highly unlikely, however, that a new franchise with only five operating units can successfully attract, screen, train and bring multiple new units on-stream in a 12-month period. If it suggests that it can, or even wants to, be properly wary. You must be confident a company has the financial and management resources necessary to pull off such a Herculean feat. If management is already thin, concentrating on attracting new units will clearly diminish the time it can and should spend supporting you. It takes many months, if not years, to develop and train a second level of management. You don't want to depend upon new hires teaching you systems and procedures they themselves know little or nothing about.

15. **Qualifications: 4,3,2,2,2,5.** This question was posed to determine which specific evaluation criteria were important to the franchisor. The franchisor was asked the following: "In qualifying a potential franchisee, please rank the following criteria from Unimportant (1) to Very Important (5)." The responses should be self-explanatory:

Financial Net Worth (Rank from 1–5)
General Business Experience (Rank from 1–5)
Specific Industry Experience (Rank from 1–5)
Formal Education (Rank from 1–5)
Psychological Profile (Rank from 1–5)
Personal Interview(s) (Rank from 1–5)

16. **Registered** refers to the 16 states that require specific formal registration at the state level before the franchisor may offer franchises in that state. State registration and disclosure to the Federal Trade Commission are separate issues that are discussed in Chapter 1.

Capital Requirements/Rights

17. **Cash Investment: $25-100K.** On average, a Blimpie franchisee will have made a cash investment of $25,000–100,000 by the time he or she finally opens the initial operating unit.

Comment: It is important that you be realistic about the amount of cash you can comfortably invest in a business. Stretching beyond your means can have grave and far-reaching consequences. Assume that you will encounter periodic set-backs and that you will have to draw on your reserves. The demands of starting a new business are harsh enough without adding the uncertainties associated with inadequate working capital. Trust the franchisor's recommendations regarding the suggested minimum cash investment. If anything, there is an incentive for setting the recommended level of investment too low, rather than too high. The franchisor will want to qualify you to the extent that you have adequate financing. No legitimate franchisor wants you to invest if there is a chance that you might fail because of a shortage of funds.

Keep in mind that you will probably not achieve a positive cash flow before you've been in business more than six months. In your discussions with the franchisor, be absolutely certain that its calculations include an adequate working capital reserve.

18. **Total Investment: $75-250K.** On average, Blimpie franchisees will invest a total of $75,000-250,000, including both cash and debt, by the time the franchise opens its doors.

Comment: The total investment should be the cash investment noted above plus any debt that you will incur in starting up the new business. Debt could be a note to the franchisor for all or part of the franchise fee, an equipment lease, building and facilities leases, etc. Make sure that the total includes all of the obligations that you assume, especially any long-term lease obligations.

Be conservative in assessing what your real exposure is. If you are leasing highly specialized equipment or if you are leasing a single-purpose building, it is naive to think that you will recoup your investment if you have to sell or sub-lease those assets in a buyer's market. If there is any specialized equipment that may have been manufactured to the franchisor's specifications, determine if the franchisor has any form of buy-back provision.

19. **Minimum Net Worth: $100K.** In this case, Blimpie feels that a potential franchisee should have a minimum net worth of $100,000. Although net worth can be defined in vastly different ways, the franchisor's response should suggest a minimum level of equity that the prospective franchisee should possess. Net worth is the combination of both liquid and illiquid assets. Again, don't think that franchisor-determined guidelines somehow don't apply to you.

20. **Fees (Franchise): $10-18K.** Blimpie requires a front-end, one-time-only payment of $10,000–18,000 to grant a franchise for a single location. As noted in Chapter One, the franchise fee is a payment to reimburse the franchisor for the incurred costs of setting the franchisee up in business — from recruiting through training and manuals. The fee usually ranges from $15,000–30,000. It is a function of competitive franchise fees and the actual out-of-pocket costs incurred by the franchisor.

Depending upon the franchisee's particular circumstances and how well the franchisor thinks he or she might fit into the system, the franchisor may finance all or part of the franchise fee. (See Section 32 below to see if a franchisor provides any direct or indirect financial assistance.)

The franchise fee is one area in which the franchisor frequently provides either direct or indirect financial support.

Comment: Ideally, the franchisor should do no more than recover its costs on the initial franchise fee. Profits come later in the form of royalty fees, which are a function of the franchisee's sales. Whether the franchise fee is $5,000 or $35,000, the total should be carefully evaluated. What are competitive fees and are they financed? How much training will you actually receive? Are the fees reflective of the franchisor's expenses? If the fees appear to be non-competitive, address your concerns with the franchisor.

Realize that a $5,000 differential in the one-time franchise fee is a secondary consideration in the overall scheme of things. You are in the relationship for the long-term.

By the same token, don't get suckered in by an extremely low fee if there is any doubt about the franchisor's ability to follow through. Franchisors need to collect reasonable fees to cover their actual costs. If they don't recoup these costs, they cannot recruit and train new franchisees on whom your own future success partially depends.

21. **Fees (Royalty): 6%** means that six percent of gross sales (or other measure, as defined in the franchise agreement) must be periodically paid directly to the franchisor in the form of royalties. This on-going expense is your cost for being part of the larger franchise system and for all of the "back-office" support you receive. In a few cases, the amount of the royalty fee is fixed rather than variable. In others, the fee decreases as the volume of sales (or other measure) increases (i.e., 6% on the first $200,000 of sales, 5% on the next $100,000 and so on). In others, the fee is held at artificially low levels during the start-up phase of the franchisee's business,

then increases once the franchisee is better able to afford it.

Comment: Royalty fees represent the mechanism by which the franchisor finally recoups the costs it has incurred in developing its business. It may take many years and many operating units before the franchisor is able to make a true operating profit.

Consider a typical franchisor who might have been in business for three years. With a staff of five, rent, travel, operating expenses, etc., assume it has annual operating costs of $300,000 (including reasonable owner's salaries). Assume also that there are 25 franchised units with average annual sales of $250,000. Each franchise is required to pay a 6% royalty fee. Total annual royalties under this scenario would total only $375,000. The franchisor is making a $75,000 profit. Then consider the personal risk the franchisor took in developing a new business and the initial years of negative cash flows. Alternatively, evaluate what it would cost you, as a sole proprietor, to provide the myriad services included in the royalty payment.

In assessing various alternative investments, the amount of the royalty percentage is a major on-going expense. Assuming average annual sales of $250,000 per annum over a 15 year period, the total royalties at 5% would be $187,500. At 6%, the cumulative fees would be $225,000. You have to be fully convinced that the $37,500 differential is justified. While this is clearly a meaningful number, what you are really evaluating is the quality of management and the competitive advantages of the goods and/or services offered by the franchisor.

22. **Fees (Advertising): 4%.** Most national or regional franchisors require their franchisees to contribute a certain percentage of their sales (or other measure, as determined in the franchise agreement) into a corporate advertising fund. These individual advertising fees are pooled to develop a corporate advertising/marketing effort that produces great economies of scale. The end result is a national or regional advertising program that promotes the franchisor's products and services. Depending upon the nature of the business, this percentage usually ranges from 2–6% and is in addition to the royalty fee.

Comment: One of the greatest advantages of a franchised system is its ability to promote, on a national or regional basis, its products and services. The promotions may be through television, radio, print medias or direct mail. The objective is name recognition and, over time, the assumption that the product and/or service has been "time-tested." An individual business owner could never justify the expense of mounting a major advertising program at the local level. For a smaller franchise that may not yet have an advertising program or fee, it is important to know when an advertising program will start, how it will be monitored and its expected cost.

23. **Earnings Claims Statement: No** means Blimpie does not provide an earnings claims statement to potential franchisees. Unfortunately, only 12–15% of franchisors provide an earnings claims statement in their Uniform Franchise Offering Circular (UFOC). The franchising industry's failure to require earnings claims statements does a serious disservice to the potential franchisee. See Chapter Two for comments on the earnings claims statement.

24. **Term of Contract (Years): 20/5.** Blimpie's initial franchise period runs for 20 years. The first renewal period runs for an additional five years. Assuming that the franchisee operates within the terms of the franchise agreement, he or she has 25 years within which to develop and, ultimately, sell the business.

Comment: The potential (discounted) value of any business (or investment) is the sum of the operating income that is generated each year plus its value upon liquidation. Given this truth, the length of the franchise agreement and any renewals are extremely important to the franchisee. It is essential that he or she has adequate time to develop the business to its full potential. At that time, he or she will have maximized the value of the business as an on-going concern. The value of the business to a potential buyer, however, is largely a function of how long the franchise agreement runs. If there are only two years remaining before the agreement expires, or if the terms of an extension(s) are vague, the business will be worth only a fraction of the value assigned to a business with 15 years to go. For the most part, the longer the agreement and the subsequent extension, the better. (The same logic applies to a lease. If your sales are largely a function of your location and traffic count, then it is important that you have options to extend the lease under known terms. Your lease should never be longer than the remaining term of your franchise agreement, however.)

Assuming the length of the agreement is acceptable, be clear under what circumstances renewals might not be granted. Similarly, know the circumstances under which a franchise agreement might be prematurely and unilaterally canceled by the franchisor. I strongly recommend you have an experienced lawyer review this section of the franchise agreement. It would be devastating if, after spending years developing your business, there were a loophole in the contract that allowed the franchisor to arbitrarily cancel the relationship.

25. **Avg. # of Employees: 4 FT, 8 PT.** The question was asked "Including the owner/operator, how many employees are recommended to properly staff the average franchised unit?" In Blimpie's case, four full-time employees and eight part-time employees are required.

Comment: Most entrepreneurs start a new business based on their intuitive feel that it will be "fun" and that their talents and experience will be put to good use. They will be doing what they enjoy and what they are good at. Times change. Your business prospers. The number of employees increases. You are spending an increasing percentage of your time taking care of personnel problems and less and less on the fun parts of the business. In Chapter One, the importance of conducting a realistic self-appraisal was stressed. If you found that you really are not good at managing people, or you don't have the patience to manage a large minimum wage staff, cut your losses before you are locked into doing just that.

26. **Passive Ownership: Discouraged.** Depending on the nature of the business, many franchisors are indifferent as to whether you manage the business directly or hire a full-time manager. Others are insistent that, at least for the initial franchise, the franchisee be a full-time owner/operator. Blimpie discourages franchisees from hiring full-time managers to run their outlets.

Comment: Unless you have a great deal of experience in the business you have chosen or in managing similar businesses, I feel strongly that you should initially commit your personal time and energies to make the system work. After you have developed a full understanding of the business and have competent, trusted staff members who can assume day-to-day operations, then consider delegating these responsibilities. Running the business through a manager can be fraught with peril unless you have mastered all aspects of the business and there are strong economic incentives and sufficient safeguards to ensure the manager will perform as desired.

27. **Conversions Encouraged: Yes.** This section pertains primarily to sole proprietorships or "mom and pop" operations. To the extent that there truly are centralized operating savings associated with the franchise, the most logical people to join a franchise system are sole practitioners who are working hard but only eking out a living. The implementation of proven systems and marketing clout could significantly reduce operating costs and increase profits.

Comment: The franchisor has the option of 1) actively encouraging such independent operators to become members of the franchise team, 2) seeking out franchisees with limited or no applied experience or 3) going after both groups. Concerned that it will be very difficult to break independent operators of the bad habits they have picked up over the years, many only choose course two. "They will continue to do things their way. They won't, or can't, accept corporate direction," they might say to themselves. Others are simply selective in the conversions they allow. In many cases, the franchise fee is reduced or eliminated for conversions.

28. **Area Development Agreements: Yes** means that Blimpie offers an area development agreement. Area development agreements are more fully described in Chapter One. Essentially, they allow an investor or investment group to develop an entire area or region. The schedule

for development is clearly spelled out in the area development agreement. (Note: "Var." means varies and "Neg." means negotiable.)

Comment: Area development agreements represent an opportunity for the franchisor to choose a single franchisee or investment group to develop an entire area. The franchisee's qualifications should be strong and include proven business experience and the financial depth to pull it off. An area development agreement represents a great opportunity for an investor to tie up a large geographical area and develop a concept that may not have proven itself on a national basis. Keep in mind that this is a quantum leap from making an investment in a single franchise and is relevant only to those with development experience and deep pockets.

29. **Sub-Franchising Contracts: Yes.** Blimpie grants sub-franchising agreements. (See Chapter One for a more thorough explanation.) Like area development agreements, sub-franchising allows an investor or investment group to develop an entire area or region. The difference is that the sub-franchisor becomes a self-contained business, responsible for all relations with franchisees within its area, from initial training to on-going support. Franchisees pay their royalties to the sub-franchisor, who in turn pays a portion to the master franchisor.

Comment: Sub-franchising is used primarily by smaller franchisors who have a relatively easy concept and who are prepared to sell a portion of the future growth of their business to someone for some front-end cash and a percentage of the future royalties they receive from their franchisees.

30. **Expand in Territory: Yes.** Under conditions spelled out in the franchise agreement, Blimpie will allow its franchisees to expand within their exclusive territory.

Comment: Some franchisors define the franchisee's exclusive territory so tightly that there would never be room to open additional outlets within an area. Others provide a larger area in the hopes that the franchisee will do well and have the incentive to open additional units. There are clearly economic benefits to both parties from having franchisees with multiple units. There is no question that it is in your best interest to have the option to expand once you have proven to both yourself and the franchisor that you can manage the business successfully. Many would concur that the real profits in franchising come from managing multiple units rather than being locked into a single franchise in a single location. Additional fees may or may not be required with these additional units.

31. **Space Needs: 12,000 SF; FS, SF, SC, RM.** The average Blimpie's retail outlet will require 12,000 square feet in a Free-Standing (FS) building, Storefront (SF), Strip Center (SC) or Regional Mall (RM). Other types of leased space might be a Convenience Store (C-store) location, Executive Suite (ES), Home-Based (HB), Industrial Park (IP), Kiosk (KI), Office Building (OB), Power Center (PC), or Warehouse (WH).

Comment: Armed with the rough space requirements, you can better project your annual occupancy costs. It should be relatively easy to get comparable rental rates for the type of space required. As annual rent and related expenses can be as high as 15% of your annual sales, be as accurate as possible in your projections.

Franchisor Support and Training Provided

32. **Financial Assistance Provided: Yes (I)** notes that Blimpie is indirectly (I) involved in providing financial assistance. Indirect assistance might include making introductions to the franchisor's financial contacts, providing financial templates for preparing a business plan or actually assisting in the loan application process. In some cases, the franchisor becomes a co-signer on a financial obligation (equipment lease, space lease, etc.). Other franchisors are (D) directly involved in the process. In this case, the assistance may include a lease or loan made directly by the franchisor. Any loan would generally be secured by some form of collateral. A very common form of assistance is a note for all or part of the initial franchise fee. Yes (B) indicates that the franchisor provides both direct and indirect financial assistance. The level of assistance will generally depend upon the relative strengths of the franchisee.

Comment: The best of all possible worlds is one in which the franchisor has enough confidence in the business and in you to co-sign notes on the building and equipment leases and allow you to pay off the franchise fee over a specified period of time. Depending upon your qualifications, this could happen. Most likely, however, the franchisor will only give you some assistance in raising the necessary capital to start the business. Increasingly, franchisors are testing a franchisee's business acumen by letting him or her assume an increasing level of personal responsibility in securing financing. The objective is to find out early in the process how competent a franchisee really is.

33. **Site Selection Assistance: Yes** means that Blimpie will assist the franchisee in selecting a site location. While the phrase "location, location, location" may be hackneyed, its importance should not be discounted, especially when a business depends upon retail traffic counts and accessibility. If a business is home- or warehouse-based, assistance in this area is of negligible or minor importance.

Comment: Since you will be locked into a lease for a minimum of three, and probably five, years, optimal site selection is absolutely essential. Even if you were somehow able to sublease and extricate yourself from a bad lease or bad location, the franchise agreement may not allow you to move to another location. Accordingly, it is imperative that you get it right the first time.

If a franchisor is truly interested in your success, it should treat your choice of a site with the same care it would use in choosing a company-owned site. Keep in mind that many firms provide excellent demographic data on existing locations at a very reasonable cost.

34. **Lease Negotiations Assistance: Yes.** Once a site is selected, Blimpie will be actively involved in negotiating the terms of the lease.

Comment: Given the complexity of negotiating a lease, an increasing number of franchisors are taking an active role in lease negotiations. There are far too many trade-offs that must be considered — terms, percentage rents, tenant improvements, pass-throughs, kick-out clauses, etc. This responsibility is best left to the professionals. If the franchisor doesn't have the capacity to support you directly, enlist the help of a well-recommended broker. The penalties for signing a bad long-term lease are very severe.

35. **Co-operative Advertising: Yes.** This refers to the existence of a joint advertising program in which the franchisor and franchisees each contribute to promote the company's products and/or services (usually within the franchisee's specific territory).

Comment: Co-op advertising is a common and mutually-beneficial effort. By agreeing to split part of the advertising costs, whether for television, radio or direct mail, the franchisor is not only supporting the franchisee, but guaranteeing itself royalties from the incremental sales. A franchisor that is not intimately involved with the advertising campaign — particularly when it is an important part of the business — may not be fully committed to your overall success.

36. **Franchisee Assoc./Member: Yes/Yes.** This response notes that the Blimpie system does include an active association made up of Blimpie franchisees and that the franchisor is also a member of the franchisee association.

Comment: The empowerment of franchisees has become a major rallying cry within the industry over the past three years. Various states have recently passed laws favoring franchisee rights, and the subject has been widely discussed in congressional staff hearings. Political groups even represent franchisee rights on a national basis. Similarly, the IFA is now actively courting franchisees to become active members. Whether they are equal members remains to be seen.

Franchisees have also significantly increased their clout with respect with the franchisor. If a franchise is to grow and be successful in the long term, it is critical that the franchisor and its franchisees mutually agree they are partners rather than adversaries.

37. **Size of Corporate Staff: 109.** Blimpie has 109 full-time employees on its staff to support its 1,956 operating units.

Comment: There are no magic ratios that tell you whether the franchisor has enough staff to provide the proper level of support. It would appear, however, that Blimpie's staff of 109 is adequate to support 1,410 operating units. Less clear is whether a staff of three, including the company president and his wife, can adequately support 15 fledgling franchisees in the field.

Many younger franchises may be managed by a skeleton staff, assisted by outside consultants who perform various management functions during the start-up phase. From the perspective of the franchisee, it is essential that the franchisor have actual in-house franchising experience, and that the franchisee not be forced to rely on outside consultants to make the system work. Whereas a full-time, salaried employee will probably have the franchisee's objectives in mind, an outside consultant may easily not have the same priorities. Franchising is a unique form of business that requires specific skills and experience — skills and experience that are markedly different from those required to manage a non-franchised business. If you are thinking about establishing a long-term relationship with a firm just starting out in franchising, you should insist that the franchisor prove that it has an experienced, professional team on board and in place to provide the necessary levels of support to all concerned.

38. **On-Going Support: B,C,D,E,F,G,H,I.** Like initial training, the on-going support services provided by the franchisor are of paramount importance. Having a solid and responsive team behind you can certainly make your life much easier and allow you to concentrate your energies on other areas. As is noted below, the franchisors were asked to indicate their support for nine separate on-going services:

Service Provided	Included in Fees	At Add'l. Cost	NA
Central Data Processing	A	a	NA
Central Purchasing	B	b	NA
Field Operations Evaluation	C	c	NA
Field Training	D	d	NA
Initial Store Opening	E	e	NA
Inventory Control	F	f	NA
Franchisee Newsletter	G	g	NA
Regional or National Meetings	H	h	NA
800 Telephone Hotline	I	i	NA

If the franchisor provides the service at no additional cost to the franchisee (as indicated by letters A–I), a capital letter was used to indicate this. If the service is provided, but only at an additional cost, a lower case letter was used. If the franchisor responded with a NA, or failed to note an answer for a particular service, the corresponding letter was omitted from the data sheet.

39. **Training: 80 Hours in Atlanta, GA; 120 Hours in Local Franchise.**

Comment: Assuming that the underlying business concept is sound and competitive, adequate training and on-going support are among the most important determinants of your success as a franchisee. The initial training should be as lengthy and as "hands-on" as necessary to allow the franchisee to operate alone and with confidence. Obviously, every potential situation cannot be covered in any training program. But the franchisee should come away with a basic understanding of how the business operates and where to go to resolve problems when they come up. Depending on the business, there should be operating manuals, procedural manuals, company policies, training videos, (800) help-lines, etc. It may be helpful at the outset to establish how satisfied recent franchisees are with a company's training. I would also have a clear understanding about how often the company updates its manuals and training programs, the cost of sending additional employees through training, etc.

Remember, you are part of an organization that you are paying (in the form of a franchise fee and on-going royalties) to support you. Training is the first step. On-going support is the second step.

Specific Expansion Plans

40. **U.S.: All United States.** Blimpie is currently focusing its growth on the entire United States. Alternatively, the franchisor could have listed particular states or regions into which it wished to expand.

41. **Canada: All Canada.** Blimpie is currently seeking additional franchisees in Canada. Specific markets or provinces could have also been indicated.

42. **Overseas: Yes.** Blimpie is currently expanding overseas.

Comment: You will note that many smaller companies with less than 15 operating units suggest that they will concurrently expand throughout the U.S., Canada and internationally. In many cases, these are the same companies that foresee a 50+% growth rate in operating units over the next 12 months. The chances of this happening are negligible. As a prospective franchisee, you should be wary of any company that thinks it can expand throughout the world without a solid base of experience, staff and financial resources. Even if adequate financing is available, the demands on existing management will be extreme. New management cannot adequately fill the void until they are able to fully understand the system and absorb the corporate culture. If management's end objective is expansion for its own sake rather than by design, the existing franchisees will suffer.

Note: The statistics noted in the profiles preceding each company's analysis are the result of data provided by the franchisors themselves by way of a detailed questionnaire. Similarly, the data in the summary comparisons in the Introduction Chapter were taken from the company profile data. The figures used throughout each company's analysis, however, were generally taken from the UFOCs. In many cases, the UFOCs, which are only printed annually, contain information that is somewhat out of date. This is especially true with regard to the number of operating units and the current level of investment. A visit to our website at www.worldfranchising.com should provide current data.

ꟿ

If you have not already done so, please invest some modest time to read Chapter 1 — 30 Minute Overview.

Recommended Reading

Chapter

3

My strong sense is that every potential franchisee should be well-versed in the underlying fundamentals of the franchising industry before he or she commits to the way of life it involves. The better you understand the industry, the better prepared you will be to take maximum advantage of the relationship with your franchisor. There is no doubt that it will also place you in a better position to negotiate the franchise agreement — the conditions of which will dictate every facet of your life as a franchisee for the term of the agreement. The few extra dollars spent on educating yourself could well translate into tens of thousand of dollars to the bottom line in the years ahead.

In addition to general franchising publications, we have included several special interest books that relate to specific, but critical, parts of the start-up and on-going management process—site selection, hiring and managing minimum wage employees, preparing accurate cash flow projections, developing comprehensive business and/or marketing plans, etc.

We have also attempted to make the purchasing process easier by allowing readers to purchase the books directly from Source Book Publications, either via our 800-line or our website at www.sourcebookpublications.com. All of the books are currently available in inventory and are generally sent the same day an order is received. A 15% discount is available on all orders over $100.00. See page 35 for an order form. Your complete satisfaction is 100% guaranteed on all books.

Background/Evaluation

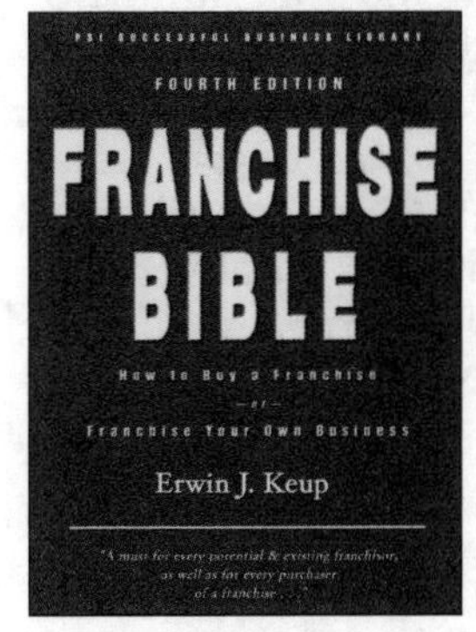

Franchise Bible: A Comprehensive Guide, 4th Edition, Keup, Oasis Press. 2000. 318 pp. $27.95.

This recently updated classic is equally useful for prospective franchisees and franchisors alike. The comprehensive guide and workbook explain in detail what the franchise system entails and the precise benefits it offers. The book features the new franchise laws that became effective January, 1995. To assist the prospective franchisee in rating a potential franchisor, Keup provides necessary checklists and forms. Also noted are the franchisor's contractual obligations to the franchisee and what the franchisee should expect from the franchisor in the way of services and support.

Tips & Traps When Buying a Franchise, Revised 2nd Edition, Tomzack, Source Book Publications. 1999. 236 pp. $19.95.

Many a novice franchisee is shocked to discover that the road to success in franchising is full of hidden costs, inflated revenue promises, reneged marketing support and worse. In this candid, hard-hitting book, Tomzack steers potential franchisees around the pitfalls and guides them in making a smart, lucrative purchase. Topics include: matching a franchise with personal finances and lifestyle, avoiding the five most common pitfalls, choosing a prime location, asking the right questions, etc.

Databases

Franchisor Database, Source Book Publications. (800) 841-0873 or (510) 839-5471.

Listing of over 2,400 active North American franchisors. 29 fields of information per company: full address, telephone/800/fax numbers, Internet address, email address, contact/title/salutation, president/title/salutation, # of franchised units, # of company-owned units, # total units, IFA/CFA Member, etc. 45 industry categories. Unlimited use. Guaranteed deliverability — $0.50 rebate for any returned mailings. $1,200 for initial database, $150 per quarter for updates.

Directories

Minority Franchise Guide — 2004 Edition, Bond/Wallace, Source Book Publications, 2004. 336 pp. $19.95.

The only minority franchising directory! Contains detailed profiles and company logos of over 550 forward-looking franchisors that encourage and actively support the inclusion of minority franchisees. It also includes a listing of resources available to prospective minority franchisees.

Earnings Claims

"How Much Can I Make?", Bond/Lee/Woo/Louie, Source Book Publications. 2005. 368 pp. $29.95.

The single most important task for a prospective investor is to prepare a realistic cash flow statement that accurately reflects the economic potential of that business. *"How Much Can I Make?"* is an invaluable insider's guide that details historical sales, expense and/or profit data on actual franchise operations, **as provided by the franchisors themselves**. Whether you plan to buy a franchise or start your own business, these actual performances statistics will ensure that you have a realistic starting point in determining how much you can expect to make in a similar business. 116 current earnings claim statements, in their entirety, are included for the food-service, retail and service-based industries. Unfortunately, less than 20% of franchisors provide such projections/guidelines to prospective franchisees. *"How Much Can I Make?"* includes roughly half of the total universe of earnings claim statements available. The list of companies includes household names such as McDonald's and Baskin Robbins to newer, smaller franchises with only a few operating units. Any serious investor would be shortsighted not to take full advantage of this extraordinary resource.

International Franchising

International Herald Tribune International Franchise Guide, Bond/Thompson, Source Book Publications. 1999. 192 pp. $29.95.

This annual publication, sponsored by the International Herald Tribune, is the definitive guide to international franchising. It lists comprehensive, in-depth profiles of major franchisors who are committed to promote and support overseas expansion. Details specific geographic areas of desired expansion for each company, country by country — as well as the number of units in each foreign country as of the date of publication. Geared specifically to the needs and requirements of prospective international area developers, master franchisees and investors. Investors must be prepared to assume responsibility for the development of large geographic areas. Also listed are international franchise consultants, attorneys and service providers. Covers 32 distinct business categories.

Franchise Rankings

Bond's Top 100 Franchises, Bond/Woo/Louie, Source Book Publications, 2004. 376 pp. $19.95.

In response to the constantly asked question, *"What are the best franchises?"*, Bond's new book focuses on the top 100 franchises broken down into three major segments — food-service, retail and service-based franchises. Within each group, a rigorous, in-depth analysis was performed on over 500 systems. Many of the companies selected are household names. Others are rapidly growing, mid-sized firms that are also strong national players. Still others are somewhat smaller systems that demonstrate sound concepts, exceptional management and an aggressive expansion system. Companies were analyzed on the basis of historical performance, brand identification, market dynamics, franchisee satisfaction, the level of training and on-going support, financial stability, etc. Detailed four to five page profiles on each company, as well as key statistics and industry overview. All companies are proven performers and most have a national presence.

Bond's Top 50 Food-Service Franchises, Bond/Schiller, Source Book Publications, 2000. 288 pp. $19.95.

In response to the constantly asked question, *"What are the best franchises?"*, Bond's book focuses on the top 50 food-service franchises. Over 500 food-service systems were evaluated for inclusion. Companies were analyzed on the basis of historical performance, brand identification, market dynamics, franchisee satisfaction, the level of training and on-going support, financial stability, etc. Detailed four to five page profiles on each company, as well as key statistics and industry overview. All companies are proven performers and most have a national presence. Excellent starting point for someone focusing on the food-service industry.

Bond's Top 50 Retail Franchises, Bond/Schiller/Tong, Source Book Publications, 2001. 288 pp. $19.95.

In response to the constantly asked question, *"What are the best franchises?"*, Bond's book focuses on the top 50 retail franchises. Over 350 retail systems were evaluated for inclusion. Companies were analyzed on the basis of historical performance, brand identification, market dynamics, franchisee satisfaction, the level of training and on-going support, financial stability, etc. Detailed four to five page profiles on each company, as well as key statistics and industry overview. All companies are proven performers and most have a national presence. Excellent starting point for someone focusing on the retail industry.

Bond's Top 50 Service-Based Franchises, Bond/ Schiller, Source Book Publications, 2001. 300 pp. $19.95.

In response to the constantly asked question, *"What are the best franchises?"*, Bond's book focuses on the top 50 service-based franchises. Over 400 service-based systems were evaluated for inclusion. Companies were analyzed on the basis of historical performance, brand identification, market dynamics, franchisee satisfaction, the level of training and ongoing support, financial stability, etc. Detailed four to five page profiles on each company, as well as key statistics and industry overview. All companies are proven performers and most have a national presence. Excellent starting point for someone focusing on the service-based industry.

Site Selection

Location, Location, Location: How to Select the Best Site for Your Business, Salvaneschi, Oasis Press. 2000. 252 pp. $24.95.

Whether you are searching for a new business site or relocating an existing business, you have the power to dramatically increase your profits by choosing the right location. For any business that depends on a customer's ability to find it, location is the most important ingredient for success. Learn how to: spot the essential characteristics of the best location; understand why and how people move from one point to another; analyze and learn from your competitor's business; and learn about the retail trading zone and how to use it to capture the most customers.

The Franchise Bookstore
Order Form

Call (800) 841-0873 or (510) 839-5471; or FAX (510) 839-2104

Title	Price	Qty.	Total
		Basic postage (1 Book)	$7.00
		Each additional book add $4.00	
		California tax @ 8.25% (if CA resident)	
		Total due in U.S. dollars	
		Deduct 15% if total due is over $100.00	
		Net amount due in U.S. dollars	

Please include credit card number and expiration date for all charge card orders! Checks should be made payable to Source Book Publications. All prices are in U.S. dollars.

Mailing Information: All books shipped by USPS Priority Mail (2nd Day Air). Please print clearly and include your phone number in case we need to contact you. Postage and handling rates are for shipping within the U.S. Please call for international rates.

❑ Check enclosed or

Charge my:

❑ MasterCard ❑ VISA ❑ American Express

Card #: ____________________

Expiration Date: ________________

Signature: ____________________

Name: ____________________

Company: ____________________

Address: ____________________

City: ____________________

Title: ____________________

Telephone No.: (____)________________

State/Prov.: ________ Zip: ____________

Special Offer — Save 15%

If your total order above exceeds $100.00, deduct 15% from your bill.

Please send order to:

Source Book Publications

1814 Franklin St., Ste. 820, Oakland, CA 94612

Satisfaction Guaranteed. If not fully satisfied, return for a prompt, 100% refund.

Automotive Products & Services

Chapter 4

AUTOMOTIVE PRODUCTS & SERVICES INDUSTRY PROFILE

Total # Franchisors in Industry Group	151
Total # Franchised Units in Industry Group	24,530
Total # Company-Owned Units in Industry Group	2,438
Total # Operating Units in Industry Group	26,968
Average # Franchised Units/Franchisor	162.5
Average # Company-Owned Units/Franchisor	16.1
Average # Total Units/Franchisor	178.6
Ratio of Total # Franchised Units/Total # Company-Owned Units	10.1:1
Industry Survey Participants	76
Representing % of Industry	50.3%
Average Franchise Fee*:	$23.2K
Average Total Investment*:	$186.6K
Average On-Going Royalty Fee*:	5.3%

*If a range was provided, the mid-point of the range was used. See detailed profiles for actual ranges.

FIVE LARGEST PARTICIPANTS IN SURVEY

Company	# Franchised Units	# Co-Owned Units	# Total Units	Franchise Fee	On-Going Royalty	Total Investment
1. Midas	2,571	73	2,644	$20K	10%	$360-487K
2. Novus Auto Glass	2,200	6	2,206	$7.5K	7-8%	$37.0-169.1K
3. Meineke Car Care Centers	883	1	884	$30K	3-7%	$180-365K
4. Valvoline Instant Oil Change	310	362	672	$30K	6%	$96-201.8K
5. Big O Tires	570	0	570	$30K	2%	NR

All of the data provided are proprietary and should not be quoted without acknowledging *Bond's Franchise Guide.*

ABRA AUTO BODY & GLASS

6601 Shingle Creek Pkwy., # 200
Brooklyn Center, MN 55430
Tel: (888) 872-2272 (763) 561-7220
E-Mail: mwahlin@abraauto.com
Web Site: www.abraauto.com
Mr. Mark Wahlin, Director of Franchising

One of the first automobile collision and glass franchises. Operating company and franchised auto body collision and auto glass replacement shops. We offer support with marketing, business management, equipment and material purchases. Investment opportunities for qualifying owners and managers.

BACKGROUND:
Established: 1984; 1st Franchised: 1987
Franchised Units: 36
Company-Owned Units: 18
Total Units: 54
Dist.: US-54; CAN-0; O'seas-0
North America: 12 States
Density: 28 in MN, 7 in TN, 6 in WI
Projected New Units (12 Months): 12
Qualifications: 5, 5, 5, 3, 3, 5
Registered: IL,IN,MI,MN,ND,SD,WI

FINANCIAL/TERMS:
Cash Investment: $60-100K
Total Investment: $229.6-422.6K
Minimum Net Worth: $500K
Fees: Franchise - $22.5K
Royalty - 5%; Ad. - 3%
Earnings Claims Statement: Yes
Term of Contract (Years): 10/10
Avg. # Of Employees: NR
Passive Ownership: Allowed
Encourage Conversions: Yes
Area Develop. Agreements: Yes/Varies
Sub-Franchising Contracts: No
Expand In Territory: Yes
Space Needs: 8,000-15,000 SF; FS, SF

SUPPORT & TRAINING:
Financial Assistance Provided: No
Site Selection Assistance: Yes
Lease Negotiation Assistance: Yes
Co-Operative Advertising: NA
Franchisee Assoc./Member: NR
Size Of Corporate Staff: 53
On-Going Support: a,B,C,D,E,F,g,h,I
Training: 2-4 Weeks ABRA Training Center, Minneapolis, MN; 6 Weeks On-Site.

SPECIFIC EXPANSION PLANS:
US: Central, South, Southeast
Canada: No
Overseas: No

<< >>

ACTIVE GREEN + ROSS TIRE & AUTOMOTIVE CENTRE

580 Evans Ave.
Toronto, ON M8W 2W1 CANADA
Tel: (416) 255-5581
Fax: (416) 255-4793
E-Mail: andychiodo@activegreenross.com
Web Site: www.activegreenross.com
Mr. Andy Chiodo, Marketing Manager

Tire and automotive sales and service. The company currently has locations in Toronto and surrounding area and is one of the largest independent groups of tire and automotive service centers in Canada. Company operations began in 1982. Franchised first outlet in 1983; Training provided for up to 2 months; Dealers elect representatives on Dealer Advisory Committee.

BACKGROUND:
Established: 1982; 1st Franchised: 1983
Franchised Units: 25
Company-Owned Units: 5
Total Units: 30
Dist.: US-0; CAN-29; O'seas-0
North America: 1 Province
Density: 29 in ON
Projected New Units (12 Months): NR
Qualifications: 4, 4, 4, 4, 4, 4
Registered: None

FINANCIAL/TERMS:
Cash Investment: NR
Total Investment: $115-200K
Minimum Net Worth: $250K
Fees: Franchise - $25K
Royalty - 5%; Ad. - 2.5%
Earnings Claims Statement: No
Term of Contract (Years): 5/5
Avg. # Of Employees: 4+ FT
Passive Ownership: Not Allowed
Encourage Conversions: Yes
Area Develop. Agreements: No
Sub-Franchising Contracts: Yes
Expand In Territory: Yes
Space Needs: 3,000-5,000 SF; NR

SUPPORT & TRAINING:
Financial Assistance Provided: Yes(I)
Site Selection Assistance: Yes
Lease Negotiation Assistance: NA
Co-Operative Advertising: Yes
Franchisee Assoc./Member: Yes
Size Of Corporate Staff: 9
On-Going Support: NR
Training: Head Office and On-Site.

SPECIFIC EXPANSION PLANS:
US: N/A
Canada: ON
Overseas: No

<< >>

AERO-COLOURS

10824 Nesbitt Ave. S.
Bloomington, MN 55437
Tel: (800) 696-2376 (952) 942-0490
Fax: (952) 942-0628
E-Mail: dadelstein@aerocolours.com
Web Site: www.aerocolours.com
Mr. Dan Adelstein, Franchise Development

AERO-COLOURS is an exclusive mobile automotive paint repair process, providing service to dealerships, fleet operations and individual vehicle owners. Our solid support system, complemented by our industry-leading training, allows our franchisees to provide unmatched service. We will show you how to operate, market and grow your own business.

BACKGROUND:
Established: 1985; 1st Franchised: 1993
Franchised Units: 210
Company-Owned Units: 8
Total Units: 218
Dist.: US-208; CAN-0; O'seas-10
North America: 30 States
Density: 56 in CA, 25 in FL, 22 in TX
Projected New Units (12 Months): 12
Qualifications: 5, 3, 5, 3, 5, 5
Registered: CA,FL,IL,IN,MD,MI,MN, OR,VA,WI

FINANCIAL/TERMS:
Cash Investment: $5-30K
Total Investment: $5-60K
Minimum Net Worth: $100K
Fees: Franchise - $25K
Royalty - 7%; Ad. - 0%
Earnings Claims Statement: No
Term of Contract (Years): 10/10
Avg. # Of Employees: 4-5 FT
Passive Ownership: Allowed
Encourage Conversions: No
Area Develop. Agreements: No
Sub-Franchising Contracts: Yes
Expand In Territory: Yes
Space Needs: 1,800 SF; Warehouse

SUPPORT & TRAINING:
Financial Assistance Provided: Yes(I)
Site Selection Assistance: Yes
Lease Negotiation Assistance: Yes
Co-Operative Advertising: No
Franchisee Assoc./Member: Yes/Yes
Size Of Corporate Staff: 6
On-Going Support: A,B,C,D,E,G,H,I
Training: 6 Days Minneapolis, MN; 5 Days Territory.

SPECIFIC EXPANSION PLANS:

US: All United States
Canada: All Canada
Overseas: No

<< >>

AIRBAG SERVICE

9675 SE 36th St., # 100
Mercer Island, WA 98040
Tel: (800) 224-7224 (206) 275-4105
Fax: (206) 275-4122
E-Mail: marketing@airbagservice.com
Web Site: www.airbagservice.com
Mr. Peter Smith, Sales/Marketing Manager

Automotive service company, specializing in airbag system repair. Our mobile service supplies a needed expertise to the automotive collision repair industry. Specialized software and tools allow us to work on any system right on site for increased efficiency.

BACKGROUND:
Established: 1992; 1st Franchised: 1995
Franchised Units: 40
Company-Owned Units: 1
Total Units: 41
Dist.: US-37; CAN-2; O'seas-0
North America: 20 States, 2 Provinces
Density: 7 in TX, 4 in CA, 3 in WA
Projected New Units (12 Months): 18
Qualifications: 3, 5, 4, 1, 1, 4
Registered: CA,FL,HI,IL,IN,MD,MI,NY,VA

FINANCIAL/TERMS:
Cash Investment: $50-100K
Total Investment: $50-125K
Minimum Net Worth: $75K
Fees: Franchise - $25-30K
Royalty - 8.5% Net; Ad. - 2% Net
Earnings Claims Statement: No
Term of Contract (Years): 10/5+5
Avg. # Of Employees: 2 FT
Passive Ownership: Discouraged
Encourage Conversions: NA
Area Develop. Agreements: Yes/10
Sub-Franchising Contracts: No
Expand In Territory: Yes
Space Needs: 1,000 SF; Commercial Office

SUPPORT & TRAINING:
Financial Assistance Provided: Yes(I)
Site Selection Assistance: No
Lease Negotiation Assistance: No
Co-Operative Advertising: Yes
Franchisee Assoc./Member: No
Size Of Corporate Staff: 10
On-Going Support: C,D,G,H,I
Training: 3 Weeks Seattle, WA.

SPECIFIC EXPANSION PLANS:
US: All United States
Canada: No
Overseas: No

<< >>

ALTRACOLOR SYSTEMS

113 23rd St.
Kenner, LA 70062
Tel: (800) 678-5220 (504) 454-7233
Fax: (985) 863-9962
E-Mail: altra@altracolor.com
Web Site: www.altracolor.com
Mr. Jeff Richards, President

ALTRACOLOR SYSTEMS is the state-of-the-art mobile, on-site touch-up and spot repair system for automotive paint repair.

BACKGROUND: IFA MEMBER
Established: 1988; 1st Franchised: 1991
Franchised Units: 82
Company-Owned Units: 92
Total Units: 174
Dist.: US-174; CAN-0; O'seas-0
North America: 27 States
Density: 14 in NC, 13 in VA, 13 in SC
Projected New Units (12 Months): 23
Qualifications: 3, 3, 1, 1, 2, 4
Registered:CA,FL,IN,MI,MN,NY,OR,VA,WA,WI,DC

FINANCIAL/TERMS:
Cash Investment: $5-11.7K
Total Investment: $16.9-25.2K
Minimum Net Worth: NA
Fees: Franchise - $9.95K
Royalty - $95/Wk.; Ad. - 0%
Earnings Claims Statement: Yes
Term of Contract (Years): 15/5
Avg. # Of Employees: 1 FT
Passive Ownership: Not Allowed
Encourage Conversions: Yes
Area Develop. Agreements: Yes/15
Sub-Franchising Contracts: Yes
Expand In Territory: Yes
Space Needs: NA SF; Mobile Bus

SUPPORT & TRAINING:
Financial Assistance Provided: Yes(D)
Site Selection Assistance: NA
Lease Negotiation Assistance: NA
Co-Operative Advertising: NA
Franchisee Assoc./Member: No
Size Of Corporate Staff: 5
On-Going Support: C,D,G,H,I
Training: 1 Week in Metairie, LA.

SPECIFIC EXPANSION PLANS:
US: All United States
Canada: No
Overseas: No

<< >>

AMERICAN BRAKE SERVICE

200 Hempstead Turnpike, # 110
W. Hempstead, NY 11552
Tel: (800) TILDENS (516) 746-7911
Fax: (516) 746-1288
E-Mail: info@tildencarcare.com
Web Site: www.tildencarcare.com
Mr. Jason Baskind, Dir. Franchise Development

We're not just brakes. The total care concept allows you to offer a full menu of automotive services for maximum customer procurement - rather than a limited niche market. You benefit from a management team whose concept system and training were proven and perfected before we even considered offering franchises.

BACKGROUND:
Established: 1923; 1st Franchised: 1996
Franchised Units: 60
Company-Owned Units: 0
Total Units: 60
Dist.: US-60; CAN-0; O'seas-0
North America: 13 States
Density: 24 in FL, 15 in NY, 6 in GA
Projected New Units (12 Months): 10
Qualifications: 3, 4, 3, 3, 3, 4
Registered: CA,FL,IL,IN,MN,NY,VA,WA

FINANCIAL/TERMS:
Cash Investment: $50-60K
Total Investment: $131-171K
Minimum Net Worth: $150K
Fees: Franchise - $25K
Royalty - 6%/$350/Wk.;
Ad. - 3%/$250/Wk.
Earnings Claims Statement: No
Term of Contract (Years): 20/20
Avg. # Of Employees: 4 FT, 2 PT
Passive Ownership: Discouraged
Encourage Conversions: Yes
Area Develop. Agreements: Yes/10
Sub-Franchising Contracts: No
Expand In Territory: Yes
Space Needs: 3,500 SF; FS, Auto Mall

SUPPORT & TRAINING:
Financial Assistance Provided: Yes(I)
Site Selection Assistance: Yes
Lease Negotiation Assistance: Yes
Co-Operative Advertising: Yes
Franchisee Assoc./Member: Yes/Yes
Size Of Corporate Staff: 4
On-Going Support: C,d,E,F,G,H,I
Training: 2 Weeks Home Office.

SPECIFIC EXPANSION PLANS:
US: All United States
Canada: All Canada
Overseas: No

AMERICAN ENGINE INSTALLATIONS

2357 W. Northwest Hwy., # 1302
Dallas, TX 75077
Tel: (800) 269-9270 (888) 959-7242
Fax: (214) 350-0902
E-Mail: aeidallas@aol.com
Web Site: www.engineinstallation.com
Mr. Greg Eyster, VP Franchise Sales

AEI specializes in the installation of automotive engines. Initial management training, site selection, advertising evaluation and recommendation are provided. Continuing on-going training is also available. Note: National call center SELLS JOBS FOR YOU! Financing packages are available upon request.

BACKGROUND:
Established: 1994; 1st Franchised: 2002
Franchised Units: 5
Company-Owned Units: 10
Total Units: 15
Dist.: US-15; CAN-0; O'seas-0
North America: 14 States
Density: 2 in TX, 1 in OH, 1 in KY
Projected New Units (12 Months): 12
Qualifications: 5, 4, 3, 3, 3, 5
Registered: CA,FL,IL,IN.MD,MI,MN,NY, ND,RI,SD,VA,WI,DC

FINANCIAL/TERMS:
Cash Investment: $50-100K
Total Investment: $137.5K
Minimum Net Worth: $100K
Fees: Franchise - $37.5K
Royalty - 7%; Ad. - 0%
Earnings Claims Statement: Yes
Term of Contract (Years): 10/10
Avg. # Of Employees: 5 FT
Passive Ownership: Allowed
Encourage Conversions: No
Area Develop. Agreements: Yes/2.5+
Sub-Franchising Contracts: No
Expand In Territory: Yes
Space Needs: 1,200 SF; FS, SC, RM

SUPPORT & TRAINING:
Financial Assistance Provided: Yes(I)
Site Selection Assistance: Yes
Lease Negotiation Assistance: No
Co-Operative Advertising: Var.
Franchisee Assoc./Member: Yes/Yes
Size Of Corporate Staff: 12
On-Going Support: C,d,E,F,G,H
Training: 3 Weeks Champaign, IL; 3 Weeks Ann Arbor, MI.

SPECIFIC EXPANSION PLANS:
US: East and Southeast
Canada: No
Overseas: No

ATL INTERNATIONAL

8334 Veterans Hwy.
Millersville, MD 21108-2543
Tel: (800) 935-8863 (410) 987-1011
Fax: (410) 987-9080
E-Mail: sales@alltuneandlube.com
Web Site: www.alltuneandlube.com
Mr. Louis Kibler, VP Franchise Development

ALL TUNE AND LUBE is the leader in 'One Stop' total car care. Our full-service centers provide vehicle maintenance and repair, such as engine performance, brakes, ride control and oil changes. Franchise owners also have the option of adding the ATL MOTOR MATE franchise, which specializes in engine installation, and the ALL TUNE TRANSMISSIONS franchise, which provides transmission service. This co-branding concept provides three times the potential at one location.

BACKGROUND:
Established: 1985; 1st Franchised: 1985
Franchised Units: 450
Company-Owned Units: 0
Total Units: 450
Dist.: US-448; CAN-2; O'seas-0
North America: 34 States
Density: 50 in CA, 35 in TX, 30 in MD
Projected New Units (12 Months): 450
Qualifications: 3, 4, 1, 2, 1, 4
Registered: All States

FINANCIAL/TERMS:
Cash Investment: $25K
Total Investment: $120-130K
Minimum Net Worth: $75K
Fees: Franchise - $25K
Royalty - 7%; Ad. - 8%
Earnings Claims Statement: No
Term of Contract (Years): 15/3x5
Avg. # Of Employees: 4-6 FT
Passive Ownership: Not Allowed
Encourage Conversions: Yes
Area Develop. Agreements: No
Sub-Franchising Contracts: No
Expand In Territory: Yes
Space Needs: 3,000 SF; FS, SC, Auto Mall

SUPPORT & TRAINING:
Financial Assistance Provided: Yes(B)
Site Selection Assistance: Yes
Lease Negotiation Assistance: Yes
Co-Operative Advertising: Yes
Franchisee Assoc./Member: No
Size Of Corporate Staff: 75
On-Going Support: B,C,D,E,F,G,H,I
Training: 2 Weeks Corporate Office; 1 Week in Center.

SPECIFIC EXPANSION PLANS:
US: All United States
Canada: All Canada
Overseas: All Countries

AUTO-LAB DIAGNOSTIC & TUNE-UP CENTERS

1050 W. Columbia Ave., # B
Battle Creek, MI 49015
Tel: (877) 349-4968 (269) 966-0500
Fax: (269) 441-1825
E-Mail: autolabfmc@aol.com
Web Site: www.autolabusa.com
Mr. Daniel J. Kiefer, President

Full service automotive repair facility, performing all aspects of auto service and repair. Our specialty is in the diagnostics and repair of computerized and electrical systems. Our goal is to be a professional alternative to auto dealer repair shops.

BACKGROUND:
Established: 1984; 1st Franchised: 1989
Franchised Units: 25
Company-Owned Units: 1
Total Units: 26
Dist.: US-40; CAN-0; O'seas-0
North America: 2 States
Density: 25 in MI, 1 in OH
Projected New Units (12 Months): 18
Qualifications: 3, 2, 3, 3, 2, 5
Registered: IN,MI

FINANCIAL/TERMS:
Cash Investment: $35-75K
Total Investment: $110-175K
Minimum Net Worth: $250K
Fees: Franchise - $19.5K
Royalty - 6%; Ad. - 3%
Earnings Claims Statement: No
Term of Contract (Years): 15/15
Avg. # Of Employees: 5 FT, 1 PT
Passive Ownership: Discouraged
Encourage Conversions: Yes
Area Develop. Agreements: Yes/15
Sub-Franchising Contracts: No
Expand In Territory: Yes
Space Needs: 3,000+ SF; FS

SUPPORT & TRAINING:

Financial Assistance Provided: No
Site Selection Assistance: Yes
Lease Negotiation Assistance: Yes
Co-Operative Advertising: Yes
Franchisee Assoc./Member: No
Size Of Corporate Staff: 10
On-Going Support: a,b,C,D,E,G,H,I
Training: 2 Weeks Grand Rapids, MI; 2-4 Weeks Battle Creek, MI.

SPECIFIC EXPANSION PLANS:
US: MW & E. to Gulf of Mexico
Canada: All Canada
Overseas: All Countries

<< >>

BATTERIES PLUS

925 Walnut Ridge Dr., # 100
Hartland, WI 53029-9389
Tel: (262) 369-0690
Fax: (262) 369-0215
E-Mail: franchising@batteriesplus.com
Web Site: www.batteriesplus.com
Mr. Rod Tremelling, Franchise Sales

BATTERIES PLUS is America's Battery Experts (TM), providing 1,000's of batteries for 1,000's of items, serving both retail and commercial customers. The $19 billion battery market, growing 6.5% annually, is driven by technology and lifestyles. BATTERIES PLUS is a unique opportunity in this growth industry not yet saturated with competitors. Our turn-key program includes a unique store design, graphics, signage and product brands and proven operating methods.

BACKGROUND: IFA MEMBER
Established: 1988; 1st Franchised: 1992
Franchised Units: 255
Company-Owned Units: 16
Total Units: 271
Dist.: US-271; CAN-0; O'seas-0
North America: 41 States
Density: 16 in WI, 15 in MN, 14 in MI
Projected New Units (12 Months): 35
Qualifications: 5, 5, 2, 3, 2, 3
Registered: All Except HI

FINANCIAL/TERMS:
Cash Investment: $100K
Total Investment: $173-216K
Minimum Net Worth: $400K
Fees: Franchise - $25K
Royalty - 4%; Ad. - 1%
Earnings Claims Statement: No
Term of Contract (Years): 10/10
Avg. # Of Employees: 3-4 FT
Passive Ownership: Not Allowed
Encourage Conversions: No
Area Develop. Agreements: Yes
Sub-Franchising Contracts: No
Expand In Territory: No
Space Needs: 1,800-2,000 SF; FS, SF, SC

SUPPORT & TRAINING:
Financial Assistance Provided: Yes(I)
Site Selection Assistance: Yes
Lease Negotiation Assistance: Yes
Co-Operative Advertising: No
Franchisee Assoc./Member: No
Size Of Corporate Staff: 65
On-Going Support: C,D,E,F,G,I
Training: 3 Weeks Corporate Training Center; 2 Weeks On-Site Franchisee's Store.

SPECIFIC EXPANSION PLANS:
US: All United States
Canada: No
Overseas: No

<< >>

BIG O TIRES

12650 E. Briarwood Ave., # 2D
Centennial, CO 80112-6734
Tel: (800) 622-2446 (303) 728-5500
Fax: (303) 728-5700
E-Mail: lbrown@bigotires.com
Web Site: www.bigotires.com
Ms. Lisa Brown, Franchise Qual. Specialist

BIG O TIRES is the fastest-growing retail tire and under-car service center franchisor in North America. We offer over 30 years' experience and proven success, site selection assistance, comprehensive training and on-going field support, protected territory, exclusive product lines, consistent product supply, unique marketing programs, contemporary building designs, effective advertising support, and proven business systems.

BACKGROUND: IFA MEMBER
Established: 1962; 1st Franchised: 1967
Franchised Units: 570
Company-Owned Units: 0
Total Units: 570
Dist.: US-569; CAN-1; O'seas-0
North America: 20 States, 1 Province
Density: 200 in CA, 65 in CO, 60 AZ
Projected New Units (12 Months): 40
Qualifications: 5, 5, 1, 2, 1, 5
Registered: NR

FINANCIAL/TERMS:
Cash Investment: $150K
Total Investment: NR
Minimum Net Worth: $500K
Fees: Franchise - $30K
Royalty - 2%; Ad. - 4%
Earnings Claims Statement: No
Term of Contract (Years): 10
Avg. # Of Employees: NR
Passive Ownership: Discouraged
Encourage Conversions: Yes
Area Develop. Agreements: Yes/Varies
Sub-Franchising Contracts: Yes
Expand In Territory: Yes
Space Needs: NR SF; FS

SUPPORT & TRAINING:
Financial Assistance Provided: Yes(I)
Site Selection Assistance: Yes
Lease Negotiation Assistance: Yes
Co-Operative Advertising: Yes
Franchisee Assoc./Member: NR
Size Of Corporate Staff: 100
On-Going Support: A,B,C,d,E,F,G,h,I
Training: 7 Weeks Littleton, CO.

SPECIFIC EXPANSION PLANS:
US: All United States
Canada: BC and AB
Overseas: No

<< >>

BRAKE MASTERS

6179 E. Broadway Blvd.
Tucson, AZ 85711
Tel: (800) 888-5545 (520) 512-0000
Fax: (520) 512-1000
E-Mail: moshei@brakemasters.com
Web Site: www.brakemasters.com
Mr. Moshe Issaharov, Dir. Franchise Development

Brake repair, brake-related services and maintenance services

BACKGROUND:
Established: 1983; 1st Franchised: 1994
Franchised Units: 40
Company-Owned Units: 42
Total Units: 82
Dist.: US-82; CAN-0; O'seas-0
North America: 9 States
Density: 31 in CA, 27 in AZ, 11 in TX
Projected New Units (12 Months): NR
Qualifications: , , , , ,
Registered: CA,IL,IN,WA

FINANCIAL/TERMS:
Cash Investment: $80-100K
Total Investment: $175-400K
Minimum Net Worth: NR
Fees: Franchise - $22.95K
Royalty - 5%; Ad. - 1%
Earnings Claims Statement: No
Term of Contract (Years): 20
Avg. # Of Employees: 6 FT, 2 PT
Passive Ownership: Discouraged

Encourage Conversions: Yes
Area Develop. Agreements: Yes/20
Sub-Franchising Contracts: Yes
Expand In Territory: Yes
Space Needs: 4,000 SF; FS

SUPPORT & TRAINING:
Financial Assistance Provided: NR
Site Selection Assistance: Yes
Lease Negotiation Assistance: Yes
Co-Operative Advertising: Yes
Franchisee Assoc./Member: NR
Size Of Corporate Staff: 30
On-Going Support: B,C,D,E,F,I
Training: 2 Weeks Tucson, AZ; 2 Weeks Location Near Franchisee.

SPECIFIC EXPANSION PLANS:
US: West, SW, NW, Midwest.
Canada: NR
Overseas: NR

CARTEX LIMITED

42816 Mound Rd.
Sterling Heights, MI 48314-3256
Tel: (800) 421-7328 (586) 739-4330
Fax: (586) 739-4331
E-Mail: crismar@aol.com
Web Site: www.fabrion.net
Mr. Lawrence P. Klukowski, Chief Executive Officer

CARTEX LIMITED, better known as Fabrion, is a mobile service business, specializing in automotive interior repair. The Fabrion repair process electrostatically repairs auto cloth, velour and carpet. Due to our specialization, we have revolutionized auto upholstery repair. Updating on current (OEM) original equipment materials and providing the tools to match all current patterns being used in auto interiors are our strong points.

BACKGROUND:
Established: 1980; 1st Franchised: 1988
Franchised Units: 105
Company-Owned Units: 0
Total Units: 105
Dist.: US-104; CAN-1; O'seas-0
North America: 36 States
Density: 13 in CA, 10 in FL, 8 in TX
Projected New Units (12 Months): 20
Qualifications: 3, 3, 3, 3, 3, 3
Registered:CA,FL,HI,IL,MD,MI,MN,NY,OR,VA,WA,DC,AB

FINANCIAL/TERMS:
Cash Investment: $23.5-36.5K
Total Investment: $23.5-36.5K
Minimum Net Worth: NA
Fees: Franchise - $23.5-36.5K
Royalty - 7%,min month fee; Ad. - NA
Earnings Claims Statement: No
Term of Contract (Years): 5/5
Avg. # Of Employees: 3 FT
Passive Ownership: Discouraged
Encourage Conversions: Yes
Area Develop. Agreements: No
Sub-Franchising Contracts: No
Expand In Territory: Yes
Space Needs: NA SF; NA

SUPPORT & TRAINING:
Financial Assistance Provided: Yes
Site Selection Assistance: NA
Lease Negotiation Assistance: NA
Co-Operative Advertising: NA
Franchisee Assoc./Member: No
Size Of Corporate Staff: 8
On-Going Support: B,C,D,G,H,I
Training: 3 Weeks On-Site Under Development.

SPECIFIC EXPANSION PLANS:
US: All United States
Canada: All Canada
Overseas: All Countries

CAR-X AUTO SERVICE

1375 E. Woodfield Rd., # 500
Schaumburg, IL 60173
Tel: (800) 359-2359
Fax: (847) 619-3310
E-Mail: kbauer@carx.com
Web Site: www.carx.com
Mr. Kim Bauer, Director Franchise Devel.

Retail auto repair specialists providing service in brakes, exhaust, road handling, tune-ups, steering systems, air conditioning, tires oil changes and more for all makes of cars and light trucks.

BACKGROUND:
Established: 1971; 1st Franchised: 1973
Franchised Units: 154
Company-Owned Units: 29
Total Units: 183
Dist.: US-186; CAN-0; O'seas-0
North America: 10 States
Density: 59 in IL, 27 in MN, 23 in MO
Projected New Units (12 Months): 8
Qualifications: 5, 3, 2, 2, 2, 5
Registered: FL,IL,IN,MI,MN,SD,WI

FINANCIAL/TERMS:
Cash Investment: $75-100K
Total Investment: $232-342K
Minimum Net Worth: $250K
Fees: Franchise - $25K
Royalty - 5%; Ad. - 5-7%
Earnings Claims Statement: Yes
Term of Contract (Years): 15/5
Avg. # Of Employees: 4 FT
Passive Ownership: Discouraged
Encourage Conversions: Yes
Area Develop. Agreements: Yes
Sub-Franchising Contracts: No
Expand In Territory: Yes
Space Needs: 5,000 SF; FS

SUPPORT & TRAINING:
Financial Assistance Provided: Yes(I)
Site Selection Assistance: Yes
Lease Negotiation Assistance: Yes
Co-Operative Advertising: No
Franchisee Assoc./Member: Yes/No
Size Of Corporate Staff: 24
On-Going Support: C,D,E,F,G,H,I
Training: 5 Weeks Headquarters; 2 Weeks at Franchisee's Shop.

SPECIFIC EXPANSION PLANS:
US: MW, SW
Canada: No
Overseas: No

CERTIGARD (PETRO-CANADA)

2489 North Sheridan Way
Mississauga, ON L5K 1A8 CANADA
Tel: (800) 668-0220 (905) 804-4555
Fax: (905) 804-4595
E-Mail: bridger@petro-canada.ca
Web Site: www.certigard.com
Mr. Antonio Valencia, Director of Franchising

Petro-Canada is a major integrated oil and gasoline company in Canada. CERTIGARD is Petro-Canada's franchise organization of automotive repair/service outlets across Canada. In operation since 1987, the CERTIGARD franchisee network is supported by a team of dedicated, corporate specialists. The top sales performers now measure annual sales/bay in excess of $260,000. Competitive pricing; convenient locations; national warranties on repairs, lifetime on certain products.

BACKGROUND:
Established: 1975; 1st Franchised: 1987
Franchised Units: 156
Company-Owned Units: 0
Total Units: 156
Dist.: US-0; CAN-155; O'seas-0
North America: 9 Provinces
Density: 53 in ON, 30 in BC, 24 in AB
Projected New Units (12 Months): 6
Qualifications: 4, 5, 4, 3, 3, 4
Registered: AB

FINANCIAL/TERMS:
Cash Investment: $40-60K
Total Investment: $100-150K
Minimum Net Worth: $30K
Fees: Franchise - $20K
Royalty - 5%; Ad. - 2%
Earnings Claims Statement: No
Term of Contract (Years): 5/5
Avg. # Of Employees: 6 FT
Passive Ownership: Not Allowed
Encourage Conversions: Yes
Area Develop. Agreements: No
Sub-Franchising Contracts: No
Expand In Territory: Yes
Space Needs: 4,000 SF; FS
SUPPORT & TRAINING:
Financial Assistance Provided: No
Site Selection Assistance: Yes
Lease Negotiation Assistance: No
Co-Operative Advertising: Yes
Franchisee Assoc./Member: Yes/Yes
Size Of Corporate Staff: 25
On-Going Support: C,D,E,F,G,H,I
Training: 3 Days System Training at Local Classroom; 3 Days Automation Training (Class & On-Site).
SPECIFIC EXPANSION PLANS:
US: No
Canada: All Canada
Overseas: No

<< >>

CHAMPION AUTO STORES

2565 Kasota Ave.
St. Paul, MN 55108
Tel: (800) 899-6528 (651) 643-3809
Fax: (651) 855-0919
E-Mail: daveb@mwapd.com
Web Site: www.championauto.com
Mr. Dave Bock, VP of Associate Sales

CHAMPION AUTO STORES is a retailer of automotive parts and service to the do-it-yourself (DIY) and do-it-for-me (DIFM) customer. CHAMPION AUTO STORES provides state-of-the-art inventory control and mechandising programs, which maximize ownership investment in this turn-key business opportunity.

BACKGROUND:
Established: 1956; 1st Franchised: 1961
Franchised Units: 28
Company-Owned Units: 0
Total Units: 28
Dist.: US-28; CAN-0; O'seas-0
North America: 10 States
Density: 18 in MN, 4 in WI, 2 in NE
Projected New Units (12 Months): 10
Qualifications: 5, 4, 3, 3, 2, 4
Registered: NR
FINANCIAL/TERMS:
Cash Investment: $100-200K
Total Investment: $225-400K
Minimum Net Worth: $200K
Fees: Franchise - $0
Royalty - 0%; Ad. - 0%
Earnings Claims Statement: No
Term of Contract (Years): Negot.
Avg. # Of Employees: 4 FT, 5 PT
Passive Ownership: Discouraged
Encourage Conversions: Yes
Area Develop. Agreements: No
Sub-Franchising Contracts: No
Expand In Territory: Yes
Space Needs: 5,000-8,000 SF; FS, SF, SC
SUPPORT & TRAINING:
Financial Assistance Provided: Yes(I)
Site Selection Assistance: Yes
Lease Negotiation Assistance: Yes
Co-Operative Advertising: Yes
Franchisee Assoc./Member: Yes/No
Size Of Corporate Staff: 23
On-Going Support: a,B,C,D,E,f,G,H,I
Training: 2 Weeks On-Site in Owner's Location.
SPECIFIC EXPANSION PLANS:
US: MN, IA, ND, SD, NE, MT, WY, WI
Canada: No
Overseas: No

<< >>

CLUTCH DOCTORS

2701 NW Vaughn St., # 438
Portland, OR 97210
Tel: (888) 258-8248 (503) 525-5808
Fax: (503) 525-5812
E-Mail: bill@clutchdoctor.com
Web Site: www.clutchdoctor.com
Mr. Bill Nootenboom, Chief Executive Officer

CLUTCH DOCTORS is the leading, innovative automotive clutch and brake repair franchise, offering our exclusive QuoteBase clutch pricing software, state-of-the-art POS system, in-house book-keeping and nationally and internationally award-winning advertising program. We offer complete training for the franchisee and employees, site selection assistance and a proven profitable automotive repair facility.

BACKGROUND:
Established: 1995; 1st Franchised: 2000
Franchised Units: 9
Company-Owned Units: 2
Total Units: 11
Dist.: US-11; CAN-0; O'seas-0
North America: 2 States
Density: 6 in OR, 5 in WA
Projected New Units (12 Months): 6
Qualifications: 3, 2, 1, 2, 3, 5
Registered: CA,WA
FINANCIAL/TERMS:
Cash Investment: $10K
Total Investment: $60-130K
Minimum Net Worth: $100K
Fees: Franchise - $20K
Royalty - 8%; Ad. - 7%
Earnings Claims Statement: Yes
Term of Contract (Years): 5/5
Avg. # Of Employees: 3 FT
Passive Ownership: Not Allowed
Encourage Conversions: Yes
Area Develop. Agreements: No
Sub-Franchising Contracts: No
Expand In Territory: Yes
Space Needs: 2,000 SF; RM
SUPPORT & TRAINING:
Financial Assistance Provided: No
Site Selection Assistance: Yes
Lease Negotiation Assistance: Yes
Co-Operative Advertising: Yes
Franchisee Assoc./Member: No
Size Of Corporate Staff: 9
On-Going Support: a,C,D,E,F,G,H,I
Training: 3 Weeks in Portland, OR; 2 Weeks On-Site.
SPECIFIC EXPANSION PLANS:
US: Pacific NW
Canada: No
Overseas: No

<< >>

COLOR SEAL WAX NO MORE

P.O. Box 2302
Brandon, FL 33509-2302
Tel: (888) 801-0333 (813) 643-0320
Fax: (813) 689-7522
E-Mail: whb7337@aol.com
Web Site: www.colorsealusa.com
Mr. Bill Henry, Consultant

With the COLOR SEAL WAX NO MORE SYSTEM 2-step process, using orbital polishers, we remove over spray, oxidized cars, trucks, boats, planes, RVs and any other painted surface. The Teflon PTFE COLOR SEAL SEALANT provides a mirror gloss finish , which is guaranteed in writing for 1 or 5 years. We offer both a mobile and shop set up in an automotive complex. We also set up in parking garages. The COLOR SEAL Extractor will clean, sanitize and deodorize interiors.

We are not a multi-level.

BACKGROUND:
Established: 1954; 1st Franchised: 1998
Franchised Units: 373
Company-Owned Units: 0
Total Units: 373
Dist.: US-373; CAN-0; O'seas-0
North America: NR
Density: 37 in FL
Projected New Units (12 Months): 50
Qualifications: 3, 3, 3, 3, 3, 3
Registered: All States
FINANCIAL/TERMS:
Cash Investment: $20K
Total Investment: $20-25K
Minimum Net Worth: $25K
Fees: Franchise - $15
Royalty - 0%; Ad. - 0%
Earnings Claims Statement: Yes
Term of Contract (Years): 1/1
Avg. # Of Employees: 1 FT, 3 PT
Passive Ownership: Allowed
Encourage Conversions: NA
Area Develop. Agreements: Yes
Sub-Franchising Contracts: Yes
Expand In Territory: Yes
Space Needs: 1,500 SF; FS, SC
SUPPORT & TRAINING:
Financial Assistance Provided: No
Site Selection Assistance: Yes
Lease Negotiation Assistance: Yes
Co-Operative Advertising: No
Franchisee Assoc./Member: No
Size Of Corporate Staff: 3
On-Going Support: B,C,D,E,F,I
Training: 1 Week Franchisee's City; 1 Week with Master Licensee.
SPECIFIC EXPANSION PLANS:
US: All United States
Canada: All Canada
Overseas: All Countries

<< >>

COLORS ON PARADE
642 Century Cir.
Conway, SC 29526
Tel: (800) 726-5677 (843) 347-8818
Fax: (843) 347-0349
E-Mail: hemingwati@colorsfranchise.com
Web Site: www.colorsfranchise.com
Ms. Isha Hemingway, Franchises Sales/ Marketing

We use our patented and proprietary techniques to make minor auto body damage disappear. We perform our quick and economical services on-site for dealers and fleet operators. COLORS ON PARADE franchisees ranked number one in financial satisfaction in the Success Magazine Gold 100 Survey. Extensive training and support provided. Major metropolitan markets available.

BACKGROUND: IFA MEMBER
Established: 1988; 1st Franchised: 1991
Franchised Units: 267
Company-Owned Units: 10
Total Units: 277
Dist.: US-360; CAN-0; O'seas-0
North America: 26 States
Density: 35 in CA, 34 in FL, 18 in TX
Projected New Units (12 Months): 50
Qualifications: 3, 3, 2, 3, 5, 5
Registered: All States
FINANCIAL/TERMS:
Cash Investment: $7.5-75K
Total Investment: $50K+
Minimum Net Worth: $50-250K
Fees: Franchise - $5K
Royalty - Varies; Ad. - 0%
Earnings Claims Statement: No
Term of Contract (Years): 10/5
Avg. # Of Employees: 4 FT
Passive Ownership: Discouraged
Encourage Conversions: Yes
Area Develop. Agreements: Yes/10
Sub-Franchising Contracts: No
Expand In Territory: Yes
Space Needs: NA SF; NA
SUPPORT & TRAINING:
Financial Assistance Provided: Yes(I)
Site Selection Assistance: NA
Lease Negotiation Assistance: NA
Co-Operative Advertising: Yes
Franchisee Assoc./Member: Yes/No
Size Of Corporate Staff: 21
On-Going Support: A,B,C,D,F,G,H,I
Training: 2 Weeks Conway, SC.
SPECIFIC EXPANSION PLANS:
US: All United States
Canada: All Canada
Overseas: Mexico

<< >>

Cottman TRANSMISSION

Top 100

COTTMAN TRANSMISSION SYSTEMS
201 Gibraltar Rd., # 150
Horsham, PA 19044
Tel: (800) 394-6116 + 120 (215) 643-5885
Fax: (801) 640-7923
E-Mail: barry@cottman.com
Web Site: www.cottman.com
Mr. Barry Auchenbach, VP Franchise Development

Automotive service franchise with centers nationwide. A market leader with opportunities for solid growth. A highly supportive company that offers intensive training, outstanding advertising and on-site support. A forty-year reputation of treating customers with fairness, integrity and honesty. No automotive experience required.

BACKGROUND: IFA MEMBER
Established: 1962; 1st Franchised: 1964
Franchised Units: 411
Company-Owned Units: 5
Total Units: 416
Dist.: US-410; CAN-4; O'seas-2
North America: 43 States, 2 Provinces
Density: 48 in TX, 47 in PA, 22 in NJ
Projected New Units (12 Months): 60
Qualifications: 4, 4, 1, 2, 3, 3
Registered:CA,FL,IL,IN,MD,MI,MN,NY, OR,RI,SD,VA,WA,WI,DC,AB
FINANCIAL/TERMS:
Cash Investment: $60K
Total Investment: $165-180K
Minimum Net Worth: $150K
Fees: Franchise - $31.5K
Royalty - 7.5%; Ad. - $730/Wk.
Earnings Claims Statement: Yes
Term of Contract (Years): 15/15
Avg. # Of Employees: 3 FT
Passive Ownership: Not Allowed
Encourage Conversions: Yes
Area Develop. Agreements: Yes/4
Sub-Franchising Contracts: Yes
Expand In Territory: Yes
Space Needs: 3,000 SF; FS,SC,SC, Auto Mall
SUPPORT & TRAINING:
Financial Assistance Provided: Yes(I)
Site Selection Assistance: Yes
Lease Negotiation Assistance: Yes
Co-Operative Advertising: No
Franchisee Assoc./Member: No
Size Of Corporate Staff: 70
On-Going Support: C,D,E,F,G,H,I
Training: 3 Weeks Home Office; 1 Week Franchise Location.
SPECIFIC EXPANSION PLANS:
US: All United States
Canada: All Canada
Overseas: Open

<< >>

DENT DOCTOR

11301 W. Markham St.
Little Rock, AR 72211
Tel: (800) 946-3368 (501) 224-0500
Fax: (501) 224-0507
E-Mail: scook@dentdoctor.com
Web Site: www.dentdoctor.com
Mr. Skip Cook, Manager, Franchise Sales

DENT DOCTOR gives you a strategy to succeed. Earn extraordinary rewards removing minor dents, door dings and hail damage from vehicles without painting. Customers receive same day service. No automotive experience is required. You can operate from a retail shop along with providing mobile service.

BACKGROUND: IFA MEMBER
Established: 1988; 1st Franchised: 1990
Franchised Units: 34
Company-Owned Units: 4
Total Units: 38
Dist.: US-37; CAN-1; O'seas-0
North America: 24 States, 1 Province
Density: 5 in CO, 4 in TN, 3 in TX
Projected New Units (12 Months): 20
Qualifications: 4, 4, 2, 3, 4, 5
Registered: CA,FL,IL,IN,MI,NY,WA,WI

FINANCIAL/TERMS:
Cash Investment: $9.9-49.9K
Total Investment: $22.9-79.9K
Minimum Net Worth: $25K
Fees: Franchise - $9.9-22.8K
Royalty - 6%; Ad. - 0%
Earnings Claims Statement: No
Term of Contract (Years): 10/20
Avg. # Of Employees: 4 FT
Passive Ownership: Allowed
Encourage Conversions: Yes
Area Develop. Agreements: Yes/10
Sub-Franchising Contracts: No
Expand In Territory: Yes
Space Needs: 1,200 SF; FS, SF

SUPPORT & TRAINING:
Financial Assistance Provided: No
Site Selection Assistance: Yes
Lease Negotiation Assistance: Yes
Co-Operative Advertising: Yes
Franchisee Assoc./Member: No
Size Of Corporate Staff: 6
On-Going Support: B,C,E,G,H,I
Training: 4 Weeks Little Rock, AR; 1 Week Franchisee's Home Area (Optional).

SPECIFIC EXPANSION PLANS:
US: All United States
Canada: All Canada
Overseas: All Countries

<< >>

DRIVE 1

6951 Cintas Blvd.
Mason, OH 45040
Tel: (888) 801-8888 (513) 459-8188 + 207
Fax: (513) 459-3045
E-Mail: bbender@drive1.com
Web Site: www.drive1.com
Mr. Robert Bender, Vice President

DRIVE 1 is a growing network of used car dealers. DRIVE 1 provides many of the items you will need to get started, such as initial training program, operations manual, dealership specifications, business and financial planning, start-up materials and supplies. Our franchisees enjoy several exclusive programs, including vehicle acquisition and consumer financing options. Other benefits include a certified vehicle program and quarterly conference meetings.

BACKGROUND:
Established: 1987; 1st Franchised: 1988
Franchised Units: 8
Company-Owned Units: 0
Total Units: 8
Dist.: US-0; CAN-0; O'seas-0
North America: 7 States
Density: 2 in VA, 1 in AZ, 1 in GA
Projected New Units (12 Months):
Qualifications: NR
Registered: NR

FINANCIAL/TERMS:
Cash Investment: Varies
Total Investment: $47.1-806.9K
Minimum Net Worth: Varies
Fees: Franchise - $25K
Royalty - $50/Sold Unit; Ad. - $25/Unit
Earnings Claims Statement: Yes
Term of Contract (Years): 7
Avg. # Of Employees: 6 FT
Passive Ownership: Discouraged
Encourage Conversions: Yes
Area Develop. Agreements: No
Sub-Franchising Contracts: No
Expand In Territory: No
Space Needs: Varies SF; FS

SUPPORT & TRAINING:
Financial Assistance Provided: Yes
Site Selection Assistance: Yes
Lease Negotiation Assistance: Yes
Co-Operative Advertising: No
Franchisee Assoc./Member: No
Size Of Corporate Staff: 3
On-Going Support:
Training: 3 Days Mason, OH; 3 Days New Franchise Location.

SPECIFIC EXPANSION PLANS:
US: All United States
Canada: NR
Overseas: NR

<< >>

ECONO LUBE N' TUNE

4911 Birch St.
Newport Beach, CA 92660
Tel: (949) 851-2259
Fax: (714) 852-6688
E-Mail: davids@econolube.com
Web Site: www.econolube.com
Mr. Dave Schaefers, VP Franchise Development

Turn-key automotive service franchise. Lubrications, tune-ups, brake and other general services. Drive-through oil change

BACKGROUND:
Established: 1974; 1st Franchised: 1974
Franchised Units: 173
Company-Owned Units: 95
Total Units: 268
Dist.: US-281; CAN-0; O'seas-0
North America: NR
Density: NR
Projected New Units (12 Months): 10
Qualifications: 4, 4, 2, 4, 3, 5
Registered: CA,FL,VA,WA

FINANCIAL/TERMS:
Cash Investment: $50-100K
Total Investment: $200K
Minimum Net Worth: $300-500K
Fees: Franchise - $49.5K
Royalty - 5%/$500; Ad. - 5%/.5% Natl
Earnings Claims Statement: Yes
Term of Contract (Years): 15/5
Avg. # Of Employees: 6-7 FT
Passive Ownership: Discouraged
Encourage Conversions: NA
Area Develop. Agreements: No
Sub-Franchising Contracts: No
Expand In Territory: Yes
Space Needs: NR SF; NR

SUPPORT & TRAINING:
Financial Assistance Provided: Yes(D)
Site Selection Assistance: NA
Lease Negotiation Assistance: NR
Co-Operative Advertising: NR
Franchisee Assoc./Member: Yes/No
Size Of Corporate Staff: 100
On-Going Support: B,C,D,E,F,G,H,I
Training: 1 Week Ontario, CA; 1 Week Cypress, CA.

SPECIFIC EXPANSION PLANS:
US: East Coast, VA,NC,SC,GA
Canada: No
Overseas: No

<< >>

EXPRESS OIL CHANGE

190 W. Valley Ave.
Birmingham, AL 35209-3621
Tel: (888) 945-1771 (205) 945-1771
Fax: (205) 940-6026
E-Mail: kfeazell@expressoil.com
Web Site: www.expressoil.com
Mr. R. Kent Feazell, VP Franchise Development

We are among the top ten fast oil change chains in the world. Per unit, sales out-pace our competitors by over 40%. Attractive, state-of-the-art facilities offer expanded, highly profitable services in addition to our ten minute oil change. We also provide transmission service, air conditioning service, brake repair, tire rotation and balancing and miscellaneous light repairs... Most extensive training and franchise support in the industry.

BACKGROUND: IFA MEMBER
Established: 1979; 1st Franchised: 1986
Franchised Units: 130
Company-Owned Units: 13
Total Units: 143
Dist.: US-143; CAN-0; O'seas-0
North America: 5 States
Density: 62 in AL, 35 in GA, 6 in TN
Projected New Units (12 Months): 15
Qualifications: 5, 5, 1, 3, 3, 5
Registered: NR

FINANCIAL/TERMS:
Cash Investment: $115-249K
Total Investment: $130K-1.1MM
Minimum Net Worth: $450K
Fees: Franchise - $17.5K
Royalty - 5%; Ad. - 3%
Earnings Claims Statement: Yes
Term of Contract (Years): 10/10
Avg. # Of Employees: 7 FT
Passive Ownership: Allowed
Encourage Conversions: Yes
Area Develop. Agreements: Yes
Sub-Franchising Contracts: No
Expand In Territory: Yes
Space Needs: 22,000 SF; FS

SUPPORT & TRAINING:
Financial Assistance Provided: Yes(I)
Site Selection Assistance: Yes
Lease Negotiation Assistance: Yes
Co-Operative Advertising: Yes
Franchisee Assoc./Member: No
Size Of Corporate Staff: 37
On-Going Support: A,B,C,D,E,F,G,H,I
Training: 8 Weeks Closest Training Center; 1 Yr. On-Site, Post-OpeningTraining; Continuous Training.

SPECIFIC EXPANSION PLANS:
US: Southeast
Canada: No
Overseas: No

<< >>

GEARHEAD TRANSMISSIONS

3365 Silica Rd.
Sylvania, OH 43560
Tel: (877) 546-3330 (419) 841-6099
Fax: (419) 841-9158
E-Mail: sales@gearheadfranchise.com
Web Site: www.gearheadfranchise.com
Mr. Brian T. Zak, VP Franchise Development

GEARHEAD TRANSMISSIONS is the industry leader of remanufactured transmissions sales direct to the wholesale and consumer market. Our new transmission shop franchise opportunity is the most affordable start-up expense and the lowest operating cost in the $4.1 billion/year transmission service business. GEARHEAD provides a wide range of training and support, including financing support, customer support at our call center, product support at our remanufacturing facility, advertising support, etc.

BACKGROUND:
Established: 2001; 1st Franchised: 2004
Franchised Units: 1
Company-Owned Units: 0
Total Units: 1
Dist.: US-1; CAN-0; O'seas-0
North America: 1 State
Density: 1 in OH
Projected New Units (12 Months): 12
Qualifications: 2, 1, 1, 1, 1, 3
Registered: All States

FINANCIAL/TERMS:
Cash Investment: $10K
Total Investment: $47.5-57.3K
Minimum Net Worth: $15K
Fees: Franchise - $10K
Royalty - None; Ad. - $1,950/Mo.
Earnings Claims Statement: Yes
Term of Contract (Years): 10/5
Avg. # Of Employees: 1 FT, 0 PT
Passive Ownership: Allowed
Encourage Conversions: Yes
Area Develop. Agreements: No
Sub-Franchising Contracts: No
Expand In Territory: Yes
Space Needs: 2,500 SF; Ind./Manu.

SUPPORT & TRAINING:
Financial Assistance Provided: Yes(D)
Site Selection Assistance: Yes
Lease Negotiation Assistance: Yes
Co-Operative Advertising: Yes
Franchisee Assoc./Member: No
Size Of Corporate Staff: 12
On-Going Support: A,B,C,D,E,H,I
Training: 3 Weeks On-Site.

SPECIFIC EXPANSION PLANS:
US: All United States
Canada: No
Overseas: No

<< >>

GLASS DOCTOR

1020 N. University Parks Dr.
Waco, TX 76707
Tel: (800) 280-9858 (254) 745-2439
Fax: (800) 209-7621
E-Mail: gena.reid@dwyergroup.com
Web Site: www.glassdoctor.com
Mr. Mike Hawkins, VP Franchising

GLASS DOCTOR is an exclusive, worldwide glass replacement franchise organization. The bulk of our business is replacing auto windshields and tempered glass.

BACKGROUND: IFA MEMBER
Established: 1962; 1st Franchised: 1977
Franchised Units: 132
Company-Owned Units: 0
Total Units: 132
Dist.: US-131; CAN-1; O'seas-0
North America: 27 States, 1 Province
Density: NR
Projected New Units (12 Months): 36
Qualifications: 3, 4, 2, 3, 3, 5
Registered: All States

FINANCIAL/TERMS:
Cash Investment: $50-100K
Total Investment: $107.6-259.6K
Minimum Net Worth: Varies
Fees: Franchise - $19.9K/100KPop
Royalty - 4-7%; Ad. - 2%
Earnings Claims Statement: Yes

Term of Contract (Years): 10/10
Avg. # Of Employees: 4 FT
Passive Ownership: NR
Encourage Conversions: Yes
Area Develop. Agreements: NR
Sub-Franchising Contracts: No
Expand In Territory: Yes
Space Needs: 1,500 SF; NR

SUPPORT & TRAINING:
Financial Assistance Provided: Yes
Site Selection Assistance: No
Lease Negotiation Assistance: No
Co-Operative Advertising: NR
Franchisee Assoc./Member: No
Size Of Corporate Staff: 25
On-Going Support: C,D,E,F,G,H,I
Training: 1 Week in Headquarters in Waco, TX.

SPECIFIC EXPANSION PLANS:
US: All United States
Canada: All Canada
Overseas: No

<< >>

GREASE MONKEY INTERNATIONAL

633 17th St., # 400
Denver, CO 80202
Tel: (800) 364-0352 (303) 308-1660
Fax: (303) 308-5908
E-Mail: mikeb@greasemonkeyintl.com
Web Site: www.greasemonkeyintl.com
Mr. Michael J. Brunetti, VP Franchise Sales/Dev.

GREASE MONKEY Centers provide convenient vehicle preventive maintenance services. We provide comprehensive technical training for all franchisees, including instruction performing all GREASE MONKEY approved services thoroughly and safely. You will also learn basic accounting, computer marketing and customer satisfaction techniques to help you operate your business.

BACKGROUND:
Established: 1978; 1st Franchised: 1979
Franchised Units: 186
Company-Owned Units: 44
Total Units: 230
Dist.: US-183; CAN-0; O'seas-34
North America: 28 States
Density: 57 in CO, 14 in CA, 13 in WA
Projected New Units (12 Months): 20
Qualifications: 5, 4, 2, 2, 3, 5
Registered: All States Except HI,SD

FINANCIAL/TERMS:
Cash Investment: $120-220K
Total Investment: $300K
Minimum Net Worth: $300K
Fees: Franchise - $28K
Royalty - 5%; Ad. - 6%
Earnings Claims Statement: Yes
Term of Contract (Years): 15/15
Avg. # Of Employees: 3 FT, 3 PT
Passive Ownership: Discouraged
Encourage Conversions: Yes
Area Develop. Agreements: Yes/Negot.
Sub-Franchising Contracts: No
Expand In Territory: Yes
Space Needs: 1,800 SF; FS, SC

SUPPORT & TRAINING:
Financial Assistance Provided: Yes(I)
Site Selection Assistance: Yes
Lease Negotiation Assistance: Yes
Co-Operative Advertising: Yes
Franchisee Assoc./Member: Yes
Size Of Corporate Staff: 45
On-Going Support: A,B,C,D,E,F,G,H,I
Training: 1 Week Corporate Headquarters, Denver, CO; 1 Week Market Center.

SPECIFIC EXPANSION PLANS:
US: All United States
Canada: No
Overseas: Mexico

<< >>

LEE MYLES TRANSMISSIONS AUTOCARE

650 From Rd., S. Lobby, 4th Fl.
Paramus, NJ 07652
Tel: (800) 251-8250
Fax: (480) 502-0404
E-Mail: info@leemyles.com
Web Site: www.leemyles.com
Mr. Mark Savel, Dir. Natl. Franchise Develop.

We offer and support franchises for LEE MYLES TRANSMISSIONS businesses that provide servicing, repair and replacements of standard and automatic transmission, as well as preventative maintenance and specialty general automotive repair and related services and products.

BACKGROUND:
Established: 1947; 1st Franchised: 1964
Franchised Units: 106
Company-Owned Units: 0
Total Units: 106
Dist.: US-106; CAN-0; O'seas-0
North America: 19 States
Density: 26 in NY, 14 in AZ, 13 in NJ
Projected New Units (12 Months): 10
Qualifications: 4, 4, 4, 5, 5, 5
Registered: CA,FL,MD,NY,OR,RI,VA, WA,DC

FINANCIAL/TERMS:
Cash Investment: $70-90K
Total Investment: $122-175K
Minimum Net Worth: $200K
Fees: Franchise - $27.5K
Royalty - 7%; Ad. - 5-10%
Earnings Claims Statement: Yes
Term of Contract (Years): 15/15
Avg. # Of Employees: 4 FT
Passive Ownership: Not Allowed
Encourage Conversions: Yes
Area Develop. Agreements: Yes/15
Sub-Franchising Contracts: No
Expand In Territory: Yes
Space Needs: 2,500 - 3,000 SF; FS, SC, Auto Mall

SUPPORT & TRAINING:
Financial Assistance Provided: NA
Site Selection Assistance: Yes
Lease Negotiation Assistance: Yes
Co-Operative Advertising: Yes
Franchisee Assoc./Member: No
Size Of Corporate Staff: 15
On-Going Support: C,D,E,G,H,I
Training: 1-2 Weeks Corporate Office; 1 Week In-Store Training.

SPECIFIC EXPANSION PLANS:
US: All US Exc. AK and HI
Canada: All Canada
Overseas: No

<< >>

LENTZ USA SERVICE CENTERS

1001 Riverview Dr.
Kalamazoo, MI 49048
Tel: (800) 354-2131 (269) 342-2200
Fax: (269) 342-9461
E-Mail: quietcar@LENTZusa.com
Web Site: www.lentzusa.com
Mr. Gary R. Thomas, Franchise Liaison

Vehicle repair service centers. Brakes, mufflers, steering systems and more.

BACKGROUND: IFA MEMBER
Established: 1972; 1st Franchised: 1989
Franchised Units: 12
Company-Owned Units: 11
Total Units: 23

Dist.: US-23; CAN-0; O'seas-0
North America: 2 States
Density: 21 in MI, 2 in FL
Projected New Units (12 Months): 6
Qualifications: 4, 3, 1, 3, 4, 5
Registered: FL,IN,MI

FINANCIAL/TERMS:
Cash Investment: $35-70K
Total Investment: $112-120K
Minimum Net Worth: $100K
Fees: Franchise - $20K
Royalty - 0-7%; Ad. - 0%
Earnings Claims Statement: No
Term of Contract (Years): 10/10
Avg. # Of Employees: 3-5 FT
Passive Ownership: Discouraged
Encourage Conversions: Yes
Area Develop. Agreements: Yes/10
Sub-Franchising Contracts: No
Expand In Territory: Yes
Space Needs: 3,600 SF; FS, SC

SUPPORT & TRAINING:
Financial Assistance Provided: Yes(I)
Site Selection Assistance: Yes
Lease Negotiation Assistance: Yes
Co-Operative Advertising: No
Franchisee Assoc./Member: No
Size Of Corporate Staff: 10
On-Going Support: B,C,D,E,F,G,I
Training: 2 Weeks Kalamazoo, MI; 1 Week Franchise Site.

SPECIFIC EXPANSION PLANS:
US: All United States
Canada: All Canada
Overseas: Middle East, India, Europe

≺≺ ≻≻

LINE-X SPRAY-ON TRUCK BEDLINERS

2400 S. Garnsey St.
Santa Ana, CA 92707
Tel: (800) 831-3232 (714) 850-1662
Fax: (714) 850-8759
E-Mail: sales@linexcorp.com
Web Site: www.goline-x.com
Mr. J. B. Burtin, President

A LINE-X franchisee operates a retail/industrial location that applies sprayed on coatings. LINE-X has a number of applications from flooring to industrial applications. LINE-X is in a growing, new and unsaturated market with extraordinary opportunities for minority entrepreneurs.

BACKGROUND:
Established: 1993; 1st Franchised: 1998
Franchised Units: 108
Company-Owned Units: 0
Total Units: 108
Dist.: US-334; CAN-0; O'seas-27
North America: 50 States
Density: 20 in CA, 15 in WA, 10 in GA
Projected New Units (12 Months): NR
Qualifications: , , , , ,
Registered: All States

FINANCIAL/TERMS:
Cash Investment: $25K
Total Investment: $68-147K
Minimum Net Worth: $20K
Fees: Franchise - $20K
Royalty - 0%; Ad. - 1.5%
Earnings Claims Statement: No
Term of Contract (Years): 5/15
Avg. # Of Employees: 2 FT
Passive Ownership: Discouraged
Encourage Conversions: NR
Area Develop. Agreements: Yes
Sub-Franchising Contracts: Yes
Expand In Territory: Yes
Space Needs: 2,500 SF; Industrial/Commercial

SUPPORT & TRAINING:
Financial Assistance Provided: NR
Site Selection Assistance: Yes
Lease Negotiation Assistance: Yes
Co-Operative Advertising: No
Franchisee Assoc./Member: No
Size Of Corporate Staff: 14
On-Going Support: C,D,E,G,H,I
Training: Up to 5 Days at Our Location; up to 7 Days at Franchisee's Location.

SPECIFIC EXPANSION PLANS:
US: All United States
Canada: All Canada
Overseas: All Countries

≺≺ ≻≻

LUBEPRO'S INTERNATIONAL, INC.

1630 Colonial Pkwy.
Inverness, IL 60067
Tel: (800) 654-5823 (847) 776-2500
Fax: (847) 776-2542
E-Mail: michelled@lubepros.com
Web Site: www.lubepros.com

Our building design, our training program and our unique approach to marketing truly set us ahead of our competitors.

BACKGROUND:
Established: 1978; 1st Franchised: 1985
Franchised Units: 22
Company-Owned Units: 14
Total Units: 36
Dist.: US-36; CAN-0; O'seas-0
North America: 4 States
Density: 28 in IL, 6 in WI
Projected New Units (12 Months): 4
Qualifications: 4, 3, 1, 2, 2, 4
Registered: IL,IN,MN,WI

FINANCIAL/TERMS:
Cash Investment: $100K
Total Investment: $170-200K
Minimum Net Worth: $300K
Fees: Franchise - $25K
Royalty - 5%; Ad. - 5%
Earnings Claims Statement: No
Term of Contract (Years): 20/10/10
Avg. # Of Employees: 6 FT
Passive Ownership: Allowed
Encourage Conversions: NA
Area Develop. Agreements: No
Sub-Franchising Contracts: No
Expand In Territory: Yes
Space Needs: 1,800 SF; FS

SUPPORT & TRAINING:
Financial Assistance Provided: No
Site Selection Assistance: Yes
Lease Negotiation Assistance: No
Co-Operative Advertising: Yes
Franchisee Assoc./Member: No
Size Of Corporate Staff: 7
On-Going Support: C,D,E,G,H,I
Training: 10 Days Rockford, IL.

SPECIFIC EXPANSION PLANS:
US: Central, North Central
Canada: No
Overseas: No

≺≺ ≻≻

MAACO AUTO PAINTING & BODYWORKS

381 Brooks Rd.
King of Prussia, PA 19406-3169
Tel: (800) 296-2226 (610) 265-6606
Fax: (610) 337-6176
E-Mail: bberman@maaco.com
Web Site: www.maaco.com
Mr. Bob E. Berman, VP Franchise Development

MAACO has developed a system relating to the establishment and operation of centers specializing in auto painting and body repair. The system includes market analysis, research and development, sales and merchandising methods, training, record keeping, advertising and business management, all of which are constantly being improved, up-dated and further developed by a fully staffed and knowledgeable corporate structure to service its owners.

BACKGROUND: IFA MEMBER
Established: 1972; 1st Franchised: 1972

Franchised Units: 456
Company-Owned Units: 0
Total Units: 456
Dist.: US-510; CAN-42; O'seas-4
North America: 47 States, 7 Provinces
Density: 42 in CA, 26 in NJ, 21 in PA
Projected New Units (12 Months): 50
Qualifications: 3, 3, 1, 1, 3, 5
Registered: All States

FINANCIAL/TERMS:
Cash Investment: $60K
Total Investment: $249K
Minimum Net Worth: $250K
Fees: Franchise - $30K
Royalty - 8%; Ad. - $850/Wk.
Earnings Claims Statement: No
Term of Contract (Years): 15/5
Avg. # Of Employees: 10 FT
Passive Ownership: Not Allowed
Encourage Conversions: No
Area Develop. Agreements: No
Sub-Franchising Contracts: No
Expand In Territory: Yes
Space Needs: 7,500-10,000 SF; FS

SUPPORT & TRAINING:
Financial Assistance Provided: Yes(I)
Site Selection Assistance: Yes
Lease Negotiation Assistance: Yes
Co-Operative Advertising: Yes
Franchisee Assoc./Member: No
Size Of Corporate Staff: 125
On-Going Support: A,B,C,D,E,F,G,H,I
Training: 4 Weeks King of Prussia, PA; 3 Weeks On-Site.

SPECIFIC EXPANSION PLANS:
US: All United States
Canada: All Canada
Overseas: No

<< >>

MAACO AUTO PAINTING & BODYWORKS (CANADA)

10 Kingsbridge Garden Cir., # 501
Mississauga, ON L5R 3K6 CANADA
Tel: (800) 387-6780 (905) 501-1212
Fax: (905) 501-1218
E-Mail: hdelisle@maaco.com
Web Site: www.maaco.com
Mr. Hermann Delisle, Mgr. Franchise Development

Production car painting and bodyworks center.

BACKGROUND:
Established: 1972; 1st Franchised: 1972
Franchised Units: 560
Company-Owned Units: 0
Total Units: 560
Dist.: US-515; CAN-45; O'seas-0
North America: 47 States, 7 Provinces
Density: 18 in ON, 7 in AB, 6 in BC
Projected New Units (12 Months): 6-8
Qualifications: 4, 4, 1, 3, 3, 3
Registered: All States and AB

FINANCIAL/TERMS:
Cash Investment: $80K
Total Investment: $240K
Minimum Net Worth: NR
Fees: Franchise - $25K
Royalty - 8%; Ad. - $700/Wk.
Earnings Claims Statement: No
Term of Contract (Years): 15/5
Avg. # Of Employees: 8 FT
Passive Ownership: Not Allowed
Encourage Conversions: Yes
Area Develop. Agreements: NR
Sub-Franchising Contracts: Yes
Expand In Territory: Yes
Space Needs: 8,000 SF; FS, SF, SC

SUPPORT & TRAINING:
Financial Assistance Provided: NA
Site Selection Assistance: Yes
Lease Negotiation Assistance: Yes
Co-Operative Advertising: Yes
Franchisee Assoc./Member: No
Size Of Corporate Staff: 10
On-Going Support: A,B,C,D,E,F,G,H,I
Training: 3 Weeks in King of Prussia, PA; 2 Weeks On-Site.

SPECIFIC EXPANSION PLANS:
US: No
Canada: All Canada
Overseas: No

<< >>

MASTER MECHANIC, THE

1989 Dundas St. E.
Mississauga, ON L4X 1M1 CANADA
Tel: (800) 383-8523 (905) 629-3773
Fax: (905) 629-3864
E-Mail: andrew@mastermechanic.ca
Web Site: www.mastermechanic.ca
Mr. Andrew Wanie, President

General auto repair and emission testing center, with a reputation in high-tech automotive excellence that provides to its customers the convenience of one-stop shopping for all of their automotive maintenance and repair needs.

BACKGROUND:
Established: 1979; 1st Franchised: 1983
Franchised Units: 35
Company-Owned Units: 1
Total Units: 36
Dist.: US-0; CAN-36; O'seas-0
North America: 1 Province
Density: 36 in ON
Projected New Units (12 Months): 4
Qualifications: 4, 3, 4, 3, 4, 5
Registered: NR

FINANCIAL/TERMS:
Cash Investment: $60-80K
Total Investment: $125-175K
Minimum Net Worth: $200K
Fees: Franchise - $25K
Royalty - 6%; Ad. - 3% (Varies)
Earnings Claims Statement: Yes
Term of Contract (Years): 20/Open
Avg. # Of Employees: 3-5 FT, 1-2 PT
Passive Ownership: Discouraged
Encourage Conversions: Yes
Area Develop. Agreements: Yes/20
Sub-Franchising Contracts: Yes
Expand In Territory: Yes
Space Needs: 4,000 SF; FS, SF, SC, RM

SUPPORT & TRAINING:
Financial Assistance Provided: Yes(I)
Site Selection Assistance: Yes
Lease Negotiation Assistance: Yes
Co-Operative Advertising: Yes
Franchisee Assoc./Member: Yes/Yes
Size Of Corporate Staff: 5
On-Going Support: a,B,C,D,E,F,G,H,I
Training: 1 Week Classroom; 4 Weeks Training Shop; On-Going -- 2 Weeks/Yr. On-Site.

SPECIFIC EXPANSION PLANS:
US: No
Canada: ON
Overseas: No

<< >>

meineke® car care center

Top 100

MEINEKE CAR CARE CENTERS

128 S. Tryon St., # 900
Charlotte, NC 28202-5001
Tel: (800) 275-5200 (704) 377-8855
Fax: (704) 372-4826
E-Mail: franchise.info@meineke.com
Web Site: www.ownameineke.com
Ms. Sharon Johnson, Franchise Sales Coordinator

MEINEKE has been offering superior automotive repair services at discount prices for over 30 years. We are a nationally-recognized brand with a proven system. Brand recognition, comprehensive training and on-going technical and operational support are some of the benefits enjoyed by MEINEKE franchisees.

BACKGROUND: IFA MEMBER
Established: 1972; 1st Franchised: 1973
Franchised Units: 883
Company-Owned Units: 1
Total Units: 884
Dist.: US-841; CAN-22; O'seas-21
North America: 49 States, 5 Provinces
Density: 73 in NY, 73 in PA, 55 in TX
Projected New Units (12 Months): 65
Qualifications: 4, 3, 3, 2, 2, 5
Registered: All States

FINANCIAL/TERMS:
Cash Investment: $50K
Total Investment: $180-365K
Minimum Net Worth: $150K
Fees: Franchise - $30K
Royalty - 3-7%; Ad. - 8%
Earnings Claims Statement: Yes
Term of Contract (Years): 15/15
Avg. # Of Employees: 4 FT
Passive Ownership: Not Allowed
Encourage Conversions: Yes
Area Develop. Agreements: Yes/Varies
Sub-Franchising Contracts: No
Expand In Territory: Yes
Space Needs: 2,880-3,880 SF; FS

SUPPORT & TRAINING:
Financial Assistance Provided: Yes(I)
Site Selection Assistance: Yes
Lease Negotiation Assistance: No
Co-Operative Advertising: Yes
Franchisee Assoc./Member: Yes/Yes
Size Of Corporate Staff: 88
On-Going Support: A,B,C,D,G,h,I
Training: 4 Weeks Charlotte, NC.

SPECIFIC EXPANSION PLANS:
US: All United States
Canada: All Canada
Overseas: All Countries

<< >>

MERLIN

1 N. River Ln., # 206
Geneva, IL 60134-2267
Tel: (800) 652-9900 + 124 (630) 208-9900
Fax: (630) 208-8601
E-Mail: mhameister@merlins.com
Web Site: www.merlins.com
Mr. Mark M. Hameister, Dir. Franchise Development

MERLIN is an upscale automotive service chain with one of the highest average sales per shop statistics in the industry. MERLIN specializes in brakes, exhaust, suspension, oil/lubrication, air conditioning, tires and related services. Marketing is based on long-term employee and customer relationships. Candidates must have significant employee management and retail/sales experience. Automotive experience is helpful. Special equity assistance is available with various programs and prospective candidates.

BACKGROUND: IFA MEMBER
Established: 1975; 1st Franchised: 1975
Franchised Units: 63
Company-Owned Units: 7
Total Units: 70
Dist.: US-65; CAN-0; O'seas-0
North America: 6 States
Density: 50 in IL, 7 in TX, 5 in GA
Projected New Units (12 Months): 6
Qualifications: 3, 5, 4, 3, 4, 5
Registered: IL,IN,MI,WI

FINANCIAL/TERMS:
Cash Investment: $20-50K
Total Investment: $185-210K
Minimum Net Worth: $75K
Fees: Franchise - $26-30K
Royalty - 6.9%; Ad. - 5%
Earnings Claims Statement: Yes
Term of Contract (Years): 20/20
Avg. # Of Employees: 3-4 FT, 1 PT
Passive Ownership: Not Allowed
Encourage Conversions: Yes
Area Develop. Agreements: No
Sub-Franchising Contracts: No
Expand In Territory: Yes
Space Needs:3,850 SF; FS, SC, RM, Other Center

SUPPORT & TRAINING:
Financial Assistance Provided: Yes(I)
Site Selection Assistance: Yes
Lease Negotiation Assistance: Yes
Co-Operative Advertising: Yes
Franchisee Assoc./Member: No
Size Of Corporate Staff: 20
On-Going Support: B,C,D,E,F,G,H,I
Training: 6 Weeks Corporate Headquarters; in Shop as Needed.

SPECIFIC EXPANSION PLANS:
US: IL, MI, GA, TX, WI, IN
Canada: No
Overseas: No

<< >>

Top 100

MIDAS

1300 Arlington Heights Rd.
Itasca, IL 60143-3174
Tel: (800) 621-0144 (630) 438-3000
Fax: (630) 438-3700
E-Mail: bkorus@midas.com
Web Site: www.midasfran.com
Ms. Barbara Korus, Franchise Recruitment Coord.

MIDAS is one of the world's largest providers of automotive service, offering exhaust, brake, steering and suspension services, as well as batteries, climate control and maintenance services at 2,700 franchised, company-owned and licensed MIDAS shops in 19 countries, including nearly 2,000 in the United States and Canada.

BACKGROUND: IFA MEMBER
Established: 1956; 1st Franchised: 1956
Franchised Units: 2,571
Company-Owned Units: 73
Total Units: 2,644
Dist.: US-1,628; CAN-220; O'seas-796
North America: NR
Density: NR
Projected New Units (12 Months): 40
Qualifications: 4, 4, 2, 2, 3, 5
Registered: All States

FINANCIAL/TERMS:
Cash Investment: $100-150K
Total Investment: $360-487K
Minimum Net Worth: $300K
Fees: Franchise - $20K
Royalty - 10%; Ad. - Incl. Roy.
Earnings Claims Statement: No
Term of Contract (Years): 20/20
Avg. # Of Employees: 6 FT, 4 PT
Passive Ownership: Discouraged
Encourage Conversions: Yes
Area Develop. Agreements: Varies
Sub-Franchising Contracts: No
Expand In Territory: Yes
Space Needs: 4,000-5,000 SF; FS

SUPPORT & TRAINING:
Financial Assistance Provided: Yes(I)
Site Selection Assistance: Yes
Lease Negotiation Assistance: Yes
Co-Operative Advertising: Yes
Franchisee Assoc./Member: Yes/Yes
Size Of Corporate Staff: NR
On-Going Support: B,C,D,e,f,G,H,I
Training: 1-2 Weeks of Self Study; 1-2 Weeks In-Shop Assignment; 3 Weeks in Palatine, IL.

SPECIFIC EXPANSION PLANS:
US: All United States
Canada: All Canada
Overseas: Select Countries

<< >>

MIGHTY DISTRIBUTING SYSTEM OF AMERICA
650 Engineering Dr.
Norcross, GA 30092-2821
Tel: (800) 829-3900 (770) 448-3900
Fax: (770) 446-8627
E-Mail: barry.teagle@mightyautoparts.com
Web Site: www.mightyfranchise.com
Mr. Barry Teagle, Vice President Franchising

Wholesale distribution of original equipment-quality, MIGHTY-branded auto parts. Franchisees operate in exclusive territories, supplying automotive maintenance and repair facilities with under-car and under-hood products, such as filters, belts, tune-up and brake parts.

BACKGROUND: IFA MEMBER
Established: 1963; 1st Franchised: 1970
Franchised Units: 117
Company-Owned Units: 5
Total Units: 122
Dist.: US-147; CAN-0; O'seas-0
North America: 45 States
Density: 12 in PA, 10 in FL, 9 in CA
Projected New Units (12 Months): 12
Qualifications: 5, 4, 3, 3, 3, 4
Registered: CA,FL,HI,IL,IN,MD,MI,MN, NY,ND,OR,RI,SD,VA,WA,WI

FINANCIAL/TERMS:
Cash Investment: $70-80K
Total Investment: $100K
Minimum Net Worth: $500K
Fees: Franchise - $5K+ $.035/Vcl
Royalty - 5%; Ad. - 0.5%
Earnings Claims Statement: Yes
Term of Contract (Years): 10
Avg. # Of Employees: 4 FT
Passive Ownership: Not Allowed
Encourage Conversions: Yes
Area Develop. Agreements: No
Sub-Franchising Contracts: No
Expand In Territory: NA
Space Needs: 2,500 SF; Warehouse

SUPPORT & TRAINING:
Financial Assistance Provided: Yes(I)
Site Selection Assistance: No
Lease Negotiation Assistance: No
Co-Operative Advertising: Yes
Franchisee Assoc./Member: Yes/No
Size Of Corporate Staff: 50
On-Going Support: C,D,F,G,h
Training: 1 Week Home Office; 1 Week On-the-Job Training.

SPECIFIC EXPANSION PLANS:
US: All United States
Canada: All Canada
Overseas: No

<< >>

MINUTE MUFFLER AND BRAKE
1600 - 3rd Ave. S.
Lethbridge, AB T1J 0L2 CANADA
Tel: (888) 646-6833 (403) 329-1020
Fax: (403) 328-9030
E-Mail: minmuff@agt.net
Web Site: www.minutemuffler.com
Mr. Leon Tokarski, VP Sales/Marketing

Retail exhaust, brake, suspension outlets with 0% royalty, 0% advertising fee. Your 65-70% average gross profit goes in your pocket, not ours. Unsurpassed support systems by actual store owner/operators. Service is our business!!

BACKGROUND:
Established: 1969; 1st Franchised: 1977
Franchised Units: 120
Company-Owned Units: 1
Total Units: 121
Dist.: US-0; CAN-119; O'seas-2
North America: NR
Density: 25 in BC, 24 in AB, 18 in ON
Projected New Units (12 Months): 12
Qualifications: 4, 3, 2, 3, 3, 5
Registered: AB

FINANCIAL/TERMS:
Cash Investment: $50-100K
Total Investment: $150-250K
Minimum Net Worth: $75-100K
Fees: Franchise - $0-25K
Royalty - 0%; Ad. - 0%
Earnings Claims Statement: No
Term of Contract (Years): On-Going
Avg. # Of Employees: 3-5 FT, 1 PT
Passive Ownership: Discouraged
Encourage Conversions: Yes
Area Develop. Agreements: No
Sub-Franchising Contracts: Yes
Expand In Territory: Yes
Space Needs: 3,200-3,500 SF; FS

SUPPORT & TRAINING:
Financial Assistance Provided: No
Site Selection Assistance: Yes
Lease Negotiation Assistance: Yes
Co-Operative Advertising: NA
Franchisee Assoc./Member: No
Size Of Corporate Staff: 13
On-Going Support: B,C,D,e,F,G,h,I
Training: 1-10 Weeks Head Office; 1-2 Weeks On-Site.

SPECIFIC EXPANSION PLANS:
US: No
Canada: All Canada
Overseas: Carribean, South/Central America, Europe

<< >>

MIRACLE AUTO PAINTING & BODY REPAIR
3157 Corporate Pl.
Hayward, CA 94545-6834
Tel: (877) 647-2253 (510) 887-2211
Fax: (510) 887-3092
E-Mail: jim@miracleautopainting.com
Web Site: www.miracleautopainting.com
Mr. Jim Jordan, Vice President

MIRACLE is a production collision repair and refinishing company that specializes in complete paint jobs. MIRACLE caters to individual vehicle owners, insurance carriers, other body shop facilities and new and used automobile dealers.

BACKGROUND: IFA MEMBER
Established: 1953; 1st Franchised: 1964
Franchised Units: 26
Company-Owned Units: 3
Total Units: 29
Dist.: US-29; CAN-0; O'seas-0
North America: 4 States
Density: 23 in CA, 5 in TX, 1 in AZ
Projected New Units (12 Months): 1
Qualifications: 3, 3, 3, 1, 2, 5
Registered: CA,OR,WA

FINANCIAL/TERMS:
Cash Investment: $75-100K
Total Investment: $215-275K
Minimum Net Worth: $400K
Fees: Franchise - $35K

Royalty - 5%; Ad. - 5%
Earnings Claims Statement: No
Term of Contract (Years): 10/10
Avg. # Of Employees: 10 FT, 2 PT
Passive Ownership: Discouraged
Encourage Conversions: Yes
Area Develop. Agreements: Yes/5
Sub-Franchising Contracts: Yes
Expand In Territory: Yes
Space Needs: 9,000-11,000 SF; FS, SF

SUPPORT & TRAINING:
Financial Assistance Provided: Yes(I)
Site Selection Assistance: Yes
Lease Negotiation Assistance: Yes
Co-Operative Advertising: No
Franchisee Assoc./Member: Yes/Yes
Size Of Corporate Staff: 20
On-Going Support: B,C,D,E,G,H
Training: 10 Days Headquarters; 10 Days On-Site.

SPECIFIC EXPANSION PLANS:
US: West, Southwest
Canada: No
Overseas: No

MISTER TRANSMISSION (INTERNATIONAL) LIMITED

9675 Yonge St.
Richmond Hill, ON L4C 1V7 CANADA
Tel: (800) 373-8432 (905) 884-1511
Fax: (905) 884-4727
E-Mail: info@mistertransmission.com
Web Site: www.MisterTransmission.com
Mr. Randall Moore, Franchise Director

With over 30 years' experience, MISTER TRANSMISSION is the established name for transmission repair service in Canada. We make sales, training, advertising, a computer program, national fleet accounts, site selection and a warranty program available to all franchisees. MISTER TRANSMISSION is Canadian-owned.

BACKGROUND:
Established: 1963; 1st Franchised: 1969
Franchised Units: 89
Company-Owned Units: 0
Total Units: 89
Dist.: US-0; CAN-89; O'seas-0
North America: 7 Provinces
Density: 63 in ON, 14 in BC, 3 in PQ
Projected New Units (12 Months): 3
Qualifications: 3, 3, 3, 2, 3, 4
Registered: NR

FINANCIAL/TERMS:
Cash Investment: $60-80K
Total Investment: $125-150K
Minimum Net Worth: $300K
Fees: Franchise - $25K
Royalty - 7%; Ad. - Varies
Earnings Claims Statement: No
Term of Contract (Years): 10/10
Avg. # Of Employees: 5 FT
Passive Ownership: Discouraged
Encourage Conversions: Yes
Area Develop. Agreements: No
Sub-Franchising Contracts: No
Expand In Territory: NR
Space Needs: 2,800 SF; FS, SC

SUPPORT & TRAINING:
Financial Assistance Provided: No
Site Selection Assistance: Yes
Lease Negotiation Assistance: Yes
Co-Operative Advertising: NA
Franchisee Assoc./Member: Yes/Yes
Size Of Corporate Staff: 12
On-Going Support: C,D,E,G,H,I
Training: 1 Week Head Office.

SPECIFIC EXPANSION PLANS:
US: No
Canada: All Canada
Overseas: No

NOVUS AUTO GLASS

10425 Hampshire Ave., S.
Minneapolis, MN 55438-2176
Tel: (800) 944-6811 (952) 946-0447
Fax: (922) 946-0481
E-Mail: michaelv@novusglass.com
Web Site: www.novusglass.com
Mr. Michael Vogel, Director Franchise Development

NOVUS invented windshield repair.

BACKGROUND: IFA MEMBER
Established: 1972; 1st Franchised: 1985
Franchised Units: 2,200
Company-Owned Units: 6
Total Units: 2,206
Dist.: US-454; CAN-46; O'seas-1,620
North America: 50 States, 8 Provinces
Density: 48 in WA, 24 in MN, 20 in KS
Projected New Units (12 Months): 8
Qualifications: 5, 3, 1, 3, 3, 5
Registered: All States

FINANCIAL/TERMS:
Cash Investment: $9.3-42.3K
Total Investment: $37.0-169.1K
Minimum Net Worth: $50K
Fees: Franchise - $7.5K
Royalty - 7-8%; Ad. - 0%
Earnings Claims Statement: No
Term of Contract (Years): 10
Avg. # Of Employees: 2 FT, 2 PT
Passive Ownership: NR
Encourage Conversions: Yes
Area Develop. Agreements: Yes/10
Sub-Franchising Contracts: No
Expand In Territory: NR
Space Needs: 3,000 SF; FS, SF, SC, RM, HB

SUPPORT & TRAINING:
Financial Assistance Provided: No
Site Selection Assistance: Yes
Lease Negotiation Assistance: No
Co-Operative Advertising: No
Franchisee Assoc./Member: Yes
Size Of Corporate Staff: 31
On-Going Support: B,D,E,G,H,I
Training: 7.5 Days Windshield Repair Minneapolis; 10 Days Replacement at Regional Training Center.

SPECIFIC EXPANSION PLANS:
US: All United States
Canada: All Canada
Overseas: All Countries

OIL BUTLER INTERNATIONAL

1599 Rte. 22 W.
Union, NJ 07083
Tel: (888) 428-8537 (908) 687-3283
Fax: (908) 687-7617
E-Mail: info@oilbutlerinternational.com
Web Site: www.oilbutlerinternational.com
Mr. Pete Rosin, VP Franchise Development

OIL BUTLER INTERNATIONAL is a mobile oil-change service and windshield repair franchise combining two money-making opportunities in one. Our uniquely designed vehicle provides the corporate image and service your customers will expect from the leader in the field of on-site service. Low-investment, low-overhead, complete training and on-going support.

BACKGROUND:
Established: 1987; 1st Franchised: 1991
Franchised Units: 149
Company-Owned Units: 1
Total Units: 150
Dist.: US-89; CAN-4; O'seas-12
North America: 22 States
Density: 21 in TX, 13 in CA, 8 in CO
Projected New Units (12 Months): 100
Qualifications: 3, 3, 2, 2, 5, 5
Registered: CA,IL,IN,MD,MI,NY,VA,WA,WI

FINANCIAL/TERMS:
Cash Investment: $8-15K

Total Investment: $9-18K
Minimum Net Worth: NR
Fees: Franchise - $4-7K
Royalty - 7%; Ad. - 2%
Earnings Claims Statement: No
Term of Contract (Years): 10/5
Avg. # Of Employees: 1 FT
Passive Ownership: Discouraged
Encourage Conversions: NA
Area Develop. Agreements: Yes
Sub-Franchising Contracts: No
Expand In Territory: Yes
Space Needs: NR SF; Mobile Unit

SUPPORT & TRAINING:
Financial Assistance Provided: Yes(I)
Site Selection Assistance: Yes
Lease Negotiation Assistance: NA
Co-Operative Advertising: Yes
Franchisee Assoc./Member: No
Size Of Corporate Staff: 9
On-Going Support: B,C,D,F,G,H
Training: 4 Days to 2 Weeks Union, NJ.

SPECIFIC EXPANSION PLANS:
US: All United States
Canada: All Canada
Overseas: All Countries

OIL CAN HENRY'S INTERNATIONAL

1200 Naito Pkwy. NW, # 690
Portland, OR 97209
Tel: (800) 765-6244 (503) 243-6311
Fax: (503) 228-5227
E-Mail: georges@oilcanhenry.com
Web Site: www.oilcanhenry.com
Mr. George Steinfurth, Dir. Franchise Development

Automotive lubrication and filter specialist. We work hard, blending the best of yesterday with the best of today to provide unbeatable service. The distinctive design of our crew uniforms and service centers evoke memories of days past when the neighbor service station provided friendly, quality service. While our centers may remind you of yesteryear, our focus is on the future. Our technicians are well-trained to provide a wide variety of valuable maintenance and safety services.

BACKGROUND: IFA MEMBER
Established: 1978; 1st Franchised: 1989
Franchised Units: 70
Company-Owned Units: 5
Total Units: 75
Dist.: US-75; CAN-0; O'seas-0
North America: 9 States
Density: 43 in OR, 17 in WA, 9 in CA
Projected New Units (12 Months): 15
Qualifications: 5, 4, 3, 3, 4, 5
Registered: CA,FL,MN,OR,WA

FINANCIAL/TERMS:
Cash Investment: $150-250K
Total Investment: $300K-1MM
Minimum Net Worth: $500K
Fees: Franchise - $25K
Royalty - 5.5%; Ad. - 1%
Earnings Claims Statement: No
Term of Contract (Years): 10/5+
Avg. # Of Employees: 4-6 FT, 5-9 PT
Passive Ownership: Not Allowed
Encourage Conversions: Yes
Area Develop. Agreements: Yes/3
Sub-Franchising Contracts: No
Expand In Territory: Yes
Space Needs: 15,000 SF; FS

SUPPORT & TRAINING:
Financial Assistance Provided: Yes(I)
Site Selection Assistance: Yes
Lease Negotiation Assistance: Yes
Co-Operative Advertising: Yes
Franchisee Assoc./Member: No
Size Of Corporate Staff: 12
On-Going Support: A,B,C,D,E,G,H,I
Training: 5 Weeks Portland, OR; 2 Weeks on Site.

SPECIFIC EXPANSION PLANS:
US: WA,OR,CA,AZ,NV,ID,MN,CO,TX
Canada: No
Overseas: No

ONE STOP UNDERCAR

2938 S. Daimler St.
Santa Ana, CA 92705
Tel: (949) 955-2600
Fax:
E-Mail: cgoldberg@onestopundercar.net
Web Site: www.onestopundercar.net
Mr. Clive Goldberg, Director Franchise Development

ONE STOP UNDERCAR outlets distribute automobile parts, accessories and equipment to automotive-repair and maintenance shops.

BACKGROUND:
Established: 1993; 1st Franchised: 1993
Franchised Units: 10
Company-Owned Units: 4
Total Units: 14
Dist.: US-14; CAN-0; O'seas-0
North America: 1 State
Density: 13 in CA
Projected New Units (12 Months): 2
Qualifications: 5, 3, 2, 3, 2, 5
Registered: CA

FINANCIAL/TERMS:
Cash Investment: $200K
Total Investment: $292-460K
Minimum Net Worth: $350K
Fees: Franchise - $40-80K
Royalty - 5%; Ad. - 3%
Earnings Claims Statement: No
Term of Contract (Years): 20/20
Avg. # Of Employees: 8 FT
Passive Ownership: Discouraged
Encourage Conversions: NR
Area Develop. Agreements: Yes/5
Sub-Franchising Contracts: No
Expand In Territory: Yes
Space Needs: 3,500 SF; Warehouse

SUPPORT & TRAINING:
Financial Assistance Provided: No
Site Selection Assistance: No
Lease Negotiation Assistance: No
Co-Operative Advertising: Yes
Franchisee Assoc./Member: NR
Size Of Corporate Staff: 7
On-Going Support: D,E,F,g,h
Training: 4 Weeks Orange County, CA.

SPECIFIC EXPANSION PLANS:
US: Southwest
Canada: No
Overseas: No

PAINT MEDIC

3111 Walden Ave.
Depew, NY 14043
Tel: (866) 446-2277 (905) 732-9770
Fax: (905) 788-1939
E-Mail: moniquefinley@paintmedic.com
Web Site: www.paintmedic.com
Ms. Monique Finley, VP Franchise Development

PAINT MEDIC is an automotive paint touch-up company. Our franchisees and their technicians can quickly, cost-effectively and permanently repair stone chips, scratches, plastic bumper scuffs and other minor paint blemishes. We service new and used car dealerships, rental car agencies, fleet companies and retail consumers. PAINT MEDIC operates from both fixed location retail facilities, as well as on a mobile basis. PAINT MEDIC is ideally suited for someone who loves cars and wants to be his own boss.

BACKGROUND:
Established: 1990; 1st Franchised: 1995
Franchised Units: 22

Company-Owned Units: 2
Total Units: 24
Dist.: US-2; CAN-22; O'seas-0
North America: 2 States, 3 Provinces
Density: 20 in ON, 1 in NY
Projected New Units (12 Months): 12
Qualifications: 4, 4, 2, 3, 4, 3
Registered: NR

FINANCIAL/TERMS:
Cash Investment: $30-60K
Total Investment: $30-60K
Minimum Net Worth: $50K
Fees: Franchise - $25-50K
Royalty - 5%/$500; Ad. - NA
Earnings Claims Statement: No
Term of Contract (Years): 10.10
Avg. # Of Employees: 3-4 FT, 1-2 PT
Passive Ownership: Not Allowed
Encourage Conversions: NA
Area Develop. Agreements: Yes/10
Sub-Franchising Contracts: No
Expand In Territory: Yes
Space Needs: 2,000 SF; FS

SUPPORT & TRAINING:
Financial Assistance Provided: No
Site Selection Assistance: Yes
Lease Negotiation Assistance: Yes
Co-Operative Advertising: NA
Franchisee Assoc./Member: No
Size Of Corporate Staff: 7
On-Going Support: B,C,D,G,h,I
Training: 3 Weeks Buffalo, NY; 1 Week in Territory.

SPECIFIC EXPANSION PLANS:
US: Focusing on NE
Canada: All Canada
Overseas: Master Franchises

PETRO STOPPING CENTERS

6080 Surety Dr.
El Paso, TX 79905
Tel: (800) 331-8809 (915) 779-4711
Fax: (915) 774-7373
E-Mail: wbowker@petrotruckstops.com
Web Site: www.petrotruckstops.com
Mr. Will Bowker, Director of Franchising

PETRO STOPPING CENTERS is a nationwide network of premier, full-service, interstate Travel Plazas. PETRO offers the Iron Skillet Restaurant, Petro Lube Truck Service, featuring Mobil Oil products and Volvo and Cummings light warranty service, Mercantile Travel Stores and quality Mobil fuels. PETRO provides the expertise and systems to help develop successful businesses.

BACKGROUND:
Established: 1975; 1st Franchised: 1985
Franchised Units: 23
Company-Owned Units: 37
Total Units: 60
Dist.: US-57; CAN-0; O'seas-0
North America: 33 States
Density: 6 in TX, 6 in PA, 4 in OH
Projected New Units (12 Months): 4
Qualifications: 5, 4, 4, 3, 3, 4
Registered: CA,FL,IL,IN,MD,MI,NY,ND, SD,VA,WA,WI

FINANCIAL/TERMS:
Cash Investment: NR
Total Investment: NR
Minimum Net Worth: NR
Fees: Franchise - NR
Royalty - NR; Ad. - NR
Earnings Claims Statement: No
Term of Contract (Years): 10/5/5
Avg. # Of Employees: 125 FT, 40 PT
Passive Ownership: Discouraged
Encourage Conversions: No
Area Develop. Agreements: No
Sub-Franchising Contracts: No
Expand In Territory: Yes
Space Needs: 20 Acres SF; Other

SUPPORT & TRAINING:
Financial Assistance Provided: No
Site Selection Assistance: No
Lease Negotiation Assistance: No
Co-Operative Advertising: Yes
Franchisee Assoc./Member: Yes/No
Size Of Corporate Staff: NR
On-Going Support: B,C,D,E,G,H,I
Training: 8 Weeks at Various US Locations.

SPECIFIC EXPANSION PLANS:
US: All US Except TX, AZ, NM
Canada: All Canada
Overseas: No

<< >>

POP-A-LOCK

1018 Harding St., # 101
Lafayette, LA 70503
Tel: (337) 233-6211
Fax: (337) 233-6655
E-Mail: info@pop-a-lock.com
Web Site: www.pop-a-lock.com
Mr. Don Marks, Chief Executive Officer

POP-A-LOCK is America's largest locksmith, car door unlocking, and roadside assistance service. We provide fast, professional, guaranteed service using our proprietary tools and opening techniques. We offer an outstanding community service through our emergency car door unlocking program. You will provide lockout and roadside assistance to the public, businesses and various motor clubs. Franchisees are presently authorized but not required to offer full locksmith services.

BACKGROUND: IFA MEMBER
Established: 1991; 1st Franchised: 1994
Franchised Units: 108
Company-Owned Units: 5
Total Units: 113
Dist.: US-112; CAN-0; O'seas-1
North America: 34 States
Density: 22 in TX, 16 in FL, 14 in LA
Projected New Units (12 Months): 75
Qualifications: 5, 4, 5, 3, 3, 3
Registered: CA,CT,FL,IL,IN,MI,MN,NY, RI,VA,WI

FINANCIAL/TERMS:
Cash Investment: NA
Total Investment: $97.6-741.5KK
Minimum Net Worth: Varies
Fees: Franchise - $22.5K+45/1000
Royalty - 6%; Ad. - 1%
Earnings Claims Statement: No
Term of Contract (Years): 10/10
Avg. # Of Employees: 2 FT, 2 PT
Passive Ownership: Allowed
Encourage Conversions: NA
Area Develop. Agreements: No
Sub-Franchising Contracts: No
Expand In Territory: Yes
Space Needs: NA SF; HB, Mobile Bus.

SUPPORT & TRAINING:
Financial Assistance Provided: No
Site Selection Assistance: Yes
Lease Negotiation Assistance: NA
Co-Operative Advertising: No
Franchisee Assoc./Member: Yes/No
Size Of Corporate Staff: 11
On-Going Support: b,C,d,E,G,h,I
Training: 10 Days in Lafayette, LA.

SPECIFIC EXPANSION PLANS:
US: All United States
Canada: Toronto
Overseas: China

PRECISION TUNE AUTO CARE CENTER

748 Miller Dr. SE
Leesburg, VA 20175
Tel: (800) 438-8863 (703) 669-2311
Fax: (703) 669-1539
E-Mail: caroline.hart@precisionac.com
Web Site: www.precisiontune.com
Ms. Caroline Hart, Franchise Sales

PRECISION TUNE AUTO CARE is

America's largest engine performance car care company, specializing in tune-up, quick oil and lube and brake services. Also offered are complete diagnostics, engine performance, fluid and maintenance services, with 20 years' experience. We provide quality support in site selection, training, marketing, operations, management, business profitability and much more. Comprehensive training program for everyone.

BACKGROUND: IFA MEMBER
Established: 1975; 1st Franchised: 1978
Franchised Units: 529
Company-Owned Units: 1
Total Units: 530
Dist.: US-403; CAN-0; O'seas-127
North America: 36 States
Density: 38 in FL, 37 in CA, 32 in GA
Projected New Units (12 Months): 45
Qualifications: 4, 5, 2, 2, 3, 5
Registered: All except HI

FINANCIAL/TERMS:
Cash Investment: $75-100K
Total Investment: $142-203K
Minimum Net Worth: NR
Fees: Franchise - $10-25K
Royalty - 7.5%; Ad. - 9.0%
Earnings Claims Statement: No
Term of Contract (Years): 10/5
Avg. # Of Employees: 6 FT, 1-2 PT
Passive Ownership: Discouraged
Encourage Conversions: Yes
Area Develop. Agreements: Yes/5
Sub-Franchising Contracts: Yes
Expand In Territory: Yes
Space Needs: 3,000 SF; FS, SF, SC

SUPPORT & TRAINING:
Financial Assistance Provided: Yes
Site Selection Assistance: Yes
Lease Negotiation Assistance: Yes
Co-Operative Advertising: Yes
Franchisee Assoc./Member: Yes
Size Of Corporate Staff: 37
On-Going Support: B,C,D,E,F,G,H,I
Training: 2 Weeks Leesburg, VA.

SPECIFIC EXPANSION PLANS:
US: All United States
Canada: All Canada
Overseas: All Countries

<< >>

RYAN ENGINE EXCHANGE

2465 W. Evans
Denver, CO 80219
Tel: (800) 466-1664 (303) 232-0012
Fax: (303) 205-0172
E-Mail: johnnywilson@ryanengineexchange.com
Web Site: www.ryanengineexchange.com
Mr. Johnny M. Wilson, President

RYAN ENGINE EXCHANGE installs and exchanges remanufactured engines. The old engine is exchanged for a new engine and the new engine is installed on the premises. Using the system developed by Ryan, the turn around time is 3 days and a factory warranty of 5 years - 50,000 miles is given.

BACKGROUND:
Established: 1987; 1st Franchised: 1999
Franchised Units: 12
Company-Owned Units: 1
Total Units: 13
Dist.: US-1; CAN-0; O'seas-0
North America: 1 State
Density: 1 in CO
Projected New Units (12 Months): 4
Qualifications: 3, 4, 2, 1, 2, 5
Registered: NR

FINANCIAL/TERMS:
Cash Investment: $40K
Total Investment: $78-112.8K
Minimum Net Worth: $50K
Fees: Franchise - $20K
Royalty - 3% or $30/engine; Ad. - 5% Local
Earnings Claims Statement: No
Term of Contract (Years): 15/5
Avg. # Of Employees: 4 FT, 1 PT
Passive Ownership: Discouraged
Encourage Conversions: Yes
Area Develop. Agreements: No
Sub-Franchising Contracts: No
Expand In Territory: Yes
Space Needs: 2,500 SF; Warehouse

SUPPORT & TRAINING:
Financial Assistance Provided: Yes(I)
Site Selection Assistance: Yes
Lease Negotiation Assistance: Yes
Co-Operative Advertising: No
Franchisee Assoc./Member: No
Size Of Corporate Staff: 3
On-Going Support: B,C,D,E,F,G,H,I
Training: 1 Week in Denver; 3 Days at Factory in Nebraska.

SPECIFIC EXPANSION PLANS:
US: All United States
Canada: No
Overseas: No

<< >>

SAF-T AUTO CENTERS

121-H N. Plains Industrial Rd.
Wallingford, CT 06492
Tel: (800) 382-7238 (203) 294-1094
Fax: (203) 269-2532
E-Mail: rbiladeau@saftauto.com
Web Site: www.saftauto.com
Mr. Richard Biladeau, President

SAF-T AUTO CENTERS is an owner-operated, general service auto repair shop dedicated to the advancement of the auto technician. Our goal is to put the very best technicians in a business opportunity where they can capitalize on their trade and maximize their talents.

BACKGROUND:
Established: 1978; 1st Franchised: 1985
Franchised Units: 5
Company-Owned Units: 1
Total Units: 6
Dist.: US-9; CAN-0; O'seas-0
North America: 1 State
Density: 6 in CT
Projected New Units (12 Months): 2
Qualifications: 1, 1, 4, 2, 4, 5
Registered: Fed. Registered Trademark

FINANCIAL/TERMS:
Cash Investment: $30K
Total Investment: $50-100K
Minimum Net Worth: $50K
Fees: Franchise - $15K
Royalty - $500/Mo.; Ad. - 1%
Earnings Claims Statement: No
Term of Contract (Years): 10/10
Avg. # Of Employees: 2 FT
Passive Ownership: Discouraged
Encourage Conversions: Yes
Area Develop. Agreements: Yes
Sub-Franchising Contracts: No
Expand In Territory: Yes
Space Needs: 2,500 SF; FS, SC

SUPPORT & TRAINING:
Financial Assistance Provided: Yes(D)
Site Selection Assistance: Yes
Lease Negotiation Assistance: Yes
Co-Operative Advertising: Yes
Franchisee Assoc./Member: No
Size Of Corporate Staff: 3
On-Going Support: A,B,C,E,F,G,H,I
Training: 1 Month On-Site.

SPECIFIC EXPANSION PLANS:
US: CT
Canada: No
Overseas: No

<< >>

SHINE FACTORY

320 Monument Pl., SE
Calgary, AB T2A 1X3 CANADA
Tel: (403) 243-3030

Fax: (403) 243-3031
E-Mail: kingv@telus.net
Web Site: www.shinefactory.ca
Mr. Bruce H. Cousens, President

A solid, proven program to put entrepreneurs into the automotive protection and detail business. Car wash combinations are available.

BACKGROUND:
Established: 1979; 1st Franchised: 1979
Franchised Units: 31
Company-Owned Units: 0
Total Units: 31
Dist.: US-0; CAN-31; O'seas-0
North America: 6 Provinces
Density: 12 in NS, 12 in AB, 4 in BC
Projected New Units (12 Months): 3-4
Qualifications: 4, 4, 3, 3, 3, 5
Registered: AB

FINANCIAL/TERMS:
Cash Investment: $100K
Total Investment: $125K
Minimum Net Worth: $60K
Fees: Franchise - $10-50K
Royalty - 8%; Ad. - 5%
Earnings Claims Statement: No
Term of Contract (Years): 5/5
Avg. # Of Employees: 3 FT, 2 PT
Passive Ownership: Discouraged
Encourage Conversions: Yes
Area Develop. Agreements: Yes/5
Sub-Franchising Contracts: Yes
Expand In Territory: Yes
Space Needs: 4,000 SF; FS, SC

SUPPORT & TRAINING:
Financial Assistance Provided: No
Site Selection Assistance: Yes
Lease Negotiation Assistance: Yes
Co-Operative Advertising: Yes
Franchisee Assoc./Member: No
Size Of Corporate Staff: 4
On-Going Support: C,D,E,F,H,I
Training: 2 Weeks Training Center; 2 Weeks On-Site.

SPECIFIC EXPANSION PLANS:
US: No
Canada: All Canada
Overseas: No

<< >>

SPEEDEE OIL CHANGE & TUNE-UP

159 Hwy. 22 East
Madisonville, LA 70447-1350
Tel: (800) 451-7461 (985) 845-1919
Fax: (985) 845-1936
E-Mail: tjones@speedeecorp.com
Web Site: www.speedeeoil.com
Ms. Tanya Jones, Dir. Franchise Development

SPEEDEE offers preventive auto maintenance services, specializing in a 17-point quick oil change, diagnostic tune-up and brake services. Also offered: fuel system cleanings, a/c services, radiator flushes, emission/smog checks and transmission/differential services. No appointment necessary. Performed while you wait. Successful franchisees are enthusiastic, have a strong commitment to customer service and people management skills. Retail experience preferred.

BACKGROUND:
Established: 1980; 1st Franchised: 1982
Franchised Units: 143
Company-Owned Units: 0
Total Units: 143
Dist.: US-121; CAN-0; O'seas-13
North America: 15 States
Density: 50 in CA, 22 in LA, 10 in MA
Projected New Units (12 Months): 14
Qualifications: 5, 5, 3, 3, 3, 4
Registered: CA,VA,FL,HI

FINANCIAL/TERMS:
Cash Investment: $100-150K
Total Investment: $186-765.5K
Minimum Net Worth: $250K
Fees: Franchise - $30K
Royalty - 6%; Ad. - 8%
Earnings Claims Statement: No
Term of Contract (Years): 21/5/5
Avg. # Of Employees: 5 FT, 2 PT
Passive Ownership: Discouraged
Encourage Conversions: Yes
Area Develop. Agreements: No
Sub-Franchising Contracts: No
Expand In Territory: Yes
Space Needs: 2,800 SF; FS

SUPPORT & TRAINING:
Financial Assistance Provided: No
Site Selection Assistance: Yes
Lease Negotiation Assistance: Yes
Co-Operative Advertising: Yes
Franchisee Assoc./Member: No
Size Of Corporate Staff: 16
On-Going Support: C,D,E,G,H
Training: 3-Day Orientation Headquarters; 2-4 Weeks Local Office; 1-2 Weeks Shop.

SPECIFIC EXPANSION PLANS:
US: All United States
Canada: All Canada
Overseas: All Countries

<< >>

SPEEDY TRANSMISSION CENTERS

74 NE 4th Ave., # 1
Delray Beach, FL 33483
Tel: (800) 336-0310 (561) 274-0445
Fax: (561) 274-6456
E-Mail: speedytrans@mindspring.com
Web Site: www.speedytransmission.com
Mr. Bob Petron, Operations Manager

Centers repair, rebuild and recondition automatic and standard transmissions. Other drive train repair services also available. Training, marketing and operational assistance. Warranties are honored throughout the U.S. and Canada.

BACKGROUND: IFA MEMBER
Established: 1974; 1st Franchised: 1974
Franchised Units: 30
Company-Owned Units: 0
Total Units: 30
Dist.: US-28; CAN-0; O'seas-0
North America: 6 States
Density: 18 in FL, 7 in GA, 2 in CA
Projected New Units (12 Months): 8
Qualifications: 3, 3, 2, 4, 4, 3
Registered: FL

FINANCIAL/TERMS:
Cash Investment: $40K
Total Investment: $80-100K
Minimum Net Worth: NR
Fees: Franchise - $19.5K
Royalty - 7%; Ad. - $100/Mo.
Earnings Claims Statement: No
Term of Contract (Years): 20/10
Avg. # Of Employees: 4 FT, 1 PT
Passive Ownership: Discouraged
Encourage Conversions: Yes
Area Develop. Agreements: Yes/10
Sub-Franchising Contracts: Yes
Expand In Territory: Yes
Space Needs: 2,400 SF; FS, SC

SUPPORT & TRAINING:
Financial Assistance Provided: Yes(I)
Site Selection Assistance: Yes
Lease Negotiation Assistance: Yes
Co-Operative Advertising: No
Franchisee Assoc./Member: Yes/Yes
Size Of Corporate Staff: 4
On-Going Support: C,D,E,F,G,H,I
Training: 2 Weeks Home Office; 1 Week On-Site.

SPECIFIC EXPANSION PLANS:
US: Southeast, Northeast
Canada: No
Overseas: Latin America

<< >>

SPOT-NOT CAR WASHES

P. O. Box 1269
Joplin, MO 64802
Tel: (800) 682-7629 (417) 781-6233
Fax: (417) 781-3906
E-Mail: doug@spot-not.com
Web Site: www.spot-not.com
Mr. Doug Myers, Executive Vice President

High-pressure spray brushless automatic car wash, complemented by full-featured, self-service wash bays. Each facility offers canopied, lighted vacuum areas. An all cash business with few employees.

BACKGROUND: IFA MEMBER
Established: 1968; 1st Franchised: 1985
Franchised Units: 36
Company-Owned Units: 0
Total Units: 36
Dist.: US-36; CAN-0; O'seas-0
North America: 6 States
Density: 10 in AR, 10 in IL, 8 in IN
Projected New Units (12 Months): 3
Qualifications: , , , , ,
Registered: IL,IN,MI,WI

FINANCIAL/TERMS:
Cash Investment: $300K
Total Investment: $622K-1.1MM
Minimum Net Worth: NR
Fees: Franchise - $25K
Royalty - 5%; Ad. - 1%
Earnings Claims Statement: No
Term of Contract (Years): 10/5/5
Avg. # Of Employees: 2 FT, 3 PT
Passive Ownership: Discouraged
Encourage Conversions: Yes
Area Develop. Agreements: Yes/Varies
Sub-Franchising Contracts: No
Expand In Territory: Yes
Space Needs: 40,000 SF; FS

SUPPORT & TRAINING:
Financial Assistance Provided: Yes(I)
Site Selection Assistance: Yes
Lease Negotiation Assistance: Yes
Co-Operative Advertising: Yes
Franchisee Assoc./Member: No
Size Of Corporate Staff: 18
On-Going Support: B,C,D,E,F,G,H,I
Training: 3 Sessions -- 17 Days Total Joplin, MO and OJT Site.

SPECIFIC EXPANSION PLANS:
US: Midwest, South and Southwest
Canada: No
Overseas: No

<< >>

SPRAYGLO AUTO REFINISHING & BODY REPAIR

1959 Parker C., # C
Stone Mountain, GA 30087-3436
Tel: (877) 286-7794 (678) 344-8065
Fax: (678) 344-7426
E-Mail: sdamron@sprayglo.com
Web Site: www.sprayglo.com
Mr. H. Stuart Damron, CEO

Painting motor vehicles at a price most anyone can afford, through the use of our "production" system. Marketed to the general public as well as used car dealers, fleet accounts, and even collision repair shops. Because we use a production system, we are able to keep costs low for our customers, while providing a high quality product and service, in turn enabling us to generate the volume that we need to insure profits.

BACKGROUND:
Established: 1986; 1st Franchised: 1994
Franchised Units: 8
Company-Owned Units: 4
Total Units: 12
Dist.: US-12; CAN-0; O'seas-0
North America: 11 States
Density: 5 in FL, 5 in GA, 1 in AL
Projected New Units (12 Months): 2
Qualifications: 3, 4, 1, 2, 4, 5
Registered: FL

FINANCIAL/TERMS:
Cash Investment: $88.5-153K
Total Investment: $88.5-153K
Minimum Net Worth: NR
Fees: Franchise - $20K
Royalty - 5%; Ad. - 2%, $150/Wk
Earnings Claims Statement: No
Term of Contract (Years): 10/10
Avg. # Of Employees: 8 FT
Passive Ownership: Allowed
Encourage Conversions: NA
Area Develop. Agreements: No
Sub-Franchising Contracts: No
Expand In Territory: Yes
Space Needs: 6,000-10,000 SF; FS

SUPPORT & TRAINING:
Financial Assistance Provided: Yes(I)
Site Selection Assistance: Yes
Lease Negotiation Assistance: Yes
Co-Operative Advertising: No
Franchisee Assoc./Member: No
Size Of Corporate Staff: 3
On-Going Support: A,B,C,D,E,F,h,I
Training: 2 Weeks Training Center; 2 Weeks Operating Location; Up to 2 Additional Weeks On Site.

SPECIFIC EXPANSION PLANS:
US: SE
Canada: No
Overseas: No

<< >>

SUPERGLASS WINDSHIELD REPAIR

6101 Chancellor Dr., # 200
Orlando, FL 32809
Tel: (888) 771-2700 (407) 240-1920
Fax: (407) 240-3266
E-Mail: david@superglass.net
Web Site: www.sgwr.com
Mr. David A. Casey, President

SUPERGLASS WINDSHIELD REPAIR is the largest repair-only franchisor in the United States, with locations in 43 states. Two weeks of training, including one week in Orlando and one week in the franchisee's exclusive territory, are provided along with all equipment, uniforms, manuals, printing and bookkeeping systems.

BACKGROUND:
Established: 1992; 1st Franchised: 1993
Franchised Units: 223
Company-Owned Units: 0
Total Units: 223
Dist.: US-182; CAN-1; O'seas-13
North America: 43 States, 1 Province
Density: 14 in GA, 13 in FL, 11 in CO
Projected New Units (12 Months): 25
Qualifications: 2, 4, 1, 2, 3, 4
Registered: CA,FL,MI,SD

FINANCIAL/TERMS:
Cash Investment: $9.5-11.5K
Total Investment: $9.5-28.5K
Minimum Net Worth: $15K
Fees: Franchise - $5.4K
Royalty - 3%; Ad. - 1%/$20 Min.
Earnings Claims Statement: No
Term of Contract (Years): 10/10
Avg. # Of Employees: 2 FT
Passive Ownership: Discouraged
Encourage Conversions: Yes
Area Develop. Agreements: Yes/10/10
Sub-Franchising Contracts: No
Expand In Territory: Yes
Space Needs: NA SF; NA

SUPPORT & TRAINING:
Financial Assistance Provided: Yes(D)
Site Selection Assistance: NA
Lease Negotiation Assistance: Yes
Co-Operative Advertising: Yes
Franchisee Assoc./Member: No
Size Of Corporate Staff: 6
On-Going Support: a,B,C,D,E,F,G,H,I
Training: 5 Days Orlando, FL; 5 Days Exclusive Franchisee Territory.

SPECIFIC EXPANSION PLANS:

US: All United States
Canada: All Canada
Overseas: Portugal, Mexico, Brazil

≺≺ ≻≻

TILDEN CAR CARE CENTERS

300 Hempstead Tpke., # 110
W. Hempstead, NY 11552
Tel: (800) 845-3367 (516) 746-7911
Fax: (516) 746-1288
E-Mail: jbaskind@tildencarcare.com
Web Site: www.tildencarcare.com
Mr. Jason Baskind, Dir. Franchise Development

We're not just brakes. The total care concept allows you to offer a full menu of automotive services for maximum customer procurement - rather than a limited niche market. You benefit from a management team whose concept system and training were proven and perfected before we even considered offering franchises.

BACKGROUND:
Established: 1923; 1st Franchised: 1996
Franchised Units: 60
Company-Owned Units: 0
Total Units: 60
Dist.: US-60; CAN-0; O'seas-0
North America: 13 States
Density: 24 in FL, 15 in NY, 5 in GA
Projected New Units (12 Months): 10
Qualifications: 3, 4, 3, 3, 3, 4
Registered: CA,FL,IL,IN,NY,VA,WA

FINANCIAL/TERMS:
Cash Investment: $50-60K
Total Investment: $131-171.5K
Minimum Net Worth: $150K
Fees: Franchise - $25K
Royalty - 6%/$350/Wk.; Ad. - 3%/$175/Wk.
Earnings Claims Statement: No
Term of Contract (Years): 20/20
Avg. # Of Employees: 2 FT, 2 PT
Passive Ownership: Discouraged
Encourage Conversions: Yes
Area Develop. Agreements: Yes/20
Sub-Franchising Contracts: No
Expand In Territory: Yes
Space Needs: 3,500+ SF; FS, Auto Mall

SUPPORT & TRAINING:
Financial Assistance Provided: Yes(I)
Site Selection Assistance: Yes
Lease Negotiation Assistance: Yes
Co-Operative Advertising: Yes
Franchisee Assoc./Member: Yes/Yes
Size Of Corporate Staff: 6
On-Going Support: A,B,C,D,E,F,G,H,I
Training: 2 Weeks Home Office.

SPECIFIC EXPANSION PLANS:
US: All United States
Canada: All Canada
Overseas: No

≺≺ ≻≻

TIRE WAREHOUSE

492 Main St., P.O. Box 486
Keene, NH 03431-4035
Tel: (800) 756-9876 (603) 352-4478
Fax: (603) 358-6620
E-Mail: franchising@tirewarehouse.net
Web Site: www.tirewarehouse.net
Mr. John Henning, VP Franchising/Real Estate

TIRE WAREHOUSE, 'Quality Tires For Less,' is a retail tire, wheel and auto parts franchise, offering quality products and services in a 'warehouse-style' setting. Franchisees will utilize the unique TW system to produce volume sales and profits. On-going training and support are provided.

BACKGROUND:
Established: 1971; 1st Franchised: 1989
Franchised Units: 25
Company-Owned Units: 25
Total Units: 50
Dist.: US-48; CAN-0; O'seas-0
North America: 6 States
Density: 18 in NH, 11 in ME, 11 in MA
Projected New Units (12 Months): 10
Qualifications: 4, 5, 1, 3, 3, 5
Registered: NY,RI

FINANCIAL/TERMS:
Cash Investment: $50-100K
Total Investment: $150-350K
Minimum Net Worth: $150K
Fees: Franchise - $0
Royalty - 3%; Ad. - 2%
Earnings Claims Statement: Yes
Term of Contract (Years): 7/5
Avg. # Of Employees: 5 FT, 2 PT
Passive Ownership: Discouraged
Encourage Conversions: Yes
Area Develop. Agreements: No
Sub-Franchising Contracts: No
Expand In Territory: Yes
Space Needs: 5,000 SF; FS

SUPPORT & TRAINING:
Financial Assistance Provided: Yes(I)
Site Selection Assistance: Yes
Lease Negotiation Assistance: Yes
Co-Operative Advertising: Yes
Franchisee Assoc./Member: No
Size Of Corporate Staff: 32
On-Going Support: A,B,C,D,E,F,G,H,I
Training: 2-4 Weeks in Keene, NH; 1-3 Weeks Field Training.

SPECIFIC EXPANSION PLANS:
US: New England
Canada: No
Overseas: No

≺≺ ≻≻

TIRES PLUS TOTAL CAR CARE

8011 34th Ave. S., # 334
Bloomington, MN 55425
Tel: (800) 754-6519 (952) 253-5968
Fax: (952) 253-5989
E-Mail: franchise@tiresplus.com
Web Site: www.tiresplus.com
Mr. John Hyduke, VP Franchise Development

TIRES PLUS is one of the fastest growing retail tire store franchisors in the U.S. We are taking a new and innovative approach to tire retailing. Our franchisees enjoy thorough education programs, in-field support, marketing and advertising assistance, name brand product lines, exclusive territories and a proven operational system.

BACKGROUND:
Established: 1976; 1st Franchised: 1981
Franchised Units: 74
Company-Owned Units: 495
Total Units: 569
Dist.: US-569; CAN-0; O'seas-0
North America: 24 States
Density: 173 in FL, 58 in MN, 49 GA
Projected New Units (12 Months): 50
Qualifications: 5, 4, 1, 3, 1, 5
Registered: IL,FL,MI,MN,ND,SD,VA,WI

FINANCIAL/TERMS:
Cash Investment: $150K
Total Investment: $462-588K
Minimum Net Worth: $500K
Fees: Franchise - $30K
Royalty - 4%; Ad. - 1%
Earnings Claims Statement: No
Term of Contract (Years): 20/20
Avg. # Of Employees: 10 FT, 5 PT
Passive Ownership: Discouraged
Encourage Conversions: Yes
Area Develop. Agreements: Yes
Sub-Franchising Contracts: No

Expand In Territory: NR
Space Needs: 6,000 SF; FS

SUPPORT & TRAINING:
Financial Assistance Provided: No
Site Selection Assistance: Yes
Lease Negotiation Assistance: Yes
Co-Operative Advertising: NR
Franchisee Assoc./Member: No
Size Of Corporate Staff: 130
On-Going Support: B,C,D,E,F,I
Training: 1 Week in Classroom; 15 Weeks at Various Store Locations.

SPECIFIC EXPANSION PLANS:
US: All United States
Canada: No
Overseas: No

<< >>

TOP VALUE CAR & TRUCK SERVICE CENTERS

36887 Schoolcraft
Livonia, MI 48150
Tel: (800) 860-8258 (734) 462-3633
Fax: (734) 462-1088
E-Mail: franchiseinfo@top-value.com
Web Site: www.top-value.com
Mr. Larry Reed, Chief Financial Officer

We fix cars. People are holding onto and maintaining their vehicles longer than ever. Our menu of repair specialization includes: brakes, exhaust, suspension, shocks, struts, air conditioning, general maintenance and general repair. We focus on customer service and franchisee satisfaction, with on-going training, strong purchasing power and field support that you can count on!

BACKGROUND:
Established: 1977; 1st Franchised: 1980
Franchised Units: 32
Company-Owned Units: 8
Total Units: 40
Dist.: US-40; CAN-0; O'seas-0
North America: 3 States
Density: 27 in MI, 3 in OH, 1 in IN
Projected New Units (12 Months): 8
Qualifications: 3, 3, 3, 3, 3, 4
Registered: MI,IN,IL

FINANCIAL/TERMS:
Cash Investment: $30-60K
Total Investment: $125K
Minimum Net Worth: $125K
Fees: Franchise - $17.5K
Royalty - 2-5%; Ad. - 3%
Earnings Claims Statement: Yes
Term of Contract (Years): 10/5
Avg. # Of Employees: 2-3 FT
Passive Ownership: Discouraged
Encourage Conversions: Yes
Area Develop. Agreements: Yes
Sub-Franchising Contracts: Yes
Expand In Territory: Yes
Space Needs: 2,500-3,500 SF; FS

SUPPORT & TRAINING:
Financial Assistance Provided: Yes(I)
Site Selection Assistance: Yes
Lease Negotiation Assistance: Yes
Co-Operative Advertising: Yes
Franchisee Assoc./Member: No
Size Of Corporate Staff: 12
On-Going Support: B,C,D,E,F,G,H,I
Training: 3 Weeks in Livonia, MI; 1 Week On-Site.

SPECIFIC EXPANSION PLANS:
US: MI, OH, IN, IL, N. KY
Canada: No
Overseas: No

<< >>

TUFFY AUTO SERVICE CENTERS

1414 Baronial Plaza Dr.
Toledo, OH 43615-7369
Tel: (800) 228-8339 (419) 865-6900
Fax: (419) 865-7343
E-Mail: jacobs@tuffy.com
Web Site: www.tuffy.com
Mr. James D. Jacobs, Director of Franchising

TUFFY AUTO SERVICE CENTERS have been ranked by Success and Entrepreneur Magazines as one of the top franchises in the country. We are an upscale automotive repair franchise specializing in brakes, exhaust, shocks, alignments, air conditioning, batteries, starting and charging, lube-oil-filter, and more. We provide initial and on-going operations, technical and marketing support. Excellent sites being developed in IN, IA, WI, VA, FL, OH, MN, ND, SD, NE and IL.

BACKGROUND: IFA MEMBER
Established: 1970; 1st Franchised: 1971
Franchised Units: 258
Company-Owned Units: 6
Total Units: 264
Dist.: US-247; CAN-0; O'seas-0
North America: 16 States
Density: 67 in MI, 63 in OH, 32 in FL
Projected New Units (12 Months): 25
Qualifications: 4, 4, 2, 2, 2, 4
Registered:FL,IL,IN,MD,MI,MN,NY,ND, VA,WI

FINANCIAL/TERMS:
Cash Investment: $75K
Total Investment: $127.5-273K
Minimum Net Worth: $250K
Fees: Franchise - $25K
Royalty - 5%; Ad. - 5%
Earnings Claims Statement: No
Term of Contract (Years): 15/10
Avg. # Of Employees: 4 FT, 1 PT
Passive Ownership: Discouraged
Encourage Conversions: Yes
Area Develop. Agreements: Yes/Negot.
Sub-Franchising Contracts: Yes
Expand In Territory: Yes
Space Needs: 3,800 SF; FS

SUPPORT & TRAINING:
Financial Assistance Provided: Yes(I)
Site Selection Assistance: Yes
Lease Negotiation Assistance: Yes
Co-Operative Advertising: Yes
Franchisee Assoc./Member: Yes/Yes
Size Of Corporate Staff: 36
On-Going Support: C,D,E,G,H,I
Training: 3-4 Weeks in Toledo, OH; 3 Weeks On-Site at Franchise.

SPECIFIC EXPANSION PLANS:
US: North Central U.S., FL
Canada: No
Overseas: No

<< >>

TUNEX INTERNATIONAL

556 East 2100 S.
Salt Lake City, UT 84106-1423
Tel: (800) 448-8639 (801) 486-8133
Fax: (801) 484-4740
E-Mail: scottm@tunex.com
Web Site: www.tunex.com
Mr. Scott Mower, Franchise Sales

We offer diagnostic, engine performance, tune-up services and repairs of engine related systems, i.e. ignition, carburetion, fuel injection, emission controls, computer controls, cooling, air conditioning, emission inspections, used-car evaluations, and lubrication services. For maximum customer satisfaction, we always analyze systems for the problem and maintenance requirements, so the customer can make service and repair decisions.

BACKGROUND: IFA MEMBER
Established: 1974; 1st Franchised: 1975
Franchised Units: 28
Company-Owned Units: 2
Total Units: 30
Dist.: US-29; CAN-0; O'seas-1
North America: 6 States
Density: 16 in UT, 4 in CO, 1 in AZ
Projected New Units (12 Months): 4
Qualifications: 4, 3, 2, 3, 2, 5

Registered: NR

FINANCIAL/TERMS:

Cash Investment: $50-60K
Total Investment: $122.5-163.1K
Minimum Net Worth: $200K
Fees: Franchise - $19K
Royalty - 5%; Ad. - $600/Mo.
Earnings Claims Statement: No
Term of Contract (Years): 10/10
Avg. # Of Employees: 4 FT
Passive Ownership: Discouraged
Encourage Conversions: NA
Area Develop. Agreements: Yes/10
Sub-Franchising Contracts: Yes
Expand In Territory: No
Space Needs: 2,750 SF; FS, SF, SC

SUPPORT & TRAINING:

Financial Assistance Provided: Yes(I)
Site Selection Assistance: Yes
Lease Negotiation Assistance: Yes
Co-Operative Advertising: Yes
Franchisee Assoc./Member: No
Size Of Corporate Staff: 5
On-Going Support: C,D,E,G,H,I
Training: 1 Week Corporate Headquarters; 1 Week On-Site.

SPECIFIC EXPANSION PLANS:

US: Inter-Mountain, Southwest
Canada: Master Franchise
Overseas: No

<< >>

VALVOLINE INSTANT OIL CHANGE

3499 Blazer Pkwy.
Lexington, KY 40509
Tel: (800) 622-6846 (859) 357-7214
Fax: (859) 357-7049
E-Mail: jjtaylor@ashland.com
Web Site: www.viocfranchise.com
Ms. Josie Taylor

Offers licenses for the establishment and operation of a business which provides a quick oil change, chassis lubrication and routine maintenance checks on automobiles. The licensor and/or its affiliates will offer (to qualified prospects) leasing programs for equipment, signage, POS systems and mortgage based financing for land, building.

BACKGROUND:

Established: 1988; 1st Franchised: 1988
Franchised Units: 310
Company-Owned Units: 362
Total Units: 672
Dist.: US-633; CAN-0; O'seas-0
North America: 35 States
Density: 73 in OH, 62 in MI, 53 in MN
Projected New Units (12 Months): 65
Qualifications: 5, 4, 2, 3, 5, 5
Registered: All States

FINANCIAL/TERMS:

Cash Investment: $150K
Total Investment: $96-201.8K
Minimum Net Worth: $200K
Fees: Franchise - $30K
Royalty - 6%; Ad. - 2%
Earnings Claims Statement: Yes
Term of Contract (Years): 15/5/5
Avg. # Of Employees: 4 FT, 2 PT
Passive Ownership: Allowed
Encourage Conversions: Yes
Area Develop. Agreements: No
Sub-Franchising Contracts: No
Expand In Territory: Yes
Space Needs: 15,000 SF; FS

SUPPORT & TRAINING:

Financial Assistance Provided: Yes(I)
Site Selection Assistance: Yes
Lease Negotiation Assistance: Yes
Co-Operative Advertising: Yes
Franchisee Assoc./Member: No
Size Of Corporate Staff: 84
On-Going Support: A,B,C,D,E,F,G,h,I
Training: 3+ Weeks Classroom/OJT/On-Site Training.

SPECIFIC EXPANSION PLANS:

US: All United States
Canada: No
Overseas: No

<< >>

VICTORY LANE QUICK OIL CHANGE

405 Little Lake Dr.
Ann Arbor, MI 48103
Tel: (734) 996-1196
Fax: (734) 996-4912
E-Mail: victorylane@aol.com
Web Site: www.victorylaneqoc.com
Mr. Dave Braun, Director Franchise Development

VICTORY LANE QUICK OIL CHANGE is a low-overhead, high-profit, drive-thru, quick oil change operation. We also perform transmission flush, fuel injection cleaning, serpentine belts, radiator flush and other high-profit services. Most franchisees are multi-shop owners.

BACKGROUND:

Established: 1980; 1st Franchised: 1986
Franchised Units: 24
Company-Owned Units: 8
Total Units: 32
Dist.: US-32; CAN-0; O'seas-0
North America: 3 States
Density: 21 in MI, OH, IN
Projected New Units (12 Months): 10
Qualifications: 3, 2, 1, 1, 1, 5
Registered: MI

FINANCIAL/TERMS:

Cash Investment: $40-80K
Total Investment: $80K
Minimum Net Worth: $80K
Fees: Franchise - $20K
Royalty - 6%; Ad. - 1%
Earnings Claims Statement: No
Term of Contract (Years): 10/10
Avg. # Of Employees: 5 FT
Passive Ownership: Discouraged
Encourage Conversions: Yes
Area Develop. Agreements: Yes/5
Sub-Franchising Contracts: Yes
Expand In Territory: Yes
Space Needs: 1,500 SF; FS, SC

SUPPORT & TRAINING:

Financial Assistance Provided: Yes(I)
Site Selection Assistance: Yes
Lease Negotiation Assistance: Yes
Co-Operative Advertising: Yes
Franchisee Assoc./Member: No
Size Of Corporate Staff: 8
On-Going Support: B,C,D,E,F,G,H
Training: 1 Week Corporate Office.

SPECIFIC EXPANSION PLANS:

US: Midwest
Canada: No
Overseas: No

<< >>

XPRESS AUTO

1200 Spears Rd., # 16
Oakville, ON L6L 2X4 CANADA
Tel: (905) 815-1121
Fax: (905) 815-1196
E-Mail: htulk@aol.com
Mr. Hugh Tulk, President

Windshield repairs. Unique opportunity. Invest in the growing auto glass repair industry. Proven track record, central insurance claims processing. (We do all the collections for you.) Affiliates itself with major automotive centers in high-traffic malls etc. (Canadian Tires.) Fleet contracts, master franchises available in Canada and U.S.

BACKGROUND:

Established: 1993; 1st Franchised: 1995
Franchised Units: 22
Company-Owned Units: 2
Total Units: 24

Dist.: US-0; CAN-44; O'seas-0
North America: 5 Provinces
Density: 27 in ON, 6 in NS, 4 in NB
Projected New Units (12 Months): 25
Qualifications: 4, 5, 1, 3, 1, 4
Registered: NR

FINANCIAL/TERMS:
Cash Investment: $25.5K
Total Investment: $30.5K
Minimum Net Worth: $50K
Fees: Franchise - $20K
Royalty - 5%; Ad. - 2%
Earnings Claims Statement: No
Term of Contract (Years): 5/15
Avg. # Of Employees: 1 FT, 1 PT
Passive Ownership: Allowed
Encourage Conversions: Yes
Area Develop. Agreements: No
Sub-Franchising Contracts: No
Expand In Territory: Yes
Space Needs: 120 SF; FS, RM

SUPPORT & TRAINING:
Financial Assistance Provided: Yes(B)
Site Selection Assistance: Yes
Lease Negotiation Assistance: Yes
Co-Operative Advertising: Yes
Franchisee Assoc./Member: No
Size Of Corporate Staff: 10
On-Going Support: a,B,C,D,E,F
Training: 1-1.5 Week(s) Home Office, Oakville, ON; 1-1.5 Week(s) On-Site.

SPECIFIC EXPANSION PLANS:
US: All United States
Canada: All Canada
Overseas: No

<< >>

ZIEBART INTERNATIONAL

1290 E. Maple Rd., P.O. Box 1290
Troy, MI 48007-1290
Tel: (800) 877-1312 (248) 588-4100
Fax: (248) 588-0718
E-Mail: rbass@ziebart.com
Web Site: www.ziebart.com
Mr. Dick Bass, Dir. Worldwide Fran. Sales

Business format consists of automobile detailing, accessories and protection services. Ultra-modern showrooms maximize the exposure for the services offered by the franchisee. The customer base consists of retail, wholesale and fleet - making ZIEBART # 1 in the world.

BACKGROUND:
Established: 1954; 1st Franchised: 1962
Franchised Units: 405
Company-Owned Units: 29
Total Units: 434
Dist.: US-265; CAN-50; O'seas-253
North America: 39 States, 7 Provinces
Density: NR
Projected New Units (12 Months): 50
Qualifications: 5, 4, 2, 3, 4, 5
Registered: All States

FINANCIAL/TERMS:
Cash Investment: $60K
Total Investment: $100-161K
Minimum Net Worth: $250K
Fees: Franchise - $24K
Royalty - 8%; Ad. - 5%
Earnings Claims Statement: No
Term of Contract (Years): 10/10
Avg. # Of Employees: 2 FT, 3 PT
Passive Ownership: Discouraged
Encourage Conversions: Yes
Area Develop. Agreements: Yes
Sub-Franchising Contracts: No
Expand In Territory: Yes
Space Needs: 500 SF; FS

SUPPORT & TRAINING:
Financial Assistance Provided: Yes(I)
Site Selection Assistance: Yes
Lease Negotiation Assistance: Yes
Co-Operative Advertising: Yes
Franchisee Assoc./Member: Yes/Yes
Size Of Corporate Staff: 100
On-Going Support: a,B,C,D,E,F,G,h,I
Training: 3-6 Weeks Sales, Management and Technical Training at Home Office.

SPECIFIC EXPANSION PLANS:
US: All United States
Canada: All Canada
Overseas: All Countries

<< >>

Auto/Truck/Trailer Rental

Chapter

5

Auto/Truck/Trailer Rental Industry Profile

Total # Franchisors in Industry Group	27
Total # Franchised Units in Industry Group	3,984
Total # Company-Owned Units in Industry Group	607
Total # Operating Units in Industry Group	4,591
Average # Franchised Units/Franchisor	147.6
Average # Company-Owned Units/Franchisor	22.5
Average # Total Units/Franchisor	170
Ratio of Total # Franchised Units/Total # Company-Owned Units	6.6:1
Industry Survey Participants	17
Representing % of Industry	63%
Average Franchise Fee*:	$21.6K
Average Total Investment*:	$226K
Average On-Going Royalty Fee*:	9%

*If a range was provided, the mid-point of the range was used. See detailed profiles for actual ranges.

Five Largest Participants in Survey

Company	# Franchised Units	# Co-Owned Units	# Total Units	Franchise Fee	On-Going Royalty	Total Investment
1. Thrifty Car Rental	849	151	1,000	Varies	3%	$200-250K
2. U-Save Auto Rental of America	454	15	469	$20K	$33.28/Vehicle	$56.5-103.5K
3. Rent-A-Wreck of America	450	0	450	$8K	$30/Car	$32.8-209K
4. Budget Rent A Car of Canada	380	8	388	$20K	7.5%	$100K+
5. Dollar Rent A Car	224	148	372	$12.5K+	8%	$100K-2MM

All of the data provided are proprietary and should not be quoted without acknowledging *Bond's Franchise Guide.*

AFFILIATED CAR RENTAL

96 Freneau Ave., # 2
Matawan, NJ 07747
Tel: (800) 367-5159 (732) 290-8300
Fax: (732) 290-8305
E-Mail: msmil@sensiblecarrental.com
Web Site: www.sensiblecarrental.com
Mr. Michael S. Miller, National Sales Manager

We offer a rental car program which provides training, insurance and management support.

BACKGROUND:
Established: 1981; 1st Franchised: 1981
Franchised Units: 150
Company-Owned Units: 0
Total Units: 150
Dist.: US-85; CAN-0; O'seas-0
North America: 15 States
Density: NR
Projected New Units (12 Months): 20
Qualifications: 2, 3, 4, 2, 2, 5
Registered: All States Except CA,WI,LA.

FINANCIAL/TERMS:
Cash Investment: $30K-50K
Total Investment: Varies
Minimum Net Worth: Varies
Fees: Franchise - $3.5K Min.
Royalty - $10-15/Car; Ad. - 0%
Earnings Claims Statement: No
Term of Contract (Years): Perpetual
Avg. # Of Employees: 1 FT, 2 PT
Passive Ownership: Not Allowed
Encourage Conversions: NA
Area Develop. Agreements: No
Sub-Franchising Contracts: No
Expand In Territory: Yes
Space Needs: NR SF; FS

SUPPORT & TRAINING:
Financial Assistance Provided: No
Site Selection Assistance: NA
Lease Negotiation Assistance: NA
Co-Operative Advertising: NA
Franchisee Assoc./Member: Yes/Yes
Size Of Corporate Staff: 9
On-Going Support: C,D,F,G,H,I
Training: 2 Days Corporate in NJ.

SPECIFIC EXPANSION PLANS:
US: All United States
Canada: No
Overseas: No

<< >>

BARGAIN BUGGIES RENT A CAR SYSTEMS

3140 N. Washington Blvd.
Arlington, VA 22201
Tel: (703) 841-0000
Fax: (703) 841-1934
E-Mail: info@bargainbuggies.com
Web Site: www.bargainbuggies.com
Mr. Patrick Cloud, Director Franchise Sales

BARGAIN BUGGIES RENT-A-CAR SYSTEMS currently operates 6 company-owned stores and 15 franchises in the Washington metropolitan area. BARGAIN BUGGIES employs 19 permanent staff members with over 200 years combined experience, who manage a fleet ranging in size from 300 to 500 vehicles. BARGAIN BUGGIES plans to continue to expand Internet capabilities and implement new marketing strategies. All of this will take place while focusing on offering exceptional customer service.

BACKGROUND:
Established: 1970; 1st Franchised: 1984
Franchised Units: 12
Company-Owned Units: 6
Total Units: 18
Dist.: US-18; CAN-0; O'seas-0
North America: NR
Density: 8 in MD, 4 in VA
Projected New Units (12 Months): 12
Qualifications: 4, 5, 4, 3, 2, 3
Registered: MD, VA, DC

FINANCIAL/TERMS:
Cash Investment: $25-75K
Total Investment: $50-250K
Minimum Net Worth: $150K
Fees: Franchise - $5-25K
Royalty - $25/Car/Mo.; Ad. - Adv. Fund
Earnings Claims Statement: No
Term of Contract (Years): 5/5
Avg. # Of Employees: 3 FT, 2 PT
Passive Ownership: Not Allowed
Encourage Conversions: Yes
Area Develop. Agreements: No
Sub-Franchising Contracts: No
Expand In Territory: Yes
Space Needs: 1,000 SF; FS, SC, Hotel, Car Dealership

SUPPORT & TRAINING:
Financial Assistance Provided: Yes(I)
Site Selection Assistance: Yes
Lease Negotiation Assistance: Yes
Co-Operative Advertising: Yes
Franchisee Assoc./Member: No
Size Of Corporate Staff: 25
On-Going Support: b,C,D,E,F,G,h,I
Training: 1 Week Corporate Headquarters; 1 Week On-Site.

SPECIFIC EXPANSION PLANS:
US: Mid-Atlantic
Canada: No
Overseas: No

<< >>

BUDGET RENT A CAR OF CANADA

3080 Yonge St., # 4000
Toronto, ON M4N 3N1 CANADA
Tel: (800) 268-8941 (416) 622-3366
Fax: (416) 622-5555
E-Mail:
Web Site: www.worldfranchising.com/website.htm
Mr. Ron Groves, Mgr. Franchising/Bus. Dev.

Car and truck rental, both in airports and local markets.

BACKGROUND:
Established: 1963; 1st Franchised: 1963
Franchised Units: 380
Company-Owned Units: 8
Total Units: 388
Dist.: US-0; CAN-388; O'seas-0
North America: NR
Density: NR
Projected New Units (12 Months): 5
Qualifications: 4, 4, 5, 3, 3, 3
Registered: AB

FINANCIAL/TERMS:
Cash Investment: $100K
Total Investment: $100K+
Minimum Net Worth: $1MM
Fees: Franchise - $20K
Royalty - 7.5%; Ad. - 0%
Earnings Claims Statement: No
Term of Contract (Years): 5/5
Avg. # Of Employees: 2 FT, 2 PT
Passive Ownership: Discouraged
Encourage Conversions: No
Area Develop. Agreements: No
Sub-Franchising Contracts: Yes
Expand In Territory: Yes
Space Needs: NR SF; FS, SF, Dealership

SUPPORT & TRAINING:
Financial Assistance Provided: No
Site Selection Assistance: Yes
Lease Negotiation Assistance: Yes
Co-Operative Advertising: No
Franchisee Assoc./Member: Yes/Yes
Size Of Corporate Staff: 40
On-Going Support: A,B,C,D,E,f,G,H,I
Training: 3 Days in Chicago, IL.

SPECIFIC EXPANSION PLANS:
US: No
Canada: AB,SK,MB,ON,PQ
Overseas: No

<< >>

DISCOUNT CAR & TRUCK RENTALS

720 Arrow Rd.
North York, ON M9M 2M1 CANADA
Tel: (800) 263-2355 (416) 744-0123
Fax: (416) 744-0624
E-Mail: jstanaitis@discountcar.com
Web Site: www.discountcar.com
Mr. John Stanaitis, Dir. Franchise Operations

DISCOUNT CAR & TRUCK RENTALS offer a unique approach to the rental business. We specialize in the replacement car market with a flair for leisure business.

BACKGROUND:

Established: 1980;	1st Franchised: 1984
Franchised Units:	180
Company-Owned Units:	23
Total Units:	203
Dist.:	US-23; CAN-170; O'seas-10
North America:	2 States, 10 Provinces
Density:	86 in ON, 36 in PQ, 12 in AZ
Projected New Units (12 Months):	10
Qualifications:	3, 5, 3, 3, 3, 5
Registered:	All States

FINANCIAL/TERMS:

Cash Investment:	$150-250K
Total Investment:	$150-250K
Minimum Net Worth:	$250K
Fees: Franchise -	Varies
Royalty - 6-8%;	Ad. - 0%
Earnings Claims Statement:	No
Term of Contract (Years):	10/5/5
Avg. # Of Employees:	3 FT, 1 PT
Passive Ownership:	Not Allowed
Encourage Conversions:	Yes
Area Develop. Agreements:	Yes/10
Sub-Franchising Contracts:	Yes
Expand In Territory:	Yes
Space Needs:	1,500 SF; FS, SF, SC

SUPPORT & TRAINING:

Financial Assistance Provided:	Yes(I)
Site Selection Assistance:	Yes
Lease Negotiation Assistance:	Yes
Co-Operative Advertising:	NA
Franchisee Assoc./Member:	Yes/Yes
Size Of Corporate Staff:	40
On-Going Support:	A,B,C,D,E,f,G,h,i
Training:	2-4 Weeks at North York, ON.

SPECIFIC EXPANSION PLANS:

US:	All United States
Canada:	All Canada
Overseas:	U.K., Australia

DOLLAR RENT A CAR

5330 E. 31st St.
Tulsa, OK 74135
Tel: (800) 555-9893 (918) 669-0000
Fax: (918) 669-3006
E-Mail: pfritz@dollar.com
Web Site: www.dollar.com
Mr. Peter Fritz, Dir. Franchise Development

DOLLAR RENT A CAR operates and licenses others to operate daily car rental operations. Established over 30 years ago, DOLLAR RENT A CAR now serves the worldwide car rental market.

BACKGROUND:

Established: 1965;	1st Franchised: 1966
Franchised Units:	224
Company-Owned Units:	148
Total Units:	372
Dist.:	US-266; CAN-76; O'seas-554
North America:	48 States
Density:	CA, TX, FL
Projected New Units (12 Months):	24
Qualifications:	5, 5, 4, 4, 4, 5
Registered:	All States

FINANCIAL/TERMS:

Cash Investment:	$100K-2MM
Total Investment:	$100K-2MM
Minimum Net Worth:	$250K
Fees: Franchise -	$12.5K+
Royalty - 8%;	Ad. - Included
Earnings Claims Statement:	No
Term of Contract (Years):	10/10
Avg. # Of Employees:	Varies
Passive Ownership:	Not Allowed
Encourage Conversions:	Yes
Area Develop. Agreements:	Yes
Sub-Franchising Contracts:	No
Expand In Territory:	Yes
Space Needs:	1,000+ SF; FS, SF, SC

SUPPORT & TRAINING:

Financial Assistance Provided:	Yes(I)
Site Selection Assistance:	No
Lease Negotiation Assistance:	No
Co-Operative Advertising:	Yes
Franchisee Assoc./Member:	No
Size Of Corporate Staff:	400
On-Going Support:	a,B,C,D,E,G,H,I
Training:	3 Days Headquarters Orientation; 2 Weeks On-Site Field Training; 1 Week Automation.

SPECIFIC EXPANSION PLANS:

US:	Not FL,MA,VT,NH,NV,AR,UT,MT
Canada:	2 Master Fran.
Overseas:	Australia, China, Southeast Asia

DOLLAR RENT A CAR (CANADA)

1027 Yonge St., 3rd Fl.
Toronto, ON M4W 2K9 CANADA
Tel: (800) 254-7561 (416) 969-1190
Fax: (416) 969-9582
E-Mail: rlewchyshyn@dtag.com
Web Site: www.worldfranchising.com/website.htm
Mr. Roman Lewchyshyn, Franchise Operations

Daily, weekly, monthly car and truck rental.

BACKGROUND:

Established: 1966;	1st Franchised: 1990
Franchised Units:	40
Company-Owned Units:	0
Total Units:	40
Dist.:	US-0; CAN-42; O'seas-0
North America:	9 Provinces
Density:	ON, BC, PQ
Projected New Units (12 Months):	20
Qualifications:	5, 5, 5, 3, 3, 3
Registered:	AB

FINANCIAL/TERMS:

Cash Investment:	$100-160K
Total Investment:	$150-300K
Minimum Net Worth:	$250K
Fees: Franchise -	$10-50K
Royalty - 7%;	Ad. - 2%
Earnings Claims Statement:	Yes
Term of Contract (Years):	5/5
Avg. # Of Employees:	3 FT, 1 PT
Passive Ownership:	Discouraged
Encourage Conversions:	Yes
Area Develop. Agreements:	Yes/3
Sub-Franchising Contracts:	Yes
Expand In Territory:	Yes
Space Needs:	1,200 SF; FS

SUPPORT & TRAINING:

Financial Assistance Provided:	Yes(I)
Site Selection Assistance:	Yes
Lease Negotiation Assistance:	Yes
Co-Operative Advertising:	Yes
Franchisee Assoc./Member:	No
Size Of Corporate Staff:	10
On-Going Support:	B,C,D,E,F,H,I
Training:	5 Days Toronto, ON.

SPECIFIC EXPANSION PLANS:

US:	No
Canada:	All Canada
Overseas:	No

<< >>

EAGLERIDER MOTORCYCLE RENTAL

11860 S. La Cienega Blvd.
Los Angeles, CA 90250-3461
Tel: (800) 501-8687 (310) 536-6777
Fax: (310) 536-6770
E-Mail: rent@eaglerider.com
Web Site: www.eaglerider.com
Mr. Marcelino Orozco, Vice President Franchising

EAGLERIDER is the world's largest motorcycle rental & tour company that specializes in Harley-Davidson motorcycles, ATVs, dirt bike, watercraft and snowmobile rentals. Why buy it when you can rent it?

BACKGROUND:

Established: 1992; 1st Franchised: 1997
Franchised Units: 21
Company-Owned Units: 4
Total Units: 25
Dist.: US-21; CAN-4; O'seas-25
North America: 11 States
Density: 6 in CA, 4 in TX, 2 FL
Projected New Units (12 Months): 10
Qualifications: 3, 2, 4, 2, 3, 5
Registered: All States

FINANCIAL/TERMS:

Cash Investment: $69.5-184K
Total Investment: $219.5-684K
Minimum Net Worth: $225K
Fees: Franchise - $30K
Royalty - 10%; Ad. - 0%
Earnings Claims Statement: No
Term of Contract (Years): 10/10
Avg. # Of Employees: 2 FT, 2 PT
Passive Ownership: Discouraged
Encourage Conversions: Yes
Area Develop. Agreements: Yes/10
Sub-Franchising Contracts: No
Expand In Territory: Yes
Space Needs: 3,500 SF; FS, SF, Industrial

SUPPORT & TRAINING:

Financial Assistance Provided: Yes(I)
Site Selection Assistance: Yes
Lease Negotiation Assistance: No
Co-Operative Advertising: No
Franchisee Assoc./Member: No
Size Of Corporate Staff: 31
On-Going Support: A,B,C,d,E,F,G,h,I
Training: 2 Weeks in Los Angeles, CA.

SPECIFIC EXPANSION PLANS:

US: All United States
Canada: All Canada
Overseas: All Tourist Destinations with 6 months or greater rental season

<< >>

PAYLESS CAR RENTAL SYSTEM

2350 34th St. N.
St. Petersburg, FL 33713
Tel: (800) 729-5255 (727) 321-6352
Fax: (727) 323-6856
E-Mail: franchise@paylesscarrental.com
Web Site: www.paylesscarrental.com
Ms. Kathleen Gassner, Dir. of Franchise Development

PAYLESS CAR RENTAL SYSTEM, Inc., has been a recognized name in the car rental industry for almost 30 years. Car rental expertise and an experienced corporate office staff give each franchisee individual assistance and the competitive edge. We offer the tools to become successful in the vehicle rental and sales business.

BACKGROUND: IFA MEMBER

Established: 1971; 1st Franchised: 1971
Franchised Units: 103
Company-Owned Units: 5
Total Units: 108
Dist.: US-68; CAN-0; O'seas-40
North America: 17 States
Density: 11 in FL, 8 in CA, 5 in AK
Projected New Units (12 Months): 70
Qualifications: 5, 4, 3, 1, 3, 5
Registered: All States

FINANCIAL/TERMS:

Cash Investment: $100K+
Total Investment: $217-6MM+
Minimum Net Worth: $500K
Fees: Franchise - $20-500K
Royalty - 4-5%; Ad. - 1-3%
Earnings Claims Statement: No
Term of Contract (Years): 5/5
Avg. # Of Employees: Varies
Passive Ownership: Discouraged
Encourage Conversions: Yes
Area Develop. Agreements: Yes/4
Sub-Franchising Contracts: Int
Expand In Territory: Yes
Space Needs: Varies SF; FS

SUPPORT & TRAINING:

Financial Assistance Provided: No
Site Selection Assistance: No
Lease Negotiation Assistance: No
Co-Operative Advertising: Yes
Franchisee Assoc./Member: Yes/Yes
Size Of Corporate Staff: 50
On-Going Support: A,B,C,D,E,G,h,I
Training: 3-5 Days Corporate Office; 3-5 Days Franchisee's Location.

SPECIFIC EXPANSION PLANS:

US: All United States
Canada: All Canada
Overseas: All Countries

<< >>

PRACTICAL RENT A CAR

4780 I-55 N., # 300
Jackson, MS 39211
Tel: (800) 424-7722 (601) 713-4333
Fax: (601) 713-4330
E-Mail: jay.mitchell@usave.net
Web Site: www.usave.net
Mr. Jay Mitchell, National Sales Director

Recruit, train and develop operators in the car rental industry as independently owned operations. National insurance program by A+ rated company, automated and voice reservation systems. Centralized purchasing, on-going support, newsletters and training.

BACKGROUND:

Established: 1989; 1st Franchised: 1989
Franchised Units: 134
Company-Owned Units: 0
Total Units: 134
Dist.: US-134; CAN-0; O'seas-0
North America: 34 States
Density: 20 in WA, 14 in PA, 10 in OK
Projected New Units (12 Months): 100
Qualifications: 5, 3, 2, 3, 4, 5
Registered: All States

FINANCIAL/TERMS:

Cash Investment: $10-25K
Total Investment: $25-100K
Minimum Net Worth: $100K
Fees: Franchise - $2.5-100K
Royalty - Flat/Car; Ad. - 0%
Earnings Claims Statement: No
Term of Contract (Years): 10/10
Avg. # Of Employees: 2 FT, 1 PT
Passive Ownership: Discouraged
Encourage Conversions: Yes
Area Develop. Agreements: No
Sub-Franchising Contracts: No
Expand In Territory: Yes
Space Needs: 1,000 SF; FS, SF, SC, Hotel

SUPPORT & TRAINING:

Financial Assistance Provided: Yes
Site Selection Assistance: Yes
Lease Negotiation Assistance: Yes
Co-Operative Advertising: No
Franchisee Assoc./Member: Yes/Yes
Size Of Corporate Staff: 8
On-Going Support: a,B,C,d,E,G,H,I
Training: 4.5 Days Headquarters.

SPECIFIC EXPANSION PLANS:

US: All United States
Canada: No
Overseas: All Countries

<< >>

RENT-A-WRECK

7710 5th St., SE, # 204
Calgary, AB T2H 2L9 CANADA
Tel: (800) 668-8591 (403) 259-6666
Fax: (403) 259-6776
E-Mail: psi@rentawreck.ca
Web Site: www.rent-a-wreck.ca
Marketing Department,

Our success is based upon teaching our franchisees how to achieve their professional goals. Our reputation is based upon providing the lowest car and truck rental rates across Canada.

BACKGROUND:
Established: 1976; 1st Franchised: 1976
Franchised Units: 59
Company-Owned Units: 0
Total Units: 59
Dist.: US-0; CAN-66; O'seas-0
North America: 8 Provinces
Density: 16 in BC, 11 in AB, 8 in NF
Projected New Units (12 Months): 21
Qualifications: 5, 5, 3, 3, 5, 5
Registered: AB

FINANCIAL/TERMS:
Cash Investment: $75K+
Total Investment: Varies
Minimum Net Worth: $75K
Fees: Franchise - $10-30K
Royalty - 6%; Ad. - 4%
Earnings Claims Statement: No
Term of Contract (Years): 5/5
Avg. # Of Employees: 3 FT, 2 PT
Passive Ownership: Discouraged
Encourage Conversions: Yes
Area Develop. Agreements: No
Sub-Franchising Contracts: No
Expand In Territory: Yes
Space Needs: 1,000 SF; SF

SUPPORT & TRAINING:
Financial Assistance Provided: Yes(I)
Site Selection Assistance: Yes
Lease Negotiation Assistance: Yes
Co-Operative Advertising: Yes
Franchisee Assoc./Member: Yes/Yes
Size Of Corporate Staff: 9
On-Going Support: C,D,E,F,G,H,I
Training: 2 Weeks Calgary, AB.

SPECIFIC EXPANSION PLANS:
US: No - US Affiliate
Canada: All Canada
Overseas: No

<< >>

RENT-A-WRECK OF AMERICA

10324 S. Dolfield Rd.
Owings Mills, MD 21117
Tel: (800) 421-7253 ex 407 (410) 581-5755
Fax: (410) 581-1566
E-Mail: dtripp@rent-a-wreck.com
Web Site: www.rent-a-wreck.com
Mr. Dale Tripp, Sales Manager

America's # 1 neighborhood car rental company, RENT-A-WRECK has attained the highest ratings in the franchising industry. For 5 successive years, Entrepreneur Magazine rated RENT-A-WRECK # 1 in its category for the prestigious Franchise 500 awards. The annual Success Magazine named RENT-A-WRECK 'one of the best-managed franchises in America.' Success surveyed over 2,800 franchise companies in all industries and ranked RENT-A-WRECK 4th.

BACKGROUND:
Established: 1973; 1st Franchised: 1978
Franchised Units: 450
Company-Owned Units: 0
Total Units: 450
Dist.: US-429; CAN-0; O'seas-21
North America: 49 States
Density: 55 in CA, 43 in NY, 34 in NJ
Projected New Units (12 Months): 73
Qualifications: 3, 5, 2, 3, 3, 3
Registered: All States

FINANCIAL/TERMS:
Cash Investment: $32.8K
Total Investment: $32.8-209K
Minimum Net Worth: $50K
Fees: Franchise - $8K
Royalty - $30/Car; Ad. - $7/Car
Earnings Claims Statement: No
Term of Contract (Years): 10/5
Avg. # Of Employees: 1 FT
Passive Ownership: Discouraged
Encourage Conversions: No
Area Develop. Agreements: No
Sub-Franchising Contracts: No
Expand In Territory: Yes
Space Needs: 1,500 SF; FS, SF, SC

SUPPORT & TRAINING:
Financial Assistance Provided: Yes(D)
Site Selection Assistance: No
Lease Negotiation Assistance: No
Co-Operative Advertising: Yes
Franchisee Assoc./Member: Yes/Yes
Size Of Corporate Staff: 25
On-Going Support: C,D,e,G,h,I
Training: 1 Week Baltimore, MD.

SPECIFIC EXPANSION PLANS:
US: All United States
Canada: No
Overseas: All Countries

<< >>

SENSIBLE CAR RENTAL

96 Freneau Ave., # 2
Matawan, NJ 07747
Tel: (800) 367-5159 (732) 583-8500
Fax: (732) 290-8305
E-Mail: corporate@sensiblecarrental.com
Web Site: www.sensiblecarrental.com
Mr. Charles A. Vitale, VP General Manager

We offer a rental car program which provides training, insurance and support. Majority of franchisee are used car dealers and other automotive related businesspersons.

BACKGROUND:
Established: 1986; 1st Franchised: 1986
Franchised Units: 140
Company-Owned Units: 0
Total Units: 140
Dist.: US-140; CAN-0; O'seas-0
North America: 22 States
Density: 25 in NY, 24 in NJ, 10 in MA
Projected New Units (12 Months): 25
Qualifications: 2, 3, 4, 2, 2, 5
Registered: All States Except CA,WI,LA

FINANCIAL/TERMS:
Cash Investment: $20-25K
Total Investment: $46.4-69.5K
Minimum Net Worth: Varies
Fees: Franchise - $6-10K
Royalty - $10-15/Car; Ad. - 0%
Earnings Claims Statement: No
Term of Contract (Years): Perpetual
Avg. # Of Employees: 1 FT, 1 PT
Passive Ownership: Not Allowed
Encourage Conversions: NA
Area Develop. Agreements: No
Sub-Franchising Contracts: No
Expand In Territory: Yes
Space Needs: NR SF; FS

SUPPORT & TRAINING:
Financial Assistance Provided: Yes
Site Selection Assistance: No
Lease Negotiation Assistance: No
Co-Operative Advertising: Yes
Franchisee Assoc./Member: Yes/Yes
Size Of Corporate Staff: 10
On-Going Support: C,d,F,G,H,I
Training: 2 Days in Matawan, NJ.

SPECIFIC EXPANSION PLANS:
US: All United States
Canada: No
Overseas: No

<< >>

THRIFTY CAR RENTAL

5310 E. 31st St.
Tulsa, OK 74135
Tel: (800) 532-3401 (918) 669-2219
Fax: (918) 669-2061
E-Mail: franchisesales@thrifty.com
Web Site: www.thrifty.com
Mr. Trey Russell, Director

THRIFTY operates in over 57 countries and territories, with over 1,000 locations throughout North and South America, Europe, the Middle East, Caribbean, Asia and the Pacific, and is one of the fastest-growing car rental company in Canada and Australia. THRIFTY has a significant presence both in the airport and local car rental markets. Approximately 66% of its business is in the airport market, 34% in the local market.

BACKGROUND:
Established: 1958; 1st Franchised: 1962
Franchised Units: 849
Company-Owned Units: 151
Total Units: 1,000
Dist.: US-374; CAN-135; O'seas-491
North America: 46 States,10 Provinces
Density: 59 in ON, 37 in FL, 34 in CA
Projected New Units (12 Months): 50-75
Qualifications: 5, 5, 5, 3, 3, 5
Registered: All States

FINANCIAL/TERMS:
Cash Investment: $150K
Total Investment: $200-250K
Minimum Net Worth: $500K
Fees: Franchise - Varies
Royalty - 3%; Ad. - 2.5-5%
Earnings Claims Statement: No
Term of Contract (Years): 10/5
Avg. # Of Employees: 4-6 FT
Passive Ownership: Not Allowed
Encourage Conversions: Yes
Area Develop. Agreements: No
Sub-Franchising Contracts: No
Expand In Territory: Yes
Space Needs: Varies SF; FS, SF, SC, RM

SUPPORT & TRAINING:
Financial Assistance Provided: No
Site Selection Assistance: No
Lease Negotiation Assistance: Yes
Co-Operative Advertising: Yes
Franchisee Assoc./Member: No
Size Of Corporate Staff: 1,000
On-Going Support: A,B,C,D,E,F,G,H,I
Training: 5 Days + Mentor Program at Headquarters in Tulsa, OK.

SPECIFIC EXPANSION PLANS:
US: Selected Markets Remaining
Canada: All Canada
Overseas: All Countries

<< >>

THRIFTY CAR RENTAL (CANADA)

6050 Indian Line
Mississauga, ON L4V 1G5 CANADA
Tel: (800) 667-5925 + 809 (905) 612-1881
Fax: (905) 612-1893
E-Mail: jforrester@dtag.com
Web Site: www.thrifty.com
Mr. Jack Forrester, Mgr. Franchise Sales

THRIFTY CAR RENTAL's high name awareness and consistent image of quality and reliable service have resulted in THRIFTY becoming one of North America's fastest-growing car rental companies. THRIFTY has over 1,200 locations in 60 countries worldwide, with approximately 145 locations in Canada. Represented at all major Canadian airport locations, also the largest off-airport car rental in the U. S. and the 5th largest in # of locations throughout North America. Full range of innovative support services.

BACKGROUND:
Established: 1958; 1st Franchised: 1984
Franchised Units: 120
Company-Owned Units: 25
Total Units: 145
Dist.: US-560; CAN-145; O'seas-500
North America: NR
Density: NR
Projected New Units (12 Months): 10
Qualifications: 5, 4, 3, 4, 3, 3
Registered: All States

FINANCIAL/TERMS:
Cash Investment: $50-300K
Total Investment: $200-500K
Minimum Net Worth: $250K
Fees: Franchise - $15K+
Royalty - 5%; Ad. - 3%
Earnings Claims Statement: No
Term of Contract (Years): 5/5
Avg. # Of Employees: 3 FT, 2 PT
Passive Ownership: Not Allowed
Encourage Conversions: Yes
Area Develop. Agreements: No
Sub-Franchising Contracts: No
Expand In Territory: Yes
Space Needs: Varies SF; FS, SF, SC, RM, Dealership

SUPPORT & TRAINING:
Financial Assistance Provided: Yes(I)
Site Selection Assistance: Yes
Lease Negotiation Assistance: Yes
Co-Operative Advertising: Yes
Franchisee Assoc./Member: Yes/Yes
Size Of Corporate Staff: 465
On-Going Support: B,C,D,e,F,G,h,I
Training: 1 Week On-Site; 1 Week at Headquarters.

SPECIFIC EXPANSION PLANS:
US: All United States
Canada: All Canada
Overseas: All Countries

<< >>

U-SAVE AUTO RENTAL OF AMERICA

4780 I-55 N., # 300
Jackson, MS 39211
Tel: (800) 438-2300 (601) 713-4333, x.146
Fax: (601) 713-4330
E-Mail: info@usave.net
Web Site: www.usave.net
Mr. Jay Mitchell, VP Franchise Sales

U-SAVE is strategically positioned as the #2 operator in the local neighborhood rental car market, providing superior customer service and affordable rental cars to consumers who need a rental car to temporarily augment their personal use vehicle, or who need a car to replace a vehicle being repaired, and to local businesses that rent vehicles on an as-needed basis.

BACKGROUND:
Established: 1979; 1st Franchised: 1979
Franchised Units: 454
Company-Owned Units: 15
Total Units: 469
Dist.: US-456; CAN-0; O'seas-6
North America: 47 States
Density: NR
Projected New Units (12 Months): NR
Qualifications: 5, 4, 3, 2, 1, 4
Registered: All States

FINANCIAL/TERMS:
Cash Investment: $60K Liquid
Total Investment: $56.5-103.5K
Minimum Net Worth: $250K
Fees: Franchise - $20K
Royalty - $33.28/Vehicle; Ad. - $0.50/Car
Earnings Claims Statement: No
Term of Contract (Years): 10/10
Avg. # Of Employees: 2 FT, 2 PT
Passive Ownership: Discouraged
Encourage Conversions: Yes
Area Develop. Agreements: No
Sub-Franchising Contracts: No
Expand In Territory: Yes

Space Needs: 1,500-2,000 SF; FS, SF, SC, Other Businesses

SUPPORT & TRAINING:

Financial Assistance Provided: Yes(D)
Site Selection Assistance: No
Lease Negotiation Assistance: No
Co-Operative Advertising: Yes
Franchisee Assoc./Member: Yes/Yes
Size Of Corporate Staff: 50
On-Going Support: B,C,D,E,F,G,H,I
Training: 5 Days Jackson, MS.

SPECIFIC EXPANSION PLANS:

US: All United States
Canada: No
Overseas: No

WHEELCHAIR GETAWAYS

P.O. Box 605
Versailles, KY 40383-0605
Tel: (800) 536-5518 (859) 873-4973
Fax: (859) 873-8039
E-Mail: corporate@wheelchairgetaways.com
Web Site: www.wheelchairgetaways.com
Mr. Richard Gatewood, President

WHEELCHAIR GETAWAYS rents wheelchair-accessible vans to wheelchair users by the day, week, month or year. We receive referrals from the major car rental companies and travel agencies. We are the leader in our field and encourage any and all applicants. We will train and continue to support you in every aspect of ownership and management. Affordable, accessible transportation is becoming a necessity as a result of the Americans With Disabilities Act.

BACKGROUND:

Established: 1988; 1st Franchised: 1989
Franchised Units: 47
Company-Owned Units: 1
Total Units: 48
Dist.: US-39; CAN-0; O'seas-0
North America: 43 States, Puerto Rico
Density: 5 in FL, 3 in NY, 2 in CA
Projected New Units (12 Months): 5
Qualifications: 3, 5, 3, 3, 4, 4
Registered: CA,FL,IL,IN,MD,MI,NY,VA, WA,DC

FINANCIAL/TERMS:

Cash Investment: $38-100K
Total Investment: $38-100K
Minimum Net Worth: $75K
Fees: Franchise - $17.5K
Royalty - $550/Van/Yr.; Ad. - $550/Van/Yr
Earnings Claims Statement: No
Term of Contract (Years): 10/10
Avg. # Of Employees: 2 FT
Passive Ownership: Discouraged
Encourage Conversions: No
Area Develop. Agreements: No
Sub-Franchising Contracts: No
Expand In Territory: Yes
Space Needs: 500 SF; FS, SF, RM, HB

SUPPORT & TRAINING:

Financial Assistance Provided: Yes(I)
Site Selection Assistance: Yes
Lease Negotiation Assistance: No
Co-Operative Advertising: NA
Franchisee Assoc./Member: No
Size Of Corporate Staff: 3
On-Going Support: E,G,h,I
Training: 1 Day Corporate Headquarters or at Franchisee Site.

SPECIFIC EXPANSION PLANS:

US: IL,WI,SC,TX,AL,OR,Northwest
Canada: All Canada
Overseas: All Countries

Building & Remodeling/Furniture & Appliance Repair

Chapter

6

Building & Remodeling/Furniture & Appliance Repair Industry Profile

Total # Franchisors in Industry Group	122
Total # Franchised Units in Industry Group	24,475
Total # Company-Owned Units in Industry Group	226
Total # Operating Units in Industry Group	24,701
Average # Franchised Units/Franchisor	200.6
Average # Company-Owned Units/Franchisor	1.9
Average # Total Units/Franchisor	202.5
Ratio of Total # Franchised Units/Total # Company-Owned Units	108.3:1
Industry Survey Participants	53
Representing % of Industry	43.4%
Average Franchise Fee*:	$22.8K
Average Total Investment*:	$202K
Average On-Going Royalty Fee*:	5.5%

*If a range was provided, the mid-point of the range was used. See detailed profiles for actual ranges.

Five Largest Participants in Survey

Company	# Franchised Units	# Co-Owned Units	# Total Units	Franchise Fee	On-Going Royalty	Total Investment
1. Epcon Communities	16,000	35	16,035	$30K	$2.5K/Home	$3-5MM
2. Furniture Medic	595	0	595	$22.5K	7%/$250 Min.	$37-81.9K
3. Kitchen Tune-Up	315	0	315	$25K	4.5-7%	$40-50K
4. Dr. Vinyl & Associates	282	2	284	$34.9K	7%	$35.9-63.4K
5. Color-Glo International	230	1	231	$7.5K	2-4%	$18-30K

All of the data provided are proprietary and should not be quoted without acknowledging *Bond's Franchise Guide.*

ABC SEAMLESS

3001 Fiechtner Dr.
Fargo, ND 58103
Tel: (800) 732-6577 (701) 293-5952
Fax: (701) 293-3107
E-Mail: theduck@abcseamless.com
Web Site: www.abcseamless.com
Mr. Veryl Vik, VP Franchise Development

Franchisor of seamless steel siding, gutters, soffit and fascia. A portable machine embosses and creates seamless siding profiles of any length on the job site.

BACKGROUND:

Established: 1978;	1st Franchised: 1978
Franchised Units:	129
Company-Owned Units:	19
Total Units:	148
Dist.:	US-132; CAN-0; O'seas-0
North America:	38 States
Density:	22 in MN, 16 in WI, 12 in IL
Projected New Units (12 Months):	10
Qualifications:	5, 4, 5, 4, 4, 4
Registered:	CA,FL,HI,IL,IN,MD,MI,MN, NY,ND,OR,RI,SD,VA,WA,WI,DC

FINANCIAL/TERMS:

Cash Investment:	$20-40K
Total Investment:	$73.8-212K
Minimum Net Worth:	$150K
Fees: Franchise -	$12K
Royalty - 2-5%;	Ad. - 0.05%
Earnings Claims Statement:	No
Term of Contract (Years):	10/10
Avg. # Of Employees:	4 FT
Passive Ownership:	Discouraged
Encourage Conversions:	No
Area Develop. Agreements:	Yes/Varies
Sub-Franchising Contracts:	No
Expand In Territory:	Yes
Space Needs:	NR SF; NR

SUPPORT & TRAINING:

Financial Assistance Provided:	Yes(I)
Site Selection Assistance:	NA
Lease Negotiation Assistance:	Yes
Co-Operative Advertising:	NA
Franchisee Assoc./Member:	No
Size Of Corporate Staff:	15
On-Going Support:	C,D,E,G,H,I
Training:	2 Weeks at Franchisee's Site; On-Going at Corporate Location.

SPECIFIC EXPANSION PLANS:

US:	All United States
Canada:	No
Overseas:	No

AIRE SERV HEATING & AIR CONDITIONING

1020 N. University Parks Dr.
Waco, TX 76707
Tel: (800) 583-2662 (254) 745-2439
Fax: (254) 745-5098
E-Mail: gena.reid@dwyergroup.com
Web Site: www.aireserv.com
Mr. Mike Hawkins, VP Franchising

Serving the heating, cooling and air balancing needs of all residential and light commercial buildings, including the repair and installation of systems and "whole house" analysis involving infiltrometer testing, duct cleaning, etc.

BACKGROUND: IFA MEMBER

Established: 1992;	1st Franchised: 1994
Franchised Units:	72
Company-Owned Units:	0
Total Units:	72
Dist.:	US-72; CAN-0; O'seas-2
North America:	31 States, 2 Provinces
Density:	5 in GA, 4 in TX, 3 in NJ
Projected New Units (12 Months):	24
Qualifications:	4, 3, 5, 3, 2, 4
Registered:	All States

FINANCIAL/TERMS:

Cash Investment:	$25-75K
Total Investment:	$31.6-119.5K
Minimum Net Worth:	Varies
Fees: Franchise -	$25K
Royalty - 2.5-4.5%;	Ad. - 2%
Earnings Claims Statement:	No
Term of Contract (Years):	10/5
Avg. # Of Employees:	Varies
Passive Ownership:	Discouraged
Encourage Conversions:	Yes
Area Develop. Agreements:	No
Sub-Franchising Contracts:	No
Expand In Territory:	No
Space Needs:	NR SF; NA

SUPPORT & TRAINING:

Financial Assistance Provided:	Yes(B)
Site Selection Assistance:	NA
Lease Negotiation Assistance:	NA
Co-Operative Advertising:	No
Franchisee Assoc./Member:	Yes
Size Of Corporate Staff:	7
On-Going Support:	C,D,E,G,h,I
Training:	6 Days Corporate Office; 3 Days On-Site.

SPECIFIC EXPANSION PLANS:

US:	All United States
Canada:	All Canada
Overseas:	U.K., Latin America

AMERICAN ASPHALT SEALCOATING

P.O. Box 600
Chesterland, OH 44026
Tel: (888) 603-7325 (440) 729-8080
Fax: (440) 729-2231
E-Mail: asphaltusa@aol.com
Web Site: www.american-sealcoating.com
Mr. John Jonz, General Manager

Get your share at the billion dollar pavement maintenance industry with our franchise. Residential, commercial and industrial sealcoating and pavement services. 94% of all pavement is asphalt that needs our service. (50 million driveways, 7+ million parking lots, 4 million miles of road.) Our expert training staff and low start-up investment of $38K will get you up and running within 60 days. Your trained crew will perform the work while you manage the business from your home-based office.

BACKGROUND:

Established: 1988;	1st Franchised: 1998
Franchised Units:	10
Company-Owned Units:	1
Total Units:	11
Dist.:	US-11; CAN-0; O'seas-0
North America:	4 States
Density:	4 in OH, 1 in VA
Projected New Units (12 Months):	10
Qualifications:	4, 3, 1, 1, 1, 3
Registered:	NR

FINANCIAL/TERMS:

Cash Investment:	$10-30K
Total Investment:	$35-50K
Minimum Net Worth:	$50K
Fees: Franchise -	$15K
Royalty - 5-7%;	Ad. - 1%
Earnings Claims Statement:	No
Term of Contract (Years):	15/15
Avg. # Of Employees:	1-2 FT, 1-2 PT
Passive Ownership:	Discouraged
Encourage Conversions:	Yes
Area Develop. Agreements:	Yes/5
Sub-Franchising Contracts:	No
Expand In Territory:	Yes
Space Needs:	NA SF; NA

SUPPORT & TRAINING:

Financial Assistance Provided:	Yes(I)
Site Selection Assistance:	Yes
Lease Negotiation Assistance:	Yes

Co-Operative Advertising: No
Franchisee Assoc./Member: No
Size Of Corporate Staff: 6
On-Going Support: B,C,d,H,I
Training: 1-3 Days.

SPECIFIC EXPANSION PLANS:
US: All United States
Canada: No
Overseas: No

<< >>

ANDY ONCALL

921 E. Main St.
Chattanooga, TN 37408
Tel: (877) 263-9662 (423) 242-0401
Fax: (423) 622-0580
E-Mail: clay@andyoncall.com
Web Site: www.andyoncall.com
Mr. H. Clay Thompson, Director Franchise Develop.

Homeowners spend over $140 billion annually on home improvements and repair. ANDY ONCALL taps into this growing market. Franchise owners do not actually perform home repairs. They advertise to consumers, recruit craftsmen, schedule orders and oversee the day-to-day operation of the business. ANDY ONCALL is in the business of connecting craftsmen who are looking for work with homeowners who need minor home repairs. We locate, qualify and supervise handymen for residential and commercial markets.

BACKGROUND: IFA MEMBER
Established: 1993; 1st Franchised: 1999
Franchised Units: 45
Company-Owned Units: 0
Total Units: 45
Dist.: US-37; CAN-0; O'seas-0
North America: 18 States
Density: 5 in TN, 5 in NC, 4 in GA
Projected New Units (12 Months): 12
Qualifications: 5, 5, 3, 3, 4, 5
Registered: CA,FL,IL,IN,MD,MI,NY,VA, WI

FINANCIAL/TERMS:
Cash Investment: $30.6-49.2K
Total Investment: $39.1-69.7K
Minimum Net Worth: $100K
Fees: Franchise - $23K
Royalty - 5%; Ad. - 0%
Earnings Claims Statement: No
Term of Contract (Years): 10/10
Avg. # Of Employees: 1 FT, 1 PT
Passive Ownership: Not Allowed
Encourage Conversions: No
Area Develop. Agreements: No
Sub-Franchising Contracts: No
Expand In Territory: Yes
Space Needs: 1,000 SF; SC

SUPPORT & TRAINING:
Financial Assistance Provided: Yes(D)
Site Selection Assistance: Yes
Lease Negotiation Assistance: Yes
Co-Operative Advertising: No
Franchisee Assoc./Member: No
Size Of Corporate Staff: 10
On-Going Support: A,B,C,D,E,G,H,I
Training: 8 Days Chattanooga, TN.

SPECIFIC EXPANSION PLANS:
US: All United States
Canada: No
Overseas: No

<< >>

ARCHADECK

2112 W. Laburnum Ave., # 100
Richmond, VA 23727
Tel: (800) 722-4668 (804) 353-6999
Fax: (804) 358-1878
E-Mail: franchising@ussi.net
Web Site: www.archadeck.com
Mr. Pete Wiggins, Vice President

ARCHADECK, founded in 1980, started the nation's first network specializing in custom-designed and built decks, porches and other outdoor products. Today, there are over 80 locally owned and operated offices in the U.S., Canada, the United Kingdom and Japan. Because construction experience is not required, our franchisees come from a variety of professional backgrounds.

BACKGROUND:
Established: 1980; 1st Franchised: 1984
Franchised Units: 84
Company-Owned Units: 1
Total Units: 85
Dist.: US-81; CAN-2; O'seas-2
North America: 27 States, 2 Provinces
Density: 6 in GA, 5 in TX, 4 in NC
Projected New Units (12 Months): 25
Qualifications: 5, 5, 1, 3, 4, 5
Registered:CA,FL,IL,IN,MD,MI,MN,NY, OR,RI,VA,WA,WI,DC

FINANCIAL/TERMS:
Cash Investment: $46-96K
Total Investment: $46-96K
Minimum Net Worth: $100K
Fees: Franchise - $28K
Royalty - 6.5%; Ad. - 1%
Earnings Claims Statement: No
Term of Contract (Years): 10/10
Avg. # Of Employees: 1 FT, 1 PT
Passive Ownership: Discouraged
Encourage Conversions: Yes
Area Develop. Agreements: No
Sub-Franchising Contracts: No
Expand In Territory: Yes
Space Needs: NA SF; Home Based

SUPPORT & TRAINING:
Financial Assistance Provided: Yes(D)
Site Selection Assistance: NA
Lease Negotiation Assistance: NA
Co-Operative Advertising: No
Franchisee Assoc./Member: Yes/Yes
Size Of Corporate Staff: 25
On-Going Support: C,D,G,H,I
Training: 20 Business Days in Richmond, VA.; 9 Days On Location.

SPECIFIC EXPANSION PLANS:
US: All United States
Canada: All Canada
Overseas: Europe

<< >>

ARTHUR RUTENBERG HOMES

13922 58th St., N.
Clearwater, FL 33760
Tel: (800) 274-6637 (727) 536-5900
Fax: (727) 538-9089
E-Mail: rjaghab@arhomes.com
Web Site: www.arhomes.com
Mr. Raja Jaghab, Senior Vice President

Home building franchisor. Master working drawings provided. All necessary forms, manuals, purchasing systems, computer software training and business planning systems provided.

BACKGROUND:
Established: 1980; 1st Franchised: 1980
Franchised Units: 26
Company-Owned Units: 1
Total Units: 27
Dist.: US-27; CAN-0; O'seas-0
North America: 1 State
Density: 27 in FL
Projected New Units (12 Months): 6

Qualifications: 5, 5, 5, 5, 5, 5
Registered: NR

FINANCIAL/TERMS:

Cash Investment: $350K
Total Investment: $250-400K
Minimum Net Worth: $100K
Fees: Franchise - $20K
Royalty - 4%; Ad. - 0%
Earnings Claims Statement: No
Term of Contract (Years): 10
Avg. # Of Employees: Varies
Passive Ownership: Allowed
Encourage Conversions: No
Area Develop. Agreements: No
Sub-Franchising Contracts: No
Expand In Territory: Yes
Space Needs: NR SF; NA

SUPPORT & TRAINING:

Financial Assistance Provided: No
Site Selection Assistance: Yes
Lease Negotiation Assistance: NA
Co-Operative Advertising: NA
Franchisee Assoc./Member: No
Size Of Corporate Staff: 75
On-Going Support: A,B,C,D,H,I
Training: Yes.

SPECIFIC EXPANSION PLANS:

US: FL
Canada: No
Overseas: No

<< >>

BATH FITTER

27 Berard Dr., # 2701
South Burlington, VT 05403-5810
Tel: (877) 422-2322 + 277 (450) 472-0027
Fax: (450) 472-9490
E-Mail: jfasoli@bathfitter.com
Web Site: www.bathfitter.com
Mr. Joe Fasoli, Franchise Sales

Since 1984, BATH FITTER has been installing custom-molded acrylic bathtub liners, shower bases and one-piece, seamless wall surrounds over existing fixtures in just a few hours in countless residential and commercial properties. We provide full training, specialized tools, marketing and technical manuals and on-going support through regular visits to your location. We award exclusive territories with enormous residential and commercial market potential to qualified franchise owners.

BACKGROUND:

Established: 1984; 1st Franchised: 1992
Franchised Units: 119
Company-Owned Units: 11
Total Units: 130
Dist.: US-88; CAN-42; O'seas-0
North America: 24 States, 8 Provinces
Density: 16 in NY, 16 in ON, 9 in PA
Projected New Units (12 Months): 24
Qualifications: 3, 3, 2, 1, 4, 5
Registered:CA,FL,IL,IN,MD,MN,MI,MN, NY,ND,OR,RI,SD,VA,WA,WI,DC

FINANCIAL/TERMS:

Cash Investment: NA
Total Investment: $120-175K
Minimum Net Worth: NA
Fees: Franchise - $30K
Royalty - 0%; Ad. - NA
Earnings Claims Statement: Yes
Term of Contract (Years): 5/5
Avg. # Of Employees: 3 FT
Passive Ownership: Not Allowed
Encourage Conversions: No
Area Develop. Agreements: Yes/Varies
Sub-Franchising Contracts: No
Expand In Territory: No
Space Needs: 2,000-2,500 SF; Industrial Park

SUPPORT & TRAINING:

Financial Assistance Provided: No
Site Selection Assistance: No
Lease Negotiation Assistance: NA
Co-Operative Advertising: NA
Franchisee Assoc./Member: No
Size Of Corporate Staff: 13
On-Going Support: B,C,D,E,G,h,I
Training: 10 Days Headquarters; 10 Days Franchisee Site.

SPECIFIC EXPANSION PLANS:

US: All United States
Canada: No
Overseas: No

BATHCREST

5195 W. 4700 South
Salt Lake City, UT 84118-6109
Tel: (800) 826-6790 (801) 957-1400
Fax: (801) 955-6499
E-Mail: info@bathcrest.com
Web Site: www.bathcrest.com
Mr. Lloyd Peterson, VP Franchise Sales

Same-day bathroom remodeling that's highly profitable. You'll get multi-surface restoration processes and products to capitalize on the booming home improvement market. Our comprehensive business system shows you how to update a bathroom in less than a day with no percentage-based royalty to hold you back. You earn it, so you get to keep it.

BACKGROUND:

Established: 1979; 1st Franchised: 1985
Franchised Units: 173
Company-Owned Units: 1
Total Units: 174
Dist.: US-166; CAN-6; O'seas-0
North America: 30 States, 3 Provinces
Density: 15 in CA, 15 in PA, 12 in FL
Projected New Units (12 Months): 12
Qualifications: 3, 4, 2, 2, 5, 4
Registered: FL,VA,WI

FINANCIAL/TERMS:

Cash Investment: $12.5-24.5K
Total Investment: $24.5-44.5K
Minimum Net Worth: $200K
Fees: Franchise - $12.5K
Royalty - $250/Mo.; Ad. - NA
Earnings Claims Statement: No
Term of Contract (Years): 15/15
Avg. # Of Employees: 3-5 FT
Passive Ownership: Allowed
Encourage Conversions: NA
Area Develop. Agreements: No
Sub-Franchising Contracts: No
Expand In Territory: No
Space Needs:500-1,200 SF; HB, Industrial Center

SUPPORT & TRAINING:

Financial Assistance Provided: Yes(D)
Site Selection Assistance: NA
Lease Negotiation Assistance: No
Co-Operative Advertising: No
Franchisee Assoc./Member: No
Size Of Corporate Staff: 11
On-Going Support: B,D,G,H,I
Training: 5 Days Headquarters; 3 Days (30-60 Days after Initial Training) Headquarters.

SPECIFIC EXPANSION PLANS:

US: All United States
Canada: All Except AB
Overseas: No

BMR BATH MASTER REGLAZING

4498 Trepanier Rd.
Peachland, BC V0H 1X3 CANADA
Tel: (877) 767-2336 (250) 767-2336
Fax: (250) 767-2718
E-Mail: sales@bathmaster.com
Web Site: www.bathmaster.com
Mr. Trevor Dixon, President

Quality bathtub, tile reglazing, acrylic bathtub liners, tub walls, porcelain restoration and countertop resurfacing with superior materials. Transform dull, worn, unsightly fixtures to a brilliant new finish in just a few hours. This system leaves no mess or odor behind and offers same day use. This franchise includes equipment, training and on-going support. We do it all!

BACKGROUND:

Established: 1989; 1st Franchised: 1992
Franchised Units: 24
Company-Owned Units: 0
Total Units: 24
Dist.: US-1; CAN-23; O'seas-0
North America: 5 Provinces
Density: 12 in ON, 6 in BC, 2 in SK
Projected New Units (12 Months): 5
Qualifications: 3, 2, 4, 3, 4, 3
Registered: NR

FINANCIAL/TERMS:

Cash Investment: $17K
Total Investment: $17-41K
Minimum Net Worth: NA
Fees: Franchise - $0
Royalty - 5%/$200/Mo.; Ad. - 2%
Earnings Claims Statement: No
Term of Contract (Years): 5/5
Avg. # Of Employees: 1 FT
Passive Ownership: Discouraged
Encourage Conversions: Yes
Area Develop. Agreements: No
Sub-Franchising Contracts: No
Expand In Territory: Yes
Space Needs: 300 SF; HB

SUPPORT & TRAINING:

Financial Assistance Provided: No
Site Selection Assistance: NA
Lease Negotiation Assistance: No
Co-Operative Advertising: NA
Franchisee Assoc./Member: Yes/Yes
Size Of Corporate Staff: 2
On-Going Support: B,C,D,F,G,H,I
Training: 15 Days Minimum Peachland, BC.

SPECIFIC EXPANSION PLANS:

US: All United States
Canada: All Canada
Overseas: No

CALIFORNIA CLOSET COMPANY

1000 Fourth St., # 800
San Rafael, CA 94901-3142
Tel: (800) 241-3222 (415) 256-8500
Fax: (415) 256-8501
E-Mail: tblackburn@calclosets.com
Web Site: www.calclosets.com
Ms. Terri Blackburn, Director Legal/Admin.

CALIFORNIA CLOSETS is the world's leading brand in the customized storage industry. Its products organize and simplify the lives of its customers in closets, home offices, garages and throughout all areas of the home. CALIFORNIA CLOSETS has sophisticated and successful programs in marketing, learning and development and all aspects of operations. Year-round communication through conventions, regional seminars, newsletters, corporate visits and the company's intranet site. Successful management team.

BACKGROUND: IFA MEMBER

Established: 1978; 1st Franchised: 1982
Franchised Units: 155
Company-Owned Units: 4
Total Units: 159
Dist.: US-127; CAN-10; O'seas-18
North America: 35 States, 5 Provinces
Density: 14 in CA, 10 in NY, 10 in FL
Projected New Units (12 Months): 4
Qualifications: , , , , ,
Registered: CA,IL,IN,MD,MI,MN,NY,RI, VA,WA,WI

FINANCIAL/TERMS:

Cash Investment: $75-225K
Total Investment: $75-225K
Minimum Net Worth: NR
Fees: Franchise - $39.5K
Royalty - 6%; Ad. - 3%
Earnings Claims Statement: No
Term of Contract (Years): 10/10
Avg. # Of Employees: 3-25 FT
Passive Ownership: Discouraged
Encourage Conversions: NA
Area Develop. Agreements: No
Sub-Franchising Contracts: No
Expand In Territory: Yes
Space Needs: 2,000-6,000 SF; Light Industrial

SUPPORT & TRAINING:

Financial Assistance Provided: Yes(I)
Site Selection Assistance: Yes
Lease Negotiation Assistance: Yes
Co-Operative Advertising: Yes
Franchisee Assoc./Member: NR
Size Of Corporate Staff: 28
On-Going Support: A,B,C,D,E,F,G,H,I
Training: 1 Week Headquarters; 2 Weeks On-Site.

SPECIFIC EXPANSION PLANS:

US: Various U.S. Locations
Canada: PQ
Overseas: Europe, Asia, Mexico, South America

CERTIRESTORE

310 North Pacific Ave.
Fargo, ND 58102
Tel: (888) 50-CERTI (701) 277-1005
Fax: (701) 277-0534
E-Mail: bmitchell@certirestore.com
Web Site: www.certirestore.com
Mr. Robert Mitchell, Vice President

CERTIRESTORE Certified Furniture Restoration is a shop-based, full-service furniture restoration and repair franchise opportunity. We focus on providing professional furniture restoration to commercial clients, moving and insurance companies, restaurants, etc. - everyone who owns furniture needs our services. CERTIRESTORE provides protected territories. We provide the tools, supplies, equipment, support and hands-on training. 12-day shop training class. Chemical-free finish removal system.

BACKGROUND: IFA MEMBER

Established: 1989; 1st Franchised: 2004
Franchised Units: 2
Company-Owned Units: 1
Total Units: 3
Dist.: US-3; CAN-0; O'seas-0
North America: 2 States
Density: 2 in ND, 1 in IA
Projected New Units (12 Months): 19
Qualifications: 2, 3, 2, 2, 3, 3
Registered: MN,ND,SD

FINANCIAL/TERMS:

Cash Investment: $39.5K
Total Investment: $53-83K
Minimum Net Worth: NA
Fees: Franchise - $29.5K
Royalty - 5-8%; Ad. - 2%
Earnings Claims Statement: No
Term of Contract (Years): 10/10
Avg. # Of Employees: 1-2 FT, 1-3 PT
Passive Ownership: Discouraged
Encourage Conversions: Yes
Area Develop. Agreements: No
Sub-Franchising Contracts: No
Expand In Territory: Yes
Space Needs: 2,000-3,000 SF; Light Industrial/Commercial

SUPPORT & TRAINING:

Financial Assistance Provided: Yes(I)
Site Selection Assistance: Yes
Lease Negotiation Assistance: Yes
Co-Operative Advertising: No
Franchisee Assoc./Member: No
Size Of Corporate Staff: 4
On-Going Support: B,C,D,E,G,H,I
Training: 12 Days Hands-On Training Fargo, ND.

SPECIFIC EXPANSION PLANS:
US: All United States
Canada: No
Overseas: No

<< >>

CLOSET & STORAGE CONCEPTS

1000 Laurel Oak Corporate Center, # 208
Voorhees, NJ 08043
Tel: (800) 862-1919 (856) 627-5700
Fax: (856) 627-7447
E-Mail: boblewis@closetandstorageconcepts.com
Web Site: www.closetandstorageconcepts.com
Mr. Bob Lewis, President

Closet & Storage Concepts designs, manufacturers and installs a wide variety of custom closet, garage, laundry room, home office and storage units. All franchisees receive complete training in all aspects of the operation of the business, both prior to opening and on an on-going basis. Call 1-800-862-1919.

BACKGROUND: IFA MEMBER
Established: 1987; 1st Franchised: 2000
Franchised Units: 21
Company-Owned Units: 1
Total Units: 22
Dist.: US-22; CAN-0; O'seas-0
North America: NR
Density: NR
Projected New Units (12 Months): 5
Qualifications: 3, 4, 1, 3, 4, 5
Registered: All States

FINANCIAL/TERMS:
Cash Investment: $20-40K
Total Investment: $103-145K
Minimum Net Worth: $100K
Fees: Franchise - $40K
Royalty - 5%; Ad. - 0%
Earnings Claims Statement: No
Term of Contract (Years): 10/10
Avg. # Of Employees: 8 FT
Passive Ownership: Discouraged
Encourage Conversions: NA
Area Develop. Agreements: No
Sub-Franchising Contracts: No
Expand In Territory: Yes
Space Needs: 4,000 SF; FS

SUPPORT & TRAINING:
Financial Assistance Provided: Yes
Site Selection Assistance: Yes
Lease Negotiation Assistance: Yes
Co-Operative Advertising: NA
Franchisee Assoc./Member: Yes
Size Of Corporate Staff: 6
On-Going Support: C,D,E,G,H,I
Training: 2 Weeks in NJ.

SPECIFIC EXPANSION PLANS:
US: All United States
Canada: All Canada
Overseas: No

<< >>

CLOSET FACTORY, THE

12800 S. Broadway
Los Angeles, CA 90061-1116
Tel: (800) 318-8800 (310) 715-1000
Fax: (310) 516-8065
E-Mail: info@closetfactory.com
Web Site: www.closetfactory.com
Mr. John LaBarbara, Chief Executive Officer

Join the industry leader, ranked #1 in custom closets by Entrepreneur Magazine worldwide. Franchisees design, sell, manufacture and install custom closet systems, garage organizers, kitchen pantries, entertainment centers and custom office systems. Operate a large, vertically integrated cash business during normal business hours in an exclusive territory. A complete turn-key business through training and ongoing support. No technical experience is necessary.

BACKGROUND:
Established: 1983; 1st Franchised: 1985
Franchised Units: 90
Company-Owned Units: 27
Total Units: 117
Dist.: US-97; CAN-5; O'seas-10
North America: 39 States, 2 Provinces
Density: 14 in CA, 8 in NY, 7 in FL
Projected New Units (12 Months): 15
Qualifications: 5, 5, 2, 4, 3, 3
Registered:CA,FL,IL,IN,MD,MI,MN,NY,OR,VA,WA,WI,DC,AB

FINANCIAL/TERMS:
Cash Investment: $40-50K
Total Investment: $99.5-185K
Minimum Net Worth: $150-350K
Fees: Franchise - $28.5-39.5K
Royalty - 5.8%; Ad. - 1%
Earnings Claims Statement: No
Term of Contract (Years): 5/5
Avg. # Of Employees: 5-6 FT
Passive Ownership: Allowed
Encourage Conversions: Yes
Area Develop. Agreements: No
Sub-Franchising Contracts: No
Expand In Territory: No
Space Needs: 3,500-4,000 SF; Warehouse or Industrial Park

SUPPORT & TRAINING:
Financial Assistance Provided: Yes(I)
Site Selection Assistance: Yes
Lease Negotiation Assistance: Yes
Co-Operative Advertising: No
Franchisee Assoc./Member: No
Size Of Corporate Staff: NR
On-Going Support: B,C,D,E,G,h
Training: 2 Weeks Corporate Headquarters; 4 Weeks On-Site.

SPECIFIC EXPANSION PLANS:
US: All United States
Canada: All Canada
Overseas: All Countries

<< >>

ClosetsbyDesign

CLOSETS BY DESIGN

13151 S. Western Ave.
Gardena, CA 90249
Tel: (800) 377-5737 (310) 965-2040
Fax: (310) 527-8955
E-Mail: info@closetsbydesign.com
Web Site: www.closetsbydesign.com
Mr. Gerald Egner, President

Sell, design, manufacture and install custom closet organizers, garage cabinets, in-home office systems, wall units, pantries and more . . .

BACKGROUND: IFA MEMBER
Established: 1982; 1st Franchised: 1997
Franchised Units: 38
Company-Owned Units: 6
Total Units: 44
Dist.: US-44; CAN-0; O'seas-0
North America: 8 States
Density: 5 in OH, 3 in Il, 3 in NY
Projected New Units (12 Months): 6
Qualifications: 5, 5, 1, 4, 1, 5
Registered: FL,IN,MI,NY,RI,VA,WI

FINANCIAL/TERMS:
Cash Investment: $100-341K
Total Investment: $275-341K
Minimum Net Worth: $500K
Fees: Franchise - $34.9K
Royalty - 6%; Ad. - 3%
Earnings Claims Statement: No
Term of Contract (Years): 5/5
Avg. # Of Employees: 7-50 FT
Passive Ownership: Discouraged
Encourage Conversions: Yes
Area Develop. Agreements: No
Sub-Franchising Contracts: No
Expand In Territory: Yes
Space Needs: 8,000-14,000 SF; Business Park

SUPPORT & TRAINING:
Financial Assistance Provided: No
Site Selection Assistance: Yes
Lease Negotiation Assistance: No
Co-Operative Advertising: Yes
Franchisee Assoc./Member: Yes
Size Of Corporate Staff: 10
On-Going Support: C,D,E,h,I
Training: 2 Weeks Corporate HQ; 1 Week To Be Determined; 2 Weeks On-Site.

SPECIFIC EXPANSION PLANS:
US: States not currently in.
Canada: ON, BC and PQ
Overseas: No

<< >>

CLOSETTEC

55 Carnegie Row
Norwood, MA 02062
Tel: (800) 365-2021 (781) 769-9997
Fax: (781) 769-9996
E-Mail: closettec@closettec.com
Web Site: www.closettec.com
Mr. David Rogers, President

CLOSETTEC sells, manufactures and installs residential and commercial storage systems, using the finest melamine laminates and exclusive European hardware. We offer comprehensive training, field support, site selection, sales/marketing programs and on-going design assistance to every franchisee. Exclusive CAD and database programs.

BACKGROUND:
Established: 1985; 1st Franchised: 1986
Franchised Units: 35
Company-Owned Units: 0
Total Units: 35
Dist.: US-35; CAN-0; O'seas-0
North America: NR
Density: 4 in MA, 2 in NY, 2 in OH
Projected New Units (12 Months): 2
Qualifications: 4, 4, 2, 3, 3, 5
Registered: NR

FINANCIAL/TERMS:
Cash Investment: NR
Total Investment: $128-240K
Minimum Net Worth: NR
Fees: Franchise - $30K
Royalty - 4.5%; Ad. - NR
Earnings Claims Statement: No
Term of Contract (Years): 15/15
Avg. # Of Employees: 3-5 FT
Passive Ownership: Discouraged
Encourage Conversions: Yes
Area Develop. Agreements: No
Sub-Franchising Contracts: No
Expand In Territory: Yes
Space Needs: 2,500-3,000 SF; Light Industrial

SUPPORT & TRAINING:
Financial Assistance Provided: No
Site Selection Assistance: Yes
Lease Negotiation Assistance: Yes
Co-Operative Advertising: No
Franchisee Assoc./Member: No
Size Of Corporate Staff: 9
On-Going Support: C,D,E,H,I
Training: 2 Weeks Norwood, MA.

SPECIFIC EXPANSION PLANS:
US: All United States
Canada: No
Overseas: No

<< >>

COLOR-GLO INTERNATIONAL

7111-7115 Ohms Ln.
Minneapolis, MN 55439-2158
Tel: (800) 333-8523 (952) 835-1338
Fax: (952) 835-1395
E-Mail: info@color-glo.com
Web Site: www.color-glo.com
Mr. Scott L. Smith, VP Franchise Sales

The leader in the leather and fabric restoration and repair industry. From automotive to marine to aircraft to all-leather furniture, COLOR-GLO leads the way with innovative products and protected application techniques. We serve all US and foreign car manufacturers.

BACKGROUND: IFA MEMBER
Established: 1975; 1st Franchised: 1984
Franchised Units: 230
Company-Owned Units: 1
Total Units: 231
Dist.: US-188; CAN-1; O'seas-21
North America: NR
Density: 15 in FL, 12 in OR, 10 in CA
Projected New Units (12 Months): 50
Qualifications: 4, 4, 3, 4, 3, 3
Registered: All States

FINANCIAL/TERMS:
Cash Investment: $15-20K
Total Investment: $18-30K
Minimum Net Worth: $20K
Fees: Franchise - $7.5K
Royalty - 2-4%; Ad. - 0%
Earnings Claims Statement: Yes
Term of Contract (Years): 10/5
Avg. # Of Employees: 1 FT
Passive Ownership: Allowed
Encourage Conversions: NA
Area Develop. Agreements: Yes/10
Sub-Franchising Contracts: Yes
Expand In Territory: Yes
Space Needs: NA SF; NA

SUPPORT & TRAINING:
Financial Assistance Provided: Yes(I)
Site Selection Assistance: NA
Lease Negotiation Assistance: NA
Co-Operative Advertising: Yes
Franchisee Assoc./Member: Yes/Yes
Size Of Corporate Staff: 20
On-Going Support: B,C,D,G,H,I
Training: 2 Weeks On-Location.

SPECIFIC EXPANSION PLANS:
US: All United States
Canada: All Canada
Overseas: All Countries

<< >>

COMPAGNIA DEL MOBILE

4100 NE 2nd Ave., # 106
Miami, FL 33137
Tel: (305) 573-2500
Fax: (305) 573-2555
E-Mail: fdimise@compagiadelmobileusa.com
Web Site: www.compagiadelmobileusa.com
Mr. Francisco Di Mise, Director

Internationally famous home design/furnishing company establishing its presence in the United States with brand kitchen cabinet furniture, wardrobes, children's furniture and other design products. Stores operate in Europe, Asia, Middle East and America.

BACKGROUND:
Established: 1939; 1st Franchised: 1998
Franchised Units: 60
Company-Owned Units: 2
Total Units: 62
Dist.: US-3; CAN-0; O'seas-59
North America: 2 States

Density: 2 in FL, 1 in VA
Projected New Units (12 Months):
Qualifications: , , , , ,
Registered:

FINANCIAL/TERMS:

Cash Investment: $10-40K
Total Investment: $60-250K
Minimum Net Worth: $80K
Fees: Franchise - $5K
Royalty - 2%; Ad. - 5%
Earnings Claims Statement: NR
Term of Contract (Years): 5/5
Avg. # Of Employees: 2 FT
Passive Ownership: Allowed
Encourage Conversions:
Area Develop. Agreements: Yes/2
Sub-Franchising Contracts: Yes
Expand In Territory: Yes
Space Needs: 2,500 SF

SUPPORT & TRAINING:

Financial Assistance Provided:
Site Selection Assistance: Yes
Lease Negotiation Assistance: No
Co-Operative Advertising: Yes
Franchisee Assoc./Member: No
Size Of Corporate Staff: 300
On-Going Support: A,B,c,D,E,F,h
Training: 2 Wks. Franchisee Location; 1 Week Italy; 3 Days Miami, FL.

SPECIFIC EXPANSION PLANS:

US: All United States
Canada: NR
Overseas: NR

<< >>

CRACK TEAM, THE

11694 Lackland Rd.
St. Louis, MO 63146
Tel: (866) 905-5200 (314) 426-0900
Fax: (314) 426-0915
E-Mail: franchise@thecrackteam.com
Web Site: www.thecrackteam.com
Mr.Tim Church, Franchise Director

THE CRACK TEAM offers a unique specialty service repairing cracks in foundation walls. Cracked and leaking basements can be repaired permanently, quickly and inexpensively using our proven marketing strategies and exclusively formulated materials.

BACKGROUND: IFA MEMBER
Established: 1985; 1st Franchised: 2001
Franchised Units: 16
Company-Owned Units: 0
Total Units: 16
Dist.: US-16; CAN-0; O'seas-0
North America: 5 States
Density: 8 in MO, 2 in IL
Projected New Units (12 Months): 24
Qualifications: 5, 3, 1, 2, 2, 3
Registered: IL,IN,MI,NY

FINANCIAL/TERMS:

Cash Investment: $60K
Total Investment: $50-78K
Minimum Net Worth: $75-100K
Fees: Franchise - $25K
Royalty - 6%; Ad. - 2%
Earnings Claims Statement: No
Term of Contract (Years): 10/10
Avg. # Of Employees: 2 FT
Passive Ownership: Discouraged
Encourage Conversions: No
Area Develop. Agreements: No
Sub-Franchising Contracts: No
Expand In Territory: No
Space Needs: 300 SF; HB

SUPPORT & TRAINING:

Financial Assistance Provided: No
Site Selection Assistance: Yes
Lease Negotiation Assistance: NA
Co-Operative Advertising: No
Franchisee Assoc./Member: No
Size Of Corporate Staff: 8
On-Going Support: A,B,C,D,E,F,G,h,I
Training: NR

SPECIFIC EXPANSION PLANS:

US: Midwest, East Coast
Canada: All Canada
Overseas: No

<< >>

CREATIVE COLORS INTERNATIONAL

5550 W. 175th St.
Tinley Park, IL 60477
Tel: (800) 933-2656 (708) 614-7786
Fax: (708) 614-9685
E-Mail: mark@creativecolorsintl.com
Web Site: www.creativecolorsintl.com
Mr. Mark J. Bollman, President

The ULTIMATE in on-site restoration and dyeing of leather, vinyl, fabrics and plastics. Mobile units providing repair and restoration in all markets that have leather, vinyl, fabric, velour, plastics and fiberglass. These markets include car dealerships (new and used), furniture retailers and manufactures, hotels, airports, car rental agencies and company fleet cars.

BACKGROUND: IFA MEMBER
Established: 1980; 1st Franchised: 1991
Franchised Units: 60
Company-Owned Units: 2
Total Units: 62
Dist.: US-61; CAN-1; O'seas-0
North America: 23 States, 1 Province
Density: IL, FL, OH
Projected New Units (12 Months): 10+
Qualifications: 4, 4, 3, 4, 4, 5
Registered: CA,FL,IL,IN,MI,NY,OR,WI, AB

FINANCIAL/TERMS:

Cash Investment: $27.5K
Total Investment: $27.5K
Minimum Net Worth: $50K
Fees: Franchise - $27.5K
Royalty - 6%/$175/Mo.; Ad. - 1%
Earnings Claims Statement: Yes
Term of Contract (Years): 10
Avg. # Of Employees: 3-4 FT
Passive Ownership: Discouraged
Encourage Conversions: Yes
Area Develop. Agreements: Yes/10
Sub-Franchising Contracts: No
Expand In Territory: Yes
Space Needs: NA SF; HB

SUPPORT & TRAINING:

Financial Assistance Provided: Yes(D)
Site Selection Assistance: Yes
Lease Negotiation Assistance: NA
Co-Operative Advertising: Yes
Franchisee Assoc./Member: Yes/Yes
Size Of Corporate Staff: 10
On-Going Support: A,B,C,D,E,F,G,H,I
Training: 3 Weeks Headquarters, Tinley Park, IL; 1 Week in Franchisee's Territory.

SPECIFIC EXPANSION PLANS:

US: All United States
Canada: All Canada
Overseas: All Countries

<< >>

DECKARE SERVICES

1501 Raff Rd., SW
Canton, OH 44710-2356
Tel: (800) 711-3325 (877) 433-2527
Fax: (330) 478-0311

E-Mail: deckcare1@aol.com
Web Site: www.deckcare.com
Mr. Dan Fuline, Jr., VP Communications

Rejuvenating exterior wood surfaces such as decks, fences, docks, gazebos and bridges with a total commitment to being the first nationally recognized franchise based on image and quality. Franchisees will receive complete business and field training with on-going support services.

BACKGROUND:
Established: 1995; 1st Franchised: 1997
Franchised Units: 40
Company-Owned Units: 0
Total Units: 40
Dist.: US-25; CAN-0; O'seas-0
North America: 16 States
Density: 4 in OH, 3 in MO, 3 in TN
Projected New Units (12 Months): 40
Qualifications: 5, 4, 3, 3, 2, 5
Registered: CA,IL,IN,MD,MI,MN,NY,VA

FINANCIAL/TERMS:
Cash Investment: $25K
Total Investment: $45K
Minimum Net Worth: $50K
Fees: Franchise - $14.5K
Royalty - 5%; Ad. - NA
Earnings Claims Statement: No
Term of Contract (Years): 5/5
Avg. # Of Employees: 1 FT, 1 PT
Passive Ownership: Allowed
Encourage Conversions: No
Area Develop. Agreements: No
Sub-Franchising Contracts: No
Expand In Territory: Yes
Space Needs: NR SF; HB

SUPPORT & TRAINING:
Financial Assistance Provided: No
Site Selection Assistance: NA
Lease Negotiation Assistance: NA
Co-Operative Advertising: NA
Franchisee Assoc./Member: No
Size Of Corporate Staff: 5
On-Going Support: C,D,G,H,I
Training: 5 Days at Corporate Office; 4 Days Franchisee's Location.

SPECIFIC EXPANSION PLANS:
US: All United States
Canada: No
Overseas: No

<< >>

DR. VINYL & ASSOCIATES
201 NW Victoria Dr.
Lee's Summit, MO 64086-9381
Tel: (800) 531-6600 (816) 525-6060
Fax: (816) 525-6333
E-Mail: tbuckley@drvinyl.com
Web Site: www.drvinyl.com
Mr. Tom Buckley, Jr., Franchise Devel. Director

DR. VINYL is consistently ranked among the best in its industry by national, independent surveys. Not only do we provide top quality vinyl, leather, fabric, hard plastic, windshield and vinyl siding repair, but we offer extensive training, on-going support, research and development of new products and techniques, a national advertising program and more. Customize your business to suit the local market-install automotive aftermarket accessories, add paint touch-up, upholstery, paintless dent removal.

BACKGROUND: IFA MEMBER
Established: 1972; 1st Franchised: 1981
Franchised Units: 282
Company-Owned Units: 2
Total Units: 284
Dist.: US-232; CAN-0; O'seas-50
North America: 50 States, Puerto Rico
Density: 25 in MO, 13 in NC, 13 in IL
Projected New Units (12 Months): 30
Qualifications: 3, 5, 2, 3, 3, 5
Registered: CA,FL,IL,IN,MD,MI,NY,OR,VA,WI

FINANCIAL/TERMS:
Cash Investment: $15-20K
Total Investment: $35.9-63.4K
Minimum Net Worth: $50K
Fees: Franchise - $34.9K
Royalty - 7%; Ad. - 1%
Earnings Claims Statement: No
Term of Contract (Years): 10/10
Avg. # Of Employees: 1 FT
Passive Ownership: Not Allowed
Encourage Conversions: NA
Area Develop. Agreements: Yes/10
Sub-Franchising Contracts: No
Expand In Territory: Yes
Space Needs: NA SF; NA

SUPPORT & TRAINING:
Financial Assistance Provided: Yes(B)
Site Selection Assistance: NA
Lease Negotiation Assistance: NA
Co-Operative Advertising: Yes
Franchisee Assoc./Member: No
Size Of Corporate Staff: 14
On-Going Support: C,D,G,H,I
Training: 2 Weeks Lee's Summit, MO; 1 Week Franchisee's Location, 1 Additional Week if needed.

SPECIFIC EXPANSION PLANS:
US: All United States
Canada: All Canada
Overseas: All Countries

<< >>

DREAMMAKER BATH & KITCHEN REMODELING
1020 N. University Parks Dr.
Waco, TX 76707
Tel: (800) 583-9099 (254) 745-2477
Fax: (254) 745-2588
E-Mail: karen.cagle@dwyergroup.com
Web Site: www.dreammaker-remodel.com
Ms. Karen Cagle, VP Franchising

DREAMMAKER BATH & KITCHEN is a full-service kitchen, bath and interior remodeling franchise. DREAMMAKER provides proven business systems, brand name and image, group buying power and remodeling options to help you grow your business and experience the strong margins and quality of life you deserve. Support includes training, research and development, marketing and one-on-one coaching.

BACKGROUND: IFA MEMBER
Established: 1970; 1st Franchised: 1971
Franchised Units: 180
Company-Owned Units: 0
Total Units: 180
Dist.: US-110; CAN-0; O'seas-70
North America: 50 States
Density: 9 in TX, 8 in CA, 5 in IL
Projected New Units (12 Months): 30
Qualifications: 4, 3, 5, 2, 2, 5
Registered: All States

FINANCIAL/TERMS:
Cash Investment: $35-65K
Total Investment: $70-180K
Minimum Net Worth: $100K
Fees: Franchise - $27K
Royalty - 6-3%; Ad. - 2-1%
Earnings Claims Statement: No
Term of Contract (Years): 10/10

Avg. # Of Employees: 4 FT
Passive Ownership: Discouraged
Encourage Conversions: Yes
Area Develop. Agreements: No
Sub-Franchising Contracts: No
Expand In Territory: Yes
Space Needs: 700-2,500 SF; SF

SUPPORT & TRAINING:
Financial Assistance Provided: Yes(B)
Site Selection Assistance: Yes
Lease Negotiation Assistance: Yes
Co-Operative Advertising: No
Franchisee Assoc./Member: Yes/Yes
Size Of Corporate Staff: 14
On-Going Support: B,C,D,E,G,H,I
Training: 8 Days Headquarters, Waco, TX - Basic Business; 5 Days Tech. Training after 12 Months.

SPECIFIC EXPANSION PLANS:
US: All United States
Canada: All Except PQ
Overseas: No

DRY-B-LO DESIGNER DECK DRAIN SYSTEM

475 Tribble Gap Rd., # 305
Cumming, GA 30040
Tel: (800) 437-9256 (770) 781-4754
Fax: (770) 886-7408
E-Mail: gmoore@dry-b-lo.com
Web Site: www.dry-b-lo.com
Mr. Grant Moore, President/CEO

DRY-B-LO Designer Deck Drain System is one of the nation's fastest-growing franchise companies in the booming home improvement industry. We currently offer "exclusive territory" opportunities to qualified individuals. Our comprehensive training program provides business management, sales and technical instruction and a strong, on-going support system. No construction or trade experience is required.

BACKGROUND: IFA MEMBER
Established: 1993; 1st Franchised: 1997
Franchised Units: 29
Company-Owned Units: 0
Total Units: 29
Dist.: US-29; CAN-0; O'seas-0
North America: 7 States
Density: 6 in SC, 5 in GA, 4 in NC
Projected New Units (12 Months): 15
Qualifications: 4, 4, 2, 4, 1, 5
Registered: FL,IN,MD,MI,NY,OR,VA,WA,WI,DC

FINANCIAL/TERMS:
Cash Investment: $65.7-147.8K
Total Investment: $65.7-147.8K
Minimum Net Worth: $250K
Fees: Franchise - $15K and 25K
Royalty - 7.5%; Ad. - 0%
Earnings Claims Statement: No
Term of Contract (Years): 5/5/5
Avg. # Of Employees: 3 FT
Passive Ownership: Discouraged
Encourage Conversions: NA
Area Develop. Agreements: No
Sub-Franchising Contracts: No
Expand In Territory: Yes
Space Needs: NA SF; HB

SUPPORT & TRAINING:
Financial Assistance Provided: 3rdPty
Site Selection Assistance: NA
Lease Negotiation Assistance: NA
Co-Operative Advertising: NA
Franchisee Assoc./Member: No
Size Of Corporate Staff: 4
On-Going Support: B,C,D,G,h,I
Training: 1 Week Atlanta, GA; 1 Week Denver, CO.

SPECIFIC EXPANSION PLANS:
US: All United States
Canada: No
Overseas: No

EPCON COMMUNITIES

500 Stonehenge Dr.
Dublin, OH 43017
Tel: (800) 783-3838 (614) 761-1010
Fax: (614) 761-2672
E-Mail: noverly@epmarkinc.com
Web Site: www.epmarkinc.com
Ms. Nanette Overly, Director Sales/Marketing

We put our franchisees in the homebuilding business. EPCON provides a comprehensive homebuilding development system targeted at the industry's largest market - active adults. As an EPCON franchisee, you receive not only the rights to build our proven, award-winning floor plans, but also on-going training for yourself and your team. National account purchasing power, standards and specification on building and selling the homes, marketing support, POP materials and support with industry experts.

BACKGROUND: IFA MEMBER
Established: 1985; 1st Franchised: 1995
Franchised Units: 16,000
Company-Owned Units: 35
Total Units: 16,035
Dist.: US-16,035; CAN-0; O'seas-0
North America: 26 States
Density: 3,620 OH, 1,208 GA, 918 VA
Projected New Units (12 Months): 3,000
Qualifications: 5, 5, 3, 3, 3, 5
Registered: All Except ND

FINANCIAL/TERMS:
Cash Investment: $~$1MM
Total Investment: $3-5MM
Minimum Net Worth: Varies
Fees: Franchise - $30K
Royalty - $2.5K/Home; Ad. - NA
Earnings Claims Statement: Yes
Term of Contract (Years): 2/Varies
Avg. # Of Employees: 5 FT
Passive Ownership: Not Allowed
Encourage Conversions: NA
Area Develop. Agreements: No
Sub-Franchising Contracts: No
Expand In Territory: Yes
Space Needs: NA SF; NA

SUPPORT & TRAINING:
Financial Assistance Provided: Yes(I)
Site Selection Assistance: Yes
Lease Negotiation Assistance: No
Co-Operative Advertising: No
Franchisee Assoc./Member: No
Size Of Corporate Staff: 12
On-Going Support: C,D,G,H
Training: 5 Days Orientation; 3 Days BOLT Selling; 4 Days Sales/Construction - all Columbus, OH.

SPECIFIC EXPANSION PLANS:
US: All United States
Canada: No
Overseas: No

<< >>

FOUR SEASONS SUNROOMS

5005 Veterans Memorial Hwy.
Holbrook, NY 11741
Tel: (800) 521-0179 (516) 563-4000
Fax: (516) 563-4010
E-Mail: tonyr@four-seasons-sunrooms.com
Web Site: www.four-seasons-sunrooms.com

Mr. Tony Russo,

FOUR SEASONS SUNROOMS is the largest manufacturer of sunrooms, conservatories and solariums in the Unites States. The FOUR SEASONS franchise opportunity is targeted to the $121 billion remodeling industry. We offer comprehensive training and exclusive products.

BACKGROUND:
Established: 1974; 1st Franchised: 1985
Franchised Units: 200
Company-Owned Units: 3
Total Units: 203
Dist.: US-188; CAN-12; O'seas-47
North America: 48 States, 5 Provinces
Density: 17 in CA, 21 in NY, 16 in PA
Projected New Units (12 Months): 24
Qualifications: 2, 5, 4, 3, 3, 4
Registered: All States

FINANCIAL/TERMS:
Cash Investment: $10-25K
Total Investment: $13.3-82.5K
Minimum Net Worth: $100K
Fees: Franchise - $7.5-15K
Royalty - 0%; Ad. - 0%
Earnings Claims Statement: No
Term of Contract (Years): 10/10
Avg. # Of Employees: 2 FT, 1 PT
Passive Ownership: Not Allowed
Encourage Conversions: Yes
Area Develop. Agreements: No
Sub-Franchising Contracts: No
Expand In Territory: Yes
Space Needs: 750 SF; FS, SF

SUPPORT & TRAINING:
Financial Assistance Provided: No
Site Selection Assistance: Yes
Lease Negotiation Assistance: Yes
Co-Operative Advertising: Yes
Franchisee Assoc./Member: Yes
Size Of Corporate Staff: 250
On-Going Support: C,D,E,F,G,H,I
Training: 5 Days Holbrook, NY; 5 Days Hayward, CA; 5 Days Regionally.

SPECIFIC EXPANSION PLANS:
US: All United States
Canada: All Canada
Overseas: U.K., Spain, France, Germany, Italy

<< >>

Top 100

FURNITURE MEDIC
3839 Forest Hill-Irene Rd.
Memphis, TN 38125-2502
Tel: (800) 255-9687 (901) 597-8600
Fax: (901) 597-8660
E-Mail: dmessenger@smclean.com
Web Site: www.furnituremedicfranchise.com
Mr. David Messenger, VP Market Expansion

FURNITURE MEDIC is a division of The ServiceMaster Company. It is the largest furniture and wood repair and restoration company in the world with over 600 franchises. Furniture Medic has unique products and processes which enable much of the work to be done on-site, reducing costs and saving time for its residential and commercial customers. Financing is provided for the initial franchise fees, start-up equipment and vehicles to qualified candidates through ServiceMaster Acceptance Company.

BACKGROUND: IFA MEMBER
Established: 1992; 1st Franchised: 1992
Franchised Units: 595
Company-Owned Units: 0
Total Units: 595
Dist.: US-420; CAN-71; O'seas-104
North America: 47 States,10 Provinces
Density: 38 in FL, 27 in CA, 22 in VA
Projected New Units (12 Months): 50
Qualifications: 4, 4, 2, 3, 3, 5
Registered: All States

FINANCIAL/TERMS:
Cash Investment: $15-25K
Total Investment: $37-81.9K
Minimum Net Worth: $50K
Fees: Franchise - $22.5K
Royalty - 7%/$250 Min.; Ad. - 1%/$50 Min.
Earnings Claims Statement: No
Term of Contract (Years): 5/5
Avg. # Of Employees: 1 FT, 1 PT
Passive Ownership: Not Allowed
Encourage Conversions: NA
Area Develop. Agreements: No
Sub-Franchising Contracts: No
Expand In Territory: Yes
Space Needs: NR SF; NA

SUPPORT & TRAINING:
Financial Assistance Provided: Yes(D)
Site Selection Assistance: NA
Lease Negotiation Assistance: No
Co-Operative Advertising: No
Franchisee Assoc./Member: Yes/Yes
Size Of Corporate Staff: 21
On-Going Support: A,B,G,h,I
Training: 3 Weeks Memphis, TN.

SPECIFIC EXPANSION PLANS:
US: Most metropolitan markets in US.
Canada: All Canada
Overseas: All Countries

<< >>

GROUT DOCTOR
7923 E. Palm Ln.
Mesa, AZ 85207
Tel: (877) 476-8800 (480) 924-2271
Fax: (877) 615-2173
E-Mail: opportunity@groutdoctor.com
Web Site: www.groutdoctor.com
Ms. Robin Rotella, Director Franchise Development

For many years there has been a strong demand for someone to provide repair and maintenance services for existing grout and tile installations. The GROUT DOCTOR is the founder and leader of this fast-growing industry! Our uncomplicated business has much to offer including: home-based, low overhead, no inventory, flexible schedule, no experience, no accounts receivables, thorough training, comprehensive support system, unlimited marketing & technical support, optional employees and it's "family friendly!"

BACKGROUND: IFA MEMBER
Established: 1992; 1st Franchised:
Franchised Units: 45
Company-Owned Units: 0
Total Units: 45
Dist.: US-45; CAN-0; O'seas-0
North America: 18 States
Density: 7 in AZ, 6 in TX, 5 in FL
Projected New Units (12 Months): 14
Qualifications: 3, 3, 2, 1, 5, 4
Registered: CA,FL,HI,IL,IN,MI,MN,NY, WI

FINANCIAL/TERMS:
Cash Investment: $12.7-29.4K
Total Investment: $12.7-29.4K
Minimum Net Worth: NA
Fees: Franchise - $8.5-18.8K
Royalty - 9% or Flat Fee; Ad. - NA
Earnings Claims Statement: Yes
Term of Contract (Years): 7/7
Avg. # Of Employees: 1 PT
Passive Ownership: Not Allowed

Encouraging Conversions: NA
Area Develop. Agreements: Yes/1-7
Sub-Franchising Contracts: No
Expand In Territory: No
Space Needs: NA SF; HB

SUPPORT & TRAINING:
Financial Assistance Provided: Yes(D)
Site Selection Assistance: NA
Lease Negotiation Assistance: NA
Co-Operative Advertising: NA
Franchisee Assoc./Member: No
Size Of Corporate Staff: 4
On-Going Support: A,B,C,d,G,h,I
Training: 5 Days Mesa, AZ (Phoenix); 5 Days St. Charles, IL (Chicago); 5 Days Pineville, NC (Charlotte).

SPECIFIC EXPANSION PLANS:
US: All United States
Canada: No
Overseas: No

<< >>

GUARDSMAN FURNITUREPRO

4999 36th St. SE
Grand Rapids, MI 49512
Tel: (800) 496-6377 (616) 285-7864
Fax: (616) 285-7882
E-Mail: tziegler@valspar.com
Web Site: www.guardsmanfurniturepro.com
Mr. Tony Ziegler

Partner and profit with a world leader. As a business unit of Lilly Industries, the largest manufacturer of furniture finishes in N. America, GUARDSMAN WOODPRO is the premier choice of residential and commercial customers alike for furniture repair and refinishing services. Lilly has been involved in the furniture industry for 130 years, supplying finishes, furniture care products and now furniture repair services. If you want to be in the furniture business, you want to be with us.

BACKGROUND:
Established: 1865; 1st Franchised: 1994
Franchised Units: 123
Company-Owned Units: 0
Total Units: 123
Dist.: US-110; CAN-14; O'seas-0
North America: 36 States, 2 Provinces
Density: 9 in MI, 6 in OH, 6 in TX
Projected New Units (12 Months): 36
Qualifications: 4, 4, 4, 3, 5, 5
Registered: All States

FINANCIAL/TERMS:
Cash Investment: $10-25K
Total Investment: $7-25K
Minimum Net Worth: $50K
Fees: Franchise - $7K
Royalty - Fixed; Ad. - Fixed
Earnings Claims Statement: No
Term of Contract (Years): 5/5
Avg. # Of Employees: 1-3 FT, 1-2 PT
Passive Ownership: Discouraged
Encourage Conversions: Yes
Area Develop. Agreements: Yes/2-5 Yrs.
Sub-Franchising Contracts: Yes
Expand In Territory: Yes
Space Needs: NR SF; HB

SUPPORT & TRAINING:
Financial Assistance Provided: Yes(D)
Site Selection Assistance: NA
Lease Negotiation Assistance: NA
Co-Operative Advertising: Yes
Franchisee Assoc./Member: Yes/Yes
Size Of Corporate Staff: 80
On-Going Support: A,C,D,G,H,I
Training: 2 Weeks Grand Rapids, MI.

SPECIFIC EXPANSION PLANS:
US: All United States
Canada: All Canada
Overseas: All Countries

HANDYMAN CONNECTION

10250 Alliance Rd., # 100
Cincinnati, OH 45242
Tel: (800) 466-5530 + 103 (513) 771-3003
Fax: (513) 771-6439
E-Mail: fharms@handymanconnection.com
Web Site: www.handymanconnection.com
Mr. Fred Harms, VP Corporate Development

HANDYMAN CONNECTION specializes in the small to medium size home repair and remodeling industry. We offer a turnkey package that includes marketing, advertising and a complete training program.

BACKGROUND: IFA MEMBER
Established: 1990; 1st Franchised: 1993
Franchised Units: 137
Company-Owned Units: 2
Total Units: 139
Dist.: US-114; CAN-25; O'seas-0
North America: 37 States
Density: 38 in CA, 8 in FL, 7 in OH
Projected New Units (12 Months): 12
Qualifications: 4, 4, 2, 3, 2, 5
Registered: CA,FL,IL,IN,MI,MN,NY,ND,OR,RI,VA,WA,WI

FINANCIAL/TERMS:
Cash Investment: $65-130K
Total Investment: $70-190K
Minimum Net Worth: $250K
Fees: Franchise - Varies
Royalty - 5%; Ad. - 2%
Earnings Claims Statement: Yes
Term of Contract (Years): 10/5
Avg. # Of Employees: 3 FT
Passive Ownership: Discouraged
Encourage Conversions: NA
Area Develop. Agreements: No
Sub-Franchising Contracts: No
Expand In Territory: Yes
Space Needs: 750-1,500 SF; FS, Industrial Warehouse

SUPPORT & TRAINING:
Financial Assistance Provided: Yes
Site Selection Assistance: NA
Lease Negotiation Assistance: No
Co-Operative Advertising: No
Franchisee Assoc./Member: Yes/Yes
Size Of Corporate Staff: 14
On-Going Support: B,C,D,E,G,h,I
Training: 2 Weeks Headquarters (Cincinnati, OH); 1 Week Franchisee Location.

SPECIFIC EXPANSION PLANS:
US: All United States
Canada: All Canada
Overseas: All Countries

<< >>

HANDYPRO HANDYMAN

995 S. Main St.
Plymouth, MI 48170-2048
Tel: (800) 942-6394 (734) 254-9160
Fax: (734) 254-9171
E-Mail: handypro@comcast.net
Web Site: www.handypro.com
Mr. Niles Redden, Dir. Business Development

Professional handyman service. Specializing in minor home repairs and improvements. Our business is focused on top-quality customer service.

BACKGROUND:
Established: 1996; 1st Franchised: 2000
Franchised Units: 5
Company-Owned Units: 1
Total Units: 6
Dist.: US-6; CAN-0; O'seas-0
North America: 4 States
Density: 2 in MI, 1 in TX, 1 in MN

Projected New Units (12 Months): 13
Qualifications: 4, 4, 2, 3, 4, 5
Registered: MI

FINANCIAL/TERMS:
Cash Investment: $36.5-65.5K
Total Investment: $29K
Minimum Net Worth: $36.5K
Fees: Franchise - $25K
Royalty - $600-1,500/Mo.; Ad. - 1%
Earnings Claims Statement: No
Term of Contract (Years): 7/7
Avg. # Of Employees: 10 FT, 1 PT
Passive Ownership: Discouraged
Encourage Conversions: NA
Area Develop. Agreements: No
Sub-Franchising Contracts: No
Expand In Territory: Yes
Space Needs: NA SF; HB, Office

SUPPORT & TRAINING:
Financial Assistance Provided: No
Site Selection Assistance: Yes
Lease Negotiation Assistance: Yes
Co-Operative Advertising: Yes
Franchisee Assoc./Member: Yes/Yes
Size Of Corporate Staff: 3
On-Going Support: A,b,C,D,E,G,H,I
Training: 1 Week Corporate Office. 30 Hours/Year On-Site.

SPECIFIC EXPANSION PLANS:
US: All United States
Canada: No
Overseas: No

<< >>

HOUSE DOCTORS HANDYMAN SERVICE

575 Chamber Dr.
Milford, OH 45150
Tel: (800) 319-3359 (513) 469-2443
Fax: (513) 469-2226
E-Mail: scohen@housedoctors.com
Web Site: www.housedoctors.com
Mr. Steve M. Cohen, President

There's big money in house calls. Millions of dollars are being spent every day on those odd jobs around the house that people don't have the time or skill to do. You don't need a screwdriver or hammer to own this franchise. Financing and training provided.

BACKGROUND: IFA MEMBER
Established: 1994; 1st Franchised: 1995
Franchised Units: 225
Company-Owned Units: 0
Total Units: 225
Dist.: US-224; CAN-0; O'seas-1
North America: 42 States
Density: 10 in OH, 9 in IN, 9 in IL
Projected New Units (12 Months): 30
Qualifications: 2, 3, 2, 2, 4, 5
Registered:CA,FL,IL,IN,MD,MI,MN,NY, ND,OR,RI,VA,WA,WI

FINANCIAL/TERMS:
Cash Investment: $14-28K
Total Investment: $26-54K
Minimum Net Worth: $26K
Fees: Franchise - $12-30K
Royalty - 6%; Ad. - 3%
Earnings Claims Statement: No
Term of Contract (Years): 10/10/10
Avg. # Of Employees: 3 FT, 2 PT
Passive Ownership: Discouraged
Encourage Conversions: Yes
Area Develop. Agreements: Yes/10
Sub-Franchising Contracts: No
Expand In Territory: No
Space Needs: NA SF; NA

SUPPORT & TRAINING:
Financial Assistance Provided: Yes(D)
Site Selection Assistance: NA
Lease Negotiation Assistance: NA
Co-Operative Advertising: NA
Franchisee Assoc./Member: No
Size Of Corporate Staff: 12
On-Going Support: A,B,C,D,E,G,H,I
Training: 1 Week Cincinnati, OH.

SPECIFIC EXPANSION PLANS:
US: All United States
Canada: All Canada
Overseas: All Countries

<< >>

JET-BLACK SEALCOATING & REPAIR

25 West Cliff Rd., # 103
Burnsville, MN 55337
Tel: (888) 538-2525 (952) 890-8343
Fax: (952) 890-7022
E-Mail: rc@earthlink.net
Web Site: www.jet-black.com
Mr. Rick Clark, Franchise Development

We provide blacktop driveway sealcoating, hot-rubber crack and joint filling, heat-treat oil spots, grass edging and patching. We beautify and protect driveways.

BACKGROUND: IFA MEMBER
Established: 1988; 1st Franchised: 1993
Franchised Units: 106
Company-Owned Units: 0
Total Units: 106
Dist.: US-106; CAN-0; O'seas-0
North America: 24 States
Density: NR
Projected New Units (12 Months): 80
Qualifications: 3, 3, 3, 3, 5, 5
Registered: All States

FINANCIAL/TERMS:
Cash Investment: $20K
Total Investment: $49K
Minimum Net Worth: $50K
Fees: Franchise - $15K
Royalty - 8%; Ad. - NA
Earnings Claims Statement: Yes
Term of Contract (Years): 15/15
Avg. # Of Employees: 1 FT
Passive Ownership: Not Allowed
Encourage Conversions: No
Area Develop. Agreements: No
Sub-Franchising Contracts: No
Expand In Territory: Yes
Space Needs: NR SF; HB

SUPPORT & TRAINING:
Financial Assistance Provided: Yes(I)
Site Selection Assistance: Yes
Lease Negotiation Assistance: NA
Co-Operative Advertising: Yes
Franchisee Assoc./Member: Yes
Size Of Corporate Staff: 3
On-Going Support: A,B,C,D,E,F,G,H
Training: 1 Week Burnsville, MN.

SPECIFIC EXPANSION PLANS:
US: All United States
Canada: All Canada
Overseas: No

<< >>

KITCHEN SOLVERS

401 Jay St.
La Crosse, WI 54601-4064
Tel: (800) 845-6779 (608) 791-5518
Fax: (608) 784-2917
E-Mail: jason@kitchensolvers.com
Web Site: www.kitchensolvers.com

Ms. Jeanne Plunkett, Dir. Franchise Development

Specialize or diversify... It's your option. Two different models to choose from. Six different profit centers. We are the most experienced kitchen and bath remodeling franchise in the US. Home-based business with no inventory required. Complete start-up and on-going support. Personalized marketing strategies. Experienced technical training and support.

BACKGROUND: IFA MEMBER
Established: 1982; 1st Franchised: 1984
Franchised Units: 132
Company-Owned Units: 0
Total Units: 132
Dist.: US-114; CAN-4; O'seas-0
North America: 32 States, 4 Provinces
Density: 17 in IL, 15 in WI, 12 in IA
Projected New Units (12 Months): 20
Qualifications: 2, 2, 2, 2, , 5
Registered:CA,FL,IL,IN,MD,MI,MN,ND, NY,OR,SD,VA,WA,WI,AB

FINANCIAL/TERMS:
Cash Investment: $40-60.2K
Total Investment: $48-82K
Minimum Net Worth: $250K
Fees: Franchise - $27.5-32.0K
Royalty - 6%; Ad. - 1%
Earnings Claims Statement: Yes
Term of Contract (Years): 10/10
Avg. # Of Employees: 1 FT
Passive Ownership: Not Allowed
Encourage Conversions: Yes
Area Develop. Agreements: No
Sub-Franchising Contracts: No
Expand In Territory: Yes
Space Needs: NA SF; HB

SUPPORT & TRAINING:
Financial Assistance Provided: Yes(D)
Site Selection Assistance: NA
Lease Negotiation Assistance: NA
Co-Operative Advertising: NA
Franchisee Assoc./Member: Yes/Yes
Size Of Corporate Staff: 10
On-Going Support: a,B,C,D,G,h,I
Training: 2 Weeks LaCrosse, WI Corporate Headquarters.

SPECIFIC EXPANSION PLANS:
US: All United States
Canada: All Canada
Overseas: No

KITCHEN TUNE-UP

813 Circle Dr.
Aberdeen, SD 57401-2670
Tel: (800) 333-6385 (605) 225-4049
Fax: (605) 225-1371
E-Mail: craig@kitchentuneup.com
Web Site: www.kitchentuneup.com
Mr. Craig Green, Franchise Director

America's #1 home improvement franchise. We offer 'Kitchen Solutions For Any Budget.' Cabinet and wood restoration, cabinet refacing, custom cabinetry, no-sanding wood finishing, acrylic bath tub lining systems and closet organizers. We offer six businesses in one! Excellent initial and on-going training and support. High residential and commercial potential. No experience needed. Home-based and retail location programs available.

BACKGROUND: IFA MEMBER
Established: 1975; 1st Franchised: 1988
Franchised Units: 315
Company-Owned Units: 0
Total Units: 315
Dist.: US-314; CAN-1; O'seas-0
North America: 38 States, 1 Province
Density: 13 in CA, 9 in IL, 8 in MN
Projected New Units (12 Months): 25
Qualifications: 4, 5, 1, 3, 2, 4
Registered: All States Except HI

FINANCIAL/TERMS:
Cash Investment: $25-30K
Total Investment: $40-50K
Minimum Net Worth: $75K
Fees: Franchise - $25K
Royalty - 4.5-7%; Ad. - 0%
Earnings Claims Statement: Yes
Term of Contract (Years): 10/10
Avg. # Of Employees: 2-3 FT, 1 PT
Passive Ownership: Discouraged
Encourage Conversions: Yes
Area Develop. Agreements: Yes/10
Sub-Franchising Contracts: No
Expand In Territory: Yes
Space Needs: 500-2,500 SF; FS, SF, SC, RM, HB

SUPPORT & TRAINING:
Financial Assistance Provided: Yes(D)
Site Selection Assistance: Yes
Lease Negotiation Assistance: Yes
Co-Operative Advertising: No
Franchisee Assoc./Member: Yes
Size Of Corporate Staff: 13
On-Going Support: A,B,d,G,h,I
Training: 2-3 Wks. Pre-Train.; 8 Days Corp. Office; 12 Wks. Home Study; 3-4 OJT Training. On-Going.

SPECIFIC EXPANSION PLANS:
US: All United States
Canada: Masters Only
Overseas: No

MARBLELIFE

5470 E. Loop 820 S., # 110
Fort Worth, TX 76119-6515
Tel: (800) 627-4569 (817) 478-4437
Fax: (817) 478-6954
E-Mail: jfreitag@marblelife.com
Web Site: www.marblelife.com
Mr. John Freitag, Franchise Director

Specializes in the restoration, preservation and maintenance services for natural stones and other surfaces.

BACKGROUND:
Established: 1987; 1st Franchised: 1993
Franchised Units: 49
Company-Owned Units: 0
Total Units: 49
Dist.: US-39; CAN-1; O'seas-9
North America: 38 States, 1 Province
Density: 3 in TX, 3 in CA, 3 in FL
Projected New Units (12 Months): 10
Qualifications: 4, 4, 2, 2, 2, 4
Registered: CA,FL,IL,NY,VA,WI

FINANCIAL/TERMS:
Cash Investment: $50K+
Total Investment: $15-100K
Minimum Net Worth: Varies/Terr.
Fees: Franchise - $5K/100K pop.
Royalty - 6%; Ad. - 2%
Earnings Claims Statement: No
Term of Contract (Years): 10/10
Avg. # Of Employees: 3+ FT
Passive Ownership: Discouraged
Encourage Conversions: Yes
Area Develop. Agreements: Yes
Sub-Franchising Contracts: No
Expand In Territory: No
Space Needs: NA SF; NA

SUPPORT & TRAINING:
Financial Assistance Provided: Yes(I)
Site Selection Assistance: NA
Lease Negotiation Assistance: No
Co-Operative Advertising: No
Franchisee Assoc./Member: Yes/Yes
Size Of Corporate Staff: 12
On-Going Support: C,D,E,G,H,I
Training: 2 Weeks at Grand Prairie, TX.

SPECIFIC EXPANSION PLANS:
US: All United States
Canada: All Canada
Overseas: All Europe and Middle East

MIRACLE METHOD SURFACE RESTORATION

4239 N. Nevada, # 115
Colorado Springs, CO 80907
Tel: (800) 444-8827 (719) 594-9196
Fax: (719) 594-9282
E-Mail: sales@miraclemethod.com
Web Site: www.miraclemethod.com
Mr. Chuck Pistor, President

Make money in the growing remodeling industry by running your own bath and kitchen refinishing business. Save customers money by refinishing instead of replacing. Bathtubs, tile, showers, counter tops and more. Excellent income potential!

BACKGROUND:
Established: 1979; 1st Franchised: 1980
Franchised Units: 100
Company-Owned Units: 0
Total Units: 100
Dist.: US-90; CAN-0; O'seas-10
North America: 30 States
Density: 20 in CA, 7 in TX, 3 in MA
Projected New Units (12 Months): 12+
Qualifications: 3, 5, 4, 3, 3, 5
Registered: CA,IL,FL,MD,MI,MN,NY,VA,WA

FINANCIAL/TERMS:
Cash Investment: $15.8-40K
Total Investment: $25K
Minimum Net Worth: $20K
Fees: Franchise - $18.5K
Royalty - 5%; Ad. - 1.5%
Earnings Claims Statement: Yes
Term of Contract (Years): 5
Avg. # Of Employees: 5 FT, 1 PT
Passive Ownership: Discouraged
Encourage Conversions: Yes
Area Develop. Agreements: No
Sub-Franchising Contracts: No
Expand In Territory: No
Space Needs: NA SF; HB

SUPPORT & TRAINING:
Financial Assistance Provided: Yes(D)
Site Selection Assistance: No
Lease Negotiation Assistance: No
Co-Operative Advertising: Yes
Franchisee Assoc./Member: Yes
Size Of Corporate Staff: 3
On-Going Support: C,D,G,H,I
Training: 2 Weeks at Company Location.

SPECIFIC EXPANSION PLANS:
US: All United States
Canada: All Canada
Overseas: Western Europe

<< >>

Top 100

MR. APPLIANCE CORPORATION

1020 N. University Parks Dr., P.O. Box 3146
Waco, TX 76707
Tel: (800) 290-1422 (254) 745-2439
Fax: (800) 209-7621
E-Mail: gena.reid@dwyergroup.com
Web Site: www.mrappliance.com
Mr. Mike Hawkins, VP Franchising

Full-service appliance repair service for all brands; residential and commercial business.

BACKGROUND: IFA MEMBER
Established: 1996; 1st Franchised: 1997
Franchised Units: 81
Company-Owned Units: 0
Total Units: 81
Dist.: US-77; CAN-2; O'seas-2
North America: 15 States
Density: 9 in TX, 4 in FL, 2 in CA
Projected New Units (12 Months): 48
Qualifications: 4, 4, 4, 2, 3, 4
Registered: All States

FINANCIAL/TERMS:
Cash Investment: $20-50K
Total Investment: $32.2-68.9
Minimum Net Worth: Varies
Fees: Franchise - $15.9K/100KPop
Royalty - 3-7%; Ad. - 2%
Earnings Claims Statement: No
Term of Contract (Years): 10/10
Avg. # Of Employees: Depends on Sales
Passive Ownership: Discouraged
Encourage Conversions: Yes
Area Develop. Agreements: No
Sub-Franchising Contracts: No
Expand In Territory: Yes
Space Needs: NR SF; NA

SUPPORT & TRAINING:
Financial Assistance Provided: Yes(I)
Site Selection Assistance: NA
Lease Negotiation Assistance: NA
Co-Operative Advertising: NA
Franchisee Assoc./Member: No
Size Of Corporate Staff: 7
On-Going Support: A,C,D,E,F,G,H,I
Training: 1 Week Waco, TX.

SPECIFIC EXPANSION PLANS:
US: All United States
Canada: Master Franchise
Overseas: Master Franchise Only

<< >>

MR. ELECTRIC
EXPERT ELECTRICAL SERVICE

Top 100

MR. ELECTRIC CORP.

1020 N. University Parks Dr., P.O. Box 3146
Waco, TX 76707
Tel: (800) 805-0575 (254) 745-2439
Fax: (800) 209-7621
E-Mail: gena.reid@dwyergroup.com
Web Site: www.mrelectric.com
Mr. Mike Hawkins, VP Franchising

Serving the electrical repair needs of residential and light commercial establishments, in addition to offering other electrical products to the 'same user,' including such items as surcharge protectors, communication and data cabling, ceiling fans, decorative light fixtures, security and landscape lighting, etc.

BACKGROUND: IFA MEMBER
Established: 1994; 1st Franchised: 1994
Franchised Units: 126
Company-Owned Units: 0
Total Units: 126
Dist.: US-121; CAN-2; O'seas-3
North America: 37 States, 2 Provinces
Density: 11 in CA, 5 in IL, 4 in TX
Projected New Units (12 Months): 18
Qualifications: 3, 2, 5, 3, 2, 4
Registered: All States

FINANCIAL/TERMS:
Cash Investment: $30.2-68K
Total Investment: $64-155K
Minimum Net Worth: Varies
Fees: Franchise - $19.5K/100KPop
Royalty - 3-6%; Ad. - 2%
Earnings Claims Statement: No
Term of Contract (Years): 10/5
Avg. # Of Employees: 3 FT, 1 PT
Passive Ownership: Discouraged
Encourage Conversions: Yes
Area Develop. Agreements: No
Sub-Franchising Contracts: No
Expand In Territory: Yes
Space Needs: 500-1,000 SF; FS, HB

SUPPORT & TRAINING:
Financial Assistance Provided: Yes(B)

Site Selection Assistance: NA
Lease Negotiation Assistance: NA
Co-Operative Advertising: No
Franchisee Assoc./Member: No
Size Of Corporate Staff: 13
On-Going Support: C,D,E,G,h,I
Training: 5 Business Days at Corporate Offices; 3 Business Days On-Site in Business.

SPECIFIC EXPANSION PLANS:
US: All United States
Canada: Not This Year
Overseas: Most Latin American and Asian Countries

MR. HANDYMAN

3948 Ranchero Dr.
Ann Arbor, MI 48108-2775
Tel: (800) 289-4600 + 790 (734) 822-6340
Fax: (734) 822-6888
E-Mail: t.burns@servicebrands.com
Web Site: www.mrhandyman.com
Ms. Jenn Osness, Licensing Coordinator

Seeking a business with tremendous consumer demand? Stop right here. MR. HANDYMAN is the solution to today's fix-it problems for millions of time-starved families. An affordable investment gives you a franchise catering to 100 million homeowners and commercial customers needing property maintenance and repair. Technicians do the work. You manage the business.

BACKGROUND: IFA MEMBER
Established: 2000; 1st Franchised: 2000
Franchised Units: 142
Company-Owned Units: 0
Total Units: 142
Dist.: US-10; CAN-0; O'seas-0
North America: 10 States
Density: NR
Projected New Units (12 Months): 25
Qualifications: 3, 3, 1, 3, 4, 5
Registered:CA,FL,IL,IN,MD,MI,MN,NY,OR,RI,VA,WA,WI,DC

FINANCIAL/TERMS:
Cash Investment: $10-20K
Total Investment: $47-76K
Minimum Net Worth: $150K
Fees: Franchise - $6.9K
Royalty - 7%; Ad. - 0%
Earnings Claims Statement: No
Term of Contract (Years): 10/10
Avg. # Of Employees: 6 FT
Passive Ownership: Discouraged
Encourage Conversions: Yes
Area Develop. Agreements: No
Sub-Franchising Contracts: No
Expand In Territory: Yes
Space Needs: 200 SF; HB

SUPPORT & TRAINING:
Financial Assistance Provided: Yes(I)
Site Selection Assistance: NA
Lease Negotiation Assistance: NA
Co-Operative Advertising: NA
Franchisee Assoc./Member: No
Size Of Corporate Staff: 15
On-Going Support: C,D,E,G,h,I
Training: 4 Days Home Office; 1 Day Field; 6 Months Right Start Program; 2 Days Franchise Location.

SPECIFIC EXPANSION PLANS:
US: All United States
Canada: All Canada
Overseas: All Countries

<< >>

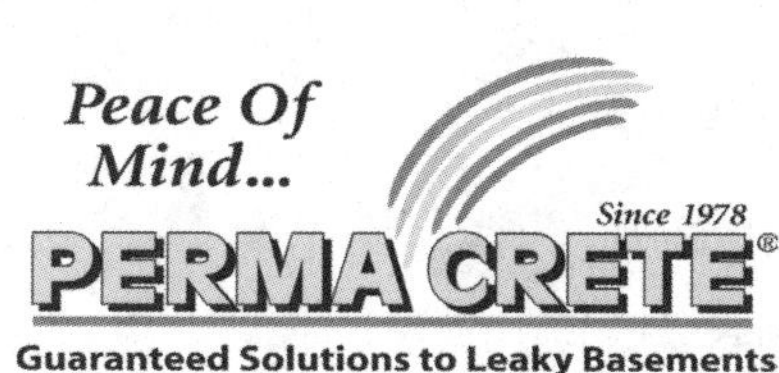

PERMACRETE SYSTEMS

850 Main St.
Dartmouth, NS B2W 3Y1 CANADA
Tel: (800) 565-5325 (902) 468-1700
Fax: (902) 468-7474
E-Mail: sales@permacrete.ca
Web Site: www.permacrete.ca
Ms. Colleen Cole, Franchise Sales

Provision of services in the restoration of concrete surfaces and structures, using products and following a repair system prescribed and developed by the franchisor. These crack repair and concrete specialists are encouraged to expand and diversify their business in any area where concrete products are used or repairs are required.

BACKGROUND:
Established: 1980; 1st Franchised: 1990
Franchised Units: 21
Company-Owned Units: 1
Total Units: 22
Dist.: US-5; CAN-16; O'seas-1
North America: 4 States, 5 Provinces
Density: 7 in NS, 4 in NB, 3 in ON
Projected New Units (12 Months): 6
Qualifications: 3, 3, 3, 2, 5, 5
Registered: AB

FINANCIAL/TERMS:
Cash Investment: $18.5-25K
Total Investment: $18.5-35K
Minimum Net Worth: NA
Fees: Franchise - $18.5K
Royalty - 5%; Ad. - 0%
Earnings Claims Statement: Yes
Term of Contract (Years): 5/5
Avg. # Of Employees: 1 FT, 1 PT
Passive Ownership: Discouraged
Encourage Conversions: NA
Area Develop. Agreements: No
Sub-Franchising Contracts: No
Expand In Territory: Yes
Space Needs:NR SF; HB, Garage Storage

SUPPORT & TRAINING:
Financial Assistance Provided: Yes(I)
Site Selection Assistance: NA
Lease Negotiation Assistance: No
Co-Operative Advertising: Yes
Franchisee Assoc./Member: No
Size Of Corporate Staff: 7
On-Going Support: A,C,D,G,H,I
Training: 2 Weeks Minimum at Head Office in Dartmouth, NS.

SPECIFIC EXPANSION PLANS:
US: All United States
Canada: All Canada
Overseas: Great Britain

<< >>

PERMA-GLAZE

1638 S. Research Loop Rd., # 160
Tucson, AZ 85710
Tel: (800) 332-7397 (520) 722-9718
Fax: (520) 296-4393
E-Mail: permaglaze@theriver.com
Web Site: www.permaglaze.com
Mr. Dale R. Young, President/CEO

PERMA GLAZE specializes in multi-surface restoration of bathtubs, sinks, countertops, appliances, porcelain, metal, acrylics, cultured marble and more. PERMA GLAZE licensed representatives provide valued services to hotels/motels, private residences, apartments, schools, hospitals, contractors, property managers and many others.

BACKGROUND: IFA MEMBER
Established: 1978; 1st Franchised: 1981
Franchised Units: 146
Company-Owned Units: 2

Total Units: 148
Dist.: US-104; CAN-2; O'seas-42
North America: 36 States, 3 Provinces
Density: 15 in CA, 7 in AZ, 6 in PA
Projected New Units (12 Months): 20
Qualifications: 4, 2, 1, 3, 4, 3
Registered:CA,IL,IN,MD,MI,MN,NY,ND, OR,SD,VA,WA,WI

FINANCIAL/TERMS:
Cash Investment: $2.5-3K
Total Investment: NR
Minimum Net Worth: $21.5K
Fees: Franchise - $21.5K+
Royalty - 6/5/4%/$200 Min.; Ad. - NR
Earnings Claims Statement: Yes
Term of Contract (Years): 10/10
Avg. # Of Employees: 1 FT
Passive Ownership: Allowed
Encourage Conversions: NA
Area Develop. Agreements: Yes/10
Sub-Franchising Contracts: No
Expand In Territory: Yes
Space Needs: NA SF; HB

SUPPORT & TRAINING:
Financial Assistance Provided: Yes
Site Selection Assistance: Yes
Lease Negotiation Assistance: NA
Co-Operative Advertising: NA
Franchisee Assoc./Member: Yes
Size Of Corporate Staff: 6
On-Going Support: C,D,G,H,I
Training: 5 Days Tucson, AZ.

SPECIFIC EXPANSION PLANS:
US: All United States
Canada: All Canada
Overseas: All Countries

<< >>

PRECISION CONCRETE CUTTING

3191 N. Canyon Rd.
Provo, UT 84604
Tel: (800) 833-7770 (801) 373-3990
Fax: (801) 373-6088
E-Mail: matt@pccfranchise.com
Web Site: www.pccfranchise.com
Mr. Matthew Haney, Franchise Development

PRECISION CONCRETE CUTTING specializes in removing trip hazards from sidewalks. Trip hazards occur when tree roots or ground settling causes the slabs of concrete to become uneven. Our proprietary equipment and process allow us to bring sidewalks into full compliance with the Americans With Disabilities Act requirements. Clients include municipalities, school districts, apartment complex owners. No experience necessary.

BACKGROUND:
Established: 1992; 1st Franchised: 2001
Franchised Units: 9
Company-Owned Units: 1
Total Units: 10
Dist.: US-10; CAN-0; O'seas-4
North America: 4 States
Density: 6 in CA, 2 in WA, 1 in AZ
Projected New Units (12 Months):
Qualifications: , , , , ,
Registered: NR

FINANCIAL/TERMS:
Cash Investment: $45-50K
Total Investment: $95-105K
Minimum Net Worth: NA
Fees: Franchise - $45K
Royalty - 4%; Ad. - 0%
Earnings Claims Statement: No
Term of Contract (Years): 10/10
Avg. # Of Employees: 2 FT, 2 PT
Passive Ownership: Discouraged
Encourage Conversions:
Area Develop. Agreements: No
Sub-Franchising Contracts: No
Expand In Territory: No
Space Needs: NA SF; Trailer

SUPPORT & TRAINING:
Financial Assistance Provided:
Site Selection Assistance: Yes
Lease Negotiation Assistance: NA
Co-Operative Advertising: NA
Franchisee Assoc./Member: No
Size Of Corporate Staff: 4
On-Going Support: A,B,C,D,G,I
Training: 5 Days Provo, UT.

SPECIFIC EXPANSION PLANS:
US: South & Southeast
Canada: NR
Overseas: NR

<< >>

PRECISION DOOR SERVICE

571 Haverty Court, # W
Rockledge, FL 32955
Tel: (888) 833-3494 (321) 433-3494
Fax: (321) 433-3417
E-Mail: jwellbeloved@precisiondoor.net
Web Site: www.precisiondoor.net
Mr. Jim T. Wellbeloved, Mgr. Franchise Admin.

PRECISION DOOR SERVICE franchise businesses principally sell garage door repair services. Franchisees also sell and install new garage doors. Business operates 24/7 and provides a lifetime warranty on all parts and labor. Trucks carry parts and supplies to repair every garage door system in the market place.

BACKGROUND: IFA MEMBER
Established: 1997; 1st Franchised: 1999
Franchised Units: 55
Company-Owned Units: 6
Total Units: 61
Dist.: US-61; CAN-0; O'seas-0
North America: 38 States
Density: 7 in CA, 7 in FL, 4 in SC
Projected New Units (12 Months):
Qualifications: , , , , ,
Registered: NR

FINANCIAL/TERMS:
Cash Investment: $150-250K
Total Investment: $73.5K-1.0MM
Minimum Net Worth: $150K
Fees: Franchise - $25-800K
Royalty - 1-1.3K.Wk.; Ad. - 0%
Earnings Claims Statement: No
Term of Contract (Years): 10/5/5/5
Avg. # Of Employees: 3-4 FT, 1 PT
Passive Ownership: Discouraged
Encourage Conversions:
Area Develop. Agreements: No
Sub-Franchising Contracts: No
Expand In Territory: No
Space Needs: 1,200 - 2,000 SF; Industrial Complex

SUPPORT & TRAINING:
Financial Assistance Provided:
Site Selection Assistance: No
Lease Negotiation Assistance: No
Co-Operative Advertising: Yes
Franchisee Assoc./Member: Yes/Yes
Size Of Corporate Staff: 20
On-Going Support: C,D,E,F,G,H,I
Training: 2 Weeks Rockledge, FL.

SPECIFIC EXPANSION PLANS:
US: All United States
Canada: NR
Overseas: NR

<< >>

RE-BATH CORPORATION

1055 S. Country Club Dr.
Mesa, AZ 85210-4613
Tel: (800) 426-4573 (480) 844-1575
Fax: (480) 833-7199
E-Mail: jhausner@re-bath.com
Web Site: www.re-bath.com
Mr. John Hausner, VP Sales & Marketing

Acrylic tubs, shower bases, and wall systems that retrofit old ones. We have innovated the one day bath remodeling program.

BACKGROUND: IFA MEMBER
Established: 1979; 1st Franchised: 1991
Franchised Units: 153
Company-Owned Units: 0
Total Units: 153
Dist.: US-149; CAN-2; O'seas-2
North America: 39 States, 2 Provinces
Density: 12 in NY, 12 in PA, 9 in OH
Projected New Units (12 Months): 25
Qualifications: 4, 4, 3, 3, 4, 5
Registered: All States

FINANCIAL/TERMS:
Cash Investment: $6.5-40K
Total Investment: $33-150K
Minimum Net Worth: $100K
Fees: Franchise - $3.5-40K
Royalty - $25/Unit; Ad. - 0%
Earnings Claims Statement: No
Term of Contract (Years): 5/5
Avg. # Of Employees: 3 FT
Passive Ownership: Discouraged
Encourage Conversions: NR
Area Develop. Agreements: No
Sub-Franchising Contracts: No
Expand In Territory: Yes
Space Needs: 500 SF; SF, Showroom

SUPPORT & TRAINING:
Financial Assistance Provided: No
Site Selection Assistance: Yes
Lease Negotiation Assistance: Yes
Co-Operative Advertising: Yes
Franchisee Assoc./Member: Yes/Yes
Size Of Corporate Staff: 14
On-Going Support: C,D,E,F,G,h,I
Training: 9 Days Pheonix, AZ.

SPECIFIC EXPANSION PLANS:
US: All United States
Canada: All Canada
Overseas: England and Others

<< >>

RECEIL IT CEILING RESTORATION

175-B Liberty St.
Copiaque, NY 11726-1207
Tel: (800) 234-5464 (631) 842-0099
Fax: (631) 980-7668
E-Mail: info@receilit.com
Web Site: www.receilit.com
Mr. Glenn Scheel, President

RECEIL IT provides expert restoration and/or cleaning in commercial locations (schools, hospitals, supermarkets, office building, department stores, etc.) of drop ceilings and acoustical tiles using proprietary coatings and cleaners. Work is done at a fraction of the cost and time necessary for ceiling replacement. Your RECEIL IT franchise can be run as a small, home-based operation with minimal personnel or built into a large profile operation.

BACKGROUND: IFA MEMBER
Established: 1992; 1st Franchised: 2003
Franchised Units: 2
Company-Owned Units: 1
Total Units: 3
Dist.: US-3; CAN-0; O'seas-0
North America: 2 States
Density: 2 in NY, 1 in CA
Projected New Units (12 Months): 4
Qualifications: 3, 3, 2, 3, 4, 5
Registered: CA,FL,MD,NY,DC

FINANCIAL/TERMS:
Cash Investment: $38.9-58.9K
Total Investment: $50-70K
Minimum Net Worth: Varies
Fees: Franchise - $17.5K
Royalty - 7%; Ad. - 0%
Earnings Claims Statement: No
Term of Contract (Years): 10/5
Avg. # Of Employees: 2 FT
Passive Ownership: Not Allowed
Encourage Conversions: No
Area Develop. Agreements: No
Sub-Franchising Contracts: No
Expand In Territory: No
Space Needs: NA SF; HB

SUPPORT & TRAINING:
Financial Assistance Provided: No
Site Selection Assistance: NA
Lease Negotiation Assistance: NA
Co-Operative Advertising: NA
Franchisee Assoc./Member: No
Size Of Corporate Staff: 4
On-Going Support: a,B,C,D,H,I
Training: 5-6 Days Copiaque, NY.

SPECIFIC EXPANSION PLANS:
US: NY, NJ, PA, CT
Canada: No
Overseas: No

<< >>

SCREEN MACHINE

4173 First St.
Livermore, CA 94551
Tel: (877) 505-1985 (925) 443-9981
Fax: (925) 443-9983
E-Mail: screens@screen-machine.com
Web Site: www.screen-machine.com
Mr. Jeff Flannigan, Director of Sales

A mobile repair and replacement service for window and door screens. Unique mobile workshop complete with all tools, materials and supplies including a portable generator and chop saw, allows franchisees to quickly take care of customers screen repairs at the customer's home. Very limited competition. High profit margins, low material costs.

BACKGROUND: IFA MEMBER
Established: 1986; 1st Franchised: 1988
Franchised Units: 22
Company-Owned Units: 1
Total Units: 23
Dist.: US-23; CAN-0; O'seas-0
North America: 1 State
Density: 23 in CA
Projected New Units (12 Months): 5
Qualifications: 3, 2, 1, 1, 4, 4
Registered: CA, FL, VA

FINANCIAL/TERMS:
Cash Investment: $20-30K
Total Investment: $44-73K
Minimum Net Worth: $50K
Fees: Franchise - $25K
Royalty - 5%; Ad. - 0%
Earnings Claims Statement: No
Term of Contract (Years): 10/10
Avg. # Of Employees: 1 FT, 3 PT
Passive Ownership: Discouraged
Encourage Conversions: Yes
Area Develop. Agreements: Yes/10
Sub-Franchising Contracts: Yes
Expand In Territory: Yes
Space Needs: 800 SF; HB, Warehouse

SUPPORT & TRAINING:
Financial Assistance Provided: Yes(I)
Site Selection Assistance: NA
Lease Negotiation Assistance: No
Co-Operative Advertising: No
Franchisee Assoc./Member: No
Size Of Corporate Staff: 3
On-Going Support: c,d,G,h,I
Training: 7 Days Walnut Creek, CA.

SPECIFIC EXPANSION PLANS:
US: SE, SW
Canada: No
Overseas: No

<< >>

SCREENMOBILE

72-050A Corporate Way
Thousand Palms, CA 92276
Tel: (866) 540-5800 (760) 343-3500
Fax: (760) 343-7543
E-Mail: salesmail@screenmobile.com
Web Site: www.screenmobile.com
Mr. Shelby Wilson, Director of Sales

SCREENMOBILE provides quality window and door screens. SCREENMOBILE is a mobile outdoor service business offering custom design and installations of high-quality screening products right at the job site on the very first visit.

BACKGROUND:
Established: 1982; 1st Franchised: 1984
Franchised Units: 85
Company-Owned Units: 1
Total Units: 86
Dist.: US-86; CAN-0; O'seas-0
North America: 21 States
Density: CA, AZ, CO, OH
Projected New Units (12 Months): 50
Qualifications: 3, 1, 1, 1, 3, 5
Registered: CA,FL,HI,MD,VA,WA

FINANCIAL/TERMS:
Cash Investment: $25K
Total Investment: $99K
Minimum Net Worth: $104K
Fees: Franchise - $30K
Royalty - $350-1,000; Ad. - $150/Mo.
Earnings Claims Statement: No
Term of Contract (Years): 10
Avg. # Of Employees: 1 FT
Passive Ownership: Not Allowed
Encourage Conversions: No
Area Develop. Agreements: No
Sub-Franchising Contracts: No
Expand In Territory: Yes
Space Needs: 400 SF; HB

SUPPORT & TRAINING:
Financial Assistance Provided: Yes(I)
Site Selection Assistance: Yes
Lease Negotiation Assistance: No
Co-Operative Advertising: Yes
Franchisee Assoc./Member: No
Size Of Corporate Staff: 11
On-Going Support: C,D,E,F,G,H,I
Training: 10 Days Palm Springs, CA.

SPECIFIC EXPANSION PLANS:
US: All United States
Canada: No
Overseas: No

<< >>

SUPERIOR WALLS OF AMERICA
937 E. Earl Rd.
New Holland, PA 17557-9597
Tel: (800) 452-9255 (717) 351-9255
Fax: (717) 351-9263
E-Mail: hawthorne@superiorwalls.com
Web Site: www.superiorwalls.com
Mr. Lee B. Hawthorne, Vice President

We provide license agreements to manufacturer, sell and install the patented SUPERIOR WALLS SYSTEM, a pre-cast, insulated, studded, waterproof concrete foundation wall for new residential and light commercial construction.

BACKGROUND: IFA MEMBER
Established: 1981; 1st Franchised: 1985
Franchised Units: 23
Company-Owned Units: 0
Total Units: 23
Dist.: US-19; CAN-0; O'seas-1
North America: 10 States
Density: 6 in PA, 2 in MI, 2 in WI
Projected New Units (12 Months): 3
Qualifications: 5, 4, 5, 3, 2, 3
Registered: IN,NY

FINANCIAL/TERMS:
Cash Investment: $500K
Total Investment: $2-3MM
Minimum Net Worth: $500K
Fees: Franchise - $30K
Royalty - 4%; Ad. - 0%
Earnings Claims Statement: No
Term of Contract (Years): 10/10/10
Avg. # Of Employees: 8 FT, 2 PT
Passive Ownership: Discouraged
Encourage Conversions: No
Area Develop. Agreements: No
Sub-Franchising Contracts: No
Expand In Territory: Yes
Space Needs: ~30,000 SF; 28' Ceilings, O/H Crane

SUPPORT & TRAINING:
Financial Assistance Provided: Yes(I)
Site Selection Assistance: Yes
Lease Negotiation Assistance: NA
Co-Operative Advertising: Yes
Franchisee Assoc./Member: No
Size Of Corporate Staff: 20+
On-Going Support: B,c,D,G,H,I
Training: 2 Weeks Corporate Office; 3 Weeks Field Location.

SPECIFIC EXPANSION PLANS:
US: All United States
Canada: All Canada
Overseas: England, Philippines

<< >>

SURFACE DOCTOR
4239 N. Nevada Ave., # 115
Colorado Springs, CO 80907-4380
Tel: (800) 735-5055 (719) 594-4112
Fax: (719) 594-9282
E-Mail: cpistor@miraclemethod.com
Web Site: www.surfacedoctor.com
Mr. Charles Pistor, President

SURFACE DOCTOR provides an alternative to conventional remodeling, saving our customers up to 70% over the cost of conventional renovation. Services include: cabinet refacing, resurfacing of cabinets, counter tops, appliances and bathroom fixtures. We provide services to both residential and a variety of commercial markets. SURFACE DOCTOR can give almost any fixture a new look, for a fraction of the cost of replacement.

BACKGROUND:
Established: 1993; 1st Franchised: 1994
Franchised Units: 14
Company-Owned Units: 0
Total Units: 14
Dist.: US-84; CAN-6; O'seas-3
North America: 42 States, 5 Provinces
Density: 7 in NC, 6 in GA, 5 in FL
Projected New Units (12 Months): 50
Qualifications: 3, 3, 3, 3, 3, 3
Registered: All States

FINANCIAL/TERMS:
Cash Investment: $20-30K
Total Investment: $20-30K
Minimum Net Worth: NA
Fees: Franchise - $19.5K
Royalty - 6%; Ad. - 2%
Earnings Claims Statement: No
Term of Contract (Years): 10/10
Avg. # Of Employees: 5 FT
Passive Ownership: Not Allowed
Encourage Conversions: NA
Area Develop. Agreements: No
Sub-Franchising Contracts: No
Expand In Territory: Yes
Space Needs: 1,000 +/- SF; Small Office Warehouse

SUPPORT & TRAINING:
Financial Assistance Provided: No
Site Selection Assistance: No
Lease Negotiation Assistance: No
Co-Operative Advertising: No
Franchisee Assoc./Member: No
Size Of Corporate Staff: 55
On-Going Support: G,H,I
Training: 2 Weeks Charlotte, NC.

SPECIFIC EXPANSION PLANS:
US: All United States
Canada: All Canada
Overseas: All Countries

<< >>

SURFACE SPECIALISTS SYSTEMS
621-B Stallings Rd.
Matthews, NC 28105
Tel: (866) 239-8707 (704) 821-3380
Fax: (704) 821-2097
E-Mail: amy@surfacespecialists.com
Web Site: www.surfacespecialists.com

Ms. Amy Irali, Marketing/Sales Director

SURFACE SPECIALISTS franchisees specialize in repairing and refinishing kitchen and bathroom surfaces. These surfaces include acrylic spas, fiberglass tubs and showers, porcelain tubs, cultured marble, Formica countertops, and PVC/ABS (plastic). Become a factory authorized warranty service provider for more than 34 manufacturers nationwide. We are the only franchisor in the industry providing full service to the new construction market. Excellent opportunity of high profit potential at low investment.

BACKGROUND:

Established: 1981;	1st Franchised: 1982
Franchised Units:	38
Company-Owned Units:	0
Total Units:	38
Dist.:	US-38; CAN-0; O'seas-0
North America:	16 States
Density:	6 in MN, 6 in WI, 5 in IA
Projected New Units (12 Months):	4
Qualifications:	4, 3, 2, 3, 3, 5
Registered:	FL,IL,MI,DC

FINANCIAL/TERMS:

Cash Investment:	$10-15K
Total Investment:	$24.5-33.4K
Minimum Net Worth:	$90K
Fees: Franchise -	$19.5K
Royalty - 5%;	Ad. - NA
Earnings Claims Statement:	Yes
Term of Contract (Years):	10/10
Avg. # Of Employees:	2 FT, 2 PT
Passive Ownership:	Discouraged
Encourage Conversions:	Yes
Area Develop. Agreements:	Yes
Sub-Franchising Contracts:	No
Expand In Territory:	Yes
Space Needs:	300 SF; HB

SUPPORT & TRAINING:

Financial Assistance Provided:	Yes(D)
Site Selection Assistance:	NA
Lease Negotiation Assistance:	NA
Co-Operative Advertising:	No
Franchisee Assoc./Member:	No
Size Of Corporate Staff:	4
On-Going Support:	B,c,D,G,h,I
Training:	3 Weeks Matthews, SC.

SPECIFIC EXPANSION PLANS:

US:	All United States
Canada:	No
Overseas:	No

<< >>

UBUILDIT

12006 98th Ave., NE, # 200
Kirkland, WA 98034
Tel: (800) 992-4357 (425) 821-6200
Fax: (425) 821-6876
E-Mail: franchiseinfo@ubuildit.com
Web Site: www.ubuildit.com
Mr. Kurt Kempfer, SVP Franchise Development

For over 10 years, the UBuildIt system has been assisting homeowners to act as their own general contractor for both remodeling and new home construction. By teaming a homeowner with a construction professional, the project is efficiently completed while avoiding the common pitfalls and saving thousands. Providing subcontractors, bank financing, site visits, etc., UBuildIt is a perfect complementary service for the building professional or entrepreneur looking for a huge untapped niche.

BACKGROUND:

Established: 1988;	1st Franchised: 1998
Franchised Units:	44
Company-Owned Units:	0
Total Units:	44
Dist.:	US-44; CAN-0; O'seas-0
North America:	18 States
Density:	12 in WA
Projected New Units (12 Months):	30
Qualifications:	4, 5, 4, 3, 4, 5
Registered:	CA,IN,MD,MN,VA,WA

FINANCIAL/TERMS:

Cash Investment:	$40.1-106.6K
Total Investment:	$40.1-106.6K
Minimum Net Worth:	$100K
Fees: Franchise -	$25K
Royalty - 5-7%/$300;Ad. - 2%/$50/Mo.	
Earnings Claims Statement:	No
Term of Contract (Years):	10/10
Avg. # Of Employees:	1 FT, 1 PT
Passive Ownership:	Not Allowed
Encourage Conversions:	Yes
Area Develop. Agreements:	No
Sub-Franchising Contracts:	No
Expand In Territory:	No
Space Needs:	400 SF; Class B Office

SUPPORT & TRAINING:

Financial Assistance Provided:	No
Site Selection Assistance:	No
Lease Negotiation Assistance:	No
Co-Operative Advertising:	Yes
Franchisee Assoc./Member:	No
Size Of Corporate Staff:	7
On-Going Support:	C,D,E,H,I
Training:	2 Weeks Seattle, WA.

SPECIFIC EXPANSION PLANS:

US:	All United States
Canada:	All Canada
Overseas:	No

Business: Financial Services

Chapter 7

Business: Financial Services Industry Profile

Total # Franchisors in Industry Group	48
Total # Franchised Units in Industry Group	13,286
Total # Company-Owned Units in Industry Group	6,950
Total # Operating Units in Industry Group	20,236
Average # Franchised Units/Franchisor	276.8
Average # Company-Owned Units/Franchisor	144.8
Average # Total Units/Franchisor	421.6
Ratio of Total # Franchised Units/Total # Company-Owned Units	1.9:1
Industry Survey Participants	17
Representing % of Industry	35.4%
Average Franchise Fee*:	$25K
Average Total Investment*:	$83.7K
Average On-Going Royalty Fee*:	9.5%

*If a range was provided, the mid-point of the range was used. See detailed profiles for actual ranges.

Five Largest Participants in Survey

Company	# Franchised Units	# Co-Owned Units	# Total Units	Franchise Fee	On-Going Royalty	Total Investment
1. Jackson Hewitt Tax Service	3,792	524	4,316	$25K	15%	$47.4-75.2K
2. Liberty Tax Service	1,735	34	1,769	$28K	Varies	$39.8-50.4K
3. Padgett Business Services	423	1	424	$34.5K	9-4.5%	$40-60K
4. CFOToday	241	1	242	$24K	6%	$24.4-37.4K
5. Interface Financial Group, The	168	0	168	$30K	8%	$100K

All of the data provided are proprietary and should not be quoted without acknowledging *Bond's Franchise Guide.*

CASH PLUS

3002 Dow Ave., # 120
Tustin, CA 92780-7233
Tel: (888) 707-2274 (714) 731-2274
Fax: (714) 731-2099
E-Mail: cwells@cashplusinc.com
Web Site: www.cashplusinc.com
Mr. Craig W. Wells, President/CEO

We are meeting America's changing financial needs with tasteful, attractive, retail stores that have proven to be appealing to customers across the socioeconomic spectrum. Our unique style shows genuine care for our customers - this is good for business. A powerful marketing program is designed to be cost-effective and offers support from major retailers. Shorter hours, fewer employees, computer management systems and training - it's all here for you.

BACKGROUND: IFA MEMBER
Established: 1985; 1st Franchised: 1988
Franchised Units: 75
Company-Owned Units: 3
Total Units: 78
Dist.: US-62; CAN-1; O'seas-0
North America: 8 States, 1 Province
Density: 46 in CA, 3 in NV, 3 in FL
Projected New Units (12 Months): 30
Qualifications: 4, 5, 1, 3, 4, 5
Registered: CA,MD,WA

FINANCIAL/TERMS:
Cash Investment: $50-100K
Total Investment: $124-204K
Minimum Net Worth: $200K
Fees: Franchise - $22.5K
Royalty - 6%; Ad. - 3%
Earnings Claims Statement: Yes
Term of Contract (Years): 10/10
Avg. # Of Employees: 2 FT, 2 PT
Passive Ownership: Allowed
Encourage Conversions: Yes
Area Develop. Agreements: Yes/5
Sub-Franchising Contracts: No
Expand In Territory: Yes
Space Needs: 1,200 SF; FS, SF, SC

SUPPORT & TRAINING:
Financial Assistance Provided: Yes(I)
Site Selection Assistance: Yes
Lease Negotiation Assistance: Yes
Co-Operative Advertising: Yes
Franchisee Assoc./Member: Yes/Yes
Size Of Corporate Staff: 9
On-Going Support: a,b,C,D,E,F,G,h,I
Training: 1 Week Tustin, CA; 3 Days at Franchisee Store.

SPECIFIC EXPANSION PLANS:
US: West, SW, NW, Midwest, SE
Canada: No
Overseas: No

CFOTODAY

401 St. Francis St.
Tallahassee, FL 32301
Tel: (888) 643-1348 (850) 681-1941
Fax: (850) 561-1374
E-Mail: rbaker@cfotoday.com
Web Site: www.cfotoday.com
Mr. Ron Baker, Vice President

Accounting, tax, payroll and financial services franchise, offering services to small business clients. Reports they can understand and use, professional services at affordable prices.

BACKGROUND:
Established: 1989; 1st Franchised: 1990
Franchised Units: 241
Company-Owned Units: 1
Total Units: 242
Dist.: US-239; CAN-2; O'seas-1
North America: 37 States
Density: Fl, NC, CA
Projected New Units (12 Months): 66
Qualifications: 3, 5, 5, 3, 2, 4
Registered: All States Except ND,SD

FINANCIAL/TERMS:
Cash Investment: $24.4-37.4K
Total Investment: $24.4-37.4K
Minimum Net Worth: NR
Fees: Franchise - $24K
Royalty - 6%; Ad. - 2%
Earnings Claims Statement: No
Term of Contract (Years): 10/10
Avg. # Of Employees: 1 FT
Passive Ownership: Allowed
Encourage Conversions: Yes
Area Develop. Agreements: Yes
Sub-Franchising Contracts: No
Expand In Territory: Yes
Space Needs: 400 SF; OB

SUPPORT & TRAINING:
Financial Assistance Provided: No
Site Selection Assistance: NA
Lease Negotiation Assistance: No
Co-Operative Advertising: Yes
Franchisee Assoc./Member: No
Size Of Corporate Staff: 7
On-Going Support: b,C,D,G,H
Training: 5 Days Chicago, IL.

SPECIFIC EXPANSION PLANS:
US: All United States
Canada: All Canada
Overseas: No

<< >>

CHECKCARE SYSTEMS

8900 Greenway Commons Pl., # 200
Louisville, KY 40220
Tel: (800) 673-2435 (502) 719--295
Fax: (502) 719-0300
E-Mail: joe_caruso@checkcare.com
Web Site: www.checkcare.com
Mr. Joseph E. Caruso, President

CHECKCARE SYSTEMS is the fastest-growing check guarantee and verification company in the U.S. Proprietary software and hardware configuration included in total investment. Our national account base makes this opportunity a 'must investigate.'

BACKGROUND: IFA MEMBER
Established: 1982; 1st Franchised: 1984
Franchised Units: 42
Company-Owned Units: 0
Total Units: 42
Dist.: US-71; CAN-0; O'seas-0
North America: 22 States
Density: 7 in GA, 6 in FL, 5 in TX
Projected New Units (12 Months): 3
Qualifications: 4, 3, 2, 3, 3, 3
Registered:CA,FL,IL,IN,MD,MI,MN,VA, DC

FINANCIAL/TERMS:
Cash Investment: $65-85K
Total Investment: $110-169K
Minimum Net Worth: $100K
Fees: Franchise - $12.5-45K
Royalty - 5%; Ad. - 0.5%
Earnings Claims Statement: Yes
Term of Contract (Years): 7/7
Avg. # Of Employees: 13 FT, 2 PT
Passive Ownership: Discouraged
Encourage Conversions: Yes
Area Develop. Agreements: Yes/1
Sub-Franchising Contracts: No
Expand In Territory: No
Space Needs: 2,000 SF; Office Park

SUPPORT & TRAINING:
Financial Assistance Provided: Yes
Site Selection Assistance: Yes
Lease Negotiation Assistance: No

Co-Operative Advertising: Yes
Franchisee Assoc./Member: Yes/Yes
Size Of Corporate Staff: 20
On-Going Support: b,c,d,e,f,G,h
Training: 2 Weeks Columbus, GA.

SPECIFIC EXPANSION PLANS:
US: West Coast, Northeast
Canada: All Canada
Overseas: No

<< >>

ECONOTAX

5846 Ridgewood Rd., # B-101, P.O. Box 13829
Jackson, MS 39236
Tel: (800) 748-9106 (601) 956-0500
Fax: (601) 956-0583
E-Mail: opportunity@econotax.com
Web Site: www.econotax.com
Mr. James T. Marsh, President

ECONOTAX provides full support for the establishment and operation of tax offices that provide the public individual and small business tax services, including audit representation, tax preparation, electronic tax filing, and refund loan services. This includes software for tax preparation and electronic filing and training and research services.

BACKGROUND:
Established: 1965; 1st Franchised: 1968
Franchised Units: 52
Company-Owned Units: 0
Total Units: 52
Dist.: US-52; CAN-0; O'seas-0
North America: 7 States
Density: 40 in MS, 6 in AL, 3 in FL
Projected New Units (12 Months): 5
Qualifications: 2, 3, 1, 1, 5, 5
Registered: FL

FINANCIAL/TERMS:
Cash Investment: $5-15K
Total Investment: $10-25K
Minimum Net Worth: $25K
Fees: Franchise - $10K
Royalty - 15%; Ad. - 4%
Earnings Claims Statement: Yes
Term of Contract (Years): 5/1
Avg. # Of Employees: 2 FT, 2 PT
Passive Ownership: Discouraged
Encourage Conversions: NA
Area Develop. Agreements: No
Sub-Franchising Contracts: No
Expand In Territory: Yes
Space Needs: 600 SF; SC

SUPPORT & TRAINING:
Financial Assistance Provided: Yes(D)
Site Selection Assistance: No
Lease Negotiation Assistance: Yes
Co-Operative Advertising: Yes
Franchisee Assoc./Member: No
Size Of Corporate Staff: 5
On-Going Support: A,b,C,d,G,H,I
Training: 5 Days, Jackson, MS.

SPECIFIC EXPANSION PLANS:
US: All United States
Canada: No
Overseas: No

<< >>

ELECTRONIC TAX FILERS

P. O. Box 2077
Cary, NC 27512-2077
Tel: (800) 945-9277 (919) 469-0651
Fax: (919) 460-5935
E-Mail: rachelwishon@aol.com
Web Site: www.electronictaxfilers.com
Ms. Rachel Wishon, President

We do no tax preparation! Instead, we provide a local, reasonably priced, walk-in retail location where the 51% of the taxpayers who prepare their own returns can obtain electronic filing without being pressured into tax preparation they do not need. We transmit the data from self-prepared returns to the IRS and states in order that the taxpayer may receive his refunds in days, not months, via direct deposit into his bank, mail or refund loan.

BACKGROUND:
Established: 1990; 1st Franchised: 1990
Franchised Units: 44
Company-Owned Units: 2
Total Units: 46
Dist.: US-44; CAN-0; O'seas-0
North America: 15 States
Density: NC
Projected New Units (12 Months): 6
Qualifications: 3, 4, 1, 3, , 4
Registered: All States

FINANCIAL/TERMS:
Cash Investment: $22.5K
Total Investment: $22.5K
Minimum Net Worth: $25K
Fees: Franchise - $9K
Royalty - 8%; Ad. - 4%
Earnings Claims Statement: No
Term of Contract (Years): 3/17
Avg. # Of Employees: 2 FT, 4 PT
Passive Ownership: Discouraged
Encourage Conversions: No
Area Develop. Agreements: No
Sub-Franchising Contracts: No
Expand In Territory: Yes
Space Needs: 1,000 SF; FS, SF, SC, RM

SUPPORT & TRAINING:
Financial Assistance Provided: Yes(D)
Site Selection Assistance: Yes
Lease Negotiation Assistance: Yes
Co-Operative Advertising: Yes
Franchisee Assoc./Member: No
Size Of Corporate Staff: Varies
On-Going Support: A,C,D,h,I
Training: 1 Week in Cary, NC; 2-3 Days On-Site.

SPECIFIC EXPANSION PLANS:
US: Eastern United States
Canada: No
Overseas: No

<< >>

INTERFACE FINANCIAL GROUP, THE

2182 DuPont Dr., # 221
Irvine, CA 92612-1320
Tel: (800) 387-0860 (905) 475-5701
Fax: (866) 475-8688
E-Mail: dtbanf@interfacefinancial.biz
Web Site: www.interfacefinancial.com
Mr. David T. Banfield, President

Franchise buys quality accounts receivables from client companies at a discount to provide short-term working capital to expanding businesses.

BACKGROUND:
Established: 1971; 1st Franchised: 1991
Franchised Units: 168
Company-Owned Units: 0
Total Units: 168
Dist.: US-120; CAN-47; O'seas-1
North America: 26 States, 6 Provinces
Density: 15 in CA, 7 in ON
Projected New Units (12 Months): 35
Qualifications: 3, 3, 4, 2, 2, 3
Registered:CA,FL,IL,MD,MI,MN,NY,VA, WA,WI,FTC Disclosure States

FINANCIAL/TERMS:

Cash Investment: $100K
Total Investment: $100K
Minimum Net Worth: $200K
Fees: Franchise - $30K
Royalty - 8%; Ad. - NR
Earnings Claims Statement: No
Term of Contract (Years): 10/10
Avg. # Of Employees: 1 PT
Passive Ownership: Discouraged
Encourage Conversions: NA
Area Develop. Agreements: Yes
Sub-Franchising Contracts: NR
Expand In Territory: Yes
Space Needs: NA SF; HB

SUPPORT & TRAINING:

Financial Assistance Provided: NA
Site Selection Assistance: NA
Lease Negotiation Assistance: NA
Co-Operative Advertising: No
Franchisee Assoc./Member: No
Size Of Corporate Staff: NR
On-Going Support: D,E,I
Training: 2 Days + Minimum 3 Days On-Site.

SPECIFIC EXPANSION PLANS:

US: All United States
Canada: All Canada
Overseas: All Countries

<< >>

JACKSON HEWITT TAX SERVICE

7 Sylvan Way, Fl. 2
Parsippany, NJ 07054
Tel: (800) 475-2904 (973) 496-1040
Fax: (973) 496-2760
E-Mail: william.scavone@jtax.com
Web Site: www.jacksonhewitt.com
Mr. William Scavone, SVP Franchise Sales/Devel.

JACKSON HEWITT prepares tax returns for customers throughout over 4,000 franchised offices in more than 48 states, including locations within Wal-Mart, Kmart, Staples, etc. Since its founding in 1986, JACKSON HEWITT is the fastest-growing national tax service. Offices are independently owned and operated, offering full-service individual tax preparation, electronic filing, refund anticipation loans (subj. to qualification), and audit representation. A subsidiary of Cendant Corp. since 1998.

BACKGROUND: IFA MEMBER

Established: 1960; 1st Franchised: 1986
Franchised Units: 3,792
Company-Owned Units: 524
Total Units: 4,316
Dist.: US-4,316; CAN-0; O'seas-0
North America: 48 States, DC
Density: 480 in TX, 381 in FL, 350 IL
Projected New Units (12 Months): 350
Qualifications: 5, 5, 3, 4, 4, 5
Registered: All States

FINANCIAL/TERMS:

Cash Investment: $25-50K
Total Investment: $47.4-75.2K
Minimum Net Worth: $100K
Fees: Franchise - $25K
Royalty - 15%; Ad. - 6%
Earnings Claims Statement: Yes
Term of Contract (Years): 10/10
Avg. # Of Employees: 1 FT, 6 PT
Passive Ownership: Allowed
Encourage Conversions: Yes
Area Develop. Agreements: No
Sub-Franchising Contracts: No
Expand In Territory: Yes
Space Needs: 400-1,000 SF; SF, SC, RM

SUPPORT & TRAINING:

Financial Assistance Provided: Yes(I)
Site Selection Assistance: Yes
Lease Negotiation Assistance: No
Co-Operative Advertising: Yes
Franchisee Assoc./Member: Yes/Yes
Size Of Corporate Staff: 235
On-Going Support: A,B,C,D,G,H,I
Training: 5 Days in Parsippany, NJ.

SPECIFIC EXPANSION PLANS:

US: All United States
Canada: No
Overseas: No

<< >>

LIBERTY TAX SERVICE

1716 Corporate Landing Pkwy.
Virginia Beach, VA 23454
Tel: (800) 790-3863 (757) 493-8855
Fax: (757) 301-8080
E-Mail: sales@libtax.com
Web Site: www.libertytax.com
Mr. Scott Arbuckle, Dir. Franchise Development

We're #1! LIBERTY TAX SERVICE is the fastest-growing international tax service ever! In 7 years, LIBERTY TAX SERVICE has grown to a size it took other national tax franchises 13 years to realize. LIBERTY's growth is fueled by a proven operating system that has been fine-tuned by the leadership and field support staff's 400 total years of experience. Founder/CEO John Hewitt has worked 36 tax seasons, including 12 years with H & R Block. No prior tax experience required to put this proven system to work.

BACKGROUND: IFA MEMBER

Established: 1996; 1st Franchised: 1997
Franchised Units: 1,735
Company-Owned Units: 34
Total Units: 1,769
Dist.: US-1,457; CAN-312; O'seas-0
North America: 48 States
Density: NR
Projected New Units (12 Months): 300-400
Qualifications: , , , , ,
Registered: NR

FINANCIAL/TERMS:

Cash Investment: $30K
Total Investment: $41.8-52.4K
Minimum Net Worth: $28K
Fees: Franchise - $30K
Royalty - Varies; Ad. - 5%
Earnings Claims Statement: No
Term of Contract (Years): 5/5
Avg. # Of Employees: 4-6 FT, 2 PT
Passive Ownership: Discouraged
Encourage Conversions: NR
Area Develop. Agreements: Yes/10
Sub-Franchising Contracts: No
Expand In Territory: Yes
Space Needs: 400+ SF; FS, SF, SC, RM

SUPPORT & TRAINING:

Financial Assistance Provided: NR
Site Selection Assistance: Yes
Lease Negotiation Assistance: Yes
Co-Operative Advertising: No
Franchisee Assoc./Member: No
Size Of Corporate Staff: 150+
On-Going Support: C,D,G,H,I
Training: 5 Days, VB Higher Education Center.

SPECIFIC EXPANSION PLANS:
US: All United States
Canada: NR
Overseas: NR

<< >>

MR. PAYROLL

1600 W. 7th St.
Fort Worth, TX 76102-2500
Tel: (800) 322-3250 (817) 570-1636
Fax: (817) 570-1738
E-Mail: lhurley@casham.com
Web Site: www.cashamerica.com
Mr. Scott Carskadon, Franchise Development

MR. PAYROLL provides financial services (check cashing, money orders, bill pay, wire transfer, etc.) to the un-banked

BACKGROUND: IFA MEMBER
Established: 1988; 1st Franchised: 1991
Franchised Units: 134
Company-Owned Units: 6
Total Units: 140
Dist.: US-140; CAN-0; O'seas-0
North America: 21 States
Density: 65 in TX, 16 in GA, 8 in NM
Projected New Units (12 Months):
Qualifications: , , , , ,
Registered:

FINANCIAL/TERMS:
Cash Investment: $70-120K
Total Investment: $30-45K
Minimum Net Worth: $140K
Fees: Franchise - $10-30K
Royalty - 10%; Ad. - 0%
Earnings Claims Statement: Yes
Term of Contract (Years): 10/10
Avg. # Of Employees: 1 FT, 1 PT
Passive Ownership: Discouraged
Encourage Conversions:
Area Develop. Agreements: No
Sub-Franchising Contracts: No
Expand In Territory: Yes
Space Needs: 48 SF; Inside Retail Store

SUPPORT & TRAINING:
Financial Assistance Provided:
Site Selection Assistance: Yes
Lease Negotiation Assistance: Yes
Co-Operative Advertising: Yes
Franchisee Assoc./Member: No
Size Of Corporate Staff: 3,000+
On-Going Support: A,B,C,D,E,F,G,h,I
Training: 3 Day Operations Training Ft. Worth; 1 Day Mgr. Orientation Ft. Worth; 2 Weeks at Opening.

SPECIFIC EXPANSION PLANS:
US: Northwest Southwest, SE
Canada: NR
Overseas: NR

<< >>

ONLINE TRADING ACADEMY

18004 Sky Park Circle S., # 140
Irvine, CA 92612
Tel: (888) 842-8418 (949) 475-5652
Fax: (949) 475-5656
E-Mail: john@tradingacademy.com
Web Site: www.tradingacademy.com
Mr. John O'Donnell, Chief Executive Officer

We are the global brand leader in direct access trading education for: stocks, futures and options. All students earn tuition rebates from a choice of five (5) brokers. Our classes are delivered via Web, CDROM and classroom experiences. OTA won the Voyager Award from Technology Investor Magazine for Education Excellence.

BACKGROUND:
Established: 1997; 1st Franchised: 2004
Franchised Units: 5
Company-Owned Units: 1
Total Units: 6
Dist.: US-4; CAN-0; O'seas-2
North America: 3 States
Density: 2 in CA, 1 in TZ, 1 in NV
Projected New Units (12 Months): 36
Qualifications: 3, 4, 4, 4, 5, 5
Registered: All States

FINANCIAL/TERMS:
Cash Investment: $50-100K
Total Investment: $100-150K
Minimum Net Worth: $100K
Fees: Franchise - $39.5
Royalty - 10%; Ad. - 15%
Earnings Claims Statement: No
Term of Contract (Years): 10/10
Avg. # Of Employees: 2 FT, 3 PT
Passive Ownership: Discouraged
Encourage Conversions: Yes
Area Develop. Agreements: Yes/10
Sub-Franchising Contracts: No
Expand In Territory: Yes
Space Needs: 3,000 SF; Office Bldg.

SUPPORT & TRAINING:
Financial Assistance Provided: Yes(I)
Site Selection Assistance: Yes
Lease Negotiation Assistance: Yes
Co-Operative Advertising: Yes
Franchisee Assoc./Member: Yes
Size Of Corporate Staff: 12
On-Going Support: a,C,D,E,G,H,I
Training: 2 Weeks Plus 2 Weeks for Instructors at Irvine, CA.

SPECIFIC EXPANSION PLANS:
US: All United States
Canada: All Canada
Overseas: Europe First, then Asia

<< >>

PADGETT BUSINESS SERVICES

160 Hawthorne Park
Athens, GA 30606-2147
Tel: (800) 723-4388 (706) 548-1040
Fax: (706) 543-8537
E-Mail: musry@smallbizpros.com
Web Site: www.smallbizpros.com
Mr. Michael Usry,

America's top-rated and fastest-growing tax and accounting franchise - serving the fastest-growing segment of the economy - America's small business owners. Initial training. Specialized software. On-going support.

BACKGROUND: IFA MEMBER
Established: 1966; 1st Franchised: 1975
Franchised Units: 423
Company-Owned Units: 1
Total Units: 424
Dist.: US-304; CAN-120; O'seas-0
North America: 45 States, 8 Provinces
Density: 67 in ON, 38 in QC, 26 in GA
Projected New Units (12 Months): 25
Qualifications: 3, 3, 4, 4, 2, 4
Registered: All States

FINANCIAL/TERMS:
Cash Investment: $15-35K
Total Investment: $40-60K
Minimum Net Worth: $60K
Fees: Franchise - $34.5K
Royalty - 9-4.5%; Ad. - 0%
Earnings Claims Statement: No
Term of Contract (Years): 20/20
Avg. # Of Employees: 1 FT, 2 PT
Passive Ownership: Discouraged
Encourage Conversions: Yes
Area Develop. Agreements: No
Sub-Franchising Contracts: No
Expand In Territory: Yes
Space Needs: 200-400 SF; HB, OB, ES

SUPPORT & TRAINING:
Financial Assistance Provided: Yes(I)
Site Selection Assistance: NA
Lease Negotiation Assistance: NA
Co-Operative Advertising: NA
Franchisee Assoc./Member: Yes/No
Size Of Corporate Staff: 20
On-Going Support: C,D,G,H,I
Training: 2.5 Weeks Athens, GA; 3 (2.5 Day) Site Visits.
SPECIFIC EXPANSION PLANS:
US: All United States
Canada: All Canada
Overseas: No

PEOPLES INCOME TAX

1801 Libbie Ave., # 100
Richmond, VA 23236
Tel: (800) 984-1040 (804) 204-1040
Fax: (804) 213-4248
E-Mail: cmccabe@peoplestax.com
Web Site: www.peoplestax.com
Mr. Charles E. McCabe, President/CEO

Professional income tax preparation service specializing in middle-income and upwardly mobile individual and small business taxpayers. Proven marketing and operating methods. Income tax school. Business training and support provided. Minimal start-up cost.

BACKGROUND:
Established: 1987; 1st Franchised: 1998
Franchised Units: 0
Company-Owned Units: 16
Total Units: 16
Dist.: US-0; CAN-0; O'seas-0
North America: 1 State
Density: 13 in VA
Projected New Units (12 Months): NR
Qualifications: , , , , ,
Registered: NR
FINANCIAL/TERMS:
Cash Investment: $40-60K
Total Investment: $51-86K
Minimum Net Worth: $100K
Fees: Franchise - $16K
Royalty - 9%; Ad. - 6%
Earnings Claims Statement: No
Term of Contract (Years): 5
Avg. # Of Employees: 1 Ft, 9 PT (seasonal)
Passive Ownership: Not Allowed
Encourage Conversions: NR
Area Develop. Agreements: No
Sub-Franchising Contracts: No
Expand In Territory: Yes
Space Needs: 600-1,000 SF; SF, SC, RM
SUPPORT & TRAINING:
Financial Assistance Provided: NR
Site Selection Assistance: Yes
Lease Negotiation Assistance: Yes
Co-Operative Advertising: No
Franchisee Assoc./Member: No
Size Of Corporate Staff: 10
On-Going Support: C,d,E,G,H,I
Training: 25 Hours Richmond, VA.
SPECIFIC EXPANSION PLANS:
US: VA Only
Canada: NR
Overseas: NR

PROFIT-TELL INTERNATIONAL

15 Spinning Wheel Rd., # 114
Hinsdale, IL 60521-2914
Tel: (888) 366-4653 + 131 (630) 655-3700 + 131
Fax: (630) 655-4542
E-Mail: info@profit-tell.com
Web Site: www.profit-tell.com
Mr. Michael Johnson, Dir. Franchise Development

PROFIT-TELL is a leader in providing audio marketing solutions to businesses through message-on-hold, enhancement of existing Websites with streaming audio, in-store overhead announcements and more cutting-edge audio marketing solutions. We teach franchisees how to build a solid and loyal customer base with immediate cash flow and no receivables. Our program includes: low investment/low overhead. Every business needs our service. No evenings or weekends.

BACKGROUND: IFA MEMBER
Established: 1993; 1st Franchised: 2002
Franchised Units: 17
Company-Owned Units: 1
Total Units: 18
Dist.: US-18; CAN-0; O'seas-0
North America: 11 States
Density: 4 in CA, 3 in IL
Projected New Units (12 Months): 18
Qualifications: , , , , ,
Registered: All States
FINANCIAL/TERMS:
Cash Investment: $25K
Total Investment: $25-35K
Minimum Net Worth: $125K
Fees: Franchise - $22.5K
Royalty - 0%; Ad. - 5%
Earnings Claims Statement: Yes
Term of Contract (Years): 20/20
Avg. # Of Employees: 2 FT
Passive Ownership: Discouraged
Encourage Conversions: N/A
Area Develop. Agreements: No
Sub-Franchising Contracts: No
Expand In Territory: Yes
Space Needs: NA SF; HB
SUPPORT & TRAINING:
Financial Assistance Provided: Yes(I)
Site Selection Assistance: NA
Lease Negotiation Assistance: NAN
Co-Operative Advertising: No
Franchisee Assoc./Member: No
Size Of Corporate Staff: 10
On-Going Support: A,B,C,d,F,G,h,I
Training: 6 Days Hinsdale, IL; 6 month Curriculum.
SPECIFIC EXPANSION PLANS:
US: All United States
Canada: All Canada
Overseas: No

TAX CENTERS OF AMERICA

1611 E. Main St.
Russellville, AR 72801-5328
Tel: (800) 364-2012 (479) 968-4796
Fax: (479) 968-8012
E-Mail: info@tcoa.net
Web Site: www.tcoa.net
Mr. Gordon Thornsberry, Franchise Manager

TAX CENTERS OF AMERICA is a tax preparation and electronic filing company with franchises in over 15 states. Our franchisees are provided with all the training and knowledge, and full-time support, to become successful. We are innovative in offering franchise opportunities to individuals desiring to become self-employed and businesses searching for a significant income stream. Franchises have unlimited expansion with our unique satellite system. The entrepreneurial spirit is a fundamental motivation.

BACKGROUND:
Established: 1995; 1st Franchised: 1996
Franchised Units: 121
Company-Owned Units: 2
Total Units: 123
Dist.: US-123; CAN-0; O'seas-0
North America: 16 States
Density: 67 in AR, 10 in LA, 8 in NE
Projected New Units (12 Months):
Qualifications: , , , , ,
Registered:

FINANCIAL/TERMS:
Cash Investment: $23.2-28.9
Total Investment: $23.2-28.9
Minimum Net Worth: NA
Fees: Franchise - $15.5K
Royalty - $17/Return; Ad. - NA
Earnings Claims Statement: No
Term of Contract (Years): 10/5
Avg. # Of Employees: 4 FT, 2 PT
Passive Ownership: Discouraged
Encourage Conversions:
Area Develop. Agreements: No
Sub-Franchising Contracts: No
Expand In Territory: Yes
Space Needs: 800-1,200 SF; FS, SF
SUPPORT & TRAINING:
Financial Assistance Provided:
Site Selection Assistance: Yes
Lease Negotiation Assistance: No
Co-Operative Advertising: Yes
Franchisee Assoc./Member: No
Size Of Corporate Staff: 13
On-Going Support: A,d,G,h,I
Training: 4 Days Russellville, AR.
SPECIFIC EXPANSION PLANS:
US: All United States
Canada: NR
Overseas: NR

TAX SMART AMERICA
7520 El Cajon Blvd., # 106
La Mesa, CA 91941
Tel: (619) 469-5800
Fax: (619) 465-7193
E-Mail: jharnsberger@taxsmartamerica.biz
Web Site: www.taxsmartamerica.biz
Mr. Jim Harnsberger, President

Full-service business method franchise for existing tax professionals. Extensive professional education, video conference support, practice management and marketing materials.

BACKGROUND:
Established: 1999; 1st Franchised: 2001
Franchised Units: 17
Company-Owned Units: 0
Total Units: 17
Dist.: US-17; CAN-0; O'seas-0
North America: 1 State
Density: 17 in CA
Projected New Units (12 Months): 30
Qualifications: 3, 3, 4, 3, 4, 4
Registered: CA
FINANCIAL/TERMS:
Cash Investment: $7.5K
Total Investment: $30-500K
Minimum Net Worth: $20K
Fees: Franchise - $30K
Royalty - 8.0%; Ad. - 0%
Earnings Claims Statement: No
Term of Contract (Years): 5/5
Avg. # Of Employees: 1 FT, 1 PT
Passive Ownership: Allowed
Encourage Conversions: Yes
Area Develop. Agreements: No
Sub-Franchising Contracts: No
Expand In Territory: Yes
Space Needs: 800+ SF; SF, SC, HB
SUPPORT & TRAINING:
Financial Assistance Provided: Yes(I)
Site Selection Assistance: No
Lease Negotiation Assistance: No
Co-Operative Advertising: No
Franchisee Assoc./Member: No
Size Of Corporate Staff: 7
On-Going Support: C,D,H,I
Training: 3 Days Corporate Center La Mesa, CA.
SPECIFIC EXPANSION PLANS:
US: CA, TX, MO, NV
Canada: No
Overseas: No

UNITED CHECK CASHING
400 Market St., # 1030
Philadelphia, PA 19106
Tel: (800) 626-0787 (215) 238-0300
Fax: (215) 238-9056
E-Mail: wbarry@unitedfsg.com
Web Site: www.unitedfsg.com
Mr. Wayne Barry, Vice President Development

It may be surprising to most people that 20 to 30% of Americans have no formal banking relationship. Most of these hard working people need a service that will give them immediate access to the cash they need. Even those Americans with established banking patterns are discovering the convenience of the alternative financial services industry. Our customers need more convenient hours than most banks provide. Our industry is happy to provide for these customers.

BACKGROUND: IFA MEMBER
Established: 1977; 1st Franchised: 1992
Franchised Units: 139
Company-Owned Units: 3
Total Units: 142
Dist.: US-142; CAN-0; O'seas-0
North America: 15 States
Density: 45 in PA, 43 in NJ, 9 in TX
Projected New Units (12 Months): 25
Qualifications: 5, 5, 2, 2, 4, 5
Registered:CA,FL,MD,NY,RI,VA,WA,DC
FINANCIAL/TERMS:
Cash Investment: $70-100K
Total Investment: $175-250K
Minimum Net Worth: $350K
Fees: Franchise - $27.5K
Royalty - 0.002% of Volume; Ad. - 3% Income
Earnings Claims Statement: Yes
Term of Contract (Years): 15/15
Avg. # Of Employees: 1 FT, 2 PT
Passive Ownership: Allowed
Encourage Conversions: Yes
Area Develop. Agreements: Yes/Negot.
Sub-Franchising Contracts: No
Expand In Territory: Yes
Space Needs: 1,000 SF; FS, SF, SC, RM
SUPPORT & TRAINING:
Financial Assistance Provided: Yes(I)
Site Selection Assistance: Yes
Lease Negotiation Assistance: Yes
Co-Operative Advertising: Yes
Franchisee Assoc./Member: Yes/Yes
Size Of Corporate Staff: 16
On-Going Support: C,D,E,F,G,H,I
Training: 2 Weeks Corporate Headquarters Philadelphia, PA.
SPECIFIC EXPANSION PLANS:
US: Mid-Atlantic, NE, FL, CA, MO, AZ, CO, NW
Canada: No
Overseas: No

Business: Advertising & Promotion

Chapter 8

Business: Advertising & Promotion Industry Profile

Total # Franchisors in Industry Group	26
Total # Franchised Units in Industry Group	1,373
Total # Company-Owned Units in Industry Group	70
Total # Operating Units in Industry Group	1,443
Average # Franchised Units/Franchisor	52.8
Average # Company-Owned Units/Franchisor	2.7
Average # Total Units/Franchisor	55.5
Ratio of Total # Franchised Units/Total # Company-Owned Units	19.6:1
Industry Survey Participants	9
Representing % of Industry	34.6%
Average Franchise Fee*:	$21.3K
Average Total Investment*:	$57.7K
Average On-Going Royalty Fee*:	2.6%

*If a range was provided, the mid-point of the range was used. See detailed profiles for actual ranges.

Five Largest Participants in Survey

Company	# Franchised Units	# Co-Owned Units	# Total Units	Franchise Fee	On-Going Royalty	Total Investment
1. Adventures in Advertising	405	0	405	$5-27.5K	4-7%	$11.9-47.7K
2. Money Mailer	244	8	252	$25-35K	Varies	$37-71.5K
3. Super Coups	223	0	223	$32K	$148/Mailing	$41K
4. Valpak Direct Marketing	200	9	209	$15K	0%	$40-225K
5. RSVP Publications	80	0	80	$30K	7%	$35-70K+

All of the data provided are proprietary and should not be quoted without acknowledging *Bond's Franchise Guide.*

ADVENTURES IN ADVERTISING

400 Crown Colony Dr.
Quincy, MA 02169
Tel: (800) 432-6332 (617) 472-9900
Fax: (617) 472-9976
E-Mail: david.wood@advinadv.com
Web Site: www.discoveraia.com
Mr. David Wood, Chief Executive Officer

Adventures in Advertising Franchise, Inc. (AIAFI) is an international network of over 450 individually owned and operated, professional promotional product distributorships. Ranked in Entrepreneur Magazine as the #1 franchise in its category, AIAFI offers unlimited capital to grow your business, a complete training and education program, and support from top industry professionals.

BACKGROUND:

Established: 1980; 1st Franchised: 1993
Franchised Units: 405
Company-Owned Units: 0
Total Units: 405
Dist.: US-350; CAN-55; O'seas-0
North America: 44 States
Density: 26 in CA, 18 in FL, 16 in TX
Projected New Units (12 Months): 60
Qualifications: 3, 3, 3, 2, 5, 5
Registered: All States and AB

FINANCIAL/TERMS:

Cash Investment: $5-35K
Total Investment: $11.9-47.7K
Minimum Net Worth: $10K
Fees: Franchise - $5-27.5K
Royalty - 4-7%; Ad. - .25-1%
Earnings Claims Statement: No
Term of Contract (Years): 5/5
Avg. # Of Employees: 1-2 FT
Passive Ownership: Discouraged
Encourage Conversions: Yes
Area Develop. Agreements: No
Sub-Franchising Contracts: No
Expand In Territory: Yes
Space Needs: NA SF; HB

SUPPORT & TRAINING:

Financial Assistance Provided: Yes(D)
Site Selection Assistance: No
Lease Negotiation Assistance: No
Co-Operative Advertising: Yes
Franchisee Assoc./Member: Yes/Yes
Size Of Corporate Staff: 60
On-Going Support: A,B,C,D,G,H,I
Training: NR

SPECIFIC EXPANSION PLANS:

US: All United States
Canada: All Canada
Overseas: No

<< >>

COUPON-CASH SAVER

325 N. Milwaukee Ave., # J
Wheeling, IL 60990
Tel: (847) 537-6420
Fax: (847) 537-6499
E-Mail: coupon@poweruser.com
Web Site: www.couponcashsaver.com
Ms. Myrna O'Reilly, President

Co-operative direct mail coupon company and internet coupons. We specialize in designing ads for our customers that increase their sales. We have about 70% repeat customers in our publications. Our system teaches franchisees how to get and keep customers.

BACKGROUND:

Established: 1984; 1st Franchised: 1990
Franchised Units: 2
Company-Owned Units: 10
Total Units: 12
Dist.: US-12; CAN-0; O'seas-0
North America: 1 State
Density: 12 in IL
Projected New Units (12 Months): 1
Qualifications: 2, 3, 3, 1, 4, 4
Registered: FL,IL

FINANCIAL/TERMS:

Cash Investment: $10K
Total Investment: $24.4-52.8K
Minimum Net Worth: $150K
Fees: Franchise - $9.5K
Royalty - 6% or $400/Zone; Ad. - 0%
Earnings Claims Statement: No
Term of Contract (Years): 20
Avg. # Of Employees: 1 FT
Passive Ownership: Discouraged
Encourage Conversions: NR
Area Develop. Agreements: No
Sub-Franchising Contracts: No
Expand In Territory: Yes
Space Needs: NR SF; HB, OB

SUPPORT & TRAINING:

Financial Assistance Provided: No
Site Selection Assistance: Yes
Lease Negotiation Assistance: NA
Co-Operative Advertising: Yes
Franchisee Assoc./Member: No
Size Of Corporate Staff: 1
On-Going Support: A,b,C,D,E,H
Training: 1 Week in Deerfield, IL; 3 Days at Franchisee's Store.

SPECIFIC EXPANSION PLANS:

US: NW, SW
Canada: No
Overseas: No

<< >>

MERCHANT ADVERTISING SYSTEMS

4115 Tiverton Rd.
Randallstown, MD 21133-2019
Tel: (410) 655-3201
Fax: (410) 655-0262
E-Mail: merchantatm@comcast.net
Web Site: www.worldfranchising.com/website.htm
Mr. Don Goldvarg, President

Local merchant display centers for supermarkets and malls. Utilize as customer information centers. Co-op advertising with local merchants. Large custom-made sign and literature dispensers sold to merchants for 1-year term. Unique, high visibility, cost- effective and professional advertising display. High profitability and cash flow.

BACKGROUND:

Established: 1985; 1st Franchised: 1987
Franchised Units: 2
Company-Owned Units: 9
Total Units: 11
Dist.: US-11; CAN-0; O'seas-0
North America: 4 States
Density: 5 in MD, 3 in PA, 2 in VA
Projected New Units (12 Months): 12
Qualifications: 2, 4, 3, 4, 5, 5
Registered: FL,MI,OR,VA,DC

FINANCIAL/TERMS:

Cash Investment: $13.5-25.5K
Total Investment: $17-29K
Minimum Net Worth: $50K
Fees: Franchise - $13.5-25.5K
Royalty - 0%; Ad. - 0%
Earnings Claims Statement: Yes
Term of Contract (Years): 10/10
Avg. # Of Employees: 3 FT, 1 PT
Passive Ownership: Discouraged
Encourage Conversions: NA
Area Develop. Agreements: Yes/10
Sub-Franchising Contracts: Yes
Expand In Territory: Yes
Space Needs: 5 SF; Supermarket, RM

SUPPORT & TRAINING:

Financial Assistance Provided: No
Site Selection Assistance: Yes
Lease Negotiation Assistance: Yes
Co-Operative Advertising: NA
Franchisee Assoc./Member: No
Size Of Corporate Staff: 4
On-Going Support: B,C,D,E,F,G,H,I
Training: 1 Week Headquarters; 1 Week Franchisee's Territory.

SPECIFIC EXPANSION PLANS:

US: All United States
Canada: All Canada
Overseas: No

<< >>

MONEY MAILER

14271 Corporate Dr.
Garden Grove, CA 92843-4937
Tel: (800) 819-9422 (714) 265-8494
Fax: (714) 265-8494
E-Mail: djenkins@moneymailer.com
Web Site: www.moneymailer.com
Mr. Dennis H. Jenkins, VP Franchise Licensing

MONEY MAILER is one of America's leading direct mail advertising companies with over 300 franchises in the U.S. and Canada. Over its 20 year history, MONEY MAILER has been at the forefront of introducing innovative direct mail advertising products and programs to the marketplace - helping businesses get and keep more customers and helping consumers save money everyday.

BACKGROUND: IFA MEMBER
Established: 1978; 1st Franchised: 1980
Franchised Units: 244
Company-Owned Units: 8
Total Units: 252
Dist.: US-312; CAN-6; O'seas-1
North America: NR
Density: 31 in CA, 23 in NJ, 20 in NC
Projected New Units (12 Months): 40
Qualifications: 4, 3, 4, 3, 4, 5
Registered: CA,FL,IL,IN,NY,VA,WA,WI

FINANCIAL/TERMS:
Cash Investment: $37-71.5K
Total Investment: $37-71.5K
Minimum Net Worth: Varies
Fees: Franchise - $25-35K
Royalty - Varies; Ad. - NA
Earnings Claims Statement: No
Term of Contract (Years): 10/10
Avg. # Of Employees: 1 FT, 1 PT
Passive Ownership: Not Allowed
Encourage Conversions: NA
Area Develop. Agreements: No
Sub-Franchising Contracts: Yes
Expand In Territory: Yes
Space Needs: NR SF; HB

SUPPORT & TRAINING:
Financial Assistance Provided: No
Site Selection Assistance: NA
Lease Negotiation Assistance: NA
Co-Operative Advertising: No
Franchisee Assoc./Member: Yes/Yes
Size Of Corporate Staff: 300
On-Going Support: C,D,H,I
Training: 1 Week Regional Office; 2 Weeks Corporate Headquarters; 1 Week Regional Office.

SPECIFIC EXPANSION PLANS:
US: All United States
Canada: No
Overseas: No

RSVP PUBLICATIONS

1156 NE Cleveland St.
Clearwater, FL 33755
Tel: (800) 360-7787 (727) 442-4000
Fax: (727) 441-1315
E-Mail: rsvp@rsvppublications.com
Web Site: www.rsvppublications.com
Mr. Dave Tropf, President

RSVP PUBLICATIONS, "direct mail to the upscale," is ideal for sales or marketing pros. RSVP regularly reaches 8 million of the most affluent homes in the U.S. With over 11,000 satisfied clients, we know what works and how to produce it to markets across the U.S. We offer extensive training that makes a new franchise buyer successful

BACKGROUND:
Established: 1985; 1st Franchised: 1986
Franchised Units: 80
Company-Owned Units: 0
Total Units: 80
Dist.: US-80; CAN-0; O'seas-0
North America: 30 States
Density: 18 in CA, 9 in OH, 5 in FL
Projected New Units (12 Months): 10
Qualifications: 2, 2, 3, 3, 3, 4
Registered: CA,FL,HI,IL,IN,MI,MN,NY,OR,RI,VA,WA,WI,DC

FINANCIAL/TERMS:
Cash Investment: $30-60K
Total Investment: $35-70K+
Minimum Net Worth: $35K
Fees: Franchise - $30K
Royalty - 7%; Ad. - 0%
Earnings Claims Statement: No
Term of Contract (Years): 10/10
Avg. # Of Employees: 2 FT, 1 PT
Passive Ownership: Discouraged
Encourage Conversions: NA
Area Develop. Agreements: No
Sub-Franchising Contracts: No
Expand In Territory: Yes
Space Needs: NA SF; HB

SUPPORT & TRAINING:
Financial Assistance Provided: Yes(D)
Site Selection Assistance: NA
Lease Negotiation Assistance: NA
Co-Operative Advertising: NA
Franchisee Assoc./Member: No
Size Of Corporate Staff: N/R
On-Going Support: B,D,H,I
Training: 2 Weeks in Tampa, FL.

SPECIFIC EXPANSION PLANS:
US: MW, NE
Canada: All Canada
Overseas: No

SUPER COUPS

350 Revolutionary Dr.
E. Taunton, MA 02718
Tel: (800) 626-2620 (508) 580-4340
Fax: (508) 977-0644
E-Mail: opportunities@supercoups.com
Web Site: www.supercoups.com
Mr. Bill Matthews, VP Franchise Development

SUPER COUPS is one of the top co-op direct mail companies in America. We specialize in developing an integrated marketing solution for local and regional businesses, featuring co-op coupon mailings, co-op TV and internet advertising. We are known for our personalized training, outstanding field support and state-of-the-art production facilities.

BACKGROUND: IFA MEMBER
Established: 1984; 1st Franchised: 1983
Franchised Units: 223
Company-Owned Units: 0
Total Units: 223
Dist.: US-438; CAN-0; O'seas-0
North America: 29 States
Density: 47 in MA, 38 in NY, 38 in NJ
Projected New Units (12 Months): 50
Qualifications: 5, 5, 4, 3, 1, 5
Registered:CA,DC,FL,IL,IN,MD,MI,MN,NY,ND,OR,SD,VA,WA,WI

FINANCIAL/TERMS:
Cash Investment: $5-10K
Total Investment: $41K
Minimum Net Worth: $50K
Fees: Franchise - $32K
Royalty - $148/Mailing; Ad. - $500/Yr.
Earnings Claims Statement: Yes
Term of Contract (Years): 10/10
Avg. # Of Employees: 1 FT

Passive Ownership: Not Allowed
Encourage Conversions: Yes
Area Develop. Agreements: No
Sub-Franchising Contracts: Yes
Expand In Territory: Yes
Space Needs: NA SF; HB

SUPPORT & TRAINING:
Financial Assistance Provided: Yes(I)
Site Selection Assistance: No
Lease Negotiation Assistance: No
Co-Operative Advertising: Yes
Franchisee Assoc./Member: Yes/Yes
Size Of Corporate Staff: 180
On-Going Support: C,D,F,G,H,I
Training: 1 Week Headquarters, Avon, MA; 1 Week in Field.

SPECIFIC EXPANSION PLANS:
US: All United States
Canada: All Canada
Overseas: No

<< >>

TRIMARK

P. O. Box 10530
Wilmington, DE 19850-0530
Tel: (888) 321-MARK (302) 322-2143
Fax: (302) 322-9910
E-Mail: dwayne.dreger@aimtrimark.com
Web Site: www.trimark.com
Mr. Dwayne Dreger, VP Communications

Multiple-unit TRIMARK master franchises offer excellent opportunities for former corporate executives and entrepreneurs with the desire to build a big and profitable business in the growing, dynamic direct-mail advertising industry. No store-front real estate or inventory. Low start-up costs, low overhead and full corporate support. An outstanding franchise business. Single unit franchises also available.

BACKGROUND:
Established: 1969; 1st Franchised: 1978
Franchised Units: 33
Company-Owned Units: 0
Total Units: 33
Dist.: US-34; CAN-0; O'seas-0
North America: 18 States
Density: 4 in PA, 3 in NY, 3 in FL
Projected New Units (12 Months): 12
Qualifications: 4, 5, 3, 3, 3, 5
Registered: FL,HI,MI,NY

FINANCIAL/TERMS:
Cash Investment: $25-100K
Total Investment: $31-122K
Minimum Net Worth: $50-150K
Fees: Franchise - $Included
Royalty - 0%; Ad. - NA
Earnings Claims Statement: No
Term of Contract (Years): 10/10
Avg. # Of Employees: 1 FT, 1 PT
Passive Ownership: Allowed
Encourage Conversions: No
Area Develop. Agreements: Yes/2
Sub-Franchising Contracts: Yes
Expand In Territory: Yes
Space Needs: NR SF; HB

SUPPORT & TRAINING:
Financial Assistance Provided: No
Site Selection Assistance: NA
Lease Negotiation Assistance: NA
Co-Operative Advertising: NA
Franchisee Assoc./Member: No
Size Of Corporate Staff: 15
On-Going Support: b,c,D,G,h
Training: 40-80 Hours Corporate Headquarters; 80 Hours On-Site.

SPECIFIC EXPANSION PLANS:
US: All United States
Canada: All Except AB
Overseas: U.K.

<< >>

VALPAK DIRECT MARKETING

8605 Largo Lakes Dr.
Largo, FL 33773
Tel: (800) 237-6266 + 3121 (727) 393-1270
Fax: (727) 392-0049
E-Mail: richard_folsom@valpak.com
Web Site: www.valpak.com
Mr. Richard Folsom, Franchise Sales Manager

Valpak Direct Marketing Systems, Inc. ("Valpak") is the largest cooperative direct mail envelope company in the US and is an indirect subsidiary of Atlanta-based Cox Enterprises, Inc. who was named by Advertising Age as the 5th largest media company in the U.S. More than 215 franchises in the U.S., Canada and Puerto Rico mail over 16 billion coupons to more than 500 million households annually.

BACKGROUND: IFA MEMBER
Established: 1968; 1st Franchised: 1989
Franchised Units: 200
Company-Owned Units: 9
Total Units: 209
Dist.: US-193; CAN-22; O'seas-0
North America: 46 States, 6 Provinces
Density: 27 in FL, 17 in CA, 13 in VA
Projected New Units (12 Months): 10-20
Qualifications: 3, 4, 1, 2, 3, 4
Registered: All States

FINANCIAL/TERMS:
Cash Investment: $15K
Total Investment: $40-225K
Minimum Net Worth: Varies
Fees: Franchise - $15K
Royalty - 0%; Ad. - 0%
Earnings Claims Statement: NA
Term of Contract (Years): 10/5
Avg. # Of Employees: Varies
Passive Ownership: Discouraged
Encourage Conversions: NA
Area Develop. Agreements: No
Sub-Franchising Contracts: No
Expand In Territory: Yes
Space Needs: NA SF; HB, SF, ES

SUPPORT & TRAINING:
Financial Assistance Provided: Yes(D)
Site Selection Assistance: NA
Lease Negotiation Assistance: NA
Co-Operative Advertising: NA
Franchisee Assoc./Member: Yes
Size Of Corporate Staff: 1,500
On-Going Support: A,C,D,E,G,H,I
Training: 2 Weeks Largo, FL; 4 Days NFI Office; 4 Days Coupon "U" (Site Varies).

SPECIFIC EXPANSION PLANS:
US: All United States
Canada: All Canada
Overseas: No

<< >>

Business: Internet/Telecommunications/Miscellaneous

Chapter 9

Business: Internet/Telecommunications/ Miscellaneous Industry

Total # Franchisors in Industry Group	71
Total # Franchised Units in Industry Group	8,247
Total # Company-Owned Units in Industry Group	863
Total # Operating Units in Industry Group	9,110
Average # Franchised Units/Franchisor	116.2
Average # Company-Owned Units/Franchisor	12.2
Average # Total Units/Franchisor	128.3
Ratio of Total # Franchised Units/Total # Company-Owned Units	9.6:1

Industry Survey Participants	27
Representing % of Industry	38%
Average Franchise Fee*:	$23.8K
Average Total Investment*:	$79.5K
Average On-Going Royalty Fee*:	17.9%

*If a range was provided, the mid-point of the range was used. See detailed profiles for actual ranges.

Five Largest Participants in Survey

Company	# Franchised Units	# Co-Owned Units	# Total Units	Franchise Fee	On-Going Royalty	Total Investment
1. WSI Internet Consulting & Education	1,674	1	1,675	$49.7K	10%	$49.7K+
2. Action International	550	0	550	$45K	5%	$72.2-84K
3. Resource Associates Corp.	500	0	500	$0K	0%	$1-35K
4. FIDUCIAL	464	27	491	$12.5-25K	1.5-6%	$44.4-115.5K
5. Sunbelt Business Advisors Network	350	1	351	$5-10K	$3-6K/Yr.	$5-50K

All of the data provided are proprietary and should not be quoted without acknowledging *Bond's Franchise Guide.*

Top 100

ACTION INTERNATIONAL

5670 Wynn Rd., # C
Las Vegas, NV 89118-2356
Tel: (888) 483-2828 (702) 795-3188
Fax: (702) 795-3183
E-Mail: actionusa@action-international.com
Web Site: www.action-international.com
Mr. Richard Bernstein, U.S. Sales Manager

ACTION INTERNATIONAL is one of the fastest-growing franchises (#16 Entrepreneur Mag., 2/04) and is the largest business coaching company in the world. The company was established in 1993 in Australia by Brad Sugars. Brad recognized early that most owners of small- to medium-sized businesses were unaware of how to effectively grow their businesses and achieve their goals. He developed a comprehensive system and methodology to assist this group. There are now 550 franchisees in 19 countries.

BACKGROUND: IFA MEMBER
Established: 1993; 1st Franchised: 1997
Franchised Units: 550
Company-Owned Units: 0
Total Units: 550
Dist.: US-180; CAN-60; O'seas-310
North America: 25 States, 3 Provinces
Density: 23 in PA, 22 in NJ, 14 in GA
Projected New Units (12 Months): 180
Qualifications: 4, 3, 3, 3, 4, 5
Registered:FL,IL,IN,MD,MI,MN,NY,RI,SD,VA,WI,DC

FINANCIAL/TERMS:
Cash Investment: $72.2-84K
Total Investment: $72.2-84K
Minimum Net Worth: $100K
Fees: Franchise - $45K
Royalty - 5%; Ad. - 5%
Earnings Claims Statement: No
Term of Contract (Years): 5/5
Avg. # Of Employees: 1 FT
Passive Ownership: Not Allowed
Encourage Conversions: NA
Area Develop. Agreements: Yes
Sub-Franchising Contracts: No
Expand In Territory: Yes
Space Needs: NA SF; HB

SUPPORT & TRAINING:
Financial Assistance Provided: Yes(I)
Site Selection Assistance: NA
Lease Negotiation Assistance: NA
Co-Operative Advertising: No
Franchisee Assoc./Member: No
Size Of Corporate Staff: 8
On-Going Support: A,B,C,D,E,F,G,H,I
Training: 10 Days Las Vegas, NV.

SPECIFIC EXPANSION PLANS:
US: All United States Except CA
Canada: All Canada
Overseas: AU, UK, Ireland, GR, FR, MX, Singapore, India, Malaysia

<< >>

Helping Businesses Succeed Since 1990

Top 100

ALTERNATIVE BOARD, THE (TAB)

1640 Grant St., # 200
Denver, CO 80203
Tel: (800) 727-0126 + 125 (303) 839-1200
Fax: (303) 839-0012
E-Mail: salesinfo@tabboards.com
Web Site: www.tabboards.com
Ms. Kris Vollrath, Franchise Support Manager

THE ALTERNATIVE BOARD (TAB) is seeking entrepreneurs, business consultants or transitioning executives who are looking to start or expand their own business. As a TAB-certified Facilitator, you will chair monthly group meetings of owners, CEOs and presidents of privately-owned companies. In addition to facilitating these monthly meetings, you will provide individual coaching sessions using proprietary processes and tools.

BACKGROUND: IFA MEMBER
Established: 1990; 1st Franchised: 1994
Franchised Units: 117
Company-Owned Units: 6
Total Units: 123
Dist.: US-111; CAN-11; O'seas-1
North America: 33 States, 5 Provinces
Density: NR
Projected New Units (12 Months): 50
Qualifications: 3, 5, 5, 5, 4, 5
Registered: All Except ND,SD

FINANCIAL/TERMS:
Cash Investment: $37.3-98.7K
Total Investment: $37.3-98.7K
Minimum Net Worth: $75-100K
Fees: Franchise - $17-47K
Royalty - 35%/$1.5-4.5K/Mo; Ad. - 1%/$100-400
Earnings Claims Statement: No
Term of Contract (Years): 10/10
Avg. # Of Employees: 1 FT
Passive Ownership: Not Allowed
Encourage Conversions: NA
Area Develop. Agreements: No
Sub-Franchising Contracts: No
Expand In Territory: Yes
Space Needs: NA SF; HB, Exec.Suite

SUPPORT & TRAINING:
Financial Assistance Provided: No
Site Selection Assistance: NA
Lease Negotiation Assistance: NA
Co-Operative Advertising: No
Franchisee Assoc./Member: Yes/Yes
Size Of Corporate Staff: 25
On-Going Support: A,C,D,G,H,I
Training: 6 Days Denver, CO.

SPECIFIC EXPANSION PLANS:
US: All United States
Canada: All Canada
Overseas: All Countries

COMM PLUS

317 NE Killingsworth St., # A
Portland, OR 97211
Tel: (800) 735-1422 (503) 936-0687
Fax: (503) 735-0482
E-Mail: mikeh@commplus2.com
Web Site: www.commplus2.com
Mr. Mike Harrison, Chief Executive Officer

Total communication paging cellular local dial tone internet access web design discount computer systems repair and service.

BACKGROUND:
Established: 1993; 1st Franchised: 1998
Franchised Units: 12
Company-Owned Units: 6
Total Units: 18
Dist.: US-18; CAN-0; O'seas-0
North America: 3 States
Density: OR, WA, SC
Projected New Units (12 Months): 4
Qualifications: 3, 4, 3, 2, 3, 3
Registered: CA,OR,WA

FINANCIAL/TERMS:
Cash Investment: $15K
Total Investment: $15-30K
Minimum Net Worth: $85K
Fees: Franchise - $5K
Royalty - None; Ad. - 2%
Earnings Claims Statement: Yes
Term of Contract (Years): 5/5
Avg. # Of Employees: 1 FT, 2 PT
Passive Ownership: Discouraged
Encourage Conversions: Yes
Area Develop. Agreements: No
Sub-Franchising Contracts: No
Expand In Territory: Yes
Space Needs:800 SF; FS, SF, SC, RM, HB
SUPPORT & TRAINING:
Financial Assistance Provided: Yes
Site Selection Assistance: No
Lease Negotiation Assistance: Yes
Co-Operative Advertising: Yes
Franchisee Assoc./Member: NR
Size Of Corporate Staff: 10
On-Going Support: A,B,c,D,e,f,G,H,I
Training: 3 Weeks at Corporate Headquarters in Portland, OR.
SPECIFIC EXPANSION PLANS:
US: NR
Canada: NR
Overseas: NR

CORPORATE MINUTES MADE FRANCHISING

5631 E. Le Mauche Ave.
Scottsdale, AZ 85265
Tel: (480) 510-9000
Fax: (480) 473-2323
E-Mail: dsmith@cmm.cox.net
Web Site: www.franchise1.net
Mr. Dale Smith, President

Our franchises sell corporate minutes to their clients. Truly home-based opportunity with low investment and very high potential return. No inventory, employees, leases or franchisor performance reporting necessary. Personal computer, printer, telephone and fax required. Territory protected. Founder offers 24 years of experience. Software provided.

BACKGROUND:
Established: 1995; 1st Franchised: 1995
Franchised Units: 17
Company-Owned Units: 0
Total Units: 17
Dist.: US-17; CAN-0; O'seas-0
North America: 6 States
Density: 6 in WS, 2 in CA, 2 in AZ
Projected New Units (12 Months): NR
Qualifications: , , , , ,
Registered: NR
FINANCIAL/TERMS:
Cash Investment: NR
Total Investment: $12.5-17.5
Minimum Net Worth: NA
Fees: Franchise - $12.5K
Royalty - $250/Mo.; Ad. - 0%
Earnings Claims Statement: No
Term of Contract (Years): 10/10
Avg. # Of Employees: 1 FT
Passive Ownership: Discouraged
Encourage Conversions: NR
Area Develop. Agreements: NR
Sub-Franchising Contracts: No
Expand In Territory: Yes
Space Needs: NR SF; NR
SUPPORT & TRAINING:
Financial Assistance Provided: NR
Site Selection Assistance: NA
Lease Negotiation Assistance: NA
Co-Operative Advertising: No
Franchisee Assoc./Member: No
Size Of Corporate Staff: NR
On-Going Support: NR
Training: Optional Half-Day, Scottsdale, AZ.
SPECIFIC EXPANSION PLANS:
US: All United States
Canada: NR
Overseas: NR

THE ENTREPRENEUR'S SOURCE®
"Your success is our only business"

ENTREPRENEUR'S SOURCE, THE

900 Main St. S., Bldg. # 2
Southbury, CT 06488
Tel: (800) 289-0086 (203) 264-2006
Fax: (203) 264-3516
E-Mail: info@theesource.com
Web Site: www.theesource.com
Mr. Brad Smith, Sr. Franchise Licensing Mgr.

We provide consulting, education and guidance to people exploring self-employment as an additional career option. Using a unique profiling system, ENTREPRENEUR'S SOURCE consultants help people discover the best options for them.

BACKGROUND: IFA MEMBER
Established: 1984; 1st Franchised: 1997
Franchised Units: 300
Company-Owned Units: 0
Total Units: 300
Dist.: US-292; CAN-3; O'seas-0
North America: 40 States
Density: 27 in CA, 19 in IL
Projected New Units (12 Months): 42
Qualifications: 4, 4, 1, 1, 2, 5
Registered: CA,FL,MD,MI,MN,NY,VA,WA,WI
FINANCIAL/TERMS:
Cash Investment: $75K
Total Investment: $87.5-95K
Minimum Net Worth: $250K
Fees: Franchise - $49K
Royalty - 0%; Ad. - $750/Mo.
Earnings Claims Statement: No
Term of Contract (Years): 10/10
Avg. # Of Employees: 1 FT
Passive Ownership: Not Allowed
Encourage Conversions: Yes
Area Develop. Agreements: No
Sub-Franchising Contracts: Yes
Expand In Territory: Yes
Space Needs: NR SF; NA
SUPPORT & TRAINING:
Financial Assistance Provided: Yes(I)
Site Selection Assistance: NA
Lease Negotiation Assistance: NA
Co-Operative Advertising: Yes
Franchisee Assoc./Member: No
Size Of Corporate Staff: 17
On-Going Support: D,H,I
Training: 8 Days in CT. Initial and On-Going
SPECIFIC EXPANSION PLANS:
US: All United States
Canada: All Canada
Overseas: Most Countries

EXPETEC TECHNOLOGY SERVICES

12 2nd Ave. SW
Aberdeen, SD 57402-0487
Tel: (888) 209-3951 (605) 225-4122 + 3019
Fax: (605) 225-5176
E-Mail: sales@expetec.biz
Web Site: www.expetec.com
Ms. Lisa Hinz, Franchise Development

EXPETEC franchisees provide mobile, on-site, high-level technology services to business and consumer customers. For more information, email us at sales@expetec.biz or call (888) 209-3951.

BACKGROUND: IFA MEMBER
Established: 1992; 1st Franchised: 1996
Franchised Units: 151
Company-Owned Units: 0
Total Units: 151
Dist.: US-151; CAN-0; O'seas-0
North America: 30 States
Density: 19 in FL
Projected New Units (12 Months): 50
Qualifications: , , , , ,
Registered: NR

FINANCIAL/TERMS:
Cash Investment: $6.5K
Total Investment: $8.1-9.5K
Minimum Net Worth: $6.5K
Fees: Franchise - $6.5K
Royalty - 15%; Ad. - $50/Wk.
Earnings Claims Statement: No
Term of Contract (Years): 10
Avg. # Of Employees: 1 FT
Passive Ownership: Discouraged
Encourage Conversions: NR
Area Develop. Agreements: Yes/10
Sub-Franchising Contracts: Yes
Expand In Territory: Yes
Space Needs: NR SF; HB, OB, ES

SUPPORT & TRAINING:
Financial Assistance Provided: No
Site Selection Assistance: No
Lease Negotiation Assistance: No
Co-Operative Advertising: No
Franchisee Assoc./Member: Yes/Yes
Size Of Corporate Staff: 20
On-Going Support: A,C,D,G,H,I
Training: 1-2 Weeks in Aberdeen, SD.

SPECIFIC EXPANSION PLANS:
US: All United States
Canada: No
Overseas: No

<< >>

FIDUCIAL

10480 Little Patuxent Pkwy., # 300
Columbia, MD 21044
Tel: (800) 323-9000 (410) 910-5860
Fax: (410) 910-5903
E-Mail: howard.margolis@fiducial.com
Web Site: www.fiducial.com
Mr. Howard J. Margolis, Director Field Support/Devel.

A FIDUCIAL franchise is a business which provides small businesses and individuals with back office support and accounting and financial management services, tax services, financial services, business counseling services and payroll services. Franchise offices operate out of commercial spaces furnished in such a manner that clients walking in immediately realize that their business, financial and tax needs will be taken care of by qualified individuals who will be there for them year after year.

BACKGROUND: IFA MEMBER
Established: 1999; 1st Franchised: 1999
Franchised Units: 464
Company-Owned Units: 27
Total Units: 491
Dist.: US-491; CAN-0; O'seas-0
North America: 48 States
Density: N/A
Projected New Units (12 Months): 30
Qualifications: 5, 4, 5, 2, 3, 4
Registered: All States

FINANCIAL/TERMS:
Cash Investment: $60-75K
Total Investment: $44.4-115.5K
Minimum Net Worth: $150K
Fees: Franchise - $12.5-25K
Royalty - 1.5-6%; Ad. - 2%
Earnings Claims Statement: No
Term of Contract (Years): 10/5
Avg. # Of Employees: 1-8 FT, 1-2 PT
Passive Ownership: Discouraged
Encourage Conversions: Yes
Area Develop. Agreements: No
Sub-Franchising Contracts: No
Expand In Territory: No
Space Needs: 800-3,200 SF; OB

SUPPORT & TRAINING:
Financial Assistance Provided: Yes(I)
Site Selection Assistance: Yes
Lease Negotiation Assistance: No
Co-Operative Advertising: Yes
Franchisee Assoc./Member: No
Size Of Corporate Staff: 82
On-Going Support: a,b,C,D,g,h,I
Training: 10-15 Days in Columbia, MD.

SPECIFIC EXPANSION PLANS:
US: All United States
Canada: No
Overseas: No

<< >>

FULL CIRCLE IMAGE

6256 34th Ave., NW
Rochester, MN 55901
Tel: (800) 584-7244 (507) 280-0136
Fax: (507) 280-4425
E-Mail: fullinfo@fullcircleimage.com
Web Site: www.fullcircleimage.com
Mr. Charles Benson, President

FULL CIRCLE IMAGE is a direct sales franchise specializing in remanufactured laser toner, ink jet and printer ribbon cartridges. Tap into the $15 billion industry of imaging products used in every business every day. Help reduce waste through recycling while presenting your customers with guaranteed product with guaranteed savings.

BACKGROUND:
Established: 1991; 1st Franchised: 1997
Franchised Units: 31
Company-Owned Units: 0
Total Units: 31
Dist.: US-23; CAN-0; O'seas-3
North America: NR
Density: 11 in MN, 2 in WI
Projected New Units (12 Months): 20
Qualifications: 2, 2, 1, 1, 1, 3
Registered:CA,FL,IL,IN,MD,MI,MN,NY, ND,OR,SD,WI

FINANCIAL/TERMS:
Cash Investment: $3K
Total Investment: $20-25K
Minimum Net Worth: $20K
Fees: Franchise - $20K
Royalty - 5%; Ad. - 3%
Earnings Claims Statement: No
Term of Contract (Years): 10/10
Avg. # Of Employees: 1 FT
Passive Ownership: Not Allowed
Encourage Conversions: NA
Area Develop. Agreements: No
Sub-Franchising Contracts: No
Expand In Territory: Yes
Space Needs: NR SF; NA

SUPPORT & TRAINING:
Financial Assistance Provided: Yes(I)
Site Selection Assistance: NA
Lease Negotiation Assistance: NA
Co-Operative Advertising: Yes
Franchisee Assoc./Member: No
Size Of Corporate Staff: 30
On-Going Support: a,B,C,D,F,G,h,I
Training: 1 Week at Home Office; 1 Week at Your Center Location.

SPECIFIC EXPANSION PLANS:
US: All United States
Canada: All Canada
Overseas: Panama, Costa Rica, Mexico, Guatemala, El Slavador, Venezuela, Columbia

<< >>

GEEKS ON CALL

814 Kempsville Rd., # 106
Norfolk, VA 23502
Tel: (888) 667-4577 + 320 (757) 466-3448
Fax: (866) 516-3513
E-Mail: info@geeksoncall.com
Web Site: www.geeksoncallfranchise.com
Ms. Deneen Wiley, Exec. Asst. of Franchise Devel

On-site computer support includes troubleshooting, virus/spyware removal, repairs, upgrades, wired/wireless networking, one-on-one training and custom-built PCs. Franchisee needs only business experience, however, only certified technicians may perform computer services. Mobile business concept. Low overhead, coupled with central dispatching, advertising, marketing campaigns and proven support make GEEKS ON CALL the logical choice. Single and multi-units available. Highly ranked in Entrepreneur Magazine

BACKGROUND: IFA MEMBER
Established: 1999; 1st Franchised: 2001
Franchised Units: 246
Company-Owned Units: 0
Total Units: 246
Dist.: US-246; CAN-0; O'seas-0
North America: NR
Density:63 in VA/DC, 28 in TX, 22 AZ
Projected New Units (12 Months): 175
Qualifications: 4, 4, 1, 4, 4, 5
Registered: All Except AB

FINANCIAL/TERMS:
Cash Investment: $18-20K
Total Investment: $53.4-82.2K
Minimum Net Worth: $50K
Fees: Franchise - $25K
Royalty - 11%; Ad. - $250/Wk.
Earnings Claims Statement: Yes
Term of Contract (Years): 10/10
Avg. # Of Employees: 1 FT
Passive Ownership: Not Allowed
Encourage Conversions: NA
Area Develop. Agreements: Yes/10
Sub-Franchising Contracts: No
Expand In Territory: No
Space Needs: NA SF; HB

SUPPORT & TRAINING:
Financial Assistance Provided: Yes(I)
Site Selection Assistance: NA
Lease Negotiation Assistance: NA
Co-Operative Advertising: NA
Franchisee Assoc./Member: No
Size Of Corporate Staff: 54
On-Going Support: C,D,G,H,I
Training: 4 Days Norfolk, VA; 1-3 Days in Franchise Territory.

SPECIFIC EXPANSION PLANS:
US: All United States
Canada: No
Overseas: No

<< >>

IMPRESSIONS ON HOLD

4880 S. Lewis Ave., # 200
Tulsa, OK 74105-5100
Tel: (800) 580-4653 (918) 744-0988
Fax: (918) 744-0989
E-Mail: danaj@iohi.com
Web Site: www.impressionsonhold.com
Ms. Dana Justin, Director of Operations

We are an advertising company tied to the telecommunications industry. We enable businesses to use the "on-hold" time of their phone system as a marketing tool. Our franchisees market and sell the "on-hold" service to businesses on a local level, and corporate offices then custom-produce the work that is sold on behalf of the franchise owner.

BACKGROUND:
Established: 1991; 1st Franchised: 1994
Franchised Units: 74
Company-Owned Units: 10
Total Units: 84
Dist.: US-75; CAN-0; O'seas-0
North America: NR
Density: NR
Projected New Units (12 Months): 18
Qualifications: 3, 4, 3, 3, 3, 5
Registered:CA,FL,HI,MD,MI,NY,VA,WA

FINANCIAL/TERMS:
Cash Investment: $47K
Total Investment: $50K
Minimum Net Worth: $150K
Fees: Franchise - $47K
Royalty - 4%; Ad. - 1%
Earnings Claims Statement: No
Term of Contract (Years): 10/10
Avg. # Of Employees: NR
Passive Ownership: Discouraged
Encourage Conversions: NA
Area Develop. Agreements: No
Sub-Franchising Contracts: No
Expand In Territory: Yes
Space Needs: NR SF; HB

SUPPORT & TRAINING:
Financial Assistance Provided: Yes(I)
Site Selection Assistance: NA
Lease Negotiation Assistance: NA
Co-Operative Advertising: NA
Franchisee Assoc./Member: Yes
Size Of Corporate Staff: 50
On-Going Support: A,B,C,D,G,h,I
Training: 5 Days at Corporate Office; 2 Days On-Site.

SPECIFIC EXPANSION PLANS:
US: All United States
Canada: All Canada
Overseas: No

<< >>

INTELLIGENT OFFICE, THE

4450 Arapahoe Ave.
Boulder, CO 80303-9123
Tel: (800) 800-1956 (303) 447-9000
Fax: (303) 415-2500
E-Mail: dennisballen@aol.com
Web Site: www.intelligentoffice.com
Mr. Dennis A. Ballen, Exclusive Agent

This highly evolved alternative to the traditional office provides a prestigious address, anywhere communications and a live receptionist for businesses, corporate executives and professionals, releasing them from the limitations and expense of a residential office. THE INTELLIGENT OFFICE offers private offices, conference rooms and professional office services on an as-needed basis and at only a fraction of the cost of a traditional office.

BACKGROUND: IFA MEMBER
Established: 1999; 1st Franchised: 1999
Franchised Units: 17
Company-Owned Units: 3
Total Units: 20
Dist.: US-2; CAN-0; O'seas-0
North America: 3 States
Density: 9 in FL, 2 in CO
Projected New Units (12 Months): 18
Qualifications: 1, 5, 1, 3, 1, 1
Registered: NR

FINANCIAL/TERMS:
Cash Investment: $120K+
Total Investment: $350-500
Minimum Net Worth: NA
Fees: Franchise - $38K
Royalty - 5%; Ad. - $250/Mo.
Earnings Claims Statement: No
Term of Contract (Years): 20/20
Avg. # Of Employees: 5 FT
Passive Ownership: Allowed
Encourage Conversions: No
Area Develop. Agreements: Yes

Sub-Franchising Contracts: Yes
Expand In Territory: Yes
Space Needs: 4,500-6,500 SF; OB

SUPPORT & TRAINING:
Financial Assistance Provided: Yes(I)
Site Selection Assistance: Yes
Lease Negotiation Assistance: Yes
Co-Operative Advertising: Yes
Franchisee Assoc./Member: Yes/IFA
Size Of Corporate Staff: 6
On-Going Support: C,D,E,H,G
Training: 1 Week Boulder, CO; 1 Week On-Site.

SPECIFIC EXPANSION PLANS:
US: All United States
Canada: All Canada
Overseas: All Countries

Area Develop. Agreements: Yes
Sub-Franchising Contracts: No
Expand In Territory: Yes
Space Needs: Varies SF; HB

SUPPORT & TRAINING:
Financial Assistance Provided: Yes(D)
Site Selection Assistance: No
Lease Negotiation Assistance: No
Co-Operative Advertising: No
Franchisee Assoc./Member: No
Size Of Corporate Staff: 5
On-Going Support: A,C,D,G,h
Training: 1 Week Joliet, IL.

SPECIFIC EXPANSION PLANS:
US: All United States
Canada: No
Overseas: No

Area Develop. Agreements: No
Sub-Franchising Contracts: No
Expand In Territory: Yes
Space Needs: NR SF; NA

SUPPORT & TRAINING:
Financial Assistance Provided: NA
Site Selection Assistance: Yes
Lease Negotiation Assistance: Yes
Co-Operative Advertising: Yes
Franchisee Assoc./Member: No
Size Of Corporate Staff: 20
On-Going Support: a,E,G,H,I
Training: 8-10 Days Chicago, IL.

SPECIFIC EXPANSION PLANS:
US: All United States
Canada: All Canada
Overseas: No

JAY ROBERTS & ASSOCIATES

608 Mack St.
Joliet, IL 60435
Tel: (815) 726-9359
Fax: (815) 726-9359
E-Mail: jayroberts_sbs@msn.com
Web Site: www.worldfranchising.com/website.htm
Mr. John S. Meers, President

JAY ROBERTS & ASSOCIATES is a management/financial consultant firm started in 1965. It specializes in start-up, general and turn-around consulting to small and medium-sized businesses. An emphasis is put on loan brokerage, particularly government loans.

BACKGROUND:
Established: 1965; 1st Franchised: 1981
Franchised Units: 30
Company-Owned Units: 2
Total Units: 32
Dist.: US-32; CAN-0; O'seas-0
North America: 16 States
Density: 2 in IL, 2 in NY, 2 in CA
Projected New Units (12 Months): 12
Qualifications: 3, 4, 2, 3, 4, 3
Registered: NR

FINANCIAL/TERMS:
Cash Investment: $25-50K
Total Investment: Varies
Minimum Net Worth: NR
Fees: Franchise - $2K
Royalty - Varies; Ad. - NA
Earnings Claims Statement: No
Term of Contract (Years): Open/Open
Avg. # Of Employees: 2 FT
Passive Ownership: Not Allowed
Encourage Conversions: NA

MANUFACTURING MANAGEMENT ASSOCIATES

700 Commerce Dr., Fl. 5
Oak Brook, IL 60523-8736
Tel: (800) 574-0308 (630) 574-0300
Fax: (630) 574-0309
E-Mail: franchising@consult-mma.com
Web Site: www.consult-mma.com
Mr. Roger Dykstra, President

Manufacturing consulting: for the small- and medium-size company. Teaching you the market development and sales techniques that made the 'big guys' big. We use your experience and knowledge with our proven methodologies to deliver a quality service.

BACKGROUND:
Established: 1982; 1st Franchised: 1992
Franchised Units: 10
Company-Owned Units: 0
Total Units: 10
Dist.: US-8; CAN-2; O'seas-0
North America: 6 States
Density: 2 in IN, 2 in IL
Projected New Units (12 Months): 4
Qualifications: 4, 5, 4, 4, 3, 5
Registered: IL,MI,KS

FINANCIAL/TERMS:
Cash Investment: $10-15K
Total Investment: $15-25K
Minimum Net Worth: $25-50K
Fees: Franchise - $6-8K
Royalty - 5%; Ad. - 1%/$500
Earnings Claims Statement: No
Term of Contract (Years): 10/10
Avg. # Of Employees: 1 FT
Passive Ownership: Not Allowed
Encourage Conversions: Yes

MISTER MONEY - USA

2057 Vermont Dr.
Ft. Collins, CO 80525-2913
Tel: (800) 827-7296 + 137 (970) 493-0574
Fax: (970) 490-2099
E-Mail: joshl@mistermoney.commattw@mistermoney.com
Web Site: www.mistermoney.com
Mr. Matt Will, National Sales Manager

MISTER MONEY - USA franchises offer pawn loans, payday loans, check cashing, money orders, and other financial services. Franchisees operate full-service retail stores or loan only outlets. MISTER MONEY - USA stores are modern, customer friendly and located in solid blue collar areas.

BACKGROUND:
Established: 1976; 1st Franchised: 1996
Franchised Units: 35
Company-Owned Units: 14
Total Units: 49
Dist.: US-48; CAN-0; O'seas-2
North America: 11 States
Density: 13 in IA, 9 in CO, 4 in WI
Projected New Units (12 Months): 12
Qualifications: 5, 4, 3, 3, 5, 5
Registered: FL,IL,IN,MN,ND,WI

FINANCIAL/TERMS:
Cash Investment: $65-150K
Total Investment: $65-200K
Minimum Net Worth: $65K
Fees: Franchise - $21.5-24.5K
Royalty - 3-5%; Ad. - 3%
Earnings Claims Statement: Yes
Term of Contract (Years): 5/5
Avg. # Of Employees: 3 FT, 1 PT
Passive Ownership: Discouraged

Encourage Conversions: Yes
Area Develop. Agreements: No
Sub-Franchising Contracts: Yes
Expand In Territory: Yes
Space Needs: 4,000-10,000 SF; FS, SF, SC

SUPPORT & TRAINING:

Financial Assistance Provided: Yes(D)
Site Selection Assistance: Yes
Lease Negotiation Assistance: Yes
Co-Operative Advertising: Yes
Franchisee Assoc./Member: Yes/Yes
Size Of Corporate Staff: 25
On-Going Support: a,B,C,D,E,F,G,I
Training: 10-14 Days Fort Collins, CO.

SPECIFIC EXPANSION PLANS:

US: All United States
Canada: No
Overseas: Mexico

MONEY CONCEPTS (CANADA)

180 Attwell Dr., # 501
Toronto, ON M9W 6A9 CANADA
Tel: (800) 661-7296 (416) 674-0450
Fax: (416) 674-4785
E-Mail: rsylvester@moneyconcepts.ca
Web Site: www.moneyconcepts.ca
Mr. Rob Sylvester, President

MONEY CONCEPTS offers financial planning control. We are the fastest-growing independent franchise in financial services in Canada, specializing in complete financial planning and searching the market for financial products to implement our plan.

BACKGROUND:

Established: 1984; 1st Franchised: 1985
Franchised Units: 94
Company-Owned Units: 0
Total Units: 94
Dist.: US-0; CAN-94; O'seas-0
North America: 8 Provinces
Density: 53 in ON, 21 in BC, 5 in NB
Projected New Units (12 Months): 25
Qualifications: 3, 4, 1, 2, 4, 5
Registered: AB

FINANCIAL/TERMS:

Cash Investment: $50K
Total Investment: $80K
Minimum Net Worth: $200K+
Fees: Franchise - $49.5K
Royalty - Varies; Ad. - 2%/$5K Max.
Earnings Claims Statement: No
Term of Contract (Years): 5/1
Avg. # Of Employees: 4 FT
Passive Ownership: Discouraged
Encourage Conversions: NA
Area Develop. Agreements: Yes/5
Sub-Franchising Contracts: No
Expand In Territory: Yes
Space Needs: 750-1,000 SF; NA

SUPPORT & TRAINING:

Financial Assistance Provided: No
Site Selection Assistance: Yes
Lease Negotiation Assistance: No
Co-Operative Advertising: Yes
Franchisee Assoc./Member: Yes/Yes
Size Of Corporate Staff: 25
On-Going Support: A,b,C,D,G,H,I
Training: 2 Weeks Head Office.

SPECIFIC EXPANSION PLANS:

US: No
Canada: All Canada
Overseas: No

NETSPACE

2801 NE 208 Ter., Fl. 2
Miami, FL 33180
Tel: (800) 638-7722 (305) 931-4000
Fax: (305) 931-7772
E-Mail: dellray@netspace.info
Web Site: www.netspace.info
Mr. DellrayLefevere, Vice President

Netspace consults with companies in assisting them in building their business by using technology available through the Internet. All of our products increase sale, lower costs and improve customer communications. These products deliver on-going recurring income to the franchisee. A marketing director and sales coach are part of your success team assisting you in building the business of your dreams. Initial and quarterly training keep you current with the most recent technology.

BACKGROUND: IFA MEMBER

Established: 1996; 1st Franchised: 2000
Franchised Units: 96
Company-Owned Units: 0
Total Units: 96
Dist.: US-60; CAN-0; O'seas-32
North America: 59 States
Density: 3 in NJ, 3 in NY
Projected New Units (12 Months): 20
Qualifications: 5, 5, 3, 4, 5, 5
Registered: All States

FINANCIAL/TERMS:

Cash Investment: $60-80K
Total Investment: $60-80K
Minimum Net Worth: $150K
Fees: Franchise - $39.5K
Royalty - 10%; Ad. - 1%
Earnings Claims Statement: No
Term of Contract (Years): 10/5
Avg. # Of Employees: 3 FT
Passive Ownership: Not Allowed
Encourage Conversions: Yes
Area Develop. Agreements: Yes
Sub-Franchising Contracts: Yes
Expand In Territory: Yes
Space Needs: NR SF; Office

SUPPORT & TRAINING:

Financial Assistance Provided: No
Site Selection Assistance: Yes
Lease Negotiation Assistance: No
Co-Operative Advertising: No
Franchisee Assoc./Member: Yes/Yes
Size Of Corporate Staff: 30
On-Going Support: A,B,C,D,e,f,G,H,I
Training: 1 Week Miami, FL.

SPECIFIC EXPANSION PLANS:

US: All United States
Canada: All Canada
Overseas: Europe and UK

PROVENTURE BUSINESS GROUP

P. O. Box 338
Needham Heights, MA 02494
Tel: (781) 444-8278
Fax: (781) 444-0565
E-Mail: proventure@aol.com
Web Site: www.worldfranchising.com/website.htm
Mr. William J. Tedoldi, President

PROVENTURE is an all-inclusive, New England-based business brokerage, consulting and management company. The group lists and sells going businesses including franchises (up to $100 million in value), and other business opportunities on a fee basis. We also offer a moderately priced consulting service for new franchise start-ups.

BACKGROUND:

Established: 1979; 1st Franchised: 1981
Franchised Units: 9
Company-Owned Units: 4
Total Units: 13
Dist.: US-9; CAN-0; O'seas-0
North America: 2 States
Density: 8 in MA, 1 in NH
Projected New Units (12 Months): 2
Qualifications: 3, 5, 3, 3, 4, 4
Registered: NR

FINANCIAL/TERMS:

Cash Investment: $35K
Total Investment: $35-50K
Minimum Net Worth: NA
Fees: Franchise - $10K

Royalty - 6%; Ad. - 0%
Earnings Claims Statement: No
Term of Contract (Years): 10/10
Avg. # Of Employees: 2 FT, 2 PT
Passive Ownership: Discouraged
Encourage Conversions: Yes
Area Develop. Agreements: No
Sub-Franchising Contracts: No
Expand In Territory: Yes
Space Needs: 500 SF; OB

SUPPORT & TRAINING:
Financial Assistance Provided: No
Site Selection Assistance: Yes
Lease Negotiation Assistance: Yes
Co-Operative Advertising: No
Franchisee Assoc./Member: No
Size Of Corporate Staff: 2
On-Going Support: C,D,E,G,h
Training: 1 Week Headquarters.

SPECIFIC EXPANSION PLANS:
US: New England
Canada: PQ, ON
Overseas: Mexico, Europe, Asia

QUIK INTERNET

129 Cbrillo St., # 100
Costa Mesa, CA 92627-3053
Tel: (888) 784-5266 (949) 548-2171
Fax: (949) 548-0569
E-Mail: jack@quik.com
Web Site: www.quik.com
Mr. Jack Reynolds, President

QUIK INTERNET is the world's first and largest Internet services franchise, with over 200 franchises worldwide. Provide highly demanded Internet services in your local community, including Internet access, Web design, on-line marketing and more. Prime territories, low fees - apply today!

BACKGROUND: IFA MEMBER
Established: 1996; 1st Franchised: 1996
Franchised Units: 240
Company-Owned Units: 0
Total Units: 240
Dist.: US-80; CAN-4; O'seas-156
North America: NR
Density: CA, TX, FL
Projected New Units (12 Months): 50
Qualifications: 5, 5, 1, 4, 4, 4
Registered: All States and AB

FINANCIAL/TERMS:
Cash Investment: $60-65K
Total Investment: $60-65K
Minimum Net Worth: NA
Fees: Franchise - $35K
Royalty - 10%; Ad. - 5%
Earnings Claims Statement: No
Term of Contract (Years): 10/10
Avg. # Of Employees: 1 FT
Passive Ownership: NR
Encourage Conversions: NA
Area Develop. Agreements: NR
Sub-Franchising Contracts: No
Expand In Territory: NA
Space Needs: NA SF; NA

SUPPORT & TRAINING:
Financial Assistance Provided: No
Site Selection Assistance: NA
Lease Negotiation Assistance: NA
Co-Operative Advertising: No
Franchisee Assoc./Member: No
Size Of Corporate Staff: 30
On-Going Support: A,B,C,D,F
Training: 1 Week Costa Mesa, CA.

SPECIFIC EXPANSION PLANS:
US: All United States
Canada: All Canada
Overseas: All Countries

RESOURCE ASSOCIATES CORP.

31 Hickory Rd.
Mohnton, PA 19540
Tel: (800) 799-6227 (610) 775-5222
Fax: (610) 775-9686
E-Mail: success@rac-tqi.com
Web Site: www.rac-tqi.com
Mr. William L. Sweney, VP Development

RESOURCE ASSOCIATES CORP. is a network of independent consultants working in the areas of strategic planning, people development, process improvement, coaching and youth leadership. RESOURCE ASSOCIATES CORP. is a business opportunity, not a franchise.

BACKGROUND:
Established: 1978; 1st Franchised: NR
Franchised Units: 500
Company-Owned Units: 0
Total Units: 500
Dist.: US-500; CAN-0; O'seas-0
North America: 45 States
Density: NJ, CA, PA
Projected New Units (12 Months): 100
Qualifications: 3, 5, 1, 1, 1, 5
Registered: NA

FINANCIAL/TERMS:
Cash Investment: $1-35K
Total Investment: $1-35K
Minimum Net Worth: NA
Fees: Franchise - $0K
Royalty - 0%; Ad. - 0%
Earnings Claims Statement: No
Term of Contract (Years): NA
Avg. # Of Employees: 0 FT, 0 PT
Passive Ownership: Discouraged
Encourage Conversions: NA
Area Develop. Agreements: NA
Sub-Franchising Contracts: No
Expand In Territory: Yes
Space Needs: NA SF; NA

SUPPORT & TRAINING:
Financial Assistance Provided: No
Site Selection Assistance: NA
Lease Negotiation Assistance: NA
Co-Operative Advertising: NA
Franchisee Assoc./Member: No
Size Of Corporate Staff: 30
On-Going Support: G,H,I
Training: Optional.

SPECIFIC EXPANSION PLANS:
US: All United States
Canada: All Canada
Overseas: No

<< >>

SUNBELT BUSINESS ADVISORS NETWORK

474 Wando Park Blvd., # 204
Mt. Pleasant, SC 29464
Tel: (800) 771-7866 (843) 853-4781
Fax: (843) 284-2419
E-Mail: etp@sunbeltnetwork.com
Web Site: www.sunbeltnetwork.com
Mr. Edward Pendarvis, President

We offer business brokerage/merger and acquisition franchises. SUNBELT is the largest and fastest-growing business brokerage firm in the world. Our success comes from our name recognition, quality training programs and hands-on assistance. We are the leaders in computerized office management, networking and Internet technology. We take no percentage fees. All of our services are covered in our low semi-annual fee.

BACKGROUND: IFA MEMBER
Established: 1978; 1st Franchised: 1993
Franchised Units: 350
Company-Owned Units: 1
Total Units: 351
Dist.: US-199; CAN-0; O'seas-6

North America: 38 States
Density: 16 in FL, 10 in NC, 10 in VA
Projected New Units (12 Months): 50
Qualifications: , , , , ,
Registered: CA,FL,HI,IL,IN,MD,MI,MN, NY,OR,RI,SD,VA,WA,WI

FINANCIAL/TERMS:
Cash Investment: $5-15K
Total Investment: $5-50K
Minimum Net Worth: NA
Fees: Franchise - $5-10K
Royalty - $3-6K/Yr.; Ad. - 0%
Earnings Claims Statement: No
Term of Contract (Years): On-Going
Avg. # Of Employees: Independent Contrac.
Passive Ownership: Not Allowed
Encourage Conversions: Yes
Area Develop. Agreements: No
Sub-Franchising Contracts: No
Expand In Territory: Yes
Space Needs: 1,000 SF; FS

SUPPORT & TRAINING:
Financial Assistance Provided: Yes(D)
Site Selection Assistance: NA
Lease Negotiation Assistance: NA
Co-Operative Advertising: NA
Franchisee Assoc./Member: Yes/Yes
Size Of Corporate Staff: 9
On-Going Support: C,D,G,H,I
Training: 4 Days Various Regional Centers.

SPECIFIC EXPANSION PLANS:
US: All United States
Canada: All Canada
Overseas: All Countries

<< >>

VR BUSINESS BROKERS/ MERGERS & ACQUISITIONS

2601 E. Oakland Park Blvd., # 301
Ft. Lauderdale, FL 33306
Tel: (800) 377-8722 (954) 565-1555
Fax: (954) 565-6855
E-Mail: vrbb@vrbusinessbrokers.com
Web Site: www.vrbusinessbrokers.com
Ms. JoAnn Lombardi, President

International network of business brokers and intermediaries, specializing in the sale of small to mid-size companies. Extensive training, support and marketing materials make it possible to become a full-time professional in our industry. VR has sold more businesses in North America than anyone ®. Of the 11 million businesses in America, 20% change hands every year for you to sell. Since 1979, VR has sold free enterprise. Now it's your turn.

BACKGROUND: IFA MEMBER
Established: 1979; 1st Franchised: 1979
Franchised Units: 103
Company-Owned Units: 0
Total Units: 103
Dist.: US-101; CAN-1; O'seas-11
North America: 37 States
Density: 12 in FL, 10 in CA, 5 in NC
Projected New Units (12 Months): 25
Qualifications: 4, 4, 1, 2, 3, 3
Registered: All States

FINANCIAL/TERMS:
Cash Investment: $40-75K
Total Investment: $40-75K
Minimum Net Worth: $150K
Fees: Franchise - $17.5K
Royalty - 6%; Ad. - $150/Mo.
Earnings Claims Statement: No
Term of Contract (Years): 10/10
Avg. # Of Employees: 2 FT, 1 PT
Passive Ownership: Allowed
Encourage Conversions: Yes
Area Develop. Agreements: No
Sub-Franchising Contracts: No
Expand In Territory: No
Space Needs: 1,200 SF; OB

SUPPORT & TRAINING:
Financial Assistance Provided: Yes(B)
Site Selection Assistance: Yes
Lease Negotiation Assistance: Yes
Co-Operative Advertising: Yes
Franchisee Assoc./Member: Yes/No
Size Of Corporate Staff: 12
On-Going Support: A,B,C,D,E,G,H,I
Training: 1 Week Dallas, TX.

SPECIFIC EXPANSION PLANS:
US: All United States
Canada: All Canada
Overseas: All Countries

<< >>

WIRELESS TOYZ

23399 Commerce Dr.
Farmington Hills, MI 48335
Tel: (866) 2-FRANCHISE (248) 426-8200
Fax: (248) 671-0346
E-Mail: franchise@wirelesstoyz.com
Web Site: www.wirelesstoyz.com
Mr. Richard Simtob, VP Franchise Development

One-stop shop wireless store. All the major cellular carriers and satellite carriers are available. Customers are guaranteed the best price and service.

BACKGROUND: IFA MEMBER
Established: 1995; 1st Franchised: 2001
Franchised Units: 68
Company-Owned Units: 2
Total Units: 70
Dist.: US-70; CAN-0; O'seas-0
North America: 19 States
Density: 24 in MI, 8 in TX, 4 in IN
Projected New Units (12 Months): 90
Qualifications: 4, 5, 2, 1, 3, 5
Registered: CA,FL,IL,IN,MD,MI,VA,WA, WI

FINANCIAL/TERMS:
Cash Investment: $60-75K
Total Investment: $200-300K
Minimum Net Worth: $100K
Fees: Franchise - $30K
Royalty - 13%/Activation; Ad. - 0%
Earnings Claims Statement: Yes
Term of Contract (Years): 10/10
Avg. # Of Employees: 2 FT, 2 PT
Passive Ownership: Not Allowed
Encourage Conversions: Yes
Area Develop. Agreements: Yes/5
Sub-Franchising Contracts: No
Expand In Territory: Yes
Space Needs: 2,000 SF; FS, SC

SUPPORT & TRAINING:
Financial Assistance Provided: Yes(I)
Site Selection Assistance: Yes
Lease Negotiation Assistance: Yes
Co-Operative Advertising: Yes
Franchisee Assoc./Member: No
Size Of Corporate Staff: 20
On-Going Support: A,B,C,D,E,F,G,H,I
Training: Minimum 4 Weeks Michigan Office/Store; 3 Days On-Site.

SPECIFIC EXPANSION PLANS:
US: All United States
Canada: No
Overseas: No

<< >>

wireless ZONE®

WIRELESS ZONE

2101 Belair Rd., # 102
Fallston, MD 21047

Tel: (443) 243-0549
Fax: (410) 877-7955
E-Mail: ronb@wirelesszone.com
Web Site: www.wirelesszone.com
Mr. Ron Bender, VP Franchise Development

WIRELESS ZONE stores are primarily retail, with strong emphasis on local ownership, networking and community involvement. Franchise provides local field support staff, centralized advertising and purchasing, initial and on-going training and strong commissions and residual income from Verizon Wireless phones, service, accessories, wireless email, etc. Join a winning team!

BACKGROUND: IFA MEMBER
Established: 1988; 1st Franchised: 1989
Franchised Units: 245
Company-Owned Units: 0
Total Units: 245
Dist.: US-226; CAN-0; O'seas-0
North America: 13 States
Density: 46 in CT, 38 in PA, 23 in NY
Projected New Units (12 Months): 65
Qualifications: 2, 4, 3, 2, 1, 5
Registered: MD,NY,RI,VA

FINANCIAL/TERMS:
Cash Investment: $40-50K
Total Investment: $60-80K
Minimum Net Worth: NA
Fees: Franchise - $8.5-25K
Royalty - 10%; Ad. - $800/Mo.
Earnings Claims Statement: No
Term of Contract (Years): 7/7
Avg. # Of Employees: 2 FT, 1 PT
Passive Ownership: Discouraged
Encourage Conversions: Yes
Area Develop. Agreements: No
Sub-Franchising Contracts: Yes
Expand In Territory: Yes
Space Needs: 1,000 SF; SC, SC, RM

SUPPORT & TRAINING:
Financial Assistance Provided: Yes(D)
Site Selection Assistance: Yes
Lease Negotiation Assistance: Yes
Co-Operative Advertising: Yes
Franchisee Assoc./Member: Yes/Yes
Size Of Corporate Staff: 64
On-Going Support: B,C,D,E,G,H
Training: 2 Days with 3rd Party Trainer New Store; Up to 1 Week Existing Store; 2 Weeks in Store. 2 Days with Executive Trainer.

SPECIFIC EXPANSION PLANS:
US: FL and VA to ME
Canada: No
Overseas: No

WSI CONSULTING & EDUCATION

5915 Airport Rd., # 300
Mississauga, ON L4V 1T1 CANADA
Tel: (888) 678-7588 (905) 678-7588
Fax: (905) 678-7242
E-Mail: ralvarado@wsicorporate.com
Web Site: www.wsicorporate.com/business.asp?id=77263
Mr. Roberto Alvarado, Media Director

WSI INTERNET business is proud to have been rated in the Top 100 Franchises by Entrepreneur Magazine. You can be part of this successful franchise and profit from the Internet! Own the #1 rated internet franchise. Proven business system. No specific business experience is required. Home- or office-based. Complete training and support. The WSI Formula is simple- Successful Franchise Owners + Successful Clients - Successful Franchise Opportunity.

BACKGROUND:
Established: NR; 1st Franchised: NR
Franchised Units: 1,674
Company-Owned Units: 1
Total Units: 1,675
Dist.: US-NR; CAN-NR; O'seas-NR
North America: NR
Density: NR
Projected New Units (12 Months): 400
Qualifications: 2, 2, 3, 3, 4, 5
Registered: NR

FINANCIAL/TERMS:
Cash Investment: $49.7K+
Total Investment: $49.7K+
Minimum Net Worth: NR
Fees: Franchise - $49.7K
Royalty - 10%; Ad. - NR
Earnings Claims Statement: No
Term of Contract (Years): 5/5
Avg. # Of Employees: 1-2 FT
Passive Ownership: Allowed
Encourage Conversions: NA
Area Develop. Agreements: No
Sub-Franchising Contracts: No
Expand In Territory: Yes
Space Needs: NA SF; HB

SUPPORT & TRAINING:
Financial Assistance Provided: No
Site Selection Assistance: NA
Lease Negotiation Assistance: NA
Co-Operative Advertising: NR
Franchisee Assoc./Member: NR
Size Of Corporate Staff: 100
On-Going Support: a,b,c,e,G,H,I
Training: 1 Week Mississauga, ON.

SPECIFIC EXPANSION PLANS:
US: All United States
Canada: All Canada
Overseas: All Countries

Child Development/Education/Products

Chapter 10

Child Development/Education/Products Industry Profile

Total # Franchisors in Industry Group	85
Total # Franchised Units in Industry Group	6,849
Total # Company-Owned Units in Industry Group	820
Total # Operating Units in Industry Group	7,669
Average # Franchised Units/Franchisor	80.6
Average # Company-Owned Units/Franchisor	9.6
Average # Total Units/Franchisor	90.2
Ratio of Total # Franchised Units/Total # Company-Owned Units	8.4:1

Industry Survey Participants	36
Representing % of Industry	42.4%
Average Franchise Fee*:	$26.4K
Average Total Investment*:	$282.3K
Average On-Going Royalty Fee*:	16.6%

*If a range was provided, the mid-point of the range was used. See detailed profiles for actual ranges.

Five Largest Participants in Survey

Company	# Franchised Units	# Co-Owned Units	# Total Units	Franchise Fee	On-Going Royalty	Total Investment
1. Kumon North America	1,501	22	1,523	$1K	$30-33K	$9.3-29.3K
2. Gymboree Play & Music	508	9	517	$45K	6%	$141-287K
3. Little Gym, The	332	0	332	$57.5K	8%	$150-225K
4. Fourth R, The	275	0	275	$16K	$400/Mo./5%Sale	$69-85K
5. FasTracKids International Ltd.	220	0	220	$21.5K	Varies	$32.5-87.5K

All of the data provided are proprietary and should not be quoted without acknowledging *Bond's Franchise Guide.*

ABRAKADOODLE
1800 Robert Fulton Dr., # 250
Reston, VA 22066
Tel: (703) 871-7356
Fax: (703) 766-3606
E-Mail: info@abrakadoodle.com
Web Site: www.abrakadoodle.com
Ms. Rosemarie Hartnett, Vice President

ABRAKADOODLE is a remarkable arts education program for children that combines high-quality Crayola paints, pastels, modeling compounds and other products with imaginative learning activities. The ABRAKADOODLE program has been designed by notable educators and artists.

BACKGROUND: IFA MEMBER
Established: 2002; 1st Franchised: 2004
Franchised Units: 38
Company-Owned Units: 2
Total Units: 40
Dist.: US-40; CAN-0; O'seas-0
North America: 24 States
Density: NR
Projected New Units (12 Months): NR
Qualifications: 4, 4, 2, 4, , 5
Registered: All States Except HI, ND and SD

FINANCIAL/TERMS:
Cash Investment: $3-9K
Total Investment: $40.7-72.5K
Minimum Net Worth: $100K
Fees: Franchise - $32.5K
Royalty - 8%; Ad. - 1%
Earnings Claims Statement: No
Term of Contract (Years): 10/10
Avg. # Of Employees: 1 FT, Varies
Passive Ownership: Not Allowed
Encourage Conversions: NA
Area Develop. Agreements: No
Sub-Franchising Contracts: No
Expand In Territory: Yes
Space Needs: NA SF; NA

SUPPORT & TRAINING:
Financial Assistance Provided: No
Site Selection Assistance: NA
Lease Negotiation Assistance: NA
Co-Operative Advertising: No
Franchisee Assoc./Member: Yes
Size Of Corporate Staff: 6
On-Going Support: a,b,c,d,h
Training: 5 Days Reston, VA.

SPECIFIC EXPANSION PLANS:
US: All States Where Registered.
Canada: No
Overseas: No

<< >>

BABY NEWS CHILDRENS STORES
6909 Las Positas Rd., Unit A
Livermore, CA 94550
Tel: (925) 245-1320
Fax: (925) 245-1376
E-Mail: info@stanforddistributing.com
Web Site: www.babynewsstores.com
Mr. Roger O'Callaghan, President

BABY NEWS is the oldest established association of individually owned baby stores.

BACKGROUND:
Established: 1950; 1st Franchised: 1961
Franchised Units: 54
Company-Owned Units: 1
Total Units: 55
Dist.: US-45; CAN-0; O'seas-10
North America: 35 States
Density: 20 in CA
Projected New Units (12 Months): 2
Qualifications: 5, 3, 3, 3, 3, 5
Registered: CA

FINANCIAL/TERMS:
Cash Investment: $100K
Total Investment: $150-250K
Minimum Net Worth: NR
Fees: Franchise - $15K
Royalty - 1%; Ad. - 0%
Earnings Claims Statement: Yes
Term of Contract (Years): 5/5
Avg. # Of Employees: 3 FT, 4 PT
Passive Ownership: Not Allowed
Encourage Conversions: Yes
Area Develop. Agreements: No
Sub-Franchising Contracts: No
Expand In Territory: Yes
Space Needs: 5,000 SF; FS, SC, RM

SUPPORT & TRAINING:
Financial Assistance Provided: No
Site Selection Assistance: Yes
Lease Negotiation Assistance: Yes
Co-Operative Advertising: Yes
Franchisee Assoc./Member: No
Size Of Corporate Staff: 16
On-Going Support: A,B,C,d,E,F,G,H
Training: 1-2 Weeks at Various Locations.

SPECIFIC EXPANSION PLANS:
US: All United States
Canada: All Canada
Overseas: All Countries

<< >>

BABY USA
793 Springer Dr.
Lombard, IL 60148
Tel: (630) 652-0600
Fax: (630) 652-9080
E-Mail: franchise@usababy.com
Web Site: www.usababy.com
Mr. James L. Courtney, Sr. Dir. Market Devel.

USA BABY is North America's leading specialty retailer of infant and juvenile furniture and accessories. Franchisees receive market evaluation, site selection, store design, financing, opening, advertising, merchandising and on-going operational support. Exclusive territories and substantial single, multi-unit and area development opportunities exist for candidates with a passion for serving customers, developing employee teams and participating in a proven retail environment.

BACKGROUND: IFA MEMBER
Established: 1975; 1st Franchised: 1986
Franchised Units: 70
Company-Owned Units: 0
Total Units: 70
Dist.: US-67; CAN-0; O'seas-3
North America: 22 States
Density: 8 in IL, 7 in NY, 6 in OH
Projected New Units (12 Months): 12
Qualifications: 4, 4, 1, 3, 2, 5
Registered: CA,FL,HI,IL,IN,MD,MI,MN, NY,VA,WA,WI

FINANCIAL/TERMS:
Cash Investment: $120-170K

Total Investment: $450-650K
Minimum Net Worth: $180K
Fees: Franchise - $42.5K
Royalty - 3%; Ad. - 5%
Earnings Claims Statement: Yes
Term of Contract (Years): 10/10
Avg. # Of Employees: 5 FT, 4 PT
Passive Ownership: Not Allowed
Encourage Conversions: Yes
Area Develop. Agreements: Yes/Varies
Sub-Franchising Contracts: No
Expand In Territory: Yes
Space Needs: 10,000-12,000 SF; SC

SUPPORT & TRAINING:
Financial Assistance Provided: Yes(I)
Site Selection Assistance: Yes
Lease Negotiation Assistance: Yes
Co-Operative Advertising: NA
Franchisee Assoc./Member: Yes/Yes
Size Of Corporate Staff: 18
On-Going Support: C,D,E,G,H,I
Training: 14 Days Corporate Office/Store; 4 Days Pre-Opening; 4 Days Opening; 4-5 Days Post-Opening.

SPECIFIC EXPANSION PLANS:
US: All United States
Canada: All Canada
Overseas: No

CHILDREN'S LIGHTHOUSE LEARNING CENTERS
101 S. Jennings, # 209
Fort Worth, TX 76104-1112
Tel: (888) 338-4466 (817) 338-1332
Fax: (817) 338-2716
E-Mail: lighthouse209@aol.com
Web Site: www.childrenslighthouse.com
Ms. Nancy Spears, Franchise Administrator

CHILDREN'S LIGHTHOUSE is one of the newest and brightest concepts in the child care industry in the last decade. State-of-the-art 10,000 square foot centers, with keycard entry and cameras in each room so a parent can view their child from anywhere in the world.

BACKGROUND: IFA MEMBER
Established: 1999; 1st Franchised: 1999
Franchised Units: 3
Company-Owned Units: 5
Total Units: 8
Dist.: US-8; CAN-0; O'seas-0
North America: 4 States
Density: 3 in TX
Projected New Units (12 Months): 6
Qualifications: 4, 4, 4, 3, 3, 4
Registered: CA,FL,MI,NY,DC

FINANCIAL/TERMS:
Cash Investment: $225K
Total Investment: $1.4MM
Minimum Net Worth: NA
Fees: Franchise - $50K
Royalty - 7%; Ad. - 1%
Earnings Claims Statement: Yes
Term of Contract (Years): 20/10
Avg. # Of Employees: 25 FT
Passive Ownership: Allowed
Encourage Conversions: No
Area Develop. Agreements: Yes
Sub-Franchising Contracts: Yes
Expand In Territory: Yes
Space Needs: 10,000 SF; FS

SUPPORT & TRAINING:
Financial Assistance Provided: Yes(I)
Site Selection Assistance: Yes
Lease Negotiation Assistance: NA
Co-Operative Advertising: Yes
Franchisee Assoc./Member: No
Size Of Corporate Staff: 8
On-Going Support: B,C,D,E,I
Training: 40 Hours Corporate Office Ft. Worth, TX; 80 Hours On Site.

SPECIFIC EXPANSION PLANS:
US: All United States
Canada: All Canada
Overseas: No

CHILDREN'S ORCHARD
900 Victor's Way, # 200
Ann Arbor, MI 48108
Tel: (800) 999-5437 (734) 994-9199 + 222
Fax: (734) 994-9323
E-Mail: franchisesales@childorch.com
Web Site: www.childorch.com
Ms. Lisa Morgan, Franchise Development Director

Upscale children's retail/resale stores, featuring clothing, toys, furniture, equipment, books and parenting products. We buy top-brand items from area families by appointment, and re-sell in boutique-style stores, along with top-quality new children's items from nearly 200 suppliers. These are large volume stores selling thousands of items per week.

BACKGROUND: IFA MEMBER
Established: 1980; 1st Franchised: 1985
Franchised Units: 92
Company-Owned Units: 1
Total Units: 93
Dist.: US-93; CAN-0; O'seas-0
North America: 23 States
Density: 23 in CA, 14 in MA, 7 in MI
Projected New Units (12 Months): 15
Qualifications: 5, 3, 2, 4, 2, 5
Registered: All Except HI,ND,RI,SD

FINANCIAL/TERMS:
Cash Investment: $20-30K
Total Investment: $69-145K
Minimum Net Worth: $150K
Fees: Franchise - $22.5K
Royalty - 5%; Ad. - 1.0%
Earnings Claims Statement: No
Term of Contract (Years): 10
Avg. # Of Employees: 1 FT, 3 PT
Passive Ownership: Discouraged
Encourage Conversions: Yes
Area Develop. Agreements: Yes/Open
Sub-Franchising Contracts: No
Expand In Territory: No
Space Needs: 1,200-2,000 SF; SF, SC

SUPPORT & TRAINING:
Financial Assistance Provided: Yes(I)
Site Selection Assistance: Yes
Lease Negotiation Assistance: Yes
Co-Operative Advertising: Yes
Franchisee Assoc./Member: Yes/Yes
Size Of Corporate Staff: 15
On-Going Support: B,C,D,E,F,G,H,I
Training: 12 Days Training in Ann Arbor, MI.

SPECIFIC EXPANSION PLANS:
US: All US Except HI, AK
Canada: No
Overseas: No

CHILDREN'S TECHNOLOGY WORKSHOP, THE
109 Vanderhoof Ave., # 101A
Toronto, ON M4G 2H7 CANADA
Tel: (866) 704-2267 + 24 (416) 425-2289
Fax: (647) 439-0890
E-Mail: franchise@ctworkshop.com
Web Site: www.ctworkshop.com
Mr. John Graham, Director Business Development

THE CHILDREN'S TECHNOLOGY WORKSHOP develops and delivers interactive, applied, technology camp programs and workshops for children. During these camps, children aged 7-12 learn video game programming, animation and LEGO robotics through individualized activities structured around exciting adventure themes. If your passion includes educating and encouraging children to learn, explore and create using technology, then we want to speak with you.

BACKGROUND: IFA MEMBER
Established: 1997; 1st Franchised: 2004
Franchised Units: 12
Company-Owned Units: 1
Total Units: 13
Dist.: US-0; CAN-9; O'seas-0
North America: 1 Province
Density: 9 in ON
Projected New Units (12 Months): 25
Qualifications: 3, 3, 4, 4, 5, 5
Registered: AB

FINANCIAL/TERMS:
Cash Investment: $20K
Total Investment: $35-50K
Minimum Net Worth: $40K
Fees: Franchise - $20K
Royalty - 10%; Ad. - 3%
Earnings Claims Statement: No
Term of Contract (Years): 5/5
Avg. # Of Employees: 1 PT
Passive Ownership: Discouraged
Encourage Conversions: Yes
Area Develop. Agreements: No
Sub-Franchising Contracts: No
Expand In Territory: Yes
Space Needs: NA SF; HB, ST Rental Space

SUPPORT & TRAINING:
Financial Assistance Provided: No
Site Selection Assistance: Yes
Lease Negotiation Assistance: NA
Co-Operative Advertising: NA
Franchisee Assoc./Member: No
Size Of Corporate Staff: 7
On-Going Support: AMGMHMI
Training: 1 Week Toronto, ON.

SPECIFIC EXPANSION PLANS:
US: All United States
Canada: All Canada
Overseas: No

<< >>

COMPUTERTOTS/COMPUTER EXPLORERS, INC.

12715 Telge Rd.
Cypress, TX 77429-2289
Tel: (888) 638-8722 (281) 256-4100
Fax: (281) 256-4178
E-Mail: ctsales@iced.net
Web Site: www.computertots.com
Mr. Donald Averitt, VP Franchise Sales

The newest member of the ICED family of franchises provides educational technology training for childcare centers, preschools and elementary schools. Two models: Owner-Operator (owner as primary teacher) and Owner-Manager (owner hires teaching staff). Having taught more than three million classes, we seek entrepreneurs who wish to build a thriving business while providing quality computer education and curriculum for children.

BACKGROUND: IFA MEMBER
Established: 1983; 1st Franchised: 1988
Franchised Units: 92
Company-Owned Units: 0
Total Units: 92
Dist.: US-87; CAN-0; O'seas-5
North America: 30 States
Density: 6 in CA, 6 in IL, 6 in NJ
Projected New Units (12 Months): NR
Qualifications: , , , , ,
Registered: All States

FINANCIAL/TERMS:
Cash Investment: $17.5K
Total Investment: $25.3-31.4K
Minimum Net Worth: NR
Fees: Franchise - $25K
Royalty - 8%; Ad. - 1%
Earnings Claims Statement: No
Term of Contract (Years): 10/10
Avg. # Of Employees: 1 FT, 5 PT
Passive Ownership: Discouraged
Encourage Conversions: NA
Area Develop. Agreements: No
Sub-Franchising Contracts: No
Expand In Territory: No
Space Needs: NA SF; HB

SUPPORT & TRAINING:
Financial Assistance Provided: No
Site Selection Assistance: NA
Lease Negotiation Assistance: NA
Co-Operative Advertising: NA
Franchisee Assoc./Member: Yes/Yes
Size Of Corporate Staff: NR
On-Going Support: b,c,d,g,h,I
Training: 2 Weeks Headquarters.

SPECIFIC EXPANSION PLANS:
US: All United States
Canada: No
Overseas: No

DIGIKIDS®

9463 Hwy. 377 South, # 111
Fort Worth, TX 76126
Tel: (800) 505-7380
Fax:
E-Mail: robert@digikids-id.com
Web Site: www.digikids-id.com
Mr. Robert Wakefield, Territorial Development

More than 2,000 children are reported lost or missing each day in the United States. DIGIKIDS® offers a unique, high-tech solution to aid in the recovery of those children. With a DIGIKIDS® franchise, you'll enjoy great earning potential and very low overhead, while providing a much-needed and highly respected service for your community.

BACKGROUND:
Established: 2003; 1st Franchised: 2004
Franchised Units: 6
Company-Owned Units: 0
Total Units: 6
Dist.: US-3; CAN-0; O'seas-0
North America: 3 States
Density: 4 in TX, 1 in OK, 1 in KY
Projected New Units (12 Months): 15
Qualifications: 2, 1, 1, 2, 3, 5
Registered: FL, MI

FINANCIAL/TERMS:
Cash Investment: $30-35K
Total Investment: $32-48K
Minimum Net Worth: $100K
Fees: Franchise - $26.5K
Royalty - 2%; Ad. - 2%
Earnings Claims Statement: Yes
Term of Contract (Years): 10/10
Avg. # Of Employees: 1 FT, 1 PT
Passive Ownership: Allowed
Encourage Conversions: Yes
Area Develop. Agreements: Yes
Sub-Franchising Contracts: No
Expand In Territory: Yes
Space Needs: NA SF; HB

SUPPORT & TRAINING:
Financial Assistance Provided: Yes(I)
Site Selection Assistance: NA
Lease Negotiation Assistance: NA
Co-Operative Advertising: No
Franchisee Assoc./Member: No
Size Of Corporate Staff: 3
On-Going Support: B,C,D,E,F,G,H,I
Training: 4 Days Corporate Headquarters;

As Agreed On-Site.
SPECIFIC EXPANSION PLANS:
US: All United States
Canada: No
Overseas: All Countries

<< >>

DRAMA KIDS INTERNATIONAL

3225-B Corporate Ct.
Ellicott City, MD 21042
Tel: (877) 543-7456 (410) 480-2015
Fax: (410) 480-2026
E-Mail: info@dramakids.com
Web Site: www.dramakids.com
Mr. Doug Howard, President

DRAMA KIDS and its international affiliates, Helen O'Grady Drama Academy, is the largest after-school drama program in the world, with over 40,000 children currently enrolled. Our award-winning drama curriculum uses a wide variety of fun and creative drama activities that are new each week. We teach skills that are not being taught in most schools today, skills critical for ongoing success in life. Franchise owners enjoy a home-based business and a flexible lifestyle. Drama experience is NOT required.

BACKGROUND: IFA MEMBER
Established: 1979; 1st Franchised: 1989
Franchised Units: 122
Company-Owned Units: 4
Total Units: 126
Dist.: US-26; CAN-0; O'seas-100
North America: 16 States,10 Countries
Density: NR
Projected New Units (12 Months): 10
Qualifications: 3, 3, 1, 4, 3, 5
Registered: All States
FINANCIAL/TERMS:
Cash Investment: $30-40K
Total Investment: $30-40K
Minimum Net Worth: $50K
Fees: Franchise - $27.5K
Royalty - 10%; Ad. - 1%
Earnings Claims Statement: Yes
Term of Contract (Years): 5/5
Avg. # Of Employees: 1 FT, 2 PT
Passive Ownership: Not Allowed
Encourage Conversions: NA
Area Develop. Agreements: No
Sub-Franchising Contracts: No
Expand In Territory: Yes
Space Needs: NA SF; HB
SUPPORT & TRAINING:
Financial Assistance Provided: No
Site Selection Assistance: Yes
Lease Negotiation Assistance: Yes
Co-Operative Advertising: Yes
Franchisee Assoc./Member: No
Size Of Corporate Staff: 5
On-Going Support: B,C,D,E,F,G,H,I
Training: 1 Week Baltimore, MD.
SPECIFIC EXPANSION PLANS:
US: SW, SE, NE and Mid-Atlantic
Canada: No
Overseas: No

<< >>

FASTRACKIDS INTERNATIONAL LTD.

6900 E. Belleview Ave., 1st Fl.
Greenwood Village, CO 80111-1619
Tel: (888) 576-6888 (303) 224-0200
Fax: (303) 224-0222
E-Mail: david.fryatt@fastrackids.com
Web Site: www.fastrackids.com
Mr. Kevin Krause, Dir. Franchise Development

FASTRACKIDS® INTERNATIONAL, recognized last year as one of the Top 10 New Franchises by Entrepreneur Magazine, has appointed over 220 licensees in 32 countries. Thousands of children have benefitted from the technologically advanced FASTRACKIDS curriculum. Developed for children ages 3-6, FASTRACKIDS is designed to increase thinking and reasoning abilities while enhancing communication skills and self-esteem.

BACKGROUND: IFA MEMBER
Established: 1998; 1st Franchised: 1998
Franchised Units: 220
Company-Owned Units: 0
Total Units: 220
Dist.: US-81; CAN-4; O'seas-135
North America: 21 States
Density: NR
Projected New Units (12 Months): 55
Qualifications: 4, 4, 4, 4, 5, 5
Registered: All States
FINANCIAL/TERMS:
Cash Investment: $32.5-87.5K
Total Investment: $32.5-87.5K
Minimum Net Worth: NR
Fees: Franchise - $21.5K
Royalty - Varies; Ad. - 0%
Earnings Claims Statement: Yes
Term of Contract (Years): 5/5
Avg. # Of Employees: 1-5 FT
Passive Ownership: Discouraged
Encourage Conversions: NA
Area Develop. Agreements: Yes/5
Sub-Franchising Contracts: No
Expand In Territory: Yes
Space Needs: 700 SF; NA
SUPPORT & TRAINING:
Financial Assistance Provided: No
Site Selection Assistance: Yes
Lease Negotiation Assistance: No
Co-Operative Advertising: Yes
Franchisee Assoc./Member: No
Size Of Corporate Staff: 12
On-Going Support: C,G,h,I
Training: 5 Days in Denver, CO.
SPECIFIC EXPANSION PLANS:
US: All United States
Canada: All Canada
Overseas: All Countries

<< >>

FOURTH R, THE

11410 NE 124th St., # 142
Kirkland, WA 98034-4399
Tel: (800) 821-8653 (425) 814-1001
Fax: (425) 814-8117
E-Mail: bob@fourthr.com
Web Site: www.fourthr.com
Mr. Robert L. McCauley, President

Computers have changed virtually all aspects of our lives. As we move into the information age, many experts agree that computer literacy has become THE FOURTH R in education today. As an international leader in computer training, THE FOURTH R is one of the fastest-growing companies in the computer training sector and has been highlighted in prominent national publications as one of the top franchisors both in the U. S. and abroad.

BACKGROUND:
Established: 1991; 1st Franchised: 1992
Franchised Units: 275
Company-Owned Units: 0
Total Units: 275
Dist.: US-45; CAN-8; O'seas-191
North America: 21 States, 2 Provinces
Density: 6 in CA, 6 in PA, 5 in WA,
Projected New Units (12 Months): 54

Qualifications: 2, 4, 3, 4, 2, 3
Registered:CA,HI,IL,IN,MD,MI,MN,NY, OR,VA,WA,WI,DC,AB

FINANCIAL/TERMS:
Cash Investment: NA
Total Investment: $69-85K
Minimum Net Worth: $None
Fees: Franchise - $16K
Royalty - $400/Mo./5%Sale; Ad. - 0%
Earnings Claims Statement: No
Term of Contract (Years): 5/5
Avg. # Of Employees: Varies
Passive Ownership: Allowed
Encourage Conversions: Yes
Area Develop. Agreements: Yes/5
Sub-Franchising Contracts: No
Expand In Territory: Yes
Space Needs: 800-3,000 SF; SF, SC, HB, Commercial

SUPPORT & TRAINING:
Financial Assistance Provided: Yes(I)
Site Selection Assistance: Yes
Lease Negotiation Assistance: Yes
Co-Operative Advertising: Yes
Franchisee Assoc./Member: Yes/Yes
Size Of Corporate Staff: 7
On-Going Support: B,C,G,H,I
Training: 5 Days Seattle, WA.

SPECIFIC EXPANSION PLANS:
US: All United States
Canada: All Canada
Overseas: All Countries

<< >>

GUARDIAN, THE CHILD SUPPORT PEOPLE

14121 NW Fwy., # B-1
Houston, TX 77040
Tel: (800) 829-3335 (713) 462-7622
Fax: (713) 462-8177
E-Mail: info@911guardian.com
Web Site: www.911guardian.com
Mr. Francis J. Welch, President

We assist custodial parents in collecting their unpaid child support. We offer a contingency fee-based service, so the custodial parent does not have any out-of-pocket, up-front expenses or fees to pay.

BACKGROUND:
Established: 1999; 1st Franchised: 2000
Franchised Units: 6
Company-Owned Units: 1
Total Units: 7
Dist.: US-7; CAN-0; O'seas-0
North America: 3 States
Density: 3 in TX, 3 in FL
Projected New Units (12 Months): 10
Qualifications: 3, 4, 1, 3, 3, 5
Registered: FL

FINANCIAL/TERMS:
Cash Investment: $35K+
Total Investment: $50.6-77.1K
Minimum Net Worth: $150K
Fees: Franchise - $25K
Royalty - Varies; Ad. - Varies
Earnings Claims Statement: No
Term of Contract (Years): 5/5
Avg. # Of Employees: 2 FT
Passive Ownership: Not Allowed
Encourage Conversions: NA
Area Develop. Agreements: No
Sub-Franchising Contracts: No
Expand In Territory: Yes
Space Needs: 700 SF; SF, SC

SUPPORT & TRAINING:
Financial Assistance Provided: No
Site Selection Assistance: Yes
Lease Negotiation Assistance: Yes
Co-Operative Advertising: Yes
Franchisee Assoc./Member: No
Size Of Corporate Staff: 17
On-Going Support: A,B,C,D,E,G,h,I
Training: 3 Weeks Corporate Site; 1 Week/Quarter Franchisee Location.

SPECIFIC EXPANSION PLANS:
US: South and Southeast
Canada: No
Overseas: No

<< >>

GYMBOREE Play & Music

Top 100

GYMBOREE PLAY & MUSIC

500 Howard St.
San Francisco, CA 94105
Tel: (800) 520-7529 (415) 278-7000
Fax: (415) 278-7452
E-Mail: cms_gymboree@ifxonline.com
Web Site: www.gymboree.com
Ms. Eva Crosland, Manager Franchise Development

GYMBOREE, the world's largest development play and music program, offers weekly classes to parents and their children, ages newborn through 4 years, with custom-designed equipment. The program is based on sensory integration theory, positive parenting, child development principles and the importance of play. GYMBOREE has recently rolled out a new Arts Program designed to support your child's development through an array of enriching experiences and Fun!

BACKGROUND: IFA MEMBER
Established: 1976; 1st Franchised: 1978
Franchised Units: 508
Company-Owned Units: 9
Total Units: 517
Dist.: US-337; CAN-19; O'seas-161
North America: 42 States, 3 Provinces
Density: 45 in CA, 27 in NY, 27 in NJ
Projected New Units (12 Months): 15
Qualifications: 4, 4, 3, 3, 2, 4
Registered: CA,FL,HI,IL,IN,MD,MI,MN, NY,OR,RI,SD,VA,WA,WI,DC,AB

FINANCIAL/TERMS:
Cash Investment: $70K
Total Investment: $141-287K
Minimum Net Worth: $250K
Fees: Franchise - $45K
Royalty - 6%; Ad. - 2.25%
Earnings Claims Statement: No
Term of Contract (Years): 10/10
Avg. # Of Employees: 1 FT, 3 PT
Passive Ownership: Not Allowed
Encourage Conversions: No
Area Develop. Agreements: No
Sub-Franchising Contracts: No
Expand In Territory: Yes
Space Needs: 2,400 SF; SF, SC, RM

SUPPORT & TRAINING:
Financial Assistance Provided: No
Site Selection Assistance: Yes
Lease Negotiation Assistance: Yes
Co-Operative Advertising: Yes
Franchisee Assoc./Member: Yes
Size Of Corporate Staff: 19
On-Going Support: B,D,G,h,I
Training: 7 Days Headquarters.

SPECIFIC EXPANSION PLANS:
US: All United States
Canada: All Canada
Overseas: India, Europe

<< >>

HIGH TOUCH-HIGH TECH

12352 Wiles Rd.
Coral Springs, FL 33076
Tel: (800) 444-4968 (954) 755-2900
Fax: (954) 755-1242
E-Mail: info@hightouch-hightech.com
Web Site: www.hightouch-hightech.com
Mr. Daniel Shaw, President/CEO

Provides hands-on science experiences that go right into the classroom. We provide in-school field trips. We also provide fun, science-oriented birthday parties.

BACKGROUND:
Established: 1992; 1st Franchised: 1994
Franchised Units: 88
Company-Owned Units: 2
Total Units: 90
Dist.: US-21; CAN-0; O'seas-1
North America: 12 States
Density: 5 in FL, 2 in NJ, 2 in IL
Projected New Units (12 Months): 8-10
Qualifications: 5, 5, 3, 5, 3, 3
Registered: CA,FL,IL,NY,VA,WI

FINANCIAL/TERMS:
Cash Investment: $5-8K
Total Investment: $28-42K
Minimum Net Worth: NR
Fees: Franchise - $20-35K
Royalty - 7%; Ad. - 0%
Earnings Claims Statement: Yes
Term of Contract (Years): 10/10
Avg. # Of Employees: 2-3 PT
Passive Ownership: NR
Encourage Conversions: NA
Area Develop. Agreements: No
Sub-Franchising Contracts: Yes
Expand In Territory: Yes
Space Needs: NR SF; HB

SUPPORT & TRAINING:
Financial Assistance Provided: Yes(D)
Site Selection Assistance: Yes
Lease Negotiation Assistance: NA
Co-Operative Advertising: NA
Franchisee Assoc./Member: No
Size Of Corporate Staff: 6
On-Going Support: D,G,H,I
Training: 5 Full Days National Programming Offices.

SPECIFIC EXPANSION PLANS:
US: All United States, Global
Canada: All Canada
Overseas: Europe, Asia, Pacific Region

<< >>

JACADI

70 West Red Oak Ln.
White Plains, NY 10604
Tel: (914) 697-7684
Fax: (914) 697-7679
E-Mail: info@jacadiusa.com
Web Site: www.jacadiusa.com
Ms. Peggy Waldo, President/CEO

JACADI is a childrenswear retail company whose collections include clothing, shoes, accessories, furniture and nursery items in newborn through size 12 for both boys and girls. The merchandise is a European-style which adapts the latest trends to classic design and allows the customer to mix and match the various styles and color groups. JACADI also strives to give excellent customer service and the highest price/quality ratio.

BACKGROUND: IFA MEMBER
Established: 1988; 1st Franchised: 1992
Franchised Units: 22
Company-Owned Units: 3
Total Units: 25
Dist.: US-32; CAN-4; O'seas-375
North America: 10 States, 1 Province
Density: 8 in CA, 7 in NY, 3 in FL
Projected New Units (12 Months): 8
Qualifications: 5, 3, 1, 2, 4, 5
Registered: CA,FL,IL,MD,NY,VA

FINANCIAL/TERMS:
Cash Investment: $120-250K
Total Investment: $183-313K
Minimum Net Worth: $750K Liquid
Fees: Franchise - $20K
Royalty - 4%; Ad. - 1%
Earnings Claims Statement: No
Term of Contract (Years): 7/7
Avg. # Of Employees: 2-3 FT, 2-3 PT
Passive Ownership: Not Allowed
Encourage Conversions: NA
Area Develop. Agreements: Yes/7
Sub-Franchising Contracts: No
Expand In Territory: Yes
Space Needs: 1,100 SF; FS, SF, RM

SUPPORT & TRAINING:
Financial Assistance Provided: No
Site Selection Assistance: Yes
Lease Negotiation Assistance: Yes
Co-Operative Advertising: No
Franchisee Assoc./Member: No
Size Of Corporate Staff: 4
On-Going Support: B,C,d,E,f,G,h
Training: 3-5 Days in Subsidiary Shop; 3 Days Franchisee's Shop Before Opening; On-Going Corporate.

SPECIFIC EXPANSION PLANS:
US: All United States
Canada: All Canada
Overseas: All Countries

<< >>

KID TO KID

452 E. 500 S.
Salt Lake City, UT 84111
Tel: (888) 543-2543 (801) 359-0071
Fax: (801) 359-3207
E-Mail: brent@kidtokid.com
Web Site: www.kidtokid.com
Mr. Brent Sloan, President

KID TO KID is an up-scale children's resale store based on the premise that 'kids grow faster than paychecks.' Parents buy and sell better-quality used children's clothing, toys, equipment and accessories. If you enjoy working with people and want to increase your financial security as you grow your own business, call KID TO KID today!

BACKGROUND: IFA MEMBER
Established: 1992; 1st Franchised: 1994
Franchised Units: 38
Company-Owned Units: 5
Total Units: 43
Dist.: US-41; CAN-0; O'seas-1
North America: 13 States
Density: 12 in UT, 8 in TX, 3 in PA
Projected New Units (12 Months): 10
Qualifications: 4, 3, 1, 2, 4, 5
Registered: All States

FINANCIAL/TERMS:
Cash Investment: $30-40K
Total Investment: $97-127K
Minimum Net Worth: $150K
Fees: Franchise - $25K
Royalty - 5%; Ad. - 0.5%
Earnings Claims Statement: No
Term of Contract (Years): 10/5
Avg. # Of Employees: 2 FT, 2 PT
Passive Ownership: Discouraged
Encourage Conversions: Yes
Area Develop. Agreements: Yes/Varies
Sub-Franchising Contracts: Yes
Expand In Territory: No
Space Needs: 2,000 SF; FS, SF, SC

SUPPORT & TRAINING:
Financial Assistance Provided: Yes(I)
Site Selection Assistance: Yes
Lease Negotiation Assistance: Yes
Co-Operative Advertising: Yes
Franchisee Assoc./Member: No
Size Of Corporate Staff: 5
On-Going Support: B,C,d,E,f,G,H
Training: 11 Days Salt Lake City, UT.

SPECIFIC EXPANSION PLANS:
US: All United States
Canada: All Canada
Overseas: English & Spanish-Speaking Countries

<< >>

KIDDIE ACADEMY INTERNATIONAL

108 Wheel Rd., # 200
Bel Air, MD 21015
Tel: (800) 554-3343 (410) 515-0788 + 245
Fax: (410) 569-2729
E-Mail: ccommarota@kiddieacademy.

com
Web Site: www.kiddieacademy.com
Mr. Chris Commorata, VP Franchise Development

We offer comprehensive training and support without additional cost. KIDDIE ACADEMY's step-by-step program assists with staff recruitment, training, accounting support, site selection, marketing, advertising and curriculum. A true turnkey opportunity that provides on-going support so you can focus on running a successful business.

BACKGROUND: IFA MEMBER
Established: 1981; 1st Franchised: 1992
Franchised Units: 89
Company-Owned Units: 12
Total Units: 101
Dist.: US-51; CAN-0; O'seas-0
North America: 10 States
Density: 15 in MD, 5 in NJ, 4 in IL
Projected New Units (12 Months): 100
Qualifications: 4, 4, 2, 3, 2, 4
Registered:CA,FL,IL,IN,MD,MI,MN,NY,OR,RI,VA,WI,DC

FINANCIAL/TERMS:
Cash Investment: $60K
Total Investment: $180-260K
Minimum Net Worth: $250K
Fees: Franchise - $40K
Royalty - 7%; Ad. - 0%
Earnings Claims Statement: No
Term of Contract (Years): 10/5
Avg. # Of Employees: 10-20 FT, 2 PT
Passive Ownership: Discouraged
Encourage Conversions: No
Area Develop. Agreements: Yes/10
Sub-Franchising Contracts: No
Expand In Territory: Yes
Space Needs: 6,500-12,000 SF; FS, SF, SC

SUPPORT & TRAINING:
Financial Assistance Provided: Yes(I)
Site Selection Assistance: Yes
Lease Negotiation Assistance: Yes
Co-Operative Advertising: Yes
Franchisee Assoc./Member: No
Size Of Corporate Staff: 30
On-Going Support: a,B,C,D,E,G,I
Training: 2 Weeks Owner Train., Corp. HQ; 1 Wk. Director Train., Corp. HQ; 3-5 Day Staff Training.

SPECIFIC EXPANSION PLANS:
US: All United States
Canada: No
Overseas: No

<< >>

KIDZART
1327 Dime Box Circle
New Braunfels, TX 78130
Tel: (800) 379-8302 (830) 626-1959
Fax: (800) 379-8302
E-Mail: shell@kidzart.com
Web Site: www.kidzart.com
Ms. Shell Herman, Chief Executive Officer

KIDZART offers a unique and proven program - a blueprint for your success. As a KIDZART franchise owner, you will receive on-going support with unparalleled expertise in our business. We offer you the competitive advantage by joining THE leading drawing/art franchise anywhere. Our franchise owners are turning an affordable low investment into an exciting business venture doing what they love and making a difference in their communities. Visit www.kidzart.com or call (800) 379-8302.

BACKGROUND: IFA MEMBER
Established: 1997; 1st Franchised: 2002
Franchised Units: 33
Company-Owned Units: 2
Total Units: 35
Dist.: US-29; CAN-1; O'seas-0
North America: 29 States
Density: r in CA, 4 in GA, 4 in NC
Projected New Units (12 Months):
Qualifications: , , , , ,
Registered:

FINANCIAL/TERMS:
Cash Investment: $21.9K
Total Investment: $21.9-31K
Minimum Net Worth: $100K
Fees: Franchise - $21.9K
Royalty - 7%/$150 Min.; Ad. - 3%
Earnings Claims Statement: No
Term of Contract (Years): 10/10
Avg. # Of Employees: 1-2 FT, 1 PT
Passive Ownership: Not Allowed
Encourage Conversions:
Area Develop. Agreements: No
Sub-Franchising Contracts: No
Expand In Territory: No
Space Needs: NA SF; HB

SUPPORT & TRAINING:
Financial Assistance Provided:
Site Selection Assistance: Yes
Lease Negotiation Assistance: NA
Co-Operative Advertising: NA
Franchisee Assoc./Member: Yes/Yes
Size Of Corporate Staff: 3
On-Going Support: b,C,D,E,G,h,I
Training: 4 Days New Braunfels, TX.

SPECIFIC EXPANSION PLANS:
US: All States Exc. Registration
Canada: NR
Overseas: NR

<< >>

KINDERDANCE INTERNATIONAL
1333 Gateway Dr., # 1003
Melbourne, FL 32901
Tel: (800) 554-2334 (321) 984-4448
Fax: (321) 984-4490
E-Mail: kindercorp@kinderdance.com
Web Site: www.kinderdance.com
Mr. Jerry M. Perch, VP Sales/Marketing

KINDERDANCE franchisees are trained to teach 4 developmentally unique dance and motor development programs: KINDERDANCE (TM), KINDERGYM (TM), KINDERTOTS (TM) and KINDERCOMBO (TM), which are designed for boys and girls ages 2-8. They learn the basics of ballet, tap, gymnastics and creative dance, as well as learning numbers, colors, shapes and words. No studio or dance experience required. Franchisee teaches at child care centers and other viable locations.

BACKGROUND: IFA MEMBER
Established: 1979; 1st Franchised: 1985
Franchised Units: 112
Company-Owned Units: 1
Total Units: 113
Dist.: US-110; CAN-1; O'seas-2
North America: 33 States, 3 Provinces
Density: 11 in TX, 9 in FL, 8 in CA
Projected New Units (12 Months): 20
Qualifications: 2, 2, 1, 2, 2, 5
Registered:CA,FL,HI,IL,MD,MI,MN,NY,OR,VA,WA,DC,AB

FINANCIAL/TERMS:
Cash Investment: $9.4-27K
Total Investment: $13-27.1K
Minimum Net Worth: NA
Fees: Franchise - $10-21K
Royalty - 6-15%; Ad. - 3%
Earnings Claims Statement: No
Term of Contract (Years): 10/10
Avg. # Of Employees: 1 PT
Passive Ownership: Discouraged

Encourage Conversions: Yes
Area Develop. Agreements: No
Sub-Franchising Contracts: No
Expand In Territory: Yes
Space Needs: NR SF; NR

SUPPORT & TRAINING:
Financial Assistance Provided: Yes(D)
Site Selection Assistance: NA
Lease Negotiation Assistance: NA
Co-Operative Advertising: Yes
Franchisee Assoc./Member: Yes/Yes
Size Of Corporate Staff: 8
On-Going Support: A,B,C,D,E,F,G,H,I
Training: 6 Days in Melbourne, FL and On-Site.

SPECIFIC EXPANSION PLANS:
US: All United States
Canada: All Canada
Overseas: No

<< >>

KUMON NORTH AMERICA

300 Frank W. Burr Blvd., Fl. 5
Teaneck, NJ 07666-6703
Tel: (866) 633-0740 (201) 928-0444 + 303
Fax: (201) 928-0044
E-Mail: mmele@kumon.com
Web Site: www.kumon.com
Mr. Mark Mele, Vice President Franchising

Kumon is the world's largest provider of supplemental math and reading programs. Our neighborhood learning centers serve students of all ages and abilities, from preschool through high school.

BACKGROUND:
Established: 1958; 1st Franchised: 1980
Franchised Units: 1,501
Company-Owned Units: 22
Total Units: 1,523
Dist.: US-1,178; CAN-345; O'seas-20,705
North America: 50 States, 9 Provinces
Density: 232 in CA, 93 in NY, 92 NJ
Projected New Units (12 Months): 150
Qualifications: 4, 3, 3, 4, 4, 4
Registered: All States

FINANCIAL/TERMS:
Cash Investment: NR
Total Investment: $9.3-29.3K
Minimum Net Worth: NR
Fees: Franchise - $1K
Royalty - $30-33K; Ad. - NA
Earnings Claims Statement: No
Term of Contract (Years): 2/5
Avg. # Of Employees: 1 FT, 1-3 PT
Passive Ownership: Not Allowed
Encourage Conversions: NA
Area Develop. Agreements: No
Sub-Franchising Contracts: No
Expand In Territory: No
Space Needs: Varies SF; FS, SF, SC, RM

SUPPORT & TRAINING:
Financial Assistance Provided: NA
Site Selection Assistance: Yes
Lease Negotiation Assistance: Yes
Co-Operative Advertising: NA
Franchisee Assoc./Member: Yes
Size Of Corporate Staff: 300
On-Going Support: B,C,D,E,G,H,I
Training: 9-12 Weeks Local Branch Office; 9-12 Weeks Local Kumon Center.

SPECIFIC EXPANSION PLANS:
US: All United States
Canada: All Canada
Overseas: All Countries

<< >>

LEARNING EXPERIENCE, THE

10 Sylvan Way, # 110
Parsippany, NJ 07054
Tel: (888) 865-7775 (973) 539-5392 + 240
Fax: (973) 539-5979
E-Mail: rft@tlecorp.com
Web Site: www.thelearningexperience.com
Mr. Ronald Triefler, Sr. Franchise Consultant

We build and deliver a complete turn-key, 10,000 square foot freestanding child development center. Low upfront cost, lowest royalty payment in the industry, with a proven franchisor that has over 23 years of direct industry experience. We want the best for your child, don't you?

BACKGROUND:
Established: 2002; 1st Franchised: 2003
Franchised Units: 18
Company-Owned Units: 6
Total Units: 24
Dist.: US-7; CAN-0; O'seas-0
North America: 3 States
Density: 5 in NJ, 1 in NY, 1 in PA
Projected New Units (12 Months): 8
Qualifications: 4, 5, 2, 3, 4, 4
Registered: FL,IL,NY

FINANCIAL/TERMS:
Cash Investment: $100K
Total Investment: $400-600K
Minimum Net Worth: $400K
Fees: Franchise - $50K
Royalty - 6%, 5%,4%; Ad. - 1.5%
Earnings Claims Statement: No
Term of Contract (Years): 15/1`0
Avg. # Of Employees: 10 FT, 12 PT
Passive Ownership: Allowed
Encourage Conversions: Yes
Area Develop. Agreements: Yes/25
Sub-Franchising Contracts: Yes
Expand In Territory: Yes
Space Needs: 10,000 SF; FS

SUPPORT & TRAINING:
Financial Assistance Provided: Yes(I)
Site Selection Assistance: Yes
Lease Negotiation Assistance: Yes
Co-Operative Advertising: Yes
Franchisee Assoc./Member: Yes/Yes
Size Of Corporate Staff: 25-30
On-Going Support: A,C,D,E,F,G,H,I
Training: 2 Weeks Parsippany, NJ; 4 Weeks Operating Unit; 3-4 Months Franchise Unit.

SPECIFIC EXPANSION PLANS:
US: Northeast
Canada: All Canada
Overseas: All Countries

<< >>

LEARNING EXPRESS

29 Buena Vista St.
Ayer, MA 01432-5026
Tel: (800) 924-2296 (978) 889-1000
Fax: (978) 889-1010
E-Mail: info@learningexpress.com
Web Site: www.learningexpress.com
Ms. Jessica Hopp, Marketing Assistant

Largest franchisor of specialty toy stores in the United states, currently operating in 20 states. Average sales significantly out-performs independent operators. Comprehensive training and turn-key services by franchisor.

BACKGROUND: IFA MEMBER
Established: 1987; 1st Franchised: 1990
Franchised Units: 117
Company-Owned Units: 0
Total Units: 117

Dist.: US-63; CAN-0; O'seas-0
North America: 20 States
Density: 14 in MA, 6 in TX, 6 in NJ
Projected New Units (12 Months): 38
Qualifications: 4, 3, 2, 3, 2, 4
Registered: All Except HI

FINANCIAL/TERMS:
Cash Investment: $75-125K
Total Investment: $203-354K
Minimum Net Worth: $300K
Fees: Franchise - $30K
Royalty - 5%; Ad. - 2%
Earnings Claims Statement: No
Term of Contract (Years): 10/5
Avg. # Of Employees: 2 FT, 8-10 PT
Passive Ownership: Discouraged
Encourage Conversions: NA
Area Develop. Agreements: Yes/10
Sub-Franchising Contracts: No
Expand In Territory: NR
Space Needs: 3,000 SF; FS, SF, SC, RM

SUPPORT & TRAINING:
Financial Assistance Provided: Yes(I)
Site Selection Assistance: Yes
Lease Negotiation Assistance: Yes
Co-Operative Advertising: No
Franchisee Assoc./Member: No
Size Of Corporate Staff: 12
On-Going Support: C,D,E,F,G,H,I
Training: 1 Week Brookline, MA; 1 Week Sunnyvale, CA; 1 Week Dallas, TX.

SPECIFIC EXPANSION PLANS:
US: All United States
Canada: No
Overseas: No

<< >>

LITTLE GYM, THE
8970 E. Raintree Dr., # 200
Scottsdale, AZ 85260-7300
Tel: (888) 228-2878 (480) 948-2878
Fax: (480) 948-2765
E-Mail: sales@thelittlegym.com
Web Site: www.thelittlegym.com
Mr. J. Ruk Adams, SVP Franchise Development

THE LITTLE GYM child development centers are for children 4 months to 12 years, and offer a unique, integrated approach to child development. THE LITTLE GYM'S highly motivational and individualized programs are curriculum-based and provide physical, social and intellectual development. Classes develop basic motor skills, build self-esteem and encourage risk-taking through gymnastics, karate and sports skills development.

BACKGROUND: IFA MEMBER
Established: 1992; 1st Franchised: 1992
Franchised Units: 332
Company-Owned Units: 0
Total Units: 332
Dist.: US-262; CAN-15; O'seas-55
North America: 35 States, DC
Density: 28 in TX, 26 in CA, 19 in NY
Projected New Units (12 Months): 40
Qualifications: 5, 5, 2, 3, 5, 5
Registered: CA,FL,IL,IN,MD,MI,MN,NY,OR,WA

FINANCIAL/TERMS:
Cash Investment: $60K
Total Investment: $150-225K
Minimum Net Worth: $200K
Fees: Franchise - $57.5K
Royalty - 8%; Ad. - 1%
Earnings Claims Statement: Yes
Term of Contract (Years): 10/10/10
Avg. # Of Employees: 2 FT, 2-3 PT
Passive Ownership: Discouraged
Encourage Conversions: Yes
Area Develop. Agreements: Yes/10
Sub-Franchising Contracts: No
Expand In Territory: Yes
Space Needs: 4,000 SF; SC, Destination

SUPPORT & TRAINING:
Financial Assistance Provided: Yes(I)
Site Selection Assistance: Yes
Lease Negotiation Assistance: Yes
Co-Operative Advertising: No
Franchisee Assoc./Member: No
Size Of Corporate Staff: 27
On-Going Support: C,D,G,H,I
Training: 2 Weeks Scottsdale, AZ; 1 Week Internship at Site To Be Determined.

SPECIFIC EXPANSION PLANS:
US: All United States
Canada: All Canada
Overseas: Asia, Australia, Europe, Mexico

<< >>

LITTLE SCIENTISTS
14 Selden St.
Woodbridge, CT 06525-2208
Tel: (800) 322-8386 (203) 732-3522
Fax: (203) 397-2165
E-Mail: dr_heidi@little-scientists.com
Web Site: www.little-scientists.com
Ms. Heidi Van Borkin, VP Franchise Development

LITTLE SCIENTISTS is a leader in hands-on science education for children ages 3 to 9. Nearly 200 hands-on lessons make up a innovative science curriculum. The curriculum has been developed by renowned scientists and educators. The market is growing at a remarkable rate. Owning a LITTLE SCIENTIST franchise is a highly profitable endeavor yielding great community benefits.

BACKGROUND:
Established: 1993; 1st Franchised: 1996
Franchised Units: 27
Company-Owned Units: 2
Total Units: 29
Dist.: US-17; CAN-0; O'seas-1
North America: 7 States
Density: 5 in CT, 2 in NJ
Projected New Units (12 Months): 14
Qualifications: 3, 5, 4, 4, 5, 5
Registered: CA,FL,IL,NY,VA,WI

FINANCIAL/TERMS:
Cash Investment: $25K
Total Investment: $35K
Minimum Net Worth: $50K
Fees: Franchise - $20K
Royalty - 6%/$250/Mo.; Ad. - 1%
Earnings Claims Statement: No
Term of Contract (Years): 10/10
Avg. # Of Employees: 2 FT, 6-10 PT
Passive Ownership: Discouraged
Encourage Conversions: Yes
Area Develop. Agreements: Yes/10
Sub-Franchising Contracts: Yes
Expand In Territory: Yes
Space Needs: 500 SF; HB

SUPPORT & TRAINING:
Financial Assistance Provided: Yes(I)
Site Selection Assistance: NA
Lease Negotiation Assistance: NA
Co-Operative Advertising: NA
Franchisee Assoc./Member: Yes/Yes
Size Of Corporate Staff: 15
On-Going Support: A,B,C,D,G,H,I
Training: 1 Week at HQ; 1-3 Day Seminars/Training 2 Times/Year at HQ; 2-4 Times/Year On Site.

SPECIFIC EXPANSION PLANS:
US: All United States
Canada: All Canada
Overseas: All Countries Except Korea

<< >>

MAD SCIENCE GROUP, THE
8360 Bougainville, # 201
Montreal, PQ H4P 2G1 CANADA

Tel: (800) 586-5231 + 104 (514) 344-4181
Fax: (514) 344-6695
E-Mail: joel@madscience.org
Web Site: www.madscience.org
Mr. Joel Lazarovitz, Sales/Marketing Coordinator

Your staff provides hands-on, interactive science shows for children ages 4-12. Turn kids onto science! Home based, profitable, rewarding.

BACKGROUND: IFA MEMBER
Established: 1985; 1st Franchised: 1995
Franchised Units: 198
Company-Owned Units: 0
Total Units: 198
Dist.: US-120; CAN-10; O'seas-25
North America: 30 States, 8 Provinces
Density: 12 in CA, 5 in NJ, 4 in BC
Projected New Units (12 Months): 20
Qualifications: 2, 5, 3, 3, 5, 5
Registered: All States

FINANCIAL/TERMS:
Cash Investment: $10K
Total Investment: $55K
Minimum Net Worth: $23.5K
Fees: Franchise - $23.5K
Royalty - 8%; Ad. - 0%
Earnings Claims Statement: Yes
Term of Contract (Years): 10/5
Avg. # Of Employees: 1 FT, 3-5 PT
Passive Ownership: Not Allowed
Encourage Conversions: NA
Area Develop. Agreements: No
Sub-Franchising Contracts: No
Expand In Territory: Yes
Space Needs: NR SF; HB

SUPPORT & TRAINING:
Financial Assistance Provided: Yes(I)
Site Selection Assistance: NA
Lease Negotiation Assistance: NA
Co-Operative Advertising: NA
Franchisee Assoc./Member: Yes/Yes
Size Of Corporate Staff: 30
On-Going Support: A,b,C,D,E,F,G,h,i
Training: 2 Weeks Montreal, PQ.

SPECIFIC EXPANSION PLANS:
US: All United States
Canada: All Canada
Overseas: All Countries

≺≺ ≻≻

MY GYM CHILDREN'S FITNESS CENTER

15300 Ventura Blvd., # 423
Sherman Oaks, CA 91403
Tel: (800) 469-4967 (818) 907-6966
Fax: (818) 907-0735
E-Mail: info@maretcorp.com
Web Site: www.my-gym.com
Mr. Michael Chalovich, Chief Operating Officer

MY GYM CHILDREN'S FITNESS CENTER's structured, age-appropriate weekly classes incorporates music, dance, relays, games, special rides, gymnastics, sports and other original activities. MY GYM kids have so much fun as they gain strength, balance, gross motor skills, agility, flexibility and social skills. Our programs' biggest benefit is the building of confidence and self esteem. We help design our state-of-the-art facility and assist in every aspect of getting you started.

BACKGROUND: IFA MEMBER
Established: 1983; 1st Franchised: 1994
Franchised Units: 130
Company-Owned Units: 8
Total Units: 138
Dist.: US-117; CAN-0; O'seas-3
North America: 29 States
Density: 24 in CA, 18 in FL, 8 in IL
Projected New Units (12 Months): 40
Qualifications: 2, 3, 3, 3, 4, 5
Registered: All States Except ND and SD

FINANCIAL/TERMS:
Cash Investment: $30-60K
Total Investment: $130-220K
Minimum Net Worth: NA
Fees: Franchise - $49.4K
Royalty - 6%; Ad. - 1%
Earnings Claims Statement: No
Term of Contract (Years): 12/12
Avg. # Of Employees: 3 FT, 4 PT
Passive Ownership: Discouraged
Encourage Conversions: NA
Area Develop. Agreements: Yes/12
Sub-Franchising Contracts: No
Expand In Territory: Yes
Space Needs: 2,400 SF; SF, SC

SUPPORT & TRAINING:
Financial Assistance Provided: Yes(I)
Site Selection Assistance: Yes
Lease Negotiation Assistance: Yes
Co-Operative Advertising: Yes
Franchisee Assoc./Member: No
Size Of Corporate Staff: 15
On-Going Support: B,C,D,E,F,I
Training: 19 Days Corporate Headquarters in Los Angeles, CA; Regional Pre-and Post-Training.

SPECIFIC EXPANSION PLANS:
US: All United States
Canada: All Canada
Overseas: All Countries

≺≺ ≻≻

ONCE UPON A CHILD

4200 Dahlberg Dr., # 100
Minneapolis, MN 55422-4837
Tel: (800) 453-7750 (763) 520-8490
Fax: (763) 520-8501
E-Mail: ouac-franchise-development@winmarkcorporation.com
Web Site: www.ouac.com
Franchise Development Dept.,

ONCE UPON A CHILD stores sell and buy used and new children's clothing, toys, furniture, equipment and accessories. Customers have the opportunity to sell their used children's wear to a ONCE UPON A CHILD store when outgrown and to purchase quality used items at prices lower than new merchandise.

BACKGROUND: IFA MEMBER
Established: 1985; 1st Franchised: 1993
Franchised Units: 215
Company-Owned Units: 1
Total Units: 216
Dist.: US-198; CAN-18; O'seas-0
North America: 37 States, 5 Provinces
Density: 33 in OH, 21 in CA, 14 in IN
Projected New Units (12 Months): 15
Qualifications: 5, 4, 2, 2, 2, 4
Registered: All States and AB

FINANCIAL/TERMS:
Cash Investment: $37-65K
Total Investment: $134-218K
Minimum Net Worth: $225K
Fees: Franchise - $20K
Royalty - 5%; Ad. - $250/Yr.
Earnings Claims Statement: Yes
Term of Contract (Years): 10/10
Avg. # Of Employees: 3 FT, 2 PT
Passive Ownership: Not Allowed
Encourage Conversions: No
Area Develop. Agreements: No
Sub-Franchising Contracts: No
Expand In Territory: No
Space Needs: 2,500-3,000 SF; SC

SUPPORT & TRAINING:
Financial Assistance Provided: No
Site Selection Assistance: Yes
Lease Negotiation Assistance: Yes
Co-Operative Advertising: No
Franchisee Assoc./Member: No
Size Of Corporate Staff: 97
On-Going Support: B,C,D,E,F,G,H,I
Training: 3 Days Minneapolis, MN; 3 Days Minneapolis, MN; 5-6 Days Minneapolis, MN.

SPECIFIC EXPANSION PLANS:
US: All United States

Canada: All Canada
Overseas: No

<< >>

PEE WEE WORKOUT

34976 Aspenwood Ln.
Willoughby, OH 44094
Tel: (800) 356-6261 (440) 946-7888
Fax: (440) 946-7888
E-Mail: peeweework@aol.com
Web Site: www.peeweeworkout.com
Ms. Margaret J. Carr, President

Mission Statement: to reach and educate children about the benefits of healthy living. Program teaches healthy living to preschoolers and grade school children. Classes consist of movement to original music that covers components of fitness and concludes with educational lessons. Trained instructors have weekly visits to day schools and recreation departments.

BACKGROUND:
Established: 1986; 1st Franchised: 1987
Franchised Units: 16
Company-Owned Units: 1
Total Units: 17
Dist.: US-37; CAN-1; O'seas-1
North America: 18 States
Density: NR
Projected New Units (12 Months): 5
Qualifications: 2, 4, 5, 3, 5, 5
Registered: NR

FINANCIAL/TERMS:
Cash Investment: NR
Total Investment: $3-3.5K
Minimum Net Worth: NA
Fees: Franchise - $2K
Royalty - 10%; Ad. - 0%
Earnings Claims Statement: Yes
Term of Contract (Years): 5/5
Avg. # Of Employees: 1 PT
Passive Ownership: Discouraged
Encourage Conversions: NA
Area Develop. Agreements: No
Sub-Franchising Contracts: Yes
Expand In Territory: Yes
Space Needs: NR SF; HB

SUPPORT & TRAINING:
Financial Assistance Provided: No
Site Selection Assistance: No
Lease Negotiation Assistance: NA
Co-Operative Advertising: No
Franchisee Assoc./Member: No
Size Of Corporate Staff: NR
On-Going Support: B,G,I
Training: Video Based.

SPECIFIC EXPANSION PLANS:
US: All United States
Canada: All Canada
Overseas: All Countries

<< >>

PRE-FIT

10926 S. Western Ave.
Chicago, IL 60643
Tel: (773) 233-7771
Fax: (773) 233-7121
E-Mail: prefit@ameritech.net
Web Site: www.pre-fit.com
Ms. Latrice Lee, Franchise Director

PRE-FIT, INC offers America's premier sports, exercise and health systems for children. These systems include: PRE-FIT, a mobile preschool fitness program; FITNESS IS ELEMENTARY, our mobile elementary physical education program; and CHEC, the Children's Health and Executive Club. All of these programs are offered through our success-oriented franchise system that provides marketing, administrative and instructional training, an exclusive territory, and continuous support.

BACKGROUND:
Established: 1987; 1st Franchised: 1992
Franchised Units: 50
Company-Owned Units: 2
Total Units: 52
Dist.: US-40; CAN-1; O'seas-0
North America: 13 States
Density: 19 in IL, 6 in PA, 2 in MI
Projected New Units (12 Months): 10
Qualifications: 4, 4, 4, 3, 3, 5
Registered:CA,FL,IL,MD,MI,MN,VA,WA

FINANCIAL/TERMS:
Cash Investment: $10-41K
Total Investment: $10-118.2K
Minimum Net Worth: $25K
Fees: Franchise - $8.5-24.5K
Royalty - 8-10%; Ad. - 2%
Earnings Claims Statement: No
Term of Contract (Years): 10/10
Avg. # Of Employees: 1-2 FT, 2-5 PT
Passive Ownership: Discouraged
Encourage Conversions: NA
Area Develop. Agreements: No
Sub-Franchising Contracts: No
Expand In Territory: Yes
Space Needs:2,000-4,000 SF; SC, RM, HB

SUPPORT & TRAINING:
Financial Assistance Provided: Yes(I)
Site Selection Assistance: Yes
Lease Negotiation Assistance: Yes
Co-Operative Advertising: No
Franchisee Assoc./Member: No
Size Of Corporate Staff: 6
On-Going Support: D,E,G,h,I
Training: Chicago, IL.

SPECIFIC EXPANSION PLANS:
US: All United States
Canada: All Canada
Overseas: All Countries

<< >>

PRIMROSE SCHOOLS FRANCHISING COMPANY

2660 Cedarcrest Rd.
Atworth, GA 30101
Tel: (800) 291-2555 (770) 529-4100
Fax: (770) 529-1551
E-Mail: kmusso@primroseschools.com
Web Site: www.primroseschools.com
Ms. Kim Musso, Dir. Franchise Recruitment

Educational child-care franchise, offering a traditional pre-school curriculum and programs while also providing quality childcare services. Site selection assistance, extensive training, operations manuals, building plans, marketing plans and on-going support.

BACKGROUND: IFA MEMBER
Established: 1982; 1st Franchised: 1989
Franchised Units: 116
Company-Owned Units: 1
Total Units: 117
Dist.: US-117; CAN-0; O'seas-0
North America: 13 States
Density: 37 in GA, 37 in TX, 10 in NC
Projected New Units (12 Months): 15
Qualifications: 5, 5, 1, 4, 5, 5
Registered: All Except HI,ND,RI,WA,WI and AB

FINANCIAL/TERMS:
Cash Investment: $200-250K
Total Investment: $2.0-2.4MM
Minimum Net Worth: $500K
Fees: Franchise - $50K
Royalty - 7%; Ad. - 1%
Earnings Claims Statement: Yes
Term of Contract (Years): 11/10/10
Avg. # Of Employees: 25 FT, 5 PT
Passive Ownership: Not Allowed
Encourage Conversions: NA
Area Develop. Agreements: No
Sub-Franchising Contracts: No
Expand In Territory: No
Space Needs: 8,500 SF; FS

SUPPORT & TRAINING:
Financial Assistance Provided: Yes(I)
Site Selection Assistance: Yes

Lease Negotiation Assistance: Yes
Co-Operative Advertising: Yes
Franchisee Assoc./Member: Yes/Yes
Size Of Corporate Staff: 35
On-Going Support: A,C,D,E,f,G,h,I
Training: 1 Week Home Office; 1 Week at Existing School; 1 Week at Franchisee's New School.

SPECIFIC EXPANSION PLANS:

US: SW, SE, TX, OH, CO
Canada: No
Overseas: No

Rainbow Station

RAINBOW STATION

3307 Church Rd., # 205
Richmond, VA 23233
Tel: (888) 747-1552 (804) 740-0892
Fax: (804) 747-8016
E-Mail: info@rainbowstation.org
Web Site: www.rainbowstation.org
Mr. Earl Johnson, Vice President

High-end, accredited pre-school and after-school recreation programs with registered nurse on site in sick child care facility (Get Well Place). Programs are accredited by National Association of Early Childhood Programs and based in 18,000 SF of state-of-the-art structures with Standards of Learning based curriculum - fully developed in-house. The pre-school will accommodate 158 children from 0 to pre-school, while the after-school program will accommodate 175 children up to 14 years of age.

BACKGROUND: IFA MEMBER

Established: 1989; 1st Franchised: 1999
Franchised Units: 2
Company-Owned Units: 3
Total Units: 5
Dist.: US-5; CAN-0; O'seas-0
North America: 2 States
Density: 3 in VA, 2 in TX
Projected New Units (12 Months): 1
Qualifications: 5, 4, 3, 4, 4, 5
Registered: FL

FINANCIAL/TERMS:

Cash Investment: $100-700K
Total Investment: $2.75-3.5MM
Minimum Net Worth: $350K
Fees: Franchise - $50K
Royalty - 7%; Ad. - 1%
Earnings Claims Statement: No
Term of Contract (Years): 10/5
Avg. # Of Employees: 40 FT, 35 PT
Passive Ownership: Not Allowed
Encourage Conversions: No
Area Develop. Agreements: No
Sub-Franchising Contracts: No
Expand In Territory: Yes
Space Needs: 18,000 SF; FS

SUPPORT & TRAINING:

Financial Assistance Provided: Yes(I)
Site Selection Assistance: Yes
Lease Negotiation Assistance: Yes
Co-Operative Advertising: NA
Franchisee Assoc./Member: No
Size Of Corporate Staff: 5
On-Going Support: C,D,E,G,I
Training: 2 Weeks Headquarters; Approximately 2 Weeks On-Site.

SPECIFIC EXPANSION PLANS:

US: All United States
Canada: No
Overseas: No

SOCCERTOTS

E. 7311 Nora, # 103
Spokane, WA 99212
Tel: (509) 290-1028
Fax: (509) 922-8611
E-Mail: info@soccertots.net
Web Site: www.soccertots.net
Mr. Kent Gold, President

SOCCERTOTS is a child development program designed to be operated from an indoor sports facility. It uses soccer as the main motor skill development tool, but also uses a variety of props and methods for general athletic development. This program can be taught out of an indoor sports facility, a gym, a roller skating rink or any large indoor space. The start-up costs are low and the income potential is high.

BACKGROUND:

Established: 2002; 1st Franchised: 2003
Franchised Units: 15
Company-Owned Units: 1
Total Units: 16
Dist.: US-16; CAN-0; O'seas-0
North America: 9 States
Density: 4 in OR, 2 in NY, 2 in TX
Projected New Units (12 Months): NR
Qualifications: , , , , ,
Registered: NR

FINANCIAL/TERMS:

Cash Investment: $2.5-4.0K
Total Investment: NR4-6K
Minimum Net Worth: NR
Fees: Franchise - $3.5K
Royalty - 6%; Ad. - 1%
Earnings Claims Statement: No
Term of Contract (Years): 5/5
Avg. # Of Employees: 1 FT, 5 PT
Passive Ownership: Allowed
Encourage Conversions: NR
Area Develop. Agreements: No
Sub-Franchising Contracts: No
Expand In Territory: Yes
Space Needs: 0 SF; HB

SUPPORT & TRAINING:

Financial Assistance Provided: NR
Site Selection Assistance: Yes
Lease Negotiation Assistance: Yes
Co-Operative Advertising: No
Franchisee Assoc./Member: No
Size Of Corporate Staff: 3
On-Going Support: a,B,C,D,E,f,,G,I
Training: 2 Days Corporate Headquarters; 2 Days at Site.

SPECIFIC EXPANSION PLANS:

US: All United States
Canada: NR
Overseas: NR

STRETCH-N-GROW INTERNATIONAL

14399 87th Ave.
Seminole, FL 33776-1927
Tel: (800) 348-0166 (727) 596-7614
Fax:
E-Mail: info@stretch-n-grow.com
Web Site: www.stretch-n-grow.com
Ms. Karyn Burnier, Franchise Sales

STRETCH-N-GROW is a comprehensive mobile fitness program for children ages 2 1/2 to 8. It is taught primarily in child care facilities. We provide a corporate marketing system and a curriculum package which covers health-related issues and exercise that is age-appropriate, but adaptable to the age ranges above. The investment and time demands are minimal, the rewards, both financial and personal, immense.

BACKGROUND:

Established: 1992; 1st Franchised: 1994
Franchised Units: 173
Company-Owned Units: 0
Total Units: 173
Dist.: US-67; CAN-1; O'seas-0

North America: 24 States, 1 Province
Density: 10 in TX, 5 in NY, 5 in PA
Projected New Units (12 Months): 12
Qualifications: 3, 3, 4, 4, , 5
Registered: CA,FL,NY

FINANCIAL/TERMS:
Cash Investment: $7.6-12.6K
Total Investment: $8.3-13.3K
Minimum Net Worth: NA
Fees: Franchise - $7.6-12.6K
Royalty - $100/Mo.; Ad. - $100/Yr.
Earnings Claims Statement: No
Term of Contract (Years): NA
Avg. # Of Employees: 1 FT, 1-2 PT
Passive Ownership: Discouraged
Encourage Conversions: NA
Area Develop. Agreements: No
Sub-Franchising Contracts: No
Expand In Territory: No
Space Needs: NA SF; HB

SUPPORT & TRAINING:
Financial Assistance Provided: No
Site Selection Assistance: NA
Lease Negotiation Assistance: NA
Co-Operative Advertising: Yes
Franchisee Assoc./Member: No
Size Of Corporate Staff: 2
On-Going Support: b,D,G,h,I
Training: 3 Days in Dallas, TX.

SPECIFIC EXPANSION PLANS:
US: All United States
Canada: No
Overseas: Australia

<< >>

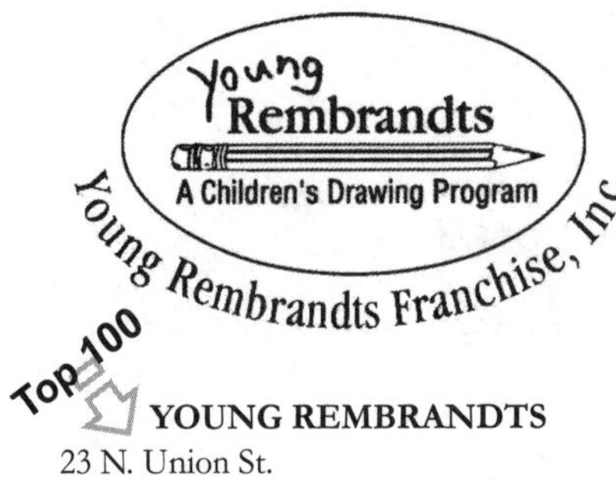

YOUNG REMBRANDTS
23 N. Union St.
Elgin, IL 60123
Tel: (866) 300-6010 (847) 742-6966
Fax: (847) 742-7197
E-Mail: contact@youngrembrandts.com
Web Site: www.youngrembrandts.com/franchise_opportunities.htm
Ms. Kim Swanson, Director Franchise Operations

YOUNG REMBRANDTS is a home-based business offering a well-organized, high-quality program that teaches a valuable drawing curriculum to children at off-site locations. An ideal candidate should possess: good people skills, management experience, sales and marketing insight and community and school involvement. No artistic or teaching background is necessary.

BACKGROUND: IFA MEMBER
Established: 1988; 1st Franchised: 2001
Franchised Units: 45
Company-Owned Units: 1
Total Units: 46
Dist.: US-46; CAN-0; O'seas-0

North America: 21 States
Density: 7 in IL, 6 in CA
Projected New Units (12 Months):
Qualifications: , , , , ,
Registered:

FINANCIAL/TERMS:
Cash Investment: $31.5K
Total Investment: $35.9-48.8K
Minimum Net Worth: $50K
Fees: Franchise - $31.5K
Royalty - 10%/8%; Ad. - NR
Earnings Claims Statement: NR
Term of Contract (Years): 10
Avg. # Of Employees: NR
Passive Ownership: NR
Encourage Conversions:
Area Develop. Agreements: Yes
Sub-Franchising Contracts: No
Expand In Territory: Yes
Space Needs: NA SF; HB

SUPPORT & TRAINING:
Financial Assistance Provided: No
Site Selection Assistance: NA
Lease Negotiation Assistance: NA
Co-Operative Advertising: NR
Franchisee Assoc./Member: Yes
Size Of Corporate Staff: 15
On-Going Support: C,H,I
Training: 5 Days Elgin, IL.

SPECIFIC EXPANSION PLANS:
US: All United States
Canada: NR
Overseas: NR

Education/Personal Development/Training

EDUCATION/PERSONAL DEVELOPMENT/TRAINING INDUSTRY PROFILE

Total # Franchisors in Industry Group	53
Total # Franchised Units in Industry Group	3,820
Total # Company-Owned Units in Industry Group	858
Total # Operating Units in Industry Group	4,678
Average # Franchised Units/Franchisor	72.1
Average # Company-Owned Units/Franchisor	16.2
Average # Total Units/Franchisor	88.3
Ratio of Total # Franchised Units/Total # Company-Owned Units	4.5:1
Industry Survey Participants	24
Representing % of Industry	45.3%
Average Franchise Fee*:	$35.3K
Average Total Investment*:	$137.7K
Average On-Going Royalty Fee*:	7.7%

*If a range was provided, the mid-point of the range was used. See detailed profiles for actual ranges.

FIVE LARGEST PARTICIPANTS IN SURVEY

Company	# Franchised Units	# Co-Owned Units	# Total Units	Franchise Fee	On-Going Royalty	Total Investment
1. Sylvan Learning Centers	900	150	1,050	$38-46K	8-9%	$121.1-219.3K
2. Berlitz International	80	350	430	$30-50K	10%	$150-300K
3. Huntington Learning Center	234	33	267	$40K	8%/$1.5K Min.	$190-290K
4. New Horizons Computer Learning Center	231	25	256	$25-75K	6%	$400-500K
5. Dale Carnegie Training	192	3	195	$25(US)-50K	12%	$150-200K

All of the data provided are proprietary and should not be quoted without acknowledging *Bond's Franchise Guide.*

ACADEMY FOR MATHEMATICS & SCIENCE

30 Glen Cameron Rd., # 200
Thornhill, ON L3T 1N7 CANADA
Tel: (800) 809-5555 (905) 709-3233
Fax: (905) 709-3045
E-Mail: info@acadfor.com
Web Site: www.acadfor.com
Mr. Balti Sauer, President/CEO

Licensees provide math, science, English and computer tutoring to school age children from kindergarten to the end of high school. Individualized, self-paced learning is provided in learning centers located in major malls, using a unique audio-visual learning program.

BACKGROUND:
Established: 1992; 1st Franchised: 1993
Franchised Units: 35
Company-Owned Units: 5
Total Units: 40
Dist.: US-0; CAN-40; O'seas-0
North America: 3 Provinces
Density: 29 in ON, 6 in BC, 5 in AB
Projected New Units (12 Months): 6
Qualifications: 2, 3, 1, 4, 1, 5
Registered: AB

FINANCIAL/TERMS:
Cash Investment: $70-100K
Total Investment: $70-100K
Minimum Net Worth: NA
Fees: Franchise - $35K
Royalty - 10-12%; Ad. - 2%
Earnings Claims Statement: No
Term of Contract (Years): 5/5
Avg. # Of Employees: 2 FT, 6 PT
Passive Ownership: Not Allowed
Encourage Conversions: NA
Area Develop. Agreements: Yes/10
Sub-Franchising Contracts: Yes
Expand In Territory: Yes
Space Needs: 1,000 SF; SC, RM

SUPPORT & TRAINING:
Financial Assistance Provided: Yes(I)
Site Selection Assistance: Yes
Lease Negotiation Assistance: Yes
Co-Operative Advertising: Yes
Franchisee Assoc./Member: Yes
Size Of Corporate Staff: 14
On-Going Support: C,D,E,G,H,I
Training: 2 Weeks Corporate Office; 1 Week Training Center.

SPECIFIC EXPANSION PLANS:
US: In Progress
Canada: All Canada
Overseas: All Countries

<< >>

BARBIZON SCHOOLS OF MODELING

3111 N. University Dr., # 406
Coral Springs, FL 33065
Tel: (888) 999-9404 (954) 345-4140
Fax: (954) 345-8055
E-Mail: franchise@barbizonmodeling.com
Web Site: www.barbizonmodeling.com
Mr. Tom Blangiardo, President

Proprietary, private schools of modeling and related creative arts.

BACKGROUND: IFA MEMBER
Established: 1939; 1st Franchised: 1968
Franchised Units: 60
Company-Owned Units: 0
Total Units: 60
Dist.: US-56; CAN-1; O'seas-3
North America: 27 States
Density: 7 in CA, 5 in NY, 5 in NJ
Projected New Units (12 Months): 7
Qualifications: 4, 3, 1, 4, 2, 5
Registered: CA,HI,IL,MD,MN,NY,VA, WA

FINANCIAL/TERMS:
Cash Investment: $30-50K
Total Investment: $47-67.5K
Minimum Net Worth: NR
Fees: Franchise - $35K
Royalty - 7.5%; Ad. - 2.5%
Earnings Claims Statement: No
Term of Contract (Years): 10/10
Avg. # Of Employees: NR
Passive Ownership: Discouraged
Encourage Conversions: Yes
Area Develop. Agreements: No
Sub-Franchising Contracts: No
Expand In Territory: Yes
Space Needs: NR SF; NR

SUPPORT & TRAINING:
Financial Assistance Provided: Yes(D)
Site Selection Assistance: Yes
Lease Negotiation Assistance: Yes
Co-Operative Advertising: NA
Franchisee Assoc./Member: Yes/Yes
Size Of Corporate Staff: NR
On-Going Support: C,D,E,G,H
Training: Varies Home Office; Varies On-Site.

SPECIFIC EXPANSION PLANS:
US: All United States
Canada: All Canada
Overseas: All Countries

<< >>

BERLITZ INTERNATIONAL

400 Alexander Park Dr.
Princeton, NJ 08540-6306
Tel: (800) 626-6419 (609) 514-3046
Fax: (609) 514-9675
E-Mail: charles.gilbert@berlitz.com
Web Site: www.berlitz.com
Mr. Charles J. Gilbert, Dir. Worldwide Franchise

Language instruction, publishing and translation services

BACKGROUND: IFA MEMBER
Established: 1900; 1st Franchised: 1996
Franchised Units: 80
Company-Owned Units: 350
Total Units: 430
Dist.: US-61; CAN-11; O'seas-328
North America: NR
Density: 18 in NY, 18 in CA, 18 in FL
Projected New Units (12 Months): 50
Qualifications: 4, 5, 2, 3, 4, 5
Registered: CA,FL,IL,MD,MI,NY,OR,VA,WA

FINANCIAL/TERMS:
Cash Investment: $150-300K
Total Investment: $150-300K
Minimum Net Worth: $300K
Fees: Franchise - $30-50K
Royalty - 10%; Ad. - 2%
Earnings Claims Statement: No
Term of Contract (Years): 10/10
Avg. # Of Employees: 1 FT, 1 PT
Passive Ownership: Discouraged
Encourage Conversions: Yes
Area Develop. Agreements: Yes/10
Sub-Franchising Contracts: No
Expand In Territory: No
Space Needs: 1,500-3,000 SF; NA

SUPPORT & TRAINING:
Financial Assistance Provided: No
Site Selection Assistance: Yes
Lease Negotiation Assistance: Yes
Co-Operative Advertising: No
Franchisee Assoc./Member: No
Size Of Corporate Staff: 7000
On-Going Support: B,C,D,E,F,G,H
Training: 2 Weeks Home Office; 2 Weeks Division Training; 2 Weeks On-Site.

SPECIFIC EXPANSION PLANS:
US: Southeast, West
Canada: NB
Overseas: Africa, Central Asia, Asia

<< >>

BOSTON BARTENDERS SCHOOL ASSOCIATES

P. O. Box 176
Wilbraham, MA 01095
Tel: (800) 357-3210 (413) 596-4600

Fax: (413) 596-4630
E-Mail: bill@bostonbartenders.com
Web Site: www.bostonbartenders.com
Mr. William Green, Chief Operating Officer

BBS offers a 35-hour course in Mixology and alcohol awareness to men and women ages 18 and up. College students, people in-between or changing jobs or those moving to a new area will be interested in a job bartending. It's easy, fun, quick and affordable. The program takes one or two weeks of evenings to complete. The program costs $400-600, paid up front.

BACKGROUND:

Established: 1968;	1st Franchised: 1995
Franchised Units:	10
Company-Owned Units:	3
Total Units:	13
Dist.:	US-9; CAN-0; O'seas-0
North America:	NR
Density:	4 in MA, 2 in CT, 2 in RI
Projected New Units (12 Months):	3
Qualifications:	1, 1, 1, 1, 1, 4
Registered:	RI

FINANCIAL/TERMS:

Cash Investment:	$30K
Total Investment:	$30K
Minimum Net Worth:	$50K
Fees: Franchise -	$6.9K
Royalty - 10%;	Ad. - NR
Earnings Claims Statement:	No
Term of Contract (Years):	10/10
Avg. # Of Employees:	2 FT, 1 PT
Passive Ownership:	Discouraged
Encourage Conversions:	NA
Area Develop. Agreements:	No
Sub-Franchising Contracts:	No
Expand In Territory:	Yes
Space Needs:	1,000 SF; NA

SUPPORT & TRAINING:

Financial Assistance Provided:	No
Site Selection Assistance:	Yes
Lease Negotiation Assistance:	Yes
Co-Operative Advertising:	NA
Franchisee Assoc./Member:	No
Size Of Corporate Staff:	2
On-Going Support:	A,E,F,H,I
Training:	2 Weeks in Springfield, MA.

SPECIFIC EXPANSION PLANS:

US:	All United States
Canada:	All Canada
Overseas:	No

<< >>

COMPUTER U LEARNING CENTERS

75850 Osage Trl.
Indian Wells, CA 92210
Tel: (888) 708-7877 (760) 340-2453
Fax: (760) 340-0306
E-Mail: info@computeru.com
Web Site: www.computeru.com
Mr. Russ Beckner, Vice President

COMPUTER U LEARNING CENTERS provides computer training to mature adults through classroom instruction and private tutoring. We teach in the context of mid-life and retirement, with tested programs developed especially for adults ago 50 and over. We make it simple to learn computers. We keep it simple for our franchise partners with comprehensive training and continuing on-line support. Come GROW with us!

BACKGROUND:

Established: 1992;	1st Franchised: 1997
Franchised Units:	9
Company-Owned Units:	6
Total Units:	15
Dist.:	US-15; CAN-0; O'seas-0
North America:	4 States
Density:	CA, NV, FL
Projected New Units (12 Months):	10
Qualifications:	3, 3, 1, 4, 5, 5
Registered:	CA,FL,MI,OR,WI,DC

FINANCIAL/TERMS:

Cash Investment:	$30-40K
Total Investment:	$30-40K
Minimum Net Worth:	NA
Fees: Franchise -	$20K
Royalty - 6%;	Ad. - 1%
Earnings Claims Statement:	Yes
Term of Contract (Years):	10/5
Avg. # Of Employees:	1 FT, 2 PT
Passive Ownership:	Allowed
Encourage Conversions:	NA
Area Develop. Agreements:	Yes
Sub-Franchising Contracts:	No
Expand In Territory:	Yes
Space Needs:	400 SF; NA

SUPPORT & TRAINING:

Financial Assistance Provided:	No
Site Selection Assistance:	Yes
Lease Negotiation Assistance:	Yes
Co-Operative Advertising:	No
Franchisee Assoc./Member:	No
Size Of Corporate Staff:	4
On-Going Support:	NR
Training:	2 Days On-Site; 6 Days Headquarters, Palm Springs, CA.

SPECIFIC EXPANSION PLANS:

US:	Where Registered
Canada:	No
Overseas:	No

<< >>

CRESTCOM INTERNATIONAL, LTD.

6900 E. Belleview Ave., # 300
Greenwood Village, CO 80111-1619
Tel: (888) 273-7826 (303) 267-8200
Fax: (303) 267-8207
E-Mail: franchiseinfo@crestcom.com
Web Site: www.crestcom.com
Mr. Kelly Krause, VP International Marketing

CRESTCOM franchisees market and deliver world-renowned training in leadership, customer service, sales and management development. CRESTCOM uses a unique combination of video instruction and live facilitation to teach these skills. Thousands of organizations use CRESTCOM training, from multi-national giants to small, local firms. The company is active in 45+ countries and has materials in over 20 languages.

BACKGROUND: IFA MEMBER

Established: 1987;	1st Franchised: 1992
Franchised Units:	143
Company-Owned Units:	0
Total Units:	143
Dist.:	US-64; CAN-10; O'seas-69
North America:	25 States, 4 Provinces
Density:	NR
Projected New Units (12 Months):	35
Qualifications:	4, 5, 2, 4, 5, 5
Registered:	All States

FINANCIAL/TERMS:

Cash Investment:	$39.5-59.5K
Total Investment:	$54.8-88.9K
Minimum Net Worth:	NR
Fees: Franchise -	$39.5-59.5K
Royalty - 1.5%;	Ad. - NA
Earnings Claims Statement:	Yes
Term of Contract (Years):	7/7/7
Avg. # Of Employees:	2-5 FT
Passive Ownership:	Discouraged
Encourage Conversions:	NA
Area Develop. Agreements:	No
Sub-Franchising Contracts:	No
Expand In Territory:	Yes
Space Needs:	NR SF; SF, HB

SUPPORT & TRAINING:

Financial Assistance Provided: Yes
Site Selection Assistance: NA
Lease Negotiation Assistance: NA
Co-Operative Advertising: No
Franchisee Assoc./Member: Yes
Size Of Corporate Staff: 15
On-Going Support: D,G,H
Training: 7-10 Days Denver, CO, Phoenix, AZ or Sacramento, CA.

SPECIFIC EXPANSION PLANS:
US: All United States
Canada: All Canada
Overseas: All Countries

DALE CARNEGIE TRAINING®

DALE CARNEGIE TRAINING

290 Motor Pkwy.
Hauppaguge, NY 11788-5105
Tel: (631) 415-9378
Fax: (631) 415-9358
E-Mail: joe_garcia@dalecarnegie.com
Web Site: www.dalecarnegie.com
Mr. Joseph Garcia, SVP Franchising

If you're committed to being the premier, local human resources development partner of a business with global reach and recognition, then DALE CARNEGIE TRAINING is an exceptional opportunity for you. DALE CARNEGIE TRAINING services thousands of organizations throughout the world, providing effective business solutions that can be tailored to meet a client's specific needs.

BACKGROUND: IFA MEMBER
Established: 1912; 1st Franchised: 1999
Franchised Units: 192
Company-Owned Units: 3
Total Units: 195
Dist.: US-94; CAN-5; O'seas-96
North America: NR
Density: NR
Projected New Units (12 Months): 7-10
Qualifications: 4, 5, 2, 4, 2, 5
Registered: All States and AB

FINANCIAL/TERMS:
Cash Investment: $100K
Total Investment: $150-200K
Minimum Net Worth: $200K
Fees: Franchise - $25(US)-50K
Royalty - 12%; Ad. - 3%-US
Earnings Claims Statement: No
Term of Contract (Years): 15/10
Avg. # Of Employees: 4 FT, 0 PT
Passive Ownership: Not Allowed
Encourage Conversions: NA
Area Develop. Agreements: Yes/15
Sub-Franchising Contracts: No
Expand In Territory: Yes
Space Needs: NA SF; NA

SUPPORT & TRAINING:
Financial Assistance Provided: No
Site Selection Assistance: NA
Lease Negotiation Assistance: NA
Co-Operative Advertising: NR
Franchisee Assoc./Member: Yes/Yes
Size Of Corporate Staff: 70
On-Going Support: a,B,C,D,E,G,H
Training: 7-10 Days Headquarters; Varies On-Site; As Needed On-Site and Headquarters.

SPECIFIC EXPANSION PLANS:
US: No
Canada: No
Overseas: Japan, Poland, Denmark, Portugal, Australia, Turkey

Sales Training Systems
"We Understand Sales"

DEI FRANCHISE SYSTEMS

888 7th Ave., 9th Fl.
New York, NY 10106
Tel: (800) 224-2140 (212) 581-7390 + 223
Fax: (212) 245-7897
E-Mail: franchise@dei-sales.com
Web Site: www.dei-sales.com
Mr. Scott Forman, Franchise Sales

DEI Management offers you an exciting business opportunity - the chance to own your own firm in the $7.6 billion sales training industry. At the same time, you will enjoy the benefits of an outstanding franchising company with a proven selling system.

BACKGROUND:
Established: 1979; 1st Franchised: 2003
Franchised Units: 31
Company-Owned Units: 1
Total Units: 32
Dist.: US-28; CAN-2; O'seas-2
North America: 18 States
Density: 2 in NY
Projected New Units (12 Months): 50
Qualifications: 3, 2, 2, 3, 3, 3
Registered: CA,IN,MI,SD,DC

FINANCIAL/TERMS:
Cash Investment: $50K
Total Investment: $60-75K
Minimum Net Worth: NA
Fees: Franchise - $50K
Royalty - 7%; Ad. - 2+4%=6%
Earnings Claims Statement: No
Term of Contract (Years): 5/5/5/5
Avg. # Of Employees: 1 FT
Passive Ownership: Discouraged
Encourage Conversions: Yes
Area Develop. Agreements: Yes
Sub-Franchising Contracts: No
Expand In Territory: Yes
Space Needs: 900 SF; HB

SUPPORT & TRAINING:
Financial Assistance Provided: No
Site Selection Assistance: Yes
Lease Negotiation Assistance: NA
Co-Operative Advertising: NA
Franchisee Assoc./Member: No
Size Of Corporate Staff: 20
On-Going Support: A,B,C,D,E,F,G,H,I
Training: 2 Weeks Homebased; 2 Weeks at Headquarters.

SPECIFIC EXPANSION PLANS:
US: All United States
Canada: All Canada
Overseas: All Countries

ELS LANGUAGE CENTERS

400 Alexander Park
Princeton, NJ 08540-6306
Tel: (800) 468-8978 (609) 750-3508
Fax: (609) 750-3596
E-Mail: info@els.com
Web Site: www.els.com
Mr. Charles J. Gilbert, Director Worldwide Fran. Supp.

Leader in teaching English to the world. Franchises English-language schools overseas, students learn business English, conversational English, TOEFL and other programs. Franchisees also offer study-abroad programs and university placement assistance.

BACKGROUND: IFA MEMBER
Established: 1956; 1st Franchised: 1978
Franchised Units: 51
Company-Owned Units: 34
Total Units: 85
Dist.: US-33; CAN-1; O'seas-50
North America: 21 States, 1 Province

Density: 5 in CA, 2 in NY, 2 in FL
Projected New Units (12 Months): Unsure
Qualifications: 4, 4, 4, 3, 4, 5
Registered: None

FINANCIAL/TERMS:
Cash Investment: $100-300K
Total Investment: $100-300K
Minimum Net Worth: $250K
Fees: Franchise - $30K
Royalty - 5%; Ad. - 0%
Earnings Claims Statement: No
Term of Contract (Years): 10/10
Avg. # Of Employees: 6-20 FT
Passive Ownership: Discouraged
Encourage Conversions: Yes
Area Develop. Agreements: Yes/10-20
Sub-Franchising Contracts: No
Expand In Territory: Yes
Space Needs: Feasible SF; NA

SUPPORT & TRAINING:
Financial Assistance Provided: No
Site Selection Assistance: Yes
Lease Negotiation Assistance: No
Co-Operative Advertising: Yes
Franchisee Assoc./Member: No
Size Of Corporate Staff: 65
On-Going Support: C,D,G,H
Training: 2 Weeks Princeton, NJ.

SPECIFIC EXPANSION PLANS:
US: No
Canada: No
Overseas: Case by Case Basis

<< >>

EWF INTERNATIONAL

4900 Richmond Sq., # 105
Oklahoma City, OK 73118
Tel: (866) 831-3934 (405) 843-3934
Fax: (405) 843-3933
E-Mail: darcie@ewfinternational.com
Web Site: www.ewfinternational.com
Ms. Darcie Harris, Co-Owner

At EWF INTERNATIONAL, our focus is on professional women who are looking for something more. Our service is peer advisory groups for women executives and business owners. Our clients are professional women with business goals to achieve. Our franchisees quickly become valuable business resources. We offer business management, operational/sales training, ongoing mentoring, and access to our other franchisees who can provide 'been there, done that' assistance. It's the 'more' you've been dreaming of!

BACKGROUND: IFA MEMBER
Established: 1998; 1st Franchised: 2002
Franchised Units: 2
Company-Owned Units: 1
Total Units: 3
Dist.: US-3; CAN-0; O'seas-0
North America: 2 States
Density: 2 in OK, 1 in TX
Projected New Units (12 Months): 3
Qualifications: 2, 4, 5, 4, 5, 5
Registered: FL

FINANCIAL/TERMS:
Cash Investment: $25-30K
Total Investment: $25-30K
Minimum Net Worth: $40K
Fees: Franchise - $25K
Royalty - 15%; Ad. - 2%
Earnings Claims Statement: Yes
Term of Contract (Years): 5/5
Avg. # Of Employees: 1 FT, 1 PT
Passive Ownership: Not Allowed
Encourage Conversions: No
Area Develop. Agreements: No
Sub-Franchising Contracts: No
Expand In Territory: No
Space Needs: NA SF; HB

SUPPORT & TRAINING:
Financial Assistance Provided: No
Site Selection Assistance: NA
Lease Negotiation Assistance: NA
Co-Operative Advertising: No
Franchisee Assoc./Member: No
Size Of Corporate Staff: 2
On-Going Support: C,D,G,H,I
Training: 1 Week Corporate Headquarters Oklahoma City, OK; additional field training.

SPECIFIC EXPANSION PLANS:
US: All United States
Canada: No
Overseas: No

<< >>

EXECUTRAIN

11770 Haynes Bridge Rd., # 205
Alpharetta, GA 30004-1970
Tel: (800) 437-2034 (865) 458-6184
Fax: (770) 664-2006
E-Mail: rick@executrain.com
Web Site: www.executrain.com
Mr. Rich Karakis, Vice President Franchising

EXECUTRAIN is the world's leading computer-training franchise. EXECUTRAIN offers over 800+ courses in the most popular business-applications software in order to increase the productivity of business people from all levels. This is achieved through instructor-led, hands-on training in a classroom setting.

BACKGROUND:
Established: 1984; 1st Franchised: 1986
Franchised Units: 116
Company-Owned Units: 35
Total Units: 151
Dist.: US-173; CAN-4; O'seas-41
North America: NR
Density: NR
Projected New Units (12 Months): 18
Qualifications: 5, 5, 3, 3, 1, 5
Registered: All States

FINANCIAL/TERMS:
Cash Investment: $200K
Total Investment: $200-250K
Minimum Net Worth: $250K
Fees: Franchise - $30K
Royalty - 6-9%; Ad. - 1.5%
Earnings Claims Statement: No
Term of Contract (Years): 7/7
Avg. # Of Employees: 15-20 FT/PT
Passive Ownership: Discouraged
Encourage Conversions: No
Area Develop. Agreements: No
Sub-Franchising Contracts: No
Expand In Territory: Yes
Space Needs: 3,500 SF; FS

SUPPORT & TRAINING:
Financial Assistance Provided: Yes(D)
Site Selection Assistance: Yes
Lease Negotiation Assistance: Yes
Co-Operative Advertising: No
Franchisee Assoc./Member: NR
Size Of Corporate Staff: 110
On-Going Support: NR
Training: 5 Days GM Training; 5 Days Instructor Training; 5 Days Sale Training -- all Atlanta, GA.

SPECIFIC EXPANSION PLANS:
US: No
Canada: All Canada
Overseas: All Countries

<< >>

GROWTH COACH, THE

10700 Montgomery Rd., # 300
Cincinnati, OH 45242
Tel: (888) 292-7992 (513) 563-0570
Fax: (513) 563-2691
E-Mail: inquiry@thegrowthcoach.com
Web Site: www.thegrowthcoach.com

Mr. Daniel Murphy, President

Business coaching, with emphasis on a refined strategic process for business owners, executives and self-employed, to drive success while balancing life.

BACKGROUND: IFA MEMBER
Established: 2002; 1st Franchised: 2003
Franchised Units: 70
Company-Owned Units: 0
Total Units: 70
Dist.: US-69; CAN-1; O'seas-0
North America: NR
Density: NR
Projected New Units (12 Months): 60
Qualifications: 2, 3, 1, 3, 3, 4
Registered: All States

FINANCIAL/TERMS:
Cash Investment: $10K
Total Investment: $22.5-34.9K
Minimum Net Worth: $10K
Fees: Franchise - $21.9K
Royalty - 6%; Ad. - 0%
Earnings Claims Statement: No
Term of Contract (Years): 10/10/10
Avg. # Of Employees: 1 FT
Passive Ownership: Not Allowed
Encourage Conversions: Yes
Area Develop. Agreements: Yes
Sub-Franchising Contracts: No
Expand In Territory: Yes
Space Needs: NA SF; HB

SUPPORT & TRAINING:
Financial Assistance Provided: Yes(D)
Site Selection Assistance: NA
Lease Negotiation Assistance: NA
Co-Operative Advertising: NA
Franchisee Assoc./Member: No
Size Of Corporate Staff: 10
On-Going Support: B,C,D,E,G,H,I
Training: 5 Business Days Cincinnati, OH.

SPECIFIC EXPANSION PLANS:
US: All United States
Canada: All Canada
Overseas: All Countries

<< >>

Top 100

HUNTINGTON LEARNING CENTER
496 Kinderkamack Rd.
Oradell, NJ 07649-1512
Tel: (800) 653-8400 (201) 261-8400
Fax: (201) 261-3233
E-Mail: franchise@huntingtonlearning.com
Web Site: www.huntingtonlearning.com/franchise
Mr. Russ Miller, VP Business Development

Offers tutoring to 5-19 year-olds, and occasionally to adults, in reading, writing, language development study skills and mathematics, as well as programs to prepare for standardized entrance exams. Instruction is offered in a tutorial setting and is predominately remedial in nature, although some enrichment is offered. SAT Prep.

BACKGROUND: IFA MEMBER
Established: 1977; 1st Franchised: 1985
Franchised Units: 234
Company-Owned Units: 33
Total Units: 267
Dist.: US-267; CAN-0; O'seas-0
North America: 34 States
Density: 26 in NY, 21 in CA, 20 in FL
Projected New Units (12 Months): 40
Qualifications: 5, 3, 1, 3, 1, 5
Registered: All Except HI, ND, SD

FINANCIAL/TERMS:
Cash Investment: $60K
Total Investment: $190-290K
Minimum Net Worth: $250K
Fees: Franchise - $40K
Royalty - 8%/$1.5K Min.; Ad. - 2%/$500 Min
Earnings Claims Statement: Yes
Term of Contract (Years): 10/10
Avg. # Of Employees: 2-4 FT, 12-20 PT
Passive Ownership: Not 1st Yr.
Encourage Conversions: No
Area Develop. Agreements: Yes
Sub-Franchising Contracts: No
Expand In Territory: No
Space Needs: 2,000-2,500 SF; SF, SC, RM

SUPPORT & TRAINING:
Financial Assistance Provided: Yes(D)
Site Selection Assistance: Yes
Lease Negotiation Assistance: Yes
Co-Operative Advertising: Yes
Franchisee Assoc./Member: Yes/Yes
Size Of Corporate Staff: 70
On-Going Support: B,C,D,E,F,G,h,I
Training: 4 Weeks at Oradell, NJ (Corporate Headquarters). On-Going Regional.

SPECIFIC EXPANSION PLANS:
US: Contiguous US
Canada: No
Overseas: No

JOHN CASABLANCAS MODELING AND CAREER CENTERS
648 Trade Center Blvd.
Chesterfield, MO 63005
Tel: (636) 536-6100
Fax: (636) 536-4352
E-Mail: info@jcasablancas.com
Web Site: www.jc-centers.com
Ms. Charyn Parker Urban, Dir. Franchise Development

Our franchised schools and in-house modeling agencies provide cutting-edge professional modeling, personal image development and film and TV acting programs and workshops. Created by John Casablancas, former Chairman of Elite Model Management.

BACKGROUND: IFA MEMBER
Established: 1979; 1st Franchised: 1979
Franchised Units: 49
Company-Owned Units: 0
Total Units: 49
Dist.: US-41; CAN-1; O'seas-7
North America: 25 States, 1 Province
Density: 5 in FL
Projected New Units (12 Months): 2
Qualifications: 5, 5, 5, 4, 5, 5
Registered: CA,FL,HI,IL,IN,MD,MN.NB,NY,RI,VA,WA,WI

FINANCIAL/TERMS:
Cash Investment: $90-195K
Total Investment: $90-200K
Minimum Net Worth: NR
Fees: Franchise - $40K
Royalty - 7%; Ad. - 3%
Earnings Claims Statement: No
Term of Contract (Years): 10/10
Avg. # Of Employees: 4 FT, 6-8 PT
Passive Ownership: Not Allowed
Encourage Conversions: Yes
Area Develop. Agreements: No
Sub-Franchising Contracts: No
Expand In Territory: Yes
Space Needs: 1,800-2,500 SF; SC, RM

SUPPORT & TRAINING:
Financial Assistance Provided: No
Site Selection Assistance: Yes
Lease Negotiation Assistance: Yes
Co-Operative Advertising: Yes
Franchisee Assoc./Member: No
Size Of Corporate Staff: 8
On-Going Support: b,C,D,E,g,h
Training: 2-3 Days NY; 3 Days in Field.

SPECIFIC EXPANSION PLANS:
US: All United States
Canada: All Canada

Overseas: Far East, Europe, Latin America

<< >>

LEADERSHIP MANAGEMENT, INC.

4567 Lake Shore Dr.
Waco, TX 76710
Tel: (800) 568-1241
Fax: (254) 757-4600
E-Mail: info@lmi-inc.com
Web Site: www.lmi-bus.com
Mr. Tony Stigliano, Dir. Development Opportunities

Own a professional training dealership that helps companies achieve success. Producing measurable results for clients since 1966; interface with business executives; programs and a process to develop leaders, managers and executives; proven success system; long-term client relationships; national network. Call (800) 365-7437 or send resume.

BACKGROUND:
Established: 1965; 1st Franchised: 1965
Franchised Units: 177
Company-Owned Units: 0
Total Units: 177
Dist.: US-365; CAN-0; O'seas-0
North America: NR
Density: NR
Projected New Units (12 Months): 60
Qualifications: , , , , ,
Registered: All States

FINANCIAL/TERMS:
Cash Investment: NR
Total Investment: NA
Minimum Net Worth: NR
Fees: Franchise - NR
Royalty - 0%; Ad. - 0%
Earnings Claims Statement: No
Term of Contract (Years): 1
Avg. # Of Employees: Varies
Passive Ownership: Discouraged
Encourage Conversions: NA
Area Develop. Agreements: No
Sub-Franchising Contracts: No
Expand In Territory: No
Space Needs: NR SF; NR

SUPPORT & TRAINING:
Financial Assistance Provided: Yes(D)
Site Selection Assistance: NA
Lease Negotiation Assistance: NA
Co-Operative Advertising: NA
Franchisee Assoc./Member: NR
Size Of Corporate Staff: 25
On-Going Support: D,C,H,I
Training: 1-3 Weeks.

SPECIFIC EXPANSION PLANS:
US: All United States
Canada: All Canada
Overseas: No

<< >>

NEW HORIZONS COMPUTER LEARNING CENTER

1900 S. State College Blvd., # 200
Anaheim, CA 92806
Tel: (714) 940-8230
Fax: (714) 938-6008
E-Mail: ralph.loberger@newhorizons.com
Web Site: www.newhorizons.com
Mr. Ralph Loberger, VP Franchise Development

NEW HORIZONS COMPUTER LEARNING CENTERS, Inc. is the world's largest independent IT training company, meeting the needs of more than 2.4 million students each year. NEW HORIZONS offers a variety of flexible training choices: instructor-led classes, Web-based training, computer-based training, computer labs, certification exam preparation tools and 24-hour, 7-day-a-week help-desk support.

BACKGROUND: IFA MEMBER
Established: 1982; 1st Franchised: 1992
Franchised Units: 231
Company-Owned Units: 25
Total Units: 256
Dist.: US-139; CAN-1; O'seas-116
North America: 42 States, 1 Province
Density: 14 in CA, 9 in FL, 6 in NY
Projected New Units (12 Months): 10
Qualifications: 5, 5, 2, 3, 3, 5
Registered: All States

FINANCIAL/TERMS:
Cash Investment: $150-200K
Total Investment: $400-500K
Minimum Net Worth: $500K
Fees: Franchise - $25-75K
Royalty - 6%; Ad. - 1%
Earnings Claims Statement: No
Term of Contract (Years): 10/5
Avg. # Of Employees: 15 FT
Passive Ownership: Discouraged
Encourage Conversions: Yes
Area Develop. Agreements: Yes/10
Sub-Franchising Contracts: Yes
Expand In Territory: Yes
Space Needs: 4,000-5,000 SF; FS, OB, IP, Business Park

SUPPORT & TRAINING:
Financial Assistance Provided: Yes(D)
Site Selection Assistance: Yes
Lease Negotiation Assistance: Yes
Co-Operative Advertising: Yes
Franchisee Assoc./Member: Yes/Yes
Size Of Corporate Staff: 200+
On-Going Support: B,C,D,E,G,H
Training: 2 Weeks Headquarters; 1 Week Franchise Location; 2 Days Regional.

SPECIFIC EXPANSION PLANS:
US: All United States
Canada: All Canada
Overseas: All Countries

<< >>

OXFORD LEARNING

747 Hyde Park Rd., # 230
London, ON N6H 3S3 CANADA
Tel: (888) 559-2212 (519) 473-1207 + 101
Fax: (519) 473-6086
E-Mail: rkipp@oxfordlearning.com
Web Site: www.oxfordlearning.com
Mr. Ron Kipp, Director Franchise Development

Join the leaders in supplemental education. Our proprietary curriculum developed over the past 20 years, ensures that your students will make impressive academic gains while developing higher self-esteem. Successful, confident students and happy parents mean referrals and a growing business. We will assist you every step of the way, providing the proven training, marketing, and business expertise you will need. Excellent territories available.

BACKGROUND: IFA MEMBER
Established: 1984; 1st Franchised: 1990
Franchised Units: 94
Company-Owned Units: 4
Total Units: 98
Dist.: US-18; CAN-79; O'seas-1
North America: 10 States, 7 Provinces
Density: 52 in ON, 6 in NJ
Projected New Units (12 Months): 30
Qualifications: 4, 3, 2, 3, 4, 5

Registered: CA,MI,MD,NY,VA

FINANCIAL/TERMS:

Cash Investment: $50-75K
Total Investment: $125-215K
Minimum Net Worth: $200K
Fees: Franchise - $39.5K
Royalty - 10%; Ad. - 3%
Earnings Claims Statement: No
Term of Contract (Years): 10/10
Avg. # Of Employees: 3 FT, 5 PT
Passive Ownership: Not Allowed
Encourage Conversions: No
Area Develop. Agreements: Yes
Sub-Franchising Contracts: No
Expand In Territory: Yes
Space Needs: 1,600-2,000 SF; SF, SC

SUPPORT & TRAINING:

Financial Assistance Provided: No
Site Selection Assistance: Yes
Lease Negotiation Assistance: Yes
Co-Operative Advertising: Yes
Franchisee Assoc./Member: Yes/Yes
Size Of Corporate Staff: 21
On-Going Support: B,C,D,E,F,G,H,I
Training: 2 Weeks London, ON.

SPECIFIC EXPANSION PLANS:

US: Northeast South East Central
Canada: All Canada
Overseas: India, Hong Kong, Japan, Germany, Korea

<< >>

PERSONAL BEST KARATE

250 E. Main St.
Norton, MA 02766-2436
Tel: (508) 285-5425 + 101
Fax: (508) 285-7064
E-Mail: founder@personalbestkarate.com
Web Site: www.personalbestkarate.com
Mr. Christopher Rappold, Chief Executive Officer

PERSONAL BEST KARATE is a one-of-a-kind franchise opportunity that combines physical fitness, character education and self-defense into a well-designed business format. If you enjoy bringing out the best in people, both physically and mentally, this is the opportunity for you.

BACKGROUND: IFA MEMBER

Established: 1991; 1st Franchised: 1999
Franchised Units: 3
Company-Owned Units: 2
Total Units: 5
Dist.: US-5; CAN-0; O'seas-0
North America: 1 State
Density: 5 in MA
Projected New Units (12 Months): 5
Qualifications: 4, 4, 3, 3, 4, 4
Registered: NR

FINANCIAL/TERMS:

Cash Investment: $63-113K
Total Investment: $63-113K
Minimum Net Worth: $100K
Fees: Franchise - $34K
Royalty - 10%; Ad. - 6%
Earnings Claims Statement: NR
Term of Contract (Years): 5/5/5/5
Avg. # Of Employees: 2 FT, 1 PT
Passive Ownership: Not Allowed
Encourage Conversions: Yes
Area Develop. Agreements: No
Sub-Franchising Contracts: No
Expand In Territory: Yes
Space Needs: 3,000 SF; FS, SF, SC

SUPPORT & TRAINING:

Financial Assistance Provided: No
Site Selection Assistance: Yes
Lease Negotiation Assistance: Yes
Co-Operative Advertising: Yes
Franchisee Assoc./Member: No
Size Of Corporate Staff: 2
On-Going Support: C,D,E,F,H
Training: 8 Half-Day Training Sessions at Norton, MA Headquarters.

SPECIFIC EXPANSION PLANS:

US: MA Only
Canada: No
Overseas: No

<< >>

PROFESSIONAL DYNAMETRIC PROGRAMS/PDP

750 E. Hwy. 24, Bldg. I
Woodland Park, CO 80863
Tel: (719) 687-6074
Fax: (719) 687-8587
E-Mail: brenth@pdpnet.com
Web Site: www.pdpnet.com
Mr. Brent W. Hubby, President

PDP is a business-to-business license that offers independence with lucrative opportunity in the executive management market. Sell, train, consult and service large and small businesses in highly successful and proven programs for hiring, motivating, stress managing and evaluating. There is automatic, repeat business, low overhead, no inventory and no leases.

BACKGROUND:

Established: 1978; 1st Franchised: 1980
Franchised Units: 24
Company-Owned Units: 0
Total Units: 24
Dist.: US-17; CAN-4; O'seas-3
North America: 28 States, 3 Provinces
Density: 4 in TX, 3 in CO, 2 in CA.
Projected New Units (12 Months): 5
Qualifications: 4, 4, 4, 4, 5, 4
Registered: CA

FINANCIAL/TERMS:

Cash Investment: $5-19.5K
Total Investment: $31.5-49.5K
Minimum Net Worth: $250K
Fees: Franchise - $29.5K
Royalty - 0%; Ad. - 0%
Earnings Claims Statement: No
Term of Contract (Years): 7
Avg. # Of Employees: 1 FT
Passive Ownership: Discouraged
Encourage Conversions: NA
Area Develop. Agreements: No
Sub-Franchising Contracts: Yes
Expand In Territory: Yes
Space Needs: NA SF; HB, ES, OB

SUPPORT & TRAINING:

Financial Assistance Provided: No
Site Selection Assistance: NA
Lease Negotiation Assistance: NA
Co-Operative Advertising: NA
Franchisee Assoc./Member: No
Size Of Corporate Staff: 7
On-Going Support: c,d,F,G,h,i,
Training: 1 Week Corporate; 2 Days Field; 3 Days Corporate.

SPECIFIC EXPANSION PLANS:

US: All United States
Canada: All Canada
Overseas: All Countries

<< >>

RENAISSANCE EXECUTIVE FORUMS

7855 Ivanhoe Ave., # 300
La Jolla, CA 92037-4500
Tel: (858) 551-6600
Fax: (858) 551-8777
E-Mail: pete@executiveforums.com
Web Site: www.executiveforums.com
Mr. Pete Clancey, Director Business Development

RENAISSANCE EXECUTIVE FORUMS bring together top executives from similarly sized, non-competing companies into an advisory board process in which thousands of chief executives throughout the world participate. These CEOs, presidents and owners meet once a month in small groups of approximately eight to fourteen individuals. The meetings provide an environment designed to address the opportunities and challenges they face as individuals and leaders of their respective organizations.

BACKGROUND: IFA MEMBER
Established: 1994; 1st Franchised: 1994
Franchised Units: 42
Company-Owned Units: 0
Total Units: 42
Dist.: US-34; CAN-2; O'seas-6
North America: 19 States
Density: 8 in CA, 3 in FL
Projected New Units (12 Months): 6
Qualifications: 4, 5, 4, 4, 4, 5
Registered: All States

FINANCIAL/TERMS:
Cash Investment: $39.5-76K
Total Investment: $70-110K
Minimum Net Worth: $500K
Fees: Franchise - $39.5K
Royalty - 20%; Ad. - 0%
Earnings Claims Statement: No
Term of Contract (Years): 10/10
Avg. # Of Employees: 1 FT
Passive Ownership: Not Allowed
Encourage Conversions: NA
Area Develop. Agreements: Yes/10
Sub-Franchising Contracts: No
Expand In Territory: Yes
Space Needs: NA SF; Executive Suite

SUPPORT & TRAINING:
Financial Assistance Provided: No
Site Selection Assistance: No
Lease Negotiation Assistance: No
Co-Operative Advertising: No
Franchisee Assoc./Member: Yes/Yes
Size Of Corporate Staff: 15
On-Going Support: A,a,B,b,C,c,D,G,H,h
Training: 7 Days La Jolla, CA.

SPECIFIC EXPANSION PLANS:
US: All United States
Canada: All Canada
Overseas: All Countries

<< >>

SANDLER SALES INSTITUTE

10411 Stevenson Rd.
Stevenson, MD 21153
Tel: (800) 669-3537 (410) 559-2033
Fax: (410) 358-7858
E-Mail: rtaylor@sandler.com
Web Site: www.sandler.com
Mr. Ron Taylor, Director of Franchising

SANDLER SALES INSTITUTE offers a distinctive style of training to companies and individuals in the fields of sales, management consulting and leadership development through on-going seminars and workshops. SANDLER SALES INSTITUTE provides intensive training, a unique lead generation program, on-going day-to-day support and protected territories to help you succeed in business.

BACKGROUND: IFA MEMBER
Established: 1967; 1st Franchised: 1983
Franchised Units: 175
Company-Owned Units: 0
Total Units: 175
Dist.: US-157; CAN-15; O'seas-3
North America: NR
Density: 14 in OH, 13 in CA, 13 in PA
Projected New Units (12 Months): 20
Qualifications: 3, 5, 5, 3, 1, 5
Registered: All States Except HI,AB

FINANCIAL/TERMS:
Cash Investment: $50K
Total Investment: $56.4-73.2K
Minimum Net Worth: NA
Fees: Franchise - $50K
Royalty - $1160/Mo.; Ad. - NA
Earnings Claims Statement: No
Term of Contract (Years): 5/5/5/5
Avg. # Of Employees: 1 FT, 1 PT
Passive Ownership: Discouraged
Encourage Conversions: NA
Area Develop. Agreements: No
Sub-Franchising Contracts: No
Expand In Territory: Yes
Space Needs: NA SF; NA

SUPPORT & TRAINING:
Financial Assistance Provided: No
Site Selection Assistance: Yes
Lease Negotiation Assistance: NA
Co-Operative Advertising: No
Franchisee Assoc./Member: Yes/Yes
Size Of Corporate Staff: 26
On-Going Support: g,H,I
Training: 5 Days Home Office/Other; 1 Day Home Office/Other.

SPECIFIC EXPANSION PLANS:
US: All United States
Canada: All Canada
Overseas: All Countries

<< >>

SCOOTER'S PLACE

221 Bonita Ave., # 240
Piedmont, CA 94611
Tel: (510) 839-5471
Fax: (510) 839-2104
E-Mail: rob@worldfranchising.com
Web Site: www.scootersplace.com
Mr. Jeffrey A. Scooter, President

Unique opportunity in the highly profitable, growth business of removing unwanted facial and body hair. Specializing in Scooter's Bikini Cuts, guaranteed to last 3 months. Custom merkin fitting. Free initial consultation. Average customer spends $225 per year for services. Great customer loyalty. Complete turn-key operation. Initial investment under $25,000.

BACKGROUND:
Established: 1982; 1st Franchised: 1986
Franchised Units: 28
Company-Owned Units: 10
Total Units: 38
Dist.: US-12; CAN-4; O'seas-5
North America: 5 States, 1 Province
Density: 7 in CA, 2 in KY, 1 in TN
Projected New Units (12 Months): 3
Qualifications: , , , , ,
Registered: NR

FINANCIAL/TERMS:
Cash Investment: $25-45K
Total Investment: $35-75K
Minimum Net Worth: NR
Fees: Franchise - $12K
Royalty - 4%; Ad. - 1%
Earnings Claims Statement: Yes
Term of Contract (Years): 10/10
Avg. # Of Employees: 2 FT, 3 PT
Passive Ownership: Discouraged
Encourage Conversions: Yes
Area Develop. Agreements: Yes/10
Sub-Franchising Contracts: No
Expand In Territory: No
Space Needs: 1,500-1,800 SF; FS, SF, SC, RM

SUPPORT & TRAINING:
Financial Assistance Provided: Yes(D)
Site Selection Assistance: Yes
Lease Negotiation Assistance: Yes
Co-Operative Advertising: Yes
Franchisee Assoc./Member: NR
Size Of Corporate Staff: 5
On-Going Support: A,C,D,G,H,I
Training: 4 Weeks Headquarters; 2 Weeks On-Site.

SPECIFIC EXPANSION PLANS:
US: All United States

Canada: BC, ON
Overseas: No

<< >>

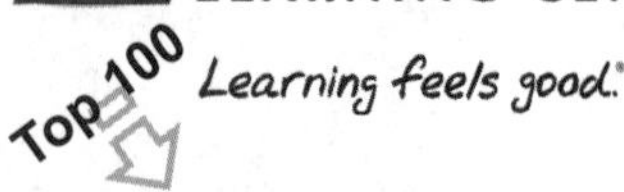

SYLVAN LEARNING CENTERS

1001 Fleet St.
Baltimore, MD 21202-4382
Tel: (800) 627-4276 + 8768 (410) 843-8000
Fax: (410) 843-6265
E-Mail: pete.lorenzo@educate.com
Web Site: www.sylvanfranchise.com
Mr. Pete Lorenzo, Director Franchise Development

SYLVAN is the leading provider of educational services to families, schools and industry. SYLVAN services kindergarten through adult-levels from more than 1,000 SYLVAN LEARNING CENTERS worldwide.

BACKGROUND: IFA MEMBER
Established: 1979; 1st Franchised: 1980
Franchised Units: 900
Company-Owned Units: 150
Total Units: 1,050
Dist.: US-971; CAN-75; O'seas-4
North America: 50 States
Density: CA, TX, NY
Projected New Units (12 Months): 50
Qualifications: 4, 4, 2, 3, 2, 5
Registered: All States

FINANCIAL/TERMS:
Cash Investment: $101.1-171.3K
Total Investment: $121.1-219.3K
Minimum Net Worth: $250K
Fees: Franchise - $38-46K
Royalty - 8-9%; Ad. - 5-13%
Earnings Claims Statement: Yes
Term of Contract (Years): 10/10
Avg. # Of Employees: 2 FT, 5 PT
Passive Ownership: Not Allowed
Encourage Conversions: No
Area Develop. Agreements: Yes/Varies
Sub-Franchising Contracts: No
Expand In Territory: Yes
Space Needs: 1,600-2,500 SF; FS, SF, SC

SUPPORT & TRAINING:
Financial Assistance Provided: Yes(B)
Site Selection Assistance: Yes
Lease Negotiation Assistance: No
Co-Operative Advertising: Yes
Franchisee Assoc./Member: Yes
Size Of Corporate Staff: 500
On-Going Support: B,C,D,E,G,H,I
Training: 6 Days Baltimore, MD; 5 Days in Various Other Locations.

SPECIFIC EXPANSION PLANS:
US: All United States
Canada: All Canada
Overseas: Asia, Europe, South America

<< >>

VELOCITY SPORTS PERFORMANCE

3650 Brookside Pkwy., # 300
Alpharetta, GA 30022
Tel: (866) 955-0400 (678) 990-2555
Fax: (678) 990-2560
E-Mail: info@velocitysp.com
Web Site: www.velocitysp.com
Mr. Tom Camplese, Executive Vice President

VELOCITY SPORTS PERFORMANCE provides people who are passionate about kids and sports the opportunity to combine that with their passion for business. By investing in a VELOCITY SPORTS PERFORMANCE training center, franchise owners offer athletes of all ages and skill sets the chance to train in state-of-the-art facilities, under professional, certified coaches and ultimately give them the chance to take their athletic performance to the highest levels.

BACKGROUND: IFA MEMBER
Established: 1999; 1st Franchised: 2002
Franchised Units: 43
Company-Owned Units: 1
Total Units: 44
Dist.: US-43; CAN-1; O'seas-0
North America: 23 States
Density: 7 in TX, 4 in NC, 4 in VA
Projected New Units (12 Months): ~50
Qualifications: 5, 5, 2, 4, 3, 5
Registered: All States

FINANCIAL/TERMS:
Cash Investment: $150K
Total Investment: $250-650K
Minimum Net Worth: $300-500K
Fees: Franchise - $54K
Royalty - 2-6%; Ad. - $2.5K/Mo.
Earnings Claims Statement: No
Term of Contract (Years): 10/10
Avg. # Of Employees: 8 FT
Passive Ownership: Discouraged
Encourage Conversions: NA
Area Develop. Agreements: Yes/10
Sub-Franchising Contracts: Yes
Expand In Territory: Yes
Space Needs: 15,000-20,000 SF; FS, SF, SC, RM

SUPPORT & TRAINING:
Financial Assistance Provided: Yes(I)
Site Selection Assistance: Yes
Lease Negotiation Assistance: Yes
Co-Operative Advertising: No
Franchisee Assoc./Member: Yes/Yes
Size Of Corporate Staff: 22
On-Going Support: a,B,C,D,E,G,H,I
Training: 2 Weeks Alpharetta, GA.

SPECIFIC EXPANSION PLANS:
US: All United States
Canada: All Canada
Overseas: Australia and others

<< >>

Employment & Personnel

Chapter 12

Employment & Personnel Industry Profile

Total # Franchisors in Industry Group	65
Total # Franchised Units in Industry Group	4,848
Total # Company-Owned Units in Industry Group	3,228
Total # Operating Units in Industry Group	8,076
Average # Franchised Units/Franchisor	74.6
Average # Company-Owned Units/Franchisor	49.7
Average # Total Units/Franchisor	124.2
Ratio of Total # Franchised Units/Total # Company-Owned Units	1.5:1
Industry Survey Participants	34
Representing % of Industry	52.3%
Average Franchise Fee*:	$24.6K
Average Total Investment*:	$102.3K
Average On-Going Royalty Fee*:	9.2%

*If a range was provided, the mid-point of the range was used. See detailed profiles for actual ranges.

Five Largest Participants in Survey

Company	# Franchised Units	# Co-Owned Units	# Total Units	Franchise Fee	On-Going Royalty	Total Investment
1. Management Recruiters/Sales Consultants	1,000	32	1,032	$72.5K	7%	$110-145K
2. Spherion	155	523	678	$10-15K	3-6%/25%	$68.3-391.7K
3. Express Personnel Services	457	0	457	$25K	8-9%	$120-170K
4. Home Instead Senior Care	448	2	450	$23.5K	5%	$30-39K
5. Home Helpers	325	0	325	$18.9K	6-4% Varies	$22.5-35.9K

All of the data provided are proprietary and should not be quoted without acknowledging *Bond's Franchise Guide.*

@WORK PERSONNEL SERVICES

3215 John Sevier Hwy.
Knoxville, TN 37920
Tel: (800) 233-6846 (865) 609-6911
Fax: (865) 573-1171
E-Mail: rmitchell@atworkpersonnel.com
Web Site: www.atworkpersonnel.com
Mr. Robert Mitchell, Director Franchise Sales

ATWORK PERSONNEL SERVICES announces its new 3-for-1 Franchise Program. For the cost of one franchise, ATWORK offers temporary help, staff leasing and permanent placement programs for its franchisees. Here are some benefits of becoming a member of ATWORK's network: franchise fee - $11,500; training fee - $2,500; sliding volume discount sale for royalty and service fees. Call our franchise sales department today to receive our information package.

BACKGROUND: IFA MEMBER
Established: 1990; 1st Franchised: 1992
Franchised Units: 62
Company-Owned Units: 1
Total Units: 63
Dist.: US-40; CAN-0; O'seas-0
North America: 12 States
Density: 15 in TN, 3 in NC, 2 in ME
Projected New Units (12 Months): 24
Qualifications: 3, 2, 3, 2, 3, 3
Registered: All States

FINANCIAL/TERMS:
Cash Investment: $15K
Total Investment: $35-75K
Minimum Net Worth: $75K
Fees: Franchise - $1K
Royalty - 8%; Ad. - 0%
Earnings Claims Statement: No
Term of Contract (Years): 10/5
Avg. # Of Employees: 3 FT, 1 PT
Passive Ownership: Discouraged
Encourage Conversions: Yes
Area Develop. Agreements: No
Sub-Franchising Contracts: No
Expand In Territory: Yes
Space Needs: 800 SF; FS, SF, SC, RM

SUPPORT & TRAINING:
Financial Assistance Provided: Yes
Site Selection Assistance: Yes
Lease Negotiation Assistance: No
Co-Operative Advertising: No
Franchisee Assoc./Member: No
Size Of Corporate Staff: 15
On-Going Support: A,C,D,H,I
Training: 4-5 Days in Corporate Office.

SPECIFIC EXPANSION PLANS:
US: All United States
Canada: No
Overseas: No

<< >>

AAA EMPLOYMENT

5533 Central Ave.
St. Petersburg, FL 33710
Tel: (800) 801-5627 (727) 343-3044
Fax: (727) 343-2953
E-Mail: aaaemployment@ij.net
Web Site: www.aaaemployment.net
Ms. Colleen Rounds, President

Employment agencies - permanent and temp to perm. A great business for women to help others secure their future while at the same time having their own business. A great way to develop financial security and business savvy. Trained to be successful - strong support system.

BACKGROUND:
Established: 1957; 1st Franchised: 1967
Franchised Units: 11
Company-Owned Units: 0
Total Units: 11
Dist.: US-11; CAN-0; O'seas-0
North America: 3 States
Density: 9 in FL, 1 in GA, 1 in MS
Projected New Units (12 Months): 10
Qualifications: 5, 3, 3, 4, 4, 4
Registered: FL

FINANCIAL/TERMS:
Cash Investment: $20K
Total Investment: $25K
Minimum Net Worth: $50K
Fees: Franchise - $25K
Royalty - 10%; Ad. - 0%
Earnings Claims Statement: Yes
Term of Contract (Years): 10/10
Avg. # Of Employees: 2-3 FT
Passive Ownership: Discouraged
Encourage Conversions: Yes
Area Develop. Agreements: Yes/2
Sub-Franchising Contracts: No
Expand In Territory: Yes
Space Needs: 400-800 SF; FS, SG, SC

SUPPORT & TRAINING:
Financial Assistance Provided: Yes(I)
Site Selection Assistance: Yes
Lease Negotiation Assistance: Yes
Co-Operative Advertising: No
Franchisee Assoc./Member: Yes/No
Size Of Corporate Staff: 1
On-Going Support: C,D,E,G,H,I
Training: 2 Weeks-30 Days in FL.

SPECIFIC EXPANSION PLANS:
US: All United States, SE First.
Canada: All Canada
Overseas: No

<< >>

ACCOUNTANTS INC.

111 Anza Blvd., # 400
Burlingame, CA 94010-1932
Tel: (800) 491-9411 (650) 579-1111
Fax: (650) 579-1927
E-Mail: driha@accountantsinc.com
Web Site: www.accountantsinc.com
Ms. DeAnna Riha, Franchise Development Manager

Temporary and full time placement of accounting and finance professionals.

BACKGROUND: IFA MEMBER
Established: 1986; 1st Franchised: 1994
Franchised Units: 16
Company-Owned Units: 21
Total Units: 37
Dist.: US-40; CAN-0; O'seas-0
North America: 13 States
Density: 19 in CA, 3 in WA
Projected New Units (12 Months): 5
Qualifications: 4, 5, 1, 1, 1, 5
Registered:CA,FL,IL,IN,MD,MI,MN,NY,OR,VA,WA,WI

FINANCIAL/TERMS:
Cash Investment: $174.5-224K
Total Investment: NR
Minimum Net Worth: $145-200K
Fees: Franchise - $30K
Royalty - 7.5-10%/4K; Ad. - 2.5 w/Co-Op
Earnings Claims Statement: Yes
Term of Contract (Years): 10/10
Avg. # Of Employees: 4 FT
Passive Ownership: Not Allowed
Encourage Conversions: NR
Area Develop. Agreements: NR
Sub-Franchising Contracts: No
Expand In Territory: Yes
Space Needs: NR SF; Class A Office

SUPPORT & TRAINING:
Financial Assistance Provided: No
Site Selection Assistance: Yes
Lease Negotiation Assistance: Yes
Co-Operative Advertising: Yes
Franchisee Assoc./Member: No
Size Of Corporate Staff: 35
On-Going Support: E,h,I
Training: Burlingame, CA; Franchisee's Location.

SPECIFIC EXPANSION PLANS:
US: All United States
Canada: No
Overseas: No

<< >>

AHEAD HUMAN RESOURCES
2209 Heather Ln.
Louisville, KY 40218
Tel: (877) 485-5858 (502) 485-1000
Fax: (502) 485-0801
E-Mail: franchise@aheadhr.com
Web Site: www.aheadhr.com
Ms. Suzie Taylor, Director Franchise

AHEAD HR brings a totally unique concept to the human resource franchise industry. SEE OUR WEBSITE! We're offering an industry-leading, top-flight temporary staffing franchise AND a PEO/HR outsourcing franchise, which is one-of-a-kind in the nation. If you want to be on the cutting edge of THE growth industry, SEE OUR WEBSITE!

BACKGROUND: IFA MEMBER
Established: 1995; 1st Franchised: 2001
Franchised Units: 11
Company-Owned Units: 2
Total Units: 13
Dist.: US-13; CAN-0; O'seas-0
North America: 8 States
Density: 2 in WI, 2 in CT, 2 in KY
Projected New Units (12 Months): 23
Qualifications: 5, 5, 3, 3, 2, 5
Registered: All Except CA,IL,HI,MD,MN,ND,RI,SD,UT,VA
FINANCIAL/TERMS:
Cash Investment: $17.7-23.7K
Total Investment: $105-171.6K
Minimum Net Worth: Varies
Fees: Franchise - $17.7-23.7K
Royalty - Varies; Ad. - Varies
Earnings Claims Statement: No
Term of Contract (Years): 5/5
Avg. # Of Employees: 1 FT, 1 PT
Passive Ownership: Discouraged
Encourage Conversions: NR
Area Develop. Agreements: No
Sub-Franchising Contracts: No
Expand In Territory: Yes
Space Needs: 100-1,500 SF; SF, SC, HB, Office
SUPPORT & TRAINING:
Financial Assistance Provided: NR
Site Selection Assistance: No
Lease Negotiation Assistance: No
Co-Operative Advertising: No
Franchisee Assoc./Member: Yes/Yes
Size Of Corporate Staff: 22
On-Going Support: A,C,D,I
Training: 2 Weeks Louisville, KY.
SPECIFIC EXPANSION PLANS:
US: All United States
Canada: No
Overseas: No

<< >>

AMERICAN RECRUITERS
6400 N. Andrews, # 100
Ft. Lauderdale, FL 33309-2075
Tel: (800) 493-9201 (954) 492-4592
Fax: (954) 958-3925
E-Mail: roy@arcimail.com
Web Site: www.americanrecruiters.com
Mr. Roy Lantz, VP Franchising

AMERICAN RECRUITERS offers retained and contingent executive search services, personnel placement and human resources consulting and training services. We provide exceptional training services and a state-of-the-art recruiting information system to get franchises up and running quickly. We also provide a universal database of clients, job orders and candidates which is uniquely shared by all franchises.

BACKGROUND:
Established: 1982; 1st Franchised: 1999
Franchised Units: 6
Company-Owned Units: 2
Total Units: 8
Dist.: US-8; CAN-0; O'seas-0
North America: 8 States
Density: 2 in FL, 1 in GA, 2 in VA
Projected New Units (12 Months): 12
Qualifications: 4, 5, 3, 3, 2, 5
Registered: FL,IL,IN,VA
FINANCIAL/TERMS:
Cash Investment: $75-100K
Total Investment: $100-150K
Minimum Net Worth: $250K
Fees: Franchise - $50K
Royalty - 7%; Ad. - NA
Earnings Claims Statement: No
Term of Contract (Years): 5/5
Avg. # Of Employees: 4-6 FT
Passive Ownership: Not Allowed
Encourage Conversions: NA
Area Develop. Agreements: No
Sub-Franchising Contracts: No
Expand In Territory: Yes
Space Needs: NA SF; NA
SUPPORT & TRAINING:
Financial Assistance Provided: No
Site Selection Assistance: Yes
Lease Negotiation Assistance: Yes
Co-Operative Advertising: Yes
Franchisee Assoc./Member: Yes/Yes
Size Of Corporate Staff: 50
On-Going Support: A,C,d,e,G,H,I
Training: 15 Business Days Ft. Lauderdale, FL.
SPECIFIC EXPANSION PLANS:
US: East Coast
Canada: No
Overseas: No

<< >>

ATC HEALTH CARE SERVICES
1983 Marcus Ave., # E122
New Hyde Park, NY 11042-1016
Tel: (800) 444-4633 (516) 750-1600
Fax: (516) 358-3678
E-Mail: pbarry@atchealthcare.com
Web Site: www.atchealthcare.com
Mr. Peter Barry, VP Franchising

ATC HEALTH CARE SERVICES provide temporary staffing and T. L. C.

BACKGROUND: IFA MEMBER
Established: 1984; 1st Franchised: 1995
Franchised Units: 37
Company-Owned Units: 0
Total Units: 37
Dist.: US-40; CAN-0; O'seas-0
North America: NR
Density: 5 in Ga, 5 in TN, 3 in PA
Projected New Units (12 Months): 15
Qualifications: 4, 4, 4, 5, 2, 5
Registered: All States
FINANCIAL/TERMS:
Cash Investment: $30-50K
Total Investment: $110K
Minimum Net Worth: $150K
Fees: Franchise - $19.5K
Royalty - Varies; Ad. - 0%
Earnings Claims Statement: No
Term of Contract (Years): 10/5/5
Avg. # Of Employees: 3 FT, 2 PT
Passive Ownership: Allowed
Encourage Conversions: Yes
Area Develop. Agreements: Yes/20
Sub-Franchising Contracts: No
Expand In Territory: Yes
Space Needs: 1,000 SF; FS, SF, SC
SUPPORT & TRAINING:
Financial Assistance Provided: Yes(D)
Site Selection Assistance: Yes
Lease Negotiation Assistance: No
Co-Operative Advertising: No
Franchisee Assoc./Member: No
Size Of Corporate Staff: 35
On-Going Support: A,B,C,D,E,G,H
Training: 1 Week Corporate Headquarters.
SPECIFIC EXPANSION PLANS:
US: All United States
Canada: All Canada

Overseas: No

<< >>

ATS PERSONNEL

9700 Philips Hwy., # 101
Jacksonville, FL 32256
Tel: (800) 346-5574 (904) 645-9505
Fax: (904) 645-0390
E-Mail: carl@ats-services.com
Web Site: www.ats-services.com
Mr. Carl Carver, Chief Operating Officer

ATS offers a unique franchise opportunity with three niche businesses in the temporary staffing industry. With over 19 years' experience, we've perfected systems for the temporary and permanent placement of office clerical, light industrial, professional and health-related positions. The three niche areas are: ATS PERSONNEL for clerical and light industrial staffing, ATS PROFESSIONAL SERVICES for accounting and technical staffing and ATS HEALTH.

BACKGROUND:
Established: 1978; 1st Franchised: 1991
Franchised Units: 5
Company-Owned Units: 9
Total Units: 14
Dist.: US-14; CAN-0; O'seas-0
North America: 6 States
Density: 7 in GA, 2 in SC, 2 in LA
Projected New Units (12 Months): 4
Qualifications: 4, 5, 3, 3, 4, 5
Registered: FL,NY

FINANCIAL/TERMS:
Cash Investment: $35-50K
Total Investment: $75-110K
Minimum Net Worth: $100K
Fees: Franchise - $12.5K
Royalty - 6.9%; Ad. - 0.5%
Earnings Claims Statement: No
Term of Contract (Years): 10/5
Avg. # Of Employees: 2 FT, 1 PT
Passive Ownership: Not Allowed
Encourage Conversions: No
Area Develop. Agreements: No
Sub-Franchising Contracts: No
Expand In Territory: Yes
Space Needs: 1,000 SF; SC

SUPPORT & TRAINING:
Financial Assistance Provided: Yes(I)
Site Selection Assistance: Yes
Lease Negotiation Assistance: Yes
Co-Operative Advertising: No
Franchisee Assoc./Member: No
Size Of Corporate Staff: 17
On-Going Support: A,B,C,D,E,F,G,h,I
Training: 2 Weeks at Corporate Office; 2 Weeks On-Site.

SPECIFIC EXPANSION PLANS:
US: FL, NC
Canada: No
Overseas: No

<< >>

CAREERS USA

6501 Congress Ave., # 200
Boca Raton, Fl 33487-2829
Tel: (888) 227-3375 (561) 995-7000
Fax: (561) 995-7001
E-Mail: tfeldman@careersusa.com
Web Site: www.careersusa.com
Ms. Trudy Feldman, EVP Franchcise Development

CAREERS USA provides temporary, temp to hire, and permanent personnel to businesses and corporations in your market area. CAREERS USA's proprietary computer software program computes the franchisee's temporary payroll, taxes and insurance. You, the franchisee, can download and analyze your sales, margins, rates, cash flow, etc. CAREERS USA finances 100% of your temporary payroll and 100% of your accounts receivable, helping you eliminate cash flow problems. Territories available nationally.

BACKGROUND: IFA MEMBER
Established: 1981; 1st Franchised: 1987
Franchised Units: 4
Company-Owned Units: 17
Total Units: 21
Dist.: US-23; CAN-0; O'seas-0
North America: 8 States
Density: 5 in PA, 5 in FL, 3 in IL
Projected New Units (12 Months): 12
Qualifications: 3, 4, 2, 3, 3, 4
Registered: All States

FINANCIAL/TERMS:
Cash Investment: $40-50K
Total Investment: $84-130K
Minimum Net Worth: $150K
Fees: Franchise - $14.5K
Royalty - 7%/Varies; Ad. - NA
Earnings Claims Statement: No
Term of Contract (Years): 10/5
Avg. # Of Employees: 3 FT
Passive Ownership: Discouraged
Encourage Conversions: Yes
Area Develop. Agreements: NA
Sub-Franchising Contracts: No
Expand In Territory: Yes
Space Needs: 1,000-1,500 SF; OB

SUPPORT & TRAINING:
Financial Assistance Provided: No
Site Selection Assistance: Yes
Lease Negotiation Assistance: Yes
Co-Operative Advertising: Yes
Franchisee Assoc./Member: No
Size Of Corporate Staff: 38
On-Going Support: A,b,C,D,E,G,H,I
Training: 2 Weeks Boca Raton, FL Headquarters; 1 Week Your Center Location.

SPECIFIC EXPANSION PLANS:
US: All United States
Canada: All Canada
Overseas: All Countries

<< >>

CHECKMATE SYSTEMS

661 St. Andrews Blvd.
Charleston, SC 29407
Tel: (800) 964-6298 (843) 763-9393
Fax: (843) 571-1851
E-Mail: checkmate@checkmatepeo.com
Web Site: www.checkmatepeo.com
Mr. Ed Arrington, VP Marketing

Employee leasing companies, also known as professional employers, are growing at over 33% per year. This new and largely untapped market has little competition and CHECKMATE is the only franchise in this new field which allows you to operate independently.

BACKGROUND:
Established: 1992; 1st Franchised: 1993
Franchised Units: 19
Company-Owned Units: 0
Total Units: 19
Dist.: US-19; CAN-0; O'seas-0
North America: 11 States
Density: 4 in LA, 2 in SC, 2 in AZ
Projected New Units (12 Months): 8
Qualifications: 3, 5, 1, 3, 4, 4
Registered: NR

FINANCIAL/TERMS:
Cash Investment: $35-85K
Total Investment: $30-75K
Minimum Net Worth: $100K
Fees: Franchise - $27.5K
Royalty - 7.5%; Ad. - 0%
Earnings Claims Statement: No
Term of Contract (Years): 10/5
Avg. # Of Employees: 3 FT, 1-2 PT
Passive Ownership: Not Allowed
Encourage Conversions: Yes
Area Develop. Agreements: No
Sub-Franchising Contracts: No
Expand In Territory: Yes
Space Needs: NA SF; HB, Rented Office

SUPPORT & TRAINING:
Financial Assistance Provided: No
Site Selection Assistance: NA
Lease Negotiation Assistance: NA
Co-Operative Advertising: NA
Franchisee Assoc./Member: No
Size Of Corporate Staff: 7
On-Going Support: G,h,I
Training: 1 Week New Orleans, LA.
SPECIFIC EXPANSION PLANS:
US: All United States
Canada: No
Overseas: No

<< >>

COMFORCARE SENIOR SERVICES
2510 Telegraph Rd., # 100
Bloomfield Hills, MI 48302
Tel: (800) 886-4044 (248) 745-9700
Fax: (248) 745-9763
E-Mail: home@comforcare.com
Web Site: www.comforcare.com
Ms. Janine Savoie, Franchise Assistant

Non-medical home care services for seniors and physically challenged individuals of all ages. Turnkey home care franchise operations for aspiring professionals. The broadest array of non-medical home care services in the field. Largest protected territories in the industry - up to 500,000 at no additional cost. Daily support of new franchises.

BACKGROUND: IFA MEMBER
Established: 1996; 1st Franchised: 2001
Franchised Units: 44
Company-Owned Units: 1
Total Units: 45
Dist.: US-45; CAN-0; O'seas-0
North America: 14 States
Density: 8 in CA , 4 in LA, 4 in OH
Projected New Units (12 Months): 24
Qualifications: 5, 4, 2, 3, 3, 5
Registered: CA,FL,HI,IL,IN,MI,MN,NY, OR,VA,WA,WI,DC
FINANCIAL/TERMS:
Cash Investment: $20-30K
Total Investment: $40-55
Minimum Net Worth: NA
Fees: Franchise - $15.5K
Royalty - 5-3% (Decl.); Ad. - 0%
Earnings Claims Statement: No
Term of Contract (Years): 10/10
Avg. # Of Employees: 12 FT
Passive Ownership: Discouraged
Encourage Conversions: Yes
Area Develop. Agreements: Yes/Varies
Sub-Franchising Contracts: No
Expand In Territory: Yes
Space Needs:250-450 SF; FS, Office Suite
SUPPORT & TRAINING:
Financial Assistance Provided: Yes(I)
Site Selection Assistance: Yes
Lease Negotiation Assistance: Yes
Co-Operative Advertising: Yes
Franchisee Assoc./Member: No
Size Of Corporate Staff: 12
On-Going Support: A,B,C,D,E,G,H,I
Training: 1 Week Bloomfield Hills, MI.
SPECIFIC EXPANSION PLANS:
US: All United States
Canada: No
Overseas: No

<< >>

DUNHILL STAFFING SYSTEMS
9190 Priority Way W. Dr., # 201
Indianapolis, IN 46240
Tel: (800) 386-7823 (631) 952-3000
Fax: (317) 818-4910
E-Mail: rrs@dunhillstaff.com
Web Site: www.dunhillstaff.com
Mr. Robert Stidham, VP Business Development

DUNHILL offers Professional Search and Temporary Staffing franchises. Our franchisees provide permanent executives, mid-level management, professionals, technical staffing and temporaries. Professional Search franchisees benefit from the industry's best interview-to-placement ratio and leading edge computerized placement matching system. All DUNHILL executives have 'front line' industry experience. Our temporary offices are supported with back-office accounting, including payroll and accounts receivable.

BACKGROUND:
Established: 1952; 1st Franchised: 1961
Franchised Units: 150
Company-Owned Units: 25
Total Units: 175
Dist.: US-151; CAN-4; O'seas-0
North America: 50 States
Density: 21 in TX, 19 in IN, 12 in CT
Projected New Units (12 Months): 12
Qualifications: 4, 3, 1, 3, 3, 5
Registered: All States
FINANCIAL/TERMS:
Cash Investment: $15-38K
Total Investment: $70-140K
Minimum Net Worth: $250K
Fees: Franchise - $15-38K
Royalty - 7% Perm./Varies; Ad. - 1% Perm.
Earnings Claims Statement: No
Term of Contract (Years): 10/10/5
Avg. # Of Employees: 2-3 FT
Passive Ownership: Discouraged
Encourage Conversions: Yes
Area Develop. Agreements: No
Sub-Franchising Contracts: No
Expand In Territory: Yes
Space Needs: 700-1,500 SF; FS, SF, SC, RM, Suites
SUPPORT & TRAINING:
Financial Assistance Provided: Yes(D)
Site Selection Assistance: Yes
Lease Negotiation Assistance: Yes
Co-Operative Advertising: Yes
Franchisee Assoc./Member: Yes
Size Of Corporate Staff: 45
On-Going Support: A,B,C,D,E,G,H,I
Training: 1-2 Weeks Corporate; 1-2 Weeks Field.
SPECIFIC EXPANSION PLANS:
US: All United States
Canada: All Canada
Overseas: No

<< >>

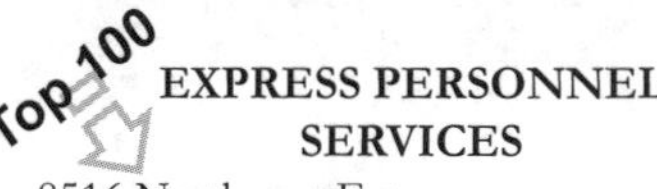

EXPRESS PERSONNEL SERVICES
8516 Northwest Expy.
Oklahoma City, OK 73162-5145
Tel: (877) 652-6400 (405) 840-5000
Fax: (405) 717-5665
E-Mail: franchising@expresspersonnel.com
Web Site: www.expressfranchising.com
Ms. Diane Carter, Manager of Franchise Admin.

EXPRESS PERSONNEL SERVICES is leading the industry in sales growth (2002 - 2004 YTD). EXPRESS PERSONNEL SERVICES offers an excellent franchise package, including temporary direct hire and professional/contract staffing.

BACKGROUND: IFA MEMBER
Established: 1983; 1st Franchised: 1985
Franchised Units: 457
Company-Owned Units: 0
Total Units: 457
Dist.: US-425; CAN-18; O'seas-12
North America: 45 States
Density: 44 in TX, 32 in OK, 23 in CA
Projected New Units (12 Months): 120
Qualifications: 4, 4, 3, 4, 4, 4
Registered: All States

FINANCIAL/TERMS:
Cash Investment: $120-170K
Total Investment: $120-170K
Minimum Net Worth: $100K
Fees: Franchise - $25K
Royalty - 8-9%; Ad. - 0.6%
Earnings Claims Statement: No
Term of Contract (Years): 5
Avg. # Of Employees: 3 FT
Passive Ownership: Not Allowed
Encourage Conversions: Yes
Area Develop. Agreements: No
Sub-Franchising Contracts: No
Expand In Territory: Yes
Space Needs: 1,200 SF; SC

SUPPORT & TRAINING:
Financial Assistance Provided: No
Site Selection Assistance: Yes
Lease Negotiation Assistance: Yes
Co-Operative Advertising: Yes
Franchisee Assoc./Member: No
Size Of Corporate Staff: 170
On-Going Support: A,C,D,E,G,H,I
Training: 2 Weeks Oklahoma City, OK; Plus 1 Week Certified Training Office (In Field).

SPECIFIC EXPANSION PLANS:
US: All United States
Canada: All Except AB
Overseas: UK, Australia.

<< >>

FPC (F-O-R-T-U-N-E PERSONNEL CONSULTANTS)

1140 Avenue of the Americas, 5th Fl.
New York, NY 10036-2711
Tel: (800) 886-7839 (212) 302-1141
Fax: (212) 302-2422
E-Mail: rherzog@fpcnational.com
Web Site: www.fpcnational.com
Mr. Ron Herzog, Executive Vice President

As one of the largest and most successful executive recruiting firms in the world, F-O-R-T-U-N-E PERSONNEL CONSULTANTS has set a distinguished standard of leadership and integrity in the executive placement industry. Franchisees enjoy all of today's technologies, along with good old-fashioned service. Intensive training and unparalleled support by industry experienced professionals securely places qualified candidates in their own professional business. Extensive on-going training.

BACKGROUND:
Established: 1959; 1st Franchised: 1973
Franchised Units: 80
Company-Owned Units: 1
Total Units: 81
Dist.: US-81; CAN-0; O'seas-0
North America: 28 States
Density: 7 in FL, 7 in MA, 7 in NJ
Projected New Units (12 Months): 12-15
Qualifications: 4, 3, 3, 4, 2, 4
Registered: All Except AB

FINANCIAL/TERMS:
Cash Investment: $31.4-63.9K
Total Investment: $83.1-128.6K
Minimum Net Worth: $250K
Fees: Franchise - $40K
Royalty - 7%; Ad. - 1%
Earnings Claims Statement: Yes
Term of Contract (Years): 20/10
Avg. # Of Employees: 3-5 FT, 1-2 PT
Passive Ownership: Discouraged
Encourage Conversions: NA
Area Develop. Agreements: No
Sub-Franchising Contracts: No
Expand In Territory: Yes
Space Needs: 1,000 SF; Commercial Office

SUPPORT & TRAINING:
Financial Assistance Provided: Yes(D)
Site Selection Assistance: Yes
Lease Negotiation Assistance: Yes
Co-Operative Advertising: Yes
Franchisee Assoc./Member: Yes
Size Of Corporate Staff: 15
On-Going Support: A,B,C,D,E,F,G,H,I
Training: 2 Weeks Home Office, New York, NY: 5 Days Franchise Location.

SPECIFIC EXPANSION PLANS:
US: All United States
Canada: All Canada
Overseas: No

<< >>

HOME HELPERS

10700 Montgomery Rd., # 300
Cincinnati, OH 45242
Tel: (800) 216-4196 (513) 563-8339
Fax: (513) 563-2691
E-Mail: inquiry@homehelpers.cc
Web Site: www.homehelpers.cc
Mr. John Buckles, President

Home-based, non-medical and personal care for seniors, new mothers and those recuperating from illness or sickness.

BACKGROUND: IFA MEMBER
Established: 1997; 1st Franchised: 1997
Franchised Units: 325
Company-Owned Units: 0
Total Units: 325
Dist.: US-325; CAN-0; O'seas-0
North America: 28 States
Density: NR
Projected New Units (12 Months): 100
Qualifications: 2, 3, 1, 2, 3, 4
Registered: All States

FINANCIAL/TERMS:
Cash Investment: $10K
Total Investment: $22.5-35.9K
Minimum Net Worth: $10K
Fees: Franchise - $18.9K
Royalty - 6-4% Varies; Ad. - 0%
Earnings Claims Statement: No
Term of Contract (Years): 10/10/10
Avg. # Of Employees: NA
Passive Ownership: Not Allowed
Encourage Conversions: Yes
Area Develop. Agreements: Yes
Sub-Franchising Contracts: No
Expand In Territory: Yes
Space Needs: NA SF; HB

SUPPORT & TRAINING:
Financial Assistance Provided: Yes(D)
Site Selection Assistance: NA
Lease Negotiation Assistance: NA
Co-Operative Advertising: NA
Franchisee Assoc./Member: No
Size Of Corporate Staff: 20
On-Going Support: B,C,D,G,H,I
Training: 5 Business Days Cincinnati, OH.

SPECIFIC EXPANSION PLANS:
US: All United States
Canada: All Canada
Overseas: All Countries

<< >>

HOME INSTEAD SENIOR CARE

604 N. 109th Ct.
Omaha, NE 68154-1716
Tel: (888) 484-5759 (402) 498-4466
Fax: (402) 498-5757
E-Mail: homeinstead@franconnect.com
Web Site: www.homeinstead.com
Ms. Jamie Meyer, Franchise Develop. Coordinator

HOME INSTEAD SENIOR CARE is the world's largest, most successful, non-medical companionship and home care franchise. Entrepreneur and other leading business publications have ranked us one of the top opportunities in all of franchising. The elderly market we serve is the fastest-growing segment of the population. Services such as companionship, light housework, errands and meal preparation assist the elderly in remaining in their homes rather than being institutionalized.

BACKGROUND: IFA MEMBER
Established: 1994; 1st Franchised: 1995
Franchised Units: 448
Company-Owned Units: 2
Total Units: 450
Dist.: US-413; CAN-10; O'seas-27
North America: 45 States, 3 Provinces
Density: 53 in CA, 27 in FL, 24 in TX
Projected New Units (12 Months): 70
Qualifications: 4, 3, 1, 3, 1, 5
Registered: All States and AB

FINANCIAL/TERMS:
Cash Investment: $23.5K
Total Investment: $30-39K
Minimum Net Worth: Varies
Fees: Franchise - $23.5K
Royalty - 5%; Ad. - 0%
Earnings Claims Statement: Yes
Term of Contract (Years): 10/10
Avg. # Of Employees: 2 FT, 45 PT
Passive Ownership: Discouraged
Encourage Conversions: Yes
Area Develop. Agreements: No
Sub-Franchising Contracts: No
Expand In Territory: Yes
Space Needs: 300-500 SF; Industrial/Office

SUPPORT & TRAINING:
Financial Assistance Provided: No
Site Selection Assistance: Yes
Lease Negotiation Assistance: No
Co-Operative Advertising: No
Franchisee Assoc./Member: No
Size Of Corporate Staff: 45
On-Going Support: B,C,D,E,F,G,H,I
Training: 1 Week Corporate Headquarters; 3 Days Field Visit Franchise Office.

SPECIFIC EXPANSION PLANS:
US: All United States
Canada: All Canada
Overseas: All Countries

<< >>

HUNT PERSONNEL

666 Cherbrooke W., # 1004
Montreal, PQ H3A 1E7 CANADA
Tel: (514) 985-0660
Fax: (514) 985-9150
E-Mail: jpourreaux@hunt.ca
Web Site: www.hunt.ca
Ms. Jacqueline Pourreaux, General Manager

Established in 1967, we have an unequalled reputation for quality service. Prefer local industry experience or conversion. Specialization encouraged.

BACKGROUND:
Established: 1967; 1st Franchised: 1974
Franchised Units: 12
Company-Owned Units: 0
Total Units: 12
Dist.: US-0; CAN-12; O'seas-0
North America: 4 Provinces
Density: 7 in ON, 3 in PQ, 1 in BC
Projected New Units (12 Months): 3
Qualifications: 5, 5, 5, 3, 4, 4
Registered: NR

FINANCIAL/TERMS:
Cash Investment: $100K
Total Investment: $150K
Minimum Net Worth: $200K
Fees: Franchise - Varies
Royalty - Varies; Ad. - ~0.25%
Earnings Claims Statement: No
Term of Contract (Years): 5/5
Avg. # Of Employees: 3+ FT
Passive Ownership: Not Allowed
Encourage Conversions: Yes
Area Develop. Agreements: No
Sub-Franchising Contracts: Yes
Expand In Territory: Yes
Space Needs: 1,200 SF; OB

SUPPORT & TRAINING:
Financial Assistance Provided: No
Site Selection Assistance: Yes
Lease Negotiation Assistance: Yes
Co-Operative Advertising: No
Franchisee Assoc./Member: No
Size Of Corporate Staff: 4
On-Going Support: a,B,C,D,G,H
Training: 2-3 Weeks Local.

SPECIFIC EXPANSION PLANS:
US: No
Canada: ON,PQ,AB,MB,SKMR
Overseas: No

INTERIM HOMESTYLE SERVICES

1601 Sawgrass Corporate Pkwy.
Sunrise, FL 33323
Tel: (800) 338-7786 + 2699 (954) 858-2699
Fax: (954) 858-2720
E-Mail: johnmarquez@interimhealthcare.com
Web Site: www.interimhealthcare.com
Mr. John Marquez, Senior Director

INTERIM HOMESTYLE SERVICES is the brand name for non-medical services provided by INTERIM HEALTHCARE, the country's oldest health care franchise organization. Interim franchise owners have one of the highest records of stability with an average collective of 20 years.

BACKGROUND:
Established: 1956; 1st Franchised: 1966
Franchised Units: 267
Company-Owned Units: 22
Total Units: 289
Dist.: US-289; CAN-0; O'seas-0
North America: 39 States
Density: 27 in NC, 26 in OH, 24 in FL
Projected New Units (12 Months): 5
Qualifications: 5, 5, 2, 3, 3, 5
Registered: All States

FINANCIAL/TERMS:
Cash Investment: $35-70K
Total Investment: $35-70K
Minimum Net Worth: $100K
Fees: Franchise - $10K
Royalty - 5%; Ad. - 0.25%
Earnings Claims Statement: No
Term of Contract (Years): 5/10
Avg. # Of Employees: 3 FT
Passive Ownership: Discouraged
Encourage Conversions: Yes
Area Develop. Agreements: No
Sub-Franchising Contracts: No
Expand In Territory: Yes
Space Needs: 1,000-1,20060 SF; HB, Executive Suite

SUPPORT & TRAINING:
Financial Assistance Provided: Yes(I)
Site Selection Assistance: Yes
Lease Negotiation Assistance: Yes
Co-Operative Advertising: No
Franchisee Assoc./Member: Yes
Size Of Corporate Staff: 100
On-Going Support: A,B,C,D,E,G,H,I
Training: 1 Week Sunrise, FL

SPECIFIC EXPANSION PLANS:
US: All United States
Canada: No
Overseas: Latin America, Mexico, Europe

LABOR FINDERS INTERNATIONAL

3910 RCA Blvd., # 1001
Palm Beach Gardens, FL 33410-4220
Tel: (800) 864-7749 (561) 627-6507
Fax: (561) 627-1910

E-Mail: lfi@laborfinders.com
Web Site: www.laborfinders.com
Mr. Robert R. Gallagher, VP Marketing

LABOR FINDERS is a specialized labor staffing service that supplies highly productive skilled, semi-skilled and unskilled workers to companies in construction, industrial and commercial business segments.

BACKGROUND: IFA MEMBER
Established: 1975; 1st Franchised: 1975
Franchised Units: 177
Company-Owned Units: 13
Total Units: 190
Dist.: US-190; CAN-0; O'seas-0
North America: 25 States
Density: 46 in FL, 19 in CA, 18 in GA
Projected New Units (12 Months): 15
Qualifications: 4, 4, 3, 3, 4, 4
Registered: CA,FL,IL,IN,MD,MN,VA,WA,WI

FINANCIAL/TERMS:
Cash Investment: $75-100K
Total Investment: $68.5-115.8K
Minimum Net Worth: $500K
Fees: Franchise - $10K
Royalty - % Billable Wages; Ad. - 0%
Earnings Claims Statement: No
Term of Contract (Years): 10/10/10
Avg. # Of Employees: 2 FT, 1 PT
Passive Ownership: Discouraged
Encourage Conversions: Yes
Area Develop. Agreements: No
Sub-Franchising Contracts: No
Expand In Territory: Yes
Space Needs: 800-1,000 SF; FS, SF, SC

SUPPORT & TRAINING:
Financial Assistance Provided: Yes(D)
Site Selection Assistance: Yes
Lease Negotiation Assistance: No
Co-Operative Advertising: Yes
Franchisee Assoc./Member: Yes/Yes
Size Of Corporate Staff: 24
On-Going Support: C,D,E,G,h,I
Training: 2 Weeks Operating Unit; 2 Weeks On-Site; 1 Week Classroom.

SPECIFIC EXPANSION PLANS:
US: NE, NW, Midwest
Canada: All Canada
Overseas: No

LINK STAFFING SERVICES
1800 Bering Dr., # 800
Houston, TX 77057-3151
Tel: (800) 848-5465 (713) 784-4400 + 1065
Fax: (713) 784-4454
E-Mail: franchise@linkstaffing.com
Web Site: www.linkstaffing.com
Mr. Donald Lawrence, VP Franchise Development

LINK STAFFING SERVICES provides a wide variety of flexible staffing/productivity solutions. We allow our clients to build their own business while providing them the staff they need; they tell us one thing that sets us apart from other staffing services is our comprehensive screening process, which consistently delivers higher quality workers. Many field staff have accepted full-time positions with our clients. Join a team with top-notch employees and the experience to support you all the way to success!

BACKGROUND: IFA MEMBER
Established: 1980; 1st Franchised: 1994
Franchised Units: 34
Company-Owned Units: 7
Total Units: 41
Dist.: US-41; CAN-0; O'seas-0
North America: 13 States
Density: 18 in TX, 6 in CA, 3 in FL
Projected New Units (12 Months): 6
Qualifications: 3, 4, 2, 4, 4, 5
Registered: All Except HI,AB

FINANCIAL/TERMS:
Cash Investment: $50K
Total Investment: $85.5-156K
Minimum Net Worth: NA
Fees: Franchise - $17K
Royalty - Varies; Ad. - 0%
Earnings Claims Statement: No
Term of Contract (Years): 10/5/5/5
Avg. # Of Employees: 2 FT
Passive Ownership: Discouraged
Encourage Conversions: Yes
Area Develop. Agreements: No
Sub-Franchising Contracts: No
Expand In Territory: Yes
Space Needs: 1,200-1,800 SF; SF, SC, Industrial Office Park

SUPPORT & TRAINING:
Financial Assistance Provided: Yes(I)
Site Selection Assistance: Yes
Lease Negotiation Assistance: Yes
Co-Operative Advertising: Yes
Franchisee Assoc./Member: Yes/Yes
Size Of Corporate Staff: 40
On-Going Support: A,B,C,D,E,G,H,I
Training: 4 Days Existing Franchise; 5 Days (Sales), 5 Days (Operations) Support Center, TX.

SPECIFIC EXPANSION PLANS:
US: All United States
Canada: No
Overseas: No

LLOYD STAFFING
445 Broadhollow Rd., # 119
Melville, NY 11747-3601
Tel: (888) 292-6678 (631) 777-7600
Fax: (631) 777-7620
E-Mail: jbondi@lloydstaffing.com
Web Site: www.lloydstaffing.com
Ms. Jeanine L. Bondi, VP Natl. Fran. Ops.

Since 1971, we have successfully served thousands of employers, job seekers and temporary employees. Our blended service concept truly embodies the entire spectrum of staffing, including temporary personnel, consultant referrals, contingency placement and executive search. And because we recognize that the field of human resources has significantly changed its structure and focus over the years, we've added several complimentary and compatible staffing components to enhance the support we provide.

BACKGROUND: IFA MEMBER
Established: 1971; 1st Franchised: 1986
Franchised Units: 8
Company-Owned Units: 7
Total Units: 15
Dist.: US-11; CAN-0; O'seas-0
North America: NR
Density: 5 in NY, 2 in NJ, 2 in CT
Projected New Units (12 Months): 3
Qualifications: 4, 5, 4, 3, 3, 5
Registered: FL,MD

FINANCIAL/TERMS:
Cash Investment: $75-100K
Total Investment: $85-150K
Minimum Net Worth: $100-150K
Fees: Franchise - $15-22K
Royalty - 60/40-7%; Ad. - NA
Earnings Claims Statement: No

Term of Contract (Years): 10/10
Avg. # Of Employees: 4 FT
Passive Ownership: Not Allowed
Encourage Conversions: No
Area Develop. Agreements: No
Sub-Franchising Contracts: No
Expand In Territory: Yes
Space Needs: 1,500 SF; FS, SF, SC

SUPPORT & TRAINING:
Financial Assistance Provided: Yes(I)
Site Selection Assistance: Yes
Lease Negotiation Assistance: Yes
Co-Operative Advertising: No
Franchisee Assoc./Member: No
Size Of Corporate Staff: 123
On-Going Support: A,C,D,E,g,h,I
Training: 2 Weeks in Melville, NY; 1 Week at Your Location.

SPECIFIC EXPANSION PLANS:
US: Southeast, Northeast
Canada: No
Overseas: No

<< >>

MANAGEMENT RECRUITERS/ SALES CONSULTANTS

200 Public Sq., 31st Fl.
Cleveland, OH 44114-2301
Tel: (800) 875-4000 (216) 416-8245
Fax: (216) 696-6612
E-Mail: jennifer.wood@brilliantpeople.com
Web Site: www.brilliantpeople.com
Mr. Dan Nemunaitis, Franchise Operations

Complete range of recruitment and human resource services, including: permanent executive, mid-management, professional, marketing, sales management and sales placement; temporary professional and sales staffing; video-conferencing; permanent and temporary office support personnel; with coverage on all continents. Franchises available outside of North America through our wholly owned subsidiary, the Humana Group International.

BACKGROUND: IFA MEMBER
Established: 1957; 1st Franchised: 1965
Franchised Units: 1,000
Company-Owned Units: 32
Total Units: 1,032
Dist.: US-829; CAN-0; O'seas-1
North America: 48 States
Density: 64 in FL, 62 in CA,60 in NC
Projected New Units (12 Months): 50
Qualifications: 3, 4, 1, 4, 3, 3
Registered: All States

FINANCIAL/TERMS:
Cash Investment: $110-145K
Total Investment: $110-145K
Minimum Net Worth: NA
Fees: Franchise - $72.5K
Royalty - 7%; Ad. - 0.5%
Earnings Claims Statement: Yes
Term of Contract (Years): 5-20/10
Avg. # Of Employees: 3-4 FT
Passive Ownership: Discouraged
Encourage Conversions: Yes
Area Develop. Agreements: No
Sub-Franchising Contracts: No
Expand In Territory: Yes
Space Needs: 600-1,000 SF; FS

SUPPORT & TRAINING:
Financial Assistance Provided: Yes(I)
Site Selection Assistance: Yes
Lease Negotiation Assistance: Yes
Co-Operative Advertising: NA
Franchisee Assoc./Member: Yes
Size Of Corporate Staff: 91
On-Going Support: C,D,E,G,H,I
Training:
3 Weeks Headquarters, Cleveland, OH; 10 Days Franchisee's Location.

SPECIFIC EXPANSION PLANS:
US: All United States
Canada: No
Overseas: No

<< >>

NURSEFINDERS

1701 E. Lamar Blvd., # 200
Arlington, TX 76006
Tel: (800) 445-0459 (817) 460-1181
Fax: (817) 462-9139
E-Mail: ed.mcguinness@nursefinders.com
Web Site: www.nursefinders.com
Mr. Ed McGuinness, VP Franchising

Largest provider in United States of temporary medical staffing to hospitals and other health care facilities. Ranked Number 1 in category by Entrepreneur Magazine. We also provide the full spectrum of home health care.

BACKGROUND:
Established: 1974; 1st Franchised: 1978
Franchised Units: 54
Company-Owned Units: 68
Total Units: 122
Dist.: US-113; CAN-0; O'seas-0
North America: 31 States
Density: 14 in FL, 8 in IL, 7 in CA
Projected New Units (12 Months): 10
Qualifications: , , , , ,
Registered: All States

FINANCIAL/TERMS:
Cash Investment: $50-100K
Total Investment: $110-200K
Minimum Net Worth: $250K
Fees: Franchise - $19.6K
Royalty - 7%; Ad. - 0%
Earnings Claims Statement: No
Term of Contract (Years): 10/5/5
Avg. # Of Employees: 5 FT, 100 PT
Passive Ownership: Discouraged
Encourage Conversions: Yes
Area Develop. Agreements: Yes/5/5
Sub-Franchising Contracts: No
Expand In Territory: Yes
Space Needs: 1,500-2,000 SF; Profess. Office. Bldg.

SUPPORT & TRAINING:
Financial Assistance Provided: Yes(D)
Site Selection Assistance: Yes
Lease Negotiation Assistance: Yes
Co-Operative Advertising: NA
Franchisee Assoc./Member: No
Size Of Corporate Staff: 62
On-Going Support: A,B,C,D,E,G,h,I
Training: 2 Weeks Arlington, TX; 1 Week Company Office; 2 Weeks On-Site.

SPECIFIC EXPANSION PLANS:
US: All United States
Canada: No
Overseas: No

<< >>

PRIDESTAFF

6780 N. West Ave., # 103
Fresno, CA 93711-1393
Tel: (800) 774-3316 (559) 432-7780 + 116
Fax: (559) 432-4371
E-Mail: jblocker@pridestaff.com
Web Site: www.pridestaff.com
Ms. Jane Blocker, EVP/Chief Operating Officer

We specialize in supplemental staffing (temporary help), outsourcing and full-time placement. PRIDESTAFF fills administrative, clerical, customer service, data entry, word processing and light industrial positions. The staffing industry is one of the fastest-growing industries in the United States.

BACKGROUND:
Established: 1974; 1st Franchised: 1994
Franchised Units: 20
Company-Owned Units: 7
Total Units: 27
Dist.: US-34; CAN-0; O'seas-0
North America: 13 States
Density: 12 in CA, 4 in AZ, 4 in IL

Projected New Units (12 Months): NR
Qualifications: , , , , ,
Registered: NR

FINANCIAL/TERMS:

Cash Investment: $75-100K
Total Investment: $80.4-126.9K
Minimum Net Worth: NA
Fees: Franchise - $12.5K
Royalty - 65%Gross Margin; Ad. - NA
Earnings Claims Statement: No
Term of Contract (Years): 10/5/5/5
Avg. # Of Employees: 2 FT
Passive Ownership: Not Allowed
Encourage Conversions: NR
Area Develop. Agreements: No
Sub-Franchising Contracts: No
Expand In Territory: Yes
Space Needs:1,200 SF; Single Story Office Building

SUPPORT & TRAINING:

Financial Assistance Provided: NR
Site Selection Assistance: Yes
Lease Negotiation Assistance: Yes
Co-Operative Advertising: NA
Franchisee Assoc./Member: No
Size Of Corporate Staff: 16
On-Going Support: A,C,D,E,G,H,I
Training: 1 Week in Fresno, CA; 1 Week at Branch Office.

SPECIFIC EXPANSION PLANS:

US: All United States
Canada: NR
Overseas: NR

<< >>

REMEDY INTELLIGENT STAFFING

101 Enterprise, # 100
Aliso Viejo, CA 92656
Tel: (800) 736-3392 (949) 425-7600
Fax: (800) 291-2060
E-Mail: natalie@remedystaff.com
Web Site: www.remedystaff.com
Ms. Natalie Jordan, AVP Franchise Development

A national full-service staffing company, providing contingent workers in the disciplines of law, accounting, professional office auditing, clerical and light industrial. Fully automated office, with exclusive, validated behavioral testing. Entire back-office support and exclusive territories.

BACKGROUND: IFA MEMBER
Established: 1965; 1st Franchised: 1988
Franchised Units: 108
Company-Owned Units: 130
Total Units: 255
Dist.: US-277; CAN-0; O'seas-0
North America: 40 States
Density: 88 in CA, 24 in FL, 18 in TX
Projected New Units (12 Months): 30
Qualifications: 4, 4, 4, 3, 4, 5
Registered: CA,FL,HI,IL,IN,MD,MI,MN, NY,OR,RI,VA,WA,WI,DC,AB

FINANCIAL/TERMS:

Cash Investment: $30-60K
Total Investment: $95-150K
Minimum Net Worth: $250K
Fees: Franchise - $18K
Royalty - Varies; Ad. - 0%
Earnings Claims Statement: No
Term of Contract (Years): 10/5
Avg. # Of Employees: 5 FT, 1 PT
Passive Ownership: Discouraged
Encourage Conversions: Yes
Area Develop. Agreements: Yes/10
Sub-Franchising Contracts: No
Expand In Territory: Yes
Space Needs: 1,400 SF; OB

SUPPORT & TRAINING:

Financial Assistance Provided: Yes(I)
Site Selection Assistance: Yes
Lease Negotiation Assistance: Yes
Co-Operative Advertising: Yes
Franchisee Assoc./Member: Yes/Yes
Size Of Corporate Staff: 160
On-Going Support: A,C,D,E,G,H,I
Training: 2 Weeks Home Office; 1 Week On-Site.

SPECIFIC EXPANSION PLANS:

US: All Except CA,WA,OR,NM,CO
Canada: All Canada
Overseas: No

<< >>

SALES CONSULTANTS

200 Public Sq., 31st Fl.
Cleveland, OH 44114-2301
Tel: (800) 875-4000 (216) 416-8467
Fax: (216) 696-6612
E-Mail: mary.costanzo@brilliantpeople.com
Web Site: www.brilliantpeople.com
Ms. Mary Costanzo, Franchise Sales Rep.

Complete range of recruitment and human resource services for sales, sales management and marketing professionals, including permanent placement, interim staffing; video-conferencing; with coverage on all continents through strategic alliances with leading search firms.

BACKGROUND: IFA MEMBER
Established: 1957; 1st Franchised: 1966
Franchised Units: 170
Company-Owned Units: 17
Total Units: 187
Dist.: US-226; CAN-0; O'seas-0
North America: 39 States
Density: 20 in CA, 15 in FL, 14 in MI
Projected New Units (12 Months): 20
Qualifications: 3, 4, 1, 4, 3, 3
Registered: All States

FINANCIAL/TERMS:

Cash Investment: $113-154K
Total Investment: $113-154K
Minimum Net Worth: NA
Fees: Franchise - $75-80K
Royalty - 7%; Ad. - 1%
Earnings Claims Statement: Yes
Term of Contract (Years): 10-20/5
Avg. # Of Employees: 3-4 FT or PT
Passive Ownership: Discouraged
Encourage Conversions: Yes
Area Develop. Agreements: No
Sub-Franchising Contracts: No
Expand In Territory: Yes
Space Needs: 600-1,000 SF; FS

SUPPORT & TRAINING:

Financial Assistance Provided: Yes(I)
Site Selection Assistance: Yes
Lease Negotiation Assistance: Yes
Co-Operative Advertising: NA
Franchisee Assoc./Member: Yes
Size Of Corporate Staff: 128
On-Going Support: C,D,E,G,H,I
Training: 3 Weeks Headquarters, Cleveland, OH; 2 Weeks Franchisee's Location.

SPECIFIC EXPANSION PLANS:

US: All United States
Canada: No
Overseas: No

<< >>

SANFORD ROSE ASSOCIATES

3737 Embassy Pkwy., # 200
Akron, OH 44333-8369
Tel: (800) 731-7724 (330) 670-9797 + 102
Fax: (330) 670-9798
E-Mail: hq@sanfordrose.com
Web Site: www.sanfordrose.com
Mr. Mark A. Sweeterman, Dir. Franchise Development

We represent companies and institutions around the world in finding high-quality executives, managers and professionals for important position openings through our proprietary Dimensional Search process.

BACKGROUND: IFA MEMBER
Established: 1959; 1st Franchised: 1970
Franchised Units: 57

Company-Owned Units: 1
Total Units: 58
Dist.: US-53; CAN-0; O'seas-5
North America: 22 States
Density: 11 in OH, 7 in CA, 5 in IL
Projected New Units (12 Months): 12
Qualifications: 4, 5, 4, 3, 4, 5
Registered: CA,FL,IL,MI,NY

FINANCIAL/TERMS:

Cash Investment: $63-103K
Total Investment: $77-103K
Minimum Net Worth: $80K
Fees: Franchise - $45K
Royalty - 7-3%; Ad. - 0%
Earnings Claims Statement: Yes
Term of Contract (Years): 10/1
Avg. # Of Employees: 3 FT, 1 PT
Passive Ownership: Not Allowed
Encourage Conversions: Yes
Area Develop. Agreements: No
Sub-Franchising Contracts: No
Expand In Territory: No
Space Needs: 600-1,000 SF; FS, SC

SUPPORT & TRAINING:

Financial Assistance Provided: Yes(D)
Site Selection Assistance: Yes
Lease Negotiation Assistance: Yes
Co-Operative Advertising: No
Franchisee Assoc./Member: Yes/Yes
Size Of Corporate Staff: 7
On-Going Support: C,D,G,H,I
Training: 12.5 Days Corporate Heqdquarters; 5 Days On Site.

SPECIFIC EXPANSION PLANS:

US: All United States
Canada: All Canada
Overseas: All Countries

<< >>

SNELLING PERSONNEL SERVICES

12801 N. Central Expy., # 700
Dallas, TX 75243
Tel: (800) 766-5556
Fax: (972) 383-3855
E-Mail: franchise.sales@snelling.com
Web Site: www.snelling.com
Mr. Wm. Fred Bartliff, VP Franchise Sales

SNELLING helps you live the American dream - To Own Your Own Business. Our full-service staffing franchise offers temporary, temp-to-hire and career placement opportunities to both people needing jobs and companies needing good people. SNELLING has been helping others achieve the success they desire for neary 50 years and has one of the most recognized names in the industry. We offer: a proven operating system; comprehensive training and on-going support; fully computerized payroll financing, etc. Call today.

BACKGROUND: IFA MEMBER

Established: 1951; 1st Franchised: 1955
Franchised Units: 150
Company-Owned Units: 52
Total Units: 202
Dist.: US-196; CAN-0; O'seas-1
North America: 43 States
Density: 32 in TX, 18 in MI, 17 in IL
Projected New Units (12 Months): 12
Qualifications: 5, 5, 1, 3, 1, 5
Registered: All States Except HI and RI.

FINANCIAL/TERMS:

Cash Investment: $99.1K
Total Investment: $140-180.7K
Minimum Net Worth: $250K
Fees: Franchise - $20K
Royalty - % Gr. Margin; Ad. - 0.5-2%
Earnings Claims Statement: No
Term of Contract (Years): 5/Options
Avg. # Of Employees: 4-6 FT
Passive Ownership: Discouraged
Encourage Conversions: Yes
Area Develop. Agreements: Yes
Sub-Franchising Contracts: No
Expand In Territory: Yes
Space Needs: 1,000-1,400 SF; FS, SF, SC

SUPPORT & TRAINING:

Financial Assistance Provided: Yes
Site Selection Assistance: Yes
Lease Negotiation Assistance: Yes
Co-Operative Advertising: NR
Franchisee Assoc./Member: Yes/Yes
Size Of Corporate Staff: 122
On-Going Support: A,b,C,D,E,G,H,I
Training: 2 Weeks Snelling University.

SPECIFIC EXPANSION PLANS:

US: All US Except HI and RI
Canada: No
Overseas: No

<< >>

Top 100

SPHERION

925 North Point Pkwy., # 100
Alpharetta, GA 30005
Tel: (678) 867-3702
Fax: (678) 867-3190
E-Mail: robertamarcantonio@spherion.com
Web Site: www.spherion.com
Ms. Roberta Marcantonio, VP Market Expansion

SPHERION franchise/license opportunities provide individuals a chance to join an exciting and rewarding industry: temporary staffing. We placed millions of workers in flexible and full-time jobs during our nearly 60 years in business. Continuous innovation and decades of growth have helped SPHERION become an industry leader. Entrepreneur Magazine ranked SPHERION Best Staffing Service for five straight years. Our franchisees contribute their talent, commitment and passion to building our brand.

BACKGROUND: IFA MEMBER

Established: 1946; 1st Franchised: 1956
Franchised Units: 155
Company-Owned Units: 523
Total Units: 678
Dist.: US-646; CAN-32; O'seas-0
North America: 46 States, 8 Provinces
Density: 29 in CA, 29 in FL, 27 in OH
Projected New Units (12 Months): 10
Qualifications: 5, 5, 2, 3, 4, 5
Registered: All States

FINANCIAL/TERMS:

Cash Investment: Varies
Total Investment: $68.3-391.7K
Minimum Net Worth: Varies
Fees: Franchise - $10-15K
Royalty - 3-6%/25%; Ad. - 0.25%
Earnings Claims Statement: No
Term of Contract (Years): 10/5
Avg. # Of Employees: 5 FT
Passive Ownership: Not Allowed
Encourage Conversions: Yes
Area Develop. Agreements: No
Sub-Franchising Contracts: No
Expand In Territory: Yes
Space Needs: 1,500 SF; SF, RM

SUPPORT & TRAINING:

Financial Assistance Provided: No
Site Selection Assistance: Yes
Lease Negotiation Assistance: Yes
Co-Operative Advertising: Yes
Franchisee Assoc./Member: No
Size Of Corporate Staff: 4,000
On-Going Support: a,B,C,D,E,G,H,I
Training: Extensive Training - Over

112 Hours In-Office Instruction; Addl. Self-Paced Instruction.

SPECIFIC EXPANSION PLANS:

US: Targeted Cities in US.
Canada: No
Overseas: No

TALENT TREE

9703 Richmond Ave., # 216
Houston, TX 77042-4620
Tel: (800) 999-1515 + 7304 (713) 361-7304
Fax: (713) 974-6507
E-Mail: franchise@talenttree.com
Web Site: www.talenttree.com
Mr. Mark Dermott, SVP Franchise Group

TALENT TREE offers full-service staffing franchise opportunities with the placement of clerical, administrative, technical support and light industrial staff. Franchisees are offered intensive on-going training and hands-on support by industry experts. Our franchisees have the advantage of our proven system and innovative, proprietary programs.

BACKGROUND: IFA MEMBER
Established: 1976; 1st Franchised: 1990
Franchised Units: 13
Company-Owned Units: 43
Total Units: 56
Dist.: US-234; CAN-0; O'seas-0
North America: 30 States
Density: 32 in CA, 14 in TX, 14 in GA
Projected New Units (12 Months): 3-5
Qualifications: 4, 4, 5, 1, 2, 4
Registered: All States

FINANCIAL/TERMS:

Cash Investment: $100-150K
Total Investment: $120-170K
Minimum Net Worth: $150-250K
Fees: Franchise - $20K
Royalty - Varies; Ad. - 0%
Earnings Claims Statement: No
Term of Contract (Years): 10/5
Avg. # Of Employees: 2 FT
Passive Ownership: Allowed
Encourage Conversions: Yes
Area Develop. Agreements: Yes
Sub-Franchising Contracts: No
Expand In Territory: Yes
Space Needs: 1,000 SF; FS, SF, SC

SUPPORT & TRAINING:

Financial Assistance Provided: Yes(I)
Site Selection Assistance: Yes
Lease Negotiation Assistance: Yes
Co-Operative Advertising: Yes
Franchisee Assoc./Member: No
Size Of Corporate Staff: 180
On-Going Support: A,B,C,D,E,H,I
Training: 3-4 Weeks at Corporate Office & On-Going; 1st 120 Days and as Needed at Franchise.

SPECIFIC EXPANSION PLANS:

US: All United States
Canada: No
Overseas: No

TODAYS STAFFING

18111 Preston Rd., # 700
Dallas, TX 75252-4383
Tel: (877) 586-3297 (972) 380-9380
Fax: (972) 713-4198
E-Mail: rick.munzesheimer@todays.com
Web Site: www.todays.com
Mr. Rick Munzesheimer, Franchise Manager

TODAYS STAFFING is a full-service, high-quality, office clerical temporary employment service, utilizing a distinctive sales, service, promotional, quality control and accounting procedure known as the TODAYS WAY method of operating a temporary employment service business. TODAYS is a national company, awarding franchisees an exclusive major market territory. TODAYS finances 100% of employees' payroll and accounts receivable.

BACKGROUND:
Established: 1982; 1st Franchised: 1983
Franchised Units: 22
Company-Owned Units: 97
Total Units: 119
Dist.: US-108; CAN-11; O'seas-0
North America: 28 States, 2 Provinces
Density: 28 in TX, 11 in MO, 9 in FL
Projected New Units (12 Months): 6
Qualifications: 5, 5, 4, 4, 5, 5
Registered: CA,IN,MI,NY

FINANCIAL/TERMS:

Cash Investment: $90-145K
Total Investment: $90-145K
Minimum Net Worth: $150K
Fees: Franchise - $20K
Royalty - Varies; Ad. - 0%
Earnings Claims Statement: Yes
Term of Contract (Years): 5/5/5
Avg. # Of Employees: 3 FT
Passive Ownership: Not Allowed
Encourage Conversions: Yes
Area Develop. Agreements: Yes
Sub-Franchising Contracts: No
Expand In Territory: Yes
Space Needs: 1,200 SF; Class A Office

SUPPORT & TRAINING:

Financial Assistance Provided: No
Site Selection Assistance: Yes
Lease Negotiation Assistance: No
Co-Operative Advertising: No
Franchisee Assoc./Member: Yes/Yes
Size Of Corporate Staff: 85
On-Going Support: A,C,D,E,G,H,I
Training: 2 Weeks at Dallas, TX; 2 Weeks Field.

SPECIFIC EXPANSION PLANS:

US: All United States
Canada: No
Overseas: No

Food: Donuts/Cookies/Bagels

Chapter 13

FOOD: DONUTS/COOKIES/BAGELS INDUSTRY PROFILE

Total # Franchisors in Industry Group	61
Total # Franchised Units in Industry Group	12,586
Total # Company-Owned Units in Industry Group	1,077
Total # Operating Units in Industry Group	13,663
Average # Franchised Units/Franchisor	206.3
Average # Company-Owned Units/Franchisor	17.7
Average # Total Units/Franchisor	224
Ratio of Total # Franchised Units/Total # Company-Owned Units	11.7:1
Industry Survey Participants	29
Representing % of Industry	47.5%
Average Franchise Fee*:	$25.7K
Average Total Investment*:	$229.5K
Average On-Going Royalty Fee*:	5.1%

*If a range was provided, the mid-point of the range was used. See detailed profiles for actual ranges.

FIVE LARGEST PARTICIPANTS IN SURVEY

Company	# Franchised Units	# Co-Owned Units	# Total Units	Franchise Fee	On-Going Royalty	Total Investment
1. Dunkin' Donuts	5,000	0	5,000	$50K	5.9%	$255.7-1139.7K
2. Cinnabon	616	0	616	$35K	5%	$150-250K
3. Panera Bread Company	356	184	540	$35K	5%	$550-650K
4. Mrs. Fields Cookies	317	75	392	$30K	6%	$162.4-247.1K
5. Coffee Time Donuts	320	10	330	$NR	4.5%	$160-250K

All of the data provided are proprietary and should not be quoted without acknowledging *Bond's Franchise Guide.*

Top 100

BIG APPLE BAGELS

500 Lake Cook Rd., # 475
Deerfield, IL 60015
Tel: (800) 251-6101 (847) 948-7520
Fax: (847) 948-7521
E-Mail: tcervini@babcorp.com
Web Site: www.babcorp.com
Mr. Anthony S. Cervini, Director of Development

Bakery-café featuring three brands, fresh-from-scratch Big Apple Bagels and My Favorite Muffin, and freshly roasted Brewster's specialty coffee. Our product offering covers many day parts with a delicious assortment of made-to-order gourmet sandwiches, salads, soups, espresso beverages, and fruit smoothies. Franchisees can develop beyond their stores with corporate catering and gift basket opportunities, as well as wholesaling opportunities within their market area.

BACKGROUND: IFA MEMBER
Established: 1992; 1st Franchised: 1993
Franchised Units: 175
Company-Owned Units: 4
Total Units: 179
Dist.: US-171; CAN-0; O'seas-8
North America: 27 States
Density: 34 in MI, 28 in WI, 23 in IL
Projected New Units (12 Months): 20
Qualifications: 3, 4, 3, 3, 3, 5
Registered: All States

FINANCIAL/TERMS:
Cash Investment: $60K
Total Investment: $174.8-349.5K
Minimum Net Worth: $250K
Fees: Franchise - $25K
Royalty - 5%; Ad. - 1%
Earnings Claims Statement: No
Term of Contract (Years): 10/10
Avg. # Of Employees: 3 FT, 11 PT
Passive Ownership: Allowed
Encourage Conversions: Yes
Area Develop. Agreements: Yes/Varies
Sub-Franchising Contracts: No
Expand In Territory: Yes
Space Needs: 1,500-1,800 SF; SC

SUPPORT & TRAINING:
Financial Assistance Provided: No
Site Selection Assistance: Yes
Lease Negotiation Assistance: Yes
Co-Operative Advertising: No
Franchisee Assoc./Member: No
Size Of Corporate Staff: 23
On-Going Support: C,D,E,F,G,H,I
Training: 2 Weeks Milwaukee, WI.

SPECIFIC EXPANSION PLANS:
US: All United States
Canada: All Canada
Overseas: All Countries

<< >>

BLUE CHIP COOKIES

157 Barnwood Dr.
Edgewood, KY 41017
Tel: (800) 888-9866 (859) 331-7600
Fax: (859) 331-7604
E-Mail: bluechip@fuse.net
Web Site: www.bluechipcookies.com
Mr. Mark D. Hannahan, President/CEO

BLUE CHIP COOKIES brings pleasure to our customers by making the world's best gourmet cookies and brownies, fresh from scratch, everyday, at every one of our retail locations. We have won numerous awards, and our wonderful cookies and brownies continue to bring joy to young and old alike!

BACKGROUND:
Established: 1983; 1st Franchised: 1986
Franchised Units: 10
Company-Owned Units: 10
Total Units: 20
Dist.: US-20; CAN-0; O'seas-0
North America: 7 States
Density: 5 in CA, 5 in OH, 2 in NJ
Projected New Units (12 Months): 4
Qualifications: 5, 4, 4, 3, 1, 5
Registered: NA

FINANCIAL/TERMS:
Cash Investment: $50-100K
Total Investment: $120-200K
Minimum Net Worth: $200K
Fees: Franchise - $19.5K
Royalty - 6%; Ad. - 0%
Earnings Claims Statement: No
Term of Contract (Years): 10/10
Avg. # Of Employees: 2-3 FT, 4-8 PT
Passive Ownership: Allowed
Encourage Conversions: Yes
Area Develop. Agreements: No
Sub-Franchising Contracts: No
Expand In Territory: Yes
Space Needs: 600+ SF; SC, RM, Airport, Tourist Site

SUPPORT & TRAINING:
Financial Assistance Provided: No
Site Selection Assistance: Yes
Lease Negotiation Assistance: Yes
Co-Operative Advertising: No
Franchisee Assoc./Member: No
Size Of Corporate Staff: 6
On-Going Support: C,D,E,G,H,I
Training: 1-2 Weeks Cincinnati, OH.

SPECIFIC EXPANSION PLANS:
US: All United States
Canada: Would Consider
Overseas: Would Consider

<< >>

BREADSMITH

409 E. Silver Spring Dr.
Whitefish Bay, WI 53217
Tel: (888) BREADS-1 (414) 962-1965
Fax: (414) 962-5888
E-Mail: albert@breadsmith.com
Web Site: www.breadsmith.com
Mr. Albert Hasse, President

Award-winning, European, hearth-bread bakery, featuring fresh-from-scratch crusty breads, scones, muffins, gourmet jams and oils. Open kitchen concept reveals a six-ton, stone hearth oven imported from Europe used to bake the hand-crafted loaves each morning. BREADSMITH has been ranked by Bon Appetit, Best in 11 cities across the country.

BACKGROUND: IFA MEMBER
Established: 1993; 1st Franchised: 1994
Franchised Units: 35
Company-Owned Units: 1
Total Units: 36
Dist.: US-38; CAN-0; O'seas-0
North America: 10 States
Density: 10 in MI, 7 in IL
Projected New Units (12 Months): 5
Qualifications: 4, 4, 2, 4, 4, 5
Registered: CA,FL,IL,IN,MI,MN,NY,OR, SD,VA,WA,WI

FINANCIAL/TERMS:
Cash Investment: $100-250K
Total Investment: $200-400K
Minimum Net Worth: $500K
Fees: Franchise - $30K
Royalty - 7/6/5%; Ad. - 0%
Earnings Claims Statement: Yes
Term of Contract (Years): 15/15
Avg. # Of Employees: 6 FT, 12 PT
Passive Ownership: Not Allowed
Encourage Conversions: NA
Area Develop. Agreements: Varies
Sub-Franchising Contracts: No

Expand In Territory: Yes
Space Needs: 1,800 SF; FS, SF, SC
SUPPORT & TRAINING:
Financial Assistance Provided: Yes(I)
Site Selection Assistance: Yes
Lease Negotiation Assistance: Yes
Co-Operative Advertising: Yes
Franchisee Assoc./Member: Yes
Size Of Corporate Staff: 10
On-Going Support: C,D,E,F,G,H,I
Training: 4 Weeks Corporate Store; 1 Week Franchisee Store.
SPECIFIC EXPANSION PLANS:
US: All United States
Canada: All Canada
Overseas: No

<< >>

BRUEGGER'S

159 Bank St., 3rd Fl.
Burlington, VT 05401
Tel: (866) 660-4104 (802) 652-9276
Fax: (802) 660-4034
E-Mail: franchise@brueggers.com
Web Site: www.brueggers.com
Mr. Kevin Hogan, Franchise Recruiter

Our mission is to be the dominant, first choice, neighborhood bagel bakery in all markets where we operate.

BACKGROUND: IFA MEMBER
Established: 1983; 1st Franchised: 1993
Franchised Units: 110
Company-Owned Units: 135
Total Units: 245
Dist.: US-242; CAN-0; O'seas-0
North America: 18 States
Density: 35 in NY, 29 in MA, 25 in OH
Projected New Units (12 Months): 25
Qualifications: 4, 3, 5, 1, 4, 5
Registered:CA,FL,IN,MD,MI,MN,NY,RI, VA,WA,WI
FINANCIAL/TERMS:
Cash Investment: $200-600K
Total Investment: $250-477.5K
Minimum Net Worth: $400K
Fees: Franchise - $25K
Royalty - 5%; Ad. - 2-4%
Earnings Claims Statement: Yes
Term of Contract (Years): 10/5
Avg. # Of Employees: NR
Passive Ownership: Discouraged
Encourage Conversions: Yes
Area Develop. Agreements: Yes
Sub-Franchising Contracts: No
Expand In Territory: Yes
Space Needs: 1,500-2,200 SF; SF, SC, RM
SUPPORT & TRAINING:
Financial Assistance Provided: No
Site Selection Assistance: Yes
Lease Negotiation Assistance: No
Co-Operative Advertising: Yes
Franchisee Assoc./Member: No
Size Of Corporate Staff: 20
On-Going Support: a,b,C,D,E,f,G,H
Training: NR
SPECIFIC EXPANSION PLANS:
US: All United States
Canada: No
Overseas: No

<< >>

BUNS MASTER BAKERY SYSTEMS

2 E. Beaver Creek Rd., Bldg. #1
Richmond Hill, ON L4B 2N3 CANADA
Tel: (905) 764-7066
Fax: (905) 764-7634
E-Mail: youngj@countrystyle.ca
Web Site: www.countrystyle.ca
Mr. Jeff Young, Director of Franchising

Retail and commercial bakery, with a wide variety of self-serve products made and baked fresh on-site.

BACKGROUND:
Established: 1970; 1st Franchised: 1977
Franchised Units: 106
Company-Owned Units: 0
Total Units: 106
Dist.: US-1; CAN-105; O'seas-0
North America: 1 State, 9 Provinces
Density: 50 in ON, 30 in BC, 9 in SK
Projected New Units (12 Months): 10
Qualifications: 4, 4, 1, 2, , 5
Registered: AB
FINANCIAL/TERMS:
Cash Investment: $95K
Total Investment: $275K
Minimum Net Worth: NR
Fees: Franchise - $25K
Royalty - 5%; Ad. - 1%
Earnings Claims Statement: No
Term of Contract (Years): 20
Avg. # Of Employees: 6 FT, 12 PT
Passive Ownership: Not Allowed
Encourage Conversions: Yes
Area Develop. Agreements: No
Sub-Franchising Contracts: No
Expand In Territory: Yes
Space Needs: NR SF; SC
SUPPORT & TRAINING:
Financial Assistance Provided: Yes(I)
Site Selection Assistance: Yes
Lease Negotiation Assistance: Yes
Co-Operative Advertising: Yes
Franchisee Assoc./Member: No
Size Of Corporate Staff: 44
On-Going Support: A,B,C,D,E,F,G,h,I
Training: 7 Days Head Office; 14 Days On-Site.
SPECIFIC EXPANSION PLANS:
US: All United States
Canada: All Canada
Overseas: No

<< >>

CINDY'S CINNAMON ROLLS

P. O. Box 1480
Fallbrook, CA 92028
Tel: (800) 468-7655 (760) 723-1121
Fax: (760) 723-4143
E-Mail: cindyscin@aol.com
Web Site: www.worldfranchising.com/website.htm
Mr. Thomas Harris, President

Fresh-baked cinnamon rolls and muffins. All shops in major shopping malls. Great family business. All products made in the shop and baked fresh all day.

BACKGROUND:
Established: 1985; 1st Franchised: 1986
Franchised Units: 30
Company-Owned Units: 0
Total Units: 30
Dist.: US-29; CAN-0; O'seas-3
North America: 14 States
Density: 8 in NY, 3 in CA, 2 in NJ
Projected New Units (12 Months): 5
Qualifications: 3, 3, 3, 3, 3, 3
Registered: NY,CA
FINANCIAL/TERMS:
Cash Investment: $130K
Total Investment: $130K
Minimum Net Worth: $100K
Fees: Franchise - $25K
Royalty - 5%; Ad. - 0%
Earnings Claims Statement: No
Term of Contract (Years): 10/10
Avg. # Of Employees: 8 FT
Passive Ownership: Allowed
Encourage Conversions: Yes
Area Develop. Agreements: No
Sub-Franchising Contracts: No
Expand In Territory: Yes
Space Needs: 800 SF; RM
SUPPORT & TRAINING:
Financial Assistance Provided: No
Site Selection Assistance: Yes
Lease Negotiation Assistance: Yes
Co-Operative Advertising: No
Franchisee Assoc./Member: No
Size Of Corporate Staff: 3
On-Going Support: B,C,D,E,F,G,H,I

Training: 1 Week New York, NY; 4 Days in Store.
SPECIFIC EXPANSION PLANS:
US: All United States
Canada: All Canada
Overseas: All Countries

<< >>

CINNABON
200 Glenridge Point Pkwy., # 200
Atlanta, GA 30342
Tel: (800) 639-3826 (404) 255-3250
Fax: (404) 255-4978
E-Mail: rjangla@focusbrands.com
Web Site: www.cinnabon.com
Ms. Rukmi Jangla, Fran. Sales Market. Specialist

Commitment to premium ingredients and quality baking - served hot. No more than 30 minutes out of oven.

BACKGROUND: IFA MEMBER
Established: 1985; 1st Franchised: 1986
Franchised Units: 616
Company-Owned Units: 0
Total Units: 616
Dist.: US-444; CAN-23; O'seas-149
North America: NR
Density: 34 in CA, 28 in FL, 24 in OH
Projected New Units (12 Months): 50
Qualifications: 5, 5, 5, 4, 4, 5
Registered: HI,IL,MD,MN,ND,RI,SD,VA,WA,WI
FINANCIAL/TERMS:
Cash Investment: $300K-3 Units
Total Investment: $150-250K
Minimum Net Worth: $600K
Fees: Franchise - $35K
Royalty - 5%; Ad. - 1.5%
Earnings Claims Statement: No
Term of Contract (Years): 10/5
Avg. # Of Employees: 6 FT
Passive Ownership: Not Allowed
Encourage Conversions: Yes
Area Develop. Agreements: Yes
Sub-Franchising Contracts: No
Expand In Territory: Yes
Space Needs: 850 SF; RM
SUPPORT & TRAINING:
Financial Assistance Provided: NA
Site Selection Assistance: Yes
Lease Negotiation Assistance: Yes
Co-Operative Advertising: Yes
Franchisee Assoc./Member: Yes/Yes
Size Of Corporate Staff: 52
On-Going Support: E,G
Training: CRT Location 4 Weeks.
SPECIFIC EXPANSION PLANS:
US: LA, NY, AL, MS, AR, MO
Canada: No
Overseas: All Countries

<< >>

COFFEE TIME DONUTS
477 Ellesmere Rd.
Toronto, ON M1R 4E5 CANADA
Tel: (416) 288-8515
Fax: (416) 288-8895
E-Mail: cioannou@coffeetime.ca
Web Site: www.coffeetime.ca
Mr. Chris Ioannou, Director of Franchising

A quick-service restaurant-type donut chain, with great-tasting coffee, muffins, donuts, salads and sandwiches. Fresh, quality products are what set us apart from the competition.

BACKGROUND:
Established: 1982; 1st Franchised: 1987
Franchised Units: 320
Company-Owned Units: 10
Total Units: 330
Dist.: US-0; CAN-324; O'seas-0
North America: 3 Provinces
Density: 319 in ON, 3 in MB, 1 in AB
Projected New Units (12 Months): 65
Qualifications: 3, 3, 2, 2, 3, 5
Registered: NR
FINANCIAL/TERMS:
Cash Investment: NR
Total Investment: $160-250K
Minimum Net Worth: $150K
Fees: Franchise - NR
Royalty - 4.5%; Ad. - 2%
Earnings Claims Statement: No
Term of Contract (Years): NR
Avg. # Of Employees: 6 FT, 4 PT
Passive Ownership: Not Allowed
Encourage Conversions: Yes
Area Develop. Agreements: NR
Sub-Franchising Contracts: No
Expand In Territory: Yes
Space Needs: NR SF; FS, SF, RM
SUPPORT & TRAINING:
Financial Assistance Provided: NR
Site Selection Assistance: NR
Lease Negotiation Assistance: NA
Co-Operative Advertising: NR
Franchisee Assoc./Member: No
Size Of Corporate Staff: 50
On-Going Support: b,C,D,E,F,G,H
Training: 3-6 Weeks Scarborough, ON.
SPECIFIC EXPANSION PLANS:
US: All United States
Canada: All Canada
Overseas: All Countries

<< >>

COOKIES BY DESIGN / COOKIE BOUQUET
1865 Summit Ave., # 605
Plano, TX 75074-8147
Tel: (800) 945-2665 (972) 398-9536
Fax: (972) 398-9542
E-Mail: frandevelopment@mgwmail.com
Web Site: www.cookiesbydesign.com/index.cfm
Mr. David Patterson, Exec. Dir. Franchise Devel.

Unique retail opportunity! Gift bakery, specializing in hand-decorated cookie arrangements and gourmet cookies, decorated for special events, holidays, centerpieces, etc. Clientele include both individual and corporate customers. A wonderfully delicious alternative to flowers or balloons.

BACKGROUND: IFA MEMBER
Established: 1983; 1st Franchised: 1987
Franchised Units: 249
Company-Owned Units: 0
Total Units: 249
Dist.: US-249; CAN-0; O'seas-0
North America: 44 States
Density: 34 in TX, 23 in CA, 21 in FL
Projected New Units (12 Months): 20
Qualifications: 3, 5, 4, 4, 4, 5
Registered: CA,FL,HI,IL,IN,MD,MI,NY,OR,RI,SD,VA,WA,WI
FINANCIAL/TERMS:
Cash Investment: $90-175K
Total Investment: $90-175K
Minimum Net Worth: NR
Fees: Franchise - $25K
Royalty - 6%; Ad. - 1%
Earnings Claims Statement: No
Term of Contract (Years): 5/5
Avg. # Of Employees: 3 FT, 2 PT
Passive Ownership: Discouraged
Encourage Conversions: No
Area Develop. Agreements: Yes
Sub-Franchising Contracts: No
Expand In Territory: Yes
Space Needs: 1,200-1,500 SF; SC
SUPPORT & TRAINING:
Financial Assistance Provided: No
Site Selection Assistance: Yes
Lease Negotiation Assistance: Yes
Co-Operative Advertising: Yes
Franchisee Assoc./Member: No
Size Of Corporate Staff: 25
On-Going Support: C,D,E,G,h,I
Training: 2 Weeks Dallas, TX.

SPECIFIC EXPANSION PLANS:
US: All United States
Canada: No
Overseas: No

<< >>

COOKIES IN BLOOM

12700 Hillcrest Rd., # 251
Dallas, TX 75230
Tel: (800) 222-3104 (972) 490-8644
Fax: (972) 490-8646
E-Mail: cibinc@swbell.net
Web Site: www.cookiesinbloom.com
Mr. Robert E. Pinac, Vice President

Exciting retail opportunity featuring cookie gift baking shop, offering hand-decorated cookies, cookie arrangements and gourmet cookies for all holidays and special occasions. We specialize in birthday, baby, thank you, get well and anniversary arrangements for both individual and corporate customers. Instead of flowers, think COOKIES IN BLOOM.

BACKGROUND:
Established: 1988; 1st Franchised: 1992
Franchised Units: 20
Company-Owned Units: 0
Total Units: 20
Dist.: US-20; CAN-0; O'seas-0
North America: 14 States
Density: 8 in TX, 2 in CA, 2 in FL
Projected New Units (12 Months): 4
Qualifications: 4, 4, 1, 3, 3, 4
Registered: CA,FL,IL,MD,MI,NY,VA,WA
FINANCIAL/TERMS:
Cash Investment: $75-116K
Total Investment: $75-116K
Minimum Net Worth: $100K
Fees: Franchise - $19.5K
Royalty - 5%; Ad. - 2%
Earnings Claims Statement: No
Term of Contract (Years): 5/5
Avg. # Of Employees: 3 FT, 2 PT
Passive Ownership: Discouraged
Encourage Conversions: No
Area Develop. Agreements: Yes/5
Sub-Franchising Contracts: No
Expand In Territory: Yes
Space Needs: 1,000-1,500 SF; SC
SUPPORT & TRAINING:
Financial Assistance Provided: No
Site Selection Assistance: Yes
Lease Negotiation Assistance: Yes
Co-Operative Advertising: Yes
Franchisee Assoc./Member: Yes/Yes
Size Of Corporate Staff: 2
On-Going Support: b,C,D,E,G,H,I
Training: 2 Weeks in Phoenix, AZ.
SPECIFIC EXPANSION PLANS:
US: All United States
Canada: All Canada
Overseas: UK, Australia, New Zealand, Mexico

<< >>

DONUT DELITE CAFE

3380 S. Service Rd.
Burlington, ON L7N 3J5 CANADA
Tel: (905) 681-8448
Fax: (905) 637-7745
E-Mail: rstraker@aftonfood.com
Web Site: www.worldfranchising.com/website.htm
Mr. Richard Straker, Director of Franchising

Cafe setting for fresh donuts, bagels, soup and sandwiches with a gourmet and specialty coffee program.

BACKGROUND:
Established: 1984; 1st Franchised: 1986
Franchised Units: 22
Company-Owned Units: 0
Total Units: 22
Dist.: US-0; CAN-22; O'seas-0
North America: 1 Province
Density: 22 in ON
Projected New Units (12 Months): 6
Qualifications: 3, 4, 3, 3, 3, 5
Registered: NR
FINANCIAL/TERMS:
Cash Investment: $40-60K
Total Investment: $110-150K
Minimum Net Worth: $100K
Fees: Franchise - $20K
Royalty - 6%; Ad. - 2%
Earnings Claims Statement: Yes
Term of Contract (Years): 10/5
Avg. # Of Employees: 3 FT, 7 PT
Passive Ownership: Discouraged
Encourage Conversions: Yes
Area Develop. Agreements: Yes/10
Sub-Franchising Contracts: Yes
Expand In Territory: Yes
Space Needs: 1,500-2,000 SF; FS, SF, SC
SUPPORT & TRAINING:
Financial Assistance Provided: Yes(I)
Site Selection Assistance: Yes
Lease Negotiation Assistance: Yes
Co-Operative Advertising: Yes
Franchisee Assoc./Member: No
Size Of Corporate Staff: 10
On-Going Support: B,C,D,E,F,G,H
Training: 1 Week Classroom; 2 Weeks Training Store; 1 Week Own Store.
SPECIFIC EXPANSION PLANS:
US: All United States
Canada: All Canada
Overseas: No

<< >>

Top 100

DUNKIN' DONUTS

14 Pacella Park Dr., P.O. Box 317
Randolph, MA 02368-0317
Tel: (800) 777-9983 (781) 961-4020
E-Mail: dlarose@adrus.com
Web Site: www.dunkin-baskin.com
Mr. Don Larose, Director Franchise Services

DUNKIN' DONUTS is the world's largest coffee and doughnut chain. We offer a full array of quick-service menu items, including muffins, bagels and donuts. In some markets DUNKIN' DONUTS, together with TOGO's and/or BASKIN-ROBBINS, offers multiple brand combinations of the three brands. TOGO's, BASKIN-ROBBINS, and DUNKIN' DONUTS are all subsidiaries of Allied Domecq PLC.

BACKGROUND: IFA MEMBER
Established: 1950; 1st Franchised: 1955
Franchised Units: 5,000
Company-Owned Units: 0
Total Units: 5,000
Dist.: US-3,390; CAN-500; O'seas-1,110
North America: 39 States
Density: 490 in MA, 359 in NY, 237 IL
Projected New Units (12 Months): 350
Qualifications: 5, 4, 2, 2, 5, 4
Registered:CA,FL,IL,IN,MD,MI,MN,NY,OR,RI,VA,WA,WI,DC
FINANCIAL/TERMS:
Cash Investment: $200K
Total Investment: $255.7-1139.7K
Minimum Net Worth: $400K/unit
Fees: Franchise - $50K
Royalty - 5.9%; Ad. - 5%
Earnings Claims Statement: Yes
Term of Contract (Years): 20
Avg. # Of Employees: NR
Passive Ownership: Allowed
Encourage Conversions: Yes
Area Develop. Agreements: Yes/3-5
Sub-Franchising Contracts: No
Expand In Territory: Yes
Space Needs: NR SF; FS, SF, SC, RM

SUPPORT & TRAINING:
Financial Assistance Provided: Yes(I)
Site Selection Assistance: NA
Lease Negotiation Assistance: Yes
Co-Operative Advertising: Yes
Franchisee Assoc./Member: Yes/No
Size Of Corporate Staff: NR
On-Going Support: B,C,E,G,H,I
Training: 51 Days in Randolph, MA; 3.5 Days in another Location.
SPECIFIC EXPANSION PLANS:
US: All Regions
Canada: PQ, ON
Overseas: All Countries

<< >>

GREAT AMERICAN BAGEL, THE

519 N. Cass Ave., # 1W
Westmont, IL 60559
Tel: (888) 224-3563 (630) 963-3393
Fax: (630) 963-7799
E-Mail: greatambgl@aol.com
Web Site: www.greatamericanbagel.com
Mr. Chris Lettieri, President

Bagel bakery and restaurant, specializing in freshly made bagels - made daily from scratch on the store premises. Stores feature monthly specials along with 28 varieties of bagels daily. In addition, each store also prepares it's own fresh cream cheeses!

BACKGROUND:
Established: 1987; 1st Franchised: 1994
Franchised Units: 201
Company-Owned Units: 14
Total Units: 215
Dist.: US-40; CAN-0; O'seas-0
North America: 10 States
Density: 25 in IL, 3 in WA, 2 in IN
Projected New Units (12 Months): 20
Qualifications: 5, 3, 2, 3, 4, 5
Registered: FL,IL,IN,MI,MN,ND,WA,WI
FINANCIAL/TERMS:
Cash Investment: $60-80K
Total Investment: $230-280K
Minimum Net Worth: $250K
Fees: Franchise - $20K
Royalty - 4%; Ad. - 2%
Earnings Claims Statement: No
Term of Contract (Years): 20/5
Avg. # Of Employees: 3 FT, 9 PT
Passive Ownership: Not Allowed
Encourage Conversions: NA
Area Develop. Agreements: No
Sub-Franchising Contracts: No
Expand In Territory: Yes
Space Needs: 2,000 SF; FS, SF, SC, RM
SUPPORT & TRAINING:
Financial Assistance Provided: No
Site Selection Assistance: Yes
Lease Negotiation Assistance: Yes
Co-Operative Advertising: NA
Franchisee Assoc./Member: Yes
Size Of Corporate Staff: NR
On-Going Support: B,C,D,E,g,h
Training: 4 Weeks Western Springs, IL.
SPECIFIC EXPANSION PLANS:
US: All United States
Canada: No
Overseas: No

<< >>

Great American Cookies

GREAT AMERICAN COOKIES

2855 E. Cottonwood Pkwy., # 400
Salt Lake City, UT 84121-7037
Tel: (800) 343-5377 + 2399
Fax: (801) 736-5936
E-Mail: donl@mrsfields.com
Web Site: www.greatamericancookies.com
Mr. Don Lewandowski, VP of Development Bakery

'Share the Fun of Cookies.' Established cookie concept with a great old family recipe, attractive retail price point, unique cookie cake program, available in store formats for traditional and non-traditional venues.

BACKGROUND: IFA MEMBER
Established: 1977; 1st Franchised: 1977
Franchised Units: 231
Company-Owned Units: 49
Total Units: 280
Dist.: US-279; CAN-0; O'seas-1
North America: 34 States
Density: 53 in TX, 25 in GA, 24 in FL
Projected New Units (12 Months): 7
Qualifications: 5, 3, 1, 1, 3, 5
Registered: All States Except VA
FINANCIAL/TERMS:
Cash Investment: $122-493K
Total Investment: $116.5-274K
Minimum Net Worth: $150K/75K LIQ
Fees: Franchise - $30K
Royalty - 6%; Ad. - 1%
Earnings Claims Statement: Yes
Term of Contract (Years): W/ Lease
Avg. # Of Employees: 3 FT, 2 PT
Passive Ownership: Discouraged
Encourage Conversions: Yes
Area Develop. Agreements: No
Sub-Franchising Contracts: No
Expand In Territory: Yes
Space Needs: 200-1,000 SF; NR
SUPPORT & TRAINING:
Financial Assistance Provided: No
Site Selection Assistance: Yes
Lease Negotiation Assistance: Yes
Co-Operative Advertising: No
Franchisee Assoc./Member: Yes
Size Of Corporate Staff: 100+
On-Going Support: B,C,D,E,G,H,I
Training: In Salt Lake City, Utah.
SPECIFIC EXPANSION PLANS:
US: All United States
Canada: No
Overseas: NR

<< >>

GREAT CANADIAN BAGEL, THE

270 Central Pkwy. W., # 301
Mississauga, ON L5C 4P4 CANADA
Tel: (905) 566-1903
Fax: (905) 566-1402
E-Mail: edk@greatcanadianbagel.com
Web Site: www.greatcanadianbagel.com
Mr. Ed Kwiatkowski, President

Canada's largest chain devoted to bagels has elevated the bagel to a new culinary experience. The chain offers a healthy way to enjoy a sandwich, snack or meal, while providing an alternative to higher fat, fast-food establishments. The bagel has become the ideal convenience food of the 90's - low in fat, high in taste, nutritious and now, convenient, thanks to the expansion of THE GREAT CANADIAN BAGEL.

BACKGROUND:
Established: 1993; 1st Franchised: 1994
Franchised Units: 101
Company-Owned Units: 3
Total Units: 104
Dist.: US-0; CAN-152; O'seas-4
North America: 9 Provinces
Density: 90 in ON, 24 in BC, 13 Marit
Projected New Units (12 Months): 20
Qualifications: 5, 4, 3, 3, 2, 5
Registered: AB
FINANCIAL/TERMS:
Cash Investment: $100K
Total Investment: $260-300K
Minimum Net Worth: $10K
Fees: Franchise - $30K
Royalty - 6%; Ad. - 1.5%
Earnings Claims Statement: Yes
Term of Contract (Years): 10/5

Avg. # Of Employees: 7 FT, 5 PT
Passive Ownership: Discouraged
Encourage Conversions: No
Area Develop. Agreements: No
Sub-Franchising Contracts: Yes
Expand In Territory: Yes
Space Needs: 2,000 SF; NA

SUPPORT & TRAINING:
Financial Assistance Provided: Yes
Site Selection Assistance: Yes
Lease Negotiation Assistance: NA
Co-Operative Advertising: Yes
Franchisee Assoc./Member: Yes/Yes
Size Of Corporate Staff: NR
On-Going Support: A,B,C,D,E,F,G,h
Training: 4-6 Weeks Toronto, ON.

SPECIFIC EXPANSION PLANS:
US: See The Great American Bagel
Canada: All Canada
Overseas: All Countries

GREAT HARVEST BREAD CO.

28 S. Montana St.
Dillon, MT 59725-2434
Tel: (800) 442-0424 + 252 (406) 683-6842 + 252
Fax: (406) 683-5537
E-Mail: dawne@greatharvest.com
Web Site: www.greatharvest.com
Ms. Dawn Eisenzimer, Dir. New Franchise Devel.

GREAT HARVEST BREAD CO. stores are neighborhood, retail bread bakeries, specializing in the best tasting, made-from-scratch, naturally fresh whole wheat breads you ever had. These unique stores also serve scratch-made cookies, scones, muffins, specialty breads, coffee and an inviting and fun environment for customers.

BACKGROUND:
Established: 1976; 1st Franchised: 1978
Franchised Units: 207
Company-Owned Units: 0
Total Units: 207
Dist.: US-180; CAN-0; O'seas-0
North America: 39 States
Density: 16 in MI, 13 in UT, 11 in IL
Projected New Units (12 Months): 24
Qualifications: 4, 4, 3, 4, 5, 4
Registered: All States

FINANCIAL/TERMS:
Cash Investment: $60-80K
Total Investment: $108-352K
Minimum Net Worth: $250K
Fees: Franchise - $30K
Royalty - 5-7%; Ad. - 0%
Earnings Claims Statement: Yes
Term of Contract (Years): 10/10
Avg. # Of Employees: 3 FT, 6 PT
Passive Ownership: Discouraged
Encourage Conversions: NA
Area Develop. Agreements: Yes/2
Sub-Franchising Contracts: No
Expand In Territory: Yes
Space Needs: 1,500-2,200 SF; SC

SUPPORT & TRAINING:
Financial Assistance Provided: Yes(I)
Site Selection Assistance: Yes
Lease Negotiation Assistance: Yes
Co-Operative Advertising: No
Franchisee Assoc./Member: Yes/Yes
Size Of Corporate Staff: 28
On-Going Support: B,C,D,E,G,H,I
Training: 1 Wk Dillon, MT; 1 Wk ea. 2 Host Trainings; 3-5 Days Store Opening; 5-10 Days 3 Trainers.

SPECIFIC EXPANSION PLANS:
US: All United States
Canada: All Canada
Overseas: No

HOUSE OF BREAD

858 Higuera St.
San Luis Obispo, CA 93401
Tel: (800) 545-5146 (805) 542-0257
Fax: (805) 542-0257
E-Mail: smccann@slonet.org
Web Site: www.houseofbread.com
Ms. Sheila McCann, Chief Executive Officer

Healthy, premium bread bakery, with over 20 varieties of delicious breads - from traditional honey whole wheat to irresistible sourdough pesto artichoke or the decadent triple chocolate bread. HOUSE OF BREAD's unique recipes use no dairy, refined sugar or fat, yet taste incredible.

BACKGROUND:
Established: 1996; 1st Franchised: 1998
Franchised Units: 21
Company-Owned Units: 2
Total Units: 23
Dist.: US-9; CAN-0; O'seas-0
North America: 2 States
Density: 7 in CA
Projected New Units (12 Months): 6
Qualifications: 3, 3, 1, 3, 3, 5
Registered: CA

FINANCIAL/TERMS:
Cash Investment: $24-65K
Total Investment: $75-204K
Minimum Net Worth: $50K
Fees: Franchise - $24K
Royalty - 6%; Ad. - 2%
Earnings Claims Statement: No
Term of Contract (Years): 10/10
Avg. # Of Employees: 2 FT, 8 PT
Passive Ownership: Discouraged
Encourage Conversions: NR
Area Develop. Agreements: Yes
Sub-Franchising Contracts: NR
Expand In Territory: Yes
Space Needs: 1,500 SF; SC, RM

SUPPORT & TRAINING:
Financial Assistance Provided: Yes(B)
Site Selection Assistance: Yes
Lease Negotiation Assistance: Yes
Co-Operative Advertising: Yes
Franchisee Assoc./Member: No
Size Of Corporate Staff: 2
On-Going Support: C,D,E,F,G,H,I
Training: Minimum 9 Days San Luis Obispo, CA; Minimum 7 Days Franchisee Location.

SPECIFIC EXPANSION PLANS:
US: All United States
Canada: All Canada
Overseas: All Countries

LAMAR'S DONUTS

6551 S. Revere Pkwy., # 250
Centennial, CO 80111
Tel: (800) 533-7489 (303) 792-9200
Fax: (303) 790-0708
E-Mail: franinfo@lamars.com
Web Site: www.lamars.com
Ms. Cheri Emerson, Franchise Sales Inquiries

LAMAR'S DONUTS is a rapidly growing chain of retail donut shops, founded in Kansas City, specializing in 53 varieties of handmade donuts and specialties since 1933, served in an atmosphere rich in hospitality and authenticity. A K.C. institution and Chamber of Commerce tourist attraction, LAMAR's has received acclaim nationwide, creating what critics call "the perfect donut."

BACKGROUND: IFA MEMBER
Established: 1933; 1st Franchised: 1993
Franchised Units: 21
Company-Owned Units: 3
Total Units: 24
Dist.: US-27; CAN-0; O'seas-0
North America: 8 States
Density: 11 in MO, 6 in KS, 2 in VA

Projected New Units (12 Months): 10-20
Qualifications: 4, 5, 3, 2, 5, 5
Registered: FL,VA

FINANCIAL/TERMS:
Cash Investment: Varies
Total Investment: $200-240K
Minimum Net Worth: Varies
Fees: Franchise - $26.5K
Royalty - 5%; Ad. - 2%
Earnings Claims Statement: No
Term of Contract (Years): 10/10
Avg. # Of Employees: 4-6 FT, 5-10 PT
Passive Ownership: Allowed
Encourage Conversions: Yes
Area Develop. Agreements: Yes/Negot.
Sub-Franchising Contracts: Yes
Expand In Territory: Yes
Space Needs: 2,000 SF; SF, SC

SUPPORT & TRAINING:
Financial Assistance Provided: Yes(I)
Site Selection Assistance: Yes
Lease Negotiation Assistance: Yes
Co-Operative Advertising: Yes
Franchisee Assoc./Member: No
Size Of Corporate Staff: 10
On-Going Support: a,b,C,D,E,F,G,H,I
Training: 2-4 Weeks Training Store in Kansas City; 3-5 On-Site in Franchise Store.

SPECIFIC EXPANSION PLANS:
US: All U.S., Midwest, Southeast
Canada: No
Overseas: No

LOX OF BAGELS
11801 Prestwick Rd.
Potomac, MD 20854
Tel: (800) 879-6927
Fax:
E-Mail: loxofbagels@msn.com
Web Site: www.bagelfranchises.com
Mr. Ted Taylor, Manager

Retail bagel bakery with gourmet coffees, espresso, juices and specialty breads.

BACKGROUND:
Established: 1986; 1st Franchised: 1995
Franchised Units: 13
Company-Owned Units: 0
Total Units: 13
Dist.: US-13; CAN-0; O'seas-0
North America: NR
Density: NR
Projected New Units (12 Months): 25
Qualifications: 4, 2, 1, 1, 5, 4
Registered: All States

FINANCIAL/TERMS:
Cash Investment: $50K
Total Investment: $168-200K
Minimum Net Worth: NR
Fees: Franchise - $24.5K
Royalty - 0%; Ad. - 0%
Earnings Claims Statement: No
Term of Contract (Years): 5/5
Avg. # Of Employees: 3 FT, 3 PT
Passive Ownership: Allowed
Encourage Conversions: Yes
Area Develop. Agreements: Yes/20
Sub-Franchising Contracts: No
Expand In Territory: Yes
Space Needs: 900-2,500 SF; FS, SF, SC

SUPPORT & TRAINING:
Financial Assistance Provided: No
Site Selection Assistance: Yes
Lease Negotiation Assistance: Yes
Co-Operative Advertising: No
Franchisee Assoc./Member: No
Size Of Corporate Staff: 4
On-Going Support: C,D,E,F,I
Training: 4 Days On-Site.

SPECIFIC EXPANSION PLANS:
US: All United States
Canada: All Canada
Overseas: Europe

MANHATTAN BAGEL COMPANY
100 Horizon Center Blvd.
Hamilton, NJ 08691
Tel: (800) 308-2457 (609) 631-7000
Fax: (609) 631-7067
E-Mail: wbarry@nwrgi.com
Web Site: www.newworldrestaurantgroup.com
Mr. Wayne Barry, Dir. Franchise Development

MANHATTAN BAGEL CO. offers upscale, efficient, bagel eateries, offering authentic New York bagels in 21 varieties, as well as gourmet spreads and deli items, plus full breakfast fare. Stores are configured 100% turn-key, including site selection and negotiation. We have comprehensive training with a detailed operations manual and continuing assistance in marketing, merchandising and food preparation. No baking experience is required.

BACKGROUND: IFA MEMBER
Established: 1987; 1st Franchised: 1988
Franchised Units: 260
Company-Owned Units: 8
Total Units: 268
Dist.: US-311; CAN-0; O'seas-0
North America: 21 States
Density: 33 in NJ, 18 in PA, 17 in CA
Projected New Units (12 Months): 35
Qualifications: 3, 3, 1, 1, 3, 5
Registered: All States

FINANCIAL/TERMS:
Cash Investment: $80-100K
Total Investment: $150-337K
Minimum Net Worth: $150K
Fees: Franchise - $20K
Royalty - 5%; Ad. - 2.5-4%
Earnings Claims Statement: No
Term of Contract (Years): 10/10
Avg. # Of Employees: 3 FT, 9 PT
Passive Ownership: Discouraged
Encourage Conversions: Yes
Area Develop. Agreements: Yes
Sub-Franchising Contracts: Yes
Expand In Territory: Yes
Space Needs: 1,200-1,600 SF; FS, SC

SUPPORT & TRAINING:
Financial Assistance Provided: No
Site Selection Assistance: Yes
Lease Negotiation Assistance: Yes
Co-Operative Advertising: Yes
Franchisee Assoc./Member: Yes
Size Of Corporate Staff: 313
On-Going Support: B,C,D,E,F,G,h
Training: 2 Weeks in Corporate Office; 1 Week in Store.

SPECIFIC EXPANSION PLANS:
US: All United States
Canada: No
Overseas: Middle East, Iceland

MMMARVELLOUS MMMUFFINS (CANADA)
400 Steeprock Dr.
Toronto, ON M3J2XI CANADA
Tel: (800) 827-1039 + 273 (416) 638-3333 + 273
Fax: (416) 236-0054
E-Mail: timothym@timothys.com
Web Site: www.mmmuffins.com
Mr. Tim Martin, Franchise Director

Fresh, high-quality specialty baked goods including over 100 varieties of muffins as well as scones, cinnamon swirls, cookies and streusel cakes. In addition, we offer a selection of gourmet coffee, teas, and fruit juices.

BACKGROUND:
Established: 1979; 1st Franchised: 1980
Franchised Units: 85
Company-Owned Units: 5
Total Units: 90
Dist.: US-0; CAN-116; O'seas-6

North America: 8 Provinces
Density: 43 in ON, 26 in PQ, 13 in BC
Projected New Units (12 Months): 10
Qualifications: 5, 4, 3, 3, 4, 5
Registered: AB

FINANCIAL/TERMS:
Cash Investment: $40-60K+
Total Investment: $160K
Minimum Net Worth: $200K
Fees: Franchise - $25K
Royalty - 7%; Ad. - 1%
Earnings Claims Statement: No
Term of Contract (Years): 10/10
Avg. # Of Employees: 2-3 FT, 4-7 PT
Passive Ownership: Not Allowed
Encourage Conversions: Yes
Area Develop. Agreements: Yes (I'ntl.)
Sub-Franchising Contracts: Yes
Expand In Territory: Yes
Space Needs: 300 SF; SF, SC, RM

SUPPORT & TRAINING:
Financial Assistance Provided: Yes(I)
Site Selection Assistance: Yes
Lease Negotiation Assistance: Yes
Co-Operative Advertising: Yes
Franchisee Assoc./Member: No
Size Of Corporate Staff: 35
On-Going Support: A,B,C,D,E,F,G,h
Training: 4 Weeks Toronto, ON.

SPECIFIC EXPANSION PLANS:
US: N/A
Canada: All Canada
Overseas: Asia, Eastern Europe, Middle East, South America

<< >>

Mrs. Fields

Top 100

MRS. FIELDS COOKIES
2855 E. Cottonwood Pkwy., # 400
Salt Lake City, UT 84121-7050
Tel: (800) 343-5377 + 2399
Fax: (801) 736-5936
E-Mail: donl@mrsfields.com
Web Site: www.mrsfields.com
Mr. Don Lewandowski, VP of Development Bakery

Premier retail cookie business with 'uncompromising quality,' 94% brand recognition, easy to operate, flexible designs and store options that operate in traditional and non-traditional venues.

BACKGROUND: IFA MEMBER
Established: 1977; 1st Franchised: 1990
Franchised Units: 317
Company-Owned Units: 75
Total Units: 392
Dist.: US-393; CAN-0; O'seas-77
North America: 43 States, 1 Province
Density: 103 in CA, 30 in MI,25 in IL
Projected New Units (12 Months): 38
Qualifications: 4, 4, 2, 2, 2, 5
Registered: All States Except VA

FINANCIAL/TERMS:
Cash Investment: $10-73.5K
Total Investment: $162.4-247.1K
Minimum Net Worth: $150K/75K LIQ
Fees: Franchise - $30K
Royalty - 6%; Ad. - 1%
Earnings Claims Statement: Yes
Term of Contract (Years): 7/7
Avg. # Of Employees: 3 FT, 2 PT
Passive Ownership: Not Allowed
Encourage Conversions: Yes
Area Develop. Agreements: No
Sub-Franchising Contracts: No
Expand In Territory: Yes
Space Needs: 600-900 SF; RM, SC, SF, Stadium

SUPPORT & TRAINING:
Financial Assistance Provided: No
Site Selection Assistance: Yes
Lease Negotiation Assistance: Yes
Co-Operative Advertising: No
Franchisee Assoc./Member: Yes/Yes
Size Of Corporate Staff: 100+
On-Going Support: A,B,C,D,E,F,G,H,I
Training: In Salt Lake City, UT.

SPECIFIC EXPANSION PLANS:
US: All United States
Canada: All Canada
Overseas: NR

<< >>

MRS. POWELL'S BAKERY EATERY
3380 S. Service Rd.
Burlington, ON L7N 3J5 CANADA
Tel: (905) 681-8448
Fax: (905) 637-7745
E-Mail: rstraker@aftonfood.com
Web Site: www.aftonfood.com
Mr. Richard Straker, Director of Franchising

Production and baking of fresh cinnamon rolls, custom sandwiches, European-style sandwiches, soup, desserts and assorted beverages.

BACKGROUND:
Established: 1984; 1st Franchised: 1986
Franchised Units: 13
Company-Owned Units: 0
Total Units: 13
Dist.: US-23; CAN-0; O'seas-2
North America: 14 States
Density: 6 in ID, 3 in WA, 3 in CA
Projected New Units (12 Months): 8
Qualifications: 3, 4, 2, 3, 3, 4
Registered: IN,WA,AB

FINANCIAL/TERMS:
Cash Investment: $50K
Total Investment: $125-160K
Minimum Net Worth: $100K
Fees: Franchise - $25K
Royalty - 5%; Ad. - 3%
Earnings Claims Statement: No
Term of Contract (Years): 10/10
Avg. # Of Employees: 2 FT, 4 PT
Passive Ownership: Discouraged
Encourage Conversions: Yes
Area Develop. Agreements: Yes/20
Sub-Franchising Contracts: Yes
Expand In Territory: Yes
Space Needs: 500-2,000 SF; SF, SC, RM

SUPPORT & TRAINING:
Financial Assistance Provided: No
Site Selection Assistance: Yes
Lease Negotiation Assistance: Yes
Co-Operative Advertising: No
Franchisee Assoc./Member: No
Size Of Corporate Staff: 10
On-Going Support: C,D,E,F,G,h
Training: 1 Week Head Office; 1 Week Franchised Store; 1 Week Own Store.

SPECIFIC EXPANSION PLANS:
US: All United States
Canada: All Canada
Overseas: Europe, Far East

<< >>

MY FAVORITE MUFFIN
500 Lake Cook Rd., # 475
Deerfield, IL 60015
Tel: (800) 251-6101 (773) 380-6100
Fax: (773) 380-6183
E-Mail: tcervini@babcorp.com
Web Site: www.babholdings.com
Mr. Tony Cervini, Director Development

As a MY FAVORITE MUFFIN franchisee, you get to create and sell over 300 varieties of our special muffins in both regular and fat-free varieties. Where applicable, you can add BIG APPLE BAGELS and BREWSTER'S COFFEE to complement your wonderful muffins.

BACKGROUND:
Established: 1987; 1st Franchised: 1988
Franchised Units: 31
Company-Owned Units: 0
Total Units: 31
Dist.: US-71; CAN-0; O'seas-0
North America: 19 States
Density: 18 in NJ, 10 in PA, 8 in FL
Projected New Units (12 Months): 15
Qualifications: 3, 3, 5, 2, 2, 5
Registered: All States
FINANCIAL/TERMS:
Cash Investment: NR
Total Investment: $234-382.3K
Minimum Net Worth: $50K Min.
Fees: Franchise - $25K
Royalty - 5%; Ad. - 2%
Earnings Claims Statement: No
Term of Contract (Years): 10/10
Avg. # Of Employees: 3 FT, 15 PT
Passive Ownership: Discouraged
Encourage Conversions: NA
Area Develop. Agreements: Yes
Sub-Franchising Contracts: No
Expand In Territory: Yes
Space Needs: 1,800-2,200 SF; FS, SC, RM
SUPPORT & TRAINING:
Financial Assistance Provided: Yes(I)
Site Selection Assistance: Yes
Lease Negotiation Assistance: Yes
Co-Operative Advertising: No
Franchisee Assoc./Member: NR
Size Of Corporate Staff: 34
On-Going Support: B,C,D,E,F,G,H,I
Training: 2 Weeks Milwaukee, WI; 5 Days Store Location Prior to Opening.
SPECIFIC EXPANSION PLANS:
US: All United States
Canada: All Canada
Overseas: All Countries

<< >>

PANERA BREAD COMPANY
6710 Clayton Rd.
Richmond Heights, MO 63117
Tel: (800) 301-5566 (314) 633-7100
Fax: (314) 633-7200
E-Mail: peter.wright@panerabread.com
Web Site: www.panerabread.com
Mr. Peter Wright, Dir. Franchise Administration

Founded in Saint Louis in 1987, SAINT LOUIS BREAD has expanded into new markets over the past few years, with strong consumer acceptance for its unique concept. Each SAINT LOUIS BREAD bakery-cafe features a comfortable neighborhood setting where residents can relax and enjoy a wide range of fresh-baked sourdough breads, along with other fresh-baked goods, bagels and hearty made-to-order sandwiches, salads and soups.

BACKGROUND:
Established: 1987; 1st Franchised: 1993
Franchised Units: 356
Company-Owned Units: 184
Total Units: 540
Dist.: US-104; CAN-0; O'seas-0
North America: 14 States
Density: 36 in MO, 25 in IL, 8 in GA
Projected New Units (12 Months): 108
Qualifications: 5, 5, 5, 3, 3, 4
Registered: All States
FINANCIAL/TERMS:
Cash Investment: $135-165K
Total Investment: $550-650K
Minimum Net Worth: $3MM
Fees: Franchise - $35K
Royalty - 5%; Ad. - Up to 5%
Earnings Claims Statement: Yes
Term of Contract (Years): 20/Agrmt.
Avg. # Of Employees: 17 FT, 17 PT
Passive Ownership: Not Allowed
Encourage Conversions: No
Area Develop. Agreements: Yes/3-13
Sub-Franchising Contracts: No
Expand In Territory: No
Space Needs: 3,500 SF; FS, SF, SC, RM
SUPPORT & TRAINING:
Financial Assistance Provided: No
Site Selection Assistance: Yes
Lease Negotiation Assistance: No
Co-Operative Advertising: Yes
Franchisee Assoc./Member: No
Size Of Corporate Staff: 54
On-Going Support: B,C,D,E,F,H,I
Training: 10 Weeks St. Louis, MO.
SPECIFIC EXPANSION PLANS:
US: All United States
Canada: No
Overseas: No

<< >>

SAINT CINNAMON BAKE SHOPPE
350 Esna Park Dr.
Markham, ON L3R 1A5 CANADA
Tel: (877) 490-5916 (905) 470-1517
Fax: (905) 470-8112
E-Mail: info@saintcinnamon.com
Web Site: www.saintcinnamon.com
Mr. Mark Halpern, Executive Vice President

Largest cinnamon-roll franchise in Canada. The rolls are made and baked daily at each location. The franchisee is given two weeks of intensive training in all aspects of the business.

BACKGROUND:
Established: 1986; 1st Franchised: 1986
Franchised Units: 125
Company-Owned Units: 1
Total Units: 126
Dist.: US-3; CAN-70; O'seas-34
North America: 3 States, 3 Provinces
Density: 42 in ON, 25 in PQ, 3 in NB
Projected New Units (12 Months): 15
Qualifications: 4, 4, 4, 4, 4, 5
Registered: NR
FINANCIAL/TERMS:
Cash Investment: $40-75K
Total Investment: $144-265K
Minimum Net Worth: NR
Fees: Franchise - $25K
Royalty - 6%; Ad. - 3%
Earnings Claims Statement: No
Term of Contract (Years): 10/5
Avg. # Of Employees: 2 FT, 5 PT
Passive Ownership: Not Allowed
Encourage Conversions: NA
Area Develop. Agreements: Yes/10
Sub-Franchising Contracts: Yes
Expand In Territory: Yes
Space Needs: 300-600 SF; RM
SUPPORT & TRAINING:
Financial Assistance Provided: NA
Site Selection Assistance: Yes
Lease Negotiation Assistance: Yes
Co-Operative Advertising: No
Franchisee Assoc./Member: No
Size Of Corporate Staff: 7
On-Going Support: A,B,C,D,e,F,G,h
Training: 2 Weeks in ON.
SPECIFIC EXPANSION PLANS:
US: All United States
Canada: All Canada
Overseas: Middle East, Europe, South America

<< >>

SOUTHERN MAID DONUTS
3615 Cavalier Dr.
Garland, TX 75042-7599
Tel: (800) 936-6887 (972) 272-6425
Fax: (972) 276-3549
E-Mail: dunker1@gte.net
Web Site: www.southernmaiddonuts.com
Mr. Les Franklin, Vice President

Since 1937, we have offered personal service to assist each franchisee in producing the finest-quality donuts at low initial cost and continuing fees. Our motto is 'The Taste You Remember - Since 1937. SOUTHERN MAID DONUTS.'

BACKGROUND:
Established: 1937; 1st Franchised: 1941
Franchised Units: 86
Company-Owned Units: 0
Total Units: 86
Dist.: US-85; CAN-0; O'seas-0
North America: 12 States
Density: 65 in TX, 10 in LA, 3 in WA
Projected New Units (12 Months): 12
Qualifications: 3, 3, 1, 1, 3, 5
Registered: CA,OR,VA

FINANCIAL/TERMS:
Cash Investment: $50K+
Total Investment: $50-125K
Minimum Net Worth: $50K+
Fees: Franchise - $5K
Royalty - 0%; Ad. - 0%
Earnings Claims Statement: No
Term of Contract (Years): 10/10
Avg. # Of Employees: 4 FT,2 PT
Passive Ownership: Allowed
Encourage Conversions: Yes
Area Develop. Agreements: Yes/5
Sub-Franchising Contracts: No
Expand In Territory: Yes
Space Needs: 1,000-1,500 SF; SF, SC

SUPPORT & TRAINING:
Financial Assistance Provided: Yes(I)
Site Selection Assistance: Yes
Lease Negotiation Assistance: Yes
Co-Operative Advertising: No
Franchisee Assoc./Member: No
Size Of Corporate Staff: 6
On-Going Support: B,C,D,e,I
Training: 7 Days at Franchisee's Location (Not Included in Initial Fee.)

SPECIFIC EXPANSION PLANS:
US: All United States
Canada: All Canada
Overseas: All Countries

TREATS

418 Preston St.
Ottawa, ON K1S 4N2 CANADA
Tel: (800) 461-4003 (613) 563-4073
Fax: (613) 563-1982
E-Mail: sadams@treats.com
Web Site: www.treats.com
Ms. Shirley Adams, Franchise Relations

Micro-bakery concept, featuring gourmet and specialty coffees and fresh-baked, on-site baked goods, including muffins, cookies and bagels. Three concept variations are available: TREATS BAKERY (~400 SF) serves the base menu offering; TREATS CAFE (~1,200 SF) also serves sandwiches (baguettes), soups and salads; TREATS COFFEE EMPORIUM (~1,200 SF) also offers coffee beans, coffee-related merchandise and sandwiches.

BACKGROUND:
Established: 1977; 1st Franchised: 1979
Franchised Units: 97
Company-Owned Units: 3
Total Units: 100
Dist.: US-5; CAN-140; O'seas-0
North America: 3 States, 9 Provinces
Density: 75 in ON, 25 in PQ, 10 in AB
Projected New Units (12 Months): 12
Qualifications: 3, 3, 3, 2, 3, 5
Registered:CA,FL,IL,IN,MD,MI,MN,NY, OR,RI,VA,WA,WI,DC,AB

FINANCIAL/TERMS:
Cash Investment: $40-50K
Total Investment: $100-150K
Minimum Net Worth: $200K
Fees: Franchise - $25K
Royalty - 7%; Ad. - 1%
Earnings Claims Statement: No
Term of Contract (Years): Lease
Avg. # Of Employees: 3 FT, 2 PT
Passive Ownership: Discouraged
Encourage Conversions: Yes
Area Develop. Agreements: Yes/15
Sub-Franchising Contracts: Yes
Expand In Territory: Yes
Space Needs: 500-1,500 SF; SF, SC, RM

SUPPORT & TRAINING:
Financial Assistance Provided: No
Site Selection Assistance: Yes
Lease Negotiation Assistance: Yes
Co-Operative Advertising: Yes
Franchisee Assoc./Member: No
Size Of Corporate Staff: 15
On-Going Support: B,C,D,E,G,H,I
Training: 2 Weeks Training Center; 1 Week On-Site.

SPECIFIC EXPANSION PLANS:
US: East Coast
Canada: All Canada
Overseas: Chile, Brazil, Middle East

For a full explanation of the data provided in the Franchisor Profiles, please refer to *Chapter 2, "How to Use the Data."*

Food: Coffee

Chapter **14**

Food: Coffee Industry Profile

Total # Franchisors in Industry Group	35
Total # Franchised Units in Industry Group	1,785
Total # Company-Owned Units in Industry Group	469
Total # Operating Units in Industry Group	2,254
Average # Franchised Units/Franchisor	51
Average # Company-Owned Units/Franchisor	13.4
Average # Total Units/Franchisor	64.4
Ratio of Total # Franchised Units/Total # Company-Owned Units	3.8:1

Industry Survey Participants	15
Representing % of Industry	42.9%
Average Franchise Fee*:	$23.9K
Average Total Investment*:	$253.6K
Average On-Going Royalty Fee*:	6%

*If a range was provided, the mid-point of the range was used. See detailed profiles for actual ranges.

Five Largest Participants in Survey

Company	# Franchised Units	# Co-Owned Units	# Total Units	Franchise Fee	On-Going Royalty	Total Investment
1. Gloria Jean's Gourmet Coffees	397	20	417	$15-35K	6%	$130-457K
2. Second Cup, The	391	8	399	$25K	9%	$~335K
3. Coffee Beanery, The	169	5	174	$27.5K	6%	$300-400K
4. Chock Full O'Nuts Café	65	0	65	$25K	5%	$260-310K
5. It's A Grind Coffee House	44	4	48	$30K	6%	$196-323K

All of the data provided are proprietary and should not be quoted without acknowledging *Bond's Franchise Guide.*

ARABICA COFFEEHOUSE

5755 Granger Rd., # 200
Independence, OH 44131-1410
Tel: (800) 837-9599 (216) 351-1000
Fax: (216) 398-0707
E-Mail: rkrieger@mrhero.com
Web Site: www.arabicacoffeeinc.com
Mr. Bob Kreiger, Director Franchise Development

Built to reflect the personality of the community, an ARABICA COFFEEHOUSE is more than a place to enjoy 50 flavors of coffee, specialty drinks, unique teas, health-conscious sandwiches, decadent pastries and desserts. Superior food and beverages in well-appointed, comfortable surroundings is a perfect venue for any purpose.

BACKGROUND:

Established: 1994; 1st Franchised: 1994
Franchised Units: 46
Company-Owned Units: 1
Total Units: 47
Dist.: US-47; CAN-0; O'seas-0
North America: 1 State
Density: 47 in OH
Projected New Units (12 Months): 25
Qualifications: 5, 3, 3, 2, 3, 5
Registered: NR

FINANCIAL/TERMS:

Cash Investment: $75K
Total Investment: $126-363K
Minimum Net Worth: $300K
Fees: Franchise - $22.5K
Royalty - 5.5%; Ad. - 2.5%
Earnings Claims Statement: No
Term of Contract (Years): 10/10
Avg. # Of Employees: 4 FT, 6 PT
Passive Ownership: Discouraged
Encourage Conversions: Yes
Area Develop. Agreements: Yes/3-5
Sub-Franchising Contracts: Yes
Expand In Territory: Yes
Space Needs: 2,500 SF; FS, SF, SC, RM, Co-Brand

SUPPORT & TRAINING:

Financial Assistance Provided: Yes(I)
Site Selection Assistance: Yes
Lease Negotiation Assistance: Yes
Co-Operative Advertising: Yes
Franchisee Assoc./Member: No
Size Of Corporate Staff: 40
On-Going Support: B,C,D,E,F,G,H,I
Training: 3 Weeks Cleveland, OH.

SPECIFIC EXPANSION PLANS:

US: MI, OH, PA, KY, IN
Canada: No
Overseas: No

<< >>

BAD ASS COFFEE OF HAWAII

166 W. 2700 South
Salt Lake City, UT 84115
Tel: (888) 422-3277 (801) 463-1966
Fax: (801) 463-2606
E-Mail: haroldh@badasscoffee.com
Web Site: www.badasscoffee.com
Mr. Harold J. Hill, Director of Franchising

The BAD ASS COMPANY is the premier destination when you go to get yourself or a friend some of the world's best coffee and to experience the friendly aloha spirit while immersed in a unique, exciting, inviting Hawaiian atmosphere.

BACKGROUND:

Established: 1989; 1st Franchised: 1999
Franchised Units: 36
Company-Owned Units: 1
Total Units: 37
Dist.: US-33; CAN-4; O'seas-0
North America: 1 State
Density: NR
Projected New Units (12 Months): 10
Qualifications: 5, 3, 3, 3, 1, 2
Registered: CA,FL,HI,IL,IN,MI,OR,RI,VA,AB

FINANCIAL/TERMS:

Cash Investment: $50K
Total Investment: $150-200K
Minimum Net Worth: $500K
Fees: Franchise - $20K
Royalty - 6%; Ad. - 2%
Earnings Claims Statement: No
Term of Contract (Years): 5/20
Avg. # Of Employees: 3 FT, 4 PT
Passive Ownership: Discouraged
Encourage Conversions: Yes
Area Develop. Agreements: Yes(10)
Sub-Franchising Contracts: No
Expand In Territory: Yes
Space Needs: 1,500 SF; FS

SUPPORT & TRAINING:

Financial Assistance Provided: No
Site Selection Assistance: Yes
Lease Negotiation Assistance: Yes
Co-Operative Advertising: Yes
Franchisee Assoc./Member: No
Size Of Corporate Staff: 6
On-Going Support: B,C,D,E,G,H,I
Training: 1 Week Salt Lake City, UT.

SPECIFIC EXPANSION PLANS:

US: All United States
Canada: All Canada
Overseas: All Countries

<< >>

BEANER'S GOURMET COFFEE

115 W. Allegan St., 6th Fl.
Lansing, MI 48933
Tel: (877) 4BEANERS (517) 482-8145
Fax: (517) 482-8625
E-Mail: info@beaners.com
Web Site: www.beaners.com
Mr. Michael J. McFall, President

Italian style espresso café including a limited lunch offering, with extraordinary effort put into the development of the beverages. Exceptional attention has been put into brand development and our operating philosophy to ensure quick consumer ID of BEANER's and an unparalleled consumer retention rate.

BACKGROUND:

Established: 1994; 1st Franchised: 1999
Franchised Units: 18
Company-Owned Units: 8
Total Units: 26
Dist.: US-26; CAN-0; O'seas-0
North America: 3 States
Density: 16 in MI, 9 in OH, I in IN
Projected New Units (12 Months): 20
Qualifications: 5, 4, 1, 1, 3, 5
Registered: IN, MI

FINANCIAL/TERMS:

Cash Investment: $40-100K
Total Investment: $200-250K
Minimum Net Worth: $200K
Fees: Franchise - $22.5K
Royalty - 5%; Ad. - 2%
Earnings Claims Statement: No
Term of Contract (Years): 10/10
Avg. # Of Employees: 4 FT, 12 PT
Passive Ownership: Not Allowed
Encourage Conversions: Yes
Area Develop. Agreements: Yes/5
Sub-Franchising Contracts: No
Expand In Territory: Yes
Space Needs: 1,750 SF; FS, SF, SC, RM

SUPPORT & TRAINING:

Financial Assistance Provided: No
Site Selection Assistance: Yes
Lease Negotiation Assistance: Yes
Co-Operative Advertising: Yes
Franchisee Assoc./Member: No
Size Of Corporate Staff: 6
On-Going Support: A,C,D,E,G,h,I
Training: 3 Weeks in Lansing, MI; 2 Weeks On-Site.

SPECIFIC EXPANSION PLANS:

US: All United States
Canada: No
Overseas: No

<< >>

BLENZ COFFEE

535 Thurlow St., # 300
Vancouver, BC V6E 3L2 CANADA
Tel: (604) 682-2995
Fax: (604) 684-2542
E-Mail: admin@blenz.com
Web Site: www.blenzcoffee.com
Mr. Mark West, Operations Manager

Retailer of specialty coffees and teas in a warm, service-oriented environment. Capitalizing on the consumer trend towards better service and quality coffee-based beverages.

BACKGROUND:
Established: 1990; 1st Franchised: 1991
Franchised Units: 25
Company-Owned Units: 2
Total Units: 27
Dist.: US-0; CAN-15; O'seas-1
North America: 1 Province
Density: 15 in BC
Projected New Units (12 Months): 6
Qualifications: 3, 2, 2, 1, 5, 5
Registered: NR

FINANCIAL/TERMS:
Cash Investment: $40-75K
Total Investment: $135-190K
Minimum Net Worth: NR
Fees: Franchise - $25K
Royalty - 8%; Ad. - 2%
Earnings Claims Statement: Yes
Term of Contract (Years): 10
Avg. # Of Employees: 4 FT, 10 PT
Passive Ownership: Not Allowed
Encourage Conversions: No
Area Develop. Agreements: Yes/20
Sub-Franchising Contracts: Yes
Expand In Territory: Yes
Space Needs: 750-2,000 SF; FS, SF, SC, RM

SUPPORT & TRAINING:
Financial Assistance Provided: Yes(I)
Site Selection Assistance: Yes
Lease Negotiation Assistance: Yes
Co-Operative Advertising: Yes
Franchisee Assoc./Member: Yes/No
Size Of Corporate Staff: 4
On-Going Support: A,B,C,D,E,H
Training: 2 Weeks Exisitng Operation; 2 Weeks New Location.

SPECIFIC EXPANSION PLANS:
US: All United States
Canada: All Canada
Overseas: All Countries

<< >>

CHOCK FULL O'NUTS CAFÉ

500 Mamaroneck Ave.
Harrison, NY 10528
Tel: (800) 381-6303 (781) 718-8392
Fax: (914) 670-3500
E-Mail: gpelissier@saraleecoffee.com
Web Site: www.chockcafe.com
Mr. Gerry Pelissier, Vice President Development

We have created a unique coffee concept - a quick-serve coffee café! Our many formats are designed for speed of service with a café which includes specialty hot and frozen signature beverages, freshly baked on-site muffins, bagels and pastries - all targeting the consumer on the go. We even serve a signature egg sandwich and omelette to go. We are backed by our parent company, Sara Lee, and serve New York's classic coffee, CHOCK FULL O'NUTS.

BACKGROUND:
Established: 1932; 1st Franchised: 1994
Franchised Units: 65
Company-Owned Units: 0
Total Units: 65
Dist.: US-65; CAN-0; O'seas-0
North America: 10 States
Density: 24 in NY, 11 in MA, 4 in RI
Projected New Units (12 Months): 17
Qualifications: 5, 5, 3, 2, 4, 5
Registered: FL,MD,NY,RI,VA

FINANCIAL/TERMS:
Cash Investment: $85K
Total Investment: $260-310K
Minimum Net Worth: $350K
Fees: Franchise - $25K
Royalty - 5%; Ad. - 4%
Earnings Claims Statement: No
Term of Contract (Years): 10/10
Avg. # Of Employees: 2 FT, 12 PT
Passive Ownership: Discouraged
Encourage Conversions: Yes
Area Develop. Agreements: Yes/20
Sub-Franchising Contracts: No
Expand In Territory: Yes
Space Needs: 1,200 SF; FS, SF

SUPPORT & TRAINING:
Financial Assistance Provided: No
Site Selection Assistance: Yes
Lease Negotiation Assistance: Yes
Co-Operative Advertising: No
Franchisee Assoc./Member: Yes/Yes
Size Of Corporate Staff: 8
On-Going Support: B,C,D,E,F,G,H,I
Training: 2 Weeks Harrison, NY.

SPECIFIC EXPANSION PLANS:
US: East Coast
Canada: No
Overseas: No

<< >>

the coffee beanery

COFFEE BEANERY, THE

3429 Pierson Pl.
Flushing, MI 48433-2413
Tel: (800) 728-2326 (810) 733-1020
Fax: (810) 733-0374
E-Mail: info@coffeebeanery.com
Web Site: www.coffeebeanery.com
Mr. Kurt Shaw, VP Franchise Sales

THE COFFEE BEANERY, LTD. offers a variety of investment levels with storefront cafes being the main growth vehicle in the future. The cornerstone and foundation of the business is the exceptional quality of its own hand-roasted coffee. Our customers enjoy the best coffee and assorted products available from a network of over 180 opened franchised and corporate locations. Our operations department and training are superb.

BACKGROUND: IFA MEMBER
Established: 1976; 1st Franchised: 1985
Franchised Units: 169
Company-Owned Units: 5
Total Units: 174
Dist.: US-159; CAN-0; O'seas-15
North America: 30 States
Density: 32 in MI, 12 in FL, 16 in NY
Projected New Units (12 Months): 25
Qualifications: 5, 5, 1, 1, 1, 5
Registered: CA,FL,IL,IN,MD,MI,MN,NY,VA

FINANCIAL/TERMS:
Cash Investment: $100-125K
Total Investment: $300-400K
Minimum Net Worth: $300K
Fees: Franchise - $27.5K
Royalty - 6%; Ad. - 2%
Earnings Claims Statement: No
Term of Contract (Years): 5,10,15+
Avg. # Of Employees: 2-3 FT, 10-15 PT
Passive Ownership: Not Allowed
Encourage Conversions: Yes
Area Develop. Agreements:Yes/5,10,15+
Sub-Franchising Contracts: No
Expand In Territory: Yes
Space Needs: 1,600 SF; FS, SF, SC, RM

SUPPORT & TRAINING:

Financial Assistance Provided: Yes(I)
Site Selection Assistance: Yes
Lease Negotiation Assistance: Yes
Co-Operative Advertising: Yes
Franchisee Assoc./Member: Yes/Yes
Size Of Corporate Staff: 40
On-Going Support: B,C,D,E,F,G,H,I
Training: 21 Days Café; 14 Days Mall at Michigan Corporate Center.

SPECIFIC EXPANSION PLANS:
US: All United States
Canada: No
Overseas: Yes, Guam (2)

<< >>

GLORIA JEAN'S GOURMET COFFEES

28 Executive Park, # 200
Irvine, CA 92614
Tel: (949) 260-1600
Fax: (949) 260-6745
E-Mail: kdavenport@gloriajeans.com
Web Site: www.gloriajeans.com
Ms. Kathy Davenport, Manager Franchise Sales

American's largest retail gourmet coffee franchisor offers the highest-quality gourmet coffees, teas and accessories. Our unique store design and exclusive coffee bean counter are the focal points of our nationally honored company. Each store has up to 64 varieties of coffees.

BACKGROUND: IFA MEMBER
Established: 1979; 1st Franchised: 1986
Franchised Units: 397
Company-Owned Units: 20
Total Units: 417
Dist.: US-417; CAN-0; O'seas-96
North America: 38 States
Density: 38 in CA, 28 in IL, 9 in WI
Projected New Units (12 Months): 20
Qualifications: 4, 4, 3, 3, 4, 5
Registered: All States

FINANCIAL/TERMS:
Cash Investment: $75K
Total Investment: $130-457K
Minimum Net Worth: $350K
Fees: Franchise - $15-35K
Royalty - 6%; Ad. - 2%
Earnings Claims Statement: No
Term of Contract (Years): 10 /Lease
Avg. # Of Employees: 2 FT, 8 PT
Passive Ownership: Discouraged
Encourage Conversions: NA
Area Develop. Agreements: No
Sub-Franchising Contracts: No
Expand In Territory: Yes
Space Needs: 200-1,000 SF; RM

SUPPORT & TRAINING:
Financial Assistance Provided: Yes(I)
Site Selection Assistance: Yes
Lease Negotiation Assistance: Yes
Co-Operative Advertising: Yes
Franchisee Assoc./Member: Yes/Yes
Size Of Corporate Staff: 150
On-Going Support: B,C,D,E,G,H,I
Training: 4-5 Weeks at Corporate Training Store

SPECIFIC EXPANSION PLANS:
US: All United States
Canada: No
Overseas: All Countries

<< >>

IT'S A GRIND COFFEE HOUSE

6272 E. Pacific Coast Hwy., # E
Long Beach, CA 90803
Tel: (866) IAG-JAVA (562) 594-5600 + 256
Fax: (562) 594-4100
E-Mail: franchise@itsagrind.com
Web Site: www.itsagrind.com
Mr. Steve Olson, SVP Franchise Development

Own an easy-to-operate business that can be enjoyable and rewarding. IT'S A GRIND is the fastest-growing coffee franchise in the U.S., with 141 franchises under development in CA, AZ, CO, MI, NV, TX and TN. An up-scale, neighborhood coffee house with a blues and jazz motif, our stores feature the highest-quality espresso and iced blended coffee drinks, bagels, muffins, scones and assorted bakery items.

BACKGROUND: IFA MEMBER
Established: 1994; 1st Franchised: 2001
Franchised Units: 44
Company-Owned Units: 4
Total Units: 48
Dist.: US-35; CAN-0; O'seas-0
North America: 6 States
Density: 27 in CA, 3 in NV, 2 in AZ
Projected New Units (12 Months): 40
Qualifications: , , , , ,
Registered: FL,MI,OR,DC

FINANCIAL/TERMS:
Cash Investment: $100K
Total Investment: $196-323K
Minimum Net Worth: $375K
Fees: Franchise - $30K
Royalty - 6%; Ad. - 1%
Earnings Claims Statement: Yes
Term of Contract (Years): 10/Varies
Avg. # Of Employees: 3 FT, 10 PT
Passive Ownership: Not Allowed
Encourage Conversions: No
Area Develop. Agreements: Yes/10
Sub-Franchising Contracts: No
Expand In Territory: NR
Space Needs: 1,000-1,500 SF; FS, SF, SC, RM

SUPPORT & TRAINING:
Financial Assistance Provided: Yes(I)
Site Selection Assistance: Yes
Lease Negotiation Assistance: Yes
Co-Operative Advertising: Yes
Franchisee Assoc./Member: Yes/Yes
Size Of Corporate Staff: 16
On-Going Support: A,B,C,D,E,F,G,H,I
Training: 2 Weeks Long Beach, CA Headquarters.

SPECIFIC EXPANSION PLANS:
US: Most States in US
Canada: No
Overseas: No

<< >>

JAVA DAVE'S COFFEE

6239 E. 15th St.
Tulsa, OK 74112
Tel: (800) 725-7315 (918) 836-5570
Fax: (918) 835-4348
E-Mail: davebeans@aol.com
Web Site: www.javadavescoffee.com
Mr. Mike Tiernan, Dir. Franchise Operations

We are a multi-concept system that features gourmet coffee, real fruit smoothies, gourmet ice cream and fat-free frozen yogurts. With three concepts inside one location, the franchisee is better diversified. We feature the world's finest Arabia bean coffees, teas, cocoas and cappuccino mixes. We strive for drive-thru locations or mall locations with heavy foot traffic.

BACKGROUND:
Established: 1981; 1st Franchised: 1993
Franchised Units: 12
Company-Owned Units: 2
Total Units: 14
Dist.: US-14; CAN-0; O'seas-0
North America: 2 States
Density: 12 in OK, 1 in TX
Projected New Units (12 Months): 2
Qualifications: 5, 3, 1, 3, 1, 4
Registered: NR

FINANCIAL/TERMS:
Cash Investment: $150K
Total Investment: $150-250K
Minimum Net Worth: $200K

Fees: Franchise - $17.5K
Royalty - 3%; Ad. - 2%
Earnings Claims Statement: No
Term of Contract (Years): 10/10
Avg. # Of Employees: 2 FT, 4-5 PT
Passive Ownership: Not Allowed
Encourage Conversions: Yes
Area Develop. Agreements: Yes/10
Sub-Franchising Contracts: No
Expand In Territory: Yes
Space Needs: 1,000-1,500 SF; SC, RM, Drive-Thru

SUPPORT & TRAINING:
Financial Assistance Provided: No
Site Selection Assistance: Yes
Lease Negotiation Assistance: Yes
Co-Operative Advertising: Yes
Franchisee Assoc./Member: Yes/Yes
Size Of Corporate Staff: 60
On-Going Support: C,D,E,G,I
Training: 1 Week in Tulsa, OK; 2 Days On-Site.

SPECIFIC EXPANSION PLANS:
US: MW, SE,SW
Canada: No
Overseas: No

<< >>

JO TO GO THE DRIVE THRU ESPRESSO BAR

Franchise Support Center, 1263 Main St.
Green Bay, WI 54313
Tel: (920) 884-6601 + 108
Fax: (920) 435-5444
E-Mail: jonl@jotogo.com
Web Site: www.jotogo.com
Mr. Jonathan Lukens, Director of Marketing

Full-service, gourmet double-drive-thru, serving premium coffee and espresso-based drinks, smoothies, tea, chai, fresh bakery. Run your business with as few as six employees. Have fun in a fast-growing industry that's immensely profitable.

BACKGROUND:
Established: 1998; 1st Franchised: 2001
Franchised Units: 5
Company-Owned Units: 4
Total Units: 9
Dist.: US-9; CAN-0; O'seas-0
North America: 1 State
Density: 9 in WI
Projected New Units (12 Months): 9
Qualifications: 4, 5, 3, 3, 5, 5
Registered: IL,MI,MN,WI

FINANCIAL/TERMS:
Cash Investment: NA
Total Investment: $82.5-786K
Minimum Net Worth: NA
Fees: Franchise - $25K
Royalty - 7%; Ad. - 1%
Earnings Claims Statement: Yes
Term of Contract (Years): 15/10
Avg. # Of Employees: 3 FT, 4 PT
Passive Ownership: Discouraged
Encourage Conversions: NA
Area Develop. Agreements: Yes
Sub-Franchising Contracts: No
Expand In Territory: Yes
Space Needs: 500 SF; Prototype

SUPPORT & TRAINING:
Financial Assistance Provided: NR
Site Selection Assistance: Yes
Lease Negotiation Assistance: Yes
Co-Operative Advertising: Yes
Franchisee Assoc./Member: No
Size Of Corporate Staff: 3
On-Going Support: C,D,E,F,G,H
Training: 10 Days, Corporate Office & Local Store.

SPECIFIC EXPANSION PLANS:
US: All U.S (Where Registered)
Canada: No
Overseas: No

NEW WORLD COFFEE

1687 Cole Blvd.
Golden, CO 07724-2206
Tel: (877) 853-2856
Fax: (303) 568-8199
E-Mail: gpowell@nwrgi.com
Web Site: www.nwcb.com
Mr. Greg Powell, Dir. Franchise Development

Full service bagel bakery - Manhattan Bagel. Upscale coffee bar/espresso - New World Coffee.

BACKGROUND: IFA MEMBER
Established: 1987; 1st Franchised: 1990
Franchised Units: 43
Company-Owned Units: 0
Total Units: 43
Dist.: US-380; CAN-0; O'seas-5
North America: NR
Density: NR
Projected New Units (12 Months): 40
Qualifications: 5, 3, 1, 1, 4, 5
Registered: All States

FINANCIAL/TERMS:
Cash Investment: $50-75K
Total Investment: $150-350K
Minimum Net Worth: $225K+
Fees: Franchise - $20K
Royalty - 5%; Ad. - 2.5-4%
Earnings Claims Statement: No
Term of Contract (Years): 10/10
Avg. # Of Employees: 3 FT, 5 PT
Passive Ownership: Allowed
Encourage Conversions: Yes
Area Develop. Agreements: Yes
Sub-Franchising Contracts: No
Expand In Territory: Yes
Space Needs: NR SF; FS, SF, SC, RM

SUPPORT & TRAINING:
Financial Assistance Provided: Yes(I)
Site Selection Assistance: Yes
Lease Negotiation Assistance: Yes
Co-Operative Advertising: Yes
Franchisee Assoc./Member: Yes
Size Of Corporate Staff: 200+
On-Going Support: C,D,E,G,H
Training: NR

SPECIFIC EXPANSION PLANS:
US: All United States
Canada: All Canada
Overseas: All Countries

<< >>

P. A. M.'S COFFEE & TEA CO.

2900 John St., # 202
Markham, ON L3R 5G3 CANADA
Tel: (905) 763-0763
Fax: (905) 305-9597
E-Mail:
Web Site: www.worldfranchising.com/website.htm
Mr. Gregory MacCormack, VP Leasing/Franchising

This specialty coffee business is a social, friendly one conducted in a clean and attractive retail environment. Our products are prestigious and bought by people with a refined sense of taste; to these people, a good cup of coffee is an affordable luxury in good times and bad.

BACKGROUND:
Established: 1981; 1st Franchised: 1991
Franchised Units: 19
Company-Owned Units: 1
Total Units: 20
Dist.: US-0; CAN-20; O'seas-0

North America: 1 Province
Density: 20 in ON
Projected New Units (12 Months): 5
Qualifications: 4, 3, 3, 3, 3, 5
Registered: NR

FINANCIAL/TERMS:
Cash Investment: $75-100K
Total Investment: $165-200K
Minimum Net Worth: NA
Fees: Franchise - $25K
Royalty - 8%; Ad. - 2%
Earnings Claims Statement: No
Term of Contract (Years): Lease
Avg. # Of Employees: 3 FT, 8 PT
Passive Ownership: Not Allowed
Encourage Conversions: No
Area Develop. Agreements: No
Sub-Franchising Contracts: No
Expand In Territory: Yes
Space Needs: 500-1,200 SF; FS, SF, SC, RM

SUPPORT & TRAINING:
Financial Assistance Provided: No
Site Selection Assistance: Yes
Lease Negotiation Assistance: Yes
Co-Operative Advertising: Yes
Franchisee Assoc./Member: Yes/Yes
Size Of Corporate Staff: 10
On-Going Support: B,C,D,E,G
Training: 1 Week at Head Office; 2 Weeks In Store.

SPECIFIC EXPANSION PLANS:
US: N/A for Now
Canada: ON
Overseas: No

P. J.'S COFFEE & TEA

1110 Poydras St., # 1150
New Orleans, LA 70163-1101
Tel: (800) 749-5547 (504) 582-2264
Fax: (504) 486-2345
E-Mail: tmareno@pjscoffee.com
Web Site: www.pjscoffee.com
Ms. Tonya Mareno, Dir. Franchise Operations

P. J.'S COFFEE & TEA has long been regarded as a leader in the specialty coffee industry in the southeast. Our neighborhood-based cafes are set apart from others because we roast and distribute only the highest-quality coffee and serve it in warm, comfortable settings. Our customer base is extremely varied. We provide an unusually high level of service to our franchisees because quality is of the utmost importance to us.

BACKGROUND: IFA MEMBER
Established: 1978; 1st Franchised: 1987
Franchised Units: 18
Company-Owned Units: 4
Total Units: 22
Dist.: US-22; CAN-0; O'seas-0
North America: 4 States
Density: 17 in LA, 2 in MS, 2 in FL
Projected New Units (12 Months): 7
Qualifications: 5, 5, 3, 3, 2, 3
Registered: FL

FINANCIAL/TERMS:
Cash Investment: $30-40K
Total Investment: $100-190K
Minimum Net Worth: $120K
Fees: Franchise - $20K
Royalty - 5%; Ad. - 1%
Earnings Claims Statement: No
Term of Contract (Years): 10/10
Avg. # Of Employees: 1 FT, 6 PT
Passive Ownership: Allowed
Encourage Conversions: Yes
Area Develop. Agreements: Yes/Varies
Sub-Franchising Contracts: No
Expand In Territory: Yes
Space Needs: 1,200 SF; SF, SC

SUPPORT & TRAINING:
Financial Assistance Provided: No
Site Selection Assistance: Yes
Lease Negotiation Assistance: Yes
Co-Operative Advertising: Yes
Franchisee Assoc./Member: No
Size Of Corporate Staff: 74
On-Going Support: B,C,D,E,G,h,I
Training: 2 Days Corporate Office; 10 Days Corporate Store; 3 Days On-Location Sites.

SPECIFIC EXPANSION PLANS:
US: Southeast
Canada: No
Overseas: No

<< >>

ROCKTONIC JUICE & COFFEE

11448 Deerfield Dr., # 2, PMB 201
Truckee, CA 96161
Tel: (877) ROCKTONIC (530) 550-9919
Fax: (530) 579-3209
E-Mail: info@rocktonic.com
Web Site: www.rocktonic.com
Mr. Ted Cohn, Chief Executive Officer

ROCKTONIC is a modern, urban juice and coffee fusion experience for customers, providing the highest-quality ingredients and proprietary recipes, outstanding coffee and exciting branding - all geared to compete strongly with industry leaders. ROCKTONIC provides comprehensive training, operating manuals, a complete support network and is poised for explosive growth.

BACKGROUND: IFA MEMBER
Established: 2002; 1st Franchised: 2003
Franchised Units: 0
Company-Owned Units: 2
Total Units: 2
Dist.: US-2; CAN-0; O'seas-0
North America: 2 States
Density: 1 in CA
Projected New Units (12 Months): 4
Qualifications: 5, 4, 2, 4, 3, 5
Registered: CA,FL

FINANCIAL/TERMS:
Cash Investment: $50-105K
Total Investment: $175-350K
Minimum Net Worth: $200K
Fees: Franchise - $24K
Royalty - 5%/$1,500/Mo.; Ad. - 1%/$300/Mo.
Earnings Claims Statement: No
Term of Contract (Years): 10/10
Avg. # Of Employees: 1-2 FT, 6 PT
Passive Ownership: Allowed
Encourage Conversions: No
Area Develop. Agreements: No
Sub-Franchising Contracts: No
Expand In Territory: Yes
Space Needs: 1,100 SF; SF, SC, RM

SUPPORT & TRAINING:
Financial Assistance Provided: No
Site Selection Assistance: Yes
Lease Negotiation Assistance: Yes
Co-Operative Advertising: Yes
Franchisee Assoc./Member: Yes/Yes
Size Of Corporate Staff: 2
On-Going Support: b,C,d,E,f,G,I
Training: 10 Days South Lake Tahoe, CA.

SPECIFIC EXPANSION PLANS:
US: All United States
Canada: No
Overseas: Australia

<< >>

Food: Ice Cream/Yogurt

Chapter 15

Food: Ice Cream/Yogurt Industry Profile

Total # Franchisors in Industry Group	55
Total # Franchised Units in Industry Group	18,142
Total # Company-Owned Units in Industry Group	1,157
Total # Operating Units in Industry Group	19,299
Average # Franchised Units/Franchisor	329.9
Average # Company-Owned Units/Franchisor	21
Average # Total Units/Franchisor	350.9
Ratio of Total # Franchised Units/Total # Company-Owned Units	15.7:1

Industry Survey Participants	26
Representing % of Industry	47.3%
Average Franchise Fee*:	$25.8K
Average Total Investment*:	$189.7K
Average On-Going Royalty Fee*:	4.5%

*If a range was provided, the mid-point of the range was used. See detailed profiles for actual ranges.

Five Largest Participants in Survey

Company	# Franchised Units	# Co-Owned Units	# Total Units	Franchise Fee	On-Going Royalty	Total Investment
1. Yogen Fruz	5,196	33	5,229	$25K	6%	$130-250K
2. Baskin-Robbins	4,500	0	4,500	$40K	5-5.9%	$145.7-527.8K
3. I Can't Believe It's Yogurt	400	940	1,340	$15K	0%	$110-203K
4. TCBY	1,262	49	1,311	$25K	4%	$142.3-347.2K
5. Cold Stone Creamery	921	18	939	$42K	6%	$269-399K

All of the data provided are proprietary and should not be quoted without acknowledging *Bond's Franchise Guide.*

2 SCOOPS CAFÉ

4561 36th St., # 600
Orlando, FL 32811
Tel: (866) 272-6677 (407) 381-0378
Fax: (407) 996-1214
E-Mail: info@2scoopscafe.com
Web Site: www.2scoopscafe.com
Ms. MaryAnn Kilgallon, President

SCOOPS of opportunities. 2 SCOOPS CAFÉ serves only the best, premium hand-dipped ice cream, subs and tasty wraps in a bright, fun, upbeat atmosphere. Come join our rapidly-growing team today and become a successful entrepreneur tomorrow in this ground-floor opportunity.

BACKGROUND: IFA MEMBER
Established: 2002; 1st Franchised: 2003
Franchised Units: 1
Company-Owned Units: 1
Total Units: 2
Dist.: US-2; CAN-0; O'seas-0
North America: 1 State
Density: 2 in FL
Projected New Units (12 Months): 10
Qualifications: 4, 3, 1, 3, 4, 5
Registered: FL

FINANCIAL/TERMS:
Cash Investment: $35K
Total Investment: $79-102K
Minimum Net Worth: $150K
Fees: Franchise - $28K
Royalty - 6%; Ad. - 2%
Earnings Claims Statement: No
Term of Contract (Years): 5/5
Avg. # Of Employees: 2 FT, 6 PT
Passive Ownership: Discouraged
Encourage Conversions: Yes
Area Develop. Agreements: Yes/5
Sub-Franchising Contracts: No
Expand In Territory: Yes
Space Needs: 1,200 SF; SC, RM

SUPPORT & TRAINING:
Financial Assistance Provided: Yes(I)
Site Selection Assistance: Yes
Lease Negotiation Assistance: Yes
Co-Operative Advertising: Yes
Franchisee Assoc./Member: No
Size Of Corporate Staff: 4
On-Going Support: B,C,D,e,F,G,H,I
Training: 1 Week Franchise Café; 1 Week Corporate Office.

SPECIFIC EXPANSION PLANS:
US: Southeast
Canada: No
Overseas: No

<< >>

ALL AMERICAN SPECIALTY RESTAURANTS

812 SW Washington St., # 1110
Portland, OR 97205-3222
Tel: (800) 311-3930 (503) 224-6199
Fax: (503) 224-5042
E-Mail: crduffie@allamericanrestaurants.com
Web Site: www.allamericanrestaurants.com
Mr. C. R. Duffie, Jr., President

Multi-concept franchise for better utilization of labor and overhead expenses with higher unit volumes vs. single product QSRs. Majority of stores located in regional malls. Upscale interior design. Choose deli, ice cream or specialty coffee - one, two or three concepts - all under one simple franchise and one investment structure.

BACKGROUND:
Established: 1986; 1st Franchised: 1987
Franchised Units: 28
Company-Owned Units: 0
Total Units: 28
Dist.: US-28; CAN-0; O'seas-0
North America: 6 States
Density: 14 in OR, 5 in WA, 3 in NV
Projected New Units (12 Months): 6
Qualifications: 4, 4, 2, 4, 3, 5
Registered: CA,MN,OR,WA

FINANCIAL/TERMS:
Cash Investment: $35-45K
Total Investment: $90-225K
Minimum Net Worth: $250K
Fees: Franchise - $25K
Royalty - 5%; Ad. - 1%
Earnings Claims Statement: No
Term of Contract (Years): 10/10
Avg. # Of Employees: 1 FT, 5 PT
Passive Ownership: Discouraged
Encourage Conversions: Yes
Area Develop. Agreements: Yes/10
Sub-Franchising Contracts: No
Expand In Territory: Yes
Space Needs: 1,400 SF; SC, RM

SUPPORT & TRAINING:
Financial Assistance Provided: Yes(I)
Site Selection Assistance: Yes
Lease Negotiation Assistance: Yes
Co-Operative Advertising: No
Franchisee Assoc./Member: Yes
Size Of Corporate Staff: 4
On-Going Support: B,C,D,E,F,G,I
Training: 1 Week Corporate Office Portland, OR; 2 Weeks Onsite (Store).

SPECIFIC EXPANSION PLANS:
US: West and Inter-Mountain States Only.
Canada: No
Overseas: No

<< >>

BASKIN-ROBBINS

14 Pacella Park Dr.
Randolph, MA 02368
Tel: (800) 777-9983 (818) 996-9361
Fax: (818) 996-5163
E-Mail: jlitton@adrus.com
Web Site: www.dunkin-baskin.com
Ms. Janet Litton

BASKIN-ROBBINS develops, operates and franchises retail stores that sell ice cream, frozen yogurt and other approved services. In some markets, BASKIN-ROBBINS, together with TOGO'S and/or DUNKIN' DONUTS, offers multiple brand combinations of the three brands. TOGO'S, BASKIN-ROBBINS and DUNKIN' DONUTS are all subsidiaries of Allied Domecq PLC.

BACKGROUND: IFA MEMBER
Established: 1946; 1st Franchised: 1948
Franchised Units: 4,500
Company-Owned Units: 0
Total Units: 4,500
Dist.: US-2,286; CAN-620; O'seas-1,594
North America: 41 States
Density: 554 in CA, 195 in IL, 181 NY
Projected New Units (12 Months): 27
Qualifications: , , , , ,
Registered: All States

FINANCIAL/TERMS:
Cash Investment: $145.8-527.8K
Total Investment: $145.7-527.8K
Minimum Net Worth: $400K/unit
Fees: Franchise - $40K
Royalty - 5-5.9%; Ad. - 5%
Earnings Claims Statement: Yes
Term of Contract (Years): 20
Avg. # Of Employees: NA

Passive Ownership: Allowed
Encourage Conversions: NR
Area Develop. Agreements: Yes/3-5
Sub-Franchising Contracts: No
Expand In Territory: Yes
Space Needs: NR SF; FS, SF, SC, RM

SUPPORT & TRAINING:
Financial Assistance Provided: Yes(I)
Site Selection Assistance: NA
Lease Negotiation Assistance: Yes
Co-Operative Advertising: Yes
Franchisee Assoc./Member: Yes/No
Size Of Corporate Staff: NA
On-Going Support: B,C,D,G,H,I
Training: 51 Days in Randolph, MA; 3.5 Days at another Location.

SPECIFIC EXPANSION PLANS:
US: All Regions
Canada: All Canada
Overseas: All Countries

BEN & JERRY'S

30 Community Dr.
South Burlington, VT 05403-6809
Tel: (802) 846-1500 + 7840
Fax: (802) 846-1538
E-Mail: franchiseinfo@benjerry.com
Web Site: www.benjerry.com
Mr. Eric Thomas, Franchise Sales Coordinator

BEN & JERRY'S was started in 1978 in a renovated gas station in Burlington, VT, by childhood friends Ben Cohen and Jerry Greenfield. They soon became popular for their funky, chunky flavors, made from fresh Vermont milk and cream. The scoop shops feature a fun environment with a varied menu including cakes, gifts, baked goods and coffee drinks created from ice cream, frozen yogurt and sorbet flavors. Community involvement is an important element in being a successful BEN & JERRY'S franchisee.

BACKGROUND: IFA MEMBER
Established: 1978; 1st Franchised: 1981
Franchised Units: 400
Company-Owned Units: 10
Total Units: 410
Dist.: US-290; CAN-9; O'seas-111
North America: 31 States, 2 Provinces
Density: 46 in CA, 18 in NY, 14 in FL
Projected New Units (12 Months): 75
Qualifications: 5, 4, 5, 3, 4, 5
Registered:CA,FL,IL,IN,MD,MI,MN,NY, OR,RI,VA,WA

FINANCIAL/TERMS:
Cash Investment: $86K+
Total Investment: $123.5-286K
Minimum Net Worth: $200K
Fees: Franchise - $30K
Royalty - 1.5%; Ad. - 4%
Earnings Claims Statement: Yes
Term of Contract (Years): 10/10
Avg. # Of Employees: 2 FT, 10 PT
Passive Ownership: Not Allowed
Encourage Conversions: Yes
Area Develop. Agreements: Yes
Sub-Franchising Contracts: No
Expand In Territory: No
Space Needs: 1,200 Avg. SF; FS, SF, SC, RM, KI

SUPPORT & TRAINING:
Financial Assistance Provided: No
Site Selection Assistance: Yes
Lease Negotiation Assistance: No
Co-Operative Advertising: Yes
Franchisee Assoc./Member: Yes
Size Of Corporate Staff: 20
On-Going Support: C,D,E,F,G,H,I
Training: 10 Days in VT.

SPECIFIC EXPANSION PLANS:
US: Various Markets
Canada: No
Overseas: Call International Division

BRUSTER'S OLD-FASHIONED ICE CREAM & YOGURT

730 Mulberry St.
Bridgewater, PA 15009
Tel: (724) 774-4250
Fax: (724) 774-0666
E-Mail: lori@brusters.net
Web Site: www.brusters.com
Ms. Lori Molnar, Franchise Development

BRUSTER'S ICE CREAM features fresh, delicious homemade ice cream which is made fresh daily on-site at each of our stores. Quality products and exceptional customer service are our main goals. Our products feature only the best ingredients - whole nuts, cherries and the best caramels and fudges. Homemade waffle cones are a great complement to our homemade ice cream.

BACKGROUND:
Established: 1989; 1st Franchised: 1993
Franchised Units: 85
Company-Owned Units: 4
Total Units: 89
Dist.: US-45; CAN-0; O'seas-0
North America: 8 States
Density: 21 in PA, 15 in GA, 2 in OH
Projected New Units (12 Months): 30
Qualifications: 3, 2, 1, 1, 4, 4
Registered: IN,NY,VA

FINANCIAL/TERMS:
Cash Investment: $150K
Total Investment: $150-761K
Minimum Net Worth: $None
Fees: Franchise - $30K
Royalty - 5%; Ad. - Up to 3%
Earnings Claims Statement: No
Term of Contract (Years): 10/10/10
Avg. # Of Employees: 2-3 FT, 25 PT
Passive Ownership: Discouraged
Encourage Conversions: No
Area Develop. Agreements: Yes/Varies
Sub-Franchising Contracts: No
Expand In Territory: Yes
Space Needs: 988 SF; FS

SUPPORT & TRAINING:
Financial Assistance Provided: No
Site Selection Assistance: Yes
Lease Negotiation Assistance: Yes
Co-Operative Advertising: Yes
Franchisee Assoc./Member: No
Size Of Corporate Staff: 10
On-Going Support: B,C,D,E,G,H
Training: 4 Weeks Western PA or Atlanta, GA.

SPECIFIC EXPANSION PLANS:
US: Eastern United States
Canada: No
Overseas: No

Top 100

CARVEL CORPORATION

200 Glenridge Point Pkwy., # 200
Atlanta, GA 30342-1450
Tel: (800) 227-8353 (404) 255-3250
Fax: (404) 255-4978
E-Mail: ghill@carvel.com
Web Site: www.carvel.com
Mr. Geoff Hill, SVP Franchise Sales

The nation's first retail ice cream franchise, CARVEL is the leading manufacturer of uniquely shaped ice cream cakes, and a leading provider of premium soft serve and hand-dipped ice cream products. Since the company's founding in 1934, CARVEL has become one of the best-loved and most recognized names in the industry. With products made fresh daily in the store, CARVEL has more than 470 franchised and foodservice locations, as well as its famous ice cream cakes in over 7,000 supermarket outlets.

BACKGROUND: IFA MEMBER
Established: 1934; 1st Franchised: 1947
Franchised Units: 534
Company-Owned Units: 0
Total Units: 534
Dist.: US-510; CAN-3; O'seas-21
North America: 25 States, 1 Province
Density: 217 in NY, 52 in NJ,29 in CT
Projected New Units (12 Months): 100
Qualifications: 5, 5, 3, 3, 3, 5
Registered: CA,MD,NY,RI,VA

FINANCIAL/TERMS:
Cash Investment: $70-125K
Total Investment: $200-270K
Minimum Net Worth: $250K
Fees: Franchise - $30K
Royalty - $1.77/Gal.; Ad. - $1.57/Gal.
Earnings Claims Statement: Yes
Term of Contract (Years): 20
Avg. # Of Employees: 2 FT, 6 PT
Passive Ownership: Not Allowed
Encourage Conversions: Yes
Area Develop. Agreements: No
Sub-Franchising Contracts: No
Expand In Territory: Yes
Space Needs:1,200-1,500 SF; FS, SC, RM, KI, PC

SUPPORT & TRAINING:
Financial Assistance Provided: Yes(I)
Site Selection Assistance: Yes
Lease Negotiation Assistance: No
Co-Operative Advertising: Yes
Franchisee Assoc./Member: Yes/Yes
Size Of Corporate Staff: 50
On-Going Support: B,C,D,E,G,H,I
Training: 10 Days Atlanta, GA.

SPECIFIC EXPANSION PLANS:
US: All Exc.WA,OR,ID,UT,MT,WY,ND,SD,KS,MS,NM
Canada: All Canada
Overseas: China, Mexico, Caribbean

<< >>

COLD STONE CREAMERY

16101 N. 82nd St., # A-4
Scottsdale, AZ 85260
Tel: (888) 218-3349 (480) 348-1704
Fax: (480) 348-1718
E-Mail: abreen@coldstonecreamery.com
Web Site: www.coldstonecreamery.com
Mr. Adam Breen, Franchise Devel./Intl. Support

Imagine providing The Ultimate Ice Cream Experience®. At COLD STONE CREAMERY, our super-premium ice cream, waffle cones and brownies are made fresh each day in every store. After that, it's all about the show that differentiates us from other scoop shops! Ranked #25 in the Entrepreneur 2004 Fastest Growing Franchise list, COLD STONE CREAMERY is the fastest growing concept in the super-premium ice cream field. We were founded in 1988; we then awarded our first franchise in 1994.

BACKGROUND: IFA MEMBER
Established: 1988; 1st Franchised: 1995
Franchised Units: 921
Company-Owned Units: 18
Total Units: 939
Dist.: US-1959; CAN-0; O'seas-0
North America: 47 States
Density: 248 in CA, 53 in TX,50 in FL
Projected New Units (12 Months): 414
Qualifications: 2, 3, 1, 1, 3, 5
Registered: All States

FINANCIAL/TERMS:
Cash Investment: $50K
Total Investment: $269-399K
Minimum Net Worth: NR
Fees: Franchise - $42K
Royalty - 6%; Ad. - 3%
Earnings Claims Statement: No
Term of Contract (Years): 10/5/5/5
Avg. # Of Employees: 3 FT, 9 PT
Passive Ownership: Discouraged
Encourage Conversions: NR
Area Develop. Agreements: Yes
Sub-Franchising Contracts: No
Expand In Territory: Yes
Space Needs: 1,200 SF; SC

SUPPORT & TRAINING:
Financial Assistance Provided: No
Site Selection Assistance: Yes
Lease Negotiation Assistance: Yes
Co-Operative Advertising: Yes
Franchisee Assoc./Member: No
Size Of Corporate Staff: 180
On-Going Support: C,D,E,G,H
Training: 10 Days Scottsdale, AZ.

SPECIFIC EXPANSION PLANS:
US: All United States
Canada: All Canada
Overseas: All Countries

<< >>

DIPPIN' DOTS ICE CREAM OF THE FUTURE

P. O. Box 9207, 5110 Charter Oak Dr.
Paducah, KY 42003
Tel: (270) 575-6990
Fax: (270) 575-6997
E-Mail: vanril@dippindots.com
Web Site: www.dippindots.com
Ms. Vanessa Riley, Franchise Devel. Specialist

DIPPIN' DOTS are those tiny beads of ice cream that are super-cold, creamy, and delicious. Here's your invitation to look at our exciting alternative to traditional ice cream, yogurt, and flavored ice products.

BACKGROUND: IFA MEMBER
Established: 1988; 1st Franchised: 1999
Franchised Units: 569
Company-Owned Units: 2
Total Units: 571
Dist.: US-571; CAN-0; O'seas-0
North America: 42 States
Density: 49 in TX, 37 in CA, 29 in FL
Projected New Units (12 Months): Unknown
Qualifications: 5, 4, 2, 3, 3, 5
Registered: All States

FINANCIAL/TERMS:
Cash Investment: $75K
Total Investment: $45.6-189.8K
Minimum Net Worth: $250K
Fees: Franchise - $12.5K
Royalty - 4%; Ad. - .05%
Earnings Claims Statement: No
Term of Contract (Years): 5/5/5
Avg. # Of Employees: 1 FT
Passive Ownership: Discouraged
Encourage Conversions: No
Area Develop. Agreements: No
Sub-Franchising Contracts: No
Expand In Territory: Yes
Space Needs: 100 SF; RM

SUPPORT & TRAINING:
Financial Assistance Provided: No
Site Selection Assistance: Yes
Lease Negotiation Assistance: Yes
Co-Operative Advertising: No
Franchisee Assoc./Member: No
Size Of Corporate Staff: 15
On-Going Support: B,C,D,E,G,H
Training: 2 Days in Paducah, KY; 2 Days On-Site.

SPECIFIC EXPANSION PLANS:
US: All United States
Canada: No
Overseas: No

EMACK & BOLIO'S ICE CREAM & YOGURT

P. O. Box 703
Brookline Village, MA 02447
Tel: (617) 739-7995
Fax: (617) 232-1102
E-Mail: info@emackandbolios.com
Web Site: www.emackandbolios.com
Mr. Bob Rook, President

Best ice cream specialty shop in NYC Zagat Survey 2004. Best Ice Cream NYC 2003. Resident Newspaper. Best Smoothie in Boston Boston Globe and Boston Magazine. Visit our stores in the Hard Rock Hotel Orlando, FL. We rock. No fees or royalties. 30 years' experience.

BACKGROUND:
Established: 1975; 1st Franchised: 1977
Franchised Units: 37
Company-Owned Units: 2
Total Units: 39
Dist.: US-39; CAN-0; O'seas-0
North America: 8 States
Density: 22 in MA, 8 in NY, 3 in FL
Projected New Units (12 Months): 10
Qualifications: 3, 3, 1, 2, 4, 5
Registered: All States
FINANCIAL/TERMS:
Cash Investment: $100-175K
Total Investment: $100-175K
Minimum Net Worth: NA
Fees: Franchise - $0
Royalty - 0%; Ad. - 0%
Earnings Claims Statement: No
Term of Contract (Years): 20/10
Avg. # Of Employees: 2 FT, 5 PT
Passive Ownership: Allowed
Encourage Conversions: Yes
Area Develop. Agreements: Yes/30
Sub-Franchising Contracts: Yes
Expand In Territory: Yes
Space Needs: 1,500 SF; SF, SC
SUPPORT & TRAINING:
Financial Assistance Provided: No
Site Selection Assistance: No
Lease Negotiation Assistance: Yes
Co-Operative Advertising: No
Franchisee Assoc./Member: No
Size Of Corporate Staff: 5
On-Going Support: A,B,C,D,E,F
Training: 1 Week Boston, MA or New York, NY.
SPECIFIC EXPANSION PLANS:
US: East of Mississippi
Canada: No
Overseas: No

<< >>

FROOTS SMOOTHIES

3325 Hollywood Blvd., # 303
Hollywood, FL 33021
Tel: (877) FROOTS-1 (954) 964-9820
Fax: (877) FROOTS-X
E-Mail: sales@frootssmoothies.com
Web Site: www.frootssmoothies.com
Ms. Christina Cavallo, Marketing Support

FROOTS offers an exciting business opportunity for individuals to own a franchise unit in the fast-growing smoothie and juice bar industry. Customers of all FROOTS locations enjoy a delicious,sweet and tangy menu, including salads and wraps provided by an experienced, customer-friendly company with a unique business system. FROOTS has two business models to choose from - an In-Line Store or Kiosk operation.

BACKGROUND: IFA MEMBER
Established: 2001; 1st Franchised: 2003
Franchised Units: 5
Company-Owned Units: 5
Total Units: 10
Dist.: US-10; CAN-0; O'seas-0
North America: 1 State
Density: 10 in FL
Projected New Units (12 Months): 25
Qualifications: 5, 5, 2, 3, 4, 4
Registered: CA,FL,NY
FINANCIAL/TERMS:
Cash Investment: $50-100K
Total Investment: $100-225K
Minimum Net Worth: $50K
Fees: Franchise - $15-25K
Royalty - 5%; Ad. - 2%
Earnings Claims Statement: Yes
Term of Contract (Years): 5/5
Avg. # Of Employees: 3 FT, 6 PT
Passive Ownership: Discouraged
Encourage Conversions: Yes
Area Develop. Agreements: Yes/5-10
Sub-Franchising Contracts: No
Expand In Territory: Yes
Space Needs:1,000 SF; SF, SC, RM, Kiosk
SUPPORT & TRAINING:
Financial Assistance Provided: Yes(I)
Site Selection Assistance: Yes
Lease Negotiation Assistance: Yes
Co-Operative Advertising: Yes
Franchisee Assoc./Member: No
Size Of Corporate Staff: 6
On-Going Support: A,B,C,D,E,F,G,H,I
Training: 1-2 Days Hollywood, FL; 5-7 Days Orlando, FL.
SPECIFIC EXPANSION PLANS:
US: All United States
Canada: All Canada
Overseas: No

<< >>

HAPPY & HEALTHY PRODUCTS

1600 S. Dixie Hwy., # 200
Boca Raton, FL 33432
Tel: (800) 764-6114 (561) 866-5136
Fax: (561) 368-5267
E-Mail: franchiseinfo@fruitfull.com
Web Site: www.fruitfull.com
Ms. Katie E. Waite, Franchise Development Director

A wholesale distributorship for the sale of FRUITFULL ® frozen fruit bars and other delicious novelties through dedicated freezers placed in retail locations or in retailer's own freezers. Super Grand, Grand and Standard wholesale franchisees will receive the services of a marketing consultant who will provide on-site training in identifying and negotiating agreements to place freezers. Training includes stocking, collection and route service procedures . International distributorships avalable.

BACKGROUND: IFA MEMBER
Established: 1991; 1st Franchised: 1993
Franchised Units: 100

Company-Owned Units: 0
Total Units: 100
Dist.: US-100; CAN-0; O'seas-0
North America: 39 States
Density: 11 in CA, 7 in NJ, 5 in IL
Projected New Units (12 Months): 12
Qualifications: 5, 5, 3, 3, 3, 5
Registered: All States Except ND,SD,WA

FINANCIAL/TERMS:

Cash Investment: $29-65K
Total Investment: $29-65K
Minimum Net Worth: $29K
Fees: Franchise - $21K
Royalty - 0%; Ad. - $300/Yr.
Earnings Claims Statement: No
Term of Contract (Years): 10/5
Avg. # Of Employees: 1 FT, 1 PT
Passive Ownership: Discouraged
Encourage Conversions: No
Area Develop. Agreements: No
Sub-Franchising Contracts: No
Expand In Territory: Yes
Space Needs: NA SF; NA

SUPPORT & TRAINING:

Financial Assistance Provided: No
Site Selection Assistance: NA
Lease Negotiation Assistance: NA
Co-Operative Advertising: NA
Franchisee Assoc./Member: No
Size Of Corporate Staff: 10
On-Going Support: B,C,D,G,I
Training: 1 or 2 Weeks in Franchise MSA.

SPECIFIC EXPANSION PLANS:

US: All Except WA,LA,ND,ME,SD
Canada: No
Overseas: No

<< >>

I CAN'T BELIEVE IT'S YOGURT

4175 Veterans Hwy.
Ronkonkoma, NY 11779
Tel: (800) 528-0727
E-Mail: cbarnett@coolbrandsww.com
Web Site: www.yogenfruz.com
Mr. Joe Arancio, VP Business Development

We are the leading premier yogurt franchisor domestically and internationally. I CAN'T BELIEVE IT'S YOGURT is noted for developing smooth, creamy, sweet-tasting frozen yogurt in more than 100 self-serve flavor combinations in original, non-fat, and sugar- free varieties.

BACKGROUND:

Established: 1977; 1st Franchised: 1983
Franchised Units: 400
Company-Owned Units: 940
Total Units: 1,340
Dist.: US-1,025; CAN-0; O'seas-317
North America: 33 States
Density: 33 in TX, 16 in NC, 15 in FL
Projected New Units (12 Months): NR
Qualifications: 4, 2, 3, 2, 2, 4
Registered: CA,IL,IN,MN,OR,RI,WA,WI,DC

FINANCIAL/TERMS:

Cash Investment: $50K
Total Investment: $110-203K
Minimum Net Worth: $200K
Fees: Franchise - $15K
Royalty - 0%; Ad. - 2.3%
Earnings Claims Statement: NR
Term of Contract (Years): 10/10
Avg. # Of Employees: 2 FT, 6 PT
Passive Ownership: Discouraged
Encourage Conversions: Yes
Area Develop. Agreements: Yes
Sub-Franchising Contracts: Yes
Expand In Territory: Yes
Space Needs: 1,200 SF; SC, RM

SUPPORT & TRAINING:

Financial Assistance Provided: No
Site Selection Assistance: Yes
Lease Negotiation Assistance: Yes
Co-Operative Advertising: NA
Franchisee Assoc./Member: Yes
Size Of Corporate Staff: 60
On-Going Support: E,G
Training: 10 Days Corporate Headquarters; 1 Week Store.

SPECIFIC EXPANSION PLANS:

US: All United States
Canada: No
Overseas: All Countries

<< >>

ICE CREAM CHURN

4175 Veterans Hwy.
Ronkonkoma, NY 11779
Tel: (800) 423-2763 (631) 737-9700
Fax: (516) 737-9792
E-Mail: cbarrett@coolbrands.com
Web Site: www.yogenfruz.com
Ms. Clarice Barrett, Franchise Services

ICE CREAM CHURN's concept is to add an old-fashioned ice cream parlor within another existing location, such as delis, bakeries, video stores, convenience stores, truckstops. ICE CREAM CHURN sets up location, trains employees, installs exterior signs and supports location with on-going promotions and training. 32 flavors of ice cream and yogurt are available. Master franchise available. New mall kiosk also available!

BACKGROUND:

Established: 1973; 1st Franchised: 1979
Franchised Units: 470
Company-Owned Units: 0
Total Units: 470
Dist.: US-516; CAN-0; O'seas-10
North America: 32 States
Density: 117 in FL, 83 in AR, 42 AL
Projected New Units (12 Months): 100
Qualifications: , , , , ,
Registered: FL,IL,IN,MD,RI,VA,DC

FINANCIAL/TERMS:

Cash Investment: $5-35K
Total Investment: $5-35K
Minimum Net Worth: NR
Fees: Franchise - $5K
Royalty - $1.40/Tub; Ad. - $0.25/Tub
Earnings Claims Statement: No
Term of Contract (Years): 10/5
Avg. # Of Employees: 1 PT
Passive Ownership: Allowed
Encourage Conversions: Yes
Area Develop. Agreements: No
Sub-Franchising Contracts: Yes
Expand In Territory: Yes
Space Needs: 135 SF; Existing Business

SUPPORT & TRAINING:

Financial Assistance Provided: Yes
Site Selection Assistance: Yes
Lease Negotiation Assistance: Yes
Co-Operative Advertising: Yes
Franchisee Assoc./Member: No
Size Of Corporate Staff: 7
On-Going Support: D,E,F,G,I
Training: As Needed.

SPECIFIC EXPANSION PLANS:

US: Seeking Master Franchisees
Canada: All Canada
Overseas: All Countries

<< >>

KOHR BROS. FROZEN CUSTARD

2115 Berkmar Dr.
Charlottesville, VA 22901
Tel: (888) 527-9783 (434) 975-1500
Fax: (434) 975-1505
E-Mail: dennispoletti@kohrbros.com
Web Site: www.kohrbros.com
Mr. Dennis G. Poletti, Executive Director Franchising

KOHR BROS. is the original frozen custard since 1919. Our stores, which are bright and easily maintained, offer a simple and unique frozen dessert concept.

BACKGROUND:

Established: 1919; 1st Franchised: 1994
Franchised Units: 37

Company-Owned Units: 11
Total Units: 48
Dist.: US-39; CAN-0; O'seas-0
North America: 11 States
Density: 10 in NJ, 6 in VA, 5 in FL
Projected New Units (12 Months): 24
Qualifications: 5, 5, 2, 4, 4, 5
Registered: FL,MD,MI,NY,VA

FINANCIAL/TERMS:
Cash Investment: $75K
Total Investment: $145.9-277.5K
Minimum Net Worth: $300K
Fees: Franchise - $27.5K
Royalty - 5%; Ad. - 1%
Earnings Claims Statement: No
Term of Contract (Years): 5/3/5
Avg. # Of Employees: 6 FT, 4 PT
Passive Ownership: Allowed
Encourage Conversions: Yes
Area Develop. Agreements: Yes
Sub-Franchising Contracts: No
Expand In Territory: Yes
Space Needs: 500 SF; FS, SC, RM, Kiosk

SUPPORT & TRAINING:
Financial Assistance Provided: Yes(I)
Site Selection Assistance: Yes
Lease Negotiation Assistance: Yes
Co-Operative Advertising: Yes
Franchisee Assoc./Member: No
Size Of Corporate Staff: 11
On-Going Support: A,B,C,D,E,F,G,H,I
Training: 6 Days in Corporate Offices; 3 Days at Franchisee Unit.

SPECIFIC EXPANSION PLANS:
US: All United States
Canada: No
Overseas: No

<< >>

MAGGIEMOO'S INTERNATIONAL

10025 Governor Warfield Pkwy., # 301
Columbia, MD 21044
Tel: (800) 949-8114 + 142 (410) 740-2100 + 142
Fax: (410) 740-1500
E-Mail: pauls@maggiemoos.com
Web Site: www.maggiemoos.com
Mr. Paul Stratmeyer, Dir. Franchise Recuiting

Unique and exciting retail shop, featuring homemade, super-premium ice cream, non-fat ice cream, custom-made cones, sorbet, smoothies, plus a line of specialty merchandise. We make our ice cream fresh in the store and serve it in fresh- baked waffle cones. Featuring over 40 mix-ins and folded in on a frozen granite mixing table to create 1,000s of great combos. Association with a marketable spokes character - MAGGIE MOO - in a fun, contemporary store design.

BACKGROUND: IFA MEMBER
Established: 1996; 1st Franchised: 1996
Franchised Units: 160
Company-Owned Units: 3
Total Units: 163
Dist.: US-75; CAN-0; O'seas-0
North America: 23 States
Density: 15 in TX, 8 in OH, 6 in VA
Projected New Units (12 Months): 60
Qualifications: 4, 5, 3, 2, 3, 5
Registered:CA,FL,IL,IN,MD,MI,MN,OR, RI,SD,VA,WA,WI,DC

FINANCIAL/TERMS:
Cash Investment: $75K
Total Investment: $166-256K
Minimum Net Worth: $300K
Fees: Franchise - $26K
Royalty - 6%; Ad. - 2%
Earnings Claims Statement: No
Term of Contract (Years): 10/5/5
Avg. # Of Employees: 3 FT, 8 PT
Passive Ownership: Discouraged
Encourage Conversions: Yes
Area Develop. Agreements: Yes/3
Sub-Franchising Contracts: No
Expand In Territory: Yes
Space Needs: 900-1,400 SF; SC

SUPPORT & TRAINING:
Financial Assistance Provided: No
Site Selection Assistance: Yes
Lease Negotiation Assistance: Yes
Co-Operative Advertising: Yes
Franchisee Assoc./Member: Yes/Yes
Size Of Corporate Staff: 14
On-Going Support: B,C,D,E,F,G,h,I
Training: 10 Days Columbia, MD; 6 Days Grand Opening On-Site.

SPECIFIC EXPANSION PLANS:
US: All United States
Canada: No
Overseas: No

MARBLE SLAB CREAMERY

3100 S. Gessner Dr., # 305
Houston, TX 77063-3760
Tel: (713) 780-3601
Fax: (713) 780-0264
E-Mail: tlinderman@marbleslab.com
Web Site: www.marbleslab.com
Mr. Tim Linderman,

Retail ice cream stores, featuring super-premium homemade ice cream, cones baked fresh daily, frozen yogurt, frozen pies and cakes, homemade cookies and brownies and specialty coffees. Ice cream is custom-designed for customer on frozen marble slab and made daily in the store.

BACKGROUND: IFA MEMBER
Established: 1983; 1st Franchised: 1984
Franchised Units: 400
Company-Owned Units: 1
Total Units: 401
Dist.: US-396; CAN-5; O'seas-0
North America: 30 States
Density: 150 in TX, 60 in CA, 40 FL
Projected New Units (12 Months): 120
Qualifications: 5, 3, 1, 3, 3, 5
Registered: All States

FINANCIAL/TERMS:
Cash Investment: $60K
Total Investment: $205-313K
Minimum Net Worth: $250K
Fees: Franchise - $28K
Royalty - 6%; Ad. - 2%
Earnings Claims Statement: Yes
Term of Contract (Years): 10/10
Avg. # Of Employees: 2 FT, 8 PT
Passive Ownership: Discouraged
Encourage Conversions: Yes
Area Develop. Agreements: No
Sub-Franchising Contracts: No
Expand In Territory: No
Space Needs: 500-1,800 SF; SC, RM

SUPPORT & TRAINING:
Financial Assistance Provided: No
Site Selection Assistance: Yes
Lease Negotiation Assistance: Yes
Co-Operative Advertising: Yes
Franchisee Assoc./Member: Yes/No
Size Of Corporate Staff: 30
On-Going Support: B,C,D,E,H
Training: 10 Days Franchisor Location; 6 Days Franchisee Site.

SPECIFIC EXPANSION PLANS:
US: All United States
Canada: All Canada
Overseas: All Countries

<< >>

RITA'S ITALIAN ICE

1525 Ford Rd.
Bensalem, PA 19020-4505

Tel: (800) 677-7482 (215) 633-9899
Fax: (215) 633-9922
E-Mail: s.miele@ritascorp.com
Web Site: www.ritasice.com
Mr. Steve Miele, Franchise Licensing Manager

Retail outlets selling Italian ices.

BACKGROUND: IFA MEMBER
Established: 1984; 1st Franchised: 1989
Franchised Units: 317
Company-Owned Units: 1
Total Units: 318
Dist.: US-318; CAN-0; O'seas-0
North America: 9 States
Density: PA, NJ, MD
Projected New Units (12 Months): 38
Qualifications: 5, 3, 2, 3, 5, 5
Registered: RI,MD,NY,VA

FINANCIAL/TERMS:
Cash Investment: $75K
Total Investment: $161.9-337.5K
Minimum Net Worth: $250K
Fees: Franchise - $27.5K
Royalty - 6.5%; Ad. - 2.5%
Earnings Claims Statement: Yes
Term of Contract (Years): 10/10
Avg. # Of Employees: 1 FT, 9 PT
Passive Ownership: Discouraged
Encourage Conversions: Yes
Area Develop. Agreements: Yes
Sub-Franchising Contracts: No
Expand In Territory: Yes
Space Needs: 600-1,500 SF; FS

SUPPORT & TRAINING:
Financial Assistance Provided: Yes(I)
Site Selection Assistance: Yes
Lease Negotiation Assistance: Yes
Co-Operative Advertising: Yes
Franchisee Assoc./Member: No
Size Of Corporate Staff: 45
On-Going Support: B,C,D,E,G,h
Training: 6 Days Corporate Office; 2-4 Days On-Site.

SPECIFIC EXPANSION PLANS:
US: FL,MD,OH,VA,PA,NY,SC,WV,CT,NJ,DE
Canada: No
Overseas: No

<< >>

RITTER'S FROZEN CUSTARD

12400 N. Meridian St., # 190
Carmel, IN 46032
Tel: (317) 819-0700
Fax: (317) 819-0261
E-Mail: info@ritters.com
Web Site: www.ritters.com
Mr. Robert Ritter, Ice President Franchising

Our mission is to serve a product and experience that people constantly claim as their favorite ice cream ever. The RITTER'S brand has captured the imagination and fanatic loyalties of customers and franchisees alike. As a RITTER'S franchisee, you'll receive comprehensive training, including the importance of our philosophy and brand position. We have systems in place to help maximize franchisee sales, profits and net worth. Our core values have resulted in a diverse and successful franchise system.

BACKGROUND: IFA MEMBER
Established: 1990; 1st Franchised: 1994
Franchised Units: 49
Company-Owned Units: 2
Total Units: 51
Dist.: US-51; CAN-0; O'seas-0
North America: 8 States
Density: 20 in IN, 7 in OH, 5 in MI
Projected New Units (12 Months):
Qualifications: , , , , ,
Registered:

FINANCIAL/TERMS:
Cash Investment: $75-100K
Total Investment: $220-300K
Minimum Net Worth: $200K
Fees: Franchise - $25K
Royalty - 5%; Ad. - 2%
Earnings Claims Statement: Yes
Term of Contract (Years): 10/10
Avg. # Of Employees: 4 FT, 15 PT
Passive Ownership: Discouraged
Encourage Conversions:
Area Develop. Agreements: Yes/5
Sub-Franchising Contracts: No
Expand In Territory: Yes
Space Needs: 1,200-1,500 SF; FS, SF, SC, RM, Airport

SUPPORT & TRAINING:
Financial Assistance Provided:
Site Selection Assistance: Yes
Lease Negotiation Assistance: Yes
Co-Operative Advertising: Yes
Franchisee Assoc./Member: Yes/Yes
Size Of Corporate Staff: 12
On-Going Support: A,B,C,D,E,F,G,H
Training: 3 Weeks Indianapolis, IN; 3 Weeks Port Orange, FL.

SPECIFIC EXPANSION PLANS:
US: East of Mississippi River
Canada: No
Overseas: No

<< >>

SCOOPERS ICE CREAM

22 Woodrow Ave.
Youngstown, OH 44512-3306
Tel: (330) 758-3857
Fax: (330) 758-4405
E-Mail: scoopers01@aol.com
Web Site: www.worldfranchising.com/website.htm
Mr. Norman J. Hughes, Jr., President

SCOOPERS ICE CREAM is a made-fresh-daily concept at each location. Using only the finest ingredients in a homemade, low over-run, high-butterfat, gourmet ice cream. As many as 100 flavors and yogurts and sherbets are made fresh at your location.

BACKGROUND:
Established: 1980; 1st Franchised: 1990
Franchised Units: 8
Company-Owned Units: 2
Total Units: 10
Dist.: US-10; CAN-0; O'seas-0
North America: 3 States
Density: 7 in PA, 2 in OH, 1 in FL
Projected New Units (12 Months): 8
Qualifications: 2, 1, 1, 2, 3, 3
Registered: NR

FINANCIAL/TERMS:
Cash Investment: $50K
Total Investment: $60-180K
Minimum Net Worth: $75K
Fees: Franchise - $15K
Royalty - 5%; Ad. - 0%
Earnings Claims Statement: No
Term of Contract (Years): 10/10
Avg. # Of Employees: 2 FT, 20 PT
Passive Ownership: Allowed
Encourage Conversions: Yes
Area Develop. Agreements: Yes/5
Sub-Franchising Contracts: Yes
Expand In Territory: Yes
Space Needs: 700-1,200 SF; FS, SF, SC, RM

SUPPORT & TRAINING:
Financial Assistance Provided: No
Site Selection Assistance: Yes
Lease Negotiation Assistance: Yes
Co-Operative Advertising: Yes
Franchisee Assoc./Member: No
Size Of Corporate Staff: 5
On-Going Support: E
Training: 2-4 Days at Main Store Location; 1 Day at Store Opening.

SPECIFIC EXPANSION PLANS:
US: All United States
Canada: All Canada
Overseas: NR

<< >>

SHAKE'S FROZEN CUSTARD

244 W. Dickson St.
Fayetteville, AR 72701-5221
Tel: (479) 587-9115
Fax: (479) 587-0780
E-Mail: to@shakesfrozencustard.com
Web Site: www.shakesfrozencustard.com
Mr. Todd Osborne, Vice President Operations/CFO

SHAKE'S FROZEN CUSTARD is where friends gather, couples fall in love, and people of all ages come to enjoy the vibrant nostalgic atmosphere of the 50's. Featuring an extensive menu consisting of our one-of-a-kind, delicious frozen custard and a wide variety of innovative concepts, SHAKE'S is a rapidly growing franchise system. With intensive training and continuous support, we will always ensure your business is operating to its maximum potential.

BACKGROUND:
Established: 1991; 1st Franchised: 1999
Franchised Units: 37
Company-Owned Units: 2
Total Units: 39
Dist.: US-39; CAN-0; O'seas-0
North America: 8 States
Density: 12 in AR, 8 in MO, 7 in TX
Projected New Units (12 Months): 25
Qualifications: 4, 4, 2, 1, 3, 5
Registered: FL,IL,IN,VA,WI

FINANCIAL/TERMS:
Cash Investment: $50-250K
Total Investment: $166-800K
Minimum Net Worth: $250K
Fees: Franchise - $30K
Royalty - 5%; Ad. - 3%
Earnings Claims Statement: Yes
Term of Contract (Years): 15/5
Avg. # Of Employees: 3 FT, 12 PT
Passive Ownership: Discouraged
Encourage Conversions: No
Area Develop. Agreements: Yes/15
Sub-Franchising Contracts: No
Expand In Territory: Yes
Space Needs: 1,200 SF; FS

SUPPORT & TRAINING:
Financial Assistance Provided: Yes(I)
Site Selection Assistance: Yes
Lease Negotiation Assistance: Yes
Co-Operative Advertising: Yes
Franchisee Assoc./Member: Yes
Size Of Corporate Staff: 10
On-Going Support: A,B,C,D,E,F,G,h
Training: 2 Weeks in Fayetteville, AR.

SPECIFIC EXPANSION PLANS:
US: South, SE, SW, Midwest
Canada: No
Overseas: No

<< >>

TCBY

2855 E. Cottonwood Pkwy., # 400
Salt Lake City, UT 84121-7037
Tel: (800) 343-5377 + 7379
Fax: (801) 736-5936
E-Mail: KeithB@mrsfields.com
Web Site: www.tcby.com
Mr. Keith Bakker, VP of Development TCBY

TCBY shops offer yogurt, sorbet and ice cream products, as well as a complete line of pies and cakes. TCBY Systems, LLC offers franchises for traditional locations, and for 'combined concept' locations, wherein TCBY shops are operated within another business.

BACKGROUND: IFA MEMBER
Established: 1981; 1st Franchised: 1982
Franchised Units: 1,262
Company-Owned Units: 49
Total Units: 1,311
Dist.: US-1,220; CAN-0; O'seas-205
North America: 50 States, 2 Provinces
Density: 136 in FL,107 in TX,96 in CA
Projected New Units (12 Months): 74
Qualifications: 5, 3, 2, 2, 2, 4
Registered: All States Except VA

FINANCIAL/TERMS:
Cash Investment: NA
Total Investment: $142.3-347.2K
Minimum Net Worth: $150K/75K LIQ
Fees: Franchise - $25K
Royalty - 4%; Ad. - 3%
Earnings Claims Statement: Yes
Term of Contract (Years): 10/10
Avg. # Of Employees: 2 FT, 8 PT
Passive Ownership: Discouraged
Encourage Conversions: Yes
Area Develop. Agreements: No
Sub-Franchising Contracts: No
Expand In Territory: Yes
Space Needs: 100-1,600 SF; FS, SF, SC, RM, C-Store, QSR

SUPPORT & TRAINING:
Financial Assistance Provided: No
Site Selection Assistance: Yes
Lease Negotiation Assistance: Yes
Co-Operative Advertising: Yes
Franchisee Assoc./Member: Yes/Yes
Size Of Corporate Staff: 100+
On-Going Support: C,D,E,G,H,I
Training: In Salt Lake City, Utah

SPECIFIC EXPANSION PLANS:
US: All United States
Canada: All Canada
Overseas: NR

<< >>

Tropicana®
SMOOTHIES,JUICES&MORE!

TROPICANA SMOOTHIES, JUICES & MORE!

4175 Veterans Hwy., # 303
Ronkonkoma, NY 11779
Tel: (800) 528-0727 + 1
Fax: (631) 737-9792
E-Mail: joearancio@aol.com
Web Site: www.tropsmoothies.com
Mr. Joe Arancio, VP Business Development

TROPICANA SMOOTHIES, JUICES & MORE! is a co-branding concept with premium-quality smoothies, nationally-branded ice cream and frozen yogurt. Concept will be sold as exclusive Territory Development Agreements for markets with a minimum of 500,000 population, with a development commitment of 5 stores in 10 years for established food-service and retail owners/operators.

BACKGROUND:
Established: 1949; 1st Franchised: 2004
Franchised Units: 8
Company-Owned Units: 2
Total Units: 10
Dist.: US-10; CAN-0; O'seas-0

North America: 7 States
Density: 2 in NV, 2 in IL
Projected New Units (12 Months): 12
Qualifications: 5, 5, 4, 4, 4, 5
Registered: All States

FINANCIAL/TERMS:
Cash Investment: $100-150K
Total Investment: $175-225K/Unit
Minimum Net Worth: $500K
Fees: Franchise - $75K/Territory
Royalty - 6%; Ad. - 1%
Earnings Claims Statement: No
Term of Contract (Years): 10/10
Avg. # Of Employees: 3-4 FT, 2-4 PT
Passive Ownership: Not Allowed
Encourage Conversions: Yes
Area Develop. Agreements: No
Sub-Franchising Contracts: No
Expand In Territory: Yes
Space Needs: 600-900 SF; RM, Power/Upscale Ctrs.

SUPPORT & TRAINING:
Financial Assistance Provided: No
Site Selection Assistance: Yes
Lease Negotiation Assistance: Yes
Co-Operative Advertising: No
Franchisee Assoc./Member: No
Size Of Corporate Staff: 100+
On-Going Support: B,C,D,E,G,H,I
Training: Las Vegas, NV.

SPECIFIC EXPANSION PLANS:
US: All United States
Canada: All Canada
Overseas: No

<< >>

YOGEN FRUZ

4175 Veterans Hwy.
Ronkonkoma, NY 11779
Tel: (800) 528-0727
Fax:
E-Mail: yogenfruz@yogenfruz.com
Web Site: www.yogenfruz.com
Mr. Joe Arancio, VP Business Development

YOGEN FRUZ is a frozen yogurt franchise chain. Frozen yogurt and fresh fruit are blended in front of the customer's eyes! We also sell shakes, pies, juices, ice cream, smoothies and fruity ice.

BACKGROUND:
Established: 1986; 1st Franchised: 1987
Franchised Units: 5,196
Company-Owned Units: 33
Total Units: 5,229
Dist.: US-1,687; CAN-795; O'seas-2,747
North America: 50 States,10 Provinces
Density: 375 in ON, 200 in TX
Projected New Units (12 Months): 500
Qualifications: 5, 4, 1, 1, 3, 5
Registered: All States and AB

FINANCIAL/TERMS:
Cash Investment: $50% Total Inv
Total Investment: $130-250K
Minimum Net Worth: $200K
Fees: Franchise - $25K
Royalty - 6%; Ad. - 3%
Earnings Claims Statement: No
Term of Contract (Years): 5-10/5-10
Avg. # Of Employees: 2 FT, 4 PT
Passive Ownership: Not Allowed
Encourage Conversions: Yes
Area Develop. Agreements: Yes/10
Sub-Franchising Contracts: Yes
Expand In Territory: No
Space Needs: 150-1,500 SF; SF, SC, RM

SUPPORT & TRAINING:
Financial Assistance Provided: Yes(I)
Site Selection Assistance: Yes
Lease Negotiation Assistance: Yes
Co-Operative Advertising: Yes
Franchisee Assoc./Member: Yes/No
Size Of Corporate Staff: 60
On-Going Support: C,D,E,F,G,H
Training: 2 Weeks in Dallas, TX; 1.5 Weeks in Toronto, ON.

SPECIFIC EXPANSION PLANS:
US: All United States
Canada: All Canada
Overseas: All Countries

For a full explanation of the data provided in the Franchisor Profiles, please refer to *Chapter 2, "How to Use the Data."*

Food: Quick Service/Take-Out

Chapter

16

Food: Quick Service/Take-Out Industry Profile

Total # Franchisors in Industry Group	390
Total # Franchised Units in Industry Group	132,824
Total # Company-Owned Units in Industry Group	28,581
Total # Operating Units in Industry Group	161,405
Average # Franchised Units/Franchisor	340.6
Average # Company-Owned Units/Franchisor	73.3
Average # Total Units/Franchisor	413.9
Ratio of Total # Franchised Units/Total # Company-Owned Units	4.6:1
Industry Survey Participants	156
Representing % of Industry	40%
Average Franchise Fee*:	$22.3K
Average Total Investment*:	$377K
Average On-Going Royalty Fee*:	4.9%

*If a range was provided, the mid-point of the range was used. See detailed profiles for actual ranges.

Five Largest Participants in Survey

Company	# Franchised Units	# Co-Owned Units	# Total Units	Franchise Fee	On-Going Royalty	Total Investment
1. McDonald's	22,213	8,105	30,318	$45K	12.5%	$506K-1.63MM
2. Subway Restaurants	21,153	1	21,154	$12.5K	8%	$86.3-213.5K
3. KFC	9,916	2,962	12,878	$25K	4% or $600/Mo.	$1.1-1.7MM
4. Burger King Corporation	10,144	1,079	11,223	$50K	4.5%	$Varies/UFOC
5. Taco Bell	4,600	3,044	7,644	$45K	5.5%	$236-503K

All of the data provided are proprietary and should not be quoted without acknowledging *Bond's Franchise Guide.*

Top 100

A & W RESTAURANTS

P. O. Box 34550, 1900 Colonel Sanders Ln.
Louisville, KY 40213
Tel: (866) 2YUM-YUM
Fax: (502) 874-8848
E-Mail: 2yumyum@yum.com
Web Site: www.yumfranchises.com
Ms. Nikki Weiss, Franchise Coordinator

A & W has been a successful, all-American icon for more than 80 years. Since repositioning A & W as the home of 'All American Food' with a menu of burgers, hot dogs, coney dogs, french fries, onion rings, and our signature A & W Root Beer and Root Beer floats, we have entered the ranks of the most rapidly growing quick-service restaurants in the world. Opportunities to develop are now even greater with our new co-branded restaurants that combine A & W and our sister brand, LONG JOHN SILVER'S.

BACKGROUND: IFA MEMBER
Established: 1919; 1st Franchised: 1925
Franchised Units: 679
Company-Owned Units: 80
Total Units: 759
Dist.: US-; CAN-; O'seas-
North America: 48 States
Density: NR
Projected New Units (12 Months): 300
Qualifications: 5, 5, 3, 4, 5, 5
Registered: All States Except DC,HI

FINANCIAL/TERMS:
Cash Investment: $
Total Investment: $1.0-1.2MMK
Minimum Net Worth: $1MM
Fees: Franchise - $30-50K
Royalty - 6% Gr. Receipts; Ad. - 4% Gr. Rec.
Earnings Claims Statement: Yes
Term of Contract (Years): 20
Avg. # Of Employees: 50-60 FT & PT
Passive Ownership: Allowed
Encourage Conversions: Yes
Area Develop. Agreements: NR
Sub-Franchising Contracts: NR
Expand In Territory: Yes
Space Needs: 1,200+ SF; FS, SF, SC, RM, Non-Tradit.

SUPPORT & TRAINING:
Financial Assistance Provided: No
Site Selection Assistance: Yes
Lease Negotiation Assistance: Yes
Co-Operative Advertising: Yes
Franchisee Assoc./Member: Yes/Yes
Size Of Corporate Staff: 300
On-Going Support: B,C,D,E,F,G,H,I
Training: 13 Weeks Prior to Opening.

SPECIFIC EXPANSION PLANS:
US: All United States
Canada: No
Overseas: All Countries

<< >>

AMECI PIZZA & PASTA

6603 Independence Ave., # B
Canoga Park, CA 91303
Tel: (818) 712-0110
Fax: (818) 712-0792
E-Mail: nandrisano@aol.com
Web Site: www.imal.com
Mr. Nick Andrisano, President

Italian fast foods, such as pizza, pasta, salads and subs.

BACKGROUND:
Established: 1979; 1st Franchised: 1987
Franchised Units: 41
Company-Owned Units: 2
Total Units: 43
Dist.: US-43; CAN-0; O'seas-0
North America: 1 State
Density: 43 in CA
Projected New Units (12 Months): 5
Qualifications: 5, 2, 1, 2, 2, 5
Registered: CA

FINANCIAL/TERMS:
Cash Investment: $185K
Total Investment: $135-235K
Minimum Net Worth: $250K
Fees: Franchise - $25K
Royalty - 4%; Ad. - 2%
Earnings Claims Statement: No
Term of Contract (Years): 10/10
Avg. # Of Employees: 4 FT, 5 PT
Passive Ownership: Discouraged
Encourage Conversions: Yes
Area Develop. Agreements: Yes/10/10
Sub-Franchising Contracts: No
Expand In Territory: Yes
Space Needs: 1,200 SF; SC

SUPPORT & TRAINING:
Financial Assistance Provided: No
Site Selection Assistance: Yes
Lease Negotiation Assistance: Yes
Co-Operative Advertising: Yes
Franchisee Assoc./Member: No
Size Of Corporate Staff: 7
On-Going Support: A,B,C,D,E,F,G,H,I
Training: 4 Weeks of School at Home Office; 2 Weeks at Unit Location.

SPECIFIC EXPANSION PLANS:
US: NR
Canada: No
Overseas: All Latin Countries

<< >>

ANDERSON'S RESTAURANTS

6075 Main St.
Williamsville, NY 14221
Tel: (716) 633-2302
Fax: (716) 633-2671
E-Mail: info@andersonscustard.com
Web Site: www.andersonscustard.com
Mr. Kirk P. Wildermuth, President

A Western New York tradition, serving award-winning roast beef, BBQ, chicken and ham sandwiches. Also, we are famous for our one-of-a-kind frozen custard, plus homemade ice cream. We also specialize in ice cream cakes and pies. We are the Northeast's premium lunch, dinner and dessert fast casual concept.

BACKGROUND:
Established: 1946; 1st Franchised: 1996
Franchised Units: 8
Company-Owned Units: 3
Total Units: 11
Dist.: US-10; CAN-0; O'seas-0
North America: 1 State
Density: 9 in NY
Projected New Units (12 Months): NR
Qualifications: , , , , ,
Registered: NR

FINANCIAL/TERMS:
Cash Investment: $400-500K
Total Investment: $900K-1.1MM
Minimum Net Worth: $500K
Fees: Franchise - $30K
Royalty - 4%; Ad. - 2%
Earnings Claims Statement: No
Term of Contract (Years): 20
Avg. # Of Employees: 10 FT, 25 PT
Passive Ownership: Not Allowed
Encourage Conversions: NR
Area Develop. Agreements: Yes/20
Sub-Franchising Contracts: No
Expand In Territory: Yes
Space Needs: 3,800 SF; FS, End Cap

SUPPORT & TRAINING:
Financial Assistance Provided: NR
Site Selection Assistance: Yes
Lease Negotiation Assistance: Yes
Co-Operative Advertising: Yes

Franchisee Assoc./Member: No
Size Of Corporate Staff: 7
On-Going Support: B,C,D,E,G
Training: 12-16 Weeks Buffalo, NY.
SPECIFIC EXPANSION PLANS:
US: OH, NY, PA
Canada: NR
Overseas: NR

<< >>

ANGEL'S HOT DOGS & MARBLE TOP ICE CREAM

37252 Hwy 26
Seaside, OR 97138
Tel: (503) 717-9560
Fax: (503) 717-9558
E-Mail: terry@angelsfranchise.com
Web Site: www.angelsfranchise.com
Mr. Terry Hoard, Director of Operations

ANGEL'S gourmet hot dogs and ice cream. Snow ANGEL'S funnel cake.

BACKGROUND:
Established: 2002; 1st Franchised: 2003
Franchised Units: 2
Company-Owned Units: 0
Total Units: 2
Dist.: US-2; CAN-0; O'seas-0
North America: 2 States
Density: 1 in CA, 1 in OR
Projected New Units (12 Months): 10
Qualifications: 3, 3, 3, 3, 3, 5
Registered: CA,FL,OR,WA
FINANCIAL/TERMS:
Cash Investment: $50K
Total Investment: $140-250K
Minimum Net Worth: $50K+
Fees: Franchise - $19.9K
Royalty - 5%; Ad. - 2%
Earnings Claims Statement: No
Term of Contract (Years): 10/10
Avg. # Of Employees: 4 FT, 4 PT
Passive Ownership: Discouraged
Encourage Conversions: NA
Area Develop. Agreements: Yes/10
Sub-Franchising Contracts: Yes
Expand In Territory: Yes
Space Needs: 1,000 SF; FS, SF, SC, RM
SUPPORT & TRAINING:
Financial Assistance Provided: Yes(I)
Site Selection Assistance: Yes
Lease Negotiation Assistance: Yes
Co-Operative Advertising: NA
Franchisee Assoc./Member: No
Size Of Corporate Staff: 2
On-Going Support: a,B,C,D,E,F,G,H
Training: 1-2 Weeks at a Working Store; 1 Week at Franchisee's New Store Location.
SPECIFIC EXPANSION PLANS:
US: All United States
Canada: All Canada
Overseas: All Countries

<< >>

ARBY'S

1000 Corporate Dr.
Ft. Lauderdale, FL 33334-3655
Tel: (800) 487-2729 + 5200 (954) 351-5100
Fax: (954) 351-5222
E-Mail: phultgren@arbys.com
Web Site: www.arbys.com
Mr. Peter Hultgren, VP Franchise Sales

The leader in the roast beef segment, ARBY'S offers cut above menu options including a complete line of roast beef and chicken sandwiches, chicken fingers, a light sandwich menu, salads and three fry varieties. Development opportunities available. An experienced brand with over 3,400 locations.

BACKGROUND: IFA MEMBER
Established: 1964; 1st Franchised: 1965
Franchised Units: 3,232
Company-Owned Units: 237
Total Units: 3,469
Dist.: US-3,335; CAN-125; O'seas-9
North America: 48 States, 8 Provinces
Density: 277 in OH, 167 in CA, 166 MI
Projected New Units (12 Months): 150
Qualifications: 5, 5, 4, 3, 3, 5
Registered: All States
FINANCIAL/TERMS:
Cash Investment: $0-2,378.2K
Total Investment: $108.3K-2.37MM
Minimum Net Worth: $1.0MM
Fees: Franchise - $37.5K
Royalty - 4%; Ad. - Min 3.7%
Earnings Claims Statement: Yes
Term of Contract (Years): 20/Varies
Avg. # Of Employees: 15 FT, 25 PT
Passive Ownership: Allowed
Encourage Conversions: Yes
Area Develop. Agreements: Yes/Varies
Sub-Franchising Contracts: No
Expand In Territory: Yes
Space Needs: 2,000-3,000 SF; FS
SUPPORT & TRAINING:
Financial Assistance Provided: No
Site Selection Assistance: Yes
Lease Negotiation Assistance: No
Co-Operative Advertising: Yes
Franchisee Assoc./Member: Yes/Yes
Size Of Corporate Staff: 150
On-Going Support: B,C,D,E,G,I
Training: 5 Weeks MTP-Certified Training Locations.
SPECIFIC EXPANSION PLANS:
US: NE, W, S
Canada: All Canada
Overseas: Canada, Mexico, Australia, U.K., Middle East

<< >>

ARIZONA PIZZA COMPANY

350 SE 15th Ave.
Pompano Beach, FL 33060
Tel: (954) 942-9424
Fax: (954) 783-5177
E-Mail: fdiintl@bellsouth.net
Web Site: www.arizonapizzaco.com
Ms. Linda Biciocchi, Director

Full service, casual dining restaurant, offering eat-in and take-out service. A full-service bar attracts singles, couples, males and females. Our wood-fired pizza oven is the central focus. We feature gourmet and traditional pasta entrees, plus appetizers, salads, wraps, calzones and other popular items, e.g. hamburgers, sandwiches. Cable TV sets at the tables attracts families and is a favorite for the children.

BACKGROUND:
Established: 2002; 1st Franchised: 2003
Franchised Units: 4
Company-Owned Units: 1
Total Units: 5
Dist.: US-4; CAN-0; O'seas-0
North America: 1 State
Density: 4 in MA
Projected New Units (12 Months): 6
Qualifications: 4, 4, 3, 3, 3, 5
Registered: CA,FL,MD,MI,NY,VA
FINANCIAL/TERMS:
Cash Investment: $125K
Total Investment: $256-397K
Minimum Net Worth: $400K
Fees: Franchise - $25K
Royalty - 4%; Ad. - 2-4%
Earnings Claims Statement: No
Term of Contract (Years): 10/10
Avg. # Of Employees: 10 FT, 10 PT
Passive Ownership: Allowed
Encourage Conversions: Yes
Area Develop. Agreements: Yes/5
Sub-Franchising Contracts: No
Expand In Territory: Yes
Space Needs: 3,500 SF; FS, SC
SUPPORT & TRAINING:
Financial Assistance Provided: Yes(I)
Site Selection Assistance: Yes

Lease Negotiation Assistance: Yes
Co-Operative Advertising: Yes
Franchisee Assoc./Member: No
Size Of Corporate Staff: 10
On-Going Support: C,D,E,F
Training: 3-4 Weeks Corporate Location in MA.

SPECIFIC EXPANSION PLANS:
US: All United States
Canada: No
Overseas: No

<< >>

ARTHUR TREACHER'S FISH & CHIPS

5 Dakota Dr., # 302
Lake Success, NY 11042
Tel: (516) 358-0600
Fax: (516) 358-5076
E-Mail: abernstein@trufoods.com
Web Site: www.arthurtreachersinc.com
Mr. Alan J. Bernstein, Concept Director

In 1969, ARTHUR TREACHER'S purchased the original fish and chips recipe from a London restaurant called Malin's of Bow (dating back to the 1860s), and with it, the original fish and chips recipe. Since then, we've adjusted the menu to accommodate American tastes and expanded it to include shrimp, clams, fried chicken and side orders including tasty hush puppies and our unique coleslaw. All of which makes ARTHUR TREACHER'S DISH & CHIPS the English meal perfect for today's all-American appetite.

BACKGROUND: IFA MEMBER
Established: 1969; 1st Franchised: 1969
Franchised Units: 203
Company-Owned Units: 0
Total Units: 203
Dist.: US-202; CAN-0; O'seas-1
North America: 21 States
Density: 77 in FL, 71 in NY, 26 in OH
Projected New Units (12 Months): 50
Qualifications: 5, 4, 4, 2, 3, 5
Registered: FL,MI,NY

FINANCIAL/TERMS:
Cash Investment: $75-100K
Total Investment: $175-250K
Minimum Net Worth: $250K
Fees: Franchise - $30K
Royalty - 5%; Ad. - 3%
Earnings Claims Statement: No
Term of Contract (Years): 10/10
Avg. # Of Employees: 3 FT, 8 PT
Passive Ownership: Discouraged
Encourage Conversions: Yes
Area Develop. Agreements: Yes/5
Sub-Franchising Contracts: No
Expand In Territory: Yes
Space Needs: 500-2,000 SF; FS, SF, SC, RM

SUPPORT & TRAINING:
Financial Assistance Provided: Yes(I)
Site Selection Assistance: Yes
Lease Negotiation Assistance: Yes
Co-Operative Advertising: Yes
Franchisee Assoc./Member: Yes/Yes
Size Of Corporate Staff: 50
On-Going Support: A,B,C,D,E,F,G,H,I
Training: 10 Days Long Island, NY.

SPECIFIC EXPANSION PLANS:
US: All United States
Canada: All Canada
Overseas: All Countries

<< >>

BACK YARD BURGERS

1657 N. Shelby Oaks Dr., # 105
Memphis, TN 38134
Tel: (800) 292-6939 (901) 367-0888 + 1204
Fax: (901) 367-0999
E-Mail: mpearce@backyardburgers.com
Web Site: www.backyardburgers.com
Mr. Scott Prewitt, Franchisee Association

BACK YARD BURGERS operates and franchises quick casual restaurants, serving 1/3 lb. gourmet hamburgers, boneless, skinless chicken fillet sandwiches, fresh lemonade, hand-dipped shakes and malts and other menu items. Our theme emphasizes charbroiled, fresh, great-tasting food as the customers would cook in their own back yard.

BACKGROUND: IFA MEMBER
Established: 1987; 1st Franchised: 1988
Franchised Units: 86
Company-Owned Units: 43
Total Units: 129
Dist.: US-105; CAN-0; O'seas-0
North America: 17 States
Density: 32 in TN, 12 in AR, 10 in NC
Projected New Units (12 Months): 15
Qualifications: 4, 4, 3, 2, 1, 3
Registered: FL,IL,IN,MI,VA

FINANCIAL/TERMS:
Cash Investment: $200-300K
Total Investment: $400K-1.2MM
Minimum Net Worth: $300K
Fees: Franchise - $25K
Royalty - 4%; Ad. - 1%
Earnings Claims Statement: No
Term of Contract (Years): 10/5
Avg. # Of Employees: 8 FT, 22 PT
Passive Ownership: Discouraged
Encourage Conversions: Yes
Area Develop. Agreements: Yes/12
Sub-Franchising Contracts: No
Expand In Territory: Yes
Space Needs: 2,500 SF; FS

SUPPORT & TRAINING:
Financial Assistance Provided: Yes(I)
Site Selection Assistance: Yes
Lease Negotiation Assistance: Yes
Co-Operative Advertising: Yes
Franchisee Assoc./Member: Yes/Yes
Size Of Corporate Staff: 30
On-Going Support: B,C,D,E,F,G,H
Training: 8 Weeks Corporate Headquarters.

SPECIFIC EXPANSION PLANS:
US: SE, MW, Mid-Atlantic, SW
Canada: No
Overseas: No

<< >>

BAJA SOL TORTILLA GRILL

7173 Oak Pointe Curve
Bloomington, MN 55438
Tel: (612) 280-1467
Fax: (952) 944-2001
E-Mail: mikeplatt@aol.com
Web Site: www.bajasol.us
Mr. Mike Platt, President

BAJA SOL TORTILLA GRILL is a growing casual fresh Mexican restaurant concept, featuring fresh-made tortillas and an extensive salsa bar.

BACKGROUND:
Established: 1995; 1st Franchised: 1999
Franchised Units: 5
Company-Owned Units: 5
Total Units: 10
Dist.: US-10; CAN-0; O'seas-0
North America: 1 State
Density: 10 in MN
Projected New Units (12 Months):
Qualifications: , , , , ,
Registered:

FINANCIAL/TERMS:
Cash Investment: NA
Total Investment: $166-400K
Minimum Net Worth: NA
Fees: Franchise - $25K
Royalty - 4.5%; Ad. - 1%
Earnings Claims Statement: No
Term of Contract (Years): 10/10
Avg. # Of Employees: 3-4 FT, 2-5 PT
Passive Ownership: Not Allowed
Encourage Conversions:

Area Develop. Agreements: Yes/10
Sub-Franchising Contracts: No
Expand In Territory: Yes
Space Needs: 2,200 SF; SF, SC, RM

SUPPORT & TRAINING:
Financial Assistance Provided:
Site Selection Assistance: Yes
Lease Negotiation Assistance: Yes
Co-Operative Advertising: Yes
Franchisee Assoc./Member: No
Size Of Corporate Staff: 2
On-Going Support: C,D,E
Training: 10 Days Minneapolis, MN.

SPECIFIC EXPANSION PLANS:
US: MN and other states (TBD).
Canada: NR
Overseas: NR

<< >>

BALDINOS GIANT JERSEY SUBS
3823 Roswell Rd., # 204
Marietta, GA 30062
Tel: (770) 971-9441
Fax: (770) 977-1083
E-Mail: baldinossubs@bellsouth.net
Web Site: www.worldfranchising.com/website.htm
Mr. Bill Baer, President/CEO

Quality submarine sandwiches with in-store bakery. All subs sliced fresh as ordered in full view of customer, served on freshly baked rolls. Built for volume business at a 'fast-food' pace by use of multi-production lines. Variety of 20 hot and cold subs and freshly baked gourmet cookies.

BACKGROUND:
Established: 1975; 1st Franchised: 1984
Franchised Units: 13
Company-Owned Units: 6
Total Units: 19
Dist.: US-19; CAN-0; O'seas-0
North America: 3 States
Density: 13 in GA, 5 in NC, 1 in SC
Projected New Units (12 Months): 3
Qualifications: , , , , ,
Registered: FL

FINANCIAL/TERMS:
Cash Investment: NR
Total Investment: $100-200K
Minimum Net Worth: NR
Fees: Franchise - $10K
Royalty - 4.5%; Ad. - 0.5%
Earnings Claims Statement: No
Term of Contract (Years): 15/10
Avg. # Of Employees: 8 FT, 12 PT
Passive Ownership: Not Allowed
Encourage Conversions: Yes
Area Develop. Agreements: Yes/15+
Sub-Franchising Contracts: Yes
Expand In Territory: Yes
Space Needs: 1,800-2,400 SF; FS

SUPPORT & TRAINING:
Financial Assistance Provided: No
Site Selection Assistance: Yes
Lease Negotiation Assistance: Yes
Co-Operative Advertising: Yes
Franchisee Assoc./Member: NR
Size Of Corporate Staff: 4
On-Going Support: B,C,D,E,F,G,H,I
Training: 4 Weeks Headquarters.

SPECIFIC EXPANSION PLANS:
US: GA, SC, NC
Canada: No
Overseas: No

<< >>

BIG TOWN HERO
912 SW Third Ave.
Portland, OR 97204
Tel: (503) 228-4376
Fax: (503) 228-8778
E-Mail: rick@bth.com
Web Site: www.bth.com
Mr. Rick Olson, Director of Franchising

Sub sandwich franchise. We bake our bread from scratch everyday. We have the "Ultimate Sandwich" and the "Ultimate Franchise."

BACKGROUND:
Established: 1982; 1st Franchised: 1987
Franchised Units: 36
Company-Owned Units: 0
Total Units: 36
Dist.: US-36; CAN-0; O'seas-0
North America: 3 States
Density: 34 in OR, 1 in CA, 1 in WA
Projected New Units (12 Months): 12
Qualifications: 5, 4, 3, 1, 1, 5
Registered: CA, HI, OR, WA

FINANCIAL/TERMS:
Cash Investment: $25-70K
Total Investment: $25-125K
Minimum Net Worth: $100K
Fees: Franchise - $14.5K
Royalty - 6%; Ad. - $300/Mo.
Earnings Claims Statement: No
Term of Contract (Years): 5/5
Avg. # Of Employees: 1 FT, 4 PT
Passive Ownership: Not Allowed
Encourage Conversions: No
Area Develop. Agreements: Yes/10
Sub-Franchising Contracts: No
Expand In Territory: Yes
Space Needs: 1,500 SF; FS, SF, SC, RM

SUPPORT & TRAINING:
Financial Assistance Provided: No
Site Selection Assistance: Yes
Lease Negotiation Assistance: Yes
Co-Operative Advertising: No
Franchisee Assoc./Member: No
Size Of Corporate Staff: 6
On-Going Support: C,D,E,F,G,h
Training: 3 Weeks in Portland, OR.

SPECIFIC EXPANSION PLANS:
US: NW, SW
Canada: No
Overseas: No

<< >>

Blimpie SUBS & SALADS

Top 100

BLIMPIE SUBS AND SALADS
180 Interstate North Pkwy., SE, # 500
Atlanta, GA 30339
Tel: (800) 447-6256 + 3 (770) 984-2707
Fax: (770) 933-6109
E-Mail: jarcher@blimpie.com
Web Site: www.blimpie.com
Ms. J. Archer, VP Franchise Development

International submarine sandwich chain, serving fresh-sliced, high-quality meats and cheeses on fresh-baked bread. Also offering an assortment of fresh-made salads and other quality products.

BACKGROUND: IFA MEMBER
Established: 1964; 1st Franchised: 1977
Franchised Units: 1,390
Company-Owned Units: 20
Total Units: 1,410
Dist.: US-1,349; CAN-0; O'seas-61
North America: 50 States, 4 Provinces
Density: 209 in FL, 193 in GA
Projected New Units (12 Months): NR
Qualifications: 4, 3, 2, 2, 2, 5
Registered: CA,FL,HI,IL,IN,MI,MN,NY,ND,OR,RI,SD,WA,WI

FINANCIAL/TERMS:
Cash Investment: $25-100K
Total Investment: $75-250K
Minimum Net Worth: $100K
Fees: Franchise - $10-18K
Royalty - 6%; Ad. - 4%
Earnings Claims Statement: No
Term of Contract (Years): 20/5
Avg. # Of Employees: 4 FT, 8 PT
Passive Ownership: Discouraged

Encourage Conversions: Yes
Area Develop. Agreements: Yes
Sub-Franchising Contracts: Yes
Expand In Territory: Yes
Space Needs: 1,200 SF; FS, SF, SC, RM

SUPPORT & TRAINING:

Financial Assistance Provided: Yes(I)
Site Selection Assistance: Yes
Lease Negotiation Assistance: Yes
Co-Operative Advertising: Yes
Franchisee Assoc./Member: Yes/Yes
Size Of Corporate Staff: 109
On-Going Support: B,C,D,E,F,G,H,I
Training: 80 Hours in Atlanta, GA; 120 Hours in Local Franchise.

SPECIFIC EXPANSION PLANS:

US: All United States
Canada: All Canada
Overseas: All Except Anti-American Countries

<< >>

BOARDWALK FRIES

8980 Route 108, # J
Columbia, MD 21045
Tel: (410) 715-0500
Fax: (410) 715-0711
E-Mail: brandedbwf@aol.com
Web Site: www.boardwalkfries.com
Mr. David DiFerdinando, President

We specialize in serving gourmet fries, fresh-cut and cooked in peanut oil with assorted toppings, prepared on location. We also have hot dogs, hamburgers, assorted sub sandwiches, drinks, fresh-squeezed lemonade. Our locations range from fries-only to full-menu restaurants.

BACKGROUND:

Established: 1981; 1st Franchised: 1981
Franchised Units: 25
Company-Owned Units: 1
Total Units: 26
Dist.: US-25; CAN-1; O'seas-26
North America: 26 States
Density: 8 in MD, 6 in PA, 3 in IL
Projected New Units (12 Months): 18-24
Qualifications: 4, 3, 3, 3, 5, 5
Registered: MD

FINANCIAL/TERMS:

Cash Investment: $30-90K
Total Investment: $30-150K
Minimum Net Worth: $100K
Fees: Franchise - $15-25K
Royalty - 5-7%; Ad. - 0-2%
Earnings Claims Statement: No
Term of Contract (Years): 10/10
Avg. # Of Employees: Varies
Passive Ownership: Not Allowed
Encourage Conversions: Yes
Area Develop. Agreements: Yes/10
Sub-Franchising Contracts: No
Expand In Territory: Yes
Space Needs: 400-1,200 SF; RM

SUPPORT & TRAINING:

Financial Assistance Provided: Yes(I)
Site Selection Assistance: Yes
Lease Negotiation Assistance: Yes
Co-Operative Advertising: Yes
Franchisee Assoc./Member: No
Size Of Corporate Staff: 9
On-Going Support: C,D,E,F
Training: 6 Days in MD.

SPECIFIC EXPANSION PLANS:

US: East Coast
Canada: No
Overseas: Korea

<< >>

BOJANGLES' FAMOUS CHICKEN 'N BISCUITS

9432 Southern Pine Blvd.
Charlotte, NC 28273-5553
Tel: (800) 366-9921 (704) 940-8621
Fax: (704) 523-6803
E-Mail: cbailey@bojangles.com
Web Site: www.bojanglesfranchise.com
Mr. Chris Bailey, Dir. Franchise Development

BOJANGLES OPERATES DURING ALL 3 DAY-PARTS. Breakfast items are available all day long. Our menu in unique, and flavorful, with chicken prepared either spicy or traditional Southern-style. Restaurants operate in traditional locations and non-traditional locations in convenience stores.

BACKGROUND: IFA MEMBER

Established: 1977; 1st Franchised: 1979
Franchised Units: 214
Company-Owned Units: 135
Total Units: 349
Dist.: US-286; CAN-0; O'seas-3
North America: 10 States
Density: 130 in NC, 55 in SC,18 in GA
Projected New Units (12 Months): 30
Qualifications: 5, 4, 4, 3, 3, 5
Registered: FL,IL,MD,VA

FINANCIAL/TERMS:

Cash Investment: $225-350K
Total Investment: $740K
Minimum Net Worth: $750K
Fees: Franchise - $12-20K
Royalty - 4%; Ad. - 1%
Earnings Claims Statement: No
Term of Contract (Years): 20/10
Avg. # Of Employees: 12 FT, 20 PT
Passive Ownership: Discouraged
Encourage Conversions: Yes
Area Develop. Agreements: Yes/10
Sub-Franchising Contracts: No
Expand In Territory: Yes
Space Needs: 2,000+ SF; FS

SUPPORT & TRAINING:

Financial Assistance Provided: No
Site Selection Assistance: Yes
Lease Negotiation Assistance: No
Co-Operative Advertising: Yes
Franchisee Assoc./Member: Yes/Yes
Size Of Corporate Staff: 80
On-Going Support: B,C,D,E,F,G,H,I
Training: 5 Weeks Training in Training Units.

SPECIFIC EXPANSION PLANS:

US: Southeast, Midwest
Canada: No
Overseas: Central America, Caribbean Areas

BOX LUNCH, THE

50 Briar Ln.
Wellfleet, MA 02667
Tel: (508) 349-3509
Fax: (508) 349-3661
E-Mail: owen@boxlunch.com
Web Site: www.boxlunch.com
Mr. Owen MacNutt, President

We are Darwin's theory applied to the sandwich. We have served only rolled pita sandwiches (Rollwiches) for 23 years. No cooking, no fried food, yet we are fast enough to feed 200+ people per hour, each Rollwich custom-made from over 40 selections. Voted best on Cape Cod last 6 years.

BACKGROUND:

Established: 1977; 1st Franchised: 1986
Franchised Units: 10
Company-Owned Units: 1
Total Units: 11
Dist.: US-11; CAN-0; O'seas-0
North America: 2 States
Density: 10 in MA, 1 in CT
Projected New Units (12 Months): 3
Qualifications: 4, 3, 1, 2, 2, 5
Registered: NA

FINANCIAL/TERMS:

Cash Investment: $60-100K
Total Investment: $125-200K
Minimum Net Worth: $500K
Fees: Franchise - $15K

Royalty - 4.5%; Ad. - 3%
Earnings Claims Statement: No
Term of Contract (Years): 5/5
Avg. # Of Employees: 4 FT, 2 PT
Passive Ownership: Not Allowed
Encourage Conversions: NA
Area Develop. Agreements: Yes/10
Sub-Franchising Contracts: No
Expand In Territory: No
Space Needs: 1,200 SF; FS, SF, SC, RM

SUPPORT & TRAINING:
Financial Assistance Provided: No
Site Selection Assistance: Yes
Lease Negotiation Assistance: Yes
Co-Operative Advertising: Yes
Franchisee Assoc./Member: No
Size Of Corporate Staff: 2
On-Going Support: A,B,C,d,E,F,G,H,i
Training: 2-4 Weeks Wellfleet, MA.

SPECIFIC EXPANSION PLANS:
US: Northeast, New England
Canada: All Canada
Overseas: No

BREADEAUX PIZZA

P. O. Box 6158, Fairleigh Station
St. Joseph, MO 64506
Tel: (800) 835-6534 (816) 364-1088
Fax: (816) 364-3739
E-Mail: shannon@breadeauxpizza.com
Web Site: www.breadeauxpizza.com
Ms. Shannon Gilliland, VP Sales/Marketing

BREADEAUX PIZZA is a growing regional chain, stressing quality and service. Our acclaimed pizza is made with a double raised crust that is chewy and sweet like fine french bread and our meat toppings have no fillers or additives. We also offer pastas, subs, baked potatoes, hot wings and salads to give customers plenty of variety. Our customers say 'Best Pizza in Town.'

BACKGROUND:
Established: 1985; 1st Franchised: 1985
Franchised Units: 100
Company-Owned Units: 3
Total Units: 103
Dist.: US-95; CAN-3; O'seas-0
North America: 8 States, 1 Province
Density: 45 in IA, 28 MO, 6 KS
Projected New Units (12 Months): 10
Qualifications: 3, 5, 2, 2, 3, 5
Registered: IL,MI,SD,WI

FINANCIAL/TERMS:
Cash Investment: $30-80K
Total Investment: $58-313K
Minimum Net Worth: $50K
Fees: Franchise - $15K
Royalty - 5%; Ad. - 3%
Earnings Claims Statement: Yes
Term of Contract (Years): 15/15
Avg. # Of Employees: 2 FT, 12 PT
Passive Ownership: Discouraged
Encourage Conversions: Yes
Area Develop. Agreements: Yes/10
Sub-Franchising Contracts: Yes
Expand In Territory: Yes
Space Needs: 1,200-2,500 SF; FS, SF, SC, RM

SUPPORT & TRAINING:
Financial Assistance Provided: Yes(I)
Site Selection Assistance: Yes
Lease Negotiation Assistance: Yes
Co-Operative Advertising: No
Franchisee Assoc./Member: Yes/Yes
Size Of Corporate Staff: 14
On-Going Support: A,B,C,D,E,F,G,H,I
Training: 2 Weeks Corporate Headquarters; 1 Week Franchisee Location; On-Going as Needed.

SPECIFIC EXPANSION PLANS:
US: Midwest
Canada: All Canada
Overseas: No

BROWN'S CHICKEN & PASTA

489 W. Fullerton Ave.
Elmhurst, IL 60126
Tel: (630) 617-8800
Fax:
E-Mail: frankportillo@brownschicken.com
Web Site: www.brownschicken.com
Mr. Frank Portillo, Jr., President

High-quality, quick-service franchisor of BROWN'S CHICKEN & PASTA RESTAURANTS. Featuring various fresh-made side dishes. Stores can have take-out, dine-in and drive-up service. Our products, service and franchisee support exceed both customer and franchisee expectations. Expanded into corporate and home catering. Oven-baked chicken and full-service grill and pan pasta catering.

BACKGROUND:
Established: 1965; 1st Franchised: 1965
Franchised Units: 70
Company-Owned Units: 24
Total Units: 94
Dist.: US-74; CAN-0; O'seas-0
North America: 3 States
Density: 80 in IL, 5 in FL
Projected New Units (12 Months): 3-5
Qualifications: 3, 3, 2, 3, 5, 5
Registered: FL,IL,IN

FINANCIAL/TERMS:
Cash Investment: $25K
Total Investment: $150-160K
Minimum Net Worth: $200K
Fees: Franchise - $25K
Royalty - 5%; Ad. - 4%
Earnings Claims Statement: Yes
Term of Contract (Years): 15/5
Avg. # Of Employees: 3 FT, 12 PT
Passive Ownership: Not Allowed
Encourage Conversions: Yes
Area Develop. Agreements: Yes/15
Sub-Franchising Contracts: No
Expand In Territory: No
Space Needs: 1,500 SF; FS, SC

SUPPORT & TRAINING:
Financial Assistance Provided: No
Site Selection Assistance: Yes
Lease Negotiation Assistance: Yes
Co-Operative Advertising: Yes
Franchisee Assoc./Member: Yes/Yes
Size Of Corporate Staff: 12
On-Going Support: B,C,D,E,F,G,H,I
Training: 6 Weeks Oakbrook, IL Corporate Office.

SPECIFIC EXPANSION PLANS:
US: FL, IL, IN
Canada: No
Overseas: Russia, Asia

BUCK'S PIZZA

P. O. Box 405
DuBois, PA 15801
Tel: (800) 310-8848 (814) 371-3076
Fax: (814) 371-4214
E-Mail: neil@buckspizza.com
Web Site: www.buckspizza.com
Mr. Neil Shindledecker, Sales & Marketing

We at BUCK'S PIZZA pride ourselves on the best-quality pizza we can prepare. To do that, we buy only select ingredients and prepare them in our own special way. BUCK'S PIZZA is a delicious blend of natural ingredients delicately, flavored with special spices. We have expanded to 22 states in a few short years. Towns of any size offer the opportunity for BUCK'S low start-up costs and low overhead concept. When you are ready, BUCK'S is ready to train and then support you in your business!

BACKGROUND:
Established: 1994; 1st Franchised: 1994
Franchised Units: 83
Company-Owned Units: 0
Total Units: 83
Dist.: US-80; CAN-0; O'seas-0
North America: 22 States
Density: 21 in TX, 10 in GA, 10 in SC
Projected New Units (12 Months): 24
Qualifications: 3, 4, 5, 3, 3, 5
Registered:FL,IL,MD,MN,NY,VA,WA,WI

FINANCIAL/TERMS:
Cash Investment: $15-30K
Total Investment: $100-120K
Minimum Net Worth: $30-40K
Fees: Franchise - $10K
Royalty - 3%; Ad. - 2%
Earnings Claims Statement: No
Term of Contract (Years): 10/10
Avg. # Of Employees: 4 FT, 11 PT
Passive Ownership: Discouraged
Encourage Conversions: Yes
Area Develop. Agreements: Yes/Varies
Sub-Franchising Contracts: No
Expand In Territory: Yes
Space Needs: 1,000 SF; FS, SF, SC

SUPPORT & TRAINING:
Financial Assistance Provided: Yes(I)
Site Selection Assistance: Yes
Lease Negotiation Assistance: Yes
Co-Operative Advertising: Yes
Franchisee Assoc./Member: No
Size Of Corporate Staff: 10
On-Going Support: B,C,d,E,F,h,I
Training: 1-2 Day(s) Seminar in Headquarters; 10-14 Days On-Site.

SPECIFIC EXPANSION PLANS:
US: All United States
Canada: No
Overseas: No

<< >>

BUMPERS DRIVE-IN

1554 West Peace St.
Canton, MS 39046
Tel: (888) 840-6601 (601) 855-0146
Fax: (601) 855-0516
E-Mail: sethi@bumpersdrivein.com
Web Site: www.worldfranchising.com/website.htm
Ms. Monica Harrigill, VP Operations

Fast food drive-in providing quality hamburgers, chicken, catfish, hot dogs, ice creams, shakes, french fries, potato pearls (tots), soft drinks, tea, coffee and desserts, namely apple pies, banana splits, short cakes with various toppings with the friendliest service possible.

BACKGROUND:
Established: 1985; 1st Franchised: 1985
Franchised Units: 5
Company-Owned Units: 25
Total Units: 30
Dist.: US-30; CAN-0; O'seas-0
North America: 3 States
Density: 28 in MS, 1 in TN, 1 in TX
Projected New Units (12 Months): 1
Qualifications: , , , , ,
Registered: NR

FINANCIAL/TERMS:
Cash Investment: $75-125K
Total Investment: $400-550K
Minimum Net Worth: $300K
Fees: Franchise - $10K
Royalty - 4%; Ad. - 6%
Earnings Claims Statement: No
Term of Contract (Years): 20/10
Avg. # Of Employees: 8 FT, 12 PT
Passive Ownership: Not Allowed
Encourage Conversions: NR
Area Develop. Agreements: Yes/10
Sub-Franchising Contracts: No
Expand In Territory: Yes
Space Needs: 24,000 SF; FS

SUPPORT & TRAINING:
Financial Assistance Provided: NR
Site Selection Assistance: Yes
Lease Negotiation Assistance: Yes
Co-Operative Advertising: Yes
Franchisee Assoc./Member: No
Size Of Corporate Staff: 70+
On-Going Support: a,B,C,D,E,F,G,h,I
Training: Nine Weeks (Two Hours Each) in Classroom; Five Weeks In-store Training.

SPECIFIC EXPANSION PLANS:
US: All United States
Canada: NR
Overseas: NR

<< >>

BURGER KING (CANADA)

401 The West Mall, 7th Fl.
Etobicoke, ON M9C 5J4 CANADA
Tel: (416) 626-7444
Fax: (416) 626-6691
E-Mail: bkfranchise@whopper.com
Web Site: www.burgerking.com
Mr. Jeff Weinman, Senior Development Manager

Do you enjoy food cooked over an open flame? So do millions of others. Come join the second largest hamburger restaurant chain in the world and become part of a well-respected and highly successful organization. BURGER KING is continuing its expansion throughout Canada and the time to join our team is now. BURGER KING provides the support to help make your restaurant successful.

BACKGROUND: IFA MEMBER
Established: 1954; 1st Franchised: 1969
Franchised Units: 236
Company-Owned Units: 129
Total Units: 365
Dist.: US-0; CAN-365; O'seas-0
North America: 10 Provinces
Density: 170 in ON, 70 in PQ, 38 BC
Projected New Units (12 Months): 15
Qualifications: 5, 4, 2, 3, 1, 5
Registered: AB

FINANCIAL/TERMS:
Cash Investment: $400K - C
Total Investment: $740-1K-1.1MMC
Minimum Net Worth: $800K - C
Fees: Franchise - $55K - C
Royalty - 4%; Ad. - 4%
Earnings Claims Statement: No
Term of Contract (Years): 20/20
Avg. # Of Employees: 15 FT, 35 PT
Passive Ownership: Allowed
Encourage Conversions: Yes
Area Develop. Agreements: No
Sub-Franchising Contracts: No
Expand In Territory: Yes
Space Needs: 3,600 SF; FS, SF, RM

SUPPORT & TRAINING:
Financial Assistance Provided: Yes(I)
Site Selection Assistance: Yes
Lease Negotiation Assistance: Yes
Co-Operative Advertising: Yes
Franchisee Assoc./Member: Yes/Yes
Size Of Corporate Staff: 70
On-Going Support: B,C,D,E,F,H
Training: 400 Hours in Restaurant; 300 Hours Classroom.

SPECIFIC EXPANSION PLANS:
US: No
Canada: All Canada
Overseas: No

<< >>

BURGER KING ® CORPORATION

5505 Blue Lagoon Dr.
Miami, FL 33126
Tel: (305) 378-7579
Fax: (305) 378-7721
E-Mail: dleonardo@whopper.com
Web Site: www.burgerking.com
Mr. David Leonardo, Manager, US Franchising

Our Vision: We proudly serve the best burgers in the business, plus a variety of real, authentic foods - all freshly prepared - just the way you want it! BURGER KING ® Corporation operates more than 11,220 restaurants in all 50 states and in 60 countries around the world. 90% of the BURGER KING ® restaurants are owned and operated by independent franchisees, many of them family-owned operations that have been in business for decades.

BACKGROUND: IFA MEMBER
Established: 1954; 1st Franchised: 1961
Franchised Units: 10,144
Company-Owned Units: 1,079
Total Units: 11,223
Dist.: US-7,679; CAN-; O'seas-3,544
North America: 50 States, 9 Provinces
Density:
Projected New Units (12 Months):
Qualifications: , , , , ,
Registered: All States and AB

FINANCIAL/TERMS:
Cash Investment: Varies/UFOC
Total Investment: Varies/UFOC
Minimum Net Worth: $1.5MM
Fees: Franchise - $50K
Royalty - 4.5%; Ad. - 4%
Earnings Claims Statement: Yes
Term of Contract (Years): 20
Avg. # Of Employees: 15 FT, 35 PT
Passive Ownership: Allowed
Encourage Conversions: Yes
Area Develop. Agreements: No
Sub-Franchising Contracts: No
Expand In Territory: Yes
Space Needs: 3,600 SF; FS, SF, RM

SUPPORT & TRAINING:
Financial Assistance Provided: Yes(I)
Site Selection Assistance: Yes
Lease Negotiation Assistance: Yes
Co-Operative Advertising: No
Franchisee Assoc./Member: Yes/Yes
Size Of Corporate Staff: 928
On-Going Support: B,C,D,E,F,H
Training: 400 Hours in Restaurant; 300 Hours Classroom.

SPECIFIC EXPANSION PLANS:
US: All United States
Canada: All Canada
Overseas: All Countries

<< >>

CALIFORNIA TORTILLA

20 Courthouse Sq., # 206
Rockville, MD 20850
Tel: (301) 545-0035
Fax: (301) 545-0051
E-Mail: franchising@californiatortilla.com
Web Site: www.californiatortilla.com
Mr. Dane J. Cherry, VP Franchise Development

This popular eatery features quick, friendly (some would say downright spunky) service and a mouthwatering menu of freshly prepared items, such as fajitas, quesadillas, tacos and burritos, including their signature dish and best seller, the Blackened Chicken Caesar Burrito. CALIFORNIA TORTILLA is also known for its quirky promotions such as the Monday Night Mystery Price Burrito Wheel, Freeze Pop Day, Jungle Noise Day and Pop Tart Day, as well as Taco Walk - their popular burrito newsletter.

BACKGROUND:
Established: 1995; 1st Franchised: 2003
Franchised Units: 12
Company-Owned Units: 3
Total Units: 15
Dist.: US-15; CAN-0; O'seas-0
North America: 3 States
Density: 11 in MD, 2 in VA, 2 in DC
Projected New Units (12 Months): 12
Qualifications: 4, 5, 4, 3, 4, 5
Registered: MD, NY, VA

FINANCIAL/TERMS:
Cash Investment: $200K
Total Investment: $316.5-585.5K
Minimum Net Worth: $1MM
Fees: Franchise - $25K
Royalty - 5%; Ad. - 2%
Earnings Claims Statement: Yes
Term of Contract (Years): 10/10
Avg. # Of Employees: 10 FT, 15 PT
Passive Ownership: Discouraged
Encourage Conversions: Yes
Area Develop. Agreements: Yes/3-5
Sub-Franchising Contracts: No
Expand In Territory: No
Space Needs: 2,500 SF; SF, SC

SUPPORT & TRAINING:
Financial Assistance Provided: No
Site Selection Assistance: Yes
Lease Negotiation Assistance: Yes
Co-Operative Advertising: Yes
Franchisee Assoc./Member: Yes/Yes
Size Of Corporate Staff: 9
On-Going Support: B,C,D,E,F,G,H
Training: 4 Weeks Potomac, MD.

SPECIFIC EXPANSION PLANS:
US: Mid-Atlantic Region
Canada: No
Overseas: No

<< >>

CAMILLE'S SIDEWALK CAFÉ

8801 S. Yale, # 400
Tulsa, OK 74137
Tel: (800) 230-7004 (703) 549-5332
Fax: (703) 549-0740
E-Mail: staceyg@fransmart.com
Web Site: www.camillescafe.com
Ms. Stacey Gallagher, Marketing Manager

CAMILLE'S SIDEWALK CAFÉ is one of the quickest-growing cafes in the US today, opening a new unit nearly every other week. Serving gourmet sandwiches, Italian panini, fresh soups and salads, smoothies, gourmet coffees and espresso, as well as pastries and baked goods, CAMILLE'S is poised to meet any customer's cravings from the health-conscious to the small child. Low start-up costs, simple operations. Simple to run, no bakeries, hoods, fryers or grease traps. Easily replicable.

BACKGROUND: IFA MEMBER
Established: 1996; 1st Franchised: 1999
Franchised Units: 50
Company-Owned Units: 1
Total Units: 51
Dist.: US-51; CAN-0; O'seas-0
North America: 18 States

Density: 8 in TX, 7 in OK, 6 in IL
Projected New Units (12 Months): 75
Qualifications: 5, 3, 4, 3, 4, 5
Registered: All States

FINANCIAL/TERMS:
Cash Investment: $250K
Total Investment: $210-470K
Minimum Net Worth: $500K
Fees: Franchise - $25K
Royalty - 5%; Ad. - 1%
Earnings Claims Statement: No
Term of Contract (Years): 20/10
Avg. # Of Employees: 15 FT, 10 PT
Passive Ownership: Allowed
Encourage Conversions: Yes
Area Develop. Agreements: Yes
Sub-Franchising Contracts: No
Expand In Territory: Yes
Space Needs: 2,500 SF; SF, SC

SUPPORT & TRAINING:
Financial Assistance Provided: Yes(I)
Site Selection Assistance: Yes
Lease Negotiation Assistance: Yes
Co-Operative Advertising: Yes
Franchisee Assoc./Member: Yes/Yes
Size Of Corporate Staff: 25
On-Going Support: a,B,C,D,e,F,G,H,I
Training: 3 Weeks Tulsa, OK; 1 Week Franchisee Store Location.

SPECIFIC EXPANSION PLANS:
US: All United States
Canada: No
Overseas: No

CAPTAIN TONY'S PIZZA & PASTA EMPORIUM

2607 S. Woodland Blvd., # 300
Deland, FL 32720
Tel: (800) 332-8669 (386) 736-9855
Fax: (386) 736-7237
E-Mail: captain-tonys@wati.com
Web Site: www.captain-tonys.wati.com
Mr. Michael J. Martella, President

We have pizza, pasta, etc. for take-out, delivery and dining-in.

BACKGROUND:
Established: 1985; 1st Franchised: 1985
Franchised Units: 10
Company-Owned Units: 0
Total Units: 10
Dist.: US-10; CAN-0; O'seas-2
North America: NR
Density: 2 in CA, 3 in OH
Projected New Units (12 Months): NR
Qualifications: 3, 3, 2, 3, 3, 5
Registered: FL,NY

FINANCIAL/TERMS:
Cash Investment: $25-75K
Total Investment: $65-250K
Minimum Net Worth: $250K
Fees: Franchise - $10-20K
Royalty - 4.5% $500/Wk cap; Ad. - 0%
Earnings Claims Statement: No
Term of Contract (Years): 20
Avg. # Of Employees: NR
Passive Ownership: Discouraged
Encourage Conversions: Yes
Area Develop. Agreements: NR
Sub-Franchising Contracts: NR
Expand In Territory: NR
Space Needs: 1,200 SF; NR

SUPPORT & TRAINING:
Financial Assistance Provided: Yes(I)
Site Selection Assistance: Yes
Lease Negotiation Assistance: Yes
Co-Operative Advertising: No
Franchisee Assoc./Member: No
Size Of Corporate Staff: NR
On-Going Support: D,E,I
Training: 3 Weeks Orlando, FL.

SPECIFIC EXPANSION PLANS:
US: All United States
Canada: No
Overseas: All Countries

CARL'S JR.

6307 Carpinteria Ave., # A
Carpinteria, CA 93013
Tel: (866) 253-7655 (805) 745-7842
Fax: (714) 780-6320
E-Mail: chopkins@ckr.com
Web Site: www.ckr.com
Mr. Craig Hopkins, VP Franchise Sales

CARL'S JR. restaurants are located predominantly in the Western United States and have long been known as the place to go for premium quality, juicy and delicious charbroiled burgers. CARL'S JR. restaurants offer superior food quality, a diverse menu focused on burgers, premium dining selections at reasonable prices and attentive customer service to create a quality dining experience for its customers.

BACKGROUND: IFA MEMBER
Established: 1979; 1st Franchised: 1984
Franchised Units: 580
Company-Owned Units: 426
Total Units: 1,006
Dist.: US-; CAN-; O'seas-
North America: NR
Density: NR
Projected New Units (12 Months): NR
Qualifications: 4, 4, 4, 2, 2, 5
Registered: CA,OR,WA

FINANCIAL/TERMS:
Cash Investment: $300K
Total Investment: $788K-1.159MM
Minimum Net Worth: $1MM
Fees: Franchise - $35K
Royalty - 4%; Ad. - 5.25%
Earnings Claims Statement: No
Term of Contract (Years): 10
Avg. # Of Employees: 12 FT, 4 PT
Passive Ownership: Not Allowed
Encourage Conversions: Yes
Area Develop. Agreements: Yes/Varies
Sub-Franchising Contracts: No
Expand In Territory: No
Space Needs: NR SF; NR

SUPPORT & TRAINING:
Financial Assistance Provided: No
Site Selection Assistance: No
Lease Negotiation Assistance: No
Co-Operative Advertising: Yes
Franchisee Assoc./Member: No
Size Of Corporate Staff: NR
On-Going Support: B,C,D,E,G,H,I
Training: 12 Weeks.

SPECIFIC EXPANSION PLANS:
US: All United States
Canada: All Canada
Overseas: All Countries

CENTRAL PARK DOUBLE DRIVE-THRU

537 Market St., # 301
Chattanooga, TN 37402
Tel: (800) 454-7891 (423) 267-6575
Fax: (423) 267-4361
E-Mail: bmendez@ufsi.net
Web Site: www.centralparkamerica.com
Ms. Beth Mendez, Director Marketing/Commun.

Double drive-thru burger/chicken chain. High quality - low price leader in QSR burgers. Reasonable start-up - ease of operation. Low over head.

BACKGROUND:
Established: 1982; 1st Franchised: 1983

Franchised Units: 38
Company-Owned Units: 1
Total Units: 39
Dist.: US-39; CAN-0; O'seas-0
North America: 8 States
Density: 20 in TN, 8 in GA, 5 in SC
Projected New Units (12 Months): NR
Qualifications: , , , , ,
Registered: NR

FINANCIAL/TERMS:
Cash Investment: $50-100K
Total Investment: $150-400K
Minimum Net Worth: Varies
Fees: Franchise - $20K
Royalty - 6%; Ad. - 2%
Earnings Claims Statement: No
Term of Contract (Years): 15/15
Avg. # Of Employees: NR
Passive Ownership: Discouraged
Encourage Conversions: NR
Area Develop. Agreements: Yes
Sub-Franchising Contracts: No
Expand In Territory: Yes
Space Needs: 500 SF; NR

SUPPORT & TRAINING:
Financial Assistance Provided: NR
Site Selection Assistance: Yes
Lease Negotiation Assistance: Yes
Co-Operative Advertising: Yes
Franchisee Assoc./Member: Yes/Yes
Size Of Corporate Staff: 6
On-Going Support: A,B,C,D,E,F,G,H,I
Training: 2 Weeks Chattanooga, TN; 2 Weeks On-Site.

SPECIFIC EXPANSION PLANS:
US: Southeast
Canada: NR
Overseas: NR

<< >>

CHECKERS DRIVE-IN RESTAURANTS

4300 W. Cypress St., # 600
Tampa, FL 33607-4159
Tel: (888) 913-9135 (813) 283-7000
Fax: (813) 283-7208
E-Mail: fransales@checkers.com
Web Site: www.checkers.com
Mr. Ted Fumia, Dir. Franchise Development

Quick-service, fast-food restaurant (double drive-thru). Total below reflect ownership of both CHECKERS and RALLY'S brands.

BACKGROUND: IFA MEMBER
Established: 1986; 1st Franchised: 1989
Franchised Units: 585
Company-Owned Units: 191
Total Units: 776
Dist.: US-781; CAN-0; O'seas-3
North America: 40 States
Density: 191 in FL, 85 in GA, 32 AL
Projected New Units (12 Months): 35
Qualifications: 5, 4, 5, 4, 4, 4
Registered: FL,IL,IN,MD,MI,MN,NY,VA, WA,WI,DC

FINANCIAL/TERMS:
Cash Investment: $100-250K
Total Investment: $351.5-637.5K
Minimum Net Worth: $250K
Fees: Franchise - $30K
Royalty - 4%; Ad. - 0.25%+4.75%
Earnings Claims Statement: No
Term of Contract (Years): 20/Agrmt.
Avg. # Of Employees: 4 FT, 20 PT
Passive Ownership: Not Allowed
Encourage Conversions: No
Area Develop. Agreements: Yes
Sub-Franchising Contracts: No
Expand In Territory: Yes
Space Needs: 21,000 SF; FS

SUPPORT & TRAINING:
Financial Assistance Provided: No
Site Selection Assistance: Yes
Lease Negotiation Assistance: NA
Co-Operative Advertising: Yes
Franchisee Assoc./Member: Yes
Size Of Corporate Staff: ~100
On-Going Support: A,B,C,D,E,F,G,H,I
Training: 4-6 WeeksTampa, FL.

SPECIFIC EXPANSION PLANS:
US: All United States
Canada: All Canada
Overseas: All Countries

<< >>

CHEEBURGER CHEEBURGER RESTAURANTS

15951 McGregor Blvd., # 2A
Fort Myers, FL 33908
Tel: (800) 487-6211 (941) 437-1611
Fax: (941) 437-1512
E-Mail: msantel@cheeburger.com
Web Site: www.cheeburger.com
Mr. Mike Santel, Director Franchise Development

Full-service, gourmet, specialty-sandwich restaurant, serving high-quality, freshly prepared products and featuring burgers in various sizes, fresh-cut fries and big, thick milk shakes.

BACKGROUND: IFA MEMBER
Established: 1986; 1st Franchised: 1990
Franchised Units: 45
Company-Owned Units: 1
Total Units: 46
Dist.: US-37; CAN-0; O'seas-0
North America: 10 States
Density: 11 in FL, 2 in AR
Projected New Units (12 Months): 15
Qualifications: 5, 5, 3, 3, 4, 5
Registered: MI,NY

FINANCIAL/TERMS:
Cash Investment: $150-200K
Total Investment: $250-350K
Minimum Net Worth: $350K Liquid
Fees: Franchise - $27.5K
Royalty - 4.5%; Ad. - 1%
Earnings Claims Statement: No
Term of Contract (Years): 10/5
Avg. # Of Employees: 10 FT, 20 PT
Passive Ownership: NR
Encourage Conversions: Yes
Area Develop. Agreements: Yes
Sub-Franchising Contracts: No
Expand In Territory: Yes
Space Needs: 2,000 SF; FS, SF, SC

SUPPORT & TRAINING:
Financial Assistance Provided: No
Site Selection Assistance: Yes
Lease Negotiation Assistance: Yes
Co-Operative Advertising: Yes
Franchisee Assoc./Member: Yes
Size Of Corporate Staff: 5
On-Going Support: C,D,E,F,H,I,G
Training: 17 Days.

SPECIFIC EXPANSION PLANS:
US: All United States
Canada: No
Overseas: No

<< >>

CHESTER'S INTERNATIONAL

3500 Colonade Pkwy., # 325
Birmingham, AL 35213
Tel: (800) 288-1555 (334) 272-3528

Fax: (205) 298-0332
E-Mail: franchising@chestersinternational.com
Web Site: www.chestersinternational.com
Mr. Rankin Belkofer, Franchise Business Devel.

CHESTER'S offers consumers a high-quality chicken product, cooked to perfection, with a unique taste and style. The Company's secret is a breading recipe and process that has been successful for more than 30 years. CHESTER'S uses only chicken that is specially marinated and offers double-breaded bone-in, tender and potato wedges as well as sandwiches, salads and breakfast. Great opportunity to enter the QSR industry with flexible locations and store design. * 1,449 units are non-franchised.

BACKGROUND: IFA MEMBER
Established: 1952; 1st Franchised: 2004
Franchised Units: 1,449
Company-Owned Units: 1
Total Units: 1,450
Dist.: US-1,449; CAN-225; O'seas-50
North America: 50 States, 11 Province
Density: NR
Projected New Units (12 Months): 49
Qualifications: 3, 3, 2, 2, 3, 4
Registered: All States and AB

FINANCIAL/TERMS:
Cash Investment: $50-100K
Total Investment: $50-400.4K
Minimum Net Worth: $100K
Fees: Franchise - $5-15K
Royalty - NR; Ad. - NR
Earnings Claims Statement: No
Term of Contract (Years): 7-10/7-10
Avg. # Of Employees: 2 FT, 4 PT
Passive Ownership: Allowed
Encourage Conversions: Yes
Area Develop. Agreements: Yes
Sub-Franchising Contracts: No
Expand In Territory: Yes
Space Needs: 400-1,400 SF; SF, SC, RM, C-Store

SUPPORT & TRAINING:
Financial Assistance Provided: Yes(I)
Site Selection Assistance: Yes
Lease Negotiation Assistance: No
Co-Operative Advertising: NA
Franchisee Assoc./Member: No
Size Of Corporate Staff: 13
On-Going Support: C,D,E,H,I
Training: 1 Week Birmingham, AL; 4 Days Franchisee Location.

SPECIFIC EXPANSION PLANS:
US: All United States
Canada: All Canada
Overseas: All Countries

<< >>

CHICKEN DELIGHT

395 Berry St.
Winnipeg, MB R3J 1N6 CANADA
Tel: (204) 885-7570
Fax: (204) 831-6176
E-Mail: lmillar@chickendelight.com
Web Site: www.chickendelight.com
Mr. Larry Millar, Marketing Manager

CHICKEN DELIGHT has been in business for 50 years, featuring our famous pressure-fried chicken, BBQ ribs and fresh dough pizzas. We cater to the fast-food market with dine-in, take-out, delivery and drive-thru. Our focus on 3 staple products for take-out and delivery broadens your market potential.

BACKGROUND:
Established: 1952; 1st Franchised: 1952
Franchised Units: 35
Company-Owned Units: 15
Total Units: 50
Dist.: US-10; CAN-38; O'seas-2
North America: 2 States, 4 Provinces
Density: 33 in MB, 3 in SK, 1 in ON
Projected New Units (12 Months): 3
Qualifications: 4, 5, 3, 4, 3, 5
Registered: CA, AB

FINANCIAL/TERMS:
Cash Investment: $70-100K
Total Investment: $275-600K
Minimum Net Worth: $70K
Fees: Franchise - $25K
Royalty - 5%; Ad. - 3%
Earnings Claims Statement: No
Term of Contract (Years): 10/10
Avg. # Of Employees: 6 FT, 6 PT
Passive Ownership: Discouraged
Encourage Conversions: Yes
Area Develop. Agreements: Yes/10
Sub-Franchising Contracts: No
Expand In Territory: Yes
Space Needs: 1,600 SF; SC

SUPPORT & TRAINING:
Financial Assistance Provided: No
Site Selection Assistance: Yes
Lease Negotiation Assistance: Yes
Co-Operative Advertising: Yes
Franchisee Assoc./Member: No
Size Of Corporate Staff: 20
On-Going Support: C,D,e,F,G,h
Training: Minimum 1 Month Winnipeg, MB.

SPECIFIC EXPANSION PLANS:
US: All United States
Canada: All Canada
Overseas: Any Master License

<< >>

CHURCHS CHICKEN

980 Hammond Dr. NE, # 1100, Bldg. # 2
Atlanta, GA 30328
Tel: (800) 639-3495 (770) 350-3800
Fax: (770) 512-3920
E-Mail: hmyers@afce.com
Web Site: www.churchs.com
Mr. John McGowan, Business Support

CHURCHS is the 2nd largest chicken restaurant chain in the country. CHURCHS offers Southern fried chicken with signature side items such as fried okra, corn-on-the-cob, jalapenos and honey butter biscuits. CHURCHS has a proven business system niche customer base, low square footage requirements (as little as 750 square feet) and world class franchise support.

BACKGROUND: IFA MEMBER
Established: 1952; 1st Franchised: 1972
Franchised Units: 761
Company-Owned Units: 468
Total Units: 1,229
Dist.: US-1,032; CAN-80; O'seas-107
North America: 28 States
Density: 416 in TX, 103 in GA, 74 CA
Projected New Units (12 Months): 125
Qualifications: 5, 4, 3, 3, 3, 5
Registered: All States

FINANCIAL/TERMS:
Cash Investment: $200K
Total Investment: $194-750K
Minimum Net Worth: $400K
Fees: Franchise - $5-15K
Royalty - 5%; Ad. - 4%
Earnings Claims Statement: No
Term of Contract (Years): 20/10
Avg. # Of Employees: 15 FT, 6 PT
Passive Ownership: Discouraged
Encourage Conversions: Yes
Area Develop. Agreements: Yes/Varies
Sub-Franchising Contracts: No
Expand In Territory: Yes
Space Needs: 750-22,000 SF; FS, C-Store

SUPPORT & TRAINING:
Financial Assistance Provided: No
Site Selection Assistance: Yes
Lease Negotiation Assistance: Yes
Co-Operative Advertising: Yes
Franchisee Assoc./Member: Yes/Yes
Size Of Corporate Staff: 70

On-Going Support: C,D,E,F,G,h,I
Training: 6 Weeks Regional.
SPECIFIC EXPANSION PLANS:
US: All United States
Canada: All Canada
Overseas: Europe, Asia, Middle East, Australia

<< >>

CICI'S PIZZA

1080 W. Bethel Rd.
Coppell, TX 75019-4427
Tel: (972) 745-4200
Fax: (972) 745-4204
E-Mail: jsheahan@cicispizza.com
Web Site: www.cicispizza.com
Mr. Jim Sheahan, Dir. Franchise Sales

CICI'S PIZZA provides its guests with delicious pizza, pasta, salad and dessert on an all-you-can-eat buffet for only $3.99 for adults and $2.29 for kids (prices vary by location). Our low price, combined with quality food, great service and sparkling clean restaurants is making CICI'S among the fastest-growing franchises in America. Awarded Highest Rated Pizza Chain in America 2 years in a row by Restaurants and Institutions Magazine and Pizza Chain of the Year by Pizza Today's .

BACKGROUND: IFA MEMBER
Established: 1985; 1st Franchised: 1987
Franchised Units: 393
Company-Owned Units: 24
Total Units: 417
Dist.: US-417; CAN-0; O'seas-0
North America: 20 States
Density: NR
Projected New Units (12 Months): 70
Qualifications: 5, 4, 1, 1, 3, 5
Registered: FL,IN,MI,VA
FINANCIAL/TERMS:
Cash Investment: $116.9-148.4K
Total Investment: $390-495K
Minimum Net Worth: NR
Fees: Franchise - $30K
Royalty - 4%; Ad. - 3%/$2.3K/Mo
Earnings Claims Statement: Yes
Term of Contract (Years): 10
Avg. # Of Employees: 8 FT, 15 PT
Passive Ownership: Not Allowed
Encourage Conversions: No
Area Develop. Agreements: Yes
Sub-Franchising Contracts: No
Expand In Territory: Yes
Space Needs: 4,200 SF; FS, SC
SUPPORT & TRAINING:
Financial Assistance Provided: Yes(I)
Site Selection Assistance: Yes
Lease Negotiation Assistance: Yes
Co-Operative Advertising: Yes
Franchisee Assoc./Member: No
Size Of Corporate Staff: 48
On-Going Support: B,C,D,E,F,G,H
Training: 7-11 Weeks in Dallas, TX.
SPECIFIC EXPANSION PLANS:
US: South, Southeast, N. Central
Canada: No
Overseas: No

<< >>

COUSINS SUBS

N83 W13400 Leon Rd.
Menomenee Falls, WI 53051
Tel: (800) 238-9736 (262) 253-7700
Fax: (262) 253-7710
E-Mail: betterfranchise@cousinssubs.com
Web Site: www.cousinssubs.com
Ms. Kerry Espich, Franchise Recruit. Specialist

Thirty-two years of commitment to excellence is rolled into the COUSINS SUBS distinctive quick service, volume oriented, "Eastern Style" submarine sandwich concept. Exceptional freshly baked bread and quality ingredients highlight our hot and cold subs, which may be enjoyed with our delicious soups and garden fresh salads. The value and portability of our products promote leveraging outside sales to the bottom line. We offer single and multi-unit franchises, area development rights and master licenses.

BACKGROUND: IFA MEMBER
Established: 1972; 1st Franchised: 1985
Franchised Units: 148
Company-Owned Units: 35
Total Units: 183
Dist.: US-183; CAN-0; O'seas-0
North America: 10 States
Density: 114 in WI, 17 in AZ, 16 MN
Projected New Units (12 Months): 24
Qualifications: 5, 4, 3, 3, 3, 4
Registered: AZ,CA,CO,IA,IL,IN,MI,MN, ND,SD,WI
FINANCIAL/TERMS:
Cash Investment: $50-100K
Total Investment: $159-287K
Minimum Net Worth: $300K
Fees: Franchise - $20K
Royalty - 6%; Ad. - 2%
Earnings Claims Statement: Yes
Term of Contract (Years): 10/10
Avg. # Of Employees: 2 FT, 12 PT
Passive Ownership: Allowed
Encourage Conversions: Yes
Area Develop. Agreements: Yes
Sub-Franchising Contracts: Yes
Expand In Territory: Yes
Space Needs: 1,600 SF; FS, SF, SC, C-Store
SUPPORT & TRAINING:
Financial Assistance Provided: Yes(D)
Site Selection Assistance: Yes
Lease Negotiation Assistance: Yes
Co-Operative Advertising: Yes
Franchisee Assoc./Member: No
Size Of Corporate Staff: 40
On-Going Support: C,D,E,G,h,I
Training:
3 Days Headquarters; 30 Days Training Store; 10 Days Franchisee Store.
SPECIFIC EXPANSION PLANS:
US: AZ,ND,MN,WI,IL,IN,MI
Canada: No
Overseas: No

<< >>

CULVERS FROZEN CUSTARD

540 Water St.
Prairie du Sac, WI 53578
Tel: (608) 644-2130
Fax: (608) 644-1552
E-Mail: grud@culvers.com
Web Site: www.culvers.com
Mr. Gary L. Rudsinski, Franchise Development Manager

CULVERS FROZEN CUSTARD specializes in ButterBurgers and Frozen Custard. All food items are prepared to order and delivered to the customer's table in about five minutes. Our system is based on franchisees as owner/operators with the operator working full time in their restaurant to ensure guest satisfaction and involvement in the local community.

BACKGROUND: IFA MEMBER
Established: 1984; 1st Franchised: 1988
Franchised Units: 265
Company-Owned Units: 5
Total Units: 270
Dist.: US-270; CAN-0; O'seas-0
North America: 14 States
Density: 102 in WI, 49 in IL, 36 MN
Projected New Units (12 Months): 50
Qualifications: 5, 3, 3, 3, 1, 5
Registered: Midwest States

FINANCIAL/TERMS:
Cash Investment: $250-400K
Total Investment: $400K-2.9MM
Minimum Net Worth: $500K
Fees: Franchise - $55K
Royalty - 4%; Ad. - 2%
Earnings Claims Statement: Yes
Term of Contract (Years): 15/10
Avg. # Of Employees: 18 FT, 52 PT
Passive Ownership: Not Allowed
Encourage Conversions: Yes
Area Develop. Agreements: No
Sub-Franchising Contracts: No
Expand In Territory: No
Space Needs: 4,200-5,300 SF; FS

SUPPORT & TRAINING:
Financial Assistance Provided: No
Site Selection Assistance: Yes
Lease Negotiation Assistance: No
Co-Operative Advertising: No
Franchisee Assoc./Member: No
Size Of Corporate Staff: 75
On-Going Support: B,C,D,E,F,G,H
Training: 16 Weeks in South Central, WI.

SPECIFIC EXPANSION PLANS:
US: Midwest, TX
Canada: No
Overseas: No

<< >>

DAIRY BELLE FREEZE

P. O. Box 360830
Milpitas, CA 95036-0830
Tel: (408) 433-9337
Fax: (408) 433-9395
E-Mail: stone557@aol.com
Web Site: www.dairybelle.com
Ms. Patricia (Pat) Souza, President

Locally owned and operated since 1957, DAIRY BELLE restaurants have provided quality food that is cooked to order to ensure the satisfaction of each customer. Our menu has expanded from soft-serve cones, hamburgers, fries and soft drinks to now include specialty sandwiches, Mexican food and a variety of soft-serve desserts.

BACKGROUND:
Established: 1957; 1st Franchised: 1981
Franchised Units: 13
Company-Owned Units: 0
Total Units: 13
Dist.: US-13; CAN-0; O'seas-0
North America: 1 State
Density: 13 in CA
Projected New Units (12 Months): 2
Qualifications: 5, 3, 4, 2, 2, 5
Registered: CA

FINANCIAL/TERMS:
Cash Investment: $50-100K
Total Investment: $50-200K
Minimum Net Worth: $100K
Fees: Franchise - $12.5K
Royalty - 4.5%/$600; Ad. - 2%
Earnings Claims Statement: Yes
Term of Contract (Years): 10/10
Avg. # Of Employees: 4 FT, 3-10 PT
Passive Ownership: Not Allowed
Encourage Conversions: Yes
Area Develop. Agreements: No
Sub-Franchising Contracts: No
Expand In Territory: Yes
Space Needs: 1,500 SF; FS

SUPPORT & TRAINING:
Financial Assistance Provided: Yes(I)
Site Selection Assistance: Yes
Lease Negotiation Assistance: Yes
Co-Operative Advertising: Yes
Franchisee Assoc./Member: No
Size Of Corporate Staff: 6
On-Going Support: B,C,D,E,H
Training: 2-3 Weeks at Existing Franchisee's Restaurant; 2-3 Weeks at New Franchisee's Restaurant.

SPECIFIC EXPANSION PLANS:
US: Northern CA
Canada: No
Overseas: No

<< >>

DAIRY QUEEN

P. O. Box 39286
Minneapolis, MN 55439-0286
Tel: (800) 679-6556 (952) 830-0200
Fax: (952) 830-0450
E-Mail: thomas.dambrine@idq.com
Web Site: www.dairyqueen.com
Mr. Thomas Dambrine, Dir. Intl. Development

A subsidiary of Berkshire Hathaway, Inc., DAIRY QUEEN offers several franchise concepts and development programs from single unit to multi-unit agreements. Our concepts are designed for various location types -- from free-standing restaurants to regional shopping malls. With over sixty years and 6000 units we offer great experience and brand recognition.

BACKGROUND:
Established: 1940; 1st Franchised: 1940
Franchised Units: 5,960
Company-Owned Units: 60
Total Units: 6,020
Dist.: US-5,166; CAN-635; O'seas-294
North America: 49 States,12 Provinces
Density: 629 in TX, 287 in IL, 282 OH
Projected New Units (12 Months): 100
Qualifications: 5, 4, 5, 3, , 4
Registered: All States

FINANCIAL/TERMS:
Cash Investment: $200-300K
Total Investment: $200-950K
Minimum Net Worth: $200-500K
Fees: Franchise - $20-35K
Royalty - 4-6%; Ad. - 3-6%
Earnings Claims Statement: No
Term of Contract (Years): 20/10
Avg. # Of Employees: Varies
Passive Ownership: Allowed
Encourage Conversions: Yes
Area Develop. Agreements: Yes/Varies
Sub-Franchising Contracts: Yes
Expand In Territory: No
Space Needs: 40,000 SF; FS, RM

SUPPORT & TRAINING:
Financial Assistance Provided: No
Site Selection Assistance: Yes
Lease Negotiation Assistance: Yes
Co-Operative Advertising: Yes
Franchisee Assoc./Member: Yes/No
Size Of Corporate Staff: 470
On-Going Support: C,D,E,G,H,I
Training: 4 Weeks in Existing Restaurants; 1-2 Weeks at Headquarters; 1-2 Weeks On-Site.

SPECIFIC EXPANSION PLANS:
US: All United States
Canada: BC, AB, ON
Overseas: Mexico

DEL TACO

25521 Commercentre Dr.

Lake Forest, CA 92630-8872
Tel: (949) 462-7319
Fax: (949) 462-7311
E-Mail: mmushkin@deltaco.com
Web Site: www.deltaco.com
Mr. J. Marc Mushkin, Director Franchise Sales

Mexican-American fast-food restaurant. Second largest Mexican brand in U. S. sales.

BACKGROUND: IFA MEMBER
Established: 1964; 1st Franchised: 1967
Franchised Units: 167
Company-Owned Units: 266
Total Units: 433
Dist.: US-433; CAN-0; O'seas-3
North America: 13 States
Density: 327 in CA, 38 in AZ, 32 NV
Projected New Units (12 Months): 40
Qualifications: 5, 3, 5, 2, 1, 5
Registered: CA,IL,WA
FINANCIAL/TERMS:
Cash Investment: $300K
Total Investment: $800K
Minimum Net Worth: $1MM
Fees: Franchise - $25K
Royalty - 5%; Ad. - 4%
Earnings Claims Statement: Yes
Term of Contract (Years): 20/15
Avg. # Of Employees: 2 FT, 24 PT
Passive Ownership: Not Allowed
Encourage Conversions: No
Area Develop. Agreements: Yes/Varies
Sub-Franchising Contracts: No
Expand In Territory: Yes
Space Needs: 2,100 SF; FS
SUPPORT & TRAINING:
Financial Assistance Provided: No
Site Selection Assistance: Yes
Lease Negotiation Assistance: Yes
Co-Operative Advertising: Yes
Franchisee Assoc./Member: No
Size Of Corporate Staff: 110
On-Going Support: B,C,E,G,H
Training: 4 Weeks Certified Training Restaurant; 1 Week Corporate Headquarters.
SPECIFIC EXPANSION PLANS:
US: W, SW, Midwest, Pacific NW
Canada: No
Overseas: No

DIAMOND DAVE'S TACO COMPANY

201 S. Clinton St., # 281
Iowa City, IA 52240
Tel: (319) 337-7690
Fax: (319) 337-4707
E-Mail: diamonddaves@mcleodusa.net
Web Site: www.diamonddaves.com
Mr. Stanley J. White, President

DIAMOND DAVE'S TACO COMPANY is a regional restaurant chain, featuring great family priced Mexican/American cuisine. Opportunities include full-service restaurant/bar concept. Locations available in enclosed regional malls, strip centers and free-standing units.

BACKGROUND:
Established: 1980; 1st Franchised: 1981
Franchised Units: 22
Company-Owned Units: 5
Total Units: 27
Dist.: US-36; CAN-0; O'seas-0
North America: 5 States
Density: 14 in IA, 9 in IL, 5 in WI
Projected New Units (12 Months): 2
Qualifications: , , , , ,
Registered: IL,MN,SD,WI
FINANCIAL/TERMS:
Cash Investment: $50-75K
Total Investment: $150-250K
Minimum Net Worth: NR
Fees: Franchise - $15K
Royalty - 4%; Ad. - 1%
Earnings Claims Statement: No
Term of Contract (Years): 10/10
Avg. # Of Employees: 5 FT, 15 PT
Passive Ownership: Discouraged
Encourage Conversions: Yes
Area Develop. Agreements: Yes
Sub-Franchising Contracts: No
Expand In Territory: Yes
Space Needs: 2,000-3,000 SF; SC, RM
SUPPORT & TRAINING:
Financial Assistance Provided: NA
Site Selection Assistance: Yes
Lease Negotiation Assistance: Yes
Co-Operative Advertising: Yes
Franchisee Assoc./Member: NR
Size Of Corporate Staff: 4
On-Going Support: C,D,E,F,G,H
Training: 2-4 Weeks Local Restaurant.
SPECIFIC EXPANSION PLANS:
US: Midwest Only
Canada: No
Overseas: No

DOMINO'S PIZZA

30 Frank Lloyd Wright Dr., P.O. Box 997
Ann Arbor, MI 48106-0997
Tel: (800) 564-4918 (734) 930-3030
Fax: (734) 930-3664
E-Mail: deverej@dominos.com
Web Site: www.dominos.com
Mr. Jim Betts, Sr. Director Fran. Services

DOMINO'S PIZZA is the recognized world leader in pizza delivery, with more than 43 years of experience. We operate a network of more than 7,000 stores in the US and 50 countries around the world.

BACKGROUND: IFA MEMBER
Established: 1960; 1st Franchised: 1967
Franchised Units: 4,334
Company-Owned Units: 576
Total Units: 4,910
Dist.: US-4,200; CAN-233; O'seas-2,000
North America: 50
Density: 264 in CA. 250 in DC, 215 NY
Projected New Units (12 Months):
Qualifications: , , , , ,
Registered:
FINANCIAL/TERMS:
Cash Investment: $30K
Total Investment: NR
Minimum Net Worth: NA
Fees: Franchise - $3.2K
Royalty - 5.5%; Ad. - 3%
Earnings Claims Statement: No
Term of Contract (Years): 10/10
Avg. # Of Employees: NR
Passive Ownership: Not Allowed
Encourage Conversions:
Area Develop. Agreements: Yes/1-3
Sub-Franchising Contracts: No
Expand In Territory: Yes
Space Needs: 1,200 SF; FS, SF, SC
SUPPORT & TRAINING:
Financial Assistance Provided:
Site Selection Assistance: Yes
Lease Negotiation Assistance: Yes
Co-Operative Advertising: Yes
Franchisee Assoc./Member: Yes/Yes
Size Of Corporate Staff: NA
On-Going Support: B,C,D,E,G,H,I
Training: 6-8 Weeks Local/Regional.
SPECIFIC EXPANSION PLANS:
US: All United States
Canada: NR
Overseas: NR

DONATOS PIZZA

935 Taylor Station Rd.
Columbus, OH 43230
Tel: (800) 366-2867 (614) 416-7700
Fax: (614) 416-7701
E-Mail: boaks@donatos.com
Web Site: www.donatos.com

Mr. Brian Oaks, Exec. Dir. Franchise Devel.

DONATOS PIZZA is a retail outlet specializing in the sale of pizzas, subs and salads, featuring delivery, carryout and dine-in service. DONATOS is committed to serving the best pizza and promoting goodwill through product, principle and people. DONATOS PIZZA strives to be the best pizza on the block where the stores are located.

BACKGROUND: IFA MEMBER
Established: 1963; 1st Franchised: 1991
Franchised Units: 46
Company-Owned Units: 83
Total Units: 129
Dist.: US-114; CAN-0; O'seas-0
North America: 4 States
Density: 94 in OH, 13 in IN, 4 in KY
Projected New Units (12 Months): 25
Qualifications: 5, 4, 5, 3, 2, 4
Registered: FL,IL,IN,MD,MI,MN,VA,DC

FINANCIAL/TERMS:
Cash Investment: $25% of Total
Total Investment: $250-600K
Minimum Net Worth: $350K
Fees: Franchise - $30K
Royalty - 4%; Ad. - 4%
Earnings Claims Statement: Yes
Term of Contract (Years): 20/5
Avg. # Of Employees: 15 FT, 20 PT
Passive Ownership: Discouraged
Encourage Conversions: Yes
Area Develop. Agreements: Yes/Varies
Sub-Franchising Contracts: No
Expand In Territory: Yes
Space Needs: 2,000 SF; FS, SF, SC

SUPPORT & TRAINING:
Financial Assistance Provided: No
Site Selection Assistance: Yes
Lease Negotiation Assistance: Yes
Co-Operative Advertising: Yes
Franchisee Assoc./Member: No
Size Of Corporate Staff: 90
On-Going Support: B,C,D,E,G,H,I
Training: 6-8 Weeks Colombus, OH.

SPECIFIC EXPANSION PLANS:
US: Midwest, Southeast
Canada: No
Overseas: No

≺≺ ≻≻

EAST OF CHICAGO PIZZA COMPANY

318 W. Walton Rd.
Willard, OH 44890
Tel: (419) 935-3033
Fax: (419) 935-3278
E-Mail: mbruno@eastofchicago.com
Web Site: www.eastofchicago.com
Mr. Mike Bruno, Vice President

EAST OF CHICAGO PIZZA COMPANY is a young, determined franchising company that utilizes dine-in and delivery/carry-out units to achieve market dominance. Established in 1990, EOC has grown to over 100 units, with plans to expand. Combining proven marketing and operational systems, with ideal franchisee strategic partnerships, EOC meets demands of customers with unique products, which, when combined with superior customer service, creates an atmosphere of tremendous customer loyalty/repeat business.

BACKGROUND:
Established: 1990; 1st Franchised: 1991
Franchised Units: 135
Company-Owned Units: 5
Total Units: 140
Dist.: US-128; CAN-0; O'seas-0
North America: 5 States
Density: 115 in OH, 9 in IN, 4 in PA
Projected New Units (12 Months): 30
Qualifications: 4, 3, 3, 3, 4, 4
Registered: FL,IN,VA

FINANCIAL/TERMS:
Cash Investment: $50K
Total Investment: $150-300K
Minimum Net Worth: NA
Fees: Franchise - $20K
Royalty - 5%; Ad. - 2%
Earnings Claims Statement: Yes
Term of Contract (Years): 10/10
Avg. # Of Employees: 10 FT, 10 PT
Passive Ownership: Allowed
Encourage Conversions: Yes
Area Develop. Agreements: No
Sub-Franchising Contracts: No
Expand In Territory: No
Space Needs: 1,200-3,000 SF; FS, SC

SUPPORT & TRAINING:
Financial Assistance Provided: No
Site Selection Assistance: Yes
Lease Negotiation Assistance: No
Co-Operative Advertising: Yes
Franchisee Assoc./Member: Yes/Yes
Size Of Corporate Staff: 40
On-Going Support: A,B,C,D,E,F,G,H
Training: 4 Weeks in Willard, OH.

SPECIFIC EXPANSION PLANS:
US: OH, IN, PA, FL, VA Only.
Canada: No
Overseas: No

≺≺ ≻≻

EL POLLO LOCO

3333 Michelson Dr., # 550
Irvine, CA 92612-0625
Tel: (800) 997-6556 (949) 399-2055
Fax: (949) 399-2025
E-Mail: smiller@elpolloloco.com
Web Site: www.elpolloloco.com
Ms. Stacy Miller, Franchise Development

EL POLLO LOCO is the nation's leading quick-service restaurant chain specializing in flame-grilled chicken. Offering a fresh, wholesome alternative to traditional fast food, EL POLLO LOCO serves its famous citrus-marinated, flame-grilled chicken with steaming tortillas, fresh salsas and a variety of accompaniments. Fresh entrees (signature burritos, Pollo Bowls, Pollo Salads, etc.) also served. All feature the mouth-watering citrus-marinated, flame-grilled chicken that put EL POLLO LOCO on the map.

BACKGROUND: IFA MEMBER
Established: 1975; 1st Franchised: 1983
Franchised Units: 182
Company-Owned Units: 140
Total Units: 322
Dist.: US-318; CAN-0; O'seas-4
North America: 4 States
Density: 286 in CA, 11 in AZ, 10 NV
Projected New Units (12 Months): 15-20
Qualifications: 5, 5, 5, 3, 3, 5
Registered: All States Except VA

FINANCIAL/TERMS:
Cash Investment: $350K
Total Investment: $722K-1.1MM
Minimum Net Worth: $1.5MM
Fees: Franchise - $40K
Royalty - 4%; Ad. - 5%
Earnings Claims Statement: Yes
Term of Contract (Years): 20
Avg. # Of Employees: 8 FT, 17 PT
Passive Ownership: Discouraged
Encourage Conversions: Yes
Area Develop. Agreements: Yes/Varies
Sub-Franchising Contracts: No
Expand In Territory: Yes
Space Needs: 2,400 SF; FS, SF, SC

SUPPORT & TRAINING:
Financial Assistance Provided: Yes
Site Selection Assistance: Yes
Lease Negotiation Assistance: No
Co-Operative Advertising: No
Franchisee Assoc./Member: Yes/Yes
Size Of Corporate Staff: 125
On-Going Support: B,C,D,E,G,H,I
Training: 6 Weeks in Southern CA.
SPECIFIC EXPANSION PLANS:
US: West,Southwest,Upper Midwest
Canada: No
Overseas: No

<< >>

ERBERT & GERBERT'S SUBS & CLUBS
205 E. Grand Ave
Eau Claire, WI 54701
Tel: (800) 283-5241 (715) 833-1375
Fax: (715) 833-8523
E-Mail: info@erbertandgerberts.com
Web Site: www.erbertandgerberts.com
Mr. Kevin Schippers, President/CEO

ERBERT AND GERBERT'S SUBS & CLUBS offer the gourmet sandwich product in the fast-food niche. Growing rapidly, the market is wide open for this top-quality, service-oriented company. Immaculate shops and outstanding service complement the gourmet product.

BACKGROUND:
Established: 1987; 1st Franchised: 1992
Franchised Units: 25
Company-Owned Units: 1
Total Units: 26
Dist.: US-26; CAN-0; O'seas-0
North America: 3 States
Density: 14 in WI, 11 in MN, 1 in ND
Projected New Units (12 Months): 10
Qualifications: 4, 5, 1, 3, 4, 5
Registered: FL,IL,MN,ND,SD,WI
FINANCIAL/TERMS:
Cash Investment: $30-35K
Total Investment: $194-356K
Minimum Net Worth: $250K
Fees: Franchise - $25K
Royalty - 6%; Ad. - 2%
Earnings Claims Statement: Yes
Term of Contract (Years): 15/5
Avg. # Of Employees: 2-3 FT, 10 PT
Passive Ownership: Discouraged
Encourage Conversions: Yes
Area Develop. Agreements: Yes/Varies
Sub-Franchising Contracts: No
Expand In Territory: NR
Space Needs: 1,000-2,000 SF; SF, SC

SUPPORT & TRAINING:
Financial Assistance Provided: Yes(I)
Site Selection Assistance: Yes
Lease Negotiation Assistance: Yes
Co-Operative Advertising: Yes
Franchisee Assoc./Member: Yes
Size Of Corporate Staff: 10
On-Going Support: C,D,d,E,G,H,I
Training: 3 Weeks Home Office; 1 Week On-Site during Opening.
SPECIFIC EXPANSION PLANS:
US: All U.S., Primarily Midwest
Canada: No
Overseas: No

<< >>

FAMILY PIZZA
318 105th St. E., Bay 10
Saskatoon, SK S7N 1Z3 CANADA
Tel: (306) 955-0215
Fax: (306) 955-1864
E-Mail: family.pizza@shaw.ca
Web Site: www.worldfranchising.com/website.htm
Mr. Hal Schmidt, President

2-for-1 gourmet pizza and pasta. Take-out and delivery - 39 minute guarantee or your order is free.

BACKGROUND:
Established: 1983; 1st Franchised: 1987
Franchised Units: 17
Company-Owned Units: 7
Total Units: 24
Dist.: US-0; CAN-24; O'seas-0
North America: 3 Provinces
Density: 13 in SK, 5 in AB, 5 in BC
Projected New Units (12 Months): 10
Qualifications: 3, 3, 2, 3, 3, 4
Registered: AB
FINANCIAL/TERMS:
Cash Investment: $40K
Total Investment: $75-120K
Minimum Net Worth: $50K
Fees: Franchise - $15K
Royalty - 4%; Ad. - 5%
Earnings Claims Statement: Yes
Term of Contract (Years): 5/5
Avg. # Of Employees: 5 FT, 10 PT
Passive Ownership: Discouraged
Encourage Conversions: No
Area Develop. Agreements: Yes/5
Sub-Franchising Contracts: No
Expand In Territory: Yes
Space Needs: 900-1,500 SF; FS, SC
SUPPORT & TRAINING:
Financial Assistance Provided: Yes(I)
Site Selection Assistance: Yes
Lease Negotiation Assistance: Yes
Co-Operative Advertising: Yes
Franchisee Assoc./Member: No
Size Of Corporate Staff: 3
On-Going Support: A,B,C,D,E,F,G,H
Training: 2-4 Weeks in Store.
SPECIFIC EXPANSION PLANS:
US: No
Canada: All Canada
Overseas: No

<< >>

FARMER BOYS HAMBURGERS
3452 University Ave.
Riverside, CA 92501
Tel: (888) 930-3276 (909) 275-9900
Fax: (909) 275-9930
E-Mail: bfoss@farmerboys.com
Web Site: www.farmerboys.com
Mr. Bill Foss, Franchise Development Manager

FARMER BOYS RESTAURANTS fill a unique food service niche by offering greater choice to both fast food and traditional sit-down restaurant customers. Concept offers over 100 fresh breakfast, lunch or dinner items, prepared and cooked to order in 5 - 7 minutes - with a choice of sit-down, take-out or drive-thru service.

BACKGROUND: IFA MEMBER
Established: 1981; 1st Franchised: 1997
Franchised Units: 42
Company-Owned Units: 11
Total Units: 53
Dist.: US-53; CAN-0; O'seas-0
North America: 1 State
Density: 53 in CA
Projected New Units (12 Months): 10
Qualifications: 4, 4, 2, 3, 1, 5
Registered: CA
FINANCIAL/TERMS:
Cash Investment: $350K
Total Investment: $1.2MM
Minimum Net Worth: $750K
Fees: Franchise - $40K
Royalty - 5%; Ad. - 2%
Earnings Claims Statement: Yes
Term of Contract (Years): 20/10/10
Avg. # Of Employees: 7-10 FT, 10-15 PT
Passive Ownership: Not Allowed

Encourage Conversions: No
Area Develop. Agreements: Yes/Varies
Sub-Franchising Contracts: No
Expand In Territory: Yes
Space Needs: 3,000-3,200 SF; FS

SUPPORT & TRAINING:
Financial Assistance Provided: Yes
Site Selection Assistance: Yes
Lease Negotiation Assistance: Yes
Co-Operative Advertising: Yes
Franchisee Assoc./Member: Yes
Size Of Corporate Staff: 25
On-Going Support: B,C,D,E,F,I
Training: 3 Months at Company-Operated Unit.

SPECIFIC EXPANSION PLANS:
US: Western United States
Canada: No
Overseas: No

FAST EDDIE'S

102 - 129 Wellington St.
Brantford, ON N3R 4R6 CANADA
Tel: (877) HOT-FRYS (519) 758-0111
Fax: (519) 758-1393
E-Mail: fasteddies@fasteddies.ca
Web Site: www.fasteddies.ca
Ms. Nicki Straza, Franchise Director

FAST EDDIE'S is a hamburger-based, fast-food, double-drive-thru restaurant with no inside seating. We have 100% pure-beef, quality hamburgers with shakes and fries to go. Try our crazy fries!

BACKGROUND:
Established: 1989; 1st Franchised: 2000
Franchised Units: 6
Company-Owned Units: 4
Total Units: 10
Dist.: US-0; CAN-10; O'seas-0
North America: 1 Province
Density: 10 in ON
Projected New Units (12 Months): 2
Qualifications: 5, 5, 4, 3, 3, 5
Registered: None

FINANCIAL/TERMS:
Cash Investment: $60-100K
Total Investment: $200-400K
Minimum Net Worth: $200-300K
Fees: Franchise - $25K
Royalty - 4%; Ad. - 2%
Earnings Claims Statement: Yes
Term of Contract (Years): 1-/5
Avg. # Of Employees: 3 FT, 15 PT
Passive Ownership: Not Allowed
Encourage Conversions: No
Area Develop. Agreements: No
Sub-Franchising Contracts: No
Expand In Territory: Yes
Space Needs: 900 SF; FS

SUPPORT & TRAINING:
Financial Assistance Provided: Yes(I)
Site Selection Assistance: Yes
Lease Negotiation Assistance: Yes
Co-Operative Advertising: Yes
Franchisee Assoc./Member: Yes/Yes
Size Of Corporate Staff: 18
On-Going Support: C,D,E,F
Training: 2 Weeks Brantford, ON.

SPECIFIC EXPANSION PLANS:
US: No
Canada: Ontario
Overseas: No

FATBURGER

1218 Third St. Promenade
Santa Monica, CA 90401-1308
Tel: (310) 319-1850
Fax: (310) 319-1863
E-Mail: mwilkins@fatburger.com
Web Site: www.fatburger.com
Ms. Michelle G. Wilkins, Director Franchise Relations

The classic hamburger stand, serving cooked-to-order burgers at an open grill since 1952. Also serving grilled chicken-breast sandwiches, freshly made onion rings and real milkshakes in a fun environment with a unique R & B jukebox.

BACKGROUND: IFA MEMBER
Established: 1952; 1st Franchised: 1980
Franchised Units: 33
Company-Owned Units: 25
Total Units: 58
Dist.: US-58; CAN-0; O'seas-0
North America: 7 States
Density: 39 in CA, 10 in NV
Projected New Units (12 Months): 8
Qualifications: 4, 5, 3, 2, 5, 5
Registered: CA,IL,MD,NY,WA

FINANCIAL/TERMS:
Cash Investment: $750K+
Total Investment: $370-730K
Minimum Net Worth: $1.25MM
Fees: Franchise - $40K
Royalty - 6%; Ad. - 2%
Earnings Claims Statement: Yes
Term of Contract (Years): 15/10/10
Avg. # Of Employees: 16-40 PT
Passive Ownership: Allowed
Encourage Conversions: Yes
Area Develop. Agreements: Yes/10
Sub-Franchising Contracts: No
Expand In Territory: No
Space Needs: 1,800-2,000 SF; FS, SF, SC

SUPPORT & TRAINING:
Financial Assistance Provided: No
Site Selection Assistance: Yes
Lease Negotiation Assistance: Yes
Co-Operative Advertising: No
Franchisee Assoc./Member: No
Size Of Corporate Staff: 30
On-Going Support: C,D,E,H
Training: 8 Weeks Certified Training Centers; 7-10 Days On-Site.

SPECIFIC EXPANSION PLANS:
US: All United States
Canada: All Canada
Overseas: No

FIGARO'S PIZZA

1500 Liberty St., S. E., # 160
Salem, OR 97302-4392
Tel: (888) 344-2767 (503) 371-9318
Fax: (503) 363-5364
E-Mail: figaros@figaros.com
Web Site: www.figaros.com
Mr. Steve Nilsby, Dir. Franchise Development

A Figaro's Pizza franchise is a complete business system. It's easy to run, has low initial investment, low labor costs, simple equipment package and low-cost locations. Figaro's is unique because it offers the consumer the choice of fresh, made-to-order "Take-and-Bake" pizza made with the freshest, highest quality ingredients or one that is "Baked-to-Order" in the store and ready-to-eat. And most importantly, pizza delivers an excellent profit margin.

BACKGROUND: IFA MEMBER
Established: 1981; 1st Franchised: 1986
Franchised Units: 100
Company-Owned Units: 0
Total Units: 100
Dist.: US-87; CAN-0; O'seas-0
North America: 7 States
Density: 64 in OR, 17 in WA, 6 in ID
Projected New Units (12 Months): 25
Qualifications: 5, 4, 2, 3, 4, 5
Registered: CA,FL,IN,MN,ND,OR,SD,TX,UT,WA

FINANCIAL/TERMS:
Cash Investment: $50-65K
Total Investment: $104-298K
Minimum Net Worth: $150-225K
Fees: Franchise - $20K
Royalty - 5%; Ad. - 3%
Earnings Claims Statement: No

Term of Contract (Years): 5/5/5/5
Avg. # Of Employees: 1 FT, 12 PT
Passive Ownership: Discouraged
Encourage Conversions: Yes
Area Develop. Agreements: Yes
Sub-Franchising Contracts: Yes
Expand In Territory: Yes
Space Needs: 1,200 SF; FS, SF, SC

SUPPORT & TRAINING:
Financial Assistance Provided: Yes
Site Selection Assistance: Yes
Lease Negotiation Assistance: Yes
Co-Operative Advertising: Yes
Franchisee Assoc./Member: Yes
Size Of Corporate Staff: 27
On-Going Support: B,C,D,E,G,H,I
Training: 14 Days Salem, OR.

SPECIFIC EXPANSION PLANS:
US: All United States
Canada: No
Overseas: No

<< >>

FIREHOUSE SUBS

3410 Kori Rd.
Jacksonville, FL 32257
Tel: (800) 388-3473 (904) 886-8300
Fax: (904) 886-2111
E-Mail: sjoost@firehousesubs.com
Web Site: www.firehousesubs.com
Mr. Stephen Joost, VP Franchising

FIREHOUSE SUBS has expended considerable time and effort developing a sandwich restaurant system specializing in serving large portion, steaming hot submarine-style sandwiches in a unique firehouse atmosphere and décor, at an economical price.

BACKGROUND: IFA MEMBER
Established: 1995; 1st Franchised: 1995
Franchised Units: 145
Company-Owned Units: 30
Total Units: 175
Dist.: US-175; CAN-0; O'seas-0
North America: 10 States
Density: FL, NC, AL
Projected New Units (12 Months): 90
Qualifications: , , , , ,
Registered:

FINANCIAL/TERMS:
Cash Investment: $156.3-480.5K
Total Investment: $156.3-480.5K
Minimum Net Worth: $50K
Fees: Franchise - $20K
Royalty - 6%; Ad. - 3%
Earnings Claims Statement: Yes
Term of Contract (Years): 10/5
Avg. # Of Employees: 305 Ft, 15-20 PT
Passive Ownership: Not Allowed
Encourage Conversions:
Area Develop. Agreements: Yes/10
Sub-Franchising Contracts: Yes
Expand In Territory: Yes
Space Needs: 1,500 SF; SC

SUPPORT & TRAINING:
Financial Assistance Provided:
Site Selection Assistance: Yes
Lease Negotiation Assistance: No
Co-Operative Advertising: Yes
Franchisee Assoc./Member: No
Size Of Corporate Staff: 45
On-Going Support: a,B,C,D,E,F,G,I
Training: 4-6 Weeks Various Regional Centers; 2 Weeks Jacksonville, FL Final Training.

SPECIFIC EXPANSION PLANS:
US: SE and Mid-Atlantic.
Canada: NR
Overseas: NR

<< >>

FLAMERS CHARBROILED HAMBURGERS & CHICKEN

500 S. 3rd St.
Jacksonville Beach, FL 32250
Tel: (800) 952-7645 (904) 322-1781
Fax: (904) 302-4335
E-Mail: fdarabi@attbi.com
Web Site: www.flamersgrill.com
Mr. Faszin Darabi, President/CEO

Gourmet, charbroiled hamburgers, chicken, grilled fish and steaks restaurant, which operates in both food-court environments and neighborhood open-air centers, featuring food products cooked over an open-flame, just like you would cook them on your own backyard grill.

BACKGROUND:
Established: 1987; 1st Franchised: 1988
Franchised Units: 76
Company-Owned Units: 8
Total Units: 84
Dist.: US-79; CAN-0; O'seas-5
North America: 24 States
Density: 21 in FL, 11 in DC, 7 in PA
Projected New Units (12 Months): 10-15
Qualifications: 5, 3, 3, 4, 3, 4
Registered: CA,FL,HI,IL,IN,MD,MI,NY, OR,RI,VA,WA,WI,DC

FINANCIAL/TERMS:
Cash Investment: $60-90K
Total Investment: $180-210K
Minimum Net Worth: $350K
Fees: Franchise - $25K
Royalty - 5%; Ad. - 1%
Earnings Claims Statement: No
Term of Contract (Years): 10/10/10
Avg. # Of Employees: 3-4 FT, 7-10 PT
Passive Ownership: Allowed
Encourage Conversions: Yes
Area Develop. Agreements: Yes/20
Sub-Franchising Contracts: Yes
Expand In Territory: Yes
Space Needs: 500-2,000 SF; SF, SC, RM

SUPPORT & TRAINING:
Financial Assistance Provided: Yes(I)
Site Selection Assistance: Yes
Lease Negotiation Assistance: Yes
Co-Operative Advertising: Yes
Franchisee Assoc./Member: No
Size Of Corporate Staff: 11
On-Going Support: a,B,C,D,E,F,G,H,I
Training:
2 Weeks at Company Unit in Boston, MA; 2 Weeks Franchisee's Store.

SPECIFIC EXPANSION PLANS:
US: All United States
Canada: All Canada
Overseas: Europe, Middle East

<< >>

FOUR STAR PIZZA

P. O. Box W
Claysville, PA 15323
Tel: (800) 628-3398 (412) 484-9235
Fax: (724) 484-9235
E-Mail: fourstarza@aol.com
Web Site: www.fourstarpizza.net
Mr. David Roderick, President

Four Star Pizza is looking for aggressive, hard-driving entrepreneur as a four star franchisee you will feature a popular premium quality product, a great location, and an unbeatable, low start-up cost. Add a dash of entrepreneurial spirit and you're on your way to an exciting and profitable future.

BACKGROUND:
Established: 1981; 1st Franchised: 1985
Franchised Units: 14
Company-Owned Units: 0
Total Units: 14
Dist.: US-19; CAN-0; O'seas-0
North America: 5 States
Density: 10 in PA, 4 in MO, 2 in OH

Projected New Units (12 Months): 6
Qualifications: 3, 4, 2, 3, 1, 5
Registered: MD,NY,VA

FINANCIAL/TERMS:
Cash Investment: NR
Total Investment: $47.5-142K
Minimum Net Worth: NR
Fees: Franchise - $7K
Royalty - 5%; Ad. - 1%
Earnings Claims Statement: No
Term of Contract (Years): 10/10
Avg. # Of Employees: 3 FT, 4-10 PT
Passive Ownership: Discouraged
Encourage Conversions: Yes
Area Develop. Agreements: Yes
Sub-Franchising Contracts: No
Expand In Territory: Yes
Space Needs: 800-1,200 SF; FS, SC

SUPPORT & TRAINING:
Financial Assistance Provided: Yes(I)
Site Selection Assistance: No
Lease Negotiation Assistance: Yes
Co-Operative Advertising: Yes
Franchisee Assoc./Member: No
Size Of Corporate Staff: 3
On-Going Support: B,C,D,E,H,I
Training: 1-2 Weeks Varied Location.

SPECIFIC EXPANSION PLANS:
US: PA, VA, OH, WV, MD
Canada: No
Overseas: No

<< >>

FOX'S PIZZA DEN

3243 Old Frankstown Rd.
Pittsburgh, PA 15239
Tel: (800) 899-3697 (724) 733-7888
Fax: (724) 325-5479
E-Mail: foxs@alltel.net
Web Site: www.foxspizza.com
Mr. James R. Fox, President

FOX'S PIZZA DEN believes in one philosophy - you earned it, you keep it! FOX'S royalties are $200 a month - no percentages of sales. FOX'S PIZZA DENS offers the finest pizza, specialty sandwiches, salads and sides and our house special - the 'wedgie.'

BACKGROUND:
Established: 1971; 1st Franchised: 1974
Franchised Units: 218
Company-Owned Units: 0
Total Units: 218
Dist.: US-205; CAN-0; O'seas-0
North America: 19 States
Density: 105 in PA, 42 in WV, 12 OH
Projected New Units (12 Months): 30
Qualifications: 2, 4, 4, 2, 2, 5
Registered: FL,MD,MI,NY,VA

FINANCIAL/TERMS:
Cash Investment: $50-80K
Total Investment: $50-80K
Minimum Net Worth: NA
Fees: Franchise - $8K
Royalty - $200/Mo.; Ad. - 0%
Earnings Claims Statement: No
Term of Contract (Years): 5/5
Avg. # Of Employees: 2-3 FT, 8-10 PT
Passive Ownership: Discouraged
Encourage Conversions: Yes
Area Develop. Agreements: Yes
Sub-Franchising Contracts: Yes
Expand In Territory: Yes
Space Needs: 1,000-2,000 SF; FS, SF, SC

SUPPORT & TRAINING:
Financial Assistance Provided: Yes(I)
Site Selection Assistance: Yes
Lease Negotiation Assistance: No
Co-Operative Advertising: Yes
Franchisee Assoc./Member: NR
Size Of Corporate Staff: 8
On-Going Support: B,C,D,E,F,G,H,I
Training: 7 Days On-Site.

SPECIFIC EXPANSION PLANS:
US: All United States
Canada: No
Overseas: No

<< >>

FRULLATI CAFÉ & BAKERY

7730 E. Greenway Rd., # 104
Scottsdale, AZ 85260
Tel: (800) 438-2590 (480) 443-0200
Fax: (480) 443-0972
E-Mail: nrayborn@kahalacorp.com
Web Site: www.kahalacorp.com
Ms. Nicole Rayborn, Franchise Director

FRULLATI CAFÉ & BAKERY, the fresh franchise alternative in fast food. Featuring something fresh for every taste, FRULLATI's lite fare menu includes: fruit smoothies, frozen yogurt, deli sandwiches, healthy snacks, fresh baked bread, cookies and gourmet coffee. If the taste of success by owning one or a chain of FRULLATI CAFÉs sounds appetizing, here's the opportunity for you. We have FRULLATI CAFÉ & BAKERY franchise opportunities coming to your neighborhood.

BACKGROUND: IFA MEMBER
Established: 1985; 1st Franchised: 1994
Franchised Units: 57
Company-Owned Units: 37
Total Units: 94
Dist.: US-100; CAN-0; O'seas-0
North America: 14 States
Density: 29 in TX, 12 in IL, 7 in FL
Projected New Units (12 Months): 28
Qualifications: 5, 4, , 3, , 5
Registered:CA,FL,IL,IN,MD,MI,MN,ND,OR,VA,WA,WI

FINANCIAL/TERMS:
Cash Investment: $50K
Total Investment: $150-275K
Minimum Net Worth: $150K
Fees: Franchise - $20K
Royalty - 6%; Ad. - 1%
Earnings Claims Statement: Yes
Term of Contract (Years): 10/10
Avg. # Of Employees: 3 FT, 5 PT
Passive Ownership: Discouraged
Encourage Conversions: Yes
Area Develop. Agreements: Yes/Varies
Sub-Franchising Contracts: No
Expand In Territory: Yes
Space Needs: 600 SF; RM

SUPPORT & TRAINING:
Financial Assistance Provided: Yes(I)
Site Selection Assistance: Yes
Lease Negotiation Assistance: Yes
Co-Operative Advertising: Yes
Franchisee Assoc./Member: Yes/Yes
Size Of Corporate Staff: 350
On-Going Support: C,D,E,G,H,I
Training: 3 Weeks Dallas, TX.

SPECIFIC EXPANSION PLANS:
US: All United States
Canada: No
Overseas: No

<< >>

GODFATHER'S PIZZA

9140 W. Dodge Rd., # 300
Omaha, NE 68114
Tel: (800) 456-8347 (402) 391-1452
Fax: (402) 255-2685
E-Mail: brucec@godfathers.com
Web Site: www.godfathers.com
Mr. Bruce N. Cannon, VP Franchising

GODFATHER'S PIZZA is consistently recognized by consumers and independent research as having a superior quality product. Couple this with consistent operations, innovative new products, attention to service and full support services and GODFATHER'S PIZZA is positioned to retain its reputation for high quality and service.

BACKGROUND:
Established: 1973; 1st Franchised: 1974
Franchised Units: 480

Company-Owned Units: 111
Total Units: 591
Dist.: US-590; CAN-1; O'seas-0
North America: 38 States
Density: 67 in WA, 60 in IA, 39 in MN
Projected New Units (12 Months): 27
Qualifications: 5, 5, 5, 3, ,
Registered: CA,FL,IL,IN,MD,MI,MN,OR,SD,WA

FINANCIAL/TERMS:
Cash Investment: $55-120K
Total Investment: $82.5-358K
Minimum Net Worth: $200K
Fees: Franchise - $20K
Royalty - 5%; Ad. - 0%
Earnings Claims Statement: No
Term of Contract (Years): 15/10
Avg. # Of Employees: 6 FT, 20 PT
Passive Ownership: Discouraged
Encourage Conversions: Yes
Area Develop. Agreements: Yes/5
Sub-Franchising Contracts: No
Expand In Territory: Yes
Space Needs: 3,500 SF; FS, SC

SUPPORT & TRAINING:
Financial Assistance Provided: No
Site Selection Assistance: Yes
Lease Negotiation Assistance: No
Co-Operative Advertising: Yes
Franchisee Assoc./Member: Yes
Size Of Corporate Staff: 92
On-Going Support: D,G,I
Training: 35 Days Omaha, NE.

SPECIFIC EXPANSION PLANS:
US: All United States
Canada: No
Overseas: No

<< >>

GOLDEN CHICK

11488 Luna Rd., # 100B
Dallas, TX 75234-9430
Tel: (972) 831-0911
Fax: (972) 831-0401
E-Mail: gcinfo@goldenchick.com
Web Site: www.goldenchick.com
Mr. Kelly Creighton, President

GOLDEN CHICK is a fast-food chicken restaurant, offering indoor dining, drive-thru, carry-out and delivery service. GC's menu consists of fresh, golden fried chicken, roasted chicken, golden tenders, fried catfish, fresh-baked yeast rolls, country-style biscuits, gravy, french fries, coleslaw, mashed potatoes, corn on the cob, green beans, mac & cheese, sandwiches and fountain soft drinks.

BACKGROUND:
Established: 1967; 1st Franchised: 1972
Franchised Units: 64
Company-Owned Units: 10
Total Units: 74
Dist.: US-74; CAN-0; O'seas-0
North America: 3 States
Density: 72 in TX, 2 in OK
Projected New Units (12 Months): 6
Qualifications: 4, 4, 5, 2, 2, 5
Registered: AR, OK, TX

FINANCIAL/TERMS:
Cash Investment: $50-200K
Total Investment: $400-750K
Minimum Net Worth: $100K
Fees: Franchise - $15K
Royalty - 4%; Ad. - 1%
Earnings Claims Statement: No
Term of Contract (Years): 20/N/A
Avg. # Of Employees: 15
Passive Ownership: Not Allowed
Encourage Conversions: Yes
Area Develop. Agreements: No
Sub-Franchising Contracts: No
Expand In Territory: Yes
Space Needs: 1,800 SF; FS

SUPPORT & TRAINING:
Financial Assistance Provided: No
Site Selection Assistance: Yes
Lease Negotiation Assistance: No
Co-Operative Advertising: Yes
Franchisee Assoc./Member: No
Size Of Corporate Staff: 12
On-Going Support: a,B,C,D,d,E,F,G,H
Training: 6 Weeks Dallas, TX.

SPECIFIC EXPANSION PLANS:
US: South, Southwest
Canada: No
Overseas: No

<< >>

GRANDY'S

997 Grandy's Ln.
Lewisville, TX 75077-2507
Tel: (877) 457-8145 (972) 317-8086
Fax: (972) 317-8174
E-Mail: bgilbert@grandys.com
Web Site: www.grandys.com
Mr. Brian Gilbert, Franchise Development

GRANDY'S is one of America's most distinctive quick-service chains. GRANDY'S offers an unparalleled opportunity for potential franchisees. Our unique niche in the market, coupled with a solid 30-year history and our menu of delicious Home-style Food, including country-style breakfasts, chicken fried steaks, southern fried chicken and grilled chicken and a variety of homestyle vegetables - provide a great recipe for success.

BACKGROUND: IFA MEMBER
Established: 1973; 1st Franchised: 1977
Franchised Units: 77
Company-Owned Units: 7
Total Units: 84
Dist.: US-84; CAN-0; O'seas-0
North America: 9 States
Density: 60 in TX, 9 in OK, 6 in IN
Projected New Units (12 Months): 6
Qualifications: 5, 5, 4, 3, 4, 4
Registered: FL,IL,IN

FINANCIAL/TERMS:
Cash Investment: $150K
Total Investment: $800K-1.5MM
Minimum Net Worth: $350K
Fees: Franchise - $30K
Royalty - 5%; Ad. - Up to 2.5%
Earnings Claims Statement: No
Term of Contract (Years): 15/10
Avg. # Of Employees: 6 FT, 15 PT
Passive Ownership: Allowed
Encourage Conversions: Yes
Area Develop. Agreements: Yes/TBD
Sub-Franchising Contracts: No
Expand In Territory: Yes
Space Needs: 2,700 SF; FS

SUPPORT & TRAINING:
Financial Assistance Provided: No
Site Selection Assistance: Yes
Lease Negotiation Assistance: Yes
Co-Operative Advertising: Yes
Franchisee Assoc./Member: Yes
Size Of Corporate Staff: 25
On-Going Support: B,C,D,E,G,h
Training: 6-8 Weeks Lewisville, TX.

SPECIFIC EXPANSION PLANS:
US: TX,OK,AR,FL,GA,IN,LA,NC,SC
Canada: All Canada
Overseas: All Countries

<< >>

GREAT OUTDOOR SUB SHOPS

3910 Hwy. 67

Mesquite, TX 75150
Tel: (888) 260-3354 (972) 698-7505
Fax: (972) 698-7545
E-Mail: gail@greatoutdoorsubs.com
Web Site: www.greatoutdoorsubs.com
Ms. Gail Voelcker, President

G. O. FRANCHISE, INC. is a quick-service restaurant which offers freshly prepared submarine sandwiches, salads and ice cream under the trade name GREAT OUTDOOR SUB SHOP. Over the last 26 years, we have excelled and perfected the system and are now offering G. O. FRANCHISE opportunities to qualified individuals who are interested in the franchise restaurant industry.

BACKGROUND:
Established: 1973; 1st Franchised: 1996
Franchised Units: 3
Company-Owned Units: 6
Total Units: 9
Dist.: US-9; CAN-0; O'seas-0
North America: 1 State
Density: 9 in TX
Projected New Units (12 Months): 3
Qualifications: 3, 4, 4, 3, 4, 5
Registered: NR

FINANCIAL/TERMS:
Cash Investment: $75-265K
Total Investment: $75-265K
Minimum Net Worth: $150K
Fees: Franchise - $25K
Royalty - 4%; Ad. - 3%
Earnings Claims Statement: Yes
Term of Contract (Years): 10/10
Avg. # Of Employees: 6 FT, 5 PT
Passive Ownership: Not Allowed
Encourage Conversions: Yes
Area Develop. Agreements: Yes/10
Sub-Franchising Contracts: No
Expand In Territory: Yes
Space Needs: 1,800-2,200 SF; FS, SC

SUPPORT & TRAINING:
Financial Assistance Provided: No
Site Selection Assistance: Yes
Lease Negotiation Assistance: Yes
Co-Operative Advertising: No
Franchisee Assoc./Member: No
Size Of Corporate Staff: 8
On-Going Support: b,C,d,E,f
Training: 8 Weeks Dallas, TX.

SPECIFIC EXPANSION PLANS:
US: TX, SW
Canada: No
Overseas: No

<< >>

GREAT WRAPS
4 Executive Park E., # 315
Atlanta, GA 30329
Tel: (888) 489-7277 (404) 248-9900 + 16
Fax: (404) 248-0180
E-Mail: ckoestner@greatwraps.com
Web Site: www.greatwraps.com
Ms. Chris Koestner, Director Franchise Development

GREAT WRAPS is the #1 Hot Wrapped Sandwich & Grilled Sub Franchise, and is experiencing rapid growth. That's because we offer a franchise opportunity that is unique and proven . . . and provides tremendous growth potential. We feature a powerful menu that is fresher and tastier than traditional fast food . . .like the Santa Fe Chicken Wrap, our signature GyroWrap, Grilled (hot deli) Rollers, etc. Our operation is extremely efficient, and is so simple to learn, you don't even need prior food experience.

BACKGROUND: IFA MEMBER
Established: 1978; 1st Franchised: 1986
Franchised Units: 80
Company-Owned Units: 1
Total Units: 81
Dist.: US-81; CAN-0; O'seas-0
North America: 16 States
Density: 28 in GA, 6 in FL, 4 in TX
Projected New Units (12 Months): 35
Qualifications: 5, 3, 3, 3, 4, 4
Registered: CA,IL,MD,MI,NY,VA

FINANCIAL/TERMS:
Cash Investment: $60-80K
Total Investment: $175-240K
Minimum Net Worth: $250K
Fees: Franchise - $19.5K
Royalty - 5%; Ad. - 1%
Earnings Claims Statement: No
Term of Contract (Years): 15/10
Avg. # Of Employees: 5 FT, 6 PT
Passive Ownership: Discouraged
Encourage Conversions: Yes
Area Develop. Agreements: Yes/15 Yrs.+
Sub-Franchising Contracts: Yes
Expand In Territory: Yes
Space Needs: 600-1,500 SF; RM, SC, Airport, Univer.

SUPPORT & TRAINING:
Financial Assistance Provided: Yes(I)
Site Selection Assistance: Yes
Lease Negotiation Assistance: Yes
Co-Operative Advertising: Yes
Franchisee Assoc./Member: Yes
Size Of Corporate Staff: 13
On-Going Support: B,C,D,E,G,H
Training: 3 Weeks Atlanta, GA.

SPECIFIC EXPANSION PLANS:
US: NE, SE, SW, MW
Canada: No
Overseas: No

GRECO PIZZA DONAIR
P. O. Box 1040
Truro, NS B2N 5G9 CANADA
Tel: (902) 893-4141 + 8
Fax: (902) 895-7635
E-Mail:
Web Site: www.greco.ca
Mr. Dwayne Boudreau, VP Franchising

Atlantic Canada's largest home delivery pizza chain, specializing in pizza, donair products, oven sub sandwiches and pita-wrapped sandwiches.

BACKGROUND:
Established: 1977; 1st Franchised: 1981
Franchised Units: 101
Company-Owned Units: 2
Total Units: 103
Dist.: US-0; CAN-54; O'seas-0
North America: 4 Provinces
Density: 21 in NB, 23 in NS, 5 in NF
Projected New Units (12 Months): 5
Qualifications: , , , , ,
Registered: NR

FINANCIAL/TERMS:
Cash Investment: $40K
Total Investment: $150-180K
Minimum Net Worth: $40K
Fees: Franchise - $15K
Royalty - 5%; Ad. - 3%
Earnings Claims Statement: No
Term of Contract (Years): 10/5/5
Avg. # Of Employees: 5 FT, 10 PT
Passive Ownership: Discouraged
Encourage Conversions: Yes
Area Develop. Agreements: Yes/Varies
Sub-Franchising Contracts: Yes
Expand In Territory: Yes
Space Needs: 1,200 SF; FS, SF, SC, RM

SUPPORT & TRAINING:
Financial Assistance Provided: No
Site Selection Assistance: Yes
Lease Negotiation Assistance: Yes
Co-Operative Advertising: Yes

Franchisee Assoc./Member: NR
Size Of Corporate Staff: 19
On-Going Support: a,b,C,D,E,F,G,h,I
Training: 4 Weeks Correspondence; 2 Days Headquarters; 3 Weeks On-Site.

SPECIFIC EXPANSION PLANS:
US: No
Canada: PQ, Atlantic CAN
Overseas: No

<< >>

HAMBURGER MARY'S BAR & GRILLE

P. O. Box 456
Corona Del Mar, CA 92625
Tel: (888) 834-6279 (949) 729-8000
Fax: (949) 675-9979
E-Mail: hamburgermary@cox.net
Web Site: www.hamburgermarys.net
Mr. Darren Woolsey, Vice President

Hamburger Mary's Bar & Grille is the only and the largest restaurant franchise catering to the Gay and Lesbian community (as well as the general public). With over 32 years of successful operations, we have totally re-organized under HMI to become a major franchise. 14 franchised stores have been sold across the U.S. Our Owner's Manual, Bar Guide/Recipe book, Ad program and In-store training program are just a few of the plus features offered. Eat, Drink . . and be Mary!

BACKGROUND:
Established: 1972; 1st Franchised: 1997
Franchised Units: 14
Company-Owned Units: 1
Total Units: 15
Dist.: US-15; CAN-0; O'seas-0
North America: 8 States, DC
Density: 5 in CA, 1 in AZ, 1 in OH
Projected New Units (12 Months): NR
Qualifications: , , , , ,
Registered: NR

FINANCIAL/TERMS:
Cash Investment: $50K (Fee)
Total Investment: $200-950K
Minimum Net Worth: $150K
Fees: Franchise - $50K
Royalty - 5%; Ad. - 2%
Earnings Claims Statement: No
Term of Contract (Years): 15/5/5/5
Avg. # Of Employees:35-40 FT, 5-10 PT
Passive Ownership: Not Allowed
Encourage Conversions: NR
Area Develop. Agreements: Yes/Lifetime
Sub-Franchising Contracts: Yes
Expand In Territory: Yes
Space Needs: 4,000+ SF; FS

SUPPORT & TRAINING:
Financial Assistance Provided: NR
Site Selection Assistance: Yes
Lease Negotiation Assistance: Yes
Co-Operative Advertising: No
Franchisee Assoc./Member: No
Size Of Corporate Staff: 3 FT,
On-Going Support: B,C,D,E,f,H,I
Training: 2 Weeks Orange County (CA) Corp. Restaurant.

SPECIFIC EXPANSION PLANS:
US: All United States
Canada: NR
Overseas: Australia, Europe

<< >>

HAPPY JOE'S PIZZA & ICE CREAM PARLOR

2705 Happy Joe Dr.
Bettendorf, IA 52722
Tel: (800) 640-2834 (563) 332-8811
Fax: (563) 332-5822
E-Mail: tima@happyjoes.com
Web Site: www.happyjoes.com
Mr. Tim Anderson, Director Franchising

Pizza and ice cream in a fun atmosphere. Birthday party packages available. Very involved with special programs for youth in the community. Diversified pizza, pasta, sandwiches, salad bar and ice cream menu, candy, soft drinks and beer. Several parlors offer Family Fun Centers with redemption games and adventure-style golf.

BACKGROUND:
Established: 1972; 1st Franchised: 1973
Franchised Units: 58
Company-Owned Units: 7
Total Units: 65
Dist.: US-65; CAN-0; O'seas-0
North America: 6 States, 1 Province
Density: 33 in IA, 16 in IL, 7 in WI
Projected New Units (12 Months): 3
Qualifications: 5, 4, 3, 3, 3, 4
Registered: IL,ND,WI

FINANCIAL/TERMS:
Cash Investment: $300K
Total Investment: $300K-1.5MM
Minimum Net Worth: $200K
Fees: Franchise - $25K
Royalty - 4.5%; Ad. - 1%
Earnings Claims Statement: No
Term of Contract (Years): 15/10
Avg. # Of Employees: 4 FT, 30 PT
Passive Ownership: Discouraged
Encourage Conversions: Yes
Area Develop. Agreements: Yes/15
Sub-Franchising Contracts: No
Expand In Territory: Yes
Space Needs: 3,500 SF; FS, SF, SC

SUPPORT & TRAINING:
Financial Assistance Provided: Yes(I)
Site Selection Assistance: Yes
Lease Negotiation Assistance: Yes
Co-Operative Advertising: Yes
Franchisee Assoc./Member: Yes/Yes
Size Of Corporate Staff: 30
On-Going Support: B,C,D,E,G,h
Training: 6-12 Weeks in IA.

SPECIFIC EXPANSION PLANS:
US: Midwest
Canada: No
Overseas: No

<< >>

HARDEE'S

6307 Carpinteria Ave., # A
Carpinteria, CA 93013
Tel: (866) 253-7655 (805) 745-7842
Fax: (714) 780-6320
E-Mail: chopkins@ckr.com
Web Site: www.ckr.com
Mr. Craig Hopkins, VP Franchise Sales

HARDEE'S restaurants are located predominantly in the Midwest and Eastern United States and are known as the place to go for premium quality, juicy and delicious Thickburgers. HARDEE'S restaurants offer superior food quality, a diverse menu focused on burgers, premium dining selections at reasonable prices and attentive customer service to create a quality dining experience for its customers.

BACKGROUND: IFA MEMBER
Established: 1961; 1st Franchised: 1962
Franchised Units: 1,400
Company-Owned Units: 721
Total Units: 2,121
Dist.: US-; CAN-; O'seas-
North America: 38 States
Density: 315 in NC, 207 in VA,186 SC
Projected New Units (12 Months): NR
Qualifications: 4, 4, 4, 2, 2, 5
Registered: All States

FINANCIAL/TERMS:
Cash Investment: $300K
Total Investment: $796K-1.1MM
Minimum Net Worth: $1MM
Fees: Franchise - $35K
Royalty - 4%; Ad. - 5% Min.
Earnings Claims Statement: No
Term of Contract (Years): 10
Avg. # Of Employees: 12 FT, 4 PT
Passive Ownership: Not Allowed
Encourage Conversions: Yes
Area Develop. Agreements: Yes/Varies
Sub-Franchising Contracts: No
Expand In Territory: No
Space Needs: 2,000 SF; FS, SC, RM, Univer.

SUPPORT & TRAINING:
Financial Assistance Provided: No
Site Selection Assistance: No
Lease Negotiation Assistance: No
Co-Operative Advertising: Yes
Franchisee Assoc./Member: No
Size Of Corporate Staff: 300
On-Going Support: B,C,D,E,G,H,I
Training: 12 Weeks Training.

SPECIFIC EXPANSION PLANS:
US: All United States
Canada: All Canada
Overseas: NR

<< >>

HARTZ CHICKEN

14451 Cornerstone Village Dr., # 250
Houston, TX 77014
Tel: (281) 583-0020
Fax: (281) 580-3752
E-Mail: hartz@hartz-chicken.com
Web Site: www.hartz-chicken.com
Mr. John Bergeron, Controller

All-you-can-eat chicken buffet restaurant, featuring crispy and rotisserie chicken, Southern-style fish, fresh steamed vegetables, cold salads, casseroles, homestyle desserts and fresh homemade yeast rolls. Drive-thru and take-out service available at units. Delivery available in 1/3 of the domestic units. International program expanding - units open in Malaysia, Indonesia and China.

BACKGROUND:
Established: 1972; 1st Franchised: 1975
Franchised Units: 50
Company-Owned Units: 1
Total Units: 51
Dist.: US-42; CAN-0; O'seas-9
North America: 2 States
Density: 41 in TX, 1 in MS
Projected New Units (12 Months): 20
Qualifications: 4, 5, 3, 1, 3, 5
Registered: NR

FINANCIAL/TERMS:
Cash Investment: $250K
Total Investment: $300K-1MM
Minimum Net Worth: $250K
Fees: Franchise - $20K
Royalty - 4%; Ad. - 2-3%
Earnings Claims Statement: Yes
Term of Contract (Years): 20/5
Avg. # Of Employees: 7 FT, 6 PT
Passive Ownership: Discouraged
Encourage Conversions: Yes
Area Develop. Agreements: Yes
Sub-Franchising Contracts: Yes
Expand In Territory: Yes
Space Needs: 3,000 SF; FS

SUPPORT & TRAINING:
Financial Assistance Provided: No
Site Selection Assistance: Yes
Lease Negotiation Assistance: Yes
Co-Operative Advertising: Yes
Franchisee Assoc./Member: Yes
Size Of Corporate Staff: 10
On-Going Support: B,C,D,E,G,I
Training: 6 Weeks in Houston, TX.

SPECIFIC EXPANSION PLANS:
US: South
Canada: No
Overseas: Far East, Asia

<< >>

HO-LEE-CHOW

658 Danforth Ave., # 201
Toronto, ON M4J 5B9 CANADA
Tel: (800) HO-LEE-CHOW (416) 778-8028
Fax: (416) 778-6818
E-Mail: holeechow@holeechow.com
Web Site: www.holeechow.com
Mr. Jake Cappiello, President

Great Chinese food delivered fast and fresh. Each entree in our restaurants is cooked-to-order with no added MSG or preservatives. Each order is delivered in under 45 minutes. All locations are brightly lit and have our open kitchen concept so customers can view their food being cooked in the most pristine kitchens.

BACKGROUND:
Established: 1989; 1st Franchised: 1989
Franchised Units: 19
Company-Owned Units: 2
Total Units: 21
Dist.: US-0; CAN-22; O'seas-0
North America: 1 Province
Density: 22 in ON
Projected New Units (12 Months): 15
Qualifications: 3, 3, 1, 2, 3, 5
Registered: NR

FINANCIAL/TERMS:
Cash Investment: $50-75K
Total Investment: $150-175K
Minimum Net Worth: $100K
Fees: Franchise - $Included
Royalty - 6%; Ad. - 3%
Earnings Claims Statement: Yes
Term of Contract (Years): 5/15
Avg. # Of Employees: 3 FT, 1 PT
Passive Ownership: Discouraged
Encourage Conversions: Yes
Area Develop. Agreements: Yes/10
Sub-Franchising Contracts: Yes
Expand In Territory: Yes
Space Needs: 900 SF; FS, SF, SC

SUPPORT & TRAINING:
Financial Assistance Provided: Yes(I)
Site Selection Assistance: Yes
Lease Negotiation Assistance: Yes
Co-Operative Advertising: Yes
Franchisee Assoc./Member: Yes/Yes
Size Of Corporate Staff: 50+
On-Going Support: A,B,C,D,E,F,G,H,I
Training: 1 Week Head Office in Toronto, ON; 4 Weeks On-Site.

SPECIFIC EXPANSION PLANS:
US: All United States
Canada: ON
Overseas: No

<< >>

HOT 'N NOW HAMBURGERS

4205 Charlar, # 3
Holt, MI 48842
Tel: (888) 350-3146 (517) 694-4240
Fax: (517) 694-6370
E-Mail: tomv@voyager.net
Web Site: www.worldfranchising.com/website.htm
Mr. Tom VanAlstine, Vice President/CFO

Hot 'N Now operates and franchises drive thru only quick service restaurants, with the goal of serving great food fast. By keeping our operations as simple as possible we are able to keep our focus on what is really important, customer service.

BACKGROUND:
Established: 1984; 1st Franchised: 1987
Franchised Units: 30
Company-Owned Units: 32
Total Units: 62
Dist.: US-62; CAN-0; O'seas-0

North America: 3 States
Density: 55 in MI, 3 in IN, 4 in WI
Projected New Units (12 Months): NR
Qualifications: , , , , ,
Registered: NR

FINANCIAL/TERMS:
Cash Investment: $50K+
Total Investment: $400K-1MM
Minimum Net Worth: $100K
Fees: Franchise - $22K
Royalty - 4%; Ad. - .5%
Earnings Claims Statement: No
Term of Contract (Years): 20/20
Avg. # Of Employees: 4 FT, 15 PT
Passive Ownership: Discouraged
Encourage Conversions: NR
Area Develop. Agreements: Yes/Varies
Sub-Franchising Contracts: No
Expand In Territory: Yes
Space Needs: 1,000 SF; FS

SUPPORT & TRAINING:
Financial Assistance Provided: NR
Site Selection Assistance: NA
Lease Negotiation Assistance: Yes
Co-Operative Advertising: Yes
Franchisee Assoc./Member: No
Size Of Corporate Staff: 10
On-Going Support: B,C,D,E,G,H,I
Training: Eight Hours at a To Be Determined Location.

SPECIFIC EXPANSION PLANS:
US: Midwest
Canada: NR
Overseas: NR

<< >>

HUNGRY HOWIE'S PIZZA & SUBS

30300 Stephenson Hwy., # 200
Madison Heights, MI 48071-1600
Tel: (800) 624-8122 (248) 414-3300 + 223
Fax: (248) 414-3301
E-Mail: bcuffaro@hungryhowies.com
Web Site: www.hungryhowies.com
Mr. Bob Cuffaro, Dir. Franchise Development

HUNGRY HOWIE'S, the innovator of the award-winning Flavored-Crust Pizza, is the nation's 9th largest carry-out / delivery pizza company. Menu offerings include 8 varieties of Flavored-Crust pizzas, delicious oven-baked subs and fresh and crispy salads.

BACKGROUND: IFA MEMBER
Established: 1973; 1st Franchised: 1982
Franchised Units: 475
Company-Owned Units: 0
Total Units: 475
Dist.: US-434; CAN-1; O'seas-0
North America: 19 States, 1 Province
Density: 180 in FL, 180 in MI, 15 CA
Projected New Units (12 Months): 20
Qualifications: 4, 3, 2, 3, 4, 5
Registered:CA,FL,IL,IN,MD,MI,MN,NY, OR,RI,VA,WA,WI,DC

FINANCIAL/TERMS:
Cash Investment: $50K
Total Investment: $85-125K
Minimum Net Worth: $150K
Fees: Franchise - $15K
Royalty - 5%; Ad. - 3%
Earnings Claims Statement: No
Term of Contract (Years): 20/20
Avg. # Of Employees: 4 FT, 8 PT
Passive Ownership: Discouraged
Encourage Conversions: Yes
Area Develop. Agreements: Yes/20
Sub-Franchising Contracts: Yes
Expand In Territory: Yes
Space Needs: 1,200 SF; SC

SUPPORT & TRAINING:
Financial Assistance Provided: Yes(I)
Site Selection Assistance: Yes
Lease Negotiation Assistance: Yes
Co-Operative Advertising: Yes
Franchisee Assoc./Member: No
Size Of Corporate Staff: 20
On-Going Support: B,C,D,E,F,G,h
Training: 5 Weeks Madison Heights, MI.

SPECIFIC EXPANSION PLANS:
US: All United States
Canada: No
Overseas: No

<< >>

INTERSTATE DAIRY QUEEN

8555 16th St., # 850
Silver Spring, MD 20910
Tel: (800) 546-5923, x 223 (301) 587-4411
Fax: (301) 585-8997
E-Mail: wtellegen@interstatedq.com
Web Site: www.interstatedq.com
Mr. Walt Tellegen, President

Fast food treat franchisor on interstate highways. `

BACKGROUND:
Established: 1977; 1st Franchised: 1978
Franchised Units: 170
Company-Owned Units: 0
Total Units: 170
Dist.: US-170; CAN-0; O'seas-0
North America: 29 States
Density: 25 in GA, 10 in NC, 10 in FL
Projected New Units (12 Months): 13
Qualifications: 4, 5, 2, 2, 2, 5
Registered: CA,FL,IL,IN,MD,MI,NY,RI

FINANCIAL/TERMS:
Cash Investment: $100-300K
Total Investment: Varies
Minimum Net Worth: Varies
Fees: Franchise - $25K
Royalty - 4-7%; Ad. - 3-5%
Earnings Claims Statement: No
Term of Contract (Years): 20/Option
Avg. # Of Employees: Varies
Passive Ownership: Allowed
Encourage Conversions: Yes
Area Develop. Agreements: No
Sub-Franchising Contracts: No
Expand In Territory: Yes
Space Needs: 1,000-3,000 SF; FS, SC, Travel Plaza

SUPPORT & TRAINING:
Financial Assistance Provided: No
Site Selection Assistance: Yes
Lease Negotiation Assistance: Yes
Co-Operative Advertising: No
Franchisee Assoc./Member: Yes/No
Size Of Corporate Staff: 15
On-Going Support: a,B,C,D,e,F,G,H,I
Training: 2-4 Weeks in Minneapolis, MN.

SPECIFIC EXPANSION PLANS:
US: Eastern United States
Canada: No
Overseas: No

<< >>

JERRY'S SUBS & PIZZA

15942 Shady Grove Rd.
Gaithersburg, MD 20877-1315
Tel: (800) 990-9176 + 155 (301) 921-8777 + 155
Fax: (301) 948-3508
E-Mail: robbinb@jerrysusa.com
Web Site: www.jerrysusa.com
Ms. Robbin E. Brinkhoff, Dir. Franchise Development

High-volume, high-traffic locations are selected, featuring our 'overstuffed' subs and NY-style pizza. Decor is bright and up-scale and provides a warm, friendly environment.

BACKGROUND:
Established: 1954; 1st Franchised: 1980
Franchised Units: 140
Company-Owned Units: 2
Total Units: 142
Dist.: US-142; CAN-0; O'seas-0
North America: 7 States
Density: MD, VA, DC
Projected New Units (12 Months): 15
Qualifications: 4, 2, 1, 1, 4, 2

Registered: MD,VA,DC

FINANCIAL/TERMS:

Cash Investment: $50-75K
Total Investment: $225-350K
Minimum Net Worth: $250K
Fees: Franchise - $25K
Royalty - 6%; Ad. - 3%
Earnings Claims Statement: No
Term of Contract (Years): 20/Open
Avg. # Of Employees: NR
Passive Ownership: Discouraged
Encourage Conversions: Yes
Area Develop. Agreements: Yes/20
Sub-Franchising Contracts: No
Expand In Territory: Yes
Space Needs: 1,500-2,000 SF; FS, SC, RM

SUPPORT & TRAINING:

Financial Assistance Provided: Yes
Site Selection Assistance: Yes
Lease Negotiation Assistance: Yes
Co-Operative Advertising: Yes
Franchisee Assoc./Member: No
Size Of Corporate Staff: 25
On-Going Support: B,C,D,E,F,G,H,I
Training: 6 Weeks Aspen Hill, MD.

SPECIFIC EXPANSION PLANS:

US: East Coast
Canada: No
Overseas: No

<< >>

JERSEY MIKE'S SUBMARINES & SALADS

1973 Hwy. 34, # E 21
Wall, NJ 07719
Tel: (800) 321-7676 (732) 282-2323
Fax: (732) 282-2233
E-Mail: franchisedevelopment@jerseymikes.com
Web Site: www.jerseymikes.com
Mr. Ed Yancey, Jr.,

JERSEY MIKE'S is a submarine sandwich franchise company which prides itself on producing the freshest submarine sandwich in the industry. They bake bread daily in the store. Roast beefs are cooked on premises and meats and cheeses are sliced in front of the customer. Awards include 'Best Sub' in Nashville, Charlotte, RTP, Wilmington, Greenville and Ocean/Monmouth, NJ.

BACKGROUND:

Established: 1956; 1st Franchised: 1986
Franchised Units: 235
Company-Owned Units: 5
Total Units: 240
Dist.: US-131; CAN-0; O'seas-0
North America: 13 States
Density: 83 in NC, 25 in OH, 15 in TN
Projected New Units (12 Months): NR
Qualifications: , , , , ,
Registered: NR

FINANCIAL/TERMS:

Cash Investment: NR
Total Investment: $150-200K
Minimum Net Worth: NR
Fees: Franchise - $18.5K
Royalty - 5.5%; Ad. - 3.5%
Earnings Claims Statement: NR
Term of Contract (Years): 10/10
Avg. # Of Employees: 7 FT, 8 PT
Passive Ownership: Discouraged
Encourage Conversions: NR
Area Develop. Agreements: Yes/10
Sub-Franchising Contracts: No
Expand In Territory: NR
Space Needs: 1,500 SF; FS, SC

SUPPORT & TRAINING:

Financial Assistance Provided: NR
Site Selection Assistance: Yes
Lease Negotiation Assistance: Yes
Co-Operative Advertising: Yes
Franchisee Assoc./Member: No
Size Of Corporate Staff: 30
On-Going Support: B,C,D,E,G,H,I
Training: 3-4 Weeks Nashville, TN.

SPECIFIC EXPANSION PLANS:

US: All United States
Canada: NR
Overseas: NR

<< >>

JIMBOY'S TACOS

JIMBOY'S TACOS

1830 Sierra Gardens Dr., # 80
Roseville, CA 95661
Tel: (800) 546-2697 (916) 788-9770
Fax: (916) 788-9776
E-Mail: jlanni@jimboys.com
Web Site: www.jimboys.com
Mr. John Lanni, Director Franchise Marketing

JIMBOY'S TACOS - famous, award-winning tacos. Maintaining a proven conept through 50 years of commitment to excellent food and service. Cooked fresh daily using high-quality ingredients. Our franchisees are given a very thorough and extensive hands-on classroom training program. Strong on-going, in-store support. Franchisees required to attend our classroom training every other month at our corporate office. We offer free-standing concepts with drive-up windows, also end-cap concepts in strip centers.

BACKGROUND:

Established: 1954; 1st Franchised: 1965
Franchised Units: 38
Company-Owned Units: 2
Total Units: 40
Dist.: US-40; CAN-0; O'seas-0
North America: 2 States
Density: 33 in CA, 7 in NV
Projected New Units (12 Months): 8
Qualifications: 5, 4, 3, 3, 4, 5
Registered: CA

FINANCIAL/TERMS:

Cash Investment: Varies
Total Investment: $203-587K
Minimum Net Worth: NR
Fees: Franchise - $36K
Royalty - 4%; Ad. - 3%
Earnings Claims Statement: No
Term of Contract (Years): 15/5/5
Avg. # Of Employees: 4-10 FT, 6-12 PT
Passive Ownership: Discouraged
Encourage Conversions: Yes
Area Develop. Agreements: No
Sub-Franchising Contracts: No
Expand In Territory: Yes
Space Needs: 2,000 SF; FS, SC

SUPPORT & TRAINING:

Financial Assistance Provided: NR
Site Selection Assistance: Yes
Lease Negotiation Assistance: Yes
Co-Operative Advertising: Yes
Franchisee Assoc./Member: No
Size Of Corporate Staff: 7
On-Going Support: C,DD,E,G,H,I
Training: 96 Hours Corporate Training Rest. Folsom, CA; 32 Hours Corporate Office, Roseville, CA.

SPECIFIC EXPANSION PLANS:

US: California, Nevada
Canada: No
Overseas: No

<< >>

JIMMY JOHN'S GOURMET SANDWICHES

600 Tollgate Rd., # B
Elgin, IL 60123-9342
Tel: (800) 546-6904 (847) 888-7206

Fax: (847) 888-7070
E-Mail: bmorena@jimmyjohns.com
Web Site: www.jimmyjohns.com
Mr. Bob Morena, Sales Associate

World's greatest gourmet sandwich shop. All the sandwiches are made on fresh-baked french bread or 7-grain honey wheat bread. We only use the highest-quality meats available with garden fresh veggies that are brought in and sliced each morning.

BACKGROUND: IFA MEMBER
Established: 1983; 1st Franchised: 1993
Franchised Units: 237
Company-Owned Units: 15
Total Units: 252
Dist.: US-246; CAN-0; O'seas-6
North America: 25 States
Density: 78 in IL, 32 in MI, 22 in WI
Projected New Units (12 Months): 25
Qualifications: 5, 4, 2, 4, 4, 5
Registered: FL,IL,IN,MI,MN,RI,VA,WI,DC

FINANCIAL/TERMS:
Cash Investment: $80K+
Total Investment: $127-353K
Minimum Net Worth: $300K
Fees: Franchise - $20-30K
Royalty - 6%; Ad. - 4.5%
Earnings Claims Statement: Yes
Term of Contract (Years): 10/5/5
Avg. # Of Employees: 2 FT, 20 PT
Passive Ownership: Discouraged
Encourage Conversions: NA
Area Develop. Agreements: Yes/Varies
Sub-Franchising Contracts: No
Expand In Territory: Yes
Space Needs: 800-1,200 SF; FS, SC, SF

SUPPORT & TRAINING:
Financial Assistance Provided: No
Site Selection Assistance: Yes
Lease Negotiation Assistance: Yes
Co-Operative Advertising: Yes
Franchisee Assoc./Member: Yes
Size Of Corporate Staff: 20
On-Going Support: C,D,E,F,G,H,I
Training: 3 Weeks in Champaign, IL.

SPECIFIC EXPANSION PLANS:
US: All United States
Canada: All Canada
Overseas: All Countries

JOHNNY BRUSCO'S NEW YORK STYLE PIZZA

189 Chappell Rd.
Fayetteville, GA 30215
Tel:
Fax: (770) 478-5021
E-Mail: franchiseinfo@jnysp.com
Web Site: www.johnnybruscos.com
Mr. Bruce Jackson, President

JOHNNY BRUSCO'S is a true New York Style Pizzeria, specializing in authentic hand-tossed NY Style Pizza, a variety of salads, appetizers, Italian Dinners, calzones, and stromboli. A sit-down, full-service restaurant that caters to customer service and a memorable dining experience. Family-friendly establishment where kids are comfortable and parents can enjoy their favorite beverages.The atmosphere and décor reflects both the neighborhood and its surrounding interests. Truly your "neighborhood pizzeria."

BACKGROUND:
Established: 1977; 1st Franchised: 1995
Franchised Units: 43
Company-Owned Units: 0
Total Units: 43
Dist.: US-43; CAN-0; O'seas-0
North America: 2 States
Density: 40 in GA, 3 in TN
Projected New Units (12 Months): 7-10
Qualifications: 4, 3, 2, 3, 4, 5
Registered: NR

FINANCIAL/TERMS:
Cash Investment: $75-250K
Total Investment: $150-250K
Minimum Net Worth: $500K
Fees: Franchise - $27K
Royalty - 4%; Ad. - 1%
Earnings Claims Statement: No
Term of Contract (Years): 10/5/5
Avg. # Of Employees: 8 FT, 8 PT
Passive Ownership: Discouraged
Encourage Conversions: No
Area Develop. Agreements: Negotiable
Sub-Franchising Contracts: No
Expand In Territory: No
Space Needs: 2,100-2,400 SF; SC

SUPPORT & TRAINING:
Financial Assistance Provided: Yes(I)
Site Selection Assistance: Yes
Lease Negotiation Assistance: Yes
Co-Operative Advertising: Yes
Franchisee Assoc./Member: Yes/No
Size Of Corporate Staff: 4
On-Going Support: C,D,E,F,H,I
Training: 6 Weeks minimum in Atlanta, GA; 6 Weeks minimum in Memphis, TN.

SPECIFIC EXPANSION PLANS:
US: Southeast US; AL, GA, FL, NC, SC, TN
Canada: No
Overseas: No

JOHNNY ROCKETS, THE ORIGINAL HAMBURGER

26970 Aliso Viejo Pkwy., # 100
Aliso Viejo, CA 92656-2621
Tel: (949) 643-6100
Fax: (949) 643-6200
E-Mail: mghubbard@johnnyrockets.com
Web Site: www.johnnyrockets.com
Mr. Marshall Greg Hubbard, SVP Development/Franchise

Johnny Rockets is more than a restaurant. It's like taking a bite out of the good ol' days. A 1950's "magical" experience at the neighborhood malt shop. It's two straws in a shake, red vinyl bar stools, chrome, and jukeboxes at a nickel a play. It's juicy hamburgers on a seared bun, crisp golden fries and waiters that always dance on the half-hour, twirl straws and serve ketchup with a smile! Johnny Rockets is a place that feels like a stroll down memory lane back to those simpler times.

BACKGROUND: IFA MEMBER
Established: 1986; 1st Franchised: 1989
Franchised Units: 82
Company-Owned Units: 60
Total Units: 142
Dist.: US-82; CAN-0; O'seas-60
North America: 26 States, 9 Countries
Density: 38 in CA, 13 in FL, 9 in GA
Projected New Units (12 Months): NR
Qualifications: , , , , ,
Registered: NR

FINANCIAL/TERMS:
Cash Investment: $800K-1MM
Total Investment: $595-695K
Minimum Net Worth: $1MM+

Fees: Franchise - $45K
Royalty - 5% of gross sale; Ad. - 2% of Gross
Earnings Claims Statement: No
Term of Contract (Years): 10/2 or 5
Avg. # Of Employees: 1 Server/12 Guests
Passive Ownership: Allowed
Encourage Conversions: NR
Area Develop. Agreements: Yes/10
Sub-Franchising Contracts: No
Expand In Territory: Yes
Space Needs: 800-2,000 SF; FS, SF, SC, RM

SUPPORT & TRAINING:
Financial Assistance Provided: NR
Site Selection Assistance: Yes
Lease Negotiation Assistance: Yes
Co-Operative Advertising: No
Franchisee Assoc./Member: No
Size Of Corporate Staff: 40
On-Going Support: B,C,D,E,G,H,I
Training: 6 Weeks, 1 of 6 Locations.

SPECIFIC EXPANSION PLANS:
US: All United States
Canada: NR
Overseas: All Countries

<< >>

KFC
P. O. Box 34550, 1900 Colonel Sanders Ln.
Louisville, KY 40213
Tel: (866) 2YUM-YUM (502) 874-8300
Fax: (502) 874-8848
E-Mail: 2yumyum@yum.com
Web Site: www.yumfranchises.com
Ms. Nikki Weis, Franchise Coordinator

World's largest quick-service restaurant with a chicken-dominant menu. KFC offers full-service restaurants and non-traditional express units for captive markets.

BACKGROUND: IFA MEMBER
Established: 1939; 1st Franchised: 1952
Franchised Units: 9,916
Company-Owned Units: 2,962
Total Units: 12,878
Dist.: US-; CAN-; O'seas-
North America: 50 States,10 Provinces
Density: CA, TX, IL
Projected New Units (12 Months): 100
Qualifications: 5, 4, 5, 3, 3, 5
Registered: All States

FINANCIAL/TERMS:
Cash Investment: NR
Total Investment: $1.1-1.7MM
Minimum Net Worth: $1MM
Fees: Franchise - $25K
Royalty - 4% or $600/Mo.; Ad. - 5%
Earnings Claims Statement: No
Term of Contract (Years): 20
Avg. # Of Employees: 2 FT, 22 PT
Passive Ownership: Not Allowed
Encourage Conversions: No
Area Develop. Agreements: No
Sub-Franchising Contracts: No
Expand In Territory: Yes
Space Needs: 2,000-3,000 SF; FS

SUPPORT & TRAINING:
Financial Assistance Provided: No
Site Selection Assistance: Yes
Lease Negotiation Assistance: No
Co-Operative Advertising: Yes
Franchisee Assoc./Member: Yes/Yes
Size Of Corporate Staff: 820
On-Going Support: C,d,E,G,h,I
Training: 10-16 Weeks of Training.

SPECIFIC EXPANSION PLANS:
US: All United States
Canada: All Canada
Overseas: All Countries

<< >>

KOYA JAPAN
720 Broadway, # 207
Winnipeg, MB R3G 0X1 CANADA
Tel: (888) 569-2872 (204) 783-4433
Fax: (204) 783-1749
E-Mail: info@koyajapan.com
Web Site: www.koyajapan.com
Mr. Steve M. Sabbagh, President

Delicious Japanese food served fast from the freshest of ingredients and complimented by or unique sauce. What makes us successful is our cooking techniques, each meal is made to order in full view of the customer. KOYA JAPAN -- where freshness sizzles before your eyes.

BACKGROUND:
Established: 1985; 1st Franchised: 1986
Franchised Units: 24
Company-Owned Units: 0
Total Units: 24
Dist.: US-2; CAN-22; O'seas-0
North America: 6 Provinces
Density: 7 in BC, 6 in MB, 5 in ON
Projected New Units (12 Months): 12
Qualifications: 4, 4, 3, 2, 3, 5
Registered: FL

FINANCIAL/TERMS:
Cash Investment: $50% of Total
Total Investment: $165-250K
Minimum Net Worth: $100K
Fees: Franchise - $25K
Royalty - 6-7%; Ad. - 2%
Earnings Claims Statement: No
Term of Contract (Years): Up to 10
Avg. # Of Employees: 3 FT, 1 PT
Passive Ownership: Allowed
Encourage Conversions: Yes
Area Develop. Agreements: Yes/20
Sub-Franchising Contracts: No
Expand In Territory: Yes
Space Needs: 300-400 SF; RM

SUPPORT & TRAINING:
Financial Assistance Provided: No
Site Selection Assistance: Yes
Lease Negotiation Assistance: Yes
Co-Operative Advertising: Yes
Franchisee Assoc./Member: No
Size Of Corporate Staff: 3
On-Going Support: C,d,E,I
Training: Up to 1 Month in Operating Location; up to 1 Month On-Site; 2-3 Days at Head Office.

SPECIFIC EXPANSION PLANS:
US: All United States
Canada: All Canada
Overseas: Bahrain, United Arab Emirates, Kuwait, Quatar, Saudi Arabia

<< >>

KRYSTAL COMPANY, THE
1 Union Square, Fl. 9
Chattanooga, TN 37402-2505
Tel: (800) 458-5912 (423) 757-5601
Fax: (423) 757-1588
E-Mail: jspivey@krystalco.com
Web Site: www.krystal.com
Ms. Jo Spivey, Franchise Development

The KRYSTAL COMPANY, a 'cultural icon' in the Southeast, is a unique brand with 72 years of success as a niche franchisor, we provide quality service and thoughtful leadership to our franchise partners. We are an innovative, forward-looking franchisor who is looking for highly motivated operators. We offer a protected development territory, requiring a minimum 3-restaurant development agreement, minimum liquidity of $650K and a net worth of $1.2 million. KRYSTAL, fresh, hot, small and square.

BACKGROUND: IFA MEMBER
Established: 1932; 1st Franchised: 1990
Franchised Units: 188
Company-Owned Units: 245
Total Units: 433
Dist.: US-433; CAN-0; O'seas-0
North America: 15 States
Density: 104 in GA, 105 in TN, 53 AL
Projected New Units (12 Months): 25
Qualifications: 5, 4, 5, 2, 2, 5
Registered: FL,VA

FINANCIAL/TERMS:
Cash Investment: $200-300K/Rest
Total Investment: $900K-1.3MM
Minimum Net Worth: $1.2MM
Fees: Franchise - $32.5K
Royalty - 4.5%; Ad. - 4%
Earnings Claims Statement: No
Term of Contract (Years): 20/20
Avg. # Of Employees: 12-15 FT, 15 PT
Passive Ownership: Allowed
Encourage Conversions: Yes
Area Develop. Agreements: No
Sub-Franchising Contracts: No
Expand In Territory: Yes
Space Needs: 1,300-2,200 SF; FS,SC,C-Store

SUPPORT & TRAINING:
Financial Assistance Provided: No
Site Selection Assistance: Yes
Lease Negotiation Assistance: No
Co-Operative Advertising: Yes
Franchisee Assoc./Member: Yes/No
Size Of Corporate Staff: 100
On-Going Support: A,B,C,D,E,F,G,H,I
Training: 4 Weeks Company Store; 1 Week Corporate Computer Center.

SPECIFIC EXPANSION PLANS:
US: SE,TX,OK,VA,NC,SC,WV,FL
Canada: No
Overseas: No

<< >>

Top 100 **LA SALSA FRESH MEXICAN GRILL**
6307 Carpinteria Ave., # A
Carpinteria, CA 93013
Tel: (866) 253-7655 (805) 745-7843
Fax: (714) 780-6320
E-Mail: rbasinger@ckr.com
Web Site: www.lasalsa.com
Mr. Ron Basinger, VP Franchise Sales

A fast, casual restaurant chain, specializing in hand-crafted Mexican favorites and appealing to health-conscious individuals with discriminating taste.

BACKGROUND: IFA MEMBER
Established: 1979; 1st Franchised: 1989
Franchised Units: 41
Company-Owned Units: 61
Total Units: 102
Dist.: US-102; CAN-0; O'seas-0
North America: NR
Density: 62 in CA, 7 in AZ, 6 in UT
Projected New Units (12 Months): 36
Qualifications: 4, 4, 4, 2, 2, 5
Registered:CA,FL,IL,IN,MD,MI,MN,NY,VA,WA,WI

FINANCIAL/TERMS:
Cash Investment: NR
Total Investment: $431-612K
Minimum Net Worth: $1.2MM
Fees: Franchise - $20K
Royalty - 5%; Ad. - 5%
Earnings Claims Statement: No
Term of Contract (Years): 10
Avg. # Of Employees: 12 FT, 4 PT
Passive Ownership: Not Allowed
Encourage Conversions: Yes
Area Develop. Agreements: Yes/Varies
Sub-Franchising Contracts: No
Expand In Territory: No
Space Needs: 2,500 SF; SF, SC, RM

SUPPORT & TRAINING:
Financial Assistance Provided: No
Site Selection Assistance: No
Lease Negotiation Assistance: No
Co-Operative Advertising: Yes
Franchisee Assoc./Member: No
Size Of Corporate Staff: NR
On-Going Support: B,C,D,E,G,H,I
Training: 5 Weeks.

SPECIFIC EXPANSION PLANS:
US: All United States
Canada: All Canada
Overseas: NR

<< >>

LARRY'S GIANT SUBS
8616 Baymeadows Rd.
Jacksonville, FL 32256
Tel: (800) 358-6870 (904) 739-2498
Fax: (904) 739-1218
E-Mail: bigone@larryssubs.com
Web Site: www.larryssubs.com
Mr. Mitchell Raikes, Vice President

Upscale submarine sandwich franchise, featuring top-quality foods, such as USDA choice roast beef, oven-roasted turkey, white-meat chicken salad, store décor, custom table tops, laser logo steel chairs and huge ape display.

BACKGROUND:
Established: 1982; 1st Franchised: 1986
Franchised Units: 88
Company-Owned Units: 3
Total Units: 91
Dist.: US-91; CAN-0; O'seas-0
North America: 6 States
Density: 53 in FL, 28 in GA, 2 in TX
Projected New Units (12 Months): 15
Qualifications: 3, 3, 3, 3, 3, 5
Registered: FL

FINANCIAL/TERMS:
Cash Investment: $25-40K
Total Investment: $110-170K
Minimum Net Worth: $150K
Fees: Franchise - $19K
Royalty - 6%; Ad. - 2%
Earnings Claims Statement: No
Term of Contract (Years): 10/10
Avg. # Of Employees: 6 FT, 10 PT
Passive Ownership: Discouraged
Encourage Conversions: No
Area Develop. Agreements: Yes/2
Sub-Franchising Contracts: Yes
Expand In Territory: Yes
Space Needs: 1,400 SF; FS, SC

SUPPORT & TRAINING:
Financial Assistance Provided: No
Site Selection Assistance: Yes
Lease Negotiation Assistance: Yes

Co-Operative Advertising: Yes
Franchisee Assoc./Member: No
Size Of Corporate Staff: 10
On-Going Support: A,B,C,D,E,F,G,H,I
Training: 30 Days at Corporate Office; 1 - 2 Weeks Franchise Store.

SPECIFIC EXPANSION PLANS:
US: Southeast
Canada: No
Overseas: No

<< >>

LEDO PIZZA SYSTEM

2001 Tidewater Colony Way, # 203
Annapolis, MD 21401-2194
Tel: (410) 721-6887
Fax: (410) 266-6888
E-Mail: ledomarketing@ledomarketing.com
Web Site: www.ledopizza.com
Mr. Will Robinson, Director of Marketing

Ledo Pizza is a full service dining experience with a menu that features fresh salads, pastas, sandwiches, and our critically acclaimed Ledo Pizza.

BACKGROUND: IFA MEMBER
Established: 1955; 1st Franchised: 1989
Franchised Units: 51
Company-Owned Units: 0
Total Units: 51
Dist.: US-51; CAN-0; O'seas-0
North America: 5 States
Density: 41 in MD, 7 in VA, 2 in PA
Projected New Units (12 Months): NR
Qualifications: , , , , ,
Registered: NR

FINANCIAL/TERMS:
Cash Investment: $50-150K
Total Investment: $119-419K
Minimum Net Worth: Varies
Fees: Franchise - $20K
Royalty - 5%; Ad. - 2%
Earnings Claims Statement: No
Term of Contract (Years): 5/15
Avg. # Of Employees: 15 FT, 30 PT
Passive Ownership: Discouraged
Encourage Conversions: NR
Area Develop. Agreements: No
Sub-Franchising Contracts: No
Expand In Territory: Yes
Space Needs: 1,800+ SF; FS, SC, Hotels

SUPPORT & TRAINING:
Financial Assistance Provided: NR
Site Selection Assistance: Yes
Lease Negotiation Assistance: Yes
Co-Operative Advertising: Yes
Franchisee Assoc./Member: Yes/No
Size Of Corporate Staff: 12
On-Going Support: B,C,D,E,F,G,H
Training: Varies.

SPECIFIC EXPANSION PLANS:
US: NE, SE
Canada: NR
Overseas: NR

<< >>

LINDY - GERTIE'S

8437 Park Ave.
Burr Ridge, IL 60527
Tel: (630) 323-8003
Fax: (630) 323-5449
E-Mail: lyesutis@aol.com
Web Site: www.lindyschili.com
Mr. Joseph Yesutis, President

LINDY-GERTIE restaurants sell LINDY's chili, the oldest (established in 1924) chili parlor in Chicago, and GERTIE'S Ice Cream (the oldest ice cream parlor in Chicago, established in 1901).

BACKGROUND:
Established: 1986; 1st Franchised: 1987
Franchised Units: 9
Company-Owned Units: 0
Total Units: 9
Dist.: US-9; CAN-0; O'seas-0
North America: 1 State
Density: 10 in IL
Projected New Units (12 Months): 2
Qualifications: 4, 1, 1, 2, 4, 5
Registered: IL

FINANCIAL/TERMS:
Cash Investment: $40K
Total Investment: NR
Minimum Net Worth: $100K
Fees: Franchise - $9.5K
Royalty - 6%; Ad. - 2%
Earnings Claims Statement: No
Term of Contract (Years): 10/10
Avg. # Of Employees: 1 FT, 2 PT
Passive Ownership: Not Allowed
Encourage Conversions: Yes
Area Develop. Agreements: No
Sub-Franchising Contracts: No
Expand In Territory: Yes
Space Needs: NR SF; FS, SF, SC, RM

SUPPORT & TRAINING:
Financial Assistance Provided: Yes(I)
Site Selection Assistance: Yes
Lease Negotiation Assistance: Yes
Co-Operative Advertising: Yes
Franchisee Assoc./Member: No
Size Of Corporate Staff: 1
On-Going Support: D,E
Training: 1 Week 5858 S. Kedzie, Chicago, IL; 1 Week 3685 S. Archer, Chicago, IL.

SPECIFIC EXPANSION PLANS:
US: IL
Canada: No
Overseas: No

<< >>

LITTLE KING

11811 I St.
Omaha, NE 68137
Tel: (800) 788-9478 (402) 330-8019
Fax: (402) 330-3221
E-Mail: rw68137@aol.com
Web Site: www.littlekinginc.com
Mr. Bob B. Wertheim, President

Deli and sub restaurant, featuring fresh, fast-food concept - sandwiches. Products are prepared in full view of customers, breads are all baked fresh on premises. All meats are sliced fresh to order. Top-of-the-line food quality, utilizing major nationally known brands. Concept is adaptable to various locations and configurations.

BACKGROUND:
Established: 1968; 1st Franchised: 1978
Franchised Units: 30
Company-Owned Units: 0
Total Units: 30
Dist.: US-30; CAN-0; O'seas-0
North America: 5 States
Density: 29 in NE, 3 in IA, 2 in SD
Projected New Units (12 Months): 5-7
Qualifications: 5, 4, 4, 4, 1, 5
Registered: NR

FINANCIAL/TERMS:
Cash Investment: Varies
Total Investment: $75-95K
Minimum Net Worth: $100K
Fees: Franchise - $12K
Royalty - 6%; Ad. - 2.5%
Earnings Claims Statement: No
Term of Contract (Years): 10/10
Avg. # Of Employees: 1-3 FT, 6-9 PT
Passive Ownership: Discouraged
Encourage Conversions: Yes
Area Develop. Agreements: Yes
Sub-Franchising Contracts: No
Expand In Territory: Yes
Space Needs: 1,200-1,800 SF; FS, SF, SC

SUPPORT & TRAINING:
Financial Assistance Provided: Yes(I)
Site Selection Assistance: Yes
Lease Negotiation Assistance: Yes
Co-Operative Advertising: Yes
Franchisee Assoc./Member: No
Size Of Corporate Staff: 2

On-Going Support: B,C,E,F,G,H,I
Training: 15 Days Omaha, NE Headquarters; 8 Days On-Site; Follow Up Training as Needed.

SPECIFIC EXPANSION PLANS:
US: All United States
Canada: No
Overseas: No

<< >>

LONG JOHN SILVER'S

P. O. Box 34550, 1900 Colonel Sanders Ln.
Louisville, KY 40213
Tel: (866) 2YUM-YUM (502) 874-8300
Fax: (502) 874-8848
E-Mail: 2yumyum@yum.com
Web Site: www.yumfranchises.com
Ms. Nikki Weis, Franchise Coordinator

LONG JOHN SILVER'S is the largest, quick-service seafood restaurant chain in the world. We continue to aggressively grow with new units and sales. Opportunities are available in new and existing markets and with our sister brand, A & W in our new co-brand facilities.

BACKGROUND: IFA MEMBER
Established: 1969; 1st Franchised: 1969
Franchised Units: 537
Company-Owned Units: 698
Total Units: 1,235
Dist.: US-; CAN-; O'seas-
North America: 35 States
Density: 185 in TX, 114 in OH, 101 IN
Projected New Units (12 Months): NR
Qualifications: 5, 5, 3, 4, 5, 5
Registered: ALL

FINANCIAL/TERMS:
Cash Investment: NR
Total Investment: $1.0-1.3MM
Minimum Net Worth: $1MM
Fees: Franchise - $30-50K
Royalty - 6% Gr. Receipts; Ad. - 4% Gr. Rec.
Earnings Claims Statement: Yes
Term of Contract (Years): 20
Avg. # Of Employees: NR
Passive Ownership: Allowed
Encourage Conversions: NR
Area Develop. Agreements: NR
Sub-Franchising Contracts: No
Expand In Territory: Yes
Space Needs: NR SF; FS, C-Store, Food Court

SUPPORT & TRAINING:
Financial Assistance Provided: No
Site Selection Assistance: Yes
Lease Negotiation Assistance: NR
Co-Operative Advertising: Yes
Franchisee Assoc./Member: Yes
Size Of Corporate Staff: 300
On-Going Support: C,D,E,G,h,I
Training: 10-16 Weeks of Training.

SPECIFIC EXPANSION PLANS:
US: All United States
Canada: All Canada
Overseas: Asia, Europe, Caribbean, Latin America, Middle East

<< >>

MAGIC WOK

2060 Laskey Rd.
Toledo, OH 43613
Tel: (419) 471-0696
Fax: (419) 471-0405
E-Mail:
Web Site: www.worldfranchising.com/website.htm
Mr. Tommy Pipatjarasgit, Vice President

Quick-service, made-to-order, hot oriental concept. Stand alone, mall, drive-thru, delivery, school lunch and other non-traditional operations. Low barrier to entry, high return on investment. Domestic and international.

BACKGROUND:
Established: 1983; 1st Franchised: 1991
Franchised Units: 12
Company-Owned Units: 10
Total Units: 22
Dist.: US-11; CAN-0; O'seas-2
North America: 5 States
Density: 7 in OH, 3 in MI
Projected New Units (12 Months): 2
Qualifications: 3, 2, 2, 2, 2, 4
Registered: FL,IL,IN,MD,MI,VA

FINANCIAL/TERMS:
Cash Investment: $50K
Total Investment: $95-150K
Minimum Net Worth: $100K
Fees: Franchise - $12.5K
Royalty - 5%; Ad. - 3%
Earnings Claims Statement: No
Term of Contract (Years): 10/10
Avg. # Of Employees: 2 FT, 8 PT
Passive Ownership: Discouraged
Encourage Conversions: Yes
Area Develop. Agreements: Yes
Sub-Franchising Contracts: Yes
Expand In Territory: Yes
Space Needs: 1,600 SF; FS

SUPPORT & TRAINING:
Financial Assistance Provided: No
Site Selection Assistance: Yes
Lease Negotiation Assistance: Yes
Co-Operative Advertising: Yes
Franchisee Assoc./Member: No
Size Of Corporate Staff: 7
On-Going Support: C,D,E,F,H,I
Training: 3-4 Weeks Toledo, OH.

SPECIFIC EXPANSION PLANS:
US: Midwest
Canada: No
Overseas: Saudi Arabia, Mexico

<< >>

MAMMA ILARDO'S

3600 Clipper Mill Rd., # 260
Baltimore, MD 21211
Tel: (410) 662-1930
Fax: (410) 662-1936
E-Mail: john@mammailardos.com
Web Site: www.mammailardos.com
Mr. John A. Filipiak, VP Operations/Development

MAMMA ILARDO'S prepares fresh, delicious pizza. Choose from a variety of whole pies and pizza by the slice, featuring New York-style and our signature pan pizza. We offer great side items to complement our pizza, including calzones, pasta, salads and subs. Pizzeria and Express formats available -- no franchising fees, no royalty fees, no marketing fees.

BACKGROUND:
Established: 1976; 1st Franchised: 1984
Franchised Units: 48
Company-Owned Units: 2
Total Units: 50
Dist.: US-50; CAN-0; O'seas-0
North America: 16 States, DC
Density: 16 in MD, 6 in NV, 4 in NY
Projected New Units (12 Months): 40
Qualifications: 3, 4, 4, 4, 4, 5
Registered: NA

FINANCIAL/TERMS:
Cash Investment: $40-100K
Total Investment: $175-320K
Minimum Net Worth: $150K
Fees: Franchise - $0
Royalty - 0%; Ad. - 0%
Earnings Claims Statement: No
Term of Contract (Years): 10/10
Avg. # Of Employees: 8 FT, 10 PT

Passive Ownership: Discouraged
Encourage Conversions: Yes
Area Develop. Agreements: Yes/10
Sub-Franchising Contracts: Yes
Expand In Territory: Yes
Space Needs: 350-1,200 SF; SF, RM, Cart

SUPPORT & TRAINING:
Financial Assistance Provided: Yes(I)
Site Selection Assistance: Yes
Lease Negotiation Assistance: Yes
Co-Operative Advertising: NA
Franchisee Assoc./Member: No
Size Of Corporate Staff: 7
On-Going Support: B,C,D,E,F,G,H
Training: 3 Days to 3 Weeks at Corporate Office and Stores in Baltimore, MD.

SPECIFIC EXPANSION PLANS:
US: All United States
Canada: All Canada
Overseas: All Countries

MANCHU WOK (USA)

12912 Meadow Breeze Dr., # 2
Wellington, FL 33414
Tel: (800) 423-4009 (561) 798-7800
Fax: (561) 333-6663
E-Mail: david-gleason@manchuwok.com
Web Site: www.manchuwok.com
Mr. David Gleason, Non-Traditional Franchising

MANCHU WOK is one of the largest Chinese quick service franchises in North America. MANCHU WOK operates in over 225 food court locations in large regional malls. MANCHU WOK franchisees are enjoying profitable growth; many owning multiple locations.

BACKGROUND: IFA MEMBER
Established: 1980; 1st Franchised: 1980
Franchised Units: 142
Company-Owned Units: 47
Total Units: 189
Dist.: US-111; CAN-76; O'seas-2
North America: 28 States,10 Provinces
Density: 45 in ON, 14 in FL, 13 in IL
Projected New Units (12 Months): 40
Qualifications: 4, 4, 4, 3, 4, 4
Registered: All States and AB

FINANCIAL/TERMS:
Cash Investment: $100-150K
Total Investment: $265.5-316.75K
Minimum Net Worth: $100-150K
Fees: Franchise - $20K
Royalty - 7%; Ad. - 1%
Earnings Claims Statement: Yes
Term of Contract (Years): 5/5
Avg. # Of Employees: 2-3 FT, 6-10 PT
Passive Ownership: Discouraged
Encourage Conversions: Yes
Area Develop. Agreements: Yes
Sub-Franchising Contracts: No
Expand In Territory: Yes
Space Needs: 800 SF; RM

SUPPORT & TRAINING:
Financial Assistance Provided: Yes(I)
Site Selection Assistance: Yes
Lease Negotiation Assistance: Yes
Co-Operative Advertising: NA
Franchisee Assoc./Member: Yes
Size Of Corporate Staff: 500
On-Going Support: B,C,D,E,F,G,H,I
Training: 3-4 Weeks Corporate Site.

SPECIFIC EXPANSION PLANS:
US: Northeast, Southeast
Canada: All Canada
Overseas: No

MANNY AND OLGA'S PIZZA

13707 Northgate Dr.
Silver Spring, MD 20906
Tel: (866) 320-6542 (301) 588-2500
Fax: (301) 924-0081
E-Mail: bobby@mannyandolgas.com
Web Site: www.mannyandolgas.com
Mr. Bobby Athanasakis, President

MANNY AND OLGA'S PIZZA offers a full menu of pizza, subs, salads, pasta, wings, gyros and desserts - everything made fresh daily. Delivery or carry-out.

BACKGROUND:
Established: 1983; 1st Franchised: 1998
Franchised Units: 1
Company-Owned Units: 4
Total Units: 5
Dist.: US-5; CAN-0; O'seas-0
North America: 3 States
Density: NR
Projected New Units (12 Months): 4
Qualifications: 5, 2, 1, 3, 3, 3
Registered: MD,DC,VA

FINANCIAL/TERMS:
Cash Investment: $65K
Total Investment: $120-220K
Minimum Net Worth: $100K
Fees: Franchise - $25K
Royalty - 5%; Ad. - 4%
Earnings Claims Statement: No
Term of Contract (Years): 5/5
Avg. # Of Employees: 3 FT, 3 PT
Passive Ownership: Not Allowed
Encourage Conversions: Yes
Area Develop. Agreements: Yes/10
Sub-Franchising Contracts: Yes
Expand In Territory: Yes
Space Needs: 700 SF; FS, SF, SC, RM

SUPPORT & TRAINING:
Financial Assistance Provided: No
Site Selection Assistance: Yes
Lease Negotiation Assistance: Yes
Co-Operative Advertising: Yes
Franchisee Assoc./Member: No
Size Of Corporate Staff: 8
On-Going Support: E
Training: 5 Weeks Silver Spring, MD.

SPECIFIC EXPANSION PLANS:
US: Northeast
Canada: No
Overseas: No

Marco's Pizza

Top 100

MARCO'S PIZZA

5252 Monroe St.
Toledo, OH 43623
Tel: (800) 262-7267 (419) 885-7000
Fax: (419) 885-5215
E-Mail: lpalmer@marcos.com
Web Site: www.marcos.com
Ms. Lisa Palmer, Director Franchise Development

MARCO'S PIZZA offers pizza, hot sub sandwiches, Cheezybread, salad and soft drinks. There are 3 crust style - hand spun, pan and crispy thin, and 3 types of crust flavors - garlic butter, parmesan, and roma seasoning. MARCO'S PIZZA offers carry-out and fast, hot delivery.

BACKGROUND: IFA MEMBER
Established: 1978; 1st Franchised: 1979
Franchised Units: 89
Company-Owned Units: 40
Total Units: 129
Dist.: US-129; CAN-0; O'seas-0
North America: 4 States
Density: 98 in OH, 22 in MI, 7 in IN
Projected New Units (12 Months): 34
Qualifications: 5, 4, 3, 4, 3, 5
Registered: IN,MI,VA

FINANCIAL/TERMS:
Cash Investment: $60-75K
Total Investment: $118.5-204.5K
Minimum Net Worth: $100K
Fees: Franchise - $15K
Royalty - 3-5%; Ad. - 1%
Earnings Claims Statement: No
Term of Contract (Years): 10/10
Avg. # Of Employees: 4 FT, 15 PT
Passive Ownership: Not Allowed
Encourage Conversions: NA
Area Develop. Agreements: Yes/10
Sub-Franchising Contracts: No
Expand In Territory: Yes
Space Needs: 1,300-1,400 SF; SF, SC
SUPPORT & TRAINING:
Financial Assistance Provided: Yes(I)
Site Selection Assistance: Yes
Lease Negotiation Assistance: Yes
Co-Operative Advertising: Yes
Franchisee Assoc./Member: Yes
Size Of Corporate Staff: 40
On-Going Support: B,C,D,E,F,H,I
Training: 2 Weeks Toledo, OH; 6 Weeks in Store.
SPECIFIC EXPANSION PLANS:
US: Midwest
Canada: No
Overseas: No

MAUI TACOS
1775 The Exchange, # 600
Atlanta, GA 30339
Tel: (888) 628-4822 + 102 (770) 226-8226 + 102
Fax: (770) 541-2300
E-Mail: info@mauitacos.com
Web Site: www.mauitacos.com
Mr. Robert Sitkoff, President

Fast-casual "Maui-Mex" restaurant featuring Mexican Foods created by internationally recognized chef Mark Ellmao, using pineapple and lime juice marinade with island spices. Char-grilled chicken, steak, and lean beef burritos topped with unique salsas is our mainstay. This food experience is like a vacation in Maui.

BACKGROUND: IFA MEMBER
Established: 1993; 1st Franchised: 1998
Franchised Units: 10
Company-Owned Units: 1
Total Units: 11
Dist.: US-14; CAN-0; O'seas-0
North America: 2 States
Density: 8 in HI, 3 in GA
Projected New Units (12 Months): 20
Qualifications: 4, 4, 3, 3, 4, 4
Registered:CA,FL,HI,IN,MD,MI,MN,NY,ND,OR,RI,VA,WA,WI,DC
FINANCIAL/TERMS:
Cash Investment: $60-125K
Total Investment: $180-375K
Minimum Net Worth: $300K
Fees: Franchise - $20K
Royalty - 6%; Ad. - 4%
Earnings Claims Statement: Yes
Term of Contract (Years): 20/20
Avg. # Of Employees: 4 FT, 10 PT
Passive Ownership: Discouraged
Encourage Conversions: Yes
Area Develop. Agreements: Yes/50
Sub-Franchising Contracts: Yes
Expand In Territory: Yes
Space Needs: 2,000 SF; FS, SF,SC, RM, HB, Open Air
SUPPORT & TRAINING:
Financial Assistance Provided: Yes(I)
Site Selection Assistance: Yes
Lease Negotiation Assistance: Yes
Co-Operative Advertising: Yes
Franchisee Assoc./Member: Yes/Yes
Size Of Corporate Staff: 6
On-Going Support: A,B,C,D,E,F,G,h,I
Training: 160 Hours in Atlanta, GA.
SPECIFIC EXPANSION PLANS:
US: All United States
Canada: All Canada
Overseas: All Countries

MCDONALD'S
2911 Jorie Blvd.
Oak Brook, IL 60523-2114
Tel: (888) 800-7257 (630) 623-3403
Fax: (630) 623-5658
E-Mail: john.kujawa@mcd.com
Web Site: www.mcdonalds.com
Mr. John Kujawa, Vice President Franchising

Quick-service restaurant.

BACKGROUND: IFA MEMBER
Established: 1955; 1st Franchised: 1956
Franchised Units: 22,213
Company-Owned Units: 8,105
Total Units: 30,318
Dist.: US-13,638; CAN-1,354; O'seas-15,326
North America: 50 States
Density: 1,313 in CA, 1,038 TX,800 FL
Projected New Units (12 Months): NR
Qualifications: 3, 5, 3, 3, 4, 4
Registered: All States
FINANCIAL/TERMS:
Cash Investment: NR
Total Investment: $506K-1.63MM
Minimum Net Worth: NR
Fees: Franchise - $45K
Royalty - 12.5%; Ad. - 4%
Earnings Claims Statement: No
Term of Contract (Years): 20/20
Avg. # Of Employees: NR
Passive Ownership: Not Allowed
Encourage Conversions: NA
Area Develop. Agreements: No
Sub-Franchising Contracts: No
Expand In Territory: No
Space Needs: 2,000 SF; FS
SUPPORT & TRAINING:
Financial Assistance Provided: No
Site Selection Assistance: NA
Lease Negotiation Assistance: NA
Co-Operative Advertising: Yes
Franchisee Assoc./Member: Yes/Yes
Size Of Corporate Staff: NR
On-Going Support: B,C,D,E,G,H,I
Training: NR
SPECIFIC EXPANSION PLANS:
US: All United States
Canada: All Canada
Overseas: All Countries

MICHEL'S BAGUETTE
16251 Dallas Pkwy.
Addison, TX 75001
Tel: (972) 687-4091
Fax: (972) 687-4062
E-Mail: franchise@mmmuffins.com
Web Site: www.mmmuffins.com
Ms. Irene La Cota, Chief Executive Officer

European bakery/café, featuring authentic European breads, rolls, and pastries. In addition, we offer gourmet soups, salads, sandwiches, and hot entrees. We also serve a variety of beverages including espresso, gourmet coffee, teas and fruit juices. In addition to our full store, we have a "grab 'n' go" version as well.

BACKGROUND:
Established: 1980; 1st Franchised: 1984
Franchised Units: 13
Company-Owned Units: 5

Total Units: 18
Dist.: US-0; CAN-15; O'seas-0
North America: 3 Provinces
Density: 13 in ON, 3 in AB, 1 in BC
Projected New Units (12 Months): 10
Qualifications: 5, 4, 3, 3, 4, 5
Registered: AB

FINANCIAL/TERMS:
Cash Investment: $300K+
Total Investment: $750-800K
Minimum Net Worth: $500K
Fees: Franchise - $40K
Royalty - 6%; Ad. - 0.5%
Earnings Claims Statement: No
Term of Contract (Years): 10/10
Avg. # Of Employees: 10 FT, 8-12 PT
Passive Ownership: Not Allowed
Encourage Conversions: Yes
Area Develop. Agreements: Yes (Int'l.)
Sub-Franchising Contracts: Yes
Expand In Territory: Yes
Space Needs: 4,000 SF; SF, SC, RM

SUPPORT & TRAINING:
Financial Assistance Provided: No
Site Selection Assistance: Yes
Lease Negotiation Assistance: Yes
Co-Operative Advertising: Yes
Franchisee Assoc./Member: No
Size Of Corporate Staff: 35
On-Going Support: A,B,C,D,E,F,G,h
Training: 3 Months Toronto, ON or Dallas, TX.

SPECIFIC EXPANSION PLANS:
US: N/A
Canada: All Canada
Overseas: Middle East, Europe, South America

<< >>

MOE'S ITALIAN SANDWICHES

15 Constitution Dr., # 140
Bedford, NH 03110
Tel: (800) 588-6637 (603) 472-8008
Fax: (603) 218-6018
E-Mail: info@moesitaliansandwiches.com
Web Site: www.moesitaliansandwiches.com
Mr. Stanley R. DeLoid, President

High-quality sandwiches and soups, featuring our flagship sandwich 'The Original Moe.' We have a simple concept that has over 40 years of heritage in New England. Low overhead, turnkey system. Very flexible.

BACKGROUND:
Established: 1959; 1st Franchised: 1993
Franchised Units: 12
Company-Owned Units: 0
Total Units: 12
Dist.: US-12; CAN-0; O'seas-0
North America: 3 States
Density: 9 in NH, 2 in ME, 1 in MA
Projected New Units (12 Months): 2-5
Qualifications: 4, 4, 3, 3, 4, 5
Registered: None

FINANCIAL/TERMS:
Cash Investment: $30-50K
Total Investment: $60-100K
Minimum Net Worth: $250K
Fees: Franchise - $10K
Royalty - 5%; Ad. - 2%
Earnings Claims Statement: No
Term of Contract (Years): 10/5
Avg. # Of Employees: 2 FT, 4 PT
Passive Ownership: Discouraged
Encourage Conversions: Yes
Area Develop. Agreements: No
Sub-Franchising Contracts: No
Expand In Territory: Yes
Space Needs: 1,000-1,400 SF; SF, SC, RM

SUPPORT & TRAINING:
Financial Assistance Provided: Yes(I)
Site Selection Assistance: Yes
Lease Negotiation Assistance: Yes
Co-Operative Advertising: Yes
Franchisee Assoc./Member: No
Size Of Corporate Staff: 2
On-Going Support: C,D,E,F,G,H,I
Training: 2 Weeks in Store - Various Locations; 3 Days in Class.

SPECIFIC EXPANSION PLANS:
US: NE. Expansion Outside 2002
Canada: No
Overseas: No

<< >>

MR. GOODCENTS SUBS & PASTAS

8997 Commerce Dr.
DeSoto, KS 66018
Tel: (800) 648-2368 (913) 583-8400 + 216
Fax: (913) 583-3500
E-Mail: mbubien@mrgoodcents.com
Web Site: www.mrgoodcents.com
Ms. Margot A. Bubien, VP Franchise Development

Quick-service lunch and dinner restaurant, serving freshly sliced submarine sandwiches served on bread baked daily on premises, hot pasta dishes, delicious soups and fresh salads, quick-service restaurant for dine-in, carry-out, delivery or catering. Continued business consultant support and in-house 30-day training period.

BACKGROUND: IFA MEMBER
Established: 1989; 1st Franchised: 1990
Franchised Units: 136
Company-Owned Units: 4
Total Units: 140
Dist.: US-140; CAN-0; O'seas-0
North America: 13 States
Density: 43 in KS, 54 in MO, 8 in AZ
Projected New Units (12 Months): NR
Qualifications: 3, 3, 2, 2, 1, 5
Registered: All States

FINANCIAL/TERMS:
Cash Investment: $35-50K
Total Investment: $77-243K
Minimum Net Worth: NR
Fees: Franchise - $12.5K
Royalty - 5%; Ad. - 2.5%
Earnings Claims Statement: Yes
Term of Contract (Years): 10/10
Avg. # Of Employees: 1-3 FT, 10-20 PT
Passive Ownership: NA
Encourage Conversions: Yes
Area Develop. Agreements: Yes
Sub-Franchising Contracts: No
Expand In Territory: Yes
Space Needs: 1,500-2,000 SF; FS, SC

SUPPORT & TRAINING:
Financial Assistance Provided: Yes(I)
Site Selection Assistance: Yes
Lease Negotiation Assistance: Yes
Co-Operative Advertising: Yes
Franchisee Assoc./Member: No
Size Of Corporate Staff: 40
On-Going Support: A,B,C,D,E,F,G,H,I
Training: 30 Days DeSoto, KS.

SPECIFIC EXPANSION PLANS:
US: All United States
Canada: No
Overseas: No

<< >>

MR. HERO

5755 Granger Rd., # 200
Independence, OH 44131-1410
Tel: (800) 837-9599 (216) 398-1101
Fax: (216) 398-0707
E-Mail: rkrieger@mrhero.com
Web Site: www.mrhero.com
Mr. Bob Krieger, Director Franchise Development

MR. HERO®, known for cheesesteaks, burgers and subs, is an exciting alternative to the typical quick-service restaurant. The MR. HERO® difference centers on the food! MR HERO® has grilled food offerings, such as the signature Romanburgers and Ribeye Hero, the Grilled Chicken Philly, hot buttered cheesesteaks and Potato Waffer Fries. The extensive menu also boasts an assortment of deli subs, fresh salads, pasta and an array of sides and desserts. MR. HERO ® is Keepin' It Fresh!

BACKGROUND: IFA MEMBER
Established: 1969; 1st Franchised: 1969
Franchised Units: 107
Company-Owned Units: 13
Total Units: 120
Dist.: US-120; CAN-0; O'seas-0
North America: 7 States
Density: 112 in OH, 3 in NC, 2 in VA
Projected New Units (12 Months): 20
Qualifications: 5, 3, 3, 2, 5, 4
Registered: IL,IN,MD,MI,NY,VA,DC

FINANCIAL/TERMS:
Cash Investment: $40-75K
Total Investment: $75-300K
Minimum Net Worth: $250K
Fees: Franchise - $16.5K
Royalty - 5.5%; Ad. - 5%
Earnings Claims Statement: No
Term of Contract (Years): 20/20
Avg. # Of Employees: 4 FT, 8 PT
Passive Ownership: Discouraged
Encourage Conversions: Yes
Area Develop. Agreements: Yes/3-5
Sub-Franchising Contracts: Yes
Expand In Territory: Yes
Space Needs: 1,500 SF; FS, SF, SC, RM, Co-Brand

SUPPORT & TRAINING:
Financial Assistance Provided: Yes(I)
Site Selection Assistance: Yes
Lease Negotiation Assistance: Yes
Co-Operative Advertising: Yes
Franchisee Assoc./Member: No
Size Of Corporate Staff: 40
On-Going Support: A,B,C,D,E,F,G,H,I
Training: 4 Weeks Cleveland, OH.

SPECIFIC EXPANSION PLANS:
US: NE, E, SE, S, MW
Canada: No
Overseas: No

MR. JIM'S PIZZA

4276 Kellway Cir.
Addison, TX 75001
Tel: (800) 583-5960 (972) 267-5467
Fax: (972) 267-5463
E-Mail: randy@mrjimspizza.net
Web Site: www.mrjimspizza.net
Mr. Randall Wooley, Executive Director

Specializing in delivery and take-out operations. Low start-up cost of under $90,000, including franchise fee. Dallas, Ft. Worth's largest locally owned pizza franchise.

BACKGROUND:
Established: 1974; 1st Franchised: 1976
Franchised Units: 64
Company-Owned Units: 0
Total Units: 64
Dist.: US-64; CAN-0; O'seas-0
North America: NR
Density: 58 in TX, 2 in LA, 2 in VA
Projected New Units (12 Months): 6
Qualifications: 4, 4, 5, 2, 3, 4
Registered: OR,VA

FINANCIAL/TERMS:
Cash Investment: $50K
Total Investment: $56-108K
Minimum Net Worth: $100K
Fees: Franchise - $10K
Royalty - 5%; Ad. - 0%
Earnings Claims Statement: No
Term of Contract (Years): 15/15
Avg. # Of Employees: 5 FT, 15 PT
Passive Ownership: Discouraged
Encourage Conversions: Yes
Area Develop. Agreements: Yes
Sub-Franchising Contracts: No
Expand In Territory: Yes
Space Needs: 1,100 SF; SC

SUPPORT & TRAINING:
Financial Assistance Provided: No
Site Selection Assistance: Yes
Lease Negotiation Assistance: Yes
Co-Operative Advertising: Yes
Franchisee Assoc./Member: No
Size Of Corporate Staff: 6
On-Going Support: B,C,D,E,G,H
Training: 2 Months.

SPECIFIC EXPANSION PLANS:
US: All Except FL, MI
Canada: No
Overseas: No

MY FRIEND'S PLACE

904 Bombay Ln.
Roswell, GA 30076
Tel: (800) 882-9436 (770) 817-4200
Fax:
E-Mail: franchise@myfriendsplace.com
Web Site: www.my-friends-place.com
Mr. John Thomas, Dir. Franchise Sales

A quality franchise opportunity for your financial independence and future. Our restaurants cater to the quality-oriented customer interested in a quick, yet light and healthy lunch, specializing in sandwiches, salads, soups and home-made desserts. MY FRIEND'S PLACE is a 'Fresh Food Express!'

BACKGROUND:
Established: 1980; 1st Franchised: 1990
Franchised Units: 16
Company-Owned Units: 2
Total Units: 18
Dist.: US-13; CAN-0; O'seas-0
North America: 1 State
Density: 13 in GA
Projected New Units (12 Months): 4
Qualifications: 3, 4, 3, 3, 2, 5
Registered: NR

FINANCIAL/TERMS:
Cash Investment: $95-175K
Total Investment: $95-175K
Minimum Net Worth: $200K
Fees: Franchise - $17.5K
Royalty - Flat; Ad. - Flat
Earnings Claims Statement: No
Term of Contract (Years): 15/10
Avg. # Of Employees: 2 FT, 2 PT
Passive Ownership: Not Allowed
Encourage Conversions: Yes
Area Develop. Agreements: No
Sub-Franchising Contracts: Yes
Expand In Territory: Yes
Space Needs: 1,400 SF; SC, FS

SUPPORT & TRAINING:
Financial Assistance Provided: Yes(I)
Site Selection Assistance: Yes
Lease Negotiation Assistance: Yes
Co-Operative Advertising: Yes
Franchisee Assoc./Member: No
Size Of Corporate Staff: 4
On-Going Support: C,d,E,f
Training: 12 Business Days Headquarters; 12 Business Days Franchisee Site.

SPECIFIC EXPANSION PLANS:
US: SE Only, GA,FL,AL,IN,SC,TX
Canada: No
Overseas: No

NATHAN'S FAMOUS

1400 Old Country Rd., # 400
Westbury, NY 11590
Tel: (800) NATHANS (516) 338-8500
Fax: (516) 338-7220
E-Mail: cpaley@nathansfamous.com
Web Site: www.nathansfamous.com
Mr. Carl Paley, Senior Vice President

Fast-food restaurant, featuring premium-quality, all beef hot dogs, fresh-cut fries, plus a large variety of menu items - 9 prototypes, ranging from carts, counter modules, food courts and full-service restaurants. Franchise license and area development opportunities available worldwide.

BACKGROUND:

Established: 1916; 1st Franchised: 1979
Franchised Units: 165
Company-Owned Units: 9
Total Units: 174
Dist.: US-214; CAN-0; O'seas-0
North America: 37 States
Density: 27 in NY, 19 in NJ, 17 in FL
Projected New Units (12 Months): 35
Qualifications: 5, 3, 4, 2, 3, 5
Registered: CA,FL,HI,IL,IN,MD,MI,MN, NY,VA,WA,WI,DC

FINANCIAL/TERMS:

Cash Investment: $50-250K
Total Investment: $50-550K
Minimum Net Worth: $400K
Fees: Franchise - $15-30K
Royalty - 4.5%; Ad. - 2.5%
Earnings Claims Statement: No
Term of Contract (Years): 20/15
Avg. # Of Employees: 6-7 FT, 10-15 PT
Passive Ownership: Discouraged
Encourage Conversions: Yes
Area Develop. Agreements: Yes/Varies
Sub-Franchising Contracts: Yes
Expand In Territory: Yes
Space Needs: 500-2,500 SF; SF, RM

SUPPORT & TRAINING:

Financial Assistance Provided: Yes(I)
Site Selection Assistance: Yes
Lease Negotiation Assistance: Yes
Co-Operative Advertising: Yes
Franchisee Assoc./Member: No
Size Of Corporate Staff: 42
On-Going Support: B,C,D,E,F,G,H,I
Training: 2-4 Weeks in Long Island, NY and in Store.

SPECIFIC EXPANSION PLANS:

US: All United States
Canada: PQ, ON
Overseas: Europe, Asia

<< >>

NATURE'S TABLE

800 N. Magnolia Ave.
Orlando, FL 32803
Tel: (800) 222-6090 (407) 481-2544
Fax: (407) 843-6057
E-Mail: info@naturestable.com
Web Site: www.naturestable.com
Mr. Michael W. Karr, Franchise Agent

NATURE'S TABLE is an expanding Florida-based chain with 20 years of experience. Our menu features healthy food such as vegetarian chili, homemade soups, harvest salads, frozen yogurt, smoothies and a variety of sandwiches.

BACKGROUND:

Established: 1977; 1st Franchised: 1985
Franchised Units: 42
Company-Owned Units: 6
Total Units: 48
Dist.: US-48; CAN-0; O'seas-0
North America: 1 State
Density: 34 in FL
Projected New Units (12 Months): 12
Qualifications: 5, 3, 3, 4, 5, 4
Registered: FL,MD,MI,MN,VA,WI,DC

FINANCIAL/TERMS:

Cash Investment: $100-175K
Total Investment: $100-175K
Minimum Net Worth: $100K
Fees: Franchise - $25K
Royalty - 5%; Ad. - 1%
Earnings Claims Statement: No
Term of Contract (Years): 10/5
Avg. # Of Employees: 2 FT, 2-4 PT
Passive Ownership: Allowed
Encourage Conversions: NA
Area Develop. Agreements: Yes/10
Sub-Franchising Contracts: No
Expand In Territory: No
Space Needs: 500-750 SF; RM

SUPPORT & TRAINING:

Financial Assistance Provided: No
Site Selection Assistance: Yes
Lease Negotiation Assistance: Yes
Co-Operative Advertising: No
Franchisee Assoc./Member: Yes
Size Of Corporate Staff: 7
On-Going Support: C,D,E,F,G,h,I
Training: 2 Weeks Orlando, FL; On-Site.

SPECIFIC EXPANSION PLANS:

US: Southeast United States
Canada: No
Overseas: No

<< >>

NEW YORK BURRITO GOURMET WRAPS

300 International Pkwy., # 100
Heathrow, FL 32746
Tel: (800) 711-4036 (480) 503-3363
Fax: (480) 503-1850
E-Mail: bmendez@ufsi.net
Web Site: www.newyorkburrito.com
Ms. Beth Mendez, Marketing

Casual/up-scale, quick-serve restaurants serving multi-cultural gourmet wraps (burritos). Some restaurants feature breakfast, fruit smoothies, and/or beer and wine. Menu items prepared daily with the highest-quality and variety meats and veggies. Giant tortillas offered in a variety of flavors: tomato basil, whole wheat, spinach, jalapeno and white flour. Low start-up cost and ease of operation. Join the hottest new food trend of the 90s with the leader of the pack.

BACKGROUND:

Established: 1995; 1st Franchised: 1996
Franchised Units: 40
Company-Owned Units: 0
Total Units: 40
Dist.: US-79; CAN-0; O'seas-0
North America: 27 States
Density: 8 in CA, 8 in CO, 5 in UT
Projected New Units (12 Months): 15
Qualifications: 4, 4, 2, 3, 3, 4
Registered: CA,FL,IN,MI,MN,NY,OR,SD,WI

FINANCIAL/TERMS:

Cash Investment: $25-35K
Total Investment: $75-135K
Minimum Net Worth: Varies
Fees: Franchise - $15K
Royalty - 7%; Ad. - 2%
Earnings Claims Statement: No
Term of Contract (Years): Perpetual
Avg. # Of Employees: Varies
Passive Ownership: Discouraged
Encourage Conversions: NA
Area Develop. Agreements: Yes
Sub-Franchising Contracts: No
Expand In Territory: Yes
Space Needs: 1,500-2,500 SF; FS, SC, RM

SUPPORT & TRAINING:

Financial Assistance Provided: Yes
Site Selection Assistance: Yes
Lease Negotiation Assistance: Yes
Co-Operative Advertising: Yes
Franchisee Assoc./Member: No
Size Of Corporate Staff: 9+
On-Going Support: A,B,C,D,E,F,G,H,I
Training: 5 Days at Headquarters/Training Center; 5 Days at Franchise Store.

SPECIFIC EXPANSION PLANS:

US: All United States
Canada: All Except AB
Overseas: No

<< >>

OBEE'S SOUP-SALAD-SUBS

1777 Tamiami Trail, # 206
Port Charlotte, FL 33948
Tel: (866) 623-3462 (941) 625-0773
Fax: (941) 625-0052
E-Mail: dfuller@obees.com
Web Site: www.obees.com
Mr. Dennis G. Fuller, Executive Vice

President

World's greatest fresh food restaurant. Our subs are made from the highest quality meats, cheeses, and condiments available. The vegetables that go into our subs are sliced daily. We use real Italian break baked fresh daily. In addition to the mouth-watering subs, O'Bee's also offers a variety of soups, salads, desserts and soft drinks.

BACKGROUND: IFA MEMBER
Established: 1995; 1st Franchised: 2000
Franchised Units: 75
Company-Owned Units: 0
Total Units: 75
Dist.: US-75; CAN-0; O'seas-0
North America: 21 States
Density: 25 in FL, 18 in TX, 4 in CA
Projected New Units (12 Months): 60
Qualifications: , , , , ,
Registered: All States

FINANCIAL/TERMS:
Cash Investment: $30-40K
Total Investment: $100-138K
Minimum Net Worth: NR
Fees: Franchise - $20K
Royalty - 5-6%; Ad. - 2%
Earnings Claims Statement: No
Term of Contract (Years): 10/10
Avg. # Of Employees: 3 FT, 8 PT
Passive Ownership: Discouraged
Encourage Conversions: NR
Area Develop. Agreements: Yes/50
Sub-Franchising Contracts: No
Expand In Territory: Yes
Space Needs: 1,100-1,400 SF; SF, SC

SUPPORT & TRAINING:
Financial Assistance Provided: NR
Site Selection Assistance: Yes
Lease Negotiation Assistance: Yes
Co-Operative Advertising: Yes
Franchisee Assoc./Member: No
Size Of Corporate Staff: 19
On-Going Support: B,C,D,E,F,G,H,I
Training: 2 Weeks in Store; 1 Week HQ Classroom; 2 Weeks at Opening.

SPECIFIC EXPANSION PLANS:
US: All United States
Canada: No
Overseas: No

<< >>

ORION FOOD SYSTEMS

2930 W. Maple Ave., P.O. Box 780
Sioux Falls, SD 57101
Tel: (800) 648-6227 (605) 336-6961
Fax: (605) 336-0141
E-Mail: tom.kasper@orionfoodsys.com
Web Site: www.orionfoodsys.com
Mr. Tom Kasper, VP Franchise Development

Franchise offers 9 separate brands covering all popular fast food categories: HOT STUFF PIZZA, EDDIE PEPPERS GREAT AMERICAN, CINNAMON STREET BAKERY + COFFEE COMPANY, MEAN GENE'S BURGERS, MACGREGOR'S MARKET SUBS, SMASH HITS SUBS, JOEY PAGODA'S ORIENTAL EXPRESS, CHIX THE CHICKEN STATION.

BACKGROUND:
Established: 1984; 1st Franchised: 1986
Franchised Units: 1,058
Company-Owned Units: 7
Total Units: 1,065
Dist.: US-1,493; CAN-7; O'seas-1
North America: 50 States, 2 Provinces
Density: 89 in MN, 38 in SD, 34 in WI
Projected New Units (12 Months): 240
Qualifications: 4, 4, 4, 3, 3, 5
Registered: All States and AB

FINANCIAL/TERMS:
Cash Investment: $20K
Total Investment: $35-300K
Minimum Net Worth: $30K
Fees: Franchise - $0
Royalty - 0%; Ad. - 0%
Earnings Claims Statement: No
Term of Contract (Years): 5/5
Avg. # Of Employees: 4 FT, 10 PT
Passive Ownership: Allowed
Encourage Conversions: Yes
Area Develop. Agreements: No
Sub-Franchising Contracts: No
Expand In Territory: Yes
Space Needs: 700 SF; RM

SUPPORT & TRAINING:
Financial Assistance Provided: Yes(I)
Site Selection Assistance: Yes
Lease Negotiation Assistance: Yes
Co-Operative Advertising: No
Franchisee Assoc./Member: Yes/Yes
Size Of Corporate Staff: 700
On-Going Support: B,C,D,E,F,G,I
Training: 2 Weeks at New Franchisee's Site.

SPECIFIC EXPANSION PLANS:
US: All United States
Canada: All Canada
Overseas: No

<< >>

PASTEL'S CAFE

1121 Centre St. N., # 440
Calgary, AB T2E 7K6 CANADA
Tel: (800) 361-1151 (403) 230-1151
Fax: (403) 230-2182
E-Mail: info@comac.ca
Web Site: www.comac.ca
Mr. Andrew Alintino, Division Manager

PASTEL'S CAFE features a full menu of the finest-quality gourmet sandwiches, a mouth-watering array of specialty salads and hearty homemade soups, all prepared with FRESH, healthy ingredients and presented with style.

BACKGROUND:
Established: 1980; 1st Franchised: 1982
Franchised Units: 20
Company-Owned Units: 0
Total Units: 20
Dist.: US-0; CAN-20; O'seas-0
North America: 2 Provinces
Density: 15 in BC
Projected New Units (12 Months): 3
Qualifications: , , , , ,
Registered: AB

FINANCIAL/TERMS:
Cash Investment: $75-95K
Total Investment: $160-250K
Minimum Net Worth: $175K
Fees: Franchise - $25K
Royalty - 5%; Ad. - 0%
Earnings Claims Statement: Yes
Term of Contract (Years): 10/10
Avg. # Of Employees: 2 FT, 5 PT
Passive Ownership: Discouraged
Encourage Conversions: Yes
Area Develop. Agreements: No
Sub-Franchising Contracts: No
Expand In Territory: Yes
Space Needs: 1,100 SF; SF, SC, RM

SUPPORT & TRAINING:
Financial Assistance Provided: Yes(I)
Site Selection Assistance: Yes
Lease Negotiation Assistance: Yes
Co-Operative Advertising: Yes
Franchisee Assoc./Member: Yes
Size Of Corporate Staff: 12
On-Going Support: C,D,E,f,G,h
Training: 21 Days Comprehensive Hands-On Training.

SPECIFIC EXPANSION PLANS:
US: No
Canada: All Canada
Overseas: No

<< >>

PENN STATION/EAST COAST SUBS

8276 Beechmont Ave.
Cincinnati, OH 45255-3153
Tel: (513) 474-5957
Fax: (513) 474-7116
E-Mail:
Web Site: www.penn-station.com
Mr. Mark Partusch, Dir. Sales/Development

Retail sale of authentic 'East Coast-style' submarines, including the original Philadelphia cheesesteak, all prepared fresh before the customer. Fresh-cut fries, flash fried in peanut oil, and fresh-squeezed lemonade.

BACKGROUND:
Established: 1985; 1st Franchised: 1987
Franchised Units: 79
Company-Owned Units: 4
Total Units: 83
Dist.: US-70; CAN-0; O'seas-0
North America: 4 States
Density: 41 in OH, 14 in IN, 13 in KY
Projected New Units (12 Months): 25
Qualifications: 3, 5, 3, 4, 4, 5
Registered: IN

FINANCIAL/TERMS:
Cash Investment: $40-82.5K
Total Investment: $182.8-328.7K
Minimum Net Worth: Varies
Fees: Franchise - $17.5K
Royalty - 4-7.5%; Ad. - 1%
Earnings Claims Statement: Yes
Term of Contract (Years): 5/5/5/5
Avg. # Of Employees: 11 FT, 10 PT
Passive Ownership: Allowed
Encourage Conversions: No
Area Develop. Agreements: Yes
Sub-Franchising Contracts: No
Expand In Territory: Yes
Space Needs: 1,600-1,800 SF; FS, SC

SUPPORT & TRAINING:
Financial Assistance Provided: No
Site Selection Assistance: Yes
Lease Negotiation Assistance: Yes
Co-Operative Advertising: Yes
Franchisee Assoc./Member: Yes/Yes
Size Of Corporate Staff: 13
On-Going Support: C,D,E,F,G,H
Training: 2 Weeks Penn Station in Cincinnati, OH; 2-3 Days On-Site Training Prior to Grand Opening.

SPECIFIC EXPANSION PLANS:
US: Midwest, Southeast, South
Canada: No
Overseas: No

<< >>

PHILLY CONNECTION

120 Interstate N. Pkwy., E., # 112
Atlanta, GA 30339-2164
Tel: (800) 886-8826 (770) 952-6152
Fax: (770) 952-3168
E-Mail: phillyconnection@mindspring.com
Web Site: www.phillyconnection.com
Mr. John D. Pollock, SVP Franchise Development

Quick service restaurant and ice cream parlor. "The Cheesesteak Champion" serves fresh, high quality products prepared to order in front of customers. On premises, take out, drive though, delivery. May operate in strip shopping centers, convenience stores, free-standing buildings and "end cap" space. Franchisor helps in site location, lease negotiation, equipment purchasing, grand opening, initial and on-going training, toll free helpline.

BACKGROUND: IFA MEMBER
Established: 1984; 1st Franchised: 1987
Franchised Units: 119
Company-Owned Units: 1
Total Units: 120
Dist.: US-120; CAN-0; O'seas-0
North America: 7 States
Density: 68 in GA, 19 in TX, 10 in FL
Projected New Units (12 Months): 40
Qualifications: 4, 3, 3, 2, 2, 3
Registered: FL,IL,IN,VA

FINANCIAL/TERMS:
Cash Investment: $35-50K
Total Investment: $130-198.5K
Minimum Net Worth: $150K
Fees: Franchise - $20K
Royalty - 6%; Ad. - 4%
Earnings Claims Statement: No
Term of Contract (Years): 10/5
Avg. # Of Employees: 2 FT, 10 PT
Passive Ownership: Discouraged
Encourage Conversions: Yes
Area Develop. Agreements: Yes/15
Sub-Franchising Contracts: No
Expand In Territory: No
Space Needs: 1,100-1,600 SF; SC

SUPPORT & TRAINING:
Financial Assistance Provided: Yes(I)
Site Selection Assistance: Yes
Lease Negotiation Assistance: Yes
Co-Operative Advertising: Yes
Franchisee Assoc./Member: No
Size Of Corporate Staff: 15
On-Going Support: C,E,I
Training: 80 Hours Atlanta, GA.

SPECIFIC EXPANSION PLANS:
US: SE,TX,IL,VA,KY,IN,OH,NJ Only
Canada: No
Overseas: No

<< >>

PICKERMAN'S SOUP & SANDWICHES

5714 Nordic Dr., # 400
Cedar Falls, IA 50613-6958
Tel: (800) 273-2172 (319) 266-7141
Fax: (319) 277-1201
E-Mail: mark@pickermans.com
Web Site: www.pickermans.com
Mr. Mark Chiattello, Director Franchise Development

Pickerman's is a low investment, high-return restaurant that sells distinctive soups, sandwiches and salads. Our service fee is on 4% without hidden fees. We help keep your investment low by providing you with an efficient food system requiring minimal space and capital. The total investment range is generally between $165,000-$185,000.

BACKGROUND:
Established: 1998; 1st Franchised: 1998
Franchised Units: 39
Company-Owned Units: 0
Total Units: 39
Dist.: US-39; CAN-0; O'seas-0
North America: 8 States
Density: 12 in IA, 12 in IL, 5 in MN
Projected New Units (12 Months): 100
Qualifications: 2, 2, 1, 2, 3, 3
Registered: IL,MN

FINANCIAL/TERMS:
Cash Investment: $42-46K
Total Investment: $165-185K
Minimum Net Worth: NA
Fees: Franchise - $10K
Royalty - 4%; Ad. - 0%
Earnings Claims Statement: No
Term of Contract (Years): 10/10
Avg. # Of Employees: 2 FT, 10 PT
Passive Ownership: Discouraged
Encourage Conversions: Yes
Area Develop. Agreements: No
Sub-Franchising Contracts: No
Expand In Territory: Yes
Space Needs: 1,300-2,000 SF; SC, RM

SUPPORT & TRAINING:
Financial Assistance Provided: Yes(I)
Site Selection Assistance: Yes
Lease Negotiation Assistance: Yes
Co-Operative Advertising: No
Franchisee Assoc./Member: No
Size Of Corporate Staff: 24
On-Going Support: C,D,E,G

Training: 1 Week Corporate Office; 1 Week Another Store; 1 Week Franchisee's Store.

SPECIFIC EXPANSION PLANS:

US: Midwest
Canada: No
Overseas: No

<< >>

PIZZA FACTORY

P. O. Box 989, 49430 Road 426, # D
Oakhurst, CA 93644
Tel: (800) 654-4840 (559) 683-3377
Fax: (559) 683-6879
E-Mail: pfinc@sierratel.com
Web Site: www.pizzafactoryinc.com
Ms. Nikki Van Velson, Operations Director

'We Toss 'em, They're Awesome.' PIZZA FACTORY has a proven track record with 107 restaurants in 12 states, The franchisee has a strong support system which includes site location, lease negotiating, on-site training and on-going support from headquarters. Call for brochure. Serving homemade pizza, pasta, sandwiches, beer and wine.

BACKGROUND:

Established: 1979; 1st Franchised: 1985
Franchised Units: 116
Company-Owned Units: 0
Total Units: 116
Dist.: US-197; CAN-0; O'seas-8
North America: 12 States
Density: 61 in CA, 17 in WA, 10 in ID
Projected New Units (12 Months): 10
Qualifications: 5, 4, 4, 2, 2, 3
Registered: AZ,CA,CO,FL,ID,MN,OR,SD,WA

FINANCIAL/TERMS:

Cash Investment: $65-80K
Total Investment: $70-262K
Minimum Net Worth: $150K
Fees: Franchise - $20K
Royalty - 5%; Ad. - 2%
Earnings Claims Statement: No
Term of Contract (Years): 20
Avg. # Of Employees: 3 FT, 12-15 PT
Passive Ownership: Allowed
Encourage Conversions: Yes
Area Develop. Agreements: Yes/Varies
Sub-Franchising Contracts: No
Expand In Territory: Yes
Space Needs: 200-1,500 Var SF; SC

SUPPORT & TRAINING:

Financial Assistance Provided: No
Site Selection Assistance: Yes
Lease Negotiation Assistance: Yes
Co-Operative Advertising: Yes
Franchisee Assoc./Member: NR
Size Of Corporate Staff: 7
On-Going Support: C,D,E,G,H,I
Training: 325 Hours Training Stores, Training Fee: $2,500.

SPECIFIC EXPANSION PLANS:

US: All United States
Canada: All Canada
Overseas: All Countries; China

<< >>

PIZZA INN

3551 Plano Pkwy.
The Colony, TX 75056
Tel: (800) 284-3466 (469) 384-5250
Fax: (469) 384-5062
E-Mail: fran_opps@pizzainn.com
Web Site: www.pizzainn.com
Mr. Ward Olgreen, SVP Franchise Operations

For Pizza Out, it's PIZZA INN! Our variety of great pizzas, pasta, salad, sandwiches and dessert pizza options will bring customers to your door! PIZZA INN has franchise opportunities for single and multiple locations in the Southeast US. We offer a reasonable, well-structured franchise program with a comprehensive training program and on-going marketing and operational support for our Buffet, Delivery/Carry-Out and Express restaurants. Join our team-we're right beside you.

BACKGROUND: IFA MEMBER

Established: 1960; 1st Franchised: 1963
Franchised Units: 405
Company-Owned Units: 2
Total Units: 407
Dist.: US-342; CAN-0; O'seas-65
North America: 19 States
Density: 114 in TX, 55 in NC, 26 MS
Projected New Units (12 Months):
Qualifications: , , , , ,
Registered:

FINANCIAL/TERMS:

Cash Investment: $50-125K
Total Investment: $49K-1.3MM
Minimum Net Worth: $100-200K
Fees: Franchise - $5-20K
Royalty - 4-6%; Ad. - 1%
Earnings Claims Statement: No
Term of Contract (Years): 10-20/10
Avg. # Of Employees: Depends
Passive Ownership: Allowed
Encourage Conversions:
Area Develop. Agreements: Yes
Sub-Franchising Contracts: Yes
Expand In Territory: Yes
Space Needs: Varies SF; FS, C-Store

SUPPORT & TRAINING:

Financial Assistance Provided:
Site Selection Assistance: Yes
Lease Negotiation Assistance: Yes
Co-Operative Advertising: Yes
Franchisee Assoc./Member: Yes/No
Size Of Corporate Staff: NR
On-Going Support: B,C,D,E,F,G,h,I
Training: 24 Days - MIT Class The Colony, TX; 5 days - Express Class, The Colony, TX

SPECIFIC EXPANSION PLANS:

US: Southeast and Southwest
Canada: NR
Overseas: NR

PIZZA MAN

6930 1/2 Tujunga Ave.
North Hollywood, CA 91605
Tel: (818) 766-4395
Fax: (818) 766-1496
E-Mail: ecfpizaman@aol.com
Web Site: www.worldfranchising.com/website.htm
Mr. Robert Ohanian, President/CEO

Pizza, chicken, ribs, Italian dishes. Delivery and fast food.

BACKGROUND:

Established: 1964; 1st Franchised: 1973
Franchised Units: 48
Company-Owned Units: 0
Total Units: 48
Dist.: US-50; CAN-0; O'seas-0
North America: 1 State
Density: 50 in CA
Projected New Units (12 Months): 3
Qualifications: 3, 5, 5, 4, 5, 5
Registered: All States

FINANCIAL/TERMS:

Cash Investment: $70K
Total Investment: $100K
Minimum Net Worth: $150K
Fees: Franchise - $25K
Royalty - 4%/$140/Wk.; Ad. - 4%/$140/Wk.
Earnings Claims Statement: No
Term of Contract (Years): 1+/1+
Avg. # Of Employees: 3 FT, 2 PT
Passive Ownership: Discouraged
Encourage Conversions: Yes
Area Develop. Agreements: Yes/2
Sub-Franchising Contracts: No
Expand In Territory: Yes
Space Needs: 1,000 SF; SF, SC

SUPPORT & TRAINING:
Financial Assistance Provided: Yes(I)
Site Selection Assistance: Yes
Lease Negotiation Assistance: Yes
Co-Operative Advertising: Yes
Franchisee Assoc./Member: No
Size Of Corporate Staff: 8
On-Going Support: b,C,D,e,f,H
Training: 3 Weeks Los Angeles, CA.
SPECIFIC EXPANSION PLANS:
US: All United States
Canada: All Canada
Overseas: All Countries

<< >>

PIZZA PIZZA INTERNATIONAL

580 Jarvis St.
Toronto, ON M4Y 2H9 CANADA
Tel: (800) 263-5556 (416) 967-1010
Fax: (416) 967-9865
E-Mail: sfuschini@pizzapizza.ca
Web Site: www.pizzapizza.ca
Mr. Sebastian Fushini, VP Franchising

In business over 34 years and established as Ontario's market leader in QSR sector specializing in pizza, chicken and oven-baked sandwiches. Offering state-of-the-art order processing systems, top-ranked training programs and marketing strategies that are second to none.

BACKGROUND:
Established: 1968; 1st Franchised: 1974
Franchised Units: 212
Company-Owned Units: 122
Total Units: 334
Dist.: US-0; CAN-324; O'seas-0
North America: 2 Provinces
Density: 318 in ON, 6 in PQ
Projected New Units (12 Months): 7
Qualifications: 3, 1, 4, 3, 4, 5
Registered: OR
FINANCIAL/TERMS:
Cash Investment: $50-100K
Total Investment: $100-400K
Minimum Net Worth: $200K
Fees: Franchise - $30K
Royalty - 6%; Ad. - 6%
Earnings Claims Statement: No
Term of Contract (Years): 5/5
Avg. # Of Employees: 4 FT, 6 PT
Passive Ownership: Discouraged
Encourage Conversions: NA
Area Develop. Agreements: No
Sub-Franchising Contracts: No
Expand In Territory: Yes
Space Needs: 2,300 SF; FS,SF,SC,RM
SUPPORT & TRAINING:
Financial Assistance Provided: Yes(I)
Site Selection Assistance: Yes
Lease Negotiation Assistance: NA
Co-Operative Advertising: Yes
Franchisee Assoc./Member: No
Size Of Corporate Staff: 200+
On-Going Support: A,B,C,D,E,F,G,h,I
Training: 12 Weeks Toronto, Ontario.
SPECIFIC EXPANSION PLANS:
US: N/A
Canada: Ontario
Overseas: No

<< >>

PIZZA PRO

2107 North 2nd St., P.O. Box 1285
Cabot, AR 72023
Tel: (800) 777-7554 (501) 605-1175
Fax: (501) 605-1204
E-Mail: scott@pizzapro.com
Web Site: www.pizzapro.com
Ms. Katy Brown, Franchise Services

Our goal at PIZZA PRO is to offer the highest quality food product and customer satisfaction at the best possible price. PIZZA PRO was founded in 1985 by its current President, Scott Stevens, while in search of a higher quality, more superior product over that of the national chains. Constant research and development keep that consistent and superior quality product today.

BACKGROUND:
Established: 1985; 1st Franchised: 1992
Franchised Units: 438
Company-Owned Units: 9
Total Units: 447
Dist.: US-447; CAN-0; O'seas-0
North America: 15 States
Density: 135 in AR, 125 in TX, 41 MO
Projected New Units (12 Months): 125
Qualifications: 4, 4, 3, 1, 3, 5
Registered: CA,FL,IL,SD
FINANCIAL/TERMS:
Cash Investment: $8-75K
Total Investment: Varies
Minimum Net Worth: Varies
Fees: Franchise - $2-5K
Royalty - 5%; Ad. - 2%
Earnings Claims Statement: No
Term of Contract (Years): 10/10
Avg. # Of Employees: Varies
Passive Ownership: Discouraged
Encourage Conversions: Yes
Area Develop. Agreements: Yes/10
Sub-Franchising Contracts: Yes
Expand In Territory: Yes
Space Needs: Varies SF; Varies
SUPPORT & TRAINING:
Financial Assistance Provided: No
Site Selection Assistance: No
Lease Negotiation Assistance: No
Co-Operative Advertising: No
Franchisee Assoc./Member: No
Size Of Corporate Staff: NR
On-Going Support: d,E,G,I
Training: 14 Days Cabot, AR.
SPECIFIC EXPANSION PLANS:
US: All United States
Canada: No
Overseas: No

PIZZA RANCH, THE

1121 Main St., Box 823
Hull, IA 51239
Tel: (800) 321-3401 (712) 439-1150
Fax: (712) 439-1125
E-Mail: jmoss@pizzaranch.com
Web Site: www.pizzaranch.com
Mr. John Moss, Dir. Advert./Marketing

THE PIZZA RANCH is a family restaurant, specializing in pizza, pasta and chicken.

BACKGROUND:
Established: 1981; 1st Franchised: 1984
Franchised Units: 95
Company-Owned Units: 0
Total Units: 95
Dist.: US-85; CAN-0; O'seas-0
North America: 6 States
Density: 40 in IA, 20 in MN, 16 in SD
Projected New Units (12 Months): 12
Qualifications: 3, 3, 3, 3, 2, 5
Registered: IL,MI,MN,ND,SD, WI
FINANCIAL/TERMS:
Cash Investment: $20-50K
Total Investment: $200-500K
Minimum Net Worth: $25K
Fees: Franchise - $10K
Royalty - 4%; Ad. - $1.7-2.2K
Earnings Claims Statement: No
Term of Contract (Years): 10/10/10
Avg. # Of Employees: 2 FT, 20 PT
Passive Ownership: Allowed
Encourage Conversions: Yes
Area Develop. Agreements: Yes
Sub-Franchising Contracts: Yes
Expand In Territory: Yes
Space Needs: 4,000 SF; Any
SUPPORT & TRAINING:
Financial Assistance Provided: Yes(I)
Site Selection Assistance: Yes
Lease Negotiation Assistance: Yes

Co-Operative Advertising: Yes
Franchisee Assoc./Member: No
Size Of Corporate Staff: 15
On-Going Support: C,D,E,F,G,H,I
Training: 2 Weeks Sioux Center, IA.; 1 Week On-Site.

SPECIFIC EXPANSION PLANS:
US: Midwest
Canada: No
Overseas: No

PIZZA ROYALE

650 Graham Bell, # 217
Sainte-Foy, PQ G1N 4H5 CANADA
Tel: (418) 682-5744
Fax: (418) 682-2684
E-Mail: administration@pizzaroyale.com
Web Site: www.pizzaroyale.com
Mr. Rejean Samson, President

PIZZA ROYALE is a chain of Italian restaurants, specializing in pizza cooked in an open wood oven fire in the serving area. It also offers a salad bar and a pasta bar. Take-out orders and delivery are also available. Healthy food and warm atmosphere are the main features of a concept that has proven successful over the years.

BACKGROUND:
Established: 1980; 1st Franchised: 1985
Franchised Units: 7
Company-Owned Units: 3
Total Units: 10
Dist.: US-0; CAN-10; O'seas-0
North America: 1 Province
Density: 10 in PQ
Projected New Units (12 Months): 1
Qualifications: , , , , ,
Registered: NR

FINANCIAL/TERMS:
Cash Investment: $100-125K
Total Investment: $250-300K
Minimum Net Worth: NR
Fees: Franchise - $30K
Royalty - 4%; Ad. - 2%
Earnings Claims Statement: NR
Term of Contract (Years): 10/10
Avg. # Of Employees: 20 FT, 5 PT
Passive Ownership: Discouraged
Encourage Conversions: Yes
Area Develop. Agreements: Yes
Sub-Franchising Contracts: No
Expand In Territory: Yes
Space Needs: 3,500 SF; FS, SC, RM

SUPPORT & TRAINING:
Financial Assistance Provided: Yes(I)
Site Selection Assistance: Yes
Lease Negotiation Assistance: Yes
Co-Operative Advertising: Yes
Franchisee Assoc./Member: NR
Size Of Corporate Staff: 6
On-Going Support: B,C,d,E,F,H
Training: 2 Weeks Headquarters; 2 Weeks On-Site.

SPECIFIC EXPANSION PLANS:
US: NE, Master Franchises Avail.
Canada: PQ, ON, Master
Overseas: No

<< >>

POPEYES CHICKEN & BISCUITS

5555 Glenridge Connector NE, # 300
Atlanta, GA 30342-4759
Tel: (800) 639-3780 (404) 459-4450
Fax: (404) 459-4523
E-Mail: popeyesfranchising@afce.com
Web Site: www.popeyesfranchising.com
Ms. Diane Phibbs, Business Development

POPEYES CHICKEN & BISCUITS, the world's second-largest chicken chain, is owned by AFC Enterprises, Inc., one of the world's largest restaurant parent companies and the winner of the 1997 MUFSO Operator of the Year and Golden Chain awards. POPEYES is famous for its New Orleans-style chicken, buttermilk biscuits and signature side items. The brand name has a presence in 41 states and 20 countries worldwide. 1999 system sales were more than $1 billion.

BACKGROUND: IFA MEMBER
Established: 1972; 1st Franchised: 1976
Franchised Units: 1,664
Company-Owned Units: 95
Total Units: 1,759
Dist.: US-945; CAN-12; O'seas-257
North America: 41 States, 2 Provinces
Density: NR
Projected New Units (12 Months): 120
Qualifications: 5, 4, 5, 3, , 3
Registered: All States

FINANCIAL/TERMS:
Cash Investment: $600K
Total Investment: $500K-1.2MM
Minimum Net Worth: $1.2MM
Fees: Franchise - $20K
Royalty - 5%; Ad. - 3%
Earnings Claims Statement: No
Term of Contract (Years): 20/10
Avg. # Of Employees: 15-25 FT
Passive Ownership: Discouraged
Encourage Conversions: Yes
Area Develop. Agreements: Varies
Sub-Franchising Contracts: No
Expand In Territory: Yes
Space Needs: 2,200 SF; FS, SC, RM, Airport, Univer.

SUPPORT & TRAINING:
Financial Assistance Provided: Yes(I)
Site Selection Assistance: Yes
Lease Negotiation Assistance: Yes
Co-Operative Advertising: Yes
Franchisee Assoc./Member: Yes/Yes
Size Of Corporate Staff: NR
On-Going Support: B,C,D,E,F,G,H,I
Training: 4 Weeks Atlanta, GA.

SPECIFIC EXPANSION PLANS:
US: All United States
Canada: All Canada
Overseas: All Countries

PORT OF SUBS

5365 Mae Anne Ave., # A-29
Reno, NV 89523-1840
Tel: (800) 245-0245 (775) 747-0555
Fax: (775) 747-1510
E-Mail: vcrisologo@portofsubs.com
Web Site: www.portofsubs.com
Ms. Victoria Crisologo, Development Coordinator

Port of Subs is an established fast-casual submarine sandwich chain with over 30 years of proven operating systems. Port of Subs specializes in fresh, quality, deli-style products and sandwiches. We serve breakfast, lunch and dinner, and offer catering and special event planning. We offer an assortment of made-to-order submarine type sandwiches, hot sandwiches, salads, pastries, party platters, beverages and other quick service food items for the on-premises consumption or take-out.

BACKGROUND: IFA MEMBER
Established: 1975; 1st Franchised: 1985
Franchised Units: 120
Company-Owned Units: 19
Total Units: 139
Dist.: US-139; CAN-0; O'seas-0
North America: 5 States
Density: 69 in NV, 45 in CA, 11 in AZ
Projected New Units (12 Months): 25
Qualifications: , , , , ,
Registered: CA,HI,WA

FINANCIAL/TERMS:
Cash Investment: $75-80K
Total Investment: $181.8-270.5K

Minimum Net Worth: $250K
Fees: Franchise - $16K
Royalty - 5.5%; Ad. - 1%
Earnings Claims Statement: No
Term of Contract (Years): 10/10
Avg. # Of Employees: 2-3 FT, 6-7 PT
Passive Ownership: Discouraged
Encourage Conversions: Yes
Area Develop. Agreements: Yes/Varies
Sub-Franchising Contracts: No
Expand In Territory: Yes
Space Needs: 1,200-1,500 SF; SF, SC, Power Center

SUPPORT & TRAINING:
Financial Assistance Provided: No
Site Selection Assistance: Yes
Lease Negotiation Assistance: Yes
Co-Operative Advertising: Yes
Franchisee Assoc./Member: Yes
Size Of Corporate Staff: 27
On-Going Support: A,B,C,D,E,F,G,H,I
Training: 3 Weeks Reno, NV.

SPECIFIC EXPANSION PLANS:
US: W, NW, SW
Canada: No
Overseas: No

PUDGIE'S FAMOUS CHICKEN

5 Dakota Dr., # 302
Lake Success, NY 11042
Tel: (516) 358-0600
Fax: (516) 358-5076
E-Mail: abernstein@trufoods.com
Web Site: www.trufoods.com
Mr. Alan J. Bernstein, Concept Director

Skinless fried chicken. Please see our Website at www.trufoods.com for more information.

BACKGROUND: IFA MEMBER
Established: 1981; 1st Franchised: 1981
Franchised Units: 29
Company-Owned Units: 0
Total Units: 29
Dist.: US-28; CAN-0; O'seas-1
North America: 3 States
Density: 24 in NY, 3 in NJ, 1 in CT
Projected New Units (12 Months): 20
Qualifications: 5, 4, 4, 2, 3, 5
Registered: NY

FINANCIAL/TERMS:
Cash Investment: $75-100K
Total Investment: $175-225K
Minimum Net Worth: $250K
Fees: Franchise - $30K
Royalty - 5%; Ad. - 3%
Earnings Claims Statement: Yes
Term of Contract (Years): 10/10
Avg. # Of Employees: 4 FT, 6 PT
Passive Ownership: Discouraged
Encourage Conversions: Yes
Area Develop. Agreements: Yes
Sub-Franchising Contracts: No
Expand In Territory: Yes
Space Needs:1,000-1,200 SF; SF, SC, Shop Ctr.

SUPPORT & TRAINING:
Financial Assistance Provided: Yes(I)
Site Selection Assistance: Yes
Lease Negotiation Assistance: Yes
Co-Operative Advertising: Yes
Franchisee Assoc./Member: Yes/Yes
Size Of Corporate Staff: 50
On-Going Support: A,B,C,D,E,F,G,H,I
Training: 1 Week - 10 Days Long Island, NY.

SPECIFIC EXPANSION PLANS:
US: Northeast, Southeast
Canada: No
Overseas: No

QUIZNOS SUB

1475 Lawrence St., # 400
Denver, CO 80202
Tel: (800) 335-4782 (720) 359-3300
Fax: (720) 359-3393
E-Mail: hstarr@quiznos.com
Web Site: www.quiznos.com
Ms. Heather Starr, Logistics Manager

Toasted subs are the key to QUIZNOS SUB's success. QUIZNOS SUB is dedicated to growing the brand by building financially successful franchises and serving the best sub sandwich in the market.

BACKGROUND: IFA MEMBER
Established: 1981; 1st Franchised: 1984
Franchised Units: 3,241
Company-Owned Units: 12
Total Units: 3,253
Dist.: US-2,921; CAN-285; O'seas-47
North America: 50 States, 6 Provinces
Density: 437 in CA, 265 in TX, 187 in
Projected New Units (12 Months): 400
Qualifications: 5, 4, 2, 2, 2, 5
Registered: All States

FINANCIAL/TERMS:
Cash Investment: $70K
Total Investment: $176-227K
Minimum Net Worth: $125K
Fees: Franchise - $25K
Royalty - 7%; Ad. - 4%
Earnings Claims Statement: No
Term of Contract (Years): 7/7
Avg. # Of Employees: 15-20 FT
Passive Ownership: Discouraged
Encourage Conversions: Yes
Area Develop. Agreements: Varies
Sub-Franchising Contracts: Yes
Expand In Territory: Yes
Space Needs: 1,200-1,800 SF; FS, SF, SC, RM

SUPPORT & TRAINING:
Financial Assistance Provided: Yes(I)
Site Selection Assistance: Yes
Lease Negotiation Assistance: Yes
Co-Operative Advertising: Yes
Franchisee Assoc./Member: Yes
Size Of Corporate Staff: 485
On-Going Support: E,G,H,I
Training: 3 Weeks Regional Market; 1 Week Corporate Office Denver, CO.

SPECIFIC EXPANSION PLANS:
US: All US, Limited in MD and S. CA.
Canada: All Canada
Overseas: All Countries

RANCH *1

7730 E. Greenway Rd., # 104
Scottsdale, AZ 85260
Tel: (800) 438-2590 (480) 443-0200
Fax: (480) 443-1972
E-Mail: sjlacroix@kahalacorp.com
Web Site: www.kahalacorp.com
Ms. Stephanie J. LaCroix, VP Franchise Sales

Up-scale - QSR features - fresh, never-frozen, grilled chicken sandwiches, salads, pasta and wraps.

BACKGROUND: IFA MEMBER
Established: 1993; 1st Franchised: 1993
Franchised Units: 43
Company-Owned Units: 3
Total Units: 46
Dist.: US-35; CAN-0; O'seas-0
North America: 3 States
Density: 32 in NY, 2 in MD, 1 in CA
Projected New Units (12 Months): 25
Qualifications: 4, 4, 5, 1, 3, 4
Registered: All States and AB

FINANCIAL/TERMS:
Cash Investment: $150-200K
Total Investment: $200-350K
Minimum Net Worth: $200K
Fees: Franchise - $40K
Royalty - 5%; Ad. - 3%
Earnings Claims Statement: No
Term of Contract (Years): 15/5
Avg. # Of Employees: 3 FT, 20 PT
Passive Ownership: Discouraged

Encourage Conversions: Yes
Area Develop. Agreements: Yes/3
Sub-Franchising Contracts: No
Expand In Territory: No
Space Needs: 1,500-2,000 SF; FS, SF, SC, RM

SUPPORT & TRAINING:
Financial Assistance Provided: Yes(I)
Site Selection Assistance: Yes
Lease Negotiation Assistance: No
Co-Operative Advertising: Yes
Franchisee Assoc./Member: Yes/Yes
Size Of Corporate Staff: 34
On-Going Support: C,D,E,F,G,H,I
Training: 6 Weeks at New York Ranch *1; 2 Weeks on Site.

SPECIFIC EXPANSION PLANS:
US: All United States
Canada: All Canada
Overseas: Europe, Asia

RENZIOS

4690 S. Yosemite St.
Greenwood Village, CO 80111-1227
Tel: (303) 267-0300
Fax: (303) 267-0088
E-Mail:
Web Site: www.renzios.com
Mr. Thomas D. Rentzios, President

You don't have to be Greek to own this unique, fast-service Greek restaurant franchise, operating in a variety of locations such as regional mall food courts, strip centers and gas stations, with future plans in airports and free-standing. RENZIOS fills the gap between fast-food and full-service restaurants. Designed to be easily operated with minimum staff and minimum restaurant experience. Featuring the best all beef or chicken gyros pitas.

BACKGROUND:
Established: 1986; 1st Franchised: 1993
Franchised Units: 9
Company-Owned Units: 9
Total Units: 18
Dist.: US-25; CAN-0; O'seas-0
North America: 8 States
Density: 10 in CO, 2 in NV, 4 in TX
Projected New Units (12 Months): 30
Qualifications: 5, 5, 1, 3, 5, 5
Registered: None

FINANCIAL/TERMS:
Cash Investment: $60K
Total Investment: $130-199K
Minimum Net Worth: $100K
Fees: Franchise - $15K
Royalty - 5%; Ad. - 2%
Earnings Claims Statement: No
Term of Contract (Years): 10/5/5
Avg. # Of Employees: 3 FT, 5 PT
Passive Ownership: Discouraged
Encourage Conversions: Yes
Area Develop. Agreements: Yes/10
Sub-Franchising Contracts: No
Expand In Territory: Yes
Space Needs: 500-800 SF; SC, RM

SUPPORT & TRAINING:
Financial Assistance Provided: Yes(I)
Site Selection Assistance: Yes
Lease Negotiation Assistance: Yes
Co-Operative Advertising: Yes
Franchisee Assoc./Member: No
Size Of Corporate Staff: 8
On-Going Support: B,C,D,E,F,G,H,I
Training: 21 Days Corporate Training Center; 5 Days On-Location.

SPECIFIC EXPANSION PLANS:
US: All United States
Canada: All Canada
Overseas: No

ROLI BOLI

109 Main St.
Sayreville, NJ 08872
Tel: (732) 257-8100
Fax: (732) 257-3255
E-Mail:
Web Site: www.worldfranchising.com/website.htm
Mr. Anthony Felicetta, President

Specialty sandwich - combines a french bread dough stuffed with a selection of 24 different ingredients to choose from, along with related items.

BACKGROUND:
Established: 1987; 1st Franchised: 1987
Franchised Units: 11
Company-Owned Units: 3
Total Units: 14
Dist.: US-13; CAN-0; O'seas-0
North America: 6 States
Density: 8 in NJ, 1 in CA, 1 in NC
Projected New Units (12 Months): 6
Qualifications: 1, 1, 1, 1, 1, 1
Registered: CA,FL,NY

FINANCIAL/TERMS:
Cash Investment: $50-75K
Total Investment: $130-195K
Minimum Net Worth: NR
Fees: Franchise - $20K
Royalty - 5%; Ad. - 0%
Earnings Claims Statement: No
Term of Contract (Years): 10/10
Avg. # Of Employees: 2 FT, 4 PT
Passive Ownership: Not Allowed
Encourage Conversions: NA
Area Develop. Agreements: Yes
Sub-Franchising Contracts: No
Expand In Territory: Yes
Space Needs: 600 SF; RM

SUPPORT & TRAINING:
Financial Assistance Provided: No
Site Selection Assistance: Yes
Lease Negotiation Assistance: Yes
Co-Operative Advertising: Yes
Franchisee Assoc./Member: NR
Size Of Corporate Staff: 6
On-Going Support: C,D,E,F,G
Training: 2 Weeks Company Store; 1 Week Franchisee Location.

SPECIFIC EXPANSION PLANS:
US: All United States
Canada: All Canada
Overseas: All Countries

<< >>

ROTELLI PIZZA & PASTA

9045 La Fontana Blvd., # B-1
Boca Raton, FL 33434
Tel: (877) 768-3554 (561) 477-8300
Fax: (561) 451-1970
E-Mail: info@rotellipizzapasta.com
Web Site: www.rotellipizzapasta.com
Mr. Jeffrey R. Smith, Chief Operating Officer

ROTELLI is a fast-casual pizza and pasta restaurant that offers superior yet affordable products, prepared fresh to order, and artistically presented in a warm, upscale environment. Whether it's dine-in, take-out or delivery, our menu contains products with mass appeal that are made from only the finest, freshest ingredients and include traditional and gourmet pizza, fresh pasta made to order. Our stores can range from 1,800-2,500 square feet and are generally located in high traffic shopping plazas.

BACKGROUND: IFA MEMBER
Established: 1999; 1st Franchised: 1999
Franchised Units: 31
Company-Owned Units: 0
Total Units: 31
Dist.: US-30; CAN-0; O'seas-1
North America: 5 States
Density: 15 in FL, 3 in PA, 1 in NC
Projected New Units (12 Months): 15
Qualifications: 3, 4, 2, 3, 2, 4
Registered:CA,FL,IL,IN,MD,MI,MN,NY,

OR,RI,VA,WA,WI,DC

FINANCIAL/TERMS:

Cash Investment: $100-150K
Total Investment: $300-450K
Minimum Net Worth: $100K
Fees: Franchise - $25K
Royalty - 6.0%; Ad. - 3%
Earnings Claims Statement: No
Term of Contract (Years): 20/10
Avg. # Of Employees: 30 FT
Passive Ownership: Discouraged
Encourage Conversions: Yes
Area Develop. Agreements: Yes/20
Sub-Franchising Contracts: No
Expand In Territory: Yes
Space Needs: NR SF; SF, SC, End Cap

SUPPORT & TRAINING:

Financial Assistance Provided: No
Site Selection Assistance: Yes
Lease Negotiation Assistance: Yes
Co-Operative Advertising: Yes
Franchisee Assoc./Member: No
Size Of Corporate Staff: 6
On-Going Support: a,B,C,d,E,F,G,h,I
Training: 4-6 Weeks Instore at Area Developer; 10 Days Boca Raton, FL.

SPECIFIC EXPANSION PLANS:

US: All United States
Canada: No
Overseas: No

<< >>

ROY ROGERS

4 S. McCain Dr.
Frederick, MD 21703
Tel: (301) 695-8563
Fax: (301) 695-5066
E-Mail: franchise@royrogersrestaurants.com
Web Site: www.royrogersrestaurants.com
Ms. Dee Dee Barsy, Franchise Administrator

ROY ROGERS is a quick-service restaurant that is a "cut above" fast food, with a cult-like following. Our concept focuses on quality, variety and choice, targeted primarily for an adult audience.Our favorite foods include the "Big Three" - roast beef, chicken and burgers. Our "Choose Any Side" option includes french fries, baked and mashed potatoes, cole slaw, tossed salad and baked beans. The ROY ROGERS Fixin's Bar includes multiple complimentary condiments. Guests customize their our sandwiches.

BACKGROUND: IFA MEMBER

Established: 1979; 1st Franchised: 2003
Franchised Units: 41
Company-Owned Units: 15
Total Units: 56
Dist.: US-56; CAN-0; O'seas-0
North America: 9 States
Density: 18 in MD, 11 in NY, 9 in NJ
Projected New Units (12 Months): 3
Qualifications: 4, 5, 4, 3, 3, 5
Registered: MD,NY,VA

FINANCIAL/TERMS:

Cash Investment: $250-300K
Total Investment: $885-1,344K
Minimum Net Worth: $1.4MM
Fees: Franchise - $30K
Royalty - 5%; Ad. - 2%
Earnings Claims Statement: Yes
Term of Contract (Years): 15/5
Avg. # Of Employees: 10-12 FT, 25-30 PT
Passive Ownership: Discouraged
Encourage Conversions: Yes
Area Develop. Agreements: No
Sub-Franchising Contracts: No
Expand In Territory: Yes
Space Needs: 3,200-3,700 SF; FS

SUPPORT & TRAINING:

Financial Assistance Provided: No
Site Selection Assistance: Yes
Lease Negotiation Assistance: No
Co-Operative Advertising: NA
Franchisee Assoc./Member: No
Size Of Corporate Staff: 21
On-Going Support: B,C,D,E,F,H,I
Training: 8-10 Weeks Corporate Training Store, 7 Days Corporate Offices

SPECIFIC EXPANSION PLANS:

US: MD,DC,VA,DE,NJ,CT,MA,OH
Canada: No
Overseas: No

SIMPLE SIMON'S PIZZA

6650 S. Lewis
Tulsa, OK 74136
Tel: (800) 261-6375 (918) 496-1272
Fax: (918) 493-6516
E-Mail: tmiller@simple-simon.com
Web Site: www.simple-simon.com
Mr. Todd Miller, Executive Vice President

SIMPLE SIMON'S PIZZA and its related concepts focus on operations and return on investment. The low start-up costs and low royalty cost allow its franchisees to make good returns on all sales levels. The customer receives a high-quality pizza and a great value. The concepts fit almost any location and market. Its simple operations, customer value, low entry cost and great profit potential make SIMPLE SIMON'S PIZZA a strong investment for any motivated business owner.

BACKGROUND:

Established: 1982; 1st Franchised: 1984
Franchised Units: 230
Company-Owned Units: 7
Total Units: 237
Dist.: US-237; CAN-0; O'seas-0
North America: 8 States
Density: 80 in OK, 40 in TX, 20 in AR
Projected New Units (12 Months):
Qualifications: , , , , ,
Registered:

FINANCIAL/TERMS:

Cash Investment: $20-40K
Total Investment: $80-120K
Minimum Net Worth: $20K
Fees: Franchise - $5-15K
Royalty - 3-5%; Ad. - 1%
Earnings Claims Statement: No
Term of Contract (Years): 10/10
Avg. # Of Employees: 2 FT, 10 PT
Passive Ownership: Discouraged
Encourage Conversions:
Area Develop. Agreements: No
Sub-Franchising Contracts: No
Expand In Territory: Yes
Space Needs: 2,000 SF; FS, SF, SC

SUPPORT & TRAINING:

Financial Assistance Provided:
Site Selection Assistance: Yes
Lease Negotiation Assistance: Yes
Co-Operative Advertising: NA
Franchisee Assoc./Member: No
Size Of Corporate Staff: 10
On-Going Support: B,C,D,E,G
Training: 1 Week Tulsa, OK Area.

SPECIFIC EXPANSION PLANS:

US: South, Mid-Southwest
Canada: NR
Overseas: NR

<< >>

SKYLINE CHILI

4180 Thunderbird Ln.
Fairfield, OH 45014-2235
Tel: (800) 443-4371 (513) 874-1188
Fax: (513) 874-3591

E-Mail: pmlewis@skylinechili.com
Web Site: www.skylinechili.com
Mr. Phillip Lewis, Jr., Corporate Vice President

Fast-casual restaurant concept that delivers great Cincinnati style chili in the speed of fast food. Sit down unit with table service that is ideal for owner/operators. Concept has a fanatical following by consumers and is one of the simplest restaurant concepts to run.

BACKGROUND: IFA MEMBER
Established: 1949; 1st Franchised: 1965
Franchised Units: 83
Company-Owned Units: 41
Total Units: 124
Dist.: US-124; CAN-0; O'seas-0
North America: 5 States
Density: 94 in OH, 19 in KY, 6 in IN
Projected New Units (12 Months): 12
Qualifications: 5, 4, 4, 3, 4, 5
Registered: FL,IN,MI

FINANCIAL/TERMS:
Cash Investment: $60-200K
Total Investment: $300K-1MM
Minimum Net Worth: $650K
Fees: Franchise - $20K
Royalty - 4%; Ad. - 4%
Earnings Claims Statement: Yes
Term of Contract (Years): 20/20
Avg. # Of Employees: 15 FT, 20 PT
Passive Ownership: Discouraged
Encourage Conversions: Yes
Area Develop. Agreements: Yes/5-10
Sub-Franchising Contracts: No
Expand In Territory: Yes
Space Needs: 2,800 SF; FS, SF, SC, End Cap

SUPPORT & TRAINING:
Financial Assistance Provided: No
Site Selection Assistance: Yes
Lease Negotiation Assistance: Yes
Co-Operative Advertising: Yes
Franchisee Assoc./Member: Yes/No
Size Of Corporate Staff: 40
On-Going Support: a,B,C,D,E,G,I
Training: 6-8 Weeks in Cincinnati, OH.

SPECIFIC EXPANSION PLANS:
US: OH, KY, IN, MI, FL, PA, WV
Canada: No
Overseas: No

SMOOTHIE KING
2400 Veterans Blvd., # 110
Kenner, LA 70062
Tel: (800) 577-4200 (504) 467-4006 + 232
Fax: (504) 469-1274
E-Mail: mpowers@smoothieking.com
Web Site: www.smoothieking.com
Mr. Michael C. Powers, EVP New Business Develop.

SMOOTHIE KING is the original nutritional smoothie bar and health marketplace since 1973. Our brand is recognized by Entrepreneur Magazine as being # 1 in our category for 15 consecutive years and has steadily grown to 360 stores. Brand loyalty and recognition, corporate support and innovation are some reasons why SMOOTHIE KING is in the front of the industry.

BACKGROUND: IFA MEMBER
Established: 1973; 1st Franchised: 1989
Franchised Units: 359
Company-Owned Units: 1
Total Units: 360
Dist.: US-360; CAN-0; O'seas-0
North America: 10 States
Density: 116 in TX, 81 in LA, 42 FL
Projected New Units (12 Months): 75
Qualifications: 4, 4, 3, 3, 5, 4
Registered: All States

FINANCIAL/TERMS:
Cash Investment: $50K
Total Investment: $120-220K
Minimum Net Worth: $100K
Fees: Franchise - $25K
Royalty - 6%; Ad. - 1%
Earnings Claims Statement: No
Term of Contract (Years): 10/5/5/5
Avg. # Of Employees: 2 FT, 6 PT
Passive Ownership: Discouraged
Encourage Conversions: Yes
Area Develop. Agreements: No
Sub-Franchising Contracts: No
Expand In Territory: Yes
Space Needs: 800-1,000 SF; SC

SUPPORT & TRAINING:
Financial Assistance Provided: NA
Site Selection Assistance: Yes
Lease Negotiation Assistance: Yes
Co-Operative Advertising: Yes
Franchisee Assoc./Member: No
Size Of Corporate Staff: 50+
On-Going Support: B,C,D,E,F,G,h,I
Training: 7 Days New Orleans, LA.

SPECIFIC EXPANSION PLANS:
US: All United States
Canada: No
Overseas: No

SNAPPY TOMATO PIZZA
7230 Turfway Rd.
Florence, KY 41042
Tel: (888) 463-7627 (859) 525-4680
Fax: (859) 525-4686
E-Mail: bwitte@snappytomato.com
Web Site: www.snappytomato.com
Mr. Bret Witte, Director of Marketing

We offer the best in pizza, subs and salads. We have a variety of concepts to offer to our franchisee. We are the pizza of choice in the new millennia.

BACKGROUND:
Established: 1982; 1st Franchised: 1985
Franchised Units: 53
Company-Owned Units: 2
Total Units: 55
Dist.: US-38; CAN-4; O'seas-9
North America: 7 States, 1 Province
Density: 17 in KY, 5 in FL, 5 in TN
Projected New Units (12 Months): 20
Qualifications: 3, 3, 3, 2, 1, 3
Registered: FL,IN,IL

FINANCIAL/TERMS:
Cash Investment: $20-30K
Total Investment: $70-150K
Minimum Net Worth: NR
Fees: Franchise - $15K
Royalty - 5.5%/$200; Ad. - 2.5%
Earnings Claims Statement: Yes
Term of Contract (Years): 15/15
Avg. # Of Employees: 2 FT, 10 PT
Passive Ownership: Discouraged
Encourage Conversions: Yes
Area Develop. Agreements: Yes/15
Sub-Franchising Contracts: Yes
Expand In Territory: Yes
Space Needs: 400-2,000 SF; FS, SF, SC, RM, C-Store

SUPPORT & TRAINING:
Financial Assistance Provided: No
Site Selection Assistance: Yes
Lease Negotiation Assistance: Yes
Co-Operative Advertising: Yes
Franchisee Assoc./Member: No
Size Of Corporate Staff: 5
On-Going Support: A,B,C,D,E,G,H,I

Training: 3 Days to 2 Weeks KY, TN or FL..

SPECIFIC EXPANSION PLANS:

US: SE, SE, Mid-Atl., Midwest
Canada: All Canada
Overseas: Japan, China, Caribbean, Middle East

SONIC DRIVE-IN

300 Johnny Bench Dr.
Oklahoma City, OK 73104
Tel: (800) 569-6656 (405) 280-7654
Fax: (405) 290-7404
E-Mail: dvernon@sonicdrivein.com
Web Site: www.sonicdrivein.com
Mr. David Vernon, VP Franchise Sales

SONIC DRIVE-INS offer made-to-order hamburgers and other sandwiches, and feature signature items, such as extra-long cheese coneys, hand-breaded onion rings, tater tots, fountain favorites, including cherry limeades, slushes and a full ice-cream dessert menu.

BACKGROUND: IFA MEMBER
Established: 1953; 1st Franchised: 1959
Franchised Units: 2,177
Company-Owned Units: 494
Total Units: 2,671
Dist.: US-2,667; CAN-0; O'seas-4
North America: 30 States
Density:739 In TX, 234 in OK, 191 TN
Projected New Units (12 Months): 185
Qualifications: 5, 5, 5, 2, 2, 4
Registered: CA,FL,IL,IN,OR,VA,WA,DC

FINANCIAL/TERMS:

Cash Investment: $500K
Total Investment: $700K-2.3MM
Minimum Net Worth: $1MM
Fees: Franchise - $30K
Royalty - 1-5%; Ad. - 4%
Earnings Claims Statement: No
Term of Contract (Years): 20/10
Avg. # Of Employees: 35 FT
Passive Ownership: Not Allowed
Encourage Conversions: No
Area Develop. Agreements: Yes/Varies
Sub-Franchising Contracts: No
Expand In Territory: Yes
Space Needs: 1,450 SF; FS

SUPPORT & TRAINING:

Financial Assistance Provided: Yes(I)
Site Selection Assistance: Yes
Lease Negotiation Assistance: Yes
Co-Operative Advertising: Yes
Franchisee Assoc./Member: Yes/Yes
Size Of Corporate Staff: 210
On-Going Support: B,C,D,E,F,G,H,I
Training: 1 Week Oklahoma City, OK; 11 Weeks at Local Market.

SPECIFIC EXPANSION PLANS:

US: SW, SE, West, Midwest
Canada: No
Overseas: Mexico, Puerto Rico

STEAK ESCAPE

222 Neilston St.
Columbus, OH 43215
Tel: (866) 247-8325 (614) 224-0300
Fax: (614) 224-6460
E-Mail: lallen@steakescape.com
Web Site: www.steakescape.com
Mr. Shane Pratt, VP Franchise Development

STEAK ESCAPE prides itself on serving delicious grilled sandwiches, freshly cut fries and freshly squeezed lemonade. All of these items are created from fresh ingredients and are prepared in full view of customers using our own unique method of exhibition-style cooking. STEAK ESCAPE's signature item is The Genuine Philadelphia Cheesesteak Sandwich. Today we have opportunities available in free-standing locations, strip center locations and in mall locations!

BACKGROUND:
Established: 1982; 1st Franchised: 1983
Franchised Units: 165
Company-Owned Units: 0
Total Units: 165
Dist.: US-166; CAN-0; O'seas-1
North America: 35 States
Density: 18 un CA, 16 in CO, 14 in OH
Projected New Units (12 Months): 40-45
Qualifications: 4, 4, 3, 1, 3, 4
Registered: All States

FINANCIAL/TERMS:

Cash Investment: $70-250K
Total Investment: $180-1.25MM
Minimum Net Worth: $100K
Fees: Franchise - $25K
Royalty - 6-5%; Ad. - 0.5%
Earnings Claims Statement: No
Term of Contract (Years): 20/Varies
Avg. # Of Employees: 4 FT, 12 PT
Passive Ownership: Allowed
Encourage Conversions: Yes
Area Develop. Agreements: Yes
Sub-Franchising Contracts: Yes
Expand In Territory: Yes
Space Needs: 300-2,400 SF; FS, SF, SC, RM

SUPPORT & TRAINING:

Financial Assistance Provided: Yes(I)
Site Selection Assistance: Yes
Lease Negotiation Assistance: Yes
Co-Operative Advertising: Yes
Franchisee Assoc./Member: Yes/Yes
Size Of Corporate Staff: 28
On-Going Support: A,B,C,D,e,F,G,H,I
Training: 3 Weeks in Colombus, OH.

SPECIFIC EXPANSION PLANS:

US: All United States
Canada: All Canada
Overseas: Western Hemisphere

STEAK 'N SHAKE

38 S. Pennsylvania St., # 500
Indianapolis, IN 46204
Tel: (317) 633-4100
Fax: (317) 656-4500
E-Mail: brad.manns@steaknshake.com
Web Site: www.steaknshake.com
Mr. Brad Manns, Vice President Franchising

STEAK N' SHAKE is a unique restaurant concept, serving the mid-scale, casual dining segment of the market with a menu that features steakburgers, thin and crispy french fries and hand-dipped milk shakes. STEAK N' SHAKE offers full waitress service with food served on china, 24 hours a day.

BACKGROUND:
Established: 1934; 1st Franchised: 1939
Franchised Units: 45
Company-Owned Units: 380
Total Units: 425
Dist.: US-249; CAN-0; O'seas-0
North America: 14 States
Density: 60 in MO, 51 in IN, 46 in IL
Projected New Units (12 Months): 45
Qualifications: 4, 4, 5, 3, 3, 5
Registered: FL,IL,IN,MI,VA

FINANCIAL/TERMS:

Cash Investment: $200-400K
Total Investment: $1.1-2.4MM
Minimum Net Worth: $500K
Fees: Franchise - $30K
Royalty - 4%; Ad. - 5%
Earnings Claims Statement: No
Term of Contract (Years): 20/20
Avg. # Of Employees: 20-25 FT, 30-40 PT
Passive Ownership: NR
Encourage Conversions: No
Area Develop. Agreements: Yes/3-6
Sub-Franchising Contracts: No
Expand In Territory: Yes

Space Needs: 3,630 SF; FS
SUPPORT & TRAINING:
Financial Assistance Provided: No
Site Selection Assistance: No
Lease Negotiation Assistance: No
Co-Operative Advertising: No
Franchisee Assoc./Member: No
Size Of Corporate Staff: 60
On-Going Support: NR
Training: 6-8 Weeks Operating Steak n' Shake.
SPECIFIC EXPANSION PLANS:
US: Midwest, Southeast
Canada: No
Overseas: No

STUFT PIZZA
50855 Washington St., # 210
La Quinta, CA 92253-2891
Tel: (760) 777-1660
Fax: (760) 777-1660
E-Mail: noelle@stuftpizza.com
Web Site: www.stuftpizza.com
Ms. Noelle Bertram, VP Sales & Marketing

Take-outs to full service with pasta and micro-brewery.

BACKGROUND:
Established: 1976; 1st Franchised: 1985
Franchised Units: 26
Company-Owned Units: 1
Total Units: 27
Dist.: US-27; CAN-0; O'seas-0
North America: 2 States
Density: 26 in CA, 1 in OR
Projected New Units (12 Months): 5
Qualifications: 4, 3, 2, 3, 3, 4
Registered: CA,OR
FINANCIAL/TERMS:
Cash Investment: $75-150K
Total Investment: $150-750K
Minimum Net Worth: $250K
Fees: Franchise - $25K
Royalty - 3%; Ad. - 0%
Earnings Claims Statement: No
Term of Contract (Years): 10/10
Avg. # Of Employees: 3 FT, 8+ PT
Passive Ownership: Discouraged
Encourage Conversions: Yes
Area Develop. Agreements: Yes
Sub-Franchising Contracts: Yes
Expand In Territory: Yes
Space Needs: 1,800+ SF; FS, SF, SC, RM
SUPPORT & TRAINING:
Financial Assistance Provided: NA
Site Selection Assistance: Yes
Lease Negotiation Assistance: Yes
Co-Operative Advertising: No
Franchisee Assoc./Member: No
Size Of Corporate Staff: 4
On-Going Support: C,D,E,G,H
Training: 2 Weeks San Clemente, CA.
SPECIFIC EXPANSION PLANS:
US: West
Canada: No
Overseas: No

<< >>

SUB STATION II
425 N. Main St.
Sumter, SC 29150
Tel: (800) 779-2970 (803) 773-4711
Fax: (803) 775-2220
E-Mail: franchises@substationii.com
Web Site: www.substationii.com
Ms. Susan H. Vaden, Vice President

SUB STATION II is a chain of submarine sandwich franchises. We currently have 90 stores located in 9 states. Our sandwich shops offer a variety of over 25 submarine sandwiches, along with specialty sandwiches and salads. We have developed an efficient method of preparing each sandwich to the customer's specifications. The emphasis is on high-quality food and cleanliness. We provide our franchisee's with training and on-going support, layout, etc.

BACKGROUND:
Established: 1975; 1st Franchised: 1976
Franchised Units: 82
Company-Owned Units: 2
Total Units: 84
Dist.: US-90; CAN-0; O'seas-0
North America: 9 States
Density: 40 in SC, 20 in NC, 15 in CA
Projected New Units (12 Months): 15
Qualifications: 5, 4, 2, 3, 2, 4
Registered: CA,FL,VA
FINANCIAL/TERMS:
Cash Investment: $40-70K
Total Investment: $75-150K
Minimum Net Worth: $200K
Fees: Franchise - $10.5K
Royalty - 4%; Ad. - 2%
Earnings Claims Statement: No
Term of Contract (Years): 10/10
Avg. # Of Employees: 4 FT, 8 PT
Passive Ownership: Allowed
Encourage Conversions: Yes
Area Develop. Agreements: No
Sub-Franchising Contracts: Yes
Expand In Territory: Yes
Space Needs: 1,500 SF; FS, SF, SC, RM
SUPPORT & TRAINING:
Financial Assistance Provided: Yes(I)
Site Selection Assistance: Yes
Lease Negotiation Assistance: Yes
Co-Operative Advertising: Yes
Franchisee Assoc./Member: No
Size Of Corporate Staff: 8
On-Going Support: B,C,D,E,G,h
Training: 7-10 Days Corporate Store; 7-10 Days Franchisee Location.
SPECIFIC EXPANSION PLANS:
US: Southeast, Southern CA
Canada: No
Overseas: No

<< >>

SUBWAY RESTAURANTS
325 Bic Dr.
Milford, CT 06460-3072
Tel: (800) 888-4848 (203) 877-4281
Fax: (203) 783-7325
E-Mail: franchise@subway.com
Web Site: www.subway.com
Mr. Donald Fertman, Franchise Director

For more than 39 years, SUBWAY RESTAURANTS has been offering entrepreneurs an opportunity to build and succeed in their own business through a proven, well-structured franchise system. SUBWAY is the world's largest submarine sandwich franchise and the largest restauarant chain in N. America. In 2004, Entrepreneur Magazine again chose SUBWAY as the overall number one franchise opportunity, making it the 12th time in the past 16 years. Over 21,000 independently-owned and operated location in 75 counties.

BACKGROUND: IFA MEMBER
Established: 1965; 1st Franchised: 1974
Franchised Units: 21,153
Company-Owned Units: 1
Total Units: 21,154
Dist.: US-17,156; CAN-1,916; O'seas-2,082
North America: All States & Provinces
Density: 1,545 CA, 1,273 TX, 1,016 FL
Projected New Units (12 Months): 1,000+
Qualifications: 5, 4, 3, 4, 3, 3
Registered: All States
FINANCIAL/TERMS:
Cash Investment: $Not Required

Total Investment: $86.3-213.5K
Minimum Net Worth: $Not Required
Fees: Franchise - $12.5K
Royalty - 8%; Ad. - 4.5%
Earnings Claims Statement: No
Term of Contract (Years): 20/20
Avg. # Of Employees: 2-3 FT, 6-10 PT
Passive Ownership: Not Allowed
Encourage Conversions: NA
Area Develop. Agreements: Yes/20
Sub-Franchising Contracts: No
Expand In Territory: Yes
Space Needs: 300-2,000 SF; FS, SF, SC, RM, C-Store

SUPPORT & TRAINING:
Financial Assistance Provided: Yes(D)
Site Selection Assistance: Yes
Lease Negotiation Assistance: Yes
Co-Operative Advertising: No
Franchisee Assoc./Member: Yes/Yes
Size Of Corporate Staff: 700
On-Going Support: A,B,C,D,E,F,G,H,I
Training: 2 Weeks Milford, CT; 2 Weeks Miami, FL; 2 Weeks Montreal, PQ.

SPECIFIC EXPANSION PLANS:
US: All United States
Canada: All Canada
Overseas: All Countries

TACO BELL

P. O. Box 34550, 1900 Colonel Sanders Ln.
Louisville, KY 40213
Tel: (866) 2YUM-YUM (502) 874-8300
Fax: (502) 874-8848
E-Mail: 2yumyum@yum.com
Web Site: www.yumfranchises.com
Ms. Nikki Weis, Franchise Coordinator

TACO BELL has been the world's largest Mexican quick-service franchise for the past 38 years.

BACKGROUND: IFA MEMBER
Established: 1962; 1st Franchised: 1964
Franchised Units: 4,600
Company-Owned Units: 3,044
Total Units: 7,644
Dist.: US-1,597; CAN-600; O'seas-5,447
North America: 50 States
Density: 232 in CA, 151 in OH, 150 FL
Projected New Units (12 Months): NR
Qualifications: , , , , ,
Registered: All States

FINANCIAL/TERMS:
Cash Investment: NR
Total Investment: $236-503K
Minimum Net Worth: NR
Fees: Franchise - $45K
Royalty - 5.5%; Ad. - 4.5%
Earnings Claims Statement: No
Term of Contract (Years): 20
Avg. # Of Employees: NR
Passive Ownership: Allowed
Encourage Conversions: NR
Area Develop. Agreements: Yes
Sub-Franchising Contracts: No
Expand In Territory: Yes
Space Needs: NR SF; FS, SF, RM, Other

SUPPORT & TRAINING:
Financial Assistance Provided: Yes
Site Selection Assistance: Yes
Lease Negotiation Assistance: Yes
Co-Operative Advertising: Yes
Franchisee Assoc./Member: NR
Size Of Corporate Staff: NR
On-Going Support: NR
Training: 18 Weeks at Approved Training Restaurant.

SPECIFIC EXPANSION PLANS:
US: All United States
Canada: All Canada
Overseas: All Countries

TACO JOHN'S INTERNATIONAL

808 W. 20th St.
Cheyenne, WY 82001
Tel: (800) 854-0819 + 9701 (307) 635-0101 + 9701
Fax: (307) 638-0603
E-Mail: bmiller@tacojohns.com
Web Site: www.tacojohns.com
Dr. Brett D. Miller, Director of Development

Mexican fast-food restaurant franchisor.

BACKGROUND:
Established: 1969; 1st Franchised: 1969
Franchised Units: 401
Company-Owned Units: 9
Total Units: 410
Dist.: US-410; CAN-0; O'seas-0
North America: 27 States
Density: 66 in MN, 62 in IA, 38 in SD
Projected New Units (12 Months): 28
Qualifications: 4, 5, 3, 3, 1, 5
Registered: All States Except DC

FINANCIAL/TERMS:
Cash Investment: $150K
Total Investment: $495-814K
Minimum Net Worth: $400K
Fees: Franchise - $25K
Royalty - 4%; Ad. - 3.5%
Earnings Claims Statement: No
Term of Contract (Years): 20/10
Avg. # Of Employees: 15-25
Passive Ownership: Discouraged
Encourage Conversions: Yes
Area Develop. Agreements: Yes/Varies
Sub-Franchising Contracts: No
Expand In Territory: Yes
Space Needs: 1,200-2,300 SF; FS, SC, RM

SUPPORT & TRAINING:
Financial Assistance Provided: No
Site Selection Assistance: No
Lease Negotiation Assistance: Yes
Co-Operative Advertising: Yes
Franchisee Assoc./Member: Yes/No
Size Of Corporate Staff: 60
On-Going Support: B,C,D,E,G,H,I
Training: 4 Weeks Cheyenne, Wyoming.

SPECIFIC EXPANSION PLANS:
US: Upper Midwest, Central US
Canada: No
Overseas: No

<< >>

TACO MAKER, THE

P. O. Box 150650
Ogden, UT 84415
Tel: (801) 476-9780
Fax: (801) 476-9788
E-Mail: ttm@tacomaker.com
Web Site: www.tacomaker.com
Mr. Bob Strong, Franchising Director

International Mexican fast-food franchise, specializing in fast, friendly service and a complete menu with made-from-scratch and fresh ingredients. Centralized purchasing, corporate marketing and promotional support and progressive store design provide for the most comprehensive and fun investment opportunity. Available in free-standing, mall or strip center locations and also convenience stores, truck stops and co-branding opportunities.

BACKGROUND:
Established: 1978; 1st Franchised: 1978
Franchised Units: 127
Company-Owned Units: 3
Total Units: 130
Dist.: US-84; CAN-0; O'seas-73
North America: 32 States
Density: 13 in UT, 10 in WA, 5 in NY
Projected New Units (12 Months): 50
Qualifications: 4, 4, 5, 2, 4, 4
Registered: All States

FINANCIAL/TERMS:
Cash Investment: $20-140K
Total Investment: $75-650K
Minimum Net Worth: NR
Fees: Franchise - $5-22.5K
Royalty - 5-7%; Ad. - 3%
Earnings Claims Statement: No
Term of Contract (Years): 15/15
Avg. # Of Employees: 2-6 FT, 5-20 PT
Passive Ownership: Discouraged
Encourage Conversions: Yes
Area Develop. Agreements: Yes/15
Sub-Franchising Contracts: Yes
Expand In Territory: Yes
Space Needs: 200-3,000 SF; FS
SUPPORT & TRAINING:
Financial Assistance Provided: Yes(I)
Site Selection Assistance: Yes
Lease Negotiation Assistance: Yes
Co-Operative Advertising: Yes
Franchisee Assoc./Member: No
Size Of Corporate Staff: 30
On-Going Support: B,C,D,E,F,I
Training: 12-15 Days UT.
SPECIFIC EXPANSION PLANS:
US: All United States
Canada: All Canada
Overseas: All Countries

TACO MAYO

10405 Greenbriar Pl.
Oklahoma City, OK 73159
Tel: (405) 691-8226
Fax: (405) 691-2572
E-Mail:
Web Site: www.tacomayo.com
Ms. Debbie Jackson, Qualifications Specialist

Southwest-based, privately held chain of quick-service restaurants, serving Tex-Mex favorites, including tacos, nachos, salads, burritos, etc. Almost 100 restaurants in 5 states, with active advertising co-ops, centralized purchasing, distribution, training and field service representatives. Free-standing limits (conversion and remodeled) feature drive-thru and dining room seating.

BACKGROUND:
Established: 1978; 1st Franchised: 1980
Franchised Units: 61
Company-Owned Units: 30
Total Units: 91
Dist.: US-91; CAN-0; O'seas-0
North America: 5 States
Density: 83 in OK, 8 in TX, 3 in KS
Projected New Units (12 Months): 18
Qualifications: 5, 4, 2, 3, 5, 5
Registered: NR
FINANCIAL/TERMS:
Cash Investment: $100K
Total Investment: $99-499K
Minimum Net Worth: $200K
Fees: Franchise - $15K
Royalty - 4%; Ad. - 3%
Earnings Claims Statement: No
Term of Contract (Years): 10/10
Avg. # Of Employees: 5 FT, 16 PT
Passive Ownership: Not Allowed
Encourage Conversions: Yes
Area Develop. Agreements: Yes/10
Sub-Franchising Contracts: No
Expand In Territory: Yes
Space Needs: 900-2,200 SF; FS
SUPPORT & TRAINING:
Financial Assistance Provided: Yes(I)
Site Selection Assistance: Yes
Lease Negotiation Assistance: Yes
Co-Operative Advertising: Yes
Franchisee Assoc./Member: Yes/Yes
Size Of Corporate Staff: 23
On-Going Support: a,B,C,D,E,G,H
Training: 3 Weeks at Store in Tulsa or Oklahoma City, OK; 2 Weeks at Franchise Store.
SPECIFIC EXPANSION PLANS:
US: OK, KS, AR, MO, N.TX
Canada: No
Overseas: No

TACO PALACE

814 E. Hwy. 60, P.O. Box 87
Monett, MO 65708
Tel: (417) 235-6595
Fax: (573) 216-1739
E-Mail: larry@tacopalace.com
Web Site: www.tacopalace.com
Mr. Larry Faria, President

Our concept is targeted at people that normally could not afford the cost and expense that other franchises require. Our low overhead concept translates to more profit to the franchisee. We offer more flexibility. Fresh Tex-Mex food at "down to earth" prices!

BACKGROUND:
Established: 1985; 1st Franchised: 1999
Franchised Units: 14
Company-Owned Units: 2
Total Units: 16
Dist.: US-15; CAN-1; O'seas-0
North America: 9 States
Density: 8 in MO, 2 in TX, 2 in OK
Projected New Units (12 Months): 6
Qualifications: , , , , ,
Registered: FL,MN,WI,VA
FINANCIAL/TERMS:
Cash Investment: $69K
Total Investment: $132-170K
Minimum Net Worth: $50-65K
Fees: Franchise - $33.5
Royalty - 0%; Ad. - 0%
Earnings Claims Statement: Yes
Term of Contract (Years): Unlimited
Avg. # Of Employees: 8 FT, 2 PT
Passive Ownership: Allowed
Encourage Conversions: Yes
Area Develop. Agreements: Yes
Sub-Franchising Contracts: Yes
Expand In Territory: Yes
Space Needs: 1,000+ SF; FS, SF, SC, RM
SUPPORT & TRAINING:
Financial Assistance Provided: NR
Site Selection Assistance: Yes
Lease Negotiation Assistance: Yes
Co-Operative Advertising: No
Franchisee Assoc./Member: No/No
Size Of Corporate Staff: 4
On-Going Support: C,D,E,F
Training: Unlimited Days in Monett, MO; 10-20 Days with Trainers at Franchisee's Location.
SPECIFIC EXPANSION PLANS:
US: All United States
Canada: All Canada
Overseas: All Countries

TACO TIME INTERNATIONAL

7730 E. Greenway Rd., # 104
Scottsdale, AZ 85260
Tel: (800) 438-2590 (480) 443-0200
Fax: (480) 443-1972
E-Mail: sjlacroix@kahalacorp.com
Web Site: www.kahalacorp.com
Ms. Stephanie J. LaCroix, VP Franchise Sales

TACO TIME continues to provide and improve our system for quick-service Mexican restaurants that have stood the test of time for 40 years. TACO TIME quality, focus on customer service, franchisee support and existing new products make us the innovative leader of high-quality Mexican food.

BACKGROUND: IFA MEMBER
Established: 1959; 1st Franchised: 1960
Franchised Units: 284
Company-Owned Units: 4

Total Units: 288
Dist.: US-194; CAN-112; O'seas-9
North America: 14 States, 7 Provinces
Density: 74 in OR, 42 in UT, 34 in BC
Projected New Units (12 Months): 20
Qualifications: 5, 4, 3, 4, 5, 5
Registered: All States Except MD,RI,AB

FINANCIAL/TERMS:
Cash Investment: $100K
Total Investment: $150-200K
Minimum Net Worth: $300K
Fees: Franchise - $25K
Royalty - 5%; Ad. - 4%
Earnings Claims Statement: No
Term of Contract (Years): 15/10
Avg. # Of Employees: 2-3 FT, 15-20 PT
Passive Ownership: Not Allowed
Encourage Conversions: Yes
Area Develop. Agreements: Yes
Sub-Franchising Contracts: Yes
Expand In Territory: Yes
Space Needs: 1,500-2,160 SF; FS, RM

SUPPORT & TRAINING:
Financial Assistance Provided: No
Site Selection Assistance: Yes
Lease Negotiation Assistance: Yes
Co-Operative Advertising: Yes
Franchisee Assoc./Member: Yes/Yes
Size Of Corporate Staff: 25
On-Going Support: B,C,D,E,F,G,h,I
Training: Up to 6 Weeks at Corporate Office.

SPECIFIC EXPANSION PLANS:
US: All United States
Canada: Western Province
Overseas: Master Licensing Agreement -- Asia

<< >>

TACO VILLA

3710 Chesswood Dr., # 220
North York, ON M3J 2W4 CANADA
Tel: (416) 636-9348
Fax: (416) 636-9162
E-Mail: tacovilla@on.aibn.com
Web Site: www.worldfranchising.com/website.htm
Ms. Wendy J. MacKinnon, Franchise Director

TACO VILLA is a quick-service Mexican-food concept. With over 16 years' experience, we offer franchisees a dynamic design concept, full turn-key operation, proven menu and procedures, full training and marketing. We provide today's consumer with a high-quality, high-value food experience. TACO VILLA continues to expand.

BACKGROUND:
Established: 1983; 1st Franchised: 1985
Franchised Units: 20
Company-Owned Units: 1
Total Units: 21
Dist.: US-0; CAN-21; O'seas-0
North America: 1 Province
Density: 21 in ON
Projected New Units (12 Months): 10-15
Qualifications: 5, 3, 2, 3, 4, 4
Registered: NR

FINANCIAL/TERMS:
Cash Investment: $40-50K
Total Investment: $140-150K
Minimum Net Worth: $150K
Fees: Franchise - $20K
Royalty - 6%; Ad. - 2%
Earnings Claims Statement: No
Term of Contract (Years): 10/10
Avg. # Of Employees: 3 FT, 5 PT
Passive Ownership: Not Allowed
Encourage Conversions: Yes
Area Develop. Agreements: No
Sub-Franchising Contracts: Yes
Expand In Territory: Yes
Space Needs: 350-400 SF; RM

SUPPORT & TRAINING:
Financial Assistance Provided: Yes(I)
Site Selection Assistance: Yes
Lease Negotiation Assistance: Yes
Co-Operative Advertising: Yes
Franchisee Assoc./Member: NR
Size Of Corporate Staff: 7
On-Going Support: A,B,C,D,E,G,I
Training: 1 Week Head Office; 3 Weeks In Store.

SPECIFIC EXPANSION PLANS:
US: Eastern Seaboard, New Eng.
Canada: All Canada
Overseas: No

<< >>

TACONE

950 Flower St., # 105
Los Angeles, CA 90015
Tel: (877) 482-2663 (213) 236-0950
Fax: (213) 236-0951
E-Mail: craig@tacone.com
Web Site: www.tacone.com
Mr. Craig Albert, President

Franchisor of quick-service restaurants serving fresh soups, sandwiches, salads, smoothies and catering.

BACKGROUND:
Established: 1995; 1st Franchised: 1998
Franchised Units: 60
Company-Owned Units: 0
Total Units: 60
Dist.: US-60; CAN-0; O'seas-0
North America: 6 States
Density: 9 in CA
Projected New Units (12 Months): NR
Qualifications: , , , , ,
Registered: NR

FINANCIAL/TERMS:
Cash Investment: $75K
Total Investment: $200-350K
Minimum Net Worth: $100K
Fees: Franchise - $25K
Royalty - 6%; Ad. - 1%
Earnings Claims Statement: No
Term of Contract (Years): 10
Avg. # Of Employees: 1 FT, 5-7 PT
Passive Ownership: Allowed
Encourage Conversions: NR
Area Develop. Agreements: Yes/10
Sub-Franchising Contracts: Yes
Expand In Territory: Yes
Space Needs: 400-1,500 SF; SF, SC, RM

SUPPORT & TRAINING:
Financial Assistance Provided: Yes(I)
Site Selection Assistance: Yes
Lease Negotiation Assistance: Yes
Co-Operative Advertising: Yes
Franchisee Assoc./Member: Yes
Size Of Corporate Staff: 10
On-Going Support: A,B,C,D,E,F,G,H,I
Training: 3 Weeks Corporate Training in Downtown Los Angeles, CA.

SPECIFIC EXPANSION PLANS:
US: All United States
Canada: NR
Overseas: NR

<< >>

TASTEE-FREEZ

48380 Van Dyke Ave.
Utica, MI 48317
Tel: (586) 739-5520
Fax: (586) 739-8351
E-Mail: tfiint@aol.com
Web Site: www.tastee-freez.com
Mr. Bob Lerash, Dir. Operations/Development

Restaurant franchise with the flexibility to offer a full menu from chicken, burgers and fries plus hand-dipped and soft serve ice cream treats to offering a very streamlined soft serve treats-only menu for a co-brand or limited space location.

BACKGROUND:
Established: 1950; 1st Franchised: 1950
Franchised Units: 250
Company-Owned Units: 0

Total Units: 250
Dist.: US-253; CAN-0; O'seas-7
North America: NR
Density: NR
Projected New Units (12 Months): 40-50
Qualifications: 3, 3, 3, 3, 3, 3
Registered:
CA,FL,IN,MD,MI,MN,ND,VA,WI

FINANCIAL/TERMS:
Cash Investment: $20-250K
Total Investment: $30K-1MM
Minimum Net Worth: NA
Fees: Franchise - $5-15K
Royalty - 4-5%; Ad. - 1%
Earnings Claims Statement: No
Term of Contract (Years): 10/10
Avg. # Of Employees: Varies
Passive Ownership: Discouraged
Encourage Conversions: Yes
Area Develop. Agreements: NA
Sub-Franchising Contracts: NA
Expand In Territory: Possible
Space Needs: NR SF; FS, SF, SC, Co-Brand

SUPPORT & TRAINING:
Financial Assistance Provided: No
Site Selection Assistance: No
Lease Negotiation Assistance: No
Co-Operative Advertising: No
Franchisee Assoc./Member: No
Size Of Corporate Staff: 7
On-Going Support: B,C,D,E,F,G,H
Training: Varies.

SPECIFIC EXPANSION PLANS:
US: All United States
Canada: No
Overseas: No

<< >>

THUNDERCLOUD SUBS

1102 W. 6th St.
Austin, TX 78703
Tel: (800) 256-7895 (512) 479-8805
Fax: (512) 479-8806
E-Mail: thunder@onr.com
Web Site: www.thundercloud.com
Mr. David E. Cohen, Director Franchising

Fresh, fast and healthy sub sandwiches, salads, soup, etc. in a casual atmosphere without the fast-food look. A distinctive trademark, system and product, each store having a unique decor that ties in to the local community. Definitely not a cookie cutter franchise. We train our people to capture the essence of the THUNDERCLOUD experience. The customer service and atmosphere play a large part in overall customer satisfaction. We offer a great value.

BACKGROUND:
Established: 1975; 1st Franchised: 1989
Franchised Units: 15
Company-Owned Units: 10
Total Units: 25
Dist.: US-38; CAN-0; O'seas-0
North America: 2 States
Density: 37 in TX
Projected New Units (12 Months): 8-12
Qualifications: 4, 4, 3, 3, 4, 5
Registered: NR

FINANCIAL/TERMS:
Cash Investment: $25-50K
Total Investment: $60-100K
Minimum Net Worth: $100K
Fees: Franchise - $10K
Royalty - 4%; Ad. - Varies
Earnings Claims Statement: No
Term of Contract (Years): 10+8/4/4
Avg. # Of Employees: 2 FT, 6-12 PT
Passive Ownership: Discouraged
Encourage Conversions: Yes
Area Develop. Agreements: Yes/Varies
Sub-Franchising Contracts: No
Expand In Territory: Yes
Space Needs: 1,000-1,500 SF; FS, SF, SC

SUPPORT & TRAINING:
Financial Assistance Provided: No
Site Selection Assistance: Yes
Lease Negotiation Assistance: Yes
Co-Operative Advertising: NA
Franchisee Assoc./Member: No
Size Of Corporate Staff: 5
On-Going Support: C,D,E,F,G,h,I
Training: 1-2 Weeks at Corporate Headquarters in Austin, TX; 5-10 Days at Franchisee's Store.

SPECIFIC EXPANSION PLANS:
US: Primarily Southwest
Canada: No
Overseas: No

<< >>

TOGO'S EATERY

14 Pacella Park Dr., P.O. Box 317
Randolph, MA 02368-0317
Tel: (800) 777-9983 (781) 961-4020
Fax: (781) 585-2760
E-Mail: dlarose@adrus.com
Web Site: www.dunkin-baskin-togos.com
Mr. Don Larose, Director Franchise Services

As part of Allied Domecq's team of international franchise leaders, TOGO'S joins BASKIN-ROBBINS and DUNKIN' DONUTS in franchising for the future - multi-branding. Allied Domecq's strategic plan includes territorial development.

BACKGROUND: IFA MEMBER
Established: 1971; 1st Franchised: 1977
Franchised Units: 399
Company-Owned Units: 0
Total Units: 399
Dist.: US-0; CAN-1; O'seas-0
North America: 1 Province
Density: 1 in BC
Projected New Units (12 Months): 12
Qualifications: 5, 5, 4, 4, 4, 5
Registered: NR

FINANCIAL/TERMS:
Cash Investment: $125-150K
Total Investment: $225-250K
Minimum Net Worth: $500K
Fees: Franchise - $25K
Royalty - 5%; Ad. - 5%
Earnings Claims Statement: No
Term of Contract (Years): 10/10
Avg. # Of Employees: 4 FT, 8 PT
Passive Ownership: Discouraged
Encourage Conversions: No
Area Develop. Agreements: Yes/3
Sub-Franchising Contracts: No
Expand In Territory: No
Space Needs: 1,400-4,400 SF; FS, SF, SC, RM

SUPPORT & TRAINING:
Financial Assistance Provided: No
Site Selection Assistance: Yes
Lease Negotiation Assistance: Yes
Co-Operative Advertising: No
Franchisee Assoc./Member: Yes/Yes
Size Of Corporate Staff: 30
On-Going Support: B,C,d,E,G,H,I
Training: 4 Weeks CA.

SPECIFIC EXPANSION PLANS:
US: All United States
Canada: BC, ON, PQ
Overseas: No

<< >>

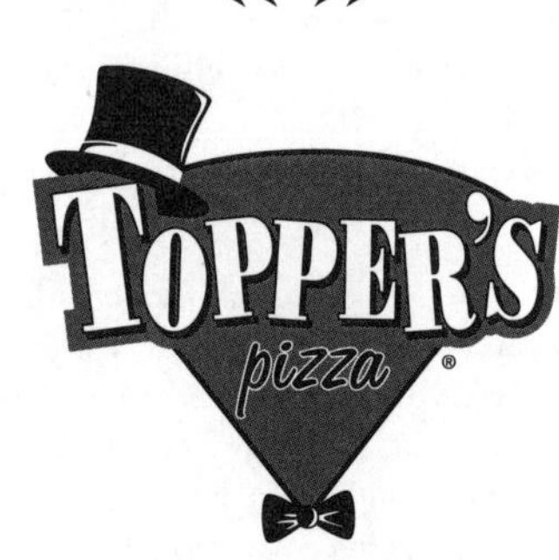

TOPPER'S PIZZA

261 S. Fourth St.
Whitewater, WI 53190
Tel: (888) 586-7737 (262) 473-6666 + 304
Fax: (262) 473-6697
E-Mail: siversen@toppers.com
Web Site: www.toppers.com
Mr. Scott Iversen, Director Franchise Sales

TOPPER'S PIZZA's vision is to provide customers with a unique, high-end pizza AND fast, free delivery. Our menu is superior because we use fresh, hand-prepared ingredients. We cut our own vegetables and sell only the highest-quality meats and real Wisconsin cheeses. We prepare our dough and sauce fresh, from scratch, in each store's kitchen. The cornerstone of our menu is variety. We have developed efficient systems that can be easily taught. Solid strategy and systematized business formula.

BACKGROUND: IFA MEMBER
Established: 1991; 1st Franchised: 2000
Franchised Units: 16
Company-Owned Units: 0
Total Units: 16
Dist.: US-16; CAN-0; O'seas-0
North America: 3 States
Density: 10 in WI, 4 in MN, 3 in NC
Projected New Units (12 Months): 6
Qualifications: 4, 3, 2, 2, 2, 5
Registered: IL,IN,MI,MN,WI

FINANCIAL/TERMS:
Cash Investment: $50-100K
Total Investment: $150-275K
Minimum Net Worth: $150K
Fees: Franchise - $20K
Royalty - 5%; Ad. - 1%
Earnings Claims Statement: Yes
Term of Contract (Years): 5/5
Avg. # Of Employees: 5-10 FT, 20-30 PT
Passive Ownership: Discouraged
Encourage Conversions: Yes
Area Develop. Agreements: No
Sub-Franchising Contracts: No
Expand In Territory: Yes
Space Needs: 1,500 SF; FS, SC, RM

SUPPORT & TRAINING:
Financial Assistance Provided: No
Site Selection Assistance: Yes
Lease Negotiation Assistance: Yes
Co-Operative Advertising: NA
Franchisee Assoc./Member: Yes/Yes
Size Of Corporate Staff: 7
On-Going Support: A,B,C,D,E,F,G,H,I
Training: Program is 30 Days in Whitewater/Madison, WI and is flexible, based on needs; 75% conducted in Store, 25% Classroom.

SPECIFIC EXPANSION PLANS:
US: WI, MN, IL, IA, IN, MI, OH, NC, SC
Canada: No
Overseas: No

<< >>

TUBBY'S SUB SHOPS

35807 Moravian
Clinton Township, MI 48035
Tel: (800) 752-0644 (586) 792-2369 + 3035
Fax: (586) 792-4250
E-Mail: info@tubby.com
Web Site: www.tubby.com
Ms. Jennifer Ciampa, Director Franchise Development

Deli-style and grilled-to-perfection submarine sandwiches, along with soups, healthy salads, various side items, including fries and freshly-baked desserts and bread.

BACKGROUND:
Established: 1968; 1st Franchised: 1978
Franchised Units: 86
Company-Owned Units: 1
Total Units: 87
Dist.: US-87; CAN-0; O'seas-0
North America: 2 States
Density: 86 in MI, 1 in FL
Projected New Units (12 Months): 10
Qualifications: 5, 3, 2, 2, 3, 4
Registered: FL,MI

FINANCIAL/TERMS:
Cash Investment: $50-75K
Total Investment: $50-150K
Minimum Net Worth: $300K
Fees: Franchise - $12.5-15K
Royalty - 6%or $200/Wk.; Ad. - 4%/$150/Wk.
Earnings Claims Statement: Yes
Term of Contract (Years): 10/5
Avg. # Of Employees: 2-4 FT, 3-5 PT
Passive Ownership: Allowed
Encourage Conversions: Yes
Area Develop. Agreements: Yes/0
Sub-Franchising Contracts: No
Expand In Territory: Yes
Space Needs: 1,200-1,500 SF; FS,SC, Gas Stat.

SUPPORT & TRAINING:
Financial Assistance Provided: Yes(I)
Site Selection Assistance: Yes
Lease Negotiation Assistance: No
Co-Operative Advertising: No
Franchisee Assoc./Member: No
Size Of Corporate Staff: 15
On-Going Support: A,b,C,D,E,G,I
Training: 3 Weeks/120 Hours Clinton Township, MI.

SPECIFIC EXPANSION PLANS:
US: Michigan Only.
Canada: No
Overseas: No

<< >>

VILLA PIZZA/COZZOLI'S

17 Elm St.
Morristown, NJ 07960-4158
Tel: (973) 285-4800
Fax: (973) 285-5252
E-Mail: atorine@villaenterprises.com
Web Site: www.villapizza.com
Mr. Adam Torine, VP Business Development

Quick-service pizza and Italian restaurant chain, primarily located in regional malls and outlet centers either in food courts or in-line locations. We use only the freshest cheeses, seasonings, vegetables, homemade sauces and other ingredients. Our large, tantalizing food display offers customers a wide variety of homemade dishes.

BACKGROUND:
Established: 1964; 1st Franchised: 1995
Franchised Units: 75
Company-Owned Units: 128
Total Units: 203
Dist.: US-194; CAN-0; O'seas-11
North America: 38 States
Density: 27 in FL, 23 in TX, 15 in CA
Projected New Units (12 Months): 25
Qualifications: 4, 4, 5, 3, 3, 4
Registered: All States

FINANCIAL/TERMS:
Cash Investment: $100-250K
Total Investment: $190-400K
Minimum Net Worth: $150K
Fees: Franchise - $25K
Royalty - 6%; Ad. - 0%
Earnings Claims Statement: No
Term of Contract (Years): 10
Avg. # Of Employees: 2 FT, 4-7 PT
Passive Ownership: Not Allowed
Encourage Conversions: Yes
Area Develop. Agreements: No
Sub-Franchising Contracts: No
Expand In Territory: Yes

Space Needs: 650-2,500 SF; RM, Non-Traditional

SUPPORT & TRAINING:

Financial Assistance Provided: Yes(I)
Site Selection Assistance: Yes
Lease Negotiation Assistance: Yes
Co-Operative Advertising: NA
Franchisee Assoc./Member: No
Size Of Corporate Staff: 25
On-Going Support: B,C,D,E,F,G,I
Training: 3 Weeks.

SPECIFIC EXPANSION PLANS:

US: All United States
Canada: All Canada
Overseas: England, Italy, Spain, Kuwait, Russia

<< >>

VOCELLI PIZZA

2101 Greentree Rd., # A-202
Pittsburgh, PA 15220-1400
Tel: (866) 279-9100 (412) 279-9100
Fax: (412) 279-9781
E-Mail: bmontanari@vocellipizza.com
Web Site: www.vocellipizza.com
Mr. Bob Montanari, Dir. Franchise Sales/Dev.

VOCELLI PIZZA provides delivery and carry-out service of pizza, subs, wings, breadsticks and drinks. Streamlined operations and a compact menu provide for low start-up costs and ease of operation. On-going support at every level is provided, including a marketing effort with a national focus.

BACKGROUND:

Established: 1988; 1st Franchised: 1994
Franchised Units: 135
Company-Owned Units: 31
Total Units: 166
Dist.: US-106; CAN-0; O'seas-0
North America: 5 States
Density: 83 in PA, 11 in VA, 6 in WV
Projected New Units (12 Months): 15
Qualifications: 5, 4, 4, 2, 2, 4
Registered: NR

FINANCIAL/TERMS:

Cash Investment: $25-50K
Total Investment: $95-185K
Minimum Net Worth: $75K
Fees: Franchise - $15K
Royalty - 4%; Ad. - 1%
Earnings Claims Statement: Yes
Term of Contract (Years): 10/5
Avg. # Of Employees: 8 FT, 12 PT
Passive Ownership: Not Allowed
Encourage Conversions: Yes
Area Develop. Agreements: Yes/Varies
Sub-Franchising Contracts: No
Expand In Territory: Yes
Space Needs: 1,200 SF; FS, SF, SC

SUPPORT & TRAINING:

Financial Assistance Provided: No
Site Selection Assistance: Yes
Lease Negotiation Assistance: No
Co-Operative Advertising: Yes
Franchisee Assoc./Member: No
Size Of Corporate Staff: 38
On-Going Support: B,C,D,E,F,G,H,I
Training: 4 Weeks Corporate Office; 1 Week On-Site during Opening.

SPECIFIC EXPANSION PLANS:

US: OH, PA, WV, VA
Canada: No
Overseas: No

WARD'S RESTAURANTS

7 Professional Pkwy.
Hattiesburg, MS 39402
Tel: (800) 748-9273 (601) 268-9273
Fax: (601) 268-9283
E-Mail: wfsinc@netdoor.com
Web Site: www.wardsrestaurants.com
Mr. Kenneth R. Hrdlica, President

Fast-food restaurant, both traditional and non-traditional, featuring chili-burgers, chili-dogs and frosted mugs of homemade root beer. Menu is complemented by full breakfast line and a variety of sandwiches, side orders and beverages. Seating of up to 60 and drive-thru facilities are part of the building package.

BACKGROUND:

Established: 1985; 1st Franchised: 1985
Franchised Units: 18
Company-Owned Units: 1
Total Units: 19
Dist.: US-19; CAN-0; O'seas-0
North America: 2 States
Density: 14 in MS, 5 in AL
Projected New Units (12 Months): 2
Qualifications: 5, 4, 3, 3, 3, 4
Registered: NR

FINANCIAL/TERMS:

Cash Investment: $100K
Total Investment: $300-500K
Minimum Net Worth: $100K
Fees: Franchise - $20K
Royalty - 4-5%; Ad. - NR
Earnings Claims Statement: No
Term of Contract (Years): Varies
Avg. # Of Employees: 8 FT, 7 PT
Passive Ownership: Discouraged
Encourage Conversions: Yes
Area Develop. Agreements: Yes/Varies
Sub-Franchising Contracts: No
Expand In Territory: Yes
Space Needs: 2,000 SF; FS

SUPPORT & TRAINING:

Financial Assistance Provided: No
Site Selection Assistance: Yes
Lease Negotiation Assistance: No
Co-Operative Advertising: No
Franchisee Assoc./Member: No
Size Of Corporate Staff: 4
On-Going Support: a,C,D,E,f,G,h,I
Training: 4 Weeks Home Office.

SPECIFIC EXPANSION PLANS:

US: All United States, Southeast
Canada: No
Overseas: No

<< >>

WIENERSCHNITZEL / TASTEE FREEZ

4440 Von Karman Ave., # 222
Newport Beach, CA 92660
Tel: (800) 764-9353 + 609 (949) 851-2609
Fax: (949) 851-2618
E-Mail: fcoyle@galardigroup.com
Web Site: www.wienerschnitzel.com
Mr. Frank R. Coyle, Franchise Sales Director

WIENERSCHNITZEL is the world's largest quick service hot dog restaurant chain with over 350 locations selling 90 million hot dogs annually. We are interested in developing new franchisees throughout California, the Southwest and Pacific Northwest.

BACKGROUND: IFA MEMBER

Established: 1961; 1st Franchised: 1965
Franchised Units: 370
Company-Owned Units: 0
Total Units: 370
Dist.: US-364; CAN-0; O'seas-0
North America: 11 States
Density: 228 in CA, 51 in TX, 14 in A
Projected New Units (12 Months): 35
Qualifications: 4, 3, 3, 2, 1, 4
Registered: CA,IL,OR,WA

FINANCIAL/TERMS:
Cash Investment: $150-250K
Total Investment: $135K-1.2MM
Minimum Net Worth: $500-700K
Fees: Franchise - $36K
Royalty - 5%; Ad. - 3-5%
Earnings Claims Statement: No
Term of Contract (Years): 20/1-20
Avg. # Of Employees: 1-3 FT, 25-30 PT
Passive Ownership: Discouraged
Encourage Conversions: Yes
Area Develop. Agreements: No
Sub-Franchising Contracts: No
Expand In Territory: Yes
Space Needs: 20,000 SF; FS

SUPPORT & TRAINING:
Financial Assistance Provided: Yes(I)
Site Selection Assistance: Yes
Lease Negotiation Assistance: No
Co-Operative Advertising: Yes
Franchisee Assoc./Member: Yes/Yes
Size Of Corporate Staff: 48
On-Going Support: A,B,C,D,E,F,G,H,I
Training: NR

SPECIFIC EXPANSION PLANS:
US: SW, W, NW
Canada: No
Overseas: No

<< >>

WING MACHINE

246 Parliament St.
Toronto, ON M5A 3A4 CANADA
Tel: (416) 362-4589
Fax: (416) 362-8217
E-Mail: wingmachine@netscape.net
Web Site: www.worldfranchising.com/website.htm
Mr. Frank Schiavone, President

Fast-food service, specializing in chicken wings and pizza, servicing the metropolitan Toronto area. Our wings are oven-baked in our special oven for delicious flavor. Chicken is a growing business in the 90's due to the new health-conscious consumer.

BACKGROUND:
Established: 1965; 1st Franchised: 1987
Franchised Units: 11
Company-Owned Units: 1
Total Units: 12
Dist.: US-0; CAN-12; O'seas-0
North America: 1 Province
Density: 12 in ON
Projected New Units (12 Months): 3
Qualifications: 4, 4, 3, 2, 2, 3
Registered: NR

FINANCIAL/TERMS:
Cash Investment: $50K
Total Investment: $102-204K
Minimum Net Worth: $50K
Fees: Franchise - $10K
Royalty - 6%; Ad. - 3%
Earnings Claims Statement: Yes
Term of Contract (Years): 5/5
Avg. # Of Employees: 4 FT, 2 PT
Passive Ownership: Discouraged
Encourage Conversions: NA
Area Develop. Agreements: Yes
Sub-Franchising Contracts: Yes
Expand In Territory: Yes
Space Needs: 1,000 SF; SF

SUPPORT & TRAINING:
Financial Assistance Provided: Yes
Site Selection Assistance: Yes
Lease Negotiation Assistance: Yes
Co-Operative Advertising: Yes
Franchisee Assoc./Member: No
Size Of Corporate Staff: 25
On-Going Support: A,B,C,D,E,F,G,H
Training: 6 Weeks at Corporate Store.

SPECIFIC EXPANSION PLANS:
US: All United States
Canada: All Canada
Overseas: Asia

<< >>

Top 100

WING ZONE

900 Circle 75 Pkwy., # 930
Atlanta, GA 30339-3084
Tel: (877) 946-4966 (404) 875-5045
Fax: (404) 875-6631
E-Mail: stan@wingzone.com
Web Site: www.wingzone.com
Mr. Stan Friedman, Executive Vice President

Take-out/delivery of 25 taste-tempting flavors of fresh, cooked-to-order Buffalo wings. Also featuring grilled or fried chicken sandwiches, chicken fingers, 1/2 lb. burgers, salads, onion rings, fries, appetizers and desserts, delivered hot and fresh to your door. A great opportunity in urban and suburban markets, near apartments, campuses, bases or hospitals and offices.

BACKGROUND: IFA MEMBER
Established: 1991; 1st Franchised: 1999
Franchised Units: 101
Company-Owned Units: 2
Total Units: 103
Dist.: US-67; CAN-0; O'seas-0
North America: 24 States
Density: 13 in TX, 7 in LA, 6 in FL
Projected New Units (12 Months): 30
Qualifications: 5, 5, 5, 5, 1, 5
Registered: FL,MD,MI,NY,OR,RI,VA,WA,DC

FINANCIAL/TERMS:
Cash Investment: $60-75K
Total Investment: $179.5-229.5K
Minimum Net Worth: $150K
Fees: Franchise - $25K
Royalty - 5%; Ad. - 0.5%
Earnings Claims Statement: Yes
Term of Contract (Years): 10/10
Avg. # Of Employees: 5 FT, 10 PT
Passive Ownership: Not Allowed
Encourage Conversions: No
Area Develop. Agreements: No
Sub-Franchising Contracts: No
Expand In Territory: Yes
Space Needs: 1,200 SF; SF, SC

SUPPORT & TRAINING:
Financial Assistance Provided: Yes(I)
Site Selection Assistance: Yes
Lease Negotiation Assistance: Yes
Co-Operative Advertising: No
Franchisee Assoc./Member: Yes/Yes
Size Of Corporate Staff: 12
On-Going Support: B,C,D,E,F,G,H,I
Training: 12 Days Atlanta, GA; 10 Days In-Store.

SPECIFIC EXPANSION PLANS:
US: SE, NE, MW, SW
Canada: Near Border
Overseas: No

<< >>

WINGSTOP RESTAURANTS

1234 Northwest Hwy.
Garland, TX 75041-5834
Tel: (972) 686-6500
Fax: (972) 686-6502
E-Mail: info@wingstop.com
Web Site: www.wingstop.com
Mr. Bruce Evans, Business Development

The Arlington Morning News wrote: ' With the somewhat rough-and-ready air of an early century barnstormers' aircraft hanger, WINGSTOP treads the line between neighborhood hang and a casual, laid-back dinner-snack spot. The place's signature chicken wings, however, are righteously assertive, distinctive and anything but bland . . .' WINGSTOP is fun! WINGSTOP is focused! WINGSTOP is growing fast!

BACKGROUND: IFA MEMBER
Established: 1994; 1st Franchised: 1997
Franchised Units: 72
Company-Owned Units: 2
Total Units: 74
Dist.: US-101; CAN-0; O'seas-0
North America: 13 States
Density: 63 in TX, 5 in FL, 4 in LA
Projected New Units (12 Months): 90
Qualifications: 2, 3, 2, 2, 1, 5
Registered: All States Except ND, SD

FINANCIAL/TERMS:
Cash Investment: $60-70K
Total Investment: $250K
Minimum Net Worth: $100K
Fees: Franchise - $20K
Royalty - 5%; Ad. - 2%
Earnings Claims Statement: Yes
Term of Contract (Years): 10/10
Avg. # Of Employees: 2 FT, 4 PT
Passive Ownership: Discouraged
Encourage Conversions: NA
Area Develop. Agreements: No
Sub-Franchising Contracts: No
Expand In Territory: Yes
Space Needs: 1,200-1,500 SF; SF, SC

SUPPORT & TRAINING:
Financial Assistance Provided: Yes(I)
Site Selection Assistance: Yes
Lease Negotiation Assistance: Yes
Co-Operative Advertising: Yes
Franchisee Assoc./Member: Yes/Yes
Size Of Corporate Staff: 16
On-Going Support: A,B,C,D,E,H
Training: 2 Weeks Corporate Store; 1 Week Franchise Store.

SPECIFIC EXPANSION PLANS:
US: All United States
Canada: All Canada
Overseas: All Countries

<< >>

WOODY'S BAR-B-Q

4745 Sutton Park Ct., # 301
Jacksonville, FL 32224
Tel: (904) 992-0556 + 12
Fax: (904) 992-0551
E-Mail: admin@woodysbarbq.com
Web Site: www.woodysbarbq.com
Mr. Steve David, VP Franchise Development/COO

WOODY'S BAR-B-Q is a full-service family restaurant, serving 'southern classic' ribs, chicken, pork and beef since 1981. WOODY'S support system includes full training, purchasing, site selection, marketing, opening team and field support. WOODY'S roadhouse décor is generally located in shopping center sites and is a great conversion at a low entry cost.

BACKGROUND:
Established: 1981; 1st Franchised: 1989
Franchised Units: 40
Company-Owned Units: 2
Total Units: 42
Dist.: US-40; CAN-0; O'seas-0
North America: 3 States
Density: 37 in FL, 2 in GA, 1 in AL
Projected New Units (12 Months): 8
Qualifications: 4, 3, 4, 3, 1, 5
Registered: FL

FINANCIAL/TERMS:
Cash Investment: $100-175K
Total Investment: $250-450K
Minimum Net Worth: $250K
Fees: Franchise - $35K
Royalty - 4%; Ad. - 1%
Earnings Claims Statement: No
Term of Contract (Years): 10/10
Avg. # Of Employees: 10 FT, 14 PT
Passive Ownership: Allowed
Encourage Conversions: Yes
Area Develop. Agreements: Yes/Varies
Sub-Franchising Contracts: No
Expand In Territory: Yes
Space Needs: 4,000 SF; FS, SC

SUPPORT & TRAINING:
Financial Assistance Provided: Yes(I)
Site Selection Assistance: Yes
Lease Negotiation Assistance: Yes
Co-Operative Advertising: Yes
Franchisee Assoc./Member: No
Size Of Corporate Staff: 9
On-Going Support: B,C,d,E,G,H
Training: 6 Weeks Jacksonville, FL.

SPECIFIC EXPANSION PLANS:
US: Southeast
Canada: No
Overseas: No

<< >>

YAYA'S FLAME BROILED CHICKEN

521 S. Dort Hwy.
Flint, MI 48503
Tel: (800) 754-1242 (810) 235-6550
Fax: (810) 235-5210
E-Mail: yayas@yayas.com
Web Site: www.yayas.com
Mr. John D. Chinonis, President

Flamed-broiled chicken, health oriented with great flavor. No freezers or fryers in restaurant. Dine-in or take-out. Locations in strips centers or free-standing buildings.

BACKGROUND:
Established: 1985; 1st Franchised: 1988
Franchised Units: 14
Company-Owned Units: 5
Total Units: 19
Dist.: US-20; CAN-0; O'seas-0
North America: 2 States
Density: 14 in MI, 6 in FL
Projected New Units (12 Months): 5
Qualifications: 4, 4, 3, 3, 4, 4
Registered: FL,MI,MN

FINANCIAL/TERMS:
Cash Investment: $233-336K
Total Investment: $233-336K
Minimum Net Worth: $500K
Fees: Franchise - $15K
Royalty - 4%; Ad. - 4%
Earnings Claims Statement: No
Term of Contract (Years): 10/10
Avg. # Of Employees: 7 FT, 7 PT
Passive Ownership: Not Allowed
Encourage Conversions: NA
Area Develop. Agreements: Yes/10
Sub-Franchising Contracts: No
Expand In Territory: Yes
Space Needs: 2,800 SF; FS, SF, SC

SUPPORT & TRAINING:
Financial Assistance Provided: No
Site Selection Assistance: NA
Lease Negotiation Assistance: NA
Co-Operative Advertising: Yes
Franchisee Assoc./Member: No
Size Of Corporate Staff: 6
On-Going Support: C,D,E,F,H,I
Training: 3 Weeks Flint, MI.

SPECIFIC EXPANSION PLANS:
US: All United States
Canada: All Canada
Overseas: No

<< >>

ZERO'S SUBS

2859 VA Beach Blvd., # 105
Virginia Beach, VA 23452
Tel: (800) 588-0782 (757) 486-8338
Fax: (757) 486-9755
E-Mail: zeros@zeros.com
Web Site: www.zeros.com
Ms. Kristy Pardee,

Quick service restaurant specializing in hot, oven-baked submarines, philly cheesesteaks, and pizzas. We cater to families and offer kids meals. Catering and party subs complement any special event. Our uniqueness brings customers back again and again.

BACKGROUND:
Established: 1967; 1st Franchised: 1993
Franchised Units: 65
Company-Owned Units: 0
Total Units: 65
Dist.: US-64; CAN-0; O'seas-1
North America: 7 States
Density: 45 in VA, 8 in NC, 5 in SC
Projected New Units (12 Months): 12
Qualifications: 3, 4, 5, 3, 3, 5
Registered: FL, MD, VA

FINANCIAL/TERMS:
Cash Investment: $50-75K
Total Investment: $50-150K
Minimum Net Worth: $150K
Fees: Franchise - $15K
Royalty - 6%; Ad. - 2%
Earnings Claims Statement: No
Term of Contract (Years): 15/15
Avg. # Of Employees: 4 FT, 3 PT
Passive Ownership: Discouraged
Encourage Conversions: Yes
Area Develop. Agreements: Yes/25
Sub-Franchising Contracts: Yes
Expand In Territory: Yes
Space Needs: 1,500 SF; FS, SF, SC

SUPPORT & TRAINING:
Financial Assistance Provided: Yes(I)
Site Selection Assistance: Yes
Lease Negotiation Assistance: Yes
Co-Operative Advertising: Yes
Franchisee Assoc./Member: No
Size Of Corporate Staff: 10
On-Going Support: C,d,E,F,H,I
Training: 2-3 Weeks in Virginia Beach, VA.

SPECIFIC EXPANSION PLANS:
US: East Coast and SW
Canada: No
Overseas: No

<< >>

ZOUP! FRESH SOUP COMPANY
23231 Woodward Ave.
Ferndale, MI 48220
Tel: (800) 778-7687 (248) 434-4123
Fax: (248) 339-6505
E-Mail: franchise@zoup.com
Web Site: www.zoup.com
Mr. Eric Ersher, Managing Partner

ZOUP! FRESH SOUP COMPANY, named one of Inc. Magazine's '500 fastest-growing companies,' is the country's leading quick-casual soup restaurant - defining the category with its fresh, handcrafted and all-natural soups, sandwiches, salads and smoothies. Best known for 'taking soup to the next level,' ZOUP! has used its 'everything matters' philosophy to build the state-of-the-art infrastructure, systems and support programs that make franchisees successful. Offering geographic areas to motivated people.

BACKGROUND: IFA MEMBER
Established: 1997; 1st Franchised: 2003
Franchised Units: 6
Company-Owned Units: 5
Total Units: 11
Dist.: US-11; CAN-0; O'seas-0
North America: 1 State
Density: 11 in MI
Projected New Units (12 Months): 12
Qualifications: 5, 4, 2, 3, 4, 5
Registered: IL,IN,WI

FINANCIAL/TERMS:
Cash Investment: $150-300K
Total Investment: $300-400K
Minimum Net Worth: $300K
Fees: Franchise - $25K
Royalty - 5%; Ad. - 1%
Earnings Claims Statement: Yes
Term of Contract (Years): 10/5
Avg. # Of Employees: 6 FT, 6 PT
Passive Ownership: Discouraged
Encourage Conversions: Yes
Area Develop. Agreements: Yes
Sub-Franchising Contracts: no
Expand In Territory: Yes
Space Needs: 2,200 SF; FS, SF, SC, RM

SUPPORT & TRAINING:
Financial Assistance Provided: Yes(I)
Site Selection Assistance: Yes
Lease Negotiation Assistance: Yes
Co-Operative Advertising: Yes
Franchisee Assoc./Member: No
Size Of Corporate Staff: 6
On-Going Support: A,B,C,D,E,F,G,H,I
Training: 1-2 Days Corporte Office; 10-14 Days Training Store; 1 Week or More New-Site Opening.

SPECIFIC EXPANSION PLANS:
US: MI, OH, IL, PA, MO, IN
Canada: No
Overseas: No

<< >>

Food: Restaurants/Family-Style

Chapter 17

Food: Restaurants/Family-Style Industry Profile

Total # Franchisors in Industry Group	171
Total # Franchised Units in Industry Group	18,753
Total # Company-Owned Units in Industry Group	9,020
Total # Operating Units in Industry Group	27,773
Average # Franchised Units/Franchisor	109.7
Average # Company-Owned Units/Franchisor	52.7
Average # Total Units/Franchisor	162.4
Ratio of Total # Franchised Units/Total # Company-Owned Units	2.1:1
Industry Survey Participants	67
Representing % of Industry	39.2%
Average Franchise Fee*:	$32.2K
Average Total Investment*:	$1,021.2K
Average On-Going Royalty Fee*:	4.4%

*If a range was provided, the mid-point of the range was used. See detailed profiles for actual ranges.

Five Largest Participants in Survey

Company	# Franchised Units	# Co-Owned Units	# Total Units	Franchise Fee	On-Going Royalty	Total Investment
1. Denny's	1,048	552	1,600	$40K	4%	$971K-1.8MM
2. Applebee's International	1,201	383	1,584	$35K/Unit	4%	$1.74-3.17MM
3. Big Boy Restaurant & Bakery	596	104	700	$40K	3%	$600K-1.8MM
4. Round Table Pizza Restaurant	517	19	536	$25K	4%	$420-496K
5. Friendly's Restaurants	188	348	536	$30-35K	4%	$592K-1.94MM

All of the data provided are proprietary and should not be quoted without acknowledging *Bond's Franchise Guide.*

APPLEBEE'S INTERNATIONAL

4551 W. 107th St., # 100
Overland Park, KS 66207
Tel: (913) 967-4000
Fax: (913) 967-4135
E-Mail: dave.goebel@applebees.com
Web Site: www.applebees.com
Mr. Dave Goebel, President/COO

Everyone's favorite neighbor is definitely APPLEBEE'S neighborhood grill and bar. This distinguished casual-dining restaurant has a comfortable individuality which reflects the neighborhood in which it is located, making the APPLEBEE'S concept appealing wherever it is built.

BACKGROUND: IFA MEMBER
Established: 1980; 1st Franchised: 1988
Franchised Units: 1,201
Company-Owned Units: 383
Total Units: 1,584
Dist.: US-889; CAN-5; O'seas-8
North America: 47 States, 3 Provinces
Density: 62 in FL, 54 in CA, 48 in OH
Projected New Units (12 Months): 125
Qualifications: 5, 5, 5, , , 5
Registered: All Except AB

FINANCIAL/TERMS:
Cash Investment: $1MM-50% Liq.
Total Investment: $1.74-3.17MM
Minimum Net Worth: NR
Fees: Franchise - $35K/Unit
Royalty - 4%; Ad. - 3%
Earnings Claims Statement: No
Term of Contract (Years): 20/5
Avg. # Of Employees: 75-100 FT
Passive Ownership: Not Allowed
Encourage Conversions: No
Area Develop. Agreements: Yes
Sub-Franchising Contracts: No
Expand In Territory: Yes
Space Needs: 5,000-5,400 SF; FS, SC, RM

SUPPORT & TRAINING:
Financial Assistance Provided: No
Site Selection Assistance: Yes
Lease Negotiation Assistance: Yes
Co-Operative Advertising: Yes
Franchisee Assoc./Member: Yes
Size Of Corporate Staff: 300
On-Going Support: A,B,C,D,E,G,H,I
Training: 8-12 Weeks Certified Training Unit; 3-Day Seminars at Headquarters.

SPECIFIC EXPANSION PLANS:
US: NY, LA, HI, AK
Canada: All Canada
Overseas: All Countries

<< >>

BEEF O'BRADY'S FAMILY SPORTS PUBS

5510 W. LaSalle St., # 200
Tampa, FL 33607
Tel: (800) 728-8878 + 322 (813) 226-2333 + 322
Fax: (813) 226-0030
E-Mail: scott@beefobradys.com
Web Site: www.beefobradys.com
Mr. Scott Taylor, VP Franchise Sales/Ops.

BEEF O'BRADY'S FAMILY SPORTS PUBS are family-friendly, community-oriented, casual sports pubs. BEEF's features their signature crispy buffalo-style chicken wings, great burgers, sandwiches, salads and kids' meals. Large selection of beers and wines - no hard liquor. Satellite TV. Our concept is built on the owner/operator model, where the day-to-day operations in every BEEF's is conducted by the owner. The concept is simple enough to operate that most of our partners have no prior restaurant experience.

BACKGROUND: IFA MEMBER
Established: 1985; 1st Franchised: 1998
Franchised Units: 129
Company-Owned Units: 1
Total Units: 130
Dist.: US-130; CAN-0; O'seas-0
North America: 9 States
Density: 90 in FL, 16 in GA, 12 in SC
Projected New Units (12 Months): 40
Qualifications: 3, 4, 2, 2, 4, 4
Registered: FL

FINANCIAL/TERMS:
Cash Investment: $80K
Total Investment: $250-350K
Minimum Net Worth: $150K
Fees: Franchise - $30K
Royalty - 4%; Ad. - 1.5%
Earnings Claims Statement: No
Term of Contract (Years): 10/5/5
Avg. # Of Employees: 15 FT, 10 PT
Passive Ownership: Not Allowed
Encourage Conversions: Yes
Area Develop. Agreements: Yes/5
Sub-Franchising Contracts: Yes
Expand In Territory: Yes
Space Needs: 3,000 SF; SC

SUPPORT & TRAINING:
Financial Assistance Provided: Yes(I)
Site Selection Assistance: Yes
Lease Negotiation Assistance: Yes
Co-Operative Advertising: NA
Franchisee Assoc./Member: No
Size Of Corporate Staff: 20
On-Going Support: B,C,D,E,G,H,I
Training: 6 Weeks in Approved Location.

SPECIFIC EXPANSION PLANS:
US: SE and Midwest
Canada: No
Overseas: No

<< >>

BENIHANA OF TOKYO

8685 NW 53rd Ter., # 201
Miami, FL 33166
Tel: (800) 327-3369 (305) 593-0770
Fax: (305) 592-6371
E-Mail: tvrabel@benihana.com
Web Site: www.benihana.com
Mr. Tom Vrabel, Director Franchising

BENIHANA is not only an internationally famous Japanese steak and seafood restaurant, it is also a genuine 'dining experience.' Both first-time and frequent visitors to BENIHANA are immediately drawn to the unique table top hibachi-style of cuisine, where mouth-watering dishes are prepared before their very eyes.

BACKGROUND:
Established: 1964; 1st Franchised: 1970
Franchised Units: 23
Company-Owned Units: 57
Total Units: 80
Dist.: US-57; CAN-1; O'seas-8
North America: 20 States, 1 Province
Density: 15 in CA, 6 in FL, 3 in IL
Projected New Units (12 Months): 3
Qualifications: 5, 4, 3, 2, 2, 4
Registered: CA,HI,NY

FINANCIAL/TERMS:
Cash Investment: $550-650K
Total Investment: $1.3-1.8MM
Minimum Net Worth: $1K
Fees: Franchise - $50K
Royalty - 6%; Ad. - 0.5%
Earnings Claims Statement: No
Term of Contract (Years): 15/Varies
Avg. # Of Employees: 35 FT, 7 PT
Passive Ownership: Discouraged
Encourage Conversions: Yes
Area Develop. Agreements: Yes/15
Sub-Franchising Contracts: No
Expand In Territory: No
Space Needs: 6,000+ SF; FS

SUPPORT & TRAINING:
Financial Assistance Provided: No
Site Selection Assistance: Yes
Lease Negotiation Assistance: NA
Co-Operative Advertising: Yes
Franchisee Assoc./Member: No
Size Of Corporate Staff: 51
On-Going Support: a,C,d,E,F,H,I

Training: 12-15 Weeks in Miami, FL.
SPECIFIC EXPANSION PLANS:
US: PA,MD,MI,NC,OH,AZ,TX,NY
Canada: All Canada
Overseas: Europe, Pacific Rim

<< >>

BENNIGAN'S GRILL & TAVERN

6500 International Pkwy., # 1000
Plano, TX 75093
Tel: (800) 543-9670 (972) 588-5654
Fax: (972) 588-5806
E-Mail: etaylor@metrogroup.com
Web Site: www.bennigans.com
Mr. Eric Taylor, Director Franchise Development

BENNIGAN'S is a leading casual restaurant chain known for the warm hospitality of an Irish pub and the great taste of fun American foods. Established in 1976, BENNIGAN'S has expanded beyond its original tavern image to become more food-focused. Today, each restaurant serves a wide assortment of moderately priced, quality food, as well as a wide selection of beverages.

BACKGROUND:
Established: 1976; 1st Franchised: 1995
Franchised Units: 127
Company-Owned Units: 181
Total Units: 308
Dist.: US-285; CAN-0; O'seas-23
North America: 34 States
Density: 61 in TX, 44 in FL, 23 in IL
Projected New Units (12 Months): 28
Qualifications: 5, 5, 4, 4, 4, 5
Registered: All States
FINANCIAL/TERMS:
Cash Investment: NR
Total Investment: $1.4-2.6MM
Minimum Net Worth: $3MM
Fees: Franchise - $65K
Royalty - 4%; Ad. - 4%
Earnings Claims Statement: Yes
Term of Contract (Years): 15/NR
Avg. # Of Employees: 5 FT, 65 PT
Passive Ownership: Not Allowed
Encourage Conversions: No
Area Develop. Agreements: No
Sub-Franchising Contracts: No
Expand In Territory: Yes
Space Needs: 6,689 SF; FS, SC
SUPPORT & TRAINING:
Financial Assistance Provided: No
Site Selection Assistance: No
Lease Negotiation Assistance: No
Co-Operative Advertising: Yes
Franchisee Assoc./Member: Yes/NA
Size Of Corporate Staff: 23
On-Going Support: A,B,C,D,E,F,G,H,I
Training: 13 Weeks at a Certified Training Restaurant.
SPECIFIC EXPANSION PLANS:
US: NW, SW, SE, HI
Canada: All Canada
Overseas: Germany, Italy, Portugal, Spain, Caribbean, Brazil, China

<< >>

BIG BOY RESTAURANT & BAKERY

4199 Marcy Dr.
Warren, MI 48091
Tel: (800) 837-3003 (586) 759-6000
Fax: (586) 757-4737
E-Mail: dknitter@bigboy.com
Web Site: www.bigboy.com
Mr. Dave Knitter, Franchise Development Manager

Full-service family restaurant with over 60 years of success. BIG BOY'S comprehensive menu features a daily breakfast and fruit buffet, soup, salad and fruit bar, instore bakery and award-winning desserts, in addition to traditional favorites. Industry leader in managed profitability.

BACKGROUND: IFA MEMBER
Established: 1936; 1st Franchised: 1952
Franchised Units: 596
Company-Owned Units: 104
Total Units: 700
Dist.: US-373; CAN-0; O'seas-100
North America: 17 States
Density: 142 in MI, 102 in OH, 25 KY
Projected New Units (12 Months): 7
Qualifications: 5, 5, 4, 3, 4, 5
Registered: All States
FINANCIAL/TERMS:
Cash Investment: $250K
Total Investment: $600K-1.8MM
Minimum Net Worth: $700K
Fees: Franchise - $40K
Royalty - 3%; Ad. - 3%
Earnings Claims Statement: Yes
Term of Contract (Years): 20
Avg. # Of Employees: 10 FT, 25 PT
Passive Ownership: Discouraged
Encourage Conversions: Yes
Area Develop. Agreements: Yes/20
Sub-Franchising Contracts: No
Expand In Territory: Yes
Space Needs: 5,200 SF; FS
SUPPORT & TRAINING:
Financial Assistance Provided: Yes(I)
Site Selection Assistance: Yes
Lease Negotiation Assistance: Yes
Co-Operative Advertising: Yes
Franchisee Assoc./Member: Yes/Yes
Size Of Corporate Staff: 165
On-Going Support: A,B,C,D,E,F,G,H,I
Training: 6-8 Weeks In-Unit; 1-2 Weeks at Corporate Headquarters.
SPECIFIC EXPANSION PLANS:
US: All United States
Canada: All Canada
Overseas: All Countries

<< >>

BOSTON PIZZA INTERNATIONAL

5500 Parkwood Way
Richmond, BC V6V 2M4 CANADA
Tel: (604) 270-1108
Fax: (604) 270-4168
E-Mail: villalpr@bostonpizza.com
Web Site: www.bostonpizza.com
Mr. Rick Villalpando, Dir. Franchising & Real Estate

BOSTON PIZZA is Canada's most successful casual dining pizza and pasta franchise operation, with over 170 locations in North America and system-wide sales in excess of 300 million. Boston Pizza appeals to four sectors: families at early evening, business people at lunch, after movies and takeout and delivery.

BACKGROUND:
Established: 1963; 1st Franchised: 1968
Franchised Units: 168
Company-Owned Units: 5
Total Units: 173
Dist.: US-11; CAN-162; O'seas-0
North America: 7 States, 9 Provinces
Density: 71 in AB, 46 in BC, 20 in ON
Projected New Units (12 Months): 25
Qualifications: 5, 5, 3, 3, 4, 5
Registered: All States
FINANCIAL/TERMS:
Cash Investment: $300-600K
Total Investment: $1.2-2.2MM
Minimum Net Worth: $1MM
Fees: Franchise - $35K
Royalty - 5%; Ad. - 2.5%
Earnings Claims Statement: Yes
Term of Contract (Years): 10/10
Avg. # Of Employees: 40 FT, 40 PT
Passive Ownership: Not Allowed
Encourage Conversions: No
Area Develop. Agreements: Yes/10
Sub-Franchising Contracts: No
Expand In Territory: Yes

Space Needs: 5,620 SF; FS

SUPPORT & TRAINING:

Financial Assistance Provided: Yes(I)
Site Selection Assistance: Yes
Lease Negotiation Assistance: Yes
Co-Operative Advertising: Yes
Franchisee Assoc./Member: Yes/Yes
Size Of Corporate Staff: 123
On-Going Support: B,C,D,E,F,G,H,I
Training: 6 Weeks Corporate Training Center; 2 Weeks Richmond, BC, Head Office.

SPECIFIC EXPANSION PLANS:

US: All United States
Canada: All Canada
Overseas: No

<< >>

BUFFALO WILD WINGS GRILL & BAR

1600 Utica Ave., S., # 700
Minneapolis, MN 55416-1470
Tel: (800) 499-9586 (952) 593-9943
Fax: (952) 593-9787
E-Mail: bill@buffalowildwings.com
Web Site: www.buffalowildwings.com
Mr. Bill McClintock, VP Franchise Development

Sports theme, family friendly restaurant, world-famous buffalo wings with 12 proprietary sauces, great burgers & sandwiches, full bar, 40+ TV's, National Trivia Network.

BACKGROUND: IFA MEMBER

Established: 1982; 1st Franchised: 1991
Franchised Units: 140
Company-Owned Units: 76
Total Units: 216
Dist.: US-216; CAN-0; O'seas-0
North America: 27 States
Density: 70 in OH, 20 in IN, 10 in TX
Projected New Units (12 Months): 50
Qualifications: 5, 4, 4, 3, 3, 5
Registered: All States

FINANCIAL/TERMS:

Cash Investment: $250K
Total Investment: $900K-1.0MM
Minimum Net Worth: $800K/Store
Fees: Franchise - $40K
Royalty - 5%; Ad. - 3-5%
Earnings Claims Statement: Yes
Term of Contract (Years): 15/10/5
Avg. # Of Employees: 3 FT, 50 PT
Passive Ownership: Not Allowed
Encourage Conversions: Yes
Area Develop. Agreements: Yes/10
Sub-Franchising Contracts: No
Expand In Territory: Yes
Space Needs: 5,000-6,000 SF; FS, SC

SUPPORT & TRAINING:

Financial Assistance Provided: Yes
Site Selection Assistance: Yes
Lease Negotiation Assistance: Yes
Co-Operative Advertising: Yes
Franchisee Assoc./Member: Yes/Yes
Size Of Corporate Staff: 65
On-Going Support: A,B,C,D,E,F,G,H,I
Training: 5 Weeks in Store/Classroom.

SPECIFIC EXPANSION PLANS:

US: All United States
Canada: No
Overseas: No

<< >>

BUFFALO'S SOUTHWEST CAFÉ

707 Whitlock Ave. SW, # 13
Marietta, GA 30064-3033
Tel: (800) 459-4647 (770) 420-1800
Fax: (770) 420-1811
E-Mail: teague@buffaloscafe.com
Web Site: www.buffaloscafe.com
Ms. Teri Teague, Franchise Administrator

At the value-end of the casual dining segment, our menu appeals to singles, families, groups. . . We feature Southwest entrees, world-famous wings, salads, burgers, full bar, party platters, take-out and catering. Our interior, featuring artifacts and antiques from the Old West, hardwood floor and rustic metal ceiling, adds to the overall Southwest dining experience.

BACKGROUND:

Established: 1985; 1st Franchised: 1991
Franchised Units: 42
Company-Owned Units: 9
Total Units: 51
Dist.: US-50; CAN-0; O'seas-1
North America: 6 States, Puerto Rico
Density: 32 in GA, 5 in SC, 3 in NC
Projected New Units (12 Months): 6
Qualifications: 4, 4, 4, 3, 3, 4
Registered: IN,MI

FINANCIAL/TERMS:

Cash Investment: $250-300K
Total Investment: $1.3MM
Minimum Net Worth: $2.0MM
Fees: Franchise - $35K
Royalty - 5%; Ad. - 2%
Earnings Claims Statement: No
Term of Contract (Years): 10/10
Avg. # Of Employees: 30 FT, 10 PT
Passive Ownership: Discouraged
Encourage Conversions: No
Area Develop. Agreements: Yes/Varies
Sub-Franchising Contracts: No
Expand In Territory: Yes
Space Needs: 4,700 SF; FS, End-Cap

SUPPORT & TRAINING:

Financial Assistance Provided: Yes(I)
Site Selection Assistance: Yes
Lease Negotiation Assistance: Yes
Co-Operative Advertising: Yes
Franchisee Assoc./Member: No
Size Of Corporate Staff: 16
On-Going Support: C,D,E,G,h,I
Training: 2-Day Owner Orientation; 2 Days Atlanta, GA; 28 Days Corporate Facility.

SPECIFIC EXPANSION PLANS:

US: All United States
Canada: All Canada
Overseas: All Countries

BULLWINKLE'S RESTAURANT & THE FAMILY FUN CENTERS

18300 Von Karman, # 900
Irvine, CA 92612
Tel: (949) 261-0404
Fax: (949) 261-1414
E-Mail: rowens@palaceentertainment.com
Web Site: www.bullwinkles.com
Mr. Russ Owens, Director of Acquisitions

There's only one family entertainment concept that combines great food and fun center attractions. 'Gadzooks', you say? Well, all this plus merchandise, animated shows, go-karts, soft play areas, miniature golf, games and hard rides, too.

BACKGROUND:

Established: 1982; 1st Franchised: 1994
Franchised Units: 2
Company-Owned Units: 7
Total Units: 9
Dist.: US-8; CAN-0; O'seas-1
North America: 2 States
Density: 6 in CA, 1 in OR
Projected New Units (12 Months): 3
Qualifications: 4, 5, 3, 4, 4, 4
Registered: CA,FL,NY,OR,

FINANCIAL/TERMS:

Cash Investment: $40%
Total Investment: $1.1-5.5MM
Minimum Net Worth: $650K
Fees: Franchise - $25-75K
Royalty - 4%; Ad. - 3.5%
Earnings Claims Statement: Yes
Term of Contract (Years): 15/15
Avg. # Of Employees: 40 PT, 40 FT

Passive Ownership: Discouraged
Encourage Conversions: Yes
Area Develop. Agreements: Yes/15
Sub-Franchising Contracts: No
Expand In Territory: No
Space Needs: 10,000 SF; FS

SUPPORT & TRAINING:

Financial Assistance Provided: Yes(I)
Site Selection Assistance: Yes
Lease Negotiation Assistance: Yes
Co-Operative Advertising: Yes
Franchisee Assoc./Member: No
Size Of Corporate Staff: 6
On-Going Support: A,C,D,E,F,G,H
Training: 5 Weeks Upland, CA; 3 Weeks On-Site.

SPECIFIC EXPANSION PLANS:

US: All United States
Canada: All Canada
Overseas: Middle East

≺≺ ≻≻

CHARLEY'S STEAKERY

2500 Farmers Dr., # 140
Columbus, OH 43235-5706
Tel: (800) 437-8325 (614) 923-4700
Fax: (614) 923-4701
E-Mail: franchising@charleyssteakery.com
Web Site: www.charleyssteakery.com
Mr. Ted Chang, Dir. Regional Development

CHARLEY'S STEAKERY is a progressive quick-service restaurant with over 100 locations across the United States and Canada. The heart of CHARLEY'S menu consists of freshly grilled Steak and Chicken Subs, fresh-cut fries and freshly squeezed lemonade. CHARLEY'S open kitchen environment and freshly prepared products are unique in the fast-food industry.

BACKGROUND:

Established: 1986; 1st Franchised: 1991
Franchised Units: 106
Company-Owned Units: 12
Total Units: 118
Dist.: US-96; CAN-8; O'seas-2
North America: 27 States, 1 Province
Density: 15 in OH, 8 in FL,8 in ON
Projected New Units (12 Months): 60
Qualifications: 4, 5, 2, 2, 2, 5
Registered: CA,FL,HI,IL,IN,MD,MI,NY,VA,WI

FINANCIAL/TERMS:

Cash Investment: NR
Total Investment: $124.5-294.5K
Minimum Net Worth: $200K
Fees: Franchise - $19.5K
Royalty - 5% or $200/Mo.; Ad. - 0.25%
Earnings Claims Statement: Yes
Term of Contract (Years): 10/10
Avg. # Of Employees: NR
Passive Ownership: Discouraged
Encourage Conversions: Yes
Area Develop. Agreements: Yes/10
Sub-Franchising Contracts: Yes
Expand In Territory: Yes
Space Needs: NR SF; SC, RM

SUPPORT & TRAINING:

Financial Assistance Provided: Yes(I)
Site Selection Assistance: Yes
Lease Negotiation Assistance: Yes
Co-Operative Advertising: Yes
Franchisee Assoc./Member: Yes/Yes
Size Of Corporate Staff: 18
On-Going Support: B,C,D,e(required),G,h,I
Training: 3 Weeks at Columbus, OH.

SPECIFIC EXPANSION PLANS:

US: All United States
Canada: ON
Overseas: No

≺≺ ≻≻

CHEDDAR'S CASUAL CAFÉ

616 Six Flags Dr., # 116
Arlington, TX 76011
Tel: (817) 640-4344
Fax: (817) 633-4452
E-Mail: cheddarsinc@aol.com
Web Site: www.cheddarscasualcafe.com
Mr. Douglas Rogers, President

Full-service restaurant. Terrific price/value, with traditional menu, in pleasing ambiance.

BACKGROUND:

Established: 1978; 1st Franchised: 1984
Franchised Units: 24
Company-Owned Units: 18
Total Units: 42
Dist.: US-30; CAN-0; O'seas-0
North America: 10 States
Density: 12 in TX, 6 in IL, 3 in OH
Projected New Units (12 Months): 5-7
Qualifications: 5, 4, 5, 2, 3, 5
Registered: NR

FINANCIAL/TERMS:

Cash Investment: $300K
Total Investment: $1.5-1.9MM+
Minimum Net Worth: $750K
Fees: Franchise - $30K
Royalty - 3%; Ad. - 0%
Earnings Claims Statement: No
Term of Contract (Years): 20/20
Avg. # Of Employees: 60FT, 40 PT
Passive Ownership: Not Allowed
Encourage Conversions: NR
Area Develop. Agreements: Yes/Varies
Sub-Franchising Contracts: No
Expand In Territory: NR
Space Needs: 7,700 SF; FS

SUPPORT & TRAINING:

Financial Assistance Provided: No
Site Selection Assistance: Yes
Lease Negotiation Assistance: Yes
Co-Operative Advertising: No
Franchisee Assoc./Member: No
Size Of Corporate Staff: 20
On-Going Support: B,C,D,E,F,G,H
Training: 12 Weeks Arlington, TX.

SPECIFIC EXPANSION PLANS:

US: All United States
Canada: All Canada
Overseas: All Countries

≺≺ ≻≻

COLTER'S BAR-B-Q

7502 Greenville Ave., # 500
Dallas, TX 75231
Tel: (888) 265-8377 (214) 987-5910
Fax: (214) 987-5938
E-Mail: therealstuff@mindspring.com
Web Site: www.coltersbbq.com
Mr. Mitch Johnson,

Casual, family, cafeteria-style barbeque restaurant, serving Texas barbecue in a western setting.

BACKGROUND:

Established: 1982; 1st Franchised: 1994
Franchised Units: 9
Company-Owned Units: 6
Total Units: 15
Dist.: US-13; CAN-0; O'seas-0
North America: 1 State
Density: 13 in TX
Projected New Units (12 Months): 2-4
Qualifications: 5, 4, 4, 3, 4, 3
Registered: NR

FINANCIAL/TERMS:

Cash Investment: $156-250K
Total Investment: $730K-1.03MM
Minimum Net Worth: $1-1.5MM
Fees: Franchise - $30K
Royalty - 4%; Ad. - 0.5%
Earnings Claims Statement: No
Term of Contract (Years): 20/10-20
Avg. # Of Employees: 3 FT, 25 PT
Passive Ownership: Discouraged
Encourage Conversions: No
Area Develop. Agreements: Yes/Open

Sub-Franchising Contracts: No
Expand In Territory: Yes
Space Needs: 4,600 SF; FS

SUPPORT & TRAINING:
Financial Assistance Provided: Yes(I)
Site Selection Assistance: Yes
Lease Negotiation Assistance: NA
Co-Operative Advertising: Yes
Franchisee Assoc./Member: No
Size Of Corporate Staff: 10
On-Going Support: B,C,D,E,F,H,I
Training: 8 Weeks at Dallas, TX.

SPECIFIC EXPANSION PLANS:
US: Southwest, Northeast
Canada: No
Overseas: No

<< >>

COUNTRY KITCHEN INTERNATIONAL

801 Deming Way
Madison, WI 53717-1918
Tel: (888) 359-3235 (608) 833-9633
Fax: (608) 826-9080
E-Mail: cmocco@countrykitchen.net
Web Site: www.countrykitchenrestaurant.net
Mr. Charles L. Mocco, Sr. Dir. Franchise Development

COUNTRY KITCHEN INTERNATIONAL, rated the # 1 family dining restaurant franchise, develops, operates and franchises COUNTRY KITCHEN RESTAURANTS, one of the most aggressive and growth-oriented family dining chains in the U. S. They have developed an outstanding reputation for the depth of their support system at all levels.

BACKGROUND:
Established: 1939; 1st Franchised: 1965
Franchised Units: 146
Company-Owned Units: 33
Total Units: 179
Dist.: US-179; CAN-0; O'seas-0
North America: 26 States
Density: 42 in WI, 23 in MO, 21 in MN
Projected New Units (12 Months): NR
Qualifications: , , , , ,
Registered: NR

FINANCIAL/TERMS:
Cash Investment: $150-300K
Total Investment: $670K - 1.6MM
Minimum Net Worth: $300K
Fees: Franchise - $40K
Royalty - 4%; Ad. - Up to 3%
Earnings Claims Statement: No
Term of Contract (Years): 10.5.5
Avg. # Of Employees: 20 FT, 20 PT
Passive Ownership: Allowed
Encourage Conversions: NR
Area Develop. Agreements: No
Sub-Franchising Contracts: Yes
Expand In Territory: Yes
Space Needs: NR SF; FS, SF, SC, RM, Casino

SUPPORT & TRAINING:
Financial Assistance Provided: NR
Site Selection Assistance: No
Lease Negotiation Assistance: Yes
Co-Operative Advertising: Yes
Franchisee Assoc./Member: No
Size Of Corporate Staff: 26
On-Going Support: B,C,D,E,F,G,H
Training: 10 Weeks Madison, WI.

SPECIFIC EXPANSION PLANS:
US: All United States
Canada: NR
Overseas: NR

<< >>

CRABBY BOB'S SEAFOOD GRILL

997 Grandy's Ln.
Lewisville, TX 75077-2507
Tel: (877) 457-8145 (972) 317-8086
Fax: (972) 317-8174
E-Mail: bgilbert@grandys.com
Web Site: www.crabbybobs.com
Mr. Brian Gilbert, Franchise Development

CRABBY BOB'S SEAFOOD GRILLs are family-friendly restaurants, known as 'Home of Seriously Fun, Fresh Seafood,' represent an excellent franchise opportunity. CRABBY BOB'S is a full-service seafood concept that offers a variety of fresh fish, crab, lobster and ribs in a relaxing, comfortable setting decorated with whimsical nautical artifacts. Families love our delicious seafood and fun environment, while adults enjoy our Blue Lagoon Lounge that also serves our full menu.

BACKGROUND:
Established: 1997; 1st Franchised: 1998
Franchised Units: 0
Company-Owned Units: 2
Total Units: 2
Dist.: US-2; CAN-0; O'seas-0
North America: 1 State
Density: 2 in CA
Projected New Units (12 Months): 3-6
Qualifications: 5, 5, 4, 4, 4, 4
Registered: CA

FINANCIAL/TERMS:
Cash Investment: $250K
Total Investment: $1.5-3.5MM
Minimum Net Worth: $1MM
Fees: Franchise - $50K
Royalty - 5%; Ad. - Up To 2%
Earnings Claims Statement: No
Term of Contract (Years): 15/10
Avg. # Of Employees: 8 FT, 25 PT
Passive Ownership: Allowed
Encourage Conversions: Yes
Area Develop. Agreements: TBD
Sub-Franchising Contracts: No
Expand In Territory: Yes
Space Needs: 9,500 SF; FS, SC

SUPPORT & TRAINING:
Financial Assistance Provided: No
Site Selection Assistance: Yes
Lease Negotiation Assistance: Yes
Co-Operative Advertising: Yes
Franchisee Assoc./Member: Yes
Size Of Corporate Staff: 25
On-Going Support: B,C,D,E,G,h
Training: 8-10 Weeks Irvine, CA; 8-10 Weeks TBD.

SPECIFIC EXPANSION PLANS:
US: All United States
Canada: All Canada
Overseas: All Countries

<< >>

DENNY'S

203 E. Main St.
Spartanburg, SC 29319-9912
Tel: (800) 653-4128 (864) 597-7781
Fax: (864) 597-7708
E-Mail: ddjerf@dennys.com
Web Site: www.dennys.com
Ms. Dory Djerf, Franchise Recruiting/Devel.

DENNY'S is America's restaurant. As the undisputed leader in full-service, family dining, DENNY'S enjoys a 99% national brand awareness and a 15% national market share. We have the greatest number of restaurants and the largest advertising budget in the family restaurant segment. Our mission is to profitably grow the company by providing our guests with great food, service and hospitality, in a clean, comfortable restaurant, 24 hours a day.

BACKGROUND: IFA MEMBER
Established: 1953; 1st Franchised: 1963
Franchised Units: 1,048
Company-Owned Units: 552
Total Units: 1,600
Dist.: US-1,574; CAN-53; O'seas-24
North America: 49 States, 5 Provinces
Density: 401 in CA, 184 in FL, 156 in
Projected New Units (12 Months): 25
Qualifications: 5, 4, 5, 3, , 5
Registered: All States

FINANCIAL/TERMS:
Cash Investment: Varies
Total Investment: $971K-1.8MM
Minimum Net Worth: $1MM
Fees: Franchise - $40K
Royalty - 4%; Ad. - 3%
Earnings Claims Statement: Yes
Term of Contract (Years): 20/NA
Avg. # Of Employees: Varies
Passive Ownership: Not Allowed
Encourage Conversions: Yes
Area Develop. Agreements: Yes/Varies
Sub-Franchising Contracts: No
Expand In Territory: Yes
Space Needs: 3,370-5,085 SF; FS

SUPPORT & TRAINING:
Financial Assistance Provided: No
Site Selection Assistance: Yes
Lease Negotiation Assistance: No
Co-Operative Advertising: Yes
Franchisee Assoc./Member: Yes/No
Size Of Corporate Staff: 10
On-Going Support: C,D,e,G,I
Training: Up to 10 Weeks at Nearest Training Restaurant to the Franchisee.

SPECIFIC EXPANSION PLANS:
US: All United States
Canada: All Canada
Overseas: No

<< >>

DICKEY'S BARBECUE PIT RESTAURANTS

4514 Cole Ave., # 1000
Dallas, TX 75205
Tel: (866) 340-6188 (972) 248-9899
Fax: (972) 248-8667
E-Mail: info@dickeys.com
Web Site: www.dickeys.com
Ms. Debra Maher, Director Franchise Sales/Devel

Fast casual barbecue restaurant. Simple, efficient operating system. Am,ple training and on-going support. Unique counter service and drive-thru, quick-serve concept with great food - and great sales. We have a great family of franchisees that are about half minority operators. We are growing fast. Come join us and join in the profit.

BACKGROUND: IFA MEMBER
Established: 1941; 1st Franchised: 1994
Franchised Units: 54
Company-Owned Units: 5
Total Units: 59
Dist.: US-59; CAN-0; O'seas-0
North America: 5 States
Density: 53 in TX, 2 in CO, 1 in NJ
Projected New Units (12 Months): 20
Qualifications: 5, 4, 1, 4, 1, 5
Registered: NR

FINANCIAL/TERMS:
Cash Investment: $150-350K
Total Investment: $508K-1.8MM
Minimum Net Worth: $500K
Fees: Franchise - $25/30K
Royalty - 4%; Ad. - 4%
Earnings Claims Statement: Yes
Term of Contract (Years): 10/20
Avg. # Of Employees: 14 FT
Passive Ownership: Discouraged
Encourage Conversions: Yes
Area Develop. Agreements: No
Sub-Franchising Contracts: No
Expand In Territory: No
Space Needs: 3,000 SF; FS, SC, RM, Conversions

SUPPORT & TRAINING:
Financial Assistance Provided: No
Site Selection Assistance: Yes
Lease Negotiation Assistance: Yes
Co-Operative Advertising: Yes
Franchisee Assoc./Member: No
Size Of Corporate Staff: 12
On-Going Support: B,C,D,E,F,G,H,,I
Training: 30 Days Dallas, TX.

SPECIFIC EXPANSION PLANS:
US: All United States
Canada: All Canada
Overseas: Europe, Pacific Rim

<< >>

DUKE SANDWICH COMPANY

1001 Poinsett Hwy.
Greenville, SC 29609
Tel: (877) 308-2343 (864) 331-0703
Fax: (864) 232-0706
E-Mail: franchise@dukesandwich.com
Web Site: www.dukesandwich.com
Ms. Jennifer Stephens, Marketing/Relations Director

We are a family-owned and operated sandwich company with superb sandwich spreads, a superior business system and nearly 90 years of quality, tradition and experience.

BACKGROUND: IFA MEMBER
Established: 1917; 1st Franchised: 2004
Franchised Units: 0
Company-Owned Units: 3
Total Units: 3
Dist.: US-3; CAN-0; O'seas-0
North America: 1 State
Density: 3 in SC
Projected New Units (12 Months): NR
Qualifications: 4, 3, 3, 3, 3, 4
Registered:

FINANCIAL/TERMS:
Cash Investment: $60-100K
Total Investment: $90-240K
Minimum Net Worth: $400K
Fees: Franchise - $25K
Royalty - 6%; Ad. - 2%
Earnings Claims Statement: No
Term of Contract (Years): 5/20
Avg. # Of Employees: 3 FT, 4 PT
Passive Ownership: NR
Encourage Conversions: Yes
Area Develop. Agreements: Yes/5
Sub-Franchising Contracts: No
Expand In Territory: Yes
Space Needs: 1,800-2,400 SF; SC

SUPPORT & TRAINING:
Financial Assistance Provided: No
Site Selection Assistance: Yes
Lease Negotiation Assistance: No
Co-Operative Advertising: NR
Franchisee Assoc./Member: No
Size Of Corporate Staff: 5
On-Going Support: A,C,D,E,G,H,I
Training: 3-4 Weeks at Headquarters or Specified Training Site.

SPECIFIC EXPANSION PLANS:
US: Southeast
Canada: No
Overseas: No

<< >>

EATZA PIZZA

4800 N. Scottsdale Rd., # 3000
Scottsdale, AZ 85251-7631
Tel: (800) 596-8464 (480) 941-5200
Fax: (480) 941-5202
E-Mail: rcordova@eatzapizza.com
Web Site: www.eatzapizza.com
Mr. Ronn Cordova, Franchise Devel. Director

EATZA PIZZA is an all-you-can-eat pizza, pasta, salad and dessert family buffet restaurant. The combination of a great concept, lower than average investment requirements, outstanding systems and franchisee support makes for the ultimate recipe for success!

BACKGROUND: IFA MEMBER
Established: 1999; 1st Franchised: 1999
Franchised Units: 49
Company-Owned Units: 13
Total Units: 62
Dist.: US-21; CAN-0; O'seas-0
North America: 5 States
Density: 14 in AZ, 4 in UT, 2 in WA
Projected New Units (12 Months): 13
Qualifications: 3, 4, 4, 3, 5, 5
Registered: CA,IN,MI,OR,WA,WI

FINANCIAL/TERMS:
Cash Investment: $55.5-104K
Total Investment: $185.1-347.5K
Minimum Net Worth: $250K
Fees: Franchise - $25K
Royalty - 5%; Ad. - 4%
Earnings Claims Statement: No
Term of Contract (Years): 10/10
Avg. # Of Employees: 2-4 FT, 12-24 PT
Passive Ownership: NR
Encourage Conversions: No
Area Develop. Agreements: Yes
Sub-Franchising Contracts: Yes
Expand In Territory: Yes
Space Needs: 5,200 SF; FS, SC

SUPPORT & TRAINING:
Financial Assistance Provided: Yes(I)
Site Selection Assistance: Yes
Lease Negotiation Assistance: Yes
Co-Operative Advertising: No
Franchisee Assoc./Member: No
Size Of Corporate Staff: 9
On-Going Support: B,C,D,e,F,G,H,I
Training: 3 Weeks Phoenix, AZ.

SPECIFIC EXPANSION PLANS:
US: West, Great Lakes, Upper/Central US
Canada: No
Overseas: No

<< >>

EDO JAPAN

4838 32nd St. SE
Calgary, AB T2B 2S6 CANADA
Tel: (888) 336-9888 (403) 215-8800
Fax: (403) 215-8801
E-Mail: simon@edojapan.com
Web Site: www.edojapan.com
Mr. Simon Lileikis, Director of Operations

EDO JAPAN originated the concept of preparing Japanese Teppan Meals inexpensively through fast-food outlets more than 20 years ago. Since that time, EDO has maintained its popularity in the food courts due to EDO's menu placing emphasis on freshness, nutrition, service and very reasonable prices.

BACKGROUND:
Established: 1977; 1st Franchised: 1986
Franchised Units: 93
Company-Owned Units: 3
Total Units: 96
Dist.: US-46; CAN-55; O'seas-3
North America: 13 States, 5 Provinces
Density: 28 in AB, 16 in ON, 14 in CA
Projected New Units (12 Months): 6
Qualifications: 5, 4, 4, 3, 4, 5
Registered: CA,FL,HI,MD,OR,WA,AB

FINANCIAL/TERMS:
Cash Investment: NR
Total Investment: $160-350K
Minimum Net Worth: NR
Fees: Franchise - $20K
Royalty - 6%; Ad. - 0-2%
Earnings Claims Statement: No
Term of Contract (Years): Lease
Avg. # Of Employees: 2 FT, 4 PT
Passive Ownership: Discouraged
Encourage Conversions: NA
Area Develop. Agreements: Yes/Varies
Sub-Franchising Contracts: Yes
Expand In Territory: Yes
Space Needs: 350-650 SF; RM

SUPPORT & TRAINING:
Financial Assistance Provided: No
Site Selection Assistance: Yes
Lease Negotiation Assistance: Yes
Co-Operative Advertising: Yes
Franchisee Assoc./Member: No
Size Of Corporate Staff: 10
On-Going Support: B,C,D,E,F,G,H
Training: 2 Weeks Calgary, AB; 10 Days Opening Assistance On-Site.

SPECIFIC EXPANSION PLANS:
US: All United States
Canada: No
Overseas: No

<< >>

EL CHICO CAFÉ

12200 Stemmons Fwy., # 100
Dallas, TX 75234
Tel: (800) 275-1337 (972) 241-5500
Fax: (214) 888-8198
E-Mail: info-web@croinc.com
Web Site: www.croinc.com
Mr. Adam Mandel, Director of Franchising

EL CHICO has been serving top-quality Mexican food favorites since 1940. Today we offer two exciting concepts. EL CHICO CAFÉ serves delicious, freshly-prepared tex-mex dishes. The strength of EL CHICO CAFÉ comes from the fact that we have been in this business so long that we know how to improve traditional favorites and how to introduce our guests to the next level of great Mexican food. Our other concept is CANTINA LAREDO, which serves authentic Mexico City-style dishes in a sophisticated atmosphere.

BACKGROUND:
Established: 1940; 1st Franchised: 1969
Franchised Units: 25
Company-Owned Units: 66
Total Units: 91
Dist.: US-91; CAN-0; O'seas-0
North America: 12 States
Density: 41 in TX, 18 in OK, 8 in LA
Projected New Units (12 Months): 10
Qualifications: 5, 5, 5, 3, 2, 5
Registered: NR

FINANCIAL/TERMS:
Cash Investment: $300-600K

Total Investment: $1.4-2.6MM
Minimum Net Worth: $1MM
Fees: Franchise - $35-50K
Royalty - 5%; Ad. - NR
Earnings Claims Statement: Yes
Term of Contract (Years): 15/10
Avg. # Of Employees: NR
Passive Ownership: Discouraged
Encourage Conversions: Yes
Area Develop. Agreements: Yes
Sub-Franchising Contracts: No
Expand In Territory: Yes
Space Needs: NR SF; FS, SC, RM

SUPPORT & TRAINING:
Financial Assistance Provided: Yes(I)
Site Selection Assistance: Yes
Lease Negotiation Assistance: Yes
Co-Operative Advertising: No
Franchisee Assoc./Member: Yes
Size Of Corporate Staff: 74
On-Going Support: B,C,D,E,F,H,I
Training: 6 Weeks Dallas, TX; 3 Weeks On-Site.

SPECIFIC EXPANSION PLANS:
US: All United States
Canada: All Canada
Overseas: All Countries

<< >>

ELMER'S BREAKFAST/LUNCH/ DINNER

11802 SE Stark St.
Portland, OR 97216
Tel: (800) 325-5188 (503) 252-1485
Fax: (503) 252-6706
E-Mail: jerryscott@worldnet.att.net
Web Site: www.elmers-restaurants.com
Mr. Jerry Scott, VP Operations/Franchising

Full-service, family oriented restaurant serving three meals a day. All menu items served all day. Banquet facilities.

BACKGROUND: IFA MEMBER
Established: 1960; 1st Franchised: 1966
Franchised Units: 22
Company-Owned Units: 10
Total Units: 32
Dist.: US-32; CAN-0; O'seas-0
North America: 6 States
Density: 17 in OR, 5 in WA, 5 in ID
Projected New Units (12 Months): 5
Qualifications: 5, 4, 1, 1, 3, 5
Registered: CA,FL,IL,OR,WA,WI

FINANCIAL/TERMS:
Cash Investment: $100-400K
Total Investment: $400K-1.2MM
Minimum Net Worth: Varies
Fees: Franchise - $35K
Royalty - 4%; Ad. - 1%
Earnings Claims Statement: No
Term of Contract (Years): 25
Avg. # Of Employees: 15 FT, 35 PT
Passive Ownership: Discouraged
Encourage Conversions: Yes
Area Develop. Agreements: Yes/5
Sub-Franchising Contracts: No
Expand In Territory: Yes
Space Needs: 5,500 SF; FS, SC, RM

SUPPORT & TRAINING:
Financial Assistance Provided: Yes(I)
Site Selection Assistance: Yes
Lease Negotiation Assistance: Yes
Co-Operative Advertising: Yes
Franchisee Assoc./Member: No
Size Of Corporate Staff: 20
On-Going Support: a,B,C,D,E,F,G,H,I
Training: 8-12 Weeks Portland, OR.

SPECIFIC EXPANSION PLANS:
US: Northwest, Southwest
Canada: No
Overseas: No

<< >>

FAMOUS DAVE'S

8091 Wallace Rd.
Eden Prairie, MN 55344-2224
Tel: (800) 210-4040 + 1343 (952) 294-1343
Fax: (952) 294-0242
E-Mail: jim.schwitzer@famousdaves.com
Web Site: www.famousdaves.com
Mr. Jim Schwitzer, Director Franchise Sales/Devel

FAMOUS DAVE'S develops, owns, operates and franchises barbecue-style restaurants. We feature award-winning barbecued and grilled meats and other unique menu items in a fun environment. The company currently has 55 franchised units and 38 Company-owned units.

BACKGROUND: IFA MEMBER
Established: 1994; 1st Franchised: 1998
Franchised Units: 55
Company-Owned Units: 38
Total Units: 93
Dist.: US-93; CAN-0; O'seas-0
North America: 23 States
Density: 19 in MN, 13 in IL, 6 in VA
Projected New Units (12 Months): 25
Qualifications: 5, 4, 5, 3, 3, 5
Registered: All States Except RI

FINANCIAL/TERMS:
Cash Investment: $250-950K
Total Investment: $650K-3.2MM
Minimum Net Worth: $750K
Fees: Franchise - $40K
Royalty - 5%/$5K/Mo.; Ad. - 2%
Earnings Claims Statement: Yes
Term of Contract (Years): 20/10
Avg. # Of Employees: 20 FT, 45 PT
Passive Ownership: Discouraged
Encourage Conversions: Yes
Area Develop. Agreements: Yes/5
Sub-Franchising Contracts: No
Expand In Territory: Yes
Space Needs: 6,100 SF; FS, SC

SUPPORT & TRAINING:
Financial Assistance Provided: Yes(I)
Site Selection Assistance: Yes
Lease Negotiation Assistance: Yes
Co-Operative Advertising: Yes
Franchisee Assoc./Member: Yes/Yes
Size Of Corporate Staff: 78
On-Going Support: A,B,C,D,E,G,H,I
Training: Varies. 35 Days Minimum.

SPECIFIC EXPANSION PLANS:
US: Selected States
Canada: No
Overseas: No

<< >>

FAMOUS FAMIGLIA

199 Main St., 8th Fl.
White Plains, NY 10601
Tel: (914) 328-4444
Fax: (914) 328-4479
E-Mail: info@famousfamiglia.com
Web Site: www.famousfamiglia.com
Mr. Giorgio Kolaj, Executive Vice President

FAMOUS FAMIGLIA is an award-winning national pizza brand with leading sales in the pizza segment. Operating nationwide, FAMOUS FAMIGLIA has earned several leading industry awards that herald its unsurpassed product quality and unparalleled customer service. Our expansion plans include high-profile markets and locations, such as: leading airports, universities, travel plazas, etc. We have a successful franchise program in place and we offer a number of high-caliber locations nationwide.

BACKGROUND: IFA MEMBER

Established: 1986; 1st Franchised: 2002
Franchised Units: 17
Company-Owned Units: 23
Total Units: 40
Dist.: US-40; CAN-0; O'seas-0
North America: 11 States
Density: 15 in NY, 6 in PA, 4 in IL
Projected New Units (12 Months): 15
Qualifications: , , , , ,
Registered:All States Except ND, OR and SD.

FINANCIAL/TERMS:
Cash Investment: $200K
Total Investment: $250-500K
Minimum Net Worth: $500K
Fees: Franchise - $35K
Royalty - 6%; Ad. - 1%
Earnings Claims Statement: No
Term of Contract (Years): 10/5-10
Avg. # Of Employees: 4 FT, 8 PT
Passive Ownership: Discouraged
Encourage Conversions: Yes
Area Develop. Agreements: No
Sub-Franchising Contracts: No
Expand In Territory: Yes
Space Needs:1,000 SF; SF, SC, RM, Food Court

SUPPORT & TRAINING:
Financial Assistance Provided: No
Site Selection Assistance: Yes
Lease Negotiation Assistance: Yes
Co-Operative Advertising: Yes
Franchisee Assoc./Member: No
Size Of Corporate Staff: 12
On-Going Support: a,B,C,D,E,F,G,H,I
Training: 2-3 Weeks Corporate Headquarters, NY.

SPECIFIC EXPANSION PLANS:
US: All United States
Canada: All Canada
Overseas: All Countries

<< >>

Friendly's

Top 100

FRIENDLY'S RESTAURANTS
1855 Boston Rd.
Wilbraham, MA 01095-1002
Tel: (800) 576-8088 (413) 543-2400
Fax: (413) 543-2820
E-Mail: laurel.adams@friendlys.com
Web Site: www.friendlys.com
Ms. Laurel Adams, Franchise Development Manager

FRIENDLY'S is a full-service restaurant chain with ice cream a key point of difference. FRIENDLY'S has experienced growth in every year since 2000. The franchisee will receive support, including training, marketing, site selection, store openings and on-going operational assistance.

BACKGROUND: IFA MEMBER
Established: 1935; 1st Franchised: 1997
Franchised Units: 188
Company-Owned Units: 348
Total Units: 536
Dist.: US-536; CAN-0; O'seas-0
North America: 16 States
Density: 122 in MA, 115 in NY, 66 PA
Projected New Units (12 Months): 15
Qualifications: , , , , ,
Registered: FL,IL,IN,MD,NY,RI,VA

FINANCIAL/TERMS:
Cash Investment: $400-500K
Total Investment: $592K-1.94MM
Minimum Net Worth: $1.5MM-650Liq
Fees: Franchise - $30-35K
Royalty - 4%; Ad. - 3%
Earnings Claims Statement: Yes
Term of Contract (Years): 20/10-20
Avg. # Of Employees: 40 FT, 35 PT
Passive Ownership: Not Allowed
Encourage Conversions: Yes
Area Develop. Agreements: Yes
Sub-Franchising Contracts: No
Expand In Territory: Yes
Space Needs: 4,100-5,000 SF; FS

SUPPORT & TRAINING:
Financial Assistance Provided: No
Site Selection Assistance: Yes
Lease Negotiation Assistance: No
Co-Operative Advertising: No
Franchisee Assoc./Member: No
Size Of Corporate Staff: 350
On-Going Support: A,b,C,d,E,F,G,h
Training: 12 Weeks at the Corporate Training Center and in Individual Training Units.

SPECIFIC EXPANSION PLANS:
US: SE, NE, Mid-Atlantic
Canada: No
Overseas: No

<< >>

FUDDRUCKERS
4407 Monterey Oaks Blvd., Bldg. 1, # 101
Austin, TX 78749
Tel: (512) 275-0426
Fax: (512) 275-0670
E-Mail: dino.chavez@fuddruckers.com
Web Site: www.fuddruckers.com
Mr. Dino Chavez, Franchise Sales Manager

It's an exciting time at FUDDRUCKERS. Our relentless commitment to freshness makes us "Home of the World's Greatest Hamburgers". Our in-house butcher shops and bakeries provide our guests with the freshest products available. FUDDRUCKERS' menu includes not only our famous 1/3 and 1/2 pound hamburgers but now features a 1-lb. burger. We have also added Big Bowl salads, new Steakhouse Platters and fantastic desserts like our Brownie Blast Sundae. We also have a new 50's and 60's rock and roll image.

BACKGROUND: IFA MEMBER
Established: 1980; 1st Franchised: 1983
Franchised Units: 110
Company-Owned Units: 111
Total Units: 221
Dist.: US-204; CAN-1; O'seas-21
North America: 30 States, 1 Province
Density: 44 in TX, 16 in CA, 12 in VA
Projected New Units (12 Months): 30
Qualifications: 5, 5, 4, 3, 2, 5
Registered: CA,FL,HI,IL,IN,MD,MI,MN, NY,ND,RI,SD,VA,WA,DC

FINANCIAL/TERMS:
Cash Investment: $550K
Total Investment: $740K-1.48MM
Minimum Net Worth: $1.5MM
Fees: Franchise - $50K
Royalty - 5%; Ad. - 0-4%
Earnings Claims Statement: Yes
Term of Contract (Years): 10 & 20
Avg. # Of Employees: 15 FT, 30 PT
Passive Ownership: Discouraged
Encourage Conversions: Yes
Area Develop. Agreements: Yes/Varies
Sub-Franchising Contracts: No
Expand In Territory: Yes
Space Needs: 6,200-7,000 SF; FS

SUPPORT & TRAINING:
Financial Assistance Provided: No
Site Selection Assistance: Yes
Lease Negotiation Assistance: No
Co-Operative Advertising: Yes
Franchisee Assoc./Member: No
Size Of Corporate Staff: 70
On-Going Support: C,D,E,G,H
Training: 6-8 Weeks at Regional Training Locations.

SPECIFIC EXPANSION PLANS:
US: All United States
Canada: All Canada
Overseas: All Countries

<< >>

GARFIELD'S RESTAURANT & PUB

1220 S. Santa Fe Ave.
Edmond, OK 73003-5904
Tel: (405) 705-5000
Fax: (405) 705-5004
E-Mail: heidiv@eats-inc.com
Web Site: www.eats-inc.com
Ms. Heidi Valenzuela, Franchise Marketing Manager

A friendly casual dining restaurant serving an American menu of convenience, quality and value.

BACKGROUND:
Established: 1984; 1st Franchised: 1987
Franchised Units: 11
Company-Owned Units: 47
Total Units: 58
Dist.: US-58; CAN-0; O'seas-0
North America: 26 States
Density: 8 in IN, 6 in OK, 4 in MO
Projected New Units (12 Months): 12
Qualifications: 5, 3, 5, 3, 3, 5
Registered:CA,FL,IL,IN,MD,MI,MN,NY, ND,OR,RI,SD,VA,WA,WI

FINANCIAL/TERMS:
Cash Investment: $300-500K
Total Investment: $1.2-2.0MM
Minimum Net Worth: $1MM
Fees: Franchise - $30K
Royalty - 4%; Ad. - 3.5%
Earnings Claims Statement: No
Term of Contract (Years): 20/5
Avg. # Of Employees: 50 FT, 25 PT
Passive Ownership: Not Allowed
Encourage Conversions: Yes
Area Develop. Agreements: Yes/Negot.
Sub-Franchising Contracts: No
Expand In Territory: Yes
Space Needs: 4,500-5,000 SF; FS,SC,RM

SUPPORT & TRAINING:
Financial Assistance Provided: No
Site Selection Assistance: Yes
Lease Negotiation Assistance: No
Co-Operative Advertising: Yes
Franchisee Assoc./Member: Yes
Size Of Corporate Staff: 48
On-Going Support: a,C,D,E
Training: 8 Weeks in Edmond, OK.

SPECIFIC EXPANSION PLANS:
US: All United States
Canada: No
Overseas: No

GOLDEN CORRAL FAMILY STEAKHOUSE

P. O. Box 29502
Raleigh, NC 27626-0502
Tel: (800) 284-5673 (919) 881-5128
Fax: (919) 881-5252
E-Mail: tsullivan@goldencorral.net
Web Site: www.goldencorralfranchise.com
Mrs. Tammy Sullivan, Franchise Development

Golden Corral family restaurants feature 'steaks, buffet and bakery.' The 'Golden Choice Buffet' offers 150 hot and cold items, including all you care to eat steak. A special feature is 'The Brass Bell Bakery' which prepares made-from-scratch rolls, cookies, muffins, brownies and pizza. Steak, chicken and fish entrees are also available. Value-driven concept with a $7.80 per person check average in 2004. Open lunch and dinner - 7 days; Breakfast Buffet - weekends or holidays.

BACKGROUND: IFA MEMBER
Established: 1973; 1st Franchised: 1986
Franchised Units: 345
Company-Owned Units: 120
Total Units: 465
Dist.: US-465; CAN-0; O'seas-0
North America: 38 States
Density: TX, OK, NC
Projected New Units (12 Months): 25
Qualifications: , , , , ,
Registered: All States Except HI

FINANCIAL/TERMS:
Cash Investment: $350K
Total Investment: $1.7-4.0MM
Minimum Net Worth: $1.5MM
Fees: Franchise - $40K
Royalty - 4%; Ad. - 2%
Earnings Claims Statement: Yes
Term of Contract (Years): 15/5
Avg. # Of Employees: 80 FT, 40 PT
Passive Ownership: Not Allowed
Encourage Conversions: No
Area Develop. Agreements: Yes/Varies
Sub-Franchising Contracts: No
Expand In Territory: Yes
Space Needs: 7,780-11,900 SF; FS

SUPPORT & TRAINING:
Financial Assistance Provided: No
Site Selection Assistance: Yes
Lease Negotiation Assistance: No
Co-Operative Advertising: Yes
Franchisee Assoc./Member: NR
Size Of Corporate Staff: 200
On-Going Support: C,D,E,G
Training: 12 Weeks Headquarters and Field.

SPECIFIC EXPANSION PLANS:
US: All United States
Canada: No
Overseas: No

<< >>

GREAT STEAK & POTATO COMPANY, THE

7730 E. Greenway Rd., # 104
Scottsdale, AZ 85260
Tel: (480) 443-0200
Fax: (480) 443-0972
E-Mail: roger@thegreatsteak.com
Web Site: www.kahalacorp.com
Mr. Roger J. Burrin, Vice President of Development

America's premier fresh grilled cheesesteak franchisor, serving hand-cut french fries (cooked in peanut oil), baked potatoes with various toppings, grilled topped salads, homemade soups and fresh-squeezed lemonade.

BACKGROUND:
Established: 1982; 1st Franchised: 1984
Franchised Units: 242
Company-Owned Units: 9
Total Units: 251
Dist.: US-214; CAN-12; O'seas-4
North America: 31 States, 1 Province
Density: 32 in OH, 27 in CA, 25 in IL
Projected New Units (12 Months): 24
Qualifications: 4, 4, 3, 2, 3, 4
Registered: All States

FINANCIAL/TERMS:
Cash Investment: $75-100K
Total Investment: $200-800K
Minimum Net Worth: $200K
Fees: Franchise - $20K
Royalty - 5%; Ad. - 2%
Earnings Claims Statement: No
Term of Contract (Years): 10/10
Avg. # Of Employees: 2 FT, 15 PT
Passive Ownership: Allowed
Encourage Conversions: Yes
Area Develop. Agreements: Yes/10
Sub-Franchising Contracts: Yes
Expand In Territory: Yes
Space Needs:600-2,000 SF; FS,SF,SC,RM,

Airports,Univ.

SUPPORT & TRAINING:

Financial Assistance Provided: Yes(I)
Site Selection Assistance: Yes
Lease Negotiation Assistance: Yes
Co-Operative Advertising: Yes
Franchisee Assoc./Member: No
Size Of Corporate Staff: 28
On-Going Support: a,B,C,D,E,F,G,H
Training: 2 Weeks Hamilton, OH.

SPECIFIC EXPANSION PLANS:

US: All United States
Canada: All Canada
Overseas: No

<< >>

GROUND ROUND, THE

703 Granite St.
Braintree, MA 02184-9078
Tel: (800) 229-7005 (781) 380-3125
Fax: (781) 380-3244
E-Mail: info@groundround.com
Web Site: www.groundround.com
Ms. Michele R. Inglese, Franchcise Devel. Coord

THE GROUND ROUND GRILL & BAR has a solid plan for success. Whether you wish to diversify or add to your portfolio, we are currently developing exciting franchise opportunities in the country's most desirable markets. The GROUND ROUND is a proven casual dining concept that profits from its vision, commitment and energy. Call or click today and start building a growth plan that can really pay dividends.

BACKGROUND:

Established: 1969; 1st Franchised: 1970
Franchised Units: 73
Company-Owned Units: 60
Total Units: 133
Dist.: US-132; CAN-1; O'seas-0
North America: 24 States, 1 Province
Density: 19 in NY, 19 in MA, 16 in PA
Projected New Units (12 Months): 15
Qualifications: 5, 5, 4, 3, 3, 4
Registered: CA,FL,HI,IL,IN,MD,MI,MN, NY,ND,RI,SD,VA,WA,WI

FINANCIAL/TERMS:

Cash Investment: $125-200K
Total Investment: $1.0-1.9MM
Minimum Net Worth: $800K
Fees: Franchise - $40K
Royalty - 4%; Ad. - 3%
Earnings Claims Statement: Yes
Term of Contract (Years): 20/5/5/5
Avg. # Of Employees: 15 FT, 52 PT
Passive Ownership: Not Allowed
Encourage Conversions: Yes
Area Develop. Agreements: Yes
Sub-Franchising Contracts: No
Expand In Territory: No
Space Needs:43,560 Min. SF; FS, SC, RM

SUPPORT & TRAINING:

Financial Assistance Provided: Yes(I)
Site Selection Assistance: Yes
Lease Negotiation Assistance: No
Co-Operative Advertising: Yes
Franchisee Assoc./Member: Yes/Yes
Size Of Corporate Staff: 58
On-Going Support: B,C,d,e G,h,I
Training: 6-10 Weeks at Regional Training Unit.

SPECIFIC EXPANSION PLANS:

US: NE, MW, Atl. States, Grt Lks
Canada: No
Overseas: No

<< >>

HARVEY'S RESTAURANTS

6303 Airport Rd.
Mississauga, ON L4V 1R8 CANADA
Tel: (905) 405-6771
Fax: (905) 405-6667
E-Mail: jattwood@cara.com
Web Site: www.cara.com
Ms. Jocelyn Attwood, Franchise Coordinator

Foodservice. Quick-service restaurants.

BACKGROUND:

Established: 1900; 1st Franchised: 1982
Franchised Units: 290
Company-Owned Units: 60
Total Units: 350
Dist.: US-0; CAN-350; O'seas-0
North America: NR
Density: ON, PQ, AB
Projected New Units (12 Months): 42
Qualifications: 5, 4, 3, 3, 1, 5
Registered: AB

FINANCIAL/TERMS:

Cash Investment: $155-200K
Total Investment: $510-600K
Minimum Net Worth: $300K
Fees: Franchise - $50-75K
Royalty - 5%; Ad. - 4%
Earnings Claims Statement: Yes
Term of Contract (Years): 20/5x4
Avg. # Of Employees: 3 FT, 40 PT
Passive Ownership: Not Allowed
Encourage Conversions: Yes
Area Develop. Agreements: No
Sub-Franchising Contracts: No
Expand In Territory: Yes
Space Needs: 2,600 SF; FS

SUPPORT & TRAINING:

Financial Assistance Provided: NA
Site Selection Assistance: Yes
Lease Negotiation Assistance: Yes
Co-Operative Advertising: Yes
Franchisee Assoc./Member: Yes/Yes
Size Of Corporate Staff: 200
On-Going Support: C,D,E,G,h,I
Training: 6-8 Weeks Toronto, ON.

SPECIFIC EXPANSION PLANS:

US: No
Canada: All Canada
Overseas: No

<< >>

HUDDLE HOUSE RESTAURANTS

2969 E. Ponce de Leon Ave.
Decatur, GA 30030
Tel: (800) 868-5700 (404) 377-5700
Fax: (404) 377-0497
E-Mail: franchise@huddlehouse.com
Web Site: www.huddlehouse.com
Ms. Brianne Skinner, Franchise Development Admin.

HUDDLE HOUSE RESTAURANTS are open 24 hours a day, serving delicious meals, cooked to order - a place where hungry folks gather to enjoy good food, good friends and good hospitality. HUDDLE HOUSE RESTAURANTS offer any meal, any time from our broad menu of breakfast, lunch and dinner entrees, featuring, 'Big House' platters, which are our signature 'Big Meals for Big Appetites.'

BACKGROUND: IFA MEMBER

Established: 1964; 1st Franchised: 1966
Franchised Units: 361
Company-Owned Units: 26387
Total Units: 382
Dist.: US-382; CAN-0; O'seas-0
North America: 14 States
Density: 166 in GA, 60 in SC, 34 AL
Projected New Units (12 Months): 40
Qualifications: 5, 5, 4, 3, 3, 4
Registered: FL,IL,IN,VA

FINANCIAL/TERMS:

Cash Investment: $200K

Total Investment: $300-750K
Minimum Net Worth: $250K
Fees: Franchise - $20K
Royalty - 4%; Ad. - 1%
Earnings Claims Statement: Yes
Term of Contract (Years): 15/5x3
Avg. # Of Employees: 18 FT, 6 PT
Passive Ownership: Discouraged
Encourage Conversions: Yes
Area Develop. Agreements: Yes/Varies
Sub-Franchising Contracts: No
Expand In Territory: Yes
Space Needs: 2,000 SF; FS,SF,SC, Co-Brand, C-Stores

SUPPORT & TRAINING:

Financial Assistance Provided: No
Site Selection Assistance: Yes
Lease Negotiation Assistance: Yes
Co-Operative Advertising: Yes
Franchisee Assoc./Member: Yes/No
Size Of Corporate Staff: 120
On-Going Support: b,C,D,E,f,h,I
Training: 7 Weeks Metro Atlanta, GA.

SPECIFIC EXPANSION PLANS:

US: Southeast, Midwest
Canada: No
Overseas: No

<< >>

HUDSON'S GRILL OF AMERICA

16970 Dallas Pkwy., # 402
Dallas, TX 75248-1928
Tel: (972) 931-9237
Fax: (972) 931-1326
E-Mail: sacco@hudsonsgrill.com
Web Site: www.hudsonsgrill.com
Mr. Tom Sacco, VP Franchising

A casual-style, full-service, high-energy, late 50's and early 60's rock 'n' roll theme restaurant and bar. Burgers, chicken sandwiches, salads, desserts and specialty items, such as fajitas. TV monitors throughout restaurant and bar show sporting events while the bubbling Wurlitzer juke box beats out Elvis Presley and Beatles' tunes, bridging the past with the present.

BACKGROUND:

Established: 1985; 1st Franchised: 1986
Franchised Units: 17
Company-Owned Units: 2
Total Units: 19
Dist.: US-17; CAN-0; O'seas-0
North America: 4 States
Density: 10 in CA, 4 in TX, 2 in MI
Projected New Units (12 Months): 4
Qualifications: 5, 3, 1, 3, 3, 5
Registered: All Except RI

FINANCIAL/TERMS:

Cash Investment: $125K
Total Investment: $100K-1MM
Minimum Net Worth: $250K
Fees: Franchise - $25K
Royalty - 4%; Ad. - 1%
Earnings Claims Statement: Yes
Term of Contract (Years): 20/20
Avg. # Of Employees: 12 FT, 38 PT
Passive Ownership: Allowed
Encourage Conversions: No
Area Develop. Agreements: Yes/5
Sub-Franchising Contracts: Yes
Expand In Territory: Yes
Space Needs: 4,500 SF; FS

SUPPORT & TRAINING:

Financial Assistance Provided: Yes(I)
Site Selection Assistance: Yes
Lease Negotiation Assistance: Yes
Co-Operative Advertising: Yes
Franchisee Assoc./Member: No
Size Of Corporate Staff: 7
On-Going Support: B,C,D,E,F,H
Training: 5-6 Weeks CA; 5-6 Weeks TX.

SPECIFIC EXPANSION PLANS:

US: All United States
Canada: BC,AB,ON,PQ,NS
Overseas: Latin America, South America, Pacific Rim, Europe

<< >>

KELSEY'S RESTAURANTS

6303 Airport Rd.
Mississauga, ON L4V 1R8 CANADA
Tel: (905) 405-6500
Fax: (905) 405-6777
E-Mail: lsantolini@hq.kelseys.ca
Web Site: www.kelseys.ca
Mr. Larry Santolini, Director Franchising

Approaching its 20th anniversary, KELSEY'S has been bringing outstanding food, unrivaled service and its celebrated 'good times' to communities throughout Canada since 1998. KELSEY'S new menu features more than 100 exciting items. KELSEY'S warm, friendly decor and fast service make it an appealing place for lunch crowds, the after work gang, as well as families at dinner and late evening adult patrons who come for the good times in a neighborhood atmosphere.

BACKGROUND:

Established: 1978; 1st Franchised: 1983
Franchised Units: 28
Company-Owned Units: 77
Total Units: 105
Dist.: US-0; CAN-54; O'seas-0
North America: 5 Provinces
Density: 42 in ON, 8 in AB, 1 in SK
Projected New Units (12 Months): 10
Qualifications: 5, 4, 4, 2, 2, 5
Registered: AB

FINANCIAL/TERMS:

Cash Investment: $250-300K
Total Investment: $600-750K
Minimum Net Worth: $600K
Fees: Franchise - $40K
Royalty - 5%; Ad. - 0.5%
Earnings Claims Statement: No
Term of Contract (Years): 10/5/5
Avg. # Of Employees: 70-90 FT & PT
Passive Ownership: Not Allowed
Encourage Conversions: No
Area Develop. Agreements: NR
Sub-Franchising Contracts: No
Expand In Territory: Yes
Space Needs: 5,000 SF; FS

SUPPORT & TRAINING:

Financial Assistance Provided: Yes(I)
Site Selection Assistance: Yes
Lease Negotiation Assistance: Yes
Co-Operative Advertising: Yes
Franchisee Assoc./Member: Yes/Yes
Size Of Corporate Staff: 30
On-Going Support: a,B,C,D,E,F,G,I
Training: 12 Weeks in Restaurant; 1 Week Office.

SPECIFIC EXPANSION PLANS:

US: NA
Canada: ON, AB, BC
Overseas: Philippines, Western Europe, Australia

<< >>

KRIEGER'S YOUR HOMETOWN SPORTS GRILL

744-F Spirit of St. Louis Blvd.
Chesterfield, MO 63005
Tel: (636) 530-1395
Fax: (636) 530-6890
E-Mail: info@kriegerspub.com
Web Site: www.kriegerspub.com
Mr. Al Genovesse, Director Franchise Devel.

KRIEGER'S YOUR HOMETOWN SPORTS GRILL is a neighborhood establishment where friends and family join to eat and drink in a sports-themed atmosphere. KRIEGER'S has family dining. Our staff treats you like family, caters to every need and offers over 70 menu items. Your dining experience is enhanced by 25 TVs featuring the best sports events on Direct TV. KRIEGER'S was voted "The Best Place To Take the Kids," "The Best Wings," "Best Happy Hour," "Best Menu," "Best Casual Lunch."

BACKGROUND:
Established: 1991; 1st Franchised: 2002
Franchised Units: 7
Company-Owned Units: 6
Total Units: 13
Dist.: US-13; CAN-0; O'seas-0
North America: 2 States
Density: 8 in MO, 5 in Il
Projected New Units (12 Months): 6
Qualifications: 5, 5, 3, 3, 4, 5
Registered: IL

FINANCIAL/TERMS:
Cash Investment: $250K
Total Investment: $450K-1.5MM
Minimum Net Worth: $750K
Fees: Franchise - $30K
Royalty - 5%; Ad. - 1%
Earnings Claims Statement: Yes
Term of Contract (Years): 15/15
Avg. # Of Employees: 10 FT, 50 PT
Passive Ownership: Discouraged
Encourage Conversions: Yes
Area Develop. Agreements: Yes
Sub-Franchising Contracts: No
Expand In Territory: Yes
Space Needs: 4,000 SF; FS, SF, SC, RM

SUPPORT & TRAINING:
Financial Assistance Provided: No
Site Selection Assistance: Yes
Lease Negotiation Assistance: Yes
Co-Operative Advertising: Yes
Franchisee Assoc./Member: No
Size Of Corporate Staff: 10
On-Going Support: A,B,C,D,E,F,G,H
Training: 8 Weeks St. Louis, MO.

SPECIFIC EXPANSION PLANS:
US: Northern & Southern Midwest
Canada: No
Overseas: No

<< >>

LE PEEP

4 W. Dry Creek Circle, # 201
Littleton, CO 80120
Tel: (303) 730-6300
Fax: (303) 730-7105
E-Mail: lepeep4west@lepeep.com
Web Site: www.lepeep.com
Ms. Amanda Rhoads, Licensing Manager

LE PEEP is a licenser of a breakfast, brunch and lunch concept, featuring an award-winning menu, decor and coffee and juice bar.

BACKGROUND:
Established: 1992; 1st Franchised: 1981
Franchised Units: 68
Company-Owned Units: 5
Total Units: 73
Dist.: US-73; CAN-0; O'seas-0
North America: 17 States
Density: 25 in CO, 8 in TX, 5 in GA
Projected New Units (12 Months): 8
Qualifications: 5, 3, 5, 3, 3, 5
Registered: NA

FINANCIAL/TERMS:
Cash Investment: $100-350K
Total Investment: $150-550K
Minimum Net Worth: NR
Fees: Franchise - $0
Royalty - 3%; Ad. - 0%
Earnings Claims Statement: Yes
Term of Contract (Years): 15/10
Avg. # Of Employees: 10 FT, 10 PT
Passive Ownership: NA
Encourage Conversions: Yes
Area Develop. Agreements: No
Sub-Franchising Contracts: No
Expand In Territory: Yes
Space Needs: 2,500-3,500 SF; FS, SF, SC, RM

SUPPORT & TRAINING:
Financial Assistance Provided: No
Site Selection Assistance: No
Lease Negotiation Assistance: No
Co-Operative Advertising: No
Franchisee Assoc./Member: No
Size Of Corporate Staff: 5
On-Going Support: b,c,d,e
Training: 8 Weeks in Denver, CO.

SPECIFIC EXPANSION PLANS:
US: All United States
Canada: All Canada
Overseas: U.K., France, Australia

<< >>

MADE IN JAPAN...A TERIYAKI EXPERIENCE

700 Kerr St.
Oakville, ON L6K 3W5 CANADA
Tel: (800) 555-5726 (905) 337-7777
Fax: (905) 337-0331
E-Mail: adudnik@donatogroup.com
Web Site: www.donatofood.com
Mr. Alex Dudnik, Director of Operations

Japanese quick service restaurant located in major mall food courts, airports, universities, hospitals, theme parks, strip plazas and other similar high traffic settings.

BACKGROUND: IFA MEMBER
Established: 1986; 1st Franchised: 1987
Franchised Units: 70
Company-Owned Units: 2
Total Units: 72
Dist.: US-0; CAN-50; O'seas-5
North America: 4 Provinces
Density: 36 in ON, 7 in PQ, 4 in BC
Projected New Units (12 Months): 6
Qualifications: 5, 2, 2, 2, 3, 4
Registered: IL,AB

FINANCIAL/TERMS:
Cash Investment: $50-100K
Total Investment: $175-250K
Minimum Net Worth: $200K
Fees: Franchise - $25K
Royalty - 6%; Ad. - 1.5%
Earnings Claims Statement: No
Term of Contract (Years): 8-10/5-10
Avg. # Of Employees: 3 FT, 6 PT
Passive Ownership: Discouraged
Encourage Conversions: Yes
Area Develop. Agreements: Yes/15
Sub-Franchising Contracts: Yes
Expand In Territory: Yes
Space Needs: 400-1,800 SF; SC, RM

SUPPORT & TRAINING:
Financial Assistance Provided: Yes(I)
Site Selection Assistance: Yes
Lease Negotiation Assistance: Yes
Co-Operative Advertising: NA
Franchisee Assoc./Member: No/No
Size Of Corporate Staff: 40
On-Going Support: B,C,D,E,G,H,I
Training: 3-4 Days at Company HQ; 3-4 Days at the Store; 1 Week during your Grand Opening.

SPECIFIC EXPANSION PLANS:
US: All United States
Canada: All Canada
Overseas: All Countries

<< >>

MAX & ERMA'S RESTAURANTS

4849 Evanswood Dr.
Columbus, OH 43229
Tel: (614) 431-5800
Fax: (614) 854-7957
E-Mail: rob@max-ermas.com
Web Site: www.maxandermas.com
Mr. Rob Lindeman, VP Franchising

MAX & ERMA'S RESTAURANTS is famous for gourmet burgers, overstuffed sandwiches, homemade pasta dishes, char-grilled chicken specialties, super salads and taste-tempting munchies. Antiques artifacts and local paraphernalia make MAX & ERMA'S a fun, unique place to take friends and family. We work hard every day to help our guests enjoy their total dining experience so they can't wait to come back. And, we believe that experience starts with our food. We use only the freshest, highest-quality ingredients.

BACKGROUND:
Established: 1972; 1st Franchised: 1997
Franchised Units: 14
Company-Owned Units: 70
Total Units: 84
Dist.: US-67; CAN-0; O'seas-0
North America: 9 States
Density: 22 in OH, 8 in MI, 7 in IL
Projected New Units (12 Months): 10
Qualifications: 3, 4, 4, 2, 3, 5
Registered: VA,WI

FINANCIAL/TERMS:
Cash Investment: $400-500K
Total Investment: $800K-2.7MM
Minimum Net Worth: $3MM
Fees: Franchise - $40K
Royalty - 4%; Ad. - 2%
Earnings Claims Statement: No
Term of Contract (Years): 20/10
Avg. # Of Employees: 40 FT, 50 PT
Passive Ownership: Allowed
Encourage Conversions: Yes
Area Develop. Agreements: Yes
Sub-Franchising Contracts: No
Expand In Territory: Yes
Space Needs: 5,000-6,900 SF; FS, RM

SUPPORT & TRAINING:
Financial Assistance Provided: No
Site Selection Assistance: Yes
Lease Negotiation Assistance: Yes
Co-Operative Advertising: NA
Franchisee Assoc./Member: No
Size Of Corporate Staff: 55
On-Going Support: B,C,D,E,F,G,H
Training: 14 Weeks Manager Training; 2-6 Weeks Staff Training; 2-3 Weeks Opening Training.

SPECIFIC EXPANSION PLANS:
US: All United States
Canada: No
Overseas: No

The Melting Pot®
a fondue restaurant

Top 100

MELTING POT RESTAURANTS, THE

8810 Twin Lakes Blvd.
Tampa, FL 33614
Tel: (800) 783-0867 + 108 (813) 881-0055
Fax: (813) 889-9361
E-Mail: dana@meltingpot.com
Web Site: www.meltingpot.com
Mr. Dan N. Addison, Franchise Sales

The largest fondue-based restaurant system in the world. Franchise provides numerous areas of expertise and assistance to new and established owners. Large percentage of existing owners become multi-unit operators. A unique dining format that is often referred to as a "fun and gotta be experienced" event.

BACKGROUND: IFA MEMBER
Established: 1975; 1st Franchised: 1984
Franchised Units: 81
Company-Owned Units: 4
Total Units: 85
Dist.: US-85; CAN-0; O'seas-0
North America: 31 States
Density: 16 in FL, 6 in NC, 4 in VA
Projected New Units (12 Months): 20
Qualifications: 5, 5, 3, 3, 3, 5
Registered:CA,FL,IL,IN,MD,MI,MN,NY, OR,RI,VA,WA,WI,DC

FINANCIAL/TERMS:
Cash Investment: $200-250K
Total Investment: $595K-1.1MM
Minimum Net Worth: NA
Fees: Franchise - $35K
Royalty - 4.5%; Ad. - 1.5%
Earnings Claims Statement: Yes
Term of Contract (Years): 10/10
Avg. # Of Employees:10-20 FT, 5-20 PT
Passive Ownership: Not Allowed
Encourage Conversions: No
Area Develop. Agreements: Yes
Sub-Franchising Contracts: No
Expand In Territory: No
Space Needs: 4,000-6,000 SF; FS, SC

SUPPORT & TRAINING:
Financial Assistance Provided: Yes(I)
Site Selection Assistance: Yes
Lease Negotiation Assistance: Yes
Co-Operative Advertising: Yes
Franchisee Assoc./Member: No
Size Of Corporate Staff: 32
On-Going Support: A,b,C,D,E,F,G,h,I
Training: 8-12 Weeks, Tampa, FL.

SPECIFIC EXPANSION PLANS:
US: All US Except ND,SD,HI
Canada: No
Overseas: No

MONTANA MIKE'S STEAK HOUSE

2908 N. Plum St.
Hutchinson, KS 67502
Tel: (620) 669-9372
Fax: (620) 669-0531
E-Mail: madisonj@stockadecompanies.com
Web Site: www.stockadecompanies.com
Mr. Madison Jobe, VP Franchise Development

MONTANA MIKE'S STEAK HOUSE is a sit-down, full-service restaurant serving alcohol and a bar area. We are known for very large portions at affordable prices. Open for lunch and dinner Thursday through Sunday.

BACKGROUND: IFA MEMBER
Established: 1984; 1st Franchised: 1984
Franchised Units: 10
Company-Owned Units: 3
Total Units: 13
Dist.: US-13; CAN-0; O'seas-0
North America: 6 States
Density: 5 in KS, 3 in TX
Projected New Units (12 Months): 4
Qualifications: 5, 4, 4, 3, 2, 4
Registered: IL,IN,VA

FINANCIAL/TERMS:
Cash Investment: $250-350K
Total Investment: $1.2-2.2MM
Minimum Net Worth: $1MM
Fees: Franchise - $15K
Royalty - 3%; Ad. - 1%
Earnings Claims Statement: Yes
Term of Contract (Years): 15/5
Avg. # Of Employees: 20 FT, 50 PT
Passive Ownership: Discouraged
Encourage Conversions: Yes
Area Develop. Agreements: Not Now
Sub-Franchising Contracts: No
Expand In Territory: Yes
Space Needs: 10,000 SF; FS

SUPPORT & TRAINING:
Financial Assistance Provided: No
Site Selection Assistance: Yes
Lease Negotiation Assistance: No
Co-Operative Advertising: No

Franchisee Assoc./Member: NR
Size Of Corporate Staff: 16
On-Going Support: B,C,D,E,G,h,i
Training: 6-8 Weeks Training.

SPECIFIC EXPANSION PLANS:
US: All United States
Canada: No
Overseas: No

<< >>

MONTANA'S COOKHOUSE SALOON

6303 Airport Rd.
Mississauga, ON L4V 1R8 CANADA
Tel: (905) 405-6500
Fax: (905) 405-6777
E-Mail: info@cara.com
Web Site: www.kelseys.ca
Mr. Andy Gunkler, VP Franchise Development

Montana's offers the guest a rustic, Western lodge setting with fresh country-style cooking. Montana's offers guests a menu of approximately 60 selections featuring rotisserie chicken, turkey, beef and pork. The average adult check is $9-12 with kid's meals starting at $2.99. Montana's is casual dining at affordable prices.

BACKGROUND:
Established: 1978; 1st Franchised: 1983
Franchised Units: 36
Company-Owned Units: 83
Total Units: 119
Dist.: US-1; CAN-118; O'seas-0
North America: 1 State, 5 Provinces
Density: 42 in ON, 8 in AB, 2 in NY
Projected New Units (12 Months): 22
Qualifications: 5, , 5, 1, 2, 5
Registered: NR

FINANCIAL/TERMS:
Cash Investment: $300-400K
Total Investment: $400K-1.2MM
Minimum Net Worth: $5 MM
Fees: Franchise - $35K
Royalty - 4%; Ad. - 1.5%
Earnings Claims Statement: No
Term of Contract (Years): 20/10
Avg. # Of Employees: 70-90 FT & PT
Passive Ownership: Discouraged
Encourage Conversions: Yes
Area Develop. Agreements: Yes
Sub-Franchising Contracts: No
Expand In Territory: Yes
Space Needs: 5,200 SF; FS

SUPPORT & TRAINING:
Financial Assistance Provided: Yes(I)
Site Selection Assistance: Yes
Lease Negotiation Assistance: No
Co-Operative Advertising: Yes
Franchisee Assoc./Member: No
Size Of Corporate Staff: 50
On-Going Support: B,C,D,E,F,G,h
Training: 12 Weeks in Toronto, ON.

SPECIFIC EXPANSION PLANS:
US: All United States
Canada: All Canada
Overseas: No

<< >>

MOUNTAIN MIKE'S PIZZA

4212 N. Freeway Blvd., # 6
Sacramento, CA 95834
Tel: (916) 929-3946
Fax: (916) 929-6018
E-Mail: rvogel@mountainmikes.com
Web Site: www.mountainmikes.com
Mr. Randy Vogel, President

Casual dining in a family oriented restaurant, featuring counter service, delivery and take-out, lunch buffet, self-service beverages and video game room. Our pizzas are made-to-order, using only the freshest-quality ingredients available.

BACKGROUND:
Established: 1978; 1st Franchised: 1978
Franchised Units: 79
Company-Owned Units: 0
Total Units: 79
Dist.: US-79; CAN-0; O'seas-0
North America: 6 States
Density: 63 in CA, 1 in NV, 1 in OR
Projected New Units (12 Months): 40
Qualifications: 4, 4, 2, 2, 3, 5
Registered: CA,FL,IL,IN,MD,MI,MN,OR,VA,WI

FINANCIAL/TERMS:
Cash Investment: $75-100K
Total Investment: $150-250K
Minimum Net Worth: $150K
Fees: Franchise - $20K
Royalty - 5%/$1K; Ad. - 3%
Earnings Claims Statement: Yes
Term of Contract (Years): 15/15
Avg. # Of Employees: 2 FT, 15 PT
Passive Ownership: Not Allowed
Encourage Conversions: Yes
Area Develop. Agreements: Yes/15
Sub-Franchising Contracts: No
Expand In Territory: Yes
Space Needs: 2,500 SF; SF, SC

SUPPORT & TRAINING:
Financial Assistance Provided: Yes(I)
Site Selection Assistance: Yes
Lease Negotiation Assistance: Yes
Co-Operative Advertising: Yes
Franchisee Assoc./Member: No
Size Of Corporate Staff: 10
On-Going Support: A,B,C,D,E,F,H,I
Training: 3 Weeks Boulder, CO/Northern CA; 2 Weeks On-Site at Opening.

SPECIFIC EXPANSION PLANS:
US: All United States
Canada: No
Overseas: No

<< >>

MR. MIKE'S WEST COAST GRILL

631 Carnarvon St.
New Westminster, BC V3M 1E3
CANADA
Tel: (800) 668-MIKE (604) 515-1190
Fax: (604) 515-1197
E-Mail: wmaillet@stonewatergroup.ca
Web Site: www.mrmikes.ca
Mr. Wayne Maillet, VP Franchising

Founded in 1960, MR. MIKE'S WEST COAST GRILL is a full-service casual dining restaurant experience. Our primary focus is beef. We provide "affordable indulgence" of premium spirits and quality grilled entrees in a refreshing restaurant environment that is relaxed and inviting. A full support franchise system. Proven results, a fresh approach - all uniquely West Coast.

BACKGROUND:
Established: 1960; 1st Franchised: 1961
Franchised Units: 4
Company-Owned Units: 4
Total Units: 8
Dist.: US-0; CAN-8; O'seas-0
North America: 2 Provinces
Density: 7 in BC, 1 in AB
Projected New Units (12 Months): 2
Qualifications: 5, 5, 3, 2, 2, 5
Registered: NR

FINANCIAL/TERMS:
Cash Investment: $300-700K
Total Investment: $650K-1.0MM
Minimum Net Worth: $300K
Fees: Franchise - $37.5K
Royalty - 5%; Ad. - 2%
Earnings Claims Statement: No
Term of Contract (Years): 10/5
Avg. # Of Employees: 10 FT, 30 PT
Passive Ownership: Discouraged
Encourage Conversions: Yes
Area Develop. Agreements: No
Sub-Franchising Contracts: No
Expand In Territory: No
Space Needs: 3,500-5,000 SF; FS, SC

SUPPORT & TRAINING:

Financial Assistance Provided: Yes
Site Selection Assistance: Yes
Lease Negotiation Assistance: Yes
Co-Operative Advertising: Yes
Franchisee Assoc./Member: No
Size Of Corporate Staff: 10
On-Going Support: A,B,C,D,E,F,G,H,I
Training: 8-12 Weeks in Corporate Store; 2 Weeks On-Site.

SPECIFIC EXPANSION PLANS:

US: None
Canada: BC
Overseas: No

<< >>

NANCY'S PIZZERIA

8200 W. 185th St., # J
Tinley Park, IL 60477
Tel: (800) 626-2977 (708) 444-4411
Fax: (708) 444-4422
E-Mail: eileenh@chicagofranchise.com
Web Site: www.nancyspizza.com
Ms. Eileen Holly, VP Franchise Development

NANCY'S PIZZERIA is expanding nationally; we have 66 franchisees with stores located in Illinois, Iowa and Michigan. More coming soon in Florida and Indiana. We offer the following advantages: original inventor of stuffed pizza, protected territories, comprehensive classroom and in-store training, pre and past-opening support provided by our "operations" support staff, teamed with the product voted "The Best Pizza in Chicago" by Chicago Magazine and lauded by other publications.

BACKGROUND:

Established: 1974; 1st Franchised: 1993
Franchised Units: 66
Company-Owned Units: 0
Total Units: 66
Dist.: US-66; CAN-0; O'seas-0
North America: 3 States
Density: 36 in IL, 1 in IA, 1 in MI
Projected New Units (12 Months): 12
Qualifications: 5, 4, 3, 3, 5, 5
Registered: CA,FL,IL,IN,MD,MI,VA,WI

FINANCIAL/TERMS:

Cash Investment: $50-120K
Total Investment: $190-250K
Minimum Net Worth: $250K
Fees: Franchise - $20K
Royalty - 5%; Ad. - 2%
Earnings Claims Statement: No
Term of Contract (Years): 10/10
Avg. # Of Employees: 3 FT, 15 PT
Passive Ownership: Discouraged
Encourage Conversions: Yes
Area Develop. Agreements: Yes/1-5
Sub-Franchising Contracts: No
Expand In Territory: Yes
Space Needs: 800-1,400 SF; SF

SUPPORT & TRAINING:

Financial Assistance Provided: No
Site Selection Assistance: Yes
Lease Negotiation Assistance: Yes
Co-Operative Advertising: Yes
Franchisee Assoc./Member: No
Size Of Corporate Staff: 12
On-Going Support: b,C,D,E,F,G,H
Training: 230 Hours of Hands-On Training; 40 Hours Office Training.

SPECIFIC EXPANSION PLANS:

US: All United States
Canada: No
Overseas: No

<< >>

NATIONAL SPORTS GRILL

997 Grandy's Ln.
Lewisville, TX 75077-2507
Tel: (877) 457-8145 (972) 317-8086
Fax: (972) 317-8174
E-Mail: bgilbert@grandys.com
Web Site: www.nationalsportsgrill.com
Mr. Brian Gilbert, Franchise Development

The NATIONAL SPORTS GRILL chain is a winning franchise concept that beats the competition year after year. Our restaurants are the premier place to watch and participate in sporting events and enjoy some of the best food in town in a fun, casual environment. NSG franchisees gain access to our successful team formula of food, fun, sports and live simulcast sporting events. Voted Best Sports Grill in S. CA 10 years in a row. Largest sports entertainment chain on the West Coast.

BACKGROUND: IFA MEMBER

Established: 1991; 1st Franchised: 1999
Franchised Units: 1
Company-Owned Units: 4
Total Units: 5
Dist.: US-4; CAN-0; O'seas-1
North America: 1 State
Density: 4 in CA
Projected New Units (12 Months): 3-6
Qualifications: 5, 5, 4, 4, 4, 4
Registered: NR

FINANCIAL/TERMS:

Cash Investment: $250K
Total Investment: $1.5-3.5MM
Minimum Net Worth: $1MM
Fees: Franchise - $75K
Royalty - 5%; Ad. - Up to 2%
Earnings Claims Statement: No
Term of Contract (Years): 15/10
Avg. # Of Employees: 8 FT, 30 PT
Passive Ownership: Allowed
Encourage Conversions: Yes
Area Develop. Agreements: Yes/TBD
Sub-Franchising Contracts: No
Expand In Territory: Yes
Space Needs: 12,000 SF; FS, SC

SUPPORT & TRAINING:

Financial Assistance Provided: No
Site Selection Assistance: Yes
Lease Negotiation Assistance: Yes
Co-Operative Advertising: Yes
Franchisee Assoc./Member: Yes
Size Of Corporate Staff: 25
On-Going Support: B,C,D,E,G,h
Training: 8-10 Weeks Irvine, CA; 8-10 Weeks TBD.

SPECIFIC EXPANSION PLANS:

US: All United States
Canada: All Canada
Overseas: All Countries

<< >>

PEPE'S MEXICAN RESTAURANT

1325 W. 15th St.
Chicago, IL 60608
Tel: (312) 733-2500
Fax: (312) 733-2564
E-Mail: bobptak@pepes.com
Web Site: www.worldfranchising.com/website.htm
Mr. Robert Ptak, President

A full-service Mexican restaurant, serving a complete line of Mexican food, with liquor, beer and wine. Complete training and help in remodeling, site selection, equipment purchasing and running the restaurant provided.

BACKGROUND:

Established: 1967; 1st Franchised: 1968
Franchised Units: 55

Company-Owned Units: 0
Total Units: 55
Dist.: US-55; CAN-0; O'seas-0
North America: 3 States
Density: 44 in IL, 11 in IN
Projected New Units (12 Months): 4
Qualifications: 3, 3, 2, 2, 1, 4
Registered: IL,IN,VA

FINANCIAL/TERMS:

Cash Investment: $30-100K
Total Investment: $75-300K
Minimum Net Worth: NR
Fees: Franchise - $15K
Royalty - 4%; Ad. - 3%
Earnings Claims Statement: Yes
Term of Contract (Years): 20
Avg. # Of Employees: 8 FT, 5 PT
Passive Ownership: Discouraged
Encourage Conversions: Yes
Area Develop. Agreements: Yes/Varies
Sub-Franchising Contracts: No
Expand In Territory: No
Space Needs: 3,000 SF; FS, SF, SC

SUPPORT & TRAINING:

Financial Assistance Provided: No
Site Selection Assistance: Yes
Lease Negotiation Assistance: Yes
Co-Operative Advertising: Yes
Franchisee Assoc./Member: NR
Size Of Corporate Staff: 15
On-Going Support: B,C,D,E,F,G,H
Training: 4 Weeks Headquarters.

SPECIFIC EXPANSION PLANS:

US: Midwest
Canada: No
Overseas: No

<< >>

Total Units: 497
Dist.: US-485; CAN-15; O'seas-0
North America: 36 States
Density: 72 in MN, 58 in FL, 57 in PA
Projected New Units (12 Months): 20
Qualifications: 5, 3, 5, 3, 3, 4
Registered: All States Except RI

FINANCIAL/TERMS:

Cash Investment: $100-600K
Total Investment: $1.1-2.0MM
Minimum Net Worth: $750K
Fees: Franchise - $40K
Royalty - 4%; Ad. - 3%
Earnings Claims Statement: Yes
Term of Contract (Years): 20
Avg. # Of Employees: 20 FT, 40 PT
Passive Ownership: Discouraged
Encourage Conversions: Yes
Area Develop. Agreements: Yes/3-8
Sub-Franchising Contracts: No
Expand In Territory: Yes
Space Needs: 5,000 SF; FS, SC, PC, SF

SUPPORT & TRAINING:

Financial Assistance Provided: No
Site Selection Assistance: Yes
Lease Negotiation Assistance: Yes
Co-Operative Advertising: Yes
Franchisee Assoc./Member: No
Size Of Corporate Staff: 224
On-Going Support: a,B,C,D,E,F,G,H,I
Training: 8-12 Weeks Management Training at Various Locations.

SPECIFIC EXPANSION PLANS:

US: All United States
Canada: All Canada
Overseas: No

<< >>

Dist.: US-0; CAN-107; O'seas-0
North America: 6 Provinces
Density: 82 in Atlantic, 25 in ON
Projected New Units (12 Months): 15
Qualifications: 5, 3, 2, 2, 4, 5
Registered: AB

FINANCIAL/TERMS:

Cash Investment: $50-150K
Total Investment: $150-350K
Minimum Net Worth: $250K
Fees: Franchise - $10-20K
Royalty - 6%; Ad. - 3%
Earnings Claims Statement: No
Term of Contract (Years): 10/10
Avg. # Of Employees: 5-10 FT, 5-10 PT
Passive Ownership: Not Allowed
Encourage Conversions: Yes
Area Develop. Agreements: Yes/20
Sub-Franchising Contracts: Yes
Expand In Territory: Yes
Space Needs: 1,000-4,000 SF; Varies

SUPPORT & TRAINING:

Financial Assistance Provided: Yes(I)
Site Selection Assistance: Yes
Lease Negotiation Assistance: Yes
Co-Operative Advertising: Yes
Franchisee Assoc./Member: No
Size Of Corporate Staff: 25
On-Going Support: a,B,C,D,E,F,G,H,i
Training: 12 Days Head Office; 10 Days On-the-Job Training; 3 Days a Year of Continuous Training.

SPECIFIC EXPANSION PLANS:

US: No
Canada: Quebec, Alberta
Overseas: No

<< >>

PERKINS RESTAURANT & BAKERY

6075 Poplar Ave., # 800
Memphis, TN 38119-4717
Tel: (800) 877-7375 (901) 766-6400
Fax: (901) 766-6482
E-Mail: franchise@perkinsrestaurants.com
Web Site: www.perkinsrestaurants.com
Mr. Robert J. Winters, VP Franchise Development

Full-service family style restaurant, offering breakfast, lunch and dinner, along with proprietary bakery items at moderate prices.

BACKGROUND:

Established: 1958; 1st Franchised: 1958
Franchised Units: 343
Company-Owned Units: 154

PIZZA DELIGHT

774 Main St., 4th FL
Moncton, NB E1C 9Y3 CANADA
Tel: (877) 853-0990 (506) 853-4131
Fax: (506) 853-4131
E-Mail: pfurness@pizzadelight.ca
Web Site: www.pizzadelight.com
Mr. Pier T. Furness, VP Development

PIZZA DELIGHT is a family/mid-scale dining brand, featuring pizza, pasta, salads and rotisserie chicken. Started in 1968 in Shediac, New Brunswick, PIZZA DELIGHT is now the largest family restaurant chain in Atlantic Canada.

BACKGROUND:

Established: 1968; 1st Franchised: 1970
Franchised Units: 103
Company-Owned Units: 4
Total Units: 107

PONDEROSA/BONANZA STEAKHOUSES

6500 International Pkwy., # 1000
Plano, TX 75093
Tel: (800) 527-6832 (321) 773-2788
Fax: (321) 773-2675
E-Mail: etaylor@metrogroup.com
Web Site: www.ponderosasteakhouses.com
Mr. Eric Taylor,

PONDEROSA and BONANZA FAMILY STEAKHOUSES serve great-tasting, family priced steaks and entrees, accompanied by a large variety of all-you-can-eat salad items, soups, appetizers, hot vegetables, breads, sundae and dessert bar and other tasty food. All steaks and entrees come with the salad bar, buffet and dessert bar at no extra cost.

BACKGROUND:
Established: 1965; 1st Franchised: 1966
Franchised Units: 398
Company-Owned Units: 85
Total Units: 483
Dist.: US-417; CAN-8; O'seas-58
North America: 31 States
Density: 60 in OH, 36 in MI, 32 in IN
Projected New Units (12 Months): 5
Qualifications: 5, 5, 4, 4, 4, 5
Registered: All States and AB

FINANCIAL/TERMS:
Cash Investment: $750K
Total Investment: $1.3-2.1MM
Minimum Net Worth: $3MM
Fees: Franchise - $40K
Royalty - 4%; Ad. - 4%
Earnings Claims Statement: No
Term of Contract (Years): 20
Avg. # Of Employees: 10 FT, 50 PT
Passive Ownership: Not Allowed
Encourage Conversions: No
Area Develop. Agreements: No
Sub-Franchising Contracts: No
Expand In Territory: Yes
Space Needs: 6,000-8,000 SF; FS, SC

SUPPORT & TRAINING:
Financial Assistance Provided: No
Site Selection Assistance: No
Lease Negotiation Assistance: No
Co-Operative Advertising: Yes
Franchisee Assoc./Member: Yes/NA
Size Of Corporate Staff: 125
On-Going Support: A,B,C,D,E,F,G,H,I
Training: 9 Weeks at Certified Training Restaurant.

SPECIFIC EXPANSION PLANS:
US: All United States
Canada: ON,QB,NB,BC,AB
Overseas: Brazil, Canada, China, Hong Kong, Japan, Venezuela, Mexico

RED HOT & BLUE

1701 Clarendon Blvd., # 105
Arlington, VA 22209
Tel: (800) 723-0745 (703) 276-8833
Fax: (703) 528-4789
E-Mail: dknutsen@rhbri.com
Web Site: www.redhotandblue.com
Mr. Dave Knutsen, Dir. Franchise Operations

RED HOT & BLUE restaurants serve Memphis-style ribs, pork, beef, chicken plus salads, burgers and a full menu in a casual dining environment, featuring blues memorabilia and recorded blues music. Service is Southern hospitality.

BACKGROUND:
Established: 1988; 1st Franchised: 1991
Franchised Units: 32
Company-Owned Units: 6
Total Units: 38
Dist.: US-35; CAN-0; O'seas-0
North America: 10 States
Density: 6 in NC, 5 in TX, 5 in VA
Projected New Units (12 Months): 6
Qualifications: 5, 5, 5, 4, 3, 5
Registered: All States Except RI,SD

FINANCIAL/TERMS:
Cash Investment: $347.7-868K
Total Investment: $397.75K
Minimum Net Worth: $1MM
Fees: Franchise - $35K
Royalty - 5%; Ad. - $375/Mo.
Earnings Claims Statement: No
Term of Contract (Years): 20/10
Avg. # Of Employees: 30 FT, 20 PT
Passive Ownership: Not Allowed
Encourage Conversions: Yes
Area Develop. Agreements: Yes/Varies
Sub-Franchising Contracts: No
Expand In Territory: No
Space Needs: 2,400-5,000 SF; FS, SC

SUPPORT & TRAINING:
Financial Assistance Provided: No
Site Selection Assistance: Yes
Lease Negotiation Assistance: No
Co-Operative Advertising: Yes
Franchisee Assoc./Member: Yes/Yes
Size Of Corporate Staff: 18
On-Going Support: C,D,E,f,G,h
Training: 3 Weeks at Home Office; 2 Weeks On-Site.

SPECIFIC EXPANSION PLANS:
US: All United States
Canada: All Canada
Overseas: No

ROUND TABLE PIZZA RESTAURANT

1320 Willow Pass Rd., # 600
Concord, CA 94520
Tel: (925) 969-3900
Fax: (925) 969-3978
E-Mail: krogers@roundtablepizza.com
Web Site: www.roundtablepizza.com
Ms. Kim Rogers, Franchise Sales Manager

ROUND TABLE FRANCHISE CORP. offers franchisees the opportunity to establish and operate a ROUND TABLE PIZZA RESTAURANT, which provides the public with pizza and related products in a wholesome, family restaurant setting. ROUND TABLE PIZZA is the nation's fourth largest pizza franchise chain, providing restaurant, take-out and delivery service.

BACKGROUND:
Established: 1959; 1st Franchised: 1962
Franchised Units: 517
Company-Owned Units: 19
Total Units: 536
Dist.: US-536; CAN-0; O'seas-17
North America: 11 States
Density: NR
Projected New Units (12 Months): 10
Qualifications: , , , , ,
Registered: CA,HI,OR,WA

FINANCIAL/TERMS:
Cash Investment: $135K
Total Investment: $420-496K
Minimum Net Worth: $450K
Fees: Franchise - $25K
Royalty - 4%; Ad. - 4%
Earnings Claims Statement: No
Term of Contract (Years): 10/10
Avg. # Of Employees: 5-7 FT, 10-15 PT
Passive Ownership: Discouraged
Encourage Conversions: Yes
Area Develop. Agreements: Yes/Varies
Sub-Franchising Contracts: Yes
Expand In Territory: Yes
Space Needs: 2,800 SF; SC, RM

SUPPORT & TRAINING:
Financial Assistance Provided: No
Site Selection Assistance: Yes
Lease Negotiation Assistance: Yes
Co-Operative Advertising: Yes
Franchisee Assoc./Member: NR
Size Of Corporate Staff: 70
On-Going Support: C,D,E,G,H,I
Training: 2 Weeks Headquarters; 2 Weeks Field.

SPECIFIC EXPANSION PLANS:
US: Northwest, Southwest
Canada: No
Overseas: All Countries

ROYAL WAFFLE KING

P. O. Box 1025
Alpharetta, GA 30009
Tel: (770) 442-3800
Fax: (877) 640-5977
E-Mail: royalwaffleking@mindspring.com
Web Site: www.royalwaffleking.com
Mr. Chad Maynard, Dir. Franchcise Devel./Recruit

ROYAL WAFFLE KING is a 24-hour, full-service restaurant in the Southeast. ROYAL WAFFLE KING sets itself apart by allowing individuals to become single unit operators with the opportunity to become a multi-unit operator. With very little overhead, the opportunities are endless.

BACKGROUND:

Established: 1986;	1st Franchised: 1989
Franchised Units:	25
Company-Owned Units:	8
Total Units:	33
Dist.:	US-33; CAN-0; O'seas-0
North America:	4 States
Density:	22 in GA, 7 in AL, 3 in KY
Projected New Units (12 Months):	NR
Qualifications:	, , , , ,
Registered:	

FINANCIAL/TERMS:

Cash Investment:	$50-100K
Total Investment:	$150-400K
Minimum Net Worth:	$500K
Fees: Franchise -	$20K
Royalty - 4%;	Ad. - NA
Earnings Claims Statement:	No
Term of Contract (Years):	15/5/5/5
Avg. # Of Employees:	14 FT
Passive Ownership:	Not Allowed
Encourage Conversions:	NR
Area Develop. Agreements:	Yes
Sub-Franchising Contracts:	No
Expand In Territory:	Yes
Space Needs:	2,000 SF; FS, C-Store

SUPPORT & TRAINING:

Financial Assistance Provided:	NR
Site Selection Assistance:	Yes
Lease Negotiation Assistance:	Yes
Co-Operative Advertising:	NA
Franchisee Assoc./Member:	No
Size Of Corporate Staff:	75
On-Going Support:	B,C,D,E,F,G,H,I
Training:	NR

SPECIFIC EXPANSION PLANS:

US:	Southeast
Canada:	NR
Overseas:	NR

<< >>

SANDWICH TREE RESTAURANTS

535 Thurlow St.
Vancouver, BC V6E 3L2 CANADA
Tel: (604) 435-4012
Fax: (604) 684-2542
E-Mail:
Web Site: www.sandwichtree.ca
Mr. Tony Cardarelli, Director Operations

Famous for our custom sandwiches, creative salads, hearty soups, catering and much more, SANDWICH TREE is a limited-hours operation located in shopping centers, commercial towers and industrial centres. Our quality food, served in our attractive surroundings, makes SANDWICH TREE a number one investment opportunity.

BACKGROUND:

Established: 1978;	1st Franchised: 1979
Franchised Units:	31
Company-Owned Units:	0
Total Units:	31
Dist.:	US-0; CAN-43; O'seas-0
North America:	6 Provinces
Density:	19 in BC, 7 in NS, 5 in ON
Projected New Units (12 Months):	4
Qualifications:	, , , , ,
Registered:	NR

FINANCIAL/TERMS:

Cash Investment:	$35-55K
Total Investment:	$90-120K
Minimum Net Worth:	NR
Fees: Franchise -	$10-17.5K
Royalty - 5%;	Ad. - 3%
Earnings Claims Statement:	Yes
Term of Contract (Years):	5/5
Avg. # Of Employees:	4 FT, 7 PT
Passive Ownership:	Discouraged
Encourage Conversions:	Yes
Area Develop. Agreements:	Yes/10
Sub-Franchising Contracts:	Yes
Expand In Territory:	Yes
Space Needs:	300+ SF; SF, RM, Industrial Park

SUPPORT & TRAINING:

Financial Assistance Provided:	Yes(I)
Site Selection Assistance:	Yes
Lease Negotiation Assistance:	Yes
Co-Operative Advertising:	Yes
Franchisee Assoc./Member:	NR
Size Of Corporate Staff:	6
On-Going Support:	a,B,C,D,E,F,G,H,I
Training:	2 Weeks Headquarters.

SPECIFIC EXPANSION PLANS:

US:	No
Canada:	All Canada
Overseas:	All Countries

<< >>

SHAKEY'S

2200 W. Valley Blvd.
Alhambra, CA 91803
Tel: (800) 540-0737 (626) 576-0737
Fax: (626) 576-2114
E-Mail: info@shakeys.com
Web Site: www.shakeys.com
Dr. Joe Remsa, Executive Vice President

SHAKEY'S offers a wide selection of freshly-prepared foods, consisting of a variety of pizzas, chicken and pasta and more than 50 freshly-prepared lunch and dinner items. SHAKEY'S features both pizza and fried chicken and the Bunch of Lunch all-you-can-eat buffet. Serves beer and wine and every store has a game room with approximately 15 redemption games. 64 restaurants in the US and 250 worldwide. Current prototype store has 6,000 SF and seats 200 customers. Average check was $7.25 in 2003.

BACKGROUND: IFA MEMBER

Established: 1954;	1st Franchised: 1958
Franchised Units:	44
Company-Owned Units:	20
Total Units:	64
Dist.:	US-64; CAN-0; O'seas-0
North America:	7 States
Density:	56 in CA
Projected New Units (12 Months):	10
Qualifications:	4, 4, 4, 2, 2, 5
Registered:	All States in Process.

FINANCIAL/TERMS:

Cash Investment:	NR
Total Investment:	$750K
Minimum Net Worth:	NR
Fees: Franchise -	$25K
Royalty - 5%;	Ad. - 6%-5% Local
Earnings Claims Statement:	No
Term of Contract (Years):	10/5/5
Avg. # Of Employees:	10-24 FT, 45% PT
Passive Ownership:	Discouraged
Encourage Conversions:	No
Area Develop. Agreements:	Yes
Sub-Franchising Contracts:	No
Expand In Territory:	Yes
Space Needs:	4,000-6,000 SF; FS, SC

SUPPORT & TRAINING:

Financial Assistance Provided:	No
Site Selection Assistance:	Yes
Lease Negotiation Assistance:	Yes
Co-Operative Advertising:	Yes
Franchisee Assoc./Member:	Yes/No
Size Of Corporate Staff:	6
On-Going Support:	B,C,D,E,F,G,h
Training:	6 Weeks CA.

SPECIFIC EXPANSION PLANS:

US:	All United States
Canada:	No
Overseas:	No

<< >>

SIRLOIN STOCKADE

2908 N. Plum St.
Hutchinson, KS 67502
Tel: (620) 669-9372
Fax: (620) 669-0531
E-Mail: madisonj@stockadecompanies.com
Web Site: www.stockadecompanies.com
Mr. Madison Jobe, VP Franchise Development

SIRLOIN STOCKADE features a selection of top-quality steaks, chicken and fish, a self-service salad bar, hot food buffet and display bakery at affordable prices. Free-standing buildings of approximately 10,000 square feet, seating 300+ and 70,000 square feet of land required.

BACKGROUND: IFA MEMBER
Established: 1984; 1st Franchised: 1984
Franchised Units: 51
Company-Owned Units: 1
Total Units: 52
Dist.: US-39; CAN-0; O'seas-13
North America: 10 States
Density: 12 in TX, 8 in KS, 6 in OK
Projected New Units (12 Months): 4
Qualifications: 5, 4, 4, 3, 2, 4
Registered: IL,IN,VA

FINANCIAL/TERMS:
Cash Investment: $250-350K
Total Investment: $1.2-2.2MM
Minimum Net Worth: $1MM
Fees: Franchise - $15K
Royalty - 3%; Ad. - 1%
Earnings Claims Statement: No
Term of Contract (Years): 15/5
Avg. # Of Employees: 20 FT, 50 PT
Passive Ownership: Discouraged
Encourage Conversions: Yes
Area Develop. Agreements: Yes/Varies
Sub-Franchising Contracts: No
Expand In Territory: Yes
Space Needs: 10,000 SF; FS

SUPPORT & TRAINING:
Financial Assistance Provided: No
Site Selection Assistance: Yes
Lease Negotiation Assistance: No
Co-Operative Advertising: No
Franchisee Assoc./Member: NR
Size Of Corporate Staff: 16
On-Going Support: B,C,D,E,G,h,i
Training: 6-8 Weeks Training.

SPECIFIC EXPANSION PLANS:
US: All United States
Canada: No
Overseas: Mexico

STRAW HAT PIZZA

18 Crow Canyon Ct., # 150
San Ramon, CA 94583-1669
Tel: (925) 837-3400
Fax: (925) 820-1080
E-Mail: info@strawhatpizza.com
Web Site: www.strawhatpizza.com
Mr. Joshua V. Richman, President/CEO

STRAW HAT PIZZA is a cooperative owned by a membership made up of individual store owners. Royalty fees are very low and more than offset by purchasing, insurance and marketing advantages. Stores operate under a detailed system, yet are allowed a great deal of flexibility. Store owners participate in the operation of the parent company.

BACKGROUND: IFA MEMBER
Established: 1959; 1st Franchised: 1969
Franchised Units: 45
Company-Owned Units: 0
Total Units: 45
Dist.: US-44; CAN-0; O'seas-0
North America: 2 States
Density: 44 in CA, 1 in NV
Projected New Units (12 Months): 4
Qualifications: 4, 4, 3, 3, 4, 4
Registered: CA,HI,WA

FINANCIAL/TERMS:
Cash Investment: $100-200K
Total Investment: $150-600K
Minimum Net Worth: $250K
Fees: Franchise - $10K
Royalty - 2%; Ad. - 0.75%
Earnings Claims Statement: No
Term of Contract (Years): 10/5
Avg. # Of Employees: 3-5 FT, 8-15 PT
Passive Ownership: Discouraged
Encourage Conversions: Yes
Area Develop. Agreements: No
Sub-Franchising Contracts: No
Expand In Territory: Yes
Space Needs: 4,000 SF; FS,SC

SUPPORT & TRAINING:
Financial Assistance Provided: Yes(I)
Site Selection Assistance: No
Lease Negotiation Assistance: No
Co-Operative Advertising: Yes
Franchisee Assoc./Member: No
Size Of Corporate Staff: 5
On-Going Support: B,C,D,F,G,h
Training: 4 Weeks Long Beach, CA

SPECIFIC EXPANSION PLANS:
US: West
Canada: No
Overseas: No

STRINGS ITALIAN CAFE

11344 Coloma Rd., # 545
Gold River, CA 95670
Tel: (916) 635-3990
Fax: (916) 631-9775
E-Mail: al@stringscafe.com
Web Site: www.stringscafe.com
Mr. Al DeCaprio, President

STRINGS ITALIAN CAFE is a full-service, casual restaurant, with a menu focusing on a variety of pasta entrees, pizza, salads, desserts and espresso. A central kitchen/commissary provides most of the product requirements.

BACKGROUND:
Established: 1987; 1st Franchised: 1989
Franchised Units: 17
Company-Owned Units: 3
Total Units: 20
Dist.: US-18; CAN-2; O'seas-0
North America: 3 States, 1 Province
Density: 24 in CA, 2 in PQ, 1 in NV
Projected New Units (12 Months): 4
Qualifications: 4, 4, 5, 3, 3, 4
Registered: CA,FL,OR,WA

FINANCIAL/TERMS:
Cash Investment: $100K
Total Investment: $325K
Minimum Net Worth: $400K
Fees: Franchise - $37.5K
Royalty - 5%; Ad. - 2%
Earnings Claims Statement: No
Term of Contract (Years): 10/5
Avg. # Of Employees: 4-6 FT, 15 PT
Passive Ownership: Discouraged
Encourage Conversions: Yes
Area Develop. Agreements: Yes/5
Sub-Franchising Contracts: No
Expand In Territory: Yes
Space Needs: 2,500 SF; SC, RM

SUPPORT & TRAINING:
Financial Assistance Provided: No
Site Selection Assistance: Yes
Lease Negotiation Assistance: Yes
Co-Operative Advertising: Yes
Franchisee Assoc./Member: No
Size Of Corporate Staff: 12
On-Going Support: C,D,E,F,G,H
Training: 6 Weeks Gold River, CA; 3 Weeks On-Site.

SPECIFIC EXPANSION PLANS:
US: All United States
Canada: No
Overseas: No

<< >>

SUNSHINE CAFE

7112 Zionsville Rd.
Indianapolis, IN 46268-4153
Tel: (800) 808-4774 (317) 299-3391
Fax: (317) 299-3390
E-Mail: sqsinc@aol.com
Web Site: www.worldfranchising.com/website.htm
Mr. James Frederick, Chief Executive Officer

A bright and cheerful, casual restaurant which reflects family dining at its best. Full table service is offered. Menu offers breakfast, lunch and dinner fare available throughout the day with local special entrees each day. Widely varied menu features American, Mexican, Italian and Oriental fare with fresh salad selections, signature items and desserts. Franchise has option to offer alcoholic beverages (beer, wine only) as market demands.

BACKGROUND:
Established: 1965; 1st Franchised: 1985
Franchised Units: 12
Company-Owned Units: 2
Total Units: 14
Dist.: US-14; CAN-0; O'seas-0
North America: 2 States
Density: 13 in IN, 1 in OH
Projected New Units (12 Months): 6
Qualifications: 5, 5, 5, 2, 4, 5
Registered: IL,IN,MI,WI

FINANCIAL/TERMS:
Cash Investment: $150K+
Total Investment: $150K-1MM
Minimum Net Worth: $500K
Fees: Franchise - $25K
Royalty - 4%; Ad. - 3%
Earnings Claims Statement: No
Term of Contract (Years): 5/5
Avg. # Of Employees: 50 FT, 10 PT
Passive Ownership: Allowed
Encourage Conversions: Yes
Area Develop. Agreements: Yes/Varies
Sub-Franchising Contracts: No
Expand In Territory: Yes
Space Needs: 4,400-5,600 SF; FS, SC, SF

SUPPORT & TRAINING:
Financial Assistance Provided: Yes(I)
Site Selection Assistance: Yes
Lease Negotiation Assistance: Yes
Co-Operative Advertising: Yes
Franchisee Assoc./Member: No
Size Of Corporate Staff: 16
On-Going Support: B,C,D,E,F,G,H
Training: 7 Weeks Indianapolis, IN.

SPECIFIC EXPANSION PLANS:
US: Midwest, N. Central U.S.
Canada: No
Overseas: No

<< >>

SWISS CHALET/SWISS CHALET PLUS RESTAURANTS

6303 Airport Rd.
Mississauga, ON L4V 1R8 CANADA
Tel: (800) 860-4082 (905) 405-6500
Fax: (905) 405-6777
E-Mail: dtaylor@cara.com
Web Site: www.swisschalet.com
Mr. Derek Taylor, Director of Franchising

Foodservice family restaurants.

BACKGROUND:
Established: 1900; 1st Franchised: 1984
Franchised Units: 173
Company-Owned Units: 38
Total Units: 211
Dist.: US-7; CAN-146; O'seas-0
North America: NR
Density: ON, PQ, AB
Projected New Units (12 Months): 20
Qualifications: 5, 4, 3, 3, 1, 5
Registered: AB

FINANCIAL/TERMS:
Cash Investment: $300-360K
Total Investment: $1-1.2MM
Minimum Net Worth: $600K
Fees: Franchise - $75-90K
Royalty - 5%; Ad. - 4%
Earnings Claims Statement: Yes
Term of Contract (Years): 20/5x4
Avg. # Of Employees: 6 FT, 80 PT
Passive Ownership: Not Allowed
Encourage Conversions: Yes
Area Develop. Agreements: No
Sub-Franchising Contracts: No
Expand In Territory: Yes
Space Needs: 6,000 SF; FS

SUPPORT & TRAINING:
Financial Assistance Provided: No
Site Selection Assistance: Yes
Lease Negotiation Assistance: Yes
Co-Operative Advertising: Yes
Franchisee Assoc./Member: Yes/Yes
Size Of Corporate Staff: 200
On-Going Support: C,D,E,G,h,I
Training: 10-12 Weeks Toronto, ON.

SPECIFIC EXPANSION PLANS:
US: No
Canada: All Canada
Overseas: No

<< >>

TONY ROMA'S FAMOUS FOR RIBS

9304 Forest Ln., # 200
Dallas, TX 75243-8953
Tel: (800) 286-7662 (214) 343-7800
Fax: (214) 343-7860
E-Mail: kenm@romacorp.com
Web Site: www.tonyromas.com
Mr. Kenneth L. Myres, VP Franchise Development

At TONY ROMA'S, we are committed to 'World Wide - World Class.' With intense guest focus, high integrity and Great Food! Providing for a great business opportunity. We started out with one restaurant in Miami FL, and today there are 280 TONY ROMA'S on six continents. We owe our phenomenal growth to one thing - Great People! TONY ROMA'S franchisee partners are a cut above the rest and we are always looking for more people to join our success.

BACKGROUND: IFA MEMBER
Established: 1972; 1st Franchised: 1979
Franchised Units: 213
Company-Owned Units: 43
Total Units: 256
Dist.: US-111; CAN-23; O'seas-79
North America: 42 States, 3 Provinces
Density: 37 in CA, 14 in AB, 15 in MX
Projected New Units (12 Months): NR
Qualifications: 5, 5, 5, 4, 4, 5
Registered:CA,FL,IN,MD,MI,MN,NY,ND,RI,SD,WA,WI

FINANCIAL/TERMS:
Cash Investment: Varies
Total Investment: Varies
Minimum Net Worth: $3MM
Fees: Franchise - $20K
Royalty - 4%; Ad. - .5%
Earnings Claims Statement: No
Term of Contract (Years): 20/10
Avg. # Of Employees: NR
Passive Ownership: Allowed
Encourage Conversions: Yes
Area Develop. Agreements: Yes/Varies
Sub-Franchising Contracts: No
Expand In Territory: Yes
Space Needs: 6,500 SF; FS, SC

SUPPORT & TRAINING:
Financial Assistance Provided: No
Site Selection Assistance: Yes

Lease Negotiation Assistance: No
Co-Operative Advertising: Yes
Franchisee Assoc./Member: No
Size Of Corporate Staff: 35
On-Going Support: C,D,E,h,I
Training: 8 1/2 Weeks.

SPECIFIC EXPANSION PLANS:
US: All United States
Canada: All Canada
Overseas: All Countries

<< >>

Top 100

UNO CHICAGO GRILL

100 Charles Park Rd.
Boston, MA 02132-4985
Tel: (617) 218-5325
Fax: (617) 218-5376
E-Mail: randy.clifton@unos.com
Web Site: www.unos.com
Mr. Randy M. Clifton, SVP Franchising

A full-service casual theme restaurant with a brand name signature product - UNO's Original Chicago Deep Dish Pizza. A full varied menu with broad appeal featuring steak, shrimp and pasta. A flair for fun including a bar and comfortable décor in a facility that attracts guests of all ages.

BACKGROUND: IFA MEMBER
Established: 1943; 1st Franchised: 1979
Franchised Units: 86
Company-Owned Units: 126
Total Units: 212
Dist.: US-208; CAN-0; O'seas-4
North America: 32 States
Density: 28 in MA, 24 in NY, 14 in VA
Projected New Units (12 Months): 18
Qualifications: 5, 5, 5, 3, 4, 4
Registered: All States

FINANCIAL/TERMS:
Cash Investment: $700K
Total Investment: $1.3-2.7MM
Minimum Net Worth: $3MM
Fees: Franchise - $35K
Royalty - 5%; Ad. - 1%
Earnings Claims Statement: Yes
Term of Contract (Years): 20/10
Avg. # Of Employees: 40 FT, 40 PT
Passive Ownership: Allowed
Encourage Conversions: Yes
Area Develop. Agreements: Yes
Sub-Franchising Contracts: No
Expand In Territory: Yes
Space Needs: 5,800 SF; FS, SC

SUPPORT & TRAINING:
Financial Assistance Provided: Yes(I)
Site Selection Assistance: Yes
Lease Negotiation Assistance: Yes
Co-Operative Advertising: Yes
Franchisee Assoc./Member: Yes/Yes
Size Of Corporate Staff: 135
On-Going Support: a,B,C,D,E,F,G,H,I
Training: 12 Weeks in a Training Restaurant; 2 Weeks On-Site Staff Training.

SPECIFIC EXPANSION PLANS:
US: All United States
Canada: All Canada
Overseas: Asia, South and Central America, Europe

<< >>

WALL STREET DELI SYSTEMS

5 Dakota Dr., # 302
Lake Success, NY 11042
Tel: (516) 358-0600
Fax: (516) 358-5076
E-Mail: abernstein@trufoods.com
Web Site: www.trufoods.com
Mr. Alan J. Bernstein, Concept Director

Sandwich shop offering fresh salads, coffee and hot entrees. Located at commercial parks and non-traditional locations, such as airports, hospitals, college campuses and office buildings. Quality of life is very appealing to potential franchisees. Monday through Friday, 7 AM - 3 PM. We promote a captive audience.

BACKGROUND: IFA MEMBER
Established: 1967; 1st Franchised: 1987
Franchised Units: 33
Company-Owned Units: 10
Total Units: 43
Dist.: US-43; CAN-0; O'seas-0
North America: 13 States
Density: 9 in AL, 5 in TX, 5 in CA
Projected New Units (12 Months): 25
Qualifications: 5, 4, 4, 3, 2, 1
Registered: CA,IN,NY,VA,DC

FINANCIAL/TERMS:
Cash Investment: NR
Total Investment: $230-470K
Minimum Net Worth: $200K
Fees: Franchise - $30K
Royalty - 5%; Ad. - 1%
Earnings Claims Statement: Yes
Term of Contract (Years): 10/10
Avg. # Of Employees: 6 FT, 4 PT
Passive Ownership: Discouraged
Encourage Conversions: Yes
Area Develop. Agreements: Yes
Sub-Franchising Contracts: Yes
Expand In Territory: Yes
Space Needs: Varies SF; See Above

SUPPORT & TRAINING:
Financial Assistance Provided: NR
Site Selection Assistance: Yes
Lease Negotiation Assistance: Yes
Co-Operative Advertising: NR
Franchisee Assoc./Member: Yes/Yes
Size Of Corporate Staff: 30-40
On-Going Support: A,B,C,D,E,F,G,H
Training: Training is On-Site; 10 Days Follow-up in Washington, DC.

SPECIFIC EXPANSION PLANS:
US: All United States
Canada: No
Overseas: No

<< >>

WESTERN SIZZLIN'

1338 Plantation Rd.
Roanoke, VA 24012
Tel: (800) 247-8325 (540) 345-3195
Fax: (540) 345-0831
E-Mail: jplunkett@western-sizzlin.com
Web Site: www.western-sizzlin.com
Mr. Jerry Plunkett, Manager Franchise Relations

WESTERN SIZZLIN' restaurants operate a full line of steak-chicken-seafood entrees, as well as a full expanded food bar, featuring proteins, vegetables and bakery items, along with an expanded salad bar. Our focus is on making a quality statement with excellent price/value. Also offering franchises for Great American Steak & Buffet and Austin's Steakhouse and Saloon.

BACKGROUND: IFA MEMBER
Established: 1962; 1st Franchised: 1976
Franchised Units: 151
Company-Owned Units: 7
Total Units: 158
Dist.: US-163; CAN-0; O'seas-0
North America: NR
Density: 31 in AR, 18 in VA, 14 in GA
Projected New Units (12 Months): NR
Qualifications: 5, 4, 2, 3, 2, 5
Registered: CA,FL,IL,IN,MD,VA

FINANCIAL/TERMS:
Cash Investment: NR
Total Investment: $811K-2.3MM

Minimum Net Worth: NR
Fees: Franchise - $30K
Royalty - 3% Gross; Ad. - $250/Mo.
Earnings Claims Statement: Yes
Term of Contract (Years): 20/10
Avg. # Of Employees: 25 FT, 50 PT
Passive Ownership: NR
Encourage Conversions: Yes
Area Develop. Agreements: Yes/Negot.
Sub-Franchising Contracts: NR
Expand In Territory: Yes
Space Needs: 7,500-8,500 SF; FS

SUPPORT & TRAINING:
Financial Assistance Provided: No
Site Selection Assistance: Yes
Lease Negotiation Assistance: No
Co-Operative Advertising: No
Franchisee Assoc./Member: Yes
Size Of Corporate Staff: 25
On-Going Support: B,C,D,E,F,G,h,I
Training: 6 Weeks Training.

SPECIFIC EXPANSION PLANS:
US: All United States
Canada: No
Overseas: No

<< >>

WORLDLY WRAPS

221 Sequoia Rd.
Louisville, KY 40207
Tel: (510) 839-5462
Fax: (510) 839-2104
E-Mail: jlee@worldfranchising.com
Web Site: www.worldlywraps.com
Mr. Fisher A. Hamilton, President

Truly the world's best wraps! 17 different varieties. Also, smoothies ând health drinks. Low start-up cost. Exceptional training and on-going support. This is a new market that has not yet been tapped. Take advantage of our concept and our growth program. Option to expand within territory.

BACKGROUND:
Established: 1994; 1st Franchised: 1995
Franchised Units: 24
Company-Owned Units: 6
Total Units: 30
Dist.: US-21; CAN-0; O'seas-0
North America: 6 States
Density: 10 in KY, 4 in TN, 2 in IN
Projected New Units (12 Months): 4
Qualifications: , , , , ,
Registered: CA,FL,IL,MN,WA

FINANCIAL/TERMS:
Cash Investment: $90-120K
Total Investment: $200-280K
Minimum Net Worth: $100K
Fees: Franchise - $19.5K
Royalty - 6%; Ad. - 1%
Earnings Claims Statement: No
Term of Contract (Years): 10/10
Avg. # Of Employees: 2 FT, 8 PT
Passive Ownership: Not Allowed
Encourage Conversions: Yes
Area Develop. Agreements: Yes/10
Sub-Franchising Contracts: No
Expand In Territory: No
Space Needs: 3,000-4,000 SF; FS

SUPPORT & TRAINING:
Financial Assistance Provided: Yes(I)
Site Selection Assistance: Yes
Lease Negotiation Assistance: Yes
Co-Operative Advertising: Yes
Franchisee Assoc./Member: NR
Size Of Corporate Staff: 21
On-Going Support: A,B,C,D,E,F,G,H,I
Training: 8 Weeks Headquarters; 3 Weeks Pre-Opening; On-Going.

SPECIFIC EXPANSION PLANS:
US: South, Southeast
Canada: No
Overseas: No

<< >>

ZPIZZA

50 Newport Center Dr., # 630
Newport Beach, CA 92660
Tel: (800) 422-2435 (949) 719-3800
Fax: (949) 721-4053
E-Mail: zpizza@zpizza.com
Web Site: www.zpizza.com
Mr. Chris Bright, President

Gourmet pizza, pasta, salads and sandwiches in a very up-scale California style. 1,000 square feet seating for 20 to 50 guests. Start-up costs under $150,000. Over 50 units in development

BACKGROUND:
Established: 1986; 1st Franchised: 1997
Franchised Units: 10
Company-Owned Units: 12
Total Units: 22
Dist.: US-22; CAN-0; O'seas-0
North America: 4 States
Density: California, Nevada
Projected New Units (12 Months): 15
Qualifications: 4, 4, 4, 2, 4, 4
Registered: CA,VA

FINANCIAL/TERMS:
Cash Investment: $50K
Total Investment: $150K
Minimum Net Worth: $50K
Fees: Franchise - $25K
Royalty - 5%; Ad. - 1%
Earnings Claims Statement: No
Term of Contract (Years): 20/10
Avg. # Of Employees: 3 FT, 10 PT
Passive Ownership: Allowed
Encourage Conversions: Yes
Area Develop. Agreements: Yes/10
Sub-Franchising Contracts: No
Expand In Territory: Yes
Space Needs: 1,000 SF; FS, SF, SC, RM

SUPPORT & TRAINING:
Financial Assistance Provided: Yes(I)
Site Selection Assistance: Yes
Lease Negotiation Assistance: Yes
Co-Operative Advertising: Yes
Franchisee Assoc./Member: No
Size Of Corporate Staff: 5
On-Going Support: B,C,D,E,F,G,H,I
Training: Orange County, CA.

SPECIFIC EXPANSION PLANS:
US: All United States
Canada: All Canada
Overseas: No

Food: Specialty Foods

Chapter 18

Food: Specialty Foods Industry Profile

Total # Franchisors in Industry Group	105
Total # Franchised Units in Industry Group	7,650
Total # Company-Owned Units in Industry Group	780
Total # Operating Units in Industry Group	8,430
Average # Franchised Units/Franchisor	72.9
Average # Company-Owned Units/Franchisor	7.4
Average # Total Units/Franchisor	80.3
Ratio of Total # Franchised Units/Total # Company-Owned Units	9.8:1
Industry Survey Participants	36
Representing % of Industry	34.3%
Average Franchise Fee*:	$24.8K
Average Total Investment*:	$265.6K
Average On-Going Royalty Fee*:	4.8%

*If a range was provided, the mid-point of the range was used. See detailed profiles for actual ranges.

Five Largest Participants in Survey

Company	# Franchised Units	# Co-Owned Units	# Total Units	Franchise Fee	On-Going Royalty	Total Investment
1. Papa Murphy's	850	11	861	$25K	5%	$148.8-199.5K
2. Auntie Anne's Hand-Rolled Soft Pretzels	825	30	855	$30K	6%	$192.6-342K
3. Schlotzsky's Deli	641	33	674	$30K	6%	$480K-2.6MM
4. Candy Bouquet International	669	1	670	$3.6-29K	0%	$7-49K
5. Maui Wowi Hawaiian Coffees & Smoothies	310	0	310	$24.5-59.5K	0%	$70-300K

All of the data provided are proprietary and should not be quoted without acknowledging *Bond's Franchise Guide.*

ATLANTA BREAD COMPANY

1955 Lake Park Dr.
Smyrna, GA 30080
Tel: (800) 398-3728 (770) 432-0933
Fax: (770) 444-9082
E-Mail: eschmitt@atlantabread.com
Web Site: www.atlantabread.com
Mr. Eric Schmitt, Sr. Dir. Franchise Development

Let's make some bread together! The concept behind the ATLANTA BREAD COMPANY BAKERY CAFE is simple: an upscale neighborhood café serving soups, salads, sandwiches, breads and pastries. ATLANTA BREAD COMPANY is riding the crest of the hottest food concept around - and we've experienced over 450% growth in just 12 months. ABC provides a full spectrum of support, from training to real estate assistance. Franchise offer made by offering circular only.

BACKGROUND: IFA MEMBER
Established: 1993; 1st Franchised: 1995
Franchised Units: 104
Company-Owned Units: 1
Total Units: 105
Dist.: US-105; CAN-0; O'seas-0
North America: 23 States
Density: GA, NC, SC
Projected New Units (12 Months): 60
Qualifications: 5, 3, 3, 3, 4, 4
Registered: All States Except ND, SD, IA

FINANCIAL/TERMS:
Cash Investment: $120-150K
Total Investment: $533.7-718.8K
Minimum Net Worth: $500-650K
Fees: Franchise - $40K
Royalty - 5%; Ad. - 2%
Earnings Claims Statement: No
Term of Contract (Years): 10/10
Avg. # Of Employees: 34 FT
Passive Ownership: Discouraged
Encourage Conversions: NA
Area Develop. Agreements: Yes
Sub-Franchising Contracts: No
Expand In Territory: Yes
Space Needs: 4,000-4,500 SF; FS, SF, PC

SUPPORT & TRAINING:
Financial Assistance Provided: Yes(I)
Site Selection Assistance: Yes
Lease Negotiation Assistance: Yes
Co-Operative Advertising: NA
Franchisee Assoc./Member: No
Size Of Corporate Staff: 34
On-Going Support: B,C,D,E,F,H,I
Training: 7 Weeks Atlanta, GA.

SPECIFIC EXPANSION PLANS:
US: All United States
Canada: No
Overseas: No

<< >>

AUNTIE ANNE'S HAND-ROLLED SOFT PRETZELS

160-A, Rt. 41, P.O. Box 529
Gap, PA 17527
Tel: (717) 442-4766
Fax: (717) 442-4139
E-Mail: lindae@auntieannesinc.com
Web Site: www.auntieannes.com
Ms. Linda Engels, Franchise Support Rep.

Our motto is: To serve a fresh, hot, golden-brown pretzel with friendly, courteous customer service in a sparkling clean store.

BACKGROUND: IFA MEMBER
Established: 1988; 1st Franchised: 1989
Franchised Units: 825
Company-Owned Units: 30
Total Units: 855
Dist.: US-750; CAN-0; O'seas-155
North America: 44 States, 2 Provinces
Density: 75 in PA, 51 in CA, 44 in FL
Projected New Units (12 Months): 50
Qualifications: 4, 2, 2, 2, 3, 5
Registered: All States

FINANCIAL/TERMS:
Cash Investment: $192.6-342K
Total Investment: $192.6-342K
Minimum Net Worth: $300K
Fees: Franchise - $30K
Royalty - 6%; Ad. - 1%
Earnings Claims Statement: No
Term of Contract (Years): 10/10
Avg. # Of Employees: 4 FT, 4 PT
Passive Ownership: Allowed
Encourage Conversions: NA
Area Develop. Agreements: No
Sub-Franchising Contracts: No
Expand In Territory: No
Space Needs: 400-600 SF; FS

SUPPORT & TRAINING:
Financial Assistance Provided: Yes(I)
Site Selection Assistance: Yes
Lease Negotiation Assistance: Yes
Co-Operative Advertising: Yes
Franchisee Assoc./Member: Yes/Yes
Size Of Corporate Staff: 150
On-Going Support: B,C,D,E,G,H,I
Training: 2 Weeks Gap, PA.

SPECIFIC EXPANSION PLANS:
US: All United States
Canada: No
Overseas: All Countries

<< >>

BAHAMA BUCK'S ORIGINAL SHAVED ICE CO.

465 E. Chilton Dr., # 5
Chandler, AZ 85225
Tel: (480) 539-6952
Fax: (480) 539-6953
E-Mail: azlee1@aol.com
Web Site: www.bahamabucks.com
Mr. Blake Buchanan, President

BAHAMA BUCK'S offers a unique, low-cost opportunity for anyone interested in a fun, family oriented business. We concentrate on offering quality products and great customer service. Set in a tropical atmosphere, BAHAMA BUCK'S offers 61 flavors of soft, creamy shaved ice, plus over 14 non-alcoholic tropical drinks. Store layouts and sizes vary and are extremely flexible, but typically range from 1200-1500 square feet.

BACKGROUND:
Established: 1990; 1st Franchised: 1992
Franchised Units: 6
Company-Owned Units: 3
Total Units: 9
Dist.: US-10; CAN-0; O'seas-0
North America: 2 States
Density: 5 in AZ, 5 in TX
Projected New Units (12 Months): 6
Qualifications: 4, 3, 1, 3, 4, 4
Registered: NR

FINANCIAL/TERMS:
Cash Investment: $35K
Total Investment: $60-140K
Minimum Net Worth: $120K
Fees: Franchise - $15K
Royalty - 6%; Ad. - 1%
Earnings Claims Statement: No
Term of Contract (Years): 10/10
Avg. # Of Employees: 1 FT, 12 PT
Passive Ownership: Allowed
Encourage Conversions: Yes
Area Develop. Agreements: Yes/10
Sub-Franchising Contracts: No
Expand In Territory: Yes
Space Needs: 1,000-1,500 SF; FS, SC

SUPPORT & TRAINING:

Financial Assistance Provided: Yes(I)
Site Selection Assistance: Yes
Lease Negotiation Assistance: Yes
Co-Operative Advertising: Yes
Franchisee Assoc./Member: No
Size Of Corporate Staff: 5
On-Going Support: B,C,d,E,G,H,I
Training: 60-80 Hours Tempe, AZ; 2 Days On-Site.

SPECIFIC EXPANSION PLANS:
US: Southwest, South
Canada: No
Overseas: No

<< >>

BEAVERTAILS PASTRY

133 de la Commune East
Montreal, PQ K2E 7V2 CANADA
Tel: (800) 704-0351 (514) 392-2222 + 12
Fax: (514) 392-2223
E-Mail: pino@moozoo.com
Web Site: www.beavertailsinc.com
Mr. Pino Di Ioia, Franchise Sales/Support

BEAVERTAILS are a unique, wholesome pastry cooked fresh at leisure sites. We offer low entry investment, interesting locations and excellent strategic support. We are interested in development opportunities at amusement parks, sports venues, tourist destinations and ski hills across North America.

BACKGROUND:
Established: 1978; 1st Franchised: 1989
Franchised Units: 130
Company-Owned Units: 3
Total Units: 133
Dist.: US-4; CAN-99; O'seas-30
North America: 4 States, 8 Provinces
Density: 2 in TX, 1 in FL, 1 in CO
Projected New Units (12 Months): NR
Qualifications: , , , , ,
Registered: NR

FINANCIAL/TERMS:
Cash Investment: $30-50K
Total Investment: $85-150K
Minimum Net Worth: $50K
Fees: Franchise - $20K
Royalty - 5%; Ad. - 3%
Earnings Claims Statement: Yes
Term of Contract (Years): 5/15
Avg. # Of Employees: 1 FT, 2-3 PT
Passive Ownership: Discouraged
Encourage Conversions: NR
Area Develop. Agreements: Yes
Sub-Franchising Contracts: Yes
Expand In Territory: Yes
Space Needs: 200-300 SF; FS, SF, RM, Amusement.Recr.

SUPPORT & TRAINING:
Financial Assistance Provided: NR
Site Selection Assistance: Yes
Lease Negotiation Assistance: Yes
Co-Operative Advertising: Yes
Franchisee Assoc./Member: Yes/Yes
Size Of Corporate Staff: 10
On-Going Support: A,B,C,D,E,F,G,I
Training: 14 Days Ottawa, ON; 3 Days On-Site.

SPECIFIC EXPANSION PLANS:
US: Southeast, Southwest
Canada: NR
Overseas: NR

<< >>

CANDY BOUQUET INTERNATIONAL

423 E. 3rd St.
Little Rock, AR 72201
Tel: (877) 226-3901 (501) 375-9990
Fax: (501) 375-9998
E-Mail: yumyum@candybouquet.com
Web Site: www.candybouquet.com
Ms. Gina McNabb, Executive Vice President

CANDY BOUQUET franchises are as unique as the people who own them. All franchises offer floral-like arrangements that are crafted from candies and the finest of chocolates. Each bouquet includes a burst of accessories, bright cellophane accents and a unique container. CANDY BOUQUETS are fun to give, fun to receive and fun to eat. They are perfect as corporate gifts and can be shipped anywhere.

BACKGROUND: IFA MEMBER
Established: 1989; 1st Franchised: 1993
Franchised Units: 669
Company-Owned Units: 1
Total Units: 670
Dist.: US-585; CAN-37; O'seas-48
North America: 49 States, 8 Provinces
Density: 48 in AR, 46 in TX, 31 in CA
Projected New Units (12 Months): 239
Qualifications: 5, 5, 5, 5, 5, 5
Registered: All States and AB

FINANCIAL/TERMS:
Cash Investment: $7.5-49K
Total Investment: $7-49K
Minimum Net Worth: NA
Fees: Franchise - $3.6-29K
Royalty - 0%; Ad. - 0%
Earnings Claims Statement: No
Term of Contract (Years): 5/5
Avg. # Of Employees: 1 FT, 2 PT
Passive Ownership: Not Allowed
Encourage Conversions: NA
Area Develop. Agreements: Yes/10
Sub-Franchising Contracts: Yes
Expand In Territory: Yes
Space Needs: ~1,000 SF; HB, SF

SUPPORT & TRAINING:
Financial Assistance Provided: No
Site Selection Assistance: Yes
Lease Negotiation Assistance: No
Co-Operative Advertising: Yes
Franchisee Assoc./Member: No
Size Of Corporate Staff: 27
On-Going Support: b,c,d,D,e,G,h,I
Training: 5 Days Little Rock, AR.

SPECIFIC EXPANSION PLANS:
US: All United States
Canada: All Canada
Overseas: All Countries

<< >>

CANDY EXPRESS

10480 Little Patuxent Pkwy., # 400
Columbia, MD 21044
Tel: (800) 511-4438 (410) 964-5500
Fax: (410) 964-6404
E-Mail: jrosenberg@candyexpress.com
Web Site: www.candyexpress.com
Mr. Joel Rosenberg, President

The number-one ranked retail candy store franchise, offering over 1,000 varieties of candy and confections in a self-serve format. This international franchise company provides franchisees with a total turn-key opportunity that is profitable and easy to operate.

BACKGROUND:
Established: 1989; 1st Franchised: 1989
Franchised Units: 37
Company-Owned Units: 5
Total Units: 42
Dist.: US-40; CAN-0; O'seas-8
North America: 17 States
Density: 6 in MD, 5 in GA, 4 in VA
Projected New Units (12 Months): 15
Qualifications: 5, 2, 1, 1, 2, 3
Registered: All States

FINANCIAL/TERMS:
Cash Investment: $25-75K
Total Investment: $125-175K
Minimum Net Worth: $200K
Fees: Franchise - $25K
Royalty - 6%; Ad. - 1%
Earnings Claims Statement: No
Term of Contract (Years): 10/10
Avg. # Of Employees: 1 FT, 3 PT

Passive Ownership: Allowed
Encourage Conversions: Yes
Area Develop. Agreements: Yes/20
Sub-Franchising Contracts: Yes
Expand In Territory: Yes
Space Needs: 1,000 SF; SF, RM, Airport

SUPPORT & TRAINING:
Financial Assistance Provided: Yes(I)
Site Selection Assistance: Yes
Lease Negotiation Assistance: Yes
Co-Operative Advertising: Yes
Franchisee Assoc./Member: Yes/No
Size Of Corporate Staff: 10
On-Going Support: A,B,C,D,E,F,G,H
Training: 2 Weeks MD.

SPECIFIC EXPANSION PLANS:
US: All United States
Canada: All Canada
Overseas: All Countries

<< >>

DIFFERENT TWIST PRETZEL CO., THE

6052 Rte. 8, P.O. Box 334
Bakerstown, PA 15007
Tel: (724) 443-8010
Fax: (724) 443-7287
E-Mail: apmaggio@differenttwistpretzel.com
Web Site: www.differenttwistpretzel.com
Mr. August P. Maggio, President

Serving hand-rolled, fresh-baked soft pretzels in 10 different flavors. (Licensor)

BACKGROUND:
Established: 1992; 1st Franchised: 1992
Franchised Units: 23
Company-Owned Units: 2
Total Units: 25
Dist.: US-18; CAN-1; O'seas-6
North America: 8 States
Density: 4 in WV, 3 in KY, 3 in Phil.
Projected New Units (12 Months): 20
Qualifications: 4, 4, 1, 2, 1, 4
Registered: FL

FINANCIAL/TERMS:
Cash Investment: $40-80K
Total Investment: $40-80K
Minimum Net Worth: $50K
Fees: Franchise - $5K
Royalty - 5%; Ad. - NR
Earnings Claims Statement: Yes
Term of Contract (Years): 10/10
Avg. # Of Employees: 3 FT, 3 PT
Passive Ownership: Allowed
Encourage Conversions: Yes
Area Develop. Agreements: Yes
Sub-Franchising Contracts: Yes
Expand In Territory: Yes
Space Needs: 150-400 SF; SF, RM, Other

SUPPORT & TRAINING:
Financial Assistance Provided: Yes(D)
Site Selection Assistance: Yes
Lease Negotiation Assistance: Yes
Co-Operative Advertising: Yes
Franchisee Assoc./Member: No
Size Of Corporate Staff: 12
On-Going Support: b,D,e
Training: 1 Week On-Site.

SPECIFIC EXPANSION PLANS:
US: All United States
Canada: All Canada
Overseas: All Countries

<< >>

FRESH CITY

145 Rosemary St., # C
Needham, MA 02494
Tel: (888) FRESH55 (781) 453-0200 + 230
Fax: (781) 453-8686
E-Mail: jpainter@freshfoodconcepts.com
Web Site: www.freshcity.com
Ms. Joan Painter, Director of Franchising

FRESH CITY, one of Nation's Restaurant News' 'Hot Concept' award winners, 'Ones to Watch' by QSR Magazine and 'Best of Boston,' provides comfortable Fast, Fresh, Casual and Fresh Fusion cuisine. Several cooking and fusion stations provide guests with an international diversity of menu offerings, including hot and cold wraps, Asian noodles, salads, distinct sandwiches, smoothies, lattes and more - to dine in, take out or have catered.

BACKGROUND: IFA MEMBER
Established: 1998; 1st Franchised: 2003
Franchised Units: 0
Company-Owned Units: 6
Total Units: 6
Dist.: US-6; CAN-0; O'seas-0
North America: 3 States
Density: 4 in MA, 1 in NH, 1 in CT
Projected New Units (12 Months): 4
Qualifications: 5, 4, 4, 4, 1, 5
Registered: FL,IL,MD,MI,MN,NY,RI,VA,WI

FINANCIAL/TERMS:
Cash Investment: $2 MM
Total Investment: $726K-1.1MM
Minimum Net Worth: $3.5MM
Fees: Franchise - $25K
Royalty - 5%; Ad. - 2% + 2%
Earnings Claims Statement: Yes
Term of Contract (Years): 10/10
Avg. # Of Employees: 5 FT, 10-20 PT
Passive Ownership: Not Allowed
Encourage Conversions: Yes
Area Develop. Agreements: Yes/3+
Sub-Franchising Contracts: No
Expand In Territory: No
Space Needs: 3,700 SF; FS, SF, SC

SUPPORT & TRAINING:
Financial Assistance Provided: No
Site Selection Assistance: Yes
Lease Negotiation Assistance: Yes
Co-Operative Advertising: NA
Franchisee Assoc./Member: No
Size Of Corporate Staff: 12
On-Going Support: A,B,C,D,E,F,G,H,I
Training: 9 Weeks Needham, MA.

SPECIFIC EXPANSION PLANS:
US: NY,NJ,CT,IL,SE, Mid-Atlantic
Canada: No
Overseas: No

<< >>

GRAPE, THE

4300 Paces Ferry Rd., # 500A
Atlanta, GA 30339
Tel: (678) 309-9463
Fax: (678) 309-1208
E-Mail: franchise@yourgrape.com
Web Site: www.yourgrape.com
Mr. Martin A. Thallman, President

Uncork an innovative opportunity!!! Demystify wine through THE GRAPES's copyrighted wine by taste guide that combines two complementary revenue sources (wine bar and retail store). Simplify operations and keep inventory costs to a minimum. Serving in-style, gourmet food, utilizing very minimal equipment and kitchen space.

BACKGROUND: IFA MEMBER
Established: 2000; 1st Franchised: 2004
Franchised Units: 15
Company-Owned Units: 3
Total Units: 18
Dist.: US-18; CAN-0; O'seas-0
North America: 5 States
Density: 4 in GA
Projected New Units (12 Months): 6
Qualifications: 5, 5, 3, 5, 5, 5
Registered: FL,VA

FINANCIAL/TERMS:
Cash Investment: $250-300K
Total Investment: $450-600K
Minimum Net Worth: $600K
Fees: Franchise - $50K
Royalty - 6%; Ad. - 2%
Earnings Claims Statement: Yes
Term of Contract (Years): 7/5/5/5
Avg. # Of Employees: NR
Passive Ownership: Not Allowed
Encourage Conversions: Yes
Area Develop. Agreements: Yes
Sub-Franchising Contracts: No
Expand In Territory: Yes
Space Needs: 2,000 SF; FS, SF, SC, RM

SUPPORT & TRAINING:
Financial Assistance Provided: No
Site Selection Assistance: Yes
Lease Negotiation Assistance: Yes
Co-Operative Advertising: Yes
Franchisee Assoc./Member: No
Size Of Corporate Staff: 7
On-Going Support: B,C,D,E,F,H
Training: 4 Weeks Pre-Opening Atlanta, GA; 1 Week Grand Opening On-Site; As Needed On-Site.

SPECIFIC EXPANSION PLANS:
US: SE US;GA,FL,NC,SC, AL,TN,KY,DC,MS,LA
Canada: No
Overseas: No

<< >>

HARD TIMES CAFÉ

1404 King St.
Alexandria, VA 22314
Tel: (703) 683-8545
Fax: (703) 837-0057
E-Mail:
Web Site: www.hardtimes.com
Mr. Rich Kelly, Chief Executive Officer

Authentic western-style chili parlor. Featuring chili, burgers and beer.

BACKGROUND:
Established: 1980; 1st Franchised: 1992
Franchised Units: 10
Company-Owned Units: 4
Total Units: 14
Dist.: US-0; CAN-0; O'seas-0
North America: 3 States
Density: 6 in VA, 6 in MD, 2 in NC
Projected New Units (12 Months): NR
Qualifications: , , , , ,
Registered: NR

FINANCIAL/TERMS:
Cash Investment: $100-200K
Total Investment: $400-500K
Minimum Net Worth: $250K
Fees: Franchise - $30K
Royalty - 4%; Ad. - 1%
Earnings Claims Statement: No
Term of Contract (Years): 10/10
Avg. # Of Employees: 6 FT, 20 PT
Passive Ownership: Not Allowed
Encourage Conversions: NR
Area Develop. Agreements: Yes/20
Sub-Franchising Contracts: Yes
Expand In Territory: Yes
Space Needs: NR SF; FS, SC

SUPPORT & TRAINING:
Financial Assistance Provided: NR
Site Selection Assistance: Yes
Lease Negotiation Assistance: Yes
Co-Operative Advertising: Yes
Franchisee Assoc./Member: No
Size Of Corporate Staff: 10
On-Going Support: a,C,D,E,F,G,H,I
Training: 4 Weeks in Washington, DC Area.

SPECIFIC EXPANSION PLANS:
US: East Coast, Mid-Atlantic
Canada: NR
Overseas: NR

<< >>

INCREDIBLY EDIBLE DELITES

1 Summitt Ave.
Broomall, PA 19008-2519
Tel: (866) 203-7848 (610) 353-8844
Fax: (610) 359-9188
E-Mail: ied@fruitflowers.com
Web Site: www.fruitflowers.com
Mr. Melvin Messinger, VP Franchising

We are offering a franchised retail business which features the creation and delivery of sculptured fruit and vegetable bouquets. Our bouquets are provided for our customers who share our passion for sight, smell and taste of fruit and vegetables.

BACKGROUND: IFA MEMBER
Established: 1984; 1st Franchised: 1993
Franchised Units: 12
Company-Owned Units: 1
Total Units: 13
Dist.: US-13; CAN-0; O'seas-0
North America: 12 States
Density: 4 in PA, 3 in FL, 2 in NJ
Projected New Units (12 Months): 12
Qualifications: 5, 3, 1, 1, 3, 3
Registered:CA,FL,IL,IN,MD,MI,MN,NY, VA,WA,WI,DC

FINANCIAL/TERMS:
Cash Investment: $30K
Total Investment: $100-150K
Minimum Net Worth: $175K
Fees: Franchise - $25K
Royalty - 4.5%; Ad. - 1%
Earnings Claims Statement: Yes
Term of Contract (Years): 10/10
Avg. # Of Employees: 1 FT, 4 PT
Passive Ownership: Allowed
Encourage Conversions: NA
Area Develop. Agreements: No
Sub-Franchising Contracts: No
Expand In Territory: Yes
Space Needs: 1,600 SF; FS, SF, SC

SUPPORT & TRAINING:
Financial Assistance Provided: No
Site Selection Assistance: Yes
Lease Negotiation Assistance: Yes
Co-Operative Advertising: Yes
Franchisee Assoc./Member: No
Size Of Corporate Staff: 5
On-Going Support: C,D,E,G,h
Training: 3 Weeks Broomall, PA.

SPECIFIC EXPANSION PLANS:
US: All United States
Canada: All Canada
Overseas: No

<< >>

JOE CORBI'S ® PIZZA KIT FUNDRAISING PROGRAM

1430 Desoto Rd.
Baltimore, MD 21230
Tel: (888) 526-7247 (410) 525-8331
Fax: (412) 745-1272
E-Mail: joe.violi@joecorbisfundraising.com
Web Site: www.joecorbi.com
Mr. Joseph Violi,

Specializing in the sale of fund-raising pizza kits, breads and other food items, as well as related goods and ancillary services, which are marketed to charitable, municipal, civic and other organizations.

BACKGROUND:
Established: 1984; 1st Franchised: 1999
Franchised Units: 5
Company-Owned Units: 5

Total Units: 10
Dist.: US-8; CAN-0; O'seas-0
North America: 7 States
Density: 2 in PA, 1 in MD, 1 in VA
Projected New Units (12 Months): 6
Qualifications: 5, 3, 3, 3, 5, 5
Registered: MD,NY

FINANCIAL/TERMS:

Cash Investment: $40-85K
Total Investment: $50.4-105.5K
Minimum Net Worth: $50.4K
Fees: Franchise - $25-50K
Royalty - 0%; Ad. - 0%
Earnings Claims Statement: No
Term of Contract (Years): 10/10
Avg. # Of Employees: 2 FT
Passive Ownership: Discouraged
Encourage Conversions: Yes
Area Develop. Agreements: No
Sub-Franchising Contracts: No
Expand In Territory: Yes
Space Needs: NA SF; HB

SUPPORT & TRAINING:

Financial Assistance Provided: No
Site Selection Assistance: Yes
Lease Negotiation Assistance: No
Co-Operative Advertising: No
Franchisee Assoc./Member: No
Size Of Corporate Staff: 7
On-Going Support: C,d,F,G,H
Training: 3 Days at Operating Unit.

SPECIFIC EXPANSION PLANS:

US: Eastern United States
Canada: No
Overseas: No

<< >>

JUICE IT UP!

17915 Sky Park Circle, # J
Irvine, CA 92614
Tel: (888) 705-8423 (949) 475-0146
Fax: (949) 475-0137
E-Mail: lisac@juiceitup.com
Web Site: www.juiceitup.com
Ms. Lisa Casanova, Franchise Manager

JUICE IT UP! is a privately held corporation founded in California in 1995. JUICE IT UP! has successfully established itself as a leader in the juice and smoothie bar industry by providing great customer service and great products. With over 50 locations and growing, JUICE IT UP! offers a unique and exciting franchise opportunity to entrepreneurially minded individuals. JUICE IT UP! is an approved SBA franchisor.

BACKGROUND: IFA MEMBER
Established: 1995; 1st Franchised: 1998
Franchised Units: 41
Company-Owned Units: 4
Total Units: 45
Dist.: US-45; CAN-0; O'seas-0
North America: 6 States
Density: 35 in CA, 2 in FL
Projected New Units (12 Months): NR
Qualifications: , , , , ,
Registered: NR

FINANCIAL/TERMS:

Cash Investment: $50K
Total Investment: $162-247K
Minimum Net Worth: $250K
Fees: Franchise - $25K
Royalty - 6%; Ad. - 2%
Earnings Claims Statement: No
Term of Contract (Years): 10/5/5
Avg. # Of Employees: 1 FT, 8 PT
Passive Ownership: Discouraged
Encourage Conversions: NR
Area Develop. Agreements: Yes/10
Sub-Franchising Contracts: Yes
Expand In Territory: Yes
Space Needs: 1,200 SF; SF, SC,RM

SUPPORT & TRAINING:

Financial Assistance Provided: NR
Site Selection Assistance: Yes
Lease Negotiation Assistance: Yes
Co-Operative Advertising: Yes
Franchisee Assoc./Member: Yes/No
Size Of Corporate Staff: 8
On-Going Support: C,D,E,G,H,I
Training: 1-2 Weeks Corporate Store; 2 Days Corporate Office; 1 Week Franchisee Store.

SPECIFIC EXPANSION PLANS:

US: All United States
Canada: NR
Overseas: NR

<< >>

MAUI WOWI HAWAIIAN COFFEES & SMOOTHIES

Top 100

MAUI WOWI HAWAIIAN COFFEES AND SMOOTHIES

5445 DTC Parkway, # 1050
Greenwood Village, CO 80111
Tel: (888) 862-8555 + 19 (303) 781-7800 + 19
Fax: (303) 781-2438
E-Mail: leads@mauiwowi.com
Web Site: www.mauiwowi.com
Ms. Kera Vo, Franchise Devel. Mktg. Mgr.

Ranked as # 175 in Inc 500, with over 310 locations, MAUI WOWI is the #1 largest smoothie/coffee franchise in the world. With 24/7 support and extensive training, MAUI WOWI offers a simple, profitable and flexible business business model. MAUI WOWI has thousands of locations and events throughout the country waiting for a MAUI WOWI franchise owner. Because of our flexibility, low investment and variety of business models, MAUI WOWI is the fastest-growing franchise.

BACKGROUND: IFA MEMBER
Established: 1983; 1st Franchised: 1997
Franchised Units: 310
Company-Owned Units: 0
Total Units: 310
Dist.: US-300; CAN-0; O'seas-0
North America: 43 States
Density: NR
Projected New Units (12 Months): 250-300
Qualifications: 2, 2, 1, 1, 1, 5
Registered: All States

FINANCIAL/TERMS:

Cash Investment: $40K
Total Investment: $70-300K
Minimum Net Worth: $250K
Fees: Franchise - $24.5-59.5K
Royalty - 0%; Ad. - 2%
Earnings Claims Statement: Yes
Term of Contract (Years): 10
Avg. # Of Employees: 2 FT
Passive Ownership: Allowed
Encourage Conversions: Yes
Area Develop. Agreements: Yes
Sub-Franchising Contracts: No
Expand In Territory: Yes
Space Needs: 100 SF; HB, KI

SUPPORT & TRAINING:

Financial Assistance Provided: Yes(I)
Site Selection Assistance: Yes
Lease Negotiation Assistance: Yes
Co-Operative Advertising: Yes
Franchisee Assoc./Member: No
Size Of Corporate Staff: 25
On-Going Support: B,C,D,E,F,G,H,I
Training: 4 Days in Denver, CO.

SPECIFIC EXPANSION PLANS:

US: All United States
Canada: All Canada
Overseas: All Countries

<< >>

MCALISTER'S DELI

731 S. Pear Orchard Rd., # 51
Ridgeland, MS 39157-4800
Tel: (888) 855-3354 (601) 952-1107
Fax: (601) 952-1138

E-Mail: pwalls@mcalistersdeli.com
Web Site: www.mcalistersdeli.com
Mr. Patrick K. Walls, SVP Franchise Sales

Fast, casual restaurant, featuring a complete menu of gourmet deli foods, including hot and cold deli sandwiches, super-stuffed baked potatoes, salads, soups, desserts, MCALISTER'S famous sweet tea and other food and beverage products.

BACKGROUND: IFA MEMBER
Established: 1989; 1st Franchised: 1994
Franchised Units: 115
Company-Owned Units: 23
Total Units: 138
Dist.: US-138; CAN-0; O'seas-0
North America: 17 States
Density: 22 in MS, 12 in AL, 12 in NC
Projected New Units (12 Months): 30
Qualifications: 5, 5, 4, 3, 1, 3
Registered: All States

FINANCIAL/TERMS:
Cash Investment: $400-500KK
Total Investment: $329K-1.4MM
Minimum Net Worth: $1MM
Fees: Franchise - $30K
Royalty - 5%; Ad. - 2%
Earnings Claims Statement: Yes
Term of Contract (Years): 10/5/5/5
Avg. # Of Employees: 5 FT, 35 PT
Passive Ownership: Allowed
Encourage Conversions: Yes
Area Develop. Agreements: Yes/Varies
Sub-Franchising Contracts: No
Expand In Territory: No
Space Needs: 3,600 SF; FS, SC

SUPPORT & TRAINING:
Financial Assistance Provided: Yes(I)
Site Selection Assistance: Yes
Lease Negotiation Assistance: Yes
Co-Operative Advertising: Yes
Franchisee Assoc./Member: Yes
Size Of Corporate Staff: 40
On-Going Support: a,B,C,D,E,F,G,H,I
Training: 8 Weeks Jackson, MS; 10 Days Franchisee Location.

SPECIFIC EXPANSION PLANS:
US: All United States
Canada: All Canada
Overseas: No

<< >>

MOM'S BAKE AT HOME PIZZA

4457 Main St.
Philadelphia, PA 19127
Tel: (800) 311-MOMS (215) 482-1044
Fax: (215) 482-0402
E-Mail: bakehome@aol.com
Web Site: www.momsbakeathomepizza.com
Ms. Gwenn Bair, President

MOM'S PIZZA franchise 'Bake at Home' pizza stores. The franchisee purchases his or her supplies from the main office. The franchisee then retails a fresh, hand-made gourmet pizza, which is baked at the customer's convenience, in the convenience of his or her home.

BACKGROUND:
Established: 1961; 1st Franchised: 1981
Franchised Units: 13
Company-Owned Units: 0
Total Units: 13
Dist.: US-18; CAN-0; O'seas-0
North America: 2 States
Density: 12 in PA, 6 in NJ
Projected New Units (12 Months): 2
Qualifications: , , , , ,
Registered: NR

FINANCIAL/TERMS:
Cash Investment: $50K
Total Investment: $50K
Minimum Net Worth: NR
Fees: Franchise - $15K
Royalty - 0%; Ad. - 0%
Earnings Claims Statement: No
Term of Contract (Years): On-Going
Avg. # Of Employees: 1 FT, 2 PT
Passive Ownership: Not Allowed
Encourage Conversions: No
Area Develop. Agreements: No
Sub-Franchising Contracts: No
Expand In Territory: No
Space Needs: 800 SF; SC

SUPPORT & TRAINING:
Financial Assistance Provided: No
Site Selection Assistance: Yes
Lease Negotiation Assistance: Yes
Co-Operative Advertising: No
Franchisee Assoc./Member: No
Size Of Corporate Staff: 12
On-Going Support: B,C,D,E
Training: 7 Days Existing Franchise.

SPECIFIC EXPANSION PLANS:
US: PA, NJ
Canada: No
Overseas: No

<< >>

MY GIRLFRIEND'S KITCHEN

6926 Greenfield Way, # 1
Salt Lake City, UT 84121
Tel: (801) 944-5090
Fax: (801) 944-5093
E-Mail: franchise@mgfk.com
Web Site: www.mgfk.com
Ms. Jennifer Jackenthal, President

What's for dinner tonight? MY GIRLFRIEND'S KITCHEN solves that problem and our customers leave the mess in our kitchen! Imagine assembling and taking home 12 family-sized, ready-to-cook gourmet entrees without the aggravation of shopping, prep and clean up. Put them in your fridge/freezer and stop wondering what's for dinner tonight! Each menu item feeds 4-6. Vast assortment of dinner selections. Support network of recipes, menus, ordering and production systems. Comprehensive training/ongoing support.

BACKGROUND: IFA MEMBER
Established: 2003; 1st Franchised: 2004
Franchised Units: 2
Company-Owned Units: 1
Total Units: 3
Dist.: US-3; CAN-0; O'seas-0
North America: 2 States
Density: 2 in UT, 1 in SD
Projected New Units (12 Months): 20
Qualifications: 4, 4, 3, 3, 3, 5
Registered: CA,FL,MD,ND,OR,SD,VA

FINANCIAL/TERMS:
Cash Investment: $45-70K
Total Investment: $199.3-340.5K
Minimum Net Worth: $150-250K
Fees: Franchise - $35K
Royalty - 5%; Ad. - 2%
Earnings Claims Statement: Yes
Term of Contract (Years): 10/5
Avg. # Of Employees: 1 FT, 5 PT
Passive Ownership: Not Allowed
Encourage Conversions: NA
Area Develop. Agreements: No
Sub-Franchising Contracts: No
Expand In Territory: Yes
Space Needs: 1,700-2,000 SF; SC

SUPPORT & TRAINING:
Financial Assistance Provided: No
Site Selection Assistance: Yes
Lease Negotiation Assistance: Yes
Co-Operative Advertising: Yes
Franchisee Assoc./Member: No
Size Of Corporate Staff: 5
On-Going Support: A,C,D,E,F,G
Training: 2 Weeks Corporate Office and Store; Up to 5 Days at Opening.

SPECIFIC EXPANSION PLANS:

US: All United States
Canada: No
Overseas: No

<< >>

NEW YORK FRIES

1220 Yonge St., # 400
Toronto, ON M4T 1W1 CANADA
Tel: (416) 963-5005
Fax: (416) 963-4920
E-Mail: mail@newyorkfries.com
Web Site: www.newyorkfries.com
Mr. Bob Okamoto, Business Develop. Manager

Exceptional product and simplicity of operations make NEW YORK FRIES an outstanding opportunity. Specializing in fresh-cut fries and hot dogs, our concept is simply. Our standards are high. We start with fresh potatoes, hand-cut on site everyday. We cook them in 100% vegetable oil in our special process. Winner, Canada's Best managed Companies award, requalified winner 2001. Winner of numerous advertising awards. Runner-up, Franchisor of the Year award, Canadian Franchise Association 1994.

BACKGROUND:
Established: 1984; 1st Franchised: 1984
Franchised Units: 160
Company-Owned Units: 15
Total Units: 175
Dist.: US-0; CAN-171; O'seas-4
North America: 9 Provinces
Density: 94 in ON, 27 in BC, 24 in AB
Projected New Units (12 Months): 10-12
Qualifications: 4, 5, 4, 3, 1, 5
Registered: AB

FINANCIAL/TERMS:
Cash Investment: $50-75K
Total Investment: $125-175K
Minimum Net Worth: Varies
Fees: Franchise - $30K
Royalty - 6%; Ad. - 2%
Earnings Claims Statement: No
Term of Contract (Years): 10/5/5
Avg. # Of Employees: 2-3 FT, 5-6 PT
Passive Ownership: Allowed
Encourage Conversions: NA
Area Develop. Agreements: Overseas
Sub-Franchising Contracts: No
Expand In Territory: Yes
Space Needs: 350 SF; RM

SUPPORT & TRAINING:
Financial Assistance Provided: No
Site Selection Assistance: Yes
Lease Negotiation Assistance: Yes
Co-Operative Advertising: Yes
Franchisee Assoc./Member: Yes/Yes
Size Of Corporate Staff: 16
On-Going Support: B,C,D,E,G,h
Training: 7-10 Days Toronto, ON; 5-10 Week On-Site.

SPECIFIC EXPANSION PLANS:
US: No
Canada: All Canada
Overseas: England, Pacific Rim

<< >>

PAPA MURPHY'S

8000 NE Parkway Dr., # 350
Vancouver, WA 98662
Tel: (800) 257-7272 (360) 449-4016
Fax: (360) 397-6864
E-Mail: rhondam@papamurphys.com
Web Site: www.papamurphys.com
Ms. Rhonda McGrew, Manager Business Development

PAPA MURPHY'S produces a great pizza made from top-quality ingredients. Letting customers bake it themselves is smart business. Put the 2 together and you get the largest, fastest-growing Take 'N' Bake franchise in the world. PAPA MURPHY'S now has 565 stores with another 175 stores expected to open in 2000.

BACKGROUND: IFA MEMBER
Established: 1981; 1st Franchised: 1982
Franchised Units: 850
Company-Owned Units: 11
Total Units: 861
Dist.: US-640; CAN-0; O'seas-0
North America: 22 States
Density: 163 in CA,117 in WA,85 in OR
Projected New Units (12 Months): 175
Qualifications: 4, 3, 2, 3, 3, 5
Registered: CA,IL,IN,MI,MN,ND,OR,SD,WA,WI

FINANCIAL/TERMS:
Cash Investment: $80K
Total Investment: $148.8-199.5K
Minimum Net Worth: $250K
Fees: Franchise - $25K
Royalty - 5%; Ad. - 1%
Earnings Claims Statement: No
Term of Contract (Years): 10/5
Avg. # Of Employees: 2 FT, 8-10 PT
Passive Ownership: Not Allowed
Encourage Conversions: Yes
Area Develop. Agreements: No
Sub-Franchising Contracts: No
Expand In Territory: Yes
Space Needs: 1,200-1,400 SF; FS, SF, SC

SUPPORT & TRAINING:
Financial Assistance Provided: Yes(I)
Site Selection Assistance: Yes
Lease Negotiation Assistance: Yes
Co-Operative Advertising: Yes
Franchisee Assoc./Member: Yes/No
Size Of Corporate Staff: 106
On-Going Support: B,C,D,E,G,H,I
Training: 3 Days/30 Hours in the Closest Training Store; 6 Weeks in Store; 6 Days Corporate Office.

SPECIFIC EXPANSION PLANS:
US: Midwest
Canada: No
Overseas: No

<< >>

PAPA'S PIZZA TO GO

4465 Commerce Dr., # 101
Buford, GA 30518-9913
Tel: (770) 614-6676
Fax: (770) 614-9095
E-Mail: papa2go@bellsouth.net
Web Site: www.papaspizzatogo.com
Ms. Kathy Underwood, Dir. Operations/ Franchise Sale

Two business models - one for small town USA and one for metro markets. Small town - to go only to small buffets of limited serving hours. Metro markets - all day, every day with game room for kids.

BACKGROUND:
Established: 1986; 1st Franchised: 1986
Franchised Units: 72
Company-Owned Units: 13
Total Units: 85
Dist.: US-85; CAN-0; O'seas-0
North America: NR
Density: GA, NC, TN
Projected New Units (12 Months): NR
Qualifications: , , , , ,
Registered:

FINANCIAL/TERMS:
Cash Investment: $40-130K
Total Investment: $130-350K
Minimum Net Worth: $90K
Fees: Franchise - $9.5-12.5K
Royalty - 5%; Ad. - 5%
Earnings Claims Statement: Yes
Term of Contract (Years): 10/10
Avg. # Of Employees: 3 FT, 7 PT
Passive Ownership: Allowed
Encourage Conversions: NR
Area Develop. Agreements: No
Sub-Franchising Contracts: No
Expand In Territory: Yes
Space Needs: 1,000-4,200 SF; SF, SC

SUPPORT & TRAINING:

Financial Assistance Provided: NR
Site Selection Assistance: Yes
Lease Negotiation Assistance: Yes
Co-Operative Advertising: yes
Franchisee Assoc./Member: No
Size Of Corporate Staff: 12
On-Going Support: B,C,D,E,F,G,H
Training: 10 Days Cherryville, NC; 10 Days Calhoune, GA.

SPECIFIC EXPANSION PLANS:
US: Southeast
Canada: NR
Overseas: NR

<< >>

PIZZA NOVA

2247 Midland Ave.
Scarborough, ON M1P 4R1 CANADA
Tel: (416) 439-0051
Fax: (416) 299-3558
E-Mail: marsha@pizzanova.com
Web Site: www.pizzanova.com
Mr. Frank Macri, Franchise Director

PIZZA NOVA specializes in traditional Italian pizza, pastas and chicken wings. All menu items are prepared fresh daily and are available for take-out or delivery. We pride ourselves on quality and service.

BACKGROUND:
Established: 1963; 1st Franchised: 1969
Franchised Units: 85
Company-Owned Units: 2
Total Units: 87
Dist.: US-1; CAN-80; O'seas-6
North America: 1 State, 1 Province
Density: 80 in ON
Projected New Units (12 Months): 10
Qualifications: 4, 4, 4, 2, 4, 5
Registered: NR

FINANCIAL/TERMS:
Cash Investment: $40K
Total Investment: $125-135K
Minimum Net Worth: NR
Fees: Franchise - NA
Royalty - 6%; Ad. - 4%
Earnings Claims Statement: Yes
Term of Contract (Years): 5/5
Avg. # Of Employees: 4 FT, 6 PT
Passive Ownership: Not Allowed
Encourage Conversions: Yes
Area Develop. Agreements: No
Sub-Franchising Contracts: No
Expand In Territory: Yes
Space Needs: 800-1,100 SF; SF, SC, RM

SUPPORT & TRAINING:
Financial Assistance Provided: No
Site Selection Assistance: Yes
Lease Negotiation Assistance: Yes
Co-Operative Advertising: Yes
Franchisee Assoc./Member: Yes
Size Of Corporate Staff: 18
On-Going Support: A,B,C,D,E,F,G,H
Training: 3 Weeks.

SPECIFIC EXPANSION PLANS:
US: NR
Canada: ON
Overseas: All Countries

<< >>

PRETZEL TIME® FRESHNESS WITH A TWIST!™

Top 100

PRETZEL TIME

2855 E. Cottonwood Pkwy., # 400
Salt Lake City, UT 84121-7037
Tel: (800) 343-5377 + 2399
Fax: (801) 736-5936
E-Mail: donl@mrsfields.com
Web Site: www.pretzeltime.com
Mr. Don Lewandowski, VP of Development Bakery

'Freshness With A Twist.' Retail pretzel stores, offering a healthy snack alternative that is freshly mixed, rolled and baked. Store options are available for traditional and non-traditional venues.

BACKGROUND: IFA MEMBER
Established: 1991; 1st Franchised: 1992
Franchised Units: 172
Company-Owned Units: 54
Total Units: 226
Dist.: US-213; CAN-0; O'seas-4
North America: 37 States, 2 Provinces
Density: 25 in NY, 21 in CA, 15 in TX
Projected New Units (12 Months): 21
Qualifications: , , , , ,
Registered: All States

FINANCIAL/TERMS:
Cash Investment: $175-250K
Total Investment: $107-238.5K
Minimum Net Worth: $150K/75K LIQ
Fees: Franchise - $25K
Royalty - 7%; Ad. - 1%
Earnings Claims Statement: Yes
Term of Contract (Years): 7/7
Avg. # Of Employees: 3 FT, 2 PT
Passive Ownership: Discouraged
Encourage Conversions: Yes
Area Develop. Agreements: Yes/3
Sub-Franchising Contracts: No
Expand In Territory: Yes
Space Needs: 400-800 SF; RM

SUPPORT & TRAINING:
Financial Assistance Provided: No
Site Selection Assistance: Yes
Lease Negotiation Assistance: Yes
Co-Operative Advertising: No
Franchisee Assoc./Member: Yes
Size Of Corporate Staff: 100+
On-Going Support: B,C,D,E,F,G,H,I
Training: 6 Days Salt Lake City, UT.

SPECIFIC EXPANSION PLANS:
US: All United States
Canada: All Canada
Overseas: NR

<< >>

PRETZEL TWISTER, THE

322 Burgwin Wright Way
Cary, NC 27519
Tel: (888) 638-8806 (919) 387-8929
Fax: (919) 363-6945
E-Mail: bwang@pretzeltwister.com
Web Site: www.pretzeltwister.com
Mr. Bobby Wang, President

THE PRETZEL TWISTER is a gourmet, hand-rolled soft pretzel franchise. Other products sold are fresh, hand-squeezed lemonade, frozen fruit smoothies and soft drinks. The pretzels are served fresh and hot and are available in a wide variety of flavors.

BACKGROUND:
Established: 1992; 1st Franchised: 1993
Franchised Units: 45
Company-Owned Units: 0
Total Units: 45
Dist.: US-43; CAN-2; O'seas-0
North America: 14 States, 3 Provinces
Density: 14 in FL, 9 in NC, 3 in SC
Projected New Units (12 Months): NR
Qualifications: , , , , ,
Registered: NR

FINANCIAL/TERMS:
Cash Investment: NR
Total Investment: $105.2-162.5K
Minimum Net Worth: NR
Fees: Franchise - $22.5K
Royalty - 5%; Ad. - .5-1%
Earnings Claims Statement: No
Term of Contract (Years): NR
Avg. # Of Employees: NR
Passive Ownership: Allowed
Encourage Conversions: NR
Area Develop. Agreements: No
Sub-Franchising Contracts: No
Expand In Territory: Yes
Space Needs: 300-900 SF; RN, Kiosk or In-Line

SUPPORT & TRAINING:
Financial Assistance Provided: NR
Site Selection Assistance: No
Lease Negotiation Assistance: Yes
Co-Operative Advertising: No
Franchisee Assoc./Member: NR
Size Of Corporate Staff: NR
On-Going Support: C,D,E,G,h,I
Training: NR
SPECIFIC EXPANSION PLANS:
US: All United States
Canada: NR
Overseas: NR

<< >>

PRETZELMAKER
2855 E. Cottonwood Pkwy., # 400
Salt Lake City, UT 84121
Tel: (800) 343-5377 + 2399
Fax: (801) 736-5936
E-Mail: donl@mrsfields.com
Web Site: www.mrsfieldsfranchise.com
Mr. Don Lewandowski, VP of Development Bakery

The 'World's Best Soft Pretzels,' hand-rolled and served hot with high consumer acceptance and precision portion control. May be operated in both traditional and non-traditional venues.

BACKGROUND: IFA MEMBER
Established: 1991; 1st Franchised: 1992
Franchised Units: 166
Company-Owned Units: 5
Total Units: 171
Dist.: US-163; CAN-0; O'seas-38
North America: 37 States, Provinces
Density: 23 in CA, 14 in IA, 11 in CO
Projected New Units (12 Months): 11
Qualifications: 4, 4, 3, 2, 2, 5
Registered: All States Except VA
FINANCIAL/TERMS:
Cash Investment: $10-30K
Total Investment: $107-238.5K
Minimum Net Worth: $150K/75K LIQ
Fees: Franchise - $25K
Royalty - 6%; Ad. - 1.5%
Earnings Claims Statement: Yes
Term of Contract (Years): 7/7
Avg. # Of Employees: 3 FT, 2 PT
Passive Ownership: Discouraged
Encourage Conversions: Yes
Area Develop. Agreements: No
Sub-Franchising Contracts: No
Expand In Territory: Yes
Space Needs: 200-850 SF; FS, SC, RM
SUPPORT & TRAINING:
Financial Assistance Provided: No
Site Selection Assistance: Yes
Lease Negotiation Assistance: Yes
Co-Operative Advertising: No
Franchisee Assoc./Member: Yes
Size Of Corporate Staff: 100+
On-Going Support: B,C,D,E,F,G,H
Training: 5 Days Salt Lake City, UT
SPECIFIC EXPANSION PLANS:
US: All United States
Canada: All Canada
Overseas: NR

<< >>

PRETZELS PLUS
639 Frederick St.
Hanover, PA 17331
Tel: (800) 559-7927 (717) 633-7927
Fax: (717) 633-5078
E-Mail: beline@pretzelsplus.com
Web Site: www.pretzelsplus.com
Mr. Bradley L. Eline, President

PRETZELS PLUS stores sell soft, hand-rolled pretzels, soups and hearty sandwiches made on our famous pretzel dough rolls. Our mall-based stores provide ample seating for about twenty people in the cafe-styled environment. With our sandwich menu along with our pretzels, we're definitely a twist above the competition.

BACKGROUND:
Established: 1990; 1st Franchised: 1991
Franchised Units: 28
Company-Owned Units: 0
Total Units: 28
Dist.: US-30; CAN-0; O'seas-0
North America: 9 States
Density: 13 in PA, 5 in VA, 3 in NC
Projected New Units (12 Months): 24
Qualifications: 5, 2, 1, 1, 2, 2
Registered: MD,VA
FINANCIAL/TERMS:
Cash Investment: $70-90K
Total Investment: $70-90K
Minimum Net Worth: NA
Fees: Franchise - $12K
Royalty - 4%; Ad. - 0%
Earnings Claims Statement: No
Term of Contract (Years): 10/10
Avg. # Of Employees: 5 FT, 4 PT
Passive Ownership: Allowed
Encourage Conversions: Yes
Area Develop. Agreements: No
Sub-Franchising Contracts: No
Expand In Territory: Yes
Space Needs: 1,000 SF; RM
SUPPORT & TRAINING:
Financial Assistance Provided: No
Site Selection Assistance: Yes
Lease Negotiation Assistance: No
Co-Operative Advertising: No
Franchisee Assoc./Member: No
Size Of Corporate Staff: 3
On-Going Support: B,D,E,I
Training: 3 Days Before Opening.
SPECIFIC EXPANSION PLANS:
US: Eastern United States
Canada: All Canada
Overseas: No

<< >>

ROBEKS FRUIT SMOOTHIES AND HEALTHY EATS
1230 E. Rosecrans Ave., # 400
Manhattan Beach, CA 90266
Tel: (866) 4-ROBEKS (310) 727-0500 + 237
Fax: (310) 943-1877
E-Mail: franchising@robeks.com
Web Site: www.robeks.com
Mr. Corey Remington, Franchise Coordinatior

At ROBEKS, our passion is to help people lead active and healthy lifestyles by offering the highest-quality nutritional food products and supplements. Our blended-to-order pure fruit smoothies, freshly squeezed juices and other healthy eats provide more nutritious alternatives to traditional fast food. ROBEKS is rapidly expanding across the US to meet this accelerating demand for healthier products.

BACKGROUND: IFA MEMBER
Established: 1995; 1st Franchised: 2001
Franchised Units: 61
Company-Owned Units: 3
Total Units: 64
Dist.: US-64; CAN-0; O'seas-0
North America: 10 States, DC
Density: 48 in CA, 6 in AZ, 2 in OH
Projected New Units (12 Months): 49

Qualifications: 5, 5, 3, 3, 3, 5
Registered: All States Except ND, SD

FINANCIAL/TERMS:
Cash Investment: $57.2-97.4K
Total Investment: $190.8-324.6K
Minimum Net Worth: $250K
Fees: Franchise - $25K
Royalty - 7%; Ad. - 2.5%
Earnings Claims Statement: Yes
Term of Contract (Years): 10/5/5
Avg. # Of Employees: 1 FT, 6-14 PT
Passive Ownership: Not Allowed
Encourage Conversions: No
Area Develop. Agreements: Yes/10/5/5
Sub-Franchising Contracts: No
Expand In Territory: Yes
Space Needs: 800-1,200 SF; FS, SF, SC

SUPPORT & TRAINING:
Financial Assistance Provided: Yes(I)
Site Selection Assistance: Yes
Lease Negotiation Assistance: Yes
Co-Operative Advertising: Yes
Franchisee Assoc./Member: Yes/Yes
Size Of Corporate Staff: 29
On-Going Support: B,C,D,E,G,H,I
Training: 5 Days Regional or Los Angeles, CA; 5 Days Los Angeles, CA; 5 Days In-Store.

SPECIFIC EXPANSION PLANS:
US: All United States Exc. SD and ND
Canada: No
Overseas: No

ROCKY MOUNTAIN CHOCOLATE FACTORY

265 Turner Dr.
Durango, CO 81301
Tel: (800) 438-7623 (970) 259-0554
Fax: (970) 259-5895
E-Mail: pope@rmcf.net
Web Site: www.sweetfranchise.com
Mr. Greg Pope, SVP Franchise Development

Retail sale of packaged and bulk chocolates, brittles, truffles, sauces, cocoas, coffees, assorted hard candies and related chocolate and non-chocolate items. In-store preparation of fudges, caramel apples and dipped fruits via interactive cooking demonstrations. Complete line of gift and holiday items. Supplemental retail sale of soft drinks, ice cream, cookies and brewed coffee.

BACKGROUND: IFA MEMBER
Established: 1981; 1st Franchised: 1982
Franchised Units: 276
Company-Owned Units: 8
Total Units: 284
Dist.: US-202; CAN-17; O'seas-1
North America: 41 States, 3 Provinces
Density: 36 in CA, 22 in CO, 12 BC
Projected New Units (12 Months): 12-15
Qualifications: , , , , ,
Registered: CA,FL,HI,IL,IN,MD,MI,MN, NY,OR,SD,VA,WA,WI

FINANCIAL/TERMS:
Cash Investment: $50K
Total Investment: $113-213K
Minimum Net Worth: $250K
Fees: Franchise - $19.5K
Royalty - 5%; Ad. - 1%
Earnings Claims Statement: No
Term of Contract (Years): 5/5
Avg. # Of Employees: 2 FT, 4 PT
Passive Ownership: Discouraged
Encourage Conversions: NA
Area Develop. Agreements: No
Sub-Franchising Contracts: No
Expand In Territory: Yes
Space Needs: 800-1,200 SF; Factory Outlet

SUPPORT & TRAINING:
Financial Assistance Provided: Yes(I)
Site Selection Assistance: Yes
Lease Negotiation Assistance: Yes
Co-Operative Advertising: No
Franchisee Assoc./Member: Yes
Size Of Corporate Staff: 12
On-Going Support: B,C,D,E,F,G,H,I
Training: 7 Days Durango, CO; 5 Days Store Site.

SPECIFIC EXPANSION PLANS:
US: All United States
Canada: No
Overseas: All Countries

SCHAKOLAD CHOCOLATE FACTORY

5966 Lakehurst Dr.
Orlando, FL 32819
Tel: (407) 248-6400
Fax: (407) 248-1466
E-Mail: schakolad@aol.com
Web Site: www.schakolad.com
Mr. Edgar Schaked, President

Hand-made, fine chocolates made on premises for customers to watch. Over 30 years experience in chocolate making. Our goal is to become the premiere high quality chocolatier in the U.S. and international markets.

BACKGROUND: IFA MEMBER
Established: 1995; 1st Franchised: 1999
Franchised Units: 11
Company-Owned Units: 2
Total Units: 13
Dist.: US-7; CAN-0; O'seas-3
North America: 2 States
Density: 4 in FL, 2 in VA, 1 in GA
Projected New Units (12 Months): NR
Qualifications: , , , , ,
Registered: NR

FINANCIAL/TERMS:
Cash Investment: $80-110K
Total Investment: $80-110K
Minimum Net Worth: $200K
Fees: Franchise - $30K
Royalty - 4%; Ad. - 1%
Earnings Claims Statement: No
Term of Contract (Years): 10/10
Avg. # Of Employees: 3 FT
Passive Ownership: Not Allowed
Encourage Conversions: NR
Area Develop. Agreements: No
Sub-Franchising Contracts: No
Expand In Territory: Yes
Space Needs: 800-1,400 SF; SC, RM

SUPPORT & TRAINING:
Financial Assistance Provided: Yes(I)
Site Selection Assistance: Yes
Lease Negotiation Assistance: Yes
Co-Operative Advertising: Yes
Franchisee Assoc./Member: No
Size Of Corporate Staff: 2
On-Going Support: C,D,E
Training: 1-2 Weeks in Orlando, FL.

SPECIFIC EXPANSION PLANS:
US: Eastern United States
Canada: NR
Overseas: NR

≺≺ ≻≻

SCHLOTZSKY'S DELI

203 Colorado St.
Austin, TX 78701
Tel: (800) 846-2867 (512) 236-3600
Fax: (512) 236-3650
E-Mail: franchise@schlotzskys.com
Web Site: www.schlotzskys.com
Mr. Patrick Eulberg, VP Franchise Development

SCHLOTZSKY'S DELI is a leader in the fast casual upscale specialty franchised restaurant category, serving a menu of sandwiches, pizza and salads on SCHLOTZSKY'S baked-fresh-daily sourdough bread. New SCHLOTZSKY'S deli restaurants are defining fast casual, with its appealing architecture, original products and speed of service.

BACKGROUND:
Established: 1971; 1st Franchised: 1977
Franchised Units: 641
Company-Owned Units: 33
Total Units: 674
Dist.: US-653; CAN-1; O'seas-20
North America: 38 States, DC
Density: 197 in TX, 30 in GA , 30 NC
Projected New Units (12 Months): 40
Qualifications: 5, 5, 3, 3, 4, 5
Registered: All States

FINANCIAL/TERMS:
Cash Investment: NR
Total Investment: $480K-2.6MM
Minimum Net Worth: NR
Fees: Franchise - $30K
Royalty - 6%; Ad. - 4%
Earnings Claims Statement: Yes
Term of Contract (Years): 20/10
Avg. # Of Employees: 5 FT, 20 PT
Passive Ownership: Not Allowed
Encourage Conversions: No
Area Develop. Agreements: No
Sub-Franchising Contracts: No
Expand In Territory: Yes
Space Needs: 3,200 SF; FS, SC

SUPPORT & TRAINING:
Financial Assistance Provided: Yes
Site Selection Assistance: Yes
Lease Negotiation Assistance: Yes
Co-Operative Advertising: Yes
Franchisee Assoc./Member: Yes/No
Size Of Corporate Staff: 145
On-Going Support: A,C,D,E,F,G,H,I
Training: 4 Weeks in Austin, TX.

SPECIFIC EXPANSION PLANS:
US: All United States
Canada: All Canada
Overseas: Europe, Latin America, Pacific Rim

<< >>

STEAK-OUT CHAR-BROILED DELIVERY

6801 Governors Lake Pkwy., # 100
Norcross, GA 30071-1130
Tel: (877) 878-3257 (678) 533-6000
Fax: (678) 291-0222
E-Mail: jmccord@steakout.com
Web Site: www.steakout.com
Mr. Joseph M. McCord, Vice President Franchising

STEAK-OUT franchising specializes in home and office deliveries of charbroiled steaks, chicken and burgers - other menu items include salads and desserts. The only full meal delivery service expanding nationwide. Customers absolutely love our combination of quality food and delivery service. America's finest delivery.

BACKGROUND: IFA MEMBER
Established: 1986; 1st Franchised: 1987
Franchised Units: 70
Company-Owned Units: 3
Total Units: 73
Dist.: US-73; CAN-0; O'seas-0
North America: 17 States
Density: 18 in AL, 12 in TN, 8 in GA
Projected New Units (12 Months): 12
Qualifications: 4, 5, 3, 3, 3, 5
Registered:CA,FL,IL,IN,MD,MI,MN,NY, OR,SD,VA,WI

FINANCIAL/TERMS:
Cash Investment: $75-100K
Total Investment: $221-379KK
Minimum Net Worth: $300K
Fees: Franchise - $25K
Royalty - 5%; Ad. - 2%
Earnings Claims Statement: Yes
Term of Contract (Years): 10/10
Avg. # Of Employees: 2 FT, 25-30 PT
Passive Ownership: Discouraged
Encourage Conversions: Yes
Area Develop. Agreements: Yes/Varies
Sub-Franchising Contracts: No
Expand In Territory: Yes
Space Needs: 1,600 SF; FS, SF, SC

SUPPORT & TRAINING:
Financial Assistance Provided: Yes(I)
Site Selection Assistance: Yes
Lease Negotiation Assistance: Yes
Co-Operative Advertising: NA
Franchisee Assoc./Member: No
Size Of Corporate Staff: 25
On-Going Support: B,C,D,E,G,H,I
Training: 4-5 Weeks Training Center at Atlanta, GA.

SPECIFIC EXPANSION PLANS:
US: SE, MW
Canada: No
Overseas: No

<< >>

STUCKEY'S

8555 16th St., # 850
Silver Spring, MD 20910-2835
Tel: (800) 423-6171 (301) 585-8222
Fax: (301) 585-8997
E-Mail: mbolin@stuckeys.com
Web Site: www.stuckeys.com
Mr. Mike Bolin, VP Business Development

An icon of the American highways, STUCKEY'S franchises more than 200 stores located along interstates throughout the US. It began with the traditional blue-roofed, stand-alone locations, but today consists primarily of co-branded STUCKEY'S, in which a STUCKEY'S outlet is located inside other convenience stores and travel centers. STUCKEY'S sells its pecans and pecan candies (pralines, divinity, brittle and its famous Pecan Logs) along with gifts and souvenirs (t-shirts, postcards and trinkets).

BACKGROUND:
Established: 1930; 1st Franchised: 1960
Franchised Units: 199
Company-Owned Units: 2
Total Units: 201
Dist.: US-201; CAN-0; O'seas-0
North America: 20 States
Density: 10 in MS, 8 in SC, 6 in TN
Projected New Units (12 Months): 12
Qualifications: 5, 4, 4, 2, 1, 4
Registered: MD,VA

FINANCIAL/TERMS:
Cash Investment: $10-25K
Total Investment: $16.8-47K
Minimum Net Worth: NR
Fees: Franchise - $7.5KK
Royalty - $295/Mo.; Ad. - 0.5%
Earnings Claims Statement: No
Term of Contract (Years): 5/5/5
Avg. # Of Employees: Varies
Passive Ownership: Allowed
Encourage Conversions: Yes
Area Develop. Agreements: No
Sub-Franchising Contracts: No
Expand In Territory: Yes
Space Needs: Varies SF; Fuel Center

SUPPORT & TRAINING:
Financial Assistance Provided: No
Site Selection Assistance: Yes
Lease Negotiation Assistance: Yes
Co-Operative Advertising: No
Franchisee Assoc./Member: Yes/Yes
Size Of Corporate Staff: 21
On-Going Support: B,C,D,E,G,H,I
Training: 1-2 Days in Store.

SPECIFIC EXPANSION PLANS:
US: All United States
Canada: No
Overseas: No

<< >>

TROPICAL SMOOTHIE CAFÉ
1150 Eglin Pkwy.
Shalimar, FL 32579
Tel: (888) 292-2522 (850) 609-6022
Fax: (850) 609-6023
E-Mail: ts@tropicalsmoothie.com
Web Site: www.tropicalsmoothie.com
Mr. Scott Cole, Franchise Sales

At Tropical Smoothie, we believe in serving only the highest quality products to create the ultimate refreshing nutritional beverage. We offer over 40 flavors of smoothies with exact recipes to create the perfect smoothie for everyone. In addition to smoothies we offer high quality gourmet wraps, sandwiches and specialty coffee.

BACKGROUND: IFA MEMBER
Established: 1997; 1st Franchised: 1997
Franchised Units: 134
Company-Owned Units: 0
Total Units: 134
Dist.: US-132; CAN-0; O'seas-2
North America: 19 States
Density: 68 in FL, 15 in VA
Projected New Units (12 Months): 55
Qualifications: 3, 4, 2, 2, 5, 5
Registered:CA,FL,HI,MD,MI,ND,NY,VA,WA,WI,DC

FINANCIAL/TERMS:
Cash Investment: $50-60K
Total Investment: $150-225K
Minimum Net Worth: $100-150K
Fees: Franchise - $15K
Royalty - 6%; Ad. - 1+2%
Earnings Claims Statement: No
Term of Contract (Years): 20/10
Avg. # Of Employees: 2 FT, 10 PT
Passive Ownership: Discouraged
Encourage Conversions: Yes
Area Develop. Agreements: Yes/25
Sub-Franchising Contracts: Yes
Expand In Territory: Yes
Space Needs: 1,600 SF; SC

SUPPORT & TRAINING:
Financial Assistance Provided: Yes(I)
Site Selection Assistance: Yes
Lease Negotiation Assistance: Yes
Co-Operative Advertising: Yes
Franchisee Assoc./Member: No
Size Of Corporate Staff: 11
On-Going Support: A,B,C,D,E,F,G,H,I
Training: 1 Week Corporate Office; 1 Week Local Stores; 1 Week Store Opening.

SPECIFIC EXPANSION PLANS:
US: All United States
Canada: All Canada
Overseas: All Countries

<< >>

TROPIK SUN FRUIT & NUT
14052 Petronella Dr., # 102
Libertyville, IL 60048
Tel: (847) 968-4415
Fax: (847) 968-5535
E-Mail: tropikhdqr@aol.com
Web Site: www.tropiksun.com
Ms. Barbara J. Wellard, President

TROPIK SUN FRUIT & NUT is a national franchised chain of over 80 retail stores located in regional malls, featuring candies, nuts, chocolates, fresh popcorn, snacks, drinks, plush toys, balloons and gifts.

BACKGROUND:
Established: 1980; 1st Franchised: 1980
Franchised Units: 80
Company-Owned Units: 2
Total Units: 82
Dist.: US-82; CAN-0; O'seas-0
North America: 27 States
Density: 12 in TX, 5 in CT, 5 IN CA
Projected New Units (12 Months): 20
Qualifications: 4, 2, 1, 2, 2, 4
Registered: All States

FINANCIAL/TERMS:
Cash Investment: $30-50K
Total Investment: $100-190K
Minimum Net Worth: $125K
Fees: Franchise - $20K
Royalty - 6%; Ad. - 0%
Earnings Claims Statement: No
Term of Contract (Years): 5-10/5-10
Avg. # Of Employees: 0 FT, 3-6 PT
Passive Ownership: Allowed
Encourage Conversions: Yes
Area Develop. Agreements: No
Sub-Franchising Contracts: No
Expand In Territory: No
Space Needs: 160-1,000 SF; RM

SUPPORT & TRAINING:
Financial Assistance Provided: No
Site Selection Assistance: Yes
Lease Negotiation Assistance: Yes
Co-Operative Advertising: NA
Franchisee Assoc./Member: Yes/No
Size Of Corporate Staff: 9
On-Going Support: C,D,E,G,H
Training: 5 Days Franchisee's Store.

SPECIFIC EXPANSION PLANS:
US: All United States
Canada: No
Overseas: No

<< >>

WE'RE ROLLING PRETZEL COMPANY
P. O. Box 6106, 2500 W. State St.,
Alliance, OH 44601
Tel: (888) 549-7655 (330) 823-0575
Fax: (330) 821-8908
E-Mail: kkrabill@wererolling.com
Web Site: www.wererolling.com
Mr. Kevin Krabill, President

WE'RE ROLLING PRETZEL COMPANY offers fresh, hand-made pretzels, pretzel rods, pretzel sandwiches and a variety of beverages. By serving an expanded menu, creating a strong system to open and operate stores, and recruiting, training, and supporting dedicated franchisees, WE'RE ROLLING PRETZEL COMPANY can effectively meet the needs of a variety of customers.

BACKGROUND:
Established: 1996; 1st Franchised: 2000
Franchised Units: 47
Company-Owned Units: 4
Total Units: 51
Dist.: US-49; CAN-0; O'seas-0
North America: 6 States
Density: 33 in OH, 6 in KY, 4 in PA
Projected New Units (12 Months): 30
Qualifications: 4, 3, 3, 2, 5, 5
Registered: CA,FL,IA,IN,MI,NY,VA,WI

FINANCIAL/TERMS:
Cash Investment: $20-50K
Total Investment: $64-195K
Minimum Net Worth: $100K
Fees: Franchise - $15K
Royalty - 5%; Ad. - 1%
Earnings Claims Statement: No
Term of Contract (Years): 5/5
Avg. # Of Employees: 3 FT, 3 PT
Passive Ownership: Allowed
Encourage Conversions: Yes
Area Develop. Agreements: Yes

Sub-Franchising Contracts: No
Expand In Territory: Yes
Space Needs: 400-1,000 SF; RM, SF, Wal-Mart Supercenter

SUPPORT & TRAINING:
Financial Assistance Provided: No
Site Selection Assistance: Yes
Lease Negotiation Assistance: Yes
Co-Operative Advertising: Yes
Franchisee Assoc./Member: No
Size Of Corporate Staff: 9
On-Going Support: b,C,D,E,F,G,H,I
Training: 3 Days Corporate Office; 4 Days Corporate Store; 1 Week On-Site.

SPECIFIC EXPANSION PLANS:
US: All United States
Canada: No
Overseas: No

<< >>

WINE NOT INTERNATIONAL

235310 Grey Rd. 13, Box 80
Kimberley, ON N0C 1G0 CANADA
Tel: (888) 946-3668 (519) 599-7400
Fax: (519) 599-7300
E-Mail: kerrybaskey@winenot.com
Web Site: www.winenot.com
Mr. Kerry Baskey, Vice President

Commercial custom wineries, wine pubs and u-vint operations in which we provide equipment and supplies for the production of fine wines for retail and wholesale distribution.

BACKGROUND: IFA MEMBER
Established: 1993; 1st Franchised: 1995
Franchised Units: 45
Company-Owned Units: 0
Total Units: 45
Dist.: US-8; CAN-37; O'seas-1
North America: 6 States, 1 Province
Density: 38 in ON, 1 in TX, 1 in MI
Projected New Units (12 Months): 10
Qualifications: 4, 3, 2, 3, 3, 5
Registered: CA,FL,HI,IL,IN,MN,NY,OR,WA,WI

FINANCIAL/TERMS:
Cash Investment: $75-150K
Total Investment: $225-250K
Minimum Net Worth: $100-500K
Fees: Franchise - $50K
Royalty - 5%; Ad. - 2% (ON)
Earnings Claims Statement: No
Term of Contract (Years): 10/10
Avg. # Of Employees: 2 FT, 2 PT
Passive Ownership: Discouraged
Encourage Conversions: Yes
Area Develop. Agreements: Yes
Sub-Franchising Contracts: Yes
Expand In Territory: Yes
Space Needs: 2,500-3,000 SF; FS, SC

SUPPORT & TRAINING:
Financial Assistance Provided: No
Site Selection Assistance: Yes
Lease Negotiation Assistance: Yes
Co-Operative Advertising: No
Franchisee Assoc./Member: Yes/Yes
Size Of Corporate Staff: 10
On-Going Support: A,B,C,D,E,F,G,H,I
Training: 2 Weeks Home Study; 5 Days Head Office; 1-6 Days On-Site..

SPECIFIC EXPANSION PLANS:
US: All United States
Canada: BC & ON
Overseas: Caribbean

The Top 100 Franchises denoted in this book were derived from the 2005 edition of *Bond's Top 100 Franchises.* As the pre-eminent publisher of nine books on franchising, Source Book Publications evaluated hundreds of proven franchise systems to arrive at what it feels are the top 100 franchises. Companies were evaluated on the basis of historical performance, brand identification, market dynamics, franchisee satisfaction, the level of initial training and on-going support, financial stability and various other key factors.

To learn more about *Bond's Top 100 Franchises*, please visit our website at www.worldfranchising.com.

Hairstyling Salons

Chapter 19

Hairstyling Salons Industry Profile

Total # Franchisors in Industry Group	34
Total # Franchised Units in Industry Group	7,173
Total # Company-Owned Units in Industry Group	2,494
Total # Operating Units in Industry Group	9,667
Average # Franchised Units/Franchisor	211
Average # Company-Owned Units/Franchisor	73.4
Average # Total Units/Franchisor	284.3
Ratio of Total # Franchised Units/Total # Company-Owned Units	2.9:1
Industry Survey Participants	13
Representing % of Industry	38.2%
Average Franchise Fee*:	$28.6K
Average Total Investment*:	$134.8K
Average On-Going Royalty Fee*:	5.3%

*If a range was provided, the mid-point of the range was used. See detailed profiles for actual ranges.

Five Largest Participants in Survey

Company	# Franchised Units	# Co-Owned Units	# Total Units	Franchise Fee	On-Going Royalty	Total Investment
1. Great Clips	2,300	0	2,300	$25K	6%	$96.6-182.1K
2. SuperCuts	956	875	1,831	$22.5K 1st	4% Yr. 1/6%	$106.9-169.1K
3. Fantastic Sams	1,364	0	1,364	$25-30K	$236/Wk.- Varies	$138-188K
4. Cost Cutters Family Hair Care	678	182	860	$22.5K 1st.	4% Yr.1/6%	$82.3-175.1K
5. First Choice Haircutters	210	191	401	$10-25K	NR	$96-167K

All of the data provided are proprietary and should not be quoted without acknowledging *Bond's Franchise Guide.*

COST CUTTERS FAMILY HAIR CARE

7201 Metro Blvd.
Minneapolis, MN 55439-2130
Tel: (888) 888-7008 (952) 947-7777
Fax: (952) 947-7300
E-Mail: stephanie.theis@regiscorp.com
Web Site: www.regisfranchise.com
Ms. Stephanie Theis, Franchiseing Coordinator

COST CUTTERS FAMILY HAIR CARE is a value-priced, family hair salon chain offering its customers high-quality hair care services and professional products.

BACKGROUND: IFA MEMBER
Established: 1982; 1st Franchised: 1982
Franchised Units: 678
Company-Owned Units: 182
Total Units: 860
Dist.: US-860; CAN-0; O'seas-0
North America: 45 States
Density: 115 in WI, 82 in MN, 81 CO
Projected New Units (12 Months): 100
Qualifications: 5, 5, 1, 4, 2, 5
Registered: All States

FINANCIAL/TERMS:
Cash Investment: $25-50K/Unit
Total Investment: $82.3-175.1K
Minimum Net Worth: $300K/100K Liq
Fees: Franchise - $22.5K 1st
Royalty - 4% Yr.1/6%; Ad. - 4%+$190 Loc
Earnings Claims Statement: Yes
Term of Contract (Years): 15/15
Avg. # Of Employees: 6 FT, 3 PT
Passive Ownership: Discouraged
Encourage Conversions: Yes
Area Develop. Agreements: Yes/3-10 St
Sub-Franchising Contracts: No
Expand In Territory: Yes
Space Needs: 900-1,200 SF; SC

SUPPORT & TRAINING:
Financial Assistance Provided: Yes(I)
Site Selection Assistance: Yes
Lease Negotiation Assistance: Yes
Co-Operative Advertising: No
Franchisee Assoc./Member: No
Size Of Corporate Staff: 55
On-Going Support: C,D,E,G,h,I
Training: 3-5 Days Training Minneapolis, MN; 1 Week Managerial & Tech. Training. 1 Week On-Site. Consultation Available. On-Going.

SPECIFIC EXPANSION PLANS:
US: All United States
Canada: No
Overseas: No

<< >>

Top 100 **Fantastic Sams**

FANTASTIC SAMS

50 Dunham Rd., Fl. 3
Beverly, MA 01915
Tel: (800) 441-6588 (978) 232-5600
Fax: (978) 232-5601
E-Mail: franchise@fantasticsams.com
Web Site: www.fantasticsams.com
Mr. Rich Pittius, SVP Franchise Development

FANTASTIC SAMS is the world's largest full-service hair care franchise, with over 1,350 salons worldwide. Our full service salons offer quality hair care services for the entire family, including cuts, perms and color. When you join the FANTASTIC SAMS family of franchisees, you'll receive both local and national support through on-going management training, educational programs and national conferences, as well as advertising and other benefits. No hair care experience required.

BACKGROUND: IFA MEMBER
Established: 1974; 1st Franchised: 1976
Franchised Units: 1,364
Company-Owned Units: 0
Total Units: 1,364
Dist.: US-1,332; CAN-19; O'seas-13
North America: 43 States, 4 Provinces
Density: 221 in CA, 102 in FL, 99 MI
Projected New Units (12 Months): 120
Qualifications: 5, 5, 1, 4, 1, 5
Registered: All States

FINANCIAL/TERMS:
Cash Investment: $50K
Total Investment: $138-188K
Minimum Net Worth: Varies
Fees: Franchise - $25-30K
Royalty - $236/Wk.- Varies; Ad. - $109/Wk.
Earnings Claims Statement: No
Term of Contract (Years): 10/10
Avg. # Of Employees: 8 FT
Passive Ownership: Allowed
Encourage Conversions: Yes
Area Develop. Agreements: Yes/10
Sub-Franchising Contracts: Yes
Expand In Territory: Yes
Space Needs: 1,200 SF; SC

SUPPORT & TRAINING:
Financial Assistance Provided: Yes
Site Selection Assistance: Yes
Lease Negotiation Assistance: Yes
Co-Operative Advertising: Yes
Franchisee Assoc./Member: No
Size Of Corporate Staff: 40
On-Going Support: c,d,E,F,H
Training: 5 Day Salon Fundamentals Class; On-Going within Region.

SPECIFIC EXPANSION PLANS:
US: All United States
Canada: All Canada
Overseas: Pacific Rim, UK, Australia

<< >>

FIRST CHOICE HAIRCUTTERS

6465 Millcreek Dr., # 210
Mississauga, ON L5N 5R6 CANADA
Tel: (800) 617-3961 (905) 821-8555
Fax: (905) 567-7000
E-Mail: franchise@regiscorp.com
Web Site: www.firstchoice.com
Ms. Martha Lawrence, Dir. Franchise Development

We're a cutting-edge chain of price-value family hair care salons with over 400 locations across Canada and the US. Since 1980, we've built a strong, growing base of loyal customers - over 6 million last year alone. And you don't even have to have any hair experience or become a stylist. We'll provide all the training, tools and on-going support you'll need to manage your thriving salon business. At FIRST CHOICE HAIRCUTTERS, our philosophy is simple: your success is our success.

BACKGROUND: IFA MEMBER
Established: 1980; 1st Franchised: 1982
Franchised Units: 210
Company-Owned Units: 191
Total Units: 401
Dist.: US-81; CAN-320; O'seas-0
North America: 2 States, 8 Provinces
Density: 186 in ON, 50 in FL, 36 BC
Projected New Units (12 Months): 40
Qualifications: , , , , ,
Registered: NA

FINANCIAL/TERMS:
Cash Investment: $48K Min.
Total Investment: $96-167K
Minimum Net Worth: $200K

Fees: Franchise - $10-25K
Royalty - NR; Ad. - NR
Earnings Claims Statement: No
Term of Contract (Years): 10/5
Avg. # Of Employees: 5-7 FT, 2-4 PT
Passive Ownership: Not Allowed
Encourage Conversions: Yes
Area Develop. Agreements: Yes/10
Sub-Franchising Contracts: No
Expand In Territory: Yes
Space Needs: 800-1,000 SF; SC

SUPPORT & TRAINING:

Financial Assistance Provided: Yes(I)
Site Selection Assistance: Yes
Lease Negotiation Assistance: Yes
Co-Operative Advertising: Yes
Franchisee Assoc./Member: No
Size Of Corporate Staff: 20
On-Going Support: B,C,D,E,G,H,I
Training: 1 Week Classroom; 10 Days On-Site. Annual Staff Refresher.

SPECIFIC EXPANSION PLANS:

US: No
Canada: All Canada
Overseas: No

<< >>

GREAT CLIPS

7700 France Ave. S., # 425
Minneapolis, MN 55433
Tel: (800) 999-5959 (952) 893-9088
Fax: (952) 844-3443
E-Mail: jennifer.tatum@greatclips.com
Web Site: www.greatclipsfranchise.com
Ms. Jennifer Tatum, Development Coordinator

High-volume haircutting salon, specializing in haircuts for the entire family. Unique, attractive decor, with quality, comprehensive advertising programs. Strong, local support to franchisees, excellent training programs. We offer real value to our customers. Tremendous growth opportunities.

BACKGROUND: IFA MEMBER
Established: 1982; 1st Franchised: 1983
Franchised Units: 2,300
Company-Owned Units: 0
Total Units: 2,300
Dist.: US-2,200; CAN-65; O'seas-35
North America: 37 States, 2 Provinces
Density:175 in CA, 154 in OH, 149 MN
Projected New Units (12 Months): 200
Qualifications: 5, 4, 1, 3, 3, 5
Registered:CA,FL,IL,IN,MD,MI,MN,NY, ND,OR,SD,VA,WA,WI,DC,AB

FINANCIAL/TERMS:

Cash Investment: $150-250K
Total Investment: $96.6-182.1K
Minimum Net Worth: $250K
Fees: Franchise - $25K
Royalty - 6%; Ad. - 5%
Earnings Claims Statement: Yes
Term of Contract (Years): 10/5/5
Avg. # Of Employees: 3 FT, 5 PT
Passive Ownership: Allowed
Encourage Conversions: No
Area Develop. Agreements: Yes
Sub-Franchising Contracts: No
Expand In Territory: Yes
Space Needs: 1,000-1,200 SF; SF, SC

SUPPORT & TRAINING:

Financial Assistance Provided: Yes(I)
Site Selection Assistance: Yes
Lease Negotiation Assistance: Yes
Co-Operative Advertising: Yes
Franchisee Assoc./Member: Yes/Yes
Size Of Corporate Staff: 200
On-Going Support: A,B,C,D,E,f,G,H,I
Training: 5 Days Minneapolis, MN; 2.5 Weeks Local Market.

SPECIFIC EXPANSION PLANS:

US: All United States
Canada: Western Canada
Overseas: No

<< >>

HAIRCOLOREXPERTS

4850 W. Prospect Rd.
Ft. Lauderdale, FL 33309-3048
Tel: (866) HCX-HCX1 (954) 315-4900
Fax: (954) 486-5623
E-Mail: dsacks@haircolorxpress.com
Web Site: www.hcx.com
Ms. Danielle Sacks, Marketing Coordinator

HCX INTERNATIONAL is the newest innovation in hair salons, offering affordable hair color services and custom blended cosmetics at affordable prices in an up-scale salon environment.

BACKGROUND: IFA MEMBER
Established: 2000; 1st Franchised: 2001
Franchised Units: 14
Company-Owned Units: 4
Total Units: 18
Dist.: US-18; CAN-0; O'seas-0
North America: 14 States
Density: 10 in FL, 3 in NJ, 2 in MD
Projected New Units (12 Months): 250
Qualifications: 5, 4, 4, 3, 3, 5
Registered: CA,FL,HI,IL,IN,MD,MI,MN, NY,OR,RI,VA,WA,WI,DC

FINANCIAL/TERMS:

Cash Investment: $80-100K
Total Investment: $199-299K
Minimum Net Worth: $250K
Fees: Franchise - $15K
Royalty - 6%; Ad. - 3%
Earnings Claims Statement: No
Term of Contract (Years): 10/5
Avg. # Of Employees: 15 FT, 1 PT
Passive Ownership: Allowed
Encourage Conversions: Yes
Area Develop. Agreements: Yes/20
Sub-Franchising Contracts: No
Expand In Territory: Yes
Space Needs: 1,200-1,400 SF; FS, SF, SC, RM

SUPPORT & TRAINING:

Financial Assistance Provided: Yes(I)
Site Selection Assistance: Yes
Lease Negotiation Assistance: Yes
Co-Operative Advertising: Yes
Franchisee Assoc./Member: NR
Size Of Corporate Staff: 42
On-Going Support: A,B,C,D,E,F,G,H,I
Training: 10 Days Ft. Lauderdale, FL.

SPECIFIC EXPANSION PLANS:

US: All United States
Canada: All Canada
Overseas: Australia, UK, Canada

<< >>

LEMON TREE FAMILY HAIR SALON ®

One Division Ave.
Levittown, NY 11756-1310
Tel: (800) 345-9156 (516) 735-2828
Fax: (516) 735-1851
E-Mail: lemontree@lemontree.com
Web Site: www.lemontree.com
Ms. Taylor Wagner, Director Salon Relations

LEMON TREE serves the full-service haircare needs of the entire family. We offer affordable prices and quality service and use only quality, name-brand products. We provide our franchisees a strong, hands-on training program.

BACKGROUND: IFA MEMBER
Established: 1975; 1st Franchised: 1976
Franchised Units: 60
Company-Owned Units: 0
Total Units: 60
Dist.: US-60; CAN-0; O'seas-0
North America: 5 States
Density: 53 in NY, 2 in NJ, 2 in FL
Projected New Units (12 Months): 10
Qualifications: 2, 2, 1, 2, 1, 5
Registered: FLNY

FINANCIAL/TERMS:
Cash Investment: $25-30K
Total Investment: $44-75K
Minimum Net Worth: $40K
Fees: Franchise - $15K
Royalty - 6%; Ad. - $400/Mo.
Earnings Claims Statement: No
Term of Contract (Years): 15/15
Avg. # Of Employees: 5 FT, 3 PT
Passive Ownership: Discouraged
Encourage Conversions: Yes
Area Develop. Agreements: No
Sub-Franchising Contracts: No
Expand In Territory: Yes
Space Needs: 1,200 SF; SF, SC, RM

SUPPORT & TRAINING:
Financial Assistance Provided: Yes(D)
Site Selection Assistance: Yes
Lease Negotiation Assistance: Yes
Co-Operative Advertising: Yes
Franchisee Assoc./Member: No
Size Of Corporate Staff: 6
On-Going Support: B,C,D,E,F,H,I
Training: 5 Days Main Office; Minimum 5 Days Location of Franchise.

SPECIFIC EXPANSION PLANS:
US: Northeast, Southeast
Canada: No
Overseas: No

<< >>

LORD'S & LADY'S HAIR SALONS

50 Tower Rd.
Newton, MA 02464
Tel: (617) 323-4714
Fax: (617) 332-7284
E-Mail: mbarsamian@lordsandladys.com
Web Site: www.lordsandladys.com
Mr. Michael Barsamian, President

Service and retail mall locations which normally do 50% men and 50% women in sales.

BACKGROUND:
Established: 1975; 1st Franchised: 1980
Franchised Units: 22
Company-Owned Units: 0
Total Units: 22
Dist.: US-22; CAN-0; O'seas-0
North America: 3 States
Density: 18 in MA, 3 in NH, 1 in CT
Projected New Units (12 Months): 3
Qualifications: 3, 4, 5, 3, 4, 4
Registered: NR

FINANCIAL/TERMS:
Cash Investment: $50-175K
Total Investment: $50-175K
Minimum Net Worth: $200K
Fees: Franchise - $25K
Royalty - 6%; Ad. - 0%
Earnings Claims Statement: No
Term of Contract (Years): 10/10
Avg. # Of Employees: 6 FT, 8 PT
Passive Ownership: Discouraged
Encourage Conversions: Yes
Area Develop. Agreements: No
Sub-Franchising Contracts: No
Expand In Territory: Yes
Space Needs: 1,500 SF; RM

SUPPORT & TRAINING:
Financial Assistance Provided: Yes(I)
Site Selection Assistance: Yes
Lease Negotiation Assistance: Yes
Co-Operative Advertising: Yes
Franchisee Assoc./Member: No
Size Of Corporate Staff: 6
On-Going Support: A,B,C,D,E,F,H,I
Training: 2-5 Days in Boston, MA.

SPECIFIC EXPANSION PLANS:
US: Northeast
Canada: No
Overseas: No

<< >>

PRO-CUTS

7201 Metro Blvd.
Minneapolis, MN 55439-2130
Tel: (888) 888-7008 (952) 947-7777
Fax: (952) 947-7300
E-Mail: stephanie.theis@regiscorp.com
Web Site: www.regisfranchise.com
Ms. Stephanie Theis, Franchising Coordinator

PRO-CUTS provides professional haircuts for the whole family at affordable prices in a neighborhood environment. PRO-CUTS exhibits a friendly, yet professional atmosphere. Our franchisees are provided with support and training in ALL phases of operation, as well as on-going training and support for employees.

BACKGROUND: IFA MEMBER
Established: 1982; 1st Franchised: 1984
Franchised Units: 191
Company-Owned Units: 0
Total Units: 191
Dist.: US-191; CAN-0; O'seas-0
North America: 12 States
Density: 149 in TX, 18 in OK, 8 in NM
Projected New Units (12 Months): 15
Qualifications: 4, 5, 1, 3, 3, 4
Registered: All States

FINANCIAL/TERMS:
Cash Investment: $25-50K
Total Investment: $97.1-138.3K
Minimum Net Worth: $300K/100K Liq
Fees: Franchise - $22.5K 1st
Royalty - 4% Yr. 1/6%; Ad. - 5%
Earnings Claims Statement: No
Term of Contract (Years): 10/10
Avg. # Of Employees: 6 FT, 2 PT
Passive Ownership: Discouraged
Encourage Conversions: No
Area Develop. Agreements: Yes/3-10 St.
Sub-Franchising Contracts: No
Expand In Territory: Yes
Space Needs: 900-1,200 SF; FS, SC

SUPPORT & TRAINING:
Financial Assistance Provided: Yes(I)
Site Selection Assistance: Yes
Lease Negotiation Assistance: Yes
Co-Operative Advertising: No
Franchisee Assoc./Member: Yes/Yes
Size Of Corporate Staff: 100
On-Going Support: b,C,D,E,G,h,I
Training: 3-5 Days Franchise Support Office; 5 Days Field Training.

SPECIFIC EXPANSION PLANS:
US: All United States
Canada: No
Overseas: No

<< >>

ROOSTERS MEN'S GROOMING CENTERS

216 E. Genesee St.
Lapeer, MI 48446
Tel: (866) 642-2625 (810) 441-5859
Fax: (810) 667-1889
E-Mail: joe@roostersmgc.com
Web Site: www.roostersmgc.com
Mr. Joseph B. Grondin, President

ROOSTERS MEN'S GROOMING CENTERS is an upscale, male only, barber and company-licensed establishment. The only franchise to operate on a flat royalty fee. No percentage of gross. No audits, custom design and setup. The best of the best for men and with the career of the stylest the top priority.

BACKGROUND:
Established: 1999; 1st Franchised: 2003
Franchised Units: 6
Company-Owned Units: 2
Total Units: 8
Dist.: US-8; CAN-0; O'seas-0
North America: 4 States
Density: 4 in MI, 2 in TX
Projected New Units (12 Months): 5
Qualifications: 2, 3, 3, 2, 4, 5
Registered: CA,FL,IL,IN,MI

FINANCIAL/TERMS:
Cash Investment: $25-50K
Total Investment: $125-150K
Minimum Net Worth: $50K
Fees: Franchise - NR
Royalty - $600 Flat Fee; Ad. - 0%
Earnings Claims Statement: No
Term of Contract (Years): 10/10
Avg. # Of Employees: 5 FT, 3 PT
Passive Ownership: Discouraged
Encourage Conversions: Yes
Area Develop. Agreements: Yes/5
Sub-Franchising Contracts: No
Expand In Territory: Yes
Space Needs: 1,200 SF; SF, SC

SUPPORT & TRAINING:
Financial Assistance Provided: Yes(I)
Site Selection Assistance: Yes
Lease Negotiation Assistance: Yes
Co-Operative Advertising: No
Franchisee Assoc./Member: No
Size Of Corporate Staff: 4
On-Going Support: B,C,D,E,h,I
Training: 2 Weeks On-Site.

SPECIFIC EXPANSION PLANS:
US: All United States
Canada: All Canada
Overseas: All Countries

<< >>

SPORT CLIPS

110 Briarwood
Georgetown, TX 78628
Tel: (800) 872-4247 (512) 869-1201 + 239
Fax: (512) 869-0366
E-Mail: gordon@sportclips.com
Web Site: www.sportclips.com
Ms. Beth Boecker, Director of Marketing

Sports-themed haircutting salons, appealing primarily to men and boys. Unique design, proprietary haircutting system and complete support at the unit level. Retail sale of Paul Mitchell hair care products, sports apparel and memorabilia.

BACKGROUND: IFA MEMBER
Established: 1995; 1st Franchised: 1995
Franchised Units: 84
Company-Owned Units: 8
Total Units: 92
Dist.: US-62; CAN-0; O'seas-0
North America: 4 States
Density: 46 in TX, 5 in NY, 2 in OK
Projected New Units (12 Months): 40
Qualifications: 5, 3, 1, 1, 3, 5
Registered: FL,TX

FINANCIAL/TERMS:
Cash Investment: $30-50K
Total Investment: $100-150K
Minimum Net Worth: $250K
Fees: Franchise - $17.5K
Royalty - 6%; Ad. - $250/Wk.
Earnings Claims Statement: Yes
Term of Contract (Years): 5/5
Avg. # Of Employees: 8 FT, 4 PT
Passive Ownership: Allowed
Encourage Conversions: No
Area Develop. Agreements: Yes
Sub-Franchising Contracts: No
Expand In Territory: Yes
Space Needs: 1,200 SF; SC

SUPPORT & TRAINING:
Financial Assistance Provided: Yes
Site Selection Assistance: Yes
Lease Negotiation Assistance: Yes
Co-Operative Advertising: Yes
Franchisee Assoc./Member: Yes/Yes
Size Of Corporate Staff: 15
On-Going Support: B,C,D,E,F,G,H,I
Training: 3 Days in Georgetown, TX for Franchisee + 2 Weeks Locally; 2 Weeks Locally for Manager.

SPECIFIC EXPANSION PLANS:
US: SW, MW, SE
Canada: No
Overseas: No

<< >>

SUPERCUTS

7201 Metro Blvd.
Minneapolis, MN 55439-2103
Tel: (888) 888-7008 (952) 947-7777
Fax: (952) 947-7300
E-Mail: stephanie.theis@regiscorp.com
Web Site: www.regisfranchise.com
Ms. Stephanie Theis, Franchise Coordinator

SUPERCUTS salons offer its customers high-quality haircuts and professional hair care products for the family at affordable prices.

BACKGROUND: IFA MEMBER
Established: 1976; 1st Franchised: 1979
Franchised Units: 956
Company-Owned Units: 875
Total Units: 1,831
Dist.: US-1,831; CAN-0; O'seas-0
North America: 50 States
Density: NR
Projected New Units (12 Months): 100
Qualifications: 5, 5, 1, 3, 4, 5
Registered: All States

FINANCIAL/TERMS:
Cash Investment: $25-50K/Locat.
Total Investment: $106.9-169.1K
Minimum Net Worth: $300K/100K Liq
Fees: Franchise - $22.5K 1st
Royalty - 4% Yr. 1/6%; Ad. - 4%/6%
Earnings Claims Statement: No
Term of Contract (Years): Evergreen
Avg. # Of Employees: 6 FT, 4 PT
Passive Ownership: Discouraged
Encourage Conversions: Yes
Area Develop. Agreements: Yes/3-10 St.
Sub-Franchising Contracts: No
Expand In Territory: Yes
Space Needs: 900-1,200 SF; SC

SUPPORT & TRAINING:
Financial Assistance Provided: Yes(I)
Site Selection Assistance: Yes
Lease Negotiation Assistance: Yes
Co-Operative Advertising: No
Franchisee Assoc./Member: Yes/Yes
Size Of Corporate Staff: 50
On-Going Support: B,C,D,E,G,H
Training: 3-5 Days Minneapolis, MN; Outstanding support in all areas (RE, Opening, Staffing, On-Going Marketing Support).

SPECIFIC EXPANSION PLANS:
US: All United States
Canada: All Canada
Overseas: No

<< >>

Health/Fitness/Beauty

Chapter

20

Health/Fitness/Beauty Industry Profile

Total # Franchisors in Industry Group	115
Total # Franchised Units in Industry Group	19,169
Total # Company-Owned Units in Industry Group	2,087
Total # Operating Units in Industry Group	21,256
Average # Franchised Units/Franchisor	166.7
Average # Company-Owned Units/Franchisor	18.1
Average # Total Units/Franchisor	184.8
Ratio of Total # Franchised Units/Total # Company-Owned Units	9.2:1
Industry Survey Participants	32
Representing % of Industry	27.8%
Average Franchise Fee*:	$20.1K
Average Total Investment*:	$188.6K
Average On-Going Royalty Fee*:	6.1%

*If a range was provided, the mid-point of the range was used. See detailed profiles for actual ranges.

Five Largest Participants in Survey

Company	# Franchised Units	# Co-Owned Units	# Total Units	Franchise Fee	On-Going Royalty	Total Investment
1. Jazzercise	5,752	1	5,753	$0.7K	20%	$1.5-20K
2. Merle Norman Cosmetics	1,899	9	1,908	$0	0%	NR
3. Pearle Vision	421	389	810	$30K	7%	$135K-2.5MM
4. L A Weight Loss Centers	340	340	680	$20K	7%	$65-117K
5. Jenny Craig Weight Loss and Management Centres	95	548	643	$25K	7%	$122.6-301.5K

All of the data provided are proprietary and should not be quoted without acknowledging *Bond's Franchise Guide.*

ALOETTE COSMETICS

4900 Highlands Pkwy.
Smyrna, GA 30082
Tel: (800) 256-3883 (678) 444-2563
Fax: (678) 444-2564
E-Mail: snormand@aloette.com
Web Site: www.aloette.com
Ms. Sharon Normand, Franchise Administrator

ALOETTE is a direct marketer of Aloe Vera-based skin care products. Franchises provide career opportunities to beauty consultants who sell the products through home shows.

BACKGROUND: IFA MEMBER
Established: 1978; 1st Franchised: 1978
Franchised Units: 58
Company-Owned Units: 0
Total Units: 58
Dist.: US-50; CAN-32; O'seas-0
North America: 36 States,10 Provinces
Density: 18 in ON, 4 in BC, 3 in PQ
Projected New Units (12 Months): 10
Qualifications: 1, 2, 5, 2, 1, 2
Registered: NR

FINANCIAL/TERMS:
Cash Investment: $10-20K
Total Investment: $55-86.3K
Minimum Net Worth: $10K
Fees: Franchise - $20K
Royalty - 5%; Ad. - NA
Earnings Claims Statement: No
Term of Contract (Years): 5/10
Avg. # Of Employees: 3 FT
Passive Ownership: Discouraged
Encourage Conversions: NA
Area Develop. Agreements: No
Sub-Franchising Contracts: No
Expand In Territory: Yes
Space Needs: 1,000 SF; HB, Light Industrial, Retail

SUPPORT & TRAINING:
Financial Assistance Provided: Yes(D)
Site Selection Assistance: No
Lease Negotiation Assistance: No
Co-Operative Advertising: No
Franchisee Assoc./Member: No
Size Of Corporate Staff: 25
On-Going Support: C,D,E,h
Training: 2 Days Operations Training at Franchise; 2 Days Sales Training at Franchise.

SPECIFIC EXPANSION PLANS:
US: All United States
Canada: ON
Overseas: No

ANNE PENMAN LASER THERAPY

6690 Roswell Rd., # 350
Atlanta, GA 30328
Tel: (888) 64-LASER
Fax: (404) 256-2234
E-Mail: johng@annepenmanlasertherapy.com
Web Site: www.annepenmanlasertherapy.com
Mr. John Granito, VP Franchise Development

Exciting franchise opportunity using state-of-the-art, innovative low-level lasers for smoking reduction, cessation and weight loss. The method is non-invasive and has a very high success rate. Franchise includes business format, technical training, site selection, methodology, equipment and much more.

BACKGROUND:
Established: 2003; 1st Franchised: 2004
Franchised Units: 35
Company-Owned Units: 1
Total Units: 36
Dist.: US-34; CAN-0; O'seas-2
North America: 11 States
Density: 5 in GA, 4 in FL
Projected New Units (12 Months): 60
Qualifications: 4, 2, 1, 3, 5, 5
Registered: All States

FINANCIAL/TERMS:
Cash Investment: $50K
Total Investment: $30-82K
Minimum Net Worth: $Open
Fees: Franchise - $10-20K
Royalty - 10%; Ad. - 2%
Earnings Claims Statement: No
Term of Contract (Years): 5/5/5
Avg. # Of Employees: 2 FT, 1 PT
Passive Ownership: Allowed
Encourage Conversions: Yes
Area Develop. Agreements: Yes/5
Sub-Franchising Contracts: No
Expand In Territory: Yes
Space Needs: 1,000 SF; FS, SF, SC, RM

SUPPORT & TRAINING:
Financial Assistance Provided: Yes
Site Selection Assistance: Yes
Lease Negotiation Assistance: Yes
Co-Operative Advertising: Yes
Franchisee Assoc./Member: No
Size Of Corporate Staff: 18
On-Going Support: A,B,C,D,E,G,H,I
Training: 6 Days Atlanta, GA.

SPECIFIC EXPANSION PLANS:
US: All United States
Canada: All Canada
Overseas: All Countries

<< >>

ARISTOCARE

1200 N. El Dorado Pl., # A130
Tucson, AZ 85715
Tel: (866) 731-2273 (520) 731-2273
Fax: (520) 529-0862
E-Mail: info@aristocare.net
Web Site: www.aristocare.net
Ms. Cyndy Michaud, Franchise Liaison

Today the rapidly-growing senior population is fueling the demand for in-home health services. This demand has created explosive growth in the senior care industry. The ARISTOCARE private duty home care system is a full-service medical business, providing two income streams for non-medical and medical care senior services. ARISTOCARE provides excellent ownership opportunities. No previous experience in home health care is necessary. Comprehensive training.

BACKGROUND: IFA MEMBER
Established: 1999; 1st Franchised: 2003
Franchised Units: 1
Company-Owned Units: 3
Total Units: 4
Dist.: US-3; CAN-0; O'seas-0
North America: 1 State
Density: 3 in AZ
Projected New Units (12 Months): NR
Qualifications: 4, 4, 1, 3, 3, 5
Registered: FL,MI

FINANCIAL/TERMS:
Cash Investment: $60K
Total Investment: $148-250K
Minimum Net Worth: $250K
Fees: Franchise - $36K
Royalty - 6%; Ad. - NR
Earnings Claims Statement: NR
Term of Contract (Years): 10/5
Avg. # Of Employees: 2 FT, 1 PT
Passive Ownership: Allowed
Encourage Conversions: NR
Area Develop. Agreements: No

Sub-Franchising Contracts: No
Expand In Territory: Yes
Space Needs: 600 SF; SC, Exec. Suite
SUPPORT & TRAINING:
Financial Assistance Provided: NA
Site Selection Assistance: Yes
Lease Negotiation Assistance: No
Co-Operative Advertising: NR
Franchisee Assoc./Member: NR
Size Of Corporate Staff: 5
On-Going Support: A,b,C,D,E,G,H,I
Training: 2 Weeks Tucson, AZ Corporate Office; 1 Week On-Site.
SPECIFIC EXPANSION PLANS:
US: All United States
Canada: No
Overseas: No

<< >>

BEAUTY BRANDS SALON-SPA-SUPERSTORE

4600 Madison Ave., # 400
Kansas City, MO 64112-3002
Tel: (888) 725-6608 (816) 960-5759
Fax: (816)960-5890
E-Mail: franchising@beautybrands.com
Web Site: www.beautybrands.com
Mr. Steve Eckman, VP Corp. Development

BEAUTY BRANDS SALON/SPA/SUPERSTORE is the cutting-edge concept that offers consumers a "total beauty" experience. We have brought together a full-service salon and spa and have showcased it in a dynamic 6,000-7,000 square-foot retail environment offering nearly 50,000 units of product representing the top salon brands for hair, skin and nails.

BACKGROUND: IFA MEMBER
Established: 1995; 1st Franchised: 1999
Franchised Units: 2
Company-Owned Units: 34
Total Units: 36
Dist.: US-23; CAN-0; O'seas-0
North America: 5 States
Density: 4 in KS, 6 in TX, 6 in CO
Projected New Units (12 Months): 10
Qualifications: 5, 5, 5, 4, 4, 4
Registered: All States Except IL
FINANCIAL/TERMS:
Cash Investment: $100-200K
Total Investment: $594.5-936K
Minimum Net Worth: $3MM
Fees: Franchise - $25K
Royalty - 1-5%; Ad. - 1-2%
Earnings Claims Statement: Yes
Term of Contract (Years): 10/10
Avg. # Of Employees: 10, 20 PT
Passive Ownership: Not Allowed
Encourage Conversions: Yes
Area Develop. Agreements: Yes/Varies
Sub-Franchising Contracts: No
Expand In Territory: Yes
Space Needs: 5,000-7,000 SF; FS, SC
SUPPORT & TRAINING:
Financial Assistance Provided: No
Site Selection Assistance: Yes
Lease Negotiation Assistance: Yes
Co-Operative Advertising: Yes
Franchisee Assoc./Member: Yes
Size Of Corporate Staff: 50
On-Going Support: A,B,C,D,E,F,h,I
Training: 4-6 Weeks Kansas City, MO.
SPECIFIC EXPANSION PLANS:
US: All United States
Canada: No
Overseas: No

<< >>

20 MINUTE TOTAL FITNESS FOR MEN

BLITZ, THE, 20-MINUTE TOTAL FITNESS FOR MEN

980 E. Santa Fe
Gardner, KS 66030
Tel: (866) 968-2548 (913) 856-2424
Fax: (309) 424-3558
E-Mail: info@timetoblitz.com
Web Site: www.timetoblitz.com
Mr. Scott T. Smith, Founder

The world's largest and fastest-growing fitness franchise for men. THE BLITZ combines strength training with cardio boxing and martial art techniques, all inside "The BLITZ Ring" 20-minute circuit. Your low investment could yield high returns. Great opportunity for those looking for more independence.

BACKGROUND: IFA MEMBER
Established: 2002; 1st Franchised: 2002
Franchised Units: 201
Company-Owned Units: 1
Total Units: 202
Dist.: US-70; CAN-40; O'seas-92
North America: 25 States
Density: NR
Projected New Units (12 Months): NR
Qualifications: , , , , ,
Registered:
FINANCIAL/TERMS:
Cash Investment: $29.9K
Total Investment: $38-60K
Minimum Net Worth: $300K
Fees: Franchise - $29.9K
Royalty - $395/Mo.; Ad. - 0%
Earnings Claims Statement: No
Term of Contract (Years): 7/5
Avg. # Of Employees: 1 Ft, 1 PT
Passive Ownership: Discouraged
Encourage Conversions: NR
Area Develop. Agreements: Yes/Varies
Sub-Franchising Contracts: No
Expand In Territory: Yes
Space Needs: 1,800 SF; SC
SUPPORT & TRAINING:
Financial Assistance Provided: NR
Site Selection Assistance: Yes
Lease Negotiation Assistance: Yes
Co-Operative Advertising: NA
Franchisee Assoc./Member: No
Size Of Corporate Staff: 15
On-Going Support: a,B,C,D,E,f,G,h,I
Training: 4 Days Gardner, KS Headquarters.
SPECIFIC EXPANSION PLANS:
US: All United States
Canada: All Canada
Overseas: All Countries

<< >>

CELSIUS TANNERY

12142 State Line Rd.
Leawood, KS 66223
Tel: (866) 826-7400 (913) 451-7000
Fax: (913) 451-7001
E-Mail: jburandt@celsiustan.com
Web Site: www.celsiustan.com
Mr. Jim Burandt, Vice President Sales

We are the fastest growing indoor tanning franchise chain in the U.S. With the exclusive STS tanning process, we are the first tanning salon franchise inside a big box retailer. We offer motivating and educational instruction in management, sales, and marketing your salon, and help you with professional guidance as well as on-going administrative and business support. Site location, lease negotiation, construction, financial assistance and a toll-free number for support!

BACKGROUND:
Established: 1995; 1st Franchised: 2000

Franchised Units: 15
Company-Owned Units: 3
Total Units: 18
Dist.: US-18; CAN-0; O'seas-0
North America: 3 States
Density: 10 in KS, 7 in MO, 1 in NE
Projected New Units (12 Months): 8-10
Qualifications: 3, 2, 1, 1, 2, 4
Registered: FL,IL,NY,WI

FINANCIAL/TERMS:

Cash Investment: $35-100K
Total Investment: $240-600K
Minimum Net Worth: $150K
Fees: Franchise - $20-35K
Royalty - 1%/$250 Min.; Ad. - $1,200/Mo.
Earnings Claims Statement: No
Term of Contract (Years): 5/5
Avg. # Of Employees: 3 FT, 5 PT
Passive Ownership: Allowed
Encourage Conversions: Yes
Area Develop. Agreements: Yes/5
Sub-Franchising Contracts: No
Expand In Territory: Yes
Space Needs: 2,000 SF; FS, SF, SC

SUPPORT & TRAINING:

Financial Assistance Provided: Yes(I)
Site Selection Assistance: Yes
Lease Negotiation Assistance: Yes
Co-Operative Advertising: Yes
Franchisee Assoc./Member: No
Size Of Corporate Staff: 10
On-Going Support: A,B,C,D,E,F,I
Training: 1 Week at Corporate Headquarters; 3 Week On-Site.

SPECIFIC EXPANSION PLANS:

US: All United States
Canada: No
Overseas: No

<< >>

Champion Home Health Care, Inc.

CHAMPION HOME HEALTH CARE

3247 Northwest 60th St.
Boca Raton, FL 33496
Tel: (561) 843-5960
Fax: (561) 999-9608
E-Mail: rickstewart@championhome.com
Web Site: www.championhome.com
Mr. Richard G. Stewart, President

CHAMPION HOME HEALTH CARE is a licensed private pay agency that is able to provide all levels of in-home service from Companions to skilled Nursing as well as institutional staffing. We license only in Florida where we are fully conversant with the market and State Licensure requirements. Within Florida the elderly population is expanding at 20% per year. Exclusive territories are available. Our integrated personnel, client and scheduling software and back office bookkeeping service simplify operations.

BACKGROUND:

Established: 1993; 1st Franchised: 1999
Franchised Units: 4
Company-Owned Units: 0
Total Units: 4
Dist.: US-4; CAN-0; O'seas-0
North America: 1 State
Density: 4 in FL
Projected New Units (12 Months): 2
Qualifications: 4, 4, 1, 3, 3, 4
Registered: FL

FINANCIAL/TERMS:

Cash Investment: $30-50K
Total Investment: $50-75K
Minimum Net Worth: $100K
Fees: Franchise - $18K
Royalty - 8%; Ad. - 0%
Earnings Claims Statement: No
Term of Contract (Years): 5/5
Avg. # Of Employees: 2 FT
Passive Ownership: Discouraged
Encourage Conversions: No
Area Develop. Agreements: No
Sub-Franchising Contracts: No
Expand In Territory: Yes
Space Needs: 400-800 SF; FS

SUPPORT & TRAINING:

Financial Assistance Provided: No
Site Selection Assistance: Yes
Lease Negotiation Assistance: No
Co-Operative Advertising: Yes
Franchisee Assoc./Member: No/No
Size Of Corporate Staff: 4
On-Going Support: A,C,d,E
Training: 1-6 Weeks in Boca Raton, FL.

SPECIFIC EXPANSION PLANS:

US: FL
Canada: No
Overseas: No

<< >>

COMFORT KEEPERS

6640 Poe Ave., # 200
Dayton, OH 45414-2600
Tel: (800) 387-2415 (937) 264-1933 + 112
Fax: (937) 264-3103
E-Mail: admin@comfortkeepers.com
Web Site: www.comfortkeepers.com
Mr. Jeff C. Bevis, VP Franchise Development

COMFORT KEEPERS provides non-medical, in-home care, such as companionship, meal preparation, light housekeeping, grocery and clothing shopping, grooming and assistance with recreational activities for the elderly and others who need assistance in daily living.

BACKGROUND: IFA MEMBER

Established: 1999; 1st Franchised: 1999
Franchised Units: 445
Company-Owned Units: 1
Total Units: 446
Dist.: US-390; CAN-1; O'seas-0
North America: 45 States, 1 Province
Density: 38 in FL, 35 in CA, 35 in OH
Projected New Units (12 Months): 92
Qualifications: 5, 5, 2, 3, 3, 4
Registered: All States

FINANCIAL/TERMS:

Cash Investment: $40-65K
Total Investment: $40-65K Min.
Minimum Net Worth: $100K
Fees: Franchise - $18.8K
Royalty - 5/4/3%; Ad. - 0%
Earnings Claims Statement: Yes
Term of Contract (Years): 10/10
Avg. # Of Employees: 2 FT
Passive Ownership: Not Allowed
Encourage Conversions: Yes
Area Develop. Agreements: No
Sub-Franchising Contracts: No
Expand In Territory: Yes
Space Needs: 600-800 SF; HB, Office Space

SUPPORT & TRAINING:

Financial Assistance Provided: No
Site Selection Assistance: No
Lease Negotiation Assistance: No
Co-Operative Advertising: No
Franchisee Assoc./Member: No
Size Of Corporate Staff: 12
On-Going Support: B,C,D,G,h,I
Training: 1 Week Dayton, OH.

SPECIFIC EXPANSION PLANS:

US: All United States
Canada: No
Overseas: No

<< >>

CONTOURS EXPRESS

156 Imperial Way
Nicholasville, KY 40356
Tel: (877) 227-2282 (859) 885-6441
Fax: (859) 241-2234

E-Mail: daren@contoursexpress.com
Web Site: www.contoursexpress.com
Mr. Daren Carter, Chief Executive Officer

CONTOURS EXPRESS is a fitness center, designed especially for women, based on the concept of circuit training. A cue tape, with high energy music, keeps club members moving through our 16-piece circuit that alternates between strength-training machines and aerobic stations. Unlike other clubs designed for women, CONTOURS EXPRESS uses actual weight-bearing machines (vs. less efficient hydraulic machines). Franchisees also derive profits from their own pro shop and our line of weight loss supplements.

BACKGROUND: IFA MEMBER
Established: 1998; 1st Franchised: 1998
Franchised Units: 400
Company-Owned Units: 0
Total Units: 400
Dist.: US-290; CAN-10; O'seas-5
North America: 33 States
Density: 58 in MI, 30 in CA, 26 in FL
Projected New Units (12 Months): NR
Qualifications: , , , , ,
Registered:

FINANCIAL/TERMS:
Cash Investment: $10K
Total Investment: $33.2-47.2K
Minimum Net Worth: $50K
Fees: Franchise - $50K
Royalty - $395/Mo.; Ad. - 0%
Earnings Claims Statement: No
Term of Contract (Years): 10/5
Avg. # Of Employees: 1 FT, 1 PT
Passive Ownership: Allowed
Encourage Conversions: NR
Area Develop. Agreements: No
Sub-Franchising Contracts: Yes
Expand In Territory: Yes
Space Needs: 1,200 SF; FS, SC

SUPPORT & TRAINING:
Financial Assistance Provided: NR
Site Selection Assistance: Yes
Lease Negotiation Assistance: No
Co-Operative Advertising: Yes
Franchisee Assoc./Member: No
Size Of Corporate Staff: 9
On-Going Support: a,E,G,h,I
Training: 4 Days Nicholasville, KY.

SPECIFIC EXPANSION PLANS:
US: All United States
Canada: NR
Overseas: NR

DIET CENTER

395 Springside Dr.
Akron, OH 44333-2496
Tel: (800) 656-3294 (330) 655-5861
Fax: (330) 666-2197
E-Mail: info@dietcenterworldwide.com
Web Site: www.dietcenterworldwide.com
Mr. Grayden Webb, Dir. Franchise Development

DIET CENTER offers innovative weight management programs.

BACKGROUND:
Established: 1972; 1st Franchised: 1972
Franchised Units: 325
Company-Owned Units: 0
Total Units: 325
Dist.: US-238; CAN-11; O'seas-1
North America: 44 States, 4 Provinces
Density: 28 in NY, 19 in NC, 18 in CA
Projected New Units (12 Months): 8-10
Qualifications: 3, 3, 3, 2, 3, 5
Registered: All States

FINANCIAL/TERMS:
Cash Investment: $16.4-34.9K
Total Investment: $16.4-34.9K
Minimum Net Worth: $50-75K
Fees: Franchise - $15K
Royalty - 8%/$100/Wk.; Ad. - 8%/$500/Mo.
Earnings Claims Statement: No
Term of Contract (Years): 5/5
Avg. # Of Employees: 2 FT, 1 PT
Passive Ownership: Discouraged
Encourage Conversions: Yes
Area Develop. Agreements: No
Sub-Franchising Contracts: No
Expand In Territory: Yes
Space Needs: 700-1,200 SF; FS, SF, SC

SUPPORT & TRAINING:
Financial Assistance Provided: No
Site Selection Assistance: Yes
Lease Negotiation Assistance: Yes
Co-Operative Advertising: No
Franchisee Assoc./Member: No
Size Of Corporate Staff: 40
On-Going Support: C,D,E,G,H,I
Training: 3 Weeks in Akron, OH.

SPECIFIC EXPANSION PLANS:
US: All United States
Canada: All Canada
Overseas: No

ELDIRECT IN-HOME SENIOR CARE

716 W. Sycamore, # 1
Fayetteville, AR 72703
Tel: (479) 443-7173
Fax: (479) 443-0183
E-Mail: eldirecthomecare@yahoo.com
Web Site: www.eldirecthomecare.com
Franchising Department,

See the future of in-home care franchising - today. ELDIRECT IN-HOME SENIOR CARE, one of the newest, most innovative homecare opportunities, offers America's entrepreneurs the ability to be a part of the next wave of in-home care. After many years of family and industry experience, we have created a program that is unique. Multiple service and income opportunities, combined with industry-exceeding quality assurance measures, are just part of the ELDIRECT IN-HOME SENIOR CARE franchise opportunity.

BACKGROUND:
Established: 1996; 1st Franchised: 2003
Franchised Units: 0
Company-Owned Units: 2
Total Units: 2
Dist.: US-1; CAN-0; O'seas-0
North America: 1 State
Density: 1 in AR
Projected New Units (12 Months): 10-20
Qualifications: 4, 3, 3, 2, 5, 5
Registered: FL,OR,DC

FINANCIAL/TERMS:
Cash Investment: $15-20K
Total Investment: $21.9-29.7K
Minimum Net Worth: NA
Fees: Franchise - $15K
Royalty - 5%; Ad. - 0%
Earnings Claims Statement: No
Term of Contract (Years): 10/5
Avg. # Of Employees: 2 FT
Passive Ownership: Allowed
Encourage Conversions: NA
Area Develop. Agreements: No
Sub-Franchising Contracts: No
Expand In Territory: Yes
Space Needs: 300-700 SF; Office Space

SUPPORT & TRAINING:
Financial Assistance Provided: No
Site Selection Assistance: Yes
Lease Negotiation Assistance: Yes
Co-Operative Advertising: No
Franchisee Assoc./Member: No
Size Of Corporate Staff: 7
On-Going Support: A,B,C,D,E,G,I
Training: Up to 5 Days Fayetteville, AR; Up to 3 Days ELDirect Franchise Location.

SPECIFIC EXPANSION PLANS:

US: All United States
Canada: No
Overseas: No

<< >>

EXECUTIVE TANS

165 S. Union Blvd., # 785
Lakewood, CO 80228-2215
Tel: (877) 393-2826 (303) 988-9999
Fax: (303) 988-5390
E-Mail: pat@executivetans.com
Web Site: www.executivetans.com
Mr. Patrick Pounders, VP Sales & Marketing

Indoor tanning salons along with related products and services.

BACKGROUND: IFA MEMBER
Established: 1991; 1st Franchised: 1995
Franchised Units: 147
Company-Owned Units: 3
Total Units: 150
Dist.: US-26; CAN-0; O'seas-0
North America: 1 State
Density: 26 in CO
Projected New Units (12 Months): 10
Qualifications: 3, 3, 3, 4, 3, 3
Registered: IL,FL,WI

FINANCIAL/TERMS:
Cash Investment: $40-60K
Total Investment: $130-150K
Minimum Net Worth: $175K
Fees: Franchise - $15K
Royalty - $795-1,895/Mo.; Ad. - $315/Mo.
Earnings Claims Statement: No
Term of Contract (Years): 3/3
Avg. # Of Employees: 2 FT, 3 PT
Passive Ownership: Discouraged
Encourage Conversions: Yes
Area Develop. Agreements: Yes/5
Sub-Franchising Contracts: Yes
Expand In Territory: Yes
Space Needs: 1,500-6,000 SF; SC

SUPPORT & TRAINING:
Financial Assistance Provided: Yes(I)
Site Selection Assistance: Yes
Lease Negotiation Assistance: Yes
Co-Operative Advertising: Yes
Franchisee Assoc./Member: No
Size Of Corporate Staff: 4
On-Going Support: B,C,d,E,G,h,I
Training: 1 Week at Corporate Offices; 1 Week on Location.

SPECIFIC EXPANSION PLANS:
US: All United States
Canada: No
Overseas: No

<< >>

FACES COSMETICS

30 MacIntosh Blvd., Unit 6
Vaughan, ON L4K 4P1 CANADA
Tel: (877) 773-2237 (905) 760-0110 + 112
Fax: (905) 760-0901
E-Mail: michael@faces-cosmetics.com
Web Site: www.faces-cosmetics.com
Mr. Michael Lublin, Vice President

FACES is a retail cosmetics business featuring in-mall, stand-alone boutiques selling FACES' own extensive, affordable and distinct brand of prestige color cosmetics and bath, body and skin care. Twenty-five years of operating history and extensive market research enables FACES to successfully service a critical gap between mass-market merchandisers and expensive department store brands.

BACKGROUND: IFA MEMBER
Established: 1974; 1st Franchised: 1980
Franchised Units: 40
Company-Owned Units: 10
Total Units: 50
Dist.: US-0; CAN-39; O'seas-28
North America: 9 Provinces
Density: 12 in PQ, 6 in ON
Projected New Units (12 Months): NR
Qualifications: 3, 4, 3, 3, 3, 5
Registered:FL,MI,MN,NY,ND,OR,RI,SD,VA,WA,WI,DC

FINANCIAL/TERMS:
Cash Investment: $25-30K
Total Investment: $125-275K
Minimum Net Worth: Varies
Fees: Franchise - $25K
Royalty - 6%; Ad. - 2%
Earnings Claims Statement: No
Term of Contract (Years): 10/10
Avg. # Of Employees: 1 FT, 3-4 PT
Passive Ownership: Allowed
Encourage Conversions: Yes
Area Develop. Agreements: Yes/10
Sub-Franchising Contracts: Yes
Expand In Territory: Yes
Space Needs: 230-1,000 SF; SF, SC, RM

SUPPORT & TRAINING:
Financial Assistance Provided: Yes(I)
Site Selection Assistance: Yes
Lease Negotiation Assistance: Yes
Co-Operative Advertising: No
Franchisee Assoc./Member: No
Size Of Corporate Staff: 70
On-Going Support: A,B,D,E,G,h
Training: 4 Weeks Toronto, ON.

SPECIFIC EXPANSION PLANS:
US: All United States
Canada: All Canada
Overseas: All Countries in a Master Franchisee capacity

<< >>

FORM-YOU-3 INTERNATIONAL

395 Springside Dr.
Akron, OH 44333-2496
Tel: (800) 525-6315 (330) 668-1461
Fax: (330) 666-2197
E-Mail: kmccollins@hmgmail.com
Web Site: www.formyou3.com
Ms. Krishna McCollins, Dir. Franchise Development

Assisting individuals in weight loss and maintenance by utilizing a proprietary multi-level diet plan, individual and group behavior life modification programs, diet-related products and maintenance programs.

BACKGROUND:
Established: 1982; 1st Franchised: 1983
Franchised Units: 53
Company-Owned Units: 3
Total Units: 56
Dist.: US-34; CAN-0; O'seas-0
North America: 12 States
Density: 12 in OH, 7 in MI, 5 in NC
Projected New Units (12 Months): 10
Qualifications: 5, 4, 3, 3, , 5
Registered: None

FINANCIAL/TERMS:
Cash Investment: $23.1-33.7K
Total Investment: $33-43K
Minimum Net Worth: $100K
Fees: Franchise - $15K
Royalty - 6%/$150/Wk.; Ad. - 6%
Earnings Claims Statement: No
Term of Contract (Years): 5/5/5/5
Avg. # Of Employees: 2-5 FT
Passive Ownership: Not Allowed
Encourage Conversions: Yes
Area Develop. Agreements: No
Sub-Franchising Contracts: No
Expand In Territory: Yes
Space Needs: 700-1,200 SF; SC

SUPPORT & TRAINING:
Financial Assistance Provided: NA
Site Selection Assistance: Yes
Lease Negotiation Assistance: Yes
Co-Operative Advertising: Yes
Franchisee Assoc./Member: No
Size Of Corporate Staff: 45
On-Going Support: A,B,c,d,E,G,H,I
Training: 3 Weeks in Akron, OH; 1-3 Days On-Site.

SPECIFIC EXPANSION PLANS:
US: All United States
Canada: No
Overseas: No

GRANDMA'S LOVING HANDS SENIOR HOME CARE

2222 S. Linden Rd., # J
Flint, MI 48532
Tel: (877) 42-HANDS (810) 720-5700
Fax: (810) 720-5251
E-Mail: plewis@grandmaslovinghands.com
Web Site: www.grandmaslovinghands.com
Ms. Phyllis Lewis, Vice President

GRANDMA'S LOVING HANDS is an award-winning business system originating out of the work of Linda Rice, who began a home care business in 1999 as a result of her father's struggles with Alzheimer's. Ms. Rice has dedicated herself to serving the needs of families in similar situations. GRANDMA'S LOVING HANDS offers a well-developed and proven business system at an affordable initial investment. GRANDMA'S LOVING HANDS provides complete step-by-step guidance to jump-start your new operation.

BACKGROUND:
Established: 1999; 1st Franchised: 2004
Franchised Units: 0
Company-Owned Units: 1
Total Units: 1
Dist.: US-1; CAN-0; O'seas-0
North America: 1 State
Density: 1 in MI
Projected New Units (12 Months): 4
Qualifications: 4, 3, 1, 2, 5, 5
Registered: MI

FINANCIAL/TERMS:
Cash Investment: $13.2-24.9K
Total Investment: $38.3-49.9K
Minimum Net Worth: $150K
Fees: Franchise - $25K
Royalty - 6%; Ad. - 1%
Earnings Claims Statement: Yes
Term of Contract (Years): 5/5
Avg. # Of Employees: 2 FT, 2 PT
Passive Ownership: Discouraged
Encourage Conversions: No
Area Develop. Agreements: No
Sub-Franchising Contracts: No
Expand In Territory: Yes
Space Needs: 700 SF; HB

SUPPORT & TRAINING:
Financial Assistance Provided: No
Site Selection Assistance: Yes
Lease Negotiation Assistance: No
Co-Operative Advertising: No
Franchisee Assoc./Member: No
Size Of Corporate Staff: 3
On-Going Support: C,D,E,G,H,I
Training: 10 Days Michigan.

SPECIFIC EXPANSION PLANS:
US: Michigan Only
Canada: No
Overseas: No

<< >>

GRISWOLD SPECIAL CARE

717 Bethlehem Pk., # 300
Erdenheim, PA 19001
Tel: (888) 777-7630 (215) 402-0200
Fax: (215) 402-0202
E-Mail: specialcare@griswoldspecialcare.com
Web Site: www.griswoldspecialcare.com
Mr. Albert Scharbach, Manager of Development

Own a business that helps people - that is what it means to start a homecare business with GRISWOLD SPECIAL CARE. We help older adults and the disabled remain in the comfort of home by referring caregivers who provide companionship and assistance with personal care needs. We succeed because we provide the highest-quality homecare. We keep overhead low and pay our caregivers well. Our priority is to thoroughly support our existing offices, so the on-going support is unprecedented in the industry.

BACKGROUND: IFA MEMBER
Established: 1982; 1st Franchised: 1984
Franchised Units: 80
Company-Owned Units: 5
Total Units: 85
Dist.: US-78; CAN-0; O'seas-2
North America: 16 States
Density: 20 in PA, 15 in NH, 7 in MA
Projected New Units (12 Months): NR
Qualifications: , , , , ,
Registered:

FINANCIAL/TERMS:
Cash Investment: $15-23K
Total Investment: $15-23K
Minimum Net Worth: NA
Fees: Franchise - $9K
Royalty - 2.5-4.0%; Ad. - NA
Earnings Claims Statement: No
Term of Contract (Years): 7/5
Avg. # Of Employees: 2 FT, 2 PT
Passive Ownership: Not Allowed
Encourage Conversions: NR
Area Develop. Agreements: No
Sub-Franchising Contracts: Yes
Expand In Territory: Yes
Space Needs: NA SF; HB

SUPPORT & TRAINING:
Financial Assistance Provided: NR
Site Selection Assistance: Yes
Lease Negotiation Assistance: NA
Co-Operative Advertising: No
Franchisee Assoc./Member: No
Size Of Corporate Staff: 12
On-Going Support: B,C,D,G,H,I
Training: 5 Days Corporate Office; 1-2 Days Franchisee's Location; 1-2 Days Franchisee's Location.

SPECIFIC EXPANSION PLANS:
US: NE, SE, Midwest and SW
Canada: NR
Overseas: NR

<< >>

Home Care | Assistance

HOME CARE ASSISTANCE

148 Hawthorne Ave.
Palo Alto, CA 94301
Tel: (866) 454-8346 (650) 462-6900
Fax: (650) 462-6907
E-Mail: kj@homecareassistance.com
Web Site: www.homecareassistance.com
Mr. Jim Johnson,

HOME CARE ASSISTANCE specializes in offering 24/7 care to the senior market place. We offer the exclusive 'We will be there' guarantee to our clients. HOME CARE ASSISTANCE is America's leading provider of 24/7 care.

BACKGROUND: IFA MEMBER
Established: 2002; 1st Franchised: 2004
Franchised Units: 8
Company-Owned Units: 1
Total Units: 9
Dist.: US-9; CAN-0; O'seas-0
North America: 8 States
Density: 2 in TX, 1 in GA, 1 in FL
Projected New Units (12 Months): 12
Qualifications: 4, 4, 2, 3, 3, 4

Registered: FL,MI,WA

FINANCIAL/TERMS:

Cash Investment: $50-150K
Total Investment: $50-150K
Minimum Net Worth: $100K
Fees: Franchise - $20K
Royalty - 5%; Ad. - 0%
Earnings Claims Statement: Yes
Term of Contract (Years): 15/15
Avg. # Of Employees: 2 FT, 10 PT
Passive Ownership: Not Allowed
Encourage Conversions: NR
Area Develop. Agreements: No
Sub-Franchising Contracts: No
Expand In Territory: Yes
Space Needs: 1,500 SF; SC

SUPPORT & TRAINING:

Financial Assistance Provided: No
Site Selection Assistance: Yes
Lease Negotiation Assistance: NA
Co-Operative Advertising: NA
Franchisee Assoc./Member: No
Size Of Corporate Staff: 7
On-Going Support: A,B,C,D,I
Training: 1 Week Palo Alto, CA.

SPECIFIC EXPANSION PLANS:

US: All United States
Canada: No
Overseas: All Countries

<< >>

INTRIVAH HEALTH AND WELLNESS

2012 8th Ave.
Altoona, PA 16602
Tel: (800) 941-9251 (814) 941-9250
Fax: (814) 941-8260
E-Mail: info@intrivah.com
Web Site: www.intrivah.com
Mr. Michael McConnell, Vice President Franchising

INTRIVAH is an innovative, cutting-edge fitness and nutrition center with superb methodologies, an outstanding business system and a dynamic franchise opportunity. Consultants develop personalized wellness programs for people of all fitness levels in a safe, non-intimidating environment. INTRIVAH is an exciting franchise with a healthy future.

BACKGROUND:

Established: 2002; 1st Franchised: 2004
Franchised Units: 0
Company-Owned Units: 1
Total Units: 1
Dist.: US-1; CAN-0; O'seas-0
North America: 1 State
Density: 1 in PA
Projected New Units (12 Months): 10
Qualifications: 3, 2, 4, 3, 4, 5
Registered: NR

FINANCIAL/TERMS:

Cash Investment: $50-80K
Total Investment: $133.8-224.8K
Minimum Net Worth: $150K
Fees: Franchise - $30K
Royalty - 5%; Ad. - 2%
Earnings Claims Statement: No
Term of Contract (Years): 5/5
Avg. # Of Employees: 2 FT, 1 PT
Passive Ownership: Not Allowed
Encourage Conversions: NA
Area Develop. Agreements: No
Sub-Franchising Contracts: No
Expand In Territory: NO
Space Needs: 3,000 SF; SC

SUPPORT & TRAINING:

Financial Assistance Provided: Yes(I)
Site Selection Assistance: Yes
Lease Negotiation Assistance: No
Co-Operative Advertising: Yes
Franchisee Assoc./Member: No
Size Of Corporate Staff: 3
On-Going Support: C,d,E,h,I
Training: 4 -6 Weeks Altoona, PA.

SPECIFIC EXPANSION PLANS:

US: PA and Eastern OH
Canada: No
Overseas: No

<< >>

JAZZERCISE

2460 Impala Dr.
Carlsbad, CA 92008
Tel: (800) FIT IS IT (760) 476-1750
Fax: (760) 602-7180
E-Mail: jazzinc@jazzercise.com
Web Site: www.jazzercise.com
Ms. Nancy Guetzke, Franchise Coordinator

JAZZERCISE is the world's leading international dance fitness franchisor, with a multi-media division and mail-order catalog business at 1-800-FIT-IS-IT, specializing in active wear and accessories.

BACKGROUND:

Established: 1969; 1st Franchised: 1983
Franchised Units: 5,752
Company-Owned Units: 1
Total Units: 5,753
Dist.: US-4,210; CAN-101; O'seas-860
North America: 50 States, 5 Provinces
Density: 626 in CA, 296 in OH, 343 TX
Projected New Units (12 Months): 600
Qualifications: 1, 2, 4, 2, 5, 5
Registered: All States

FINANCIAL/TERMS:

Cash Investment: $1.5-3K
Total Investment: $1.5-20K
Minimum Net Worth: NA
Fees: Franchise - $700
Royalty - 20%; Ad. - NA
Earnings Claims Statement: No
Term of Contract (Years): 5/5
Avg. # Of Employees: NR
Passive Ownership: Allowed
Encourage Conversions: NA
Area Develop. Agreements: No
Sub-Franchising Contracts: No
Expand In Territory: Yes
Space Needs: 3,000 SF; Community Building

SUPPORT & TRAINING:

Financial Assistance Provided: No
Site Selection Assistance: No
Lease Negotiation Assistance: No
Co-Operative Advertising: Yes
Franchisee Assoc./Member: No
Size Of Corporate Staff: 125
On-Going Support: C,D,G,H,I
Training: 3 Days Various Locations.

SPECIFIC EXPANSION PLANS:

US: All United States
Canada: All Canada
Overseas: All Countries

<< >>

JENNY CRAIG WEIGHT AND MANAGEMENT LOSS CENTRES

5770 Fleet St.
Carlsbad, CA 92008
Tel: (888) 848-8885 (760) 696-4000
Fax: (760) 696-4708
E-Mail: franchising@jennycraig.com
Web Site: www.jennycraig.com/franchise
Mr. Victor DeSio, Dir. Franchise Development

We change lives! JENNY CRAIG provides dynamic, safe and effective weight loss and lasting management solutions, tailored to individuals who desire to look better, feel better and live healthier. The JENNY CRAIG program is a long-term solution that helps clients lose weight, create a healthy relationship with food, build an active lifestyle and develop a balanced approach to living.

BACKGROUND: IFA MEMBER
Established: 1983; 1st Franchised: 1987
Franchised Units: 95
Company-Owned Units: 548
Total Units: 643
Dist.: US-490; CAN-32; O'seas-121
North America: 46 States, 3 Provinces
Density: NR
Projected New Units (12 Months): 20
Qualifications: 5, 5, 4, 4, 5, 5
Registered: All States

FINANCIAL/TERMS:
Cash Investment: $50-150K
Total Investment: $122.6-301.5K
Minimum Net Worth: $300K
Fees: Franchise - $25K
Royalty - 7%; Ad. - 0-10%
Earnings Claims Statement: Yes
Term of Contract (Years): 10/10
Avg. # Of Employees: 4 FT
Passive Ownership: Discouraged
Encourage Conversions: NA
Area Develop. Agreements: Yes/Varies
Sub-Franchising Contracts: No
Expand In Territory: Yes
Space Needs: 1,200-1,500 SF; SC

SUPPORT & TRAINING:
Financial Assistance Provided: No
Site Selection Assistance: Yes
Lease Negotiation Assistance: Yes
Co-Operative Advertising: NA
Franchisee Assoc./Member: No
Size Of Corporate Staff: 250
On-Going Support: A,B,C,D,E,F,H,I
Training: 2-3 Weeks Corporate Office; 2 Weeks In-Centre.

SPECIFIC EXPANSION PLANS:
US: All United States
Canada: All Canada
Overseas: No

<< >>

L A WEIGHT LOSS CENTERS
747 Dresher Rd., # 150
Horsham, PA 19044-2247
Tel: (888) 258-7099 (215) 346-8762
Fax: (215) 346-8810
E-Mail: tbritt@laweightloss.com
Web Site: www.laweightloss.com
Mr. Tim Britt, VP Franchise Development

L A WEIGHT LOSS CENTERS combine personalized meal plans, using everyday foods, with professional one-on-one counseling and a line of proprietary products to create one of the hottest new business opportunities. This center-based weight loss program features the industry's leading marketing, training and operations systems.

BACKGROUND: IFA MEMBER
Established: 1989; 1st Franchised: 1998
Franchised Units: 340
Company-Owned Units: 340
Total Units: 680
Dist.: US-652; CAN-25; O'seas-3
North America: 48 States
Density: 58 in NY, 51 in PA, 38 in FL
Projected New Units (12 Months): 150
Qualifications: 3, 5, 1, 3, 3, 4
Registered: All States Except VA

FINANCIAL/TERMS:
Cash Investment: $65-117K
Total Investment: $65-117K
Minimum Net Worth: $200K
Fees: Franchise - $20K
Royalty - 7%; Ad. - NR
Earnings Claims Statement: No
Term of Contract (Years): 10/10
Avg. # Of Employees: 5 FT
Passive Ownership: Not Allowed
Encourage Conversions: NA
Area Develop. Agreements: Yes/10
Sub-Franchising Contracts: No
Expand In Territory: Yes
Space Needs: 1,200 SF; SC

SUPPORT & TRAINING:
Financial Assistance Provided: Yes(I)
Site Selection Assistance: Yes
Lease Negotiation Assistance: Yes
Co-Operative Advertising: NA
Franchisee Assoc./Member: No
Size Of Corporate Staff: 1,460
On-Going Support: A,B,C,D,E,G,H,I
Training: 1 Week Corporate Headquarters; 2 Wks. Center; 2 Wks. Classroom.

SPECIFIC EXPANSION PLANS:
US: Specific Cities Only
Canada: Montreal, Halifax, Prince Ed. Isl.
Overseas: S. America, Mexico, W. Europe, UK, Australia, New Zealand

<< >>

LADY OF AMERICA
500 E. Broward Blvd., # 1650
Ft. Lauderdale, FL 33394-3000
Tel: (800) 833-5239 (954) 527-5373
Fax: (954) 527-5436
E-Mail: wlandman@ladyofamerica.com
Web Site: www.ladyofamerica.com
Mr. Bill Landman, VP Franchising

Ladies-only health club, specializing in aerobics, weight training, personal training and the sales of related products and services.

BACKGROUND:
Established: 1984; 1st Franchised: 1985
Franchised Units: 280
Company-Owned Units: 0
Total Units: 280
Dist.: US-145; CAN-0; O'seas-0
North America: 25 States, 4 Countries
Density: 46 in FL, 25 in TX, 15 in PA
Projected New Units (12 Months): 25
Qualifications: 5, 4, 1, 3, 4, 4
Registered: CA,FL,NY

FINANCIAL/TERMS:
Cash Investment: $20-30K
Total Investment: $40-75K
Minimum Net Worth: $50K
Fees: Franchise - $12.5K
Royalty - 10%; Ad. - 0%
Earnings Claims Statement: No
Term of Contract (Years): 10/5
Avg. # Of Employees: 2 FT, 6 PT
Passive Ownership: Allowed
Encourage Conversions: Yes
Area Develop. Agreements: Yes/10
Sub-Franchising Contracts: Yes
Expand In Territory: Yes
Space Needs: 4,500 SF; SC

SUPPORT & TRAINING:
Financial Assistance Provided: Yes
Site Selection Assistance: Yes
Lease Negotiation Assistance: Yes
Co-Operative Advertising: Yes
Franchisee Assoc./Member: Yes/No
Size Of Corporate Staff: 25
On-Going Support: A,B,C,D,E,F,G,H,I
Training: 2-3 Weeks On-Site; 1-2 Weeks at Corporate Headquarters.

SPECIFIC EXPANSION PLANS:
US: All United States
Canada: All Canada
Overseas: All Countries

<< >>

MERLE NORMAN COSMETICS

9130 Bellanca Ave.
Los Angeles, CA 90045-4710
Tel: (800) 421-6648 (310) 641-3000
Fax: (310) 337-2370
E-Mail: claporta@merlenorman.com
Web Site: www.merlenorman.com
Ms. Carol LaPorta, VP Studio Development

MERLE NORMAN COSMETICS is a specialty retail store, selling scientifically developed, state-of-the-art cosmetic products, using the 'free make over' and 'try before you buy' complete customer satisfaction methods of selling.

BACKGROUND: IFA MEMBER
Established: 1931; 1st Franchised: 1989
Franchised Units: 1,899
Company-Owned Units: 9
Total Units: 1,908
Dist.: US-1,802; CAN-90; O'seas-16
North America: 50 States, 1 Province
Density: 256 in TX, 100 in GA, 95 AL
Projected New Units (12 Months): 88
Qualifications: 3, 4, 3, 3, 4, 4
Registered: All States

FINANCIAL/TERMS:
Cash Investment: NR
Total Investment: NR
Minimum Net Worth: NR
Fees: Franchise - $0
Royalty - 0%; Ad. - 0%
Earnings Claims Statement: Yes
Term of Contract (Years): Unlimited
Avg. # Of Employees: 2 FT, 2-5 PT
Passive Ownership: Discouraged
Encourage Conversions: No
Area Develop. Agreements: No
Sub-Franchising Contracts: No
Expand In Territory: Yes
Space Needs: 450-800 SF; SC, RM

SUPPORT & TRAINING:
Financial Assistance Provided: Yes(I)
Site Selection Assistance: Yes
Lease Negotiation Assistance: Yes
Co-Operative Advertising: Yes
Franchisee Assoc./Member: No
Size Of Corporate Staff: 630
On-Going Support: a,B,C,D,E,F,G,H,I
Training: 2 Weeks Los Angeles, CA.

SPECIFIC EXPANSION PLANS:
US: All United States
Canada: All Canada
Overseas: No

<< >>

PALM BEACH TAN

13800 Senlac Dr.
Framers Branch, TX 75234
Tel: (888) 725-6826 (972) 406-2400 + 1017
Fax: (972) 406-2417
E-Mail: franchise@palmbeachtan.com
Web Site: www.palmbeachtan.com
Mr. Deno Scoular, Director Franchise Sales

PALM BEACH TAN sells UV-free tanning equipment and skincare products to independently operated tanning salons, tanning services and skincare products directly to consumers and tanning salon franchises to independent operating companies.

BACKGROUND: IFA MEMBER
Established: 1990; 1st Franchised: 2002
Franchised Units: 10
Company-Owned Units: 30
Total Units: 40
Dist.: US-40; CAN-0; O'seas-0
North America: 5 States
Density: 32 in TX, 4 in NC, 2 in MD
Projected New Units (12 Months): NR
Qualifications: 5, 5, 2, 2, 2, 5
Registered: All States

FINANCIAL/TERMS:
Cash Investment: $500K
Total Investment: $345-612K
Minimum Net Worth: $1MM
Fees: Franchise - $25K
Royalty - 2%/4%/6%; Ad. - 5%
Earnings Claims Statement: Yes
Term of Contract (Years): 10/10
Avg. # Of Employees: 6 FT, 6 PT
Passive Ownership: Allowed
Encourage Conversions: No
Area Develop. Agreements: Yes/Varies
Sub-Franchising Contracts: No
Expand In Territory: Yes
Space Needs: 3,200 SF; SC

SUPPORT & TRAINING:
Financial Assistance Provided: No
Site Selection Assistance: Yes
Lease Negotiation Assistance: No
Co-Operative Advertising: No
Franchisee Assoc./Member: No
Size Of Corporate Staff: 7
On-Going Support: A,B,C,D,E,F,G,H
Training: 3 Days Franchisee Organization Dallas, TX; 4 Weeks Operator Trianing Dallas, TX.

SPECIFIC EXPANSION PLANS:
US: All United States
Canada: No
Overseas: No

<< >>

PEARLE VISION

1925 Enterprise Pkwy.
Twinsburg, OH 44087
Tel: (800) 282-3931 + 3310 (330) 486-4000 + 3310
Fax: (330) 486-3425
E-Mail: opportunities@pearlevision.com
Web Site: www.pearlevision.com
Mr. Bill Vaughan, Director Franchise Development

PEARLE VISION, the largest optical franchisor, offers the ability for qualified individuals to benefit from PEARLE's strong name recognition and operating systems developed over the past 36 years. We have been franchising for 16 years.

BACKGROUND: IFA MEMBER
Established: 1961; 1st Franchised: 1980
Franchised Units: 450
Company-Owned Units: 370
Total Units: 820
Dist.: US-637; CAN-18; O'seas-36
North America: 43 States, 2 Provinces
Density: 65 in PA, 53 in IL, 49 in TX
Projected New Units (12 Months): 45
Qualifications: 5, 4, 5, 3, 2, 4
Registered: CA,FL,HI,IL,IN,MD,MI,MN, NY,ND,OR,RI,SD,VA,WI,DC

FINANCIAL/TERMS:
Cash Investment: $110K Max.
Total Investment: $135K-2.5MM
Minimum Net Worth: Varies
Fees: Franchise - $30K
Royalty - 7%; Ad. - 9%
Earnings Claims Statement: No
Term of Contract (Years): 10/10
Avg. # Of Employees: Varies
Passive Ownership: Not Allowed
Encourage Conversions: Yes
Area Develop. Agreements: No
Sub-Franchising Contracts: No
Expand In Territory: Yes
Space Needs: 2,000-2,500 SF; FS, SC, RM

SUPPORT & TRAINING:
Financial Assistance Provided: Yes(B)
Site Selection Assistance: NR
Lease Negotiation Assistance: No
Co-Operative Advertising: No
Franchisee Assoc./Member: Yes
Size Of Corporate Staff: 250

On-Going Support: a,B,C,D,d,E,F,G,H,I
Training: Varies Dramatically with Skill Assessment of Franchisee.
SPECIFIC EXPANSION PLANS:
US: All U.S. Except CA, WA
Canada: No
Overseas: No

<< >>

PHYSICIANS WEIGHT LOSS CENTERS OF AMERICA

395 Springside Dr.
Akron, OH 44333-2496
Tel: (800) 205-7887 (330) 666-7952
Fax: (330) 666-2197
E-Mail: kmccollins@hmgmail.com
Web Site: www.pwlc.com
Ms. C. Krishna McCollins, Franchise Development

Supervised weight reduction business, offering the customer a comprehensive program, utilizing individual treatment, personal care, counseling and weight management.

BACKGROUND:
Established: 1979; 1st Franchised: 1980
Franchised Units: 58
Company-Owned Units: 2
Total Units: 60
Dist.: US-56; CAN-0; O'seas-0
North America: 12 States
Density: 20 in OH, 10 in SC, 4 in NC
Projected New Units (12 Months): 10
Qualifications: 5, 4, 3, 3, , 5
Registered: All States Except CA,HI,NY
FINANCIAL/TERMS:
Cash Investment: $21-52.1K
Total Investment: $38-70K
Minimum Net Worth: $100K
Fees: Franchise - $20K
Royalty - 5.5%/$115/Wk.; Ad. - 7%/$600/Wk.
Earnings Claims Statement: No
Term of Contract (Years): 5/5/5
Avg. # Of Employees: 2 FT, 2 PT
Passive Ownership: Not Allowed
Encourage Conversions: Yes
Area Develop. Agreements: No
Sub-Franchising Contracts: No
Expand In Territory: Yes
Space Needs: 1,200 SF; SC
SUPPORT & TRAINING:
Financial Assistance Provided: No
Site Selection Assistance: Yes
Lease Negotiation Assistance: Yes
Co-Operative Advertising: Yes
Franchisee Assoc./Member: No
Size Of Corporate Staff: 45
On-Going Support: A,B,c,d,E,G,H,I
Training: 3 Weeks Akron, OH; 1-3 Days On-Site.
SPECIFIC EXPANSION PLANS:
US: All United States
Canada: No
Overseas: No

<< >>

PLANET BEACH

5161 Taravella Rd.
Marrero, LA 70072
Tel: (888) 290-8266 (504) 361-5550
Fax: (504) 361-5540
E-Mail: franchiselead@planetbeach.com
Web Site: www.planetbeach.com
Ms. Laura Lott, Franchise Advertising Manager

For the benefit of our customers and the communities we serve, we will remain dedicated to the continued success of each PLANET BEACH franchise. Our salons provide superior customer service with an alternative, exciting atmosphere. PLANET BEACH will focus solely on the service of tanning and the sale of retail products that enhance the taning experience.

BACKGROUND: IFA MEMBER
Established: 1995; 1st Franchised: 1996
Franchised Units: 251
Company-Owned Units: 0
Total Units: 251
Dist.: US-232; CAN-18; O'seas-1
North America: 31 States
Density: 52 in LA, 29 in TX, 21 in CA
Projected New Units (12 Months): NR
Qualifications: , , , , ,
Registered:
FINANCIAL/TERMS:
Cash Investment: $100K
Total Investment: $213-370K
Minimum Net Worth: $225K
Fees: Franchise - $30K
Royalty - 6%; Ad. - 1%
Earnings Claims Statement: Yes
Term of Contract (Years): 10/5
Avg. # Of Employees: 1 FT, 2 PT
Passive Ownership: Discouraged
Encourage Conversions: NR
Area Develop. Agreements: Yes/10
Sub-Franchising Contracts: Yes
Expand In Territory: Yes
Space Needs: 1,000-1,500 SF; FS, SC
SUPPORT & TRAINING:
Financial Assistance Provided: NR
Site Selection Assistance: Yes
Lease Negotiation Assistance: Yes
Co-Operative Advertising: Yes
Franchisee Assoc./Member: Yes/No
Size Of Corporate Staff: 65
On-Going Support: A,B,C,d,G,h,I
Training: NR
SPECIFIC EXPANSION PLANS:
US: All United States
Canada: NR
Overseas: NR

<< >>

RIGHT AT HOME

11949 Q St., # 100
Omaha, NE 68137
Tel: (877) 697-7537 (402) 697-7537
Fax: (402) 697-0289
E-Mail: kristin@rightathome.net
Web Site: www.rightathome.net
Ms. Kristi Jelinek, Franchise Sales Coordinator

RIGHT AT HOME offers one of the most exciting opportunities in franchising today. RIGHT AT HOME offers in-home senior care and supplemental staffing for the healthcare industry. You double your opportunity with the same franchise system.

BACKGROUND: IFA MEMBER
Established: 1995; 1st Franchised: 2000
Franchised Units: 60
Company-Owned Units: 1
Total Units: 61
Dist.: US-61; CAN-0; O'seas-0
North America: 29 States
Density: NR
Projected New Units (12 Months): 40
Qualifications: 3, 4, 1, 1, 1, 5
Registered: All States Except RI, HI, AB
FINANCIAL/TERMS:
Cash Investment: $29.3-63.2K
Total Investment: $29.3-63.2K
Minimum Net Worth: NR
Fees: Franchise - $17.8K
Royalty - 5%; Ad. - 0%
Earnings Claims Statement: No
Term of Contract (Years): 10/5/5
Avg. # Of Employees: NR
Passive Ownership: Discouraged

Encourage Conversions: No
Area Develop. Agreements: Yes/10
Sub-Franchising Contracts: No
Expand In Territory: Yes
Space Needs: 700 SF; FS

SUPPORT & TRAINING:
Financial Assistance Provided: No
Site Selection Assistance: Yes
Lease Negotiation Assistance: No
Co-Operative Advertising: No
Franchisee Assoc./Member: No
Size Of Corporate Staff: 9
On-Going Support: C,D,G,H,I
Training: 2 Weeks Omaha, NE.

SPECIFIC EXPANSION PLANS:
US: All United States
Canada: No
Overseas: No

<< >>

SANGSTER'S HEALTH CENTRES
2218 Hanselman Ave.
Saskatoon, SK S7L 6A4 CANADA
Tel: (306) 653-4481
Fax: (306) 653-4688
E-Mail: franchise@sangsters.com
Web Site: www.sangsters.com
Ms. Wendy Sangster, VP Franchising

Health and well being are part of today's lifestyle with an enormous demand for vitamins, minerals, sports nutrition, body care and aromatherapy. SANGSTER'S HEALTH CENTRES has over 30 years of market experience and aggressive growth both in Canada and internationally. SANGSTER'S has received many awards including the CFA's 2001 Marketing Award. SANGSTER'S complete franchise system includes: Exclusive Private Label Supplements, extensive training, on-going support, and national advertising.

BACKGROUND:
Established: 1971; 1st Franchised: 1978
Franchised Units: 44
Company-Owned Units: 4
Total Units: 48
Dist.: US-0; CAN-48; O'seas-0
North America: 7 Provinces
Density: 14 in SK, 11 in ON, 8 in AB
Projected New Units (12 Months): 8
Qualifications: 3, 3, 4, 2, 3, 4
Registered: AB

FINANCIAL/TERMS:
Cash Investment: $30-50K
Total Investment: $50-165K
Minimum Net Worth: $50K
Fees: Franchise - $25K
Royalty - 5%; Ad. - 2%
Earnings Claims Statement: No
Term of Contract (Years): 5/2-5
Avg. # Of Employees: 2 FT, 1 PT
Passive Ownership: Discouraged
Encourage Conversions: Yes
Area Develop. Agreements: No
Sub-Franchising Contracts: No
Expand In Territory: Yes
Space Needs: 600-1,000 SF; SC, RM

SUPPORT & TRAINING:
Financial Assistance Provided: Yes(D)
Site Selection Assistance: Yes
Lease Negotiation Assistance: Yes
Co-Operative Advertising: Yes
Franchisee Assoc./Member: Yes
Size Of Corporate Staff: 13
On-Going Support: B,C,D,E,F,G,H
Training: 2 Weeks in Saskatoon, SK; Minimum of 1 Week at Franchisee Location.

SPECIFIC EXPANSION PLANS:
US: All United States
Canada: All Canada
Overseas: Europe, Asia

<< >>

SONA MEDSPA INTERNATIONAL
840 Crescent Centre Ct., # 260
Franklin, TN 37067
Tel: (615) 591-5040
Fax: (615) 591-5041
E-Mail: kboughnou@sonainternational.com
Web Site: www.sonamedspa.com
Ms. Karen Boughnou, Executive Director of Sales

SONA MEDSPA is the premier med-spa franchise in the US. SONA MEDSPA combines state-of-the-art technology with SONA'S patent-pending process called the 'SONA Concept,' which allows laser hair removal and other anti-aging services to be performed in less time, with better results and at fees that are affordable to the general public. All this, offered in an up-scale, spa-like atmosphere.

BACKGROUND: IFA MEMBER
Established: 1997; 1st Franchised: 2002
Franchised Units: 25
Company-Owned Units: 4
Total Units: 29
Dist.: US-29; CAN-0; O'seas-0
North America: 17 States
Density: 3 in VA, 2 in NC, 2 in MN
Projected New Units (12 Months): 55
Qualifications: 5, 5, 2, 2, 4, 5
Registered: All States Except HI and ND

FINANCIAL/TERMS:
Cash Investment: $150K
Total Investment: $382-748KK
Minimum Net Worth: $750K
Fees: Franchise - $59.5K Std.
Royalty - 10.75%; Ad. - 2%
Earnings Claims Statement: Yes
Term of Contract (Years): 15/15
Avg. # Of Employees: 5 FT, 5 PT
Passive Ownership: Not Allowed
Encourage Conversions: Yes
Area Develop. Agreements: Yes
Sub-Franchising Contracts: No
Expand In Territory: Yes
Space Needs:3,500-4,200 SF; Class A Off. Bldg.

SUPPORT & TRAINING:
Financial Assistance Provided: Yes
Site Selection Assistance: Yes
Lease Negotiation Assistance: Yes
Co-Operative Advertising: Yes
Franchisee Assoc./Member: Yes/Yes
Size Of Corporate Staff: 24
On-Going Support: B,C,D,E,G,H,I
Training: 4 Days Corporate Office; 6 Days Laser Center; 6 Days On-Site.

SPECIFIC EXPANSION PLANS:
US: All United States
Canada: All Canada
Overseas: All Countries

<< >>

SUNBANQUE ISLAND TANNING
2533A Yonge St.
Toronto, ON M4P 2H9 CANADA
Tel: (416) 488-5838
Fax: (416) 488-3712
E-Mail: sunbanq@interlog.com
Web Site: www.worldfranchising.com/website.htm
Mr. Joel Giusto, Chairman

SUNBANQUE ISLAND TANNING is a full-service suntan salon with complete and exclusive inventory control and management.

BACKGROUND:
Established: 1983; 1st Franchised: 1984
Franchised Units: 11
Company-Owned Units: 4

Total Units: 15
Dist.: US-7; CAN-8; O'seas-0
North America: 1 State, 1 Province
Density: 8 in ON, 7 in MA
Projected New Units (12 Months): 10
Qualifications: , , , , ,
Registered: NR

FINANCIAL/TERMS:
Cash Investment: $10-20K
Total Investment: $30-40K
Minimum Net Worth: NR
Fees: Franchise - $5K
Royalty - 3%; Ad. - 5%
Earnings Claims Statement: Yes
Term of Contract (Years): 5/5
Avg. # Of Employees: 2 FT, 1 PT
Passive Ownership: Discouraged
Encourage Conversions: Yes
Area Develop. Agreements: Yes/5
Sub-Franchising Contracts: Yes
Expand In Territory: Yes
Space Needs: 1,000 SF; FS, SF

SUPPORT & TRAINING:
Financial Assistance Provided: Yes(D)
Site Selection Assistance: Yes
Lease Negotiation Assistance: Yes
Co-Operative Advertising: Yes
Franchisee Assoc./Member: NR
Size Of Corporate Staff: 5
On-Going Support: A,B,C,D,E,F,G,H
Training: 1-2 Weeks Headquarters.

SPECIFIC EXPANSION PLANS:
US: All United States
Canada: All Canada
Overseas: All Countries

<< >>

TROPI-TAN FRANCHISING

5152 Commerce Rd.
Flint, MI 48507
Tel: (866) 818-1826 (810) 230-6789
Fax: (810) 230-1115
E-Mail: franchises@tropitan.biz
Web Site: www.tropitan.biz
Mr. Vince Lorraine, President

In business for 20 years, TROPI-TAN indoor sun-tanning salons are international design and decor award winners. One of the most progressive salon chains, TROPI-TAN salons also feature a full line of tanning lotions, clothing, and related accessories.

BACKGROUND: IFA MEMBER
Established: 1979; 1st Franchised: 1985
Franchised Units: 3
Company-Owned Units: 9
Total Units: 12
Dist.: US-12; CAN-0; O'seas-0
North America: 1 State
Density: 12 in MI
Projected New Units (12 Months): 25
Qualifications: 3, 3, 1, 3, 3, 5
Registered: MI

FINANCIAL/TERMS:
Cash Investment: $50-100K
Total Investment: $175-250K
Minimum Net Worth: $150K
Fees: Franchise - $20K
Royalty - 5%; Ad. - 3%
Earnings Claims Statement: No
Term of Contract (Years): 10/5
Avg. # Of Employees: 1 FT, 3 PT
Passive Ownership: Discouraged
Encourage Conversions: Yes
Area Develop. Agreements: Yes/5
Sub-Franchising Contracts: No
Expand In Territory: Yes
Space Needs: 2,500 SF; FS, SC

SUPPORT & TRAINING:
Financial Assistance Provided: Yes(I)
Site Selection Assistance: Yes
Lease Negotiation Assistance: Yes
Co-Operative Advertising: Yes
Franchisee Assoc./Member: No
Size Of Corporate Staff: 30
On-Going Support: A,B,C,D,E,F,G,H,I
Training: 80 Hours at Corporate Training Center; 40 Hours On-Site.

SPECIFIC EXPANSION PLANS:
US: All United States
Canada: All Canada
Overseas: All Countries

<< >>

For a full explanation of the data provided in the Franchisor Profiles, please refer to *Chapter 2, "How to Use the Data."*

Laundry & Dry Cleaning

Chapter 21

Laundry & Dry Cleaning Industry Profile

Total # Franchisors in Industry Group	19
Total # Franchised Units in Industry Group	2,221
Total # Company-Owned Units in Industry Group	30
Total # Operating Units in Industry Group	2,251
Average # Franchised Units/Franchisor	116.9
Average # Company-Owned Units/Franchisor	1.6
Average # Total Units/Franchisor	118.5
Ratio of Total # Franchised Units/Total # Company-Owned Units	74:1
Industry Survey Participants	10
Representing % of Industry	52.6%
Average Franchise Fee*:	$23K
Average Total Investment*:	$273.9K
Average On-Going Royalty Fee*:	4.5%

*If a range was provided, the mid-point of the range was used. See detailed profiles for actual ranges.

Five Largest Participants in Survey

Company	# Franchised Units	# Co-Owned Units	# Total Units	Franchise Fee	On-Going Royalty	Total Investment
1. Martinizing Dry Cleaning	642	0	642	$30K	4%	$250-396K
2. Comet One-Hour Cleaners	330	11	341	$25K	0%	$200-400K
3. Pressed 4 Time	180	0	180	$12.5K	6%	$15.2-22.3K
4. Eagle Cleaners	95	1	96	$15K	5%/$195	$200-250K
5. 1-800-DryClean	84	0	84	$9.9K	7%	$53-143K

All of the data provided are proprietary and should not be quoted without acknowledging *Bond's Franchise Guide.*

1-800-DRYCLEAN

3948 Ranchero Dr.
Ann Arbor, MI 48108-2775
Tel: (866) 822-6115 (734) 822-6340
Fax: (734) 822-6888
E-Mail: t.burns@1-800-dryclean.com
Web Site: www.1-800-dryclean.com
Ms. Terry Burns,

The $10 billion dry cleaning industry creates tremendous potential for 1-800-DRYCLEAN when combined with the need of busy consumers looking for convenience. Our convenient, hassle-free dry cleaning pick-up and delivery system provides consumers exceptional dry cleaning and laundry service. Business formats include the single van opportunity, the multiple van fleet option and expansion of van opportunities to either the dry cleaning plant or drop store format.

BACKGROUND: IFA MEMBER
Established: 1999; 1st Franchised: 2000
Franchised Units: 84
Company-Owned Units: 0
Total Units: 84
Dist.: US-76; CAN-0; O'seas-0
North America: 23 States
Density: 16 in CA, 5 in IL, 4 in TX
Projected New Units (12 Months): 20
Qualifications: 5, 3, 1, 2, 1, 5
Registered:CA,FL,IL,IN,MD,MI,MN,NY,OR,RI,VA,WA,WI,DC

FINANCIAL/TERMS:
Cash Investment: $30K
Total Investment: $53-143K
Minimum Net Worth: $200K
Fees: Franchise - $9.9K
Royalty - 7%; Ad. - 1%
Earnings Claims Statement: No
Term of Contract (Years): 10/10
Avg. # Of Employees: 5 FT
Passive Ownership: Discouraged
Encourage Conversions: Yes
Area Develop. Agreements: No
Sub-Franchising Contracts: No
Expand In Territory: Yes
Space Needs: 200 SF; HB

SUPPORT & TRAINING:
Financial Assistance Provided: Yes(I)
Site Selection Assistance: Yes
Lease Negotiation Assistance: Yes
Co-Operative Advertising: No
Franchisee Assoc./Member: No
Size Of Corporate Staff: 25
On-Going Support: C,D,E,G,h,I
Training: 5 Days Home Office; 5 Days Franchise Location; 4-6 Weeks Right-Start Program.

SPECIFIC EXPANSION PLANS:
US: All United States
Canada: All Canada
Overseas: No

<< >>

AWC COMMERCIAL WINDOW COVERINGS

825 W. Williamson Wy.
Fullerton, CA 92832
Tel: (800) 252-2280 (714) 879-3880
Fax: (714) 879-8419
E-Mail: jim@awc-cwc.com
Web Site: www.awc-cwc.com
Mr. Jim Cherry, Franchise Director

Mobile non-toxic drapery dry cleaning services provided on location for commercial customers; as well as sales, installation & repairs of all types of window coverings at competitive prices through centralized buying. Nationwide accounts will be serviced by the franchisees as they are established. Utilizing the customer base, references and reputation of the franchisor, developed over the past 37 years makes this an exceptional opportunity with endless possibilities and immediate credibility.

BACKGROUND:
Established: 1963; 1st Franchised: 1992
Franchised Units: 6
Company-Owned Units: 4
Total Units: 10
Dist.: US-14; CAN-0; O'seas-0
North America: 5 States
Density: 6 in CA, 1 in NJ, 1 in DC
Projected New Units (12 Months): 3
Qualifications: 3, 4, 3, 3, 4, 4
Registered: CA,DC,MD

FINANCIAL/TERMS:
Cash Investment: $25-50K
Total Investment: $112.5-181.4K
Minimum Net Worth: NA
Fees: Franchise - $25K
Royalty - 5-12.5%; Ad. - 2.5%
Earnings Claims Statement: No
Term of Contract (Years): 10/10
Avg. # Of Employees: 1 FT, PT As Needed
Passive Ownership: Not Allowed
Encourage Conversions: Yes
Area Develop. Agreements: Yes
Sub-Franchising Contracts: No
Expand In Territory: Yes
Space Needs: NA SF; HB

SUPPORT & TRAINING:
Financial Assistance Provided: Yes(I)
Site Selection Assistance: NA
Lease Negotiation Assistance: Yes
Co-Operative Advertising: Yes
Franchisee Assoc./Member: No
Size Of Corporate Staff: 8
On-Going Support: A,B,C,D,F,h,I
Training: 2 Weeks at Plant and On-Site; On-Going.

SPECIFIC EXPANSION PLANS:
US: All United States
Canada: All Canada
Overseas: All Countries

<< >>

COMET ONE-HOUR CLEANERS

406 W. Division St.
Arlington, TX 76011
Tel: (817) 461-3555
Fax: (817) 861-4779
E-Mail: cometgodfrey@msn.com
Web Site: www.cometcleaners.com
Mr. Jack D. Godfrey, Jr., President

We offer a turn-key opportunity in the laundry and dry-cleaning business. Site evaluation, complete training and installation are just a few of the services that COMET offers. There is a franchise fee of $250 per month required, as opposed to other franchisors that require a percent of your gross income per year.

BACKGROUND:
Established: 1960; 1st Franchised: 1967
Franchised Units: 330
Company-Owned Units: 11
Total Units: 341
Dist.: US-322; CAN-0; O'seas-9
North America: 15 States
Density: 206 in TX, 30 in AR, 17 in N
Projected New Units (12 Months): 20
Qualifications: 4, 4, 1, 3, 3, 4
Registered: CA

FINANCIAL/TERMS:
Cash Investment: $80-100K
Total Investment: $200-400K
Minimum Net Worth: $80K
Fees: Franchise - $25K
Royalty - 0%; Ad. - NA
Earnings Claims Statement: No
Term of Contract (Years): 5/5/5
Avg. # Of Employees: 6 FT, 2-3 PT
Passive Ownership: Discouraged
Encourage Conversions: No
Area Develop. Agreements: No
Sub-Franchising Contracts: No
Expand In Territory: Yes
Space Needs: 1,800-2,000 SF; SC

SUPPORT & TRAINING:
Financial Assistance Provided: Yes(I)

Site Selection Assistance: Yes
Lease Negotiation Assistance: Yes
Co-Operative Advertising: No
Franchisee Assoc./Member: Yes/Yes
Size Of Corporate Staff: 12
On-Going Support: c,d,D,E,G,H,I
Training: 1 Week in Waco, TX; 1 Week in Store.

SPECIFIC EXPANSION PLANS:
US: All United States
Canada: No
Overseas: No

<< >>

Site Selection Assistance: Yes
Lease Negotiation Assistance: Yes
Co-Operative Advertising: Yes
Franchisee Assoc./Member: No
Size Of Corporate Staff: 5
On-Going Support: B,C,D,E,G,H,I
Training: 10-15 Days at a Store and Headquarters.

SPECIFIC EXPANSION PLANS:
US: All United States
Canada: All Canada
Overseas: All Countries

<< >>

Lease Negotiation Assistance: Yes
Co-Operative Advertising: NA
Franchisee Assoc./Member: No
Size Of Corporate Staff: 16
On-Going Support: A,C,D,E,F,G,H,I
Training: 3 Weeks Coral Springs, FL; 1 Week Opening; 90-120 Post-Opening.

SPECIFIC EXPANSION PLANS:
US: East, Midwest
Canada: No
Overseas: Mexico, South America, Latin America

<< >>

DRY CLEANING STATION

8301 Golden Valley Rd., # 230
Minneapolis, MN 55427
Tel: (800) 655-8134 (763) 541-0832
Fax: (763) 542-2246
E-Mail: johnca@franchisemasters.com
Web Site: www.drycleaningstation.com
Mr. John A. Campbell, Chief Executive Officer

A high-quality, lower priced dry cleaner and shirt laundry, offering a special niche in the industry, including environmentally efficient equipment, proprietary unique software/computer systems and attractively designed, high-traffic stores.

BACKGROUND:
Established: 1987; 1st Franchised: 1993
Franchised Units: 48
Company-Owned Units: 0
Total Units: 48
Dist.: US-14; CAN-0; O'seas-0
North America: 7 States
Density: 5 in MN, 4 in NE
Projected New Units (12 Months): 50
Qualifications: 5, 3, 1, 2, 2, 5
Registered: FL,IL,MI,MN

FINANCIAL/TERMS:
Cash Investment: $40-120K
Total Investment: $50-350K
Minimum Net Worth: $250K
Fees: Franchise - $22.5K
Royalty - 2-5%; Ad. - 0%
Earnings Claims Statement: Yes
Term of Contract (Years): 15/2-5
Avg. # Of Employees: 4 FT, 2 PT
Passive Ownership: Discouraged
Encourage Conversions: No
Area Develop. Agreements: Yes/Open
Sub-Franchising Contracts: No
Expand In Territory: Yes
Space Needs: 2,200-4,000 SF; FS, SF, SC

SUPPORT & TRAINING:
Financial Assistance Provided: Yes(I)

EAGLE CLEANERS

1500 University Dr., # 208
Coral Springs, FL 33071
Tel: (800) 275-9751 (954) 346-9501
Fax: (954) 346-9505
E-Mail: G2eagle@aol.com
Web Site: www.worldfranchising.com/website.htm
Mr. Gerard J. Teeven, President

Franchisor of state-of-the-art dry-cleaning stores, offering turn-key plants and drop stores, complete training, site evaluation and a marketing strategy that separates us from the rest of the dry cleaning industry.

BACKGROUND:
Established: 1991; 1st Franchised: 1993
Franchised Units: 95
Company-Owned Units: 1
Total Units: 96
Dist.: US-92; CAN-0; O'seas-0
North America: 16 States
Density: CT, NY, FL
Projected New Units (12 Months): 40
Qualifications: 4, 5, 1, 4, 5, 4
Registered: FL,IL,MI,NY

FINANCIAL/TERMS:
Cash Investment: $75-110K
Total Investment: $200-250K
Minimum Net Worth: $250K
Fees: Franchise - $15K
Royalty - 5%/$195; Ad. - 3%
Earnings Claims Statement: No
Term of Contract (Years): 10/10
Avg. # Of Employees: 3 FT, 1 PT
Passive Ownership: Discouraged
Encourage Conversions: No
Area Develop. Agreements: Yes/10
Sub-Franchising Contracts: Yes
Expand In Territory: Yes
Space Needs: 1,800-2,200 SF; FS, SC

SUPPORT & TRAINING:
Financial Assistance Provided: Yes(I)
Site Selection Assistance: Yes

HANGERS CLEANERS

3505 County Road 42 W.
Burnsville, MN 55306
Tel: (866) 262-9274 (952) 882-5000
Fax: (952) 882-5175
E-Mail: tom.lorenz@hangersamerica.com
Web Site: www.co2olclean.com
Mr. Tom Lorenz, Director of Franchise

Good for you, good for your clothes and good for the environment. The world's first environmentally friendly dry cleaner, HANGERS has locations throughout N. America and is expanding into Europe. The cool odor CO2 cleaning process causes less wear on your customer's garments and provides brighter colors with no chemical smell or residue. Your investment in HANGERS will give you a unique competitive advantage. You will be able to acquire locations traditional dry cleaners are prohibited from.

BACKGROUND:
Established: 2004; 1st Franchised: 2004
Franchised Units: 28
Company-Owned Units: 0
Total Units: 28
Dist.: US-25; CAN-3; O'seas-0
North America: 11 States, 2 Provinces
Density: 6 in NC, 4 in WI
Projected New Units (12 Months): 12
Qualifications: 5, 4, 1, 1, 5, 5
Registered: All States

FINANCIAL/TERMS:
Cash Investment: $100K-1MM
Total Investment: $450,000-2MM
Minimum Net Worth: $1MM
Fees: Franchise - $50K
Royalty - 4%; Ad. - 1%
Earnings Claims Statement: No
Term of Contract (Years): 10/10
Avg. # Of Employees: 6-20 FT
Passive Ownership: Discouraged
Encourage Conversions: Yes

Area Develop. Agreements: Yes/10
Sub-Franchising Contracts: No
Expand In Territory: Yes
Space Needs: 3,500 SF; SC

SUPPORT & TRAINING:
Financial Assistance Provided: No
Site Selection Assistance: Yes
Lease Negotiation Assistance: Yes
Co-Operative Advertising: No
Franchisee Assoc./Member: No
Size Of Corporate Staff: 6
On-Going Support: C,D,e,I
Training: 24 Hours at a Designated Training Facility; 80 Hours at a Designated Training Facility; 96 Hours On-Site.

SPECIFIC EXPANSION PLANS:
US: All United States
Canada: All Canada
Overseas: All Countries

<< >>

LAPELS DRY CLEANING

962 Washington St.
Hanover, MA 02339
Tel: (866) 695-2735 (781) 829-9935
Fax: (781) 829-9546
E-Mail: lhurley@lapelsdrycleaning.com
Web Site: www.lapelsdrycleaning.com
Ms. Laura Hurley, Franchise Administrator

LAPELS is absolutely the best business opportunity available today. We provide you with a complete, turn-key dry cleaning retail store, stocked with supplies and ready to go, as well as full training and on-going support. No experience necessary, all work is processed off-site. No expensive equipment or hazardous chemicals required. The total price of $57,700 includes site location, signage, customer counters, conveyor system, computers, marketing supplies and more.

BACKGROUND:
Established: 2000; 1st Franchised: 2000
Franchised Units: 21
Company-Owned Units: 0
Total Units: 21
Dist.: US-21; CAN-0; O'seas-0
North America: 5 States
Density: 16 in MA, 2 in NH
Projected New Units (12 Months): 37
Qualifications: 3, 2, 1, 1, 3, 3
Registered: CA,FL,NY,RI

FINANCIAL/TERMS:
Cash Investment: NR
Total Investment: $57.7K
Minimum Net Worth: $80K
Fees: Franchise - $20K
Royalty - 5%; Ad. - 0%
Earnings Claims Statement: No
Term of Contract (Years): 10/10
Avg. # Of Employees: 2-3 PT
Passive Ownership: Discouraged
Encourage Conversions: Yes
Area Develop. Agreements: Yes/10
Sub-Franchising Contracts: No
Expand In Territory: Yes
Space Needs: 800-1,000 SF; FS, SF, SC

SUPPORT & TRAINING:
Financial Assistance Provided: Yes(I)
Site Selection Assistance: Yes
Lease Negotiation Assistance: Yes
Co-Operative Advertising: Yes
Franchisee Assoc./Member: Yes/Yes
Size Of Corporate Staff: 6
On-Going Support: A,B,C,D,E,F,G,H,I
Training: 10 Days Massachusetts; 2-4 Days New Location (Franchisee).

SPECIFIC EXPANSION PLANS:
US: All United States
Canada: No
Overseas: No

<< >>

Top 100 **MARTINIZING DRY CLEANING**

422 Wards Corner Rd.
Loveland, OH 45140-6950
Tel: (800) 827-0207 + 365 (513) 351-6211
Fax: (513) 731-0818
E-Mail: cleanup@martinizing.com
Web Site: www.martinizing.com
Mr. Jerald E. Laesser, Vice President

MARTINIZING is the most recognized brand name in dry cleaning. The # 1 Dry Cleaning Franchise: MARTINIZING has been ranked the # 1 dry cleaning franchise 19 out of the last 22 years by Entrepreneur Magazine.

BACKGROUND:
Established: 1949; 1st Franchised: 1949
Franchised Units: 642
Company-Owned Units: 0
Total Units: 642
Dist.: US-389; CAN-19; O'seas-234
North America: 38 States, 3 Provinces
Density: 92 in MI, 67 in CA, 36 in WI
Projected New Units (12 Months): 25
Qualifications: 5, 4, 1, 3, 1, 5
Registered: All States

FINANCIAL/TERMS:
Cash Investment: $110K
Total Investment: $250-396K
Minimum Net Worth: $225K
Fees: Franchise - $30K
Royalty - 4%; Ad. - 0.5%
Earnings Claims Statement: Yes
Term of Contract (Years): 20
Avg. # Of Employees: 2 FT, 4 PT
Passive Ownership: Discouraged
Encourage Conversions: Yes
Area Develop. Agreements: Yes/3-20
Sub-Franchising Contracts: Yes
Expand In Territory: Yes
Space Needs: 1,500-2,000 SF; FS, SC

SUPPORT & TRAINING:
Financial Assistance Provided: Yes(I)
Site Selection Assistance: Yes
Lease Negotiation Assistance: Yes
Co-Operative Advertising: Yes
Franchisee Assoc./Member: Yes/Yes
Size Of Corporate Staff: 16
On-Going Support: C,D,E,G,H,I
Training: 1 Week Classroom; 2 Weeks In-Store.

SPECIFIC EXPANSION PLANS:
US: All United States
Canada: All Except AB,ON
Overseas: Europe, Far and Middle East

<< >>

NU-LOOK 1-HR. CLEANERS

5970 SW 18th St., # 331
Boca Raton, FL 33433-7197
Tel: (800) 413-7881 (561) 362-4190
Fax: (561) 362-4229
E-Mail: marketing@nu-look.com
Web Site: www.nulookcleaners.com
Mr. Karl N. Dickey, President/CEO

Retail dry cleaner.

BACKGROUND:
Established: 1967; 1st Franchised: 1967
Franchised Units: 50
Company-Owned Units: 3
Total Units: 53
Dist.: US-41; CAN-0; O'seas-12
North America: 4 States
Density: 24 in FL, 12 in MD, 10 in VA
Projected New Units (12 Months): 25
Qualifications: 2, 4, 2, 2, 3, 4
Registered: FL,MD,VA

FINANCIAL/TERMS:

Cash Investment:	$45-75K
Total Investment:	$125-200K+
Minimum Net Worth:	$150K
Fees: Franchise -	$20K
Royalty - 2%;	Ad. - 3%
Earnings Claims Statement:	No
Term of Contract (Years):	20/10
Avg. # Of Employees:	2 FT, 2 PT
Passive Ownership:	Discouraged
Encourage Conversions:	Yes
Area Develop. Agreements:	Yes
Sub-Franchising Contracts:	Yes
Expand In Territory:	Yes
Space Needs:	1,200-1,400 SF; FS, SC

SUPPORT & TRAINING:

Financial Assistance Provided:	Yes(I)
Site Selection Assistance:	Yes
Lease Negotiation Assistance:	Yes
Co-Operative Advertising:	Yes
Franchisee Assoc./Member:	No
Size Of Corporate Staff:	4
On-Going Support:	C,D,E,G,H
Training:	4 Weeks Deerfield Beach, FL.

SPECIFIC EXPANSION PLANS:

US:	All United States
Canada:	All Canada
Overseas:	All Countries

PRESSED 4 TIME

124 Boston Post Rd.
Sudbury, MA 01776
Tel: (800) 423-8711 (978) 823-8300
Fax: (978) 443-0709
E-Mail: randy@pressed4time.com
Web Site: www.pressed4time.com
Mr. Randy Erb, Dir. Franchise Development

The nation's first and foremost dry-cleaning/shoe repair, pick-up and delivery franchise. Coast to coast, more than 50,000 customers smile when they see our franchisees. Dry-cleaning and shoe repair are performed by local merchants. Experience in the 7 billion-dollar dry-cleaning industry is not needed. If you like people and can work on your own, then this leading home-based, mobile franchise is probably for you!

BACKGROUND:

Established: 1987;	1st Franchised: 1990
Franchised Units:	180
Company-Owned Units:	0
Total Units:	180
Dist.:	US-107; CAN-4; O'seas-22
North America:	31 States, 2 Provinces
Density:	13 in PA, 7 in OH, 7 in MA
Projected New Units (12 Months):	36
Qualifications:	2, 1, 1, 3, 3, 3

Registered:CA,FL,IL,IN,MD,MI,MN,NY,OR,RI,VA,WA,WI

FINANCIAL/TERMS:

Cash Investment:	$15.2-22.3K
Total Investment:	$15.2-22.3K
Minimum Net Worth:	NA
Fees: Franchise -	$12.5K
Royalty - 6%;	Ad. - 0%
Earnings Claims Statement:	No
Term of Contract (Years):	10/10
Avg. # Of Employees:	1 FT
Passive Ownership:	Not Allowed
Encourage Conversions:	Yes
Area Develop. Agreements:	No
Sub-Franchising Contracts:	No
Expand In Territory:	Yes
Space Needs:	NA SF; HB

SUPPORT & TRAINING:

Financial Assistance Provided:	No
Site Selection Assistance:	Yes
Lease Negotiation Assistance:	NA
Co-Operative Advertising:	NA
Franchisee Assoc./Member:	No
Size Of Corporate Staff:	5
On-Going Support:	a,b,C,D,E,G,H,I
Training:	2 Days Corporate at Sudbury, MA; 2 Days at Franchise; 1 Day at Franchise.

SPECIFIC EXPANSION PLANS:

US:	All United States
Canada:	All Canada
Overseas:	No

<< >>

Lawn & Garden

Chapter 22

Lawn & Garden Industry Profile

Total # Franchisors in Industry Group	23
Total # Franchised Units in Industry Group	3,478
Total # Company-Owned Units in Industry Group	98
Total # Operating Units in Industry Group	3,576
Average # Franchised Units/Franchisor	151.2
Average # Company-Owned Units/Franchisor	4.3
Average # Total Units/Franchisor	155.5
Ratio of Total # Franchised Units/Total # Company-Owned Units	35.5:1
Industry Survey Participants	14
Representing % of Industry	60.9%
Average Franchise Fee*:	$26.4K
Average Total Investment*:	$87.2K
Average On-Going Royalty Fee*:	6.6%

*If a range was provided, the mid-point of the range was used. See detailed profiles for actual ranges.

Five Largest Participants in Survey

Company	# Franchised Units	# Co-Owned Units	# Total Units	Franchise Fee	On-Going Royalty	Total Investment
1. Kwik Kerb	2,000	0	2,000	NA	NA	$5-42K
2. Lawn Doctor	460	0	460	$0	10%	$68-74.9K
3. Weed Man	287	0	287	$20-34K	$8.8K/Vehcl.	$75K
4. U. S. Lawns	135	0	135	$29K	4%	$50-85K
5. Spring-Green Lawn Care	81	21	102	$21.9K	9-6%	$112-155K

All of the data provided are proprietary and should not be quoted without acknowledging *Bond's Franchise Guide.*

BORDER MAGIC

1503 Country Rd., 2700 N.
Rantoul, IL 61866-9705
Tel: (877) 892-2954 (217) 892-2954
Fax: (217) 893-3739
E-Mail: bordermagic@illicom.net
Web Site: www.bordermagic.com
Mr. Sam Thrush, National Sales Representative

Sell and install beautiful, seamless concrete landscape edging that has the look and feel of real brick and stone in your protected territory using the BORDER MAGIC BM 2000 extruder and the BORDER MAGIC proven method. The BM 2000 also extrudes concrete parking lot curbing for schools, restaurants and businesses of all kinds. A turnkey franchise opportunity awaits you as a licensed dealer.

BACKGROUND: IFA MEMBER
Established: 1984; 1st Franchised: 2002
Franchised Units: 81
Company-Owned Units: 0
Total Units: 81
Dist.: US-81; CAN-0; O'seas-0
North America: 24 States
Density: OH, IL, IN
Projected New Units (12 Months): 24
Qualifications: 3, 2, 2, 1, 2, 3
Registered: All States

FINANCIAL/TERMS:
Cash Investment: $7K
Total Investment: $42-65K
Minimum Net Worth: NA
Fees: Franchise - $5K
Royalty - $250/Mo.; Ad. - NA
Earnings Claims Statement: Yes
Term of Contract (Years): 5/5/5
Avg. # Of Employees: 3 FT
Passive Ownership: Allowed
Encourage Conversions: NA
Area Develop. Agreements: No
Sub-Franchising Contracts: No
Expand In Territory: Yes
Space Needs: NA SF; HB

SUPPORT & TRAINING:
Financial Assistance Provided: Yes(I)
Site Selection Assistance: NA
Lease Negotiation Assistance: NA
Co-Operative Advertising: Yes
Franchisee Assoc./Member: No
Size Of Corporate Staff: 7
On-Going Support: A,B,C,F,G,H,I
Training: 3 Days Rantoul, IL.

SPECIFIC EXPANSION PLANS:
US: All United States
Canada: NR
Overseas: NR

<< >>

CLINTAR GROUNDSKEEPING SERVICES

70 Esna Park Dr., # 1
Markham, ON L3R 1E3 CANADA
Tel: (800) 361-3542 (905) 943-9530
Fax: (905) 943-9529
E-Mail: rwilton@clintar.com
Web Site: www.clintar.com
Mr. Robert C. Wilton, President

Company provides a full-service, year-round grounds care service to Fortune 500 clients and government agencies. The average size business is $1,000,000. It provides landscape maintenance services, power sweeping, and snow and ice control services.

BACKGROUND:
Established: 1973; 1st Franchised: 1984
Franchised Units: 11
Company-Owned Units: 1
Total Units: 12
Dist.: US-0; CAN-9; O'seas-0
North America: 1 Province
Density: 9 in ON
Projected New Units (12 Months): 2
Qualifications: 4, 5, 2, 3, 4, 5
Registered: NR

FINANCIAL/TERMS:
Cash Investment: $50-75K
Total Investment: $90-150K
Minimum Net Worth: $100K
Fees: Franchise - $30K
Royalty - 8%; Ad. - 0%
Earnings Claims Statement: No
Term of Contract (Years): 10/5
Avg. # Of Employees: 10 FT, 15 PT
Passive Ownership: Not Allowed
Encourage Conversions: Yes
Area Develop. Agreements: Yes
Sub-Franchising Contracts: No
Expand In Territory: Yes
Space Needs: 3,000 SF; FS, Multi-Unit Industrial

SUPPORT & TRAINING:
Financial Assistance Provided: Yes(I)
Site Selection Assistance: Yes
Lease Negotiation Assistance: Yes
Co-Operative Advertising: Yes
Franchisee Assoc./Member: Yes/Yes
Size Of Corporate Staff: 9
On-Going Support: a,B,C,D,E,F,H,I
Training: 2 Weeks in Toronto, ON.

SPECIFIC EXPANSION PLANS:
US: Northwest (Great Lakes Area)
Canada: All Canada
Overseas: No

<< >>

ENVIRO MASTERS LAWN CARE

P. O. Box 178
Caledon East, ON L0N 1E0 CANADA
Tel: (905) 584-9592
Fax: (905) 584-0402
E-Mail: martin@enviromasters.com
Web Site: www.enviromasters.com
Mr. Martin Fielding, President

Enjoy the Great Outdoors! and be part of a great new approach to lawn care. Organic and environmentally considerate. Home based. Excellent opportunity. Protected territories. Repeat business. Full training and marketing support. Business, turf management and in-field training.

BACKGROUND:
Established: 1987; 1st Franchised: 1991
Franchised Units: 43
Company-Owned Units: 2
Total Units: 45
Dist.: US-0; CAN-45; O'seas-0
North America: NR
Density: NR
Projected New Units (12 Months): 6
Qualifications: 3, 2, 1, 2, 3, 3
Registered: NR

FINANCIAL/TERMS:
Cash Investment: $30-40K
Total Investment: $30-50K
Minimum Net Worth: $25K
Fees: Franchise - $20-30K
Royalty - 5%/$2.5K; Ad. - 2%
Earnings Claims Statement: No
Term of Contract (Years): 10/10
Avg. # Of Employees: 1 FT, 1 PT
Passive Ownership: Discouraged
Encourage Conversions: Yes
Area Develop. Agreements: Yes - US
Sub-Franchising Contracts: Yes
Expand In Territory: No
Space Needs: NR SF; HB

SUPPORT & TRAINING:
Financial Assistance Provided: Yes(D)
Site Selection Assistance: Yes
Lease Negotiation Assistance: NA
Co-Operative Advertising: Yes
Franchisee Assoc./Member: No

Size Of Corporate Staff: 4
On-Going Support: B,C,D,E,F,G,H,I
Training: 1-2 Weeks in Caledon East, ON.
SPECIFIC EXPANSION PLANS:
US: No
Canada: All Canada
Overseas: All Countries

<< >>

GREENLAND IRRIGATION

150 Ambleside Dr.
London, ON N6G 4R1 CANADA
Tel: (800) 661-0221 (519) 439-0220
Fax: (519) 433-9780
E-Mail: barrysmith@greenlandirrigation.com
Web Site: www.greenlandirrigation.com
Mr. Barry Smith, Vice President/Franchising

Installation and service for lawn sprinklers' commercial and residential application. Complete training for TORO, Hunter, Rainbird and Nelson equipment. A niche market with tremendous opportunities.

BACKGROUND:
Established: 1986; 1st Franchised: 1995
Franchised Units: 12
Company-Owned Units: 2
Total Units: 14
Dist.: US-0; CAN-14; O'seas-0
North America: 2 Provinces
Density: NR
Projected New Units (12 Months): 5
Qualifications: 4, 4, 2, 4, 4, 4
Registered: NR
FINANCIAL/TERMS:
Cash Investment: $25K
Total Investment: $25-50K
Minimum Net Worth: $100K
Fees: Franchise - $10K
Royalty - 10-3%; Ad. - 0%
Earnings Claims Statement: No
Term of Contract (Years): Lifetime
Avg. # Of Employees: 4 FT
Passive Ownership: Not Allowed
Encourage Conversions: No
Area Develop. Agreements: No
Sub-Franchising Contracts: No
Expand In Territory: Yes
Space Needs: NA SF; HB
SUPPORT & TRAINING:
Financial Assistance Provided: Yes(I)
Site Selection Assistance: Yes
Lease Negotiation Assistance: NA
Co-Operative Advertising: Yes
Franchisee Assoc./Member: No
Size Of Corporate Staff: 5
On-Going Support: A,B,C,D,E,G,H,I
Training: NR
SPECIFIC EXPANSION PLANS:
US: All United States
Canada: All Canada
Overseas: No

<< >>

KWIK KERB

100 Technology Park, # 160
Lake Mary, FL 32746
Tel: (866) 459-4553 (321) 257-2002
Fax: (321) 257-2004
E-Mail: kkinfo@kwikkerb.com
Web Site: www.kwikkerb.com
Mr. Gordon Buckland, Sales Manager

KWIK KERB concrete curbing machines and business system. This is a franchise-style business in machine-laid concrete curbing with amazing profits. We have developed an excellent business system to ensure that your entry into the exciting world of concrete curbing is fast and successful. The landscape edging business is now growing at an extraordinary rate and you can be part of it as thousands have already!

BACKGROUND:
Established: 1987; 1st Franchised: 1987
Franchised Units: 2,000
Company-Owned Units: 0
Total Units: 2,000
Dist.: US-1,000; CAN-0; O'seas-1,000
North America: NR
Density: NR
Projected New Units (12 Months): 500
Qualifications: 3, 3, 1, 3, 3, 3
Registered: NR
FINANCIAL/TERMS:
Cash Investment: $5-42K
Total Investment: $5-42K
Minimum Net Worth: $15K
Fees: Franchise - NA
Royalty - NA; Ad. - NA
Earnings Claims Statement: No
Term of Contract (Years): NR
Avg. # Of Employees: 2 FT
Passive Ownership: Allowed
Encourage Conversions: Yes
Area Develop. Agreements: No
Sub-Franchising Contracts: No
Expand In Territory: Yes
Space Needs: NA SF; NA
SUPPORT & TRAINING:
Financial Assistance Provided: Yes(I)
Site Selection Assistance: NA
Lease Negotiation Assistance: Yes
Co-Operative Advertising: Yes
Franchisee Assoc./Member: No
Size Of Corporate Staff: 60
On-Going Support: B,D,E,G,H,I
Training: 3-4 Days Vancouver, BC; 3-4 Days Orlando, FL.
SPECIFIC EXPANSION PLANS:
US: All United States
Canada: All Canada
Overseas: Europe, Asia, Africa, Carribean, New Zealand, Australia

<< >>

LAWN DOCTOR

142 Hwy. Route. 34, P.O. Box 401
Holmdel, NJ 07733-2090
Tel: (800) 452-9637 (732) 946-0029
Fax: (732) 946-0002
E-Mail: franchiseinformation@lawndoctor.com
Web Site: www.lawndoctor.com
Mr. Stephen Bucci, Dir. Franchise Development

LAWN DOCTOR is an automated lawn care service. We use all natural and regular fertilization, plus control application, using our exclusive Turf Tamer equipment, manufactured and used only by LAWN DOCTOR, supplemented by a broad range of cultural care practices, utilizing integrated Pest Control Management to develop the health and beauty of turf and landscape areas with environmentally balanced care.

BACKGROUND: IFA MEMBER
Established: 1967; 1st Franchised: 1967
Franchised Units: 460
Company-Owned Units: 0
Total Units: 460
Dist.: US-439; CAN-0; O'seas-0
North America: 34 States
Density: 63 in NJ, 37 in NY, 35 in PA
Projected New Units (12 Months): 30
Qualifications: 3, 1, 1, 2, 1, 5
Registered: All Except HI
FINANCIAL/TERMS:
Cash Investment: $33-38.9K
Total Investment: $68-74.9K
Minimum Net Worth: $150K
Fees: Franchise - $0
Royalty - 10%; Ad. - 10%
Earnings Claims Statement: No
Term of Contract (Years): 20/5/5
Avg. # Of Employees: 2 PT
Passive Ownership: Discouraged
Encourage Conversions: Yes
Area Develop. Agreements: No

Sub-Franchising Contracts: No
Expand In Territory: Yes
Space Needs: NA SF; HB

SUPPORT & TRAINING:
Financial Assistance Provided: Yes(D)
Site Selection Assistance: NA
Lease Negotiation Assistance: No
Co-Operative Advertising: Yes
Franchisee Assoc./Member: Yes/Yes
Size Of Corporate Staff: 50
On-Going Support: B,C,D,G,H,I
Training: 2 Weeks NJ.

SPECIFIC EXPANSION PLANS:
US: All Except CA,WA,OR
Canada: No
Overseas: No

NATURALAWN OF AMERICA

1 E. Church St.
Frederick, MD 21701
Tel: (800) 989-5444 + 211 (301) 694-5440
Fax: (301) 846-0320
E-Mail: franchise@nl-amer.com
Web Site: www.nl-amer.com
Mr. Randy Loeb, VP Franchise Development

NATURALAWN of America is the only nationwide lawn care franchise offering an environmentally friendly lawn care service incorporating natural, organic-based fertilizers and biological controls. Our franchise owners provide residential and commercial customers with fertilization, weed control, insect control, disease control and lawn diagnosis services using safer and healthier products, eliminating the need for harsh chemicals and pesticides.

BACKGROUND:
Established: 1987; 1st Franchised: 1989
Franchised Units: 68
Company-Owned Units: 3
Total Units: 71
Dist.: US-52; CAN-1; O'seas-0
North America: 27 States
Density: 6 in MD, 5 in PA, 5 in VA
Projected New Units (12 Months): 10-12
Qualifications: 4, 4, 1, 4, 3, 5
Registered:CA,FL,IL,IN,MD,MI,MN,NY,OR,VA,WA,WI

FINANCIAL/TERMS:
Cash Investment: $50K
Total Investment: $75-150K
Minimum Net Worth: $250K
Fees: Franchise - $29.5K
Royalty - Varies; Ad. - 0%
Earnings Claims Statement: Yes
Term of Contract (Years): 5/10
Avg. # Of Employees: 1-3 FT
Passive Ownership: Discouraged
Encourage Conversions: Yes
Area Develop. Agreements: No
Sub-Franchising Contracts: Yes
Expand In Territory: Yes
Space Needs: 1,200 SF; Warehouse

SUPPORT & TRAINING:
Financial Assistance Provided: Yes(I)
Site Selection Assistance: Yes
Lease Negotiation Assistance: Yes
Co-Operative Advertising: NA
Franchisee Assoc./Member: No
Size Of Corporate Staff: 14
On-Going Support: A,B,C,D,E,F,G,h,I
Training: 1 Week Home Office; 1 Week Field Office; 1 Week OnSite.

SPECIFIC EXPANSION PLANS:
US: All United States
Canada: All Canada
Overseas: No

NUTRI-LAWN, ECOLOGY-FRIENDLY LAWN CARE

5397 Eglinton Ave. W., # 110
Toronto, ON M9C 5K6 CANADA
Tel: (800) 396-6096 (416) 620-7100
Fax: (416) 620-7771
E-Mail: larrynutrilawn@bellnet.ca
Web Site: www.nutri-lawn.com
Mr. Larry Maydonik, President

NUTRI-LAWN offers ecology-friendly lawn care to meet increasing consumer demand. We focus on organic fertilization and reduced control product usage through our spot treating and our natural and safe lawn care product line. We create large lawn care operations through our proven program and systems.

BACKGROUND: IFA MEMBER
Established: 1985; 1st Franchised: 1987
Franchised Units: 32
Company-Owned Units: 0
Total Units: 32
Dist.: US-2; CAN-30; O'seas-0
North America: 3 States, 8 Provinces
Density: 17 in ON, 7 in BC
Projected New Units (12 Months): 2
Qualifications: 5, 4, 1, 3, 3, 5
Registered: VA

FINANCIAL/TERMS:
Cash Investment: $60-100K
Total Investment: $100-200K
Minimum Net Worth: $250K
Fees: Franchise - $40K
Royalty - 6%; Ad. - 1% US)
Earnings Claims Statement: No
Term of Contract (Years): 5/10
Avg. # Of Employees: 1 FT
Passive Ownership: Not Allowed
Encourage Conversions: Yes
Area Develop. Agreements: Yes
Sub-Franchising Contracts: No
Expand In Territory: Yes
Space Needs: NR SF; SC

SUPPORT & TRAINING:
Financial Assistance Provided: No
Site Selection Assistance: Yes
Lease Negotiation Assistance: Yes
Co-Operative Advertising: Yes
Franchisee Assoc./Member: Yes/Yes
Size Of Corporate Staff: 4
On-Going Support: B,C,D,E,G,H
Training: 1 Week Toronto, ON.

SPECIFIC EXPANSION PLANS:
US: Northeast, Northwest
Canada: All Canada
Overseas: All Countries

SCOTTS LAWN SERVICE

14111 Scottslawn Rd.
Marysville, OH 43041
Tel: (800) 221-1760 (937) 644-7297
Fax: (937) 644-7422
E-Mail: jim.miller@scotts.com
Web Site: www.scotts.com
Mr. Jim Miller, Director Franchising

SCOTTS, the leading marketer of home lawn and garden products, has entered the lawn service business, the result ... SCOTTS LAWN SERVICE. As a franchise system, we offer very strong brand name awareness, powerful sales and marketing programs, extensive training and premium products.

BACKGROUND:
Established: 1998; 1st Franchised: 1998
Franchised Units: 51
Company-Owned Units: 50
Total Units: 101
Dist.: US-101; CAN-0; O'seas-0
North America: NR
Density: 4 in OH, 3 in GA
Projected New Units (12 Months): 15
Qualifications: 4, 3, 3, 2, 2, 5
Registered:FL,IL,IN,MD,MI,MN,ND,OR,SD,VA,WA,WI

FINANCIAL/TERMS:
Cash Investment: $30-60K
Total Investment: $85.7-405.9K
Minimum Net Worth: $100-500K

Fees: Franchise - $30-250K
Royalty - 6-10%; Ad. - 0%
Earnings Claims Statement: Yes
Term of Contract (Years): 10/10
Avg. # Of Employees: 2+ FT
Passive Ownership: Discouraged
Encourage Conversions: Yes
Area Develop. Agreements: No
Sub-Franchising Contracts: No
Expand In Territory: Yes
Space Needs: 400 SF; FS, HB

SUPPORT & TRAINING:
Financial Assistance Provided: Yes(I)
Site Selection Assistance: NA
Lease Negotiation Assistance: No
Co-Operative Advertising: NA
Franchisee Assoc./Member: No
Size Of Corporate Staff: 25
On-Going Support: B,C,D,E,F,H,I
Training: 2 Weeks.

SPECIFIC EXPANSION PLANS:
US: All United States
Canada: All Canada
Overseas: No

<< >>

SPRING-GREEN.

SPRING-GREEN LAWN CARE

11909 Spaulding School Dr.
Plainfield, IL 60544-9501
Tel: (800) 435-4051 (815) 436-8777
Fax: (815) 436-9056
E-Mail: jyoung@spring-green.com
Web Site: www.spring-green.com
Mr. James Young, VP Franchise Development

SPRING-GREEN delivers lawn and tree care services nationwide. Our service is centered on the beautification of middle class and affluent neighborhoods and communities. Our customers include both residential and commercial establishments. SPRING-GREEN has been beautiying the environment for 27+ years, in now more than 20 states. SPRING-GREEN's success has continued through slow economic times. Program includes lead generation. No heavy investing in equipment and personnel. Loyal and profitable customers.

BACKGROUND: IFA MEMBER
Established: 1977; 1st Franchised: 1977
Franchised Units: 81
Company-Owned Units: 21
Total Units: 102
Dist.: US-102; CAN-0; O'seas-0
North America: 20 States
Density: 26 in IL, 13 in WI, 7 in VA
Projected New Units (12 Months): 15
Qualifications: 4, 3, 1, 3, 2, 4
Registered: IL,IN,MD,MI,MN,OR,VA,WA,WI

FINANCIAL/TERMS:
Cash Investment: $54K
Total Investment: $112-155K
Minimum Net Worth: $125K
Fees: Franchise - $21.9K
Royalty - 9-6%; Ad. - 2%
Earnings Claims Statement: Yes
Term of Contract (Years): 10/10
Avg. # Of Employees: 3 FT, 1 PT
Passive Ownership: Not Allowed
Encourage Conversions: Yes
Area Develop. Agreements: No
Sub-Franchising Contracts: No
Expand In Territory: No
Space Needs: NA SF; HB

SUPPORT & TRAINING:
Financial Assistance Provided: Yes(D)
Site Selection Assistance: NA
Lease Negotiation Assistance: NA
Co-Operative Advertising: NA
Franchisee Assoc./Member: Yes/Yes
Size Of Corporate Staff: 15
On-Going Support: A,B,C,D,E,F,G,H,I
Training: On-Line Pre-Training; 1 Week Training at Corp. HQ; 3 On-Site Visits (Min. 2 Days Each).

SPECIFIC EXPANSION PLANS:
US: All Exc. AK,AZ,CA,FL,NY,NV,ND,SD,HI
Canada: No
Overseas: No

<< >>

SUPER LAWNS

15901 Derwood Rd., P.O. Box 5677
Rockville, MD 20855
Tel: (301) 948-8181
Fax: (301) 948-8461
E-Mail: rmiller783@aol.com
Web Site: www.superlawns.com
Mr. Ron Miller, Vice President

Our system is a modern, profitable approach to lawn care. One person or many, depending upon your desire to succeed. We offer complete training and constant assistance in all areas of business. We'll try to keep you 'One step ahead of the competition.'

BACKGROUND:
Established: 1975; 1st Franchised: 1979
Franchised Units: 22
Company-Owned Units: 1
Total Units: 23
Dist.: US-23; CAN-0; O'seas-0
North America: 5 States
Density: 8 in MD, 5 in VA, 3 in DE
Projected New Units (12 Months): 4
Qualifications: 3, 3, 2, 2, 4, 5
Registered: MD,VA

FINANCIAL/TERMS:
Cash Investment: $30K
Total Investment: $60-70K
Minimum Net Worth: $60K
Fees: Franchise - $17.5K
Royalty - 10% Decreasing; Ad. - 0%
Earnings Claims Statement: No
Term of Contract (Years): 20/5
Avg. # Of Employees: 1 FT
Passive Ownership: Discouraged
Encourage Conversions: NA
Area Develop. Agreements: No
Sub-Franchising Contracts: No
Expand In Territory: Yes
Space Needs: NA SF; NA

SUPPORT & TRAINING:
Financial Assistance Provided: Yes(B)
Site Selection Assistance: NA
Lease Negotiation Assistance: NA
Co-Operative Advertising: Yes
Franchisee Assoc./Member: No
Size Of Corporate Staff: 3
On-Going Support: B,C,D,F,I
Training: 7-10 Days Rockville, MD or Elkton, MD and as Needed.

SPECIFIC EXPANSION PLANS:
US: East of Mississippi
Canada: No
Overseas: No

<< >>

U. S. LAWNS

4407 Vineland Rd., # D-15
Orlando, FL 33811
Tel: (800) 875-2967 (407) 522-1630
Fax: (407) 246-1623
E-Mail: pwolbert@uslawns.com
Web Site: www.uslawns.com
Mr. Paul C. Wolbert, VP Franchise Development

Train and support franchisees in a commercial landscape market.

BACKGROUND: IFA MEMBER
Established: 1986; 1st Franchised: 1986
Franchised Units: 140
Company-Owned Units: 0
Total Units: 140
Dist.: US-135; CAN-0; O'seas-0

North America: 25 States
Density: 30 in FL, 15 in GA, 10 in TN
Projected New Units (12 Months): 25
Qualifications: 4, 4, 2, 2, 3, 5
Registered: All States and AB

FINANCIAL/TERMS:
Cash Investment: $20K
Total Investment: $50-85K
Minimum Net Worth: $70K
Fees: Franchise - $29K
Royalty - 4%; Ad. - 1%
Earnings Claims Statement: No
Term of Contract (Years): 10/5
Avg. # Of Employees: 3 FT
Passive Ownership: Not Allowed
Encourage Conversions: Yes
Area Develop. Agreements: No
Sub-Franchising Contracts: No
Expand In Territory: Yes
Space Needs: NA SF; HB

SUPPORT & TRAINING:
Financial Assistance Provided: Yes(D)
Site Selection Assistance: NA
Lease Negotiation Assistance: No
Co-Operative Advertising: NA
Franchisee Assoc./Member: Yes/Yes
Size Of Corporate Staff: 19
On-Going Support: B,C,D,E,G,H,I
Training: 5 Days in Orlando, FL; 5 Days In Location.

SPECIFIC EXPANSION PLANS:
US: All United States
Canada: No
Overseas: No

<< >>

UNDERGROUND IRRIGATION

P. O. Box 267
Merrimack, NH 03054
Tel: (866) WET-GRASS (603) 424-3611
Fax: (603) 424-3611
E-Mail: ll1976@adelphia.net
Web Site: www.undergroundirrigation.net
Mr. Larry Leavitt, President

Unique ground-floor opportunity in the multi-billion dollar lawn sprinkler business. Low start-up costs, full training and support, exclusive territories, low overhead, full or part-time, unlimited potential.

BACKGROUND:
Established: 1998; 1st Franchised: 2001
Franchised Units: 0
Company-Owned Units: 1
Total Units: 1
Dist.: US-1; CAN-0; O'seas-0
North America: 1 State
Density: 1 in NH
Projected New Units (12 Months): 10
Qualifications: 2, 3, 1, 3, 3, 3
Registered: NR

FINANCIAL/TERMS:
Cash Investment: $20-30K
Total Investment: $20-30K
Minimum Net Worth: $$20K
Fees: Franchise - $10K
Royalty - $300-500/Mo.; Ad. - 3%
Earnings Claims Statement: No
Term of Contract (Years): 10/10
Avg. # Of Employees: 2 FT
Passive Ownership: Allowed
Encourage Conversions: NA
Area Develop. Agreements: No
Sub-Franchising Contracts: No
Expand In Territory: Yes
Space Needs: NA SF; HB

SUPPORT & TRAINING:
Financial Assistance Provided: No
Site Selection Assistance: Yes
Lease Negotiation Assistance: NA
Co-Operative Advertising: NA
Franchisee Assoc./Member: No
Size Of Corporate Staff: 3
On-Going Support: B,C,D,E,G,I
Training: 3-5 Weeks Merrimack, NH.

SPECIFIC EXPANSION PLANS:
US: All United States
Canada: No
Overseas: No

<< >>

WEED MAN

11 Grand Marshall Dr.
Toronto, ON M1B 5N6 CANADA
Tel: (888) 321-9333 (416) 269-5754 + 114
Fax: (416) 269-8233
E-Mail: turfholdings@aol.com
Web Site: www.weed-man.com
Mr. Don Dankowich, Franchise Manager

Professional lawn care services.

BACKGROUND: IFA MEMBER
Established: 1970; 1st Franchised: 1976
Franchised Units: 287
Company-Owned Units: 0
Total Units: 287
Dist.: US-167; CAN-119; O'seas-1
North America: 27 States,10 Provinces
Density: NR
Projected New Units (12 Months): 24
Qualifications: 3, 4, 1, 3, 3, 4
Registered: CA,CT,FL,IL,IN,KY,MD,MI, MN,ND,NE,NY,OR,RI,TX,WA,WI

FINANCIAL/TERMS:
Cash Investment: $25K
Total Investment: $75K
Minimum Net Worth: $50K
Fees: Franchise - $20-34K
Royalty - $8.8K/Vehcl.; Ad. - 20% Royalty
Earnings Claims Statement: Yes
Term of Contract (Years): 10/10
Avg. # Of Employees: 5 FT
Passive Ownership: Discouraged
Encourage Conversions: Yes
Area Develop. Agreements: No
Sub-Franchising Contracts: Yes
Expand In Territory: Yes
Space Needs: NR SF; HB, SC

SUPPORT & TRAINING:
Financial Assistance Provided: No
Site Selection Assistance: Yes
Lease Negotiation Assistance: No
Co-Operative Advertising: Yes
Franchisee Assoc./Member: Yes
Size Of Corporate Staff: 9
On-Going Support: B,C,D,F,G,H
Training: 2 Weeks Scarborough, ON.

SPECIFIC EXPANSION PLANS:
US: All United States
Canada: All Canada
Overseas: Australia

<< >>

Lodging

Chapter
23

Lodging Industry Profile

Total # Franchisors in Industry Group	68
Total # Franchised Units in Industry Group	27,727
Total # Company-Owned Units in Industry Group	3,484
Total # Operating Units in Industry Group	31,211
Average # Franchised Units/Franchisor	407.8
Average # Company-Owned Units/Franchisor	51.2
Average # Total Units/Franchisor	459
Ratio of Total # Franchised Units/Total # Company-Owned Units	8:1
Industry Survey Participants	25
Representing % of Industry	36.8%
Average Franchise Fee*:	$28.3K
Average Total Investment*:	$3,592K
Average On-Going Royalty Fee*:	4.4%

*If a range was provided, the mid-point of the range was used. See detailed profiles for actual ranges.

Five Largest Participants in Survey

Company	# Franchised Units	# Co-Owned Units	# Total Units	Franchise Fee	On-Going Royalty	Total Investment
1. Cendant	6,588	0	6,588	Varies	Varies	$205K-6.2MM
2. Choice Hotels International	4,810	3	4,813	$25-50K	2.75-5.1%	$2-10MM
3. InterContinental Hotels Group	2,970	580	3,550	$500/Rm,40Kmin	5%	Varies
4. Hampton Inn/Hampton Inn & Suites	1,250	36	1,286	$45K	4% Gross Rm. Rev	$4.9-8.7MM
5. Ramada Franchise Systems	893	0	893	$35Kor $350/RM	4%	$NA

All of the data provided are proprietary and should not be quoted without acknowledging *Bond's Franchise Guide.*

AFM HOSPITALITY CORPORATION

135 Queens Plate Dr., # 400
Toronto, ON M9W 6V1 CANADA
Tel: (800) 249-4656 (416) 361-1010
Fax: (416) 361-9050
E-Mail: vcuralli@afmcorp.com
Web Site: www.afmcorp.com
Mr. Vito Curalli, VP Franchise Development

Multi-tiered hotel franchise organization, with representation across Canada. 41 PLAZA INN and limited properties comprising good rooms nationwide. Franchise offers marketing, training, advertising, loyalty programs and site selection.

BACKGROUND:
Established: 1991; 1st Franchised: 1992
Franchised Units: 88
Company-Owned Units: 0
Total Units: 88
Dist.: US-0; CAN-41; O'seas-0
North America: 8 Provinces
Density: 20 in ON, 12 in BC, 4 in PQ
Projected New Units (12 Months): 8-10
Qualifications: 5, 4, 1, 5, 1, 5
Registered: AB

FINANCIAL/TERMS:
Cash Investment: $1-7MM
Total Investment: $2-20MM
Minimum Net Worth: Varies
Fees: Franchise - $35K
Royalty - 3%; Ad. - 4%
Earnings Claims Statement: No
Term of Contract (Years): 5/5/5/5
Avg. # Of Employees: 0.4/Room; 80FT, 20PT
Passive Ownership: Allowed
Encourage Conversions: Yes
Area Develop. Agreements: Yes/5
Sub-Franchising Contracts: No
Expand In Territory: Yes
Space Needs: NR SF; FS

SUPPORT & TRAINING:
Financial Assistance Provided: NA
Site Selection Assistance: Yes
Lease Negotiation Assistance: Yes
Co-Operative Advertising: Yes
Franchisee Assoc./Member: Yes/Yes
Size Of Corporate Staff: 15
On-Going Support: A,B,C,D,E,G,H,I
Training: 3-5 Days On-Site.

SPECIFIC EXPANSION PLANS:
US: No
Canada: All Canada
Overseas: No

<< >>

AMERICINN INTERNATIONAL, LLC

250 Lake Dr. E.
Chanhassen, MN 55317-9364
Tel: (800) 634-3444-Res. (952) 294-5000
Fax: (952) 294-5001
E-Mail: jkennedy@americinn.com
Web Site: www.americinn.com
Mr. Jon D. Kennedy, SVP Mktg./Franchise Dev.

The AMERICINN Lodging System is one of the fastest-growing, upscale, limited service lodging chains, with 220 properties currently open or under development. The success and savvy growth of the AMERICINN Lodging System is due to its unique product and market niche. AMERICINN competes across the luxury-economy and mid-market segments and is dedicated to the concept of providing the best lodging value for its guest.

BACKGROUND: IFA MEMBER
Established: 1984; 1st Franchised: 1984
Franchised Units: 214
Company-Owned Units: 6
Total Units: 220
Dist.: US-207; CAN-0; O'seas-0
North America: 23 States
Density: 74 in MN, 43 in WI, 26 in IA
Projected New Units (12 Months): 200
Qualifications: 5, 5, 4, 4, 4,
Registered: All States

FINANCIAL/TERMS:
Cash Investment: NR
Total Investment: $2.9-6.0MM
Minimum Net Worth: $1MM
Fees: Franchise - $35K
Royalty - 5%; Ad. - 2%
Earnings Claims Statement: No
Term of Contract (Years): 20
Avg. # Of Employees: 20 FT, 9 PT
Passive Ownership: Allowed
Encourage Conversions: NA
Area Develop. Agreements: No
Sub-Franchising Contracts: No
Expand In Territory: Yes
Space Needs: 60,000 SF; FS

SUPPORT & TRAINING:
Financial Assistance Provided: Yes(I)
Site Selection Assistance: Yes
Lease Negotiation Assistance: Yes
Co-Operative Advertising: Yes
Franchisee Assoc./Member: Yes/Yes
Size Of Corporate Staff: 75
On-Going Support: a,b,C,D,E,G,H,I
Training: 3 Different Properties, 1 Week at Each.

SPECIFIC EXPANSION PLANS:
US: All United States
Canada: All Canada
Overseas: All Countries

<< >>

BEST INNS & SUITES

13 Corporate Sq., # 250
Atlanta, GA 30329
Tel: (800) TELL-US5 (404) 321-4045
Fax: (404) 321-4482
E-Mail: mike.muir@usfsi.com
Web Site: www.bestinn.com
Mr. Mike Muir, SVP Sales and Develop.

BEST INNS & SUITES is a high-quality, mid-level, limited service hotel brand. With 107 hotels open and 6 under development as of 3/31/2004, BEST INNS & SUITES continues to expand around the country. BEST INNS & SUITES is primarily a conversion brand for existing hotel owners looking for a better way to do business. BEST offers a solution to independent hotel owners looking for a franchise brand or for current franchise hotel owners looking to reposition their property in the market place.

BACKGROUND: IFA MEMBER
Established: 1995; 1st Franchised: 1995
Franchised Units: 106
Company-Owned Units: 0
Total Units: 106
Dist.: US-105; CAN-1; O'seas-0
North America: 34 States
Density: 8 in CA, 8 in IL, 7 in GA
Projected New Units (12 Months): 50
Qualifications: 3, 4, 4, 2, 2, 3
Registered: All States

FINANCIAL/TERMS:
Cash Investment: $190-330K
Total Investment: $170-577K
Minimum Net Worth: NA
Fees: Franchise - $10K
Royalty - 2,4,5%; Ad. - 2.5%
Earnings Claims Statement: Yes
Term of Contract (Years): 10/10
Avg. # Of Employees: 11 FT
Passive Ownership: Allowed
Encourage Conversions: Yes
Area Develop. Agreements: No
Sub-Franchising Contracts: No
Expand In Territory: Yes
Space Needs: NR SF; FS

SUPPORT & TRAINING:
Financial Assistance Provided: Yes(I)
Site Selection Assistance: Yes
Lease Negotiation Assistance: No
Co-Operative Advertising: Yes

Franchisee Assoc./Member: Yes
Size Of Corporate Staff: 94
On-Going Support: C,D,E,G,I
Training: 1 Week On-Site; 1 Week Classroom Atlanta, GA; 3 Days Hands-On Reservation Training IL.

SPECIFIC EXPANSION PLANS:
US: All United States
Canada: No
Overseas: No

<< >>

CANDLEWOOD SUITES/ CAMBRIDGE SUITES

8621 E. 21st St. N., # 200
Wichita, KS 67206
Tel: (316) 631-1300
Fax: (316) 631-1333
E-Mail: carmstrong@candlewoodsuites.com
Web Site: www.candlewoodsuites.com
Mr. Chick Armstrong, VP Franchise Sales

CANDLEWOOD SUITES is a unique, high-quality, mid-priced hotel brand designed to deliver exceptional value to both owners and guests. CAMBRIDGE SUITES, established in 1998, is another tremendous opportunity to build or convert an existing hotel into the newest concept in lodging for the up-scale traveler.

BACKGROUND: IFA MEMBER
Established: 1995; 1st Franchised: 1996
Franchised Units: 35
Company-Owned Units: 78
Total Units: 113
Dist.: US-98; CAN-0; O'seas-0
North America: 32 States
Density: 14 in TX, 8 in IL, 8 in CA
Projected New Units (12 Months): NR
Qualifications: 3, 3, 2, 2, 2, 3
Registered: All States Except HI,VA

FINANCIAL/TERMS:
Cash Investment: $700K-2MM
Total Investment: $3-7MM
Minimum Net Worth: NA
Fees: Franchise - $400/Key/40K
Royalty - 4-5%RR; Ad. - 1.5%RR
Earnings Claims Statement: Yes
Term of Contract (Years): 20
Avg. # Of Employees: 6-13 FT
Passive Ownership: Allowed
Encourage Conversions: Yes
Area Develop. Agreements: No
Sub-Franchising Contracts: No
Expand In Territory: Yes
Space Needs: 56,628-108,90 SF; FS

SUPPORT & TRAINING:
Financial Assistance Provided: NR
Site Selection Assistance: No
Lease Negotiation Assistance: Yes
Co-Operative Advertising: No
Franchisee Assoc./Member: Yes/Yes
Size Of Corporate Staff: 100
On-Going Support: C,D,G,H,I
Training: Extensive Training Program.

SPECIFIC EXPANSION PLANS:
US: All United States
Canada: All Canada
Overseas: All Countries

<< >>

CENDANT

1 Sylvan Way
Parsippany, NJ 07054-3878
Tel: (800) 758-8999 (973) 428-9700
Fax: (973) 496-5915
E-Mail:
Web Site: www.cendant.com
Ms. Nicole Johnson-Reece, Dir. Diversity/ Emerging Market

Franchisees looking for a hotel franchise to serve the growing business and leisure demand often turn to the CENDANT portfolio of hotel brands. And for good reason. CENDANT is the world's largest hotel franchisor with more than 6400 hotels, nearly 540,000 rooms and 5200 lodging franchisees. CENDANT brands cover a wide cross-section of lodging markets, ranging from mid-priced, to economy to extended stay facilities, catering to both business and pleasure travelers.

BACKGROUND:
Established: 1990; 1st Franchised: 1990
Franchised Units: 6,588
Company-Owned Units: 0
Total Units: 6,588
Dist.: US-6,588; CAN-0; O'seas-0
North America: 50 States
Density: 478 in CA, 435 in TX, 423 FL
Projected New Units (12 Months): NR
Qualifications: , , , , ,
Registered: NR

FINANCIAL/TERMS:
Cash Investment: NA
Total Investment: $205K-6.2MM
Minimum Net Worth: NA
Fees: Franchise - Varies
Royalty - Varies; Ad. - Varies
Earnings Claims Statement: Yes
Term of Contract (Years): 15-20/N/A
Avg. # Of Employees: Varies
Passive Ownership: NR
Encourage Conversions: NR
Area Develop. Agreements: Yes-Int.
Sub-Franchising Contracts: NR
Expand In Territory: No
Space Needs: Varies SF; FS

SUPPORT & TRAINING:
Financial Assistance Provided: NR
Site Selection Assistance: No
Lease Negotiation Assistance: No
Co-Operative Advertising: Yes
Franchisee Assoc./Member: Yes
Size Of Corporate Staff: 724
On-Going Support: b,C,D,E,G,h,I
Training: Varies by Brand.

SPECIFIC EXPANSION PLANS:
US: All United States
Canada: NR
Overseas: NR

<< >>

CHOICE HOTELS CANADA

5090 Explorer Dr., # 500
Mississauga, ON L4W 4T9 CANADA
Tel: (905) 624-7803
Fax: (905) 624-7786
E-Mail: franchising@choicehotels.ca
Web Site: www.choicehotels.ca
Mr. Mike Jackson, President

Canada's largest hotel chain, with over 280 locations open and under development. We franchise 8 brands coast-to-coast: CLARION, QUALITY, COMFORT, COMFORT SUITES, SLEEP INN, RODEWAY INN, ECONO LODGE and MAINSTAY SUITES.

BACKGROUND:
Established: 1993; 1st Franchised: 1993
Franchised Units: 280
Company-Owned Units: 0
Total Units: 280
Dist.: US-0; CAN-280; O'seas-0
North America: 10 Provinces
Density: 100 in ON, 40 in PQ,20 in AB
Projected New Units (12 Months): 18
Qualifications: 4, 5, 4, 3, 3, 4
Registered: AB

FINANCIAL/TERMS:
Cash Investment: $50% of Total
Total Investment: $2-10MM
Minimum Net Worth: Varies

Fees: Franchise - $25-50K
Royalty - 2.5-5%; Ad. - 1.3%
Earnings Claims Statement: Yes
Term of Contract (Years): 20
Avg. # Of Employees: Varies
Passive Ownership: Allowed
Encourage Conversions: Yes
Area Develop. Agreements: No
Sub-Franchising Contracts: No
Expand In Territory: No
Space Needs: 60,000 SF; FS

SUPPORT & TRAINING:
Financial Assistance Provided: No
Site Selection Assistance: Yes
Lease Negotiation Assistance: NA
Co-Operative Advertising: Yes
Franchisee Assoc./Member: Yes/Yes
Size Of Corporate Staff: 40
On-Going Support: A,B,C,D,e,G,h
Training: 3 Days to 1 Week On-Site Opening; 1-2 Day Seminar On-Going On-Site.

SPECIFIC EXPANSION PLANS:
US: No
Canada: All Canada
Overseas: No

CHOICE HOTELS INTERNATIONAL®

CHOICE HOTELS INTERNATIONAL

10750 Columbia Pike
Silver Spring, MD 20901-4427
Tel: (800) 547-0007 (301) 592-5041
Fax: (301) 592-6135
E-Mail: brian_parker@choicehotels.com
Web Site: www.choicehotels.com
Mr. Brian Parker, Dir. Emerging Mkts./Bus. Devel

CHOICE HOTELS is the leading hotel franchisor with more than 60 years' experience in developing brands and services that optimize hotel performance. Our single focus is on enhancing the return on investment for our owners and growing our brands strategically. Brands include COMFORT INN, COMFORT SUITES, QUALITY, SLEEP INN, CLARION, MAINSTAY SUITES, ECONO LODGE, and RODEWAY INN, and our new boutique brand extension, CLARION COLLECTION. Either convert an existing location or build a new one.

BACKGROUND: IFA MEMBER
Established: 1941; 1st Franchised: 1962
Franchised Units: 4,810
Company-Owned Units: 3
Total Units: 4,813
Dist.: US-3,636; CAN-260; O'seas-914
North America: 50 States,10 Provinces
Density: 258 in TX, 251 in CA, 205 FL
Projected New Units (12 Months): 400+
Qualifications: 4, 4, 4, 2, 1, 1
Registered: All States

FINANCIAL/TERMS:
Cash Investment: $20-30% Costs
Total Investment: $2-10MM
Minimum Net Worth: Varies
Fees: Franchise - $25-50K
Royalty - 2.75-5.1%; Ad. - 1.75% Rev.
Earnings Claims Statement: Yes
Term of Contract (Years): 20/5
Avg. # Of Employees: Varies
Passive Ownership: Allowed
Encourage Conversions: Yes
Area Develop. Agreements: No
Sub-Franchising Contracts: No
Expand In Territory: Yes
Space Needs: 31,000-33,000 SF; FS

SUPPORT & TRAINING:
Financial Assistance Provided: Yes(B)
Site Selection Assistance: Yes
Lease Negotiation Assistance: Yes
Co-Operative Advertising: Yes
Franchisee Assoc./Member: Yes/Yes
Size Of Corporate Staff: 1,500
On-Going Support: A,B,C,D,F,G,h,I
Training: 1 Day (on Aspects of Operation).

SPECIFIC EXPANSION PLANS:
US: All United States
Canada: All Canada
Overseas: All Countries

COUNTRY INNS & SUITES BY CARLSON

P. O. Box 59159, Carlson Pkwy.
Minneapolis, MN 55459-8203
Tel: (800) 456-4000 (763) 212-2525
Fax: (763) 212-1338
E-Mail: njohnson@countryinns.com
Web Site: www.countryinns.com
Ms. Nancy Johnson, EVP Brand Leader

COUNTRY INNS & SUITES locations feature traditional architecture and sophisticated residential interior design with hardwood flooring and decorative ceiling borders. Each hotel welcomes guests with traditional furnishings that blend rich woods and elegant patterned fabrics. The brand is known for its consistently high-quality accommodations and personal, warm hospitality.

BACKGROUND: IFA MEMBER
Established: 1987; 1st Franchised: 1987
Franchised Units: 310
Company-Owned Units: 4
Total Units: 314
Dist.: US-288; CAN-12; O'seas-14
North America: 39 States, 7 Provinces
Density: 38 in MN, 24 in WI, 24 in GA
Projected New Units (12 Months): 45
Qualifications: 5, 5, 5, 3, 5, 5
Registered: All States

FINANCIAL/TERMS:
Cash Investment: $780K-1.45MM
Total Investment: $3.1-5.4MM
Minimum Net Worth: $1MM
Fees: Franchise - $40K
Royalty - 4.5%; Ad. - 3%
Earnings Claims Statement: Yes
Term of Contract (Years): 15/0
Avg. # Of Employees: 10 FT, 6 PT
Passive Ownership: Allowed
Encourage Conversions: Yes
Area Develop. Agreements: No
Sub-Franchising Contracts: No
Expand In Territory: No
Space Needs: 65,340 SF; FS

SUPPORT & TRAINING:
Financial Assistance Provided: Yes(I)
Site Selection Assistance: No
Lease Negotiation Assistance: No
Co-Operative Advertising: Yes
Franchisee Assoc./Member: Yes/Yes
Size Of Corporate Staff: 24
On-Going Support: B,C,D,E,G,H
Training: 1 Week Minneapolis, MN (Brand Orientation); 3 Days Opening On-Site; 3 Days New Franchisee.

SPECIFIC EXPANSION PLANS:
US: All United States
Canada: All Canada
Overseas: Europe, Asia, South and Central America

DOUBLETREE®
HOTELS·SUITES·RESORTS·CLUBS

DOUBLETREE

9336 Civic Center Dr.
Beverly Hills, CA 90210
Tel: (800) 286-0645 (310) 278-4321

Fax: (310) 205-7655
E-Mail: bill_fortier@hilton.com
Web Site: www.doubletreefranchise.com
Mr. Bill Fortier, SVP Franchise Development

DOUBLETREE HOTELS AND RESORTS, DOUBLETREE GUEST SUITES and DOUBLETREE CLUB HOTEL properties have their own unique, contemporary design reflecting the local or regional environment. Service is warm and friendly. Since the merger with HILTON, DOUBLETREE has seen a resurgence in growth and performance. Our objectives are focused on new-build and conversion opportunities. Our conversion procedures help simplify the reflagging of an existing hotel in a cost-effective manner. Convert to DOUBLETREE today!

BACKGROUND: IFA MEMBER
Established: 1989; 1st Franchised: 1989
Franchised Units: 79
Company-Owned Units: 76
Total Units: 155
Dist.: US-151; CAN-2; O'seas-2
North America: 36 States, 1 Province
Density: 23 in CA, 18 in FL, 10 in TX
Projected New Units (12 Months): NR
Qualifications: 5, 5, 5, 3, 1, 3
Registered: All States

FINANCIAL/TERMS:
Cash Investment: Varies
Total Investment: $7-40.2MM
Minimum Net Worth: $60K/Rm.
Fees: Franchise - $50K Min.
Royalty - 4% Gross Rm. Rev; Ad. - 4% Gross Rm
Earnings Claims Statement: No
Term of Contract (Years): 22/10-20
Avg. # Of Employees: 100 FT
Passive Ownership: Allowed
Encourage Conversions: Yes
Area Develop. Agreements: Yes/Varies
Sub-Franchising Contracts: No
Expand In Territory: Yes
Space Needs: 90-100 Rooms SF; FS

SUPPORT & TRAINING:
Financial Assistance Provided: Yes(I)
Site Selection Assistance: No
Lease Negotiation Assistance: No
Co-Operative Advertising: Yes
Franchisee Assoc./Member: No
Size Of Corporate Staff: 2,332
On-Going Support: a,b,C,c,D,d,E,G,H,h,I
Training: General Manager Training prior to certification for opening.

SPECIFIC EXPANSION PLANS:
US: All United States
Canada: All Canada
Overseas: Mexico, Latin America

<< >>

EMBASSY SUITES HOTELS®

EMBASSY SUITES HOTELS

9336 Civic Center Dr.
Beverly Hills, CA 90210
Tel: (800) 286-0645 (310) 278-4321
Fax: (310) 205-7655
E-Mail: bill_fortier@hilton.com
Web Site: www.embassyfranchise.com
Mr. Bill Fortier, SVP Franchise Development

As the prominent brand in the upscale all-suite market, EMBASSY SUITES HOTELS properties offer spacious 2-room suites and an impressive list of amenities adding up to more comfort, more space and a more efficient environment. With a majority market share, EMBASSY is positioned for continued solid growth. The "Tier Two" prototype with 150 rooms represents an excellent development opportunity that is more cost-efficient to build. EMBASSY has powerful incentives in the Developer's Advantage Program.

BACKGROUND: IFA MEMBER
Established: 1983; 1st Franchised: 1983
Franchised Units: 92
Company-Owned Units: 87
Total Units: 179
Dist.: US-173; CAN-1; O'seas-5
North America: 38 States, 1 Province
Density: 28 in CA, 15 in FL, 17 in TX
Projected New Units (12 Months): NR
Qualifications: 5, 5, 5, 3, 1, 3
Registered: All States

FINANCIAL/TERMS:
Cash Investment: Varies
Total Investment: $17-23MM
Minimum Net Worth: $40-60K/Rm.
Fees: Franchise - $100K Min.
Royalty - 4% Gross Rm. Rev; Ad. - 4% GrRmRev
Earnings Claims Statement: No
Term of Contract (Years): 22/10-20
Avg. # Of Employees: 75 FT
Passive Ownership: Allowed
Encourage Conversions: Yes
Area Develop. Agreements: No
Sub-Franchising Contracts: No
Expand In Territory: Yes
Space Needs: 153,000 SF; NR

SUPPORT & TRAINING:
Financial Assistance Provided: Yes(I)
Site Selection Assistance: No
Lease Negotiation Assistance: Yes
Co-Operative Advertising: Yes
Franchisee Assoc./Member: No
Size Of Corporate Staff: 2,332
On-Going Support: b,C,D,E,G,h,I
Training: 2 Weeks in Memphis, TN.

SPECIFIC EXPANSION PLANS:
US: All United States
Canada: All Canada
Overseas: Mexico, Latin America

<< >>

HAMPTON INN/ HAMPTON INN & SUITES

9336 Civic Center Dr.
Beverly Hills, CA 90210
Tel: (800) 286-0645 (310) 278-4321
Fax: (310) 205-7655
E-Mail: bill_fortier@hilton.com
Web Site: www.hamptonfranchise.com
Mr. Bill Fortier, SVP Franchise Development

HAMPTON pioneered the 100% Satisfaction Guarantee in 1989 that paid off by enhancing the brand's reputation for innovation and quality. No wonder HAMPTON is ranked #1 Mid-Price Hotel Chain (without food & beverage) by Business Travel News. Survey respondents gave HAMPTON high marks for its corporate rate programs, physical appearance, quality of business centers and the relationship of price to value. We have 3 development programs, allowing maximum flexibility at a minimum investment.

BACKGROUND: IFA MEMBER
Established: 1983; 1st Franchised: 1983
Franchised Units: 1,250
Company-Owned Units: 36
Total Units: 1,286
Dist.: US-1,262; CAN-15; O'seas-10

North America: 48 States, 5 Provinces
Density: 100 in FL, 84 in TX,80 in NC
Projected New Units (12 Months): NR
Qualifications: 5, 5, 5, 3, 1, 3
Registered: All States

FINANCIAL/TERMS:
Cash Investment: Varies
Total Investment: $4.9-8.7MM
Minimum Net Worth: $30K/Rm.
Fees: Franchise - $45K
Royalty - 4% Gross Rm. Rev; Ad. - 4% Gross Rm
Earnings Claims Statement: No
Term of Contract (Years): 22/10-20
Avg. # Of Employees: 25 FT
Passive Ownership: Allowed
Encourage Conversions: Yes
Area Develop. Agreements: No
Sub-Franchising Contracts: No
Expand In Territory: Yes
Space Needs: 1.5-3 Acres SF; FS

SUPPORT & TRAINING:
Financial Assistance Provided: Yes(I)
Site Selection Assistance: Yes
Lease Negotiation Assistance: No
Co-Operative Advertising: Yes
Franchisee Assoc./Member: No
Size Of Corporate Staff: 2,332
On-Going Support: b,C,D,E,G,H,I
Training: 2 Weeks for GM in Memphis, TN; 3 Days New Owner.

SPECIFIC EXPANSION PLANS:
US: All United States
Canada: All Canada
Overseas: Mexico & Latin America

<< >>

HAWTHORN SUITES HOTELS INTERNATIONAL

13 Corporate Sq., # 250
Atlanta, GA 30329
Tel: (404) 235-5791
Fax: (404) 235-7491
E-Mail: chick.armstrong@usfsi.com
Web Site: www.hawthorn.com
Mr. Chick Armstrong, SVP of Development

HAWTHORN SUITES is one of the fastest-growing hotel brands in the upper extended stay market. With 112 hotels open and 28 under development as of 3/30/2004, HAWTHORN continues to expand in both primary and tertiary markets. In November, 2000, HAWTHORN SUITES paretn company, U. S. Franchise Systems, was purchased by business interests of the Pritzker family. This acquisition bolstered our already strong leadership by providing powerful strategic and financial advantages.

BACKGROUND: IFA MEMBER
Established: 1995; 1st Franchised: 1995
Franchised Units: 111
Company-Owned Units: 0
Total Units: 111
Dist.: US-109; CAN-1; O'seas-1
North America: 32 States
Density: 23 in TX, 9 in CA, 5 in FL
Projected New Units (12 Months): 25
Qualifications: 4, 4, 4, 2, 2, 3
Registered: All States

FINANCIAL/TERMS:
Cash Investment: $5.6-7.4MM
Total Investment: $5.6-7.4MM
Minimum Net Worth: NA
Fees: Franchise - $40K
Royalty - 5%; Ad. - 2.5%
Earnings Claims Statement: Yes
Term of Contract (Years): 20/10
Avg. # Of Employees: 15-20 FT
Passive Ownership: Allowed
Encourage Conversions: Yes
Area Develop. Agreements: No
Sub-Franchising Contracts: No
Expand In Territory: Yes
Space Needs: NR SF; FS

SUPPORT & TRAINING:
Financial Assistance Provided: Yes(I)
Site Selection Assistance: Yes
Lease Negotiation Assistance: No
Co-Operative Advertising: Yes
Franchisee Assoc./Member: Yes
Size Of Corporate Staff: 96
On-Going Support: C,D,G,h,I
Training: 5 Days Training in Atlanta, GA; 5 Days Sales Training in Atlanta, GA.

SPECIFIC EXPANSION PLANS:
US: All United States
Canada: All Canada
Overseas: Europe, South America, Latin America.

<< >>

Top 100 Hilton™

HILTON

9336 Civic Center Dr.
Beverly Hills, CA 90210
Tel: (800) 286-0645 (310) 278-4321
Fax: (310) 205-7655
E-Mail: bill_fortier@hilton.com
Web Site: www.hiltonfranchise.com
Mr. Bill Fortier, SVP Franchise Development

Our core value is "helping each guest and team member be their best by functioning as a caring and proficient personal assistant who helps guests make the most of their stay." In addition to conversions, new HILTON construction continues. A smaller HILTON prototype has been designed to deliver upscale services in smaller, growing urban/resort markets using a compact design footprint allowing for lower construction costs and shorter building times. Also traditional, larger-scale, full-service hotels.

BACKGROUND: IFA MEMBER
Established: 1919; 1st Franchised: 1967
Franchised Units: 155
Company-Owned Units: 72
Total Units: 227
Dist.: US-214; CAN-9; O'seas-4
North America: 39 States, 4 Provinces
Density: 38 in CA, 22 in FL, 21 in TX
Projected New Units (12 Months): NR
Qualifications: 5, 5, 5, 3, 1, 3
Registered: All States

FINANCIAL/TERMS:
Cash Investment: Varies
Total Investment: $2-44.8MM
Minimum Net Worth: $60K/Rm.
Fees: Franchise - $75K Min.
Royalty - 5% Gross Rm. Rev; Ad. - 4% GrRmRev
Earnings Claims Statement: No
Term of Contract (Years): 22/10-20
Avg. # Of Employees: 150 FT
Passive Ownership: Allowed
Encourage Conversions: Yes
Area Develop. Agreements: No
Sub-Franchising Contracts: No
Expand In Territory: Yes
Space Needs: 135,000 SF; FS

SUPPORT & TRAINING:
Financial Assistance Provided: Yes(I)
Site Selection Assistance: NA
Lease Negotiation Assistance: No
Co-Operative Advertising: Yes
Franchisee Assoc./Member: No
Size Of Corporate Staff: 2,332
On-Going Support: b,C,D,d,E,e,G,H,I
Training: 4 Days Dallas, TX; 3 Days Beverly Hills, CA; 3 Days Regional Office.

SPECIFIC EXPANSION PLANS:
US: All United States
Canada: All Canada
Overseas: Mexico, Latin America

<< >>

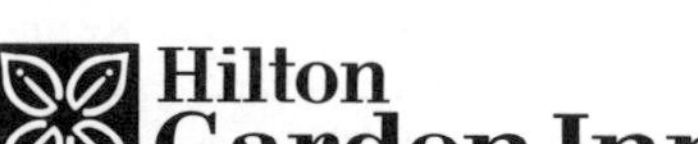

HILTON GARDEN INN

9336 Civic Center Dr.
Beverly Hills, CA 90210
Tel: (800) 286-0645 (310) 278-4321
Fax: (310) 205-7655
E-Mail: bill_fortier@hilton.com
Web Site: www.hiltongardeninnfranchise.com
Mr. Bill Fortier, SVP Franchise Development

An upscale, mid-priced, focused-service hotel concept that eliminates the costly trappings of large-scale properties, yet provides the finest quality of essential services and amenities. HILTON GARDEN INN properties are redefining this category with aggressive expansion. With more than 300 properties open or in development, HILTON GARDEN INN is the fastest-growing brand in the HILTON Family of Hotels. We are considering conversions with a focus on urban locations and other hard-to-develop markets.

BACKGROUND: IFA MEMBER
Established: 1996; 1st Franchised: 1996
Franchised Units: 208
Company-Owned Units: 8
Total Units: 216
Dist.: US-205; CAN-7; O'seas-4
North America: 41 States, 4 Provinces
Density: 25 in CA, 19 in FL, 12 in TX
Projected New Units (12 Months): NR
Qualifications: 5, 5, 5, 3, 1, 3
Registered: All States

FINANCIAL/TERMS:
Cash Investment: Varies
Total Investment: $8-11.4MM
Minimum Net Worth: $40K/Rm.
Fees: Franchise - $60K Min.
Royalty - 5% Gross Rm.;Ad. - 4% Gross Rm
Earnings Claims Statement: No
Term of Contract (Years): 22/10-20
Avg. # Of Employees: 35-50 FT, 10-15 PT
Passive Ownership: Allowed
Encourage Conversions: Yes
Area Develop. Agreements: No
Sub-Franchising Contracts: No
Expand In Territory: Yes
Space Needs: 90-250 Rooms SF; NR

SUPPORT & TRAINING:
Financial Assistance Provided: Yes(I)
Site Selection Assistance: Yes
Lease Negotiation Assistance: No
Co-Operative Advertising: Yes
Franchisee Assoc./Member: No
Size Of Corporate Staff: 2,332
On-Going Support: a,b,C,d,E,G,H,h
Training: 3 Days Owner Orientation, Beverly Hills, CA.

SPECIFIC EXPANSION PLANS:
US: All United States
Canada: All Canada
Overseas: Mexico, Latin America

<< >>

HOMEWOOD SUITES BY HILTON

9336 Civic Center Dr.
Beverly Hills, CA 90210
Tel: (800) 286-0645 (310) 278-4321
Fax: (310) 205-7655
E-Mail: bill_fortier@hilton.com
Web Site: www.homewoodfranchise.com
Mr. Bill Fortier, SVP Franchise Development

Spacious and comfortable living quarters combining the amenities of a full-service hotel with the comforts of home-all at the price of a quality, traditional 1-room hotel. In a category in which demand runs 6 times higher than supply, HOMEWOOD is solidly positioned for future growth. We have a new and improved prototype to help you build or convert to a HOMEWOOD property. Expansion has been motivated by the Developer's Edge package, which includes fee reductions, reduced royalty fees, PR support and more.

BACKGROUND: IFA MEMBER
Established: 1988; 1st Franchised: 1988
Franchised Units: 102
Company-Owned Units: 39
Total Units: 141
Dist.: US-140; CAN-1; O'seas-0
North America: 38 States, 1 Province
Density: 25 in TX, 13 in FL, 9 in OH
Projected New Units (12 Months): NR
Qualifications: 5, 5, 5, 3, 1, 3
Registered: All States

FINANCIAL/TERMS:
Cash Investment: Varies
Total Investment: $9-12.2MM
Minimum Net Worth: $40K/Rm.
Fees: Franchise - $50K Min.
Royalty - 4% Gross Rm. Rev; Ad. - 4% GrRmRev
Earnings Claims Statement: No
Term of Contract (Years): 22/10-20
Avg. # Of Employees: 25 FT
Passive Ownership: Allowed
Encourage Conversions: Yes
Area Develop. Agreements: No
Sub-Franchising Contracts: No
Expand In Territory: Yes
Space Needs: 110,000 SF; FS

SUPPORT & TRAINING:
Financial Assistance Provided: Yes(I)
Site Selection Assistance: No
Lease Negotiation Assistance: Yes
Co-Operative Advertising: Yes
Franchisee Assoc./Member: No
Size Of Corporate Staff: 2,332
On-Going Support: b,C,D,E,G,h,I
Training: 2 Weeks in Memphis, TN.

SPECIFIC EXPANSION PLANS:
US: All United States
Canada: All Canada
Overseas: Mexico, Latin America.

<< >>

HOSPITALITY INTERNATIONAL

1726 Montreal Cir.
Tucker, GA 30084
Tel: (800) 247-4677 (770) 270-1180
Fax: (770) 270-1077
E-Mail: sales@hifranchise.com
Web Site: www.bookroomsnow.com
Ms. Amy Foy, VP Franchise Development

Hotel franchisor of MASTER HOSTS INNS AND RESORTS, RED CARPET INN, SCOTTISH INNS, PASSPORT INN, DOWNTOWNER INNS, with over 252 franchised properties. HOSPITALITY INTERNATIONAL is proud of the fact that approximately 75% of its current franchisees are minorities. The company is actively pursuing the addition of new minority-owned franchises in all of the U.S.

BACKGROUND:
Established: 1982; 1st Franchised: 1982
Franchised Units: 251
Company-Owned Units: 0
Total Units: 251
Dist.: US-252; CAN-0; O'seas-0
North America: 32 States
Density: 30 in FL, 39 in GA, 18 in TN

Projected New Units (12 Months): 25
Qualifications: 3, 5, 4, 3, 2, 5
Registered: All States Except HI,WA

FINANCIAL/TERMS:

Cash Investment: $70-200K
Total Investment: $1.0-5.0MM
Minimum Net Worth: Varies
Fees: Franchise - $2.5-5K
Royalty - 3-4%; Ad. - 2%
Earnings Claims Statement: No
Term of Contract (Years): 5
Avg. # Of Employees: 6 FT, 3 PT
Passive Ownership: Allowed
Encourage Conversions: Yes
Area Develop. Agreements: No
Sub-Franchising Contracts: No
Expand In Territory: NA
Space Needs: 288/Guest SF; NA

SUPPORT & TRAINING:

Financial Assistance Provided: Yes(I)
Site Selection Assistance: Yes
Lease Negotiation Assistance: Yes
Co-Operative Advertising: Yes
Franchisee Assoc./Member: Yes/Yes
Size Of Corporate Staff: 36
On-Going Support: B,C,D,E,G,H,I
Training: 2 Days in Tucker, GA.

SPECIFIC EXPANSION PLANS:

US: All United States
Canada: All Canada
Overseas: Mexico, Asia, South America

<< >>

Top 100

INTERCONTINENTAL HOTELS GROUP

3 Ravinia Dr., # 100
Atlanta, GA 30346-2118
Tel: (770) 604-2000
Fax: (770) 604-2107
E-Mail: brown.kessler@ichotelsgroup.com
Web Site: www.ichotelsgroup.com
Mr. Brown Kessler, VP Franchise Sales/Dev.

INTERCONTINENTAL HOTELS GROUP is the world's global hotel company. Operates or franchises more than 3,500 hotels and 535,000 guest rooms in more than 100 countries. Franchisor of INTER-CONTINENTAL HOTELS, CROWNE PLAZA HOTELS, HOLIDAY INN, HOLIDAY INN EXPRESS AND STAYBRIDGE SUITES HOTELS, CANDLEWOOD SUITES and HOTEL INDIGO.

BACKGROUND: IFA MEMBER
Established: 1952; 1st Franchised: 1952
Franchised Units: 2,970
Company-Owned Units: 580
Total Units: 3,550
Dist.: US-; CAN-; O'seas-
North America: 50 States
Density: NR
Projected New Units (12 Months): 100+
Qualifications: 5, 4, 4, , ,
Registered: All States and AB

FINANCIAL/TERMS:

Cash Investment: $1-20MM
Total Investment: Varies
Minimum Net Worth: Varies
Fees: Franchise - $500/Rm,40Kmin
Royalty - 5%; Ad. - 2.5-3%
Earnings Claims Statement: Yes
Term of Contract (Years): 10/10
Avg. # Of Employees: Varies
Passive Ownership: Allowed
Encourage Conversions: Yes
Area Develop. Agreements: No
Sub-Franchising Contracts: No
Expand In Territory: Yes
Space Needs: Hotel Site SF; FS

SUPPORT & TRAINING:

Financial Assistance Provided: Yes(I)
Site Selection Assistance: Yes
Lease Negotiation Assistance: No
Co-Operative Advertising: Yes
Franchisee Assoc./Member: Yes
Size Of Corporate Staff: 1,000
On-Going Support: C,D,E,H,I
Training: 4 - 5 Days Atlanta, GA. 4 - 5 Days Regional.

SPECIFIC EXPANSION PLANS:

US: All United States
Canada: All Canada
Overseas: All Countries

<< >>

KAMPGROUNDS OF AMERICA / KOA

550 N. 31st St., FL. 4
Billings, MT 59101
Tel: (800) 548-7239 (406) 248-7444
Fax: (406) 254-7440
E-Mail: cpreble@koa.net
Web Site: www.koa.com
Ms. Carol Preble, VP Franchise Sales

KAMPGROUNDS OF AMERICA is North America's largest franchise system of open-to-the public campgrounds; no membership fees or annual dues are required. All KOA campgrounds offer RV and tent sites; 90% also offer Kamping Kabins. Nearly 2 million copies of the KOA directory are printed and distributed to campers. KOA campgrounds are located in 45 of the contiguous United States, 8 Canadian Provinces, Mexico and Japan.

BACKGROUND:
Established: 1961; 1st Franchised: 1962
Franchised Units: 458
Company-Owned Units: 14
Total Units: 472
Dist.: US-432; CAN-32; O'seas-8
North America: 45 States, 8 Provinces
Density: 27 in FL, 26 in Cam 23 in CO
Projected New Units (12 Months): 8
Qualifications: 5, 3, 2, 3, 4, 4
Registered: All States

FINANCIAL/TERMS:

Cash Investment: $150-500K
Total Investment: $200K-4MM
Minimum Net Worth: $300K
Fees: Franchise - $30/22.5/7.5K
Royalty - 8%; Ad. - 2%
Earnings Claims Statement: Yes
Term of Contract (Years): 5
Avg. # Of Employees: 5 PT (Varies)
Passive Ownership: Discouraged
Encourage Conversions: Yes
Area Develop. Agreements: No
Sub-Franchising Contracts: No
Expand In Territory: Yes
Space Needs: 10+ acres SF; NR

SUPPORT & TRAINING:

Financial Assistance Provided: No
Site Selection Assistance: Yes
Lease Negotiation Assistance: No
Co-Operative Advertising: Yes
Franchisee Assoc./Member: Yes/Yes
Size Of Corporate Staff: 65
On-Going Support: A,B,C,D,E,F,G,h,I
Training: 5 Days at Billings, MT.

SPECIFIC EXPANSION PLANS:

US: All United States
Canada: All Canada
Overseas: No

<< >>

MICROTEL INNS & SUITES

13 Corporate Sq., # 250
Atlanta, GA 30329-1906
Tel: (888) 771-7171 (404) 321-4045
Fax: (404) 321-4482
E-Mail: tim.muir@usfsi.com
Web Site: www.microtelinn.com
Mr. Mike Muir, SVP Sales/Develop.

MICROTEL INNS & SUITES is one of the fastest-growing, all-new construction budget hotel franchise brands in the economy/budget segment and has establishe a reputation for customer satisfaction in the minds of travel consumers around the country. MICROTEL is the proven leader in the economy/budget hotel market. Our concept involves offering the traveling public a high-quality product at a value rate while keeping operating and development costs to a minimum. All MICROTEL INNS are 100% new construction.

BACKGROUND: IFA MEMBER
Established: 1995; 1st Franchised: 1995
Franchised Units: 260
Company-Owned Units: 0
Total Units: 260
Dist.: US-250; CAN-0; O'seas-10
North America: 38 States
Density: 26 in NC, 20 in TX, 19 in GA
Projected New Units (12 Months): 35
Qualifications: 3, 4, 4, 2, 2, 3
Registered: All States

FINANCIAL/TERMS:
Cash Investment: $400K-1MM
Total Investment: $2.8-5.6MM
Minimum Net Worth: NA
Fees: Franchise - $35K
Royalty - 4,5,6%; Ad. - 3,2.5,2%
Earnings Claims Statement: Yes
Term of Contract (Years): 20/10
Avg. # Of Employees: 11 FT
Passive Ownership: Allowed
Encourage Conversions: No
Area Develop. Agreements: No
Sub-Franchising Contracts: No
Expand In Territory: Yes
Space Needs: NR SF; FS

SUPPORT & TRAINING:
Financial Assistance Provided: Yes(I)
Site Selection Assistance: Yes
Lease Negotiation Assistance: No
Co-Operative Advertising: Yes
Franchisee Assoc./Member: Yes
Size Of Corporate Staff: 96
On-Going Support: C,D,E,G,h,I
Training: 4 Weeks Mana./Staff On-Site; 1 Week Classroom Atlanta, GA; 3 Day Reservation Marion, IL.

SPECIFIC EXPANSION PLANS:
US: All United States
Canada: All Canada
Overseas: Europe, South America

<< >>

Top 100

MOTEL 6

4001 International Pkwy.
Carrollton, TX 75007
Tel: (888) 842-2942 (972) 360-5409
Fax: (972) 360-5567
E-Mail: arcinfo@airmail.net
Web Site: www.motel6.com
Ms. Cynthia Gartman, Sr. Dir., Franchise Admin.

With 4,000 hotels worldwide, Accor is the industry leader. Of Accor's 1,200+ N. American properties, today 280 are franchised. An integral part of our strategy will include franchise relationships with a diverse mix of entrepreneurs that share the Accor spirit of quality, fairness and respect. We received the AAFD Fair Franchising Seal of Approval. MOTEL 6 has a quality product, proven operational results and is easy to operate. Many open markets are available. MOTEL 6 is a well-established brand.

BACKGROUND: IFA MEMBER
Established: 1962; 1st Franchised: 1996
Franchised Units: 159
Company-Owned Units: 684
Total Units: 843
Dist.: US-839; CAN-4; O'seas-0
North America: 48 States
Density: 171 in CA, 120 in TX, 47 AZ
Projected New Units (12 Months): 23
Qualifications: 4, 4, 1, 1, 1, 3
Registered: All States

FINANCIAL/TERMS:
Cash Investment: $100-500K
Total Investment: $1.9-2.3MM
Minimum Net Worth: $1.5MM
Fees: Franchise - $25K
Royalty - 4%; Ad. - 3.5%
Earnings Claims Statement: Yes
Term of Contract (Years): 15/20/10
Avg. # Of Employees: 2-4 FT, 4-10 PT
Passive Ownership: Allowed
Encourage Conversions: Yes
Area Develop. Agreements: No
Sub-Franchising Contracts: No
Expand In Territory: No
Space Needs: 1.5 Acres SF; FS

SUPPORT & TRAINING:
Financial Assistance Provided: Yes(I)
Site Selection Assistance: NA
Lease Negotiation Assistance: No
Co-Operative Advertising: Yes
Franchisee Assoc./Member: Yes/Yes
Size Of Corporate Staff: 550
On-Going Support: A,b,C,d,e,h,I
Training: 2 Days Dallas, TX for Owner's Orientation; 1 Week Manager Training Dallas, TX.

SPECIFIC EXPANSION PLANS:
US: All United States
Canada: All Canada
Overseas: No

<< >>

RAMADA®
A very good place to be.℠

RAMADA FRANCHISE SYSTEMS

One Sylvan Way
Parsippany, NJ 07054
Tel: (800) 758-8999 (973) 428-9700
Fax: (800) 643-2107
E-Mail: tom.bernardo@cendant.com
Web Site: www.ramada.com
Mr. Tom P. Bernardo, EVP Franchise Sales

RAMADA is proud to have nearly 900 properties in the United States and Canada. The RAMADA brand was created in Flagstaff, AZ in 1954. In 1990, the brand was acquired by Cendant Corporation, formerly HFS Inc. RAMADA FRANCHISE SYSTEMS is a subsidiary of Cendant Corporation (NYSE: CD).

BACKGROUND: IFA MEMBER
Established: 1954; 1st Franchised: 1989
Franchised Units: 893
Company-Owned Units: 0
Total Units: 893
Dist.: US-822; CAN-71; O'seas-0
North America: 48 States, 8 Provinces
Density: 90 in CA, 67 in FL, 64 in TX
Projected New Units (12 Months): NA
Qualifications: 3, 2, 4, 1, 1, 5
Registered: All States and AB

FINANCIAL/TERMS:
Cash Investment: $384K-8.3MM
Total Investment: NA
Minimum Net Worth: NA
Fees: Franchise - $35Kor $350/RM
Royalty - 4%; Ad. - 4.5%

Earnings Claims Statement: Yes
Term of Contract (Years): 15 - 20
Avg. # Of Employees: 75% FT, 25% PT
Passive Ownership: Allowed
Encourage Conversions: Yes
Area Develop. Agreements: No
Sub-Franchising Contracts: No
Expand In Territory: No
Space Needs: 18.-2.4 Acres SF; FS

SUPPORT & TRAINING:
Financial Assistance Provided: Yes(I)
Site Selection Assistance: No
Lease Negotiation Assistance: No
Co-Operative Advertising: Yes
Franchisee Assoc./Member: Yes/Yes
Size Of Corporate Staff: NA
On-Going Support: B,C,D,G,h,I
Training: 3-6 Days On-Site Property Opening/Training.

SPECIFIC EXPANSION PLANS:
US: All United States
Canada: All Canada
Overseas: No

<< >>

Top 100

RED ROOF INNS

4001 International Pkwy.
Carrollton, TX 75007
Tel: (888) 842-2942 (972) 360-5409
Fax: (972) 360-5567
E-Mail: franchisesales@accor-na.com
Web Site: www.redroof.com
Ms. Cynthia Gartman, Sr. Dir., Franchise Admin.

With 4,000 hotels worldwide, Accor is the industry leader. Of Accor's 1,200+ N. American properties, today 280 are franchised. An integral part of our strategy will include franchise relationships with a diverse mix of entrepreneurs that share the Accor spirit of quality, fairness and respect. We received the AAFD Fair Franchising Seal of Approval. RED ROOF INNS, a well-established brand, has a quality product, proven operational results and is easy to operate. Many open markets are available.

BACKGROUND: IFA MEMBER
Established: 1972; 1st Franchised: 1996
Franchised Units: 100
Company-Owned Units: 246
Total Units: 346
Dist.: US-346; CAN-0; O'seas-0
North America: 39 States
Density: 32 in OH, 25 in TX, 22 in GA
Projected New Units (12 Months): 15
Qualifications: 4, 4, 1, 1, 1, 3
Registered: All States

FINANCIAL/TERMS:
Cash Investment: $100-500K
Total Investment: $2.6-3.9MM
Minimum Net Worth: $1.5MM
Fees: Franchise - $30K
Royalty - 4.5%; Ad. - 4%
Earnings Claims Statement: Yes
Term of Contract (Years): 15/20/10
Avg. # Of Employees: 2-4 FT, 4-10 PT
Passive Ownership: Allowed
Encourage Conversions: Yes
Area Develop. Agreements: No
Sub-Franchising Contracts: No
Expand In Territory: No
Space Needs: 15,000+ SF; FS

SUPPORT & TRAINING:
Financial Assistance Provided: Yes(I)
Site Selection Assistance: No
Lease Negotiation Assistance: No
Co-Operative Advertising: Yes
Franchisee Assoc./Member: Yes/Yes
Size Of Corporate Staff: 550
On-Going Support: A,b,C,d,e,h,I
Training: 2 Days Dallas, TX for Owner's Orientation; 2 Weeks Dallas, TX for Manager Orientation..

SPECIFIC EXPANSION PLANS:
US: All United States
Canada: All Canada
Overseas: No

<< >>

STUDIO 6

4001 International Pkwy.
Carrollton, TX 75007
Tel: (888) 842-2942 (972) 360-5409
Fax: (972) 360-5567
E-Mail: franchisesales@accor-na.com
Web Site: www.staystudio6.com
Ms. Cynthia Gartman, Sr. Dir., Franchise Admin.

With 4,000 hotels worldwide, Accor is the industry leader. Of Accor's 1,200+ N. American properties, today 280 are franchised. An integral part of our strategy will include franchise relationships with a diverse mix of entrepreneurs that share the Accor spirit of quality, fairness and respect. We received the AAFD Fair Franchising Seal of Approval. STUDIO 6 has a quality product, proven operational results and is easy to operate. Many open markets are available. STUDIO 6 is a well-established brand.

BACKGROUND: IFA MEMBER
Established: 1962; 1st Franchised: 1999
Franchised Units: 5
Company-Owned Units: 35
Total Units: 40
Dist.: US-40; CAN-0; O'seas-0
North America: 11 States
Density: 17 in TX, 4 in GA
Projected New Units (12 Months): 3
Qualifications: 4, 4, 1, 1, 1, 3
Registered: All States

FINANCIAL/TERMS:
Cash Investment: $100-500K
Total Investment: $2.7-3.4MM
Minimum Net Worth: $1.5MM
Fees: Franchise - $25K
Royalty - 5%; Ad. - 2%
Earnings Claims Statement: Yes
Term of Contract (Years): 15/20/10
Avg. # Of Employees: 2-4 FT, 4-10 PT
Passive Ownership: Allowed
Encourage Conversions: Yes
Area Develop. Agreements: No
Sub-Franchising Contracts: No
Expand In Territory: No
Space Needs: 2.5 Acres Min SF; FS

SUPPORT & TRAINING:
Financial Assistance Provided: Yes(I)
Site Selection Assistance: No
Lease Negotiation Assistance: No
Co-Operative Advertising: Yes
Franchisee Assoc./Member: No/No
Size Of Corporate Staff: 550
On-Going Support: A,b,C,d,e,h,I
Training: 2 Days in Dallas, TX for Owner's Orientation; 2 Weeks in Dallas, TX for Managers' Orientation.

SPECIFIC EXPANSION PLANS:
US: All United States
Canada: All Canada

Overseas: No

<< >>

U. S. FRANCHISE SYSTEMS

13 Corporate Sq., # 250
Atlanta, GA 30329
Tel: (404) 321-4045
Fax: (404) 321-4482
E-Mail: tim.muir@usfsi.com
Web Site: www.usfsi.com
Mr. Michael Leven, President/CEO

Hotel franchisor of MICROTEL INNS & SUITES, BEST INNS & SUITES and HAWTHORN SUITES brands. MICROTEL -- all new construction, budget. BEST INNS -- middle level limited service. HAWTHORN -- upscale, suite-oriented brand. USFS is known as the "fair franchisor" with the most 2-sided agreement, lower than average fee structure, and no-hidden fees. Brands range from low-capital requirements (MICROTEL) to high (HAWTHORN).

BACKGROUND:
Established: 1995; 1st Franchised: 1995
Franchised Units: 517
Company-Owned Units: 0
Total Units: 517
Dist.: US-430; CAN-3; O'seas-78
North America: 49 States
Density: NR
Projected New Units (12 Months): 60
Qualifications: 4, 4, 4, 3, 3, 4
Registered: All States

FINANCIAL/TERMS:
Cash Investment: $300K-1MM
Total Investment: $1.2-7MM
Minimum Net Worth: NA
Fees: Franchise - $35-40K
Royalty - 5-6%; Ad. - 2.5%
Earnings Claims Statement: Yes
Term of Contract (Years): 20/10
Avg. # Of Employees: 10-25 FT
Passive Ownership: Allowed
Encourage Conversions: Yes
Area Develop. Agreements: No
Sub-Franchising Contracts: No
Expand In Territory: Yes
Space Needs: 45,000 SF; FS, Raw land for development

SUPPORT & TRAINING:
Financial Assistance Provided: Yes(I)
Site Selection Assistance: No
Lease Negotiation Assistance: Yes
Co-Operative Advertising: No
Franchisee Assoc./Member: Yes
Size Of Corporate Staff: 150
On-Going Support: B,C,D,E,G,H,I
Training: 3-4 Days Atlanta, GA; On-Site as Needed.

SPECIFIC EXPANSION PLANS:
US: All United States
Canada: All Canada
Overseas: All Countries

YOGI BEAR'S JELLYSTONE PARK (TM) CAMP-RESORTS

50 W. TechneCenter Dr., # G
Milford, OH 45150-9798
Tel: (800) 626-3720 (513) 831-2100
Fax: (513) 576-8670
E-Mail: rschutter@leisure-systems.com
Web Site: www.campjellystone.com
Mr. Robert E. Schutter, Jr., President/COO

A unique recreation camp-resort for the entire family. YOGI BEAR and friends offer daily activities with a full amenity package, clean restrooms and YOGI BEAR souvenirs. Each camp-resort is independently owned and operated and maintains system standards.

BACKGROUND: IFA MEMBER
Established: 1969; 1st Franchised: 1969
Franchised Units: 68
Company-Owned Units: 0
Total Units: 68
Dist.: US-63; CAN-5; O'seas-0
North America: 25 States, 2 Provinces
Density: 7 in IN, 7 in MI, 7 in WI
Projected New Units (12 Months): 4
Qualifications: , , , , ,
Registered: CA,FL,IL,IN,MD,MI,MN,NY,VA,WI

FINANCIAL/TERMS:
Cash Investment: $30K
Total Investment: $30K
Minimum Net Worth: NR
Fees: Franchise - $20-30K
Royalty - 6%; Ad. - 1%
Earnings Claims Statement: NR
Term of Contract (Years): 5-20/5-10
Avg. # Of Employees: 3 FT, 25 PT
Passive Ownership: Discouraged
Encourage Conversions: Yes
Area Develop. Agreements: No
Sub-Franchising Contracts: No
Expand In Territory: No
Space Needs: NR SF; NR

SUPPORT & TRAINING:
Financial Assistance Provided: Yes(D)
Site Selection Assistance: Yes
Lease Negotiation Assistance: Yes
Co-Operative Advertising: Yes
Franchisee Assoc./Member: NR
Size Of Corporate Staff: 6
On-Going Support: B,C,D,E,G,H,I
Training: 2-3 Days On-Site; 3-4 Days Headquarters; 1-3 Days/Year On-Site.

SPECIFIC EXPANSION PLANS:
US: All United States
Canada: All Canada
Overseas: No

Maid Services & Home Cleaning

Chapter

24

Lodging Industry Profile

Total # Franchisors in Industry Group	22
Total # Franchised Units in Industry Group	3,803
Total # Company-Owned Units in Industry Group	181
Total # Operating Units in Industry Group	3,984
Average # Franchised Units/Franchisor	172.9
Average # Company-Owned Units/Franchisor	8.2
Average # Total Units/Franchisor	181.1
Ratio of Total # Franchised Units/Total # Company-Owned Units	21:1
Industry Survey Participants	14
Representing % of Industry	63.6%
Average Franchise Fee*:	$13.5K
Average Total Investment*:	$55.6K
Average On-Going Royalty Fee*:	4.9%

*If a range was provided, the mid-point of the range was used. See detailed profiles for actual ranges.

Five Largest Participants in Survey

Company	# Franchised Units	# Co-Owned Units	# Total Units	Franchise Fee	On-Going Royalty	Total Investment
1. Merry Maids	1,277	144	1,421	$19-27K	5-7%	$44-52K
2. Molly Maid	600	0	600	$6.9K	7-3%	$36-65K
3. Maids, The	540	3	543	$17.5K	3.3-7%	$56-245K
4. Maid Brigade Services	357	6	363	$19.5K	6.9-3.9%	$88-116K
5. Maid to Perfection	275	0	275	$10K	5-7%	$38-44K

All of the data provided are proprietary and should not be quoted without acknowledging *Bond's Franchise Guide.*

COTTAGECARE

6323 W. 110th St.
Overland Park, KS 66211
Tel: (800) 718-8200 (913) 469-8778
Fax: (913) 469-0822
E-Mail: mpaul@cottagecare.com
Web Site: www.cottagecare.com
Mr. Mert Paul, Dir. Franchise Licensing

Big business approach to housecleaning. We do the marketing and sign up new customers for you! You retain customers and manage the business, not clean houses. "Jumbo" exclusive territories are 4 times larger than industry standards, leading to 'Jumbo' sales.

BACKGROUND:
Established: 1988; 1st Franchised: 1989
Franchised Units: 45
Company-Owned Units: 3
Total Units: 48
Dist.: US-38; CAN-7; O'seas-0
North America: 20 States, 3 Provinces
Density: 4 in KS, 5 in AB
Projected New Units (12 Months): 15
Qualifications: 4, 4, 2, 2, 1, 5
Registered: All States

FINANCIAL/TERMS:
Cash Investment: $46K
Total Investment: $46K
Minimum Net Worth: NA
Fees: Franchise - $7K
Royalty - 5.5%; Ad. - As Needed
Earnings Claims Statement: Yes
Term of Contract (Years): 10/10
Avg. # Of Employees: 1 FT, 16 PT
Passive Ownership: Discouraged
Encourage Conversions: No
Area Develop. Agreements: Yes
Sub-Franchising Contracts: Yes
Expand In Territory: Yes
Space Needs: 400 SF; FS, SF, SC

SUPPORT & TRAINING:
Financial Assistance Provided: Yes(I)
Site Selection Assistance: Yes
Lease Negotiation Assistance: Yes
Co-Operative Advertising: Yes
Franchisee Assoc./Member: No
Size Of Corporate Staff: 10
On-Going Support: C,D,G,H
Training: 2 Weeks Overland Park, KS Headquarters.

SPECIFIC EXPANSION PLANS:
US: All United States
Canada: All Canada
Overseas: No

<< >>

DIAMOND HOME CLEANING SERVICES

4887 E. La Palma Ave., # 708
Anaheim, CA 92807
Tel: (800) 393-6243 (714) 701-9771
Fax: (714) 693-8106
E-Mail: mtgi@maintenanceinc.com
Web Site: www.diamondhomecleaning.com
Mr. Tom Devlin, President

3 franchise concepts - 1 franchise fee when you join the DIAMOND HOME CLEANING SERVICES franchise system. After completion of our extensive training program, you will be an expert in maid services, carpet cleaning and window cleaning services. Benefits include explosive 20% annual customer growth demand; home-based business; no weekends (have a life!); low investment of $25-60K, including start-up/working capital; and prime territories available.

BACKGROUND:
Established: 1993; 1st Franchised: 1997
Franchised Units: 26
Company-Owned Units: 8
Total Units: 34
Dist.: US-34; CAN-0; O'seas-0
North America: 2 States
Density: 13 in CA
Projected New Units (12 Months): 12
Qualifications: 5, 3, 1, 3, 3, 5
Registered: CA

FINANCIAL/TERMS:
Cash Investment: $25K
Total Investment: $25-61K
Minimum Net Worth: $100K
Fees: Franchise - $5K
Royalty - 4-6%; Ad. - 0%
Earnings Claims Statement: No
Term of Contract (Years): 10/5
Avg. # Of Employees: 3 FT, 24 PT
Passive Ownership: Discouraged
Encourage Conversions: Yes
Area Develop. Agreements: No
Sub-Franchising Contracts: No
Expand In Territory: Yes
Space Needs: 500 SF; HB

SUPPORT & TRAINING:
Financial Assistance Provided: Yes(I)
Site Selection Assistance: Yes
Lease Negotiation Assistance: Yes
Co-Operative Advertising: No
Franchisee Assoc./Member: No
Size Of Corporate Staff: 6
On-Going Support: B,C,D,E,F,G,H,I
Training: 1 Week Anaheim, CA.

SPECIFIC EXPANSION PLANS:
US: Southwest
Canada: No
Overseas: No

HOME CLEANING CENTERS OF AMERICA

10851 Mastin Blvd., # 130
Overland Park, KS 66210
Tel: (800) 767-1118 (913) 327-5227
Fax: (913) 327-5272
E-Mail: mcalhoon@aol.com
Web Site: www.homecleaningcenters.com
Mr. Mike Calhoon, President

Very large franchise zones. Quality Quality Quality. Owners do not clean houses. Every corporate policy is made by the franchise owners. Each and every owner is hand picked - having money is not enough. Corporate 'Mission Statement' is to have the largest grossing, highest-quality offices in the industry.

BACKGROUND: IFA MEMBER
Established: 1981; 1st Franchised: 1984
Franchised Units: 38
Company-Owned Units: 0
Total Units: 38
Dist.: US-38; CAN-0; O'seas-0
North America: 9 States
Density: 7 in MO, 4 in KS, 4 in CO
Projected New Units (12 Months): 3
Qualifications: 3, 3, 1, 3, 5, 5
Registered: CA,IL,IN,MI,MN,NY,OR

FINANCIAL/TERMS:
Cash Investment: $20-30K
Total Investment: $30-50K
Minimum Net Worth: NA
Fees: Franchise - $9.5K
Royalty - 4.5-5%; Ad. - 0%
Earnings Claims Statement: Yes
Term of Contract (Years): 10/10
Avg. # Of Employees: 12 FT
Passive Ownership: Discouraged
Encourage Conversions: No
Area Develop. Agreements: No
Sub-Franchising Contracts: No
Expand In Territory: Yes
Space Needs: 500 SF; Non-Retail

SUPPORT & TRAINING:
Financial Assistance Provided: No
Site Selection Assistance: Yes
Lease Negotiation Assistance: Yes
Co-Operative Advertising: No
Franchisee Assoc./Member: Yes/Yes
Size Of Corporate Staff: 2
On-Going Support: b,C,D,E,F,G,H,I
Training: 5 Days Denver, CO or 5 days at

St. Louis, MO.

SPECIFIC EXPANSION PLANS:
US: All United States
Canada: No
Overseas: No

<< >>

MAID BRIGADE SERVICES

4 Concourse Pkwy., # 200
Atlanta, GA 30328-5397
Tel: (800) 722-6243 + 102 (770) 551-9630
Fax: (770) 391-9092
E-Mail: chay@maidbrigade.com
Web Site: www.maidbrigade.com
Ms. Cathy Hay, VP Franchise Development

MAID BRIGADE offers the best opportunity in the industry with our 3 new Large, Major and Regional Market Franchises. Our exclusive territory sizes range from 20,000 to 150,000 qualified households. We provide unparalleled support, business development and the latest technology in the industry. Our focus is to build strong businesses. Master franchises available outside the USA.

BACKGROUND: IFA MEMBER
Established: 1979; 1st Franchised: 1984
Franchised Units: 357
Company-Owned Units: 6
Total Units: 363
Dist.: US-293; CAN-70; O'seas-2
North America: 35 States, 7 Provinces
Density: 43 in VA, 20 in TX, 18 in WA
Projected New Units (12 Months): 25
Qualifications: 4, 3, 2, 3, 2, 5
Registered:CA,FL,HI,IL,MD,MI,MN,NY,OR,VA,WA,WI,DC

FINANCIAL/TERMS:
Cash Investment: $88-116K
Total Investment: $88-116K
Minimum Net Worth: $100K
Fees: Franchise - $19.5K
Royalty - 6.9-3.9%; Ad. - 2%
Earnings Claims Statement: Yes
Term of Contract (Years): 10/10
Avg. # Of Employees: 15 FT
Passive Ownership: Discouraged
Encourage Conversions: Yes
Area Develop. Agreements: No
Sub-Franchising Contracts: No
Expand In Territory: Yes
Space Needs: 700-1,200 SF; HB, SF, SC

SUPPORT & TRAINING:
Financial Assistance Provided: Yes(I)
Site Selection Assistance: Yes
Lease Negotiation Assistance: Yes
Co-Operative Advertising: Yes
Franchisee Assoc./Member: Yes/Yes
Size Of Corporate Staff: 13
On-Going Support: A,B,C,D,E,F,G,H,I
Training: 5 Days in Atlanta, GA; 8 Days On-Site Week of Opening; Training Videos/Manuals.

SPECIFIC EXPANSION PLANS:
US: All United States
Canada: All Canada
Overseas: All Countries

<< >>

MAID TO PERFECTION

1101 Opal Ct., Fl. 2
Hagerstown, MD 21740
Tel: (800) 648-6243 (301) 790-7900
Fax: (301) 790-3949
E-Mail: maidsvc@aol.com
Web Site: www.maidtoperfectioncorp.com
Mr. Michael Katzenberger, President/CEO

MAID TO PERFECTION ® is the only major cleaning franchise that provides access to every residential and commercial service dollar, within an exclusive territory. Ranked #1 for franchisee support/satisfaction in Success Magazine; cited as one of only 15 Great, Low-Investment franchises by Black Enterprise Magazine.

BACKGROUND: IFA MEMBER
Established: 1980; 1st Franchised: 1990
Franchised Units: 275
Company-Owned Units: 0
Total Units: 275
Dist.: US-252; CAN-23; O'seas-0
North America: 22 States, 2 Provinces
Density: 50 in MD, 33 in PA, 20 in CA
Projected New Units (12 Months): 50
Qualifications: 5, 5, 2, 4, 4, 5
Registered: CA,FL,IL,HI,IN,MD,MI,MN,NY,ND,OR,RI,VA,WA,WI,DC

FINANCIAL/TERMS:
Cash Investment: $38-44K
Total Investment: $38-44K
Minimum Net Worth: $80K
Fees: Franchise - $10K
Royalty - 5-7%; Ad. - 0%
Earnings Claims Statement: No
Term of Contract (Years): 10/10
Avg. # Of Employees: 15 FT, 5 PT
Passive Ownership: Discouraged
Encourage Conversions: Yes
Area Develop. Agreements: Yes/5
Sub-Franchising Contracts: No
Expand In Territory: Yes
Space Needs: 400-800 SF; FS, HB, Non-Retail

SUPPORT & TRAINING:
Financial Assistance Provided: Yes(B)
Site Selection Assistance: Yes
Lease Negotiation Assistance: Yes
Co-Operative Advertising: No
Franchisee Assoc./Member: Yes/Yes
Size Of Corporate Staff: 17
On-Going Support: C,D,E,G,H,I
Training: 1 Week at Corporate Headquarters; 1 Week On-Site.

SPECIFIC EXPANSION PLANS:
US: All United States
Canada: All Canada
Overseas: All Countries

MAIDPRO

180 Canal St.
Boston, MA 02114
Tel: (888) 624-3776 (617) 742-8787 + 222
Fax: (617) 720-0700
E-Mail: chuck@maidpro.com
Web Site: www.maidpro.com
Mr. Charles Lynch,

MaidPro is setting the trend in the home and office cleaning industry. MaidPro has a contemporary approach to this high-growth service. With unmatched graphic design and marketing, a completely paperless office and the ability for clients to request service on the Internet, MAIDPRO's franchisees have become successful in running a larger business.

BACKGROUND: IFA MEMBER
Established: 1991; 1st Franchised: 1997
Franchised Units: 30
Company-Owned Units: 1
Total Units: 31
Dist.: US-24; CAN-0; O'seas-0
North America: 14 States
Density: 6 in MA, 3 in FL, 2 in NH
Projected New Units (12 Months): 15
Qualifications: 3, 3, 1, 2, 4, 5
Registered: All States

FINANCIAL/TERMS:

Cash Investment: $10-15K
Total Investment: $28-50K
Minimum Net Worth: NA
Fees: Franchise - $7.9K
Royalty - 3-6%; Ad. - NA
Earnings Claims Statement: No
Term of Contract (Years): 10/5
Avg. # Of Employees: 15 FT, 3 PT
Passive Ownership: Not Allowed
Encourage Conversions: Yes
Area Develop. Agreements: No
Sub-Franchising Contracts: No
Expand In Territory: Yes
Space Needs: 500-1,500 SF; SF, OB

SUPPORT & TRAINING:
Financial Assistance Provided: Yes(I)
Site Selection Assistance: Yes
Lease Negotiation Assistance: Yes
Co-Operative Advertising: Yes
Franchisee Assoc./Member: No
Size Of Corporate Staff: 5
On-Going Support: C,d,E,G,h,I
Training: 2 Weeks in Boston, MA.

SPECIFIC EXPANSION PLANS:
US: All United States
Canada: No
Overseas: No

Maids Etc.®
The Full Service People

MAIDS ETC.

4907 Hollendale Dr., # 208
Raleigh, NC 27616
Tel: (866) 578-6243 (919) 834-8215
Fax: (919) 834-7630
E-Mail: franchise@maidsetc.com
Web Site: www.maidsetc.com
Ms. LaVerne Artis, Vice President

It's time to clean up with MAIDS ETC. and create your own future in the residential and commercial cleaning industries, which are experiencing explosive growth. We are the "Full Service People," offering full-service residential and commercial Bulls-Eye Cleaning Systems. We provide our owner-operators with training, consultation, operational support and access to the latest advances in technology.

BACKGROUND:
Established: 1995; 1st Franchised: 2003
Franchised Units: 3
Company-Owned Units: 1
Total Units: 4
Dist.: US-4; CAN-0; O'seas-0
North America: 3 States
Density: 2 in NC, 1 in SC, 1 in NY
Projected New Units (12 Months): 25
Qualifications: 5, 3, 1, 3, 4, 5
Registered: FL,MI,OR

FINANCIAL/TERMS:
Cash Investment: $19-25K
Total Investment: $36-56K
Minimum Net Worth: Varies
Fees: Franchise - $10K
Royalty - 5-7%; Ad. - 0-2%
Earnings Claims Statement: No
Term of Contract (Years): 5/5
Avg. # Of Employees: 2 FT, 6 PT
Passive Ownership: Discouraged
Encourage Conversions: Yes
Area Develop. Agreements: No
Sub-Franchising Contracts: No
Expand In Territory: Yes
Space Needs: 800+ SF; FS, SF, HB

SUPPORT & TRAINING:
Financial Assistance Provided: Yes(D)
Site Selection Assistance: Yes
Lease Negotiation Assistance: NA
Co-Operative Advertising: NA
Franchisee Assoc./Member: No
Size Of Corporate Staff: 2
On-Going Support: A,B,C,D,e,F,H,I
Training: 7 Days Headquarters in Raleigh, NC.

SPECIFIC EXPANSION PLANS:
US: All United States
Canada: All Canada
Overseas: All Countries

MAIDS TO ORDER®
Residential & Commercial Cleaning Service

"The Personal Touch People"®

MAIDS TO ORDER

4000 Embassy Pkwy., # 430
Akron, OH 44333
Tel: (800) 701-6243 (330) 666-9460
Fax: (877) 666-9710
E-Mail: tpetty@maidstoorder.com
Web Site: www.maidstoorder.com
Mr. Todd Petty, Natl. Franchise Sales Manager

We offer opportunities in all related industries; residential, commercial, power washing and carpet cleaning. Our territories are typically sold by an entire county as opposed to zip codes. We provide an initial start-up package including cleaning chemicals and equipment, office supplies, uniforms, websites and e-mail for staff, marketing materials and more.

BACKGROUND: IFA MEMBER
Established: 1987; 1st Franchised: 1992
Franchised Units: 39
Company-Owned Units: 0
Total Units: 39
Dist.: US-39; CAN-0; O'seas-39
North America: 19 States
Density: 12 in OH, 3 in FL, 3 in NH
Projected New Units (12 Months): 12
Qualifications: 3, 3, 1, 3, 4, 4
Registered: CA,FL,MD,MI,NY,RI,SD,VA

FINANCIAL/TERMS:
Cash Investment: $12.5-57.5K
Total Investment: $35.1-101.5K
Minimum Net Worth: NA
Fees: Franchise - $12.5-57.5K
Royalty - 5%; Ad. - 0%
Earnings Claims Statement: Yes
Term of Contract (Years): 15/15
Avg. # Of Employees: 3 FT, 12 PT
Passive Ownership: Not Allowed
Encourage Conversions: NR
Area Develop. Agreements: No
Sub-Franchising Contracts: No
Expand In Territory: Yes
Space Needs: 500 SF; SF, SC

SUPPORT & TRAINING:
Financial Assistance Provided: Yes(D)
Site Selection Assistance: Yes
Lease Negotiation Assistance: Yes
Co-Operative Advertising: Yes
Franchisee Assoc./Member: Yes/Yes
Size Of Corporate Staff: NR
On-Going Support: A,C,D,E,G,h,I
Training: 1 Week in Akron, OH.

SPECIFIC EXPANSION PLANS:
US: All United States
Canada: All Canada
Overseas: No

MAIDS, THE

4820 Dodge St.
Omaha, NE 68132-3111
Tel: (800) 843-6243 (402) 558-5555
Fax: (402) 558-4112
E-Mail: franchising@themaids.net
Web Site: www.maids.com
Mr. Sanford L. Friedman, VP Franchise Development

AMERICA'S MAID SERVICE - THE MAIDS is the premier residential cleaning franchise. Our cleaning system is the most thorough in the industry and sets us ahead of all competition. We offer low investment, comprehensive training and on-going support that set the industry standard. Call THE MAIDS today and discover why we are AMERICA'S MAID SERVICE.

BACKGROUND: IFA MEMBER
Established: 1979; 1st Franchised: 1980
Franchised Units: 540
Company-Owned Units: 3
Total Units: 543
Dist.: US-415; CAN-13; O'seas-0
North America: 40 States, 5 Provinces
Density: 34 in CA, 23 in NY, 20 in IL
Projected New Units (12 Months): 40
Qualifications: 4, 4, 1, 3, 1, 4
Registered: All States

FINANCIAL/TERMS:
Cash Investment: $14-61K
Total Investment: $56-245K
Minimum Net Worth: $180-350K
Fees: Franchise - $17.5K
Royalty - 3.3-7%; Ad. - 1%
Earnings Claims Statement: Yes
Term of Contract (Years): 20/20
Avg. # Of Employees: 1-2 FT, 8-12 PT
Passive Ownership: Discouraged
Encourage Conversions: Yes
Area Develop. Agreements: No
Sub-Franchising Contracts: Yes
Expand In Territory: Yes
Space Needs: 200 SF; FS, SC, SF

SUPPORT & TRAINING:
Financial Assistance Provided: Yes(I)
Site Selection Assistance: Yes
Lease Negotiation Assistance: No
Co-Operative Advertising: Yes
Franchisee Assoc./Member: Yes/Yes
Size Of Corporate Staff: 35
On-Going Support: A,B,C,D,G,H,I
Training: 8 Days Each in Both Managerial and Technical Training at Headquarters; 90 Days On-Site.

SPECIFIC EXPANSION PLANS:
US: All United States
Canada: All Canada
Overseas: All Countries

Top 100

MERRY MAIDS
3839 Forest Hill-Irene Rd.
Memphis, TN 38125
Tel: (800) 798-8000 (901) 597-8100
Fax: (901) 597-8140
E-Mail: franchisesales@mmhomeoffice.com
Web Site: www.merrymaids.com
Mr. Rob Sanders, Director Market Expansion

MERRY MAIDS is the largest and most recognized company in the home cleaning industry. The company's commitment to training and on-going support is unmatched. MERRY MAIDS is highly ranked as an established and fast growing franchise opportunity according to leading national publications. We offer low investment, cross-selling promotions with our partner companies, research and development and excellent marketing support.

BACKGROUND: IFA MEMBER
Established: 1979; 1st Franchised: 1980
Franchised Units: 1,277
Company-Owned Units: 144
Total Units: 1,421
Dist.: US-915; CAN-68; O'seas-438
North America: 49 States, 7 Provinces
Density: 123 in CA, 51 in TX, 42 IL
Projected New Units (12 Months): 32
Qualifications: 5, 3, 1, 3, 4, 5
Registered: All States

FINANCIAL/TERMS:
Cash Investment: $22-25K
Total Investment: $44-52K
Minimum Net Worth: Varies
Fees: Franchise - $19-27K
Royalty - 5-7%; Ad. - 0.25-1%
Earnings Claims Statement: No
Term of Contract (Years): 5/5
Avg. # Of Employees: 2 FT, 12 PT
Passive Ownership: Discouraged
Encourage Conversions: Yes
Area Develop. Agreements: No
Sub-Franchising Contracts: No
Expand In Territory: Yes
Space Needs: 800 Minimum SF; FS

SUPPORT & TRAINING:
Financial Assistance Provided: Yes(D)
Site Selection Assistance: No
Lease Negotiation Assistance: No
Co-Operative Advertising: NA
Franchisee Assoc./Member: No
Size Of Corporate Staff: 65
On-Going Support: C,D,G,H,I
Training: 8 Days Headquarters, Memphis, TN.

SPECIFIC EXPANSION PLANS:
US: All United States
Canada: All Canada
Overseas: All Countries

MINI MAID SERVICE SYSTEMS OF CANADA
192 Shorting Rd.
Scarborough, ON M1S 3S7 CANADA
Tel: (800) 627-MINI (416) 298-7288
Fax: (416) 298-8445
E-Mail: minimaid@mindspring.com
Web Site: www.minimaid.com
Mr. David Dugas, President

A team of 4 maids clean, using own supplies and equipment. All fully trained, uniformed, insured and bonded. Arrive at customer homes in identifiable station wagons for professional image. Strong support programs from home office assures successful operation.

BACKGROUND:
Established: 1979; 1st Franchised: 1979
Franchised Units: 78
Company-Owned Units: 11
Total Units: 89
Dist.: US-0; CAN-101; O'seas-0
North America: 7 Provinces
Density: 20 in ON, 16 in BC, 9 in PQ
Projected New Units (12 Months): 3
Qualifications: , , , , ,
Registered: AB

FINANCIAL/TERMS:
Cash Investment: $14K
Total Investment: $14K
Minimum Net Worth: NR
Fees: Franchise - $10K
Royalty - 6%; Ad. - 2%
Earnings Claims Statement: No
Term of Contract (Years): 10/10
Avg. # Of Employees: 6 FT
Passive Ownership: Not Allowed
Encourage Conversions: No
Area Develop. Agreements: Yes/5
Sub-Franchising Contracts: Yes
Expand In Territory: Yes
Space Needs: NR SF; NR

SUPPORT & TRAINING:
Financial Assistance Provided: No
Site Selection Assistance: Yes
Lease Negotiation Assistance: NA
Co-Operative Advertising: Yes
Franchisee Assoc./Member: NR
Size Of Corporate Staff: 5
On-Going Support: B,C,D,G,H,I
Training: 1 Week Headquarters; Annual Seminars.

SPECIFIC EXPANSION PLANS:

US: No
Canada: All Canada
Overseas: No

MOLLY MAID

3948 Ranchero Dr.
Ann Arbor, MI 48108-2775
Tel: (800) 289-4600 + 100 (734) 822-6340
Fax: (734) 822-6888
E-Mail: rdg@mollymaid.com
Web Site: www.mollymaid.com
Mr. Rob Goggins, Franchise Director

MOLLY MAID is # 1 in the industry in residential cleaning and home care service. Ranked in INC 500, Entrepreneur's Top 100, Platinum 200, Entrepreneur 509 and Business Start-Ups As Top 200 Hottest Franchises. MOLLY MAID's technology won The Windows Worldwide Open in 1995 sponsored by Bill Gates.

BACKGROUND: IFA MEMBER

Established: 1979; 1st Franchised: 1979
Franchised Units: 600
Company-Owned Units: 0
Total Units: 600
Dist.: US-280; CAN-167; O'seas-100
North America: 36 States, 3 Provinces
Density: 146 in ON, 52 in CA, 22 MI
Projected New Units (12 Months): 40
Qualifications: 3, 3, 1, 3, 4, 5
Registered:CA,FL,IL,IN,MD,MI,MN,NY,OR,RI,VA,WA,WI,DC

FINANCIAL/TERMS:

Cash Investment: $15-25K
Total Investment: $36-65K
Minimum Net Worth: $150K
Fees: Franchise - $6.9K
Royalty - 7-3%; Ad. - $75/Qtr.
Earnings Claims Statement: Yes
Term of Contract (Years): 10/10
Avg. # Of Employees: 12 FT
Passive Ownership: Discouraged
Encourage Conversions: Yes
Area Develop. Agreements: No
Sub-Franchising Contracts: No
Expand In Territory: Yes
Space Needs: 400 SF; Other

SUPPORT & TRAINING:

Financial Assistance Provided: Yes(I)
Site Selection Assistance: Yes
Lease Negotiation Assistance: No
Co-Operative Advertising: Yes
Franchisee Assoc./Member: Yes/Yes
Size Of Corporate Staff: 33
On-Going Support: C,D,F,G,h,I
Training: 5 Days in Home Office; 6 Months in Right Start Program; 2 Days at Franchise Location.

SPECIFIC EXPANSION PLANS:

US: All United States
Canada: All Canada
Overseas: Japan, United Kingdom

WORKENDERS

4400 N. Federal Hwy., # 210
Boca Raton, FL 33431
Tel:
Fax: (561) 477-5321
E-Mail:
Web Site: www.workenders.com
Mr. Gary D. Goranson, President

Residential cleaning service. Team cleaning system, stressing efficient methods and efficient client scheduling. Strategy is to generate $25/hour per employee, including both actual cleaning time and travel time.

BACKGROUND:

Established: 1991; 1st Franchised: 1992
Franchised Units: 20
Company-Owned Units: 0
Total Units: 20
Dist.: US-20; CAN-0; O'seas-0
North America: 14 States
Density: 3 in OR, 2 in CA, 2 in NC
Projected New Units (12 Months): 6
Qualifications: 5, 4, 1, 2, 4, 3
Registered: CA,FL,MI,NY,OR,WA

FINANCIAL/TERMS:

Cash Investment: $42.9-70.1K
Total Investment: $60-100K
Minimum Net Worth: $200K
Fees: Franchise - $22.5K
Royalty - 3-6%; Ad. - 0%
Earnings Claims Statement: Yes
Term of Contract (Years): 20/10
Avg. # Of Employees: 6-30 FT
Passive Ownership: Discouraged
Encourage Conversions: No
Area Develop. Agreements: No
Sub-Franchising Contracts: No
Expand In Territory: Yes
Space Needs:600-1,000 SF; Ground Floor Office

SUPPORT & TRAINING:

Financial Assistance Provided: No
Site Selection Assistance: NA
Lease Negotiation Assistance: Yes
Co-Operative Advertising: No
Franchisee Assoc./Member: Yes/Yes
Size Of Corporate Staff: 1
On-Going Support: c,d,E,G,H,I
Training: 3 Weeks with Mentor Franchisee in AK, GA, NY or OR.

SPECIFIC EXPANSION PLANS:

US: All Except HI,MN,WI,IL,MD,VA
Canada: No
Overseas: No

<< >>

Maintenance/Cleaning/Sanitation

Chapter
25

MAINTENANCE/CLEANING/SANITATION INDUSTRY PROFILE

Total # Franchisors in Industry Group	131
Total # Franchised Units in Industry Group	45,503
Total # Company-Owned Units in Industry Group	1242
Total # Operating Units in Industry Group	46,745
Average # Franchised Units/Franchisor	347.4
Average # Company-Owned Units/Franchisor	9.5
Average # Total Units/Franchisor	356.8
Ratio of Total # Franchised Units/Total # Company-Owned Units	36.6:1
Industry Survey Participants	74
Representing % of Industry	56.5%
Average Franchise Fee*:	$20.8K
Average Total Investment*:	$66.9K
Average On-Going Royalty Fee*:	8.7%

*If a range was provided, the mid-point of the range was used. See detailed profiles for actual ranges.

FIVE LARGEST PARTICIPANTS IN SURVEY

Company	# Franchised Units	# Co-Owned Units	# Total Units	Franchise Fee	On-Going Royalty	Total Investment
1. Jani-King International	11,000	27	11,027	$8-33K	10%	$2.9-40K
2. Coverall Cleaning Concepts	8,451	0	8,451	$6.2-32.2K	5%	$6.2-36K
3. ServiceMaster Clean	4,488	0	4,488	$16.9-43K	4-10%	$18.8-100K
4. Chem-Dry Carpet & Upholstery Cleaning	3,903	0	3,903	$19.5K	$212/Mo.	$6.9-27.6K
5. Jan-Pro Cleaning Systems	3,009	0	3,009	$1-35K	8%	$2.8-44K

All of the data provided are proprietary and should not be quoted without acknowledging *Bond's Franchise Guide.*

1-800-GOT-JUNK?

200-1523 W. 3rd Ave.
Vancouver, BC V6J 1J8 CANADA
Tel: (877) 408-5865 (604) 731-5865
Fax: (801) 751-0634
E-Mail: aread@1800gotjunk.com
Web Site: www.1800gotjunk.com
Mr. Alex Read, Director Business Development

1-800-GOT-JUNK? has revolutionized customer service in junk removal for over 10 years. By setting the mark for service standards and professionalism, an industry that once operated without set rates, price lists or receipts, now has top service standards. You will have the expert advice and support that is key to success. Our intensive training program will get you on track; our on-going support and continuing education will keep you there. Centralized call center allows you to focus on your business.

BACKGROUND: IFA MEMBER
Established: 1989; 1st Franchised: 1999
Franchised Units: 120
Company-Owned Units: 1
Total Units: 121
Dist.: US-85; CAN-10; O'seas-0
North America: 35 States, 3 Provinces
Density: 5 in CA, 5 in ON, 2 in WA
Projected New Units (12 Months): 50
Qualifications: 5, 5, 1, 2, 4, 5
Registered: All States

FINANCIAL/TERMS:
Cash Investment: $45-90K
Total Investment: $45-90K
Minimum Net Worth: $150K
Fees: Franchise - $18K
Royalty - 8%; Ad. - 1%
Earnings Claims Statement: No
Term of Contract (Years): 5/15
Avg. # Of Employees: 6 FT, 4 PT
Passive Ownership: Discouraged
Encourage Conversions: No
Area Develop. Agreements: No
Sub-Franchising Contracts: No
Expand In Territory: Yes
Space Needs: 350 SF; OB

SUPPORT & TRAINING:
Financial Assistance Provided: Yes(I)
Site Selection Assistance: NA
Lease Negotiation Assistance: NA
Co-Operative Advertising: Yes
Franchisee Assoc./Member: Yes/Yes
Size Of Corporate Staff: 30
On-Going Support: a,B,C,D,G,H,I
Training: 5-10 Days Vancouver, BC; 3-5 Days in Assigned Territory.

SPECIFIC EXPANSION PLANS:
US: All United States
Canada: No
Overseas: No

<< >>

AEROWEST & WESTAIR SANITATION SERVICES

3882 Del Amo Blvd., # 3602
Torrance, CA 90503
Tel: (888) 663-6726 (310) 793-4242
Fax: (310) 793-4250
E-Mail: info@westsanitation.com
Web Site: www.westsanitation.com
Mr. Graham H. Emery, President

AEROWEST & WESTAIR franchisees provide a specialized restroom fixture service to kill unpleasant odors, provide a light fragrance in the restroom and leave the urinals and toilets sanitary. The services do not involve any janitorial work, only the 28-day service of dispensers. WEST supplies full administrative support (billing, collections, reports). Products are supplied to franchisees at WEST's cost.

BACKGROUND: IFA MEMBER
Established: 1983; 1st Franchised: 1983
Franchised Units: 55
Company-Owned Units: 17
Total Units: 72
Dist.: US-72; CAN-0; O'seas-0
North America: 30 States
Density: 14 in CA, 11 in TX, 9 in IL
Projected New Units (12 Months): 10
Qualifications: 2, 1, 4, 3, 2, 4
Registered: CA,FL,IL,IN,MD,MI,NY,OR, VE,WA,WI,DC

FINANCIAL/TERMS:
Cash Investment: $3-10K
Total Investment: $3-40K
Minimum Net Worth: $10K
Fees: Franchise - $4K
Royalty - 8%; Ad. - 4%
Earnings Claims Statement: Yes
Term of Contract (Years): 5/1
Avg. # Of Employees: 1 FT
Passive Ownership: Discouraged
Encourage Conversions: Yes
Area Develop. Agreements: NA
Sub-Franchising Contracts: No
Expand In Territory: No
Space Needs: NA SF; HB

SUPPORT & TRAINING:
Financial Assistance Provided: Yes(D)
Site Selection Assistance: NA
Lease Negotiation Assistance: NA
Co-Operative Advertising: NA
Franchisee Assoc./Member: No
Size Of Corporate Staff: 14
On-Going Support: A,B,D,G,H
Training: 7-10 Working Days Near Existing Franchisee.

SPECIFIC EXPANSION PLANS:
US: OR, MD, FL, VA
Canada: No
Overseas: No

<< >>

AIRE-MASTER OF AMERICA

1821 N. Highway CC, P.O. Box 2310
Nixa, MO 65714
Tel: (800) 525-0957 (417) 725-2691
Fax: (417) 725-5737
E-Mail: aire@airemaster.com
Web Site: www.airemaster.com
Mr. Jim M. Roudenis, Franchise Director

AIRE-MASTER is a unique system of odor control and restroom fixture cleaning. Unlike the majority of 'air-fresheners' on the market, AIRE-MASTER deodorizers and deodorant products actually eliminate odors by oxidation. You don't need prior experience in the odor control/sanitary supply industry to qualify for a franchise. Customer base is built by making sales calls and providing good customer service. Complete training. We are FDA approved and manufacture deodorants, cleaning products and hand soaps.

BACKGROUND:
Established: 1958; 1st Franchised: 1976
Franchised Units: 60
Company-Owned Units: 5
Total Units: 65
Dist.: US-63; CAN-2; O'seas-62
North America: 39 States, 2 Provinces
Density: 5 in MO, 4 in FL, 4 in CA
Projected New Units (12 Months): 14
Qualifications: 5, 5, 5, 5, 5, 5
Registered: CA,IL,MD,NY

FINANCIAL/TERMS:
Cash Investment: $31K

Total Investment: $30-80K
Minimum Net Worth: NR
Fees: Franchise - $23K
Royalty - 5%; Ad. - 0%
Earnings Claims Statement: No
Term of Contract (Years): 20/3
Avg. # Of Employees: 2-3 FT
Passive Ownership: Discouraged
Encourage Conversions: Yes
Area Develop. Agreements: No
Sub-Franchising Contracts: No
Expand In Territory: NA
Space Needs: NA SF; HB

SUPPORT & TRAINING:

Financial Assistance Provided: Yes(D)
Site Selection Assistance: NA
Lease Negotiation Assistance: Yes
Co-Operative Advertising: Yes
Franchisee Assoc./Member: Yes/Yes
Size Of Corporate Staff: 70
On-Going Support: a,B,C,D,E,G,h,I
Training: 5 Days Headquarters, Nixa, MO; 5 Days Franchisee's Location.

SPECIFIC EXPANSION PLANS:

US: All United States
Canada: All Canada
Overseas: No

<< >>

AMERICAN LEAK DETECTION

888 Research Dr., # 100, P.O. Box 1701
Palm Springs, CA 92262
Tel: (800) 755-6697 (760) 320-9991
Fax: (760) 320-1288
E-Mail: sbangs@americanleakdetection.com
Web Site: www.americanleakdetection.com
Ms. Sheila Bangs, Director Franchise Sales

Electronic detection of water, drain, waste, and sewer leaks under concrete slabs of homes, commercial buildings, pools, spas, fountains, etc. with equipment commissioned/ manufactured by company.

BACKGROUND: IFA MEMBER

Established: 1974; 1st Franchised: 1985
Franchised Units: 312
Company-Owned Units: 6
Total Units: 318
Dist.: US-243; CAN-8; O'seas-67
North America: 40 States, 3 Provinces
Density: 71 in CA, 35 in FL, 15 in TX
Projected New Units (12 Months): 4
Qualifications: 3, 3, 2, 2, 2, 3
Registered: CA,FL,HI,IL,IN,MD,MI,MN, NY,OR,RI,VA,WA,WI,DC,AB

FINANCIAL/TERMS:

Cash Investment: $58-120K
Total Investment: $85-150K
Minimum Net Worth: Varies
Fees: Franchise - $57.5K
Royalty - 6-10%; Ad. - NA
Earnings Claims Statement: No
Term of Contract (Years): 10/10
Avg. # Of Employees: 1-4 FT, 2 PT
Passive Ownership: Discouraged
Encourage Conversions: NA
Area Develop. Agreements: No
Sub-Franchising Contracts: No
Expand In Territory: Yes
Space Needs: NR SF; NR

SUPPORT & TRAINING:

Financial Assistance Provided: Yes(D)
Site Selection Assistance: NA
Lease Negotiation Assistance: NA
Co-Operative Advertising: Yes
Franchisee Assoc./Member: Yes/Yes
Size Of Corporate Staff: 37
On-Going Support: a,B,C,D,f,G,H,I
Training: 6-10 Weeks Palm Springs, CA.

SPECIFIC EXPANSION PLANS:

US: Northeast, Midwest
Canada: MB, SK
Overseas: Western Europe, South America

<< >>

AMERICARE RESTROOM HYGIENE & SUPPLY

225 Laura Dr., # A
Addison, IL 60101
Tel: (800) 745-6191 (630) 458-1990
Fax: (630) 458-1994
E-Mail: richard@americarehygiene.com
Web Site: www.americarehygiene.com
Mr. Richard F. Gac, President

Aroma enhancement plus infection control systems for retail, commercial and industrial manufacturing, specializing in full line of high profit products and services for germ killing, restroom supplies and maintenance. Also, interior non-toxic power washing of kitchens, restrooms, delis, coolers, food prep areas, etc. to eliminate cross contamination of infectious diseases. Plus, exterior, environmentally-friendly high-heat power washing of sidewalks, grease pits and dumpster areas.

BACKGROUND:

Established: 1990; 1st Franchised: 1993
Franchised Units: 30
Company-Owned Units: 10
Total Units: 40
Dist.: US-41; CAN-0; O'seas-0
North America: 3 States
Density: 36 in IL, 3 in IN, 2 in WI
Projected New Units (12 Months): 12
Qualifications: 3, 2, 1, 2, 3, 5
Registered: IL,WI

FINANCIAL/TERMS:

Cash Investment: $2.5-9.5K
Total Investment: $9.5-95K
Minimum Net Worth: $50K
Fees: Franchise - $9.5K
Royalty - 8-13%; Ad. - 2%
Earnings Claims Statement: No
Term of Contract (Years): 10/10
Avg. # Of Employees: 1 FT
Passive Ownership: Not Allowed
Encourage Conversions: NA
Area Develop. Agreements: Yes
Sub-Franchising Contracts: Yes
Expand In Territory: Yes
Space Needs: NA SF; HB

SUPPORT & TRAINING:

Financial Assistance Provided: Yes
Site Selection Assistance: Yes
Lease Negotiation Assistance: NA
Co-Operative Advertising: Yes
Franchisee Assoc./Member: No
Size Of Corporate Staff: 10
On-Going Support: A,B,C,D,E,F,G,H,I
Training: 2 Weeks in Addison, IL.

SPECIFIC EXPANSION PLANS:

US: IL, IN, MI, WI
Canada: No
Overseas: No

<< >>

ANAGO CLEANING SYSTEMS

3111 N. University Dr., # 625
Coral Springs, FL 33065
Tel: (800) 213-5857 (954) 752-3111
Fax: (954) 752-1200

E-Mail: jwalker@anagousa.net
Web Site: www.goanago.com
Ms. Judy Walker, Director Franchise Marketing

We are the digital generation of cleaning franchises. We provide you with customers!!! Plus invoicing and collection services. We provide complete training, progressive business development, equipment package and start-up. Master franchises available for select locations, as well as local unit franchises.

BACKGROUND:
Established: 1995; 1st Franchised: 2001
Franchised Units: 350
Company-Owned Units: 0
Total Units: 350
Dist.: US-350; CAN-0; O'seas-0
North America: 15 States
Density: 169 in FL, 54 in IL, 41 in O
Projected New Units (12 Months): 200
Qualifications: 3, 3, 3, 2, 2, 2
Registered: CA,FL,IL,VA,DC
FINANCIAL/TERMS:
Cash Investment: $1-50K
Total Investment: $5-325K
Minimum Net Worth: $2-100K
Fees: Franchise - $4.5-150K
Royalty - 5%; Ad. - 2%
Earnings Claims Statement: No
Term of Contract (Years): 10/10
Avg. # Of Employees: 1-2 FT, 4 PT
Passive Ownership: Discouraged
Encourage Conversions: Yes
Area Develop. Agreements: Yes/10
Sub-Franchising Contracts: Yes
Expand In Territory: Yes
Space Needs: 1,500 SF; FS
SUPPORT & TRAINING:
Financial Assistance Provided: Yes(I)
Site Selection Assistance: Yes
Lease Negotiation Assistance: Yes
Co-Operative Advertising: NA
Franchisee Assoc./Member: No
Size Of Corporate Staff: 10
On-Going Support: C,E,G,H,I
Training: 2 Weeks for Master in FL Corp. Office; 75 Hours for Unit Franchise - Master Office.
SPECIFIC EXPANSION PLANS:
US: All United States
Canada: All Canada
Overseas: All Countries

<< >>

BEARCOM BUILDING SERVICES
7022 S. 400 W.
Midvale, UT 84047
Tel: (888) 569-9533 (801) 569-9500
Fax: (801) 569-8400
E-Mail: michael@bearcomservices.com
Web Site: www.bearcomservices.com
Mr. Michael A. Jenkins, President/CEO

We train you on how to get your own janitorial accounts. We support you to help you maintain those accounts. We have software to help you manage your business. You will own and operate a cleaning business (commercial).

BACKGROUND:
Established: 1993; 1st Franchised: 1994
Franchised Units: 60
Company-Owned Units: 1
Total Units: 61
Dist.: US-63; CAN-0; O'seas-0
North America: 1 State
Density: 63 in UT
Projected New Units (12 Months): NR
Qualifications: , , , , ,
Registered:
FINANCIAL/TERMS:
Cash Investment: $3K
Total Investment: $12.8K
Minimum Net Worth: $0K
Fees: Franchise - $10K
Royalty - 6%; Ad. - 0%
Earnings Claims Statement: No
Term of Contract (Years): 5/5
Avg. # Of Employees: 3 FT, 3 PT
Passive Ownership: Allowed
Encourage Conversions: NR
Area Develop. Agreements: No
Sub-Franchising Contracts: No
Expand In Territory: No
Space Needs: NA SF; HB
SUPPORT & TRAINING:
Financial Assistance Provided: NR
Site Selection Assistance: No
Lease Negotiation Assistance: No
Co-Operative Advertising: No
Franchisee Assoc./Member: No
Size Of Corporate Staff: 7
On-Going Support: a,G,I
Training: 3 Days UT.
SPECIFIC EXPANSION PLANS:
US: All US Except. Cert Reg. States
Canada: NR
Overseas: NR

<< >>

BIOLOGIX
1561 Fairview Ave.
St. Louis, MO 63132-1324
Tel: (800) 747-1885 (314) 423-1945
Fax: (314) 423-4394
E-Mail: jjones@biologix.com
Web Site: www.biologix.com
Mr. James C. Jones, Vice PresidentP/Director

BIOLOGIX provides guaranteed environmental waste elimination services to clients in the food service and hospitality industry. This is a ground floor opportunity to purchase exclusive rights to a territory in the Biotechnology/Environmental service field. Business-to-business sales, renewable income and a positive environmental impact make BIOLOGIX a tremendous opportunity.

BACKGROUND:
Established: 1989; 1st Franchised: 1995
Franchised Units: 22
Company-Owned Units: 2
Total Units: 24
Dist.: US-2; CAN-0; O'seas-0
North America: 12 States
Density: 4 in MO, 3 in OH, 2 in TX
Projected New Units (12 Months): 22
Qualifications: 4, 4, 3, 4, 4, 5
Registered: IL,IN,MD,MI,RI,VA,WI
FINANCIAL/TERMS:
Cash Investment: $23.9-43.6K
Total Investment: NR
Minimum Net Worth: $30K
Fees: Franchise - $12.5K
Royalty - 4%; Ad. - NA
Earnings Claims Statement: No
Term of Contract (Years): 5/5
Avg. # Of Employees: 2 FT, 2 PT
Passive Ownership: Discouraged
Encourage Conversions: NA
Area Develop. Agreements: No
Sub-Franchising Contracts: No
Expand In Territory: Yes
Space Needs: NR SF; HB
SUPPORT & TRAINING:
Financial Assistance Provided: No
Site Selection Assistance: NA
Lease Negotiation Assistance: NA
Co-Operative Advertising: NA
Franchisee Assoc./Member: No
Size Of Corporate Staff: 30
On-Going Support: A,B,C,D,F,G,H,I
Training: 1 Week St. Louis, MO.
SPECIFIC EXPANSION PLANS:
US: All United States
Canada: No
Overseas: NR

<< >>

BONUS BUILDING CARE

P. O. Box 300
Indianola, OK 74442
Tel: (800) 931-1102 (918) 823-4990
Fax: (918) 823-4994
E-Mail: bonusinc@aol.com
Web Site: www.bonusbuildingcare.com
Ms. Arleen Cavanaugh, Chief Executive Officer

Commercial cleaning. Turn-key operation, with customers, training, operations assistance, equipment, business insurance and clerical support. Best cleaning franchise on the market today because of lower fees, personalized support, less restrictions and quicker start-up. We're not the biggest, but we are the best. Master franchises available. IFA Member.

BACKGROUND: IFA MEMBER
Established: 1996; 1st Franchised: 1996
Franchised Units: 830
Company-Owned Units: 3
Total Units: 833
Dist.: US-381; CAN-0; O'seas-0
North America: 7 States
Density: TN, MO, TX
Projected New Units (12 Months): 100
Qualifications: 1, 1, 2, 2, 3, 3
Registered: IL, IN

FINANCIAL/TERMS:
Cash Investment: Varies
Total Investment: Varies
Minimum Net Worth: NA
Fees: Franchise - $6.5K
Royalty - 10%; Ad. - 0%
Earnings Claims Statement: No
Term of Contract (Years): 20/20
Avg. # Of Employees: Varies
Passive Ownership: Discouraged
Encourage Conversions: Yes
Area Develop. Agreements: No
Sub-Franchising Contracts: Yes
Expand In Territory: Yes
Space Needs: NA SF; BH

SUPPORT & TRAINING:
Financial Assistance Provided: Yes(D)
Site Selection Assistance: NA
Lease Negotiation Assistance: NA
Co-Operative Advertising: NA
Franchisee Assoc./Member: Yes/No
Size Of Corporate Staff: 6
On-Going Support: B,C,D,I
Training: Minimum 20 Hours On-Site; Minimum 10 Hours Classroom; as Needed Self-Study.

SPECIFIC EXPANSION PLANS:
US: All United States
Canada: All Canada
Overseas: All Countries

<< >>

BUILDING SERVICES OF AMERICA
11900 W. 87th St., # 135
Lenexa, KS 66215
Tel: (913) 599-6200
Fax: (913) 599-4441
E-Mail: howard@buildingservicesofamerica.com
Web Site: www.buildingservicesofamerica.com
Mr. Howard Capps, President

Franchised commercial cleaning.

BACKGROUND:
Established: 1992; 1st Franchised: 1991
Franchised Units: 35
Company-Owned Units: 1
Total Units: 36
Dist.: US-36; CAN-0; O'seas-0
North America: 2 States
Density: 15 in KS, 21 in MO
Projected New Units (12 Months): 6
Qualifications: 2, 2, 1, 2, 2, 2
Registered: NR

FINANCIAL/TERMS:
Cash Investment: $1.5-15K
Total Investment: $7.5-20K
Minimum Net Worth: $0K
Fees: Franchise - $1.5-15K
Royalty - 8%; Ad. - 0%
Earnings Claims Statement: No
Term of Contract (Years): 10/10
Avg. # Of Employees: Varies
Passive Ownership: Not Allowed
Encourage Conversions: NA
Area Develop. Agreements: No
Sub-Franchising Contracts: No
Expand In Territory: Yes
Space Needs: NR SF; NA

SUPPORT & TRAINING:
Financial Assistance Provided: Yes(D)
Site Selection Assistance: No
Lease Negotiation Assistance: No
Co-Operative Advertising: No
Franchisee Assoc./Member: Yes/Yes
Size Of Corporate Staff: 7
On-Going Support: A,C,D,G,H
Training: 1-2 Weeks at Corporate Office.

SPECIFIC EXPANSION PLANS:
US: All United States
Canada: No
Overseas: No

<< >>

CAPITAL CARPET CLEANING & DYE
22410 Woodward
Ferndale, MI 48220
Tel: (586) 677-6378
Fax: (248) 542-4566
E-Mail:
Web Site: www.chemmasters.com
Mr. Michael Woods, President

CAPITAL CARPET CLEANING was developed out of an unquestionable need in the carpet and upholstery cleaning industry to provide a superior, ultra-high powered, carpet and upholstery cleaning system.

BACKGROUND:
Established: 1983; 1st Franchised: 1990
Franchised Units: 12
Company-Owned Units: 2
Total Units: 14
Dist.: US-14; CAN-0; O'seas-0
North America: 3 States
Density: 7 in FL, 4 in MN, 3 in CA
Projected New Units (12 Months): 10
Qualifications: 1, 3, 1, 3, 3, 5
Registered: CA,FL,MN

FINANCIAL/TERMS:
Cash Investment: $0-5K
Total Investment: $35-45K
Minimum Net Worth: NR
Fees: Franchise - $1-10K
Royalty - 0%; Ad. - 0%
Earnings Claims Statement: No
Term of Contract (Years): 5/5
Avg. # Of Employees: 1 FT, 1 PT
Passive Ownership: Allowed
Encourage Conversions: Yes
Area Develop. Agreements: No
Sub-Franchising Contracts: No
Expand In Territory: Yes
Space Needs: NR SF; HB

SUPPORT & TRAINING:
Financial Assistance Provided: Yes(B)
Site Selection Assistance: Yes
Lease Negotiation Assistance: Yes
Co-Operative Advertising: Yes
Franchisee Assoc./Member: No
Size Of Corporate Staff: 2
On-Going Support: C,D,E,G,H
Training: 2 Weeks FL.

SPECIFIC EXPANSION PLANS:
US: All United States
Canada: All Canada
Overseas: All Countries

<< >>

CHEM-DRY CANADA
8472 Harvard Pl.
Chilliwack, BC V2P 7Z5 CANADA

Tel: (888) CHEM-DRY (604) 795-9918
Fax: (604) 795-7071
E-Mail: jared@chemdry.ca
Web Site: www.chemdry.ca
Mr. Jared Monds, Franchise Support Manager

The world's largest carpet & upholstery franchise rated 'The Best of the Best' by Entrepreneur magazine for 12 consecutive years. Our unique patented, non-toxic, heated carbonating cleaner allows most carpets to dry in one hour. State-of-the-art equipment, 22 years experience, on-going research, in-field training, technical support, a monthly newsletter and annual conventions makes a CHEM-DRY franchise a good business.

BACKGROUND:

Established: 1977; 1st Franchised: 1978
Franchised Units: 135
Company-Owned Units: 0
Total Units: 135
Dist.: US-0; CAN-135; O'seas-0
North America: 10 Provinces
Density: 48 in ON, 28 in BC, 18 in AB
Projected New Units (12 Months): 20
Qualifications: 3, 1, 1, 1, 1, 1
Registered: AB

FINANCIAL/TERMS:

Cash Investment: $17-25K
Total Investment: $37.9K
Minimum Net Worth: $40K
Fees: Franchise - $11K
Royalty - $410/Mo.; Ad. - $0
Earnings Claims Statement: No
Term of Contract (Years): 5/5
Avg. # Of Employees: 1-5 FT, 2-4 PT
Passive Ownership: Discouraged
Encourage Conversions: NA
Area Develop. Agreements: No
Sub-Franchising Contracts: No
Expand In Territory: Yes
Space Needs: 500 SF; HB

SUPPORT & TRAINING:

Financial Assistance Provided: Yes(D)
Site Selection Assistance: NA
Lease Negotiation Assistance: Yes
Co-Operative Advertising: No
Franchisee Assoc./Member: Yes/Yes
Size Of Corporate Staff: 14
On-Going Support: B,C,D,G,H,I
Training: 1 Week Head Office.

SPECIFIC EXPANSION PLANS:

US: NA
Canada: All Canada
Overseas: No

<< >>

CHEM-DRY CARPET & UPHOLSTERY CLEANING

1530 N. 1000 West
Logan, UT 84321
Tel: (800) CHEMDRY (877) 307-8233
Fax: (435) 755-0021
E-Mail: sfinn@chemdry.com
Web Site: www.chemdry.com
Mr. Scott Finn, Dir. New Franchise Licensing

CHEM-DRY has: 1-2 hour dry times (carpet & upholstery cleaning); hot carbonating cleaning solution (safe); uses 80% less water than steam cleaning; and no harsh chemicals.

BACKGROUND: IFA MEMBER

Established: 1977; 1st Franchised: 1977
Franchised Units: 3,903
Company-Owned Units: 0
Total Units: 3,903
Dist.: US-2,495; CAN-124; O'seas-1,330
North America: 50 States,11 Provinces
Density: 421 in CA, 166 in TX, 146 FL
Projected New Units (12 Months): 2200
Qualifications: 4, 3, 1, 1, 1, 5
Registered: All States

FINANCIAL/TERMS:

Cash Investment: $10.0-14.9K
Total Investment: $6.9-27.6K
Minimum Net Worth: $10K
Fees: Franchise - $19.5K
Royalty - $212/Mo.; Ad. - 0%
Earnings Claims Statement: No
Term of Contract (Years): 5/5
Avg. # Of Employees: 1 FT
Passive Ownership: Not Allowed
Encourage Conversions: NA
Area Develop. Agreements: No
Sub-Franchising Contracts: No
Expand In Territory: No
Space Needs: NA SF; Home Based

SUPPORT & TRAINING:

Financial Assistance Provided: Yes(D)
Site Selection Assistance: NA
Lease Negotiation Assistance: No
Co-Operative Advertising: No
Franchisee Assoc./Member: No
Size Of Corporate Staff: 70
On-Going Support: B,C,D,G,H,I
Training: 5 Days Logan, UT.

SPECIFIC EXPANSION PLANS:

US: Northeast,Cenrtral,Southeast
Canada: All Canada
Overseas: Most Countries

<< >>

CHEMSTATION INTERNATIONAL

3400 Encrete Ln.
Dayton, OH 45439
Tel: (800) 554-8265 (937) 294-8265
Fax: (937) 294-5360
E-Mail: franchise@chemstation.com
Web Site: www.chemstation.com
Mr. Jeff Purks, Vice President

CHEMSTATION is an affiliation of manufacturing centers which offer their customers the unique service of custom manufactured cleaning chemicals delivered in bulk to refillable containers that eliminate the waste and inefficiencies of drums.

BACKGROUND: IFA MEMBER

Established: 1983; 1st Franchised: 1984
Franchised Units: 49
Company-Owned Units: 2
Total Units: 51
Dist.: US-50; CAN-0; O'seas-0
North America: 27 States
Density: 5 in OH, 3 in MI, 3 in IN
Projected New Units (12 Months): 4
Qualifications: 5, 4, 3, 2, 1, 5
Registered: NR

FINANCIAL/TERMS:

Cash Investment: $150-300K
Total Investment: $500-700K
Minimum Net Worth: NR
Fees: Franchise - $45K
Royalty - 4%; Ad. - 2%/$5K Max.
Earnings Claims Statement: No
Term of Contract (Years): 10/5
Avg. # Of Employees: 10 FT
Passive Ownership: Discouraged
Encourage Conversions: NA
Area Develop. Agreements: No
Sub-Franchising Contracts: No
Expand In Territory: Yes
Space Needs: 6,000 SF; Commercial/Industrial

SUPPORT & TRAINING:

Financial Assistance Provided: No
Site Selection Assistance: Yes
Lease Negotiation Assistance: Yes
Co-Operative Advertising: Yes
Franchisee Assoc./Member: Yes
Size Of Corporate Staff: 41
On-Going Support: A,B,C,D,E,F,G,H,I
Training: 1 Week Dayton, OH and On-Going.

SPECIFIC EXPANSION PLANS:

US: West, NY, Northeast
Canada: All Canada
Overseas: All Countries

<< >>

CLEANNET USA

9861 Broken Land Pkwy., # 208
Columbia, MD 21046
Tel: (800) 735-8838 (410) 720-6444
Fax: (410) 720-5307
E-Mail: elugo@cleannetusa.com
Web Site: www.cleannetusa.com
Mr. Ed Lugo, Franchise Sales

Full-service, turn-key commercial office cleaning franchise, offering guaranteed customer accounts, complete training, brand new equipment, supplies, local office support, quality control backup, billing/invoicing and services provided. Company also sells master licenses for markets with metropolitan populations of 500,000 and up.

BACKGROUND:
Established: 1987; 1st Franchised: 1988
Franchised Units: 2,591
Company-Owned Units: 6
Total Units: 2,597
Dist.: US-2,560; CAN-0; O'seas-0
North America: 13 States
Density: 366 in MD, 308 in NJ, 195 PA
Projected New Units (12 Months): 400
Qualifications: 4, 3, 2, 1, 3, 4
Registered: CA,FL,IL,MD,MI,VA

FINANCIAL/TERMS:
Cash Investment: $0-25K
Total Investment: $2.9-35.7K
Minimum Net Worth: $0-100K
Fees: Franchise - $2-25.5K
Royalty - 3%; Ad. - 0%
Earnings Claims Statement: No
Term of Contract (Years): 10/10
Avg. # Of Employees: 2 FT, 10 PT
Passive Ownership: Discouraged
Encourage Conversions: NA
Area Develop. Agreements: Yes/10
Sub-Franchising Contracts: Yes
Expand In Territory: Yes
Space Needs: 2,000 SF; Multi-Tenant

SUPPORT & TRAINING:
Financial Assistance Provided: Yes(D)
Site Selection Assistance: Yes
Lease Negotiation Assistance: Yes
Co-Operative Advertising: No
Franchisee Assoc./Member: No
Size Of Corporate Staff: 75
On-Going Support: A,B,C,D,E,G,H,I
Training: 8 Days to 2 Weeks Company Offices; 4 Days to 3 Weeks Job Site or Master Offices.

SPECIFIC EXPANSION PLANS:
US: All United States
Canada: All Canada
Overseas: South Africa, Korea, Southeast Asia, Europe, Australia, U.K.

<< >>

COIT SERVICES

897 Hinckley Rd.
Burlingame, CA 94010-1502
Tel: (800) 243-8797 + 121 (650) 697-5471
Fax: (650) 697-6117
E-Mail: nick@coit.com
Web Site: www.coit.com
Mr. Nick Granato, Vice President Franchising

Granting large, exclusive territories, COIT SERVICES provides a proven opportunity in the carpet, upholstery, drapery, area rug air-duct cleaning and hard surface renewal business. COIT franchisees enjoy use of a universal 800# (1-800-FOR-COIT), along with successful marketing and business development that have been developed in 50 years of operational experience.

BACKGROUND: IFA MEMBER
Established: 1950; 1st Franchised: 1963
Franchised Units: 60
Company-Owned Units: 10
Total Units: 70
Dist.: US-66; CAN-3; O'seas-1
North America: 26 States, 2 Provinces
Density: 16 in CA, 4 in WA, 4 in OH
Projected New Units (12 Months): 51
Qualifications: 3, 5, 4, 3, 1, 5
Registered: All States

FINANCIAL/TERMS:
Cash Investment: $40-60K
Total Investment: $100K
Minimum Net Worth: $No Minimum
Fees: Franchise - $25K
Royalty - 2-6%; Ad. - 0%
Earnings Claims Statement: Yes
Term of Contract (Years): 10/10
Avg. # Of Employees: 2 FT, 1 PT
Passive Ownership: Discouraged
Encourage Conversions: Yes
Area Develop. Agreements: No
Sub-Franchising Contracts: No
Expand In Territory: Yes
Space Needs: 1,000 SF; Industrial

SUPPORT & TRAINING:
Financial Assistance Provided: Yes(D)
Site Selection Assistance: Yes
Lease Negotiation Assistance: Yes
Co-Operative Advertising: Yes
Franchisee Assoc./Member: Yes/Yes
Size Of Corporate Staff: 19
On-Going Support: A,a,B,C,D,E,G,H,I
Training: 7 Days Corporate Headquarters; 1-2 Weeks in Field.

SPECIFIC EXPANSION PLANS:
US: Northeast, Southeast,Midwest
Canada: All Canada
Overseas: All Countries

<< >>

COUSTIC-GLO INTERNATIONAL

7115 Ohms Ln., # 7111
Minneapolis, MN 55439
Tel: (800) 333-8523 (612) 835-1338
Fax: (612) 835-1395
E-Mail: cgiinc@aol.com
Web Site: www.cousticglo.com
Mr. Scott L. Smith, Marketing

Building restoration products which enable you to clean and restore all types of ceiling and wall areas. Very specialized market which is growing as buildings age and the indoor environmental concerns continue to grow nationwide.

BACKGROUND: IFA MEMBER
Established: 1975; 1st Franchised: 1984
Franchised Units: 150
Company-Owned Units: 1
Total Units: 151
Dist.: US-210; CAN-26; O'seas-26
North America: NR
Density: 12 in GA, 6 in FL, 5 in TX
Projected New Units (12 Months): 50
Qualifications: 4, 4, 3, 3, 3, 3
Registered: All States

FINANCIAL/TERMS:
Cash Investment: $12-25K
Total Investment: $12-25K
Minimum Net Worth: $20K
Fees: Franchise - $12K
Royalty - 5%; Ad. - 1%
Earnings Claims Statement: Yes
Term of Contract (Years): 10/5
Avg. # Of Employees: 1 FT
Passive Ownership: Allowed
Encourage Conversions: NA
Area Develop. Agreements: Yes/10
Sub-Franchising Contracts: Yes
Expand In Territory: Yes
Space Needs: NA SF; NA

SUPPORT & TRAINING:
Financial Assistance Provided: Yes(I)
Site Selection Assistance: NA
Lease Negotiation Assistance: NA
Co-Operative Advertising: Yes
Franchisee Assoc./Member: Yes/Yes
Size Of Corporate Staff: 20
On-Going Support: B,C,D,G,H,I
Training: 2 Weeks On-Location.

SPECIFIC EXPANSION PLANS:
US: All United States

Canada: All Canada
Overseas: All Countries

<< >>

Top 100

COVERALL CLEANING CONCEPTS

5201 Congress Ave., # 275
Boca Raton, FL 33487
Tel: (800) 537-3371 (561) 922-2500
Fax: (561) 922-2423
E-Mail: info@coverall.com
Web Site: www.coverall.com
Mr. Jack Caughey, VP Business Development

Commercial cleaning franchise which includes comprehensive training, equipment, billing and collection services, and an initial customer base. With an affordable down payment as low as $1,500, COVERALL CLEANING CONCEPTS provides a combination of business programs and support systems that focus on meeting the franchisees and customers alike. Master and territory franchises are also available.

BACKGROUND: IFA MEMBER
Established: 1985; 1st Franchised: 1985
Franchised Units: 8,451
Company-Owned Units: 0
Total Units: 8,451
Dist.: US-7,992; CAN-201; O'seas-258
North America: 32 States, 2 Provinces
Density: 1,165 CA, 1,083 FL, 610 OH
Projected New Units (12 Months): 1817
Qualifications: 3, 3, 2, 2, 3, 5
Registered: All States Except SD

FINANCIAL/TERMS:
Cash Investment: $1.5-25.2K
Total Investment: $6.2-36K
Minimum Net Worth: $1.5K
Fees: Franchise - $6.2-32.2K
Royalty - 5%; Ad. - 0%
Earnings Claims Statement: No
Term of Contract (Years): 20/20
Avg. # Of Employees: 1-2 FT, 2-3 PT
Passive Ownership: Allowed
Encourage Conversions: Yes
Area Develop. Agreements: Yes/20
Sub-Franchising Contracts: Yes
Expand In Territory: Yes
Space Needs: NA SF; NA

SUPPORT & TRAINING:
Financial Assistance Provided: Yes(D)
Site Selection Assistance: Yes
Lease Negotiation Assistance: No
Co-Operative Advertising: Yes
Franchisee Assoc./Member: No/No
Size Of Corporate Staff: 90
On-Going Support: A,B,C,D,G,H,I
Training: 40 Hours at Local Regional Support Center.

SPECIFIC EXPANSION PLANS:
US: All United States
Canada: All Canada
Overseas: All Countries

DUCTBUSTERS

2030 Main St.
Dunedin, FL 34698
Tel: (800) 786-3828 (727) 787-7087
Fax: (727) 442-3380
E-Mail: iaqtomy@aol.com
Web Site: www.ductbusters.com
Mr. Dan Wantz, Franchise Director

DUCTBUSTERS is the largest franchisor of duct-cleaning businesses selling exclusively to air conditioning contractors. You receive a protected territory, full use of the nationally registered name and logo, the Busterlink computer software, training for production-sales-and management, 14-volume training and reference manuals, equipment recommendations and continual on-going support.

BACKGROUND:
Established: 1989; 1st Franchised: 1992
Franchised Units: 29
Company-Owned Units: 1
Total Units: 30
Dist.: US-25; CAN-0; O'seas-3
North America: 8 States
Density: 17 in FL, 3 in LA, 2 in TX
Projected New Units (12 Months): 16
Qualifications: 3, 4, 5, 2, 3, 5
Registered: CA,FL,IL,MD

FINANCIAL/TERMS:
Cash Investment: $7.5K
Total Investment: $2.5-50K
Minimum Net Worth: NA
Fees: Franchise - $7.5-24K
Royalty - 7%; Ad. - 0%
Earnings Claims Statement: No
Term of Contract (Years): 10/5
Avg. # Of Employees: 6 FT
Passive Ownership: Discouraged
Encourage Conversions: Yes
Area Develop. Agreements: NR
Sub-Franchising Contracts: NR
Expand In Territory: Yes
Space Needs: NR SF; NA

SUPPORT & TRAINING:
Financial Assistance Provided: Yes(B)
Site Selection Assistance: NA
Lease Negotiation Assistance: NA
Co-Operative Advertising: NA
Franchisee Assoc./Member: No
Size Of Corporate Staff: 6
On-Going Support: A,B,C,D,F,H,I
Training: 5 Days Clearwater, FL; 2 Days Franchisee's Facilities.

SPECIFIC EXPANSION PLANS:
US: All United States
Canada: All Canada
Overseas: All Countries

DURACLEAN INTERNATIONAL

220 Campus Dr.
Arlington Heights, IL 60004-1485
Tel: (800) 251-7070 + 130 (847) 704-7100 + 122
Fax: (847) 704-7101
E-Mail: vince@duraclean.com
Web Site: www.duraclean.com
Mr. Vince Caffarello, President

DURACLEAN offers distinct services, markets and revenue center packages to fit your needs for independence and growth. Carpet cleaning, ceiling and wall cleaning, upholstery and drapery cleaning, fire/smoke/water restoration, janitorial, pressure washing, hard surface floor care, duct cleaning and ultrasonic cleaning are all services that we offer. We are the most diversified cleaning franchise in the world.

BACKGROUND: IFA MEMBER
Established: 1930; 1st Franchised: 1945
Franchised Units: 375
Company-Owned Units: 2
Total Units: 377
Dist.: US-267; CAN-22; O'seas-59
North America: 50 States
Density: 38 in FL, 34 in IL, 30 in CA
Projected New Units (12 Months): 30
Qualifications: 4, 4, 3, 3, 3, 3
Registered: All States

FINANCIAL/TERMS:
Cash Investment: $25K
Total Investment: $54-70K
Minimum Net Worth: NA
Fees: Franchise - $10K
Royalty - 6-8%; Ad. - 0%
Earnings Claims Statement: No
Term of Contract (Years): 5/5
Avg. # Of Employees: 2 FT, 1 PT

Passive Ownership: Discouraged
Encourage Conversions: Yes
Area Develop. Agreements: No
Sub-Franchising Contracts: No
Expand In Territory: Yes
Space Needs: NA SF; HB

SUPPORT & TRAINING:
Financial Assistance Provided: Yes(D)
Site Selection Assistance: NA
Lease Negotiation Assistance: NA
Co-Operative Advertising: No
Franchisee Assoc./Member: Yes/No
Size Of Corporate Staff: 25
On-Going Support: C,D,G,H,I
Training: 6 Days Success Institute, Corp. Office; 2 Days On-Site Cleaning; Home Study Program.

SPECIFIC EXPANSION PLANS:
US: All United States
Canada: All Canada
Overseas: All Countries

<< >>

E. P. I. C. SYSTEMS

402 E. Maryland
Evansville, IN 47711
Tel: (800) 230-3742 (812) 428-7750
Fax: (812) 428-4162
E-Mail: jrs@speedex.net
Web Site: www.worldfranchising.com/website.htm
Mr. Jeffrey R. Schaperjohn, President

Complete janitorial service franchising master units for $25,000 per million population, single units for $6,500. We can assist with financing with good credit.

BACKGROUND:
Established: 1993; 1st Franchised: 1994
Franchised Units: 7
Company-Owned Units: 0
Total Units: 7
Dist.: US-7; CAN-0; O'seas-0
North America: 2 States
Density: 4 in KY, 3 in IN
Projected New Units (12 Months): 6
Qualifications: 5, 3, 4, 3, 5, 4
Registered: FL,IN

FINANCIAL/TERMS:
Cash Investment: $6.5-28.5K
Total Investment: $6.5-60K
Minimum Net Worth: $10.2-28.5K
Fees: Franchise - $6.5K
Royalty - 4-10%; Ad. - NA
Earnings Claims Statement: No
Term of Contract (Years): 10/10
Avg. # Of Employees: 1 FT, 5 PT
Passive Ownership: Discouraged
Encourage Conversions: Yes
Area Develop. Agreements: Yes/10
Sub-Franchising Contracts: Yes
Expand In Territory: Yes
Space Needs: 250-1,000 SF; HB, OB

SUPPORT & TRAINING:
Financial Assistance Provided: Yes(D)
Site Selection Assistance: Yes
Lease Negotiation Assistance: No
Co-Operative Advertising: No
Franchisee Assoc./Member: No
Size Of Corporate Staff: 4
On-Going Support: c,D,I
Training: 2 Weeks at Headquarters.

SPECIFIC EXPANSION PLANS:
US: Midwest, Southeast
Canada: No
Overseas: No

<< >>

FABRIZONE CLEANING SYSTEMS

3135 Universal Dr., # 6
Mississauga, ON L4X 2E2 CANADA
Tel: (888) 781-1123 (416) 201-1010
Fax: (905) 602-7821
E-Mail: headoffice@fabrizone.com
Web Site: www.fabrizone.com
Mr. Jerry Cunningham, Franchise Development

FABRI-ZONE offers a full-service affiliate concept to start with a turn-key system with an environmentally sensitive cleaning program, a patented dry cleaning and purification carpet cleaning process. Steam finishing process cleans upholstery and draperies. 14 profit centers mean high returns for affiliates. Recommended by carpet manufacturers.

BACKGROUND:
Established: 1981; 1st Franchised: 1984
Franchised Units: 39
Company-Owned Units: 1
Total Units: 40
Dist.: US-7; CAN-30; O'seas-3
North America: NR
Density: NR
Projected New Units (12 Months): 8
Qualifications: 3, 4, 1, 4, 4, 4
Registered: NR

FINANCIAL/TERMS:
Cash Investment: $6K
Total Investment: $14K
Minimum Net Worth: NR
Fees: Franchise - Varies
Royalty - $150/Mo.; Ad. - 0%
Earnings Claims Statement: NR
Term of Contract (Years): 3/3
Avg. # Of Employees: 2 FT, 4 PT
Passive Ownership: Not Allowed
Encourage Conversions: Yes
Area Develop. Agreements: Yes
Sub-Franchising Contracts: NR
Expand In Territory: NR
Space Needs: NA SF; Home Based

SUPPORT & TRAINING:
Financial Assistance Provided: Yes
Site Selection Assistance: NA
Lease Negotiation Assistance: NA
Co-Operative Advertising: NA
Franchisee Assoc./Member: No
Size Of Corporate Staff: 20
On-Going Support: B,C,d,e,G,H,I
Training: 8 Days Toronto, ON.

SPECIFIC EXPANSION PLANS:
US: All United States
Canada: All Canada
Overseas: All Countries

<< >>

FISH WINDOW CLEANING SERVICES

200 Enchanted Pkwy.
Manchester, MO 63021
Tel: (877) 707-3474 (636) 530-7334
Fax: (636) 530-7856
E-Mail: amanda@fishwindowcleaning.com
Web Site: www.fishwindowcleaning.com
Ms. Amanda Wright, Franchise Development Asst.

There is no glass ceiling when it comes to the potential you will have to grow your own unique service business in a large protected territory, specializing in year-round commercial and residential low-rise window cleaning. You can have the satisfaction of owning a business that requires no night or weekend work, backed by a franchisor with 27 years of experience.

BACKGROUND: IFA MEMBER
Established: 1978; 1st Franchised: 1998
Franchised Units: 179
Company-Owned Units: 1
Total Units: 180
Dist.: US-180; CAN-0; O'seas-0
North America: 35 States
Density: NR
Projected New Units (12 Months): 40
Qualifications: 4, 4, 1, 2, 3, 5
Registered: All States

FINANCIAL/TERMS:
Cash Investment: $66.4-127.6K
Total Investment: $66.4-127.6K
Minimum Net Worth: $100-200K
Fees: Franchise - $24.9-49.9K
Royalty - 8-6%; Ad. - 1%
Earnings Claims Statement: Yes
Term of Contract (Years): 10
Avg. # Of Employees: 3-12 FT
Passive Ownership: Discouraged
Encourage Conversions: Yes
Area Develop. Agreements: No
Sub-Franchising Contracts: No
Expand In Territory: Yes
Space Needs: Na SF; NA

SUPPORT & TRAINING:
Financial Assistance Provided: Yes(I)
Site Selection Assistance: Yes
Lease Negotiation Assistance: Yes
Co-Operative Advertising: Yes
Franchisee Assoc./Member: Yes
Size Of Corporate Staff: 22
On-Going Support: A,B,C,D,E,G,H,I
Training: 12 Days.

SPECIFIC EXPANSION PLANS:
US: All United States
Canada: Soon
Overseas: No

<< >>

FRESH COAT
10700 Montgomery Rd., # 300
Cincinnati, OH 45242
Tel: (800) 317-7089 (513) 587-4974
Fax: (513) 563-2691
E-Mail: inquiry@freshcoatpainters.com
Web Site: www.freshcoatpainters.com
Mr. Ralph Martin, President

All over America, homeowners spend millions of dollars everyday on painting kitchens, family rooms...every room in the house. And FRESH COAT has captured a niche within the industry that is taking the market by storm. As a Franchise, you build your business through proven marketing, expertise and a system exclusive to FRESH COAT. This business is about building an organization and managing people. No painting required. In fact, we prefer you don't own a brush.

BACKGROUND:
Established: 2004; 1st Franchised: 2005
Franchised Units: 1
Company-Owned Units: 0
Total Units: 1
Dist.: US-1; CAN-0; O'seas-0
North America: 1 State
Density: 1 in OH
Projected New Units (12 Months): 60
Qualifications: 3, 4, 1, 2, 2, 4
Registered: All States

FINANCIAL/TERMS:
Cash Investment: $17.9K
Total Investment: $29.7-44.9K
Minimum Net Worth: $10K
Fees: Franchise - $17.9K
Royalty - 6%; Ad. - $100/Mo.
Earnings Claims Statement: No
Term of Contract (Years): 10/10/10
Avg. # Of Employees: 1 FT
Passive Ownership: Discouraged
Encourage Conversions: Yes
Area Develop. Agreements: Yes
Sub-Franchising Contracts: No
Expand In Territory: NR
Space Needs: NA SF; NA

SUPPORT & TRAINING:
Financial Assistance Provided: Yes(D)
Site Selection Assistance: NA
Lease Negotiation Assistance: NA
Co-Operative Advertising: NA
Franchisee Assoc./Member: No
Size Of Corporate Staff: 27
On-Going Support: B,C,E,F,G,H,I
Training: 5 Days in Cincinnati, OH.

SPECIFIC EXPANSION PLANS:
US: All United States
Canada: All Canada
Overseas: All Countries

<< >>

HANDYMAN MATTERS
12136 W. Bayard Ave., # 105
Lakewood, CO 80228
Tel: (866) 808-8401 (303) 984-0177
Fax: (303) 984-0133
E-Mail: dan@handymanmatters.com
Web Site: www.handymanmatters.com
Mr. Dan Schafer, Director Franchise Sales

HANDYMAN MATTERS is an industry leader in the growing handyman repair and improvement category for residential and commercial properties. HANDYMAN MATTERS provides the convenience of one-call-does-it-all and is experiencing extremely high client satisfaction. We operate strictly as a time-plus-material service, choosing to employ our handymen for control, and offering our clients one handyman to perform carpentry, plumbing, electrical, drywall, masonry, roofing, and other tasks.

BACKGROUND: IFA MEMBER
Established: 1998; 1st Franchised: 2000
Franchised Units: 22
Company-Owned Units: 0
Total Units: 22
Dist.: US-21; CAN-0; O'seas-1
North America: 6 States
Density: 7 in CO, 4 in CA, 4 in WA
Projected New Units (12 Months): 25
Qualifications: 3, 4, 4, 3, 3, 5
Registered: All States

FINANCIAL/TERMS:
Cash Investment: $50K
Total Investment: $50-75K
Minimum Net Worth: $150K
Fees: Franchise - $30K
Royalty - 6%; Ad. - 2%
Earnings Claims Statement: No
Term of Contract (Years): 10/10
Avg. # Of Employees: 12 FT
Passive Ownership: Allowed
Encourage Conversions: No
Area Develop. Agreements: Yes/10
Sub-Franchising Contracts: No
Expand In Territory: Yes
Space Needs: 500 SF; WH

SUPPORT & TRAINING:
Financial Assistance Provided: Yes(I)
Site Selection Assistance: Yes
Lease Negotiation Assistance: Yes
Co-Operative Advertising: Yes
Franchisee Assoc./Member: No
Size Of Corporate Staff: 18
On-Going Support: a,C,D,E,G,h,I
Training: 1 Week in Denver, CO.

SPECIFIC EXPANSION PLANS:
US: All United States

Canada: All Canada
Overseas: Ireland

HEAVEN'S BEST CARPET/ UPHOLST. CLEANING

247 N. 1st E., P.O. Box 607
Rexburg, ID 83440
Tel: (800) 359-2095 (208) 359-1106
Fax: (208) 359-1236
E-Mail: mcoinc@heavensbest.com
Web Site: www.heavensbest.com
Mr. Cody Howard, CEO

Unique low moisture cleaning process. There is no better franchise opportunity than this. Our franchisees are happy, our customers are happy. Our franchise is very affordable. Call for our free video.

BACKGROUND:
Established: 1983; 1st Franchised: 1983
Franchised Units: 675
Company-Owned Units: 0
Total Units: 675
Dist.: US-491; CAN-4; O'seas-9
North America: 28 States
Density: 48 in CA, 46 in ID, 25 in CO
Projected New Units (12 Months): 100
Qualifications: , , , , ,
Registered: CA,IL,IN,MN,OR,WA

FINANCIAL/TERMS:
Cash Investment: $7.5-20K
Total Investment: $16-40K
Minimum Net Worth: $10K
Fees: Franchise - $2.9K
Royalty - $80/Mo.; Ad. - NR
Earnings Claims Statement: No
Term of Contract (Years): 5/5
Avg. # Of Employees: 1 FT
Passive Ownership: Allowed
Encourage Conversions: Yes
Area Develop. Agreements: No
Sub-Franchising Contracts: Yes
Expand In Territory: Yes
Space Needs: NA SF; NA

SUPPORT & TRAINING:
Financial Assistance Provided: Yes
Site Selection Assistance: NA
Lease Negotiation Assistance: NA
Co-Operative Advertising: Yes
Franchisee Assoc./Member: Yes/Yes
Size Of Corporate Staff: 7
On-Going Support: A,B,F,G,H,I
Training: 4 Days Rexburg, ID.

SPECIFIC EXPANSION PLANS:
US: All United States
Canada: All Canada
Overseas: All Countries

<< >>

HYDRO PHYSICS PIPE INSPECTION

1855 W. Union Ave., # N
Englewood, CO 80110
Tel: (800) 781-3164 (303) 781-2474
Fax: (303) 781-2474
E-Mail: hydrophys@aol.com
Web Site: www.hydrophysics.com
Mr. Pete Fitzgerald, Dir. Franchise Development

HYDRO PHYSICS specializes in the video inspection of underground pipes. By seeing exactly what and where the problems are located, we can save our customers thousands of dollars in unnecessary repair costs. We are the only franchise specializing in this type of work.

BACKGROUND:
Established: 1991; 1st Franchised: 1998
Franchised Units: 9
Company-Owned Units: 1
Total Units: 10
Dist.: US-10; CAN-0; O'seas-0
North America: 4 States
Density: 1 in CO, 1 in ID, 1 in MO
Projected New Units (12 Months): 15
Qualifications: 4, 3, 2, 2, 2, 5
Registered: CA,VA

FINANCIAL/TERMS:
Cash Investment: $25-80K
Total Investment: $68-125K
Minimum Net Worth: $250K
Fees: Franchise - $19.5K
Royalty - 7.5%; Ad. - 2%
Earnings Claims Statement: No
Term of Contract (Years): 10/10
Avg. # Of Employees: 1 FT
Passive Ownership: Not Allowed
Encourage Conversions: NA
Area Develop. Agreements: Yes/10
Sub-Franchising Contracts: No
Expand In Territory: Yes
Space Needs: NR SF; NA

SUPPORT & TRAINING:
Financial Assistance Provided: Yes(I)
Site Selection Assistance: NA
Lease Negotiation Assistance: NA
Co-Operative Advertising: NA
Franchisee Assoc./Member: No
Size Of Corporate Staff: 2
On-Going Support: B,C,D,e,F,G,H,I
Training: 2 Weeks in Englewood, CO.

SPECIFIC EXPANSION PLANS:
US: All United States
Canada: No
Overseas: No

<< >>

Top 100

JANI-KING INTERNATIONAL

16885 Dallas Pkwy.
Addison, TX 75001-5215
Tel: (800) 552-5264 (972) 991-0900
Fax: (972) 764-3651
E-Mail: gdick@janiking.com
Web Site: www.janiking.com
Mr. Gary Dick, VP Franchising

JANI-KING INTERNATIONAL is the world's largest commercial cleaning franchisor, with locations in 15 countries and over 100 regions in the U. S. and abroad. Our franchise opportunity includes initial customer contracts, training, continuous local support , administrative and accounting assistance, an equipment leasing program and national advertising. If you are searching for a flexible business opportunity, look no further.

BACKGROUND: IFA MEMBER
Established: 1969; 1st Franchised: 1974
Franchised Units: 11,000
Company-Owned Units: 27
Total Units: 11,027
Dist.: US-8,153; CAN-351; O'seas-528
North America: 39 States, 7 Provinces
Density: 880 in TX, 737 in CA, 307 FL
Projected New Units (12 Months): 1,500
Qualifications: 2, 2, 1, 2, 2, 3
Registered: CA,FL,HI,IL,IN,MI,MN,NY, OR,SD,VA,WA,WI,DC

FINANCIAL/TERMS:
Cash Investment: $2.9-33K
Total Investment: $2.9-40K
Minimum Net Worth: $2.9-33K
Fees: Franchise - $8-33K
Royalty - 10%; Ad. - 0%
Earnings Claims Statement: Yes
Term of Contract (Years): 20/20
Avg. # Of Employees: NR
Passive Ownership: Allowed
Encourage Conversions: NA
Area Develop. Agreements: Yes/20
Sub-Franchising Contracts: Yes
Expand In Territory: Yes
Space Needs: NR SF; HB

SUPPORT & TRAINING:
Financial Assistance Provided: No

Site Selection Assistance: NA
Lease Negotiation Assistance: NA
Co-Operative Advertising: NA
Franchisee Assoc./Member: Yes/Yes
Size Of Corporate Staff: 65
On-Going Support: A,B,C,D,G,H,I
Training: 2 Weeks Local Regional Office.

SPECIFIC EXPANSION PLANS:
US: All United States
Canada: All Canada
Overseas: All Countries

<< >>

JAN-PRO CLEANING SYSTEMS

383 Strand Industrial Dr.
Little River, SC 29566
Tel: (800) 668-1001 (843) 399-9895
Fax: (843) 399-9890
E-Mail: janpro1@aol.com
Web Site: www.jan-pro.com
Ms. Carol McLennan, Vice President

JAN-PRO has built a solid reputation as a quality franchise organization within the commercial cleaning industry. We have been highly ranked in magazines such as Entrepreneur, Income Opportunities, Home Business and Business Start-Up. JAN-PRO franchise owners are in business for themselves, but not by themselves.

BACKGROUND:
Established: 1991; 1st Franchised: 1992
Franchised Units: 3,009
Company-Owned Units: 0
Total Units: 3,009
Dist.: US-0; CAN-0; O'seas-0
North America: 16 States
Density: 75 in NJ, 55 in GA, 45 in IL
Projected New Units (12 Months): NR
Qualifications: , , , , ,
Registered: NR

FINANCIAL/TERMS:
Cash Investment: $1-35K
Total Investment: $2.8-44K
Minimum Net Worth: $3K
Fees: Franchise - $1-35K
Royalty - 8%; Ad. - 0%
Earnings Claims Statement: No
Term of Contract (Years): 10/20
Avg. # Of Employees: 2 FT, 2 PT
Passive Ownership: Allowed
Encourage Conversions: NR
Area Develop. Agreements: No
Sub-Franchising Contracts: Yes
Expand In Territory: Yes
Space Needs: NR SF; HB

SUPPORT & TRAINING:
Financial Assistance Provided: NR
Site Selection Assistance: NA
Lease Negotiation Assistance: NA
Co-Operative Advertising: NA
Franchisee Assoc./Member: No
Size Of Corporate Staff: NR
On-Going Support: A,B,C,D,G,H
Training: 5 On-Site Training Sessions.

SPECIFIC EXPANSION PLANS:
US: All United States
Canada: NR
Overseas: NR

<< >>

JANTIZE AMERICA

15449 Middlebelt
Livonia, MI 48154
Tel: (800) 968-9182 (734) 421-4733
Fax: (734) 421-4936
E-Mail: jerryg@jantize.com
Web Site: www.jantize.com
Mr. Jerry Grabowski, President

A JANTIZE commercial office cleaning franchise has it all - computerized procedures, audio/visual training, on-going assistance and more! Master franchises and exclusive territories are available.

BACKGROUND:
Established: 1985; 1st Franchised: 1988
Franchised Units: 27
Company-Owned Units: 1
Total Units: 28
Dist.: US-21; CAN-0; O'seas-0
North America: 3 States
Density: 13 in MI, 7 in NC, 1 in NV
Projected New Units (12 Months): 5
Qualifications: 4, 4, 3, 2, 2, 5
Registered: MI

FINANCIAL/TERMS:
Cash Investment: $9-11.5K
Total Investment: $20K
Minimum Net Worth: NR
Fees: Franchise - $3.5-75K
Royalty - 9%; Ad. - 0%
Earnings Claims Statement: No
Term of Contract (Years): 10/10
Avg. # Of Employees: 3-20 PT
Passive Ownership: Discouraged
Encourage Conversions: Yes
Area Develop. Agreements: No
Sub-Franchising Contracts: Yes
Expand In Territory: No
Space Needs: NR SF; NR

SUPPORT & TRAINING:
Financial Assistance Provided: Yes(D)
Site Selection Assistance: Yes
Lease Negotiation Assistance: No
Co-Operative Advertising: No
Franchisee Assoc./Member: NR
Size Of Corporate Staff: 8
On-Going Support: a,D,E,G,H,I
Training: 3-6 Days Headquarters; 3 Days Franchisee Location.

SPECIFIC EXPANSION PLANS:
US: All United States
Canada: All Canada
Overseas: No

<< >>

KWIK DRY INTERNATIONAL

13553 Golden Eagle Cir.
Plainfield, IL 60544
Tel: (815) 436-0333
Fax: (815) 436-7519
E-Mail: kwikdryint@hotmail.com
Web Site: www.kwikdry.com
Mr. Jim Boyd, Operations Manager

You would control your time and income, be new, yet run a business with 30 years of experience, using the dry extraction method of cleaning both carpets and furniture. KWIK DRY is very user-friendly (easy on the operator), utilizing an all natural cleaner. We put great emphasis on marketing (getting the jobs). Ideal as a second income business. Choice locations available.

BACKGROUND:
Established: 1967; 1st Franchised: 1995
Franchised Units: 16
Company-Owned Units: 2
Total Units: 18
Dist.: US-12; CAN-0; O'seas-0
North America: 5 States
Density: 6 in IL, 3 in MO
Projected New Units (12 Months): 20
Qualifications: 1, 1, 1, 1, 4, 5
Registered: IL

FINANCIAL/TERMS:
Cash Investment: $5.7K
Total Investment: $11.7K
Minimum Net Worth: $10K
Fees: Franchise - $6K
Royalty - $175/Mo.; Ad. - 0%
Earnings Claims Statement: No
Term of Contract (Years): 5/5
Avg. # Of Employees: 1 FT
Passive Ownership: Allowed
Encourage Conversions: NA
Area Develop. Agreements: No
Sub-Franchising Contracts: No
Expand In Territory: Yes
Space Needs: NR SF; HB

SUPPORT & TRAINING:
Financial Assistance Provided: Yes(D)

Site Selection Assistance: NA
Lease Negotiation Assistance: NA
Co-Operative Advertising: NA
Franchisee Assoc./Member: No
Size Of Corporate Staff: NR
On-Going Support: B,G,h
Training: 5 Days Plainsfield, IL.

SPECIFIC EXPANSION PLANS:
US: All United States
Canada: No
Overseas: No

≺≺ ≻≻

LANGENWALTER CARPET DYEING

1111 S. Richfield Rd.
Placentia, CA 92870-6790
Tel: (800) 422-4370 (714) 528-7610
Fax: (714) 528-7620
E-Mail:
Web Site: www.langdye.com
Mr. John Langenwalter, VP Franchise Development

We offer complete carpet color correction. The franchisees are carpet color correction experts. They can take care of problems such as sun fading, pet stains, bleach spots, chemical stains, etc. Complete color changes are also done to save the customer 85% of carpet replacement costs.

BACKGROUND:
Established: 1975; 1st Franchised: 1981
Franchised Units: 170
Company-Owned Units: 3
Total Units: 173
Dist.: US-152; CAN-19; O'seas-2
North America: 25 States, 3 Provinces
Density: 75 in CA, 10 in BC, 9 in MA
Projected New Units (12 Months): 50
Qualifications: 3, 2, 1, 1, 2, 4
Registered: CA,FL,IN,MD,MI,MN,NY, OR,RI,VA,WA,WI,AB

FINANCIAL/TERMS:
Cash Investment: $30K
Total Investment: $30K
Minimum Net Worth: $30K
Fees: Franchise - $18K
Royalty - $110/Mo.; Ad. - 0%
Earnings Claims Statement: No
Term of Contract (Years): 3/3
Avg. # Of Employees: 1 PT
Passive Ownership: Not Allowed
Encourage Conversions: No
Area Develop. Agreements: No
Sub-Franchising Contracts: No
Expand In Territory: Yes
Space Needs: NR SF; HB

SUPPORT & TRAINING:
Financial Assistance Provided: No
Site Selection Assistance: NA
Lease Negotiation Assistance: NA
Co-Operative Advertising: Yes
Franchisee Assoc./Member: No
Size Of Corporate Staff: 10
On-Going Support: G,h,I
Training: 5 Days Placentia, CA.

SPECIFIC EXPANSION PLANS:
US: All United States
Canada: All Canada
Overseas: All Countries

≺≺ ≻≻

MASTER CARE

555 6th St., # 327
New Westminster, BC V3L 4Y4
CANADA
Tel: (800) 889-2799 (604) 525-8221
Fax: (604) 526-2235
E-Mail: gerhard@mastercare.com
Web Site: www.mastercare.com
Mr. Gerhard Hoffman, President

Commercial janitorial services.

BACKGROUND:
Established: 1960; 1st Franchised: 1987
Franchised Units: 211
Company-Owned Units: 1
Total Units: 212
Dist.: US-0; CAN-212; O'seas-0
North America: 1 Province
Density: 108 in BC
Projected New Units (12 Months): 30
Qualifications: 3, 3, 1, 1, 2, 3
Registered: NR

FINANCIAL/TERMS:
Cash Investment: $2-75K
Total Investment: $5-200K
Minimum Net Worth: $25K
Fees: Franchise - $4.5-125K
Royalty - 5-15%; Ad. - 1%
Earnings Claims Statement: No
Term of Contract (Years): 5/5
Avg. # Of Employees: 2 FT
Passive Ownership: Discouraged
Encourage Conversions: Yes
Area Develop. Agreements: Yes/10
Sub-Franchising Contracts: Yes
Expand In Territory: Yes
Space Needs: NR SF; NA

SUPPORT & TRAINING:
Financial Assistance Provided: Yes(D)
Site Selection Assistance: Yes
Lease Negotiation Assistance: NA
Co-Operative Advertising: Yes
Franchisee Assoc./Member: Yes/Yes
Size Of Corporate Staff: 4
On-Going Support: A,B,C,D,E,G,h,I
Training: 1-6 Weeks at Head Office.

SPECIFIC EXPANSION PLANS:
US: Master Franchises Only
Canada: Master Franchise
Overseas: No

≺≺ ≻≻

MILLICARE COMMERCIAL CARPET CARE

201 Lukken Industrial Dr., W.
LaGrange, GA 30240-5913
Tel: (877) 812-8803 (706) 880-5741
Fax: (706) 880-3279
E-Mail: tracey.reina@millicare.com
Web Site: www.millicare.com
Ms. Tracey Reina, Dir. Marketing

Buy into experience and professionalism. MILLICARE ENVIRONMENTAL SERVICES is currently seeking to select people to become franchisees in select cities in North America. The MILLICARE system includes a variety of services provided to commercial facility managers including carpet maintenance, carpet recycling, panel and upholstery cleaning and entryway systems. Franchisees receive world-class training, sales and marketing programs from a strong, experienced global franchisor.

BACKGROUND: IFA MEMBER
Established: 1984; 1st Franchised: 1996
Franchised Units: 74
Company-Owned Units: 0
Total Units: 74
Dist.: US-71; CAN-7; O'seas-2
North America: NR
Density: NR
Projected New Units (12 Months): 15-20
Qualifications: 5, 4, 3, 3, 4, 5
Registered: CA,FL,HI,IL,IN,MD,MI,MN, NY,OR,RI,VA,WA,WI,DC,AB

FINANCIAL/TERMS:
Cash Investment: $30-50K
Total Investment: $70-170K
Minimum Net Worth: $100K
Fees: Franchise - $20K
Royalty - 6%; Ad. - 2%
Earnings Claims Statement: No
Term of Contract (Years): 5/5
Avg. # Of Employees: 1-20 FT
Passive Ownership: Allowed
Encourage Conversions: No
Area Develop. Agreements: Possible
Sub-Franchising Contracts: No
Expand In Territory: Possible

Space Needs: 2,000 SF; Warehouse

SUPPORT & TRAINING:

Financial Assistance Provided: Yes(I)
Site Selection Assistance: No
Lease Negotiation Assistance: NA
Co-Operative Advertising: Yes
Franchisee Assoc./Member: Yes
Size Of Corporate Staff: 6
On-Going Support: C,D,E,G,H,I
Training: 3 Days La Grange, GA; 3 Days Model Franchise Location, DE; 2 Days Franchisee's Location.

SPECIFIC EXPANSION PLANS:

US: All Major 2ndary Metro Areas
Canada: Toronto,Montreal
Overseas: Mexico

<< >>

MR. ROOTER CORP.

1020 N. University Parks Dr.
Waco, TX 76707
Tel: (800) 298-6855 (254) 745-2439
Fax: (800) 209-7621
E-Mail: gena.reid@dwyergroup.com
Web Site: www.mrrooter.com
Mr. Mike Hawkins, VP Franchising

Full-service plumbing and sewer/drain cleaning. Franchise specializing in conversion of existing trades people to our method of doing business.

BACKGROUND: IFA MEMBER

Established: 1968; 1st Franchised: 1972
Franchised Units: 300
Company-Owned Units: 0
Total Units: 300
Dist.: US-279; CAN-15; O'seas-6
North America: 41 States, 4 Provinces
Density: 35 in CA, 18 in ON, 17 in TX
Projected New Units (12 Months): 40
Qualifications: 3, 3, 5, 2, 3, 4
Registered: All States

FINANCIAL/TERMS:

Cash Investment: $35-75K
Total Investment: $46.8-120.5K
Minimum Net Worth: Varies
Fees: Franchise - $22.5K/100KPop
Royalty - 4-7%; Ad. - 2%
Earnings Claims Statement: No
Term of Contract (Years): 10/5
Avg. # Of Employees: Depends on Sales
Passive Ownership: Not Allowed
Encourage Conversions: Yes
Area Develop. Agreements: Yes/10
Sub-Franchising Contracts: No
Expand In Territory: Yes
Space Needs: NR SF; NA

SUPPORT & TRAINING:

Financial Assistance Provided: Yes(I)
Site Selection Assistance: NA
Lease Negotiation Assistance: NA
Co-Operative Advertising: No
Franchisee Assoc./Member: No
Size Of Corporate Staff: 17
On-Going Support: C,D,E,F,G,H,I
Training: 1 Week Waco, TX.

SPECIFIC EXPANSION PLANS:

US: Uncovered Areas
Canada: All Canada
Overseas: All Countries

<< >>

NATIONAL MAINTENANCE CONTRACTORS

1801 130th Ave. NE
Bellevue, WA 98005
Tel: (800) 347-7844 (425) 881-0500
Fax: (425) 883-4785
E-Mail: lyle.graddon@natmainco.com
Web Site: www.worldfranchising.com/website.htm
Mr. Lyle R. Graddon, President

NATIONAL MAINTENANCE CONTRACTORS is a janitorial business.

BACKGROUND:

Established: 1975; 1st Franchised: 1975
Franchised Units: 409
Company-Owned Units: 0
Total Units: 409
Dist.: US-409; CAN-0; O'seas-0
North America: 2 States
Density: 275 in WA, 139 in OR
Projected New Units (12 Months): 25
Qualifications: 5, 2, 5, 1, 1, 5
Registered: OR,WA

FINANCIAL/TERMS:

Cash Investment: $1-20K
Total Investment: $2-22K
Minimum Net Worth: NA
Fees: Franchise - $1-20K
Royalty - 6%; Ad. - 0%
Earnings Claims Statement: No
Term of Contract (Years): 5/5
Avg. # Of Employees: 1-4 FT
Passive Ownership: Discouraged
Encourage Conversions: Yes
Area Develop. Agreements: No
Sub-Franchising Contracts: No
Expand In Territory: Yes
Space Needs: NA SF; NR

SUPPORT & TRAINING:

Financial Assistance Provided: Yes(D)
Site Selection Assistance: NA
Lease Negotiation Assistance: NA
Co-Operative Advertising: NA
Franchisee Assoc./Member: No
Size Of Corporate Staff: 32
On-Going Support: A,C,D,G,H,I
Training: 5 Days Headquarters.

SPECIFIC EXPANSION PLANS:

US: WA, OR Only
Canada: No
Overseas: No

<< >>

NATURZONE PEST CONTROL

1899 Porter Lake Dr., #103
Sarasota, FL 34240
Tel: (877) 3-NOPEST (941) 378-3334
Fax: (941) 378-8584
E-Mail: travis@naturzone.com
Web Site: www.naturzone.com
Mr. Travis Wellbrock, President

Natural, non-allergenic pest control + lawn care/fertilization. Serves both commercial units and residential homes.

BACKGROUND:

Established: 1988; 1st Franchised: 1999
Franchised Units: 10
Company-Owned Units: 1
Total Units: 11
Dist.: US-4; CAN-0; O'seas-0
North America: 2 States
Density: 3 in FL, 1 in KY
Projected New Units (12 Months): 10
Qualifications: 3, 3, 2, 1, 3, 4
Registered: FL

FINANCIAL/TERMS:

Cash Investment: $5K
Total Investment: $25K
Minimum Net Worth: $50K
Fees: Franchise - $15K
Royalty - 5%; Ad. - NA
Earnings Claims Statement: No
Term of Contract (Years): On-Going
Avg. # Of Employees: 3 FT
Passive Ownership: Discouraged
Encourage Conversions: Yes
Area Develop. Agreements: Yes
Sub-Franchising Contracts: No
Expand In Territory: Yes
Space Needs: NR SF; FS, HB, SC

SUPPORT & TRAINING:

Financial Assistance Provided: Yes(I)
Site Selection Assistance: No
Lease Negotiation Assistance: No

Co-Operative Advertising: Yes
Franchisee Assoc./Member: No
Size Of Corporate Staff: 10
On-Going Support: C,D,h
Training: 2-3 Weeks in Sarasota, FL.

SPECIFIC EXPANSION PLANS:
US: All United States
Canada: All Canada
Overseas: All Countries

OCTOCLEAN

1760 Chicago Ave., # J-15
Riverside, CA 92507
Tel: (866) OCTOCLN (951) 683-5859
Fax: (951) 779-0270
E-Mail: info@octoclean.com
Web Site: www.octoclean.com
Mr. Charles Stowe, Chief Executive Officer

OCTOCLEAN is a dynamic, innovative janitorial franchise system. We have developed an exciting opportunity for all kinds of people to simply and quickly start their own commercial janitorial business. Low start-up, guaranteed accounts, and extensive training and support make OCTOCLEAN an attractive option for those looking for the security and growth potential option for those looking for the security and growth potential of an established franchise opportunity.

BACKGROUND:
Established: 1991; 1st Franchised: 2000
Franchised Units: 74
Company-Owned Units: 0
Total Units: 74
Dist.: US-74; CAN-0; O'seas-0
North America: 1 State
Density: 74 in CA
Projected New Units (12 Months): 60
Qualifications: 2, 1, 1, 1, 3, 5
Registered: CA

FINANCIAL/TERMS:
Cash Investment: $1.5-2K
Total Investment: $8-57.5K
Minimum Net Worth: $10K
Fees: Franchise - $8K
Royalty - 5%; Ad. - 0%
Earnings Claims Statement: Yes
Term of Contract (Years): 5/5/5
Avg. # Of Employees: 1 FT, 1 PT
Passive Ownership: Discouraged
Encourage Conversions: NA
Area Develop. Agreements: Yes/20
Sub-Franchising Contracts: Yes
Expand In Territory: Yes
Space Needs: NA SF; HB

SUPPORT & TRAINING:
Financial Assistance Provided: Yes(D)
Site Selection Assistance: NA
Lease Negotiation Assistance: NA
Co-Operative Advertising: NA
Franchisee Assoc./Member: No
Size Of Corporate Staff: 12
On-Going Support: B,C,D,G,H,I
Training: 7 Days Riverside, CA.

SPECIFIC EXPANSION PLANS:
US: California
Canada: No
Overseas: No

OMEX INTERNATIONAL

3905 Hartzdale Dr., # 506
Camp Hill, PA 17011
Tel: (800) 827-6639 (717) 737-7311
Fax: (717) 737-9271
E-Mail: kabato@omexcorp.com
Web Site: www.omexcorp.com
Ms. Karen Goss, Franchise Representative

OMEX provides commercial contract cleaning services to first class office facilities including Fortune 500 companies, large office buildings, banks and medical clinics. Seeking prospects with good management, sales or business backgrounds determined to succeed and willing to follow our system. Low investment! Low royalties! Major territories! Free franchise renewal!

BACKGROUND:
Established: 1979; 1st Franchised: 1994
Franchised Units: 12
Company-Owned Units: 1
Total Units: 13
Dist.: US-12; CAN-0; O'seas-0
North America: 9 States
Density: 4 in PA
Projected New Units (12 Months): NR
Qualifications: , , , , ,
Registered: NR

FINANCIAL/TERMS:
Cash Investment: $40K
Total Investment: $40.4-70.6K
Minimum Net Worth: $150K
Fees: Franchise - $15-25K
Royalty - 4%; Ad. - NA
Earnings Claims Statement: No
Term of Contract (Years): 10/10
Avg. # Of Employees: Varies
Passive Ownership: Discouraged
Encourage Conversions: NR
Area Develop. Agreements: No
Sub-Franchising Contracts: No
Expand In Territory: Yes
Space Needs: 800-1,200 SF; Prime Location Not Required

SUPPORT & TRAINING:
Financial Assistance Provided: NR
Site Selection Assistance: No
Lease Negotiation Assistance: Yes
Co-Operative Advertising: Yes
Franchisee Assoc./Member: No
Size Of Corporate Staff: 7
On-Going Support: A,B,C,D,E,G,H,h, I
Training: 1 Week, Corporate Headquarters; 1 Week, Franchisee's Territory.

SPECIFIC EXPANSION PLANS:
US: All United States
Canada: NR
Overseas: NR

OPENWORKS

4742 N. 24th St., # 300
Phoenix, AZ 85016-4347
Tel: (800) 777-6736 (602) 224-0440 + 149
Fax: (602) 468-3788
E-Mail: bills@penworksweb.com
Web Site: www.openworksweb.com
Mr. Bill Scheidt, Master Franchise Sales

OPENWORKS has been granting commercial cleaning franchises since 1983. Our program is centered around on-going training and support in addition to guaranteed initial customers. All franchises include a customer base, equipment and advanced business training. We also offer Master Franchises on an exclusive basis for certain metropolitan areas. Contact us today for more information.

BACKGROUND: IFA MEMBER
Established: 1983; 1st Franchised: 1983
Franchised Units: 405
Company-Owned Units: 4
Total Units: 409
Dist.: US-401; CAN-0; O'seas-0
North America: 3 States
Density: 183 in AZ, 153 in WA, 65 CA
Projected New Units (12 Months): 100
Qualifications: 3, 3, 1, 2, 4, 4
Registered: CA,WA

FINANCIAL/TERMS:
Cash Investment: $5-150K
Total Investment: $14-150K
Minimum Net Worth: $10-500K
Fees: Franchise - $5-150K
Royalty - 10%; Ad. - 1%
Earnings Claims Statement: No
Term of Contract (Years): 10/10
Avg. # Of Employees: 3+ FT
Passive Ownership: Discouraged
Encourage Conversions: Yes
Area Develop. Agreements: Yes/20
Sub-Franchising Contracts: Yes
Expand In Territory: Yes
Space Needs: 3,000(Master) SF; Master

SUPPORT & TRAINING:
Financial Assistance Provided: Yes(D)
Site Selection Assistance: No
Lease Negotiation Assistance: Yes
Co-Operative Advertising: NA
Franchisee Assoc./Member: No
Size Of Corporate Staff: 30
On-Going Support: A,B,C,D,E,G,H,I
Training: 2 Wks. Regional Office (Janitorial); 4 Wks. Regional Off. & 3 Wks. Master's Off. (Master).

SPECIFIC EXPANSION PLANS:
US: All United States
Canada: All Canada
Overseas: All Countries

<< >>

P.E.S.T. MACHINE TEAM, THE
3616 Lake Rd.
Ponca City, OK 74604-5100
Tel: (800) 654-4541 (580) 762-6614
Fax: (580) 765-4613
E-Mail: brad@parkerpestcontrol.com
Web Site: www.worldfranchising.com/website.htm
Mr. Brad Parker, President

Using patented P.E.S.T. ® Machine, treat homes for cockroaches one time with a one year guarantee. Other clients include apartment complexes (especially low rent), restaurants and health care facilities. Can also offer all other aspects of pest control.

BACKGROUND:
Established: 1963; 1st Franchised: 1987
Franchised Units: 3
Company-Owned Units: 6
Total Units: 9
Dist.: US-0; CAN-0; O'seas-0
North America: 3 States
Density: 1 in OK, 1 in KS, 1 in CA
Projected New Units (12 Months): NR
Qualifications: , , , , ,
Registered: NR

FINANCIAL/TERMS:
Cash Investment: NA
Total Investment: $25-75K
Minimum Net Worth: NR
Fees: Franchise - $25K
Royalty - 8%/150/Mo.; Ad. - NA
Earnings Claims Statement: No
Term of Contract (Years): 5/5
Avg. # Of Employees: 1 FT
Passive Ownership: Discouraged
Encourage Conversions: NR
Area Develop. Agreements: No
Sub-Franchising Contracts: No
Expand In Territory: Yes
Space Needs: NR SF; HB

SUPPORT & TRAINING:
Financial Assistance Provided: NR
Site Selection Assistance: NA
Lease Negotiation Assistance: NA
Co-Operative Advertising: No
Franchisee Assoc./Member: No
Size Of Corporate Staff: 15
On-Going Support: A,a,B,C,c,D,d,E,F,G,I
Training: 3 Weeks in Ponca City, OK; 1 Week at Franchisee's Location.

SPECIFIC EXPANSION PLANS:
US: All United States
Canada: NR
Overseas: NR

<< >>

PROFESSIONAL CARPET SYSTEMS
4211 Atlantic Ave.
Raleigh, NC 27604
Tel: (800) 925-5055 (919) 875-8871
Fax: (919) 875-9855
E-Mail: fthompson@procarpetsys.com
Web Site: www.procarpetsys.com
Mr. Fritz D. Thompson, President

PROFESSIONAL CARPET SYSTEMS is the leader in "on-site" carpet re-dyeing, servicing thousands of apartment complexes, hotels and motels worldwide. Services also include carpet cleaning, rejuvenation, repair, water and flood damage restoration and "guaranteed odor control." A total carpet care concept serving commercial and residential customers.

BACKGROUND:
Established: 1978; 1st Franchised: 1979
Franchised Units: 61
Company-Owned Units: 0
Total Units: 61
Dist.: US-114; CAN-8; O'seas-14
North America: 43 States, 6 Provinces
Density: 24 in CA, 12 in FL, 9 in NC
Projected New Units (12 Months): 15
Qualifications: , , , , ,
Registered: All States

FINANCIAL/TERMS:
Cash Investment: $10K+
Total Investment: $19.7K+
Minimum Net Worth: NR
Fees: Franchise - $14.7K
Royalty - 6%; Ad. - 0%
Earnings Claims Statement: No
Term of Contract (Years): 10/10
Avg. # Of Employees: 1 FT With Truck
Passive Ownership: Discouraged
Encourage Conversions: No
Area Develop. Agreements: No
Sub-Franchising Contracts: No
Expand In Territory: Yes
Space Needs: NR SF; HB

SUPPORT & TRAINING:
Financial Assistance Provided: No
Site Selection Assistance: Yes
Lease Negotiation Assistance: NA
Co-Operative Advertising: NA
Franchisee Assoc./Member: NR
Size Of Corporate Staff: 8
On-Going Support: A,B,C,D,F,G,H,I
Training: 2 Weeks Headquarters.

SPECIFIC EXPANSION PLANS:
US: All United States
Canada: All Canada
Overseas: All Countries

<< >>

PROFESSIONAL POLISH
5450 East Loop 820 South
Fort Worth, TX 76119
Tel: (800) 255-0488 (817) 572-7353
Fax: (817) 561-6193
E-Mail: carren@professionalpolish.com
Web Site: www.professionalpolish.com
Ms. Carren Cavanaugh, Owner

Janitorial, lawn and building repair. Alto distributor. We make our franchisor make money.

BACKGROUND:
Established: 1981; 1st Franchised: 1986
Franchised Units: 34
Company-Owned Units: 2
Total Units: 36
Dist.: US-36; CAN-0; O'seas-0
North America: 2 States
Density: 1 in TX, 1 in NC
Projected New Units (12 Months): 4
Qualifications: 5, 5, 5, 5, 5, 5
Registered: FL

FINANCIAL/TERMS:
Cash Investment: $7.5K
Total Investment: $20K
Minimum Net Worth: $25K
Fees: Franchise - $4.5K
Royalty - 15%; Ad. - 0%
Earnings Claims Statement: No
Term of Contract (Years): 20/20
Avg. # Of Employees: 2 FT, 1 PT
Passive Ownership: Discouraged
Encourage Conversions: NA
Area Develop. Agreements: No
Sub-Franchising Contracts: No
Expand In Territory: Yes
Space Needs: NA SF; NA
SUPPORT & TRAINING:
Financial Assistance Provided: NR
Site Selection Assistance: NA
Lease Negotiation Assistance: NA
Co-Operative Advertising: Yes
Franchisee Assoc./Member: No
Size Of Corporate Staff: 6
On-Going Support: A,B,C,D,F,G,H,I
Training: 2 Weeks On-Site; 1 Week Fort Worth, TX; 1 Week Followup On-Site.
SPECIFIC EXPANSION PLANS:
US: Southwest, Southeast
Canada: No
Overseas: No

PROPERTY DAMAGE APPRAISERS
6100 Southwest Blvd., # 200
Fort Worth, TX 76109-3964
Tel: (800) 749-7324 + 23 (817) 731-5555
Fax: (817) 731-5565
E-Mail: rick.cutler@pdaorg.net
Web Site: www.pdahomeoffice.com
Mr. Rick Cutler, Dir. Training/Development

The industry's largest, franchised appraisal company, with national marketing support, a computerized office management system, training and on-going management assistance. No initial franchise fee is required - only a royalty on completed business. Automobile damage appraising experience a pre-requisite.

BACKGROUND:
Established: 1963; 1st Franchised: 1963
Franchised Units: 282
Company-Owned Units: 0
Total Units: 282
Dist.: US-263; CAN-0; O'seas-0
North America: 47 States
Density: 25 in TX, 21 in CA, 15 in FL
Projected New Units (12 Months): 20
Qualifications: 3, 3, 5, 3, , 5
Registered: All States
FINANCIAL/TERMS:
Cash Investment: $9.2-23K
Total Investment: $9.2-23K
Minimum Net Worth: NR
Fees: Franchise - $0
Royalty - 15%; Ad. - 0%
Earnings Claims Statement: No
Term of Contract (Years): 3/5
Avg. # Of Employees: 2 FT
Passive Ownership: Not Allowed
Encourage Conversions: Yes
Area Develop. Agreements: No
Sub-Franchising Contracts: No
Expand In Territory: Yes
Space Needs: NR SF; NA
SUPPORT & TRAINING:
Financial Assistance Provided: No
Site Selection Assistance: Yes
Lease Negotiation Assistance: NA
Co-Operative Advertising: Yes
Franchisee Assoc./Member: No
Size Of Corporate Staff: 36
On-Going Support: A,C,D,G,H,I
Training: 1 Week Corporate Headquarters; 4 Days On-Site.
SPECIFIC EXPANSION PLANS:
US: All United States
Canada: No
Overseas: No

<< >>

PUROCLEAN
6001 Hiatus Rd., # 13
Tamarac, FL 33321
Tel: (800) 247-9047 (954) 722-6618
Fax: (954) 722-8316
E-Mail: sales@puroclean.com
Web Site: www.purocleanopportunity.com
Mr. C. Monty Smith, VP Sales & Marketing

PUROCLEAN offers an exciting service business opportunity in a $35 billion niche, recession-proof industry. PUROCLEAN franchisees provide quick-response emergency restoration services to insurance companies and homeowners based on property damage caused by smoke, fire, etc. PUROCLEAN is experiencing dynamic growth and expansion in this immense market. Expanded local market opportunities available. Registered in all states.

BACKGROUND: IFA MEMBER
Established: 1985; 1st Franchised: 1991
Franchised Units: 89
Company-Owned Units: 0
Total Units: 89
Dist.: US-89; CAN-0; O'seas-0
North America: 25 States
Density: 14 in CA, 11 in PA, 7 in NJ
Projected New Units (12 Months): 30
Qualifications: 3, 1, 1, 3, 1, 3
Registered: All States
FINANCIAL/TERMS:
Cash Investment: $25K
Total Investment: $79.3-122.2K
Minimum Net Worth: NR
Fees: Franchise - $25K
Royalty - 10-8%; Ad. - 0%
Earnings Claims Statement: No
Term of Contract (Years): 20/10
Avg. # Of Employees: 2 FT, 2 PT
Passive Ownership: Discouraged
Encourage Conversions: Yes
Area Develop. Agreements: No
Sub-Franchising Contracts: No
Expand In Territory: Yes
Space Needs: Varies SF; FS, SF, HB
SUPPORT & TRAINING:
Financial Assistance Provided: Yes(I)
Site Selection Assistance: No
Lease Negotiation Assistance: No
Co-Operative Advertising: No
Franchisee Assoc./Member: Yes/Yes
Size Of Corporate Staff: 15
On-Going Support: C,G,H,I
Training: 10 Days Ft. Lauderdale, FL; 5 Days Franchise Location.
SPECIFIC EXPANSION PLANS:
US: Southeast, Midwest, West
Canada: No
Overseas: No

<< >>

RAINBOW INTERNATIONAL CARPET CARE & RESTORATION
P. O. Box 3146, 1010 N. University Parks Dr.
Waco, TX 76707-0146
Tel: (800) 280-9963 (254) 745-2439
Fax: (800) 209-7621
E-Mail: gena.reid@dwyergroup.com
Web Site: www.rainbowintl.com

Mr. Mike Hawkins, VP Franchising

Nationally acclaimed carpet care and restoration franchisor, with 16 years of experienced, positioned to help franchisees tap into the expanding insurance restoration industry, only one of the more than ten profit centers from which franchisees can gain competitive advantage. Success of our franchisees is attributed to our proven niche marketing methods, comprehensive 12-hour technical support and consumer awareness of RAINBOW. Featured in Entrepreneur's Top 100.

BACKGROUND: IFA MEMBER
Established: 1980; 1st Franchised: 1981
Franchised Units: 460
Company-Owned Units: 0
Total Units: 460
Dist.: US-446; CAN-8; O'seas-6
North America: 42 States, 6 Provinces
Density: 50 in TX, 20 in CA, 15 in FL
Projected New Units (12 Months): 24
Qualifications: 3, 2, 1, 2, 3, 5
Registered: All States

FINANCIAL/TERMS:
Cash Investment: $25K/100K Pop.
Total Investment: $50-100K
Minimum Net Worth: Varies
Fees: Franchise - $19.9K
Royalty - 4-7%; Ad. - 2%
Earnings Claims Statement: No
Term of Contract (Years): 10/5
Avg. # Of Employees: 2 FT, 1 PT
Passive Ownership: Discouraged
Encourage Conversions: No
Area Develop. Agreements: No
Sub-Franchising Contracts: No
Expand In Territory: Yes
Space Needs: NR SF; HB

SUPPORT & TRAINING:
Financial Assistance Provided: Yes(D)
Site Selection Assistance: NA
Lease Negotiation Assistance: No
Co-Operative Advertising: No
Franchisee Assoc./Member: No
Size Of Corporate Staff: 17
On-Going Support: A,b,C,D,G,H,I
Training: 2 Weeks at Corporate Headquarters.

SPECIFIC EXPANSION PLANS:
US: All United States
Canada: All Canada
Overseas: Japan, Middle East, Europe, Latin America

<< >>

ROTO-ROOTER

300 Ashworth Rd.
West Des Moines, IA 50265-3786
Tel: (800) 575-7737 (515) 223-1343
Fax: (515) 223-6109
E-Mail: mike.higgins@rotorootercorp.com
Web Site: www.rotorooter.com
Mr. Michael Higgins, Dir. Franchise Development

World's largest plumbing repair and sewer and drain cleaning company, providing service to residential, commercial and municipal customers.

BACKGROUND: IFA MEMBER
Established: 1935; 1st Franchised: 1935
Franchised Units: 500
Company-Owned Units: 100
Total Units: 600
Dist.: US-598; CAN-23; O'seas-0
North America: 50 States, 5 Provinces
Density: 44 in CA, 28 in TX, 24 in FL
Projected New Units (12 Months): 2
Qualifications: 3, 4, 5, 2, 2, 2
Registered: All States and AB

FINANCIAL/TERMS:
Cash Investment: $15-75K
Total Investment: $25-99K
Minimum Net Worth: NA
Fees: Franchise - $10K
Royalty - Varies; Ad. - Varies
Earnings Claims Statement: No
Term of Contract (Years): 10/10
Avg. # Of Employees: NR
Passive Ownership: Discouraged
Encourage Conversions: Yes
Area Develop. Agreements: No
Sub-Franchising Contracts: No
Expand In Territory: Yes
Space Needs: NR SF; NA

SUPPORT & TRAINING:
Financial Assistance Provided: Yes(I)
Site Selection Assistance: NA
Lease Negotiation Assistance: NA
Co-Operative Advertising: Yes
Franchisee Assoc./Member: Yes/No
Size Of Corporate Staff: 25
On-Going Support: B,G,h,I
Training: N/A.

SPECIFIC EXPANSION PLANS:
US: No
Canada: No
Overseas: All Countries

<< >>

ROTO-STATIC INTERNATIONAL

90 Delta Park Blvd., Bldg. A
Brampton, ON L6T 5E7 CANADA
Tel: (905) 458-7002
Fax: (905) 458-8650
E-Mail: success@rotostatic.com
Web Site: www.rotostatic.com
Ms. Pauline Wallace, Franchise Director

Profit from offering 6 services, including a unique system of carpet cleaning, , using Static Attraction principle, water damage restoration and odor removal services. Complete training in head office. On-going support systems. A company with a proven past.

BACKGROUND:
Established: 1977; 1st Franchised: 1977
Franchised Units: 141
Company-Owned Units: 0
Total Units: 141
Dist.: US-0; CAN-141; O'seas-0
North America: 9 Provinces
Density: ON, PQ, BC
Projected New Units (12 Months): 10
Qualifications: , , , , ,
Registered: AB

FINANCIAL/TERMS:
Cash Investment: $5-20K
Total Investment: $45-60K
Minimum Net Worth: NR
Fees: Franchise - $15K
Royalty - 5%; Ad. - 2%
Earnings Claims Statement: No
Term of Contract (Years): 10/10
Avg. # Of Employees: 1-2 FT
Passive Ownership: Not Allowed
Encourage Conversions: NR
Area Develop. Agreements: Yes
Sub-Franchising Contracts: Yes
Expand In Territory: No
Space Needs: NR SF; NR

SUPPORT & TRAINING:
Financial Assistance Provided: Yes(I)
Site Selection Assistance: NA
Lease Negotiation Assistance: NA
Co-Operative Advertising: NA
Franchisee Assoc./Member: Yes
Size Of Corporate Staff: 7
On-Going Support: C,D,E,F,G,H,I
Training: 4 Days Toronto, ON.

SPECIFIC EXPANSION PLANS:
US: All United States
Canada: All Canada
Overseas: U.K., Germany, France, Australia, Japan, Mexico, Spain

<< >>

SEALMASTER

2520 S. Campbell St.
Sandusky, OH 44870

Tel: (800) 395-7325 + 146 (419) 621-8001
Fax: (419) 626-5477
E-Mail: gmuscarella@sealmaster.com
Web Site: www.sealmaster.net
Mr. Gregory Muscarella, Franchise Director

SEALMASTER is now offering manufacturing/sales opportunities in the billion dollar pavement products industry. This is a business-to-business franchise, offering pavement sealers, crack fillers, asphalt repair products, tennis court/running track coatings, traffic striping paints, tools, equipment and more. Turn-key operations available with on-going training and support.

BACKGROUND: IFA MEMBER
Established: 1969; 1st Franchised: 1993
Franchised Units: 23
Company-Owned Units: 2
Total Units: 25
Dist.: US-18; CAN-0; O'seas-0
North America: 17 States
Density: NR
Projected New Units (12 Months): 6
Qualifications: 5, 3, 2, 2, 3, 4
Registered: CA,FL,HI,IL,IN,MD,MI,MN, NY,OR,RI,VA,WA,WI,DC

FINANCIAL/TERMS:
Cash Investment: $175K
Total Investment: $223.3-426K
Minimum Net Worth: $300-500K
Fees: Franchise - $35K
Royalty - 5%; Ad. - 1.5%
Earnings Claims Statement: No
Term of Contract (Years): 10/5/5/5
Avg. # Of Employees: 3 FT, 3 PT
Passive Ownership: Discouraged
Encourage Conversions: Yes
Area Develop. Agreements: NR
Sub-Franchising Contracts: NR
Expand In Territory: NR
Space Needs: 7,000-10,000 SF; FS

SUPPORT & TRAINING:
Financial Assistance Provided: NR
Site Selection Assistance: Yes
Lease Negotiation Assistance: NR
Co-Operative Advertising: Yes
Franchisee Assoc./Member: No
Size Of Corporate Staff: 27
On-Going Support: A,B,C,D,E,G,I
Training: 2 Weeks Corporate Headquarters, OH.

SPECIFIC EXPANSION PLANS:
US: All United States
Canada: All Canada
Overseas: All Countries

<< >>

SERVICE ONE
5104 N. Orange Blossom Tr., # 114
Orlando, FL 32810
Tel: (800) 522-7111 (407) 293-7645
Fax: (407) 299-4306
E-Mail: serviceonex16@aol.com
Web Site: www.serviceonejanitorial.net
Mr. Steve Rathel, Franchise Director

We are a janitorial franchise, delivering supplies, equipment, training and customers.

BACKGROUND:
Established: 1965; 1st Franchised: 1985
Franchised Units: 185
Company-Owned Units: 0
Total Units: 185
Dist.: US-140; CAN-0; O'seas-0
North America: 20 States
Density: 87 in FL, 5 in AZ, 13 in NC
Projected New Units (12 Months): 24
Qualifications: , , , , ,
Registered: FL

FINANCIAL/TERMS:
Cash Investment: $3-9K
Total Investment: $6.1-19.3K
Minimum Net Worth: NR
Fees: Franchise - $6-18.3K
Royalty - $175/Mo.; Ad. - 0%
Earnings Claims Statement: NR
Term of Contract (Years): 10/10
Avg. # Of Employees: NR
Passive Ownership: Not Allowed
Encourage Conversions: NA
Area Develop. Agreements: No
Sub-Franchising Contracts: No
Expand In Territory: No
Space Needs: NR SF; NA

SUPPORT & TRAINING:
Financial Assistance Provided: Yes(D)
Site Selection Assistance: NA
Lease Negotiation Assistance: NA
Co-Operative Advertising: NA
Franchisee Assoc./Member: No
Size Of Corporate Staff: 6
On-Going Support: A,E,G,I
Training: 2 Days Where Convenient.

SPECIFIC EXPANSION PLANS:
US: Non-Registration States
Canada: No
Overseas: No

<< >>

Top 100

SERVICEMASTER CLEAN
3839 Forest Hill Irene Rd
Memphis, TN 38125
Tel: (800) 786-9687 (901) 597-7500
Fax: (901) 597-7580
E-Mail: dmessenger@smclean.com
Web Site: www.ownafranchise.com
Mr. David Messenger, Vice President

SERVICEMASTER CLEAN is a division of The ServiceMaster Company. With over 52 years of franchising experience and over 4,000 franchises, SERVICEMASTER CLEAN continues to grow each year and offers franchise opportunities in three distinct categories: 1) Commercial Cleaning services 2) Residential carpet and upholstery cleaning & 3) Disaster Restoration services. Financing is provided for the initial franchise fee, start-up equipment & vehicles to qualified candidates through ServiceMaster Acceptance Co.

BACKGROUND: IFA MEMBER
Established: 1947; 1st Franchised: 1952
Franchised Units: 4,488
Company-Owned Units: 0
Total Units: 4,488
Dist.: US-2,951; CAN-176; O'seas-1,398
North America: 50 States,10 Provinces
Density: 200 in IL, 155 in CA, 139 OH
Projected New Units (12 Months): 150
Qualifications: 5, 3, 2, 2, 3, 5
Registered: All States and AB

FINANCIAL/TERMS:
Cash Investment: $12K
Total Investment: $18.8-100K
Minimum Net Worth: $50K
Fees: Franchise - $16.9-43K
Royalty - 4-10%; Ad. - 0.5-1%
Earnings Claims Statement: No
Term of Contract (Years): 5/5
Avg. # Of Employees: 3 FT, 2 PT
Passive Ownership: Discouraged
Encourage Conversions: Yes
Area Develop. Agreements: No
Sub-Franchising Contracts: Yes
Expand In Territory: Yes
Space Needs: NA SF; NA

SUPPORT & TRAINING:
Financial Assistance Provided: Yes(D)
Site Selection Assistance: No
Lease Negotiation Assistance: No
Co-Operative Advertising: Yes

Franchisee Assoc./Member: Yes/Yes
Size Of Corporate Staff: 200
On-Going Support: A,B,C,D,F,G,H,I
Training: 2 Weeks Memphis, TN; 1 Week on Location.

SPECIFIC EXPANSION PLANS:
US: All United States
Canada: All Canada
Overseas: All Countries

<< >>

SERVPRO

801 Industrial Dr.
Gallatin, TN 37066
Tel: (800) 826-9586 (615) 451-0600
Fax: (615) 451-1602
E-Mail: franchise@servpronet.com
Web Site: www.servpro.com
Mr. Kevin Brown, Dir. Franchise Expansion

A completely diversified cleaning and restoration business, with multiple income opportunities. The insurance restoration market (fire, smoke and water damages) is our main focus. We also specialize in commercial and residential cleaning. SERVPRO teaches effective management, marketing and technical skills. We are seeking qualified individuals with the desire to own their own business and become part of the SERVPRO team. If you want to be the best, join the best team. Call 1-800-826-9586.

BACKGROUND:
Established: 1967; 1st Franchised: 1969
Franchised Units: 1,276
Company-Owned Units: 0
Total Units: 1,276
Dist.: US-1,276; CAN-0; O'seas-0
North America: 47 States
Density: 100 in CA, 80 in FL, 79 TX
Projected New Units (12 Months): 95
Qualifications: 3, 4, 1, 3, 4, 4
Registered: All States

FINANCIAL/TERMS:
Cash Investment: $60-70K
Total Investment: $99.3-150.4K
Minimum Net Worth: $150K
Fees: Franchise - $36K
Royalty - 3-10%; Ad. - 3%
Earnings Claims Statement: No
Term of Contract (Years): 5/5
Avg. # Of Employees: 5-10 FT, 2-4 PT
Passive Ownership: Discouraged
Encourage Conversions: Yes
Area Develop. Agreements: No
Sub-Franchising Contracts: No
Expand In Territory: No
Space Needs: 1,500+ SF; FS, HB, Warehouse

SUPPORT & TRAINING:
Financial Assistance Provided: Yes(D)
Site Selection Assistance: Yes
Lease Negotiation Assistance: No
Co-Operative Advertising: Yes
Franchisee Assoc./Member: No/No
Size Of Corporate Staff: 180
On-Going Support: B,C,D,E,G,H,I
Training: 2.5 Weeks Gallatin, TN; 1 Week Franchisee's Location.

SPECIFIC EXPANSION PLANS:
US: All United States
Canada: No
Overseas: No

SPARKLE WASH

26851 Richmond Rd.
Bedford Heights, OH 44146
Tel: (800) 321-0770 (216) 464-4212
Fax: (216) 464-8869
E-Mail: yuhas@en.com
Web Site: www.sparklewash.com
Mr. Tom Yuhas, Dir. Franchise Development

SPARKLE WASH provides mobile power-cleaning and restoration, providing broad market opportunities to our franchisees for the commercial, industrial, residential and fleet markets. SPARKLE WASH franchisees can also provide special services, including wood restoration, all using our environmentally friendly products.

BACKGROUND: IFA MEMBER
Established: 1965; 1st Franchised: 1967
Franchised Units: 173
Company-Owned Units: 1
Total Units: 174
Dist.: US-93; CAN-0; O'seas-79
North America: 32 States
Density: 13 in OH, 13 in PA, 8 in NY
Projected New Units (12 Months): 10
Qualifications: 3, 3, 1, 2, 4, 5
Registered: All States

FINANCIAL/TERMS:
Cash Investment: $19.3-21.3K
Total Investment: $50K
Minimum Net Worth: $60K
Fees: Franchise - $15K
Royalty - 3-5%; Ad. - 0%
Earnings Claims Statement: Yes
Term of Contract (Years): Continual
Avg. # Of Employees: 2 FT, 2 PT
Passive Ownership: Allowed
Encourage Conversions: Yes
Area Develop. Agreements: No
Sub-Franchising Contracts: No
Expand In Territory: Yes
Space Needs: NR SF; NA

SUPPORT & TRAINING:
Financial Assistance Provided: Yes(B)
Site Selection Assistance: NA
Lease Negotiation Assistance: NA
Co-Operative Advertising: No
Franchisee Assoc./Member: Yes/Yes
Size Of Corporate Staff: 15
On-Going Support: B,C,D,G,H,I
Training: 1 Week Headquarters; 3 Days Franchisee Location; 3 Days National/Regional Meetings.

SPECIFIC EXPANSION PLANS:
US: All United States
Canada: All Canada
Overseas: All Countries

<< >>

STEAM BROTHERS PROFESSIONAL CLEANING & RESTORATION

2124 E. Sweet Ave.
Bismarck, ND 58504
Tel: (800) 767-5064 (701) 222-1263
Fax: (701) 222-1372
E-Mail: steambrothers@gcentral.com
Web Site: www.steambrothers.com
Mr. Adam Leier, President

Residential and commercial - carpet, upholstery, drapery, wall and ceiling cleaning; furnace air duct cleaning; water, smoke and fire clean-up. Named one of the Top 100 home-based franchises in 1995.

BACKGROUND:
Established: 1977; 1st Franchised: 1983
Franchised Units: 24
Company-Owned Units: 0
Total Units: 24
Dist.: US-22; CAN-0; O'seas-0
North America: 5 States
Density: 9 in MN, 7 in ND, 3 in SD
Projected New Units (12 Months): 2-5
Qualifications: 3, 2, 1, 3, 4, 5
Registered: MN,SD

FINANCIAL/TERMS:
Cash Investment: $16-22.5K
Total Investment: $22.5-53.5K
Minimum Net Worth: NA
Fees: Franchise - $16K

Royalty - 5-6.5%; Ad. - NA
Earnings Claims Statement: No
Term of Contract (Years): 10/10
Avg. # Of Employees: 3 FT
Passive Ownership: Discouraged
Encourage Conversions: Yes
Area Develop. Agreements: No
Sub-Franchising Contracts: No
Expand In Territory: No
Space Needs: NR SF; HB

SUPPORT & TRAINING:
Financial Assistance Provided: Yes(I)
Site Selection Assistance: Yes
Lease Negotiation Assistance: Yes
Co-Operative Advertising: No
Franchisee Assoc./Member: Yes/Yes
Size Of Corporate Staff: 2
On-Going Support: B,C,D,E,F,G,H,I
Training: 5 Days Home Office; 3-5 Days Franchise Location.

SPECIFIC EXPANSION PLANS:
US: Upper Midwest States
Canada: No
Overseas: No

<< >>

STEAMATIC

303 Arthur St.
Fort Worth, TX 76107-2352
Tel: (800) 527-1295 (817) 332-1575
Fax: (817) 332-5349
E-Mail: bsims@steamatic.com
Web Site: www.steamatic.com
Mr. Bill Sims, VP International Development

The total cleaning and disaster recover franchise, serving the residential, commercial and industrial markets.Emphasis is on combating problems associated with indoor air pollution, such as cleaning/sanitation of the HVAC system, air ducts, coils, carpet cleaning, etc. Emphasis also on water and fire damage restoration of residential/commercial buildings. Plus, general cleaning of residential and commercial properties.

BACKGROUND: IFA MEMBER
Established: 1948; 1st Franchised: 1968
Franchised Units: 401
Company-Owned Units: 34
Total Units: 435
Dist.: US-361; CAN-48; O'seas-26
North America: 43 States,10 Provinces
Density: 56 in TX, 43 in CA, 26 in IL
Projected New Units (12 Months): 40
Qualifications: , , , , ,
Registered: All States

FINANCIAL/TERMS:
Cash Investment: $54-71K
Total Investment: $100-171K
Minimum Net Worth: NR
Fees: Franchise - $7-24K
Royalty - 8-5%; Ad. - 0%
Earnings Claims Statement: No
Term of Contract (Years): 10/5
Avg. # Of Employees: 5-40 FT, 3-10 PT
Passive Ownership: Discouraged
Encourage Conversions: Yes
Area Develop. Agreements: No
Sub-Franchising Contracts: No
Expand In Territory: No
Space Needs: NA SF; HB, Warehouse

SUPPORT & TRAINING:
Financial Assistance Provided: Yes(D)
Site Selection Assistance: NA
Lease Negotiation Assistance: NA
Co-Operative Advertising: NA
Franchisee Assoc./Member: Yes/Yes
Size Of Corporate Staff: 32
On-Going Support: A,B,C,D,E,F,G,H,I
Training: 3 Weeks Ft. Worth, TX.

SPECIFIC EXPANSION PLANS:
US: All United States
Canada: All Canada
Overseas: All Countries

<< >>

TOWER CLEANING SYSTEMS

P. O. Box 2468
Southeastern, PA 19399
Tel: (800) 355-4000 (610) 278-9000
Fax: (610) 275-7662
E-Mail: towerclean@aol.com
Web Site: www.toweronline.com
Mr. Chuck Lomagro, Vice President

TOWER CLEANING was rated in the top 100 franchises by "Entrepreneur"; "Inc. Magazine" says we are one of the country's fastest-growing franchises of 1997. We feature a tested, proven program with your initial clients already obtained; full start-up package, complete step-by-step and on-going training; professional administrative support (customer relations, accounting, invoicing, on-going marketing).

BACKGROUND:
Established: 1988; 1st Franchised: 1990
Franchised Units: 449
Company-Owned Units: 0
Total Units: 449
Dist.: US-1,270; CAN-0; O'seas-0
North America: 19 States
Density: 480 in PA, 235 in NJ, 225 WA
Projected New Units (12 Months): 500
Qualifications: 3, 3, 3, 2, 1, 5
Registered: All States

FINANCIAL/TERMS:
Cash Investment: $1.5-25K
Total Investment: $3.4-34K
Minimum Net Worth: $10K
Fees: Franchise - $4-33.6K
Royalty - 3%; Ad. - 0%
Earnings Claims Statement: No
Term of Contract (Years): 10/10
Avg. # Of Employees: 1-5 FT
Passive Ownership: Allowed
Encourage Conversions: Yes
Area Develop. Agreements: Yes/10
Sub-Franchising Contracts: No
Expand In Territory: Yes
Space Needs: NA SF; NR

SUPPORT & TRAINING:
Financial Assistance Provided: Yes(D)
Site Selection Assistance: NA
Lease Negotiation Assistance: NA
Co-Operative Advertising: NA
Franchisee Assoc./Member: No
Size Of Corporate Staff: 50+
On-Going Support: A,B,C,D,G,H,I
Training: 1 Week Local Office; 2-3 Days On-Site.

SPECIFIC EXPANSION PLANS:
US: All United States
Canada: All Canada
Overseas: No

<< >>

TRI-COLOR FRANCHISE SYSTEMS

603 W. Main St.
Glasgow, KY 42141
Tel: (800) 452-9065 (270) 651-7879
Fax: (270) 651-6048
E-Mail: randy@tri-color.com
Web Site: www.tri-color.com
Mr. Randy Raines, President/CEO

TRI-COLOR is a total service carpet care and restoration company for residential and commercial clients. Franchisees are trained in management, public relations and marketing with their personal franchise director to help them excel in all areas of their franchise. With 19 years in business, our franchisees are becoming industry leaders.

BACKGROUND:
Established: 1984; 1st Franchised: 1997
Franchised Units: 6
Company-Owned Units: 6
Total Units: 12

Dist.: US-12; CAN-0; O'seas-0
North America: 2 States
Density: 9 in KY, 3 in TN
Projected New Units (12 Months): 15
Qualifications: 5, 4, 3, 4, 5, 5
Registered: FL

FINANCIAL/TERMS:
Cash Investment: $10-20K
Total Investment: $45-100K
Minimum Net Worth: $50K
Fees: Franchise - $17.5K
Royalty - 5%; Ad. - 0%
Earnings Claims Statement: Yes
Term of Contract (Years): 10/5
Avg. # Of Employees: 3 FT
Passive Ownership: Not Allowed
Encourage Conversions: No
Area Develop. Agreements: Yes/10
Sub-Franchising Contracts: No
Expand In Territory: Yes
Space Needs: NA SF; NA

SUPPORT & TRAINING:
Financial Assistance Provided: Yes(B)
Site Selection Assistance: Yes
Lease Negotiation Assistance: NA
Co-Operative Advertising: No
Franchisee Assoc./Member: No
Size Of Corporate Staff: 18
On-Going Support: A,B,C,D,E,F,H,I
Training: 2 Weeks Glascow, KY Home Office; As Needed Franchisee Location.

SPECIFIC EXPANSION PLANS:
US: South, Southeast, Southwest
Canada: No
Overseas: No

<< >>

TRULY NOLEN PEST CONTROL

3636 E. Speedway Blvd.
Tucson, AZ 85716-4018
Tel: (800) 458-3664 (520) 327-3447
Fax: (520) 322-4010
E-Mail: truly@truly.com
Web Site: www.trulynolen.com
Mr. Bill Nolen, Chief Executive Officer

Pest, lawn, termite, inspection based upon a unique and memorably established business system.

BACKGROUND: IFA MEMBER
Established: 1938; 1st Franchised: 1996
Franchised Units: 10
Company-Owned Units: 67
Total Units: 77
Dist.: US-72; CAN-0; O'seas-0
North America: 13 States
Density: 42 in FL, 19 in AZ, 8 in CA
Projected New Units (12 Months): 4
Qualifications: 2, 2, 2, 2, 2, 5
Registered: CA, FL, MI, NY

FINANCIAL/TERMS:
Cash Investment: $5-100K
Total Investment: $1.5-200K
Minimum Net Worth: $25K
Fees: Franchise - $45K
Royalty - 7%; Ad. - 0%
Earnings Claims Statement: No
Term of Contract (Years): 5
Avg. # Of Employees: 10 FT, 1 PT
Passive Ownership: Discouraged
Encourage Conversions: Yes
Area Develop. Agreements: No
Sub-Franchising Contracts: No
Expand In Territory: Yes
Space Needs: NR SF; NA

SUPPORT & TRAINING:
Financial Assistance Provided: No
Site Selection Assistance: No
Lease Negotiation Assistance: No
Co-Operative Advertising: No
Franchisee Assoc./Member: No
Size Of Corporate Staff: 25
On-Going Support: C,c,D,d,h,I
Training: 1 Week in Pompano Beach, FL; On-Site as Determined.

SPECIFIC EXPANSION PLANS:
US: All United States
Canada: All Canada
Overseas: No

<< >>

UNICLEAN SYSTEMS

1010 W. Queens Rd., #200
North Vancouver, BC V7R 4S9
CANADA
Tel: (604) 986-4750
Fax: (604) 987-6838
E-Mail: info@unicleansystems.com
Web Site: www.worldfranchising.com/website.htm
Mr. Jack B. Karpowicz, President

Commercial office cleaning on a long-term contract basis.

BACKGROUND:
Established: 1976; 1st Franchised: 1981
Franchised Units: 398
Company-Owned Units: 1
Total Units: 399
Dist.: US-48; CAN-347; O'seas-0
North America: 12 States, 5 Provinces
Density: 167 in BC, 89 in ON, 35 PQ
Projected New Units (12 Months): 20
Qualifications: 2, 3, 2, 2, 4, 5
Registered: CL,IL,OR,WA

FINANCIAL/TERMS:
Cash Investment: $5.5-16.5K
Total Investment: $5.5-16.5K
Minimum Net Worth: NA
Fees: Franchise - $1.5K
Royalty - 15%; Ad. - 0-5%
Earnings Claims Statement: No
Term of Contract (Years): 3/3
Avg. # Of Employees: NA
Passive Ownership: Discouraged
Encourage Conversions: No
Area Develop. Agreements: Yes/10
Sub-Franchising Contracts: Yes
Expand In Territory: Yes
Space Needs: NA SF; HB

SUPPORT & TRAINING:
Financial Assistance Provided: Yes(I)
Site Selection Assistance: NA
Lease Negotiation Assistance: No
Co-Operative Advertising: Yes
Franchisee Assoc./Member: No
Size Of Corporate Staff: 8
On-Going Support: A,b,c,D,G,H
Training: 1-2 Weeks Home Office, North Vancouver, BC.

SPECIFIC EXPANSION PLANS:
US: All United States
Canada: All Except AB
Overseas: No

<< >>

VALUE LINE MAINTENANCE SYSTEMS

P. O. Box 6450
Great Falls, MT 59406
Tel: (800) 824-4838 (406) 761-4471
Fax: (406) 761-4486
E-Mail: wmc@sofast.net
Web Site: www.worldfranchising.com/website.htm
Mr. Jerome McAllister, General Manager

VALUE LINE MAINTENANCE offers janitorial service to large retail outlets. VALUE LINE offers technical support, sales support and maintains a supply and machine facility to help franchisees stay up to date on product development and maintain their equipment.

BACKGROUND:
Established: 1959; 1st Franchised: 1982
Franchised Units: 22
Company-Owned Units: 3
Total Units: 25
Dist.: US-25; CAN-0; O'seas-0
North America: 5 States
Density: MT, CA, WY
Projected New Units (12 Months): 2

Qualifications: 3, 4, 2, 3, 4, 4
Registered: CA

FINANCIAL/TERMS:

Cash Investment: $25K
Total Investment: $50K
Minimum Net Worth: $50K
Fees: Franchise - $30K
Royalty - 10%; Ad. - 0%
Earnings Claims Statement: No
Term of Contract (Years): 10/10
Avg. # Of Employees: 2 FT
Passive Ownership: Discouraged
Encourage Conversions: NA
Area Develop. Agreements: No
Sub-Franchising Contracts: No
Expand In Territory: Yes
Space Needs: NR SF; NA

SUPPORT & TRAINING:

Financial Assistance Provided: Yes(D)
Site Selection Assistance: Yes
Lease Negotiation Assistance: NA
Co-Operative Advertising: NA
Franchisee Assoc./Member: Yes
Size Of Corporate Staff: 12
On-Going Support: A,B,C,D,E,F,I
Training: 1 Week Corporate; 2 Weeks On-Location.

SPECIFIC EXPANSION PLANS:

US: CA
Canada: No
Overseas: No

<< >>

VANGUARD CLEANING SYSTEMS

655 Mariners Island Blvd., # 303
San Mateo, CA 94404
Tel: (800) 564-6422 + 414 (650) 287-2414
Fax: (650) 591-1545
E-Mail: wgreene@vanguardcleaning.com
Web Site: www.vanguardcleaning.com
Mr. Will Greene, Business Development Director

VANGUARD CLEANING SYSTEMS has been successfully franchising in the commercial cleaning industry since 1984. VANGUARD is currently seeking unit and master franchisees in the United States. A VANGUARD Master has 2 key responsibilities: recruiting individual unit franchisees and securing commercial cleaning accounts for them.

BACKGROUND: IFA MEMBER

Established: 1984; 1st Franchised: 1984
Franchised Units: 497
Company-Owned Units: 3
Total Units: 500
Dist.: US-500; CAN-0; O'seas-0
North America: 8 States
Density: 300 in CA
Projected New Units (12 Months): 225
Qualifications: 3, 5, 1, 3, 4, 5
Registered: CA,FL,IL,IN,MD,MI,NY,RI,VA,WA,WI

FINANCIAL/TERMS:

Cash Investment: $50K(Master)
Total Investment: $100-220K (M)
Minimum Net Worth: $400K (Master)
Fees: Franchise - $75K (M) Min.
Royalty - 4% (Master); Ad. - NR
Earnings Claims Statement: No
Term of Contract (Years): 20/20
Avg. # Of Employees: 5 FT, 2 PT
Passive Ownership: Discouraged
Encourage Conversions: Yes
Area Develop. Agreements: No
Sub-Franchising Contracts: Yes
Expand In Territory: Yes
Space Needs: NA SF; NA

SUPPORT & TRAINING:

Financial Assistance Provided: Yes(D)
Site Selection Assistance: Yes
Lease Negotiation Assistance: NA
Co-Operative Advertising: NA
Franchisee Assoc./Member: No
Size Of Corporate Staff: 20
On-Going Support: A,b,C,D,G,I
Training: 2 Weeks+ in California, on-site after opening.

SPECIFIC EXPANSION PLANS:

US: All United States
Canada: All Canada
Overseas: All Countries

<< >>

WINDOW BRIGADE

WINDOW BRIGADE

4907 Hollenden Dr., # 208
Raleigh, NC 27616
Tel: (866) 587-6243 (919) 834-8215
Fax: (919) 834-7630
E-Mail: franchise@windowbrigade.com
Web Site: www.windowbrigade.com
Ms. LaVerne Artis, Vice President

It's time to clean up with WINDOW BRIGADE and create your own future in the residential and commercial cleaning industries, which are experiencing explosive growth. We are the "Full Service People," offering full-service residential and commercial window, blind, gutter and pressure wash Bulls-Eye Cleaning Systems. We provide our owner-operators with training, consultation, operational support and access to the latest advances in technology.

BACKGROUND:

Established: 2000; 1st Franchised: 2003
Franchised Units: 3
Company-Owned Units: 1
Total Units: 4
Dist.: US-4; CAN-0; O'seas-0
North America: 2 States
Density: 3 in NC, 1 in SC
Projected New Units (12 Months): 25
Qualifications: 5, 3, 1, 3, 4, 5
Registered: FL,MI,OR

FINANCIAL/TERMS:

Cash Investment: $19-25K
Total Investment: $12-56K
Minimum Net Worth: Varies
Fees: Franchise - $6K
Royalty - 5-7%; Ad. - 0-2%
Earnings Claims Statement: No
Term of Contract (Years): 5/5
Avg. # Of Employees: 2 FT, 6 PT
Passive Ownership: Discouraged
Encourage Conversions: Yes
Area Develop. Agreements: No
Sub-Franchising Contracts: No
Expand In Territory: Yes
Space Needs: 1,000+ SF; FS, SF, HB

SUPPORT & TRAINING:

Financial Assistance Provided: Yes(D)
Site Selection Assistance: Yes
Lease Negotiation Assistance: No
Co-Operative Advertising: No
Franchisee Assoc./Member: No
Size Of Corporate Staff: 2
On-Going Support: A,B,C,D,e,F,H,I
Training: 7 Days Headquarters in Raleigh, NC.

SPECIFIC EXPANSION PLANS:

US: All United States
Canada: All Canada
Overseas: All Countries

<< >>

WINDOW GANG

405 Arendall St.
Morehead City, NC 28557
Tel: (877) WIN-GANG (252) 726-1463
Fax: (252) 726-2837
E-Mail: tim@windowgang.com
Web Site: www.windowgang.com
Mr. Tim McCullen, President

Residential/commercial window, gutter, pressure and blind cleaning company. Large, extensive markets.

BACKGROUND:
Established: 1986; 1st Franchised: 1996
Franchised Units: 151
Company-Owned Units: 0
Total Units: 151
Dist.: US-151; CAN-0; O'seas-0
North America: 10 States
Density: 46 in NC, 24 in SC, 23 in VA
Projected New Units (12 Months): NR
Qualifications: , , , , ,
Registered: NR

FINANCIAL/TERMS:
Cash Investment: $25-50K
Total Investment: $25-50K
Minimum Net Worth: $50K
Fees: Franchise - $25K+
Royalty - 6%; Ad. - 0%
Earnings Claims Statement: No
Term of Contract (Years): 10/10
Avg. # Of Employees: 5 FT, 5 PT
Passive Ownership: Discouraged
Encourage Conversions: NR
Area Develop. Agreements: No
Sub-Franchising Contracts: No
Expand In Territory: Yes
Space Needs: 1,000 SF; FS, HB

SUPPORT & TRAINING:
Financial Assistance Provided: NR
Site Selection Assistance: Yes
Lease Negotiation Assistance: Yes
Co-Operative Advertising: No
Franchisee Assoc./Member: No
Size Of Corporate Staff: 3
On-Going Support: B,C,D,E,G,h
Training: 5-10 Days Beaufort, NC.

SPECIFIC EXPANSION PLANS:
US: All United States
Canada: NR
Overseas: NR

<< >>

WINDOW GENIE

350 Gest St.
Cincinnati, OH 45203
Tel: (800) 700-0022 (513) 412-7762
Fax: (513) 412-7760
E-Mail: rik@windowgenie.com
Web Site: www.windowgenie.com
Mr. Richard (Rik) Nonelle, President

Residential window cleaning, window tint and pressure washing business.

BACKGROUND: IFA MEMBER
Established: 1994; 1st Franchised: 1998
Franchised Units: 39
Company-Owned Units: 0
Total Units: 39
Dist.: US-39; CAN-0; O'seas-0
North America: 12 States
Density: 6 in OH, 4 in CO, 3 in KY
Projected New Units (12 Months): 19
Qualifications: 4, 4, 1, 3, 3, 5
Registered:
CA,FL,IL,IN,MD,MI,NY,VA,WA

FINANCIAL/TERMS:
Cash Investment: $40-50K
Total Investment: $40-50K
Minimum Net Worth: Varies
Fees: Franchise - $19.5K
Royalty - 6%; Ad. - 1%
Earnings Claims Statement: No
Term of Contract (Years): 10/5
Avg. # Of Employees: 2 FT, 2 PT
Passive Ownership: Discouraged
Encourage Conversions: Yes
Area Develop. Agreements: No
Sub-Franchising Contracts: No
Expand In Territory: Yes
Space Needs: NA SF; NA

SUPPORT & TRAINING:
Financial Assistance Provided: No
Site Selection Assistance: NA
Lease Negotiation Assistance: NA
Co-Operative Advertising: NA
Franchisee Assoc./Member: No
Size Of Corporate Staff: 3
On-Going Support: B,C,D,E,F,G,H,I
Training: 5 Days Corporate, Cincinnati, OH; 5 Days On-Site.

SPECIFIC EXPANSION PLANS:
US: All United States
Canada: No
Overseas: No

<< >>

Medical/Optical/Dental Products & Services

Chapter 26

Medical/Optical/Dental Products & Services Industry Profile

Total # Franchisors in Industry Group	17
Total # Franchised Units in Industry Group	1,551
Total # Company-Owned Units in Industry Group	300
Total # Operating Units in Industry Group	1,851
Average # Franchised Units/Franchisor	91.2
Average # Company-Owned Units/Franchisor	17.6
Average # Total Units/Franchisor	108.9
Ratio of Total # Franchised Units/Total # Company-Owned Units	5.2:1
Industry Survey Participants	6
Representing % of Industry	35.3%
Average Franchise Fee*:	$30.3K
Average Total Investment*:	$167.8K
Average On-Going Royalty Fee*:	5.4%

*If a range was provided, the mid-point of the range was used. See detailed profiles for actual ranges.

Five Largest Participants in Survey

Company	# Franchised Units	# Co-Owned Units	# Total Units	Franchise Fee	On-Going Royalty	Total Investment
1. Miracle-Ear	930	185	1,115	$28-60K	$46.50/Unit	$100-200K
2. Option Care	147	31	178	$15-35K	Varies	NR
3. Henry Ford OptimEyes	15	22	37	$10K	8%	$150-250K
4. Hemorrhoid Clinic, The	32	1	33	$25K	6%	$140-225K
5. Women's Health Boutique	13	0	13	$20K	4-7%	$215.3-247.4K

All of the data provided are proprietary and should not be quoted without acknowledging *Bond's Franchise Guide.*

HEMORRHOID CLINIC, THE

P. O. Box 12488
Oakland, CA 94604
Tel: (510) 839-5471
Fax: (510) 839-2104
E-Mail: rob@worldfranchising.com
Web Site: www.nohemies.com
Mr. Robert A. Antonius, President

Highly efficient and automated out-patient clinics for hemorrhoid and related rectal procedures. Proprietary laser techniques developed by Dr. Anning insure painless, 20-minute procedure and minimal recuperative discomfort. Lucrative business that takes advantage of the fact that 1 in 8 adults requires rectal surgery. 12 week training at headquarters clinic. All procedures on video. Excellent opportunity to work with the best!

BACKGROUND:
Established: 1987; 1st Franchised: 1988
Franchised Units: 32
Company-Owned Units: 1
Total Units: 33
Dist.: US-27; CAN-3; O'seas-3
North America: 10 States, 2 Provinces
Density: 5 in OH, 2 in KY, 2 in MS
Projected New Units (12 Months): 2
Qualifications: , , , , ,
Registered: NR

FINANCIAL/TERMS:
Cash Investment: $80-125K
Total Investment: $140-225K
Minimum Net Worth: NR
Fees: Franchise - $25K
Royalty - 6%; Ad. - 1%
Earnings Claims Statement: Yes
Term of Contract (Years): 10/10
Avg. # Of Employees: 3 FT, 4 PT
Passive Ownership: Not Allowed
Encourage Conversions: Yes
Area Develop. Agreements: Yes/10
Sub-Franchising Contracts: Yes
Expand In Territory: Yes
Space Needs: 1,500-2,000 SF; FS, SF

SUPPORT & TRAINING:
Financial Assistance Provided: Yes(I)
Site Selection Assistance: Yes
Lease Negotiation Assistance: Yes
Co-Operative Advertising: Yes
Franchisee Assoc./Member: NR
Size Of Corporate Staff: 12
On-Going Support: C,D,E,G,H,I
Training: 12 Weeks Anning Clinic; 3 Weeks On-Site; On-Going Video Training Procedures.

SPECIFIC EXPANSION PLANS:
US: All United States
Canada: ON Only
Overseas: No

<< >>

HENRY FORD OPTIMEYES

655 W. 13 Mile Rd.
Madison Heights, MI 48071
Tel: (248) 588-9300
Fax: (248) 588-3355
E-Mail: fmarberry@optimeyes.com
Web Site: www.optimeyes.com
Ms. Frances Marberry, Director of Franchising

Sale of primary vision care services and products to correct and improve vision. Three user vision correction centers for refractive surgery, sale of eye glasses and contact lenses.

BACKGROUND:
Established: 1980; 1st Franchised: 1981
Franchised Units: 15
Company-Owned Units: 22
Total Units: 37
Dist.: US-37; CAN-0; O'seas-0
North America: 1 State
Density: NR
Projected New Units (12 Months): 5
Qualifications: 5, 3, 5, 5, 5, 5
Registered: MI

FINANCIAL/TERMS:
Cash Investment: $100K
Total Investment: $150-250K
Minimum Net Worth: $200K
Fees: Franchise - $10K
Royalty - 8%; Ad. - 5%
Earnings Claims Statement: Yes
Term of Contract (Years): 10/5
Avg. # Of Employees: 5 FT, 2 PT
Passive Ownership: Not Allowed
Encourage Conversions: Yes
Area Develop. Agreements: Yes/10
Sub-Franchising Contracts: Yes
Expand In Territory: Yes
Space Needs: 2,000 SF; FS, SD, SC, RM

SUPPORT & TRAINING:
Financial Assistance Provided: Yes(I)
Site Selection Assistance: Yes
Lease Negotiation Assistance: Yes
Co-Operative Advertising: Yes
Franchisee Assoc./Member: Yes
Size Of Corporate Staff: 25
On-Going Support: A,B,C,D,E,G,H,I
Training: 2 Weeks Roseville, MI; On-Going Field Training.

SPECIFIC EXPANSION PLANS:
US: Michigan Only
Canada: No
Overseas: No

<< >>

MIRACLE-EAR

5000 Cheshire Ln. N.
Plymouth, MN 55446
Tel: (800) 234-7714 + 4048 (763) 268-4048
Fax: (763) 268-4254
E-Mail: cjohnson@miracle-ear.com
Web Site: www.miracle-ear.com
Mr. Cecil Johnson, Franchise Director

Manufacturer and world's largest retailer of hearing systems, with 1,287 offices nationally. MIRACLE-EAR also has master franchisors in 20 foreign countries.

BACKGROUND: IFA MEMBER
Established: 1948; 1st Franchised: 1983
Franchised Units: 930
Company-Owned Units: 185
Total Units: 1,115
Dist.: US-1,267; CAN-0; O'seas-20
North America: 50 States
Density: 96 in CA, 39 in TX, 74 in FL
Projected New Units (12 Months): 125
Qualifications: 4, 4, 2, 3, 4, 4
Registered: All States

FINANCIAL/TERMS:
Cash Investment: $50-150K
Total Investment: $100-200K
Minimum Net Worth: $100K
Fees: Franchise - $28-60K
Royalty - $46.50/Unit;Ad. - $26/Inquiry
Earnings Claims Statement: No
Term of Contract (Years): 5/5
Avg. # Of Employees: 2 FT, 1 PT
Passive Ownership: Not Allowed
Encourage Conversions: NA
Area Develop. Agreements: Yes/1-1.5
Sub-Franchising Contracts: No
Expand In Territory: Yes
Space Needs: 750 SF; FS, SF, SC, RM

SUPPORT & TRAINING:
Financial Assistance Provided: NA
Site Selection Assistance: NA
Lease Negotiation Assistance: No
Co-Operative Advertising: Yes
Franchisee Assoc./Member: No
Size Of Corporate Staff: 3
On-Going Support: A,C,D,E,G,h,I
Training: 2 Weeks Corporate Headquarters; 10 Weeks On-Site.

SPECIFIC EXPANSION PLANS:
US: West, Midwest
Canada: No
Overseas: All Countries

<< >>

OPTION CARE

485 Half Day Road, # 300
Buffalo Grove, IL 60089
Tel: (800) 879-6137 (847) 615-1690
Fax: (847) 615-0326
E-Mail: tmartin@optioncare.net
Web Site: www.optioncare.net
Mr. Tom Martin, Division VP Franchise Ops.

We offer franchises for the establishment of outpatient health care businesses which operate under the service mark of OPTION CARE. Our franchises specialize in what is sometimes referred to as home infusion therapy, but the services encompass many aspects of health care in home and other outpatient settings.

BACKGROUND:

Established: 1979; 1st Franchised: 1984
Franchised Units: 147
Company-Owned Units: 31
Total Units: 178
Dist.: US-178; CAN-0; O'seas-0
North America: 37 States
Density: 16 in CA, 13 in FL, 13 in OH
Projected New Units (12 Months): 10
Qualifications: 3, 5, 5, 4, 2, 3
Registered:CA,HI,IL,IN,MD,MI,MN,NY,ND,RI,SD,VA,WA,WI

FINANCIAL/TERMS:

Cash Investment: $243.7-541.8K
Total Investment: NR
Minimum Net Worth: NR
Fees: Franchise - $15-35K
Royalty - Varies; Ad. - 1.5%
Earnings Claims Statement: No
Term of Contract (Years): 20/10
Avg. # Of Employees: NR
Passive Ownership: Allowed
Encourage Conversions: Yes
Area Develop. Agreements: No
Sub-Franchising Contracts: No
Expand In Territory: Yes
Space Needs: 1,500 SF; FS, SF, SC

SUPPORT & TRAINING:

Financial Assistance Provided: No
Site Selection Assistance: No
Lease Negotiation Assistance: No
Co-Operative Advertising: No
Franchisee Assoc./Member: No
Size Of Corporate Staff: 64
On-Going Support: B,G,H,I
Training: 4 Days Clinical Operations Chicago, IL; 4 Days Sales/Business Development Chicago, IL.

SPECIFIC EXPANSION PLANS:

US: All United States
Canada: No
Overseas: No

<< >>

WOMEN'S HEALTH BOUTIQUE

12715 Telge Rd.
Cypress, TX 77429-2289
Tel: (888) 280-2053 (281) 256-4100
Fax: (281) 256-4178
E-Mail: w-h-bsales@w-h-b.com
Web Site: www.w-h-b.com
Mr. Donald Averitt, VP Franchise Sales

WOMEN'S HEALTH BOUTIQUE provides products and services for women with special needs. A caring and compassionate staff creates a comfortable environment for individuals buying maternity and post-mastectomy products and personal care items, including compression therapy, turbans and wigs.

BACKGROUND: IFA MEMBER

Established: 1988; 1st Franchised: 1993
Franchised Units: 13
Company-Owned Units: 0
Total Units: 13
Dist.: US-13; CAN-0; O'seas-0
North America: 6 States
Density: 4 in TX, 2 in MI, 2 in CA
Projected New Units (12 Months): NR
Qualifications: 4, 4, 3, 2, 5, 5
Registered: All Except HI,ND,SD

FINANCIAL/TERMS:

Cash Investment: $35K
Total Investment: $215.3-247.4K
Minimum Net Worth: $200K
Fees: Franchise - $20K
Royalty - 4-7%; Ad. - 0%
Earnings Claims Statement: No
Term of Contract (Years): 15
Avg. # Of Employees: 2 FT
Passive Ownership: Not Allowed
Encourage Conversions: NA
Area Develop. Agreements: No
Sub-Franchising Contracts: No
Expand In Territory: Yes
Space Needs: 1,500 SF; SC, Medical Center

SUPPORT & TRAINING:

Financial Assistance Provided: Yes(I)
Site Selection Assistance: Yes
Lease Negotiation Assistance: Yes
Co-Operative Advertising: No
Franchisee Assoc./Member: Yes/Yes
Size Of Corporate Staff: NR
On-Going Support: C,D,E,G,H,I
Training: 3 Weeks Headquarters.

SPECIFIC EXPANSION PLANS:

US: All United States
Canada: No
Overseas: No

<< >>

Packaging & Mailing

Chapter 27

Packaging & Mailing Industry Profile

Total # Franchisors in Industry Group	21
Total # Franchised Units in Industry Group	10,043
Total # Company-Owned Units in Industry Group	29
Total # Operating Units in Industry Group	10,072
Average # Franchised Units/Franchisor	478.2
Average # Company-Owned Units/Franchisor	1.4
Average # Total Units/Franchisor	479.6
Ratio of Total # Franchised Units/Total # Company-Owned Units	346.3:1
Industry Survey Participants	13
Representing % of Industry	61.9%
Average Franchise Fee*:	$28.2K
Average Total Investment*:	$135.4K
Average On-Going Royalty Fee*:	5.5%

*If a range was provided, the mid-point of the range was used. See detailed profiles for actual ranges.

Five Largest Participants in Survey

Company	# Franchised Units	# Co-Owned Units	# Total Units	Franchise Fee	On-Going Royalty	Total Investment
1. UPS Store, The	5,290	0	5,290	$29.9K	5%	$143-247K
2. PostNet Postal & Business Centers	900	1	901	$29.9	4%	$160-180K
3. Packaging and Shipping Specialists	703	1	704	$28.9K	0%	$91-138K
4. Pak Mail	400	1	401	$28K	5% Sliding	$70-115K
5. Unishippers	308	0	308	$10-50K	16.5%	$40-100K

All of the data provided are proprietary and should not be quoted without acknowledging *Bond's Franchise Guide.*

AIM MAIL CENTERS

15550-D Rockfield Blvd.
Irvine, CA 92618
Tel: (800) 669-4246 (949) 837-4151
Fax: (949) 837-4537
E-Mail: franchiseinfo@aimmailcenters.com
Web Site: www.aimmailcenters.com
Mr. David Wiener, Franchise Development Manager

AIM MAIL CENTERS has developed a unique and attractive franchise opportunity designed for motivated professionals. AIM MAIL CENTERS are complete business service centers, offering a wide array of products and services to small businesses and the general consumer, including shipping with UPS, FedEx and USPS. We provide packaging, stamps, faxing, mailbox rentals, photocopies, office supplies and much more. Our advanced systems, training and field support make AIM the right choice for entrepreneurs.

BACKGROUND: IFA MEMBER
Established: 1985; 1st Franchised: 1989
Franchised Units: 110
Company-Owned Units: 0
Total Units: 110
Dist.: US-110; CAN-0; O'seas-0
North America: 22 States
Density: NR
Projected New Units (12 Months): 40
Qualifications: 5, 1, 1, 3, 5, 5
Registered: CA,FL,IL,IN,OR,VA,WI,WA

FINANCIAL/TERMS:
Cash Investment: $40K
Total Investment: $125-175K
Minimum Net Worth: $200K
Fees: Franchise - $26.9K
Royalty - 5%; Ad. - 2%
Earnings Claims Statement: No
Term of Contract (Years): 15/5
Avg. # Of Employees: 1 FT, 2 PT
Passive Ownership: Discouraged
Encourage Conversions: Yes
Area Develop. Agreements: No
Sub-Franchising Contracts: No
Expand In Territory: Yes
Space Needs: 800-1,200 SF; SC

SUPPORT & TRAINING:
Financial Assistance Provided: Yes(I)
Site Selection Assistance: Yes
Lease Negotiation Assistance: Yes
Co-Operative Advertising: Yes
Franchisee Assoc./Member: Yes/Yes
Size Of Corporate Staff: 14
On-Going Support: C,DE,F,G,H,I
Training: 2 Weeks Corporate Headquarters; 3 Days Store.

SPECIFIC EXPANSION PLANS:
US: All United States
Canada: No
Overseas: No

<< >>

CRATERS & FREIGHTERS

7000 E. 47th Ave. Dr., # 100
Denver, CO 80216-3464
Tel: (800) 949-9931 (303) 399-8190
Fax: (303) 399-9964
E-Mail: bob@cratersandfreighters.com
Web Site: www.cratersandfreighters.com
Mr. Bob Molnar, Vice President Operations

As specialty freight handlers, CRATERS & FREIGHTERS is the best-niched concept in the industry. We're the exclusive source for reliable, affordable specialty shipping services for pieces that are too big for UPS and too small for movers. We provide high-demand packing, crating and shipping with iron-clad insurance to an up-scale clientele. Serve your large territory from low overhead warehouse space.

BACKGROUND: IFA MEMBER
Established: 1990; 1st Franchised: 1991
Franchised Units: 65
Company-Owned Units: 0
Total Units: 65
Dist.: US-60; CAN-0; O'seas-0
North America: 30 States
Density: 6 in CA, 6 in FL, 5 in TX
Projected New Units (12 Months): 14
Qualifications: 5, 4, 2, 1, 3, 5
Registered: CA,FL,MD,MI

FINANCIAL/TERMS:
Cash Investment: NR
Total Investment: $88-127K
Minimum Net Worth: $150K
Fees: Franchise - $27K
Royalty - 5%; Ad. - 1%
Earnings Claims Statement: No
Term of Contract (Years): 15/15
Avg. # Of Employees: 3 FT
Passive Ownership: Discouraged
Encourage Conversions: NA
Area Develop. Agreements: No
Sub-Franchising Contracts: No
Expand In Territory: Yes
Space Needs: 2,000-2,500 SF; Warehouse

SUPPORT & TRAINING:
Financial Assistance Provided: Yes(I)
Site Selection Assistance: Yes
Lease Negotiation Assistance: Yes
Co-Operative Advertising: Yes
Franchisee Assoc./Member: Yes
Size Of Corporate Staff: 12
On-Going Support: A,B,C,D,E,G,h,I
Training: 7 Days Home Office in Denver, CO.

SPECIFIC EXPANSION PLANS:
US: All United States
Canada: All Canada
Overseas: All Countries

<< >>

MAIL BOXES ETC. (CANADA)

505 Iroquois Shore Rd., # 4
Oakville, ON L6H 2R3 CANADA
Tel: (800) 661-MBEC (905) 338-9754
Fax: (905) 338-7491
E-Mail: development@mbe.ca
Web Site: www.mbe.ca
Ms. Brenda Perpeck, Franchise Development

Business and communication services.

BACKGROUND:
Established: 1990; 1st Franchised: 1990
Franchised Units: 255
Company-Owned Units: 2
Total Units: 257
Dist.: US-0; CAN-216; O'seas-0
North America: 9 Provinces
Density: NR
Projected New Units (12 Months): 50
Qualifications: 5, 4, 3, 3, 3, 4
Registered: NR

FINANCIAL/TERMS:
Cash Investment: $60K
Total Investment: $110-135K
Minimum Net Worth: $125K
Fees: Franchise - $29.9K
Royalty - 6%; Ad. - 2%
Earnings Claims Statement: No
Term of Contract (Years): 10/10
Avg. # Of Employees: 2 FT, 1 PT
Passive Ownership: Discouraged
Encourage Conversions: Yes
Area Develop. Agreements: Yes/10
Sub-Franchising Contracts: No
Expand In Territory: Yes
Space Needs: 1,200 SF; FS, SF, SC

SUPPORT & TRAINING:

Financial Assistance Provided:	Yes
Site Selection Assistance:	Yes
Lease Negotiation Assistance:	Yes
Co-Operative Advertising:	Yes
Franchisee Assoc./Member:	Yes/No
Size Of Corporate Staff:	20
On-Going Support:	a,B,C,D,e,G,h

Training: 2 Weeks at Corporate Office; 1.5 Weeks in Center.

SPECIFIC EXPANSION PLANS:

US:	All United States
Canada:	All Canada
Overseas:	U.K. and Ireland

NAVIS PACK & SHIP CENTER

5675 DTC Blvd., # 280
Greenwood Village, CO 80111
Tel: (866) 738-6820 (303) 741-6626
Fax: (303) 741-6653
E-Mail: info@gonavis.com
Web Site: www.gonavis.com
Mr. Roy D. Billesbach, Director of Franchise Develop.

NAVIS PACK & SHIP CENTERS, established in 2001, specialize in packaging and shipping items that are fragile, large, awkward and valuable. NAVIS PACK & SHIP CENTERS is a B2B marketing-oriented concept that primarily services commercial clients with business equipment, computers, office furniture, art, and antique items. Locations are in light industrial or warehouse areas. Navis has been franchising since 1984 with Handle With Care Packaging Store, a retail entity.

BACKGROUND: IFA MEMBER

Established: 1980;	1st Franchised: 1984
Franchised Units:	66
Company-Owned Units:	0
Total Units:	66
Dist.:	US-65; CAN-1; O'seas-0
North America:	21 States, 1 Province
Density:	4 in CO, 4 in TX, 3 in IL
Projected New Units (12 Months):	24
Qualifications:	5, 5, 2, 4, 5, 5

Registered:CA,FL,IL,IN,MD,MI,MN,NY, OR,RI,SD,VA,WA,WI,DC

FINANCIAL/TERMS:

Cash Investment:	$75-95K
Total Investment:	$100-175K
Minimum Net Worth:	$75-100K
Fees: Franchise -	$32.5K
Royalty - 5%;	Ad. - 3%
Earnings Claims Statement:	Yes
Term of Contract (Years):	10/5/5
Avg. # Of Employees:	3-5 FT
Passive Ownership:	Not Allowed
Encourage Conversions:	No
Area Develop. Agreements:	No
Sub-Franchising Contracts:	No
Expand In Territory:	Yes
Space Needs:	2,000 SF; Light Industrial

SUPPORT & TRAINING:

Financial Assistance Provided:	Yes(I)
Site Selection Assistance:	Yes
Lease Negotiation Assistance:	Yes
Co-Operative Advertising:	Yes
Franchisee Assoc./Member:	Yes/Yes
Size Of Corporate Staff:	34
On-Going Support:	A,B,C,D,E,F,G,h,I

Training: 3 Wks online Pre-Training; 2 Wks Denver,CO; 1 Wk Certified Training Facility; 2-3 day Certif. visit by support staff.

SPECIFIC EXPANSION PLANS:

US:	All United States
Canada:	All Canada
Overseas:	All Countries

<< >>

PACKAGING AND SHIPPING SPECIALISTS

5211 85th St., # 104
Lubbock, TX 79424
Tel: (800) 877-8884 (806) 794-9996
Fax: (806) 794-9997
E-Mail: mike@packship.com
Web Site: www.packship.com
Mr. Mike Gallagher, President

No Royalties! We are a complete copy shop with all shipping companies - UPS, FedEx and more. We are a combination of several businesses under one roof. Copying, mailing, sign service, invitations and announcements, mail box rentals and much more. All with no royalties.

BACKGROUND:

Established: 1981;	1st Franchised: 1988
Franchised Units:	703
Company-Owned Units:	1
Total Units:	704
Dist.:	US-702; CAN-2; O'seas-0
North America:	37 States, 2 Provinces
Density:	90 in TX, 10 in NM, 9 in LA
Projected New Units (12 Months):	40
Qualifications:	3, 2, 1, 2, 2, 2
Registered:	All States

FINANCIAL/TERMS:

Cash Investment:	$20-40K
Total Investment:	$91-138K
Minimum Net Worth:	$150K
Fees: Franchise -	$28.9K
Royalty - 0%;	Ad. - 0%
Earnings Claims Statement:	Yes
Term of Contract (Years):	10/10
Avg. # Of Employees:	2 FT, 2 PT
Passive Ownership:	Allowed
Encourage Conversions:	Yes
Area Develop. Agreements:	Yes/10
Sub-Franchising Contracts:	Yes
Expand In Territory:	Yes
Space Needs:	1,600 SF; SF, SC

SUPPORT & TRAINING:

Financial Assistance Provided:	Yes(I)
Site Selection Assistance:	Yes
Lease Negotiation Assistance:	Yes
Co-Operative Advertising:	Yes
Franchisee Assoc./Member:	Yes/Yes
Size Of Corporate Staff:	18
On-Going Support:	A,b,C,D,E,F,G,h,I

Training: 14 Days in Ann Arbor, MI; 14 Days in Dallas, TX.

SPECIFIC EXPANSION PLANS:

US:	All United States
Canada:	All Canada
Overseas:	All Countries

<< >>

PAK MAIL

7173 S. Havana St., # 600
Centennial, CO 80112-3891
Tel: (800) 833-2821 (303) 957-1000
Fax: (303) 957-1015
E-Mail: cprentner@pakmail.org
Web Site: www.pakmail.com
Mr. Chuck L. Prentner, VP Franchise Development

PAK MAIL is a convenient center for packaging, shipping and business support services, offering both residential and commercial customers air, ground, and ocean carriers, custom packaging and crating, private mailbox rental, mail services, packaging and moving supplies, copy and fax service and internet access and related services. We ship anything, anywhere.

BACKGROUND: IFA MEMBER
Established: 1983; 1st Franchised: 1984
Franchised Units: 400
Company-Owned Units: 1
Total Units: 401
Dist.: US-370; CAN-8; O'seas-22
North America: 42 States
Density: 91 in FL, 41 in GA, 22 in CA
Projected New Units (12 Months): 50
Qualifications: 3, 2, 2, 2, 2, 5
Registered: All States and AB

FINANCIAL/TERMS:
Cash Investment: $30-108K
Total Investment: $70-115K
Minimum Net Worth: $100K
Fees: Franchise - $28K
Royalty - 5% Sliding; Ad. - 2%
Earnings Claims Statement: Yes
Term of Contract (Years): 10/10
Avg. # Of Employees: 1 FT, 1 PT
Passive Ownership: Discouraged
Encourage Conversions: Yes
Area Develop. Agreements: Yes/5
Sub-Franchising Contracts: No
Expand In Territory: Yes
Space Needs: 1,200 SF; SC

SUPPORT & TRAINING:
Financial Assistance Provided: Yes(I)
Site Selection Assistance: Yes
Lease Negotiation Assistance: Yes
Co-Operative Advertising: Yes
Franchisee Assoc./Member: Yes/Yes
Size Of Corporate Staff: 22
On-Going Support: B,C,D,E,F,G,H,I
Training: 10 Days in Englewood, CO; 3 Days in Existing Center; 3 Days In New Center at Opening.

SPECIFIC EXPANSION PLANS:
US: All United States
Canada: All Canada
Overseas: All Countries

<< >>

PARCEL PLUS

12715 Telge Rd.
Cypress, TX 77429-2289
Tel: (888) 280-2053 (281) 256-4100
Fax: (281) 256-4178
E-Mail: ppsales@iced.net
Web Site: www.parcelplus.com
Mr. Donald Averitt, VP Franchise Sales

PARCEL PLUS centers offer packaging, freight, cargo, crating and international shipping in a retail setting. We provide a professional way to pack-and-ship everything from fragile antiques to large cargo items. An outside sales associate and/or the center owner utilize a consultative selling program to grow the freight and cargo segments.

BACKGROUND: IFA MEMBER
Established: 1986; 1st Franchised: 1988
Franchised Units: 100
Company-Owned Units: 0
Total Units: 100
Dist.: US-100; CAN-0; O'seas-0
North America: 20 States
Density: 30 in VA, 29 in TX, 18 in MD
Projected New Units (12 Months): NR
Qualifications: , , , , ,
Registered: FL,IL,IN,MD,MI,MN,VA,DC

FINANCIAL/TERMS:
Cash Investment: $45.5K
Total Investment: $150.4-209.6K
Minimum Net Worth: NR
Fees: Franchise - $30K
Royalty - 6%; Ad. - 1%
Earnings Claims Statement: No
Term of Contract (Years): 15
Avg. # Of Employees: 2 FT, 2 PT
Passive Ownership: Discouraged
Encourage Conversions: Yes
Area Develop. Agreements: No
Sub-Franchising Contracts: No
Expand In Territory: Yes
Space Needs: 1,200 SF; SC

SUPPORT & TRAINING:
Financial Assistance Provided: Yes(I)
Site Selection Assistance: Yes
Lease Negotiation Assistance: Yes
Co-Operative Advertising: No
Franchisee Assoc./Member: Yes/Yes
Size Of Corporate Staff: NR
On-Going Support: A,B,C,D,E,F,G,H,I
Training: 2 Weeks Headquarters; 1 Week On-Site.

SPECIFIC EXPANSION PLANS:
US: All United States
Canada: No
Overseas: No

<< >>

POSTAL ANNEX+

7580 Metropolitan Dr., # 200
San Diego, CA 92108-4417
Tel: (800) 456-1525 (619) 563-4800
Fax: (619) 563-9850
E-Mail: mike@postalannex.com
Web Site: www.postalannex.com
Mr. Mike J. Watorski, VP Franchise Development

Retail business service center, providing: packaging, shipping, copying, postal, mail box rental, printing fax, notary, office supplies and more.

BACKGROUND: IFA MEMBER
Established: 1985; 1st Franchised: 1986
Franchised Units: 298
Company-Owned Units: 0
Total Units: 298
Dist.: US-229; CAN-0; O'seas-1
North America: 27 States
Density: 130 in CA, 20 in OR, 17 MI
Projected New Units (12 Months): 36
Qualifications: 5, 3, 1, 1, 3, 3
Registered:CA,FL,IL,MD,MI,NY,OR,WA,WI,DC

FINANCIAL/TERMS:
Cash Investment: $35K
Total Investment: $111.9-169.7K
Minimum Net Worth: $200K
Fees: Franchise - $29.95K
Royalty - 5%; Ad. - 2%
Earnings Claims Statement: Yes
Term of Contract (Years): 15/15
Avg. # Of Employees: 1 FT, 2 PT
Passive Ownership: Allowed
Encourage Conversions: Yes
Area Develop. Agreements: Yes/10
Sub-Franchising Contracts: No
Expand In Territory: Yes
Space Needs: 1,200 SF; Supermarket Anchored

SUPPORT & TRAINING:
Financial Assistance Provided: Yes(I)
Site Selection Assistance: Yes
Lease Negotiation Assistance: Yes
Co-Operative Advertising: Yes
Franchisee Assoc./Member: Yes/Yes
Size Of Corporate Staff: 21
On-Going Support: c,d,E,G,H,I
Training: 2 Weeks San Diego, CA; 1 Week On-Site.

SPECIFIC EXPANSION PLANS:
US: All United States
Canada: All Canada
Overseas: All Countries

<< >>

POSTAL CONNECTIONS OF AMERICA

1081 Camino del Rio S., # 109
San Diego, CA 92108
Tel: (800) 767-8257 (619) 294-7550
Fax: (619) 294-4550
E-Mail: dhurley@postalconnections.com

Web Site: www.postalconnections.com
Mr. David W. Hurley, VP Franchise Development

POSTAL CONNECTIONS OF AMERICA franchises are specialty postal and copy service centers offering a variety of services, including packing, shipping, mailbox rentals, fax, moneygrams and notary services. Our newer outlets also include state-of-the-art technology features, such as computer work stations with high speed Internet access, e-mail address, video conferencing and meeting rooms, truly making our locations "virtual offices."

BACKGROUND: IFA MEMBER
Established: 1985; 1st Franchised: 1995
Franchised Units: 70
Company-Owned Units: 4
Total Units: 74
Dist.: US-42; CAN-0; O'seas-0
North America: 13 States
Density: 13 in CA, 7 in AZ, 4 in OR
Projected New Units (12 Months): 36
Qualifications: 4, 1, 1, 3, 1, 4
Registered: All States

FINANCIAL/TERMS:
Cash Investment: $25-35K
Total Investment: $80-120K
Minimum Net Worth: $100K
Fees: Franchise - $18.9K
Royalty - 4%; Ad. - 2%
Earnings Claims Statement: No
Term of Contract (Years): 10/10
Avg. # Of Employees: 1 FT, 2 PT
Passive Ownership: Discouraged
Encourage Conversions: Yes
Area Develop. Agreements: Yes/10
Sub-Franchising Contracts: No
Expand In Territory: Yes
Space Needs: 1,200 SF; SF, SC

SUPPORT & TRAINING:
Financial Assistance Provided: Yes(I)
Site Selection Assistance: Yes
Lease Negotiation Assistance: Yes
Co-Operative Advertising: No
Franchisee Assoc./Member: No
Size Of Corporate Staff: 8
On-Going Support: B,C,d,e,h,I
Training: 7 Days Home Office, Beverly Hills, CA; 3 Days, New Location.

SPECIFIC EXPANSION PLANS:
US: All United States
Canada: All Canada
Overseas: Asia, Europe, South America

<< >>

POSTNET
CREATE • DUPLICATE • DELIVER

Top 100

POSTNET POSTAL & BUSINESS SERVICES
181 N. Arroyo Grande Blvd., # 100 A
Henderson, NV 89014-1630
Tel: (800) 841-7171 (702) 792-7100
Fax: (702) 792-7115
E-Mail: info@postnet.com
Web Site: www.postnet.com
Mr. Brian Spindel, Executive Vice President

POSTNET's franchise opportunity offers a proven method of marketing products and services, which consumers need on a daily basis. The opportunity to get in on the ground floor of a rapidly expanding business is a rarity -- POSTNET's domestic and international franchisees have the opportunity to tap into the world market, offering personal and business services including UPS and FedEx Shipping, B/W and color copy services, private mail boxes, fax, printing and much more.

BACKGROUND: IFA MEMBER
Established: 1992; 1st Franchised: 1993
Franchised Units: 900
Company-Owned Units: 1
Total Units: 901
Dist.: US-601; CAN-0; O'seas-350
North America: 39 States, 2 Provinces
Density: 17 in CA, 14 in IL, 11 in FL
Projected New Units (12 Months): 100
Qualifications: 5, 3, 1, 3, 4, 5
Registered: All States

FINANCIAL/TERMS:
Cash Investment: $35-50K
Total Investment: $160-180K
Minimum Net Worth: $250K
Fees: Franchise - $29.9K
Royalty - 4%; Ad. - 2%
Earnings Claims Statement: No
Term of Contract (Years): 15/15
Avg. # Of Employees: 2 FT, 1 PT
Passive Ownership: Not Allowed
Encourage Conversions: Yes
Area Develop. Agreements: Yes/Varies
Sub-Franchising Contracts: No
Expand In Territory: Yes
Space Needs: 1,200 SF; SC

SUPPORT & TRAINING:
Financial Assistance Provided: Yes(I)
Site Selection Assistance: Yes
Lease Negotiation Assistance: Yes
Co-Operative Advertising: No
Franchisee Assoc./Member: No
Size Of Corporate Staff: 30
On-Going Support: C,D,E,F,G,H,I
Training: 1 Week Henderson, NV; 1 Week at Store Opening; 2-3 Days Follow-Up.

SPECIFIC EXPANSION PLANS:
US: All United States
Canada: All Canada
Overseas: All Countries Not Currently Represented

<< >>

Signal Graphics.

SIGNAL GRAPHICS BUSINESS CENTER
852 Broadway, # 300
Denver, CO 80203
Tel: (800) 852-6336 + 229 (303) 779-6789 + 229
Fax: (303) 779-8445
E-Mail: info@signalgraphics.com
Web Site: www.signalgraphics.com
Mr. Joe Collins, Dir. Franchise Development

Welcome to SIGNAL GRAPHICS! For over 20 years, SIGNAL GRAPHICS has been developing entrepreneurs. Our business centers enable owners to market printing, copying, desktop publishing, packaging and shipping. Your store will be a resource center for products such as business cards, stationery, envelopes, brochures, booklets, flyers and labels. We also package and ship all around the world. You will have the latest technology in computers and digital copiers. Join us in this exciting and gratifying business.

BACKGROUND: IFA MEMBER
Established: 1974; 1st Franchised: 1982
Franchised Units: 34
Company-Owned Units: 4
Total Units: 38
Dist.: US-36; CAN-0; O'seas-0
North America: 14 States
Density: 16 in CO
Projected New Units (12 Months): 10
Qualifications: , , , , ,
Registered: All States Except HI,ND, RI,SD

FINANCIAL/TERMS:
Cash Investment: $40-60K
Total Investment: $159-201K
Minimum Net Worth: NR
Fees: Franchise - $25K

Royalty - 5%; Ad. - $200/Mo.
Earnings Claims Statement: No
Term of Contract (Years): 20
Avg. # Of Employees: 1 FT, 1 PT
Passive Ownership: Discouraged
Encourage Conversions: Yes
Area Develop. Agreements: Yes
Sub-Franchising Contracts: No
Expand In Territory: Yes
Space Needs: 1,000-1,200 SF; SC

SUPPORT & TRAINING:
Financial Assistance Provided: Yes(I)
Site Selection Assistance: Yes
Lease Negotiation Assistance: Yes
Co-Operative Advertising: Yes
Franchisee Assoc./Member: Yes/Yes
Size Of Corporate Staff: NR
On-Going Support: B,C,D,E,G,H,I
Training: 2 Weeks Headquarters; 1 Week On-Site.

SPECIFIC EXPANSION PLANS:
US: All United States
Canada: No
Overseas: No

UNISHIPPERS

746 E. Winchester St., # 200
Salt Lake City, UT 84107-8512
Tel: (800) 999-8721 (801) 487-0600 + 151
Fax: (801) 487-0623
E-Mail: debbie.brown@unishippers.com
Web Site: www.unishippers.com
Ms. Debbie Brown, Communications Program Mgr.

UNISHIPPERS is an international shipping company that provides individual solutions and personalized customer service to our customers - all at discounted prices.

BACKGROUND: IFA MEMBER
Established: 1987; 1st Franchised: 1987
Franchised Units: 308
Company-Owned Units: 0
Total Units: 308
Dist.: US-296; CAN-0; O'seas-1
North America: 50 States
Density: 27 in CA, 20 in NY, 20 in TX
Projected New Units (12 Months): 4
Qualifications: 4, 5, 1, 1, 5, 5
Registered:CA,FL,HI,IN,MD,MI,MN,NY, ND,OR,RI,SD,VA,WA,WI,DC

FINANCIAL/TERMS:
Cash Investment: $40-100K
Total Investment: $40-100K
Minimum Net Worth: NA
Fees: Franchise - $10-50K
Royalty - 16.5%; Ad. - 1% Gross
Earnings Claims Statement: Yes
Term of Contract (Years): 5/5
Avg. # Of Employees: 1 FT
Passive Ownership: Not Allowed
Encourage Conversions: NA
Area Develop. Agreements: No
Sub-Franchising Contracts: Yes
Expand In Territory: No
Space Needs: NR SF; SF, hb

SUPPORT & TRAINING:
Financial Assistance Provided: Yes
Site Selection Assistance: Yes
Lease Negotiation Assistance: Yes
Co-Operative Advertising: Yes
Franchisee Assoc./Member: No
Size Of Corporate Staff: 60
On-Going Support: D,G,h
Training: 1 Week Salt Lake City, UT; Time Varies at Franchisee's Location.

SPECIFIC EXPANSION PLANS:
US: No
Canada: All Canada
Overseas: Western Europe, Pacific Rim

Top 100

UPS STORE, THE

6060 Cornerstone Ct. W.
San Diego, CA 92121-3762
Tel: (877) 623-7253
Fax: (858) 546-7493
E-Mail: usafranchise@mbe.com
Web Site: www.theupsstore.com/franchise/fraopp.html
Ms. Rachelle Piriano, Franchise Sales

In April 2001, Mail Boxes Etc., Inc., the world's largest franchisor of retail shipping, postal and business service centers, became a subsidiary of UPS, the world's largest express carrier and package delivery company. In 2003, the company introduced The UPS STORE franchise opportunity to offer franchisees and customers the best of both businesses. With over 5,000 The UPS Store and Mail Boxes Etc., Inc. locations in more than 40 countries and territories, the network is the global leader in its market.

BACKGROUND: IFA MEMBER
Established: 1980; 1st Franchised: 1980
Franchised Units: 5,290
Company-Owned Units: 0
Total Units: 5,290
Dist.: US-3,859; CAN-269; O'seas-929
North America: 50 States,10 Provinces
Density: 556 in CA, 346 in FL, 215 TX
Projected New Units (12 Months): 500
Qualifications: 5, 4, 3, 3, 3, 5
Registered: All States

FINANCIAL/TERMS:
Cash Investment: $7.5K
Total Investment: $143-247K
Minimum Net Worth: $50K
Fees: Franchise - $29.9K
Royalty - 5%; Ad. - 3.5%
Earnings Claims Statement: No
Term of Contract (Years): 10/10
Avg. # Of Employees: 2 FT, 2+ PT
Passive Ownership: Discouraged
Encourage Conversions: Yes
Area Develop. Agreements: Yes/10
Sub-Franchising Contracts: No
Expand In Territory: No
Space Needs: 1,400 SF; SF, SC, RM, Non-Tradit.

SUPPORT & TRAINING:
Financial Assistance Provided: Yes
Site Selection Assistance: Yes
Lease Negotiation Assistance: Yes
Co-Operative Advertising: Yes
Franchisee Assoc./Member: Yes/Yes
Size Of Corporate Staff: 300
On-Going Support: A,B,C,e,G,h,I
Training: 10 Days San Diego, CA; Ongoing.

SPECIFIC EXPANSION PLANS:
US: All United States
Canada: All Canada
Overseas: All Countries

<< >>

Printing & Graphics

Chapter 28

Printing & Graphics Industry Profile

Total # Franchisors in Industry Group	16
Total # Franchised Units in Industry Group	3,379
Total # Company-Owned Units in Industry Group	60
Total # Operating Units in Industry Group	3,439
Average # Franchised Units/Franchisor	211.2
Average # Company-Owned Units/Franchisor	3.8
Average # Total Units/Franchisor	214.9
Ratio of Total # Franchised Units/Total # Company-Owned Units	56.3:1
Industry Survey Participants	12
Representing % of Industry	75%
Average Franchise Fee*:	$26.9K
Average Total Investment*:	$255.7K
Average On-Going Royalty Fee*:	6.3%

*If a range was provided, the mid-point of the range was used. See detailed profiles for actual ranges.

Five Largest Participants in Survey

Company	# Franchised Units	# Co-Owned Units	# Total Units	Franchise Fee	On-Going Royalty	Total Investment
1. Minuteman Press International	905	0	905	$44.5K	6%	$100-150K
2. Sir Speedy	600	0	600	$20K	4-6%	$316-391K
3. ProForma	600	0	600	$19.5K	9%	$22-27K
4. Allegra Print & Imaging	400	0	400	$30K	3.6-6%	$155.6-279K
5. AlphaGraphics Printshops of the Future	278	0	278	$25.9K	1.5-8%	$380-551K

All of the data provided are proprietary and should not be quoted without acknowledging *Bond's Franchise Guide.*

ALLEGRA PRINT & IMAGING

21680 Haggerty Rd.
Northville, MI 48084-7104
Tel: (888) 258-2730 (248) 396-8600
Fax: (248) 596-8601
E-Mail: meredithz@allegranetwork.com
Web Site: www.allegranetwork.com
Ms. Meredith Zielinski, Development Program Manager

As one of the largest printing franchises in the world, ALLEGRA NETWORK links more than 400 locations in the US, Canada and Japan. This January marks the 20th year that ALLEGRA has ranked among Entrepreneur Mag's Annual 500. ALLEGRA NETWORK's premier brand, ALLEGRA PRINT & IMAGING offers full-service print and graphic communications services including full-color printing, graphic design, digital color copying, mailing services, high sped output, online file transfer and many other services.

BACKGROUND: IFA MEMBER
Established: 1976; 1st Franchised: 1977
Franchised Units: 400
Company-Owned Units: 0
Total Units: 400
Dist.: US-; CAN-; O'seas-
North America: 42 States, 3 Provinces
Density: 63 in MI, 34 in IL, 31 in MN
Projected New Units (12 Months): 12
Qualifications: 5, 2, 1, 2, 2, 2
Registered: All States

FINANCIAL/TERMS:
Cash Investment: $40K+
Total Investment: $155.6-279K
Minimum Net Worth: $200K
Fees: Franchise - $30K
Royalty - 3.6-6%; Ad. - 1-2%
Earnings Claims Statement: No
Term of Contract (Years): 20/20
Avg. # Of Employees: 3 FT, 1 PT
Passive Ownership: Not Allowed
Encourage Conversions: Yes
Area Develop. Agreements: No
Sub-Franchising Contracts: Yes
Expand In Territory: Yes
Space Needs: 1,200 SF; FS, SF, SC

SUPPORT & TRAINING:
Financial Assistance Provided: Yes
Site Selection Assistance: Yes
Lease Negotiation Assistance: Yes
Co-Operative Advertising: Yes
Franchisee Assoc./Member: Yes/Yes
Size Of Corporate Staff: 50+
On-Going Support: C,D,E,F,G,h,I
Training: 2 Weeks at Home Office; 1 Week On-Site; On-Going

SPECIFIC EXPANSION PLANS:
US: All United States
Canada: All Canada
Overseas: No

<< >>

alphagraphics®
DESIGN ■ COPY ■ PRINT

Top 100

ALPHAGRAPHICS PRINTSHOPS OF THE FUTURE

268 S. State St., # 300
Salt Lake City, UT 84111-2048
Tel: (800) 955-6246 (801) 595-7270
Fax: (801) 595-7271
E-Mail: opportunity@alphagraphics.com
Web Site: www.alphagraphics.com
Mr. Keith M. Gerson, VP Sales, Marketing & Develop.

ALPHAGRAPHICS PRINTSHOPS OF THE FUTURE are the leading providers of print-related and digital publishing services for business worldwide. Our mission is to enable our customers to easily and effectively communicate in any publishing medium - anywhere in the world, any time. Our franchisees enjoy the industry's highest reported average annual sales. Services include design, high-speed duplication, single and multi-color printing, digital large format publishing, binding, CD-ROM and Web site services.

BACKGROUND: IFA MEMBER
Established: 1970; 1st Franchised: 1980
Franchised Units: 278
Company-Owned Units: 0
Total Units: 278
Dist.: US-243; CAN-0; O'seas-35
North America: 39 States
Density: 26 in IL, 26 in CA, 26 in AZ
Projected New Units (12 Months): 24
Qualifications: 4, 5, 1, 3, 3, 5
Registered: All States

FINANCIAL/TERMS:
Cash Investment: $100-150K
Total Investment: $380-551K
Minimum Net Worth: $350K
Fees: Franchise - $25.9K
Royalty - 1.5-8%; Ad. - 2.5%
Earnings Claims Statement: Yes
Term of Contract (Years): 20/20
Avg. # Of Employees: 5 FT
Passive Ownership: Not Allowed
Encourage Conversions: Yes
Area Develop. Agreements: Yes/N/A
Sub-Franchising Contracts: No
Expand In Territory: Yes
Space Needs: 2,200-3,000 SF; FS, SC, SC

SUPPORT & TRAINING:
Financial Assistance Provided: Yes(I)
Site Selection Assistance: Yes
Lease Negotiation Assistance: No
Co-Operative Advertising: Yes
Franchisee Assoc./Member: No/No
Size Of Corporate Staff: 94
On-Going Support: b,C,D,E,G,H,I
Training: 4 Weeks Salt Lake City, UT Service Center

SPECIFIC EXPANSION PLANS:
US: All United States
Canada: All Canada
Overseas: Spain, Italy, France, Germany, Benelux, Austria

<< >>

AMERICAN WHOLESALE THERMOGRAPHERS / AWT

12715 Telge Rd.
Cypress, TX 77429-2289
Tel: (888) 280-2053 (281) 256-4100
Fax: (281) 256-4178
E-Mail: awtsales@awt.com
Web Site: www.awt.com
Mr. Donald Averitt, VP Franchise Sales

AMERICAN WHOLESALE THERMOGRAPHERS / AWT provides wholesale raised letter printing to retail printers, print brokers, copy centers and business service centers. Our superior customer service and proprietary automated workflow system allow a 24-hour turnaround on most orders.

BACKGROUND: IFA MEMBER
Established: 1980; 1st Franchised: 1981
Franchised Units: 16
Company-Owned Units: 0
Total Units: 16
Dist.: US-13; CAN-3; O'seas-
North America: 13 States, 2 Provinces
Density: 3 in ON, 2 in OK, 2 in VA
Projected New Units (12 Months): NR
Qualifications: , , , , ,

Registered: FL,IL,IN,MI,NY,VA,WI

FINANCIAL/TERMS:

Cash Investment: $75K
Total Investment: $350.4-458.9K
Minimum Net Worth: NR
Fees: Franchise - $30K
Royalty - 7%; Ad. - NR
Earnings Claims Statement: No
Term of Contract (Years): 25/25
Avg. # Of Employees: 9 FT, 4 PT
Passive Ownership: Not Allowed
Encourage Conversions: No
Area Develop. Agreements: No
Sub-Franchising Contracts: No
Expand In Territory: Yes
Space Needs: 2,500-3,000 SF; Business Park, Warehouse

SUPPORT & TRAINING:

Financial Assistance Provided: Yes(B)
Site Selection Assistance: Yes
Lease Negotiation Assistance: Yes
Co-Operative Advertising: Yes
Franchisee Assoc./Member: Yes/Yes
Size Of Corporate Staff: NR
On-Going Support: B,C,D,E,G,h,I
Training: 2 Weeks Headquarters; 1 Week On-Site.

SPECIFIC EXPANSION PLANS:

US: All United States
Canada: All Canada
Overseas: No

BABIES 'N' BELLS

4489 Mira Vista Dr.
Frisco, TX 75034-7519
Tel: (888) 418-2229 (972) 335-3535
Fax: (469) 384-0138
E-Mail: franchise.east@babiesnbells.com
Web Site: www.babiesnbells.com
Ms. Cheryl Rogers, Franchise Manager

Balance family and career and work from home! BABIES 'N' BELLS uses state-of-the-art computer printing systems and proprietary design elements to produce custom announcements and invitations for all occasions. BABIES 'N' BELLS has been featured in industry publications, including Entrepreneur Magazine.

BACKGROUND:

Established: 1993; 1st Franchised: 1997
Franchised Units: 65
Company-Owned Units: 34
Total Units: 99
Dist.: US-99; CAN-0; O'seas-0
North America: 25 States
Density: 10 in TX, 7 in NY, 7 in CA
Projected New Units (12 Months): 152
Qualifications: 4, 2, 2, 3, 5,
Registered: CA,FL,IL,ME,MI,MN,NY,VA, WA

FINANCIAL/TERMS:

Cash Investment: $9-20K
Total Investment: $17-29.3K
Minimum Net Worth: NA
Fees: Franchise - $9K
Royalty - 8%; Ad. - 2%
Earnings Claims Statement: No
Term of Contract (Years): 5/5
Avg. # Of Employees: 1 FT
Passive Ownership: Not Allowed
Encourage Conversions: NA
Area Develop. Agreements: No
Sub-Franchising Contracts: No
Expand In Territory: Yes
Space Needs: 600 SF; HB

SUPPORT & TRAINING:

Financial Assistance Provided: No
Site Selection Assistance: Yes
Lease Negotiation Assistance: NA
Co-Operative Advertising: No
Franchisee Assoc./Member: No
Size Of Corporate Staff: 8
On-Going Support: A,B,c,d,E,F,G,h,I
Training: 5 Days Dallas, TX.

SPECIFIC EXPANSION PLANS:

US: All United States
Canada: No
Overseas: No

BUSINESS CARDS TOMORROW

3000 NE 30th Pl., 5th Fl.
Ft. Lauderdale, FL 33306
Tel: (800) 627-9998 + 343 (954) 563-1224 + 343
Fax: (954) 565-0742
E-Mail: bob.dolan@bctonline.net
Web Site: www.bct-net.com
Mr. Bob Dolan, VP Franchise Sales

Join the 24-year old industry-leading wholesale, manufacturing franchise with the competitive advantage. We are recession-resistant, high-volume, quick-turn around, wholesale only manufacturers, specializing in next-day delivery of thermographed and offset-printed products and rubber stamps to retail printers, mailing centers, office supply stores and other retailers. Comprehensive training, excellent support and nationally praised.

BACKGROUND: IFA MEMBER

Established: 1975; 1st Franchised: 1977
Franchised Units: 80
Company-Owned Units: 2
Total Units: 82
Dist.: US-86; CAN-7; O'seas-1
North America: 38 States, 5 Provinces
Density: 16 in CA, 7 in FL, 5 in NY
Projected New Units (12 Months): 2
Qualifications: 4, 4, 3, 3, 3, 5
Registered: All States

FINANCIAL/TERMS:

Cash Investment: $115-151K
Total Investment: $354-441K
Minimum Net Worth: $250K
Fees: Franchise - $35K
Royalty - 6%; Ad. - NA
Earnings Claims Statement: No
Term of Contract (Years): 25/10
Avg. # Of Employees: 10 FT, 6 PT
Passive Ownership: Not Allowed
Encourage Conversions: Yes
Area Develop. Agreements: No
Sub-Franchising Contracts: No
Expand In Territory: No
Space Needs: 4,000+ SF; FS, SC, Commercial Park

SUPPORT & TRAINING:

Financial Assistance Provided: Yes(I)
Site Selection Assistance: Yes
Lease Negotiation Assistance: Yes
Co-Operative Advertising: No
Franchisee Assoc./Member: Yes
Size Of Corporate Staff: 32
On-Going Support: a,B,C,d,E,G,h,I
Training: 2 Weeks Ft. Lauderdale, FL; 1 Week Pre-Opening at New-Site; 2 Weeks after and On-Going.

SPECIFIC EXPANSION PLANS:

US: NJ, NE
Canada: No
Overseas: No

COPY CLUB

12715 Telge Rd.
Cypress, TX 77429-2289
Tel: (888) 280-2053 (281) 256-4100
Fax: (281) 256-4178
E-Mail: ccsales@copyclub.com
Web Site: www.copyclub.com
Mr. Donald Averitt, VP Franchise Sales

High-traffic, high-visibility, digital printing and copying center. We offer copying, bindery and graphic design to corporations, small businesses and home offices. Outside sales consultants generate high-volume repeat business in a fast-paced, technology-driven environment.

BACKGROUND: IFA MEMBER
Established: 1992; 1st Franchised: 1994
Franchised Units: 20
Company-Owned Units: 0
Total Units: 20
Dist.: US-20; CAN-0; O'seas-0
North America: 4 States
Density: 10 in CA, 7 in TX
Projected New Units (12 Months): NR
Qualifications: , , , , ,
Registered: CA,FL,IL,NY,VA,WA

FINANCIAL/TERMS:
Cash Investment: $110K
Total Investment: $311.2-439.4K
Minimum Net Worth: NR
Fees: Franchise - $30K
Royalty - 7%; Ad. - 0%
Earnings Claims Statement: No
Term of Contract (Years): 25/25
Avg. # Of Employees: 8 FT, 5 PT
Passive Ownership: Allowed
Encourage Conversions: No
Area Develop. Agreements: No
Sub-Franchising Contracts: Yes
Expand In Territory: Yes
Space Needs: 3,000 SF; FS

SUPPORT & TRAINING:
Financial Assistance Provided: Yes(I)
Site Selection Assistance: Yes
Lease Negotiation Assistance: Yes
Co-Operative Advertising: No
Franchisee Assoc./Member: Yes/Yes
Size Of Corporate Staff: NR
On-Going Support: C,D,E,G,h,I
Training: 3 Weeks Headquarters

SPECIFIC EXPANSION PLANS:
US: All United States
Canada: No
Overseas: No

<< >>

KWIK KOPY BUSINESS CENTERS, INC.
12715 Telge Rd.
Cypress, TX 77429-2289
Tel: (800) 746-9498 (281) 256-4101
Fax: (281) 256-4178
E-Mail: kksales@kwikkopy.com
Web Site: www.kkbconline.com
Mr. Donald Averitt, VP Franchise Development

KWIK KOPY BUSINESS CENTERS use a high-tech approach to provide a full range of printing, copying, pack-and-ship and cargo services for business and retail customers. We have an extensive network of vendor partners and are members of the worldwide ICED family of more than 1,000 franchises.

BACKGROUND: IFA MEMBER
Established: 2001; 1st Franchised: 2001
Franchised Units: 12
Company-Owned Units: 0
Total Units: 12
Dist.: US-12; CAN-0; O'seas-0
North America: 8 States
Density: 4 in TX, 2 in NC
Projected New Units (12 Months): NR
Qualifications: , , , , ,
Registered: All Except SD,ND,HI

FINANCIAL/TERMS:
Cash Investment: NR
Total Investment: $187-277.7K
Minimum Net Worth: $250K
Fees: Franchise - $25K
Royalty - 7%; Ad. - 0%
Earnings Claims Statement: No
Term of Contract (Years): 15
Avg. # Of Employees: 2 FT, 1 PT
Passive Ownership: Not Allowed
Encourage Conversions: No
Area Develop. Agreements: No
Sub-Franchising Contracts: No
Expand In Territory: Yes
Space Needs: 1,500-2,000 SF; SC, SF

SUPPORT & TRAINING:
Financial Assistance Provided: Yes(D)
Site Selection Assistance: Yes
Lease Negotiation Assistance: Yes
Co-Operative Advertising: No
Franchisee Assoc./Member: Yes/Yes
Size Of Corporate Staff: NR
On-Going Support: B,C,D,E,G,h,I
Training: 4 Weeks Training.

SPECIFIC EXPANSION PLANS:
US: All United States
Canada: All Canada
Overseas: All Countries

<< >>

KWIK KOPY PRINTING CANADA
1550 16th Ave., Bldg. D
Richmond Hill, ON L4B 3K9 CANADA
Tel: (800) 387-9725 (416) 798-7007
Fax: (905) 780-0575
E-Mail: kkpcc@kwikkopy.ca
Web Site: www.kwikkopy.ca
Mr. Brett Hardine, President

Full-service print franchise, on-site printing, copying and digital printing/copying. Canada's largest and most successful print franchise. Strong support and training programs -- no industry experience necessary -- over 1,000 outlets worldwide.

BACKGROUND:
Established: 1979; 1st Franchised: 1979
Franchised Units: 68
Company-Owned Units: 2
Total Units: 70
Dist.: US-0; CAN-78; O'seas-0
North America: 9 Provinces
Density: 55 in ON, 5 in AB, 5 in BC
Projected New Units (12 Months): 6
Qualifications: 3, 4, 1, 3, 4, 5
Registered: All States and AB

FINANCIAL/TERMS:
Cash Investment: $80K
Total Investment: $175-200K
Minimum Net Worth: $200K
Fees: Franchise - $29.5K
Royalty - 7%; Ad. - 3%
Earnings Claims Statement: No
Term of Contract (Years): 10/10
Avg. # Of Employees: 2 FT
Passive Ownership: Not Allowed
Encourage Conversions: Yes
Area Develop. Agreements: Yes/10
Sub-Franchising Contracts: No
Expand In Territory: Yes
Space Needs: 800-1,500 SF; FS, Office Tower, Ind. Park

SUPPORT & TRAINING:
Financial Assistance Provided: Yes(I)
Site Selection Assistance: Yes
Lease Negotiation Assistance: Yes
Co-Operative Advertising: Yes
Franchisee Assoc./Member: Yes/No
Size Of Corporate Staff: 15
On-Going Support: C,D,E,G,h,I
Training: 3 Weeks Houston, TX; 1 Week Toronto, ON; 1 Week On-Site.

SPECIFIC EXPANSION PLANS:
US: NA
Canada: All Canada
Overseas: Middle East, India, Asian Pacific Rim, Africa

<< >>

LAZERQUICK
29900 SW Kinsman, # 200
Wilsonville, OR 97070
Tel: (800) 477-2679 (503) 682-1322
Fax: (503) 682-1670
E-Mail: ahoeck@lazerquick.com
Web Site: www.lazerquick.com
Mr. Allan Hoeckendors, Dir. Franchise

Development

LAZERQUICK centers are complete, one-stop printing and copying centers. All centers feature state-of-the-art electronic publishing, digital graphics and imaging services that support our range of quality, fast-service offset printing, high-speed copying and related bindery and finishing services. The LAZERQUICK franchise is based on value and performance. Affiliates benefit from our unique and innovative programs.

BACKGROUND:
Established: 1968; 1st Franchised: 1990
Franchised Units: 24
Company-Owned Units: 21
Total Units: 45
Dist.: US-47; CAN-0; O'seas-0
North America: 7 States
Density: 29 in OR, 13 in WA, 1 in CA
Projected New Units (12 Months): 6
Qualifications: 4, 3, 2, 3, 3, 5
Registered:CA,FL,IL,IN,MD,MI,MN,NY, OR,VA,WA,WI

FINANCIAL/TERMS:
Cash Investment: $51.8-82.5K
Total Investment: $172.5-275K
Minimum Net Worth: NA
Fees: Franchise - $25K
Royalty - 3-5%/$500; Ad. - 1.5%/$250
Earnings Claims Statement: Yes
Term of Contract (Years): 7/7/7
Avg. # Of Employees: 2 FT, 2 PT
Passive Ownership: Not Allowed
Encourage Conversions: Yes
Area Develop. Agreements: Yes/Varies
Sub-Franchising Contracts: No
Expand In Territory: No
Space Needs: 1,400-1,800 SF; SC

SUPPORT & TRAINING:
Financial Assistance Provided: Yes(I)
Site Selection Assistance: Yes
Lease Negotiation Assistance: Yes
Co-Operative Advertising: NA
Franchisee Assoc./Member: No
Size Of Corporate Staff: 32
On-Going Support: C,D,E,G,I
Training: 5-7 Weeks at Corporate Headquarters.

SPECIFIC EXPANSION PLANS:
US: All United States
Canada: All Exc. AB,PQ
Overseas: No

<< >>

MINUTEMAN PRESS INTERNATIONAL

61 Executive Blvd.
Farmingdale, NY 11735
Tel: (800) 645-3006 (631) 249-1370
Fax: (631) 249-5618
E-Mail: info@minutemanpress.com
Web Site: www.minutemanpress.com
Mr. Mike Miller, Franchise Development

MINUTEMAN PRESS currently has over 900 full-service printing and graphic centers throughout the world. As a MINUTEMAN PRESS owner, you will have a unique place in the industry, having the capability to serve virtually all the printing needs a business may be faced with. No experience necessary. Award-winning training school. On-going technical marketing and business management support through our network of 27 regional offices. Repeatedly named the # 1 printing franchise by Entrepreneur Magazine.

BACKGROUND: IFA MEMBER
Established: 1973; 1st Franchised: 1975
Franchised Units: 905
Company-Owned Units: 0
Total Units: 905
Dist.: US-725; CAN-60; O'seas-120
North America: 46 States, 5 Provinces
Density: 75 in CA, 66 in NY, 58 in TX
Projected New Units (12 Months): 50
Qualifications: 3, 3, 1, 1, 3, 5
Registered: All States and AB

FINANCIAL/TERMS:
Cash Investment: $40-60K
Total Investment: $100-150K
Minimum Net Worth: NR
Fees: Franchise - $44.5K
Royalty - 6%; Ad. - 0%
Earnings Claims Statement: Yes
Term of Contract (Years): 35/35
Avg. # Of Employees: 3 FT (Init.)
Passive Ownership: Discouraged
Encourage Conversions: Yes
Area Develop. Agreements: No
Sub-Franchising Contracts: No
Expand In Territory: Yes
Space Needs: 1,000 SF; FS, SF, SC, RM

SUPPORT & TRAINING:
Financial Assistance Provided: Yes(I)
Site Selection Assistance: Yes
Lease Negotiation Assistance: Yes
Co-Operative Advertising: No
Franchisee Assoc./Member: No
Size Of Corporate Staff: 160
On-Going Support: B,C,D,E,F,G,H,I
Training: 2.5 Weeks Framingdale, NY; On-Site As Needed.

SPECIFIC EXPANSION PLANS:
US: All United States
Canada: All Canada
Overseas: U.K., S. Africa, Australia

<< >>

PROFORMA

8800 E. Pleasant Valley Rd.
Cleveland, OH 44131
Tel: (800) 825-1525 + 3102 (216) 520-8400
Fax: (216) 520-8444
E-Mail: jcampbell@proforma.com
Web Site: www.connectionwithproforma.com
Mr. John Campbell, Chief Franchise Officer

Home-based franchise. Franchise owners market and distribute printing and promotional products to other businesses. Major player in a $150 billion industry! Low overhead. Full marketing and administrative support. $9,500 initial investment. Expanding rapidly throughout North America.

BACKGROUND: IFA MEMBER
Established: 1978; 1st Franchised: 1985
Franchised Units: 600
Company-Owned Units: 0
Total Units: 600
Dist.: US-260; CAN-20; O'seas-0
North America: 42 States, 2 Provinces
Density: 18 in CA, 10 in OH, 10 in NY
Projected New Units (12 Months): 75
Qualifications: 3, 5, 1, 3, 1, 5
Registered: All States

FINANCIAL/TERMS:
Cash Investment: $5-10K
Total Investment: $22-27K
Minimum Net Worth: $100K
Fees: Franchise - $19.5K
Royalty - 9%; Ad. - 1%
Earnings Claims Statement: No
Term of Contract (Years): 10/10
Avg. # Of Employees: 1 FT
Passive Ownership: Not Allowed
Encourage Conversions: Yes
Area Develop. Agreements: No
Sub-Franchising Contracts: No

Expand In Territory: NA
Space Needs: NR SF; HB

SUPPORT & TRAINING:

Financial Assistance Provided: Yes(D)
Site Selection Assistance: NA
Lease Negotiation Assistance: NA
Co-Operative Advertising: Yes
Franchisee Assoc./Member: NR
Size Of Corporate Staff: 140
On-Going Support: A,C,D,F,G,H,I
Training: 1 Week Headquarters; 2 Days Regional 2 Days National; 2 Days Field Visit.

SPECIFIC EXPANSION PLANS:

US: All United States
Canada: All Canada
Overseas: No

SIR SPEEDY

26722 Plaza Dr.
Mission Viejo, CA 92691-6390
Tel: (800) 854-3321 (949) 348-5000
Fax: (949) 348-5010
E-Mail: success@sirspeedy.com
Web Site: www.sirspeedy.com
Ms. Carole Luther, Executive Assistant/ Services

A Monday through Friday business-to-business service, it provides copying, printing, digital communication and graphic design for a diverse range of corporate clients. It's global digital link facilitates instantaneous communication and transfer of material between all centers in the group.

BACKGROUND: IFA MEMBER

Established: 1968; 1st Franchised: 1968
Franchised Units: 600
Company-Owned Units: 0
Total Units: 600
Dist.: US-752; CAN-5; O'seas-125
North America: 47 States, 1 Province
Density: 86 in CA, 72 in FL, 41 in IL
Projected New Units (12 Months): 40
Qualifications: 5, 4, 1, 3, 3, 5
Registered: All States

FINANCIAL/TERMS:

Cash Investment: $100-150K
Total Investment: $316-391K
Minimum Net Worth: $300K
Fees: Franchise - $20K
Royalty - 4-6%; Ad. - 1-2%
Earnings Claims Statement: Yes
Term of Contract (Years): 20/10
Avg. # Of Employees: 5+ FT
Passive Ownership: Discouraged
Encourage Conversions: Yes
Area Develop. Agreements: No
Sub-Franchising Contracts: No
Expand In Territory: Yes
Space Needs: 2,000-12,000 SF; FS, SC

SUPPORT & TRAINING:

Financial Assistance Provided: Yes(I)
Site Selection Assistance: Yes
Lease Negotiation Assistance: Yes
Co-Operative Advertising: No
Franchisee Assoc./Member: No
Size Of Corporate Staff: 50
On-Going Support: B,C,D,E,F,G,H,I
Training: 3 Weeks in Mission Viejo, CA; 6 Weeks at Franchisee's Site.

SPECIFIC EXPANSION PLANS:

US: All United States
Canada: ON
Overseas: Most Countries

For a full explanation of the data provided in the Franchisor Profiles, please refer to *Chapter 2, "How to Use the Data."*

Publications

Chapter 29

Publications Industry Profile

Total # Franchisors in Industry Group	16
Total # Franchised Units in Industry Group	3,379
Total # Company-Owned Units in Industry Group	60
Total # Operating Units in Industry Group	3,439
Average # Franchised Units/Franchisor	211.2
Average # Company-Owned Units/Franchisor	3.8
Average # Total Units/Franchisor	214.9
Ratio of Total # Franchised Units/Total # Company-Owned Units	56.3:1
Industry Survey Participants	12
Representing % of Industry	75%
Average Franchise Fee*:	$26.9K
Average Total Investment*:	$255.7K
Average On-Going Royalty Fee*:	6.3%

*If a range was provided, the mid-point of the range was used. See detailed profiles for actual ranges.

Five Largest Participants in Survey

Company	# Franchised Units	# Co-Owned Units	# Total Units	Franchise Fee	On-Going Royalty	Total Investment
1. Minuteman Press International	905	0	905	$44.5K	6%	$100-150K
2. Sir Speedy	600	0	600	$20K	4-6%	$316-391K
3. ProForma	600	0	600	$19.5K	9%	$22-27K
4. Allegra Print & Imaging	400	0	400	$30K	3.6-6%	$155.6-279K
5. AlphaGraphics Printshops of the Future	278	0	278	$25.9K	1.5-8%	$380-551K

All of the data provided are proprietary and should not be quoted without acknowledging *Bond's Franchise Guide.*

BINGO BUGLE NEWSPAPER

P. O. Box 527
Vashon Island, WA 98070-0527
Tel: (800) 327-6437 (206) 463-5656
Fax: (206) 463-5630
E-Mail: tara@bingobugle.com
Web Site: www.bingobugle.com
Ms. Tara Snowden, President

THE BINGO BUGLE is North America's largest network of newspapers devoted to bingo & gaming. Circulation over 1 million copies monthly. Listed in Entrepreneur's Annual Franchise 500 as one of the lowest cost franchise opportunities. Franchise fees range from $1,500 to $7,000. Complete training and support. Modest investment. Call 1-800-327-6437 for details.

BACKGROUND:
Established: 1981; 1st Franchised: 1983
Franchised Units: 64
Company-Owned Units: 0
Total Units: 64
Dist.: US-66; CAN-5; O'seas-0
North America: 30 States, 2 Provinces
Density: 12 in CA, 6 in NY, 5 in FL
Projected New Units (12 Months): 6
Qualifications: 2, 4, 4, 2, 2, 1
Registered: IL,FL,SD,VA

FINANCIAL/TERMS:
Cash Investment: $1.5-6K
Total Investment: $1.5-10K
Minimum Net Worth: NR
Fees: Franchise - $1.5-10K
Royalty - 10%; Ad. - 0%
Earnings Claims Statement: No
Term of Contract (Years): 5/5
Avg. # Of Employees: 0
Passive Ownership: Allowed
Encourage Conversions: No
Area Develop. Agreements: No
Sub-Franchising Contracts: No
Expand In Territory: No
Space Needs: NA SF; NA

SUPPORT & TRAINING:
Financial Assistance Provided: No
Site Selection Assistance: NA
Lease Negotiation Assistance: No
Co-Operative Advertising: No
Franchisee Assoc./Member: Yes/Yes
Size Of Corporate Staff: 2
On-Going Support: NR
Training: 2.5 Days Seattle, WA.

SPECIFIC EXPANSION PLANS:
US: Northeast, Central US, NC
Canada: All Canada
Overseas: No

COFFEE NEWS

P. O. Box 8444
Bangor, ME 04402-8444
Tel: (207) 941-0860
Fax: (207) 941-1050
E-Mail: bill@coffeenewsusa.com
Web Site: www.coffeenewsusa.com
Mr. William A. Buckley, President

COFFEE NEWS is an international, fun-filled weekly publication produced and delivered free of charge by local franchisors to restaurants, coffee shops and the hospitality industry. Each issue contains short stories, trivia, horoscopes, interesting facts and jokes, plus a local event section edited by the franchisee. Income is derived from the sale of ads to small businesses in each community.

BACKGROUND:
Established: 1994; 1st Franchised: 1996
Franchised Units: 635
Company-Owned Units: 0
Total Units: 635
Dist.: US-288; CAN-119; O'seas-228
North America: NR
Density: 43 in TX, 33 in ME, 31 in BC
Projected New Units (12 Months): 100
Qualifications: 1, 5, 5, 3, 3, 3
Registered: CA,FL,HI,IL,IN,MI,MN,MO, ND,NY,OR,SD,VA,WA,WI,AB

FINANCIAL/TERMS:
Cash Investment: $6K
Total Investment: $6K
Minimum Net Worth: None
Fees: Franchise - $3K
Royalty - $20-75/Wk.; Ad. - 0%
Earnings Claims Statement: No
Term of Contract (Years): 4/4
Avg. # Of Employees: 3 FT
Passive Ownership: Discouraged
Encourage Conversions: NA
Area Develop. Agreements: No
Sub-Franchising Contracts: No
Expand In Territory: Yes
Space Needs: NA SF; NA

SUPPORT & TRAINING:
Financial Assistance Provided: No
Site Selection Assistance: Yes
Lease Negotiation Assistance: No
Co-Operative Advertising: No
Franchisee Assoc./Member: No
Size Of Corporate Staff: 5
On-Going Support: G
Training: Quarterly Sales Meetings in ME.

SPECIFIC EXPANSION PLANS:
US: All United States
Canada: All Canada
Overseas: All Countries

EASYCHAIR MEDIA

800 Third St.
Windsor, CO 80550-5424
Tel: (800) 741-6308 (970) 686-5805
Fax: (800) 438-2150
E-Mail: kristie@easychairmedia.com
Web Site: www.easychairmedia.com
Ms. Kristie Melendez, General Manager

EASYCHAIR MEDIA produces a quality community-based, 4-color glossy lifestyle magazine that targets the best local buyers and brings solid results to satisfied advertisers. We offer results-oriented advertising, with a proven product that makes sense in today's community-oriented economy. EASYCHAIR MEDIA can do any and/or all design, edit content, printing, labeling and mailing of a magazine tailored for your market, community and publishing requirements. All at very affordable prices.

BACKGROUND:
Established: 2000; 1st Franchised: 2003
Franchised Units: 1
Company-Owned Units: 5
Total Units: 6
Dist.: US-6; CAN-0; O'seas-0
North America: 2 States
Density: 5 in CO, 1 in NY
Projected New Units (12 Months): 10-20
Qualifications: 3, 4, 4, 2, 3, 3
Registered:

FINANCIAL/TERMS:
Cash Investment: $10-20K
Total Investment: $32.7-36.7K
Minimum Net Worth: $100K+
Fees: Franchise - $20K
Royalty - 0%; Ad. - 0%
Earnings Claims Statement: No
Term of Contract (Years): 10/10
Avg. # Of Employees: 1 FT, 1-2 PT
Passive Ownership: Allowed
Encourage Conversions: NA

Area Develop. Agreements: Yes
Sub-Franchising Contracts: No
Expand In Territory: Yes
Space Needs: NA SF; HB
SUPPORT & TRAINING:
Financial Assistance Provided: No
Site Selection Assistance: Yes
Lease Negotiation Assistance: NA
Co-Operative Advertising: No
Franchisee Assoc./Member: No
Size Of Corporate Staff: 5
On-Going Support: b,C,D,G,h,I
Training: 2-3 Weeks on Franchisee Site.
SPECIFIC EXPANSION PLANS:
US: All United States
Canada: No
Overseas: Mexico Only

<< >>

FINDERBINDER / SOURCEBOOK DIRECTORIES
5173 Waring Rd., # 8
San Diego, CA 92120
Tel: (800) 255-2575 (619) 582-8500
Fax: (619) 463-5097
E-Mail: kzwolinski@yahoo.com
Web Site: www.finderbinder.com
Ms. Kathy Zwolinski, Office Manager

The FINDERBINDER News Media Directory and the SOURCEBOOK Directory of Clubs and Associations are locally produced reference books created by existing communications firms, such as an advertising agency or public relations consultants. It is an added profit center that builds public awareness for the local company.

BACKGROUND:
Established: 1974; 1st Franchised: 1978
Franchised Units: 18
Company-Owned Units: 1
Total Units: 19
Dist.: US-22; CAN-0; O'seas-0
North America: 15 States
Density: 4 in CA
Projected New Units (12 Months): 3
Qualifications: , , , , ,
Registered: CA
FINANCIAL/TERMS:
Cash Investment: NR
Total Investment: $10-15K
Minimum Net Worth: $30K
Fees: Franchise - $1K
Royalty - 5-10%; Ad. - NA
Earnings Claims Statement: No
Term of Contract (Years): Open
Avg. # Of Employees: 2 FT, 1 PT
Passive Ownership: Discouraged
Encourage Conversions: No
Area Develop. Agreements: No
Sub-Franchising Contracts: No
Expand In Territory: Yes
Space Needs: NA SF; NA
SUPPORT & TRAINING:
Financial Assistance Provided: No
Site Selection Assistance: NA
Lease Negotiation Assistance: NA
Co-Operative Advertising: Yes
Franchisee Assoc./Member: No
Size Of Corporate Staff: 3
On-Going Support: C,D,E,G,H,I
Training: 1 Day in San Diego.
SPECIFIC EXPANSION PLANS:
US: All United States
Canada: All Canada
Overseas: U.K., Australia, New Zealand

<< >>

HOMESTEADER
Knox Trail Office Bldg., 2352 Main St.
Concord, MA 01742
Tel: (800) 941-9907 (978) 461-0028 + 3
Fax: (978) 461-0486
E-Mail: allen@thehomesteader.com
Web Site: www.thehomesteader.com
Mr. Allen Nitschelm, President

THE HOMESTEADER is a publication direct-mailed to new homeowners, one of the best target markets for businesses to reach. This is a low-cost, home-based opportunity with great income potential for anyone with a sales, publishing or business background.

BACKGROUND:
Established: 1990; 1st Franchised: 1993
Franchised Units: 18
Company-Owned Units: 7
Total Units: 25
Dist.: US-17; CAN-0; O'seas-0
North America: 4 States
Density: 11 in MA, 4 in CT, 1 in NY
Projected New Units (12 Months): 6-10
Qualifications: 3, 3, 4, 2, 4, 2
Registered: CA,FL,NY,VA
FINANCIAL/TERMS:
Cash Investment: $3.3-22K
Total Investment: $3.3-22K
Minimum Net Worth: $10K
Fees: Franchise - $3.4K
Royalty - 10%; Ad. - 0-2%
Earnings Claims Statement: Yes
Term of Contract (Years): 10/10
Avg. # Of Employees: 1 FT
Passive Ownership: Allowed
Encourage Conversions: NA
Area Develop. Agreements: No
Sub-Franchising Contracts: No
Expand In Territory: No
Space Needs: NR SF; HB
SUPPORT & TRAINING:
Financial Assistance Provided: Yes(I)
Site Selection Assistance: NA
Lease Negotiation Assistance: NA
Co-Operative Advertising: NA
Franchisee Assoc./Member: No
Size Of Corporate Staff: 4
On-Going Support: d,H
Training: 2-3 Days Framingham, MA.
SPECIFIC EXPANSION PLANS:
US: All United States
Canada: All Canada
Overseas: No

<< >>

PERFECT WEDDING GUIDE, THE
39 Skyline Dr., # 1001
Lake Mary, FL 32746-6249
Tel: (888) 222-7433 (407) 331-6212
Fax: (407) 331-5004
E-Mail: amy@pwg.com
Web Site: www.pwg.com
Ms. Amy Pedrotty, Franchise Resource Manager

THE PERFECT WEDDING GUIDE is a comprehensive buyers' guide to wedding and honeymoon products and services. As the owner of a PERFECT WEDDING GUIDE, you will publish a magazine that thousands of people will read every day. With the guidance of the nation's premier wedding magazine publisher, you will own and manage your own business!

BACKGROUND: IFA MEMBER
Established: 1991; 1st Franchised: 1998
Franchised Units: 68
Company-Owned Units: 1
Total Units: 69
Dist.: US-68; CAN-1; O'seas-0
North America: 22 States
Density: 4 in FL, 2 in TX
Projected New Units (12 Months): 24
Qualifications: 4, 3, 3, 3, 5, 5
Registered: FL
FINANCIAL/TERMS:
Cash Investment: $30-50K
Total Investment: $35-50K
Minimum Net Worth: $50K
Fees: Franchise - $25-35K
Royalty - 6%; Ad. - 1%
Earnings Claims Statement: No

Term of Contract (Years): 10/10
Avg. # Of Employees: 2 FT
Passive Ownership: Discouraged
Encourage Conversions: NR
Area Develop. Agreements: No
Sub-Franchising Contracts: No
Expand In Territory: Yes
Space Needs: NA SF; HB

SUPPORT & TRAINING:
Financial Assistance Provided: Yes(D)
Site Selection Assistance: NA
Lease Negotiation Assistance: NA
Co-Operative Advertising: No
Franchisee Assoc./Member: No
Size Of Corporate Staff: 7
On-Going Support: a,b,C,d,G,h,I
Training: 5 Days Longwood, FL; 5 Days Franchise Territory.

SPECIFIC EXPANSION PLANS:
US: All United States
Canada: All Canada
Overseas: No

Chapter

30

Real Estate Inspection Services Industry Profile

Total # Franchisors in Industry Group	21
Total # Franchised Units in Industry Group	3,016
Total # Company-Owned Units in Industry Group	364
Total # Operating Units in Industry Group	3,380
Average # Franchised Units/Franchisor	143.6
Average # Company-Owned Units/Franchisor	17.3
Average # Total Units/Franchisor	161
Ratio of Total # Franchised Units/Total # Company-Owned Units	8.3:1
Industry Survey Participants	13
Representing % of Industry	61.9%
Average Franchise Fee*:	$20.3K
Average Total Investment*:	$32.5K
Average On-Going Royalty Fee*:	7%

*If a range was provided, the mid-point of the range was used. See detailed profiles for actual ranges.

Five Largest Participants in Survey

Company	# Franchised Units	# Co-Owned Units	# Total Units	Franchise Fee	On-Going Royalty	Total Investment
1. Pillar To Post	457	0	457	$18.9-28.9K	7%	$23.9-44.5K
2. HouseMaster Home Inspections	382	0	382	$18-30K	7.5%	$20-55K
3. AmeriSpec Home Inspection Service	367	2	369	$18-26.9K	7%	$24.6-63.5K
4. HomeTeam Inspection Service, The	353	0	353	$11.9-29.9K	6%	$17.5-45K
5. National Property Inspections (NPI)	250	0	250	$21.8K	8%	$21.8K

All of the data provided are proprietary and should not be quoted without acknowledging *Bond's Franchise Guide.*

Top 100

AMERISPEC HOME INSPECTION SERVICE

889 Ridge Lake Blvd.
Memphis, TN 38120-9421
Tel: (800) 426-2270 (901) 820-8500
Fax: (901) 820-8520
E-Mail: sales@amerispec.com
Web Site: www.amerispecfranchise.com
Ms. Theresa Westphall, Sales Coordinator

AMERISPEC delivers productivity enhancing tools to our owners like feature-rich personal Websites, branded email accounts, secure web delivery for reports and contact management software specifically designed to manage a home inspection business. A private intranet permits two-way communication with and among our owners. Consider our extensive training, the acclaimed and recognized 'AMERISPEC REPORT,' our on-going educational support and the package is complete.

BACKGROUND: IFA MEMBER
Established: 1987; 1st Franchised: 1988
Franchised Units: 367
Company-Owned Units: 2
Total Units: 369
Dist.: US-287; CAN-80; O'seas-0
North America: 48 States, 8 Provinces
Density: 24 in CA, 16 in FL, 11 in IL
Projected New Units (12 Months): 25
Qualifications: 3, 3, 3, 3, 1, 5
Registered: All States

FINANCIAL/TERMS:
Cash Investment: $10-15K
Total Investment: $24.6-63.5K
Minimum Net Worth: $25K
Fees: Franchise - $18-26.9K
Royalty - 7%; Ad. - 3%
Earnings Claims Statement: No
Term of Contract (Years): 5/5
Avg. # Of Employees: 1 FT, 2 PT
Passive Ownership: Allowed
Encourage Conversions: Yes
Area Develop. Agreements: No
Sub-Franchising Contracts: No
Expand In Territory: Yes
Space Needs: NA SF; HB

SUPPORT & TRAINING:
Financial Assistance Provided: Yes(D)
Site Selection Assistance: NA
Lease Negotiation Assistance: NA
Co-Operative Advertising: Yes
Franchisee Assoc./Member: No
Size Of Corporate Staff: 45
On-Going Support: C,D,E,G,h,I
Training: 2 Weeks Memphis, TN.

SPECIFIC EXPANSION PLANS:
US: All United States
Canada: All Canada
Overseas: No

<< >>

BRICKKICKER, THE

849 N. Ellsworth St.
Naperville, IL 60563
Tel: (888) 339-5425 (630) 420-9900
Fax: (630) 420-2270
E-Mail: jallen@brickkicker.com
Web Site: www.brickkicker.com
Mr. James Allen, Dir. Marketing Services

Home and building inspections. Operating our own business since 1989 gives us a unique insight into the entrepreneurial aspects required to be an impact player in the industry. We've packaged our experience into a dynamic, aggressive program, including a heavy emphasis on 'live,' on-the-job training. Every BRICKKICKER benefits from the roll up our sleeves attitude in which we operate.

BACKGROUND:
Established: 1989; 1st Franchised: 1995
Franchised Units: 120
Company-Owned Units: 20
Total Units: 140
Dist.: US-79; CAN-0; O'seas-0
North America: 7 States
Density: 16 in MI, 8 in WI, 7 in IN
Projected New Units (12 Months): 45
Qualifications: 3, 4, 2, 3, 3, 4
Registered: All States

FINANCIAL/TERMS:
Cash Investment: $9.4-24.9K
Total Investment: $19.4-39.9K
Minimum Net Worth: $10K
Fees: Franchise - $6.9-12.9K
Royalty - 6%; Ad. - 2%
Earnings Claims Statement: No
Term of Contract (Years): 7/20
Avg. # Of Employees: 1 FT
Passive Ownership: Discouraged
Encourage Conversions: Yes
Area Develop. Agreements: No
Sub-Franchising Contracts: No
Expand In Territory: Yes
Space Needs: NR SF; NR

SUPPORT & TRAINING:
Financial Assistance Provided: Yes(D)
Site Selection Assistance: NA
Lease Negotiation Assistance: NA
Co-Operative Advertising: NA
Franchisee Assoc./Member: Yes/Yes
Size Of Corporate Staff: 7
On-Going Support: B,C,D,E,G,H,I
Training: 10 Days, Naperville, IL; 3 Days On-Site.

SPECIFIC EXPANSION PLANS:
US: All United States
Canada: All Canada
Overseas: No

<< >>

CRITERIUM ENGINEERS

22 Monument Sq., # 600
Portland, ME 04101
Tel: (800) 242-1969 (207) 828-1969
Fax: (207) 775-4405
E-Mail: phollander@criterium-engineers.com
Web Site: www.criterium-engineers.com
Mr. Peter E. Hollander, Executive Vice President

CRITERIUM ENGINEERS is a consulting franchise available to licensed professional engineers. Company specializes in building inspection and evaluation services for buyers, investors, corporations, attorneys, insurance companies, lenders and government. Services include pre-purchase inspections, insurance investigations, due diligence, maintenance planning, expert testimony, reserve studies, environmental assessments, design and construction review.

BACKGROUND:
Established: 1957; 1st Franchised: 1958
Franchised Units: 72
Company-Owned Units: 0
Total Units: 72
Dist.: US-70; CAN-2; O'seas-0
North America: 37 States
Density: 4 in CA, 3 in PA, 3 in NJ
Projected New Units (12 Months): 6
Qualifications: , , , , ,
Registered: CA,FL,IN, IL, NY,OR

FINANCIAL/TERMS:
Cash Investment: $6K
Total Investment: $30K
Minimum Net Worth: NR
Fees: Franchise - $26.5K
Royalty - 6%; Ad. - 1%
Earnings Claims Statement: Yes
Term of Contract (Years): 5/5/5
Avg. # Of Employees: 2 FT, 2 PT
Passive Ownership: Not Allowed
Encourage Conversions: NA

Area Develop. Agreements: No
Sub-Franchising Contracts: No
Expand In Territory: Yes
Space Needs: 300 SF; NR

SUPPORT & TRAINING:
Financial Assistance Provided: Yes
Site Selection Assistance: NA
Lease Negotiation Assistance: No
Co-Operative Advertising: NA
Franchisee Assoc./Member: NR
Size Of Corporate Staff: 10
On-Going Support: B,C,D,G,H,I
Training: 1 Week Headquarters.

SPECIFIC EXPANSION PLANS:
US: All Legally Permitted
Canada: All Canada
Overseas: All Countries

<< >>

CRITTER CONTROL

9435 E. Cherry Bend Rd.
Traverse City, MI 49684
Tel: (800) 451-6544 (305) 664-3080
Fax: (360) 483-1755
E-Mail: franchise@crittercontrol.com
Web Site: www.crittercontrol.com
Mr. Charlie Culver, Chief Operating Officer

Urban Wildlife Management Specialists. The nation's leading wildlife control firm. Humane animal removal, prevention and repairs of animal damage.

BACKGROUND: IFA MEMBER
Established: 1983; 1st Franchised: 1988
Franchised Units: 96
Company-Owned Units: 5
Total Units: 101
Dist.: US-94; CAN-2; O'seas-0
North America: 36 States, 2 Provinces
Density: 11 in MI, 7 in FL, 6 in OH
Projected New Units (12 Months): 14
Qualifications: 2, 3, 3, 3, 3, 4
Registered: CA,IN,MD,MI,NY,VA,WI

FINANCIAL/TERMS:
Cash Investment: $3-5K
Total Investment: $5-25K
Minimum Net Worth: NA
Fees: Franchise - $15-24K
Royalty - 6-16%; Ad. - 1-2%
Earnings Claims Statement: Yes
Term of Contract (Years): 10/10
Avg. # Of Employees: 2 FT, 1 PT
Passive Ownership: Discouraged
Encourage Conversions: NA
Area Develop. Agreements: No
Sub-Franchising Contracts: No
Expand In Territory: Yes
Space Needs: NA SF; HB

SUPPORT & TRAINING:
Financial Assistance Provided: Yes
Site Selection Assistance: Yes
Lease Negotiation Assistance: NA
Co-Operative Advertising: Yes
Franchisee Assoc./Member: Yes/Yes
Size Of Corporate Staff: 8
On-Going Support: C,D,G,H,I
Training: 1 Week Columbus, OH.

SPECIFIC EXPANSION PLANS:
US: All United States
Canada: All Canada
Overseas: No

<< >>

HOMETEAM INSPECTION SERVICE, THE

575 Chamber Dr.
Milford, OH 45150
Tel: (800) 598-5297 (513) 469-2100
Fax: (513) 469-2226
E-Mail: info@hmteam.com
Web Site: www.hmteam.com
Mr. Greg Haskett, President

Ranked #1 fastest-growing home inspection franchise in North America. Unique and field-proven marketing system that produces leads and appointments. Exclusive, protected territory. Extensive and continuous training. Sales hotline to build your business. Financing provided.

BACKGROUND: IFA MEMBER
Established: 1992; 1st Franchised: 1992
Franchised Units: 353
Company-Owned Units: 0
Total Units: 353
Dist.: US-292; CAN-5; O'seas-0
North America: 48 States, 2 Provinces
Density: 29 in FL, 20 in OH, 16 in MI
Projected New Units (12 Months): 29
Qualifications: 2, 3, 2, 3, 3, 5
Registered:CA,FL,IL,IN,MD,MI,MN,NY,ND,OR,RI,SD,VA,WA,WI,DC

FINANCIAL/TERMS:
Cash Investment: $6.5-15.7K
Total Investment: $17.5-45K
Minimum Net Worth: NA
Fees: Franchise - $11.9-29.9K
Royalty - 6%; Ad. - 3%
Earnings Claims Statement: No
Term of Contract (Years): 10/10/10
Avg. # Of Employees: 1 FT
Passive Ownership: Discouraged
Encourage Conversions: NA
Area Develop. Agreements: No
Sub-Franchising Contracts: No
Expand In Territory: Yes
Space Needs: NA SF; NA

SUPPORT & TRAINING:
Financial Assistance Provided: Yes(D)
Site Selection Assistance: NA
Lease Negotiation Assistance: NA
Co-Operative Advertising: Yes
Franchisee Assoc./Member: Yes/Yes
Size Of Corporate Staff: 20
On-Going Support: A,B,C,D,G,H,I
Training: 2 Weeks Corporate Headquarters, Cincinnati, OH.

SPECIFIC EXPANSION PLANS:
US: All United States
Canada: All Canada
Overseas: No

<< >>

HouseMaster®
Home Inspections. Done Right.℠

Top 100

HOUSEMASTER HOME INSPECTIONS

421 W. Union Ave.
Bound Brook, NJ 08805-1220
Tel: (800) 526-3939 (732) 469-6565
Fax: (732) 469-7405
E-Mail: mmurphy@housemaster.com
Web Site: www.housemaster.com
Ms. Marianne P. Murphy, VP Marketing/Development

HOUSEMASTER is the oldest and most experienced home inspection franchise. HOUSEMASTER is the recognized authority on home inspections and has been featured as such on CNN, CNBC, Our Home Show and many more! You will be impressed with the level of expertise and the unsurpassed level of support that HOUSEMASTER franchise operators enjoy.

BACKGROUND: IFA MEMBER
Established: 1979; 1st Franchised: 1979
Franchised Units: 382
Company-Owned Units: 0
Total Units: 382
Dist.: US-349; CAN-33; O'seas-0
North America: 48 States,10 Provinces
Density: 23 in NJ, 20 in NY, 18 in FL
Projected New Units (12 Months): 72
Qualifications: 4, 3, 2, 2, 5, 5
Registered: All States

FINANCIAL/TERMS:
Cash Investment: $18-40K
Total Investment: $20-55K

Minimum Net Worth: $75K
Fees: Franchise - $18-30K
Royalty - 7.5%; Ad. - 2.5%
Earnings Claims Statement: No
Term of Contract (Years): 5/5
Avg. # Of Employees: Varies
Passive Ownership: Allowed
Encourage Conversions: NA
Area Develop. Agreements: No
Sub-Franchising Contracts: No
Expand In Territory: Yes
Space Needs: NA SF; HB

SUPPORT & TRAINING:
Financial Assistance Provided: Yes(D)
Site Selection Assistance: NA
Lease Negotiation Assistance: NA
Co-Operative Advertising: NA
Franchisee Assoc./Member: Yes/Yes
Size Of Corporate Staff: 22
On-Going Support: D,G,H,I
Training: 2-3 Weeks Bound Brook, NJ.

SPECIFIC EXPANSION PLANS:
US: All United States
Canada: All Canada
Overseas: Most Countries

<< >>

INSPECT-IT 1ST PROPERTY INSPECTION

8541 E. Anderson Dr., # 102
Scottsdale, AZ 85255
Tel: (800) 510-9100
Fax: (480) 355-3255
E-Mail: joinus@inspectit1st.com
Web Site: www.inspectit1st.com
Mr. Scott Grossman, Chief Operating Officer

Before you buy, before you sell, INSPECT-IT 1ST. Providing state-of-the-art home inspections since 1991. Consistently recognized by Entrepreneur Magazine as one of their Top 500 franchises. 13 years and 60,000 inspections. We provide you with all you need: initial training, digitally-enhanced inspection reports, on-going marketing support and programs, business development CD, support center and more.

BACKGROUND: IFA MEMBER
Established: 1991; 1st Franchised: 1998
Franchised Units: 62
Company-Owned Units: 0
Total Units: 62
Dist.: US-62; CAN-0; O'seas-0
North America: NR
Density: 10 in AZ, 7 in FL, 4 in CA
Projected New Units (12 Months): NR
Qualifications: , , , , ,
Registered:

FINANCIAL/TERMS:
Cash Investment: $6-12K
Total Investment: $33-51K
Minimum Net Worth: NA
Fees: Franchise - $24.9-27.9K
Royalty - 6%/$200; Ad. - 2%/$50
Earnings Claims Statement: Yes
Term of Contract (Years): 10/10
Avg. # Of Employees: 1-3 FT
Passive Ownership: Discouraged
Encourage Conversions: NR
Area Develop. Agreements: Yes/Varies
Sub-Franchising Contracts: Yes
Expand In Territory: Yes
Space Needs: NA SF; NA

SUPPORT & TRAINING:
Financial Assistance Provided: NR
Site Selection Assistance: NA
Lease Negotiation Assistance: NA
Co-Operative Advertising: Yes
Franchisee Assoc./Member: No
Size Of Corporate Staff: 5
On-Going Support: B,c,D,E,G,H,I
Training: 2 Weeks Arizona.

SPECIFIC EXPANSION PLANS:
US: All United States
Canada: NR
Overseas: NR

NATIONAL PROPERTY INSPECTIONS®

Top 100

NATIONAL PROPERTY INSPECTIONS (NPI)

9375 Burt St., # 201
Omaha, NE 68114
Tel: (800) 333-9807 + 24 (402) 333-9807 + 24
Fax: (800) 933-2508
E-Mail: info@npiweb.com
Web Site: www.npiweb.com
Ms. Julie Erickson, Director of Franchise Sales

Nationally acclaimed residential and commercial property inspection franchise. Low start-up costs. Exclusive territories. Expansion encouraged. Intensive, interactive, 2-week classroom training , 1-week field training. On-going marketing and technical support. Fee includes state-of-the-art computer package and most everything needed to start your business. GLOBAL PROPERTY INSPECTIONS (GPI) is the operating entity in Canada.

BACKGROUND:
Established: 1987; 1st Franchised: 1987
Franchised Units: 250
Company-Owned Units: 0
Total Units: 250
Dist.: US-239; CAN-11; O'seas-0
North America: 43 States, 4 Provinces
Density: 24 in CA, 22 in FL, 13 in PA
Projected New Units (12 Months): 40
Qualifications: 3, 3, 4, 3, 4, 4
Registered: All States and AB

FINANCIAL/TERMS:
Cash Investment: $21.8K
Total Investment: $21.8K
Minimum Net Worth: NR
Fees: Franchise - $21.8K
Royalty - 8%; Ad. - 0%
Earnings Claims Statement: No
Term of Contract (Years): 10
Avg. # Of Employees: 1 FT
Passive Ownership: Discouraged
Encourage Conversions: Yes
Area Develop. Agreements: No
Sub-Franchising Contracts: No
Expand In Territory: Yes
Space Needs: NR SF; NA

SUPPORT & TRAINING:
Financial Assistance Provided: Yes(D)
Site Selection Assistance: NA
Lease Negotiation Assistance: NA
Co-Operative Advertising: NA
Franchisee Assoc./Member: No
Size Of Corporate Staff: 11
On-Going Support: D,G,H,I
Training: 2 Weeks Omaha, NE in NPI Corporate Office; 1 Week Field Training near Franchisee's Home.

SPECIFIC EXPANSION PLANS:
US: All United States
Canada: All Canada
Overseas: No

<< >>

PESTMASTER FRANCHISE NETWORK

137 E. South St.
Bishop, CA 93514
Tel: (800) 525-3268 (760) 873-8100
Fax: (760) 873-4826
E-Mail: pfn@pestmaster.com
Web Site: www.pestmaster.com
Ms. Terry K. Walker, Franchise Manager

PESTMASTER is flexible. We offer proven programs to ensure growth, starting with training and on-going support.

You'll benefit from a protected marketing territory, reduced insurance rates, as well as valuable discounts on equipment and supplies. Unlike other franchises, PESTMASTER offers a contracts department, which will consistently seek out government and commercial jobs for bid.

BACKGROUND: IFA MEMBER
Established: 1979; 1st Franchised: 1992
Franchised Units: 15
Company-Owned Units: 12
Total Units: 27
Dist.: US-27; CAN-0; O'seas-0
North America: 6 States
Density: 18 in CA, 3 in TX, 2 in FL
Projected New Units (12 Months): 4
Qualifications: 3, 4, 5, 2, 3, 4
Registered: CA,FL,NY

FINANCIAL/TERMS:
Cash Investment: $20-40K
Total Investment: $18-70K
Minimum Net Worth: $30K
Fees: Franchise - $15-30K
Royalty - 5-7%; Ad. - 0.5%
Earnings Claims Statement: No
Term of Contract (Years): 10/20
Avg. # Of Employees: 2-4 PT
Passive Ownership: Discouraged
Encourage Conversions: Yes
Area Develop. Agreements: No
Sub-Franchising Contracts: No
Expand In Territory: Yes
Space Needs: 500 SF; HB

SUPPORT & TRAINING:
Financial Assistance Provided: No
Site Selection Assistance: Yes
Lease Negotiation Assistance: No
Co-Operative Advertising: Yes
Franchisee Assoc./Member: Yes
Size Of Corporate Staff: 12
On-Going Support: a,c,D,h,I
Training: 3-5 Days Bishop, CA; 2-5 Days Franchise Site.

SPECIFIC EXPANSION PLANS:
US: All United States
Canada: No
Overseas: No

<< >>

PILLAR TO POST
13902 N. Dale Mabry Hwy., # 300
Tampa, FL 33618
Tel: (877) 963-3129 (813) 962-4461
Fax: (813) 963-5301
E-Mail: jmajirsky@pillartopost.com
Web Site: www.pillartopost.com
Mr. Jim M. Majirsky, Director Franchise Development

Program directed by specialists with over 50 years of experience. Territory development from preferred aggressive multi-inspector business levels to moderate single inspector levels available. PILLAR TO POST provides the most recognized opportunity in the home inspection industry. Imaginative, highly successful marketing designed for top performance in business development. Promotional materials, IT support, innovative website and on-going, cooperative team building operational assistance are provided.

BACKGROUND: IFA MEMBER
Established: 1994; 1st Franchised: 1994
Franchised Units: 457
Company-Owned Units: 0
Total Units: 457
Dist.: US-372; CAN-85; O'seas-0
North America: 43 States, 8 Provinces
Density: 26 in FL, 19 in NY, 18 in NJ
Projected New Units (12 Months): 90
Qualifications: 3, 3, 3, 3, 3, 3
Registered: All States and AB

FINANCIAL/TERMS:
Cash Investment: $18.9-28.9K
Total Investment: $23.9-44.5K
Minimum Net Worth: $100K
Fees: Franchise - $18.9-28.9K
Royalty - 7%; Ad. - 4%
Earnings Claims Statement: No
Term of Contract (Years): 30/5
Avg. # Of Employees: 4 FT
Passive Ownership: Not Allowed
Encourage Conversions: NA
Area Develop. Agreements: No
Sub-Franchising Contracts: Yes
Expand In Territory: Yes
Space Needs: Home-Based SF; NA

SUPPORT & TRAINING:
Financial Assistance Provided: No
Site Selection Assistance: NA
Lease Negotiation Assistance: No
Co-Operative Advertising: Yes
Franchisee Assoc./Member: No
Size Of Corporate Staff: 16
On-Going Support: A,B,C,D,G,h,I
Training: 2 Weeks Mississauga, ON.

SPECIFIC EXPANSION PLANS:
US: All United States
Canada: All Canada
Overseas: No

<< >>

Top 100

PROSPECTION
7100 E. Pleasant Valley Rd. # 260
Independence, OH 44131
Tel: (866) 328-7720 + 25 (216) 328-7720 + 25
Fax: (216) 674-0650
E-Mail: inquiry@pro-spection.com
Web Site: www.prospectionusa.com
Mr. Todd Petty, Sales Manager

Benefits of PROSPECTION include large territories, lower franchise fees, interest-free financing, training and more. You also have access to our team of marketing, technology and business development experts. Compare us to other inspection franchises and then contact us for a cost/benefit analysis. PROSPECTION is a subsidiary of Merrymeeting Inc. (MMI) an investment firm founded by John Davies, former division president of Progressive. Through its multiple franchises, MMI operates 800+ units.

BACKGROUND: IFA MEMBER
Established: 2003; 1st Franchised: 2003
Franchised Units: 9
Company-Owned Units: 0
Total Units: 9
Dist.: US-5; CAN-0; O'seas-0
North America: 5 States
Density: 1 each in CA,FL,IL,WA,WI
Projected New Units (12 Months): 25
Qualifications: 3, 2, 1, 1, 1, 5
Registered: CA,FL,IL,WA,WI

FINANCIAL/TERMS:
Cash Investment: $3-4K
Total Investment: $15.2-38.5K
Minimum Net Worth: $None
Fees: Franchise - $6K or 12K
Royalty - 7%; Ad. - 2%
Earnings Claims Statement: NR
Term of Contract (Years): 7/7
Avg. # Of Employees: 1 FT
Passive Ownership: Allowed
Encourage Conversions: NA
Area Develop. Agreements: No
Sub-Franchising Contracts: No
Expand In Territory: Yes

Space Needs: NR SF; HB

SUPPORT & TRAINING:

Financial Assistance Provided: Yes(D)
Site Selection Assistance: NA
Lease Negotiation Assistance: NA
Co-Operative Advertising: Yes
Franchisee Assoc./Member: No
Size Of Corporate Staff: 25
On-Going Support: A,B,D,G,h,I
Training: 7 Days at 8 different locations; 6 Hours Online.

SPECIFIC EXPANSION PLANS:

US: CA,FL,IL,OH,WA,NY
Canada: No
Overseas: No

WORLD INSPECTION NETWORK

6500 6th Ave., NW
Seattle, WA 98117-5099
Tel: (800) 967-8127 (206) 728-8100
Fax: (206) 441-3655
E-Mail: joinwin@wini.com
Web Site: www.winfranchise.com
Mr. Robert Riggs, Franchise Develop Consultant

WORLD INSPECTION NETWORK - the # 1 premium home inspection service in North America. Get your share of the more than 4 million home inspections performed each year. We know home inspections. With over 10 years in the industry, we give you the independence of being your own boss with the support of a powerful nationwide network of more than 200 franchisees in 31 states. We offer an unparalleled track record of success. Exclusive territories and the most extensive training, technology and support.

BACKGROUND: IFA MEMBER

Established: 1993; 1st Franchised: 1994
Franchised Units: 205
Company-Owned Units: 0
Total Units: 205
Dist.: US-205; CAN-0; O'seas-0
North America: 31 States
Density: 51 in CA, 23 in WA, 15 in NY
Projected New Units (12 Months): 59
Qualifications: 5, 5, 2, 2, 5, 5
Registered:All Except CT,HI,MA,MD,NC, ND,RI,SD,TX

FINANCIAL/TERMS:

Cash Investment: $25K
Total Investment: $41.7-49.5K
Minimum Net Worth: NA
Fees: Franchise - $25K
Royalty - 7%/$300 Min.;Ad. - 3%/$125 Min
Earnings Claims Statement: Yes
Term of Contract (Years): 5/5
Avg. # Of Employees: 1 FT
Passive Ownership: Discouraged
Encourage Conversions: Yes
Area Develop. Agreements: Yes/10
Sub-Franchising Contracts: No
Expand In Territory: Yes
Space Needs: NA SF; HB

SUPPORT & TRAINING:

Financial Assistance Provided: Yes(D)
Site Selection Assistance: Yes
Lease Negotiation Assistance: NA
Co-Operative Advertising: Yes
Franchisee Assoc./Member: Yes/Yes
Size Of Corporate Staff: 14
On-Going Support: B,C,D,G,H,I
Training: 2 Weeks Pre-Training at Home; 2 Weeks Training in Seattle, WA.

SPECIFIC EXPANSION PLANS:

US: Most of United States
Canada: No
Overseas: No

Chapter

31

Real Estate Services Industry Profile

Total # Franchisors in Industry Group	59
Total # Franchised Units in Industry Group	23,794
Total # Company-Owned Units in Industry Group	1,461
Total # Operating Units in Industry Group	25,255
Average # Franchised Units/Franchisor	403.3
Average # Company-Owned Units/Franchisor	24.8
Average # Total Units/Franchisor	428.1
Ratio of Total # Franchised Units/Total # Company-Owned Units	16.3:1

Industry Survey Participants	23
Representing % of Industry	39%
Average Franchise Fee*:	$14.2K
Average Total Investment*:	$104K
Average On-Going Royalty Fee*:	5.8%

*If a range was provided, the mid-point of the range was used. See detailed profiles for actual ranges.

Five Largest Participants in Survey

Company	# Franchised Units	# Co-Owned Units	# Total Units	Franchise Fee	On-Going Royalty	Total Investment
1. Century 21 Real Estate	7,075	0	7,075	NR	6%	$11.6-522.4K
2. RE/MAX International	5,244	28	5,272	$10-25K	Varies	$20-150K
3. Coldwell Banker Real Estate	2,728	884	3,612	NR	6%	$23.5-477.3K
4. ERA Franchise Systems	2,626	30	2,656	$0-20K	NR	$42.7-205.9K
5. GMAC Home Services	1,300	93	1,393	$7.5-20K	Varies	NR

All of the data provided are proprietary and should not be quoted without acknowledging *Bond's Franchise Guide.*

APARTMENT SELECTOR

P. O. Box 8355
Dallas, TX 75205-0060
Tel: (800) 324-3733 (214) 361-4420
Fax: (214) 361-8677
E-Mail: aptsel@aptselector.com
Web Site: www.aptselector.com
Mr. Kendall A. Laughlin, President

APARTMENT SELECTOR is the nation's oldest and largest FREE apartment and home rental service. Our fee is paid by apartment owners. Extensive training systems for agents and management. Referral network called Official Relocation Network.

BACKGROUND:
Established: 1959; 1st Franchised: 1983
Franchised Units: 24
Company-Owned Units: 0
Total Units: 24
Dist.: US-21; CAN-0; O'seas-0
North America: 6 States
Density: 8 in TX
Projected New Units (12 Months): 2
Qualifications: 3, 3, 4, 3, 1, 1
Registered: All States

FINANCIAL/TERMS:
Cash Investment: $3K+
Total Investment: NR
Minimum Net Worth: NA
Fees: Franchise - $2.5-10K
Royalty - 5%; Ad. - 1%
Earnings Claims Statement: No
Term of Contract (Years): 3/3
Avg. # Of Employees: 3 FT, 3 PT
Passive Ownership: Discouraged
Encourage Conversions: Yes
Area Develop. Agreements: No
Sub-Franchising Contracts: No
Expand In Territory: No
Space Needs: 250 SF; SC

SUPPORT & TRAINING:
Financial Assistance Provided: No
Site Selection Assistance: Yes
Lease Negotiation Assistance: No
Co-Operative Advertising: No
Franchisee Assoc./Member: No
Size Of Corporate Staff: 3
On-Going Support: c,d,E,g,h,I
Training: 1 Week Dallas, TX.

SPECIFIC EXPANSION PLANS:
US: Southeast, West
Canada: No
Overseas: No

<< >>

ASSIST-2-SELL

1610 Meadow Wood Ln.
Reno, NV 89502
Tel: (800) 528-7816 (775) 688-6060
Fax: (775) 823-8823
E-Mail: info@assist2sell.com
Web Site: www.assist2sell.com
Ms. Tara Hartsoch

America's 'full service with savings' discount real estate franchise. Real estate license required. The future of real estate will focus around a 'menu of services' concept. Lower commissions will be the norm. Don't be left behind: catch our vision and step into the future.

BACKGROUND:
Established: 1987; 1st Franchised: 1993
Franchised Units: 341
Company-Owned Units: 1
Total Units: 342
Dist.: US-337; CAN-5; O'seas-0
North America: 44 States, 3 Provinces
Density: 36 in CA, 21 in CO, 12 in MA
Projected New Units (12 Months): 170
Qualifications: 4, 4, 5, 2, 1, 1
Registered:CA,FL,IL,IN,MD,MN,NY,ND,OR,RI,SD,VA,WA,WI

FINANCIAL/TERMS:
Cash Investment: $14.5K
Total Investment: $35-57K
Minimum Net Worth: NA
Fees: Franchise - $14.5-19.5K
Royalty - 5%; Ad. - 0%
Earnings Claims Statement: No
Term of Contract (Years): 5/5
Avg. # Of Employees: 3 FT
Passive Ownership: Not Allowed
Encourage Conversions: Yes
Area Develop. Agreements: No
Sub-Franchising Contracts: No
Expand In Territory: No
Space Needs: 1,000 SF; OB

SUPPORT & TRAINING:
Financial Assistance Provided: No
Site Selection Assistance: Yes
Lease Negotiation Assistance: Yes
Co-Operative Advertising: No
Franchisee Assoc./Member: No
Size Of Corporate Staff: 24
On-Going Support: c,d,G,h,I
Training: 5 Days in Reno, NV.

SPECIFIC EXPANSION PLANS:
US: All United States
Canada: All Canada
Overseas: No

<< >>

BETTER HOMES REALTY

1777 Botelho Dr., # 390
Walnut Creek, CA 94596-8181
Tel: (800) 642-4428 (925) 937-9001
Fax: (925) 988-2770
E-Mail: denise@bhrcorp.com
Web Site: www.bhr.com
Ms. Denise Bucchianeri, Manager Franchise Sales

Established identity, legal hot line support, no institutional advertising fee, franchise cap each calendar year, excellent corporate support, free DRE renewal, corporate advertising, hands-on regional support.

BACKGROUND:
Established: 1964; 1st Franchised: 1969
Franchised Units: 42
Company-Owned Units: 0
Total Units: 42
Dist.: US-40; CAN-0; O'seas-0
North America: 1 State
Density: 39 in CA
Projected New Units (12 Months): 10
Qualifications: 3, 3, 3, 2, 1, 1
Registered: CA

FINANCIAL/TERMS:
Cash Investment: $10-60K
Total Investment: NA
Minimum Net Worth: NA
Fees: Franchise - $9.95K
Royalty - 6% w/Cap/4.5%; Ad. - 0%
Earnings Claims Statement: Yes
Term of Contract (Years): 5/5
Avg. # Of Employees: NA
Passive Ownership: Allowed
Encourage Conversions: Yes
Area Develop. Agreements: NR
Sub-Franchising Contracts: Yes
Expand In Territory: Yes
Space Needs: NA SF; NA

SUPPORT & TRAINING:
Financial Assistance Provided: Yes(I)
Site Selection Assistance: NA
Lease Negotiation Assistance: NA
Co-Operative Advertising: Yes
Franchisee Assoc./Member: No
Size Of Corporate Staff: 7
On-Going Support: b,C,D,G,H,I
Training: Varies. 0.5-1 Day.

SPECIFIC EXPANSION PLANS:
US: West
Canada: No
Overseas: No

<< >>

BUYER'S AGENT, THE

2010 Exeter Rd.
Germantown, TN 38138

Tel: (800) 444-3959 (901) 753-6400
Fax: (901) 756-9610
E-Mail: info@memphisareahomebuyers.com
Web Site: www.forbuyers.com
Mr. Tom Hathaway, Franchise Operations

The nation's oldest and largest real estate franchise in the business of exclusive buyer representation.

BACKGROUND:
Established: 1988; 1st Franchised: 1988
Franchised Units: 62
Company-Owned Units: 0
Total Units: 62
Dist.: US-70; CAN-0; O'seas-0
North America: 28 States
Density: 8 in FL, 8 in CA, 5 in TN
Projected New Units (12 Months): 50
Qualifications: 3, 3, 2, 3, 3, 3
Registered:CA,FL,HI,IN,MD,MI,MN,NY,OR,RI,VA,WA,WI

FINANCIAL/TERMS:
Cash Investment: $20-30K
Total Investment: $25-50K
Minimum Net Worth: $50K
Fees: Franchise - $14.9K
Royalty - 5%; Ad. - 1%
Earnings Claims Statement: No
Term of Contract (Years): 5/5
Avg. # Of Employees: 5-15 FT
Passive Ownership: Discouraged
Encourage Conversions: Yes
Area Develop. Agreements: Consider
Sub-Franchising Contracts: No
Expand In Territory: Yes
Space Needs: 2,000 SF; FS, SF, SC

SUPPORT & TRAINING:
Financial Assistance Provided: Yes(I)
Site Selection Assistance: Yes
Lease Negotiation Assistance: Yes
Co-Operative Advertising: Yes
Franchisee Assoc./Member: No
Size Of Corporate Staff: 12
On-Going Support: A,B,C,D,E,G,H,I
Training: 5 Days Memphis, TN.

SPECIFIC EXPANSION PLANS:
US: All United States
Canada: All Canada
Overseas: No

<< >>

Top 100

CENTURY 21 REAL ESTATE
1 Campus Dr.
Parsippany, NJ 07054
Tel: (877) 221-2765 (973) 428-9700
Fax: (973) 496-5806
E-Mail: brien.mcmahon@cendant.com
Web Site: www.century21.com
Mr. Brien McMahon, EVP Franchise Sales

With more than 131,000 broker and sales associates worldwide, the CENTURY 21 ® system is the world's largest residential real estate organization, providing comprehensive training, management, administrative and marketing support for its members.

BACKGROUND: IFA MEMBER
Established: 1972; 1st Franchised: 1972
Franchised Units: 7,075
Company-Owned Units: 0
Total Units: 7,075
Dist.: US-4,156; CAN-347; O'seas-2,572
North America: 50 States, DC
Density: 513 in CA, 357 in FL, 262 TX
Projected New Units (12 Months): NR
Qualifications: 4, 4, 5, 4, 4, 4
Registered: All States and AB

FINANCIAL/TERMS:
Cash Investment: NR
Total Investment: $11.6-522.4K
Minimum Net Worth: $25K
Fees: Franchise - NR
Royalty - 6%; Ad. - 2%
Earnings Claims Statement: No
Term of Contract (Years): 10
Avg. # Of Employees: Varies
Passive Ownership: Not Allowed
Encourage Conversions: Yes
Area Develop. Agreements: No
Sub-Franchising Contracts: No
Expand In Territory: Yes
Space Needs: 1,000 SF; FS, SF, SC

SUPPORT & TRAINING:
Financial Assistance Provided: No
Site Selection Assistance: No
Lease Negotiation Assistance: No
Co-Operative Advertising: Yes
Franchisee Assoc./Member: Yes/Yes
Size Of Corporate Staff: NR
On-Going Support: A,C,D,E,G,H,I
Training: 5 Days in Parsippany, NJ; 3-7 Sessions on Telephone; 1 Day On-Site.

SPECIFIC EXPANSION PLANS:
US: All United States
Canada: All Canada
Overseas: All Countries

<< >>

COLDWELL BANKER COMMERCIAL
1 Campus Dr.
Parsippany, NJ 07054-0656
Tel: (800) 222-2162 (973) 428-9700
Fax: (973) 496-5639
E-Mail: brien.mcmahon@cendant.com
Web Site: www.coldwellbankercommercial.com
Mr. Brien McMahon, EVP Franchise Sales

COLDWELL BANKER COMMERCIAL is one of the largest commercial franchise operations, with affiliates offering clients comprehensive buying, selling, leasing, acquisition, disposition and management services.

BACKGROUND: IFA MEMBER
Established: 1906; 1st Franchised: 1996
Franchised Units: 75
Company-Owned Units: 0
Total Units: 75
Dist.: US-75; CAN-0; O'seas-0
North America: 32 States
Density: 13 in CA, 9 in TX, 5 in PA
Projected New Units (12 Months): NR
Qualifications: 4, 4, 5, 4, 4, 4
Registered: NR

FINANCIAL/TERMS:
Cash Investment: NR
Total Investment: $37.2-529.4K
Minimum Net Worth: NR
Fees: Franchise - NR
Royalty - 6%; Ad. - $950/Mo/Off
Earnings Claims Statement: No
Term of Contract (Years): 10
Avg. # Of Employees: Varies
Passive Ownership: Not Allowed
Encourage Conversions: Yes
Area Develop. Agreements: No
Sub-Franchising Contracts: No
Expand In Territory: Yes
Space Needs: 1,000 SF; FS, SF, SC,

SUPPORT & TRAINING:
Financial Assistance Provided: No
Site Selection Assistance: No
Lease Negotiation Assistance: No
Co-Operative Advertising: Yes
Franchisee Assoc./Member: Yes
Size Of Corporate Staff: NR
On-Going Support: A,C,D,E,G,H,I
Training: 1-2 Days On-Site.

SPECIFIC EXPANSION PLANS:

US: All United States
Canada: No
Overseas: No

<< >>

Top 100

COLDWELL BANKER REAL ESTATE

1 Campus Dr.
Parsippany, NJ 07054
Tel: (973) 428-9700
Fax: (973) 496-9700
E-Mail: brien.mcmahon@cendant.com
Web Site: www.coldwellbanker.com
Mr. Brien McMahon, EVP Franchise Sales

For 99 years, the COLDWELL BANKER (TM) organization has been the premiere provider of full-service real estate. With more than 3,600 independently and company owned and operated residential real estate offices with approximately 120,000 sales associates globally, the company is an industry leader.

BACKGROUND: IFA MEMBER
Established: 1981; 1st Franchised: 1981
Franchised Units: 2,728
Company-Owned Units: 884
Total Units: 3,612
Dist.: US-3,156; CAN-217; O'seas-239
North America: 50 States, DC
Density: 380 in CA, 255 in FL, 159 TX
Projected New Units (12 Months): NR
Qualifications: 4, 4, 5, 4, 4, 4
Registered: All States and AB

FINANCIAL/TERMS:
Cash Investment: NR
Total Investment: $23.5-477.3K
Minimum Net Worth: $25K
Fees: Franchise - NR
Royalty - 6%; Ad. - 2.5%
Earnings Claims Statement: No
Term of Contract (Years): 10
Avg. # Of Employees: Varies
Passive Ownership: Not Allowed
Encourage Conversions: Yes
Area Develop. Agreements: No
Sub-Franchising Contracts: No
Expand In Territory: Yes
Space Needs: 1,000 SF; FS, SF, SC

SUPPORT & TRAINING:
Financial Assistance Provided: No
Site Selection Assistance: No
Lease Negotiation Assistance: No
Co-Operative Advertising: Yes
Franchisee Assoc./Member: Yes
Size Of Corporate Staff: 100
On-Going Support: A,C,D,E,G,H,I
Training: 4 Days in Parsippany, NJ; 1-2 Days On-Site; Varies via Internet.

SPECIFIC EXPANSION PLANS:
US: All United States
Canada: All Canada
Overseas: All Countries

<< >>

COMMISSION EXPRESS

8306 Professional Hill Dr.
Fairfax, VA 22031
Tel: (888) 560-5501 (703) 560-5500
Fax: (703) 560-5502
E-Mail: manager@commissionexpress.com
Web Site: www.commissionexpress.com
Mr. John L. Stedman, President

We are a true 'white collar' franchise. We offer 'exclusive' territories with professional customers. 9 to 5, no holidays or late nights, a normal life. High profit margin per transaction and a high 80% repeat factor.

BACKGROUND:
Established: 1992; 1st Franchised: 1996
Franchised Units: 55
Company-Owned Units: 1
Total Units: 56
Dist.: US-43; CAN-0; O'seas-0
North America: 30 States
Density: 5 in CA, 4 in FL, 4 in VA
Projected New Units (12 Months): 14
Qualifications: 4, 5, 3, 3, 3, 4
Registered: CA,FL,IL,IN,MD,MI,NY,VA,WA

FINANCIAL/TERMS:
Cash Investment: $34.4-43.7K
Total Investment: $80-180K
Minimum Net Worth: $100K
Fees: Franchise - $10-40K
Royalty - 4.5-9%; Ad. - 1%
Earnings Claims Statement: No
Term of Contract (Years): 10/5
Avg. # Of Employees: 1 FT
Passive Ownership: Discouraged
Encourage Conversions: NA
Area Develop. Agreements: No
Sub-Franchising Contracts: No
Expand In Territory: Yes
Space Needs: 400 SF; NA

SUPPORT & TRAINING:
Financial Assistance Provided: Yes(D)
Site Selection Assistance: Yes
Lease Negotiation Assistance: No
Co-Operative Advertising: Yes
Franchisee Assoc./Member: No
Size Of Corporate Staff: 4
On-Going Support: C,D,G,H,I
Training: 5 Days Fairfax, VA.

SPECIFIC EXPANSION PLANS:
US: All United States
Canada: All Canada
Overseas: No

<< >>

ELLIOTT & COMPANY APPRAISERS

3316 Battleground Ave., # A
Greensboro, NC 27410-2458
Tel: (800) 854-5889 (336) 854-3075
Fax: (336) 854-7734
E-Mail: charlie@elliottco.com
Web Site: www.appraisalsanywhere.com
Mr. Charlie W. Elliott, Jr., President

The franchisor provides a comprehensive package of services designed to assist the franchisee in marketing residential and commercial appraisals and managing the appraisal office.

BACKGROUND:
Established: 1985; 1st Franchised: 1994
Franchised Units: 7
Company-Owned Units: 3
Total Units: 10
Dist.: US-10; CAN-0; O'seas-0
North America: 2 States
Density: 7 in NC, 3 in SC
Projected New Units (12 Months): 4
Qualifications: 3, , 5, , , 4
Registered: FL,VA

FINANCIAL/TERMS:
Cash Investment: $5.1-17.1K
Total Investment: $5.1-17.1K
Minimum Net Worth: NA
Fees: Franchise - $7.5K
Royalty - 8%/$200 Min.; Ad. - 2%/$50 Min.
Earnings Claims Statement: No
Term of Contract (Years): 5/5
Avg. # Of Employees: 1 FT
Passive Ownership: Allowed
Encourage Conversions: No
Area Develop. Agreements: No
Sub-Franchising Contracts: No
Expand In Territory: Yes
Space Needs: NA SF; Commercial Office

SUPPORT & TRAINING:

Financial Assistance Provided: Yes(D)
Site Selection Assistance: Yes
Lease Negotiation Assistance: Yes
Co-Operative Advertising: Yes
Franchisee Assoc./Member: No
Size Of Corporate Staff: 3
On-Going Support: C,D,E,h,I
Training: 2 Days Greensboro, NC.

SPECIFIC EXPANSION PLANS:
US: All United States
Canada: No
Overseas: No

<< >>

ERA FRANCHISE SYSTEMS

1 Campus Dr.
Parsippany, NJ 07054
Tel: (800) 869-1260 (973) 428-9700
Fax: (973) 496-0255
E-Mail: brien.mcmahon@cendant.com
Web Site: www.era.com
Mr. Brien McMahon, EVP Franchise Sales

A network of more than 2,600 brokerages and over 33,000 brokers and sales associates in the U. S. and 26 countries. As the innovator of the popular Sellers Security Plan and the ERA Answers Book, ERA has been developing quality products and services to members and consumers alike since 1971.

BACKGROUND: IFA MEMBER
Established: 1971; 1st Franchised: 1971
Franchised Units: 2,626
Company-Owned Units: 30
Total Units: 2,656
Dist.: US-1,030; CAN-0; O'seas-1,626
North America: 48 States
Density: 124 in CA, 123 in FL, 68 NY
Projected New Units (12 Months): NR
Qualifications: 4, 4, 5, 4, 4, 4
Registered: All States

FINANCIAL/TERMS:
Cash Investment: NR
Total Investment: $42.7-205.9K
Minimum Net Worth: $25K
Fees: Franchise - $0-20K
Royalty - NR; Ad. - 2%
Earnings Claims Statement: No
Term of Contract (Years): 5/10
Avg. # Of Employees: Varies
Passive Ownership: Not Allowed
Encourage Conversions: Yes
Area Develop. Agreements: No
Sub-Franchising Contracts: No
Expand In Territory: Yes
Space Needs: 1,000 SF; FS, SF, SC

SUPPORT & TRAINING:
Financial Assistance Provided: No
Site Selection Assistance: No
Lease Negotiation Assistance: No
Co-Operative Advertising: Yes
Franchisee Assoc./Member: Yes/Yes
Size Of Corporate Staff: NR
On-Going Support: A,C,D,E,G,H,I
Training: 1 Week in Parsippany, NJ; 2-3 days On-Site

SPECIFIC EXPANSION PLANS:
US: All United States
Canada: All Canada
Overseas: All Countries

<< >>

GMAC HOME SERVICES

2021 Spring Rd., # 300
Oak Brook, IL 60523
Tel: (800) 274-7661 (630) 214-1664
Fax: (866) 432-4432
E-Mail: michael_eason@gmachs.com
Web Site: www.gmacrealestate.com
Mr. Michael Eason, Franchise Qualification Specialist

GMAC HOME SERVICES is one of the nation's largest real estate organizations, delivering Premier Service to home buyers and sellers through its three operating companies - GMAC Real Estate, GHS Mortgage and GMAC Global Relocation Services. Backed by the resources of industry giant General Motors, the GMAC HOME SERVICES network has more than 1,300 franchised and owned residential real estate offices throughout the United States.

BACKGROUND: IFA MEMBER
Established: 1998; 1st Franchised: 1998
Franchised Units: 1,300
Company-Owned Units: 93
Total Units: 1,393
Dist.: US-1,360; CAN-32; O'seas-0
North America: 50 States, 5 Provinces
Density: 114 in CA, 86 in FL, 83 in F
Projected New Units (12 Months): 28
Qualifications: 4, 4, 4, 4, 3, 4
Registered: All States

FINANCIAL/TERMS:
Cash Investment: NR
Total Investment: NR
Minimum Net Worth: NR
Fees: Franchise - $7.5-20K
Royalty - Varies; Ad. - Varies
Earnings Claims Statement: No
Term of Contract (Years): 5/7/10
Avg. # Of Employees: 4 FT
Passive Ownership: Allowed
Encourage Conversions: Yes
Area Develop. Agreements: No
Sub-Franchising Contracts: No
Expand In Territory: No
Space Needs: 1,800 SF; NR

SUPPORT & TRAINING:
Financial Assistance Provided: Yes(D)
Site Selection Assistance: No
Lease Negotiation Assistance: No
Co-Operative Advertising: No
Franchisee Assoc./Member: No
Size Of Corporate Staff: 45
On-Going Support: C,d,E,G,H,I
Training: 1 Week Oak Brook, IL.

SPECIFIC EXPANSION PLANS:
US: All United States
Canada: All Canada
Overseas: Europe

<< >>

GROUP TRANS-ACTION BROKERAGE SERVICES

550 Sherbrooke St. W., # 775, W. Tower
Montreal, PQ H3A 1B9 CANADA
Tel: (514) 288-6777
Fax: (514) 288-7543
E-Mail: gta@trans-action.qc.ca
Web Site: www.trans-action.qc.ca
Mr. Richard Payeur, General Manager

Group of independent real estate brokers everywhere in Quebec. Complete real estate services.

BACKGROUND:
Established: 1979; 1st Franchised: 1982
Franchised Units: 64
Company-Owned Units: 0
Total Units: 64
Dist.: US-0; CAN-64; O'seas-0
North America: 1 Province
Density: 55 in PQ
Projected New Units (12 Months): 6
Qualifications: , , , , ,
Registered: AB

FINANCIAL/TERMS:
Cash Investment: $10K

Total Investment: $10-50K
Minimum Net Worth: NR
Fees: Franchise - $6-17K
Royalty - Flat; Ad. - Flat
Earnings Claims Statement: No
Term of Contract (Years): 5/1
Avg. # Of Employees: 10 FT
Passive Ownership: Not Allowed
Encourage Conversions: NA
Area Develop. Agreements: Yes
Sub-Franchising Contracts: No
Expand In Territory: Yes
Space Needs: 1,000 SF; FS, SF

SUPPORT & TRAINING:

Financial Assistance Provided: Yes(I)
Site Selection Assistance: Yes
Lease Negotiation Assistance: Yes
Co-Operative Advertising: Yes
Franchisee Assoc./Member: NR
Size Of Corporate Staff: 4
On-Going Support: a,b,c,D,E,f,G,H,i
Training: 1 Week Headquarters.

SPECIFIC EXPANSION PLANS:

US: No
Canada: All Canada
Overseas: No

≺≺ ≻≻

HELP-U-SELL

6800 Jericho Tpk., # 208E
Syosset, NY 11791
Tel: (800) 366-1177 (516) 364-9650
Fax: (516) 364-8757
E-Mail: info@helpusell.com
Web Site: www.helpusell.com
Ms. Sharon Dailey, Director Franchise Sales

HELP-U-SELL is the nation's first and largest fee-for-service real estate franchise. Rated not only as one of the best franchises, but one of the fastest-growing, HELP-U-SELL is revitalizing the real estate industry with programs and strategies that allow consumers to save money and real estate professionals to achieve higher profits. With hundreds of offices throughout the country and rapidly increasing numbers, HELP-U-SELL dominates in the state-of-the-art fee-for-services category.

BACKGROUND:

Established: 1976; 1st Franchised: 1976
Franchised Units: 504
Company-Owned Units: 0
Total Units: 504
Dist.: US-504; CAN-0; O'seas-0
North America: 45 States
Density: 287 in CA, 31 in FL, 23 AZ
Projected New Units (12 Months): 350
Qualifications: 4, 4, 5, 3, 3, 4
Registered:CA,FL,HI,IN,MD,MI,OR,RI,SD,WA,WI,DC,AB

FINANCIAL/TERMS:

Cash Investment: $10K
Total Investment: $30-100K
Minimum Net Worth: NA
Fees: Franchise - $19.5K
Royalty - 6%; Ad. - 1.5%
Earnings Claims Statement: No
Term of Contract (Years): 5/5
Avg. # Of Employees: 4-10 FT
Passive Ownership: Discouraged
Encourage Conversions: Yes
Area Develop. Agreements: Yes
Sub-Franchising Contracts: Yes
Expand In Territory: Yes
Space Needs: 1,000 SF; FS, SF, SC, RM, Exec. Suite

SUPPORT & TRAINING:

Financial Assistance Provided: No
Site Selection Assistance: Yes
Lease Negotiation Assistance: No
Co-Operative Advertising: Yes
Franchisee Assoc./Member: Yes
Size Of Corporate Staff: 50
On-Going Support: c,D,e,G,h,I
Training: 4 Days San Diego, CA.

SPECIFIC EXPANSION PLANS:

US: All United States
Canada: All Canada
Overseas: No

≺≺ ≻≻

HER REAL ESTATE

77 E. Nationwide Blvd.
Columbus, OH 43215-2539
Tel: (800) 848-7400 (614) 459-7400
Fax: (614) 459-5417
E-Mail: karen.workman@herrealtors.com
Web Site: www.herrealtors.com
Ms. Karen S. Workman, Director Franchising

Personalized approach to real estate financing. Brokers keep their own identity and marks of franchisor do not detract or dominate. On-location educational opportunities. Franchisee offered exclusive territory, test-marketed, award-winning marketing tools and techniques. Support program through field representation, continuing education and other unique educational opportunities.

BACKGROUND:

Established: 1976; 1st Franchised: 1981
Franchised Units: 11
Company-Owned Units: 21
Total Units: 32
Dist.: US-32; CAN-0; O'seas-0
North America: 1 State
Density: 32 in OH
Projected New Units (12 Months): 6
Qualifications: , , , , ,
Registered: NR

FINANCIAL/TERMS:

Cash Investment: NR
Total Investment: $9.3-103K
Minimum Net Worth: NR
Fees: Franchise - $2.5-80K
Royalty - 5%; Ad. - 1%
Earnings Claims Statement: Yes
Term of Contract (Years): 5/5
Avg. # Of Employees: NR
Passive Ownership: Not Allowed
Encourage Conversions: Yes
Area Develop. Agreements: No
Sub-Franchising Contracts: Yes
Expand In Territory: Yes
Space Needs: NR SF; NA

SUPPORT & TRAINING:

Financial Assistance Provided: Yes(I)
Site Selection Assistance: NA
Lease Negotiation Assistance: No
Co-Operative Advertising: Yes
Franchisee Assoc./Member: NR
Size Of Corporate Staff: 22
On-Going Support: D,E,F,G,H,I
Training: 2 Weeks Headquarters.

SPECIFIC EXPANSION PLANS:

US: OH Only
Canada: No
Overseas: No

≺≺ ≻≻

HOMEOWNERS CONCEPT

611 N. Mayfair Rd.
Wauwatosa, WI 53226
Tel: (800) 800-9890 (414) 258-7778
Fax: (414) 258-8276
E-Mail: hoc@execpc.com
Web Site: www.homeownersconcept.com
Mr. Peter M. Skanavis, President

HOMEOWNERS CONCEPT offers a unique flat fee real estate program of consulting/sales. Extremely efficient, high-volume, very profitable operation on the cutting edge of providing "value" to the consumer. Large, exclusive territory.

BACKGROUND:

Established: 1982; 1st Franchised: 1984
Franchised Units: 34
Company-Owned Units: 0
Total Units: 34

Dist.: US-38; CAN-1; O'seas-0
North America: 8 States, 1 Province
Density: 7 in WI, 6 in OH, 4 in TX
Projected New Units (12 Months): 15
Qualifications: 2, 4, 3, 2, 4, 5
Registered: IL,WI,NY,FL,WA

FINANCIAL/TERMS:

Cash Investment: $16-20K
Total Investment: $16-20K
Minimum Net Worth: $50K
Fees: Franchise - $4.5K
Royalty - 3%; Ad. - NR
Earnings Claims Statement: No
Term of Contract (Years): 10/10
Avg. # Of Employees: 5 FT
Passive Ownership: Not Allowed
Encourage Conversions: Yes
Area Develop. Agreements: No
Sub-Franchising Contracts: No
Expand In Territory: Yes
Space Needs: 700 SF; OB

SUPPORT & TRAINING:

Financial Assistance Provided: No
Site Selection Assistance: Yes
Lease Negotiation Assistance: No
Co-Operative Advertising: No
Franchisee Assoc./Member: No
Size Of Corporate Staff: 2
On-Going Support: d,G,H,I
Training: 1 Week Milwaukee, WI.

SPECIFIC EXPANSION PLANS:

US: All United States
Canada: All Canada
Overseas: No

<< >>

HOMEVESTORS OF AMERICA

10670 N. Central Expy., # 700
Dallas, TX 75231
Tel: (888) 495-5220 (972) 761-0046
Fax: (404) 688-5081
E-Mail: hvmarketing@homevestors.com
Web Site: www.homevestors.com
Mr. Terry Demarest, Franchise Sales

HOMEVESTORS franchise owners are real estate investors that specialize in buying and selling single-family houses. The franchise provides a system to by houses wholesale; financing to purchase houses; training and other services.

BACKGROUND: IFA MEMBER

Established: 1989; 1st Franchised: 1996
Franchised Units: 245
Company-Owned Units: 0
Total Units: 245
Dist.: US-33; CAN-0; O'seas-0
North America: 6 States
Density: 13 in TX, 3 in FL, 3 in MO
Projected New Units (12 Months): 15
Qualifications: 4, 4, 3, 2, 4, 5
Registered: NR

FINANCIAL/TERMS:

Cash Investment: $75-125K
Total Investment: $151-180K
Minimum Net Worth: $100K
Fees: Franchise - $25-35K
Royalty - $775/Transaction; Ad. - $125/Trans.
Earnings Claims Statement: No
Term of Contract (Years): 5/5
Avg. # Of Employees: 3 FT, 1 PT
Passive Ownership: Discouraged
Encourage Conversions: Yes
Area Develop. Agreements: No
Sub-Franchising Contracts: No
Expand In Territory: No
Space Needs: 500 SF; SF

SUPPORT & TRAINING:

Financial Assistance Provided: No
Site Selection Assistance: Yes
Lease Negotiation Assistance: No
Co-Operative Advertising: No
Franchisee Assoc./Member: No
Size Of Corporate Staff: 14
On-Going Support: A,C,D,E,G,H
Training: 5 Days in Dallas, TX; 2 Days at Franchise Location.

SPECIFIC EXPANSION PLANS:

US: Southwest, Southeast
Canada: No
Overseas: No

<< >>

NATIONAL TENANT NETWORK

525 SW First, # 105, P.O. Box 1664
Lake Oswego, OR 97034
Tel: (800) 228-0989 (503) 635-1118
Fax: (503) 638-2450
E-Mail: ntn@ntnnet.com
Web Site: www.ntnnet.com
Mr. Edward F. Byczynski, President

NATIONAL TENANT NETWORK (NTN) is a network providing tenant screening services to the real estate industry. Through the NTN centralized data system of nationally networked servers, subscribers have instant access to the data maintained exclusively by NTN in 21 states. Automated, 24-hour a day, 7 days a week access through phone, fax, PC and modem and over the Internet. On-line service provides tenant performance data, retail credit reports, analysis, scoring, etc. On-line reports in 15-seconds.

BACKGROUND:

Established: 1980; 1st Franchised: 1987
Franchised Units: 25
Company-Owned Units: 2
Total Units: 27
Dist.: US-25; CAN-0; O'seas-0
North America: 21 States
Density: 4 in TX, 2 in CA, 2 in NJ
Projected New Units (12 Months): 4
Qualifications: 2, 3, 2, 4, 4, 3
Registered: CA,FL,IL,IN,OR,VA,WA,AB

FINANCIAL/TERMS:

Cash Investment: $40-65K
Total Investment: $80-100K
Minimum Net Worth: NA
Fees: Franchise - $25K
Royalty - 10%; Ad. - 2%
Earnings Claims Statement: No
Term of Contract (Years): 10/10
Avg. # Of Employees: 2 FT, 1 PT
Passive Ownership: Discouraged
Encourage Conversions: NA
Area Develop. Agreements: Yes/10
Sub-Franchising Contracts: No
Expand In Territory: Yes
Space Needs: 300-500 SF; FS

SUPPORT & TRAINING:

Financial Assistance Provided: Yes(D)
Site Selection Assistance: No
Lease Negotiation Assistance: No
Co-Operative Advertising: Yes
Franchisee Assoc./Member: No
Size Of Corporate Staff: 10
On-Going Support: a,B,C,D,E,G,H,I
Training: 2 Weeks Franchisee Location.

SPECIFIC EXPANSION PLANS:

US: All United States
Canada: All Canada
Overseas: No

<< >>

RE/MAX INTERNATIONAL

P. O. Box 3907
Englewood, CO 80155-3907
Tel: (800) 525-7452 (303) 770-5531
Fax: (303) 796-3599
E-Mail: petergilmour@remax.net

Web Site: www.remax.com
Mr. Peter Gilmour, VP Intl. Franchising/ Brokerage

The RE/MAX real estate franchise network, now in its 32nd year of consecutive growth, is a global system of more than 5,300 offices worldwide, engaging more than 100,000 members. RE/MAX sales associates lead the industry in professional designations, experience and production while providing real estate services in residential, commercial, referral, relocation and asset management. For more information visit www.remax.com.

BACKGROUND: IFA MEMBER
Established: 1973; 1st Franchised: 1975
Franchised Units: 5,244
Company-Owned Units: 28
Total Units: 5,272
Dist.: US-3,490; CAN-575; O'seas-1,207
North America: 50 States,12 Provinces
Density: 388 in CA, 226 in TX, 174 IL
Projected New Units (12 Months): 550
Qualifications: 3, 4, 5, 1, 4, 4
Registered: All States

FINANCIAL/TERMS:
Cash Investment: $20-200K
Total Investment: $20-150K
Minimum Net Worth: Varies
Fees: Franchise - $10-25K
Royalty - Varies; Ad. - Varies
Earnings Claims Statement: No
Term of Contract (Years): 5/5
Avg. # Of Employees: 2-4 FT, 1 PT
Passive Ownership: Discouraged
Encourage Conversions: Yes
Area Develop. Agreements: No
Sub-Franchising Contracts: Yes
Expand In Territory: Varies
Space Needs: Varies SF; FS, SF, SC, RM

SUPPORT & TRAINING:
Financial Assistance Provided: Yes(D)
Site Selection Assistance: Yes
Lease Negotiation Assistance: Yes
Co-Operative Advertising: NA
Franchisee Assoc./Member: No
Size Of Corporate Staff: 250
On-Going Support: C,D,G,h,I
Training: 40+ Hours at Headquarters in Englewood, CO.

SPECIFIC EXPANSION PLANS:
US: All United States
Canada: All Canada
Overseas: All Free World Countries. Already in 39 countries. Yet to open in Japan.

<< >>

REALTY EXECUTIVES INTERNATIONAL

2398 E. Camelback Rd., # 900
Phoenix, AZ 85016
Tel: (800) 252-3366 (602) 957-0747
Fax: (602) 224-5542
E-Mail: billpowers@realtyexecutives.com
Web Site: www.realtyexecutives.com
Mr. William A. Powers, Chief Operating Officer

The originators of the 100% Commission Concept. Awarding franchises to use the REALTY EXECUTIVES' name.

BACKGROUND:
Established: 1965; 1st Franchised: 1987
Franchised Units: 70
Company-Owned Units: 0
Total Units: 70
Dist.: US-640; CAN-35; O'seas-25
North America: 45 States, 5 Provinces
Density: NR
Projected New Units (12 Months): 150
Qualifications: 4, 5, 5, 2, 3, 4
Registered: NR

FINANCIAL/TERMS:
Cash Investment: $25K
Total Investment: $25-82.5K
Minimum Net Worth: $30-50K
Fees: Franchise - $15K
Royalty - $35-50/Agent/Mo; Ad. - $5-10/Agent
Earnings Claims Statement: No
Term of Contract (Years): 5/5
Avg. # Of Employees: 1 FT
Passive Ownership: Allowed
Encourage Conversions: Yes
Area Develop. Agreements: Yes/5
Sub-Franchising Contracts: Yes
Expand In Territory: Yes
Space Needs: NR SF; NA

SUPPORT & TRAINING:
Financial Assistance Provided: No
Site Selection Assistance: No
Lease Negotiation Assistance: No
Co-Operative Advertising: Yes
Franchisee Assoc./Member: No
Size Of Corporate Staff: 12
On-Going Support: G,h,I
Training: 4 Days at Company Headquarters in Phoenix.

SPECIFIC EXPANSION PLANS:
US: All United States
Canada: All Canada
Overseas: All Countries

<< >>

RED CARPET KEIM REAL ESTATE

189 E. Big Beaver, # 209
Troy, MI 48088
Tel: (800) 355-0744 (248) 680-7300
Fax: (248) 680-3014
E-Mail: rckeim@aol.com
Web Site: www.redcarpetrealestate.com
Ms. Betty Main, Corporate General Manager

RED CARPET REAL ESTATE is one of the oldest franchise real estate sales organizations in the nation. Founded in 1966, RED CARPET has become a trusted household name for generations. We provide our members with the latest marketing tools and training available. At RED CARPET, our goal is complete client satisfaction.

BACKGROUND:
Established: 1966; 1st Franchised: 1970
Franchised Units: 69
Company-Owned Units: 0
Total Units: 69
Dist.: US-69; CAN-0; O'seas-0
North America: 3 States
Density: 48 in MI, 20 in CA, 1 in TX
Projected New Units (12 Months): NR
Qualifications: , , , , ,
Registered:

FINANCIAL/TERMS:
Cash Investment: $7.5K
Total Investment: Varies
Minimum Net Worth: $10K
Fees: Franchise - $7.5K
Royalty - 5%; Ad. - .5%
Earnings Claims Statement: NR
Term of Contract (Years): 5/5
Avg. # Of Employees: 2 FT
Passive Ownership: Discouraged
Encourage Conversions: NR
Area Develop. Agreements: No
Sub-Franchising Contracts: No
Expand In Territory: Yes
Space Needs: NR SF; FS, SF, SC, RM

SUPPORT & TRAINING:
Financial Assistance Provided: NR
Site Selection Assistance: NA
Lease Negotiation Assistance: NA
Co-Operative Advertising: NA
Franchisee Assoc./Member: NR
Size Of Corporate Staff: 4
On-Going Support: D,G,H
Training: Qusrterly Meetings.

SPECIFIC EXPANSION PLANS:
US: All United States
Canada: NR
Overseas: NR

<< >>

REMERICA REAL ESTATE

40500 Ann Arbor Rd., # 102
Plymouth, MI 48170
Tel: (800) REM-ERICA (734) 459-4500
Fax: (734) 459-1566
E-Mail: info@remerica.com
Web Site: www.remerica.com
Mr. Jeffrey Hodges, VP Marketing

A cutting-edge residential real estate franchising organization. We offer broker, agent (experience and new), training, secretarial training, assist in recruiting, your own dynamic and interactive Website, intranet, technical support, TV and print advertising. See www.remerica.com and REMERICA FINANCIAL AND TITLE GROUP.

BACKGROUND:

Established: 1988; 1st Franchised: 1990
Franchised Units: 41
Company-Owned Units: 0
Total Units: 41
Dist.: US-32; CAN-0; O'seas-0
North America: 1 State
Density: 34 in MI
Projected New Units (12 Months): 10
Qualifications: 5, 4, 5, 4, 2, 5
Registered: NR

FINANCIAL/TERMS:

Cash Investment: $15-70K
Total Investment: $20-100K
Minimum Net Worth: $25-100K
Fees: Franchise - $10K
Royalty - 6%; Ad. - 2%
Earnings Claims Statement: No
Term of Contract (Years): 5/5
Avg. # Of Employees: NR
Passive Ownership: Discouraged
Encourage Conversions: Yes
Area Develop. Agreements: No
Sub-Franchising Contracts: No
Expand In Territory: Yes
Space Needs: NR SF; FS, SF, SC, RM

SUPPORT & TRAINING:

Financial Assistance Provided: Yes(I)
Site Selection Assistance: Yes
Lease Negotiation Assistance: Yes
Co-Operative Advertising: Yes
Franchisee Assoc./Member: No
Size Of Corporate Staff: 12
On-Going Support: A,B,C,D,E,F,G,H,I
Training: 20+ Hours Plymouth, MI.

SPECIFIC EXPANSION PLANS:

US: All United States
Canada: All Canada
Overseas: No

<< >>

TUCKER ASSOCIATES

9279 N. Meridian St., # 100
Indianapolis, IN 46260
Tel: (800) 659-0432 (317) 571-2200
Fax: (317) 571-2204
E-Mail: mbush@talktotucker.com
Web Site: www.talktotucker.com
Mr. Mark Bush, Senior Vice President

Real estate franchisor for the State of Indiana, offering marketing, recruiting, training and relocation leads for franchisees. Number one company in Indiana and recently named # 10 brand name of independently owned companies.

BACKGROUND:

Established: 1918; 1st Franchised: 1989
Franchised Units: 23
Company-Owned Units: 14
Total Units: 37
Dist.: US-37; CAN-0; O'seas-0
North America: 1 State
Density: 33 in IN
Projected New Units (12 Months): 3-4
Qualifications: 5, 5, 5, 3, 4, 5
Registered: IL,IN

FINANCIAL/TERMS:

Cash Investment: $100-200K
Total Investment: $125-250K
Minimum Net Worth: $25K
Fees: Franchise - $0
Royalty - 6%; Ad. - 0%
Earnings Claims Statement: No
Term of Contract (Years): 6/5
Avg. # Of Employees: 1-2 FT, 3 PT
Passive Ownership: Discouraged
Encourage Conversions: Yes
Area Develop. Agreements: No
Sub-Franchising Contracts: No
Expand In Territory: Yes
Space Needs: 1,500 SF; FS, SF, SC

SUPPORT & TRAINING:

Financial Assistance Provided: Yes
Site Selection Assistance: Yes
Lease Negotiation Assistance: Yes
Co-Operative Advertising: NA
Franchisee Assoc./Member: No
Size Of Corporate Staff: 3
On-Going Support: a,B,C,D,E,G,h
Training: 2 Weeks Indianapolis, IN.

SPECIFIC EXPANSION PLANS:

US: IN, Surrounding States
Canada: No
Overseas: No

<< >>

Recreation & Entertainment

Chapter 32

RECREATION & ENTERTAINMENT INDUSTRY PROFILE

Total # Franchisors in Industry Group	38
Total # Franchised Units in Industry Group	2,184
Total # Company-Owned Units in Industry Group	135
Total # Operating Units in Industry Group	2,319
Average # Franchised Units/Franchisor	57.5
Average # Company-Owned Units/Franchisor	3.6
Average # Total Units/Franchisor	61
Ratio of Total # Franchised Units/Total # Company-Owned Units	16.2:1
Industry Survey Participants	11
Representing % of Industry	28.9%
Average Franchise Fee*:	$20.9K
Average Total Investment*:	$429.2K
Average On-Going Royalty Fee*:	9.1%

*If a range was provided, the mid-point of the range was used. See detailed profiles for actual ranges.

FIVE LARGEST PARTICIPANTS IN SURVEY

Company	# Franchised Units	# Co-Owned Units	# Total Units	Franchise Fee	On-Going Royalty	Total Investment
1. American Poolplayers Association	284	0	284	Varies	20%	$11-15K
2. World Gym International	278	0	278	$13K	$7K/Yr.	$300K-1MM
3. Complete Music	161	1	162	$15.5K	8%	$15.5-35K
4. Putt-Putt Golf Courses of America	132	0	132	$25-50K	5%	$1.5K-5MM
5. Fred Astaire Dance Studios	100	0	100	$15-35K	7-8%	$138.5-357K

All of the data provided are proprietary and should not be quoted without acknowledging *Bond's Franchise Guide.*

AMERICAN DARTERS ASSOCIATION

1000 Lake St. Louis Blvd., # 310
Lake St. Louis, MO 63367
Tel: (888) 327-8752 (636) 625-8621
Fax: (636) 625-2975
E-Mail: adapres@adadarters.com
Web Site: www.adadarters.com
Mr. Glenn Remick, President

ADA franchisees offer recreational dart leagues using the Neutralizer, a copyrighted handicap system that neutralizes play. The league currently consists of 15,000 members who compete in year-round weekly play. Franchisees receive customized software, complete training, technical updates, support and networking opportunities at the national convention.

BACKGROUND:
Established: 1990; 1st Franchised: 1991
Franchised Units: 75
Company-Owned Units: 0
Total Units: 75
Dist.: US-75; CAN-0; O'seas-0
North America: 26 States
Density: TX, IL, MO
Projected New Units (12 Months): 12
Qualifications: 3, 3, 3, 3, 3, 2
Registered: All States Except OR,AB

FINANCIAL/TERMS:
Cash Investment: $1-2.3K
Total Investment: $1.5-2.8K
Minimum Net Worth: Varies
Fees: Franchise - $By Population
Royalty - 20%; Ad. - NA
Earnings Claims Statement: No
Term of Contract (Years): 1.5/5
Avg. # Of Employees: Varies
Passive Ownership: Not Allowed
Encourage Conversions: NA
Area Develop. Agreements: No
Sub-Franchising Contracts: No
Expand In Territory: Yes
Space Needs: NA SF; NA

SUPPORT & TRAINING:
Financial Assistance Provided: No
Site Selection Assistance: Yes
Lease Negotiation Assistance: NA
Co-Operative Advertising: No
Franchisee Assoc./Member: No
Size Of Corporate Staff: 2
On-Going Support: A,B,C,D,F,G,H,I
Training: 3 Days Lake Saint Louis, MO.

SPECIFIC EXPANSION PLANS:
US: All United States
Canada: No
Overseas: No

AMERICAN POOLPLAYERS ASSOCIATION

1000 Lake St. Louis Blvd., # 325
Lake St. Louis, MO 63367-1340
Tel: (800) 372-2536 (636) 625-8611 + 5118
Fax: (636) 625-2975
E-Mail: ddavis@poolplayers.com
Web Site: www.poolplayers.com
Mr. Doug Davis, Franchise Development Assist.

APA franchisees operate recreational pool leagues utilizing "The Equalizer", a unique handicap system that equalizes play. The League, previously known as the Bud Light Pool League or the Camel pool League, and now known nationally as the "APA Pool League", currently consists of over 230,000 members who compete in year-round weekly play. Franchisees receive customized software, technical updates, complete training, marketing support and networking opportunities at the annual convention.

BACKGROUND: IFA MEMBER
Established: 1980; 1st Franchised: 1982
Franchised Units: 284
Company-Owned Units: 0
Total Units: 284
Dist.: US-267; CAN-17; O'seas-0
North America: 46 States, 6 Provinces
Density: 23 in FL, 17 in IL, 15 in ON
Projected New Units (12 Months): 20
Qualifications: 3, 3, 2, 2, 1, 5
Registered: All States

FINANCIAL/TERMS:
Cash Investment: $11-15K
Total Investment: $11-15K
Minimum Net Worth: NA
Fees: Franchise - Varies
Royalty - 20%; Ad. - NA
Earnings Claims Statement: No
Term of Contract (Years): 2/5/10
Avg. # Of Employees: Varies
Passive Ownership: Not Allowed
Encourage Conversions: NA
Area Develop. Agreements: No
Sub-Franchising Contracts: No
Expand In Territory: NA
Space Needs: NA SF; HB

SUPPORT & TRAINING:
Financial Assistance Provided: No
Site Selection Assistance: Yes
Lease Negotiation Assistance: NA
Co-Operative Advertising: Yes
Franchisee Assoc./Member: Yes/No
Size Of Corporate Staff: 50
On-Going Support: A,D,G,H
Training: 6 Days APA Home Office.

SPECIFIC EXPANSION PLANS:
US: All United States
Canada: All Canada
Overseas: No

<< >>

COMPLETE MUSIC

7877 "L" St.
Omaha, NE 68127
Tel: (800) 843-3866 (402) 339-0001
Fax: (402) 898-1777
E-Mail: eric@cmusic.com
Web Site: www.cmusic.com
Mr. Eric Mass, Franchise Director

COMPLETE MUSIC is the leader in disc jockey entertainment, providing dance music for over 1 million people each year. The uniqueness of this business allows owners, who need not be entertainers, to use their skills in management to hire and book their own musically trained DJ's for all types of special events.

BACKGROUND:
Established: 1972; 1st Franchised: 1982
Franchised Units: 161
Company-Owned Units: 1
Total Units: 162
Dist.: US-140; CAN-4; O'seas-0
North America: 31 States, 1 Province
Density: 21 in TX, 11 in NE, 8 in CO
Projected New Units (12 Months): 6-12
Qualifications: 3, 4, 1, 4, 4, 3
Registered:CA,FL,IL,IN,MD,MI,MN,OR, SD,WA,WI

FINANCIAL/TERMS:
Cash Investment: $9.5-24.5K
Total Investment: $15.5-35K
Minimum Net Worth: NA
Fees: Franchise - $15.5K
Royalty - 8%; Ad. - 4%
Earnings Claims Statement: Yes
Term of Contract (Years): Lifetime
Avg. # Of Employees: 2 FT, 5-40 PT
Passive Ownership: Discouraged

Encourage Conversions: Yes
Area Develop. Agreements: No
Sub-Franchising Contracts: No
Expand In Territory: Yes
Space Needs: NA SF; HB

SUPPORT & TRAINING:
Financial Assistance Provided: Yes(D)
Site Selection Assistance: Yes
Lease Negotiation Assistance: Yes
Co-Operative Advertising: Yes
Franchisee Assoc./Member: Yes/Yes
Size Of Corporate Staff: 5
On-Going Support: B,c,D,E,F,G,h,i
Training: 9 Days Omaha, NE; 4 Days On-Site.

SPECIFIC EXPANSION PLANS:
US: All United States
Canada: All Canada
Overseas: No

<< >>

FRED ASTAIRE DANCE STUDIOS

10 Bliss Rd.
Longmeadow, MA 01106
Tel: (800) 278-2473 (413) 567-3200
Fax: (413) 565-2455
E-Mail: dancefads@aol.com
Web Site: www.fredastaire.com
Mr. Andy Kreig, Franchise Manager

FRED ASTAIRE DANCE STUDIOS (FADS) provides its franchised community with a 50+ year tradition that gives the individual franchisee worldwide name recognition identified with dance excellence unsurpassed in its industry. The original teaching methods of the great Fred Astaire are still in place today at the company that proudly bears his name. FADS provides its franchisees with extensive business and dance training, and ensures that its franchises operate under the strictest code of ethics.

BACKGROUND:
Established: 1947; 1st Franchised: 1950
Franchised Units: 100
Company-Owned Units: 0
Total Units: 100
Dist.: US-110; CAN-6; O'seas-0
North America: 28 States, 1 Province
Density: 16 in FL, 13 in NY, 12 in OH
Projected New Units (12 Months): 8-10
Qualifications: 5, 4, 3, 2, 2, 5
Registered: CA,FL,MD,MN,NY,OR,RI, VA,WI

FINANCIAL/TERMS:
Cash Investment: $125K
Total Investment: $138.5-357K
Minimum Net Worth: $150K
Fees: Franchise - $15-35K
Royalty - 7-8%; Ad. - 0.2%/$25Min
Earnings Claims Statement: No
Term of Contract (Years): 5/5
Avg. # Of Employees: 10 FT
Passive Ownership: Discouraged
Encourage Conversions: Yes
Area Develop. Agreements: No
Sub-Franchising Contracts: Yes
Expand In Territory: Yes
Space Needs: 2,500 Min. SF; FS, SC

SUPPORT & TRAINING:
Financial Assistance Provided: Yes(I)
Site Selection Assistance: Yes
Lease Negotiation Assistance: Yes
Co-Operative Advertising: Yes
Franchisee Assoc./Member: No
Size Of Corporate Staff: 9
On-Going Support: A,b,c,d,E,f,G,h,I
Training: 8 Hours Dance or Management (Franchisee's Site) or 16 Hours Management (Existing Site).

SPECIFIC EXPANSION PLANS:
US: All United States
Canada: All Canada
Overseas: Under Trade Name Megadance International

<< >>

i9 SPORTS

1723 S. Kings Ave.
Brandon, FL 33511
Tel: (800) 975-2937 (813) 662-6773
Fax: (813) 662-9114
E-Mail: FranchiseSales@i9sports.com
Web Site: www.i9sports.com
Mr. Allen Castleman, Executive Vice President

i9 SPORTS is the world's first complete amateur sports franchise for the 100 million youth and adult athletes nationwide. i9 SPORTS offers franchise opportunities for people to own and operate local amateur sports leagues, tournaments, camps, clinics, special events and corporate outings for people of all ages. i9 SPORTS provides a low-investment, low-overhead, fully-computerized business that you can run from home. Turn your love of amateur sports into a rewarding home-based business.

BACKGROUND: IFA MEMBER
Established: 2002; 1st Franchised: 2003
Franchised Units: 31
Company-Owned Units: 2
Total Units: 33
Dist.: US-33; CAN-0; O'seas-0
North America: 12 States
Density: 8 in FL, 6 in NY, 2 in PA
Projected New Units (12 Months): 30
Qualifications: 4, 4, 4, 4, 4, 4
Registered: All States

FINANCIAL/TERMS:
Cash Investment: $26-49.9K
Total Investment: $26-49.9K
Minimum Net Worth: $100K
Fees: Franchise - $12.5-18.5K
Royalty - 7.5%; Ad. - $275/Mo.
Earnings Claims Statement: Yes
Term of Contract (Years): 10/10
Avg. # Of Employees: 0-1 FT, 0-1 PT
Passive Ownership: Not Allowed
Encourage Conversions: Yes
Area Develop. Agreements: No
Sub-Franchising Contracts: No
Expand In Territory: Yes
Space Needs: NA SF; HB

SUPPORT & TRAINING:
Financial Assistance Provided: No
Site Selection Assistance: Yes
Lease Negotiation Assistance: NA
Co-Operative Advertising: Yes
Franchisee Assoc./Member: Yes/Yes
Size Of Corporate Staff: 7
On-Going Support: B,C,G,H,I
Training: 5 Days Tampa, FL.

SPECIFIC EXPANSION PLANS:
US: All United States
Canada: No
Overseas: No

OUTDOOR CONNECTION

424 Neosho
Burlington, KS 66839
Tel: (888) 548-0636 (620) 364-5500
Fax: (620) 364-5563
E-Mail: info@outdoor-connection.com
Web Site: www.outdoor-connection.com
Mr. Marc Glades, President

OUTDOOR CONNECTION franchise owners market fishing and hunting travel. Over 200 lodges, guides and charter services have been pre-inspected to ensure quality. These destinations pay OUT-

DOOR CONNECTION 15-20% of their package rates for all bookings made. An excellent support system is in place for franchise owners to tap into.

BACKGROUND:
Established: 1988; 1st Franchised: 1990
Franchised Units: 77
Company-Owned Units: 4
Total Units: 81
Dist.: US-84; CAN-0; O'seas-0
North America: 31 States
Density: 7 in WI, 6 in IL, 5 in MN
Projected New Units (12 Months): 15
Qualifications: 3, 2, 2, 2, 3, 2
Registered:CA,FL,IL,IN,,MD,MI,MN,NY, ND,OR,VA,WA,WI

FINANCIAL/TERMS:
Cash Investment: $5-9.5K
Total Investment: $9.5-14.5K
Minimum Net Worth: NA
Fees: Franchise - $9.5K
Royalty - 3-5%; Ad. - 1%
Earnings Claims Statement: No
Term of Contract (Years): 5/5
Avg. # Of Employees: 1 PT, 1 PT
Passive Ownership: Discouraged
Encourage Conversions: NA
Area Develop. Agreements: No
Sub-Franchising Contracts: No
Expand In Territory: Yes
Space Needs: 500 SF; HB

SUPPORT & TRAINING:
Financial Assistance Provided: Yes(D)
Site Selection Assistance: No
Lease Negotiation Assistance: No
Co-Operative Advertising: Yes
Franchisee Assoc./Member: No
Size Of Corporate Staff: 4
On-Going Support: B,D,E,G,H
Training: 1.5 Days at Burlington, KS.

SPECIFIC EXPANSION PLANS:
US: All United States
Canada: All Canada
Overseas: No

<< >>

PUTT-PUTT GOLF COURSES OF AMERICA

6350 Quadrangle Dr., # 210
Chapel Hill, NC 27517
Tel: (919) 493-9999 + 104
Fax: (919) 402-9902
E-Mail: bkastl@putt-putt.com
Web Site: www.putt-putt.com
Mr. Bob Kastl, Director of Sales

PUTT-PUTT GOLF is now in its 50th year of operation. It is the oldest and largest operator/franchisor of miniature golf and family entertainment centers in the world. PUTT-PUTT GOLF operates in 26 states and in 8 foreign countries and specializes in the development of PUTT-PUTT GOLF, gamerooms, batting cages, bumper cars, go-carts and laser tag.

BACKGROUND:
Established: 1954; 1st Franchised: 1955
Franchised Units: 132
Company-Owned Units: 0
Total Units: 132
Dist.: US-110; CAN-1; O'seas-21
North America: 26 States, 1 Province
Density: 21 in TX, 13 in OH, 12 in NC
Projected New Units (12 Months): 12
Qualifications: 4, 5, 2, 3, 3, 4
Registered: All States and AB

FINANCIAL/TERMS:
Cash Investment: $35K-1MM
Total Investment: $1.5K-5MM
Minimum Net Worth: $500K
Fees: Franchise - $25-50K
Royalty - 5%; Ad. - 2%
Earnings Claims Statement: No
Term of Contract (Years): 20
Avg. # Of Employees: NR
Passive Ownership: Allowed
Encourage Conversions: NA
Area Develop. Agreements: No
Sub-Franchising Contracts: No
Expand In Territory: No
Space Needs: 3-7 acres SF; NA

SUPPORT & TRAINING:
Financial Assistance Provided: Yes(I)
Site Selection Assistance: Yes
Lease Negotiation Assistance: Yes
Co-Operative Advertising: No
Franchisee Assoc./Member: No
Size Of Corporate Staff: 6
On-Going Support: C,D,G,H,I
Training: 1 Week in Training Center; 3-7 Days at Franchisee's Location.

SPECIFIC EXPANSION PLANS:
US: All United States
Canada: All Canada
Overseas: South America

<< >>

THEMED MINIATURE GOLF COURSES

P. O. Box 2435
Myrtle Beach, SC 29578-2435
Tel: (843) 249-2118
Fax: (843) 249-2118
E-Mail: chgrove2001@aol.com
Web Site: www.worldfranchising.com/website.htm
Mr. Charles H. Grove, President

Themed, contoured adventure-type miniature golf courses with lakes, streambeds and waterfalls. Lush landscaping and the very finest designed, unique, playable holes that invite repeat participation. We also design and build complete family entertainment centers.

BACKGROUND:
Established: 1977; 1st Franchised: 1985
Franchised Units: 12
Company-Owned Units: 4
Total Units: 16
Dist.: US-16; CAN-0; O'seas-0
North America: 10 States
Density: SC, FL, TX
Projected New Units (12 Months): 5
Qualifications: 5, 4, 2, 2, 3, 4
Registered: NR

FINANCIAL/TERMS:
Cash Investment: $62.5-100K
Total Investment: $250-400K
Minimum Net Worth: NA
Fees: Franchise - NA
Royalty - NA; Ad. - NA
Earnings Claims Statement: No
Term of Contract (Years): Unlimited
Avg. # Of Employees: 2 FT, 2 PT
Passive Ownership: Allowed
Encourage Conversions: NA
Area Develop. Agreements: No
Sub-Franchising Contracts: No
Expand In Territory: Yes
Space Needs: 30,000 SF; FS

SUPPORT & TRAINING:
Financial Assistance Provided: NA
Site Selection Assistance: Yes
Lease Negotiation Assistance: Yes
Co-Operative Advertising: No
Franchisee Assoc./Member: Yes/Yes
Size Of Corporate Staff: 5
On-Going Support: B,C,D
Training: NR

SPECIFIC EXPANSION PLANS:
US: All United States
Canada: All Canada
Overseas: No

<< >>

WOODY'S WOOD SHOPS

1814 Franklin St., # 820
Oakland, CA 94612
Tel: (510) 839-5462
Fax: (510) 839-2104
E-Mail: alouie@worldfranchising.com
Web Site: www.woodyswood.com
Mr. McKee A. Bermuda, President

WOODY'S WOOD SHOPS offer instruction and use of virtually all shop tools in a fully outfitted wood shop. After detailed instruction and testing, members have full use of shop and related facilities. Open 15 hours/day, 7 days/week. Also sell small tools and all power equipment at cost plus 5%. Members pay front-end fees plus dues.

BACKGROUND:
Established: 1978; 1st Franchised: 1980
Franchised Units: 28
Company-Owned Units: 14
Total Units: 42
Dist.: US-33; CAN-6; O'seas-0
North America: 7 States, 2 Provinces
Density: 16 in CA, 8 in OR, 3 in WA
Projected New Units (12 Months): 4
Qualifications: , , , , ,
Registered: NR

FINANCIAL/TERMS:
Cash Investment: $72K
Total Investment: $85-185K
Minimum Net Worth: NR
Fees: Franchise - $22K
Royalty - 6%; Ad. - 2%
Earnings Claims Statement: Yes
Term of Contract (Years): 15/15
Avg. # Of Employees: 1 FT, 4 PT
Passive Ownership: Discouraged
Encourage Conversions: Yes
Area Develop. Agreements: Yes/15
Sub-Franchising Contracts: Yes
Expand In Territory: No
Space Needs: 2,800-3,400 SF; FS, Warehouse

SUPPORT & TRAINING:
Financial Assistance Provided: Yes(D)
Site Selection Assistance: Yes
Lease Negotiation Assistance: Yes
Co-Operative Advertising: Yes
Franchisee Assoc./Member: NR
Size Of Corporate Staff: 21
On-Going Support: A,C,D,g,H,i
Training: 3 Weeks Headquarters; 2 Weeks On-Site; On-Going.

SPECIFIC EXPANSION PLANS:
US: All United States
Canada: ON Only
Overseas: No

<< >>

WORLD GYM INTERNATIONAL

3223 Washington Blvd.
Marina Del Rey, CA 90292
Tel: (800) 544-7441 (310) 827-7705
Fax: (310) 827-6355
E-Mail: info@worldgym.com
Web Site: www.worldgym.com
Ms. Karin Michael, Franchise Administrator

Service oriented fitness centers featuring circuit training, cardiovascular equipment, free weights and personal training.

BACKGROUND:
Established: 1977; 1st Franchised: 1985
Franchised Units: 278
Company-Owned Units: 0
Total Units: 278
Dist.: US-262; CAN-3; O'seas-13
North America: 34 States
Density: 30 in FL, 24 in CA, 21 in NY
Projected New Units (12 Months): 45
Qualifications: 4, 5, 3, 3, 3, 2
Registered: CA,FL,HI,IL

FINANCIAL/TERMS:
Cash Investment: $300K-1MM
Total Investment: $300K-1MM
Minimum Net Worth: $300K-1MM
Fees: Franchise - $13K
Royalty - $7K/Yr.; Ad. - 0%
Earnings Claims Statement: No
Term of Contract (Years): 5/5
Avg. # Of Employees: 8-15 FT, 5 PT
Passive Ownership: Allowed
Encourage Conversions: Yes
Area Develop. Agreements: Yes/10
Sub-Franchising Contracts: Yes
Expand In Territory: Yes
Space Needs: 6,500-40,000 SF; FS,SF,SC,RM

SUPPORT & TRAINING:
Financial Assistance Provided: Yes(I)
Site Selection Assistance: Yes
Lease Negotiation Assistance: No
Co-Operative Advertising: No
Franchisee Assoc./Member: No
Size Of Corporate Staff: 6
On-Going Support: c,d,G,H,I
Training: 2 Days Las Vegas, NV University; 2 Days Columbus, OH University.

SPECIFIC EXPANSION PLANS:
US: All United States
Canada: All Canada
Overseas: All Countries

Rental Services

Chapter

33

Rental Services Industry Profile

Total # Franchisors in Industry Group	9
Total # Franchised Units in Industry Group	2,233
Total # Company-Owned Units in Industry Group	804
Total # Operating Units in Industry Group	3,037
Average # Franchised Units/Franchisor	248.1
Average # Company-Owned Units/Franchisor	89.3
Average # Total Units/Franchisor	337.4
Ratio of Total # Franchised Units/Total # Company-Owned Units	2.8:1
Industry Survey Participants	6
Representing % of Industry	66.7%
Average Franchise Fee*:	$16.1K
Average Total Investment*:	$250.5K
Average On-Going Royalty Fee*:	3.7%

*If a range was provided, the mid-point of the range was used. See detailed profiles for actual ranges.

Five Largest Participants in Survey

Company	# Franchised Units	# Co-Owned Units	# Total Units	Franchise Fee	On-Going Royalty	Total Investment
1. Aaron's Sales & Lease Ownership	349	647	996	$35K	6%	$254-559K
2. Grand Rental Station/Taylor Rental	450	0	450	$1.5K	1.30%	$225-250K
3. Nation-Wide General Rental Centers	376	1	377	$0	0%	$80-178K
4. Colortyme	326	0	326	$25K	4%	$293-517K
5. Joe Rent All/Loue Tout	80	0	80	$20K	5%	$75-500K

All of the data provided are proprietary and should not be quoted without acknowledging *Bond's Franchise Guide.*

Top 100

AARON'S SALES & LEASE OWNERSHIP

309 E. Paces Ferry Rd., N. E.
Atlanta, GA 30305-2377
Tel: (800) 551-6015 (678) 402-3445
Fax: (678) 402-3540
E-Mail: jim.thrash@aaronrents.com
Web Site: www.aaronsfranchise.com
Mr. Jim Thrash, Director of Franchising

AARON'S SALES & LEASE OWNERSHIP is one of the fastest-growing retail companies in the U.S., specializing in furniture, electronics and appliances. AARON'S SALES & LEASE OWNERSHIP offers franchisees the expertise, advantages and support of a well-established company, plus the opportunity to realize a significant financial return in a booming market segment.

BACKGROUND: IFA MEMBER
Established: 1955; 1st Franchised: 1992
Franchised Units: 349
Company-Owned Units: 647
Total Units: 996
Dist.: US-994; CAN-2; O'seas-0
North America: 47 States
Density: TX, FL, GA
Projected New Units (12 Months): 80
Qualifications: 5, 5, 1, 4, 5, 5
Registered:CA,FL,HI,IL,IN,MI,NY,ND,OR,RI,SD,VA,WA,WI

FINANCIAL/TERMS:
Cash Investment: $300K
Total Investment: $254-559K
Minimum Net Worth: $450K
Fees: Franchise - $35K
Royalty - 6%; Ad. - 2.5%
Earnings Claims Statement: Yes
Term of Contract (Years): 10/10
Avg. # Of Employees: 6 FT
Passive Ownership: Allowed
Encourage Conversions: NA
Area Develop. Agreements: Yes/Varies
Sub-Franchising Contracts: No
Expand In Territory: Yes
Space Needs: 8,000 SF; SC

SUPPORT & TRAINING:
Financial Assistance Provided: Yes(I)
Site Selection Assistance: Yes
Lease Negotiation Assistance: Yes
Co-Operative Advertising: Yes
Franchisee Assoc./Member: Yes
Size Of Corporate Staff: 3,500
On-Going Support: A,B,C,D,E,F,H,I
Training: 3 Weeks Corporate Headquarters; 2 Weeks Minimum On-Site; On-Going Varies.

SPECIFIC EXPANSION PLANS:
US: All United States
Canada: All Canada
Overseas: All Countries

<< >>

COLORTYME

5700 Tennyson Pkwy., # 180
Plano, TX 75024-3583
Tel: (800) 411-8963 (972) 608-5376
Fax: (972) 403-4923
E-Mail: pat@colortyme.com
Web Site: www.colortyme.com
Mr. Pat Sumner, Dir. Franchise Development

The nation's largest rental-purchase franchise company, specializing in electronics, furniture, appliances and computers. We help our customers find what's right for them and give our franchisees the support needed to be successful, at the best profit margins in the industry.

BACKGROUND: IFA MEMBER
Established: 1979; 1st Franchised: 1981
Franchised Units: 326
Company-Owned Units: 0
Total Units: 326
Dist.: US-326; CAN-0; O'seas-0
North America: 41 States
Density: 57 in TX, 18 in KS, 1 in IN
Projected New Units (12 Months): 30
Qualifications: 4, 4, 4, 3, 3, 4
Registered:CA,FL,HI,IL,IN,MD,MI,NY,ND,OR,RI,SD,VA,WA,WI,DC

FINANCIAL/TERMS:
Cash Investment: $120-160K
Total Investment: $293-517K
Minimum Net Worth: $300K
Fees: Franchise - $25K
Royalty - 4%; Ad. - $250/Mo.
Earnings Claims Statement: Yes
Term of Contract (Years): 5-10/5-10
Avg. # Of Employees: 6 FT
Passive Ownership: Allowed
Encourage Conversions: Yes
Area Develop. Agreements: Yes/5
Sub-Franchising Contracts: No
Expand In Territory: Yes
Space Needs: 3,500 SF; FS, SF, SC, RM

SUPPORT & TRAINING:
Financial Assistance Provided: Yes(I)
Site Selection Assistance: Yes
Lease Negotiation Assistance: Yes
Co-Operative Advertising: Yes
Franchisee Assoc./Member: Yes/No
Size Of Corporate Staff: 21
On-Going Support: B,C,D,E,F,G,H
Training: 4 Weeks Varied Training.

SPECIFIC EXPANSION PLANS:
US: All United States
Canada: No
Overseas: No

<< >>

GRAND RENTAL STATION/ TAYLOR RENTAL

203 Jandus Rd.
Cary, IL 60013-2861
Tel: (800) 833-3004 (773) 695-5310
Fax: (847) 516-9921
E-Mail: hbrown@truserv.com
Web Site: www.truserv.com
Mr. Phil Agee, National Sales Manager

Complete equipment rental operation, specializing in light contractor, home owner and party/special occasion rentals. We provide a complete support program including market/site evaluation, store design, inventory customization, hands-on-training and on-going field and technical support.

BACKGROUND:
Established: 1910; 1st Franchised: 1985
Franchised Units: 450
Company-Owned Units: 0
Total Units: 450
Dist.: US-1272; CAN-0; O'seas-0
North America: 42 States
Density: MA, PA, NY
Projected New Units (12 Months): 60
Qualifications: 4, 4, 1, 1, 2, 4
Registered: All States

FINANCIAL/TERMS:
Cash Investment: $75-150K
Total Investment: $225-250K
Minimum Net Worth: $100K
Fees: Franchise - $1.5K
Royalty - 1.3%; Ad. - $30/Mo.
Earnings Claims Statement: No
Term of Contract (Years): 10/10
Avg. # Of Employees: 3 FT, 3 PT
Passive Ownership: Discouraged
Encourage Conversions: Yes
Area Develop. Agreements: No
Sub-Franchising Contracts: No
Expand In Territory: Yes
Space Needs: 5,000 SF; FS, SC

SUPPORT & TRAINING:
Financial Assistance Provided: No
Site Selection Assistance: Yes

Lease Negotiation Assistance: Yes
Co-Operative Advertising: Yes
Franchisee Assoc./Member: Yes/Yes
Size Of Corporate Staff: 16
On-Going Support: B,C,D,E,F,G,H,I
Training: 1 Week in Gary, IL.

SPECIFIC EXPANSION PLANS:
US: All United States
Canada: All Canada
Overseas: All Countries

<< >>

JOE RENT ALL/LOUE TOUT

28 Vanier St.
Chateauguay, PQ J6J 3W8 CANADA
Tel: (450) 692-6268
Fax: (450) 692-2848
E-Mail: mrjoe@videotron.ca
Web Site: www.joelouetout.ca
Mr. J. Maurice Bissonnette, President

Equipment rental in 4 different options: tools, recreational vehicles, special events, motorcycles. Full operating support, including school. Buying group with central billing. Specific insurance plans. Own computer program.

BACKGROUND:
Established: 1979; 1st Franchised: 1982
Franchised Units: 80
Company-Owned Units: 0
Total Units: 80
Dist.: US-0; CAN-80; O'seas-0
North America: 3 Provinces
Density: 63 in PQ, 11 in ON, 6 in NB
Projected New Units (12 Months): 8
Qualifications: 4, 4, 3, 3, 4, 3
Registered: NR

FINANCIAL/TERMS:
Cash Investment: $25-65K
Total Investment: $75-500K
Minimum Net Worth: $25K
Fees: Franchise - $20K
Royalty - 5%; Ad. - 3%
Earnings Claims Statement: Yes
Term of Contract (Years): 5/5
Avg. # Of Employees: 4 FT, 2 PT
Passive Ownership: Discouraged
Encourage Conversions: Yes
Area Develop. Agreements: No
Sub-Franchising Contracts: Yes
Expand In Territory: Yes
Space Needs: 2,000 SF; FS

SUPPORT & TRAINING:
Financial Assistance Provided: Yes(I)
Site Selection Assistance: Yes
Lease Negotiation Assistance: Yes
Co-Operative Advertising: Yes
Franchisee Assoc./Member: No
Size Of Corporate Staff: 5
On-Going Support: B,C,D,E,F,G,H,I
Training: 1 Week Head Office; 1 Month Store.

SPECIFIC EXPANSION PLANS:
US: As Master Franchisor
Canada: Ontario
Overseas: Yes, As Master Franchisor

NATION-WIDE GENERAL RENTAL CENTERS

5510 Hwy. 9 N.
Alpharetta, GA 30004
Tel: (800) 227-1643 (770) 664-7765
Fax: (770) 664-0052
E-Mail: office@nation-widerental.com
Web Site: www.worldfranchising.com/website.htm
Mr. Ike Goodvin, President

Tool and equipment rental business (since 1976) for homeowners, party and contractors. A complete turn-key package with proven equipment. No franchise fee or royalties. A complete training program with a buy-back agreement. This may be your business opportunity - act now! See our Website.

BACKGROUND:
Established: 1976; 1st Franchised: 1976
Franchised Units: 376
Company-Owned Units: 1
Total Units: 377
Dist.: US-375; CAN-0; O'seas-2
North America: 29 States
Density: NR
Projected New Units (12 Months): 18
Qualifications: 2, 1, 1, 2, 1, 5
Registered: NR

FINANCIAL/TERMS:
Cash Investment: $40-50K
Total Investment: $80-178K
Minimum Net Worth: $40-50K
Fees: Franchise - $0
Royalty - 0%; Ad. - 0%
Earnings Claims Statement: Yes
Term of Contract (Years): 3/1
Avg. # Of Employees: 1 PT
Passive Ownership: Discouraged
Encourage Conversions: No
Area Develop. Agreements: No
Sub-Franchising Contracts: No
Expand In Territory: Yes
Space Needs: 2,500 SF; FS, SF, SC

SUPPORT & TRAINING:
Financial Assistance Provided: Yes
Site Selection Assistance: Yes
Lease Negotiation Assistance: Yes
Co-Operative Advertising: No
Franchisee Assoc./Member: Yes/Yes
Size Of Corporate Staff: NR
On-Going Support: B,C,D,E,F,I
Training: 7 Days Atlanta, GA.

SPECIFIC EXPANSION PLANS:
US: All United States
Canada: All Canada
Overseas: No

<< >>

Retail: Art, Art Supplies & Framing

Chapter 34

Retail: Art, Art Supplies & Framing Industry Profile

Total # Franchisors in Industry Group	12
Total # Franchised Units in Industry Group	816
Total # Company-Owned Units in Industry Group	27
Total # Operating Units in Industry Group	843
Average # Franchised Units/Franchisor	68
Average # Company-Owned Units/Franchisor	2.3
Average # Total Units/Franchisor	70.3
Ratio of Total # Franchised Units/Total # Company-Owned Units	30.2:1

Industry Survey Participants	8
Representing % of Industry	66.7%
Average Franchise Fee*:	$30.9K
Average Total Investment*:	$127.8K
Average On-Going Royalty Fee*:	5.4%

*If a range was provided, the mid-point of the range was used. See detailed profiles for actual ranges.

Five Largest Participants in Survey

Company	# Franchised Units	# Co-Owned Units	# Total Units	Franchise Fee	On-Going Royalty	Total Investment
1. FASTFRAME	321	1	322	$25K	7.5%	$105-150K
2. Great Frame Up, The	156	0	156	$30K	6%	$138.4-188.2K
3. Deck The Walls	105	0	105	$30K	6%	$180.9-245.2K
4. Color Me Mine	99	1	100	$25K	5%	$97.5-185K
5. Framing & Art Centre	51	0	51	$30K	6%	$118-179K

All of the data provided are proprietary and should not be quoted without acknowledging *Bond's Franchise Guide.*

COLOR ME MINE

5140 Lankershim Blvd.
North Hollywood, CA 91601-3100
Tel: (888) 265-6764 (503) 254-2304
Fax: (503) 254-2306
E-Mail: maria@colormemine.com
Web Site: www.colormemine.com
Ms. Maria Baker, Exec. Dir. Franchise Devel.

COLOR ME MINE is the world's leader in contemporary ceramics and crafts studios. Our comprehensive training and support system includes glazing, firing and design techniques, construction marketing, accounting services and manufacturing plants to ensure consistency and supply.

BACKGROUND:
Established: 1992; 1st Franchised: 1996
Franchised Units: 99
Company-Owned Units: 1
Total Units: 100
Dist.: US-85; CAN-0; O'seas-15
North America: 20 States
Density: 35 in CA, 7 in NJ, 7 in PA
Projected New Units (12 Months): 30
Qualifications: 4, 3, 2, 3, 5, 5
Registered: CA,FL,HI,IL,IN,MD,MI,MN, NY,OR,VA,WA,WI,DC,AB

FINANCIAL/TERMS:
Cash Investment: $50K
Total Investment: $97.5-185K
Minimum Net Worth: $150K
Fees: Franchise - $25K
Royalty - 5%; Ad. - 1%
Earnings Claims Statement: Yes
Term of Contract (Years): 5/5/5/5
Avg. # Of Employees: 2 FT, 4 PT
Passive Ownership: Discouraged
Encourage Conversions: Yes
Area Develop. Agreements: No
Sub-Franchising Contracts: No
Expand In Territory: Yes
Space Needs:1,300-2,000 SF; SF, SC, RM, Entertainment Cent

SUPPORT & TRAINING:
Financial Assistance Provided: No
Site Selection Assistance: Yes
Lease Negotiation Assistance: Yes
Co-Operative Advertising: No
Franchisee Assoc./Member: Yes
Size Of Corporate Staff: 15
On-Going Support: A,B,C,D,E,F,G,H,I
Training: 11 Days at Home Office in North Hollywood, CA; 5 Days at Franchised Location.

SPECIFIC EXPANSION PLANS:
US: All United States
Canada: All Canada
Overseas: All Countries

<< >>

DECK THE WALLS

P. O. Box 1187
Houston, TX 77251-1187
Tel: (800) 543-3325 (281) 775-5294
Fax: (281) 872-1646
E-Mail: anance@fcibiz.com
Web Site: www.dtwfraninfo.com
Ms. Ann Nance, Director Franchise Development

DECK THE WALLS is the nation's largest specialty retailer of art, custom framing & wall décor. Each store carries a large selection of limited & open edition prints, custom frame molding & mats. Easy to learn & operate; exceptional training & support; national buying power & proven marketing programs. Stores located in high-traffic regional malls & shopping centers. Rewarding business in a growing industry.

BACKGROUND: IFA MEMBER
Established: 1979; 1st Franchised: 1981
Franchised Units: 105
Company-Owned Units: 0
Total Units: 105
Dist.: US-105; CAN-0; O'seas-0
North America: 34 States
Density: 17 in TX, 14 in PA, 12 in FL
Projected New Units (12 Months): 0
Qualifications: 4, 5, 1, 3, 3, 4
Registered: All States

FINANCIAL/TERMS:
Cash Investment: $45-80K
Total Investment: $180.9-245.2K
Minimum Net Worth: $250K
Fees: Franchise - $30K
Royalty - 6%; Ad. - 2%
Earnings Claims Statement: No
Term of Contract (Years): 10/10
Avg. # Of Employees: 2 FT, 3 PT
Passive Ownership: Allowed
Encourage Conversions: Yes
Area Develop. Agreements: No
Sub-Franchising Contracts: No
Expand In Territory: Yes
Space Needs: 1,500-2,000 SF; SC, RM

SUPPORT & TRAINING:
Financial Assistance Provided: Yes(I)
Site Selection Assistance: Yes
Lease Negotiation Assistance: Yes
Co-Operative Advertising: Yes
Franchisee Assoc./Member: Yes/Yes
Size Of Corporate Staff: 26
On-Going Support: B,C,D,E,F,G,H,I
Training: 2 Weeks St. Louis, MO; 3 Days In Store.

SPECIFIC EXPANSION PLANS:
US: All United States
Canada: No
Overseas: No

<< >>

Top 100

FASTFRAME

1200 Lawrence Dr., # 300
Newbury Park, CA 91320-1234
Tel: (800) 333-3225 (805) 498-4463
Fax: (805) 498-8983
E-Mail: mandi@fastframe.com
Web Site: www.fastframe.com
Ms. Mandi Malone, Franchise Development Support

FASTFRAME is the largest and fastest-growing custom picture framing franchise in the world. With over 300 locations, we maintain our leadership in the industry by recruiting business partners who are both qualified and passionate about our industry. We strive to provide our franchisees with an all-inclusive and uncomplicated process whereby they can easily become a part of this very enjoyable business. FASTFRAME has built its reputation of high quality craftsmanship and customer satisfaction.

BACKGROUND: IFA MEMBER
Established: 1986; 1st Franchised: 1987
Franchised Units: 321
Company-Owned Units: 1
Total Units: 322
Dist.: US-312; CAN-0; O'seas-10
North America: 35 States
Density: 76 in CA, 22 in IL, 22 in TX
Projected New Units (12 Months): 40
Qualifications: 5, 4, 1, 1, 1, 5
Registered: All States Except ND and SD.

FINANCIAL/TERMS:
Cash Investment: $40-50K
Total Investment: $105-150K
Minimum Net Worth: $150K
Fees: Franchise - $25K
Royalty - 7.5%; Ad. - 3%
Earnings Claims Statement: No
Term of Contract (Years): 10/10
Avg. # Of Employees: 1 FT, 2 PT
Passive Ownership: NR
Encourage Conversions: Yes

Area Develop. Agreements: No
Sub-Franchising Contracts: NR
Expand In Territory: Yes
Space Needs: 1,200-1,500 SF; FS, SF, SC

SUPPORT & TRAINING:
Financial Assistance Provided: Yes(I)
Site Selection Assistance: Yes
Lease Negotiation Assistance: Yes
Co-Operative Advertising: Yes
Franchisee Assoc./Member: Yes/Yes
Size Of Corporate Staff: 23
On-Going Support: A,B,C,D,E,F,G,H,I
Training: 2 Weeks at Newbury Park, CA; 1 Week at On-Site.

SPECIFIC EXPANSION PLANS:
US: All United States
Canada: No
Overseas: No

<< >>

FRAMING & ART CENTRE

12707 North Fwy., # 330
Houston, TX 77060
Tel: (800) 543-3325 (281) 775-5294
Fax: (281) 872-1646
E-Mail: anance@fcibiz.com
Web Site: www.framingartcentre.com
Ms. Ann Nance, Director Franchise Development

FRAMING & ART CENTRE is Canada's only national art & custom framing store, specializing in a hands-on, artistic environment. Each store offers a large selection of design samples, prints and posters with custom framing in a creative atmosphere. Easy to learn and operate, exceptional training and support, national buying power and proven marketing programs. Air Miles offered.

BACKGROUND: IFA MEMBER
Established: 1974; 1st Franchised: 1977
Franchised Units: 51
Company-Owned Units: 0
Total Units: 51
Dist.: US-0; CAN-51; O'seas-0
North America: 5 Provinces
Density: 29 in ON, 12 in BC, 6 in AB
Projected New Units (12 Months): 5
Qualifications: 4, 3, 3, 3, 3, 5
Registered: AB

FINANCIAL/TERMS:
Cash Investment: $30K
Total Investment: $118-179K
Minimum Net Worth: $150K
Fees: Franchise - $30K
Royalty - 6%; Ad. - 1%
Earnings Claims Statement: No
Term of Contract (Years): 10/10
Avg. # Of Employees: 2 FT, 2 PT
Passive Ownership: Discouraged
Encourage Conversions: Yes
Area Develop. Agreements: Yes
Sub-Franchising Contracts: No
Expand In Territory: Yes
Space Needs: 1,200-1,400 SF; SF, SC

SUPPORT & TRAINING:
Financial Assistance Provided: No
Site Selection Assistance: Yes
Lease Negotiation Assistance: Yes
Co-Operative Advertising: Yes
Franchisee Assoc./Member: No
Size Of Corporate Staff: 4
On-Going Support: C,D,E,G,H,I
Training: 10 Days Burlington, ON.

SPECIFIC EXPANSION PLANS:
US: No
Canada: All Canada
Overseas: No

<< >>

GREAT FRAME UP, THE

P. O. Box 1187
Houston, TX 77251-1187
Tel: (800) 543-3325 (281) 775-5262
Fax: (281) 872-1646
E-Mail: anance@fcibiz.com
Web Site: www.tgfufraninfo.com
Ms. Ann Nance, Director Franchise Development

THE GREAT FRAME UP is part of the world's largest retail franchisor of affordable, high-quality custom framing. Specializing in custom framing in a hands-on, artistic environment featuring wide selections of custom frame moldings & mat styles, a proprietary framing system, superior design center & more. Easy to learn & operate; exceptional training & support; national buying power & proven marketing programs. Growth industry.

BACKGROUND: IFA MEMBER
Established: 1971; 1st Franchised: 1975
Franchised Units: 156
Company-Owned Units: 0
Total Units: 156
Dist.: US-156; CAN-0; O'seas-0
North America: 32 States
Density: 23 in IL, 16 in CA, 16 in GA
Projected New Units (12 Months): 30
Qualifications: 4, 5, 1, 3, 3, 4
Registered: All States

FINANCIAL/TERMS:
Cash Investment: $35-50K
Total Investment: $138.4-188.2K
Minimum Net Worth: $200K
Fees: Franchise - $30K
Royalty - 6%; Ad. - 2%
Earnings Claims Statement: No
Term of Contract (Years): 10/10
Avg. # Of Employees: 1 FT, 2 PT
Passive Ownership: Allowed
Encourage Conversions: Yes
Area Develop. Agreements: Yes
Sub-Franchising Contracts: No
Expand In Territory: Yes
Space Needs: 1,500-2,000 SF; SC

SUPPORT & TRAINING:
Financial Assistance Provided: Yes(I)
Site Selection Assistance: Yes
Lease Negotiation Assistance: Yes
Co-Operative Advertising: Yes
Franchisee Assoc./Member: Yes/Yes
Size Of Corporate Staff: 26
On-Going Support: C,D,E,F,G,H,I
Training: 2 Weeks St. Louis, MO; 3 Days In Store.

SPECIFIC EXPANSION PLANS:
US: All United States
Canada: No
Overseas: No

MARAD FINE ART

992 High Ridge Rd.
Stamford, CT 06905
Tel: (203) 322-7666
Fax: (203) 329-9836
E-Mail: maradart@aol.com
Web Site: www.maradfineart.com
Mr. Dick Fierstein, President

MARAD FINE ART offers qualified individuals with a flair for sales and an appreciation of art the chance to operate their own commercial art business from their home or office. Product line contains over 15,000 of the world's best-loved art reproductions in quality, custom mattes and frames at the same low price for each piece. Comprehensive sales training, exclusive territories and a turnkey ordering/fulfillment system allow for easy start-up, operational efficiency, little overhead and NO INVENTORY.

BACKGROUND:
Established: 1938; 1st Franchised: 2002
Franchised Units: 3
Company-Owned Units: 1
Total Units: 4
Dist.: US-1; CAN-0; O'seas-0
North America: 1 State
Density: 1 in CT

Projected New Units (12 Months): 4
Qualifications: 3, 4, 2, 2, 3, 4
Registered: FL

FINANCIAL/TERMS:

Cash Investment: $35-60K
Total Investment: $35-60K
Minimum Net Worth: $100K
Fees: Franchise - $35-60K
Royalty - 4%; Ad. - 2%
Earnings Claims Statement: No
Term of Contract (Years): 10/5
Avg. # Of Employees: 1 FT
Passive Ownership: Not Allowed
Encourage Conversions: NA
Area Develop. Agreements: No
Sub-Franchising Contracts: No
Expand In Territory: Yes
Space Needs: NA SF; HB

SUPPORT & TRAINING:

Financial Assistance Provided: Yes(I)
Site Selection Assistance: NA
Lease Negotiation Assistance: NA
Co-Operative Advertising: No
Franchisee Assoc./Member: No
Size Of Corporate Staff: 1
On-Going Support: NR
Training: 1 Day Stamford CT; 1 Day Hauppage, NY.

SPECIFIC EXPANSION PLANS:

US: All United States
Canada: No
Overseas: All Countries

<< >>

Retail: Athletic Wear/Sporting Goods

Chapter 35

Retail: Athletic Wear/Sporting Goods Industry Profile

Total # Franchisors in Industry Group	17
Total # Franchised Units in Industry Group	1,821
Total # Company-Owned Units in Industry Group	44
Total # Operating Units in Industry Group	1,865
Average # Franchised Units/Franchisor	107.1
Average # Company-Owned Units/Franchisor	2.6
Average # Total Units/Franchisor	109.7
Ratio of Total # Franchised Units/Total # Company-Owned Units	41.4:1
Industry Survey Participants	13
Representing % of Industry	76.5%
Average Franchise Fee*:	$29.9K
Average Total Investment*:	$257.4K
Average On-Going Royalty Fee*:	3.8%

*If a range was provided, the mid-point of the range was used. See detailed profiles for actual ranges.

Five Largest Participants in Survey

Company	# Franchised Units	# Co-Owned Units	# Total Units	Franchise Fee	On-Going Royalty	Total Investment
1. Play It Again Sports	464	0	464	$20K	5%	$212-319K
2. Athlete's Foot, The	230	1	231	$35.5K Single	3.5 - 5%	$200-525K
3. Pro Golf of America	148	1	149	$49.5K	2.5%	$300K+
4. Golf USA	100	5	105	$34-44K	2%	$235-300K
5. Pro Image Franchise	94	0	94	$19.5K	4%	$180-200K

Top 100

ATHLETE'S FOOT, THE

1950 Vaughn Rd.
Kennesaw, GA 30144-7005
Tel: (800) 524-6444 (770) 514-4523
Fax: (770) 514-4843
E-Mail: franchiseinfo@theathletesfoot.com
Web Site: www.theathletesfoot.com
Mr. Peter Franetovich, Director Franchise Sales

THE ATHLETE'S FOOT, with more than 600 stores in 45 countries, is the leading international franchisor of name-brand athletic footwear. As a franchisee, you will benefit from headquarters' support, including training, advertising, product selection, special vendor discount programs, continual footwear research and much more.

BACKGROUND: IFA MEMBER
Established: 1971; 1st Franchised: 1972
Franchised Units: 230
Company-Owned Units: 1
Total Units: 231
Dist.: US-246; CAN-2; O'seas-381
North America: 47 States, 1 Province
Density: NR
Projected New Units (12 Months): 120
Qualifications: 4, 5, 3, 3, 2, 5
Registered: All States

FINANCIAL/TERMS:
Cash Investment: $75-125K
Total Investment: $200-525K
Minimum Net Worth: $200K
Fees: Franchise - $35.5K Single
Royalty - 3.5 - 5%; Ad. - 0.6%
Earnings Claims Statement: No
Term of Contract (Years): 10/5
Avg. # Of Employees: 2 FT, 6 PT
Passive Ownership: Discouraged
Encourage Conversions: Yes
Area Develop. Agreements: Yes/10
Sub-Franchising Contracts: Yes
Expand In Territory: Yes
Space Needs: 1,200 SF; FS, SF, SC, RM

SUPPORT & TRAINING:
Financial Assistance Provided: Yes(I)
Site Selection Assistance: Yes
Lease Negotiation Assistance: Yes
Co-Operative Advertising: No
Franchisee Assoc./Member: Yes/Yes
Size Of Corporate Staff: 25
On-Going Support: B,C,D,E,f,G,H,I
Training: 1 Week at Headquarters in Atlanta; 1 Wk. Prior to and during Opening on Location; On-Going.

SPECIFIC EXPANSION PLANS:
US: All United States
Canada: All Canada
Overseas: All Countries

<< >>

FAN-A-MANIA SPORTS AND ENTERTAINMENT

855 Cy Ave.
Casper, WY 82601-4161
Tel: (801) 253-7798
Fax: (801) 253-0931
E-Mail: fanamania1@hotmail.com
Web Site:
Mr. Mike Scheneman, Franchise Operations

Largest sport and entertainment retail franchise, great look, exciting hot products: NFL, MLB, NASCAR, NBA, NHL, WWF, Disney, Warner Brothers, Pooh, Sesame Street, Marvel Comics, Star Wars, Star Trek, and Nickelodeon apparel, novelty items and memorabilia. Malls love us and customers flock to our stores.

BACKGROUND:
Established: 1995; 1st Franchised: 1996
Franchised Units: 8
Company-Owned Units: 5
Total Units: 13
Dist.: US-5; CAN-1; O'seas-2
North America: 5 States, 1 Province
Density: NR
Projected New Units (12 Months): 3
Qualifications: 5, 3, 1, 1, 3, 5
Registered: OR,VA,AB

FINANCIAL/TERMS:
Cash Investment: $100K
Total Investment: $200K
Minimum Net Worth: $300K
Fees: Franchise - $19.5K
Royalty - 0%; Ad. - 2%
Earnings Claims Statement: No
Term of Contract (Years): 10/10
Avg. # Of Employees: 4 FT, 2 PT
Passive Ownership: Discouraged
Encourage Conversions: Yes
Area Develop. Agreements: Yes/10
Sub-Franchising Contracts: Yes
Expand In Territory: Yes
Space Needs:2,000 SF; RM, Outlet Center

SUPPORT & TRAINING:
Financial Assistance Provided: No
Site Selection Assistance: Yes
Lease Negotiation Assistance: Yes
Co-Operative Advertising: Yes
Franchisee Assoc./Member: No
Size Of Corporate Staff: 6
On-Going Support: b,C,D,E,f,G,H,I
Training: 4 Days Salt Lake City, UT; 7 Days Franchise Locations.

SPECIFIC EXPANSION PLANS:
US: All United States
Canada: All Canada
Overseas: All Countries

<< >>

FIELD OF DREAMS

5000 NW 108th Ave.
Sunrise, FL 33351
Tel: (800) 749-7529 (954) 749-8544
Fax: (954) 742-7044
E-Mail: dolarte@dreamscorp.com
Web Site: www.fieldofdreams.com
Ms. Dawna Dunn Olarte,

FIELD OF DREAMS, the ultimate sports and celebrity gift store.

BACKGROUND:
Established: 1990; 1st Franchised: 1991
Franchised Units: 38
Company-Owned Units: 0
Total Units: 38
Dist.: US-23; CAN-1; O'seas-1
North America: 18 States
Density: 3 in GA, 3 in CA, 2 in TX
Projected New Units (12 Months): 10
Qualifications: 5, 4, 5, 4, 5, 5
Registered: CA,FL,MI,OR

FINANCIAL/TERMS:
Cash Investment: $60-245K
Total Investment: $160-225K
Minimum Net Worth: $150K
Fees: Franchise - $32.5K
Royalty - 6%; Ad. - 3%
Earnings Claims Statement: No
Term of Contract (Years): Lease
Avg. # Of Employees: 1 FT, 2 PT
Passive Ownership: Discouraged
Encourage Conversions: NA
Area Develop. Agreements: Yes
Sub-Franchising Contracts: No
Expand In Territory: Yes
Space Needs: 900-1,400 SF; RM

SUPPORT & TRAINING:
Financial Assistance Provided: Yes(I)
Site Selection Assistance: Yes
Lease Negotiation Assistance: Yes
Co-Operative Advertising: Yes
Franchisee Assoc./Member: No
Size Of Corporate Staff: 9

On-Going Support: C,D,E,h,I
Training: 10 Days Orlando, FL.
SPECIFIC EXPANSION PLANS:
US: All United States
Canada: All Canada
Overseas: All Countries

GOLF ETC. OF AMERICA

2201 Commercial Ln.
Granbury, TX 76048
Tel: (800) 806-8633 (817) 279-7888
Fax: (817) 579-1793
E-Mail: sales@golfetc.com
Web Site: www.golfetc.com
Mr. Don Willingham, Dir. Franchise Development

Total turn-key golf pro shop franchise. Retail center for golf equipment, accessories, gift items and furniture. Service center built inside for precision custom fitting and repair of golf clubs. Exciting and fun sports and entertainment industry.

BACKGROUND:
Established: 1992; 1st Franchised: 1996
Franchised Units: 75
Company-Owned Units: 0
Total Units: 75
Dist.: US-75; CAN-0; O'seas-0
North America: 26 States
Density: 15 in TX, 10 in FL, 5 in LA
Projected New Units (12 Months): 24
Qualifications: , , , , ,
Registered: NR
FINANCIAL/TERMS:
Cash Investment: $50-60K
Total Investment: $200K+
Minimum Net Worth: $130-145K
Fees: Franchise - $15K
Royalty - Call; Ad. - NA
Earnings Claims Statement: No
Term of Contract (Years): NR
Avg. # Of Employees: 1 FT, 2 PT
Passive Ownership: Allowed
Encourage Conversions: NR
Area Develop. Agreements: NR
Sub-Franchising Contracts: No
Expand In Territory: NR
Space Needs: 3,000 SF; SF, SC, RM
SUPPORT & TRAINING:
Financial Assistance Provided: NR
Site Selection Assistance: Yes
Lease Negotiation Assistance: Yes
Co-Operative Advertising: No
Franchisee Assoc./Member: No
Size Of Corporate Staff: 11
On-Going Support: b,D,E,G,H,I
Training: 1 Week Granbury, TX.
SPECIFIC EXPANSION PLANS:
US: All United States
Canada: NR
Overseas: NR

GOLF USA

3705 W. Memorial Rd., # 801
Oklahoma City, OK 73134-1512
Tel: (800) 488-1107 (405) 751-0015
Fax: (405) 755-0065
E-Mail: rbenson@gusahq.com
Web Site: www.golfusa.com
Mr. Rick Benson, VP Franchising

Discount golf retail stores, complete with name-brand, pro-line equipment, apparel and accessories. Indoor driving range/ swing analyzer.

BACKGROUND: IFA MEMBER
Established: 1986; 1st Franchised: 1989
Franchised Units: 100
Company-Owned Units: 5
Total Units: 105
Dist.: US-88; CAN-3; O'seas-14
North America: 30 States, 2 Provinces
Density: 5 in TX, 5 in NC, 5 in KS
Projected New Units (12 Months): 20
Qualifications: 5, 4, 3, 3, 4, 5
Registered: All States and AB
FINANCIAL/TERMS:
Cash Investment: $75-100K
Total Investment: $235-300K
Minimum Net Worth: $300K
Fees: Franchise - $34-44K
Royalty - 2%; Ad. - 1%
Earnings Claims Statement: No
Term of Contract (Years): 15/15
Avg. # Of Employees: 2 FT, 1 PT
Passive Ownership: Discouraged
Encourage Conversions: Yes
Area Develop. Agreements: Yes/4
Sub-Franchising Contracts: Yes
Expand In Territory: Yes
Space Needs: 2,500-5,000 SF; FS, SF, SC
SUPPORT & TRAINING:
Financial Assistance Provided: Yes(I)
Site Selection Assistance: Yes
Lease Negotiation Assistance: Yes
Co-Operative Advertising: Yes
Franchisee Assoc./Member: Yes/Yes
Size Of Corporate Staff: 30
On-Going Support: A,B,C,D,E,F,G,H,I
Training: 10 Days Oklahoma City, OK; 10 Days Spain
SPECIFIC EXPANSION PLANS:
US: All United States
Canada: All Canada
Overseas: All Countries

INTERNATIONAL GOLF

9101 N. Thornydale Rd.
Tucson, AZ 85742
Tel: (800) 204-2600 (520) 744-1840
Fax: (520) 744-2076
E-Mail: info@intlgolf-ent.com
Web Site: www.intlgolf-ent.com
Ms. Sheila J. White, Franchise Director

Off-course retail golf store, with complete selection of golf and golf-related merchandise, possibly complementing tennis or ski merchandise.

BACKGROUND:
Established: 1976; 1st Franchised: 1981
Franchised Units: 64
Company-Owned Units: 6
Total Units: 70
Dist.: US-70; CAN-0; O'seas-0
North America: 17 States
Density: 12 in MI, 6 in OK, 6 in CA
Projected New Units (12 Months): 5
Qualifications: 4, 4, 3, 3, , 4
Registered: All States
FINANCIAL/TERMS:
Cash Investment: $125-150K
Total Investment: $250-300K
Minimum Net Worth: NR
Fees: Franchise - $42K
Royalty - 2%; Ad. - 0%
Earnings Claims Statement: Yes
Term of Contract (Years): 15/15
Avg. # Of Employees: 2-3 FT, 2-3 PT
Passive Ownership: Discouraged
Encourage Conversions: Yes
Area Develop. Agreements: No
Sub-Franchising Contracts: No
Expand In Territory: Yes
Space Needs: 3,500 SF; FS, SF, SC
SUPPORT & TRAINING:
Financial Assistance Provided: Yes(I)
Site Selection Assistance: Yes
Lease Negotiation Assistance: Yes
Co-Operative Advertising: Yes
Franchisee Assoc./Member: No
Size Of Corporate Staff: 15
On-Going Support: A,B,C,D,E,F,G,h,I
Training: 10-14 Days Oklahoma City, OK; 7 Days On-Site.
SPECIFIC EXPANSION PLANS:
US: All United States
Canada: All Canada
Overseas: All Countries

<< >>

NEVADA BOB'S GOLF

2000, 335 8TH Ave., SW
Calgary, AB T2P 1C9 CANADA
Tel: (877) 222-GOLF (702) 451-3333
Fax: (702) 451-9378
E-Mail: franchise@nevadabobs.com
Web Site: www.nevadabobS.com
Ms. Tracey Pegler

Join the leader in the retail golf industry! With a brand name spanning more than 25 years, NEVADA BOB'S has experience, innovation and an established track record as one of the world's largest golf specialty retailers. Entering a market with an instantly recognizable, established brand name provides you with a substantial advantage over the competition. We are positioned for growth! You can't afford to miss this opportunity!

BACKGROUND:
Established: 1974; 1st Franchised: 1974
Franchised Units: 77
Company-Owned Units: 0
Total Units: 77
Dist.: US-51; CAN-26; O'seas-0
North America: 15 States, 3 Provinces
Density: 12 in CA, 12 in BC, 6 in TN
Projected New Units (12 Months): NR
Qualifications: 4, 4, 3, 3, 4, 4
Registered: NR

FINANCIAL/TERMS:
Cash Investment: $100K
Total Investment: $300-722K
Minimum Net Worth: NR
Fees: Franchise - $50K
Royalty - 2%; Ad. - NR
Earnings Claims Statement: No
Term of Contract (Years): 10/10
Avg. # Of Employees: 2 FT, 3 PT
Passive Ownership: Discouraged
Encourage Conversions: Yes
Area Develop. Agreements: Yes/Varies
Sub-Franchising Contracts: No
Expand In Territory: Yes
Space Needs: ~5,000 SF; FS, SC

SUPPORT & TRAINING:
Financial Assistance Provided: No
Site Selection Assistance: Yes
Lease Negotiation Assistance: Yes
Co-Operative Advertising: Yes
Franchisee Assoc./Member: No
Size Of Corporate Staff: 10
On-Going Support: C,D,E,H,I
Training: Min 5 Days Calgary, AB; Whatever Required at Opening. Classroom & In-Store Support.

SPECIFIC EXPANSION PLANS:
US: All United States
Canada: All Canada
Overseas: No

<< >>

PLAY IT AGAIN SPORTS

4200 Dahlberg Dr., # 100
Minneapolis, MN 55422-4837
Tel: (800) 433-2540 (763) 520-8500
Fax: (763) 520-8501
E-Mail: rgeyer@winmarkcorporation.com
Web Site: www.playitagainsports.com
Ms. Becky Geyer, Franchising Manager

Our retail stores blend the sale of used and new, name-brand sports equipment along with promoting trade-in discounts. This sales mix creates ultra-high value for the customer while providing significantly higher gross profit margins than traditional retailers.

BACKGROUND: IFA MEMBER
Established: 1983; 1st Franchised: 1988
Franchised Units: 464
Company-Owned Units: 0
Total Units: 464
Dist.: US-402; CAN-62; O'seas-0
North America: 47 States, 8 Provinces
Density: 43 in CA, 40 in FL, 24 in MN
Projected New Units (12 Months): 15
Qualifications: 5, 4, 2, 2, 2, 4
Registered: All States and AB

FINANCIAL/TERMS:
Cash Investment: $62-96K
Total Investment: $212-319K
Minimum Net Worth: $250K
Fees: Franchise - $20K
Royalty - 5%; Ad. - $500/Yr.
Earnings Claims Statement: Yes
Term of Contract (Years): 10/10
Avg. # Of Employees: 3 FT, 2 PT
Passive Ownership: Not Allowed
Encourage Conversions: No
Area Develop. Agreements: No
Sub-Franchising Contracts: No
Expand In Territory: No
Space Needs: 2,500-3,000 SF; SC

SUPPORT & TRAINING:
Financial Assistance Provided: No
Site Selection Assistance: Yes
Lease Negotiation Assistance: Yes
Co-Operative Advertising: No
Franchisee Assoc./Member: No
Size Of Corporate Staff: 97
On-Going Support: B,C,D,E,F,G,H,I
Training: 3 Days Minneapolis, MN; 3 Days Minneapolis, MN; 5-6 Days Minneapolis, MN.

SPECIFIC EXPANSION PLANS:
US: All United States
Canada: All Canada
Overseas: No

<< >>

PRO GOLF OF AMERICA

32751 Middlebelt Rd.
Farmington Hills, MI 48334-1726
Tel: (800) 521-6388 + 226 (248) 737-0553 + 226
Fax: (248) 737-9077
E-Mail: jgriffith@progolfdiscount.com
Web Site: www.progolfamerica.com
Mr. Jeff Griffith, Director Franchise Development

PRO GOLF offers the best opportunity to make money among the golf franchise stores available today. We have the best training, the largest selection of private label and exclusive products to sell and the best name - PRO GOLF. Come visit PRO GOLF and learn how a successful retail golf store should operate.

BACKGROUND: IFA MEMBER
Established: 1962; 1st Franchised: 1974
Franchised Units: 148
Company-Owned Units: 1
Total Units: 149
Dist.: US-122; CAN-22; O'seas-4
North America: 30 States, 4 Provinces
Density: 13 in MI, 12 in CA, 9 in FL
Projected New Units (12 Months): 20
Qualifications: 5, 4, 3, 4, , 5
Registered: All States

FINANCIAL/TERMS:
Cash Investment: $100K
Total Investment: $300K+
Minimum Net Worth: $400K
Fees: Franchise - $49.5K
Royalty - 2.5%; Ad. - 0-1%
Earnings Claims Statement: No
Term of Contract (Years): 15/10
Avg. # Of Employees: 4 FT, 3 PT
Passive Ownership: Discouraged
Encourage Conversions: Yes
Area Develop. Agreements: Yes/Negot.
Sub-Franchising Contracts: No
Expand In Territory: Yes
Space Needs: 4,000-6,000 SF; FS, SC

SUPPORT & TRAINING:

Financial Assistance Provided: Yes(I)
Site Selection Assistance: Yes
Lease Negotiation Assistance: Yes
Co-Operative Advertising: Yes
Franchisee Assoc./Member: No
Size Of Corporate Staff: 15
On-Going Support: B,C,D,E,F,G,H,I
Training: 8-12 Days at the Corporate Office in MI; 4-6 Days at Your Location.

SPECIFIC EXPANSION PLANS:
US: All United States
Canada: All Canada
Overseas: All That Have Golfers

<< >>

PRO IMAGE FRANCHISE

233 N. 1250 West, # 200
Centerville, UT 84014
Tel: (888) 477-6326 (801) 296-9999
Fax: (801) 296-1319

E-Mail: charlie@proimage.net
Web Site: www.proimage.net
Mr. Charlie Parker, Director

PRO IMAGE stores carry a comprehensive variety of licensed merchandise from all of your favorite teams from the big leagues to local colleges - including NASCAR and NHL. PRO IMAGE corporate is a one-of-a-kind corporate structure. PRO IMAGE stores represent the only independent, officially-licensed sports apparel franchise outlet on the globe. PRO IMAGE franchises are also uniquely affordable, with low corporate royalty requirements.

BACKGROUND:
Established: 1985; 1st Franchised: 1986
Franchised Units: 94
Company-Owned Units: 0
Total Units: 94
Dist.: US-94; CAN-0; O'seas-0
North America: NR
Density: NR
Projected New Units (12 Months): NR
Qualifications: , , , , ,
Registered:

FINANCIAL/TERMS:
Cash Investment: $100K
Total Investment: $180-200K
Minimum Net Worth: $250K
Fees: Franchise - $19.5K
Royalty - 4%; Ad. - 0%
Earnings Claims Statement: No
Term of Contract (Years): 10/5
Avg. # Of Employees: 2 FT, 2 PT
Passive Ownership: Allowed
Encourage Conversions: NR
Area Develop. Agreements: Negotiable
Sub-Franchising Contracts: No
Expand In Territory: Yes
Space Needs: 1,200 - 1,800 SF; RM

SUPPORT & TRAINING:
Financial Assistance Provided: NR
Site Selection Assistance: Yes
Lease Negotiation Assistance: Yes
Co-Operative Advertising: yes
Franchisee Assoc./Member: No
Size Of Corporate Staff: 8
On-Going Support: A,B,C,D,E,F,G,H,I
Training: 3-4 Days Utah Corporate Office.

SPECIFIC EXPANSION PLANS:
US: All United States
Canada: NR
Overseas: NR

<< >>

SOCCER POST INTERNATIONAL

2903 Highway East 138
Wall, NJ 07719
Tel: (732) 578-1377
Fax: (732) 578-1399
E-Mail: stunis@soccerpost.com
Web Site: www.soccerpost.com
Mr. Stephen Tunis, Franchise Director

A soccer specialty retail business, featuring top-of-the-line, cutting-edge soccer equipment from Adidas, Nike, Reebok, Xara, etc. Owner of store will become the center of soccer activity in the communities they serve. Must be soccer savvy!

BACKGROUND:
Established: 1978; 1st Franchised: 1991
Franchised Units: 25
Company-Owned Units: 7
Total Units: 32
Dist.: US-32; CAN-0; O'seas-0
North America: NR
Density: 8 in PA 7 in NJ, 2 in IL
Projected New Units (12 Months): 12
Qualifications: 5, 3, 1, 3, 4, 5
Registered:CA,FL,IL,IN,MD.MI,NY,RI, WA

FINANCIAL/TERMS:
Cash Investment: $190-250K
Total Investment: $190-250K
Minimum Net Worth: $300K
Fees: Franchise - $19.5K
Royalty - 3-5%; Ad. - 1.5-3%
Earnings Claims Statement: Yes
Term of Contract (Years): 5/5
Avg. # Of Employees: 1 FT, 2-4 PT
Passive Ownership: Allowed
Encourage Conversions: Yes
Area Develop. Agreements: Yes/10
Sub-Franchising Contracts: Yes
Expand In Territory: Yes
Space Needs: 3,200 SF; SC

SUPPORT & TRAINING:
Financial Assistance Provided: Yes
Site Selection Assistance: Yes
Lease Negotiation Assistance: Yes
Co-Operative Advertising: Yes
Franchisee Assoc./Member: No
Size Of Corporate Staff: 9
On-Going Support: C,D,E,F,G,h,I
Training: 2 Weeks Plus Store, Voorhees, NJ.

SPECIFIC EXPANSION PLANS:
US: All United States
Canada: No
Overseas: No

<< >>

SPORTS TRADERS

508 Discovery St.
Victoria, BC V8T 1G8 CANADA
Tel: (800) 792-3111 (250) 383-6443
Fax: (250) 383-8481
E-Mail: sales@sportstraders.ca
Web Site: www.sportstraders.ca
Mr. Allan Mellett, President/CEO

Unique new and used retail concepts. For all sports equipment. We are a coaching franchise, not a controlling franchise, Allowing owners to run an independent store with group buying power and support.

BACKGROUND:
Established: 1983; 1st Franchised: 1987
Franchised Units: 14
Company-Owned Units: 2
Total Units: 16
Dist.: US-0; CAN-16; O'seas-0
North America: NR
Density: 7 in BC, 5 in Man, 2 in ON
Projected New Units (12 Months): 3
Qualifications: 1, 2, 3, 3, 1, 1
Registered: AB

FINANCIAL/TERMS:
Cash Investment: $25K

Total Investment: $250K+
Minimum Net Worth: $250K
Fees: Franchise - $25K
Royalty - $100/Mo.; Ad. - 0%
Earnings Claims Statement: Yes
Term of Contract (Years): 5
Avg. # Of Employees: 1 FT, 1 PT
Passive Ownership: Discouraged
Encourage Conversions: Yes
Area Develop. Agreements: Yes/10
Sub-Franchising Contracts: No
Expand In Territory: Yes
Space Needs: 2,500 SF; FS, SF, SC

SUPPORT & TRAINING:

Financial Assistance Provided: Yes(I)
Site Selection Assistance: Yes
Lease Negotiation Assistance: Yes
Co-Operative Advertising: Yes
Franchisee Assoc./Member: Yes/No
Size Of Corporate Staff: 50
On-Going Support: A,B,C,D,E,F,G,H,I
Training: 7 Days Victoria, BC Head Office; 7 Days Store Site; 2 Days Regional Buying Show.

SPECIFIC EXPANSION PLANS:

US: No
Canada: All Canada
Overseas: No

<< >>

WORLD CLASS ATHLETE

1814 Franklin St., # 820
Oakland, CA 94612
Tel: (510) 839-5462
Fax: (510) 839-2104
E-Mail: sourcebook@earthlink.net
Web Site: www.worldclass.com
Mr. Chris A. Elders, President

WORLD CLASS ATHLETE offers a unique, specialty sporting goods concept. Product mix concentrates on athletic footwear, running, tennis and swimwear. Emphasis on race sponsorship, training programs and custom fitting. All major lines of footwear, accessories, warm-up suits and bags. Custom re-soling at Company-owned distribution centers. Founded by world class athlete Jeff Bond.

BACKGROUND:

Established: 1976; 1st Franchised: 1977
Franchised Units: 42
Company-Owned Units: 12
Total Units: 54
Dist.: US-79; CAN-9; O'seas-4
North America: 15 States, 2 Provinces
Density: 25 in CA, 8 in WA, 7 in KY
Projected New Units (12 Months): 14
Qualifications: 3, 5, 4, 2, 3, 5
Registered: CA,FL,HI,IL,MN,MI,NY,OR, WA,WI,AB

FINANCIAL/TERMS:

Cash Investment: $90K
Total Investment: $150K
Minimum Net Worth: $250K
Fees: Franchise - $22K
Royalty - 6%; Ad. - 2%
Earnings Claims Statement: Yes
Term of Contract (Years): 15/15
Avg. # Of Employees: 2 FT, 4 PT
Passive Ownership: Not Allowed
Encourage Conversions: Yes
Area Develop. Agreements: Yes/15
Sub-Franchising Contracts: Yes
Expand In Territory: No
Space Needs: 1,800-2,200 SF; FS, SC, RM

SUPPORT & TRAINING:

Financial Assistance Provided: Yes(D)
Site Selection Assistance: Yes
Lease Negotiation Assistance: Yes
Co-Operative Advertising: Yes
Franchisee Assoc./Member: No
Size Of Corporate Staff: 12
On-Going Support: a,B,C,D,E,f,G,G,I
Training: 3 Weeks Headquarters; 2 Weeks On-Site; On-Going.

SPECIFIC EXPANSION PLANS:

US: All United States
Canada: All Canada
Overseas: Europe, U.K., Australia, New Zealand

<< >>

Retail: Clothing/Shoes/Accessories

Chapter 36

Retail: Clothing/Shoes/Accessories Industry Profile

Total # Franchisors in Industry Group	11
Total # Franchised Units in Industry Group	150
Total # Company-Owned Units in Industry Group	111
Total # Operating Units in Industry Group	261
Average # Franchised Units/Franchisor	13.6
Average # Company-Owned Units/Franchisor	10.1
Average # Total Units/Franchisor	23.7
Ratio of Total # Franchised Units/Total # Company-Owned Units	1.4:1
Industry Survey Participants	3
Representing % of Industry	27.3%
Average Franchise Fee*:	$26.5K
Average Total Investment*:	$244.8K
Average On-Going Royalty Fee*:	3.7%

*If a range was provided, the mid-point of the range was used. See detailed profiles for actual ranges.

Three Largest Participants in Survey

Company	# Franchised Units	# Co-Owned Units	# Total Units	Franchise Fee	On-Going Royalty	Total Investment
1. Panda Shoes	37	3	40	$25K	4%	$80-125K
2. Furla	24	12	36	$25K	2%	$284-480K
3. Educational Outfitters	16	2	18	$29.5K	5%	$250K

All of the data provided are proprietary and should not be quoted without acknowledging *Bond's Franchise Guide.*

EDUCATIONAL OUTFITTERS

8002 E. Brainerd Rd.
Chattanooga, TN 37421
Tel: (877) 814-1222 (423) 894-1222
Fax: (423) 894-9222
E-Mail: info@educationaloutfitters.com
Web Site: www.educationaloutfitters.com
Ms. Julie Batycki, Director of Development

EDUCATIONAL OUTFITTERS is a retail franchise, offering school uniforms, embroidery, corporate wear, screenprinting and promotional products through our retail locations. If it needs a logo, we can do it!

BACKGROUND: IFA MEMBER
Established: 1998; 1st Franchised: 2001
Franchised Units: 16
Company-Owned Units: 2
Total Units: 18
Dist.: US-16; CAN-0; O'seas-0
North America: 10 States
Density: 3 in NC, 3 in TN, 2 in FL
Projected New Units (12 Months): 20
Qualifications: 5, 5, 1, 4, 3, 5
Registered:CA,FL,IL,IN,MD,MI,MN,OR,VA,WA,WI,DC

FINANCIAL/TERMS:
Cash Investment: $150K
Total Investment: $250K
Minimum Net Worth: $400K
Fees: Franchise - $29.5K
Royalty - 5%; Ad. - 3%
Earnings Claims Statement: No
Term of Contract (Years): 10/5
Avg. # Of Employees: 3 FT, 5 PT
Passive Ownership: Not Allowed
Encourage Conversions: No
Area Develop. Agreements: No
Sub-Franchising Contracts: No
Expand In Territory: Yes
Space Needs: 3,000 SF; SF, SC

SUPPORT & TRAINING:
Financial Assistance Provided: No
Site Selection Assistance: Yes
Lease Negotiation Assistance: Yes
Co-Operative Advertising: Yes
Franchisee Assoc./Member: No
Size Of Corporate Staff: 5
On-Going Support: B,C,D,E,F,G,h,i
Training: 6 Days in Chattanooga, TN; 6 Days Franchise Location.

SPECIFIC EXPANSION PLANS:
US: All United States
Canada: No
Overseas: No

<< >>

FURLA

FURLA

389 Fifth Ave., # 700
New York, NY 10016
Tel: (212) 213-1177 + 15
Fax: (212) 685-5910
E-Mail: bruce@furlausa.com
Web Site: www.furlausa.com
Mr. Bruce S. Pettibone, Managing Director

FURLA designs and sells women's handbags, shoes, belts, small leather goods and related accessories. Our brand is known worldwide through 200+ boutiques around the globe. Our exclusively designed and manufactured products are primarily made in Italy and are priced in better to designer marketplace. Our shops have a distinctive design and are located in upscale retail trade areas.

BACKGROUND: IFA MEMBER
Established: 1997; 1st Franchised: 1998
Franchised Units: 24
Company-Owned Units: 12
Total Units: 36
Dist.: US-29; CAN-1; O'seas-6
North America: 5 States, 1 Province
Density: 4 in FL, 3 in NY, 2 in CA
Projected New Units (12 Months): 10
Qualifications: 3, 4, 2, 3, 5, 5
Registered: CA,FL,HI,IL,MD,MI,NY,OR,VA,WA

FINANCIAL/TERMS:
Cash Investment: $150-200K
Total Investment: $284-480K
Minimum Net Worth: $$400K
Fees: Franchise - $25K
Royalty - 2%; Ad. - 1%
Earnings Claims Statement: No
Term of Contract (Years): 7-10/7-10
Avg. # Of Employees: 3 FT, 3 PT
Passive Ownership: Not Allowed
Encourage Conversions: No
Area Develop. Agreements: No
Sub-Franchising Contracts: No
Expand In Territory: Yes
Space Needs: 900-1,200 SF; SF, RM

SUPPORT & TRAINING:
Financial Assistance Provided: Yes
Site Selection Assistance: Yes
Lease Negotiation Assistance: Yes
Co-Operative Advertising: No
Franchisee Assoc./Member: No
Size Of Corporate Staff: 13
On-Going Support: B,C,D,E,h,I
Training: 1 Week New York Offices and Stores; On-going through store visits.

SPECIFIC EXPANSION PLANS:
US: All United States
Canada: All Canada
Overseas: South America, Caribbean Basin, Central America.

<< >>

PANDA SHOES

305 Marc Aurele Fortin Blvd.
Laval, PQ H7L 2A3 CANADA
Tel: (450) 622-4833 + 201
Fax: (450) 622-2939
E-Mail: info@pandashoes.com
Web Site: www.pandashoes.com
Ms. Linda Goulet, President

Children's shoe specialist - locations in major malls across Canada - 40 stores. Complete training program, including selling, merchandising, administration, etc. National advertising. Best selection of footwear for kids.

BACKGROUND:
Established: 1972; 1st Franchised: 1974
Franchised Units: 37
Company-Owned Units: 3
Total Units: 40
Dist.: US-0; CAN-40; O'seas-0
North America: 4 Provinces
Density: 30 in PQ, 5 in ON, 4 in BC
Projected New Units (12 Months): 0
Qualifications: , , , , ,
Registered: NR

FINANCIAL/TERMS:
Cash Investment: $100K
Total Investment: $80-125K
Minimum Net Worth: NR
Fees: Franchise - $25K
Royalty - 4%; Ad. - 0.5%
Earnings Claims Statement: No
Term of Contract (Years): 5/Lease
Avg. # Of Employees: 3 FT, 2 PT
Passive Ownership: Discouraged

Encouraging Conversions: Yes
Area Develop. Agreements: No
Sub-Franchising Contracts: No
Expand In Territory: Yes
Space Needs: 800 SF; RM

SUPPORT & TRAINING:

Financial Assistance Provided: No
Site Selection Assistance: Yes
Lease Negotiation Assistance: Yes
Co-Operative Advertising: Yes
Franchisee Assoc./Member: NR
Size Of Corporate Staff: 8
On-Going Support: B,C,D,E,F,G,H
Training: 2 Weeks Toronto, ON; 2 Weeks On-Site (at Opening).

SPECIFIC EXPANSION PLANS:

US: No
Canada: All Canada
Overseas: No

<< >>

The Top 100 Franchises denoted in this book were derived from the 2005 edition of *Bond's Top 100 Franchises.* As the pre-eminent publisher of nine books on franchising, Source Book Publications evaluated hundreds of proven franchise systems to arrive at what it feels are the top 100 franchises. Companies were evaluated on the basis of historical performance, brand identification, market dynamics, franchisee satisfaction, the level of initial training and on-going support, financial stability and various other key factors.

To learn more about *Bond's Top 100 Franchises*, please visit our website at www.worldfranchising.com.

Retail: Convenience Stores/Supermarkets/Drugs

Chapter 37

Retail: Convenience Stores/Supermarkets/Drugs Industry Profile

Total # Franchisors in Industry Group	23
Total # Franchised Units in Industry Group	28,622
Total # Company-Owned Units in Industry Group	5,867
Total # Operating Units in Industry Group	34,489
Average # Franchised Units/Franchisor	1244.4
Average # Company-Owned Units/Franchisor	255.1
Average # Total Units/Franchisor	1499.5
Ratio of Total # Franchised Units/Total # Company-Owned Units	4.9:1

Industry Survey Participants	8
Representing % of Industry	34.8%
Average Franchise Fee*:	$27.5K
Average Total Investment*:	$354.5K
Average On-Going Royalty Fee*:	4.3%

*If a range was provided, the mid-point of the range was used. See detailed profiles for actual ranges.

Five Largest Participants in Survey

Company	# Franchised Units	# Co-Owned Units	# Total Units	Franchise Fee	On-Going Royalty	Total Investment
1. 7-Eleven, Inc.	19,992	2,656	22,648	$64K	NA	Varies
2. Circle K	4,400	2,400	6,800	$15K	4%	$15K-1.1MM
3. Medicine Shoppe, The	1,298	15	1,313	$10-18K	2-5.5%	$100K+
4. Health Mart	275	0	275	$50K	0%	$150-300K
5. White Hen Pantry	269	0	269	$25K	8%+	$30-80K

All of the data provided are proprietary and should not be quoted without acknowledging *Bond's Franchise Guide.*

Top 100

7-ELEVEN, INC.

2711 N. Haskell Ave., 34th Fl.
Dallas, TX 75204-2911
Tel: (800) 255-0711 (214) 828-7764
Fax: (214) 841-6776
E-Mail: jwebbj01@7-11.com
Web Site: www.7-eleven.com
Ms. Joanne Webb-Joyce, Dir.National Franchise Sales

7-ELEVEN stores were born from the simple concept of giving people 'what they want, when and where they want it.' This idea gave rise to the entire convenience store industry. While this formula still works today, customers' needs are changing at an accelerating pace. We are meeting this challenge with an infrastructure of daily distribution of fresh perishables, regional production of fresh foods and pastries and an information system that greatly improves ordering and merchandising decisions.

BACKGROUND: IFA MEMBER
Established: 1927; 1st Franchised: 1964
Franchised Units: 19,992
Company-Owned Units: 2656
Total Units: 22,648
Dist.: US-5,771; CAN-499; O'seas-16,378
North America: 36 States, 5 Provinces
Density: 1,183 in CA, 613 VA, 547 FL
Projected New Units (12 Months): 150
Qualifications: 4, 4, 3, 3, 5, 5
Registered:CA,IL,IN,MD,MI,NY,OR,RI,VA,WA,WI

FINANCIAL/TERMS:
Cash Investment: $81K
Total Investment: Varies
Minimum Net Worth: $12.5K
Fees: Franchise - $64K
Royalty - NA; Ad. - NA
Earnings Claims Statement: No
Term of Contract (Years): 10
Avg. # Of Employees: 4 FT, 4 PT
Passive Ownership: Not Allowed
Encourage Conversions: NA
Area Develop. Agreements: No
Sub-Franchising Contracts: No
Expand In Territory: No
Space Needs: 2,400 SF; FS, SC

SUPPORT & TRAINING:
Financial Assistance Provided: Yes(D)
Site Selection Assistance: NA
Lease Negotiation Assistance: NA
Co-Operative Advertising: No
Franchisee Assoc./Member: Yes/Yes
Size Of Corporate Staff: 1,000
On-Going Support: A,B,C,D,E,F,G,H,I
Training: 6 Weeks at Various Training Stores throughout US.

SPECIFIC EXPANSION PLANS:
US: NW,SW,MW,NE, Great Lakes
Canada: No
Overseas: No

<< >>

ARROW PRESCRIPTION CENTER

312 Farmington Ave.
Farmington, CT 06032-1968
Tel: (800) 203-2776 (860) 676-1222
Fax: (860) 676-1499
E-Mail: kaufmanr@familymeds.com
Web Site: www.arrowrx.com
Mr. Ron Kaufman, VP Business Development

ARROW CORPORATION is one of the nation's largest franchisors of retail pharmacies, offering opportunities in traditional and alternative settings. At the core of ARROW'S philosophy is the delivery of pharmacy services directly to the patient by the pharmacist.

BACKGROUND:
Established: 1989; 1st Franchised: 1990
Franchised Units: 48
Company-Owned Units: 22
Total Units: 70
Dist.: US-59; CAN-0; O'seas-0
North America: 6 States
Density: 42 in CT, 5 in MI, 5 in MA
Projected New Units (12 Months): 16
Qualifications: 4, 4, 5, 5, 4, 4
Registered: NR

FINANCIAL/TERMS:
Cash Investment: $20% of Total
Total Investment: Varies
Minimum Net Worth: $100K
Fees: Franchise - $15K
Royalty - 6%; Ad. - Varies
Earnings Claims Statement: No
Term of Contract (Years): 20/10
Avg. # Of Employees: 2 FT, 1-6 PT
Passive Ownership: Discouraged
Encourage Conversions: Yes
Area Develop. Agreements: Yes/5
Sub-Franchising Contracts: No
Expand In Territory: No
Space Needs: 1,500 SF; FS, SC

SUPPORT & TRAINING:
Financial Assistance Provided: Yes(B)
Site Selection Assistance: Yes
Lease Negotiation Assistance: No
Co-Operative Advertising: Yes
Franchisee Assoc./Member: Yes
Size Of Corporate Staff: 30
On-Going Support: A,C,D,E,F,G,H,I
Training: 1-2 Weeks Corporate Training Center.

SPECIFIC EXPANSION PLANS:
US: All United States
Canada: No
Overseas: No

<< >>

CIRCLE K

1130 W. Warner Rd. DC-07
Tempe, AZ 85284
Tel: (800) 813-7677 (714) 337-3404
Fax: (602) 728-5248
E-Mail: franchise@circlek.com
Web Site: www.circlek.com
Mr. Daniel D. Williams, Director Franchise Devel.

Unlike any other convenience store and petroleum company, we offer you a CIRCLE K license opportunity that helps to build a business with leading brands in both the convenience store and petroleum industries (CIRCLE K/76). Licensing leading brands in these industries provides you with the ability to offer your customers a one-of-a-kind convenience experience. We also offer superior business systems, extensive training and effective promotional tools. This unique combination is the CIRCLE K advantage.

BACKGROUND: IFA MEMBER
Established: 1951; 1st Franchised: 1995
Franchised Units: 1,603
Company-Owned Units: 577
Total Units: 2,180
Dist.: US-2,800; CAN-0; O'seas-4,000
North America: 35 States
Density: 530 in AZ, 377 in FL, 300 CA
Projected New Units (12 Months): 125
Qualifications: 5, 4, 5, 3, 3, 5
Registered: CA,FL,HI,IL,IN,MD,MI,MN,NY,ND,OR,SD,VA,WA

FINANCIAL/TERMS:
Cash Investment: $15-450K
Total Investment: $15K-1.1MM
Minimum Net Worth: $300K

Fees: Franchise - $15K
Royalty - 4%; Ad. - 2%
Earnings Claims Statement: Yes
Term of Contract (Years): 10/10
Avg. # Of Employees: 8 FT, 4 PT
Passive Ownership: Discouraged
Encourage Conversions: Yes
Area Develop. Agreements: Yes/5
Sub-Franchising Contracts: No
Expand In Territory: Yes
Space Needs: 1,500-3,000 SF; FS

SUPPORT & TRAINING:
Financial Assistance Provided: Yes(I)
Site Selection Assistance: Yes
Lease Negotiation Assistance: No
Co-Operative Advertising: NA
Franchisee Assoc./Member: No
Size Of Corporate Staff: 1,200
On-Going Support: B,C,D,E,F,G,H,I
Training: 4 Weeks in Phoenix, AZ.

SPECIFIC EXPANSION PLANS:
US: All United States
Canada: No
Overseas: Asia

HEALTH MART

1 Post St.
San Francisco, CA 94104
Tel: (800) 369-5467 (415) 983-8300
Fax: (415) 983-9353
E-Mail: stefan.linn@mckesson.com
Web Site: www.mckesson.com
Mr. Stefan Linn, President

The largest full-line pharmacy franchise for independent store owners.

BACKGROUND:
Established: 1981; 1st Franchised: 1983
Franchised Units: 275
Company-Owned Units: 0
Total Units: 275
Dist.: US-600; CAN-0; O'seas-0
North America: 34 States
Density: 83 in IL, 64 in MO, 59 in LA
Projected New Units (12 Months): 100
Qualifications: 3, 4, 5, 5, 1, 3
Registered: All States

FINANCIAL/TERMS:
Cash Investment: $5-15K
Total Investment: $150-300K
Minimum Net Worth: NR
Fees: Franchise - $50K
Royalty - 0%; Ad. - $150/Mo.
Earnings Claims Statement: Yes
Term of Contract (Years): 5/5
Avg. # Of Employees: 2 FT, 1 PT
Passive Ownership: Allowed
Encourage Conversions: Yes
Area Develop. Agreements: No
Sub-Franchising Contracts: No
Expand In Territory: Yes
Space Needs: 500+ SF; FS, SF, SC, RM

SUPPORT & TRAINING:
Financial Assistance Provided: NA
Site Selection Assistance: No
Lease Negotiation Assistance: No
Co-Operative Advertising: Yes
Franchisee Assoc./Member: No
Size Of Corporate Staff: 5
On-Going Support: b,C,D,e,G,h,I
Training: 1-3 Days On-Site.

SPECIFIC EXPANSION PLANS:
US: All United States
Canada: No
Overseas: No

MEDICAP PHARMACY

4350 Westown Pkwy., # 400
West Des Moines, IA 50266-1061
Tel: (800) 445-2244 (515) 224-8400
Fax: (515) 224-8494
E-Mail: cjames@medicaprx.com
Web Site: www.medicap.com
Mr. Calvin C. James, SVP Franchise Development

MEDICAP PHARMACY - convenient, low-cost, professional pharmacies. The stores operate in an average of 1,500-2,000 square feet. We average 90% RX and the remaining 10% over-the-counter products, including MEDICAP-brand private label. We specialize in starting new stores and converting existing full-line drug stores and independent pharmacies to the MEDICAP concept. We teach independent pharmacists how to survive in today's marketplace.

BACKGROUND: IFA MEMBER
Established: 1971; 1st Franchised: 1974
Franchised Units: 187
Company-Owned Units: 13
Total Units: 200
Dist.: US-200; CAN-0; O'seas-0
North America: 38 States
Density: 50 in IA, 23 in NC, 7 in SC
Projected New Units (12 Months): 25
Qualifications: 3, 1, 4, 5, 3, 5
Registered: CA,FL,IL,IN,MD,MN,ND,OR,SD,WA,WI

FINANCIAL/TERMS:
Cash Investment: $10-55K
Total Investment: $20-447K
Minimum Net Worth: NR
Fees: Franchise - $8.5-15K
Royalty - 2 or 3.9%; Ad. - 1%
Earnings Claims Statement: Yes
Term of Contract (Years): 20/10
Avg. # Of Employees: 2 FT
Passive Ownership: Allowed
Encourage Conversions: Yes
Area Develop. Agreements: No
Sub-Franchising Contracts: No
Expand In Territory: Yes
Space Needs: 1,500 SF; FS, SF, SC

SUPPORT & TRAINING:
Financial Assistance Provided: Yes(I)
Site Selection Assistance: Yes
Lease Negotiation Assistance: Yes
Co-Operative Advertising: NA
Franchisee Assoc./Member: NR
Size Of Corporate Staff: 62
On-Going Support: B,C,D,E,F,G,H,I
Training: 4 Days Headquarters; 3 Days On-Site; 3 Days Computer.

SPECIFIC EXPANSION PLANS:
US: All United States
Canada: All Canada
Overseas: All Countries

<< >>

MEDICINE SHOPPE, THE

1100 N. Lindbergh Blvd.
St. Louis, MO 63132-2992
Tel: (800) 325-1397 (314) 993-6000
Fax: (314) 872-5500
E-Mail: dan.lhota@cardinal.com
Web Site: www.medicineshoppe.com
Mr. Daniel P. Lhota, SVP Franchise Sales/Devel.

Medicine Shoppe International is the largest and fastest growing chain of franchised pharmacies in the world. MSI offers its owners numerous ways to enter pharmacy ownership, i.e. acquisition of existing pharmacies, new store development, supermarkets clinic locations. Diversify your portfolio and participate in the graying of America.

BACKGROUND: IFA MEMBER
Established: 1970; 1st Franchised: 1970
Franchised Units: 1,287
Company-Owned Units: 25
Total Units: 1,313
Dist.: US-1,133; CAN-0; O'seas-180
North America: 47 States
Density: 121 in PA, 111 in FL, 71 CA
Projected New Units (12 Months): 65
Qualifications: 3, 3, 4, 5, 2, 4
Registered: All States

FINANCIAL/TERMS:

Cash Investment: $10-18K
Total Investment: $100K+
Minimum Net Worth: $50K
Fees: Franchise - $10-18K
Royalty - 2-5.5%; Ad. - $200/Mo.
Earnings Claims Statement: Yes
Term of Contract (Years): 10/15
Avg. # Of Employees: 2 FT, 1 PT
Passive Ownership: Allowed
Encourage Conversions: Yes
Area Develop. Agreements: Yes
Sub-Franchising Contracts: No
Expand In Territory: Yes
Space Needs: 1,200 SF; FS, SF, SC

SUPPORT & TRAINING:

Financial Assistance Provided: Yes(D)
Site Selection Assistance: Yes
Lease Negotiation Assistance: Yes
Co-Operative Advertising: Yes
Franchisee Assoc./Member: No
Size Of Corporate Staff: 240
On-Going Support: A,B,C,D,E,F,G,H,I
Training: 6 Days St. Louis, MO.

SPECIFIC EXPANSION PLANS:

US: All United States
Canada: Master License
Overseas: All Countries

<< >>

UNCLESAM'S CONVENIENT STORE

P. O. Box 870
Elsa, TX 78543-0870
Tel: (956) 262-7273
Fax: (956) 262-7290
E-Mail:
Web Site: www.unclesamscstore.com
Mr. Jerry L. Barth, President

A turn-key convenience store franchise program available in 31 states. Affiliated with major fuel and merchandise suppliers. Attractive financing available to qualified candidates. Training, site evaluation, store design, operations manual, software package, advertising, promotions, security systems, deli, car wash and many more benefits.

BACKGROUND:

Established: 1970; 1st Franchised: 1997
Franchised Units: 1
Company-Owned Units: 52
Total Units: 53
Dist.: US-52; CAN-0; O'seas-0
North America: 1 State
Density: 52 in TX
Projected New Units (12 Months): 10
Qualifications: 4, 5, 3, 4, 3, 5
Registered: FL,OR

FINANCIAL/TERMS:

Cash Investment: $100K+
Total Investment: $800K+
Minimum Net Worth: $300K
Fees: Franchise - $25K
Royalty - 5%; Ad. - 1%
Earnings Claims Statement: No
Term of Contract (Years): 5/5/5/5/5
Avg. # Of Employees: 6 FT, 2 PT
Passive Ownership: Discouraged
Encourage Conversions: Yes
Area Develop. Agreements: Yes/5
Sub-Franchising Contracts: No
Expand In Territory: Yes
Space Needs: 2,500+ SF; FS

SUPPORT & TRAINING:

Financial Assistance Provided: Yes(I)
Site Selection Assistance: Yes
Lease Negotiation Assistance: Yes
Co-Operative Advertising: Yes
Franchisee Assoc./Member: Yes/No
Size Of Corporate Staff: 6
On-Going Support: a,B,C,d,E,F,I
Training: 4 Weeks at Corporate Headquarters.

SPECIFIC EXPANSION PLANS:

US: South, SW, SE, East, West
Canada: No
Overseas: No

<< >>

WHITE HEN PANTRY

3003 Butterfield Rd., # 300
Oak Brook, IL 60523
Tel: (800) 726-8791 (630) 366-3100
Fax: (630) 366-3447
E-Mail: gail.bosch@whitehen.com
Web Site: www.whitehen.com
Ms. Gail M. Bosch, Franchising Manager

WHITE HEN PANTRY is an up-scale neighborhood convenience store, specializing in fresh-brewed coffee, full-service deli, custom-made sandwiches and salads, fresh produce and a bakery.

BACKGROUND: IFA MEMBER

Established: 1965; 1st Franchised: 1965
Franchised Units: 269
Company-Owned Units: 0
Total Units: 269
Dist.: US-269; CAN-0; O'seas-0
North America: 3 States
Density: 215 in IL, 53 in MA, 1 in IN
Projected New Units (12 Months): 10
Qualifications: 2, 4, 3, 2, 3, 5
Registered: IL,IN,MA

FINANCIAL/TERMS:

Cash Investment: $30-50K
Total Investment: $30-80K
Minimum Net Worth: NA
Fees: Franchise - $25K
Royalty - 8%+; Ad. - Included
Earnings Claims Statement: No
Term of Contract (Years): 10/10
Avg. # Of Employees: 2 FT, 12 PT
Passive Ownership: Not Allowed
Encourage Conversions: NA
Area Develop. Agreements: No
Sub-Franchising Contracts: No
Expand In Territory: No
Space Needs: 2,500 SF; FS, SC

SUPPORT & TRAINING:

Financial Assistance Provided: Yes(D)
Site Selection Assistance: NA
Lease Negotiation Assistance: NA
Co-Operative Advertising: Yes
Franchisee Assoc./Member: Yes/Yes
Size Of Corporate Staff: 120
On-Going Support: A,C,D,E,F,G,H,I
Training: 1 Week Corporate Office; 2 Weeks On-Site.

SPECIFIC EXPANSION PLANS:

US: IL, MA, NH Only
Canada: No
Overseas: No

<< >>

Retail: Home Furnishings

Chapter 38

Retail: Home Furnishings Industry Profile

Total # Franchisors in Industry Group	43
Total # Franchised Units in Industry Group	3,131
Total # Company-Owned Units in Industry Group	229
Total # Operating Units in Industry Group	3,360
Average # Franchised Units/Franchisor	72.8
Average # Company-Owned Units/Franchisor	5.3
Average # Total Units/Franchisor	78.1
Ratio of Total # Franchised Units/Total # Company-Owned Units	13.7:1
Industry Survey Participants	21
Representing % of Industry	48.8%
Average Franchise Fee*:	$24K
Average Total Investment*:	$149.1K
Average On-Going Royalty Fee*:	4.4%

*If a range was provided, the mid-point of the range was used. See detailed profiles for actual ranges.

Five Largest Participants in Survey

Company	# Franchised Units	# Co-Owned Units	# Total Units	Franchise Fee	On-Going Royalty	Total Investment
1. Interiors by Decorating Den	465	1	466	$24.9K	7-9%	$40-70K
2. Badcock Home Furniture & More	278	55	333	$0	0%	$100-300K
3. Budget Blinds	240	0	240	$25K	4-5%	$30-45K
4. V2K The Virtual Window Fashion Store	135	0	135	$39.9K	8-6.5%	$45-55K
5. Floor To Ceiling	129	1	130	$3-6K	$350+/Mo.	Varies

All of the data provided are proprietary and should not be quoted without acknowledging *Bond's Franchise Guide.*

A SHADE BETTER

2110 W. 110th St.
Cleveland, OH 44102
Tel: (800) 722-8676 (216) 281-0640
Fax: (216) 961-9736
E-Mail: info@ashadebetter.com
Web Site: www.ashadebetter.com
Mr. James P. Prexta, President

Distinctive retail stores selling beautiful lamp shades, lamps and accessories. Franchisees will also have the opportunity to develop and service the wholesale market in their exclusive territory.

BACKGROUND:
Established: 1988; 1st Franchised: 1993
Franchised Units: 10
Company-Owned Units: 7
Total Units: 17
Dist.: US-18; CAN-0; O'seas-0
North America: 7 States
Density: 5 in OH, 3 in IL, 2 in TX
Projected New Units (12 Months): 12
Qualifications: 4, 4, 2, 2, 3, 5
Registered: CA,FL,IL,IN,MD,MI,WI

FINANCIAL/TERMS:
Cash Investment: $75-100K
Total Investment: $114-156K
Minimum Net Worth: $300K
Fees: Franchise - $35K
Royalty - 6%; Ad. - 1%
Earnings Claims Statement: No
Term of Contract (Years): 5/5/5/5
Avg. # Of Employees: 2 FT, 2 PT
Passive Ownership: Discouraged
Encourage Conversions: Yes
Area Develop. Agreements: Yes/Varies
Sub-Franchising Contracts: No
Expand In Territory: Yes
Space Needs: 1,800 SF; SC

SUPPORT & TRAINING:
Financial Assistance Provided: No
Site Selection Assistance: Yes
Lease Negotiation Assistance: Yes
Co-Operative Advertising: No
Franchisee Assoc./Member: No
Size Of Corporate Staff: 6
On-Going Support: B,C,D,E,h,I
Training: 6 Days Cleveland, OH or Phoenix, AZ; 6 Days On-Site.

SPECIFIC EXPANSION PLANS:
US: Midwest, Southwest
Canada: No
Overseas: No

BADCOCK HOME FURNITURE & MORE

P. O. Box 497
Mulberry, FL 33860
Tel: (800) 223-2625 (863) 869-7972
Fax: (863) 425-7691
E-Mail: smccorkle@badcock.com
Web Site: www.badcock.com
Mr. Scott McCorkle, Dealer Development Coordinator

W.S. BADCOCK Corp. offers dealership opportunities to qualified individuals. Dealerships are similar to franchises in that they are individually owned and operated, but require less capital (no franchise fee or monthly royalty fees) and allow for a quicker start-up than a traditional franchise. BADCOCK provides all stores with total inventory at no cost to the dealer and all account financing through the parent company.

BACKGROUND:
Established: 1904; 1st Franchised: 1928
Franchised Units: 278
Company-Owned Units: 55
Total Units: 333
Dist.: US-333; CAN-0; O'seas-0
North America: 7 States
Density: 145 in FL, 87 in GA, 35 SC
Projected New Units (12 Months): 8-12
Qualifications: 4, 4, 3, 2, 2, 4
Registered: FL

FINANCIAL/TERMS:
Cash Investment: $75-150K
Total Investment: $100-300K
Minimum Net Worth: $150K
Fees: Franchise - $0
Royalty - 0%; Ad. - 1%
Earnings Claims Statement: Yes
Term of Contract (Years): 10/5/5
Avg. # Of Employees: 4 FT, 2 PT
Passive Ownership: Discouraged
Encourage Conversions: Yes
Area Develop. Agreements: Yes/5
Sub-Franchising Contracts: No
Expand In Territory: Yes
Space Needs: ~15,000 SF; FS, SF, SC

SUPPORT & TRAINING:
Financial Assistance Provided: Yes(I)
Site Selection Assistance: Yes
Lease Negotiation Assistance: No
Co-Operative Advertising: Yes
Franchisee Assoc./Member: No
Size Of Corporate Staff: 1,100
On-Going Support: A,B,C,D,E,F,G,H,I
Training: 60-90 Days Home and Training Store

SPECIFIC EXPANSION PLANS:
US: GA, MS, SC, NC, TN, AL
Canada: No
Overseas: No

BIG BOB'S FLOORING OUTLETS

9320 W. 75th St.
Shawnee Mission, KS 66204
Tel: (877) 644-2627 (913) 789-7773
Fax: (913) 789-7126
E-Mail: BBB97inc@aol.com
Web Site: www.bigbobscarpet.com
Mr. David Elyachar, President

To provide an affordable opportunity to franchise, drawing from the unique, second, promotionals, and private lines of flowing and in turn providing an excellent margin and excellent prices to the franchisee and the customer. BIG BOB'S uses unique and proven advertising. There will be full training and counsel when needed. BIG BOB'S is like no other in the industry. We target a niche in the market that has virtually no competition.

BACKGROUND:
Established: 1983; 1st Franchised: 1993
Franchised Units: 36
Company-Owned Units: 3
Total Units: 39
Dist.: US-39; CAN-0; O'seas-0
North America: 17 States
Density: 5 in OH, 4 in CA, 4 in KS
Projected New Units (12 Months): 7
Qualifications: 2, 3, 3, 2, 4, 4
Registered:CA,FL,IL,IN,MD,MI,MN,NY,VA,WA

FINANCIAL/TERMS:
Cash Investment: $140-180K
Total Investment: $140-180K
Minimum Net Worth: $40K
Fees: Franchise - $15K
Royalty - 2-4%; Ad. - NA
Earnings Claims Statement: No
Term of Contract (Years): 5/5
Avg. # Of Employees: 3-5 FT, 1-3 PT
Passive Ownership: Discouraged
Encourage Conversions: Yes
Area Develop. Agreements: No
Sub-Franchising Contracts: No
Expand In Territory: Yes
Space Needs: 9,000-13,000 SF; FS, SF

SUPPORT & TRAINING:
Financial Assistance Provided: Yes(I)
Site Selection Assistance: Yes
Lease Negotiation Assistance: No
Co-Operative Advertising: No
Franchisee Assoc./Member: No
Size Of Corporate Staff: 5
On-Going Support: B,C,D,E,F,G,H,I

Training: Varies with Individual; 1 Week in Kansas City, KS; Other Retail Centers Optional.

SPECIFIC EXPANSION PLANS:

US: All United States
Canada: No
Overseas: No

<< >>

BLIND MAN OF AMERICA

606 Fremont Circle
Colorado Springs, CO 80919
Tel: (800) 547-9889 (719) 260-8989
Fax: (719) 272-4105
E-Mail: blindmanofamerica@msn.com
Web Site: www.blindmanofamerica.com
Ms. Linda Keller, Vice President

Sell custom-made blinds, shades, shutters and more. Our home-based, mobile showroom concept makes it easy for customers to do business with us. THE BLIND MAN'S unique approach of offering interior as well as exterior window coverings sets us apart from the competition. Not only that, but our territory sizes are normally double that of other window covering franchises. We will teach you everything you need to know, from sales to installation to office management.

BACKGROUND: IFA MEMBER

Established: 1991; 1st Franchised: 1996
Franchised Units: 6
Company-Owned Units: 1
Total Units: 7
Dist.: US-7; CAN-0; O'seas-0
North America: 4 States
Density: 4 in CO, 1 in AZ, 1 in WA
Projected New Units (12 Months): 10
Qualifications: 3, 4, 2, 1, 3, 5
Registered: WA

FINANCIAL/TERMS:

Cash Investment: $15-25K
Total Investment: $26.8-50.4K
Minimum Net Worth: $26.8K
Fees: Franchise - $15K
Royalty - 4.25%; Ad. - 0%
Earnings Claims Statement: No
Term of Contract (Years): 5/5
Avg. # Of Employees: 1-3 FT
Passive Ownership: Not Allowed
Encourage Conversions: No
Area Develop. Agreements: No
Sub-Franchising Contracts: No
Expand In Territory: NR
Space Needs: NR SF; HB

SUPPORT & TRAINING:

Financial Assistance Provided: No
Site Selection Assistance: No
Lease Negotiation Assistance: NA
Co-Operative Advertising: NA
Franchisee Assoc./Member: No
Size Of Corporate Staff: 2
On-Going Support: B,C,D,G,h,I
Training: 2 Weeks Colorado Springs, CO.

SPECIFIC EXPANSION PLANS:

US: Midwest and West Coast
Canada: No
Overseas: No

<< >>

BUDGET BLINDS

1927 N. Glassell St.
Orange, CA 92865
Tel: (800) 420-5374 (714) 637-2100
Fax: (714) 637-1400
E-Mail: todd@budgetblinds.com
Web Site: www.budgetblinds.com
Mr. Todd Jackson, Operations Manager

BUDGET BLINDS trains individuals to own and operate a home-based business that sells and installs window coverings, via a well-equipped mobile showroom. What makes our franchise unique is that we actually teach people how to run a business, versus teaching people how to do a job. By business we mean hiring, monitoring and maintaining employees, working from cash flow, profit loss and balance statements, We teach what business owners need to know, not what job operators want to know.

BACKGROUND: IFA MEMBER

Established: 1992; 1st Franchised: 1994
Franchised Units: 240
Company-Owned Units: 0
Total Units: 240
Dist.: US-240; CAN-0; O'seas-0
North America: 36 States
Density: 60 in CA, 15 in GA, 14 in AZ
Projected New Units (12 Months): 350
Qualifications: 2, 4, 1, 2, 3, 5
Registered: All States

FINANCIAL/TERMS:

Cash Investment: $50K
Total Investment: $30-45K
Minimum Net Worth: $30K
Fees: Franchise - $25K
Royalty - 4-5%; Ad. - $150
Earnings Claims Statement: Yes
Term of Contract (Years): 5/5
Avg. # Of Employees: 1-5 FT
Passive Ownership: Discouraged
Encourage Conversions: Yes
Area Develop. Agreements: No
Sub-Franchising Contracts: No
Expand In Territory: Yes
Space Needs: NR SF; HB

SUPPORT & TRAINING:

Financial Assistance Provided: Yes(I)
Site Selection Assistance: NA
Lease Negotiation Assistance: NA
Co-Operative Advertising: Yes
Franchisee Assoc./Member: No/No
Size Of Corporate Staff: 25
On-Going Support: A,B,C,D,G,H
Training: 10 Days Orange, CA.

SPECIFIC EXPANSION PLANS:

US: All United States
Canada: All Canada
Overseas: No

<< >>

CARPET NETWORK
"The Traveling Floor And Window Store" ®

Top 100

CARPET NETWORK

109 Gaither Dr., # 302
Mount Laurel, NJ 08054-1704
Tel: (800) 428-1067 (856) 273-9393
Fax: (856) 273-0160
E-Mail: info@carpetnetwork.com
Web Site: www.carpetnetwork.com
Ms. Jennifer Ostroff, VP Operations/Franchise Devel.

'The Traveling Floor and Window Store.' A mobile business offering carpet, ceramic tile, area rugs, laminate, wood, vinyl flooring and window treatments in the convenience of the consumer's home or business. Over 4,000 selections from leading manufacturers, serving today's 'time starved' consumer. Large exclusive territories, marketing strategy - training - 24-hour support - up-to-date technology and much more.

BACKGROUND:

Established: 1991; 1st Franchised: 1992
Franchised Units: 46
Company-Owned Units: 0
Total Units: 46
Dist.: US-46; CAN-0; O'seas-0
North America: 19 States
Density: 7 in PA, 6 in NJ, 5 in NY
Projected New Units (12 Months): 15
Qualifications: 5, 5, 3, 3, 5, 5
Registered: CA,FL,IL,IN,MI,MN,NY,OR,WI

FINANCIAL/TERMS:

Cash Investment: $22.2K Min.

Total Investment: $33-44.1K
Minimum Net Worth: $75K
Fees: Franchise - $21.5K
Royalty - 2-7%; Ad. - $165/Mo.
Earnings Claims Statement: No
Term of Contract (Years): 15/15
Avg. # Of Employees: 1 FT, 1 PT
Passive Ownership: Discouraged
Encourage Conversions: NA
Area Develop. Agreements: Yes
Sub-Franchising Contracts: No
Expand In Territory: Yes
Space Needs: NA SF; (Mobile) HB, WH

SUPPORT & TRAINING:
Financial Assistance Provided: Yes(D)
Site Selection Assistance: Yes
Lease Negotiation Assistance: NA
Co-Operative Advertising: NA
Franchisee Assoc./Member: Yes/Yes
Size Of Corporate Staff: 7
On-Going Support: C,D,G,H,I
Training: 2 Weeks Home Study; 1 Week Mt. Laurel, NJ Home Office.

SPECIFIC EXPANSION PLANS:
US: All United States
Canada: No
Overseas: No

<< >>

DESIGNS OF THE INTERIOR

Because every life is uniquely designed.

DOTI DESIGN STORES

18-3 E. Dundee Rd., # 208
Barrington, IL 60010
Tel: (888) 382-7488 (847) 713-2622
Fax: (847) 713-2636
E-Mail: info@doti.com
Web Site: www.doti.com
Mr. Jim Evanger, Franchise Development

Upscale home furnishings and design retail stores. DOTI DESIGN STORES offer "one-stop-shopping" for all furniture, window treatments, accessories, rugs and lights for discriminating home owners. Franchisees do NOT need industry experience - but rather a people management background and leadership ability. Huge $200 billion industry. Learn more at www.doti.com.

BACKGROUND: IFA MEMBER
Established: 1983; 1st Franchised: 2000
Franchised Units: 15
Company-Owned Units: 2
Total Units: 17
Dist.: US-17; CAN-0; O'seas-0
North America: 6 States
Density: 6 in IL, 2 in WI, 2 in FL
Projected New Units (12 Months): 10
Qualifications: 4, 5, 2, 4, 3, 5
Registered: CA,FL,IL,MI,WI

FINANCIAL/TERMS:
Cash Investment: $125-150K
Total Investment: $280-380K
Minimum Net Worth: $550K
Fees: Franchise - $36K
Royalty - 6%; Ad. - 0%
Earnings Claims Statement: Yes
Term of Contract (Years): 5/5/5/5
Avg. # Of Employees: 9 FT, 1 PT
Passive Ownership: Not Allowed
Encourage Conversions: NA
Area Develop. Agreements: Yes/3
Sub-Franchising Contracts: No
Expand In Territory: Yes
Space Needs: 5,000 SF; FS, SF, SC

SUPPORT & TRAINING:
Financial Assistance Provided: No
Site Selection Assistance: Yes
Lease Negotiation Assistance: Yes
Co-Operative Advertising: Yes
Franchisee Assoc./Member: No
Size Of Corporate Staff: 6
On-Going Support: B,C,B,E,F,G,H,I
Training: 4 Days Barrington, IL; 4 Days Barrington, IL; 7 Days On-Site.

SPECIFIC EXPANSION PLANS:
US: All United States
Canada: No
Overseas: No

<< >>

FLOOR COVERINGS INTERNATIONAL

5182 Old Dixie Hwy., # B
Forest Park, GA 30297-2612
Tel: (800) 955-4324 (404) 361-5047
Fax: (404) 366-4606
E-Mail: lcarnell@carpetvan.com
Web Site: www.floorcoveringsintl.com
Mr. Larry Carnell, Dir. Franchise Development

FLOOR COVERINGS INTERNATIONAL is the 'Flooring Store at your Door.' FCI is the first and leading mobile 'shop at home' flooring store. Customers can select from over 3,000 styles and colors of flooring right in their own home! All the right ingredients are there to simplify a buying decision. We offer all the brand names you and your customers will be familiar with. We carry all types of flooring, as well as window blinds.

BACKGROUND: IFA MEMBER
Established: 1988; 1st Franchised: 1989
Franchised Units: 90
Company-Owned Units: 0
Total Units: 90
Dist.: US-150; CAN-16; O'seas-60
North America: 43 States, 5 Provinces
Density: 15 in PA, 11 in OH, 9 in IL
Projected New Units (12 Months): 45
Qualifications: 5, 5, 4, 3, 4, 4
Registered: All States

FINANCIAL/TERMS:
Cash Investment: $25-35K
Total Investment: $31.1-41.3K
Minimum Net Worth: $50K
Fees: Franchise - $16K
Royalty - 5%/$325/Mo.; Ad. - 2%/$130/Mo.
Earnings Claims Statement: No
Term of Contract (Years): 10/10
Avg. # Of Employees: 1 FT, 1PT
Passive Ownership: Discouraged
Encourage Conversions: Yes
Area Develop. Agreements: Yes/10
Sub-Franchising Contracts: No
Expand In Territory: Yes
Space Needs: NR SF; Mobile Van

SUPPORT & TRAINING:
Financial Assistance Provided: Yes(D)
Site Selection Assistance: Yes
Lease Negotiation Assistance: NA
Co-Operative Advertising: Yes
Franchisee Assoc./Member: Yes
Size Of Corporate Staff: 15
On-Going Support: A,B,C,D,E,G,H,I
Training: 2 Weeks Home Study; 2 Weeks Atlanta, GA.

SPECIFIC EXPANSION PLANS:
US: All United States
Canada: All Canada
Overseas: U.K.

<< >>

FLOOR TO CEILING

3200 Corporate Center Dr., # 101
Burnsville, MN 55306
Tel: (952) 890-8979
Fax: (952) 890-3818
E-Mail: mscherer@floortoceiling.com
Web Site: www.floortoceiling.com
Mr. Mike Scherer, Franchise Sales Director

FLOOR TO CEILING offers a comprehensive retail franchise opportunity in the fast-growing home decorating market. FTC franchisees benefit from national buying power in floor covering, kitchen and bath and decorative products from the nation's leading manufacturers. Our service is complete with software, advertising, rebates, insurance, consumer financing, HR and much more!

BACKGROUND:
Established: 1990; 1st Franchised: 1996
Franchised Units: 129
Company-Owned Units: 1
Total Units: 130
Dist.: US-63; CAN-0; O'seas-0
North America: 9 States
Density: 23 in MN, 14 in WI, 6 in IL
Projected New Units (12 Months): 15-20
Qualifications: 5, 4, 5, 3, 4, 5
Registered: IL,IN,MN,ND,SD,WA,WI

FINANCIAL/TERMS:
Cash Investment: Varies
Total Investment: Varies
Minimum Net Worth: Varies
Fees: Franchise - $3-6K
Royalty - $350+/Mo.; Ad. - 0%
Earnings Claims Statement: Yes
Term of Contract (Years): 5/5-10
Avg. # Of Employees: 4 FT, 2 PT
Passive Ownership: Allowed
Encourage Conversions: Yes
Area Develop. Agreements: Yes/Varies
Sub-Franchising Contracts: NR
Expand In Territory: Yes
Space Needs: 8,000-14,000 SF; FS, SF, SC

SUPPORT & TRAINING:
Financial Assistance Provided: NA
Site Selection Assistance: No
Lease Negotiation Assistance: No
Co-Operative Advertising: Yes
Franchisee Assoc./Member: Yes/Yes
Size Of Corporate Staff: 10
On-Going Support: A,C,D,E,G,H
Training: Variable Amount of Time at Home Office.

SPECIFIC EXPANSION PLANS:
US: All United States
Canada: No
Overseas: No

<< >>

GOTCHA COVERED

1611 N. Stemmons Plwy., # 318
Carrollton, TX 75006
Tel: (877) 777-2544 (972) 466-2544
Fax: (972) 446-6774
E-Mail: aarong@gotchacoveredblinds.com
Web Site: www.gotchacoveredblinds.com
Mr. Aaron Gibson, Franchise Devel. Manager

GOTCHA COVERED BLINDS is listed in Entrepreneur 500 and rated # 2 in the window treatment industry. Home-based franchise with complete training and on-going support. Training is 19 weeks originally. Wide open market for growth with exclusinve areas.

BACKGROUND: IFA MEMBER
Established: 1999; 1st Franchised: 1999
Franchised Units: 101
Company-Owned Units: 0
Total Units: 101
Dist.: US-107; CAN-0; O'seas-0
North America: 28 States
Density: 19 in TX, 6 in FL, 5 in CO
Projected New Units (12 Months): NR
Qualifications: , , , , ,
Registered:

FINANCIAL/TERMS:
Cash Investment: $55K
Total Investment: $55.5-81.3K
Minimum Net Worth: $100K
Fees: Franchise - $50K
Royalty - $300/700/1K/Mo.; Ad. - $150/Mo.
Earnings Claims Statement: NR
Term of Contract (Years): 5/5
Avg. # Of Employees: 1 FT, 1 PT
Passive Ownership: Allowed
Encourage Conversions: NR
Area Develop. Agreements: No
Sub-Franchising Contracts: Yes
Expand In Territory: Yes
Space Needs: NA SF; HB

SUPPORT & TRAINING:
Financial Assistance Provided: NR
Site Selection Assistance: NA
Lease Negotiation Assistance: NA
Co-Operative Advertising: Yes
Franchisee Assoc./Member: No
Size Of Corporate Staff: 15
On-Going Support: A,B,C,D,E,F,G,H,I
Training: 2 Weeks Corporate Office Carrollton, TX; 1 Week Corporate Office Carrollton, TX.

SPECIFIC EXPANSION PLANS:
US: All United States
Canada: NR
Overseas: NR

<< >>

INTERIORS by Decorating Den™

Top 100

INTERIORS BY DECORATING DEN

8659 Commerce Dr.
Easton, MD 21601-7425
Tel: (800) 686-6393 (410) 822-9001
Fax: (410) 820-5131
E-Mail: kevina@decoratingden.com
Web Site: www.decoratingden.com
Mr. Kevin Atkinson, VP Program Development

Celebrating our 36th successful year, INTERIORS BY DECORATING DEN is the oldest international, shop-at-home interior decorating franchise in the world. Our company-trained interior decorators bring thousands of samples including window coverings, wall coverings, floor coverings, furniture and accessories to their customers' homes in our uniquely equipped COLORVAN ©. Special business features include: home-based, marketing systems, business systems, training, support and complete sampling.

BACKGROUND: IFA MEMBER
Established: 1969; 1st Franchised: 1970
Franchised Units: 465
Company-Owned Units: 1
Total Units: 466
Dist.: US-401; CAN-50; O'seas-15
North America: NR
Density: 33 in FL, 28 in NC, 27 in TX
Projected New Units (12 Months): 50
Qualifications: 5, 5, 3, 3, 5, 5
Registered: All States

FINANCIAL/TERMS:
Cash Investment: $15K
Total Investment: $40-70K
Minimum Net Worth: $40K
Fees: Franchise - $24.9K
Royalty - 7-9%; Ad. - 4%/$100 Min
Earnings Claims Statement: No
Term of Contract (Years): 10/10
Avg. # Of Employees: 1 FT
Passive Ownership: Not Allowed
Encourage Conversions: Yes
Area Develop. Agreements: Yes/10
Sub-Franchising Contracts: Yes
Expand In Territory: No
Space Needs: NA SF; HB

SUPPORT & TRAINING:
Financial Assistance Provided: Yes(D)
Site Selection Assistance: NA
Lease Negotiation Assistance: NA

Co-Operative Advertising: Yes
Franchisee Assoc./Member: Yes/Yes
Size Of Corporate Staff: 40
On-Going Support: C,D,E,G,H,I
Training: 10.5 Days in Easton, MD; Continuous.

SPECIFIC EXPANSION PLANS:
US: All United States
Canada: All Canada
Overseas: No

<< >>

LIVING LIGHTING

294 Walker Dr., # 2
Brampton, ON L6T 4Z2 CANADA
Tel: (866) 463-4124 (416) 661-9916
Fax: (905) 790-7059
E-Mail: lmorrison@franchisebancorp.com
Web Site: www.livinglighting.com
Ms. Lisa Morrison, Franchise Contact

Full line of retail lighting, home lighting and home decorating centers.

BACKGROUND:
Established: 1968; 1st Franchised: 1970
Franchised Units: 22
Company-Owned Units: 0
Total Units: 22
Dist.: US-0; CAN-28; O'seas-0
North America: 2 Provinces
Density: 27 in ON, 1 in BC
Projected New Units (12 Months): NR
Qualifications: , , , , ,
Registered: AB

FINANCIAL/TERMS:
Cash Investment: $80K
Total Investment: $200-225K
Minimum Net Worth: NR
Fees: Franchise - $30K
Royalty - 4%; Ad. - 1%
Earnings Claims Statement: Yes
Term of Contract (Years): NR
Avg. # Of Employees: NR
Passive Ownership: NR
Encourage Conversions: NR
Area Develop. Agreements: NR
Sub-Franchising Contracts: NR
Expand In Territory: NR
Space Needs: NR SF; NR

SUPPORT & TRAINING:
Financial Assistance Provided: No
Site Selection Assistance: Yes
Lease Negotiation Assistance: Yes
Co-Operative Advertising: Yes
Franchisee Assoc./Member: Yes/Yes
Size Of Corporate Staff: 18
On-Going Support: NR
Training: NR

SPECIFIC EXPANSION PLANS:
US: NR
Canada: All Canada
Overseas: No

<< >>

MORE SPACE PLACE

12555 Enterprise Blvd., # 101
Largo, FL 33773
Tel: (888) 731-3051 + 14 (727) 539-1611
Fax: (727) 524-6382
E-Mail: mjuarez@morespaceplace.com
Web Site: www.morespaceplace.com
Mr. Marty Juarez, Vice President Franchising

One of America's Top 100 Franchise Opportunities! (as listed in Bond's Top 100 Franchises, 2004). We create beautiful living spaces for our customers. Picture an elegant home office that converts into an extra bedroom. With our professionally installed Murphy bed and custom-designed office, it can happen. With us, you can fashionably design closets, entertainment centers, utility rooms and garages and turn spare bedrooms into multi-purpose rooms.

BACKGROUND:
Established: 1989; 1st Franchised: 1993
Franchised Units: 27
Company-Owned Units: 3
Total Units: 30
Dist.: US-30; CAN-0; O'seas-0
North America: 9 States
Density: 22 in FL, 2 in TX, 2 in SC
Projected New Units (12 Months): 12
Qualifications: 4, 4, 1, 3, 2, 5
Registered: FL,IL,MI,TX

FINANCIAL/TERMS:
Cash Investment: $35-65K
Total Investment: $98-183K
Minimum Net Worth: $100K
Fees: Franchise - $18-29.5K
Royalty - 4.5%; Ad. - 2.5%
Earnings Claims Statement: No
Term of Contract (Years): 10/10
Avg. # Of Employees: 3 FT, 1 PT
Passive Ownership: Discouraged
Encourage Conversions: Yes
Area Develop. Agreements: Yes/10
Sub-Franchising Contracts: No
Expand In Territory: Yes
Space Needs: 1,400-2,400 SF; FS, SF, SC

SUPPORT & TRAINING:
Financial Assistance Provided: Yes(I)
Site Selection Assistance: Yes
Lease Negotiation Assistance: Yes
Co-Operative Advertising: Yes
Franchisee Assoc./Member: Yes
Size Of Corporate Staff: 55
On-Going Support: B,C,D,E,F,G,H,I
Training: 12 Days Headquarters Largo, FL; 8 Days On-Site.

SPECIFIC EXPANSION PLANS:
US: All United States
Canada: No
Overseas: No

<< >>

NORWALK - THE FURNITURE IDEA

100 Furniture Pkwy.
Norwalk, OH 44857-9587
Tel: (888) 667-9255 (419) 668-4461
Fax: (419) 744-3212
E-Mail: mturbeville@nfcorp.com
Web Site: www.norwalkfurnitureidea.com
Mr. Mike Turbeville, Franchise Retail Development

Custom order living room specialty stores, offering consumers 1,000 fabrics and leathers available in 500 styles, with delivery in just 35 days. Low inventory investment.

BACKGROUND: IFA MEMBER
Established: 1902; 1st Franchised: 1987
Franchised Units: 60
Company-Owned Units: 17
Total Units: 77
Dist.: US-69; CAN-8; O'seas-0
North America: 30 States, 3 Provinces
Density: 13 in FL, 5 in CA, 4 in TX
Projected New Units (12 Months): 8
Qualifications: 4, 4, 2, 2, 4, 5
Registered: All States and AB

FINANCIAL/TERMS:
Cash Investment: $100K
Total Investment: $350-400K
Minimum Net Worth: $350K
Fees: Franchise - $35K
Royalty - 0%; Ad. - 0%
Earnings Claims Statement: No

Term of Contract (Years): 20/5
Avg. # Of Employees: 10 FT, 1 PT
Passive Ownership: Not Allowed
Encourage Conversions: NA
Area Develop. Agreements: Yes/1
Sub-Franchising Contracts: No
Expand In Territory: Yes
Space Needs: 4,500 SF; FS, SC

SUPPORT & TRAINING:

Financial Assistance Provided: Yes(I)
Site Selection Assistance: Yes
Lease Negotiation Assistance: Yes
Co-Operative Advertising: Yes
Franchisee Assoc./Member: Yes/Yes
Size Of Corporate Staff: 11
On-Going Support: B,C,d,E,G,h,I
Training: 3 Weeks, Cleveland; 1 Week Atlanta, GA; 2 Weeks Another Store.

SPECIFIC EXPANSION PLANS:

US: All United States
Canada: Most Provinces
Overseas: No

<< >>

SLUMBERLAND INTERNATIONAL

3060 Centerville Rd.
Little Canada, MN 55117-1105
Tel: (888) 482-7500 (651) 482-7500
Fax: (651) 490-0479
E-Mail: mlarson@slumberland.com
Web Site: www.slumberland.com
Mr. Michael Larson, Director Franchise Development

SLUMBERLAND is a home furnishings specialty retailer, featuring name-brand mattresses, sleep sofas, reclining chairs, sofas and chairs, daybeds and related bedroom furniture. SLUMBERLAND is a market-driven retailer that outpaces national averages in sales/SF and gross margins.

BACKGROUND: IFA MEMBER

Established: 1967; 1st Franchised: 1978
Franchised Units: 44
Company-Owned Units: 30
Total Units: 74
Dist.: US-67; CAN-0; O'seas-0
North America: 7 States
Density: 33 in MN, 12 in IA, 8 in SD
Projected New Units (12 Months): 8
Qualifications: , , , , ,
Registered: IL,MN,ND,SD,WI

FINANCIAL/TERMS:

Cash Investment: NR
Total Investment: $100-400K
Minimum Net Worth: NR
Fees: Franchise - $12.5K
Royalty - 3%; Ad. - 2%
Earnings Claims Statement: No
Term of Contract (Years): 10/10
Avg. # Of Employees: 4 FT, 2 PT
Passive Ownership: Discouraged
Encourage Conversions: Yes
Area Develop. Agreements: No
Sub-Franchising Contracts: No
Expand In Territory: Yes
Space Needs: 15,000 SF; FS, SC

SUPPORT & TRAINING:

Financial Assistance Provided: No
Site Selection Assistance: No
Lease Negotiation Assistance: Yes
Co-Operative Advertising: NA
Franchisee Assoc./Member: NR
Size Of Corporate Staff: NR
On-Going Support: B,c,d,G,H,i
Training: 3 Days Headquarters; 2 Weeks On-Site.

SPECIFIC EXPANSION PLANS:

US: Central Midwest
Canada: No
Overseas: No

V2K THE VIRTUAL WINDOW FASHION STORE

1127 Auraria Pkwy., # 204
Denver, CO 80204
Tel: (800) 200-0835 + 309 (303) 202-1120
Fax: (303) 202-5201
E-Mail: charlietrench@v2k.com
Web Site: www.v2k.com
Mr. Charlie Trench, Director Franchise Development

V2K sells and supports franchises in the window fashion industry, utilizing proprietary graphic software product. We go to a customer's home and on a lap top computer or the customer's digital TV, displays their walls and windows, 100% to scale, so the customer is looking at his/her windows. We can put virtually any style of window fashion treatment onto the windows, adjust, redraw and price simultaneously. Once the customer agrees, we print out the order with one keystroke. Our software is awesome.

BACKGROUND:

Established: 1997; 1st Franchised: 1997
Franchised Units: 135
Company-Owned Units: 0
Total Units: 135
Dist.: US-100; CAN-0; O'seas-0
North America: 37 States
Density: NR
Projected New Units (12 Months): 100
Qualifications: 3, 3, 2, 1, 1, 1
Registered: All States

FINANCIAL/TERMS:

Cash Investment: $50-60K
Total Investment: $45-55K
Minimum Net Worth: NA
Fees: Franchise - $39.9K
Royalty - 8-6.5%; Ad. - 2%
Earnings Claims Statement: No
Term of Contract (Years): 10/5/5
Avg. # Of Employees: 1 FT
Passive Ownership: Discouraged
Encourage Conversions: NA
Area Develop. Agreements: No
Sub-Franchising Contracts: No
Expand In Territory: Yes
Space Needs: NA SF; HB

SUPPORT & TRAINING:

Financial Assistance Provided: No
Site Selection Assistance: NA
Lease Negotiation Assistance: NA
Co-Operative Advertising: Yes
Franchisee Assoc./Member: No
Size Of Corporate Staff: 14
On-Going Support: A,B,C,D,G,h,I
Training: 2 Weeks Denver, CO.

SPECIFIC EXPANSION PLANS:

US: All United States
Canada: License Agreement
Overseas: License Agree.

<< >>

VERLO MATTRESS FACTORY STORES

W3130 Hwy 59, P.O. Box 298
Whitewater, WI 53190
Tel: (800) 229-8957 (262) 473-8957
Fax: (262) 473-4623
E-Mail: franchiseinfo@verlo.com
Web Site: www.verlofranchise.com
Mr. Bruce Major, Franchise Awards Manager

VERLO MATTRESS FACTORY STORES (R) is the nation's largest CRAFTSMAN DIRECT (R) retailer. Each franchise assembles hand-crafted mattresses to the customer's specifications.

BACKGROUND: IFA MEMBER

Established: 1958; 1st Franchised: 1981
Franchised Units: 68
Company-Owned Units: 7
Total Units: 75
Dist.: US-75; CAN-0; O'seas-0
North America: 10 States
Density: 27 in WI, 20 in IL, 4 in FL

Projected New Units (12 Months): 14
Qualifications: 4, 3, 2, 3, 4, 5
Registered: All States Except CA and HI

FINANCIAL/TERMS:

Cash Investment:	$50-100K
Total Investment:	$200-500K
Minimum Net Worth:	$300K
Fees: Franchise -	$30K
Royalty - 5%;	Ad. - $300/Mo.
Earnings Claims Statement:	Yes
Term of Contract (Years):	5/5
Avg. # Of Employees:	5 FT
Passive Ownership:	Allowed
Encourage Conversions:	Yes
Area Develop. Agreements:	Yes/Varies
Sub-Franchising Contracts:	No
Expand In Territory:	Yes
Space Needs:	3,000-10,000 SF; FS, SF

SUPPORT & TRAINING:

Financial Assistance Provided:	No
Site Selection Assistance:	Yes
Lease Negotiation Assistance:	Yes
Co-Operative Advertising:	No
Franchisee Assoc./Member:	Yes/Yes
Size Of Corporate Staff:	9
On-Going Support:	B,C,D,E,G,H,i

Training: 5-10 Days Corporate Office; 5-7 Days On-Site; On-Going.

SPECIFIC EXPANSION PLANS:

US:	All United States
Canada:	No
Overseas:	No

<< >>

WINDOW WORKS

3601 Minnesota Dr. Suite 800
Edina, MN 55435
Tel: (800) 326-2659 (952) 943-4353
Fax: (952) 921-5801
E-Mail: info@windowworks.net
Web Site: www.windowworks.net
Mr. Charlie Kanan, Chief Executive Officer

WINDOW WORKS showroom retails custom window treatments and accessories all within a 1,000 to 1,500 SF facility. Designers offer in-home consultation service, selling top-quality drapery, shutters, blinds and bedding. Exclusive Windcom software tracks day-to-day business and generates 27 reports from marketing to sales tax.

BACKGROUND:

Established: 1978; 1st Franchised: 1979

Franchised Units:	5
Company-Owned Units:	0
Total Units:	5
Dist.:	US-5; CAN-0; O'seas-0
North America:	5 States
Density:	NR
Projected New Units (12 Months):	3-4
Qualifications:	3, 2, 1, 2, 3, 4
Registered:	IL,IN,MD,MI,MN,VA,WA

FINANCIAL/TERMS:

Cash Investment:	NR
Total Investment:	$60-90K
Minimum Net Worth:	NR
Fees: Franchise -	$30K
Royalty - 4%;	Ad. - 1%
Earnings Claims Statement:	No
Term of Contract (Years):	15/15
Avg. # Of Employees:	2 FT, 1 PT
Passive Ownership:	Discouraged
Encourage Conversions:	No
Area Develop. Agreements:	No
Sub-Franchising Contracts:	No
Expand In Territory:	No
Space Needs:	1,000-1,500 SF; SC

SUPPORT & TRAINING:

Financial Assistance Provided:	No
Site Selection Assistance:	Yes
Lease Negotiation Assistance:	Yes
Co-Operative Advertising:	Yes
Franchisee Assoc./Member:	No
Size Of Corporate Staff:	5
On-Going Support:	C,D,E,G,H,I

Training: 1-2 Weeks Corporate Window Works - MN; Store Site, as Needed.

SPECIFIC EXPANSION PLANS:

US:	Most Areas; Not CA or NY
Canada:	No
Overseas:	No

<< >>

For a full explanation of the data provided in the Franchisor Profiles, please refer to *Chapter 2, "How to Use the Data."*

Retail: Home Improvement & Hardware

Chapter 39

Retail: Home Improvement & Hardware Industry Profile

Total # Franchisors in Industry Group	13
Total # Franchised Units in Industry Group	11,061
Total # Company-Owned Units in Industry Group	293
Total # Operating Units in Industry Group	11,356
Average # Franchised Units/Franchisor	850.8
Average # Company-Owned Units/Franchisor	22.5
Average # Total Units/Franchisor	873.5
Ratio of Total # Franchised Units/Total # Company-Owned Units	37.8:1
Industry Survey Participants	5
Representing % of Industry	38.5%
Average Franchise Fee*:	$30.2K
Average Total Investment*:	$344.1K
Average On-Going Royalty Fee*:	4.7%

*If a range was provided, the mid-point of the range was used. See detailed profiles for actual ranges.

Five Largest Participants in Survey

Company	# Franchised Units	# Co-Owned Units	# Total Units	Franchise Fee	On-Going Royalty	Total Investment
1. Ace Hardware	4,800	25	4,825	$35K	2%	$1.0-1.2MM
2. Snap-on Tools	4,708	85	4,793	$5K	$50/Mo.	$156-248K
3. Stained Glass Overlay	310	0	310	$45K	5%	$80K
4. Color Your World	44	130	174	$35-80K	7%	$180-300K
5. United States Seamless	87	11	98	$8.5K	$2.5K/Mach.	$49.5-147K

All of the data provided are proprietary and should not be quoted without acknowledging *Bond's Franchise Guide.*

ACE HARDWARE

2222 Kensington Ct.
Oak Brook, IL 60521-2103
Tel: (630) 990-6900
Fax: (630) 928-9179
E-Mail: myace@acehardware.com
Web Site: www.acehardware.com
Mr. John Venhuizen, Dir. Franchise Development

ACE HARDWARE is a Fortune 500 company of over 5,100 retailers selling hardware and related home improvement products. ACE is now offering franchise opportunities in selected markets nationwide. Come grow in this new endeavor with the backing of a company possessing 75 years of success, along with outstanding purchasing power, brand recognition and retail practices.

BACKGROUND: IFA MEMBER
Established: 1924; 1st Franchised: 1999
Franchised Units: 4,800
Company-Owned Units: 25
Total Units: 4,825
Dist.: US-4,825; CAN-0; O'seas-0
North America: 3 States
Density: NR
Projected New Units (12 Months): 10
Qualifications: 5, 4, 3, 3, 3, 5
Registered: All States

FINANCIAL/TERMS:
Cash Investment: $150-250K
Total Investment: $1.0-1.2MM
Minimum Net Worth: $1MM
Fees: Franchise - $35K
Royalty - 2%; Ad. - 1.3%/$6.5K
Earnings Claims Statement: No
Term of Contract (Years): 20/5
Avg. # Of Employees: 3 FT, 10-12 PT
Passive Ownership: Not Allowed
Encourage Conversions: Yes
Area Develop. Agreements: No
Sub-Franchising Contracts: No
Expand In Territory: Yes
Space Needs: 10,000-15,000 SF; FS, SC

SUPPORT & TRAINING:
Financial Assistance Provided: Yes(I)
Site Selection Assistance: Yes
Lease Negotiation Assistance: Yes
Co-Operative Advertising: Yes
Franchisee Assoc./Member: Not Yet
Size Of Corporate Staff: 5,000
On-Going Support: A,B,C,D,e,F,G
Training: 6 Weeks Oak Brook, IL.

SPECIFIC EXPANSION PLANS:
US: Selected Markets in US.
Canada: No
Overseas: No

<< >>

COLOR YOUR WORLD

2600 Steeles Ave. W.
Concord, ON L4K 3C8 CANADA
Tel: (800) 387-7311 (905) 738-7477
Fax: (905) 738-9723
E-Mail: robert_crookston@ici.com
Web Site: www.coloryourworld.com
Mr. Bob Crookston, Franchise Sales Manager

Canada's largest paint and wallpaper retailer, selling to the do-it-yourself and trade markets.

BACKGROUND:
Established: 1912; 1st Franchised: 1977
Franchised Units: 44
Company-Owned Units: 130
Total Units: 174
Dist.: US-0; CAN-276; O'seas-0
North America: 10 Provinces
Density: ON, BC, AB
Projected New Units (12 Months): NR
Qualifications: 5, 5, 2, 3, 4, 5
Registered: AB

FINANCIAL/TERMS:
Cash Investment: $90-150K
Total Investment: $180-300K
Minimum Net Worth: NA
Fees: Franchise - $35-80K
Royalty - 7%; Ad. - 4%
Earnings Claims Statement: No
Term of Contract (Years): 10/5
Avg. # Of Employees: 4 FT, 3 PT
Passive Ownership: Discouraged
Encourage Conversions: NA
Area Develop. Agreements: No
Sub-Franchising Contracts: No
Expand In Territory: No
Space Needs: 3,000 SF; FS

SUPPORT & TRAINING:
Financial Assistance Provided: NA
Site Selection Assistance: NA
Lease Negotiation Assistance: NA
Co-Operative Advertising: NA
Franchisee Assoc./Member: Yes/No
Size Of Corporate Staff: NR
On-Going Support: A,B,C,D,F,G,h,I
Training: 8 Weeks at Various Locations.

SPECIFIC EXPANSION PLANS:
US: No
Canada: All Canada
Overseas: No

<< >>

SNAP-ON TOOLS

2801 80th St.
Kenosha, WI 53141-1410
Tel: (800) 786-6600 (262) 656-6516
Fax: (262) 656-5088
E-Mail: ray.moore@snapon.com
Web Site: www.snapon.com
Mr. M. Raymond Moore, Dir. Franchise Operations

The premier solutions provider to the vehicle service industry. Premium quality products, delivered and sold with premium service. We are proud of our heritage and are boldly addressing the future needs of our customers with improved efficiency, creating products and services from hand tools to data and management systems. Contact us today for discussion.

BACKGROUND: IFA MEMBER
Established: 1920; 1st Franchised: 1991
Franchised Units: 4,708
Company-Owned Units: 85
Total Units: 4,793
Dist.: US-3,622; CAN-357; O'seas-814
North America: All States & Provinces
Density: 373 in CA, 245 in TX, 202 PA
Projected New Units (12 Months): 682
Qualifications: 3, 4, 2, 2, 5, 5
Registered: All States

FINANCIAL/TERMS:
Cash Investment: $Low Cost
Total Investment: $156-248K
Minimum Net Worth: NR
Fees: Franchise - $5K
Royalty - $50/Mo.; Ad. - 0%
Earnings Claims Statement: Yes
Term of Contract (Years): 10/5
Avg. # Of Employees: 1 FT
Passive Ownership: Not Allowed
Encourage Conversions: Yes
Area Develop. Agreements: No
Sub-Franchising Contracts: No
Expand In Territory: Yes
Space Needs: NR SF; NA

SUPPORT & TRAINING:
Financial Assistance Provided: Yes(D)
Site Selection Assistance: NA
Lease Negotiation Assistance: NA
Co-Operative Advertising: NA
Franchisee Assoc./Member: No
Size Of Corporate Staff: NR
On-Going Support: A,B,C,D,E,F,G,h,I
Training: 1 Week at Branch or Regional Office; 1 Week at Branch; 3 Weeks On-the-Job.

SPECIFIC EXPANSION PLANS:
US: All United States
Canada: All Canada
Overseas: Japan, UK, Germany, Australia, New Zealand, S. Africa

<< >>

STAINED GLASS OVERLAY

1827 North Case St.
Orange, CA 92865
Tel: (800) 944-4746 (714) 974-6124
Fax: (714) 974-6529
E-Mail: info@stainedglassoverlay.com
Web Site: www.stainedglassoverlay.com
Ms. Cathy Cooper, Franchise Services Manager

We are the leading decorative glass franchisor in the world. Combine our patented technology and proven format into a great business. Design works of SGO, for homes, business and religious institutions. We don't require that you have an artistic or glass industry background. We provide training in all required skills.

BACKGROUND: IFA MEMBER
Established: 1981; 1st Franchised: 1982
Franchised Units: 310
Company-Owned Units: 0
Total Units: 310
Dist.: US-141; CAN-14; O'seas-130
North America: 39 States, 6 Provinces
Density: 26 in CA, 7 in IL, 6 in FL
Projected New Units (12 Months): 25
Qualifications: 4, 4, 3, 2, 2, 5
Registered: All States Exc. ND and HI, plus AB

FINANCIAL/TERMS:
Cash Investment: $80K
Total Investment: $80K
Minimum Net Worth: $200K
Fees: Franchise - $45K
Royalty - 5%; Ad. - 2%
Earnings Claims Statement: No
Term of Contract (Years): 5/5
Avg. # Of Employees: 3 FT
Passive Ownership: Discouraged
Encourage Conversions: Yes
Area Develop. Agreements: No
Sub-Franchising Contracts: No
Expand In Territory: Yes
Space Needs: 1,100 SF; SC

SUPPORT & TRAINING:
Financial Assistance Provided: Yes(I)
Site Selection Assistance: Yes
Lease Negotiation Assistance: No
Co-Operative Advertising: No
Franchisee Assoc./Member: Yes/Yes
Size Of Corporate Staff: 17
On-Going Support: B,C,d,e,F,G,h,I
Training: 2 x 1 Week Sessions at Headquarters in Orange, CA.

SPECIFIC EXPANSION PLANS:
US: All United States
Canada: All CAN Exc. PQ
Overseas: Western Europe

<< >>

UNITED STATES SEAMLESS

2001 1st Ave. N.
Fargo, ND 58102-2426
Tel: (800) 615-9318 (701) 241-8888
Fax: (701) 241-9999
E-Mail: info@usseamless.com
Web Site: www.usseamless.com
Mr. David E. Hedman, National Franchise Sales

UNITED STATES SEAMLESS, ranked the #1 seamless siding franchise in America by Entrepreneur Magazine, is offering protected franchise territories for the sale and installation of seamless steel siding, gutters and vinyl replacement windows. The franchise offers 14 solid PVC colors, 12 of which have matching accessories. We also offer 7 colors in the exclusive Mountain Cedar two-tone steel siding coil, which can be produced in the standard profile plus used in our patent pending log cabin siding machine.

BACKGROUND:
Established: 1991; 1st Franchised: 1992
Franchised Units: 87
Company-Owned Units: 11
Total Units: 98
Dist.: US-98; CAN-0; O'seas-0
North America: 13 States
Density: 32 in MN, 10 in IA, 9 in ND
Projected New Units (12 Months): 11
Qualifications: 5, 5, 4, 3, 4, 5
Registered:IL,IN,MI,MN,ND,OR,SD,WA, WI

FINANCIAL/TERMS:
Cash Investment: $20-40K
Total Investment: $49.5-147K
Minimum Net Worth: $40K
Fees: Franchise - $8.5K
Royalty - $2.5K/Mach.; Ad. - $200-500/Mo
Earnings Claims Statement: No
Term of Contract (Years): 15/15
Avg. # Of Employees: 3 FT
Passive Ownership: Not Allowed
Encourage Conversions: No
Area Develop. Agreements: No
Sub-Franchising Contracts: No
Expand In Territory: Yes
Space Needs: 2,000 SF; HB, Office/Warehouse

SUPPORT & TRAINING:
Financial Assistance Provided: Yes(D)
Site Selection Assistance: Yes
Lease Negotiation Assistance: No
Co-Operative Advertising: No
Franchisee Assoc./Member: No
Size Of Corporate Staff: 10
On-Going Support: B,C,d,G,H,I
Training: 1 Week Fargo, ND.

SPECIFIC EXPANSION PLANS:
US: All United States
Canada: No
Overseas: No

<< >>

Retail: Pet Products & Services

Chapter 40

Retail: Pet Products & Services Industry Profile

Total # Franchisors in Industry Group	29
Total # Franchised Units in Industry Group	1,567
Total # Company-Owned Units in Industry Group	372
Total # Operating Units in Industry Group	1,939
Average # Franchised Units/Franchisor	54
Average # Company-Owned Units/Franchisor	12.8
Average # Total Units/Franchisor	66.9
Ratio of Total # Franchised Units/Total # Company-Owned Units	4.2:1
Industry Survey Participants	10
Representing % of Industry	34.5%
Average Franchise Fee*:	$23K
Average Total Investment*:	$143.3K
Average On-Going Royalty Fee*:	5%

*If a range was provided, the mid-point of the range was used. See detailed profiles for actual ranges.

Five Largest Participants in Survey

Company	# Franchised Units	# Co-Owned Units	# Total Units	Franchise Fee	On-Going Royalty	Total Investment
1. Aussie Pet Mobile	322	28	350	$32.5-112.5K	5%	$60-352.5K
2. Petland	160	2	162	$25K	4.50%	$180-500K
3. Bark Busters - Home Dog Training	130	0	130	$22.5	8%	$47.1-79K
4. Pet Pantry International, The	93	0	93	$8-26K	0%	$60-90K
5. Pets Are Inn	18	0	18	$15K	5-10%	$35-65K

All of the data provided are proprietary and should not be quoted without acknowledging *Bond's Franchise Guide.*

AUSSIE PET MOBILE
34189 Pacific Coast Hwy., # 203
Dana Point, CA 92629-2814
Tel: (949) 234-0680
Fax: (949) 234-0688
E-Mail: dlouy@aussiepetmobile.com
Web Site: www.aussiepetmobile.com
Mr. David Louy, VP Franchise Sales

AUSSIE PET MOBILE is an internationally proven franchise system of mobile pet grooming with new U.S. headquarters in Orange County, CA. We pride ourselves on our innovative trailer design, heated hydrobath and a 15-step grooming maintenance process. No experience is required. The AUSSIE PET MOBILE franchise package includes a comprehensive training course. Franchisees enjoy a protected territory with regional and national advertising support. Individual owner-operator and multi-unit programs available.

BACKGROUND: IFA MEMBER
Established: 1996; 1st Franchised: 1997
Franchised Units: 322
Company-Owned Units: 28
Total Units: 350
Dist.: US-278; CAN-0; O'seas-72
North America: 22 States
Density: CA, CO, VA
Projected New Units (12 Months): NR
Qualifications: 4, 4, 2, 3, 4, 5
Registered: All States Except ND

FINANCIAL/TERMS:
Cash Investment: $32.5-232.5K
Total Investment: $60-352.5K
Minimum Net Worth: $125-500K
Fees: Franchise - $32.5-112.5K
Royalty - 5%; Ad. - 3%
Earnings Claims Statement: 3.0
Term of Contract (Years): 10/10
Avg. # Of Employees: Varies
Passive Ownership: Allowed
Encourage Conversions: No
Area Develop. Agreements: Yes/10
Sub-Franchising Contracts: No
Expand In Territory: Yes
Space Needs: NR SF; NA

SUPPORT & TRAINING:
Financial Assistance Provided: Yes(I)
Site Selection Assistance: NA
Lease Negotiation Assistance: NA
Co-Operative Advertising: Yes
Franchisee Assoc./Member: Yes/Yes
Size Of Corporate Staff: 20
On-Going Support: A,B,C,D,E,F,G,H,I
Training: 10 Days for Employees; 3 Days Franchisees; 3 Days Advanced Employees.

SPECIFIC EXPANSION PLANS:
US: All United States
Canada: All Canada
Overseas: UK, Europe, Mexico

<< >>

BARK BUSTERS - HOME DOG TRAINING
250 W. Lewhow Ave., # B
Greenwood Village, CO 80110
Tel: (877) 280-7100 (303) 471-4935
Fax: (303) 283-2819
E-Mail: info@barkbusters.com
Web Site: www.barkbusters.com
Mr. Andrew Brooke, President/CEO

Unique Australian concept of in-home dog training that trains any dog, any age, any issue in two hours guaranteed. World-wide network of dog behavioral therapists that has trained in excess of 200,000 dogs. Great lifestyle! Fulfilling career!

BACKGROUND: IFA MEMBER
Established: 1989; 1st Franchised: 1994
Franchised Units: 130
Company-Owned Units: 0
Total Units: 130
Dist.: US-60; CAN-1; O'seas-69
North America: 22 States, 1 Province
Density: 9 in CO, 7 in CA, 5 in VA
Projected New Units (12 Months): 80
Qualifications: 3, 3, 1, 1, 3, 3
Registered: CA,FL,IN,MI,NY,OR,RI,VA, WA,WI,DC

FINANCIAL/TERMS:
Cash Investment: $37.5K
Total Investment: $47.1-79K
Minimum Net Worth: $100K
Fees: Franchise - $22.5K
Royalty - 8%; Ad. - 2%
Earnings Claims Statement: No
Term of Contract (Years): 5/5
Avg. # Of Employees: 1 FT
Passive Ownership: Not Allowed
Encourage Conversions: NA
Area Develop. Agreements: No
Sub-Franchising Contracts: No
Expand In Territory: No
Space Needs: NA SF; NA

SUPPORT & TRAINING:
Financial Assistance Provided: Yes(I)
Site Selection Assistance: NA
Lease Negotiation Assistance: NA
Co-Operative Advertising: NA
Franchisee Assoc./Member: Yes
Size Of Corporate Staff: 9
On-Going Support: B,C,D,E,G,h
Training: 3 Weeks Denver, CO.

SPECIFIC EXPANSION PLANS:
US: All United States
Canada: All Canada
Overseas: United Kingdom, Japan, Europe

<< >>

PET PANTRY INTERNATIONAL, THE
3719 N. Carson St.
Carson City, NV 89706
Tel: (800) 381-7387 (775) 841-9722
Fax: (775) 841-9732
E-Mail: wadew@thepetpantry.com
Web Site: www.thepetpantry.com
Mr. Wade Webster, VP Franchise Development

THE PET PANTRY affords you a spectacular growth opportunity in the pet food industry, as the forecast calls for it to continue reigning cats and dogs! No royalties; protected marketing areas; little competition; advertising and marketing support; comprehensive, on-going educational and training programs; ongoing business development support. Our free home delivery of super-premium dog and cat food is a profitable way to build your future. Call 1-800-381-7387.

BACKGROUND:
Established: 1995; 1st Franchised: 1995
Franchised Units: 93
Company-Owned Units: 0
Total Units: 93
Dist.: US-91; CAN-0; O'seas-2
North America: 34 States
Density: 7 in WA, 8 in CA, 6 in NY
Projected New Units (12 Months): 40
Qualifications: 4, 3, 1, 2, 1, 5
Registered: All States

FINANCIAL/TERMS:
Cash Investment: $40-60K
Total Investment: $60-90K
Minimum Net Worth: $200K
Fees: Franchise - $8-26K
Royalty - 0%; Ad. - 0%
Earnings Claims Statement: No

Term of Contract (Years): 7/7
Avg. # Of Employees: 1 FT
Passive Ownership: Allowed
Encourage Conversions: No
Area Develop. Agreements: No
Sub-Franchising Contracts: No
Expand In Territory: Yes
Space Needs: 1,000 SF; HB (Non-Retail)

SUPPORT & TRAINING:
Financial Assistance Provided: No
Site Selection Assistance: Yes
Lease Negotiation Assistance: No
Co-Operative Advertising: Yes
Franchisee Assoc./Member: No
Size Of Corporate Staff: 13
On-Going Support: B,C,D,F,G,H,I
Training: 5 Days in Carson City, NV (at Corporate Office).

SPECIFIC EXPANSION PLANS:
US: All United States
Canada: All Canada
Overseas: All as Master Franchisor

<< >>

PETLAND

250 Riverside St., P.O. Box 1606
Chillicothe, OH 45601-5606
Tel: (800) 221-5935 (740) 775-2464
Fax: (740) 775-2575
E-Mail: jwhitman@petland.com
Web Site: www.petland.com
Mr. Jim Whitman, Director Franchise Development

PETLAND is a full-service, pet retail store that features live animals, including tropical fish, marine fish, small mammals, reptiles, amphibians, tropical, domestically bred birds, puppies and kittens. The PETLAND concept also features over 4,000 merchandise items to support the pets sold to or already in the homes of its customers. Over 1,500 merchandise items are PETLAND brands, sold exclusively through PETLAND retail stores.

BACKGROUND:
Established: 1967; 1st Franchised: 1972
Franchised Units: 160
Company-Owned Units: 2
Total Units: 162
Dist.: US-93; CAN-46; O'seas-6
North America: 32 States, 5 Provinces
Density: 19 in OH, 14 in FL, 11 in IL
Projected New Units (12 Months): 18
Qualifications: 3, 5, 1, 3, 4, 5
Registered: AB

FINANCIAL/TERMS:
Cash Investment: $60-120K
Total Investment: $180-500K
Minimum Net Worth: $250K
Fees: Franchise - $25K
Royalty - 4.5%; Ad. - NA
Earnings Claims Statement: No
Term of Contract (Years): 20/20
Avg. # Of Employees: 5 FT, 7 PT
Passive Ownership: Discouraged
Encourage Conversions: Yes
Area Develop. Agreements: No
Sub-Franchising Contracts: No
Expand In Territory: Yes
Space Needs: 5,000 SF; FS, SC, RM

SUPPORT & TRAINING:
Financial Assistance Provided: Yes(I)
Site Selection Assistance: Yes
Lease Negotiation Assistance: Yes
Co-Operative Advertising: Yes
Franchisee Assoc./Member: No
Size Of Corporate Staff: 38
On-Going Support: B,C,D,E,F,G,H,I
Training: 1.5 Weeks Training Store, Chillicothe, OH; 1 Week Classroom; 2 Weeks New Store Location.

SPECIFIC EXPANSION PLANS:
US: All United States
Canada: All Canada
Overseas: Western Europe, Australia, South America

<< >>

PETS ARE INN

5100 Edina Blvd., # 206
Minneapolis, MN 55439
Tel: (800) 248-PETS (952) 944-8298
Fax: (952) 829-3828
E-Mail: jplatt@petsareinn.com
Web Site: www.petsareinn.com
Mr. Jim Platt, President

When a family goes on vacation, they prefer to have their pet cared for in a loving - caring - home environment. We are looking for individuals that recognize the need for PETS ARE INN in their area. An individual that has a proven track record as a professional in other areas but has made a conscious decision to change career paths - to be involved in business and in the community. Our unique niche in the hospitality/travel industry provides our customers and their pets with worry free services.

BACKGROUND:
Established: 1982; 1st Franchised: 1992
Franchised Units: 18
Company-Owned Units: 0
Total Units: 18
Dist.: US-17; CAN-0; O'seas-0
North America: NR
Density: 6 in MN, 3 in TX, 2 in WA
Projected New Units (12 Months): 4
Qualifications: 5, 4, 3, 5, 5, 4
Registered: CA,HI,IL,IN,MD,MI,MN,WA

FINANCIAL/TERMS:
Cash Investment: $20K
Total Investment: $35-65K
Minimum Net Worth: NR
Fees: Franchise - $15K
Royalty - 5-10%; Ad. - 1%
Earnings Claims Statement: Yes
Term of Contract (Years): 10/10
Avg. # Of Employees: 2 FT, 4 PT
Passive Ownership: Not Allowed
Encourage Conversions: NA
Area Develop. Agreements: No
Sub-Franchising Contracts: No
Expand In Territory: No
Space Needs: NR SF; HB

SUPPORT & TRAINING:
Financial Assistance Provided: No
Site Selection Assistance: Yes
Lease Negotiation Assistance: Yes
Co-Operative Advertising: Yes
Franchisee Assoc./Member: No
Size Of Corporate Staff: 5
On-Going Support: A,B,C,D,E,G,H,I
Training: 5 Days in Minneapolis, MN.

SPECIFIC EXPANSION PLANS:
US: Central Time Zone
Canada: No
Overseas: No

<< >>

RUFFIN'S PET CENTRES

109 Industrial Dr.
Dunnville, ON N1A 2X5 CANADA
Tel: (905) 774-7079
Fax: (905) 774-1096
E-Mail: mreynolds@ruffinspet.com
Web Site: www.ruffinspet.com
Mr. Mark Reynolds, President

RUFFIN'S PET CENTER is a unique combination of a traditional pet store and a discount, pet-food outlet. The union of these two types of stores increases the strength of both. The high traffic of a pet store increases the on-going pet food sales. This strong concept, combined with great office support, equals a successful franchise.

BACKGROUND:
Established: 1981; 1st Franchised: 1986
Franchised Units: 14
Company-Owned Units: 0

Total Units: 14
Dist.: US-0; CAN-14; O'seas-0
North America: 1 Province
Density: 14 in ON
Projected New Units (12 Months): 3
Qualifications: 4, 2, 1, 1, 2, 4
Registered: NR

FINANCIAL/TERMS:

Cash Investment: NR
Total Investment: $65-85K
Minimum Net Worth: Varies
Fees: Franchise - $20K
Royalty - 4%; Ad. - 1%
Earnings Claims Statement: No
Term of Contract (Years): 5/5
Avg. # Of Employees: 1 FT, 3 PT
Passive Ownership: Not Allowed
Encourage Conversions: Yes
Area Develop. Agreements: No
Sub-Franchising Contracts: No
Expand In Territory: No
Space Needs: 1,500 SF; SC, RM

SUPPORT & TRAINING:

Financial Assistance Provided: No
Site Selection Assistance: Yes
Lease Negotiation Assistance: Yes
Co-Operative Advertising: Yes
Franchisee Assoc./Member: No
Size Of Corporate Staff: 3
On-Going Support: B,C,D,E,f,G,H
Training: 1 Week Operating Store Close to Franchise; 1-2 Weeks Head Office; 1-2 Weeks On-Site.

SPECIFIC EXPANSION PLANS:

US: No
Canada: ON
Overseas: No

<< >>

Retail: Photographic Products & Services

Retail: Photographic Products & Services Industry Profile

Total # Franchisors in Industry Group	16
Total # Franchised Units in Industry Group	700
Total # Company-Owned Units in Industry Group	34
Total # Operating Units in Industry Group	734
Average # Franchised Units/Franchisor	43.8
Average # Company-Owned Units/Franchisor	2.1
Average # Total Units/Franchisor	45.9
Ratio of Total # Franchised Units/Total # Company-Owned Units	20.6:1
Industry Survey Participants	7
Representing % of Industry	43.8%
Average Franchise Fee*:	$21.8K
Average Total Investment*:	$121.9K
Average On-Going Royalty Fee*:	3.7%

*If a range was provided, the mid-point of the range was used. See detailed profiles for actual ranges.

Five Largest Participants in Survey

Company	# Franchised Units	# Co-Owned Units	# Total Units	Franchise Fee	On-Going Royalty	Total Investment
1. Sports Section, The	215	0	215	$10.9-30.9K	0%	$15-45K
2. MotoPhoto ®	189	2	191	$35K	6%	$225-275K
3. Glamour Shots	110	2	112	$15K	0%	$150K
4. I.N.V.U. Portraits	51	0	51	$12K	6%	$28-66K
5. Visual Image, The	17	3	20	$23.5K	0%	$35-40K

All of the data provided are proprietary and should not be quoted without acknowledging *Bond's Franchise Guide.*

CLIX

1100 Johnson Ferry Rd., # 400
Marietta, GA 30068
Tel: (888) 2GO-CLIX (770) 579-0098
Fax: (770) 234-4288
E-Mail: franchise@getyourclix.com
Web Site: www.getyourclix.com
Mr. David Asarnow, President/CEO

At CLIX, we picture you in business for yourself, not by yourself. If you're looking for a company and a franchise that is fun, friendly, hip and now, you owe it to yourself to check out CLIX. We have a proven system. The CLIX concept, launched in 1999, has a new studio look and feel that, with an image and attitude, sets CLIX apart from other portrait studios. Our 40+ years of experience stand ready to support you. We have the newest technology and a focus on service and our customer's experience.

BACKGROUND:
Established: 1999; 1st Franchised: 2005
Franchised Units: 0
Company-Owned Units: 7
Total Units: 7
Dist.: US-7; CAN-0; O'seas-0
North America: 1 State
Density: 7 in NY
Projected New Units (12 Months): 5
Qualifications: 5, 5, 1, 1, 3, 5
Registered: All States

FINANCIAL/TERMS:
Cash Investment: $75-250K
Total Investment: $240-499K
Minimum Net Worth: $300K
Fees: Franchise - $50K
Royalty - 6%; Ad. - 2% Mktg.
Earnings Claims Statement: No
Term of Contract (Years): 15/15
Avg. # Of Employees: 2 FT, 2 PT
Passive Ownership: Discouraged
Encourage Conversions: NA
Area Develop. Agreements: Yes/15
Sub-Franchising Contracts: No
Expand In Territory: Yes
Space Needs: 1,600 SF; SC

SUPPORT & TRAINING:
Financial Assistance Provided: Yes(I)
Site Selection Assistance: Yes
Lease Negotiation Assistance: Yes
Co-Operative Advertising: Yes
Franchisee Assoc./Member: No
Size Of Corporate Staff: 3
On-Going Support: B,C,D,E,G,h,I
Training: 2 Weeks Rochester, NY; 3 Weeks Franchisee Location Upon Opening.

SPECIFIC EXPANSION PLANS:
US: All United States
Canada: No
Overseas: No

<< >>

GLAMOUR SHOTS

1300 Metropolitan Ave.
Oklahoma City, OK 73108-2082
Tel: (800) 947-8747 + 323 (405) 951-7323
Fax: (405) 951-7343
E-Mail: kim@glamourshots.com
Web Site: www.glamourshots.com
Ms. Kim McElroy, Dir. Franchise Development

GLAMOUR SHOTS is more than you ever pictured. We are the industry leader in high-fashion photography. We provide pre-opening assistance, comprehensive training, operational training and systems and regional field consultants, as well as solid, on-going support. Come join the leader!

BACKGROUND: IFA MEMBER
Established: 1988; 1st Franchised: 1992
Franchised Units: 110
Company-Owned Units: 2
Total Units: 112
Dist.: US-144; CAN-5; O'seas-9
North America: 42 States, 1 Province
Density: 25 in TX, 21 in FL, 14 in CA
Projected New Units (12 Months): 25
Qualifications: 5, 1, 1, 2, 2, 5
Registered: CA,FL,HI,IL,IN,MD,MI,MN, NY,OR,RI,SD,VA,WA,WI,DC

FINANCIAL/TERMS:
Cash Investment: $15K
Total Investment: $150K
Minimum Net Worth: $200K
Fees: Franchise - $15K
Royalty - 0%; Ad. - $357/Mo.
Earnings Claims Statement: No
Term of Contract (Years): 10/10
Avg. # Of Employees: NR
Passive Ownership: Not Allowed
Encourage Conversions: Yes
Area Develop. Agreements: Yes
Sub-Franchising Contracts: No
Expand In Territory: Yes
Space Needs: 800-1,200 SF; RM

SUPPORT & TRAINING:
Financial Assistance Provided: Yes(I)
Site Selection Assistance: Yes
Lease Negotiation Assistance: Yes
Co-Operative Advertising: Yes
Franchisee Assoc./Member: Yes
Size Of Corporate Staff: NR
On-Going Support: A,B,C,D,E,G,H
Training: 1 Week at National Training Center; 4 Wks. at Training Store; As Needed at Your Location.

SPECIFIC EXPANSION PLANS:
US: All United States
Canada: All Canada
Overseas: All Countries

<< >>

GRINS 2 GO

9404 Genesee Ave., # 100
La Jolla, CA 92037
Tel: (866) GO-GRINS (858) 558-4948
Fax: (858) 558-4949
E-Mail: hbabla@grins2go.com
Web Site: www.grins2go.com
Mr. Venu Babla, Vice President

GRINS 2 GO is an innovative franchise in portrait and event photography, with two concepts - studio and on-location. Both embrace a unique approach to technology, customer service and fresh photographic styles. Opportunities for single units, multi-units and area developers available on the ground floor of this exciting new franchise.

BACKGROUND: IFA MEMBER
Established: 2004; 1st Franchised: 2004
Franchised Units: 2
Company-Owned Units: 0
Total Units: 2
Dist.: US-2; CAN-0; O'seas-0
North America: 1 State
Density: 2 in CA
Projected New Units (12 Months): 36
Qualifications: 4, 4, 1, 3, 4, 5
Registered: CA, FL (in Process), IL (in Process)

FINANCIAL/TERMS:
Cash Investment: $30-65K
Total Investment: $94.6-291.5K

Minimum Net Worth: $100K
Fees: Franchise - $17.5-25K
Royalty - 7%; Ad. - 3.5%
Earnings Claims Statement: No
Term of Contract (Years): 10/10
Avg. # Of Employees: 3 FT
Passive Ownership: Allowed
Encourage Conversions: No
Area Develop. Agreements: Yes/10
Sub-Franchising Contracts: No
Expand In Territory: Yes
Space Needs: 1,600 SF; SC, HB

SUPPORT & TRAINING:
Financial Assistance Provided: Yes(I)
Site Selection Assistance: Yes
Lease Negotiation Assistance: Yes
Co-Operative Advertising: No
Franchisee Assoc./Member: No
Size Of Corporate Staff: 5
On-Going Support: C,D,E,F,G,h,I
Training: None

SPECIFIC EXPANSION PLANS:
US: All United States
Canada: No
Overseas: No

<< >>

I.N.V.U. PORTRAITS

10880 N. 32nd St.
Phoenix, AZ 85028
Tel: (602) 996-7473
Fax: (801) 677-0010
E-Mail: ryanl@invuportraits.com
Web Site: www.invuportraits.com
Mr. Ryan Laws, VP Franchising

I.N.V.U. PORTRAITS combine heart-warming, one-of-a-kind photography with the up-scale creative touch of hand coloring and sepia toning. The resulting combination is a cherished piece. If you've ever considered owning your own home-based business and are able to put your creative talents and energies into an exciting and rewarding industry, we want to speak with you.

BACKGROUND:
Established: 1995; 1st Franchised: 1996
Franchised Units: 51
Company-Owned Units: 0
Total Units: 51
Dist.: US-51; CAN-0; O'seas-0
North America: 30 States
Density: 4 in CA, 4 in FL, 3 in VA
Projected New Units (12 Months): 60
Qualifications: 5, 4, 2, 1, 4, 5
Registered:CA,FL,IL,IN,MD,MI,MN,NY, OR,RI,VA,WA,WI,DC

FINANCIAL/TERMS:
Cash Investment: $28-66K
Total Investment: $28-66K
Minimum Net Worth: $50K
Fees: Franchise - $12K
Royalty - 6%; Ad. - 2%
Earnings Claims Statement: No
Term of Contract (Years): 10/5
Avg. # Of Employees: 4 FT
Passive Ownership: Not Allowed
Encourage Conversions: No
Area Develop. Agreements: No
Sub-Franchising Contracts: No
Expand In Territory: Yes
Space Needs: NA SF; HB

SUPPORT & TRAINING:
Financial Assistance Provided: No
Site Selection Assistance: NA
Lease Negotiation Assistance: NA
Co-Operative Advertising: NA
Franchisee Assoc./Member: No
Size Of Corporate Staff: 45
On-Going Support: b,C,D,G,h
Training: 5 Days Salt Lake City, UT.

SPECIFIC EXPANSION PLANS:
US: All United States
Canada: All Canada
Overseas: No

<< >>

MOTOPHOTO

Top 100

MOTOPHOTO ®

4444 Lake Center Dr.
Dayton, OH 45426-3868
Tel: (800) 733-6686 (937) 854-6686
Fax: (937) 854-0140
E-Mail: franchise@motophoto.com
Web Site: www.motophoto.com
Mr. Joseph M. O'Hara, VP Franchise Sales

MOTOPHOTO is a crisp, up-scale, "clicks and mortar" specialty retailer in the exploding digital photography and digital portrait studio marketplaces. Consumers and Prosumers experience the MOTOPHOTO difference through precisely blending the versatility of digital products and services with the convenience of in-store, kiosk, or on-line interactions. Nearly a quarter century of franchising experience translates to superior franchisee training and exceptional ongoing business support.

BACKGROUND: IFA MEMBER
Established: 1981; 1st Franchised: 1982
Franchised Units: 189
Company-Owned Units: 2
Total Units: 191
Dist.: US-162; CAN-29; O'seas-0
North America: 20 States, 1 Province
Density: 31 in NJ, 17 in VA, 13 in OK
Projected New Units (12 Months): 10
Qualifications: 4, 4, 1, 2, 4, 4
Registered: CA,IL,MD,MI,NY,VA

FINANCIAL/TERMS:
Cash Investment: $40-60K
Total Investment: $225-275K
Minimum Net Worth: $250K
Fees: Franchise - $35K
Royalty - 6%; Ad. - 0.5%
Earnings Claims Statement: No
Term of Contract (Years): 10/10
Avg. # Of Employees: 3 FT, 3 PT
Passive Ownership: Discouraged
Encourage Conversions: Yes
Area Develop. Agreements: No
Sub-Franchising Contracts: No
Expand In Territory: No
Space Needs: 1,200-1,400 SF; SC

SUPPORT & TRAINING:
Financial Assistance Provided: Yes(I)
Site Selection Assistance: Yes
Lease Negotiation Assistance: Yes
Co-Operative Advertising: Yes
Franchisee Assoc./Member: No
Size Of Corporate Staff: 26
On-Going Support: C,D,E,h,I
Training: 9 Days Dayton, OH; 3-5 Days Regional Training Center; 1 Week Franchisee's Store.

SPECIFIC EXPANSION PLANS:
US: All United States
Canada: ON
Overseas: No

<< >>

PORTRAIT AVENUE ™

4444 Lake Center Dr.
Dayton, OH 45426-3868
Tel: (800) 733-6686 (937) 854-6686
Fax: (937) 854-0140
E-Mail: franchise@portraitavenue.com
Web Site: www.portraitavenue.com
Mr. Joseph M. O'Hara, VP Franchise Sales

PORTRAIT AVENUE is a retail franchise in the high-touch, exciting and growing world of portrait photography. Using state-of-the-art digital technology, PORTRAIT AVENUE is uniquely positioned to capture the unclaimed opportunity that competitors leave behind. A quarter century of portrait studio and franchising experience supports the foundation of the Portrait Avenue Franchise System.

BACKGROUND: IFA MEMBER
Established: 1981; 1st Franchised: 2003
Franchised Units: 0
Company-Owned Units: 1
Total Units: 1
Dist.: US-1; CAN-0; O'seas-0
North America: 1 State
Density: 1 in OH
Projected New Units (12 Months): 19
Qualifications: 3, 3, 1, 2, 4, 4
Registered: NR

FINANCIAL/TERMS:
Cash Investment: $50-60K
Total Investment: $148-182K
Minimum Net Worth: $150K
Fees: Franchise - $25K
Royalty - 7%; Ad. - 7%
Earnings Claims Statement: Yes
Term of Contract (Years): 10/10
Avg. # Of Employees: 2 FT, 3 PT
Passive Ownership: Discouraged
Encourage Conversions: NA
Area Develop. Agreements: No
Sub-Franchising Contracts: No
Expand In Territory: No
Space Needs: 1,000 SF; RM

SUPPORT & TRAINING:
Financial Assistance Provided: Yes(I)
Site Selection Assistance: Yes
Lease Negotiation Assistance: Yes
Co-Operative Advertising: Yes
Franchisee Assoc./Member: No
Size Of Corporate Staff: 26
On-Going Support: A,b,C,D,E,G,h,I
Training: 6 Days Dayton, OH (excludes food/lodging).

SPECIFIC EXPANSION PLANS:
US: Midwest
Canada: No
Overseas: No

<< >>

SPORTS SECTION, THE

2150 Boggs Rd., # 200
Duluth, GA 30096
Tel: (866) 877-4746 (678) 740-0800
Fax: (678) 740-0808
E-Mail: jan@sports-section.com
Web Site: www.sports-section.com
Mr. Jan Rhodes, Dir. Franchise Development

'The Best in Youth & Sports Memories.' THE SPORTS SECTION franchisees earn income from 3 profit centers: youth and sports photo keepsakes, uniforms and trophies/awards. Complete training is provided. No experience in photography required. Exclusive, protected territories. No royalties. Operate from home or office, full or part-time. Finance plan available.

BACKGROUND: IFA MEMBER
Established: 1983; 1st Franchised: 1984
Franchised Units: 215
Company-Owned Units: 0
Total Units: 215
Dist.: US-165; CAN-0; O'seas-0
North America: 43 States
Density: 12 in GA, 10 in FL, 9 in CA
Projected New Units (12 Months): 30
Qualifications: 5, 4, 1, 3, 3, 4
Registered: All States

FINANCIAL/TERMS:
Cash Investment: $10.9-30.9K
Total Investment: $15-45K
Minimum Net Worth: NA
Fees: Franchise - $10.9-30.9K
Royalty - 0%; Ad. - 0%
Earnings Claims Statement: Yes
Term of Contract (Years): 10/10
Avg. # Of Employees: 2 FT, 2 PT
Passive Ownership: Discouraged
Encourage Conversions: Yes
Area Develop. Agreements: Yes (Int'l.)
Sub-Franchising Contracts: Yes
Expand In Territory: Yes
Space Needs: NA SF; HB, OB

SUPPORT & TRAINING:
Financial Assistance Provided: No
Site Selection Assistance: NA
Lease Negotiation Assistance: NA
Co-Operative Advertising: NA
Franchisee Assoc./Member: Yes/Yes
Size Of Corporate Staff: 35
On-Going Support: A,b,C,D,G,H,h,I
Training: 5 Days in Franchisee's Territory; On-Going Training.

SPECIFIC EXPANSION PLANS:
US: All United States
Canada: All Canada
Overseas: Master Franchises Only

<< >>

VISUAL IMAGE, THE

100 E. Brockman Way
Sparta, TN 38583
Tel: (800) 344-0323 (931) 836-2800
Fax: (931) 836-6279
E-Mail: tamara@childcarephotography.com
Web Site: www.thevisualimageinc.com
Ms. Tamara Staiti, Office Manager

VISUAL IMAGE combines the advantages of high mark-up photography with the low overhead of home-based business. Because we do all our photography on location, you save the high cost of retail space and the confinement of retail hours! We go to pre-schools and pet shops and take portraits for busy, working parents. Because we do studio-quality portraiture, preschools love our work and invite us back season after season. Creative, fulfilling work, financial and physical rewards.

BACKGROUND:
Established: 1984; 1st Franchised: 1994
Franchised Units: 17
Company-Owned Units: 3
Total Units: 20
Dist.: US-20; CAN-0; O'seas-0
North America: 12 States
Density: 4 in FL, 4 in TN, 2 in NC
Projected New Units (12 Months): 3
Qualifications: 3, 4, 1, 1, 3, 5
Registered: FL,MI

FINANCIAL/TERMS:
Cash Investment: $30-40K
Total Investment: $35-40K
Minimum Net Worth: $50K
Fees: Franchise - $23.5K
Royalty - 0%; Ad. - 0%
Earnings Claims Statement: Yes
Term of Contract (Years): 3/5
Avg. # Of Employees: 1 FT, 1 PT
Passive Ownership: Discouraged
Encourage Conversions: NA
Area Develop. Agreements: No
Sub-Franchising Contracts: No
Expand In Territory: Yes
Space Needs: NA SF; HB

SUPPORT & TRAINING:
Financial Assistance Provided: Yes(I)
Site Selection Assistance: NA
Lease Negotiation Assistance: NA
Co-Operative Advertising: Yes
Franchisee Assoc./Member: Yes
Size Of Corporate Staff: 3
On-Going Support: B,C,D,G,h,I
Training: 1 Week Home Base; 1 Week Training Center; I Week Training Center/Your Location.

SPECIFIC EXPANSION PLANS:
US: All United States
Canada: No
Overseas: No

<< >>

Retail: Specialty

Chapter 42

Retail: Specialty Industry Profile

Total # Franchisors in Industry Group	101
Total # Franchised Units in Industry Group	7,369
Total # Company-Owned Units in Industry Group	3,508
Total # Operating Units in Industry Group	10,877
Average # Franchised Units/Franchisor	73
Average # Company-Owned Units/Franchisor	34.7
Average # Total Units/Franchisor	107.7
Ratio of Total # Franchised Units/Total # Company-Owned Units	2.1:1

Industry Survey Participants	41
Representing % of Industry	40.6%
Average Franchise Fee*:	$26.5K
Average Total Investment*:	$188.7K
Average On-Going Royalty Fee*:	4.8%

*If a range was provided, the mid-point of the range was used. See detailed profiles for actual ranges.

Five Largest Participants in Survey

Company	# Franchised Units	# Co-Owned Units	# Total Units	Franchise Fee	On-Going Royalty	Total Investment
1. General Nutrition Centers	2,001	2,685	4,686	$40K	6%	$132.7-182K
2. Party Land	400	0	400	$35K	5%	$249-329K
3. Christmas Décor	375	0	375	$9.5-15.9K	2-4.5%	$15.9-31.9K
4. Wild Birds Unlimited	315	0	315	$18K	4%	$80-145K
5. Party America	61	230	291	$25K	4%	$335-500K

All of the data provided are proprietary and should not be quoted without acknowledging *Bond's Franchise Guide.*

ASHLEY AVERY'S COLLECTABLES

333 N. Sam Houston Plwy. E., # 690
Houston, TX 77060
Tel: (888) 310-4505 (281) 820-0789
Fax: (281) 820-2025
E-Mail: jpiana@ashleyaverys.com
Web Site: www.ashleyaverys.com
Mr. John Piana, Vice President

ASHLEY AVERY'S COLLECTABLES is America's largest chain of gifts & collectables, featuring exclusive pieces from world-renowned names such as Swarovski, Armani, Llardo, Hummel and many more. Each store features an elegant, gallery-like atmosphere with fascinating works of all kinds. Located in up-scale regional malls. Easy to learn & operate; exceptional training and support; national buying power & proven marketing programs.

BACKGROUND: IFA MEMBER
Established: 1981; 1st Franchised: 1981
Franchised Units: 40
Company-Owned Units: 1
Total Units: 41
Dist.: US-41; CAN-0; O'seas-0
North America: 13 States
Density: 17 in TX, 5 in FL, 2 in GA
Projected New Units (12 Months): 10
Qualifications: 5, 3, 3, 3, 4, 5
Registered:CA,FL,IL,IN,MD,MI,MN,NY,ND,RI,SD,VA,WA,WI

FINANCIAL/TERMS:
Cash Investment: $150K
Total Investment: $272-403K
Minimum Net Worth: $400K
Fees: Franchise - $30K
Royalty - 6%; Ad. - 2%
Earnings Claims Statement: No
Term of Contract (Years): 10
Avg. # Of Employees: 2 FT, 2 PT
Passive Ownership: Allowed
Encourage Conversions: Yes
Area Develop. Agreements: No
Sub-Franchising Contracts: No
Expand In Territory: Yes
Space Needs: 900-1,200 SF; RM, Kiosk (200sf)

SUPPORT & TRAINING:
Financial Assistance Provided: Yes(I)
Site Selection Assistance: Yes
Lease Negotiation Assistance: Yes
Co-Operative Advertising: Yes
Franchisee Assoc./Member: Yes/Yes
Size Of Corporate Staff: 7
On-Going Support: A,B,C,D,E,F,G,H,I
Training: 7 Days Houston, TX.

SPECIFIC EXPANSION PLANS:
US: All United States
Canada: No
Overseas: No

<< >>

CANDLEMAN CORPORATION

15025 Glazier Ave., # 400
Apple Valley, MN 55124
Tel: (800) 328-3453 (218) 829-0592
Fax: (800) 962-2511
E-Mail: dhuber@hubercommercial.com
Web Site: www.candleman.com
Ms. Colleen Brown, Regional Manager

Candleman is a focused franchise system is a leader in upscale retailing of unique candles and accessories. With an experienced professional management team to assist franchisees, Candleman provides an extremely comprehensive support program for its franchisees involving every aspect of setting up and operating a store. The successful franchisee is a partner couple who enjoys people, has a flair for home décor and would like working collectively with fellow franchisees.

BACKGROUND:
Established: 1991; 1st Franchised: 1992
Franchised Units: 26
Company-Owned Units: 1
Total Units: 27
Dist.: US-58; CAN-5; O'seas-0
North America: 24 States, 3 Provinces
Density: 6 in PA, 5 in MN, 4 in WA
Projected New Units (12 Months): 10
Qualifications: 4, 4, 2, 2, 4, 5
Registered: All States

FINANCIAL/TERMS:
Cash Investment: $70K
Total Investment: $150-350K
Minimum Net Worth: $200K
Fees: Franchise - $35K
Royalty - 6%; Ad. - $100/Mo.
Earnings Claims Statement: No
Term of Contract (Years): 10/10
Avg. # Of Employees: 1 FT, 4-5 PT
Passive Ownership: Not Allowed
Encourage Conversions: No
Area Develop. Agreements: No
Sub-Franchising Contracts: No
Expand In Territory: No
Space Needs: 800-1,200 SF; RM

SUPPORT & TRAINING:
Financial Assistance Provided: Yes(I)
Site Selection Assistance: Yes
Lease Negotiation Assistance: Yes
Co-Operative Advertising: No
Franchisee Assoc./Member: Yes/Yes
Size Of Corporate Staff: 13
On-Going Support: C,D,E,F,G,H,I
Training: 7 Days in Headquarters; 3 Days On-Site.

SPECIFIC EXPANSION PLANS:
US: All United States
Canada: All Canada
Overseas: Europe, Middle East, Australia, South America

<< >>

Cartridge World

Top 100

CARTRIDGE WORLD

6460 Hollis St.
Emeryville, CA 94608
Tel: (866) 473-5623 (510) 594-9900
Fax: (510) 594-9991
E-Mail: jdring@cartridgeworld.com
Web Site: www.cartridgeworldusa.com
Mr. John Dring, Executive Vice President/COO

CARTRIDGE WORLD is the leader in printer cartridge refilling. Our business strategy combines the skilled process of refilling printer cartridges for inkjet and laser printers, photocopy and fax machines with knowledgeable and fast customer service, convenient retail locations and savings to the customer of up to 50%. CARTRIDGE WORLD, which dominates its market, has become one of the fastest-growing franchise concepts in the world. Named #1 in its market by Entrepreneur Magazine.

BACKGROUND: IFA MEMBER
Established: 1997; 1st Franchised: 2002
Franchised Units: 860
Company-Owned Units: 0
Total Units: 860
Dist.: US-190; CAN-9; O'seas-661
North America: 41 States, 3 Provinces
Density: 20 in CA, 20 in TX, 15 in NJ
Projected New Units (12 Months): 350
Qualifications: 4, 5, 3, 3, 2, 5
Registered: All States and AB

FINANCIAL/TERMS:
Cash Investment: $35K

Total Investment: $104-172K
Minimum Net Worth: $250-350K
Fees: Franchise - $30K
Royalty - 6%; Ad. - 2%
Earnings Claims Statement: No
Term of Contract (Years): 10/10
Avg. # Of Employees: 1 FT, 1 PT
Passive Ownership: Discouraged
Encourage Conversions: Yes
Area Develop. Agreements: No
Sub-Franchising Contracts: Yes
Expand In Territory: Yes
Space Needs: NR SF; FS, SF, SC

SUPPORT & TRAINING:
Financial Assistance Provided: Yes(I)
Site Selection Assistance: Yes
Lease Negotiation Assistance: Yes
Co-Operative Advertising: Yes
Franchisee Assoc./Member: Yes/Yes
Size Of Corporate Staff: 30
On-Going Support: B,C,D,E,F,G,H,I
Training: 2 Weeks Emeryville, CA; 2 Weeks In-Store Field Training.

SPECIFIC EXPANSION PLANS:
US: All United States
Canada: All Canada
Overseas: All Countries

<< >>

CHRISTMAS DECOR

P. O. Box 5946
Lubbock, TX 79408
Tel: (800) 687-9551 (806) 772-1225
Fax: (806) 722-9627
E-Mail: blake@thedecorgroup.com
Web Site: www.christmasdecor.net
Mr. John Ropas, Franchise Development Director

Holiday and event decorating services provided to homes and businesses. Fun, high-margin business that offers annual income by working only 4-6 months of the year. Also, an excellent add-on business for landscape, pool and spa, electrical and other seasonal service contractors. Landscape lighting franchise available also to create year round business.

BACKGROUND: IFA MEMBER
Established: 1986; 1st Franchised: 1996
Franchised Units: 375
Company-Owned Units: 0
Total Units: 375
Dist.: US-160; CAN-5; O'seas-0
North America: 44 States, 2 Provinces
Density: 23 in TX, 14 in OH, 13 in MI
Projected New Units (12 Months): 100
Qualifications: 2, 4, 2, 3, 3, 4
Registered: All States and AB

FINANCIAL/TERMS:
Cash Investment: $6.6-9.5K
Total Investment: $15.9-31.9K
Minimum Net Worth: NA
Fees: Franchise - $9.5-15.9K
Royalty - 2-4.5%; Ad. - $180/Yr.
Earnings Claims Statement: No
Term of Contract (Years): 5/5
Avg. # Of Employees: 2-4 FT, 3-20 PT
Passive Ownership: Discouraged
Encourage Conversions: NA
Area Develop. Agreements: No
Sub-Franchising Contracts: No
Expand In Territory: No
Space Needs: Varies SF; HB, Many Add-On Businesses

SUPPORT & TRAINING:
Financial Assistance Provided: Yes(D)
Site Selection Assistance: Yes
Lease Negotiation Assistance: No
Co-Operative Advertising: No
Franchisee Assoc./Member: Yes/Yes
Size Of Corporate Staff: 18
On-Going Support: A,B,D,G,h,I
Training: 3 Days Major Cities in US; 2 Days of Continuing Education in Major Cities.

SPECIFIC EXPANSION PLANS:
US: All United States
Canada: All Canada
Overseas: All Christian Countries

<< >>

CMIT SOLUTIONS

537 Woodward St., # D
Austin, TX 78704-7324
Tel: (800) 710-2648 (512) 477-6667
Fax: (512) 692-3711
E-Mail: franchise@cmit.biz
Web Site: www.cmitsolutions.com
Mr. Victor J. Burzynski, VP Franchise Development

Offers IT service and computer support to small businesses. Franchise can be home-based, as we service the client at their place of business.

BACKGROUND: IFA MEMBER
Established: 1994; 1st Franchised: 1998
Franchised Units: 125
Company-Owned Units: 0
Total Units: 125
Dist.: US-125; CAN-0; O'seas-0
North America: 30 States
Density: NR
Projected New Units (12 Months): 60
Qualifications: 2, 3, 4, 2, 4, 4
Registered: CA,IL,IN,MD,MN,NY,RI,WA, WI

FINANCIAL/TERMS:
Cash Investment: $50-105K
Total Investment: $50-105K
Minimum Net Worth: NA
Fees: Franchise - $33.9K/Terr.
Royalty - Up to $850; Ad. - Up to $300
Earnings Claims Statement: No
Term of Contract (Years): 10/10
Avg. # Of Employees: 6-10 PT
Passive Ownership: Not Allowed
Encourage Conversions: No
Area Develop. Agreements: Yes
Sub-Franchising Contracts: No
Expand In Territory: No
Space Needs: NR SF; NA

SUPPORT & TRAINING:
Financial Assistance Provided: NR
Site Selection Assistance: NA
Lease Negotiation Assistance: NA
Co-Operative Advertising: NA
Franchisee Assoc./Member: No
Size Of Corporate Staff: 14
On-Going Support: A,B,C,d,H,I
Training: 2 Week Session in Austin, TX.

SPECIFIC EXPANSION PLANS:
US: All United States
Canada: No
Overseas: No

<< >>

COMPUTER RENAISSANCE

124 S. Florida Ave., # 202
Lakeland, FL 33801-4620
Tel: (888) 266-7736 + 25 (863) 669-1155 + 25
Fax: (800) 665-6324
E-Mail: lhennis@compren.com
Web Site: www.compren.com
Ms. Linda Hennis, Director Franchise Development

COMPUTER RENAISSANCE, a full-service retail store specializing in quality used, refurbished and new computer hardware, software and related accessories. Our stores also provide custom-built computers, system upgrades, networking, consulting and superior technical service. With constant upgrades to computers in both the hardware and software fields, you can ensure your spot in a highly innovative industry by becoming part of a continuing market demand.

BACKGROUND: IFA MEMBER
Established: 1988; 1st Franchised: 1993
Franchised Units: 100

Company-Owned Units: 0
Total Units: 100
Dist.: US-100; CAN-0; O'seas-0
North America: 34 States, 6 Provinces
Density: 9 in FL, 8 in MN, 6 in IL
Projected New Units (12 Months): 15
Qualifications: 4, 5, 2, 3, 4, 5
Registered: MI, OR, WI

FINANCIAL/TERMS:
Cash Investment: $20-50K
Total Investment: $50-150K
Minimum Net Worth: $100K
Fees: Franchise - $20K
Royalty - 4%; Ad. - .5%
Earnings Claims Statement: Yes
Term of Contract (Years): 10/10
Avg. # Of Employees: 3 FT, 2 PT
Passive Ownership: Discouraged
Encourage Conversions: Yes
Area Develop. Agreements: No
Sub-Franchising Contracts: No
Expand In Territory: Yes
Space Needs: 1,600 SF; SF, SC

SUPPORT & TRAINING:
Financial Assistance Provided: Yes(I)
Site Selection Assistance: Yes
Lease Negotiation Assistance: Yes
Co-Operative Advertising: No
Franchisee Assoc./Member: Yes/Yes
Size Of Corporate Staff: 15
On-Going Support: B,C,D,E,F,G,h,I
Training: 2 Weeks in Florida.

SPECIFIC EXPANSION PLANS:
US: All United States
Canada: No
Overseas: All Countries

<< >>

COUNTRY CLUTTER

3333 Vaca Valley Pkwy., # 900
Vacaville, CA 95688
Tel: (800) 425-8883 + 206 (707) 451-6890
Fax: (707) 451-0410
E-Mail: terry@countryclutter.com
Web Site: www.countryclutterfranchise.com
Mr. Terry Odneal, Director Franchise Development

A charming country store for gifts, collectibles and home decor. A unique business that offers old fashioned quality, selection and customer service. A complete franchise program professionally designed, computerized and planned to sell a perfected blend of country merchandise made by primarily American manufacturers and crafters. Rich arrangements and displays of textures, colors and aromas make shopping at COUNTRY CLUTTER a true sensory delight.

BACKGROUND:
Established: 1991; 1st Franchised: 1992
Franchised Units: 63
Company-Owned Units: 2
Total Units: 65
Dist.: US-65; CAN-0; O'seas-0
North America: 25 States
Density: 19 in CA, 6 in TX, 5 in GA
Projected New Units (12 Months): 10-25
Qualifications: 5, 3, 3, 2, 2, 5
Registered:CA,FL,IL,IN,MD,MI,MN,ND,NY,OR,RI,VA,WA, WI

FINANCIAL/TERMS:
Cash Investment: $65-85K
Total Investment: $200-280K
Minimum Net Worth: $200-250K
Fees: Franchise - $25K
Royalty - 5.5%; Ad. - 1%
Earnings Claims Statement: Yes
Term of Contract (Years): 10/5/5
Avg. # Of Employees: 2 FT, 4-5 PT
Passive Ownership: Discouraged
Encourage Conversions: Yes
Area Develop. Agreements: Yes/Open
Sub-Franchising Contracts: No
Expand In Territory: No
Space Needs: 850-2,200 SF; SC, RM, Outlets

SUPPORT & TRAINING:
Financial Assistance Provided: No
Site Selection Assistance: Yes
Lease Negotiation Assistance: Yes
Co-Operative Advertising: No
Franchisee Assoc./Member: Yes/Yes
Size Of Corporate Staff: 19
On-Going Support: C,D,E,F,G,H,I
Training: ~40 Hours Home Training; 5 Days Heqdquarters; 3-5 Days On-Site.

SPECIFIC EXPANSION PLANS:
US: All US But HI, AK, & SD
Canada: No
Overseas: No

<< >>

CROWN TROPHY

9 Skyline Dr.
Hawthorne, NY 10532-1402
Tel: (800) 583-8228 (914) 347-7700
Fax: (914) 347-0211
E-Mail: scott@crowntrophy.com
Web Site: www.crownfranchise.com
Mr. Scott Kelly, Executive Vice President

The only franchise of its kind in America, CROWN TROPHY is the largest supplier and fastest growing retailer of trophies and awards in the country. Crown offers a full-service facility utilizing state-of-the-art equipment along with the most innovative product line in the industry. CROWN TROPHY is truly a one of a kind, unique franchise opportunity.

BACKGROUND: IFA MEMBER
Established: 1978; 1st Franchised: 1987
Franchised Units: 131
Company-Owned Units: 0
Total Units: 131
Dist.: US-131; CAN-0; O'seas-0
North America: 37 States
Density: 16 in NY, 11 in TX, 8 in NJ
Projected New Units (12 Months): 12
Qualifications: 2, 2, 1, 3, 5, 5
Registered:CA,FL,IL,IN,MD,MI,MN,ND,NY,OR,SD,WI

FINANCIAL/TERMS:
Cash Investment: $90K
Total Investment: $135-145K
Minimum Net Worth: $100K
Fees: Franchise - $35K
Royalty - 5%; Ad. - 0%
Earnings Claims Statement: No
Term of Contract (Years): 5/5/5
Avg. # Of Employees: 1 FT, 2 PT
Passive Ownership: Discouraged
Encourage Conversions: Yes
Area Develop. Agreements: No
Sub-Franchising Contracts: No
Expand In Territory: Yes
Space Needs: 1,600-1,800 SF; SF, SC

SUPPORT & TRAINING:
Financial Assistance Provided: Yes(I)
Site Selection Assistance: Yes
Lease Negotiation Assistance: Yes
Co-Operative Advertising: No
Franchisee Assoc./Member: Yes
Size Of Corporate Staff: 10
On-Going Support: C,D,E,F,H,I
Training: 10 Days Corporate Office; 5 Days On-Site.

SPECIFIC EXPANSION PLANS:
US: All United States
Canada: No
Overseas: No

<< >>

FAST-FIX JEWELRY AND WATCH REPAIRS

1300 NW 17th Ave., # 170
Delray Beach, FL 33445
Tel: (800) 359-0407 (561) 330-6060
Fax: (561) 330-6062
E-Mail: franchise@fastfix.com
Web Site: www.fastfix.com
Mr. Mark Goldstein, VP Franchise Development

FAST-FIX JEWELRY AND WATCH REPAIRS ® is a proven business with a 20-year track record in the multi-billion dollar jewelry and watch repair industry. No experience necessary. Full training. FAST-FIX stores operate only in major regional malls, which guarantee high visibility and traffic. Most repairs can be completed within an hour while customers watch or enjoy shopping. FAST-FIX JEWELRY AND WATCH REPAIRS® has more than 135 franchise locations nationwide.

BACKGROUND: IFA MEMBER
Established: 1984; 1st Franchised: 1987
Franchised Units: 140
Company-Owned Units: 0
Total Units: 140
Dist.: US-138; CAN-2; O'seas-0
North America: 23 States, PR
Density: 19 in FL, 19 in CA, 16 in TX
Projected New Units (12 Months): 25
Qualifications: 3, 5, 1, 1, 1, 4
Registered:CA,DC,FL,IL,MD,MI,MN,NY,OR,RI,VA,WA,WI

FINANCIAL/TERMS:
Cash Investment: $40-60K
Total Investment: $113-200K
Minimum Net Worth: NA
Fees: Franchise - $30K
Royalty - 5%; Ad. - 0%
Earnings Claims Statement: No
Term of Contract (Years): 10/10
Avg. # Of Employees: 3 FT, 1 PT
Passive Ownership: Discouraged
Encourage Conversions: NR
Area Develop. Agreements: Yes/10
Sub-Franchising Contracts: Yes
Expand In Territory: Yes
Space Needs: 150-850 SF; RM

SUPPORT & TRAINING:
Financial Assistance Provided: Yes(I)
Site Selection Assistance: Yes
Lease Negotiation Assistance: Yes
Co-Operative Advertising: NA
Franchisee Assoc./Member: Yes/Yes
Size Of Corporate Staff: 9
On-Going Support: B,C,D,E,G,H,I
Training: 8 Days at National Training Center in Dallas and On-Site Training.

SPECIFIC EXPANSION PLANS:
US: All United States
Canada: All Canada
Overseas: All Countries

<< >>

FOLIAGE DESIGN SYSTEMS

4496 35th St.
Orlando, FL 32811-6504
Tel: (800) 933-7351 (407) 245-7776
Fax: (407) 245-7533
E-Mail: john@foliagedesign.com
Web Site: www.foliagedesign.com
Mr. John S. Hagood, Chairman

FOLIAGE DESIGN SYSTEMS is one of the largest interior plant maintenance companies in the U. S., according to Interiorscape Magazine. FOLIAGE DESIGN franchisees learn the business from the ground up in an intensive training program followed by training sessions in the field. Franchisees are taught design, sales and maintenance of interior foliage plants.

BACKGROUND: IFA MEMBER
Established: 1971; 1st Franchised: 1980
Franchised Units: 37
Company-Owned Units: 3
Total Units: 40
Dist.: US-40; CAN-0; O'seas-0
North America: 16 States
Density: 13 in FL, 4 in SC, 3 in MS
Projected New Units (12 Months): 3
Qualifications: 4, 5, 3, 3, 1, 5
Registered: FL

FINANCIAL/TERMS:
Cash Investment: $14.4-44.4K
Total Investment: $49.4-144.4K
Minimum Net Worth: NR
Fees: Franchise - $25-100K
Royalty - 6%; Ad. - 0%
Earnings Claims Statement: No
Term of Contract (Years): 10
Avg. # Of Employees: 4 FT, 2 PT
Passive Ownership: Discouraged
Encourage Conversions: No
Area Develop. Agreements: Yes
Sub-Franchising Contracts: No
Expand In Territory: Yes
Space Needs: 200 SF; Greenhouse, Warehouse

SUPPORT & TRAINING:
Financial Assistance Provided: No
Site Selection Assistance: Yes
Lease Negotiation Assistance: No
Co-Operative Advertising: No
Franchisee Assoc./Member: NR
Size Of Corporate Staff: 8
On-Going Support: A,B,C,D,F,G,H,I
Training: 8-10 Days Headquarters; 3-5 Days in Field.

SPECIFIC EXPANSION PLANS:
US: All United States
Canada: All Canada
Overseas: Europe, Asia, Mexico, South America

<< >>

FOOT SOLUTIONS

2359 Windy Hill Rd., # 220
Marietta, GA 30067
Tel: (866) 338-2597 (770) 955-0099
Fax: (770) 953-6270
E-Mail: fscorp@footsolutions.com
Web Site: www.footsolutions.com
Ms. Lisa Levine, Franchise Support

Health and wellness specialty retail franchise that focuses on foot care, including computer scanning of feet, proper shoe fit, especially for those with hard-to-fit shoes, custom insoles and orthotics and shoes that look and feel good. We also offer foot and shoe care products, including socks, polish and more!

BACKGROUND: IFA MEMBER
Established: 2000; 1st Franchised: 2000
Franchised Units: 140
Company-Owned Units: 1
Total Units: 141
Dist.: US-126; CAN-14; O'seas-1
North America: 29 States, 3 Provinces
Density: 13 in CA, 13 in TX, 10 in GA
Projected New Units (12 Months): 80
Qualifications: 3, 3, 1, 2, 3, 3
Registered:CA,FL,IL,IN,MD,MI,MN,NY,OR,VA,WA,WI,AB

FINANCIAL/TERMS:
Cash Investment: $50-65K
Total Investment: $173-240K
Minimum Net Worth: $300-500K
Fees: Franchise - $27.5K
Royalty - 5%; Ad. - 4%,10%/yr 1
Earnings Claims Statement: No
Term of Contract (Years): 20/10/10
Avg. # Of Employees: 2-3 FT

Passive Ownership: Allowed
Encourage Conversions: Yes
Area Develop. Agreements: Yes - Intl.
Sub-Franchising Contracts: No
Expand In Territory: Yes
Space Needs: 1,000-1,500 SF; SC

SUPPORT & TRAINING:

Financial Assistance Provided: Yes(I)
Site Selection Assistance: Yes
Lease Negotiation Assistance: Yes
Co-Operative Advertising: Yes
Franchisee Assoc./Member: Yes/Yes
Size Of Corporate Staff: 31
On-Going Support: b,C,D,E,G,H,I
Training: 2 Weeks Marietta, GA; 1 Week in Field.

SPECIFIC EXPANSION PLANS:

US: All United States
Canada: All Canada
Overseas: All Countries

<< >>

GENERAL NUTRITION CENTERS

300 Sixth Ave., Fl. 4
Pittsburgh, PA 15222-2514
Tel: (800) 766-7099 (412) 402-7121
Fax: (412) 402-7105
E-Mail: livewell@gncfranchising.com
Web Site: www.gncfranchising.com
Mr. Bruce Pollock, Sr. Dir. Franchise Development

GNC is the leading specialty retailer of vitamins, minerals, herbs and sports nutrition supplements and is uniquely positioned to capitalize on the accelerating self-care trend. As the leading provider of products and information for personal health enhancement, the company holds the largest specialty-retail share of the nutritional supplement market. GNC was ranked America's #1 retail franchise for 15 consecutive years.

BACKGROUND:

Established: 1935; 1st Franchised: 1988
Franchised Units: 2,001
Company-Owned Units: 2,685
Total Units: 4,686
Dist.: US-3,985; CAN-144; O'seas-557
North America: 50 States, 9 Provinces
Density: 392 in CA,364 in FL,300 TX
Projected New Units (12 Months): NR
Qualifications: 5, 5, 1, 1, 1, 4
Registered: All States and AB

FINANCIAL/TERMS:

Cash Investment: $65K
Total Investment: $132.7-182K
Minimum Net Worth: $100K
Fees: Franchise - $40K
Royalty - 6%; Ad. - 3%
Earnings Claims Statement: Yes
Term of Contract (Years): 10/5/5
Avg. # Of Employees: 1 FT, 3-5 PT
Passive Ownership: Not Allowed
Encourage Conversions: NR
Area Develop. Agreements: Yes/Varies
Sub-Franchising Contracts: No
Expand In Territory: Yes
Space Needs: 1,402 (avg.) SF; SF, SC, RM

SUPPORT & TRAINING:

Financial Assistance Provided: Yes(D)
Site Selection Assistance: Yes
Lease Negotiation Assistance: Yes
Co-Operative Advertising: No
Franchisee Assoc./Member: Yes/Yes
Size Of Corporate Staff: 600
On-Going Support: A,D,E,F,G,H,I
Training: 1 Wk. On-Site in Local Corporate Store; 1 Wk. in Pittsburgh, PA; 1 Wk. Opening Assistance.

SPECIFIC EXPANSION PLANS:

US: All United States
Canada: All CAN Exc. PQ
Overseas: All Countries

<< >>

GROWER DIRECT FRESH CUT FLOWERS

4220 - 98 St., # 301
Edmonton, AB T6E 6A1 CANADA
Tel: (800) 567-7258 (780) 436-7774
Fax: (780) 436-3336
E-Mail: bscott@grower.com
Web Site: www.grower.com
Mr. Bill Scott, Managing Director

As the largest floral chain retailer, our independently operated franchise locations sell the world's highest-quality fresh cut roses and other flowers in a unique 'boutique-style' setting. Product is sourced directly from the finest producers known and transported weekly to our stores via GROWER DIRECT's distribution system. Rapid product sales translate into 50-60 inventory turns annually and help make the enjoyment of FRESH CUT FLOWERS an affordable and everyday event for our customers.

BACKGROUND:

Established: 1991; 1st Franchised: 1991
Franchised Units: 121
Company-Owned Units: 1
Total Units: 122
Dist.: US-0; CAN-122; O'seas-0
North America: 10 Provinces
Density: 38 in AB, 22 in ON, 15 in BC
Projected New Units (12 Months): 12
Qualifications: 4, 4, 2, 2, 4, 4
Registered: AB

FINANCIAL/TERMS:

Cash Investment: $40K
Total Investment: $35-40K
Minimum Net Worth: $50K
Fees: Franchise - $25K
Royalty - $240/Wk.; Ad. - $15/Wk.
Earnings Claims Statement: No
Term of Contract (Years): 10/10
Avg. # Of Employees: 1 FT, 2 PT
Passive Ownership: Discouraged
Encourage Conversions: Yes
Area Develop. Agreements: No
Sub-Franchising Contracts: Yes
Expand In Territory: Yes
Space Needs: 400-1,000 SF; SC

SUPPORT & TRAINING:

Financial Assistance Provided: No
Site Selection Assistance: Yes
Lease Negotiation Assistance: Yes
Co-Operative Advertising: Yes
Franchisee Assoc./Member: Yes/Yes
Size Of Corporate Staff: 14
On-Going Support: b,C,D,E,G,H,I
Training: 5 Days in Store; 5 Days in Classroom; 5 Days Industry Tours.

SPECIFIC EXPANSION PLANS:

US: No
Canada: All Canada
Overseas: No

<< >>

HOBBYTOWN USA

6301 S. 58th St.
Lincoln, NE 68516-3676
Tel: (800) 858-7370 (402) 434-5064
Fax: (402) 434-5078
E-Mail: nichole@hobbytown.com
Web Site: www.hobbytown.com
Ms. Nichole Ernst, Associate Vice President

HOBBYTOWN USA stores are full-line hobby stores, featuring trains, models, radio-controlled vehicles, games, collectible cards, gifts, accessories and much more! The HOBBYTOWN USA system provides store owners with a comprehensive package of systems and services to be competitive in the hobby and entertainment industries.

BACKGROUND: IFA MEMBER
Established: 1969; 1st Franchised: 1986
Franchised Units: 162
Company-Owned Units: 2
Total Units: 164
Dist.: US-164; CAN-0; O'seas-0
North America: 41 States
Density: 14 in CA, 10 in TX
Projected New Units (12 Months): 30
Qualifications: 4, 3, 2, 2, 2, 5
Registered: All States

FINANCIAL/TERMS:
Cash Investment: $60-100K
Total Investment: $150-500K
Minimum Net Worth: $150K
Fees: Franchise - $19.5K
Royalty - 3-4%; Ad. - NA
Earnings Claims Statement: No
Term of Contract (Years): 10/10
Avg. # Of Employees: 1-2 FT, 2-3 PT
Passive Ownership: Discouraged
Encourage Conversions: Yes
Area Develop. Agreements: No
Sub-Franchising Contracts: No
Expand In Territory: Yes
Space Needs: 3,000 SF; SC, RM

SUPPORT & TRAINING:
Financial Assistance Provided: Yes(I)
Site Selection Assistance: Yes
Lease Negotiation Assistance: Yes
Co-Operative Advertising: Yes
Franchisee Assoc./Member: Yes
Size Of Corporate Staff: 40
On-Going Support: A,C,D,E,F,G,H,I
Training: 1 Week Home Office; 3 Weeks On-Site.

SPECIFIC EXPANSION PLANS:
US: All United States
Canada: All Canada
Overseas: No

<< >>

Your Fireplace & Barbecue Superstore

HOMETOWN HEARTH & GRILL
240 Route 10 West
Whippany, NJ 07981-0206
Tel: (888) 298-0031 (954) 429-8602
Fax: (954) 429-1389
E-Mail: dlefevere@suburbanenergy.com
Web Site: www.suburbanfranchising.com
Mr. Dellray Lefevere, National Sales Manager

A HOMETOWN HEARTH & GRILL franchised retail location offers gas grills, outdoor products, fireplaces, hearth stoves, replacement parts and accessories that transform indoor and outdoor spaces with elegance, luxury and warmth. We offer a range of products and services few retailers can match. From broad selection to expert advice, consumers can shop our stores with the confidence that they are getting the best quality, the best service and the best value. 28 years of successful experience.

BACKGROUND: IFA MEMBER
Established: 1993; 1st Franchised: 2004
Franchised Units: 0
Company-Owned Units: 13
Total Units: 13
Dist.: US-13; CAN-0; O'seas-0
North America: 9 States
Density: 2 in NJ, 2 in WA, 2 in OR
Projected New Units (12 Months): 10
Qualifications: 4, 3, 2, 3, 4, 5
Registered: All States and AB

FINANCIAL/TERMS:
Cash Investment: $80-120K
Total Investment: $300-600K
Minimum Net Worth: $300K
Fees: Franchise - $39.5K
Royalty - 5%; Ad. - 2%
Earnings Claims Statement: Yes
Term of Contract (Years): 10/5/5
Avg. # Of Employees: 3 FT, 1 PT
Passive Ownership: Not Allowed
Encourage Conversions: Yes
Area Develop. Agreements: No
Sub-Franchising Contracts: No
Expand In Territory: Yes
Space Needs: 2,500 SF; SC

SUPPORT & TRAINING:
Financial Assistance Provided: Yes(I)
Site Selection Assistance: Yes
Lease Negotiation Assistance: Yes
Co-Operative Advertising: Yes
Franchisee Assoc./Member: Yes/Yes
Size Of Corporate Staff: 4,500
On-Going Support: A,B,C,D,E,F,G,h,I
Training: 2 Weeks Whippany, NJ; On-Going In-Store.

SPECIFIC EXPANSION PLANS:
US: All United States
Canada: No
Overseas: No

<< >>

Just-A-Buck®

JUST-A-BUCK
301 N. Main St., # 5
New City, NY 10956
Tel: (800) 332-2229 (845) 291-7018
Fax: (845) 638-3878
E-Mail: rs@spyral.net
Web Site: www.just-a-buck.com
Mr. Ronald Sommers, Dir. Franchise Development

Merchandise that would sometimes cost as much as ten times more at any other store makes JUST-A-BUCK fun to shop and fun to run. America's premier franchised dollar store. Each location is neat and clean. It takes hard work but the concept is simple and it's made even easier with on-going support, training and help with everything from marketing to merchandising. IFA Member. Entrepreneur Top 500.

BACKGROUND: IFA MEMBER
Established: 1988; 1st Franchised: 1992
Franchised Units: 35
Company-Owned Units: 11
Total Units: 46
Dist.: US-46; CAN-0; O'seas-0
North America: 7 States
Density: 21 in NY, 10 in NJ, 6 in CT
Projected New Units (12 Months): 15
Qualifications: 4, 3, 2, 2, 2, 4
Registered: CA,FL,IL,MD,MI,NY,RI,VA, DC

FINANCIAL/TERMS:
Cash Investment: $40-60K
Total Investment: $126.7-265.9K
Minimum Net Worth: $150K
Fees: Franchise - $25K
Royalty - 4%; Ad. - 2%
Earnings Claims Statement: No
Term of Contract (Years): 10/20
Avg. # Of Employees: 6 FT, 10 PT
Passive Ownership: Not Allowed
Encourage Conversions: Yes
Area Develop. Agreements: Yes
Sub-Franchising Contracts: No
Expand In Territory: Yes
Space Needs: 3,000 SF; SC, RM

SUPPORT & TRAINING:
Financial Assistance Provided: Yes(I)
Site Selection Assistance: Yes
Lease Negotiation Assistance: Yes
Co-Operative Advertising: No

Franchisee Assoc./Member: No
Size Of Corporate Staff: 18
On-Going Support: A,B,C,D,E,F,G,H,I
Training: 10 Days NY State; 10 Days On-Site.

SPECIFIC EXPANSION PLANS:
US: All United States
Canada: All Canada
Overseas: All Countries

<< >>

KaBloom
The power of fresh flowers.®

Top 100

KABLOOM

200 Wildwood Ave.
Woburn, MA 01801-2031
Tel: (800) KABLOOM (781) 935-6500 + 153
Fax: (781) 935-9410
E-Mail: bgrody@kabloom.com
Web Site: www.kabloom.com
Mr. Bill Grody, Director Franchise Development

KABLOOM is the US's largest, fastest-growing and only national retail storefront florist. KABLOOM blends basic retailing fundamentals and merchandising with the European philosophy of fresh flowers in people's daily lives. With 110 stores open by 12/2004, 125+ franchisees in 30 states have bought the rights to open 350+ stores over the next few years. Flowers are FedExed to your store within 48 to 72 hours of having been cut. Strong walk-in business, weddings, funerals, weekly clients-the list is endless.

BACKGROUND: IFA MEMBER
Established: 1998; 1st Franchised: 2002
Franchised Units: 110
Company-Owned Units: 7
Total Units: 117
Dist.: US-110; CAN-0; O'seas-0
North America: 29 States, DC
Density: 32 in MA, 10 in FL, 9 in NJ
Projected New Units (12 Months): 25-50+
Qualifications: 4, 2, 1, 2, 5, 5
Registered:CA,FL,IL,IN,MD,MI,MN,NY,OR,RI,VA,WA,WI,DC

FINANCIAL/TERMS:
Cash Investment: $75K
Total Investment: $169.5-266K
Minimum Net Worth: $200K
Fees: Franchise - $30K 1st Store
Royalty - 5.5-4% Varies; Ad. - 4%
Earnings Claims Statement: No
Term of Contract (Years): 10/5/5/5
Avg. # Of Employees: 3 FT or PT
Passive Ownership: Discouraged
Encourage Conversions: No
Area Develop. Agreements: Yes/TBD
Sub-Franchising Contracts: No
Expand In Territory: Yes
Space Needs: 700-1,400 SF; FS, SF, SC

SUPPORT & TRAINING:
Financial Assistance Provided: Yes(I)
Site Selection Assistance: Yes
Lease Negotiation Assistance: Yes
Co-Operative Advertising: Yes
Franchisee Assoc./Member: No
Size Of Corporate Staff: 40
On-Going Support: A,B,C,D,E,F,G,H,I
Training: 3 Weeks Total at Brookline, MA Store and Wooburn Home Office.

SPECIFIC EXPANSION PLANS:
US: All US Exc. AK, HI, ND and SD.
Canada: No
Overseas: No

<< >>

LANDSCAPERS SUPPLY

750 Chestnut Ridge Rd.
Spring Valley, NY 10977
Tel: (800) 222-4303 (845) 356-8300
Fax: (845) 356-8593
E-Mail: rbm@landscapersupply.com
Web Site: www.landscapersupply.com
Mr. Robert B. Mytelka, President

The LANDSCAPERS SUPPLY FRANCHISE CORP. concept provides an opportunity that will give everyone from commercial contractors to home garden enthusiasts the quality equipment and supplies they need, when they need it - all at affordable prices. As a franchisee, you'll be on the front line of the vast gardening industry, offering top-notch products, tools and supplies - with a rock-solid reputation of quality, dependability and value.

BACKGROUND:
Established: 1985; 1st Franchised: 2000
Franchised Units: 0
Company-Owned Units: 8
Total Units: 8
Dist.: US-8; CAN-0; O'seas-0
North America: 5 States
Density: 3 in NY, 1 in CT, 1 in MA
Projected New Units (12 Months): 2
Qualifications: 5, 5, 5, 4, 4, 4
Registered: NY

FINANCIAL/TERMS:
Cash Investment: $65K
Total Investment: $75-225K
Minimum Net Worth: $200K
Fees: Franchise - $25K
Royalty - 4%; Ad. - 1%
Earnings Claims Statement: No
Term of Contract (Years): 10/10
Avg. # Of Employees: 1 FT, 1 PT
Passive Ownership: Discouraged
Encourage Conversions: NA
Area Develop. Agreements: NR
Sub-Franchising Contracts: No
Expand In Territory: No
Space Needs: 4,000 Min. SF; FS, SF, SC, Warehouse

SUPPORT & TRAINING:
Financial Assistance Provided: Yes(I)
Site Selection Assistance: Yes
Lease Negotiation Assistance: No
Co-Operative Advertising: Yes
Franchisee Assoc./Member: No
Size Of Corporate Staff: 28
On-Going Support: B,d,E,g,h,I
Training: Spring Valley, NY.

SPECIFIC EXPANSION PLANS:
US: Southeast, Midwest
Canada: All Canada
Overseas: No

<< >>

LATEX CITY

1814 Franklin St., # 820
Oakland, CA 94612
Tel: (510) 839-5462
Fax: (510) 839-2104
E-Mail: jlee@worldfranchising.com
Web Site: www.latexnovelty.com
Mr. Peyton A. McKee, President

Unique ground-floor specialty retailing opportunity in booming latex novelty aid business. Complete line of proprietary products. Turn-key package includes lease negotiation, fully stocked inventory, in-store merchandising/display. On-going support. LATEX CITY is ideal for aggressive couples. This is not smut - but a highly profitable, high-margin, fully legal business.

BACKGROUND:
Established: 1972; 1st Franchised: 1986
Franchised Units: 26
Company-Owned Units: 4
Total Units: 30
Dist.: US-25; CAN-2; O'seas-3
North America: 17 States, 1 Province

Density: 3 in CA, 3 in NY, 2 in OR
Projected New Units (12 Months): 10
Qualifications: , , , , ,
Registered: NR

FINANCIAL/TERMS:
Cash Investment: $65K
Total Investment: $85-235K
Minimum Net Worth: NR
Fees: Franchise - $15K
Royalty - 6%; Ad. - 2%
Earnings Claims Statement: Yes
Term of Contract (Years): 10/10
Avg. # Of Employees: 2 FT
Passive Ownership: Discouraged
Encourage Conversions: Yes
Area Develop. Agreements: Yes/5
Sub-Franchising Contracts: No
Expand In Territory: No
Space Needs: 1,000-1,400 SF; FS, SF, SC, RM

SUPPORT & TRAINING:
Financial Assistance Provided: Yes(D)
Site Selection Assistance: Yes
Lease Negotiation Assistance: Yes
Co-Operative Advertising: Yes
Franchisee Assoc./Member: NR
Size Of Corporate Staff: 6
On-Going Support: A,B,C,D,G,H
Training: 3 Weeks Headquarters; 1 Week Plant; 2 Weeks On-Site.

SPECIFIC EXPANSION PLANS:
US: All United States
Canada: Major Cities
Overseas: No

LEMSTONE BOOKS

311 S. County Farm Rd., # E
Wheaton, IL 60187
Tel: (630) 682-1400
Fax: (630) 682-1828
E-Mail: phild@lemstone.com
Web Site: www.lemstone.com
Mr. Phil Darr, VP Sales/Administration

Since 1982, LEMSTONE has been helping Christians own, operate and succeed in Christian retailing. Our franchise concept provides a 'road map for success' for Christian retailers who possess a heart for people and an entrepreneurial spirit. We currently have over 75 stores in 27 states. LEMSTONE stores are located in premier regional malls within growing markets. Our stores enjoy maximum market exposure every day as thousands of customers shop.

BACKGROUND:
Established: 1981; 1st Franchised: 1982
Franchised Units: 63
Company-Owned Units: 2
Total Units: 65
Dist.: US-77; CAN-0; O'seas-0
North America: 27 States
Density: 8 in TN, 8 in OH, 7 in IL
Projected New Units (12 Months): 12
Qualifications: 5, 2, 1, 2, 2, 4
Registered:CA,FL,IL,IN,MD,MI,MN,NY, OR,WA,WI

FINANCIAL/TERMS:
Cash Investment: $60K
Total Investment: $150-240K
Minimum Net Worth: $350K
Fees: Franchise - $30K
Royalty - 4%; Ad. - 1%
Earnings Claims Statement: NR
Term of Contract (Years): 10/10
Avg. # Of Employees: 1 FT, 4 PT
Passive Ownership: Discouraged
Encourage Conversions: No
Area Develop. Agreements: No
Sub-Franchising Contracts: No
Expand In Territory: Yes
Space Needs: 1,300-2,000 SF; RM

SUPPORT & TRAINING:
Financial Assistance Provided: No
Site Selection Assistance: Yes
Lease Negotiation Assistance: Yes
Co-Operative Advertising: Yes
Franchisee Assoc./Member: Yes/Yes
Size Of Corporate Staff: 14
On-Going Support: A,B,C,D,E,F,G,H
Training: 8 Days Headquarters; 5 Days On-Site.

SPECIFIC EXPANSION PLANS:
US: All United States
Canada: No
Overseas: No

LOVE BOUTIQUE, THE

17551 - 108 Ave. NW
Edmonton, AB T5T 3M6 CANADA
Tel: (888) 296-2588 (780) 486-0433
Fax: (780) 486-5114
E-Mail: erict@telfordinvestments.com
Web Site: www.theloveboutique.com
Mr. Eric Telford, President

Adult store franchise system, specializing in lingerie, oils, games, magazines, books, videos, toys and other products. Up-to-date selection ensures sales with better than average margin. Franchisor is Canada's complete distributor of lingerie and adult product.

BACKGROUND:
Established: 1982; 1st Franchised: 1999
Franchised Units: 2
Company-Owned Units: 19
Total Units: 21
Dist.: US-0; CAN-21; O'seas-0
North America: 1 Province
Density: 21 in Alberta
Projected New Units (12 Months): 3
Qualifications: 5, 3, 1, 1, 1, 5
Registered: AB

FINANCIAL/TERMS:
Cash Investment: $128-193K
Total Investment: $128-193K
Minimum Net Worth: NR
Fees: Franchise - $30K
Royalty - 5%; Ad. - 2%
Earnings Claims Statement: No
Term of Contract (Years): 5/5
Avg. # Of Employees: 1 FT, 2-3 PT
Passive Ownership: Not Allowed
Encourage Conversions: NA
Area Develop. Agreements: No
Sub-Franchising Contracts: No
Expand In Territory: No
Space Needs: 1,200-1,600 SF; FS, SF, SC, RM

SUPPORT & TRAINING:
Financial Assistance Provided: NA
Site Selection Assistance: Yes
Lease Negotiation Assistance: NA
Co-Operative Advertising: Yes
Franchisee Assoc./Member: No
Size Of Corporate Staff: 18
On-Going Support: A,B,C,D,E,F
Training: 1 Week Corporate Store Location.

SPECIFIC EXPANSION PLANS:
US: All United States
Canada: All Canada
Overseas: No

MERKINSTOCK

P. O. Box 12488
Oakland, CA 94604
Tel: (510) 839-5462
Fax: (510) 839-2104
E-Mail: sourcebook@earthlink.net
Web Site: www.merkinstock.com
Mr. Jeffrey A. Elder, President

World's largest selection of merkins - both natural and synthetic. Over 35 models, 15 color selections. Custom fitting in discrete environment. Also custom dyeing. Guaranteed satisfaction. 15 stores in Far East and Europe prove that concept is ripe for aggressive expansion into the U. S. market.

Looking for entrepreneurs with the desire to succeed.

BACKGROUND:
Established: 1992; 1st Franchised: 1995
Franchised Units: 52
Company-Owned Units: 7
Total Units: 59
Dist.: US-3; CAN-2; O'seas-15
North America: 2 States, 1 Province
Density: 2 in CA, 1 in NV
Projected New Units (12 Months): 10
Qualifications: 3, 5, 4, 2, 3, 5
Registered: CA

FINANCIAL/TERMS:
Cash Investment: $90K
Total Investment: $150K
Minimum Net Worth: $250K
Fees: Franchise - $20K
Royalty - 6%; Ad. - 2%
Earnings Claims Statement: Yes
Term of Contract (Years): 15/15
Avg. # Of Employees: 2 FT
Passive Ownership: Not Allowed
Encourage Conversions: Yes
Area Develop. Agreements: Yes/15
Sub-Franchising Contracts: Yes
Expand In Territory: No
Space Needs: 1,200 SF; FS, SC, RM

SUPPORT & TRAINING:
Financial Assistance Provided: Yes(D)
Site Selection Assistance: Yes
Lease Negotiation Assistance: Yes
Co-Operative Advertising: Yes
Franchisee Assoc./Member: No
Size Of Corporate Staff: 4
On-Going Support: a,B,C,D,E,f,G,G,I
Training: 3 Weeks Headquarters; 2 Weeks On-Site; On-Going.

SPECIFIC EXPANSION PLANS:
US: All United States
Canada: All Canada
Overseas: All Countries

<< >>

MUSIC GO ROUND

4200 Dahlberg Dr., # 100
Minneapolis, MN 55422-4837
Tel: (800) 269-4076 (763) 520-8582
Fax: (763) 520-8501
E-Mail: mgr-franchise-development@musicgoround.com
Web Site: www.musicgoround.com
Ms. Kathy Winslow, Administrative Assistant

MUSIC GO ROUND stores sell, buy, trade and consign used and new musical instruments, speakers, amplifiers, music-related electronics and related accessories for parents of children who play musical instruments, as well as professional and amateur musicians.

BACKGROUND: IFA MEMBER
Established: 1986; 1st Franchised: 1994
Franchised Units: 47
Company-Owned Units: 6
Total Units: 53
Dist.: US-49; CAN-0; O'seas-0
North America: 25 States
Density: 7 in MN, 3 in IA, 3 in IL
Projected New Units (12 Months): 5
Qualifications: 5, 4, 2, 2, 2, 4
Registered: All States

FINANCIAL/TERMS:
Cash Investment: $56-82K
Total Investment: $190-275K
Minimum Net Worth: $225K
Fees: Franchise - $20K
Royalty - 3%; Ad. - $250/Yr.
Earnings Claims Statement: Yes
Term of Contract (Years): 10/10
Avg. # Of Employees: 2 FT, 2 PT
Passive Ownership: Not Allowed
Encourage Conversions: No
Area Develop. Agreements: Yes/3
Sub-Franchising Contracts: No
Expand In Territory: No
Space Needs: 2,500-3,000 SF; SC

SUPPORT & TRAINING:
Financial Assistance Provided: No
Site Selection Assistance: Yes
Lease Negotiation Assistance: Yes
Co-Operative Advertising: No
Franchisee Assoc./Member: No
Size Of Corporate Staff: 97
On-Going Support: B,C,D,E,F,G,H,I
Training: 3 Days Minneapolis, MN; 3 Days Minneapolis, MN; 5-6 Days Minneapolis, MN.

SPECIFIC EXPANSION PLANS:
US: All United States
Canada: No
Overseas: No

<< >>

PARTY AMERICA

980 Atlantic Ave., # 103
Alameda, CA 94501
Tel: (510) 747-1800 + 283
Fax: (510) 747-1810
E-Mail: franchising@partyamerica.com
Web Site: www.partyamerica.com
Mr. Dave Crane, VP Franchise Development

PARTY AMERICA specialty retail stores capture the 'party experience' by offering the most comprehensive everyday and seasonal merchandise needed to throw a great party. Our fun and customer-centric stores offer a tremendous selection of balloons, gift ware, table ware, decorations, party favors and greeting cards for virtually every special occasion or seasonal theme.

BACKGROUND: IFA MEMBER
Established: 1980; 1st Franchised: 1987
Franchised Units: 61
Company-Owned Units: 230
Total Units: 291
Dist.: US-290; CAN-0; O'seas-1
North America: 46 States
Density: 40 in CA, 21 in MN, 16 in CO
Projected New Units (12 Months): 10
Qualifications: 5, 4, 3, 4, 4, 5
Registered: All States Except Hawaii

FINANCIAL/TERMS:
Cash Investment: $200K
Total Investment: $335-500K
Minimum Net Worth: $500K
Fees: Franchise - $25K
Royalty - 4%; Ad. - 1%
Earnings Claims Statement: Yes
Term of Contract (Years): 10/10
Avg. # Of Employees: 4 FT, 6 PT
Passive Ownership: Allowed
Encourage Conversions: Yes
Area Develop. Agreements: Yes/5
Sub-Franchising Contracts: Yes
Expand In Territory: Yes
Space Needs: 6,000-10,000 SF; SF, SC, Power Ctr.

SUPPORT & TRAINING:
Financial Assistance Provided: Yes(I)
Site Selection Assistance: Yes
Lease Negotiation Assistance: Yes
Co-Operative Advertising: NA
Franchisee Assoc./Member: Yes/IFA
Size Of Corporate Staff: 160
On-Going Support: C,D,E,G,H
Training: 3-5 Days Alameda, CA; 7-10 Days Corporate Store.

SPECIFIC EXPANSION PLANS:
US: All United States
Canada: All Canada
Overseas: All Countries

<< >>

PARTY LAND

5215 Militia Hill Rd.
Plymouth Meeting, PA 19462-1216
Tel: (800) 778-9563 (610) 941-6200
Fax: (610) 941-6301
E-Mail: jbarry@partyland.com
Web Site: www.partyland.com
Mr. John L. Barry, VP Franchise Sales

World's largest international retail party supply franchise, specializing in service, selection and savings. The official party store for the 'new millennium.'

BACKGROUND:
Established: 1986; 1st Franchised: 1988
Franchised Units: 400
Company-Owned Units: 0
Total Units: 400
Dist.: US-362; CAN-4; O'seas-38
North America: 23 States, 3 Provinces
Density: 20 in PA, 8 in TX, 3 in CO
Projected New Units (12 Months): 20
Qualifications: 5, 4, 2, 1, 5, 5
Registered: All States and AB

FINANCIAL/TERMS:
Cash Investment: $80K
Total Investment: $249-329K
Minimum Net Worth: $250K
Fees: Franchise - $35K
Royalty - 5%; Ad. - 4%
Earnings Claims Statement: No
Term of Contract (Years): 20/10
Avg. # Of Employees: 2 FT, 6 PT
Passive Ownership: Allowed
Encourage Conversions: Yes
Area Develop. Agreements: Yes/5
Sub-Franchising Contracts: Yes
Expand In Territory: No
Space Needs: NR SF; FS, SF, SC

SUPPORT & TRAINING:
Financial Assistance Provided: Yes(I)
Site Selection Assistance: Yes
Lease Negotiation Assistance: Yes
Co-Operative Advertising: Yes
Franchisee Assoc./Member: Yes/Yes
Size Of Corporate Staff: 30+
On-Going Support: A,B,C,D,E,F,G,H,I
Training: 1 Week Party Land University.

SPECIFIC EXPANSION PLANS:
US: All United States
Canada: All Canada
Overseas: All Countries

PINCH-A-PENNY

14480 62nd St. N.
Clearwater, FL 33760-2721
Tel: (727) 531-8913 + 237
Fax: (727) 536-8066
E-Mail: aheflin@pinchapenny.com
Web Site: www.pinchapenny.com
Mr. Adam S. Heflin, Franchise Development Manager

PINCH-A-PENNY is the nation's largest franchise retailer of swimming pool, spa and patio supplies.

BACKGROUND: IFA MEMBER
Established: 1974; 1st Franchised: 1976
Franchised Units: 160
Company-Owned Units: 2
Total Units: 162
Dist.: US-162; CAN-0; O'seas-0
North America: 3 States
Density: 159 in FL, 1 in GA, 2 in AL
Projected New Units (12 Months): 15
Qualifications: , , , , ,
Registered: FL

FINANCIAL/TERMS:
Cash Investment: NR
Total Investment: $75-594K
Minimum Net Worth: $250K
Fees: Franchise - $15-50K
Royalty - 6%; Ad. - 4%
Earnings Claims Statement: No
Term of Contract (Years): 5/20
Avg. # Of Employees: NR
Passive Ownership: Not Allowed
Encourage Conversions: No
Area Develop. Agreements: No
Sub-Franchising Contracts: No
Expand In Territory: Yes
Space Needs: 1,000-3,500 SF; SC

SUPPORT & TRAINING:
Financial Assistance Provided: No
Site Selection Assistance: Yes
Lease Negotiation Assistance: Yes
Co-Operative Advertising: NA
Franchisee Assoc./Member: NR
Size Of Corporate Staff: NR
On-Going Support: A,B,C,D,E,H,I
Training: 4 Weeks Headquarters.

SPECIFIC EXPANSION PLANS:
US: All United States
Canada: No
Overseas: No

<< >>

PLATO'S CLOSET

4200 Dahlberg Dr., # 100
Minneapolis, MN 55422-4837
Tel: (800) 269-4081 (763) 520-8500
Fax: (763) 520-8501
E-Mail: pc-franchise-development@platoscloset.com
Web Site: www.platoscloset.com
Ms. Becky Geyer, Franchise Development

PLATO'S CLOSET stores buy and sell gently used, brand-name apparel and accessories for teens and young adults. Customers have the opportunity to sell their used items to a PLATO'S CLOSET store when outgrown and to purchase quality used clothing and accessories at prices lower than new merchandise.

BACKGROUND: IFA MEMBER
Established: 1997; 1st Franchised: 1999
Franchised Units: 128
Company-Owned Units: 1
Total Units: 129
Dist.: US-129; CAN-0; O'seas-0
North America: 37 States
Density: 21 in OH, 13 in IN, 9 in GA
Projected New Units (12 Months): 30
Qualifications: 5, 4, 2, 2, 2, 4
Registered: All States

FINANCIAL/TERMS:
Cash Investment: $40-73K
Total Investment: $140-243K
Minimum Net Worth: $225K
Fees: Franchise - $20K
Royalty - 4%; Ad. - $500/Yr.
Earnings Claims Statement: Yes
Term of Contract (Years): 10/10
Avg. # Of Employees: NR
Passive Ownership: Not Allowed
Encourage Conversions: No
Area Develop. Agreements: No
Sub-Franchising Contracts: No
Expand In Territory: No
Space Needs: 2,500-3,000 SF; SC

SUPPORT & TRAINING:
Financial Assistance Provided: No
Site Selection Assistance: Yes
Lease Negotiation Assistance: Yes
Co-Operative Advertising: No
Franchisee Assoc./Member: No
Size Of Corporate Staff: 97
On-Going Support: B,C,D,E,F,G,H,I
Training: 3 Days Minneapolis, MN; 3 Days Minneapolis, MN; 5-6 Days Minneapolis, MN.

SPECIFIC EXPANSION PLANS:
US: All United States
Canada: No
Overseas: No

RAFTERS

294 Walker Dr., # 2
Brampton, ON L6T 4Z2 CANADA
Tel: (866) 463-4124 (416) 661-9916
Fax: (905) 790-7059

E-Mail: lmorrison@franchisebancorp.com
Web Site: www.franchisebancorp.com
Ms. Lisa Morrison, Franchise Contact

Full-line gift store with distinct kitchen department.

BACKGROUND:
Established: 1978; 1st Franchised: 1980
Franchised Units: 13
Company-Owned Units: 0
Total Units: 13
Dist.: US-0; CAN-16; O'seas-0
North America: 3 Provinces
Density: 8 in AB, 7 in ON, 1 in BC
Projected New Units (12 Months): NR
Qualifications: , , , , ,
Registered: AB

FINANCIAL/TERMS:
Cash Investment: $40K
Total Investment: $110K
Minimum Net Worth: NR
Fees: Franchise - $25K
Royalty - 6%; Ad. - 1%
Earnings Claims Statement: Yes
Term of Contract (Years): NR
Avg. # Of Employees: NR
Passive Ownership: NR
Encourage Conversions: NR
Area Develop. Agreements: NR
Sub-Franchising Contracts: NR
Expand In Territory: NR
Space Needs: NR SF; NR

SUPPORT & TRAINING:
Financial Assistance Provided: No
Site Selection Assistance: NR
Lease Negotiation Assistance: Yes
Co-Operative Advertising: Yes
Franchisee Assoc./Member: Yes/Yes
Size Of Corporate Staff: 18
On-Going Support: D,E,G
Training: NR

SPECIFIC EXPANSION PLANS:
US: NR
Canada: All Canada
Overseas: No

<< >>

RELAX THE BACK

17785 Center Court Dr., # 250
Cerritos, CA 90703
Tel: (800) 290-2225 (562) 860-1019
Fax: (562) 860-1312
E-Mail: michaelc@relaxtheback.com
Web Site: www.relaxtheback.com
Mr. Michael Conifliaro, Director Dranchise Sales

North America's largest specialty retailer of ergonomic and back care products. We are in the comfort business, many of our products are designed to relieve or eliminate back and neck pain.

BACKGROUND: IFA MEMBER
Established: 1983; 1st Franchised: 1989
Franchised Units: 89
Company-Owned Units: 0
Total Units: 89
Dist.: US-87; CAN-2; O'seas-0
North America: 34 States, 1 Province
Density: 22 in CA, 6 in FL, 6 in TX
Projected New Units (12 Months): 15
Qualifications: 4, 4, 3, 3, 2, 5
Registered: All States

FINANCIAL/TERMS:
Cash Investment: $100K
Total Investment: $211-329K
Minimum Net Worth: $300K
Fees: Franchise - $30K
Royalty - 4%; Ad. - 2%
Earnings Claims Statement: Yes
Term of Contract (Years): 10/10
Avg. # Of Employees: 3 FT, 1 PT
Passive Ownership: Discouraged
Encourage Conversions: NA
Area Develop. Agreements: Yes/Varies
Sub-Franchising Contracts: No
Expand In Territory: No
Space Needs: 2,600 SF; FS, SF, SC, RM

SUPPORT & TRAINING:
Financial Assistance Provided: Yes(I)
Site Selection Assistance: Yes
Lease Negotiation Assistance: Yes
Co-Operative Advertising: Yes
Franchisee Assoc./Member: Yes/Yes
Size Of Corporate Staff: 25
On-Going Support: B,C,D,E,G,H,I
Training: 8 Days Corp HQ; 1 Week On-Site.

SPECIFIC EXPANSION PLANS:
US: All United States
Canada: All Canada
Overseas: No

<< >>

RESCUECOM CORPORATION

2560 Burnet Ave.
Syracuse, NY 13206
Tel: (800) 737-2837 (315) 433-0002
Fax: (315) 433-5228
E-Mail: joinus@rescuecom.com
Web Site: www.rescuecom.com
Mr. David A. Milman, Chief Executive Officer

For the best computer technical talent, RESCUECOM offers the freedom of business ownership without the requirements (and headaches) of the mundane day to day business functions.

BACKGROUND:
Established: 1997; 1st Franchised: 1999
Franchised Units: 51
Company-Owned Units: 0
Total Units: 51
Dist.: US-5; CAN-0; O'seas-0
North America: 3 States
Density: 3 in NY, 1 in IL, 1 in CA
Projected New Units (12 Months): 3
Qualifications: 3, 3, 5, 4, 4, 4
Registered: CA,FL,IL,IN,MI,NY,AB

FINANCIAL/TERMS:
Cash Investment: $1.5-15K
Total Investment: $29.4-53.2K
Minimum Net Worth: $25K
Fees: Franchise - $15K
Royalty - 18%; Ad. - 2%
Earnings Claims Statement: Yes
Term of Contract (Years): 10/5
Avg. # Of Employees: 1-3 FT
Passive Ownership: Not Allowed
Encourage Conversions: Yes
Area Develop. Agreements: No
Sub-Franchising Contracts: No
Expand In Territory: NR
Space Needs: NA SF; HB

SUPPORT & TRAINING:
Financial Assistance Provided: Yes
Site Selection Assistance: Yes
Lease Negotiation Assistance: Yes
Co-Operative Advertising: Yes
Franchisee Assoc./Member: No
Size Of Corporate Staff: 20
On-Going Support: A,B,C,D,E,F,H,I
Training: 10 Days in Syracuse, NY.

SPECIFIC EXPANSION PLANS:
US: All United States
Canada: All Canada
Overseas: Europe

<< >>

SUCCESSORIES

2520 Diehl Rd.
Aurora, IL 60504
Tel: (800) 621-1423 (630) 820-7200
Fax: (630) 820-3856
E-Mail: olivas@successories.com
Web Site: www.successories.com
Ms. Sandra Olivas, Dir. Franchise Operations

SUCCESSORIES sells products for business and personal motivation, including over 500 proprietary products and those from other sources, such as audio tapes, time-management systems and self-improvement books. Our objective is to provide one-stop shopping for all motivational resources.

BACKGROUND:
Established: 1985; 1st Franchised: 1992
Franchised Units: 47
Company-Owned Units: 52
Total Units: 99
Dist.: US-96; CAN-3; O'seas-0
North America: 33 States, 1 Province
Density: 11 in IL, 8 in CA, 6 in FL
Projected New Units (12 Months): 6
Qualifications: 4, 4, 4, 3, 2, 3
Registered: All States

FINANCIAL/TERMS:
Cash Investment: NR
Total Investment: $144-238K
Minimum Net Worth: $250K
Fees: Franchise - $35K
Royalty - 2%; Ad. - 1%
Earnings Claims Statement: No
Term of Contract (Years): 5/5
Avg. # Of Employees: 2 FT, 2 PT
Passive Ownership: Discouraged
Encourage Conversions: NA
Area Develop. Agreements: No
Sub-Franchising Contracts: Yes
Expand In Territory: Yes
Space Needs: 800-1,200 SF; SC, RM

SUPPORT & TRAINING:
Financial Assistance Provided: NA
Site Selection Assistance: Yes
Lease Negotiation Assistance: Yes
Co-Operative Advertising: No
Franchisee Assoc./Member: Yes/Yes
Size Of Corporate Staff: 150
On-Going Support: B,C,D,E,f,h,I
Training: 5 Days in Lombard, IL.

SPECIFIC EXPANSION PLANS:
US: Various Markets
Canada: All Canada
Overseas: No

<< >>

TALKING BOOK WORLD

22272 Pepper Rd., Unit A
Lake Barrington, IL 60010
Tel: (800) 403-2933 (847) 381-9900
Fax: (847) 381-2447
E-Mail: tcl@talkingbooks.com
Web Site: www.talkingbooks.com
Mr. Geoff Hannell, Franchise Sales

TALKING BOOK WORLD is the world's largest retail chain of audiobook stores, with the widest selection of audiobooks to rent or buy anywhere. Pioneers of the concept of renting audiobooks, TBW makes audiobooks accessible and affordable - with innovative programs that give unlimited use of our library and with no due dates.

BACKGROUND:
Established: 1993; 1st Franchised: 1995
Franchised Units: 13
Company-Owned Units: 16
Total Units: 29
Dist.: US-26; CAN-3; O'seas-0
North America: 9 States, 1 Province
Density: 12 in CA, 11 in MI, 3 in ON
Projected New Units (12 Months): 10
Qualifications: 3, 3, 3, 4, 5, 5
Registered: CA,FL,IL,IN,MD,MI,NY,VA

FINANCIAL/TERMS:
Cash Investment: $150-225K
Total Investment: $150-225K
Minimum Net Worth: $100K
Fees: Franchise - $25K
Royalty - 5%; Ad. - 2%
Earnings Claims Statement: No
Term of Contract (Years): 15/5
Avg. # Of Employees: 1 FT, 2 PT
Passive Ownership: Discouraged
Encourage Conversions: Yes
Area Develop. Agreements: Yes/3
Sub-Franchising Contracts: No
Expand In Territory: Yes
Space Needs: 1,800 SF; SF, SC

SUPPORT & TRAINING:
Financial Assistance Provided: Yes(I)
Site Selection Assistance: Yes
Lease Negotiation Assistance: No
Co-Operative Advertising: Yes
Franchisee Assoc./Member: No
Size Of Corporate Staff: 6
On-Going Support: C,D,E,F,G,H,I
Training: 2 Weeks Franchisee's Store..

SPECIFIC EXPANSION PLANS:
US: All United States
Canada: All Canada
Overseas: No

<< >>

TFM

10333 - 174 St.
Edmonton, AB T5S 1H1 CANADA
Tel: (780) 483-3217
Fax: (780) 486-7528
E-Mail: aherfst@totalsound.org
Web Site: www.totalsound.com
Mr. A. J. Herfst, President

Retail sales of pre-recorded music, including compact discs, cassettes, videos and DVD, as well as related accessories and other paraphernalia. Franchisor provides full turn-key operation, inventory controls and full operational guidance.

BACKGROUND:
Established: 1974; 1st Franchised: 1985
Franchised Units: 14
Company-Owned Units: 3
Total Units: 17
Dist.: US-0; CAN-17; O'seas-0
North America: 7 Provinces
Density: 7 in AB, 5 in SK, 3 in BC
Projected New Units (12 Months): 3
Qualifications: 2, 2, 1, 2, 3, 3
Registered: AB

FINANCIAL/TERMS:
Cash Investment: $40-80K
Total Investment: $125-200K
Minimum Net Worth: NA
Fees: Franchise - $15K
Royalty - 5%; Ad. - 1%
Earnings Claims Statement: No
Term of Contract (Years): 5/5
Avg. # Of Employees: 2 FT, 4 PT
Passive Ownership: Allowed
Encourage Conversions: Yes
Area Develop. Agreements: No
Sub-Franchising Contracts: No
Expand In Territory: Yes
Space Needs: 1,400 SF; RM

SUPPORT & TRAINING:
Financial Assistance Provided: Yes(I)
Site Selection Assistance: Yes
Lease Negotiation Assistance: Yes
Co-Operative Advertising: Yes
Franchisee Assoc./Member: No
Size Of Corporate Staff: 5
On-Going Support: B,C,D,E,F,H
Training: 1 Week Headquarters; 1 Week in Store; 2 Day Refresher On-Site.

SPECIFIC EXPANSION PLANS:
US: No
Canada: Western Canada
Overseas: No

<< >>

TINDER BOX INTERNATIONAL

3 Bala Plaza East, # 102
Bala Cynwyd, PA 19004-2449
Tel: (800) 846-3372 (610) 668-4220
Fax: (610) 668-4266
E-Mail: tbiltd@tinderbox.com
Web Site: www.tinderbox.com
Mr. Rob Craft, Franchise Development

The world's largest and oldest chain of premium cigar, tobacco, smoking accessory and gift stores, with 70 years' experience as the undisputed industry leader.

BACKGROUND: IFA MEMBER
Established: 1928; 1st Franchised: 1965
Franchised Units: 104
Company-Owned Units: 3
Total Units: 107
Dist.: US-116; CAN-1; O'seas-0
North America: 50 States
Density: 17 in CA, 9 in IL, 9 in OH
Projected New Units (12 Months): 25
Qualifications: 5, 3, 1, 2, 4, 5
Registered: All Except ND,SD

FINANCIAL/TERMS:
Cash Investment: $75-100K
Total Investment: $175-250K
Minimum Net Worth: $250-300K
Fees: Franchise - $30K
Royalty - 4-5%; Ad. - 3%
Earnings Claims Statement: Yes
Term of Contract (Years): 10/5
Avg. # Of Employees: 1-2 FT, 2-3 PT
Passive Ownership: Allowed
Encourage Conversions: Yes
Area Develop. Agreements: Yes/5
Sub-Franchising Contracts: No
Expand In Territory: Yes
Space Needs: 800-1,500 SF; FS, SF, SC, RM

SUPPORT & TRAINING:
Financial Assistance Provided: Yes
Site Selection Assistance: Yes
Lease Negotiation Assistance: Yes
Co-Operative Advertising: Yes
Franchisee Assoc./Member: No
Size Of Corporate Staff: 10
On-Going Support: a,C,D,E,F,G,H,I
Training: 5 Days Home Office; 3-5 Days at Franchisee's Store; Follow-Up Store Visit within 30 Days.

SPECIFIC EXPANSION PLANS:
US: All United States
Canada: All Canada
Overseas: All Countries

<< >>

WICKS 'N' STICKS

P. O. Box 1965
Cypress, TX 77410-1965
Tel: (888) 873-3714 (713) 856-7442
Fax: (713) 856-8159
E-Mail: pparker@wicksnsticks.com
Web Site: www.wicksnsticks.com
Ms. Patty Parker, Franchise Development

Nation's largest and most respected franchised retailer of quality candles, fragrancing and related home decorative products. Franchisees are offered outstanding name recognition, comprehensive training and extensive start up and on-going support. Rated a top franchise by both Success Gold 200 and Income Opportunities Platinum 2000.

BACKGROUND:
Established: 1968; 1st Franchised: 1968
Franchised Units: 148
Company-Owned Units: 7
Total Units: 155
Dist.: US-155; CAN-0; O'seas-0
North America: 37 States
Density: 14 in TX, 14 in CA, 13 in FL
Projected New Units (12 Months): 17
Qualifications: 5, 3, 3, 3, 3, 5
Registered: CA,IL,IN,MD,MI,MN,NY, ND,OR,RI,SD,VA,WA,WI

FINANCIAL/TERMS:
Cash Investment: $65K
Total Investment: $198.5-330.72K
Minimum Net Worth: $70K Liquid
Fees: Franchise - $35K
Royalty - 2.5% (in 2002); Ad. - 0%
Earnings Claims Statement: No
Term of Contract (Years): 5+
Avg. # Of Employees: 1 FT, 6 PT
Passive Ownership: NA
Encourage Conversions: NA
Area Develop. Agreements: No
Sub-Franchising Contracts: No
Expand In Territory: Yes
Space Needs: 1,000-1,700 SF; RM

SUPPORT & TRAINING:
Financial Assistance Provided: No
Site Selection Assistance: Yes
Lease Negotiation Assistance: Yes
Co-Operative Advertising: Yes
Franchisee Assoc./Member: Yes
Size Of Corporate Staff: 21
On-Going Support: A,C,D,E,F,G,H,I
Training: 8 Days Corporate Office, Houston, TX.

SPECIFIC EXPANSION PLANS:
US: All United States
Canada: No
Overseas: No

<< >>

Top 100

WILD BIRD CENTER

7370 MacArthur Blvd.
Glen Echo, MD 20812-1200
Tel: (800) 945-3247 (301) 229-9585 + 203
Fax: (301) 320-6154
E-Mail: georgejr@wildbird.com
Web Site: www.wildbird.com
Mr. George H. Petrides, Jr., Director Franchise Development

A WBCA franchise is more than a store; it is a valued community resource. The story of THE WILD BIRD CENTERS OF AMERICA, Inc. is one of enthusiasm about wild birds and a professional approach to the birding market. The customer enjoys friendly, personal service in a peaceful environment with the feel of a relaxing backyard. The owner provides this service with the help of highly efficient systems and support.

BACKGROUND: IFA MEMBER
Established: 1985; 1st Franchised: 1988
Franchised Units: 100
Company-Owned Units: 1
Total Units: 101
Dist.: US-99; CAN-2; O'seas-0
North America: 31 States, 1 Province
Density: 10 in MD, 8 in CA, 8 in VA
Projected New Units (12 Months): 15
Qualifications: 5, 4, 2, 4, 2, 5
Registered: All Except HI

FINANCIAL/TERMS:
Cash Investment: $35-50K
Total Investment: $90-135K
Minimum Net Worth: $150K
Fees: Franchise - $15K
Royalty - 3-4%; Ad. - .5%
Earnings Claims Statement: Yes
Term of Contract (Years): 10
Avg. # Of Employees: 1 FT, 2 PT
Passive Ownership: Discouraged
Encourage Conversions: No
Area Develop. Agreements: No
Sub-Franchising Contracts: No
Expand In Territory: Yes
Space Needs: 1,500-2,400 SF; SC

SUPPORT & TRAINING:
Financial Assistance Provided: Yes(I)
Site Selection Assistance: Yes
Lease Negotiation Assistance: Yes
Co-Operative Advertising: Yes
Franchisee Assoc./Member: Yes/Yes
Size Of Corporate Staff: 15
On-Going Support: C,d,E,F,G,h,I
Training: 5 Days Home Office; 1 Day On-Site.

SPECIFIC EXPANSION PLANS:
US: All United States

Canada: All Canada
Overseas: No

<< >>

WILD BIRDS UNLIMITED

11711 N. College Ave., # 146
Carmel, IN 46032-5634
Tel: (888) 730-7108 (317) 571-7100 + 135
Fax: (317) 208-4050
E-Mail: pickettp@wbu.com
Web Site: www.wbu.com
Mr. Paul E. Pickett, Dir. Franchise Development

WILD BIRDS UNLIMITED is North America's original and largest group of retail stores catering to the backyard birdfeeding and nature enthusiast. We currently have over 300 stores in the U. S. and Canada. Stores provide birdseed, feeders, houses, optics and nature-related gifts. Additionally, stores provide extensive educational programs regarding backyard birdfeeding. Franchisees are provided an all-inclusive support system.

BACKGROUND: IFA MEMBER
Established: 1981; 1st Franchised: 1983
Franchised Units: 315
Company-Owned Units: 0
Total Units: 315
Dist.: US-302; CAN-13; O'seas-0
North America: 42 States, 3 Provinces
Density: 23 in TX, 17 in MI, 15 in IL
Projected New Units (12 Months): 15
Qualifications: 5, 5, 1, 3, 2, 5
Registered:CA,FL,IL,IN,MD,MI,MN,NY,OR,RI,VA,WA,WI,DC

FINANCIAL/TERMS:
Cash Investment: $25-35K
Total Investment: $80-145K
Minimum Net Worth: $150K
Fees: Franchise - $18K
Royalty - 4%; Ad. - .5%
Earnings Claims Statement: Yes
Term of Contract (Years): 10/5
Avg. # Of Employees: 2 FT, 4 PT
Passive Ownership: Not Allowed
Encourage Conversions: NA
Area Develop. Agreements: No
Sub-Franchising Contracts: No
Expand In Territory: Yes
Space Needs: 1,400-1,800 SF; FS, SC

SUPPORT & TRAINING:
Financial Assistance Provided: Yes(I)
Site Selection Assistance: Yes
Lease Negotiation Assistance: Yes
Co-Operative Advertising: No
Franchisee Assoc./Member: Yes/Yes
Size Of Corporate Staff: 45
On-Going Support: C,D,E,F,G,H,I
Training: 6 Days in Indianapolis, IN; 1 Day at Store Site.

SPECIFIC EXPANSION PLANS:
US: All United States
Canada: All Canada
Overseas: No

<< >>

Retail: Video/Audio/Electronics

Chapter 43

Retail: Video/Audio/Electronics Industry Profile

Total # Franchisors in Industry Group	25
Total # Franchised Units in Industry Group	4,301
Total # Company-Owned Units in Industry Group	9,834
Total # Operating Units in Industry Group	14,135
Average # Franchised Units/Franchisor	172
Average # Company-Owned Units/Franchisor	393.4
Average # Total Units/Franchisor	565.4
Ratio of Total # Franchised Units/Total # Company-Owned Units	0.4:1
Industry Survey Participants	6
Representing % of Industry	24%
Average Franchise Fee*:	$21.8K
Average Total Investment*:	$108.5K
Average On-Going Royalty Fee*:	4.1%

*If a range was provided, the mid-point of the range was used. See detailed profiles for actual ranges.

Five Largest Participants in Survey

Company	# Franchised Units	# Co-Owned Units	# Total Units	Franchise Fee	On-Going Royalty	Total Investment
1. Radio Shack Select	1,862	5,089	6,951	$39.9K	0%	$69.9K
2. Computer Troubleshooters	428	1	429	$14.5K	$240/Mo.	$22-26K
3. CD Warehouse	216	64	280	$20K	5%/4%	$122-162K
4. Videomasters	80	0	80	$20K	$750/Yr.	$20-23K
5. @Wireless	75	2	77	$7.5-15K	8% Blended	$70-130K

All of the data provided are proprietary and should not be quoted without acknowledging *Bond's Franchise Guide.*

@WIRELESS

50 Methodist Hill Dr., # 1500
Rochester, NY 14623
Tel: (800) 613-2355 (585) 359-3390
Fax: (585) 359-3253
E-Mail: maureen.hough@atwireless.com
Web Site: www.shopatwireless.com
Ms. Maureen Hough, Franchise Administrator

@WIRELESS is a retailer of innovative wireless products and services, with franchise retail stores located nationwide. We currently have agency agreements with a number of carriers. These local and national affiliations allow our franchises the opportunity to satisfy a vast array of customer needs.

BACKGROUND: IFA MEMBER
Established: 1994; 1st Franchised: 2000
Franchised Units: 75
Company-Owned Units: 2
Total Units: 77
Dist.: US-77; CAN-0; O'seas-0
North America: 17 States
Density: 17 in MI, 12 in CT, 10 in MA
Projected New Units (12 Months): 75
Qualifications: 4, 4, 4, 3, 4, 4
Registered:All Except HI,MN,ND,SD,WA

FINANCIAL/TERMS:
Cash Investment: NR
Total Investment: $70-130K
Minimum Net Worth: $100K
Fees: Franchise - $7.5-15K
Royalty - 8% Blended; Ad. - 5%
Earnings Claims Statement: No
Term of Contract (Years): 10/10
Avg. # Of Employees: 2 FT, 1 pt
Passive Ownership: NR
Encourage Conversions: Yes
Area Develop. Agreements: Yes/1+
Sub-Franchising Contracts: Yes
Expand In Territory: Yes
Space Needs: 1,000+ SF; FS, SC, RM

SUPPORT & TRAINING:
Financial Assistance Provided: No
Site Selection Assistance: Yes
Lease Negotiation Assistance: Yes
Co-Operative Advertising: Yes
Franchisee Assoc./Member: Yes/Yes
Size Of Corporate Staff: 30
On-Going Support: A,B,C,D,E,F,G,h,I
Training: 1 Week Corporate Office.

SPECIFIC EXPANSION PLANS:
US: All United States
Canada: No
Overseas: No

≺≺ ≻≻

CD WAREHOUSE

900 N. Broadway
Oklahoma City, OK 73102
Tel: (800) 641-9394 (405) 236-8742
Fax: (405) 949-2566
E-Mail:
Web Site: www.cdwarehouse.com
Mr. Matt Allen, Vice President

CD WAREHOUSE is a rapidly growing franchise, specializing in the sale of pre-owned CDs and DVDs. Our stores also buy and trade used CD's, sell top new CDs, and sell other music-related items. Our proprietary software makes it easy to buy and sell pre-owned CDs, even without prior music knowledge.

BACKGROUND:
Established: 1992; 1st Franchised: 1992
Franchised Units: 216
Company-Owned Units: 64
Total Units: 280
Dist.: US-263; CAN-7; O'seas-10
North America: 36 States, 3 Provinces
Density: 51 in TX, 21 in FL, 17 in CA
Projected New Units (12 Months): 15
Qualifications: 5, 3, 1, 2, 4, 4
Registered: CA,FL,IL,IN,MD,MI,NY,OR,RI,VA,WI

FINANCIAL/TERMS:
Cash Investment: $40-60K
Total Investment: $122-162K
Minimum Net Worth: $150K
Fees: Franchise - $20K
Royalty - 5%/4%; Ad. - 1.75%
Earnings Claims Statement: No
Term of Contract (Years): 10/10
Avg. # Of Employees: 2-3 FT, 3-4 PT
Passive Ownership: Discouraged
Encourage Conversions: NA
Area Develop. Agreements: Yes
Sub-Franchising Contracts: No
Expand In Territory: Yes
Space Needs: 1,500-2,000 SF; FS, SC

SUPPORT & TRAINING:
Financial Assistance Provided: Yes(I)
Site Selection Assistance: Yes
Lease Negotiation Assistance: Yes
Co-Operative Advertising: Yes
Franchisee Assoc./Member: Yes/No
Size Of Corporate Staff: 25
On-Going Support: C,D,E,G,H,I
Training: 5-6 Days at Oklahoma City, OK Training Center.

SPECIFIC EXPANSION PLANS:
US: All United States
Canada: All Canada
Overseas: All Countries

≺≺ ≻≻

COMPUTER TROUBLESHOOTERS

755 Commerce Dr., # 412
Decatur, GA 30030
Tel: (877) 704-1702 (770) 454-6382
Fax: (770) 234-6162
E-Mail: info@comptroub.com
Web Site: www.comptroub.com
Mr. Chip Reaves, Chief Executive Officer

COMPUTER TROUBLESHOOTERS is the world's largest and best computer service franchise. Over 420 locations in 20 countries provide personal, friendly on-site services to business and residential customers. See www.comptroub.com

BACKGROUND:
Established: 1997; 1st Franchised: 1997
Franchised Units: 428
Company-Owned Units: 1
Total Units: 429
Dist.: US-222; CAN-14; O'seas-193
North America: 33 States, 3 Provinces
Density: 20 in TX, 17 in PA, 16 in NJ
Projected New Units (12 Months): 120
Qualifications: 2, 3, 4, 3, 3, 3
Registered:CA,FL,IL,IN,MD,MI,MN,NY,OR,VA,WA,WI

FINANCIAL/TERMS:
Cash Investment: $22-26K
Total Investment: $22-26K
Minimum Net Worth: $20K
Fees: Franchise - $14.5K
Royalty - $240/Mo.; Ad. - $140/Mo.
Earnings Claims Statement: No
Term of Contract (Years): 10/10
Avg. # Of Employees: 1 FT, 0 PT
Passive Ownership: Discouraged
Encourage Conversions: Yes
Area Develop. Agreements: No
Sub-Franchising Contracts: Yes
Expand In Territory: Yes
Space Needs: NA SF; HB

SUPPORT & TRAINING:
Financial Assistance Provided: Yes(I)
Site Selection Assistance: Yes
Lease Negotiation Assistance: NA
Co-Operative Advertising: NA
Franchisee Assoc./Member: No
Size Of Corporate Staff: 5
On-Going Support: d,G,h,i
Training: 2 - 3 Days Atlanta, GA or other

facility.

SPECIFIC EXPANSION PLANS:
US: All United States
Canada: All Canada
Overseas: All Countries

<< >>

PREPLAYED ENTERTAINMENT GROUP

9 W. Aylesbury Rd., # F-G
Timoinium, MD 21093
Tel: (866) 640-7529 (410) 560-0551
Fax: (410) 560-6355
E-Mail: edg@preplayed.com
Web Site: www.preplayed.com
Mr. Ed Gieske, President

PREPLAYED is a chain of franchised stores that does more than just sell to its customers . . . it also buys directly from them. In fact, the majority of the CDs, movies, video/computer games, electronics and the gear that goes with it, all that we sell, has been obtained directly from our customers. Our stores are the largest retail concept with the greatest product diversity in the pre-owned retail industry and is backed by an experienced team with decades of experience in retail and preowned retail.

BACKGROUND: IFA MEMBER
Established: 2003; 1st Franchised: 2003
Franchised Units: 5
Company-Owned Units: 0
Total Units: 5
Dist.: US-5; CAN-0; O'seas-0
North America: 2 States
Density: 4 in WI, 1 in PA
Projected New Units (12 Months): 15
Qualifications: 5, 3, 1, 3, 1, 5
Registered: FL,HI,IL,IN,MD,MI,MN,NY,OR,RI,VA,WA,WI,DC

FINANCIAL/TERMS:
Cash Investment: $80-150K
Total Investment: $265-322K
Minimum Net Worth: $300K
Fees: Franchise - $25K
Royalty - 4%; Ad. - 2% + 2%
Earnings Claims Statement: No
Term of Contract (Years): 10/5
Avg. # Of Employees: 3 FT, 5 PT
Passive Ownership: Discouraged
Encourage Conversions: Yes
Area Develop. Agreements: Yes/Varies
Sub-Franchising Contracts: No
Expand In Territory: No
Space Needs: 5,000-6,000 SF; FS, SC

SUPPORT & TRAINING:
Financial Assistance Provided: No
Site Selection Assistance: Yes
Lease Negotiation Assistance: Yes
Co-Operative Advertising: No
Franchisee Assoc./Member: No
Size Of Corporate Staff: NR
On-Going Support: A,b,C,f
Training: 3 4 Hours Corporate Store/Headquarters; 87 Hours Corporate Store.

SPECIFIC EXPANSION PLANS:
US: All United States
Canada: No
Overseas: No

<< >>

RADIO SHACK SELECT

300 W. 3rd St., # 1600
Fort Worth, TX 76102
Tel: (800) 826-3905 (817) 415-3499
Fax: (817) 415-8651
E-Mail: paul.crump@radioshack.com
Web Site: www.radioshack.com
Mr. Paul Crump, Franchise Director/New Stores

RADIO SHACK is a consumer electronics retailer.

BACKGROUND: IFA MEMBER
Established: 1921; 1st Franchised: 1968
Franchised Units: 1,862
Company-Owned Units: 5,089
Total Units: 6,951
Dist.: US-7,091; CAN-0; O'seas-54
North America: 48 States
Density: CA, NY, IL
Projected New Units (12 Months): 150
Qualifications: 5, 5, 5, 1, 1, 4
Registered:CA,FL,IL,IN,MD,MI,MN,NY,ND,OR,SD,VA,WA,WI,DC

FINANCIAL/TERMS:
Cash Investment: $39.9K
Total Investment: $69.9K
Minimum Net Worth: NA
Fees: Franchise - $39.9K
Royalty - 0%; Ad. - 0%
Earnings Claims Statement: No
Term of Contract (Years): 10/Annual
Avg. # Of Employees: NR
Passive Ownership: Discouraged
Encourage Conversions: No
Area Develop. Agreements: No
Sub-Franchising Contracts: No
Expand In Territory: Yes
Space Needs: 600 SF; FS, SF, SC, RM

SUPPORT & TRAINING:
Financial Assistance Provided: Yes(D)
Site Selection Assistance: No
Lease Negotiation Assistance: No
Co-Operative Advertising: Yes
Franchisee Assoc./Member: Yes/Yes
Size Of Corporate Staff: 150
On-Going Support: A,B,C,D,E,F,G,H,I
Training: 5 Days On-Site.

SPECIFIC EXPANSION PLANS:
US: All States Except Hawaii and Delaware
Canada: No
Overseas: No

<< >>

VIDEOMASTERS

2200 Dunbarton Dr., # D
Chesapeake, VA 23325
Tel: (800) 836-9461 (757) 424-4272
Fax: (757) 424-8693
E-Mail: corporate@videomasters.info
Web Site: www.videomasters.info
Mr. Rory Graham, President

VIDEOMASTERS provide a unique, video-photography service to businesses and consumers. The complete package includes all equipment, training, marketing and field assistance. It can be started part-time and is ideal as a family or retirement business. VIDEOMASTERS is the largest video-taping service in North America. We also provide film-to-tape transfers and editing services.

BACKGROUND:
Established: 1981; 1st Franchised: 1984
Franchised Units: 80
Company-Owned Units: 0
Total Units: 80
Dist.: US-230; CAN-6; O'seas-0
North America: NR
Density: 24 in CA, 12 to VA, 8 in NY
Projected New Units (12 Months): 30
Qualifications: 5, 3, 1, 3, 3, 2
Registered: CA,IL,NY,VA,MI,WA

FINANCIAL/TERMS:
Cash Investment: $10-20K
Total Investment: $20-23K
Minimum Net Worth: $75K
Fees: Franchise - $20K
Royalty - $750/Yr.; Ad. - 0%
Earnings Claims Statement: No
Term of Contract (Years): 10/10
Avg. # Of Employees: 1 FT, 1 PT
Passive Ownership: Not Allowed
Encourage Conversions: NA
Area Develop. Agreements: No
Sub-Franchising Contracts: No
Expand In Territory: No
Space Needs: 200 SF; HB

SUPPORT & TRAINING:
Financial Assistance Provided: Yes(I)
Site Selection Assistance: NA
Lease Negotiation Assistance: NA
Co-Operative Advertising: NA
Franchisee Assoc./Member: Yes/No
Size Of Corporate Staff: 4
On-Going Support: B,G,H,I
Training: 3 Days San Diego, CA; 3 Days Rochester, NY.

SPECIFIC EXPANSION PLANS:
US: All United States
Canada: All Canada
Overseas: No

Retail: Miscellaneous

Retail: Miscellaneous Industry Profile

Total # Franchisors in Industry Group	16
Total # Franchised Units in Industry Group	1,555
Total # Company-Owned Units in Industry Group	124
Total # Operating Units in Industry Group	1,679
Average # Franchised Units/Franchisor	97.2
Average # Company-Owned Units/Franchisor	7.8
Average # Total Units/Franchisor	104.9
Ratio of Total # Franchised Units/Total # Company-Owned Units	12.5:1
Industry Survey Participants	9
Representing % of Industry	56.3%
Average Franchise Fee*:	$23.5K
Average Total Investment*:	$138.9K
Average On-Going Royalty Fee*:	4.1%

*If a range was provided, the mid-point of the range was used. See detailed profiles for actual ranges.

Five Largest Participants in Survey

Company	# Franchised Units	# Co-Owned Units	# Total Units	Franchise Fee	On-Going Royalty	Total Investment
1. Heel Quik!	743	0	743	$15.5-17.5K	4%	$45-95K
2. A Buck or Two Stores	269	57	326	$50K	6%	$160K
3. Your Dollar Store With More	180	4	184	$20K	4%	$150-400K
4. Dollar Discount Stores of America	165	0	165	$18K	3%	$120-130K
5. Street Corner	54	0	54	$19.9K	4.5%	$140-185K

All of the data provided are proprietary and should not be quoted without acknowledging *Bond's Franchise Guide.*

A BUCK OR TWO STORES

8200 Jane St.
Concord, ON L4K 5A7 CANADA
Tel: (800) 890-8633 (905) 738-3180 + 309
Fax: (905) 738-3176
E-Mail: jhoefel@denninghouse.com
Web Site: www.buckortwo.com
Ms. Jody Hoefel, Franchise Development Associat

We're approaching 200 fun, exciting A BUCK OR TWO locations across Canada, well defined by simplicity, offering first-quality merchandise, presented in a visually appealing format, departmentalized, at prices of $2 or less. Sales and profit are maximized with a great selection of core and seasonal merchandise, as well as aggressively priced special opportunity buys, where volume purchasing power allows franchisees to continually benefit.

BACKGROUND:
Established: 1987; 1st Franchised: 1989
Franchised Units: 269
Company-Owned Units: 57
Total Units: 326
Dist.: US-0; CAN-190; O'seas-0
North America: 9 Provinces
Density: 80 in ON, 19 in BC, 17 in NS
Projected New Units (12 Months): 25
Qualifications: 4, 5, 4, 4, 3, 5
Registered: AB
FINANCIAL/TERMS:
Cash Investment: $50-70K
Total Investment: $160K
Minimum Net Worth: $200K
Fees: Franchise - $50K
Royalty - 6%; Ad. - 1%
Earnings Claims Statement: No
Term of Contract (Years): 5/5
Avg. # Of Employees: Varies
Passive Ownership: Discouraged
Encourage Conversions: NA
Area Develop. Agreements: No
Sub-Franchising Contracts: No
Expand In Territory: Yes
Space Needs: 2,500-4,000 SF; RM
SUPPORT & TRAINING:
Financial Assistance Provided: Yes(D)
Site Selection Assistance: NA
Lease Negotiation Assistance: NA
Co-Operative Advertising: Yes
Franchisee Assoc./Member: Yes/Yes
Size Of Corporate Staff: 100
On-Going Support: a,C,D,E,G,h
Training: 1 Week Hamilton, ON; 2 Weeks Site Location.
SPECIFIC EXPANSION PLANS:
US: No
Canada: All Canada
Overseas: Mexico, South America, Europe, Australia

<< >>

DOLLAR DISCOUNT STORES OF AMERICA

1362 Naamans Creek Rd.
Boothwyn, PA 19061
Tel: (800) 227-5314 (888) 365-52 497-1991
Fax: (610) 485-6439
E-Mail: info@dollardiscount.com
Web Site: www.dollardiscount.com
Mr. Mitchel Insel, Franchise Director

Dollar stores.

BACKGROUND: IFA MEMBER
Established: 1982; 1st Franchised: 1987
Franchised Units: 165
Company-Owned Units: 0
Total Units: 165
Dist.: US-165; CAN-0; O'seas-0
North America: NR
Density: PA, MI, WI
Projected New Units (12 Months): 40
Qualifications: 3, 2, 2, 3, 3, 5
Registered: All States Except HI
FINANCIAL/TERMS:
Cash Investment: $20-30K
Total Investment: $120-130K
Minimum Net Worth: $100K
Fees: Franchise - $18K
Royalty - 3%; Ad. - 1%
Earnings Claims Statement: No
Term of Contract (Years): 10/15
Avg. # Of Employees: 1-2 FT, 5-6 PT
Passive Ownership: Discouraged
Encourage Conversions: NA
Area Develop. Agreements: No
Sub-Franchising Contracts: No
Expand In Territory: No
Space Needs: 2,000-4,000 SF; FS, SF, SC, RM
SUPPORT & TRAINING:
Financial Assistance Provided: Yes(I)
Site Selection Assistance: Yes
Lease Negotiation Assistance: Yes
Co-Operative Advertising: No
Franchisee Assoc./Member: Yes/Yes
Size Of Corporate Staff: 19
On-Going Support: A,B,C,D,E,F,G,H,I
Training: 5 Days in Boothwyn, PA.
SPECIFIC EXPANSION PLANS:
US: All United States
Canada: No
Overseas: No

<< >>

HEEL QUIK!

1730 Cumberland Point Dr., # 5
Marietta, GA 30067
Tel: (800) 255-8145 (770) 951-9440
Fax: (770) 953-6270
E-Mail: hqcorp@bellsouth.net
Web Site: www.heelquik.com
Ms. Betty Hubauer, Franchise Support

Personal services franchise opportunity with a range of services and investment levels, including shoe repair, dry cleaning, clothing alterations, monogramming, key cutting and knife and scissors sharpening.

BACKGROUND:
Established: 1983; 1st Franchised: 1984
Franchised Units: 743
Company-Owned Units: 0
Total Units: 743
Dist.: US-175; CAN-1; O'seas-567
North America: 20 States, 1 Province
Density: 78 in GA, 58 in TX, 8 in FL
Projected New Units (12 Months): 12
Qualifications: 3, 3, 1, 2, 3, 3
Registered: NR
FINANCIAL/TERMS:
Cash Investment: $15-35K
Total Investment: $45-95K
Minimum Net Worth: $25-75K
Fees: Franchise - $15.5-17.5K
Royalty - 4%; Ad. - NR
Earnings Claims Statement: No
Term of Contract (Years): 20/10/10
Avg. # Of Employees: 2 FT, 1 PT
Passive Ownership: Allowed
Encourage Conversions: Yes
Area Develop. Agreements: Yes/Varies
Sub-Franchising Contracts: Yes
Expand In Territory: Yes
Space Needs: 500 SF; SF, SC, RM
SUPPORT & TRAINING:
Financial Assistance Provided: Yes(I)
Site Selection Assistance: Yes
Lease Negotiation Assistance: Yes
Co-Operative Advertising: No
Franchisee Assoc./Member: No
Size Of Corporate Staff: 24
On-Going Support: c,d,G,I
Training: 2 Weeks Marietta, GA.
SPECIFIC EXPANSION PLANS:
US: All United States

Canada: All CAN Exc. AB
Overseas: All Countries

<< >>

NUMARKETS

816 N. Tennessee Ave.
Etowah, TN 37331
Tel: (888) NUMARKETS (423) 263-5211
Fax: (423) 506-1037
E-Mail: dboehm@numarkets.com
Web Site: www.numarkets.com
Mr. David Boehm, Franchise Director

NUMARKETS is the pioneer of eBay selling and shipping. Centers help the public and business with a new way of selling items. Just bring your items and NUMARKETS does everything else.

BACKGROUND:
Established: 2002; 1st Franchised: 2004
Franchised Units: 5
Company-Owned Units: 0
Total Units: 5
Dist.: US-5; CAN-0; O'seas-0
North America: 3 States
Density: 4 in TN, 1 in GA, 1 in NC
Projected New Units (12 Months): 500
Qualifications: 5, 5, 3, 4, 3, 5
Registered: NR

FINANCIAL/TERMS:
Cash Investment: $82K
Total Investment: $103-150K
Minimum Net Worth: $250K
Fees: Franchise - $28.9K
Royalty - 4.7%; Ad. - 2%
Earnings Claims Statement: No
Term of Contract (Years): 10/20
Avg. # Of Employees: 5 FT, 2 PT
Passive Ownership: Discouraged
Encourage Conversions: NR
Area Develop. Agreements: No
Sub-Franchising Contracts: No
Expand In Territory: Yes
Space Needs: NR SF; SC, Light Industrial

SUPPORT & TRAINING:
Financial Assistance Provided: No
Site Selection Assistance: Yes
Lease Negotiation Assistance: Yes
Co-Operative Advertising: No
Franchisee Assoc./Member: No
Size Of Corporate Staff: 31
On-Going Support: A,B,C,D,E,F,G,H,I
Training: 5 Days Etowah, TN; 5 Days Your Location at Opening.

SPECIFIC EXPANSION PLANS:
US: All United States
Canada: All Canada
Overseas: All Countries

<< >>

QUIKDROP INTERNATIONAL

3151 Airway Ave., # M-3
Costa Mesa, CA 92626
Tel: (888) 784-5266 (714) 429-1040
Fax: (714) 429-1038
E-Mail: mmead@quikdrop.com
Web Site: www.quikdrop.com
Mr. Jack Reynolds, Co-Founder

We are the first and largest eBay drop-off store franchise in the USA. We are the only eBay drop-off store franchise to operate internationally.

BACKGROUND: IFA MEMBER
Established: 2003; 1st Franchised: 2003
Franchised Units: 40
Company-Owned Units: 0
Total Units: 40
Dist.: US-20; CAN-1; O'seas-1
North America: 7 States, 1 Province
Density: 3 in CA, 3 in TX, 1 in FL
Projected New Units (12 Months): 250
Qualifications: 3, 5, 1, 3, 3, 5
Registered: CA,FL,IL,IN,MI,NY

FINANCIAL/TERMS:
Cash Investment: $60K
Total Investment: NR
Minimum Net Worth: Varies
Fees: Franchise - $15K
Royalty - $1,800/Mo.; Ad. - $450/Mo.
Earnings Claims Statement: No
Term of Contract (Years): 15/15
Avg. # Of Employees: 1 FT, 5 PT
Passive Ownership: Allowed
Encourage Conversions: Yes
Area Develop. Agreements: Yes/15
Sub-Franchising Contracts: Yes
Expand In Territory: Yes
Space Needs: 2,000 SF; SC

SUPPORT & TRAINING:
Financial Assistance Provided: Yes(I)
Site Selection Assistance: Yes
Lease Negotiation Assistance: Yes
Co-Operative Advertising: Yes
Franchisee Assoc./Member: No
Size Of Corporate Staff: 20
On-Going Support: A,B,C,D,E,F,G,H
Training: 1 Week California; 1 Week In-Store.

SPECIFIC EXPANSION PLANS:
US: All United States
Canada: All Canada
Overseas: All Countries

<< >>

SNAPPY AUCTIONS

209 10th Ave. S., # 311
Nashville, TN 37203
Tel: (800) 490-1820 (615) 400-3175
Fax: (800) 490-1820
E-Mail: franchise@snappyauctions.com
Web Site: www.snappyauctions.com
Ms. Debbie Gordon, President/CEO

SNAPPY AUCTIONS is the leading franchisor of "eBay Drop Off" Centers, where people can drop off items they would like to sell on eBay, and SNAPPY AUCTIONS handles all the details. The seller then receives a check for the amount of the sale, less a 15-35% commission. SNAPPY AUCTIONS targets people who are busy, upper middle class and relatively technology savvy. All sales are on consignment - no inventory or receivables. Low risk, low investment, very sound business model. Broad target market.

BACKGROUND: IFA MEMBER
Established: 2003; 1st Franchised: 2004
Franchised Units: 35
Company-Owned Units: 1
Total Units: 36
Dist.: US-9; CAN-0; O'seas-0
North America: 8 States
Density: 3 in GA, 2 in TN, 2 in VA
Projected New Units (12 Months): 190
Qualifications: 3, 4, 2, 3, 4, 5
Registered: All Except ND and SD.

FINANCIAL/TERMS:
Cash Investment: $34-50K
Total Investment: $35-50K
Minimum Net Worth: NA
Fees: Franchise - $15K
Royalty - 2-4%; Ad. - .5%
Earnings Claims Statement: No
Term of Contract (Years): 5/20
Avg. # Of Employees: 1 FT, 2-4 PT
Passive Ownership: Discouraged
Encourage Conversions: Yes
Area Develop. Agreements: Yes
Sub-Franchising Contracts: No
Expand In Territory: Yes
Space Needs: 1,200 SF; SF, SC

SUPPORT & TRAINING:
Financial Assistance Provided: NA

Site Selection Assistance: Yes
Lease Negotiation Assistance: Yes
Co-Operative Advertising: Yes
Franchisee Assoc./Member: No
Size Of Corporate Staff: 6
On-Going Support: A,C,D,E,G,H,I
Training: 10 Days - 5 at Corporate, 5 on Site.

SPECIFIC EXPANSION PLANS:
US: All United States
Canada: ON and BC
Overseas: No

<< >>

STREET CORNER

2945 SW Wanamaker Dr.
Topeka, KS 66614
Tel: (800) 789-NEWS (785) 272-8529 + 103
Fax: (785) 272-2384
E-Mail: kirk@streetcornernews.com
Web Site: www.streetcornernews.com
Mr. Kirk Braun, Director of Marketing/PR

STREET CORNER is the "Convenience Store in the Mall," offering the things that mall employees and mall patrons want during their shopping experiences: aspirin, fountain and bottled drinks, coffee and tea and newspapers, lottery, snacks, candy and gun, fax and copy services, cigarettes and cigars, souvenirs and gifts, office and desk supplies and other incidentals.

BACKGROUND:
Established: 1988; 1st Franchised: 1995
Franchised Units: 54
Company-Owned Units: 0
Total Units: 54
Dist.: US-54; CAN-0; O'seas-0
North America: 27 States
Density: 8 in NJ, 4 in TN, 4 in NY
Projected New Units (12 Months): 30
Qualifications: 4, 1, 1, 1, 1, 2
Registered: All States

FINANCIAL/TERMS:
Cash Investment: $45K
Total Investment: $140-185K
Minimum Net Worth: $150K
Fees: Franchise - $19.9K
Royalty - 4.5%; Ad. - 0%
Earnings Claims Statement: No
Term of Contract (Years): 7/7
Avg. # Of Employees: 2 PT
Passive Ownership: Allowed
Encourage Conversions: NA
Area Develop. Agreements: Yes
Sub-Franchising Contracts: Yes
Expand In Territory: Yes
Space Needs: 150-800 SF; RM

SUPPORT & TRAINING:
Financial Assistance Provided: Yes(I)
Site Selection Assistance: Yes
Lease Negotiation Assistance: Yes
Co-Operative Advertising: Yes
Franchisee Assoc./Member: No
Size Of Corporate Staff: 8
On-Going Support: A,C,D,E,F,G,h,I
Training: At least 40 Hours On-Site.

SPECIFIC EXPANSION PLANS:
US: All United States
Canada: No
Overseas: No

<< >>

TERRI'S CONSIGN & DESIGN FURNISHINGS

1375 W. Drivers Way
Tempe, AZ 85284
Tel: (800) 455-0400 (480) 969-1121
Fax: (480) 969-5052
E-Mail: marcusc@eterris.com
Web Site: www.eterris.com
Mr. Marcus Curtis, President

Nation's leader in consignment home furnishings. We deal in furnishings acquired from model homes, estates, factory liquidations, skilled craftsmen and fine homes. Quality brand-name furnishings, accessories, office furnishings, art and antiques. Business has high sales volume with high margin and no initial cost inventory. Ground floor opportunities still available.

BACKGROUND:
Established: 1979; 1st Franchised: 1993
Franchised Units: 8
Company-Owned Units: 8
Total Units: 16
Dist.: US-13; CAN-0; O'seas-0
North America: 5 States
Density: 7 in AZ, 2 in NV, 2 in CA
Projected New Units (12 Months): 4
Qualifications: 4, 4, 3, 3, 3, 5
Registered: CA,OR,WA

FINANCIAL/TERMS:
Cash Investment: $75-175K
Total Investment: $100-200K
Minimum Net Worth: $250K+
Fees: Franchise - $28K
Royalty - 4%; Ad. - 1%
Earnings Claims Statement: Yes
Term of Contract (Years): 10/5/5
Avg. # Of Employees: 10 FT, 3 PT
Passive Ownership: Not Allowed
Encourage Conversions: Yes
Area Develop. Agreements: Yes/10
Sub-Franchising Contracts: No
Expand In Territory: Yes
Space Needs: 20,000 SF; FS, SC, Warehouse

SUPPORT & TRAINING:
Financial Assistance Provided: Yes(I)
Site Selection Assistance: Yes
Lease Negotiation Assistance: Yes
Co-Operative Advertising: No
Franchisee Assoc./Member: No
Size Of Corporate Staff: 7
On-Going Support: C,D,E,G,H,I
Training: 1 Week Mesa, AZ; 5 Days Store Location upon Opening.

SPECIFIC EXPANSION PLANS:
US: All United States
Canada: No
Overseas: No

<< >>

Your
Dollar Store
With More

YOUR DOLLAR STORE WITH MORE

102 - 1626 Richter St.
Kelowna, BC V1Y 2M3 CANADA
Tel: (250) 860-4225
Fax: (250) 860-4215
E-Mail: ydswm@dollarstore.ca
Web Site: www.dollarstore.ca
Mr. Dave Uzelman, President

YOUR DOLLAR STORE WITH MORE targets a wide range of retail customers who are looking to purchase everyday products at a low prices. These customers want to save time and make their shopping dollars go farther. With a franchise that fits in with today's lifestyles, our franchisees are able to sell many$1 items, plus others priced higher, which allows them to create an exciting merchandise mix. We are also the only dollar store franchise in Canada that supports franchisees through a National Advert. Fund.

BACKGROUND:
Established: 1998; 1st Franchised: 1998

Franchised Units: 180
Company-Owned Units: 4
Total Units: 184
Dist.: US-0; CAN-184; O'seas-0
North America: 11 Provinces
Density: 62 in BC, 58 in AB, 26 in SK
Projected New Units (12 Months): 25
Qualifications: 4, 3, 3, 3, 4, 4
Registered: AB

FINANCIAL/TERMS:

Cash Investment: $75-200K
Total Investment: $150-400K
Minimum Net Worth: $100K
Fees: Franchise - $20K
Royalty - 4%; Ad. - .5%
Earnings Claims Statement: Yes
Term of Contract (Years): 10/10
Avg. # Of Employees: 4 FT, 4 PT
Passive Ownership: Discouraged
Encourage Conversions: Yes
Area Develop. Agreements: Yes/10
Sub-Franchising Contracts: No
Expand In Territory: Yes
Space Needs:3,000-10,000 SF; SF, SC, RM

SUPPORT & TRAINING:

Financial Assistance Provided: NR
Site Selection Assistance: Yes
Lease Negotiation Assistance: Yes
Co-Operative Advertising: No
Franchisee Assoc./Member: Yes/Yes
Size Of Corporate Staff: 15
On-Going Support: C,D,E,G,H
Training: 1 Week (5 Business Days) at Franchisee's Store Location.

SPECIFIC EXPANSION PLANS:

US: No
Canada: All Canada
Overseas: No

<< >>

The Top 100 Franchises denoted in this book were derived from the 2005 edition of *Bond's Top 100 Franchises*. As the pre-eminent publisher of nine books on franchising, Source Book Publications evaluated hundreds of proven franchise systems to arrive at what it feels are the top 100 franchises. Companies were evaluated on the basis of historical performance, brand identification, market dynamics, franchisee satisfaction, the level of initial training and on-going support, financial stability and various other key factors.

To learn more about *Bond's Top 100 Franchises*, please visit our website at www.worldfranchising.com.

Security & Safety Systems

Chapter 45

Security & Safety Systems Industry Profile

Total # Franchisors in Industry Group	19
Total # Franchised Units in Industry Group	1,017
Total # Company-Owned Units in Industry Group	105
Total # Operating Units in Industry Group	1,122
Average # Franchised Units/Franchisor	53.5
Average # Company-Owned Units/Franchisor	5.5
Average # Total Units/Franchisor	59.1
Ratio of Total # Franchised Units/Total # Company-Owned Units	9.7:1
Industry Survey Participants	4
Representing % of Industry	21.1%
Average Franchise Fee*:	$24.8K
Average Total Investment*:	$212.9K
Average On-Going Royalty Fee*:	6.8%

*If a range was provided, the mid-point of the range was used. See detailed profiles for actual ranges.

Four Largest Participants in Survey

Company	# Franchised Units	# Co-Owned Units	# Total Units	Franchise Fee	On-Going Royalty	Total Investment
1. Sonitrol	178	34	212	$20-50K	2.5%	$250-600K
2. Fire Defense Centers	19	44	63	$20.5K	10%	$47-52K
3. Safe Kids Card	33	0	33	$9.5K	$75/Mo.	$9.5-45K
4. Proshred Security	6	0	6	$35K	8%	$350K

All of the data provided are proprietary and should not be quoted without acknowledging *Bond's Franchise Guide.*

FIRE DEFENSE CENTERS

6110-20 Powers Ave.
Jacksonville, FL 32217
Tel: (904) 731-1833
Ms. I. A. La Russo, President

Dealing with national accounts on servicing of fire extinguishers, automatic restaurant hood systems, municipal supplies and first aid kits. Warranty on equipment sold to business and guaranteed fire code compliance to business. Provide consultation for businesses to comply with city and state governments.

BACKGROUND:

Established: 1973; 1st Franchised: 1986
Franchised Units: 19
Company-Owned Units: 44
Total Units: 63
Dist.: US-63; CAN-0; O'seas-0
North America: 15 States
Density: 20 in FL
Projected New Units (12 Months): 3
Qualifications: 5, 2, 1, 2, 1, 5
Registered: All States

FINANCIAL/TERMS:

Cash Investment: $47-52K
Total Investment: $47-52K
Minimum Net Worth: NR
Fees: Franchise - $20.5K
Royalty - 10%; Ad. - 0%
Earnings Claims Statement: No
Term of Contract (Years): 10/10
Avg. # Of Employees: 2-20 FT
Passive Ownership: Allowed
Encourage Conversions: No
Area Develop. Agreements: No
Sub-Franchising Contracts: No
Expand In Territory: Yes
Space Needs: 1,500 SF; Warehouse

SUPPORT & TRAINING:

Financial Assistance Provided: Yes
Site Selection Assistance: Yes
Lease Negotiation Assistance: Yes
Co-Operative Advertising: Yes
Franchisee Assoc./Member: Yes/Yes
Size Of Corporate Staff: 18
On-Going Support: A,B,C,D,E,F,G,H,I
Training: 2 Weeks Headquarters.

SPECIFIC EXPANSION PLANS:

US: All United States
Canada: No
Overseas: No

<< >>

PROSHRED SECURITY

245 Yorkland Blvd., # 100
Toronto, ON M2J 4W9 CANADA
Tel: (800) 463-1405 (416) 490-8600 + 240
Fax: (416) 490-1401
E-Mail: john.prittie@proshred.com
Web Site: www.proshred.com
Mr. Tim Shearman, Dir. Franchise Operations

PROSHRED SECURITY is a franchise for business people. Our license owners provide at-your-door document shredding services to area businesses. Customers include all levels of business and government. Operating in the U. S., Canada and Europe, PROSHRED is the largest in North America. Company management has a long, successful history in franchising.

BACKGROUND:

Established: 1985; 1st Franchised: 1990
Franchised Units: 6
Company-Owned Units: 0
Total Units: 6
Dist.: US-4; CAN-31; O'seas-0
North America: 3 States, 10 Provinces
Density: NR
Projected New Units (12 Months): 4
Qualifications: , , , , ,
Registered: CA,FL,MD,MI,OR,DC

FINANCIAL/TERMS:

Cash Investment: $200K
Total Investment: $350K
Minimum Net Worth: NR
Fees: Franchise - $35K
Royalty - 8%; Ad. - 0%
Earnings Claims Statement: No
Term of Contract (Years): 5/5/5/5
Avg. # Of Employees: 5 FT, 2 PT
Passive Ownership: Not Allowed
Encourage Conversions: Yes
Area Develop. Agreements: Yes/10
Sub-Franchising Contracts: No
Expand In Territory: Yes
Space Needs: NR SF; NA

SUPPORT & TRAINING:

Financial Assistance Provided: Yes(I)
Site Selection Assistance: NA
Lease Negotiation Assistance: NA
Co-Operative Advertising: NA
Franchisee Assoc./Member: No
Size Of Corporate Staff: 11
On-Going Support: A,C,D,E,G,H,I
Training: 9 Days Toronto, ON; 5 Days Local.

SPECIFIC EXPANSION PLANS:

US: All United States
Canada: All Canada
Overseas: Europe, Australia, Asia

SAFE KIDS CARD

17100 Bear Valley Rd., # 238
Victorville, CA 92395
Tel: (909) 486-9982
Fax: (760) 249-5751
E-Mail: jeremiah@safekidscard.com
Web Site: www.myfamilycd.com
Mr. Joe Veeser, Vice President Sales

SAFE KIDS CARD is the most advanced child, adult and pet identification card, using CD-ROMs the size of a business card with digital photos, fingerprint and lots of information for medical, law enforcement and law officials in case of an emergency. This ground-floor opportunity will change your life and give you 'protection for a lifetime.'

BACKGROUND: IFA MEMBER

Established: 2002; 1st Franchised: 2003
Franchised Units: 33
Company-Owned Units: 0
Total Units: 33
Dist.: US-32; CAN-1; O'seas-0
North America: 18 States
Density: 8 in CA, 5 in PA, 3 in TX
Projected New Units (12 Months): 30
Qualifications: 3, 3, 2, 3, 4, 4
Registered: CA,WI,VA

FINANCIAL/TERMS:

Cash Investment: $9.5K
Total Investment: $9.5-45K
Minimum Net Worth: $9.5K
Fees: Franchise - $9.5K
Royalty - $75/Mo.; Ad. - $20/Mo.
Earnings Claims Statement: No
Term of Contract (Years): 10/5
Avg. # Of Employees: 1 FT, 1 PT
Passive Ownership: Discouraged
Encourage Conversions: NA
Area Develop. Agreements: No
Sub-Franchising Contracts: No
Expand In Territory: Yes
Space Needs: 500 SF; SF, HB

SUPPORT & TRAINING:

Financial Assistance Provided: Yes(I)
Site Selection Assistance: NA
Lease Negotiation Assistance: NA
Co-Operative Advertising: NA
Franchisee Assoc./Member: No
Size Of Corporate Staff: 3
On-Going Support: b,d,e,h
Training: 1-2 Days Southern California; 2-3 Days Your Location.

SPECIFIC EXPANSION PLANS:

US: All United States
Canada: All Canada
Overseas: No

SONITROL

211 North Union, # 350
Alexandria, VA 22314-2643
Tel: (800) 328-5607 (703) 684-6606
Fax: (703) 684-6612
E-Mail: ccobb@sonitrol.com
Web Site: www.sonitrol.com
Mr. Todd Leggett, VP Business Development

SONITROL offers a broad line of security systems to commercial and residential subscribers. A majority of SONITROL products are sold to businesses which have typically been in operations for over a year. The signature system is based on a sound activated audio. This process allows for verification of alarms and has resulted in the apprehension of over 135,000 criminals.

BACKGROUND: IFA MEMBER
Established: 1964; 1st Franchised: 1965
Franchised Units: 178
Company-Owned Units: 34
Total Units: 212
Dist.: US-177; CAN-1; O'seas-2
North America: 41 States
Density: 24 in CA, 14 in FL, 11 in NY
Projected New Units (12 Months): 3
Qualifications: 4, 5, 3, 2, 5, 4
Registered: FL,IL,VA

FINANCIAL/TERMS:
Cash Investment: $100-200K
Total Investment: $250-600K
Minimum Net Worth: $250K
Fees: Franchise - $20-50K
Royalty - 2.5%; Ad. - NA
Earnings Claims Statement: No
Term of Contract (Years): 10/10
Avg. # Of Employees: Varies
Passive Ownership: Not Allowed
Encourage Conversions: NA
Area Develop. Agreements: No
Sub-Franchising Contracts: No
Expand In Territory: No
Space Needs: NR SF; NA

SUPPORT & TRAINING:
Financial Assistance Provided: NA
Site Selection Assistance: NA
Lease Negotiation Assistance: No
Co-Operative Advertising: No
Franchisee Assoc./Member: Yes/Yes
Size Of Corporate Staff: 11
On-Going Support: C,d,E,G,h,I
Training: Business Training On-Site; 1 Wk. Technical Training in Orlando; 1 Wk. Sales Tr. in Dallas.

SPECIFIC EXPANSION PLANS:
US: All United States
Canada: No
Overseas: No

For a full explanation of the data provided in the Franchisor Profiles, please refer to *Chapter 2, "How to Use the Data."*

Signs Chapter 46

Signs Industry Profile

Total # Franchisors in Industry Group	13
Total # Franchised Units in Industry Group	2,098
Total # Company-Owned Units in Industry Group	6
Total # Operating Units in Industry Group	2,104
Average # Franchised Units/Franchisor	161.4
Average # Company-Owned Units/Franchisor	0.5
Average # Total Units/Franchisor	161.8
Ratio of Total # Franchised Units/Total # Company-Owned Units	349.7:1
Industry Survey Participants	9
Representing % of Industry	69.2%
Average Franchise Fee*:	$21.8K
Average Total Investment*:	$115.1K
Average On-Going Royalty Fee*:	5.3%

*If a range was provided, the mid-point of the range was used. See detailed profiles for actual ranges.

Five Largest Participants in Survey

Company	# Franchised Units	# Co-Owned Units	# Total Units	Franchise Fee	On-Going Royalty	Total Investment
1. Sign-A-Rama	702	0	702	$39.5K	6%	$135-140K
2. FASTSIGNS	475	0	475	$20K	6%	$155.5-233K
3. Signs by Tomorrow	174	1	175	$28.5K	3-6%	$150-250K
4. Sign Biz	154	0	154	$20K	0%	$155K
5. Stork News of America	141	1	142	$7-10K	$0.50-1K	$7-12K

All of the data provided are proprietary and should not be quoted without acknowledging *Bond's Franchise Guide.*

BEYOND SIGNS

36 Apple Creek Blvd.
Markham, ON L3R 4Y4 CANADA
Tel: (800) 265-7446 (905) 415-9809
Fax: (905) 415-1583
E-Mail: gkerekes@bdimaging.com
Web Site: www.bdimaging.com
Mr. Glenn Kerekes, President

VINYLGRAPHICS is a Canadian franchisor of custom sign centers that offer interior/exterior signage, window lettering, vehicle and boat decoration, magnetic signs and more, to today's business community. The lettering for the signs is generated utilizing state-of-the-art technology and proven vinyl films.

BACKGROUND:
Established: 1983; 1st Franchised: 1990
Franchised Units: 14
Company-Owned Units: 0
Total Units: 14
Dist.: US-0; CAN-14; O'seas-0
North America: 1 Province
Density: 14 in ON
Projected New Units (12 Months): 6
Qualifications: , , , , ,
Registered: NR

FINANCIAL/TERMS:
Cash Investment: $35K
Total Investment: $90K
Minimum Net Worth: NR
Fees: Franchise - $25K
Royalty - 8%; Ad. - 0%
Earnings Claims Statement: No
Term of Contract (Years): 10/5
Avg. # Of Employees: 3 FT
Passive Ownership: Not Allowed
Encourage Conversions: Yes
Area Develop. Agreements: Yes/15
Sub-Franchising Contracts: Yes
Expand In Territory: Yes
Space Needs: 1,500 SF; SC

SUPPORT & TRAINING:
Financial Assistance Provided: Yes
Site Selection Assistance: Yes
Lease Negotiation Assistance: Yes
Co-Operative Advertising: Yes
Franchisee Assoc./Member: Yes/Yes
Size Of Corporate Staff: 8
On-Going Support: B,C,D,e,G,H,I
Training: 5 Weeks Toronto, ON.

SPECIFIC EXPANSION PLANS:
US: All United States
Canada: All Canada
Overseas: All Countries

FASTSIGNS

Top 100

FASTSIGNS

2550 Midway Rd., # 150
Carrollton, TX 75006-2357
Tel: (800) 827-7446 + 283 (214) 346-5616
Fax: (972) 248-8201
E-Mail: bill.mcpherson@fastsigns.com
Web Site: www.fastsigns.com
Mr. Bill N. McPherson, VP Franchise Sales

FASTSIGNS, the sign and graphic solutions provider for businesses worldwide, continues to receive accolades as the premier business-to-business franchise concept. FASTSIGNS was recently named the #1 sign franchise in Success Magazine's Franchisee Satisfaction Survey and has been featured in Entrepreneur for 13 years. Average per store gross sales has increased 11 of the last 12 years to $489,000 in 2003. We're proud of our franchise owners and their remarkable success stories. Come join the team!

BACKGROUND: IFA MEMBER
Established: 1985; 1st Franchised: 1986
Franchised Units: 475
Company-Owned Units: 0
Total Units: 475
Dist.: US-403; CAN-9; O'seas-56
North America: 43 States, 4 Provinces
Density: 50 in TX, 36 in CA, 24 in FL
Projected New Units (12 Months): 20
Qualifications: 5, 4, 1, 2, 3, 5
Registered: All States and AB

FINANCIAL/TERMS:
Cash Investment: $75K
Total Investment: $155.5-233K
Minimum Net Worth: $240K
Fees: Franchise - $20K
Royalty - 6%; Ad. - 2%
Earnings Claims Statement: Yes
Term of Contract (Years): 20/10
Avg. # Of Employees: 3 FT
Passive Ownership: Not Allowed
Encourage Conversions: Yes
Area Develop. Agreements: Yes
Sub-Franchising Contracts: Int
Expand In Territory: Yes
Space Needs: 1,700 SF; SC

SUPPORT & TRAINING:
Financial Assistance Provided: Yes(I)
Site Selection Assistance: Yes
Lease Negotiation Assistance: Yes
Co-Operative Advertising: Yes
Franchisee Assoc./Member: Yes
Size Of Corporate Staff: 92
On-Going Support: C,D,E,G,H,I
Training: 4 Weeks in Dallas, TX; 2 Weeks On-Site.

SPECIFIC EXPANSION PLANS:
US: All United States
Canada: All Canada
Overseas: UK, New Zealand, Australia

SIGN BIZ

24681 La Plaza, # 270
Dana Point, CA 92626
Tel: (800) 633-5580 (949) 234-0408
Fax: (949) 234-0426
E-Mail: gregs@signbiz.com
Web Site: www.signbiz.com
Mr. Greg Salzano, VP Business Development

SIGN BIZ was established in 1989 to develop entrepreneurs in the exciting field of computer-aided signmaking (CAS). The business is clean, colorful and provides great diversity. The industry continues to grow at a rate of approximately 13% per year. The SIGN BIZ Network is now the largest chain of CAS businesses worldwide in which owners pay no royalties. By assisting our stores in channeling their profits back into their local marketplace and their business, we can create phenomenal success.

BACKGROUND:
Established: 1989; 1st Franchised: 1989
Franchised Units: 154
Company-Owned Units: 0
Total Units: 154
Dist.: US-149; CAN-1; O'seas-4
North America: 40 States
Density: 44 in CA, 6 in OH, 5 in NJ
Projected New Units (12 Months): 18
Qualifications: , , , , ,
Registered:

FINANCIAL/TERMS:
Cash Investment: $45K
Total Investment: $155K
Minimum Net Worth: $100K
Fees: Franchise - $20K
Royalty - 0%; Ad. - 0%
Earnings Claims Statement: No
Term of Contract (Years): Evergreen
Avg. # Of Employees: 4 FT, 1 PT
Passive Ownership: Not Allowed
Encourage Conversions: NR
Area Develop. Agreements: No
Sub-Franchising Contracts: Yes
Expand In Territory: Yes

Space Needs: 1,500 SF; SC

SUPPORT & TRAINING:

Financial Assistance Provided: NR
Site Selection Assistance: Yes
Lease Negotiation Assistance: Yes
Co-Operative Advertising: Yes
Franchisee Assoc./Member: No
Size Of Corporate Staff: 9
On-Going Support: A,B,c,D,E,F,G,H,I
Training: 2 Weeks In-Home Study; 6 Days Dana Pt, CA; 4 Days S. California Store Training.

SPECIFIC EXPANSION PLANS:

US: All United States
Canada: All Canada
Overseas: All Countries

<< >>

SIGN-A-RAMA

1801 Australian Ave., S.
West Palm Beach, FL 33409-6465
Tel: (800) 286-8671 (561) 640-5570
Fax: (561) 478-4340
E-Mail: csimnick@signarama.com
Web Site: www.signarama.com
Mr. Christopher Simnick, Franchise Director

World's largest full-service sign franchise. Over 700 locations in 30 countries. Ranked #1 in industry. No experience needed. Full training, local back-up and support. Financing available.

BACKGROUND: IFA MEMBER

Established: 1986; 1st Franchised: 1987
Franchised Units: 702
Company-Owned Units: 0
Total Units: 702
Dist.: US-480; CAN-10; O'seas-176
North America: 44 States
Density: 67 in CA, 51 in FL, 30 in NJ
Projected New Units (12 Months): 100
Qualifications: 5, 4, 1, 1, 4, 5
Registered: All States and AB

FINANCIAL/TERMS:

Cash Investment: $40-50K
Total Investment: $135-140K
Minimum Net Worth: $60K
Fees: Franchise - $39.5K
Royalty - 6%; Ad. - 0%
Earnings Claims Statement: No
Term of Contract (Years): 35/35
Avg. # Of Employees: 3 FT
Passive Ownership: Discouraged
Encourage Conversions: Yes
Area Develop. Agreements: No Domestic
Sub-Franchising Contracts: Yes
Expand In Territory: Yes
Space Needs: 1,200 SF; SC

SUPPORT & TRAINING:

Financial Assistance Provided: Yes(I)
Site Selection Assistance: Yes
Lease Negotiation Assistance: Yes
Co-Operative Advertising: Yes
Franchisee Assoc./Member: Yes/Yes
Size Of Corporate Staff: 85
On-Going Support: A,B,C,D,E,F,G,H,I
Training: 2 Weeks West Palm Beach, FL; 2 Weeks On-Site; 1 Week On-The-Job.

SPECIFIC EXPANSION PLANS:

US: All United States
Canada: All Canada
Overseas: All Countries

<< >>

SIGNS BY TOMORROW

6460 Dobbin Rd.
Columbia, MD 21045
Tel: (800) 765-7446 (410) 992-7192
Fax: (410) 992-7675
E-Mail: sales@signsbytomorrow.com
Web Site: www.signsbytomorrow.com
Mr. Mike Cline, Dir. Franchise Development

Computer-generated, one day, signs and graphics shop. Business-to-business, high growth, high gross margins, service-oriented, multiples possible. Most extensive training and support system. Aggressive R & D program. High rate of franchisee success and satisfaction. No tech experience necessary.

BACKGROUND: IFA MEMBER

Established: 1986; 1st Franchised: 1987
Franchised Units: 174
Company-Owned Units: 1
Total Units: 175
Dist.: US-175; CAN-0; O'seas-0
North America: 34 States
Density: 16 in MD, 15 in PA, 9 in NJ
Projected New Units (12 Months): 20
Qualifications: 4, 5, 1, 4, 5, 5
Registered: All States

FINANCIAL/TERMS:

Cash Investment: $40-50K
Total Investment: $150-250K
Minimum Net Worth: $200K
Fees: Franchise - $28.5K
Royalty - 3-6%; Ad. - 1%
Earnings Claims Statement: Yes
Term of Contract (Years): 20/20
Avg. # Of Employees: 3 FT, 2 PT
Passive Ownership: Not Allowed
Encourage Conversions: No
Area Develop. Agreements: Yes/Negot.
Sub-Franchising Contracts: No
Expand In Territory: No
Space Needs: 1,800 SF; SC

SUPPORT & TRAINING:

Financial Assistance Provided: Yes(I)
Site Selection Assistance: Yes
Lease Negotiation Assistance: Yes
Co-Operative Advertising: Yes
Franchisee Assoc./Member: Yes/Yes
Size Of Corporate Staff: 27
On-Going Support: B,C,D,E,F,G,H,I
Training: 2 Weeks Headquarters; 2 Weeks in Store.

SPECIFIC EXPANSION PLANS:

US: All United States
Canada: No
Overseas: No

SIGNS FIRST

813 Ridge Lake Blvd., # 495
Memphis, TN 38120
Tel: (800) 852-2163 (901) 682-2264
Fax: (901) 682-2475
E-Mail: franchise@signsfirst.com
Web Site: www.signsfirst.com
Ms. Peggy Cahoon, Office Manager

SIGNS FIRST is the only franchise with over 25 years sign industry experience. We specialize in computer-generated, one-day temporary and permanent signs for retail, professional and commercial businesses on a cash and carry basis. Franchisee support is unparalleled with comprehensive training, on-going technological support and marketing assistance.

BACKGROUND:

Established: 1966; 1st Franchised: 1989
Franchised Units: 33
Company-Owned Units: 0
Total Units: 33
Dist.: US-42; CAN-0; O'seas-0
North America: 17 States
Density: 13 in TN, 12 in MS, 3 in CO
Projected New Units (12 Months): 5
Qualifications: 3, 4, 3, 1, 3, 5
Registered: FL

FINANCIAL/TERMS:

Cash Investment: $20K
Total Investment: $20-65K
Minimum Net Worth: $250K
Fees: Franchise - $10-15K
Royalty - 6%; Ad. - 0%
Earnings Claims Statement: No
Term of Contract (Years): 10/10
Avg. # Of Employees: 2 FT
Passive Ownership: Discouraged
Encourage Conversions: Yes
Area Develop. Agreements: Yes/10
Sub-Franchising Contracts: No
Expand In Territory: Yes
Space Needs: 1,500 SF; FS, SF, SC, RM

SUPPORT & TRAINING:

Financial Assistance Provided: NA
Site Selection Assistance: Yes
Lease Negotiation Assistance: Yes
Co-Operative Advertising: No
Franchisee Assoc./Member: No
Size Of Corporate Staff: 6
On-Going Support: B,C,D,E,F,G,I
Training: 2 Weeks Memphis, TN; 1 Week + Follow-Up Visit in Store.

SPECIFIC EXPANSION PLANS:

US: All United States
Canada: No
Overseas: No

<< >>

STORK NEWS OF AMERICA

1305 Hope Mills Rd., # A
Fayetteville, NC 28304
Tel: (800) 633-6395 (910) 426-1357
Fax: (910) 426-2473
E-Mail: no2stork@earthlink.net
Web Site: www.storknews.com
Mr. John M. Young, VP Franchise Development

The number one and the original newborn yard display business. New mothers, fathers, grandmothers and grandfathers, or any family relations want to tell the world about their new arrival. Rated in many publications as the best buy in home-operated businesses. Almost all operators are Mom's and some Mr. Mom's that don't want to have to ship their kids to day care and then go to work. With a STORK NEWS franchise, kids can go along to work, too.

BACKGROUND:

Established: 1983; 1st Franchised: 1986
Franchised Units: 141
Company-Owned Units: 1
Total Units: 142
Dist.: US-139; CAN-1; O'seas-1
North America: 33 States, 1 Province
Density: 14 in VA, 12 in FL, 11 in CA
Projected New Units (12 Months): 12
Qualifications: 1, 4, 1, 1, 3, 5
Registered: CA,FL,HI,IL,MD,MI,MN,NY,VA,WA

FINANCIAL/TERMS:

Cash Investment: $8-20K
Total Investment: $7-12K
Minimum Net Worth: NA
Fees: Franchise - $7-10K
Royalty - $0.50-1K; Ad. - NA
Earnings Claims Statement: No
Term of Contract (Years): Perpetual
Avg. # Of Employees: 1 FT
Passive Ownership: Allowed
Encourage Conversions: NA
Area Develop. Agreements: No
Sub-Franchising Contracts: No
Expand In Territory: Yes
Space Needs: NA SF; HB

SUPPORT & TRAINING:

Financial Assistance Provided: No
Site Selection Assistance: No
Lease Negotiation Assistance: No
Co-Operative Advertising: No
Franchisee Assoc./Member: No
Size Of Corporate Staff: 10
On-Going Support: D,F,G,I
Training: Manual.

SPECIFIC EXPANSION PLANS:

US: All United States
Canada: All Canada
Overseas: No

Travel

Chapter 47

Travel Industry Profile

Total # Franchisors in Industry Group	18
Total # Franchised Units in Industry Group	5,104
Total # Company-Owned Units in Industry Group	427
Total # Operating Units in Industry Group	5,531
Average # Franchised Units/Franchisor	283.6
Average # Company-Owned Units/Franchisor	23.7
Average # Total Units/Franchisor	307.3
Ratio of Total # Franchised Units/Total # Company-Owned Units	12:1
Industry Survey Participants	7
Representing % of Industry	38.9%
Average Franchise Fee*:	$17.3K
Average Total Investment*:	$60.5K
Average On-Going Royalty Fee*:	1.6%

*If a range was provided, the mid-point of the range was used. See detailed profiles for actual ranges.

Five Largest Participants in Survey

Company	# Franchised Units	# Co-Owned Units	# Total Units	Franchise Fee	On-Going Royalty	Total Investment
1. Carlson Wagonlit Travel	1,302	419	1,721	Included	Varies	$6.6-156.2K
2. Uniglobe Travel	1,100	0	1,100	$2-25K	$275-550	$21-104K
3. CruiseOne	436	0	436	$9.8K	3%	$10-22K
4. Travel Network	225	1	226	$14.9K	$350/Mo.	$120K
5. Travel Lines Express	15	1	16	$300	1%	$1-3K

All of the data provided are proprietary and should not be quoted without acknowledging *Bond's Franchise Guide.*

CARLSON WAGONLIT TRAVEL

701 Carlson Pksy
Minnetonka, MN 55305
Tel: (800) 678-8241 (763) 212-2181
Fax: (763) 212-1760
E-Mail: jrisner@carlson.com
Web Site: www.carlsontravel.com
Mr. John Risner, Director Franchise Development

Start-up and conversion travel agencies available. Preferred supplier program; national and local marketing and advertising newsletters; brochures; assistance with commercial business development; regional meetings; participation in CARLSON Selling Systems; Associate consulting service; hotel programs; 24-hour service center; centralized support department; international rate desk; and professional development programs. Leading technology to maximize efficiency.

BACKGROUND: IFA MEMBER
Established: 1900; 1st Franchised: 1984
Franchised Units: 1,302
Company-Owned Units: 419
Total Units: 1,721
Dist.: US-1,404; CAN-0; O'seas-400
North America: 49 States
Density: 160 in CA, 80 in MN, 55 TX
Projected New Units (12 Months): 100
Qualifications: 3, 4, 5, 4, 3, 4
Registered: All States Except MN,NY,DC

FINANCIAL/TERMS:
Cash Investment: $4-34.5K
Total Investment: $6.6-156.2K
Minimum Net Worth: NA
Fees: Franchise - $Included
Royalty - Varies; Ad. - Varies
Earnings Claims Statement: No
Term of Contract (Years): 3-10/3-10
Avg. # Of Employees: Varies
Passive Ownership: Discouraged
Encourage Conversions: Yes
Area Develop. Agreements: No
Sub-Franchising Contracts: No
Expand In Territory: Yes
Space Needs: NR SF; FS, SF, SC, RM, Other

SUPPORT & TRAINING:
Financial Assistance Provided: No
Site Selection Assistance: Yes
Lease Negotiation Assistance: Yes
Co-Operative Advertising: Yes
Franchisee Assoc./Member: Yes/Yes
Size Of Corporate Staff: 80
On-Going Support: d,E,g,h,i
Training: 2 Weeks in Minneapolis/On-Site for Start-Ups; 2 Days in Minneapolis for Conversions.

SPECIFIC EXPANSION PLANS:
US: All United States
Canada: No
Overseas: No

CRUISEONE

1415 NW 62nd St., # 205
Ft. Lauderdale, FL 33309-1955
Tel: (800) 892-3928 (954) 958-3701
Fax: (954) 958-3697
E-Mail: franchise@cruiseone.com
Web Site: www.cruiseone.com
Mr. Lee Mitchell,

CRUISEONE is a nationwide, home-based cruise-only franchise company representing all major cruise lines. Franchisees are professionally trained in a 7-day extensive program. How to close the sale and service the client, on-board ship inspections, sales and marketing techniques and customized software use are just the beginning. National Account Status offers consumers cruises for the lowest possible price and pays highest commissions in the industry. 1997 sales exceeded $80 million. Low start-up costs.

BACKGROUND: IFA MEMBER
Established: 1992; 1st Franchised: 1993
Franchised Units: 436
Company-Owned Units: 0
Total Units: 436
Dist.: US-430; CAN-0; O'seas-0
North America: 45 States
Density: 40 in FL, 39 in CA, 33 in TX
Projected New Units (12 Months): 120
Qualifications: 3, 4, 2, 3, 5, 4
Registered: All States

FINANCIAL/TERMS:
Cash Investment: $10-22K
Total Investment: $10-22K
Minimum Net Worth: NA
Fees: Franchise - $9.8K
Royalty - 3%; Ad. - 0%
Earnings Claims Statement: No
Term of Contract (Years): 5
Avg. # Of Employees: 1 FT
Passive Ownership: Not Allowed
Encourage Conversions: NA
Area Develop. Agreements: No
Sub-Franchising Contracts: No
Expand In Territory: Yes
Space Needs: NA SF; HB

SUPPORT & TRAINING:
Financial Assistance Provided: Yes(D)
Site Selection Assistance: NA
Lease Negotiation Assistance: NA
Co-Operative Advertising: Yes
Franchisee Assoc./Member: No
Size Of Corporate Staff: 42
On-Going Support: A,B,C,D,F,g,h,I
Training: 7 Days Ft. Lauderdale, FL.

SPECIFIC EXPANSION PLANS:
US: All United States
Canada: No
Overseas: No

TRAVEL LINES EXPRESS

19078 Skyridge Circle
Boca Raton, FL 33498
Tel: (561) 482-9557
Fax:
E-Mail: tley2k@aol.com
Web Site: www.travellinesexpress.com
Mr. David Korn, Vice President

Home-based travel agency franchise program. Full-service travel agency, offering cruises, airline tickets, hotels, car rentals, vacation packages and tours. Lowest franchise fee $300 includes state-of-the-art reservation system. Complete internet training and Website development. Lowest monthly royalty fee of 1%.

BACKGROUND: IFA MEMBER
Established: 2003; 1st Franchised: 2003
Franchised Units: 15
Company-Owned Units: 1
Total Units: 16
Dist.: US-25; CAN-0; O'seas-0
North America: 20 States
Density: NR
Projected New Units (12 Months): NR
Qualifications: , , , , ,
Registered:

FINANCIAL/TERMS:
Cash Investment: $1-3K
Total Investment: $1-3K
Minimum Net Worth: NA
Fees: Franchise - $300
Royalty - 1%; Ad. - 0%
Earnings Claims Statement: No
Term of Contract (Years): 20/20
Avg. # Of Employees: 1 FT
Passive Ownership: Discouraged
Encourage Conversions: NR
Area Develop. Agreements: No
Sub-Franchising Contracts: No
Expand In Territory: Yes
Space Needs: NA SF; HB

SUPPORT & TRAINING:
Financial Assistance Provided: NR
Site Selection Assistance: NA

Lease Negotiation Assistance: NA
Co-Operative Advertising: Yes
Franchisee Assoc./Member: No
Size Of Corporate Staff: 7
On-Going Support: D,G,H,I
Training: Complete On-Line Training.

SPECIFIC EXPANSION PLANS:
US: All United States
Canada: NR
Overseas: NR

TRAVEL NETWORK

560 Sylvan Ave.
Englewood Cliffs, NJ 07632
Tel: (800) 669-9000 (201) 567-8500
Fax: (201) 567-4405
E-Mail: info@rezconnect.com
Web Site: www.travelnetwork.com
Mr. Michael Y. Brent, President

Join the exciting travel industry with the leading travel franchisor as the owner of a TRAVEL NETWORK full-service travel agency catering to the business and leisure traveler. A TRAVEL NETWORK VACATION CENTRAL agency focuses solely on the lucrative leisure travel markets, or, as the owner of a full-service agency, catering to the business traveler as well as the leisure traveler. Our program includes complete start-up assistance, site selection and more.

BACKGROUND:
Established: 1982; 1st Franchised: 1982
Franchised Units: 225
Company-Owned Units: 1
Total Units: 226
Dist.: US-178; CAN-4; O'seas-44
North America: 35 States, 1 Province
Density: 26 in NJ, 18 in FL, 14 in CA
Projected New Units (12 Months): 30
Qualifications: 4, 4, 1, 2, 3, 4
Registered:CA,FL,IL,IN,MD,MI,MN,NY, OR,RI,VA,WA,WI,DC, AB

FINANCIAL/TERMS:
Cash Investment: $80K
Total Investment: $120K
Minimum Net Worth: $50K
Fees: Franchise - $14.9K
Royalty - $350/Mo.; Ad. - $50/Mo.
Earnings Claims Statement: No
Term of Contract (Years): 15/15
Avg. # Of Employees: 2 FT, 5 PT
Passive Ownership: Discouraged
Encourage Conversions: Yes
Area Develop. Agreements: Yes/20
Sub-Franchising Contracts: Yes
Expand In Territory: Yes
Space Needs: 600+ SF; SF

SUPPORT & TRAINING:
Financial Assistance Provided: Yes(I)
Site Selection Assistance: Yes
Lease Negotiation Assistance: Yes
Co-Operative Advertising: Yes
Franchisee Assoc./Member: Yes/No
Size Of Corporate Staff: 18
On-Going Support: a,B,C,D,E,G,H,I
Training: 1 Week in NJ; 1 Week in Orlando, FL.

SPECIFIC EXPANSION PLANS:
US: All United States
Canada: All Canada
Overseas: All Countries

UNIGLOBE TRAVEL

1199 W. Pender St., # 900
Vancouver, BC V6E 2R1 CANADA
Tel: (800) 863-1606 (604) 718-2600
Fax: (949) 623-9008
E-Mail: franchise@uniglobetravel.com
Web Site: www.uniglobefranchise.com
Mr. John Henry, SVP Global Franchise Dev.

Entrepreneur has consistently awarded UNIGLOBE TRAVEL the #1 company in travel-agency franchising. All UNIGLOBE travel agency franchisees benefit from programs and systems designed to handle the needs of both the corporate and leisure client. UNIGLOBE franchisees benefit from money-saving automation agreements and top-notch incentive commission programs with major airline, hotel, car rental, tour and cruise-line companies.

BACKGROUND: IFA MEMBER
Established: 1979; 1st Franchised: 1980
Franchised Units: 1,100
Company-Owned Units: 0
Total Units: 1,100
Dist.: US-756; CAN-200; O'seas-100
North America: 50 States, 9 Provinces
Density: 109 in CA,45 in IL,41 in OH
Projected New Units (12 Months): 100
Qualifications: 5, 4, 1, 3, 4, 5
Registered: All States

FINANCIAL/TERMS:
Cash Investment: $2-25K
Total Investment: $21-104K
Minimum Net Worth: $60K
Fees: Franchise - $2-25K
Royalty - $275-550; Ad. - $550
Earnings Claims Statement: No
Term of Contract (Years): 10/5
Avg. # Of Employees: 3 FT, 1 PT
Passive Ownership: Discouraged
Encourage Conversions: Yes
Area Develop. Agreements: Yes/5
Sub-Franchising Contracts: Yes
Expand In Territory: Yes
Space Needs: 1,200 SF; FS, SF, SC, RM, HB

SUPPORT & TRAINING:
Financial Assistance Provided: Yes
Site Selection Assistance: Yes
Lease Negotiation Assistance: Yes
Co-Operative Advertising: Yes
Franchisee Assoc./Member: Yes/No
Size Of Corporate Staff: 100
On-Going Support: B,C,D,e,G,h,I
Training: 3 -5 Days in Irvine, CA.

SPECIFIC EXPANSION PLANS:
US: All United States
Canada: All Canada
Overseas: All Countries

Miscellaneous

Chapter

48

Miscellaneous Industry Profile

Total # Franchisors in Industry Group	128
Total # Franchised Units in Industry Group	7,707
Total # Company-Owned Units in Industry Group	558
Total # Operating Units in Industry Group	8,265
Average # Franchised Units/Franchisor	60.2
Average # Company-Owned Units/Franchisor	4.4
Average # Total Units/Franchisor	64.6
Ratio of Total # Franchised Units/Total # Company-Owned Units	13.8:1
Industry Survey Participants	34
Representing % of Industry	26.6%
Average Franchise Fee*:	$36.4K
Average Total Investment*:	$175.6K
Average On-Going Royalty Fee*:	6.3%

*If a range was provided, the mid-point of the range was used. See detailed profiles for actual ranges.

Five Largest Participants in Survey

Company	# Franchised Units	# Co-Owned Units	# Total Units	Franchise Fee	On-Going Royalty	Total Investment
1. Matco Tools	1,451	8	1,459	0%	0%	$62-160
2. Culligan	647	74	721	$5K	3-5%	$103-225K
3. Color Your Carpet	256	1	257	$15K	3%	$39-49K
4. Rezcity.com	225	2	227	$1K/25K Pop.	0%	$3-40K
5. Swyrich Corportion/Hall of Names	219	0	219	$5K	Varies	$10-30K

All of the data provided are proprietary and should not be quoted without acknowledging *Bond's Franchise Guide.*

AIR BROOK LIMOUSINE

P. O. Box 123
Rochelle Park, NJ 07662
Tel: (201) 368-3974
Fax: (201) 368-2247
E-Mail: airbrook@erols.com
Web Site: www.airbrook.com
Mr. Jim Dziekonski, Franchise Director

Limousine Service / Ground Transportation.

BACKGROUND:
Established: 1969; 1st Franchised: 1971
Franchised Units: 73
Company-Owned Units: 0
Total Units: 73
Dist.: US-73; CAN-0; O'seas-0
North America: 1 State
Density: 73 in NJ
Projected New Units (12 Months): 10
Qualifications: 2, 2, 2, 2, 3, 4
Registered: NR

FINANCIAL/TERMS:
Cash Investment: $5.5-11K
Total Investment: $10.5-20K
Minimum Net Worth: NA
Fees: Franchise - $7.5-12.5K
Royalty - 35%; Ad. - 0%
Earnings Claims Statement: No
Term of Contract (Years): 10/2
Avg. # Of Employees: 2 FT
Passive Ownership: Not Allowed
Encourage Conversions: NA
Area Develop. Agreements: No
Sub-Franchising Contracts: No
Expand In Territory: Yes
Space Needs: NA SF; NA

SUPPORT & TRAINING:
Financial Assistance Provided: Yes(D)
Site Selection Assistance: NA
Lease Negotiation Assistance: NA
Co-Operative Advertising: NA
Franchisee Assoc./Member: No
Size Of Corporate Staff: 112
On-Going Support: A,B,C,D,G,H,I
Training: 5 Days Rochelle Park, NJ.

SPECIFIC EXPANSION PLANS:
US: NJ Only
Canada: No
Overseas: No

<< >>

AIT FREIGHT SYSTEMS

P. O. Box 66730
Chicago, IL 60666
Tel: (800) 323-6649 + 405 (630) 766-8300
Fax: (630) 775-1410
E-Mail: pstrompolis@aitworldwide.com
Web Site: www.aitworldwide.com
Mr. Paul Strompolis, Corporate Development

Freight forwarder - international and domestic.

BACKGROUND:
Established: 1979; 1st Franchised: 1988
Franchised Units: 17
Company-Owned Units: 10
Total Units: 27
Dist.: US-27; CAN-0; O'seas-0
North America: 16 States
Density: 2 in TX, 2 in NC, 1 in IL
Projected New Units (12 Months): 2
Qualifications: 4, 5, 5, 3, 4, 4
Registered: CA,IL,NY

FINANCIAL/TERMS:
Cash Investment: $25-50K
Total Investment: $46K
Minimum Net Worth: $46K
Fees: Franchise - $13K
Royalty - 12.8%; Ad. - 1%
Earnings Claims Statement: Yes
Term of Contract (Years): 20/10
Avg. # Of Employees: 5 FT
Passive Ownership: Discouraged
Encourage Conversions: No
Area Develop. Agreements: Yes/Contract
Sub-Franchising Contracts: No
Expand In Territory: No
Space Needs: 10,000 SF; FS

SUPPORT & TRAINING:
Financial Assistance Provided: Yes
Site Selection Assistance: Yes
Lease Negotiation Assistance: No
Co-Operative Advertising: Yes
Franchisee Assoc./Member: No
Size Of Corporate Staff: 35
On-Going Support: A,D,E,I
Training: 2 Days Chicago, IL.

SPECIFIC EXPANSION PLANS:
US: Southwest, Northeast
Canada: All Canada
Overseas: No

<< >>

ATLANTIC MOWER PARTS & SUPPLIES

13421 S.W. 14th Pl.
Ft. Lauderdale, FL 33325
Tel: (954) 474-4942
Fax: (954) 475-0414
E-Mail:
Web Site: www.ampsdist.com.com/website.htm
Mr. Gene Bettelli, President

Lawn mower replacement after-market. Parts for national brands (Snapper, Toro, MTD, Murray, etc.).

BACKGROUND:
Established: 1978; 1st Franchised: 1988
Franchised Units: 12
Company-Owned Units: 1
Total Units: 13
Dist.: US-15; CAN-0; O'seas-0
North America: 1 State
Density: 15 in FL
Projected New Units (12 Months): 5
Qualifications: 2, 3, 3, 4, 1, 5
Registered: FL

FINANCIAL/TERMS:
Cash Investment: $~45K
Total Investment: $45K
Minimum Net Worth: NR
Fees: Franchise - $15.9K
Royalty - 5%; Ad. - 0.5%
Earnings Claims Statement: No
Term of Contract (Years): 10/10
Avg. # Of Employees: 1 FT
Passive Ownership: Allowed
Encourage Conversions: Yes
Area Develop. Agreements: Yes/1
Sub-Franchising Contracts: Yes
Expand In Territory: Yes
Space Needs: 250 SF; Warehouse

SUPPORT & TRAINING:
Financial Assistance Provided: No
Site Selection Assistance: Yes
Lease Negotiation Assistance: Yes
Co-Operative Advertising: No
Franchisee Assoc./Member: NR
Size Of Corporate Staff: 3
On-Going Support: B,C,D,E
Training: 5 Days Headquarters; 5 Days On-Site.

SPECIFIC EXPANSION PLANS:
US: All United States
Canada: No
Overseas: No

<< >>

BEVINCO

505 Consumers Rd., # 510
Toronto, ON M2J 4V8 CANADA
Tel: (888) 238-4626 (416) 490-6266
Fax: (416) 490-6899
E-Mail: info@bevinco.com
Web Site: www.bevinco.com
Mr. Barry Driedger, President/CEO

Liquor inventory auditing and control service for bars and restaurants. Utilizing our computerized weighing system, franchisees will identify and resolve the shrinkage problems associated with the bar business. On-going weekly accounts make for an excellent executive income.

BACKGROUND: IFA MEMBER
Established: 1987; 1st Franchised: 1990
Franchised Units: 200
Company-Owned Units: 1
Total Units: 201
Dist.: US-139; CAN-36; O'seas-20
North America: 40 States, 7 Provinces
Density: 9 in CA, 8 in OH, 6 in TX
Projected New Units (12 Months): 50
Qualifications: 3, 4, 4, 3, 3, 3
Registered: All States

FINANCIAL/TERMS:
Cash Investment: $40K
Total Investment: $40K
Minimum Net Worth: $40K
Fees: Franchise - $39.9K
Royalty - $12/Audit; Ad. - $2/Audit
Earnings Claims Statement: No
Term of Contract (Years): 5/5
Avg. # Of Employees: 1-3 FT, 1-3 PT
Passive Ownership: Not Allowed
Encourage Conversions: NA
Area Develop. Agreements: Yes/5
Sub-Franchising Contracts: No
Expand In Territory: NA
Space Needs: NR SF; NA

SUPPORT & TRAINING:
Financial Assistance Provided: Yes(I)
Site Selection Assistance: NA
Lease Negotiation Assistance: NA
Co-Operative Advertising: NA
Franchisee Assoc./Member: Yes/Yes
Size Of Corporate Staff: 4
On-Going Support: A,b,D,G,H,I
Training: 10 Days at Head Office in Toronto; 5 Days Franchisee's Location.

SPECIFIC EXPANSION PLANS:
US: All United States
Canada: All Canada
Overseas: All Countries

<< >>

COLOR YOUR CARPET

767 Blanding Blvd., # 112
Orange Park, FL 32065
Tel: (800) 321-6567 (904) 272-6567
Fax:
E-Mail: cdimperio@carpetcolor.com
Web Site: www.coloryourcarpet.com
Ms. Connie D'Imperio, President

No competition! The ONLY on-site, 100% carpet dyeing and color restoration service in the world. Advanced technology provides cost-effective, convenient alternative to costly carpet replacement. Design dyeing, spot dyeing and color matching taught by experts. Large protected territory expansion program.

BACKGROUND:
Established: 1979; 1st Franchised: 1990
Franchised Units: 256
Company-Owned Units: 1
Total Units: 257
Dist.: US-112; CAN-48; O'seas-32
North America: 14 States, 4 Provinces
Density: 18 in FL, 12 in AB
Projected New Units (12 Months): 24
Qualifications: 3, 4, 1, 4, 5, 5
Registered: FL,HI,IL,MD,MI,MN,OR, VA,WA,DC

FINANCIAL/TERMS:
Cash Investment: $25-35K
Total Investment: $39-49K
Minimum Net Worth: $150K
Fees: Franchise - $15K
Royalty - 3%; Ad. - 0%
Earnings Claims Statement: Yes
Term of Contract (Years): 5/5
Avg. # Of Employees: 1 FT, 1 PT
Passive Ownership: Allowed
Encourage Conversions: No
Area Develop. Agreements: Yes/10
Sub-Franchising Contracts: Yes
Expand In Territory: Yes
Space Needs: NA SF; HB

SUPPORT & TRAINING:
Financial Assistance Provided: No
Site Selection Assistance: NA
Lease Negotiation Assistance: NA
Co-Operative Advertising: NA
Franchisee Assoc./Member: Yes/Yes
Size Of Corporate Staff: 6
On-Going Support: A,B,C,D,E,F,G,H,I
Training: 2 Weeks Home Study; 1 Week Orange Park, FL; 1 Week On-the-Job Existing Franchisee's Site.

SPECIFIC EXPANSION PLANS:
US: All United States
Canada: All Canada
Overseas: Primarily South America, Europe, Asia, Middle East

<< >>

COMPUTER BUILDERS WAREHOUSE

1993 Tobsal Ct.
Warren, MI 48091
Tel: (888) 668-0900 (586) 756-2600
Fax: (586) 756-8715
E-Mail: sshabander@cbwstores.com
Web Site: www.cbwstores.com
Mr. Michael Murray, Vice President Marketing

Exciting and unique franchise opportunity. Our franchisees take advantage of our state of the art manufacturing and warehouse facility. The testing center provides customers with reliable built to order computer products, while in-store service labs provide complete computer service, parts and components. A turnkey operation is provided.

BACKGROUND:
Established: 1990; 1st Franchised: 1999
Franchised Units: 10
Company-Owned Units: 3
Total Units: 13
Dist.: US-5; CAN-0; O'seas-0
North America: 1 State
Density: 5 in MI
Projected New Units (12 Months): 15
Qualifications: 5, 3, 2, 3, 3, 5
Registered: CA,FL,HI,IL,IN,MD,MI,MN, NY,ND,OR,RI,SD,VA,WA,WI,DC

FINANCIAL/TERMS:
Cash Investment: $100K
Total Investment: $300-350K
Minimum Net Worth: $200K
Fees: Franchise - $35K
Royalty - 1.5%; Ad. - 2%
Earnings Claims Statement: No
Term of Contract (Years): 10/5
Avg. # Of Employees: 7 FT, 2 PT
Passive Ownership: Not Allowed
Encourage Conversions: Yes
Area Develop. Agreements: No
Sub-Franchising Contracts: No
Expand In Territory: No
Space Needs: 3,500 SF; FS,SF,SC

SUPPORT & TRAINING:
Financial Assistance Provided: Yes(I)
Site Selection Assistance: Yes
Lease Negotiation Assistance: Yes
Co-Operative Advertising: Yes
Franchisee Assoc./Member: No
Size Of Corporate Staff: 75
On-Going Support: B,C,D,E,F,G,H
Training: 3 Weeks at Company Headquarters; 2-4 Weeks On-Site.

SPECIFIC EXPANSION PLANS:
US: All United States
Canada: No
Overseas: No

<< >>

CULLIGAN

One Culligan Pkwy.
Northbrook, IL 60062-6209

Tel: (800) CULLIGAN (847) 205-6000
Fax: (847) 205-6005
E-Mail: bweckstein@culligan.com
Web Site: www.culligan.com
Mr. Bill Weckstein, Manager Franchise Operations

CULLIGAN is looking for franchisees to start a business selling 5 gallon bottles of water for delivery to homes and offices. CULLIGAN is a manufacturer of water conditioners, filters and drinking water devices.

BACKGROUND: IFA MEMBER
Established: 1936; 1st Franchised: 1939
Franchised Units: 647
Company-Owned Units: 74
Total Units: 721
Dist.: US-673; CAN-48; O'seas-0
North America: 50 States
Density: 40 in MN, 40 in IA, 35 in WI
Projected New Units (12 Months): 8
Qualifications: 5, 5, 2, 3, 4, 4
Registered: All States

FINANCIAL/TERMS:
Cash Investment: $103-225K
Total Investment: $103-225K
Minimum Net Worth: $250K
Fees: Franchise - $5K
Royalty - 3-5%; Ad. - 0%
Earnings Claims Statement: No
Term of Contract (Years): 10/10
Avg. # Of Employees: 6 FT
Passive Ownership: Discouraged
Encourage Conversions: Yes
Area Develop. Agreements: No
Sub-Franchising Contracts: No
Expand In Territory: No
Space Needs: 2,500 SF; SF

SUPPORT & TRAINING:
Financial Assistance Provided: No
Site Selection Assistance: No
Lease Negotiation Assistance: No
Co-Operative Advertising: No
Franchisee Assoc./Member: Yes
Size Of Corporate Staff: 200
On-Going Support: C,D,G,H,I
Training: 1 Week Chicago, IL; 1 Week On-Site.

SPECIFIC EXPANSION PLANS:
US: All United States
Canada: All Canada
Overseas: Mexico, South America

<< >>

DISCOUNT IMAGING
206 Texas Ave.
Monroe, LA 71201
Tel: (800) 579-8258 (318) 324-8977
Fax: (318) 324-1211
E-Mail: paulm@discountimaging.com
Web Site: www.difcorp.com
Mr. Timothy S. Kerry, Director of Franchising

Single source providers of printer, fax and copier supplies and service to businesses of all types. Program features proprietary product line, purchasing power and other support services.

BACKGROUND: IFA MEMBER
Established: 1995; 1st Franchised: 1998
Franchised Units: 4
Company-Owned Units: 2
Total Units: 6
Dist.: US-13; CAN-0; O'seas-0
North America: 5 States
Density: 2 in AR, 1 in FL, 1 in AL
Projected New Units (12 Months): 2
Qualifications: 4, 3, 2, 1, 4, 5
Registered: FL,TX

FINANCIAL/TERMS:
Cash Investment: $25-40K
Total Investment: $56-62K
Minimum Net Worth: $75K
Fees: Franchise - $25K
Royalty - 3-6%; Ad. - 0%
Earnings Claims Statement: No
Term of Contract (Years): 10/5
Avg. # Of Employees: 4 FT, 1 PT
Passive Ownership: Discouraged
Encourage Conversions: No
Area Develop. Agreements: No
Sub-Franchising Contracts: No
Expand In Territory: Yes
Space Needs: NR SF; HB

SUPPORT & TRAINING:
Financial Assistance Provided: Yes(I)
Site Selection Assistance: Yes
Lease Negotiation Assistance: No
Co-Operative Advertising: No
Franchisee Assoc./Member: No
Size Of Corporate Staff: 6
On-Going Support: C,d,E,F,G,h,I
Training: 2 Weeks Corporate; 4 Weeks On-Site.

SPECIFIC EXPANSION PLANS:
US: South, Southeast
Canada: All Canada
Overseas: No

<< >>

EMBROIDME
1801 Australian Ave. S.
West Palm Beach, FL 33409
Tel: (800) 727-6720 (561) 868-1453
Fax: (561) 640-6062
E-Mail: csimnick@embroidme.com
Web Site: www.embroidme.com
Mr. Christopher Simnick, VP Franchise Development

The custom apparel and merchandise industry is exploding and embroidery is everywhere. To capitalize on this explosion, EMBROIDME has launched a revolution in the custom embroidery industry. At EMBROIDME, we are 'casually dressing America,' not only in our retail showrooms and through our corporate marketing program, but across the internet as well. We invite you to learn more about our unique, turn-key EMBROIDME concept, system and cutting edge franchise. Call 800/727-6720 or www.EmbroidMe.com.

BACKGROUND: IFA MEMBER
Established: 2000; 1st Franchised: 2001
Franchised Units: 205
Company-Owned Units: 0
Total Units: 205
Dist.: US-155; CAN-3; O'seas-2
North America: 21 States, 1 Province
Density: 24 in TX, 13 in CA, 12 in FL
Projected New Units (12 Months): 85
Qualifications: 3, 3, 2, 2, 1, 4
Registered: All States

FINANCIAL/TERMS:
Cash Investment: $50-60K
Total Investment: $140-145K
Minimum Net Worth: $50K
Fees: Franchise - $37.5K
Royalty - 5%; Ad. - 1%
Earnings Claims Statement: No
Term of Contract (Years): 35/35
Avg. # Of Employees: 3 FT
Passive Ownership: Discouraged
Encourage Conversions: Yes
Area Develop. Agreements: Yes/Varies
Sub-Franchising Contracts: No
Expand In Territory: Yes
Space Needs: 1,300-1,500 SF; SC

SUPPORT & TRAINING:
Financial Assistance Provided: Yes(I)
Site Selection Assistance: Yes
Lease Negotiation Assistance: Yes
Co-Operative Advertising: Yes
Franchisee Assoc./Member: No
Size Of Corporate Staff: 30
On-Going Support: C,D,E,F,G,H,I
Training: 2 Weeks West Palm Beach, FL;

2 Weeks Franchisee's Location (1 Wk. Technical, 1 Wk. Mktng.)

SPECIFIC EXPANSION PLANS:

US: All United States
Canada: All Canada
Overseas: All Countries

ENGLISH BUTLER CANADA

21 St. Clair Ave. E., # 1101
Toronto, ON M4T 1L9 CANADA
Tel: (416) 966-9802
Fax: (416) 966-9803
E-Mail: nassad@englishbutler.com
Web Site: www.englishbutler.com
Mr. Nicholas Assad, Franchise Director

Elegant, traditional gifts and home decorating accessories. Merchandise ranges from printer to pictures, afghans to table linens and collectibles to seasonal giftware.

BACKGROUND:

Established: 1984; 1st Franchised: 1994
Franchised Units: 20
Company-Owned Units: 4
Total Units: 24
Dist.: US-0; CAN-20; O'seas-0
North America: 3 Provinces
Density: 15 in ON, 3 in NB, 2 in NS
Projected New Units (12 Months): 6-8
Qualifications: 4, 4, 3, 3, 4, 5
Registered: NR

FINANCIAL/TERMS:

Cash Investment: $75K
Total Investment: $250K
Minimum Net Worth: $100K
Fees: Franchise - $25K
Royalty - 6%; Ad. - 0.5%
Earnings Claims Statement: No
Term of Contract (Years): 10/5
Avg. # Of Employees: 2 FT, 3-5 PT
Passive Ownership: Discouraged
Encourage Conversions: No
Area Develop. Agreements: No
Sub-Franchising Contracts: No
Expand In Territory: Yes
Space Needs: 2,000 SF; RM

SUPPORT & TRAINING:

Financial Assistance Provided: Yes(I)
Site Selection Assistance: Yes
Lease Negotiation Assistance: Yes
Co-Operative Advertising: Yes
Franchisee Assoc./Member: Yes/Yes
Size Of Corporate Staff: 7
On-Going Support: B,D,E,F,h
Training: 3 Weeks Corporate Stores.

SPECIFIC EXPANSION PLANS:

US: No
Canada: ON, PQ, AB
Overseas: No

FILTERFRESH

378 University Ave.
Westwood, MA 02090
Tel: (800) 332-6771 (781) 461-8734
Fax: (781) 461-8732
E-Mail: rcohen@filterfresh.com
Web Site: www.filterfresh.com
Mr. Roger Cohen, President

High-tech office coffee service, using a patented single-cup coffeemaker. FILTERFRESH brews coffee by-the-cup from fresh-ground coffee in seconds. Choice exclusive territories are available as a franchise or joint-venture with corporate. The FILTERFRESH franchise provides access to patented equipment, detailed training in sales and service, on-going support and supply services.

BACKGROUND:

Established: 1986; 1st Franchised: 1987
Franchised Units: 60
Company-Owned Units: 10
Total Units: 70
Dist.: US-49; CAN-0; O'seas-1
North America: 25 States
Density: 8 in NY, 6 in NJ, 3 in CA
Projected New Units (12 Months): 4
Qualifications: 4, 5, 2, 3, 4, 4
Registered:CA,FL,IL,IN,MD,MI,MN,NY,OR,RI,VA,WA

FINANCIAL/TERMS:

Cash Investment: $150-500K
Total Investment: $50-500K
Minimum Net Worth: $500K
Fees: Franchise - $24.5K
Royalty - 5%; Ad. - 2%
Earnings Claims Statement: No
Term of Contract (Years): 10/10
Avg. # Of Employees: 4 FT, 2 PT
Passive Ownership: Not Allowed
Encourage Conversions: NA
Area Develop. Agreements: No
Sub-Franchising Contracts: No
Expand In Territory: Yes
Space Needs: 1,500 SF; Warehouse

SUPPORT & TRAINING:

Financial Assistance Provided: Yes(I)
Site Selection Assistance: Yes
Lease Negotiation Assistance: No
Co-Operative Advertising: Yes
Franchisee Assoc./Member: Yes/No
Size Of Corporate Staff: 30
On-Going Support: A,B,C,D,E,F,G,H,I
Training: 1 Week Montreal, PQ; 2 Weeks On-Site; 1 Week Westwood, MA.

SPECIFIC EXPANSION PLANS:

US: All United States
Canada: No
Overseas: All Countries

GLASS MAGNUM

5812 Southwest Caraway Court
Portland, OR 97219
Tel: (503) 254-0047
Fax: (503) 612-9441
E-Mail: glassmagnumglassservices@yahoo.com
Web Site: www.worldfranchising.com/website.htm
Mr. Gary Cayton, President

Rock chip repair and crack repair of windshields. Restructure windscreens in planes and helicopters. Crystal and accent glass repair and restructuring. Plate glass repair - holes and cracks.

BACKGROUND:

Established: 1982; 1st Franchised: 1990
Franchised Units: 21
Company-Owned Units: 1
Total Units: 22
Dist.: US-21; CAN-0; O'seas-0
North America: 5 States
Density: 14 in OR, 2 in WA, 2 in HI
Projected New Units (12 Months): 20
Qualifications: 3, 2, 1, 1, 2, 5
Registered: HI,OR,WA

FINANCIAL/TERMS:

Cash Investment: $6-8K
Total Investment: $6-8K
Minimum Net Worth: $10K
Fees: Franchise - $5K
Royalty - 5%; Ad. - 1%
Earnings Claims Statement: No
Term of Contract (Years): 5/5
Avg. # Of Employees: 1 FT
Passive Ownership: Not Allowed
Encourage Conversions: Yes
Area Develop. Agreements: Yes/5
Sub-Franchising Contracts: Yes
Expand In Territory: Yes
Space Needs: NR SF; NA

SUPPORT & TRAINING:

Financial Assistance Provided: Yes(I)
Site Selection Assistance: NA
Lease Negotiation Assistance: NA
Co-Operative Advertising: Yes
Franchisee Assoc./Member: No
Size Of Corporate Staff: 1

On-Going Support: B,D,F,G,I
Training: 300 Hours in Beaverton, OR.
SPECIFIC EXPANSION PLANS:
US: All United States
Canada: Vancouv/Victoria
Overseas: No

<< >>

INSTANT IMPRINTS

10170 Huennekens St.
San Diego, CA 92121
Tel: (800) 542-3437 (858) 569-9937
Fax: (858) 453-6513
E-Mail: john@instantimprints.com
Web Site: www.instantimprints.com
Mr. John Canchola, Vice President

INSTANT IMPRINTS successfully merges the screen printing, embroidery, sign and promotional products industries into a "one-stop shop" with an identifiable brand name and an intelligent approach to marketing and sales. We have developed turn-key solutions for newcomers, as well as crafted benefits and new systems for seasoned industry veterans. We are determined to be # 1 in the industry.

BACKGROUND: IFA MEMBER
Established: 1992; 1st Franchised: 2002
Franchised Units: 65
Company-Owned Units: 2
Total Units: 67
Dist.: US-67; CAN-0; O'seas-0
North America: 9 States
Density: 13 in CA, 10 in CO, 7 in TX
Projected New Units (12 Months): 70
Qualifications: 3, 4, 1, 3, 3, 4
Registered: CA,FLKHI,IL,MD,MI,NY,OR,WA
FINANCIAL/TERMS:
Cash Investment: $39K
Total Investment: $150-190K
Minimum Net Worth: $150K
Fees: Franchise - $25K
Royalty - 5%; Ad. - 1.5%
Earnings Claims Statement: No
Term of Contract (Years): 15/15
Avg. # Of Employees: 2 FT, 1 PT
Passive Ownership: Discouraged
Encourage Conversions: Yes
Area Develop. Agreements: Yes/15
Sub-Franchising Contracts: Yes
Expand In Territory: Yes
Space Needs: 1,500 SF; SC
SUPPORT & TRAINING:
Financial Assistance Provided: Yes(I)
Site Selection Assistance: Yes
Lease Negotiation Assistance: No
Co-Operative Advertising: Yes
Franchisee Assoc./Member: No
Size Of Corporate Staff: 12
On-Going Support: D,E,G,h,I
Training: 2 Weeks San Diego, CA; 5 Days On-Site.
SPECIFIC EXPANSION PLANS:
US: All United States
Canada: All Canada
Overseas: Yes, with Area Development Agreement

<< >>

INTERQUEST DETECTION CANINES

21900 Tomball Pkwy.
Houston, TX 77070-1526
Tel: (800) 481-7768 (281) 320-1231
Fax: (281) 320-2512
E-Mail: mferdi@interquestfranchise.com
Web Site: www.interquestfranchise.com
Mr. Michael P. Ferdinand, VP Franchise Operations

INTERQUEST provides a home-based business opportunity incorporating the use of scent-trained canines to detect the presence of contraband in schools and industry. Limited competition, with great territories available throughout the US.

BACKGROUND: IFA MEMBER
Established: 1988; 1st Franchised: 1999
Franchised Units: 38
Company-Owned Units: 2
Total Units: 40
Dist.: US-40; CAN-0; O'seas-0
North America: NR
Density: 8 in TX, 7 in CA, 3 in LA
Projected New Units (12 Months): 5
Qualifications: 3, 3, 2, 2, 4, 4
Registered: CA,FL,HI,IL,MN,MN,WA
FINANCIAL/TERMS:
Cash Investment: $30-50K
Total Investment: $30-70K
Minimum Net Worth: $250K
Fees: Franchise - $30K
Royalty - 6%; Ad. - 1%
Earnings Claims Statement: No
Term of Contract (Years): 10/10
Avg. # Of Employees: 1-3 FT
Passive Ownership: Discouraged
Encourage Conversions: NA
Area Develop. Agreements: No
Sub-Franchising Contracts: No
Expand In Territory: Yes
Space Needs: NA SF; HB
SUPPORT & TRAINING:
Financial Assistance Provided: Yes(I)
Site Selection Assistance: Yes
Lease Negotiation Assistance: NA
Co-Operative Advertising: NA
Franchisee Assoc./Member: No
Size Of Corporate Staff: 10
On-Going Support: a,b,C,d,G,h,I
Training: 2 Weeks Houston, TX.
SPECIFIC EXPANSION PLANS:
US: Southeast, Northeast
Canada: No
Overseas: No

<< >>

MATCO TOOLS

4403 Allen Rd.
Stowe, OH 44224-1096
Tel: (800) 368-6651 (330) 929-4949
Fax: (330) 926-5325
E-Mail: matcowf@franchisehub.com
Web Site: www.matcotools.com
Ms. Angie McCartney, Franchise Administration

Sales of automotive tools, equipment and computerized diagnostic equipment to professional automotive service technicians and repair center owners. MATCO TOOLS is a home-based franchise that is owner-operated. Our business features weekly sales and service via mobile distribution. We offer exclusive territories, outstanding initial and continuing training and personalized business consultation. MATCO TOOLS and/or SBA loan financing.

BACKGROUND: IFA MEMBER
Established: 1979; 1st Franchised: 1993
Franchised Units: 1,451
Company-Owned Units: 8
Total Units: 1,459

Dist.: US-1,438; CAN-0; O'seas-0
North America: 50 States
Density: 177 in CA, 126 in TX, 75 FL
Projected New Units (12 Months): 251
Qualifications: 3, 2, 2, 2, 3, 5
Registered: All States

FINANCIAL/TERMS:
Cash Investment: $20-30K
Total Investment: $62-160K
Minimum Net Worth: $50K
Fees: Franchise - $0
Royalty - 0%; Ad. - 0%
Earnings Claims Statement: No
Term of Contract (Years): 10/10
Avg. # Of Employees: 1 FT
Passive Ownership: Discouraged
Encourage Conversions: No
Area Develop. Agreements: No
Sub-Franchising Contracts: No
Expand In Territory: Yes
Space Needs: NA SF; HB

SUPPORT & TRAINING:
Financial Assistance Provided: Yes
Site Selection Assistance: NA
Lease Negotiation Assistance: NA
Co-Operative Advertising: NA
Franchisee Assoc./Member: Yes/Yes
Size Of Corporate Staff: 185
On-Going Support: A,B,C,D,E,F,GH,I
Training: 10 Days Corporate Office, 3 Weeks On-Site/Field Training.

SPECIFIC EXPANSION PLANS:
US: All United States
Canada: No
Overseas: No

<< >>

METAL SUPERMARKETS INTERNATIONAL

170 Wilkinson Rd., # 17 &18
Brampton, ON L6T 4Z5 CANADA
Tel: (800) 807-8755 (905) 459-0466 + 227
Fax: (905) 459-3690
E-Mail: aarminen@metalsupermarkets.com
Web Site: www.metalsupermarkets.com
Mr. Andrew Arminen, VP Franchise Division

METAL SUPERMARKETS is a highly specialized supplier of small quantities of virtually all types and forms of metal. Customers are maintenance departments of all types of industries. As 'convenience stores of the metal industry,' we have no minimum order We offer fast delivery, custom cutting and can source rare metals.

BACKGROUND: IFA MEMBER
Established: 1985; 1st Franchised: 1987
Franchised Units: 60
Company-Owned Units: 21
Total Units: 81
Dist.: US-24; CAN-26; O'seas-31
North America: 24 States, 7 Provinces
Density: 13 in ON, 2 in PA, 1 in FL
Projected New Units (12 Months): 8
Qualifications: 5, 3, 3, 3, 3, 5
Registered: All States

FINANCIAL/TERMS:
Cash Investment: $125K
Total Investment: $230-270K
Minimum Net Worth: $350K
Fees: Franchise - $39.5K
Royalty - 6%; Ad. - 0%
Earnings Claims Statement: No
Term of Contract (Years): 10/10
Avg. # Of Employees: 3 FT, 1 PT
Passive Ownership: Discouraged
Encourage Conversions: Yes
Area Develop. Agreements: Yes/10
Sub-Franchising Contracts: No
Expand In Territory: Yes
Space Needs: 4,000 SF; Industrial Park

SUPPORT & TRAINING:
Financial Assistance Provided: No
Site Selection Assistance: Yes
Lease Negotiation Assistance: Yes
Co-Operative Advertising: No
Franchisee Assoc./Member: Yes/Yes
Size Of Corporate Staff: 15
On-Going Support: C,D,E,F,G,h,I
Training: 1 Week in Toronto, ON; 2 Weeks Corporate Store; 2 Weeks Own Store.

SPECIFIC EXPANSION PLANS:
US: All United States
Canada: PQ
Overseas: Europe

<< >>

PIRTEK USA

501 Haverty Ct.
Rockledge, FL 32955
Tel: (888) 774-7835 (321) 504-4422
Fax: (321) 504-4433
E-Mail: franchises@pirtekusa.com
Web Site: www.pirtekusa.com
Mr. Gwyn O'Kane, VP Franchise Development

PIRTEK is the world's leading service provider of hydraulic hoses, couplings, metric and standard fittings, and other accessories for on-site hose replacement. The PIRTEK brand is associated with the highest levels of service, responsiveness, and dependability. Hundreds of service centers and more than 1,000 mobile service vehicles worldwide. Over-the-counter service, fully-equipped mobile service vans for 24-hour emergency on-site service, and preventive maintenance programs help reduce downtime.

BACKGROUND: IFA MEMBER
Established: 1980; 1st Franchised: 1996
Franchised Units: 32
Company-Owned Units: 1
Total Units: 33
Dist.: US-32; CAN-0; O'seas-262
North America: 22 States
Density: 5 in FL, 2 in MN, 2 in TX
Projected New Units (12 Months): 10
Qualifications: 5, 3, 2, 2, 2, 4
Registered:CA,FL,IL,IN,MD,MI,MN,NY,OR,RI,VA,WA,WI

FINANCIAL/TERMS:
Cash Investment: $100K
Total Investment: $100-150K
Minimum Net Worth: $350K
Fees: Franchise - $45K
Royalty - 4%; Ad. - 1.5-3%
Earnings Claims Statement: No
Term of Contract (Years): 10/10/10
Avg. # Of Employees: 6 FT
Passive Ownership: Allowed
Encourage Conversions: NA
Area Develop. Agreements: No
Sub-Franchising Contracts: No
Expand In Territory: Yes
Space Needs: 2,500-3,000 SF; Industrial Park

SUPPORT & TRAINING:
Financial Assistance Provided: Yes(I)
Site Selection Assistance: Yes
Lease Negotiation Assistance: Yes
Co-Operative Advertising: No
Franchisee Assoc./Member: Yes/Yes
Size Of Corporate Staff: 35
On-Going Support: C,D,E,G
Training: 3 Weeks Franchisee Training; 2 Weeks Ops. Mgr./Msst Training; 1 Week Admin. Training; All in Rockledge, FL.

SPECIFIC EXPANSION PLANS:
US: All United States
Canada: No
Overseas: No

<< >>

PODS

6061 45th St. N.
St. Petersburg, FL 33714
Tel: (888) 776-7637 (727) 528-6303
Fax: (813) 354-4664
E-Mail: dlemay@podsusa.com
Web Site: www.podsusa.com
Mr. Don LeMay, Franchise Dewvelopment

Portable on demand storage. PODS utilizes a specially equipped truck and patented hydraulic lift technology to deliver, retrieve and store up to an 8x8x16 foot container. Revolutionizing the moving and storage industry

BACKGROUND: IFA MEMBER
Established: 1997; 1st Franchised: 1998
Franchised Units: 55
Company-Owned Units: 11
Total Units: 66
Dist.: US-37; CAN-0; O'seas-0
North America: 9 States
Density: FL, MN, IN
Projected New Units (12 Months): 25
Qualifications: 5, 4, 1, 1, 3, 3
Registered: FL,IN,VA
FINANCIAL/TERMS:
Cash Investment: $400K
Total Investment: $1.5MM+
Minimum Net Worth: $1MM
Fees: Franchise - $75K
Royalty - 8%/$3.5K/Mo.; Ad. - 2%
Earnings Claims Statement: No
Term of Contract (Years): 20/10
Avg. # Of Employees: 5 FT
Passive Ownership: Allowed
Encourage Conversions: NA
Area Develop. Agreements: No
Sub-Franchising Contracts: No
Expand In Territory: No
Space Needs: 20,000 SF; Warehouse
SUPPORT & TRAINING:
Financial Assistance Provided: No
Site Selection Assistance: Yes
Lease Negotiation Assistance: No
Co-Operative Advertising: No
Franchisee Assoc./Member: Yes/Yes
Size Of Corporate Staff: 110
On-Going Support: A,b,d,E,G,H,I
Training: 2 Weeks St. Petersburg, FL.
SPECIFIC EXPANSION PLANS:
US: NE, SE, Midwest
Canada: No
Overseas: No

<< >>

PURIFIED WATER TO GO

5160 S. Valley View Blvd., # 102
Las Vegas, NV 89118-1778
Tel: (800) 976-9283 (702) 895-9350
Fax: (702) 895-9306
E-Mail: mike@watertogo.com
Web Site: www.watertogo.com
Ms. Stacy Beaudoin, President

PURIFIED WATER TO GO, recently featured on NBC nightly news, is a full-service or express retail outlet, selling purified water by the gallon, purified ice and related products. As the leader in water store franchises, PURIFIED WATER TO GO answers today's need for superior quality drinking water. Water is purified on store premises, and customers are drawn to the appeal of our sparkling clean, blue and white interior design.

BACKGROUND: IFA MEMBER
Established: 1991; 1st Franchised: 1995
Franchised Units: 65
Company-Owned Units: 2
Total Units: 67
Dist.: US-33; CAN-0; O'seas-0
North America: 12 States
Density: 12 in WA, 5 in NV, 5 in NM
Projected New Units (12 Months): 15
Qualifications: 4, 2, 1, 3, 4, 5
Registered: All States
FINANCIAL/TERMS:
Cash Investment: $25-50K
Total Investment: $75-145K
Minimum Net Worth: $150K
Fees: Franchise - $23-29K
Royalty - 4-6%; Ad. - $150-200/Mo
Earnings Claims Statement: No
Term of Contract (Years): 10/10
Avg. # Of Employees: 1 FT, 1 PT
Passive Ownership: Discouraged
Encourage Conversions: NA
Area Develop. Agreements: Yes/10
Sub-Franchising Contracts: No
Expand In Territory: Yes
Space Needs: 500-1,000 SF; SF, SC
SUPPORT & TRAINING:
Financial Assistance Provided: Yes(I)
Site Selection Assistance: Yes
Lease Negotiation Assistance: Yes
Co-Operative Advertising: Yes
Franchisee Assoc./Member: Yes
Size Of Corporate Staff: 9
On-Going Support: B,C,D,E,F,G,H,I
Training: 5 Days Corporate Office in Las Vegas, NV.
SPECIFIC EXPANSION PLANS:
US: All United States
Canada: All Canada
Overseas: All Countries

<< >>

RAINSOFT

2080 E. Lunt Ave.
Elk Grove Village, IL 60007
Tel: (800) 724-6763 (847) 867-8941
Fax: (970) 663-5343
E-Mail: dmiller@aquion.com
Web Site: www.rainsoft.com
Mr. Don Miller, VP of Business Development

RAINSOFT Water Treament has enjoyed nearly constant expansion in its 51-year history. RAINSOFT provides clean, soft, luxurious great-tasting water to homes and businesses. With a lifetime warranty, one of the strongest in the industry, you know, like our one million plus clients, that you are in good hands. With Franchise-like programs and on-site support before, during and after opening, many dealers are now second-generation businesses with significant cash flow and both passive and active income.

BACKGROUND: IFA MEMBER
Established: 1953; 1st Franchised: 1959
Franchised Units: 190
Company-Owned Units: 0
Total Units: 190
Dist.: US-162; CAN-4; O'seas-24
North America: 36 States, 2 Provinces
Density: 22 in FL, 14 in TX, 10 in MI
Projected New Units (12 Months): 30
Qualifications: 4, 2, 1, 2, 3, 5
Registered: NR
FINANCIAL/TERMS:
Cash Investment: $70-100K
Total Investment: $70-100K
Minimum Net Worth: $100K
Fees: Franchise - $0K
Royalty - 0%; Ad. - 0%
Earnings Claims Statement: No
Term of Contract (Years): 2/2
Avg. # Of Employees: 15 FT, 4 PT
Passive Ownership: Not Allowed
Encourage Conversions: NA
Area Develop. Agreements: No
Sub-Franchising Contracts: No
Expand In Territory: Yes

Space Needs: 2,500 SF; SC

SUPPORT & TRAINING:

Financial Assistance Provided: No
Site Selection Assistance: Yes
Lease Negotiation Assistance: Yes
Co-Operative Advertising: No
Franchisee Assoc./Member: No
Size Of Corporate Staff: 170
On-Going Support: B,C,D,E,G,H,I
Training: One Week Chicago, IL; Up to 6 man - weeks, before/during/after opening new store; Conventions/Meetings twice a year.

SPECIFIC EXPANSION PLANS:

US: All United States
Canada: All Canada
Overseas: All Countries, Emphasis on UK, France, Russia, China

<< >>

RAPID REFILL INK INTERNATIONAL

132 E. Broadway, # 900
Eugene, OR 97401
Tel: (877) 880-4465 (541) 431-4665
Fax: (541) 431-3401
E-Mail: kelly.cahill@rapidrefillink.com
Web Site: www.rapidrefillink.com
Ms. Kelly Cahill, Marketing Director

The leader in low cost inkjet and laser toner cartridges. Fully automated remanufacturing production site with a retail storefront environment. RAPID REFILL INK INTERNATIONAL has a diversified approach to the market and product offering. With the sales strategy and marketing message we have created, we fully anticipate the ability to enter into any market region and quickly gain substantial market share.

BACKGROUND: IFA MEMBER

Established: 2002; 1st Franchised: 2004
Franchised Units: 86
Company-Owned Units: 5
Total Units: 91
Dist.: US-30; CAN-0; O'seas-0
North America: 9 States
Density: 10 in OR, 2 in WA, 2 in CO
Projected New Units (12 Months): 300
Qualifications: 3, 3, 1, 3, 4, 5
Registered: CA,FL,MI,NY,OR,WA

FINANCIAL/TERMS:

Cash Investment: $30K
Total Investment: $100-200K
Minimum Net Worth: NA
Fees: Franchise - $30K
Royalty - 5%; Ad. - 2%
Earnings Claims Statement: NR
Term of Contract (Years): 10/10
Avg. # Of Employees: 2-3 FT, 3-4 PT
Passive Ownership: Discouraged
Encourage Conversions: NA
Area Develop. Agreements: Yes/Varies
Sub-Franchising Contracts: No
Expand In Territory: Yes
Space Needs: 500-1,100 SF; FS, SF, SC

SUPPORT & TRAINING:

Financial Assistance Provided: NA
Site Selection Assistance: Yes
Lease Negotiation Assistance: NA
Co-Operative Advertising: Yes
Franchisee Assoc./Member: No
Size Of Corporate Staff: 10
On-Going Support: A,c,d,E,F,G,I
Training: 10 Days Eugene, OR.

SPECIFIC EXPANSION PLANS:

US: All United States
Canada: Alberta
Overseas: All Countries

REZCITY.COM

560 Sylvan Ave.
Englewood Cliffs, NJ 07632-3104
Tel: (800) 669-9000 + 22 (201) 567-8500 + 22
Fax: (201) 567-3265
E-Mail: mbrent@rezcity.biz
Web Site: www.rezcity.biz
Mr. Michael Y. Brent, President/CEO

REZCITY.COM is an online local city guide combined with an online travel store offering e-commerce solutions to businesses and organizations, plus travel services for 50,000 towns throughout the USA.

BACKGROUND:

Established: 2002; 1st Franchised: 2002
Franchised Units: 225
Company-Owned Units: 2
Total Units: 227
Dist.: US-224; CAN-0; O'seas-0
North America: 38 States
Density: 33 in FL, 26 in NJ, 12 in SC
Projected New Units (12 Months): 300
Qualifications: 3, 3, 3, 2, 3, 2
Registered:CA,FL,IN,MD,MI,MN,NY,OR,VA,WI,DC

FINANCIAL/TERMS:

Cash Investment: $3K
Total Investment: $3-40K
Minimum Net Worth: $10K
Fees: Franchise - $1K/25K Pop.
Royalty - 0%; Ad. - 0%
Earnings Claims Statement: No
Term of Contract (Years): 5/5
Avg. # Of Employees: 1 FT
Passive Ownership: Allowed
Encourage Conversions: NA
Area Develop. Agreements: Yes/5
Sub-Franchising Contracts: Yes
Expand In Territory: No
Space Needs: NA SF; NA

SUPPORT & TRAINING:

Financial Assistance Provided: Yes(D)
Site Selection Assistance: NA
Lease Negotiation Assistance: NA
Co-Operative Advertising: Yes
Franchisee Assoc./Member: No
Size Of Corporate Staff: 18
On-Going Support: A,B,C,d,G,h,I
Training: 15 Hours On-Line Training.

SPECIFIC EXPANSION PLANS:

US: All United States
Canada: No
Overseas: No

SHRED-IT

2794 S. Sheridan Way
Oakville, ON L6J 7T4 CANADA
Tel: (905) 829-2794
Fax: (905) 829-1999
E-Mail: info@shredit.com
Web Site: www.shredit.com
Mr. Brian MacLean, VP Franchise Devel./Ops.

Business service, offering mobile paper shredding and recycling, serving Fortune 1,000 companies, hospitals, medical facilities, banks, financial institutions, investment and professional firms and the government.

BACKGROUND:

Established: 1988; 1st Franchised: 1992
Franchised Units: 53
Company-Owned Units: 65
Total Units: 118
Dist.: US-81; CAN-12; O'seas-25
North America: 35 States, 6 Provinces
Density: 8 in CA, 5 in FL, 4 in OH
Projected New Units (12 Months): 30
Qualifications: 5, 4, 1, 2, 4, 5
Registered: CA,FL,IL,IN,MD,MI,NY,WA,

WI,DC,AB

FINANCIAL/TERMS:

Cash Investment: $200-250K
Total Investment: $400-500K
Minimum Net Worth: $500K
Fees: Franchise - $75K
Royalty - 6%; Ad. - 1.5%
Earnings Claims Statement: No
Term of Contract (Years): 10/10/10
Avg. # Of Employees: 10 FT
Passive Ownership: Not Allowed
Encourage Conversions: NA
Area Develop. Agreements: Yes/10
Sub-Franchising Contracts: No
Expand In Territory: Yes
Space Needs: 1,500 SF; Industrial Flex Space

SUPPORT & TRAINING:

Financial Assistance Provided: No
Site Selection Assistance: Yes
Lease Negotiation Assistance: Yes
Co-Operative Advertising: No
Franchisee Assoc./Member: Yes/Yes
Size Of Corporate Staff: 75
On-Going Support: B,C,D,E,H
Training: 1 Week in Oakville, ON; 1 Week On-Site.

SPECIFIC EXPANSION PLANS:

US: No
Canada: No
Overseas: Asia, E. Europe, S. America

<< >>

SUPPER THYME USA

2536 South 156th Circle
Omaha, NE 68130
Tel: (402) 933-4521
Fax: (402) 614-5900
E-Mail: brett.willenborg@supperthymeusa.com
Web Site: www.supperthymeusa.com
Mr. Brett J. Willenborg, Dir. Franchise Operations

SUPPER THYME USA Franchise Services offers you the opportunity to operate a business, providing supplies, equipment, ingredients and instructions to prepare, on the premises, ready-to-cook entrees to take home, freeze and use as needed for family meals.

BACKGROUND:

Established: 2003; 1st Franchised: 2004
Franchised Units: 2
Company-Owned Units: 1
Total Units: 3
Dist.: US-3; CAN-0; O'seas-0
North America: 2 States
Density: 2 in NE, 1 in MI
Projected New Units (12 Months): 5
Qualifications: 3, 2, 1, 3, 5, 4
Registered: IL,IN,MI,MN,SD,WI

FINANCIAL/TERMS:

Cash Investment: $25-35K
Total Investment: $110-185K
Minimum Net Worth: NA
Fees: Franchise - $35K
Royalty - 6.0%; Ad. - 1%
Earnings Claims Statement: NR
Term of Contract (Years): 5/5
Avg. # Of Employees: 1 ft, 2 pt
Passive Ownership: Not Allowed
Encourage Conversions: Yes
Area Develop. Agreements: No
Sub-Franchising Contracts: Yes
Expand In Territory: Yes
Space Needs: 1,500 SF; FS, SC

SUPPORT & TRAINING:

Financial Assistance Provided: Yes(I)
Site Selection Assistance: Yes
Lease Negotiation Assistance: Yes
Co-Operative Advertising: Yes
Franchisee Assoc./Member: No
Size Of Corporate Staff: 6
On-Going Support: a,B,C,D,E,F,G,H
Training: 2 Weeks Omaha, NE; 1 Week Franchisee city.

SPECIFIC EXPANSION PLANS:

US: Midwest
Canada: No
Overseas: No

<< >>

SUPPLY MASTER USA

6 C White Deer Plaza
Sparta, NJ 07871
Tel: (800) 582-1947 (973) 729-5006
Fax: (973) 729-1975
E-Mail: supplymasterusa@juno.com
Web Site: www.supplymasterusa.com
Mr. Bert Owens, President

Own your own Supply Master USA Mobile Business with Protected Territory for under $23,000 Total Cost. Supply Master USA is a unique mobile Distribution company specializing in High Quality Commercial and Industrial Products on a Business to Business basis. Supply Master USA provides you with the opportunity to make your own decisions to perform to your potential . . . An opportunity that allows you to enjoy the Freedom, Rewards and Personal Satisfaction of being "Your Own Boss."

BACKGROUND:

Established: 1989; 1st Franchised: 2001
Franchised Units: 3
Company-Owned Units: 1
Total Units: 4
Dist.: US-3; CAN-0; O'seas-0
North America: 4 States
Density: 1 in NJ, 1 in IN, 1 in AZ
Projected New Units (12 Months): 5
Qualifications: 3, 4, 2, 2, 4, 5
Registered: IN,NY

FINANCIAL/TERMS:

Cash Investment: $12.9-22.7K
Total Investment: $12.9-22.7K
Minimum Net Worth: $30K
Fees: Franchise - $10K
Royalty - $100/Wk.; Ad. - 1%
Earnings Claims Statement: No
Term of Contract (Years): 20/5
Avg. # Of Employees: 1 FT
Passive Ownership: Not Allowed
Encourage Conversions: NA
Area Develop. Agreements: No
Sub-Franchising Contracts: No
Expand In Territory: Yes
Space Needs: NA SF; NA

SUPPORT & TRAINING:

Financial Assistance Provided: Yes(I)
Site Selection Assistance: Yes
Lease Negotiation Assistance: NA
Co-Operative Advertising: NA
Franchisee Assoc./Member: No
Size Of Corporate Staff: 3
On-Going Support: D
Training: 4 Days New Jersey or Other Suitable Location.

SPECIFIC EXPANSION PLANS:

US: All United States
Canada: All Canada
Overseas: No

<< >>

swyrich

SWYRICH CORPORATION/ HALL OF NAMES

830 Development Dr.
Kingston, ON K7M 5V7 CANADA

Tel: (800) 265-7099 + 230 (613) 384-2257 + 230
Fax: (613) 384-0606
E-Mail: info@swyrich.com
Web Site: www.swyrich.com
Mr. Jim Whidden, Sales Manager

World leader in sales of heraldic materials. Coats of arms, surname histories, first name histories, Scottish clan badges and histories, Irish Sept histories and coats of arms. Regularly updated software. Completely user friendly and fully supported.

BACKGROUND:
Established: 1991; 1st Franchised: 1991
Franchised Units: 219
Company-Owned Units: 0
Total Units: 219
Dist.: US-84; CAN-57; O'seas-84
North America: 30 States, 9 Provinces
Density: 13 in PQ, 7 in TX, 7 in FL
Projected New Units (12 Months): 25
Qualifications: 4, 4, 2, 1, 1, 4
Registered: Lisence agreement.

FINANCIAL/TERMS:
Cash Investment: $5-10K
Total Investment: $10-30K
Minimum Net Worth: $0K
Fees: Franchise - $5K
Royalty - Varies; Ad. - 0%
Earnings Claims Statement: No
Term of Contract (Years): Indef.
Avg. # Of Employees: 1 FT, 1 PT
Passive Ownership: Allowed
Encourage Conversions: Yes
Area Develop. Agreements: No
Sub-Franchising Contracts: No
Expand In Territory: Yes
Space Needs: 50-100 SF; FS, SF, SC, TM, HB

SUPPORT & TRAINING:
Financial Assistance Provided: Yes(D)
Site Selection Assistance: NA
Lease Negotiation Assistance: NA
Co-Operative Advertising: No
Franchisee Assoc./Member: No
Size Of Corporate Staff: 20
On-Going Support: G,I
Training: On-Going On-Line Support; On-Going Telephone Support.

SPECIFIC EXPANSION PLANS:
US: All United States
Canada: All Canada
Overseas: All Countries

<< >>

TWO MEN AND A TRUCK

3400 Belle Chase Way
Lansing, MI 48911
Tel: (800) 345-1070 (517) 394-7210
Fax: (517) 394-7432
E-Mail: franchiseinfo@twomen.com
Web Site: www.twomenandatruck.com
Ms. Shirley Kefgen, Qualifying Specialist

TWO MEN AND A TRUCK is the nation's first and largest local moving franchise. Known as the "Movers Who Care," TWO MEN AND A TRUCK is committed to exceeding customers' expectations. They offer a full range of residential and commercial moving services, as well as boxes and packing supplies.

BACKGROUND: IFA MEMBER
Established: 1985; 1st Franchised: 1989
Franchised Units: 139
Company-Owned Units: 4
Total Units: 143
Dist.: US-138; CAN-0; O'seas-0
North America: 26 States
Density: 23 in MI, 13 in FL, 10 in GA
Projected New Units (12 Months): 24
Qualifications: 3, 4, 1, 3, 5, 5
Registered: CA,FL,IL,IN,MI,MN,NY,OR, RI,WA,WI

FINANCIAL/TERMS:
Cash Investment: $40K+
Total Investment: $89K
Minimum Net Worth: $100K+
Fees: Franchise - $32K
Royalty - 6%; Ad. - 1%
Earnings Claims Statement: Yes
Term of Contract (Years): 5/5
Avg. # Of Employees: 5 FT, 3 PT
Passive Ownership: Discouraged
Encourage Conversions: Yes
Area Develop. Agreements: No
Sub-Franchising Contracts: No
Expand In Territory: Yes
Space Needs: 500+ SF; Varies

SUPPORT & TRAINING:
Financial Assistance Provided: No
Site Selection Assistance: No
Lease Negotiation Assistance: No
Co-Operative Advertising: No
Franchisee Assoc./Member: Yes/Yes
Size Of Corporate Staff: 38
On-Going Support: C,D,G,h,I
Training: 3 Weeks Lansing, MI at Stick Men University.

SPECIFIC EXPANSION PLANS:
US: All United States
Canada: No
Overseas: No

<< >>

UCC TOTALHOME

8450 Broadway, P.O. Box 13006
Merrillville, IN 46410
Tel: (800) 827-6400 (219) 648-7357
Fax: (219) 755-6208
E-Mail: dbowen@ucctotalhome.com
Web Site: www.ucctotalhome.com
Ms. Debbie Bowen, Dir. Franchise Development

UCC TOTALHOME offers consumers the unparalleled opportunity to buy merchandise at manufacturer's invoice cost. Our hundreds of thousands of members purchase directly from more than 800 manufacturers. No mark-up, no middleman, no kidding. UCC TOTALHOME franchise owners enroll members through our time-tested marketing system and service these members with the support of more than 150 specialists at the UCC Corporate Support Center.

BACKGROUND: IFA MEMBER
Established: 1971; 1st Franchised: 1972
Franchised Units: 84
Company-Owned Units: 3
Total Units: 87
Dist.: US-77; CAN-15; O'seas-0
North America: 21 States, 4 Provinces
Density: 10 in MI, 8 in NY, 7 in OH
Projected New Units (12 Months): 8
Qualifications: 4, 4, 1, 3, 1, 5
Registered: All States

FINANCIAL/TERMS:
Cash Investment: $88-237K
Total Investment: $88-237K
Minimum Net Worth: $100K
Fees: Franchise - $35-55K
Royalty - 22%; Ad. - NA
Earnings Claims Statement: No
Term of Contract (Years): 12/12
Avg. # Of Employees: 12 FT, 2 PT
Passive Ownership: Discouraged
Encourage Conversions: NA
Area Develop. Agreements: No
Sub-Franchising Contracts: No
Expand In Territory: No
Space Needs: 4,000-6,000 SF; Business Park

SUPPORT & TRAINING:
Financial Assistance Provided: Yes(B)
Site Selection Assistance: Yes
Lease Negotiation Assistance: No
Co-Operative Advertising: NA
Franchisee Assoc./Member: No
Size Of Corporate Staff: 150
On-Going Support: A,B,C,D,E,G,H,h
Training: 3 Weeks Merrillville, IN; 5 Weeks in an Operating Franchise.

SPECIFIC EXPANSION PLANS:

US:	All United States
Canada:	All Canada
Overseas:	No

UNITED STATES BASKETBALL LEAGUE

46 Quirk Rd.
Milford, CT 06460
Tel: (800) THE USBL (203) 877-9508
Fax: (203) 878-8109
E-Mail: usbl96@aol.com
Web Site: www.usbl.com
Mr. Daniel Meisenheimer, III, President

The USBL is the first and only sports league structured as a franchisor and the only publicly traded sports league (OTCBB: USBL). The USBL is 19 years old with 11 teams and 136 USBL players have made the NBA. Visit the USBL Website at www.usbl.com.

BACKGROUND:

Established: 1985;	1st Franchised: 1990
Franchised Units:	11
Company-Owned Units:	0
Total Units:	11
Dist.:	US-9; CAN-0; O'seas-0
North America:	6 States
Density:	2 in NY, 2 in KS, 1 in FL
Projected New Units (12 Months):	4
Qualifications:	4, 4, 3, 3, 3, 4
Registered:	FL,NY,DC

FINANCIAL/TERMS:

Cash Investment:	$500K
Total Investment:	$500-750K
Minimum Net Worth:	$1MM
Fees: Franchise -	$300K
Royalty - 5%/$25K;	Ad. - 1%/$3K
Earnings Claims Statement:	No
Term of Contract (Years):	10/10
Avg. # Of Employees:	4 FT, 15 PT
Passive Ownership:	Not Allowed
Encourage Conversions:	NA
Area Develop. Agreements:	Yes/10
Sub-Franchising Contracts:	Yes
Expand In Territory:	Yes
Space Needs:	NA SF; FS

SUPPORT & TRAINING:

Financial Assistance Provided:	Yes(D)
Site Selection Assistance:	Yes
Lease Negotiation Assistance:	Yes
Co-Operative Advertising:	Yes
Franchisee Assoc./Member:	Yes/Yes
Size Of Corporate Staff:	8
On-Going Support:	A,b,C,d,e,f,G,h,I
Training:	2 Weeks CT or PA.

SPECIFIC EXPANSION PLANS:

US:	All U.S., East of Miss.
Canada:	All Canada
Overseas:	Europe, Far East

WE THE PEOPLE DOCUMENT SERVICES

1501 State St.
Santa Barbara, CA 93101
Tel: (805) 962-4100
Fax: (805) 962-9602
E-Mail: irad@wethepeopleusa.com
Web Site: www.wethepeopleusa.com
Ms. Melissa Soper, VP Human Resources

Legal Document Service -- alternative to lawyers. We empower people to represent themselves by preparing all the paperwork necessary for them to avoid lawyers in their uncontested legal matters. Fueled by the growing dissatisfaction of millions of Americans with our over-priced, under-responsive legal system, people who need to prepare routine legal paperwork are turning to independent paralegals like WE THE PEOPLE, instead of lawyers.

BACKGROUND: IFA MEMBER

Established: 1985;	1st Franchised: 1996
Franchised Units:	100
Company-Owned Units:	1
Total Units:	101
Dist.:	US-82; CAN-0; O'seas-0
North America:	16 States
Density:	48 in CA, 4 in CO, 3 in AZ
Projected New Units (12 Months):	30
Qualifications:	3, 2, 1, 1, 1, 5
Registered:	CA,FL,HI,IL,IN,MD,MI,MN, NY,OR,VA,WI,DC

FINANCIAL/TERMS:

Cash Investment:	NR
Total Investment:	$125-150K
Minimum Net Worth:	$250K
Fees: Franchise -	$125-150K
Royalty - 0%;	Ad. - 0%
Earnings Claims Statement:	No
Term of Contract (Years):	10/5/2
Avg. # Of Employees:	1 FT
Passive Ownership:	Allowed
Encourage Conversions:	Yes
Area Develop. Agreements:	Yes/10/5
Sub-Franchising Contracts:	Yes
Expand In Territory:	Yes
Space Needs:	NR SF; FS,SF,SC

SUPPORT & TRAINING:

Financial Assistance Provided:	No
Site Selection Assistance:	Yes
Lease Negotiation Assistance:	Yes
Co-Operative Advertising:	Yes
Franchisee Assoc./Member:	No
Size Of Corporate Staff:	60
On-Going Support:	A,B,C,D,E,F,G,H
Training:	1 Week in Santa Barbara, CA.

SPECIFIC EXPANSION PLANS:

US:	All United States, NY
Canada:	No
Overseas:	No

Franchise Attorneys

ALSCHULER GROSSMAN STEIN & KAHAN LLP

1620 26th Street, Fourth Floor, North Tower
Santa Monica, CA 90404
Tel: (310) 907-1000
Fax: (310) 907-2000
Web Site: www.agsk.com
Contact: Ms. Susan Grueneberg
Email: sgrueneberg@agsk.com

PROFILE

In addition to franchise law, the firm is known for its zealous representation in complex business litigation including class action defense, professional liability defense, securities litigation, and patent litigation. The transactional department includes expertise in real estate, intellectual property, mergers and acquisitions, securities, and commercial lending.

BACKGROUND

Firm Established In:	1952
Serving Franchising Community Since:	1971
Full-Time Employees:	250
Full-Time Professionals:	100

Major Franchise Clients in Past 3 Yrs.: The firm represents numerous franchise clients in many areas, including restaurants and food service, transportation, real estate, home services, and recreation and health. The firm also represents non-franchised distribution systems.

MR. WILLIAM A. FINKELSTEIN

Tel: (310) 255-9114
Fax: (310) 907-2114
Email: wfinkelstein@agsk.com

PROFILE

Extensive experience and expertise in all aspects of U.S. and international trademark, unfair competition and licensing law and practice as well as considerable familiarity with related franchising, copyright, marketing, branding, and electronic commerce issues.

BACKGROUND

Year Admitted to the Bar:	1970
Licensed to Practice in:	CA, NY, MA

Education/Honors: University of Virginia, B.A. with Distinction (cum laude); Boston University School of Law, J.D., Am Jur Award for Excellence in Legal History; New York University School of Law, LLM in Trade Regulation

Professional Assns./Membership: International Trademark Association - former President, Board of Directors member and chair of various committees; American Bar Association Forum on Franchising - former Governing Committee member; ABA Intellectual Property Section - former Chair of the Franchising Committee; International Franchise Association

Publications: The Franchise Trademark Handbook, Fundamentals of Franchising, Franchise Law Compliance Manual, and Fundamentals of International Franchising and articles in Franchising World and Tolley's Journal of International Franchising and Distribution Law

PROVIDE LEGAL SERVICES IN

U.S.:	Yes
Canada:	Yes
Overseas:	Yes

MS. SUSAN GRUENEBERG

Tel: (310) 255-9104
Fax: (310) 907-2104
Email: sgrueneberg@agsk.com

PROFILE

Ms. Grueneberg advises clients on laws affecting product and service distribution including franchise and business opportunity laws. This involves structuring distribution programs, regulatory compliance, preparation of disclosure documents, negotiations with franchisees, termination, nonrenewal and transfer issues, the supervision of defense of enforcement actions, litigation and other disputes.

BACKGROUND

Year Admitted to the Bar:	1980
Licensed to Practice in:	CA

Education/Honors: BA cum laude, UCLA (1973); JD, UCLA (1979); US State Department Fellowship (1976-1978); US National Academy of Sciences Fellowship (1979-1981)

Professional Assns./Membership: Chair, ABA Forum on Franchising (2001-2003); Member, IFA Legal/Legislative Committee (1996-Present); Member, Advisory Committee, NASAA Franchise Project Group

Publications: Numerous articles for publications of the America Bar Association Forum on Franchising, the International Franchise Association, the California State Bar, Continuing Education of the Bar and other groups.

PROVIDE LEGAL SERVICES IN

U.S.:	Yes
Canada:	Yes
Overseas:	Yes

MR. ROBERT L. KAHAN

Tel: (310) 255-9187
Fax: (310) 907-2187
Email: bkahan@agsk.com

PROFILE

Mr. Kahan advises and counsels clients in the areas of mergers and acquisitions, financing, and franchising.

BACKGROUND

Year Admitted to the Bar:	1970
Licensed to Practice in:	CA

Education/Honors: BA, University of California, Santa Barbara (1966); JD, UCLA (1969); Senior Editor, UCLA Law Review

Professional Assns./Membership: Member, Legal/Legislative Committee, International Franchise Association, 1983 - , Member, Franchise Development Task Force, California State Senate Select Committee on Small Business Enterprises, 1984-1986; Member, ABA Franchising Subcommittee, Small Business Committee Section of Corporation, Banking and Business Law, 1981-1983; Forum Committee on Franchising, 1981 - ; Chairman, State Bar of California Franchise Legislation Committee, Business Law Section, 1983-1985; Executive Committee, State Bar of California Business Law Section, 1986-1988; Vice Chair/South, 1988

PROVIDE LEGAL SERVICES IN

U.S.:	Yes
Canada:	Yes
Overseas:	Yes

ANGIULI, POZNANSKY, KATKIN & GENTILE, LLP

60 Bay St.
Staten Island, NY 10301
Tel: (718) 816-0005
Fax: (718) 727-5835
Web Site: www.apkgs.com
Contact: Mr. Gary C. Angiuli

PROFILE

Franchise law, commercial transactions, mortgage banking, commercial real estate development, civil litigation, workers' compensation, social security disability, estate planning and matrimonial law.

BACKGROUND

Serving Franchising Community Since:	1990
% of Billable Hrs. to Franchise Clients:	20%

Major Franchise Clients in Past 3 Yrs.: Restaurant Systems, Incorporated, Everything Yogurt, Treat Street, Greenstreet's Grille, Globe Restaurant Group, Goodfellas Pizza and Pasta, Bacchus School of Wine, Traditions and Trust Funeral Pre-Arrangement.

MR. GARY C. ANGIULI

PROFILE

Mr. Angiuli is a founding partner of Angiuli, Pozansky, Katkin & Gentile, LLP. He is highly respected for his competence and experience in commercial real estate development, real estate finance, commercial leasing, business and franchise law. Mr. Angiuli has extensive experience in the preparation of Uniform Franchise Offering Circulars and has successfully brought many start-up franchises to the market. He also has successfully negotiated numerous complex commercial leases, including leases on shopping malls, airports and office space.

BACKGROUND

Year Admitted to the Bar:	1984
Licensed to Practice in:	New York

Education/Honors: The American University, Washington College of Law, Juris Doctor 1983.

Professional Assns./Membership: NYSBA, NYSWCBA, RCBA, IFA.

BALDWIN & HASPEL, LLC

2200 Energy Centre, 1100 Poydras St.
New Orleans, LA 70163-2200
Tel: (504) 585-7711
Fax: (504) 585-7751
Web Site: www.baldwinhaspel.com
Contact: Mr. Leon H. Rittenberg, Jr.

PROFILE
General civil practice, offering comprehensive legal services to businesses and individuals, including litigation, transactional work, real estate, trusts, probate, estate planning and franchise law. Member, Commercial Law Affiliates, with independent firm in principal cities worldwide, through which the firm's clients have access to over 3,000 attorneys.

BACKGROUND
Serving Franchising Community Since: 1983

MR. LEON H. RITTENBERG, JR.

Tel: (504) 585-7855
Email: leonjr@baldwinhaspel.com

PROFILE
Leon J. Rittenberg, Jr. received his Bachelor of Science degree in Economics from the Wharton School of Business of the University of Pennsylvania in 1956 and his law degree from Tulane University in 1959. He was a member of the Tulane Law Review and Order of the Coif. He is a Certified Public Accountant, a Board Certified Tax Law Specialist, an Estate Planning and Administration Specialist and practices in the areas of franchising, commercial transactions, estate planning and litigation.

BACKGROUND
Year Admitted to the Bar: 1959
Licensed to Practice in: Louisiana

Education/Honors: AV Rating - Martindale-Hubbell. BS, University of Pennsylvania, 1956. Juris Doctor, Tulane University, 1959 - Law Review and Order of the Coif.

Professional Assns./Membership: ABA, American Institute of Certified Public Accountants, ABA Forum Committee on Franchising.

BARR & LACAVA

22 Fifth St.
Stamford, CT 06905
Tel: (800) 416-4529 (203) 356-1505
Fax: (203) 357-8397
Contact: Mr. Albert J. Barr

PROFILE
General Practice, Franchising, Franchise Law, Petroleum Marketing Practices, Litigation in all State and Federal Courts, Environmental Law, Real Estate, Corporate, Immigration, Workers' Compensation and Personal Injury.

BACKGROUND
Serving Franchising Community Since: 1981
% of Billable Hrs. to Franchise Clients: 50%

Major Franchise Clients in Past 3 Yrs.: Gasoline and Automotive Service Dealers of America, Inc., Club Sandwich, Inc., Dattilo Petroleum, Inc., Motiva Connecticut Dealers, Amoco Connecticut Dealer Committee, Connecticut Tiger Committee (Exxon Dealers), Numerous Industrial Franchises.

MR. ALBERT J. BARR

Email: AJBARR@Infolaw.com

PROFILE
Albert Barr is active in many community organizations such as the Salvation Army, Stamford Child Care Center, Wilton Youth Football, and Wilton Youth Basketball. He is a member of Legaline for the American Association of Franchises and Dealers.

BACKGROUND
Year Admitted to the Bar: 1974
Licensed to Practice in: Connecticut, US District, 2nd Circuit, US Supreme

Education/Honors: J.D. Seton Hall University School of Law (1974); B.S. in Business Administration Villanova University (1971).

Professional Assns./Membership: Connecticut UST Fund Board, Stamford/Norwalk Connecticut and American Bar Associations Member, Advisory Board, Salvation Army, Stamford Court.

Publications: Opinion-Editorial page of Stamford Advocate regarding service station franchises.

MR. JOHN J. MORGAN

Email: JMORGAN@Infolaw.com

BACKGROUND
Year Admitted to the Bar: 1992
Licensed to Practice in: Connecticut, New York, 2nd Circuit, U.S. Supreme

Education/Honors: J.D. Villanova University School of Law (1992); B.A. State University of New York at Albany (1989).

Professional Assns./Membership: American Bar Association (Litigation and Franchise), Connecticut Bar Association, Stamford/Norwalk Regional Bar Association.

≺≺ ≻≻

BLACKWELL SANDERS PEPER MARTIN

2300 Main St., # 1100
Kansas City, MO 64108
Tel: (816) 983-8000
Fax: (816) 983-9115
Contact: Mr. Donald A. Culp

PROFILE
Firm of 317 lawyers concentrates in all significant practice areas, including: franchising and distribution, intellectual property, labor and employment, securities and finance, real estate, mergers and acquisitions, creditors' rights and bankruptcy, litigation, corporate and organizations, alternative dispute resolution, employee benefits, estate planning and international. 'We Are The Law Firm That Thinks Like Your Business Partner.' SM

BACKGROUND

Serving Franchising Community Since:	1979
% of Billable Hrs. to Franchise Clients:	100%

Major Franchise Clients in Past 3 Yrs.: Batteries Plus, Home Instead Senior Care, Purina Mills, HomeVestors, Kelsey's International, CottageCare, Mr. Goodcents, Red Robin International, RentACenter, Dr. Vinyl.

MR. DONALD A. CULP

Tel: (816) 983-8115
Email: dculp@bspmlaw.com

PROFILE
Former general counsel to 2 international franchisors for 10 years. Heads franchising and distribution practice group of 317 member international firm. Skilled at taking new concepts from inception to implementation. Firm holds annual franchise seminar.

BACKGROUND

Year Admitted to the Bar:	1965
Licensed to Practice in:	Kansas, Missouri

Education/Honors: University of Kansas, JD, 1965. Best Attorneys in America - Franchising. Martindale-Hubbel -AV Rating.

Professional Assns./Membership: American Bar Association, Forum on Franchising, Kansas and Missouri Bar Associations.

PROVIDE LEGAL SERVICES IN

US:	Yes
Overseas:	Japan, Australia, Canada

≺≺ ≻≻

CARTER & TANI

402 E. Roosevelt Rd., #206
Wheaton, IL 60187
Tel: (630) 668-2135
Fax: (630) 668-9009
Web Site: www.cartertani.com
Contact: Ms. Doris Carter
Email: dcarter@cartertani.com

PROFILE
We are experienced and energetic attorneys who have spent most of our professional careers representing franchise clients. We are knowledgeable and advise our clients on structuring franchises, disclosure and nationwide franchise registration, franchise law compliance, co-branding, franchise renewals and transfers, defaults and terminations, acquisitions of franchise systems, resolving franchise disputes, leasing and general business issues. We strive to provide these services in a timely, cost-effective manner. We see the business perspective as well as the legal issues in our client's transactions and plans. We offer counsel with a "can do" attitude. Our goal is to assist you in fulfilling your business objectives within legal boundaries.

BACKGROUND

Firm Established In:	1991
Serving Franchising Community Since:	1977
% of Billable Hrs. to Franchise Clients:	75%
Full-Time Employees:	1
Full-Time Professionals:	2

Major Franchise Clients in Past 3 Yrs.: Franchisors of Restaurant "fast food" operations; Home inspection services; Children's entertainment/education services; Automotive services; Janitorial and sanitation services; Retail home furnishing stores; Decorating services; Business services; Retail Pet Stores; Convenience Stores

MS. DORIS ADKINS CARTER

Email: dcarter@cartertani.com

PROFILE
Franchise and business law as described in the firm profile.

BACKGROUND

Year Admitted to the Bar:	1980
Licensed to Practice in:	Illinois

Education/Honors: J.D. 1980 Loyola University of Chicago (Honors)

Professional Assns./Membership: American Bar Association Forum on Franchising; DuPage County Bar Association - Business Law Committee

PROVIDE LEGAL SERVICES IN

U.S.:	Yes

Canada: No
Overseas: No

MS. CHRISTINE K. TANI

Email: ctani@cartertani.com

PROFILE
Franchise and business law as described in the firm profile.

BACKGROUND
Year Admitted to the Bar: 1977
Licensed to Practice in: Illinois

Education/Honors: J.D. 1977 Chicago-Kent IIT School of Law (Honors)

Professional Assns./Membership: ABA Forum on Franchising, Illinois State Bar Association, DuPage County Bar Association

PROVIDE LEGAL SERVICES IN
U.S.: Yes
Canada: No
Overseas: No

<< >>

CORBALLY, GARTLAND & RAPPLEYEA, LLP

35 Market St.
Poughkeepsie, NY 12601
Tel: (914) 454-1111
Fax: (914) 454-4857
Web Site: www.CGRlaw.com
Contact: Mr. Vincent L. DeBiase
Other Offices In: Millbrook, NY, Rhinebeck, NY

PROFILE
Firm was founded in 1876. Serves businesses and individuals from New York City to Albany. Regularly represent national companies doing business in New York.

BACKGROUND
Firm Established In: 1876
Serving Franchising Community Since: 1982
% of Billable Hrs. to Franchise Clients: 50-60%
Full-Time Employees: 52
Full-Time Professionals: 17
Major Franchise Clients in Past 3 Yrs.: Subway, Dairy Mart Convenience Stores, Street Corner News, Golden Krust Caribbean Bakery & Grill

MR. VINCENT L. DEBIASE

Tel: (845) 454-1111
Fax: (845) 454-4857
Email: VLD@CGRlaw.com

PROFILE
Practice concentrated in licensing and franchising since 1982. Regularly represent national franchisors in New York litigation. Also represent start-up franchisors and franchise area developers.

BACKGROUND
Year Admitted to the Bar: 1975
Licensed to Practice in: New York

Education/Honors: Graduated cum laude with B.S. in Business from Northeastern University. Juris Doctor from SMU. Author of numerous articles on franchising. Firm is AV rated in Martindale-Hubbell.

Professional Assns./Membership: ABA Forum Committee on Franchising; New York Trial Lawyers.

Publications: Numerous articles on franchising. Matthew Bender; New York State Bar Journal; Practicing Law Institute.

CORY J. COVERT P.C., LAW OFFICE

1775 Expressway Drive North
Hauppauge, NY 11788
Tel: (631) 232-2544
Fax: (631) 232-4321
Contact: Mr. Cory Covert
Email: ccove@hotmail.com

PROFILE
Franchise Law, representing franchisees in the purchase and sale of franchises and franchise related litigation. Real Estate.

BACKGROUND
Firm Established In: 1992
Serving Franchising Community Since: 1993
% of Billable Hrs. to Franchise Clients: 65
Full-Time Employees: 1
Full-Time Professionals: 1
Major Franchise Clients in Past 3 Yrs.: Minuteman Press International, Speedy Sign-A-Rama. (In house Counsel).

MR. CORY J. COVERT

Email: ccove@hotmail.com

PROFILE
Franchising; Representation of perspective franchisees in the purchase of a franchise; Drafted franchise agreements, disclosure and other ancillary documents for franchisor clients. Represented both franchisors and franchisees parties in litigation concerning franchise related issues.

BACKGROUND

Year Admitted to the Bar:	1993
Licensed to Practice in:	New York, EDNY, SDNY

Professional Assns./Membership: American Bar Association, Forum on Franchising, New York State Bar Association, Committee on Franchise Law

PROVIDE LEGAL SERVICES IN

U.S.:	Yes

<< >>

DAVID L. CAHN, LAW OFFICE

20 South Charles St., #310
Baltimore, MD 21201
Tel: (410) 986-0099
Fax: (410) 986-0123
Web Site: www.marylandfranchise.com
Contact: Mr. David L. Cahn
Email: david@davidcahn.com

PROFILE
Franchising, Dispute Resolution, Business Law

BACKGROUND

Firm Established In:	2004
Serving Franchising Community Since:	1997
% of Billable Hrs. to Franchise Clients:	80%
Full-Time Employees:	1
Full-Time Professionals:	1

Major Franchise Clients in Past 3 Yrs.: David Cahn has represented franchisees or the franchisor in the following systems: Baskin Robbins, Dunkin' Donuts, Sylvan Learning Centers, All Tune & Lube, Rent-A-Wreck, UPS Stores, Church's, Maggie Moo's, It's Just Lunch, ProSource Wholesale Floor Coverings

MR. DAVID L. CAHN

Email: david@davidcahn.com

PROFILE
Drafting and negotiating franchise agreements and real estate leases, preparing and registering franchise offering circulars; preparing LLC operating agreements or corporate by-laws; representing franchisees in disputes with franchisors

BACKGROUND

Year Admitted to the Bar:	1995
Licensed to Practice in:	Maryland and District of Columbia

Education/Honors: Stanford University, B.A. 1990; University of Pennsylvania, J.D. 1995; formerly associated with Piper Rudnick LLP, 1997 - 2001

Professional Assns./Membership: Secretary, Maryland State Bar, Franchise Law Comm., Member, ABA Forum on Franchising and AAFD LegaLine

Publications: Post-Expiration Covenants Not To Compete, LJN's Franchising Business & Law Alert, 2002; Earnings Claims: The Disclosure Franchisors Should Try To Make, Franchise Law Journal, 2001

PROVIDE LEGAL SERVICES IN

U.S.:	Yes
Canada:	No
Overseas:	No

<< >>

DUELL LAW FIRM LLC

4320 Eagle Point Pkwy.
Birmingham, AL 35242-6914
Tel: (205) 408-3025
Fax: (205) 408-3029
Web Site: www.duelllawfirm.com
Contact: Mr. Richard C. Duell, III
Email: richard@duelllawfirm.com

PROFILE
Practice law, commercial law, collection law, general corporate law, trademark law and entertainment law.

BACKGROUND

Serving Franchising Community Since:	1973
% of Billable Hrs. to Franchise Clients:	100%

Major Franchise Clients in Past 3 Yrs.: Bonus of America, Inc. (dba Bonus Building Care), Carpet Network, Carpet Gang Ventures, Castle Entries Franchising, Everything Yogurt Brands, Johnny Ray Companies, Just-A-Buck Licensing, O'Carr's Franchise Management, Screenmobile, Taco Palace, Villa Pizza, Window Gang

MR. RICHARD C. DUELL, III

Tel: (205) 408-3026
Email: richard@duelllawfirm.com

PROFILE
At Duell Law Firm, we work closely with our clients through the planning and development stages of franchising their companies. It includes a willingness to build relationships with clients.

BACKGROUND
Year Admitted to the Bar: 1973
Licensed to Practice in: Alabama, 5th and 11th US Appeals, U.S. Supreme

Education/Honors: Auburn University; Cumberland School of Law, Samford University; Martindale-Hubbell AV.

Professional Assns./Membership: International Bar Association's Franchising Committee, the American Bar Association (Franchising, Section of Anti-Trust Law, Franchising Forum, Franchising of Section of Corporation, Banking and Business Laws, Small Business), Birmingham and AL Bar Ass.

PROVIDE LEGAL SERVICES IN
U.S.: Yes
Overseas: Kuwait, Puerto Rico and Japan.

MR. MARCUS L. HUNT

Tel: (205) 408-3027
Email: marcus@duelllawfirm.com

PROFILE
At Duell Law Firm, we work closely with our clients through the planning and development stages of franchising their companies. It includes a willingness to build relationships with clients.

BACKGROUND
Year Admitted to the Bar: 2004
Licensed to Practice in: Alabama

Professional Assns./Membership: International Bar Association's Franchising Committee, the American Bar Association (Franchising, Section of Anti-Trust Law, Franchising Forum, Franchising of Section of Corporation, Banking and Business Laws, Small Business), Birmingham and AL Bar Ass.

PROVIDE LEGAL SERVICES IN
U.S.: Yes
Overseas: Kuwait, Puerto Rico and Japan.

<< >>

FARRELL FRITZ, P.C.

EAB Plaza, West Tower, 14th Floor
Uniondale, NY 11556
Tel: (516) 745-0099
Fax: (516) 745-0293
Web Site: www.franchiseatty.com/farrellfritz.com
Contact: Mr. Harold L. Kestenbaum
Email: hkestenbaum@farrellfritz.com

PROFILE
We have a broad practice with a highly qualified Franchise and Distribution Practice. Under this practice group we represent franchisors, both start-up and established; we will handle any dispute resolution issues for franchisors; we do all compliance work, disclosure preparation; international representation and real estate and corporate matters.

BACKGROUND
Serving Franchising Community Since: 1977
% of Billable Hrs. to Franchise Clients: 100%
Full-Time Employees: 85
Full-Time Professionals: 70
Major Franchise Clients in Past 3 Yrs.: GarageTek, Arthur Treachers, Minuteman Press, Domino's Pizza, Camille's Sidewalk Café, Coolbrands, Carvel, Sbarro, Wall Street Deli, SeaTow International, Famous Famiglia

MR. HAROLD L. KESTENBAUM

Email: hkestenbaum@farrellfritz.com

PROFILE
I am a franchisor attorney focusing on the transactional side. I do disclosure preparation, complete start-up assistance; compliance work; I do international expansion programs. I handle start-up and established franchisors.

BACKGROUND
Year Admitted to the Bar: 1976
Licensed to Practice in: New York, New Jersey

Education/Honors: AV Rated in Martindale; List as of of the Preeminent Attorneys in franchising; J.D. from University of Richmond - Law Review

Professional Assns./Membership: ABA Forum Committee on Franchising, New York State Bar Association - Chairman of the Franchise, Licensing and Distribution Committee

Publications: Various franchise publications.

PROVIDE LEGAL SERVICES IN
U.S.: Yes
Canada: Yes - Specific Areas Only
Overseas: South Korea, Israel, Canada, Ireland

<< >>

GALLET DREYER & BERKEY LLP

845 Third Avenue - 8th Floor
New York, NY 10022
Tel: (212) 935-3131
Fax: (212) 935-4514
Web Site: www.gdblaw.com
Contact: Mr. David T. Azrin
Email: dta@gdblaw.com

PROFILE

We represent existing and start-up franchisors and franchisees in all business-related matters, including franchise disclosure documents, franchise registration, franchise litigation, leases, corporate structure, trademarks, employee issues, non-compete agreements, tax issues, and estate planning. We provide diligent representation at a reasonable cost, and close communication with our clients. The firm is AV rated by Martindale-Hubbell.

BACKGROUND

Firm Established In:	1978
Serving Franchising Community Since:	1978
% of Billable Hrs. to Franchise Clients:	20%
Full-Time Employees:	27
Full-Time Professionals:	14

Major Franchise Clients in Past 3 Yrs.: Franchisors: Perfumia, Gourmet Cajun Grill, Nemiroff, Andre's Steakhouse, Machinery Wholesalers. Franchisees: Great Clips, Burger King, Dunkin' Donuts, Mailboxes Etc., GNC, Dunhill

MR. DAVID T. AZRIN

Tel: (212) 935-3131 + 4411
Email: dta@gdblaw.com

PROFILE

I represent existing and start-up franchisors and franchisees in New York, Florida, and New Jersey in the preparation of franchise disclosure documents and registration; representation in franchise litigation and other types of business disputes, including contract disputes, fraud claims, trademark disputes, non-compete disputes, employment disputes, lease disputes; advice regarding employment issues and preparation of employment agreements; trademark registration; advice and preparation of documents concerning corporate governance.

BACKGROUND

Year Admitted to the Bar:	1988
Licensed to Practice in:	New York, Florida, New Jersey

Education/Honors: Stanford University, 1985, A.B., with honors; University of Michigan, 1988, Law Review; Phi Beta Kappa. The firm is AV rated by Martindale-Hubbell.

Professional Assns./Membership: International Franchise Association; AAFD; American Bar Association; New York Bar Association, Florida Bar

Publications: Articles on franchising published in various publications including IFA's Franchising World, Westchester County Journal News, and South Dade Newsletter

PROVIDE LEGAL SERVICES IN

U.S.:	Yes
Canada:	No
Overseas:	No

KAT TIDD, P.C., LAW OFFICE

14232 Marsh Lane, #484
Addison (Dallas), TX 75001
Tel: (972) 247-6934
Fax: (972) 247-7535
Web Site: www.tiddlaw.com
Contact: Ms. Kat Tidd
Email: k.tidd@abanet.org

PROFILE

FRANCHISING: All aspects of franchising - advice and assistance in structuring and implementation of start-up franchise systems, contract drafting, preparation of Uniform Franchise Circulars, franchise registration and compliance matters, on-going franchise operations, sales and related marketing, expansion, international franchising; franchisor-franchisee relationship counseling, problem solving for franchisors, state and federal regulatory compliance. INTELLECTUAL PROPERTY: Trademarks and licensing matters DISPUTE RESOLUTION: Counseling and representing franchisees and franchisors in problem solving and dispute resolution. REVIEW AND EVALUATION OF BUSINESS AND FRANCHISE OPPORTUNITIES: Counsel for buyers and sellers. BUSINESS AND CORPORATE: Entity formation (incorporation, LLC, LP), contracts, general transactional and business related.

BACKGROUND

Firm Established In:	1994
Serving Franchising Community Since:	1981
% of Billable Hrs. to Franchise Clients:	95%
Full-Time Employees:	varies
Full-Time Professionals:	1 plus litigator alliances

Major Franchise Clients in Past 3 Yrs.: Client references available upon request.

MS. KAT TIDD

Email: k.tidd@abanet.org

PROFILE

Kat currently advises small and medium businesses, start-up and mature franchisors and franchisees, dealers, and entrepreneurs and serves as a consultant to other attorneys on all aspects of franchise and business opportunity matters. She has worked with the franchise industry for more than 25 years, including 12 years as vice president/general counsel of franchising, licensing and distribution companies. She has negotiated and structured franchise and license arrangements at the U.S. and international levels, as well as developing and managing legal departments for franchise companies. Kat also assists in general transactional and corporate matters.

BACKGROUND

Year Admitted to the Bar:	TX 1990; OR 1981
Licensed to Practice in:	Texas, Oregon

Education/Honors: B.A. University of Oregon Honors College (with distinction); J.D. University of Oregon Law School

Professional Assns./Membership: Bar Associations: ABA Texas, Oregon, Dallas (Franchise, Business, Antitrust sections); NAWBO; Best Lawyers in America, 2005-2006 ed.

Publications: Franchise Lawyer, ABA Forum of Franchising, Legal Ethics in Texas: The Art of Ethical Winners (contribution), various seminars, bar association program papers

PROVIDE LEGAL SERVICES IN

U.S.:	Yes - Texas is primary focus
Canada	Yes - Depend on area-coordinate with local counsel

Overseas: Yes - Work with local counsel in Europe, South America, Mexico, Asia, and Australia

KENNETH G. PROTONENTIS, P.A.

1591 Gulf Boulevard, Penthouse 2
Clearwater, FL 33767-2997
Tel: (727) 596-3435
Fax: (727) 596-2076
Web Site: www.pro-franchise.net
Contact: Mr. Kenneth G. Protonentis
Email: ken.pro@gte.net

PROFILE

Kenneth G. Protonentis, P.A. has specialized in Franchise and Product Distribution Law for seventeen years and earned a national reputation as deal makers and problem solvers for both franehisors and franchisees. We provide experienced counsel for creating, managing, licensing, protecting and enforcing business relationships, product distribution systems, and dealership networks. We are known for achieving cost-effective results that serve our client's best interests, for our prompt personal attention, and for the quality and professionalism of our legal services. We serve clients through all stages of formation, development, expansion and maintenance of business relationships, including transfers, terminations and dispute resolution.

BACKGROUND

Firm Established In:	1986
Serving Franchising Community Since:	1986
% of Billable Hrs. to Franchise Clients:	90%
Full-Time Employees:	3
Full-Time Professionals:	1

Major Franchise Clients in Past 3 Yrs.: Abbey Carpet Co., Durango USA, Inc., Ident-A-Kid Services of America, Inc.; Family Industries Franchise Association, LLC; Geeks On Call America, Inc.; KnowledgePoints Franchise Development, Inc.; Mail Boxes, Etc.; Play It Again Sports Franchise Corporation; Rooney's Irish Pubs, Inc.; Sylvan Learning Corporation

MR. KENNETH G. PROTONENTIS

PROFILE

Ken concentrates on franchise development and licensing, regulation and compliance, and dispute resolution. He represents both franchisors and franchisees throughout the United States on a wide range of franchise legal matters. His practice over the past sixteen years has been a balance of transactional work and dispute resolution related to creating, managing, protecting, enforcing and terminating franchised business relationships. Ken has drafted Uniform Franchise Offering Circulars for national franchise companies in a wide variety of industries. He routinely secures and maintains franchise registrations throughout the United States and establishes in-house legal compliance systems for franchise sales teams and contract administrators.

BACKGROUND

Year Admitted to the Bar: Oregon State Bar (1984), District of Columbia (1988), and The Florida Bar (1989)
Licensed to Practice in: Florida, Oregon and District of Columbia

Education/Honors: Ken is a graduate of Northwestern School of Law of Lewis and Clark College (J.D. 1983) and Portland State University (B.A. cum laude 1980).

Professional Assns./Membership: ABA Forum on Franchising since 1984 as well as the Business Law, Litigation, and Law Practice Management Sections

Publications: Examining the Trademark Paradox Within the Franchise and Securities Laws, for Law Journal Newsletters' Franchising Business Law Alert

PROVIDE LEGAL SERVICES IN

U.S.:	Yes
Canada:	Specific Areas Only
Overseas:	No

KEUP, LAW OFFICES OF ERWIN J.

3015 Country Club Dr.
Costa Mesa, CA 92626
Tel: (714) 751-3921
Fax: (714) 751-9321
Contact: Mr. Erwin J. Keup

PROFILE
This firm concentrates on all aspects of franchise legal work including Uniform Offering Circulars, franchise agreements, registrations and trademarks.

BACKGROUND

Firm Established In:	
Serving Franchising Community Since:	1966
% of Billable Hrs. to Franchise Clients:	98%

Major Franchise Clients in Past 3 Yrs.: Amateur Bowlers Association; American Mobile Sound; American Window Coverings, Inc.; Quik Internet; Lube N Latte.

MR. ERWIN J. KEUP

PROFILE
Mr. Keup is the author of the "Franchise Bible" and numerous articles on franchising. He is the former Vice President and General Counselor for a major franchisor as well as a member of the American Bar Association's Forum on Franchising. He arbitrates many franchise matters.

BACKGROUND

Year Admitted to the Bar:	1958
Licensed to Practice in:	Ohio, California

Education/Honors: B.S., Business, Marquette University, 1953. Juris Doctor, Marquette Law School, 1958.

Professional Assns./Membership: American Bar Association, California Bar, Ohio Bar.

Publications: "Franchise Bible', numerous magazine articles.

PROVIDE LEGAL SERVICES IN

U.S.:	Yes
Canada:	Yes
Overseas:	Japan, Europe

LARKIN HOFFMAN DALY & LINDGREN LTD.

Larkin Hoffman
ATTORNEYS

1500 Wells Fargo Plaza, 7900 Xerxes Avenue South
Minneapolis, MN 55431
Tel: (952) 835-3800
Fax: (952) 896-3333
Web Site: www.larkinhoffman.com
Contact: Mr. Charles S. Modell
Email: cmodell@larkinhoffman.com

PROFILE
We assist clients in traditional areas such as corporate law, securities law, tax and taxation, banking, franchising and distributorships, commercial transactions, real estate, intellectual property, and litigation. The firm practices extensively in land use planning and development, zoning, environmental regulation, legislative lobbying and administrative law, securities and hospitality, employment law, international law, trusts and estates administration, estate planning and healthcare.

BACKGROUND

Firm Established In:	1958
Serving Franchising Community Since:	1975
Full-Time Employees:	150
Full-Time Professionals:	70

MR. JOSEPH J. FITTANTE, JR.

Email: jfittante@larkinhoffman.com

PROFILE
Mr. Fittante works in the franchising and distribution area where he advises franchisors on various topics including structuring the franchise relationship and registration and disclosure issues. Mr. Fittante also advises manufacturers creating distribution networks and routinely represents privately held companies who are buying and selling businesses. Mr. Fittante is a frequent author on franchise and distribution issues. He has published works in the ABA Franchise Journal, the Franchise Lawyer and many other publications. He has also spoken on various franchise and distribution issues for the ABA and International Franchise Association.

BACKGROUND

Year Admitted to the Bar:	1996
Licensed to Practice in:	Minnesota

Education/Honors: William Mitchell College of Law, St. Paul, MN 1996 J.D., Honors: Cum Laude; University of Wiscousin, Eau Claire, WI, 1993 B.A.

Professional Assns./Membership: American Bar Association, Minnesota State Bar Association, American Bar Association Franchise Forum

Publications: Calling All Young Lawyers: The Opportunities are in Front of You, The Franchise Lawyer, Winter 2004; Stop Losing Your Franchise Outlets - Control the Real Estate, Franchise Times, April 2004; Community of Interest: Clarity or Confusion? Franchise Law Journal, Winter 2003; The Untapped Sales Potential of Existing Franchisees, Franchise Update, April 2001

PROVIDE LEGAL SERVICES IN

U.S.:	Yes
Canada:	Yes
Overseas:	Yes

MR. CHARLES S. MODELL

Fax: (952) 896-1511
Email: cmodell@larkinhoffman.com

PROFILE

Mr. Modell spends his time primarily working with franchisors on the business aspects of franchising, including the structuring of the franchise relationship, compliance with state and federal laws and regulations, negotiations and mediations with franchisees, and the purchase and sale of franchise companies. His experience with franchise matters is national in scope. He has also represented a number of franchisors (and other non-franchise businesses) in the acquisition or sale of businesses, and is a certified commercial arbitrator for the American Arbitration Association.

BACKGROUND

Year Admitted to the Bar:	1977
Licensed to Practice in:	Minnesota

Education/Honors: University of Florida College of Law 1977 J.D., Honors: High Honors, Order of the Coif; University of Florida 1974, B.S. in Broadcasting; Martindale-Hubbell AV rating; Certified Franchise Executive

Professional Assns./Membership: ABA Forum on Franchising (Governing Committee and Financial Officer); IFA Legal-Legislative Committee

Publications: Frequent contributor to ABA's Franchise Law Journal, as well as business and legal publications on franchising and franchise law

PROVIDE LEGAL SERVICES IN

U.S.:	Yes
Canada:	No
Overseas:	No

MR. ANDREW F. PERRIN

Tel: (952) 896-3394
Fax: (952) 842-1706
Email: aperrin@larkinhoffman.com

PROFILE

Mr. Perrin's practice is devoted primarily to representing and advising franchisors in a variety of business issues, including structuring of the franchise relationship, drafting and registering franchise programs, negotiating with franchisees, and acquiring and selling franchise systems. He has written and spoken on a number of topics involving franchise matters. He is a regular speaker at franchise meetings. Mr. Perrin also represents companies in mergers and acquisitions, venture capital financing, loan transactions and general corporate matters.

BACKGROUND

Year Admitted to the Bar:	1987
Licensed to Practice in:	Georgia and Minnesota

Education/Honors: The University of Michigan Law School, Ann Arbor, MI, J.D.; Kalamazoo College, Kalamazoo, MI, B.A., Bachelors of Arts

Professional Assns./Membership: International Franchise Association's Supplier Forum; Supplier Forum Board of Advisors; Supplier Forum Executive Committee; International Franchise Association's Legal/Legislative Committee; IFA's Franchise Relations Committee; ABA Forum Committee on Franchising; Association for Corporate Growth

Publications: "Franchise Disclosure: The Breakdown in Uniformity," co-authored by Rupert M. Barkoff, March 1, 2004, Winter 2004 issue of The Franchise Lawyer; "State-Of-The-Art Franchise Agreements" International Franchise Association Legal Symposium, May 21, 2004, Washington, D.C.; "Transfers and Succession Issues," International Franchise Association Annual Meeting, March 9, 2004, Las Vegas, Nevada; "Other People's Money," American Bar Association's Forum on Franchising, October 22, 2003, Hollywood, Florida; "Enforcement of Franchise Releases: What Franchisors Ought to Know," co-authored with Genevieve A. Beck, LJN's Franchising & Business Law Alert, December 2002; "Five Methods to Expand Your Franchise System," Nova Southeastern University H. Wayne Huizenga School of Business and Entrepreneurship's "Secrets to Dynamic Franchise Expansion Conference," Fort Lauderdale, Florida, 2002; "Franchise Sales Law Compliance Roundtable," International Franchise Association Annual Meeting, Orlando, Florida, 2002; "Award of Attorney Fees Under Franchise Agreements: Specific Language is Important," LJN's Franchising & Business Law Alert, March 2002; Ask the Experts, St. Thomas University Mini MBA Franchise Program, September 2001; "Hottest Legal Topics Addressed by Franchising's Experts: Mergers and Acquisitions of Franchise Companies," Franchising World, July/August 2001; Mergers and Acquisitions of Franchise Companies, International Franchise Association Legal Symposium, Washington, D.C., 2001; "Dealing With the Underperforming Franchisee Roundtable," International Franchise Association Annual Meeting, Las Vegas, Nevada, 2001; "Franchise Sales Compliance Basics," co-presented with Joseph J. Fittante, Larkin, Hoffman, Daly & Lindgren Franchise Seminar, Minneapolis, MN, 1999; Legal Update, The University of St. Thomas Emerging Franchisor Conference, Minneapolis, Minnesota, 1999; "Advance Registration Disclosure," American Bar Association Forum on Franchising, Philadelphia, Pennsylvania, 1998; "Dealing with the Difficult or Underperforming Franchisee," International Franchise Association Annual Meeting, Las Vegas, Nevada, 1998;

Legal Update; Dealing with Franchisees, University of St. Thomas Emerging Franchisor Conference, Minneapolis, Minnesota, 1998; "What it Takes to Franchise Your Business," Co-Authored with Charles S. Modell, Minnesota Business and Opportunities, June 1995 at 24.

PROVIDE LEGAL SERVICES IN

U.S.: Yes
Canada: Yes
Overseas: Yes

MS. MARY B. STANLEY

Tel: (952) 835-3800
Email: mstanley@larkinhoffman.com

PROFILE

Ms. Stanley is a member of the Corporate Law Department at Larkin Hoffman Daly & Lindgren Ltd. She practices in areas of general corporate law, and franchise and distribution law.

BACKGROUND

Year Admitted to the Bar: 2003
Licensed to Practice in: Minnesota

Education/Honors: William Mitchell College of Law, St. Paul, MN, J.D., Honors: Cum Laude Metropolitan State University, St. Paul, MN, B.A.

Professional Assns./Membership: International Franchise Association, American Bar Association Forum on Franchising

PROVIDE LEGAL SERVICES IN

U.S.: Yes
Canada: No
Overseas: No

MR. JON S. SWIERZEWSKI

Fax: (952) 842-1736
Email: jswierzewski@larkinhoffman.com

PROFILE

Mr. Swierzewski is a well-respected and experienced practitioner in the area of franchise and distribution litigation, representing franchisors. He also practices in the area of commercial litigation, with particular emphasis on closely-held corporations and shareholders matters. Mr. Swierzewski is a frequent lecturer to special interest groups on the subjects of ethics and litigation issues.

BACKGROUND

Year Admitted to the Bar: 1978
Licensed to Practice in: Minnesota
Education/Honors: University of Minnesota Law School, Minneapolis, MN, J.D.; Carnegie-Mellon University, Pittsburg, PA M.S., Carnegie-Mellon University, Pittsburg PA B.S.

Professional Assns./Membership: Member litigation section of the ABA, Minnesota and Hennepin County Bar Associations, and Association of Professional Responsibility

Publications: Damages From Defaulting Franchisees; More Options Than You Think; Who Has Standing to Sue Franchiors?; Ethical and Professional Responsibility Issues

PROVIDE LEGAL SERVICES IN

U.S.: Yes
Canada: No
Overseas: No

MR. WILLIAM G. THORNTON

Tel: (952) 835-3800
Email: wthornton@larkinhoffman.com

PROFILE

Mr. Thornton's practice focuses on domestic and international business transactions, with an emphasis on international licensing, distribution, franchising, mergers and acquisitions, joint ventures and general commercial matters. His practice includes planning and structuring of business relationships and assisting a client's expansion into new markets, protection of intellectual property rights and building long-term relationships for growing and established businesses.

BACKGROUND

Year Admitted to the Bar: 1978
Licensed to Practice in: Minnesota

Education/Honors: Hamline University School of Law, St. Paul, MN, J.D., Honors: Honor Society Northeastern Unversity, Boston, MA, B.S., Major: Economics

Professional Assns./Membership: Member American Bar Association, Minnesota State Bar Association, Hennepin County Bar Association and Minnesota Intellectual Property Law Association

PROVIDE LEGAL SERVICES IN

U.S.: Yes
Canada: No
Overseas: No

<< >>

LAW OFFICE OF DON M. DRYSDALE

610 Newport Center Drive, # 700
Newport Beach, CA 92660-6498
Fax: (949) 760-9551
Web Site: www.dondrysdale.com
Contact: Mr. Don M. Drysdale

PROFILE

We specialize in setting up franchise concepts and registering these franchises in the U.S. and other countries. We've represented large franchisors (such as Prudential Real Estate Affiliates, Budget Blinds, New Horizons Computer Training, Closets By Design) and smaller start-ups. We've also represented franchisees and general business clients.

BACKGROUND

Serving Franchising Community Since:	1977
% of Billable Hrs. to Franchise Clients:	90%

Major Franchise Clients in Past 3 Yrs.: Prudential Real Estate Affiliates; New Horizon Computer Learning Centers; Closets By Design; Great Earth Vitamins; Budget Blinds; Super Clean Yacht Service; Pollo Campero; Red Brick Pizza; Zland (Internet Services); Splash Bath and Body.

MR. DON M. DRYSDALE

Tel: (949) 760-9677
Email: dmd@dondrysdale.com

PROFILE

I've been representing franchisors for 25 years. I was General Counsel of Coldwell Banker Real Estate when its franchise program was initiated and supervised franchise compliance for 4 years. I'm co-chair of the International Franchise Association Franchise Business Network and have lectured on franchise compliance in the U.S. and internationally.

BACKGROUND

Year Admitted to the Bar:	1976
Licensed to Practice in:	California

Education/Honors: J.D. UCLA, Member Law Review. AV Rating Martindale-Hubbell.

Professional Assns./Membership: IFA Legal/Legislative Committee; ABA Forum on Franchising; Orange County Bar Association Business and International Sections.

PROVIDE LEGAL SERVICES IN

U.S.: Yes
Overseas: Japan, UK, Canada, Mexico, Brazil, France, Germany, Australia, Spain, China.

MANNING, LEAVER, BRUDER & BERBERICH

5750 Wilshire Blvd., # 655
Los Angeles, CA 90036-3637
Tel: (323) 937-4730
Fax: (323) 937-6727
Web Site: www.manningleaver.com
Contact: Mr. Halbert B. Rasmussen

PROFILE

Representation of both automobile dealers and distributors/manufacturers in connection with motor vehicle dealer franchising, marketing, advertising and finance (retail and wholesale).

BACKGROUND

Serving Franchising Community Since:	1987
% of Billable Hrs. to Franchise Clients:	75%

Major Franchise Clients in Past 3 Yrs.: Daewoo Motor America, Miller Automotive Group, Norm Reeves Temecula, California Harley-Davidson Dealers Association.

MR. HALBERT B. RASMUSSEN

Email: Hrasmussen@manningleaver.com

PROFILE

Halbert Rasmussen was admitted to practice in California for over 17 years, specializing in franchising, regulatory compliance and specialized administrative agencies litigation in the automotive franchise area.

BACKGROUND

Year Admitted to the Bar:	1983
Licensed to Practice in:	California and Federal Courts.

Education/Honors: J.D. Loyola Law School, cum laude (1982); B.A. UCLA (1980).

Professional Assns./Membership: ABA, California State Bar, forum on franchising of the ABA, Consumer Financial Services committee of the ABA.

Publications: Several chapters of California Motor Car Dealers Association Dealer Management Guide, numerous bulletin and other articles in motor vehicle franchising related publications California Showroom.

MCGLINCHEY STAFFORD

643 Magazine St.
New Orleans, LA 70130-3477
Tel: (504) 586-1200
Fax: (504) 596-2877
Web Site: www.mcglinchey.com
Contact: Mr. James M. Fantaci

PROFILE

McGlinchey Stafford is a regional, full service firm including the following practice areas: antitrust and trade regulation; appellate; banking/financial institutions laws and regulations; bankruptcy/reorganization/creditors' rights; business litigation; corporate and general business law; employee benefits/ERISA/executive compensation; franchising; health care law and regulation; labor and employment law; products liability counseling and litigation; real estate law and litigation; and taxation.

BACKGROUND
Firm Established In:
Serving Franchising Community Since: 1988
% of Billable Hrs. to Franchise Clients: 10%
Major Franchise Clients in Past 3 Yrs.: Semolina International Pastas; Smoothie King; Aftermarket Appearance Industries, Inc. ("Altracolor"); DocuMart.

MR. JAMES M. FANTACI

Tel: (504) 596-2791
Email: jfantaci@mcglinchey.com

PROFILE
Mr. Fantaci's practice areas include preparation of franchise agreements and disclosure documents; filing of franchise documents in states with franchise registration statutes; negotiation and preparation of asset purchase, stock purchase, and merger agreements for acquisition of businesses; preparation of confidential private placement memoranda; and formation of bank holding companies. He also advises clients on incorporations, liquidations, shareholder (buy-sell) agreements, employment contracts, and other business-oriented documents.

BACKGROUND
Year Admitted to the Bar: 1971
Licensed to Practice in: Louisiana

Education/Honors: AV Rating - Martindale-Hubbell; AB, University of Rochester, 1968; Juris Doctor, University of Virginia, 1971.

Professional Assns./Membership: ABA, Business Law Section, Small Business Committee, member of Franchising Subcommittee Louisiana Bar Association, Virginia Bar Association.

Publications: Co-author: "Louisiana Limited Liability Company; Forms and Practice Manual", 1996; "Basic Corporate Law in Louisiana", National Business Institute, Inc., 1991; "Not So Boilerplate: Choice of Law, Conflict of Laws, Forum and Jurisdiction", 1990.

PROVIDE LEGAL SERVICES IN
U.S.: Yes
Overseas: No

≺≺ ≻≻

MEADOWS, ICHTER & TRIGG, P.C.

8 Piedmont Center, # 300
Atlanta, GA 30305
Tel: (404) 261-6020
Fax: (404) 261-3656
Web Site: www.mitlaw.com
Contact: Mr. Cary Ichter

PROFILE
Meadows, Ichter & Trigg is a full-service law firm with a concentration in business litigation, corporate transactional and mergers and acquisitions.

BACKGROUND
Serving Franchising Community Since: 1990
% of Billable Hrs. to Franchise Clients: 30%
Major Franchise Clients in Past 3 Yrs.: Dunkin' Donuts, Baskin Robbins, Subway, The Athlete's Foot, Discovery Point Franchising, Inc.

MR. CARY ICHTER

Email: ci@mitlaw.com

PROFILE
Cary Ichter is a founding partner of Meadows, Ichter & Trigg. Mr. Ichter has 17 years of litigation experience, focusing on franchise and distribution matters, as well as complex commercial litigation.

BACKGROUND
Year Admitted to the Bar: 1984
Licensed to Practice in: Georgia

Education/Honors: J.D. University of Georgia School of Law, magna cum laude. Order of Coif. AV Martindale Hubbell Rating.

Professional Assns./Membership: American Bar Association, ABA Forum on Franchising, Georgia Bar Association, Atlanta Bar Association.

≺≺ ≻≻

MIKA, MEYERS, BECKETT & JONES PLC

Mika Meyers Beckett & Jones PLC

900 Monroe Ave. NW
Grand Rapids, MI 49503
Tel: (616) 632-8000
Fax: (616) 632-8002
Web Site: www.mmbjlaw.com
Contact: Mr. Ben Zainea
Email: bzainea@mmbjlaw.com

PROFILE
Franchise Law, General Business Law, Real Estate Law, Estate Planning, Banking Law, Securities and Finance, Mergers and Acquisitions, Tax Law, Business Organization

BACKGROUND
Firm Established In: 1940s
Serving Franchising Community Since: mid-1990s
% of Billable Hrs. to Franchise Clients: 5%

Full-Time Employees: 75
Full-Time Professionals: 37
Major Franchise Clients in Past 3 Yrs.: We do not disclose client information.

MR. JAMES M. EARDLEY

Tel: (616) 632-8027
Fax: (616) 632-8002
Email: jeardley@mmbjlaw.com

BACKGROUND
Year Admitted to the Bar: MI - 1991; IL - 1990
Licensed to Practice in: Michigan, Illinois

Education/Honors: J.D. - University of Michigan; B.A. in Economics - University of Michigan, with High Distinction

Professional Assns./Membership: American Bar Association Franchise Law Section; University of Michigan Club of Grand Rapids

PROVIDE LEGAL SERVICES IN
U.S.: Yes - Midwest
Canada: No
Overseas: No

MR. BENJAMIN A. ZAINEA

Tel: (616) 632-8019
Fax: (616) 632-8002
Email: bzainea@mmbjlaw.com

BACKGROUND
Year Admitted to the Bar: 1999
Licensed to Practice in: Michigan

Education/Honors: J.D. - University of Michigan, 1999; B.B.A. - University of Michigan, with High Distinction, 1996

Professional Assns./Membership: American Bar Association Franchise Law Section; University of Michigan Club of Grand Rapids

PROVIDE LEGAL SERVICES IN
U.S.: Yes - Midwest
Canada: No
Overseas: No

MOHAJERIAN LAW CORPORATION

1925 Century Park East., Suite 500
Los Angeles, CA 90067
Tel: (310) 556-3800
Fax: (310) 556-3817
Web Site: www.law-up-date.com
Contact: Mr. Al Mohajerian
Email: lawyers@Mohajerian.com

PROFILE
Mohajerian Law Corporation has experience in counseling both franchisors and franchisees in all phases of the franchise operation and business relationship. We negotiate and resolve disputes between franchisors and franchisees, and, when the need arises, represent our clients in litigation and mediation to protect their interests. We represents businesses that offer goods and services through franchising and other distribution methods. Our client base is broad and diverse and includes franchisors and franchisees. We bring practical, solution-oriented legal advice and business counsel to bear on clients' problems.

BACKGROUND
Major Franchise Clients in Past 3 Yrs.: We represent multi-unit franchises in the food, hotel and staffing industries. Our representation include corporate, municipal and insurance clients in wide range of litigation and business matters. We represent lenders, bankers, brokers and financial institution in variety of disputes. Franchise Clients include: Jack-in-the-Box, Carl's Jr., Burger King, KFC, Papa John's, CoCo's, Shakey's, It's a Grind Coffee, Lloyd staffing, Remedy Intelligent Staffing, Chevron.

MR. AL MOHAJERIAN

Email: lawyers@Mohajerian.com

PROFILE
Mr. Al Mohajerian counsels corporate clients and litigates civil and business matters. He has a broad experience involving matters such as complex business litigation, franchise and distribution, intellectual property, trademark, copyright, trade dress and trade secret infringement, toxic tort, financial services, insurance coverage, labor and employment, product liability, real estate, entertainment, unfair competition and related business torts. He has represented clients in state and federal courts over complex commercial matters including Lanham Act violations, franchise terminations, contract, encroachment and antitrust liability. He is a member of the State Bar of California, American and Los Angeles County Bar Associations. He is admitted to the Federal District Courts for the Central, Northern and Eastern Districts of California. He has been recognized by Franchise Times as one of the top 100 legal eagles in 2004. This distinguished honor, based on a peer nomination process, was announced in the April 2004 issue of the Franchise Times.

BACKGROUND
Year Admitted to the Bar: 1996
Licensed to Practice in: CA, but litigate in FL and AZ

Education/Honors: Franchise Times 100 Legal Eagles, April 2004

Professional Assns./Membership: ABA, LACBA and other franchising-related associations.

Publications: Pending

<< >>

NIXON PEABODY LLP

437 Madison Ave.
New York, NY 10022-7001
Tel: (212) 940-3000
Fax: (212) 940-3111
Web Site: www.nixonpeabody.com
Contact: Ms. Maria Gray
Email: mgray@nixonpeabody.com
Other Offices In: Albany, NY; Boston, MA; Buffalo, NY; Hartford, CT; Long Island, NY; Manchester, NH; McLean, VA; New York, NY; Orange County, CA; Providence, RI; Rochester, NY; San Francisco, CA; Washington, D.C., Philadelphia, PA

PROFILE
Nixon Peabody LLP is one of the largest multi-practice law firms in the United States, with offices in 14 cities on the East and West coasts and over 600 attorneys working in 15 major practice areas. The Firm's size, diversity, and state-of-the-art technical resources enable us to offer comprehensive legal services to individuals and organizations of all sizes in local, state, national and international matters. Our clients include emerging and middle-market businesses, national and multi-national corporations, financial institutions, and individuals. Nixon Peabody adheres to the highest standards of legal excellence, and the highest standards of service.

MS. RENEE F. BERGMANN

1818 Market St., 11th Floor
Philadelphia, PA 19103-3647
Email: rbergmann@nixonpeabody.com

PROFILE
Commercial/Franchise Litigation, Vicarious Liability Litigation, Bankruptcy Litigation

BACKGROUND
Year Admitted to the Bar: 2000
Licensed to Practice in: Pennsylvania, New Jersey

Education/Honors: Rutgers-Camden J.D.; International Academy of Trial Lawyers Advocacy Award; Who's Who American Law Students; Thomas Edison State College B.S.; Arnold Fletcher Award for Independent Learning; Who's Who American Colleges and Universities

Professional Assns./Membership: ABI, ABA, ATLA, PBA, Appointed - Commisson on Women in Profession (PBA) E.D. Bank. Conf.

PROVIDE LEGAL SERVICES IN
U.S.: Yes
Canada: No
Overseas: No

MR. PETER H. DURANT

Clinton Square, P.O. Box 31051
Rochester, NY 14603
Tel: (585) 263-1227
Fax: (866) 947-1223
Email: pdurant@nixonpeabody.com

PROFILE
Mr. Durant is highly experienced in preparing franchise and other distribution agreements. He regularly counsels businesses, universities and individuals on the development, acquisition, sale, licensing, and exploitation of intellectual property and related assets. He also helps organizations establish joint ventures and outsourcing and partnering relationships with their major vendors and suppliers. Mr. Durant is also heavily involved with New Media, internet, and e-commerce issues, including privacy policies, the digital millennium copyright act, and conflicts between U.S. and European legislation and related policy.

BACKGROUND
Year Admitted to the Bar: 1980
Licensed to Practice in: New York

Professional Assns./Membership: New York State Bar Association; American Bar Association

PROVIDE LEGAL SERVICES IN
U.S.: Yes
Canada: No
Overseas: No

MS. SHANNON HAAF

401 9th Street, NW
Washington, DC 20004
Tel: (202) 585-8356
Fax: (866) 822-7781
Email: shaaf@nixonpeabody.com

BACKGROUND
Year Admitted to the Bar: 1998
Licensed to Practice in: Pennsylvania, District of Columbia

Professional Assns./Membership: District of Columbia Bar Association, ABA Forum on Franchising
PROVIDE LEGAL SERVICES IN
U.S.: Yes
Canada: Yes
Overseas: Yes - Asia, Europe, Middle-East, Central and South America

MR. JAMIE N. HAGE

889 Elm Street

Manchester, NH 03101
Tel: (603) 628-4074
Fax: (603) 628-4040
Email: jhage@nixonpeabody.com

PROFILE
Twenty-five years of experience in commercial and intellectual property litigation and business relations. He has represented franchisors and franchisees as well as high technology and emerging growth companies in intellectual property protection and licensing matters, including patent, trademark, copyright and unfair competition litigation.

BACKGROUND
Year Admitted to the Bar: 1978
Licensed to Practice in: New Hampshire and Massachusetts

Education/Honors: B.A. with Honors - Hamilton College; Research Fellow - University of Minnesota; J.D. - Pierce Law Center

Professional Assns./Membership: ABA; ATLA; AICPA; Computer Law Association; Licensing Executive Society

PROVIDE LEGAL SERVICES IN
U.S.: Yes
Canada: No
Overseas: No

MR. ANDREW P. LOEWINGER

401 9th Street, NW
Washington, DC 20004
Tel: (202) 585-8855
Fax: (866) 829-9262
Email: aloewinger@nixonpeabody.com

PROFILE
Counseling on all legal aspects of franchise programs (start-up, medium-sized and mature franchise systems); preparation of franchise agreements, offering circulars, international franchising agreements and disclosure documents; franchise relationship problems
BACKGROUND
Year Admitted to the Bar: 1984
Licensed to Practice in: District of Columbia

Professional Assns./Membership: ABA, IBA, Committee X, Forum on Franchising

PROVIDE LEGAL SERVICES IN
U.S.: Yes
Canada: Yes
Overseas: Yes - Asia-Pacific, Europe, Middle-East, Central and South America

MR. ARTHUR L. PRESSMAN

101 Federal St.
Boston, MA 02110
Tel: (417) 345-1158
Fax: (617) 345-1300
Email: apressman@nixonpeabody.com

BACKGROUND
Year Admitted to the Bar: 1971
Licensed to Practice in: Massachusetts, New York, Pennsylvania

Education/Honors: Martindale-Hubbell rating: AV; University of Pennsylvania, B.A., 1967; Temple University School of Law, 1971

Professional Assns./Membership: ABA Forum on Franchising, Governing Committee 1997-2001; First Chair, Litigation and Dispute Resolution Division; IFA Legal Legislative Committee

Publications: Numerous articles, presentations for ABA Forum on Franchising, IFA Legal Symposium, The Franchise Lawyer, Franchise Times regular column

PROVIDE LEGAL SERVICES IN
U.S.: Yes
Canada: No
Overseas: Yes - International dispute resolution

MR. CRAIG TRACTENBERG

1818 Market St., 11th Floor
Philadelphia, PA 19103
Tel: (215) 854-4020
Fax: (215) 569-0216
Email: ctractenberg@nixonpeabody.com

PROFILE
Franchise counseling, development and litigation, insolvency and bankruptcy, trademark and trade secret litigation.

BACKGROUND
Year Admitted to the Bar: 1981
Licensed to Practice in: Pennsylvania, New Jersey
Education/Honors: Martindale-Hubbell rating: AV

Professional Assns./Membership: ABA Franchise Forum, IFA Counsel of Suppliers

Publications: Articles Editor of ABA Franchise Law Journal, Franchise Columnist for the Legal Intelligencer

PROVIDE LEGAL SERVICES IN
U.S.: Yes
Canada: No
Overseas: Yes - Israel, UK, and Korea

MR. ANDREW D. ZAPPIA

1300 Clinton Square

Rochester, NY 14604
Tel: (585) 263-1214
Fax: (585) 263-1600
Email: azappia@nixonpeabody.com

PROFILE
My practice is focused on representing franchise and distribution companies on disclosure and registration issues, intellectual property dispute, licensing, franchise counseling, product pricing and distribution issues, antitrust matter, and litigation and arbitration.

BACKGROUND
Year Admitted to the Bar: 1995
Licensed to Practice in: New York and District of Columbia

Education/Honors: Phi Beta Kappa and Cumma Sum Laude Graduate of Tufts University and Order of the Coif Graduate of University of Virginia School of Law

Professional Assns./Membership: International Franchise Association, American Bar Association forum on franchising

PROVIDE LEGAL SERVICES IN
U.S.: Yes
Canada: Specific Areas Only
Overseas: No

<< >>

PERKINS COIE LLP

1899 Wynkoop St., #700
Denver, CO 80202
Tel: (303) 291-2300
Fax: (303) 291-2400
Web Site: www.perkinscoie.com
Contact: Ms. Kim I. McCullough
Email: kmccullough@perkinscoie.com

PROFILE
Perkins Coie provides clients with advice in the areas of franchising, licensing, distribution, trademark protection, intellectual property, business law, securities and corporate finance, environment and natural resources, estate planning and trust services, labor and employment, litigation, product liability, real estate and land use, regulatory and government affairs and tax law in the industries consisting of aerospace, biotech and life sciences, entertainment/arts, hotels and leisure, international companies, manufacturing, real estate and development, regulated industries, retail, technology companies and telecommunications.

BACKGROUND
Firm Established In: 1912
Serving Franchising Community Since: 2000
% of Billable Hrs. to Franchise Clients: Less than 10%
Full-Time Employees: 1,500+
Full-Time Professionals: 600
Major Franchise Clients in Past 3 Yrs.: Will not disclose.

MR. JAMES D. DEROCHE

1620 26th St., 6 Fl. S.
Santa Monica, CA 90404
Tel: (310) 788-3292
Fax: (310) 843-1280
Email: jderoche@perkinscoie.com

PROFILE
Franchise litigation including trademark, antitrust, provisional remedies, mediation, arbitration and trials.

BACKGROUND
Year Admitted to the Bar: 1976
Licensed to Practice in: California

Education/Honors: University of Santa Clara, University of the Pacific

Professional Assns./Membership: California State Bar

PROVIDE LEGAL SERVICES IN
U.S.: Yes - California
Canada: No
Overseas: No

MS. JUDITH GITTERMAN

1620 26th St., 6 Fl. S.
Santa Monica, CA 90404
Tel: (310) 788-3252
Fax: (310) 788-3399
Email: jgitterman@perkinscoie.com

PROFILE
Franchise litigation; general business litigation; appellate law

BACKGROUND
Year Admitted to the Bar: 1984
Licensed to Practice in: California

Education/Honors: University of Pennsylvania, B.A. 1978 Magna Cum Laude; Cornell Law School, J.D. 1984

Professional Assns./Membership: American Bar Association Forum on Franchising

Publications: Co-presenter, "Litigation Guide to Franchise Terminations," ABA Forum on franchising (October 2002); Author, "Y2K Disclosure Requirements for Franchisors," California Business Law News (Spring 1999); Co-author, "Best Practices: Franchising in Cyberspace," Franchise Update (Fourth Quarter 1998); Co-presenter, "Franchising and the Internet: Agreements, Regulations and Dispute Resolution," ABA Forum on Franchising (October 1998); Panelist, Federal Trade Commission Franchise

Public Workshop Conference (Seattle, WA, November 1997); Co-presenter, "Structuring Franchise Agreements After Postal Instant Press Inc. v. Scaly," 30th Annual Legal Symposium of the International Franchise Association (Washington, D.C., May 1997); Co-author, "Franchise Agreements: Contracts of Adhesion?" Franchise Law Journal (Summer 1996)

PROVIDE LEGAL SERVICES IN

U.S.: Yes
Canada: No
Overseas: No

MS. LYNNE M. HANSON

1899 Wynkoop St., #700
Denver, CO 80202
Tel: (303) 291-2300
Fax: (303) 291-2400
Email: lhanson@perkinscoie.com

PROFILE

Franchise regulatory law, trademark prosecution, franchisor-franchisee relations, franchisee representation, corporate law, business transactions

BACKGROUND

Year Admitted to the Bar: 1988
Licensed to Practice in: Colorado

Education/Honors: University of Colorado, J.D.; Carleton College, B.A.

Professional Assns./Membership: American Bar Association - Business Law Section; Forum Committee on Franchising; Colorado Bar Association; Denver Bar Association

PROVIDE LEGAL SERVICES IN

U.S.: Yes
Canada: Yes
Overseas: Yes

MS. KIM I. MCCULLOUGH

1899 Wynkoop St., #700
Denver, CO 80202
Tel: (303) 291-2300
Fax: (303) 291-2400
Email: kmccullough@perkinscoie.com

PROFILE

Franchise and distribution, initial structuring of franchise programs, franchise disclosure and registration, mergers and acquisitions, international expansion, alternative licensing and distribution, business opportunity regulation, franchise compliance and enforcement, franchise dispute and resolution, transfers and renewals, supplier relationships, franchise advisory council structure and relations, franchisee representation, trademarks and intellectual property, intellectual property counseling, trademark protection, international trademark registration, advertising issues.

BACKGROUND

Year Admitted to the Bar: 1981
Licensed to Practice in: Colorado

Education/Honors: Bachelor of Science Degree, Psychology; Juris Doctor Degree; Phi Beta Kappa; 1981 Bureau of National Affairs Award for scholastic achievement; Student Legal Aid Society Listed in The Best Lawyers in America and International Who's Who of Business Lawyers - Franchise; Martindale-Hubell rating: AV (Highest)

Professional Assns./Membership: American Bar Association; Forum Committee on Franchising; Colorado Bar Association; Denver Bar Association; Int'l Franchise Association

Publications: ABA Forum on Franchising: Annual Judicial & Legislative Update; TEA Legal Symposium: Legal Developments in E-Commerce, Vicarious Liability Developments, Franchise Transfers; CLE International Conference on Franchise Law: Hidden Franchises; Franchise Law - CLE International: Developing a Franchise Program for a Franchisor; National Business Institute, Inc.: Franchising Law in Colorado; Numerous other publications

PROVIDE LEGAL SERVICES IN

U.S.: Yes
Canada: Yes
Overseas: Yes

MR. GARRETT TUTTLE

1899 Wynkoop St., #700
Denver, CO 80202
Tel: (303) 291-2300
Fax: (303) 291-2400
Email: gtuttle@perkinscoie.com

PROFILE

Franchise: draft franchise disclosure documents, franchise agreements and related documents, franchise registration, disputes with franchise regulators, counsel clients on franchising and distribution matters. Intellectual Property: state, federal and foreign trademark registration and maintenance, enforcement and defense of federal and foreign trademark and domain name rights, including cease and desist letters and responses, opposition and cancellation proceedings, domain name administrative proceedings, trademark licensing and sale, consent to use and consent to register agreements, copyright registration and enforcement, trade secrets, asset purchase and sale transactions, confidentiality and non-compete agreements, software licenses, distribution and marketing agreements; unfair competition disputes, advertising and deceptive trade practices.

BACKGROUND

Year Admitted to the Bar: 1984
Licensed to Practice in: Colorado

Education/Honors: Masters of Business Administration, University of Colorado, Graduate School of Business Administration, Denver, CO; Beta Gamma Sigma National Scholastic Honor Society, Juris Doctor, University of Colorado School of Law, Boulder, CO; Bachelor of Arts/History, University of Virginia, Charlottesville, VA, Graduated with Distinction; Martindale-Hubell rating: AV (Highest)

Professional Assns./Membership: Denver and Colorado Bar Associations. Patent, Trademark and Copyright Section, Business Law Section and Franchise Subsection, American Bar Association. Intellectual Property Law Section and Forum on Franchising, International Franchise Association

PROVIDE LEGAL SERVICES IN

U.S.:	Yes
Canada:	Yes
Overseas:	Yes

<< >>

PITEGOFF LAW OFFICE

Ten Bank Street, Suite 540
White Plains, NY 10606
Tel: (914) 681-0100
Fax: (914) 682-7501
Web Site: www.pitlaw.com
Contact: Mr. Thomas M. Pitegoff
Email: pitegoff@pitlaw.com

PROFILE
A recognized, high quality business law boutique, Pitegoff Law Office offers corporate counsel services to companies of all sizes, locally and internationally. The firm handles business transactions, drafts and negotiates contracts, advises on intellectual property law matters and assists clients in their regulatory compliance. The firm has a strong franchise law practice, representing both franchisors and franchisees and advising companies on whether particular license or distribution arrangements constitute franchises. The firm also has a strong computer and Internet law practice.

BACKGROUND
Firm Established In: 1999, and long before that in other configurations

Serving Franchising Community Since:	Since Inception
% of Billable Hrs. to Franchise Clients:	33%
Full-Time Employees:	1 paralegal
Full-Time Professionals:	2 attorneys

Major Franchise Clients in Past 3 Yrs.: We represent several U.S. and foreign franchisors as well as franchisees of a number of different franchise brands.

MR. THOMAS M. PITEGOFF

Ten Bank Street, Suite 540
White Plains, NY 10606
Tel: (914) 681-0100
Fax: (914) 682-7501
Email: pitegoff@pitlaw.com

PROFILE
General business law, with a focus on computers and technology, franchising and international business. Services include contract drafting and negotiation, corporate transactions, intellectual property counseling, and resolving disputes before they escalate into litigation. Work includes, for franchisors, preparing franchise agreements and franchise offering circulars, and handling franchise filings and regulatory compliance. For franchisees, our work includes counseling franchisees their franchise purchases and in their corporate matters. We negotiate franchise agreements both on behalf of franchisors and franchisees, and we advise others on the question of whether particular arrangements constitute franchises.

BACKGROUND

Year Admitted to the Bar:	1977
Licensed to Practice in:	New York

Education/Honors: Martindale-Hubbell AV rating. Listed in all editions of The International Who's Who of Franchise Lawyers.

Professional Assns./Membership: Member of the executive committee of the NY State Bar Association's Business Law Section. Franchise mediator and ICANN arbitrator for domain name disputes through the CPR Institute for Dispute Resolution. Served in various leadership capacities in the Business Law Section of the American Bar Association (ABA) and as a former member of the Governing Committee of the ABA's Forum on Franchising.

Publications: Open Source, Open World: New Possibilities for Computer Software (BUSINESS LAW TODAY, American Bar Association, Sept./Oct. 2001); The Inadvertent CyberFranchisor (CYBERSPACE LAWYER April 1998); Choice of Law in Franchise Relationships (FRANCHISE LAW JOURNAL, American Bar Association, Spring 1995); Franchise Relationship Laws: A Minefield for Franchisors (BUSINESS LAWYER, American Bar Association, Nov. 1989) (reprinted in the American Bar Association's book, BUILDING FRANCHISE RELATIONSHIPS (1996, 2004); Ways to Avoid Being a Franchise (FRANCHISE LAW JOURNAL, American Bar Association, Fall 1992); Plus a number of papers prepared in conjunction with franchise law conferences.

PROVIDE LEGAL SERVICES IN
U.S.: Yes, but my practice focuses on the New York metropolitan area.
Canada: Yes, with the assistance of Canadian counsel.
Overseas: I work with foreign counsel anywhere that U.S. companies are permitted to do business.

<< >>

PLUNKETT & COONEY, P.C.

505 N. Woodward, # 3000
Bloomfield Hills, MI 48304
Tel: (248) 901-4000
Fax: (248) 901-4040
Contact: Mr. A. Benjamin Henson

PROFILE
Plunkett & Cooney is a full-service law firm with 140 attorneys and 12 offices. Our main area of concentration includes business law, general liability, insurance defense and municipal law. With respect to business law, we focus our practice in the areas of intellectual property, franchise law, banking and finance, bankruptcy, contracts, complex transactions, corporate compliance, health care, hospitality, labor and employment, mergers and acquisitions, securities, real estate, "white collar" criminal, environmental, telecommunications and Y2K matters.

BACKGROUND

Serving Franchising Community Since:	1974
% of Billable Hrs. to Franchise Clients:	30%

Major Franchise Clients in Past 3 Yrs.: Doctors Associates, Inc. (Subway); Color Tile; The Body Shop; Applebee's International, Inc.; Powerhouse Gyms International, Inc.; Mr. B's Restaurant Group; ATL International; Shields Restaurants.

MR. A. BENJAMIN HENSON

Tel: (248) 901-4036
Email: hensonbe@plunkettlaw.com

PROFILE
Mr. Henson is a shareholder who concentrates his practice in the areas of franchise law, construction litigation and commercial law. For 25 years, Mr. Henson has represented franchisors in both drafting uniform offering circulars and franchise agreements and in litigating and arbitrating disputes. Mr. Henson also represented prospective franchisees considering franchise opportunities. Mr. Henson serves as an arbitrator in franchise disputes.

BACKGROUND

Year Admitted to the Bar:	1968
Licensed to Practice in:	Michigan

Education/Honors: Juris Doctor, University of Michigan Law School, 1968; B.S., Eastern Michigan University, 1965 (Stoic Honor Society).

Professional Assns./Membership: ABA, Forum Committee on Franchising, Forum Committee on Construction Industry, AAA Large Complex Case Panel - Construction, Regional Commercial Advisory Committee of the AAA.

SONNENSCHEIN NATH & ROSENTHAL LLP

Sonnenschein®
SONNENSCHEIN NATH & ROSENTHAL LLP

8000 Sears Tower, 233 South Wacker Drive
Chicago, IL 60606
Tel: (312) 876-8000
Fax: (312) 876-3151
Web Site: www.sonnenschein.com
Other Offices In: Chicago, Kansas City, Los Angeles, New York, St. Louis, San Francisco, Short Hills, NJ, Washington D.C., West Palm Beach

PROFILE
Sonnenschein has earned a worldwide reputation as the law firm most likely to help its clients prosper and grow. Providing high-quality, innovative legal services, we help our clients identify and seize opportunities and blunt threats to their prosperity. With 700 lawyers and other professionals in nine U.S. offices and a global reach throughout Asia, Europe, the Middle East, Latin America and Canada, Sonnenschein serves many of the world's largest and best-known businesses, nonprofits and individuals. The firm is a leader in innovative legal services, serving its clients through integrated, inter-office cooperation and teamwork among practice groups to provide efficient, effective, and timely legal services and business counseling.

BACKGROUND

Firm Established In:	1906
Serving Franchising Community Since:	mid-1960s
% of Billable Hrs. to Franchise Clients:	N/A

Major Franchise Clients in Past 3 Yrs.: McDonald's Corporation; Culligan International Company; InterContinental Hotels Group PLC (Holiday Inn, Crowne Plaza, Staybridge Suites; Candlewood Suites); Pella Corporation; Sara Lee Corporation

MR. JOHN BAER

8000 Sears Tower, 233 South Wacker Drive
Chicago, IL 60606
Tel: (312) 876-2604
Fax: (312) 876-7934
Email: jbaer@sonnenschein.com

PROFILE
Mr. Baer has a broad transactional practice with extensive experience representing companies engaged in franchising, distribution, sales and commercial activities, both domestically and internationally. His wide range of experience includes Franchising & Distribution, Corporate & Commercial Practice, International Law, Sales Representatives, Product Safety, Warranties, Sales, Legislation, Administrative Law, and General Commercial.

BACKGROUND

Education/Honors: University of Illinois College of Law, J.D., 1966; University of Illinois Law Forum (Law Review) (Asst. Editor 65-66); University of Illinois, B.A. Political Science, 1963; International Who's Who of Business Lawyers, Franchise; Illinois State Bar Association; ABA; International Bar Association, InterPacific Bar Association

Professional Assns./Membership: Mr. Baer is Chair of the Illinois Attorney General's Franchise Advisory Board. He is a member of the Governing Committee of the ABA Forum on Franchising and is currently acting as the Publications Officer of the Forum. He is a member of the Legal/Legislative Committee of the International Franchise Association and on the Board of Editors of LJN's Franchising Business & Law Alert. He is also a member of the Editorial Board of the Canadian Franchise Review and a member of the Editorial Advisory Board of the International Journal of Franchising Law. Mr. Baer is currently Editor, CCH Sales Representative Law Guide (1998 - Present). He formerly served as Editor-in-Chief of the ABA Forum on Franchising's The Franchise Lawyer, Associate Editor of the ABA Forum on Franchising's Franchise Law Journal, a co-author of a quarterly column on international franchise developments for the World Franchise & Business Report, and a Vice President of the Franchising Committee of Union Internationale des Avocats.

Publications: Mr. Baer is the author of numerous articles, professional opinions and speeches, which are available upon request.

PROVIDE LEGAL SERVICES IN

U.S.:	Yes
Canada:	Yes
Overseas:	Yes

MR. ROBERT H. KING, JR.

8000 Sears Tower, 233 South Wacker Drive
Chicago, IL 60606
Tel: (312) 876-7944
Fax: (312) 876-7934
Email: rking@sonnenschein.com

PROFILE

Bob King is a partner in the Chicago office and serves as the National Chair of Franchising and Distribution Litigation within the Antitrust Marketing Practices and Franchising practice group. A widely respected commercial litigator, Mr. King has more than 25 years of trial and appellate experience in state and federal courts nationwide.

BACKGROUND

Licensed to Practice in:	Illinois, California

Education/Honors: University of Michigan, J.D. Magna Cum Laude, 1978; Visiting Student, Harvard Law, 1976-77; Dartmouth College, B.A., Magna Cum Laude, 1975

PROVIDE LEGAL SERVICES IN

U.S.:	Yes
Canada:	Yes
Overseas:	Yes

MR. ALAN H. SILBERMAN

8000 Sears Tower, 233 South Wacker Drive
Chicago, IL 60606
Tel: (312) 876-8103
Fax: (312) 876-7934
Email: asilberman@sonnenschein.com

PROFILE

Mr. Silberman is the chair of Sonnenschein's national Antitrust, Marketing Practice, Franchise/Distribution Group. He has more than 35 years' experience in antitrust and franchising litigation, counseling and related transactional representation, as well as in general commercial litigation. He has represented franchisors in a number of negotiated, litigated and arbitrated disputes with franchisees and third parties and regularly represents franchising clients in domestic and international activities.

BACKGROUND

Licensed to Practice in:	Illinois

Education/Honors: Yale Law School, LL.B., 1964; Northwestern University, B.A., 1961 with Distinction and Departmental Honors

Professional Assns./Membership: Mr. Silberman served as Chair of the American Bar Association Section of Antitrust Law for 1993-94 and as Immediate Past Chair during 1994-95. He has also held various officer positions since 1988, previously serving as a member of the Council of the ABA Section of Antitrust Law and as a member of its Special Committee on the Role of the Federal Trade Commission, and a member of the ABA House of Delegates. He has participated as a member of the Antitrust Section's Special Task Force on Competition Policy which presented views on competition and consumer protection issues to the Clinton/Gore Administration in March, 1993. A member of the Bureau of National Affairs' Antitrust and Trade Regulation Advisory Board, he is a frequent speaker on antitrust topics relating to marketing, distribution, franchising, litigation and insurance at various national and international programs and seminars. He is also a member of the Illinois Franchise Advisory Board appointed by the Attorney General of Illinois.

Publications: "US Antitrust Principles Affecting Distribution Practices" (Insight Conference - Domestic and International Perspectives on Managing Compliance in a Changing Law Environment, Toronto, 2004); "Dispositive Motions in Franchise Litigation - Summary Judgment" (American Bar Association 35th Annual Forum on Franchising, 2002).

PROVIDE LEGAL SERVICES IN

U.S.:	Yes
Canada:	Yes
Overseas:	Yes

MS. ROCHELLE SPANDORF

601 South Figueroa Street, Suite 1500
Los Angeles, CA 90017
Tel: (213) 892-5036
Fax: (213) 623-9924
Email: rspandorf@sonnenschein.com

PROFILE
Rochelle Spandorf has over 25 years' experience representing franchisors, manufacturers, licensors and suppliers in their domestic and international expansion and strategic development, concentrating on a broad spectrum of transactional and regulatory issues. She has expertise in structuring distribution, franchise, and licensing programs in all market sectors; regulatory compliance (including disclosure documents, registration filings, termination, transfer and relationship laws); mergers and acquisitions of franchise and distribution companies; and various operational and relationship issues. She counsels clients on antitrust and pricing matters, trademark protection, structuring alternatives to franchising, and contract negotiations and serves as an expert witness on franchise issues. She represents subfranchisors and area developers in the acquisition and sale of franchise rights and on transactional matters. Ms. Spandorf is the first woman to chair the ABA Forum of Franchising, the nation's leading franchise law association, and has twice chaired the California State Bar's Franchise Law Committee.

BACKGROUND

Year Admitted to the Bar:	1977
Licensed to Practice in:	CA

Education/Honors: J.D. Washington University in St. Louis (1976); B.S. Cornell University (1973) with distinction. Ms. Spandorf is listed in the International Who's Who of Franchise Lawyers and in Los Angeles Magazine's list of Super Lawyers as one of Southern California's best franchise and distribution attorneys in a survey of peers.

Professional Assns./Membership: American Bar Association (member and past Chair, Forum on Franchising; member Business Law Section; member, Antitrust Section); California State Bar (former Chair, Franchise Law Committee; member and former Executive Committee member, Business Law Section); International Bar Association (member, Legal/Legislative Committee).

Publications: Past Editor, ABA Forum on Franchising's Franchise Law Journal; co-Editor of ABA Forum on Franchising's Building Franchise Relationships; Editor, Leader's Franchising Business & Law Alert. Ms. Spandorf is a frequent speaker and author on franchise topics for various legal and other professional organizations and has developed and taught franchise courses for the University of California at Santa Barbara and California State University.

PROVIDE LEGAL SERVICES IN

U.S.:	Yes
Canada:	Yes
Overseas:	Yes

<< >>

STEPHEN A. COLLEY, APC

12760 High Buff Drive, Suite 250
San Diego, CA 92130
Tel: (858) 259-0888
Fax: (858) 259-3110
Contact: Mr. Stephen Colley
Email: colley@colleylaw.com

PROFILE
The firm concentrates on providing legal services to both franchisors and franchisees for registration and ongoing counseling. We also provide various business and transactional services.

BACKGROUND

Firm Established In:	1976
Serving Franchising Community Since:	1976
% of Billable Hrs. to Franchise Clients:	Majority
Full-Time Employees:	4
Full-Time Professionals:	2

Major Franchise Clients in Past 3 Yrs.: Expense Reduction Analysts, Inc.; Instant Imprints, Inc.; Liberty Fitness, Inc.; Copy Club West, Inc.

MR. STEPHEN A. COLLEY

12760 High Buff Drive, Suite 250
San Diego, CA 92130
Tel: (858) 259-0888
Fax: (858) 259-3110
Email: colley@colleylaw.com

PROFILE
Mr. Colley concentrates on all aspects of franchise legal work including Uniform Offering Circulars, franchise agreements registrations and ongoing counseling. As a former attorney with the Department of Corporations in the late 1970's, he has continued to provide franchise legal services for over 25 years.

BACKGROUND

Year Admitted to the Bar:	1976
Licensed to Practice in:	California

Education/Honors: BA from UCLA in 1971; CA State University at Los Angeles, Masters in Clinical Psychology, 1973; University of San Diego, J.D., 1976; Martindale-Hubbell rating: AV

Professional Assns./Membership: ABA, State Bar of CA, San Diego Co. Bar Assoc.; Former attorney with the Dept. of Corporations

PROVIDE LEGAL SERVICES IN

U.S.:	Yes - CA
Canada:	No
Overseas:	No

<< >>

SUZANNE C. CUMMINGS, LAW OFFICE

The Law Office of Suzanne C. Cummings

23 Walker Brook Dr., #44
Reading, MA 01867
Tel: (800) 982-9636 (781) 942-9221
Fax: (781) 942-0924
Web Site: www.cummingslaw.org
Contact: Ms. Suzanne C. Cummings
Email: scummings@cummingslaw.org

PROFILE

My firm's focus is franchise law. We provide legal support specifically designed for small and medium size franchisors looking to grow, including franchise system design document development and maintenance, franchise registrations, franchisor/franchisee relations and mediation.

BACKGROUND

Firm Established In:	2001
Serving Franchising Community Since:	2001
% of Billable Hrs. to Franchise Clients:	100%

MS. SUZANNE C. CUMMINGS

23 Walker Brook Dr., #44
Reading, MA 01867
Tel: (781) 942-9221
Fax: (781) 942-0924
Email: scummings@cummingslaw.org

PROFILE

I advise counsel and represent small and medium size businesses and individuals as franchise counsel in transactional matters. I prepare regulatory documents and uniform franchise offering circulars including all related contracts and exhibits. I also have over 20 years of experience as a license and franchise developer.

BACKGROUND

Year Admitted to the Bar:	2001
Licensed to Practice in:	Massachusetts and Federal

Education/Honors: Suffolk University Law School, Boston, MA - Juris Doctorate; Emmanuel College, Boston, MA - Bachelor of Science, Business Administration

Professional Assns./Membership: MA Supreme Judicial Court; U.S. District, District of MA; MA Bar Association; Essex County Bar Association; ABA's Forum on Franchising

PROVIDE LEGAL SERVICES IN

U.S.:	Yes
Canada:	No
Overseas:	Yes - Canada, United Kingdom, Korea

<< >>

THAV, GROSS, STEINWAY & BENNETT, P.C.

30150 Telegraph Road, Suite 444
Bingham Farms, MI 48025-4549
Tel: (248) 645-1700
Fax: (248) 645-8205
Web Site: www.thavgross.com
Contact: Mr. David Steinberg
Email: dsteinberg@thavgross.com
Other Offices In: Dearborn, MI

PROFILE

Franchise Offering Circular preparation, state registration, litigation/arbitration, real estate, tax representation, corporate law, mergers & acquisitions, business planning and development

BACKGROUND

Firm Established In:	1979
Serving Franchising Community Since:	1979
% of Billable Hrs. to Franchise Clients:	5%
Full-Time Employees:	21
Full-Time Professionals:	14

Major Franchise Clients in Past 3 Yrs.: Bank's Superstores Franchise Corp.; Jantize America Inc.; Handypro Handyman Services Inc.; House of Blinds and More Inc.; Cedar Promotions, Inc. (Realty Executives - Michigan); Keller-Williams, Inc.

MR. DAVID L. STEINBERG

30150 Telegraph Road, Suite 444
Bingham Farms, MI 48025-4549
Tel: (248) 645-1700
Fax: (248) 645-8205
Email: dsteinberg@thavgross.com

PROFILE

Franchise System Development, Offering Circulars, litigation/arbitration. We offer the ability to create and implement new franchise systems as well as continuing legal support to ensure compliance with state and federal regulations. Complete state registration preparation and filings as well.

BACKGROUND

Year Admitted to the Bar:	Michigan - 1980; California - 1987
Licensed to Practice in:	Michigan, California, federal courts

Education/Honors: J.D. University of Detroit School of Law; LLM - Trade Regulation, Georgetown University Law Center

Professional Assns./Membership: Cable Program Host - "Franchise Focus"; Member of ABA Franchise Forum Committee; State Bar of Michigan Antitrust/Franchise Discussion

Publications: Guest Speaker, Direct Selling Association, Washington, D.C. (February, 2004); Program Host, "Legal Talk," "Franchise Focus," "It's Your Speaking Business," Comcast Cable, 1995 to 2001; Contributor, LOS ANGELES DAILY LAW JOURNAL, 1990; "May and Steinberg, Great Expectations for Franchising: The 1984 Amendments to the Michigan Franchise Investment Law," MICHIGAN BAR JOURNAL, January 1985; "Application of the Antitrust and Labor Exemptions to Collective Bargaining of the Reserve System in Professional Baseball," WAYNE LAW REVIEW, vol. 28, p. 1301, 1982; "The Role of Section 2 of the Sherman Act in International Patent Fraud: Walk Talk and Carry a Big Stick," WASHINGTON UNIVERSITY LAW REVIEW, vol. 59, p. 123, 1981; "The National Hockey League Reserve System: A Restraint of Trade?" comment, UNIVERSITY OF DETROIT URBAN LAW REVIEW, 1979.

PROVIDE LEGAL SERVICES IN

U.S.:	Yes
Canada:	Yes
Overseas:	Yes - Canada

VINSON FRANCHISE LAW FIRM

858 Jennifer
Incline Village, NV 89451
Tel: (775) 832-5577
Fax: (775) 832-5579
Web Site: www.franchiselaw.net
Contact: Mr. Rob Vinson
Email: rob@franchiselaw.net

PROFILE
Our practice is devoted exclusively to franchise law. We specialize in representing start-up franchisors on a nationwide basis in connection with all types of franchise legal matters and transactions, except litigation. We regularly help clients with: structuring the franchise system to minimize legal and business risks; drafting franchise agreements and other agreements to be used in franchising; drafting the uniform franchise offering circular and exhibits; preparing and filing state registration forms; training staff on franchise sales compliance; and advising on state laws affecting franchise sales and relationships. We also represent established franchisors and international franchisors.

BACKGROUND

Serving Franchising Community Since:	1995
% of Billable Hrs. to Franchise Clients:	100%
Full-Time Employees:	1
Full-Time Professionals:	1

Major Franchise Clients in Past 3 Yrs.: ColorTyme Rent-to-Own, Tutoring Club, Shake's Frozen Custard, Paciugo Gelato, Bath Junkie, Cert-A-Roof International, Miracles Fitness, Discount Sport Nutrition, Dutch Bros. of California Coffee, Atlantic Pin Striping

MR. ROBERT E. VINSON, JR.

858 Jennifer Street
Incline Village, NV 89451
Tel: (775) 832-5577
Fax: (775) 832-5579
Email: rob@franchiselaw.net

PROFILE
Rob Vinson is a franchise law specialist representing start-up and existing franchisors throughout the country. He has experience with federal franchise law and with the franchise and business opportunity laws of every state. Rob handles all types of franchise legal matters and transactions, except litigation. He has international experience with inbound and outbound franchises. Rob has more than 15 years' legal experience, and is AV-rated in Martindale-Hubbell Legal Directory ("very high to preeminent legal ability and very high ethical standards"). Rob was a partner in a large Dallas law firm, but left to start his own franchise firm in 2001.

BACKGROUND

Year Admitted to the Bar:	1987
Licensed to Practice in:	California, Texas

Education/Honors: AV Rating Martindale-Hubbell; J.D., SMU School of Law 1987; B.S., Texas Tech University 1983
Professional Assns./Membership: American Bar Association's Forum on Franchising; State Bar Of Texas; California State Bar's Business Law Section; past chair of the Dallas Bar Association Franchise & Distribution Law Section (2000)

Publications: "Recent Developments in Covenants Not To Compete" IFA's Annual Legal Symposium (2000); "Marketing, Sales and Legal Requirements: How to Balance Enthusiastic Company Promotions with Legal Requirements" DSA's Legal and Ethics Seminar (2000); "The Official Rules: A Primer on Sweepstakes Law for Franchise and Distribution Systems" DBA Franchise and Distribution Law Section (1999); "Franchisor-Franchisee Relationships: The 10 Commandments from Franchise Counsel" IFA's Houston Franchise Business Network (1997)

PROVIDE LEGAL SERVICES IN

U.S.:	Yes
Canada:	Yes
Overseas:	Yes

Franchise Consultants and Service Providers

Chapter 50

AMERICAN FRANCHISEE ASSOCIATION (AFA)

53 West Jackson Blvd, Suite 205
Chicago, IL 60604
Tel: (312) 431-0545
Fax: (312) 431-1132
Web Site: www.franchisee.org
E-mail: eileen@franchisee.org
Contact: Ms. Eileen Foxman, Executive Assistant

BUSINESS FOCUS

The American Franchisee Association (AFA) is a national trade association of franchisees and dealers founded in February 1993. Fifteen thousand individuals who own over 30,000 franchised outlets in 60 different industries are members of the AFA. The AFA was formed to improve the business conditions for franchising generally, while working diligently to protect the economic interests of franchisees. The AFA accomplishes this goal by providing two additional avenues to resolve potential conflicts. First, the AFA constantly advocates the franchisee's position. Second, the AFA communicates with federal and state lawmakers about the inherent imbalance written into the contracts governing the franchisor-franchisee relationship.

Major Areas of Concentration:

1) Representation: The AFA represents the interests of franchisees to the media, the government and the public.
2) Communication: The AFA publishes the AFA E-Newsletter for its members to keep them informed on recent legal decisions and operational issues of importance to small business franchisees. AFA's Web Community provides an online forum for franchisees to communicate, buy and sell products and services, exchange ideas and post important notices.
3) Networking: AFA members can network AFA Franchisee Leadership Summits held in Chicago. At the Franchisee Leadership Summit, the leaders of independent franchisee associations are invited to spend a day sharing their experiences and discussing issues of concern. Franchisees can also network on AFA's Web Community through chat rooms, discussion forums and personal web sites.
4) Legal Referrals: AFA's Directory of Affiliate Members will put you in contact with some of the best franchisee lawyers in the country.
5) Health Insurance: AFA provides group health insurance for its members through either: 1) a Mini-Med program 2) a self-funded program; or 3) an individual program.

BACKGROUND

Business Established In:	1993
Franchise Consulting Since:	1993
% of Billable Hrs. to Franchise Clients:	100
Full-Time Employees:	3
Full-Time Professionals:	2

Major Franchising Clients in Past 3 Yrs.: Association of Kentucky Fried Chicken Franchisees, National Franchise Association (Burger King), National Coalition of 7-Eleven Franchisees, Denny's Franchisee Association, Dairy Queen Operators Association, International Organization of Little Ceasar's Franchisees, Roto Rooter Franchisee Association, National Association of Satellite Contract Owners (H&R Block) and Quizno's Franchisee Association.

AREAS CONSULT IN

U.S.:	Yes
Canada:	Yes

Overseas: Yes - We consult internationally, specifically Canada, Australia, and China.

BENETRENDS

450 B Street, Suite 1950
San Diego, CA 92101
Tel: (866) 837-6063 (619) 692-3807
Fax: (619) 858-2996
Web Site: www.benetrends.com
E-mail: lfischer@benetrendsinc.com
Contact: Mr. Len Fischer, Esq., President
Other Offices In: 1180 Welsh Road, Suite 170M, North Wales, PA 19454

BUSINESS FOCUS
At BeneTrends, Inc., we help rainy day savers become rainmakers. Using our Rainmaker Plan, you can use the funds in your 401K, IRA, profit-sharing, or annuity plans to open a franchise--and become a rainmaker--without taxes or penalties.

Major Areas of Concentration:

1) Franchise Financing
2) Small Business Financing

BACKGROUND

Full-Time Employees:	Confidential
Full-Time Professionals:	Confidential
Major Franchising Clients in Past 3 Yrs.:	Confidential

AREAS CONSULT IN

U.S.:	Yes
Canada:	No
Overseas:	No

CANAM FRANCHISE DEVELOPMENT GROUP

2607 McBain Ave.
Vancouver, BC V6L 2C7 CANADA
Tel: (604) 730-5553
Fax: (604) 876-6460
Web Site: www.canamfranchise.com
E-mail: rob@canamfranchise.com
Contact: Mr. Rob Lancit, President
Other Offices In:

BUSINESS FOCUS
CANAM Franchise Development Group helps U.S. franchisors sell franchises in Canada. We become your Canadian Franchise Sales Team. We provide franchise development services to companies wanting to franchise in Canada. With dedicated personal attention and concern for our clients, our team of experts offers a proven system that develops, packages, and launches franchise programs within the Canadian marketplace. And most importantly, we take responsibility for implementing our sales strategies and recommendations. CANAM Franchise Development Group can accelerate your company's expansion into Canada. Our vast knowledge of the Canadian marketplace and our extensive industry database, gives you immediate access to qualified individuals or corporations who are committed to franchising. We have solved the problems most franchisors are likely to experience in developing their concept in Canada. Our main goal is to make your franchise program lucrative, marketable and enduring. We believe your success is our success.

Major Areas of Concentration:

1) Sales & Marketing: 1) Provide a Canadian office 2) Planning, organizing and controlling all aspects of sales process 3) Lead Generating Programs 4) Recruitment and selection of the right franchises 5) Franchisee evaluation and profiles 6) Access to our database of corporations and entrepreneurs actively seeking franchise opportunities 7) Provide short term local management and operations services on initial stage of franchise development 8) Development of a marketing plan and budget incorporating unique, efficient, inexpensive cost strategies that yield optimum results 9) Brand awareness at Canadian exhibitions
2) Legal & Real Estate - Through our affiliation with leading franchise legal & real estate experts, CANAM offers: 1) Assistance with trademark registration 2) Advice on incorporating in Canada 3) Information about disclosure laws of Canada 4) Preparation of legal agreements and documentation 5) Lease negotiations 6) Store design and build out
3) Financing: 1) Assistance with obtaining third party financing for franchisees from finance companies that specialize in all types of financing for franchisees including start-up expenses, equipment and real estate

BACKGROUND

Business Established In:	2001
Franchise Consulting Since:	2001
% of Billable Hrs. to Franchise Clients:	100
Full-Time Employees:	2

Major Franchising Clients in Past 3 Yrs.: Discovery Computers, Precision Tune Auto Care, The Tan Company, Criterium Engineers, Quik Internet, Instant Imprints, Cleantastic International, Puckmasters, Computer Renaissance

AREAS CONSULT IN

U.S.:	Yes
Canada:	Yes

Overseas: Yes - Australia, New Zealand, Singapore, United Kingdom, Italy, The Caribbean

C-K YELLOW PAGES

733 N. Van Buren St.
Milwaukee, WI 53202
Tel: (800) 236-3574 (414) 227-3481
Fax: (414) 227-3474
Web Site: www.ckyellowpages.com
E-mail: rkennedy@c-k.com
Contact: Mr. Robert Kennedy, Vice President
Other Offices In: Baltimore, Chicago, Cincinnati, Denver, Kansas City, New York, Orlando, Phoenix, San Francisco, Twin Cities, Los Angeles, Seattle

BUSINESS FOCUS

Franchise Yellow Pages Advertising is our business. At C-K Yellow Pages we create and execute complete Yellow Pages programs that are customized to your Franchise business objectives and your local budget. Whether your program is regional, national, or international, we're dedicated to maximizing your program results and knowing which directories and ad sizes will be most effective. Handling hundreds of accounts globally, we have the experience and initiative to enhance your Franchise Yellow Pages program by taking advantage of applicable publisher incentives and discount offers. Internet Yellow Pages programs can also be coordinated to provide complementary online representation. C-K Yellow Pages is an industry leader and a Certified Marketing Representative (CMR555). Member: IFA, YPIMA, ADM, AAAA and ICOM.

Major Areas of Concentration:
Major Areas of Concentration: Franchise Program Specialists
1) Franchisor/Franchisee service contracts
2) Franchisee group ad coordination
3) Flexible billing and program reporting
4) Corporate compliant
5) Publisher incentives

BACKGROUND

Business Established In:	1898
Franchise Consulting Since:	1968
% of Billable Hrs. to Franchise Clients:	15
Full-Time Employees:	600
Full-Time Professionals:	600

Major Franchising Clients in Past 3 Yrs.: Precision Door Service; Purofirst; Jiffy Lube; Sign A Rama; Cruise One; Coit; Handyman Matters; Careers USA; Applebees; Figaros Pizza; EmbroidMe; Billboard Connection; Fish Window Cleaning; Fed USA; etc.

AREAS CONSULT IN

U.S.:	Yes
Canada:	Yes
Overseas:	No

COMPREHENSIVE LOYALTY

862 E. Wildmere
Longwood, FL 32750
Tel: (407) 339-2612
Fax: (407) 339-7412
Web Site: www.comprehensiveloyalty.com
E-mail: petertravers@earthlink.net
Contact: Mr. Peter Travers, Founder
Other Offices In: San Francisco area and Virginia Beach, VA

BUSINESS FOCUS

Comprehensive Loyalty is a team of seasoned consultants and analysts specializing in site selection studies and customer loyalty development. The name Comprehensive Loyalty was chosen because of years of working with companies who have fragmented their customer development programs by ignoring site location and modern database marketing techniques. We specialize in a comprehensive approach that incorporates store development (site selection), loyalty-based data processing, database marketing and customer profiling (RFM scores, customer segments of highest lifetime value, attrition studies), market share analysis and incentive compensation. This approach leads to achieving Marketing Alignment (TM) and a "Loyalty Transformation Process. Computerized site selection: rigorous exmination of your present customer base is carried out using regression models to determine predictive attributes. Distance decay models, competitive effect formulas, sisterstore or cannibalization formulas are all combined in a computer model. The model is cross-validated for accuracy (usually within + or - 5% to 8%m depending on sample sizes). Hundreds of potential sites are then evaluated using GIS software. Don't fly in the dark, use science to find your best location. Customer profiling for target marketing. Loyalty analysis for increased profits, and databased marketing services are all provided. Associates have combined 80 years of experience.

BACKGROUND

Full-Time Professionals:	5

Major Franchising Clients in Past 3 Yrs.: Safeway, Certified Growers, Stater Bros., Premium Pet, Yardbirds, Gap, Home Depot, Ernst Home Centers, Wickes Furniture and Sportmart. Comprehensive Loyalty is also the #1 supplier of site selection studies for RV and marine industries.

AREAS CONSULT IN

U.S.:	Yes
Canada:	Yes
Overseas:	No

CUMMINGS BUSINESS DEVELOPMENT CORP.

23 Walkers Brook Dr., #44
Reading, MA 01867
Tel: (800) 982-9636 (781) 942-9220
Fax: (781) 942-0924
Web Site: www.cummingsbiz.com
E-mail: info@cummingsbiz.com
Contact: Ms. Suzanne C. Cummings, President

BUSINESS FOCUS

We are a national franchise consulting organization providing a wide range of services to both start-up and established franchisors as well as prospective franchisees. Our services include franchise system development, franchise sales strategies, marketing/direct mail/advertising, press releases/publicity programs, franchisee relationship programs, operations manuals, business plans, document maintenance and more.

Major Areas of Concentration:

1) Franchise System Development
2) Franchise Sales Strategies
3) System Documentation Development
4) Franchise Document Maintenance

BACKGROUND

Business Established In:	1992
Franchise Consulting Since:	1992
% of Billable Hrs. to Franchise Clients:	100
Full-Time Employees:	NR
Full-Time Professionals:	NR

Major Franchising Clients in Past 3 Yrs.: Hoop Mountain, Resort Maps, Gecko Hospitality, Ideal Image, Blackjack Pasta Bar

AREAS CONSULT IN

U.S.:	Yes
Canada:	Yes - Toronto
Overseas:	Yes - United Kingdom

DAVIER CONSULTANTS INC.

438 St. Malo West
Ile Bizard, Montreal, PQ H9C 2P4 CANADA
Tel: (514) 620-3770
Fax: (514) 620-1150
Web Site: www.davierconsultants.ca
E-mail: michel@davierconsultants.ca
Contact: Mr. Michel Gagnon, President
Other Offices In: Halifax, Calgary

BUSINESS FOCUS

Davier Consultants is a Canadian firm specialized in franchising, corporate management consulting and strategic development. We offer our services to Canadian, American and international franchisors in finding the right partner, reviewing acquisition or partnership strategies, market analysis, and developing their concepts internationally. We have strategic alliances with other firms around the world. We have extensive knowledge in reviewing the potential of franchising existing companies and we will provide hands-on assistance on how to implement the strategy.

Major Areas of Concentration:

1) Developing the Canadian market
2) Franchising existing local companies
3) International development
4) Financial and management strategies

BACKGROUND

Business Established In:	1994
Franchise Consulting Since:	1994
% of Billable Hrs. to Franchise Clients:	65
Full-Time Employees:	6
Full-Time Professionals:	4

Major Franchising Clients in Past 3 Yrs.: Servicemaster, Boston Pizza, MotoPhoto, A Buck or Two, Medichair, Expense Reduction Analysts, H&R Block, Van Houtte, Tutor Doctor, Mr. Lube

AREAS CONSULT IN

U.S.:	Yes
Canada:	Yes

Overseas: Yes - South Africa, Morocco, Lebanon, Argentina, Chile, China, Romania

DIAMOND FINANCIAL SERVICES (FRANCHISE FUNDING)

262 Highway 36
West Keansburg, NJ 07734
Tel: (877) 508-2274 (732) 787-9191
Fax: (732) 495-7058

Web Site: www.franchisefunding.net
E-mail: don@franchiseloans.com
Contact: Mr. Don Johnson, President

BUSINESS FOCUS

We specialize in franchise business lending nationwide as franchise finance specialists/consultants. We have close relationships and utilize only the most aggressive business/franchise lenders for loan sizes from $100K to $3 million. Loan programs include start-ups, expansion, business acquisition, real estate, and refinance. Our specialty is SBA (Small Business Administration) financing, lending programs that are guaranteed by SBA but provided by conventional leaders. SBA programs are offered to almost anyone! We help you evaluate the possibility of buying a Franchise, assist you through the application process, professionally package your loan application and work with you until loan closing.

Major Areas of Concentration:
SBA financing can be applied for:
1) Acquisition of Business (or Buyout of Partners)
2) Franchise Businesses and Fees (for start-up or multi-locations)
3) Equipment or Equipment Refinance
4) Working Capital
5) Debt Restructuring

BACKGROUND

Business Established In: 1999
Franchise Consulting Since: 1999
% of Billable Hrs. to Franchise Clients: 90
Major Franchising Clients in Past 3 Yrs.: Subway, Quiznos, UPS Store, Coldstone Creamery, The Coffee Beanery, Maggie Moos, Cottman Transmission, Midas, Cartridge World, Executive Tans

AREAS CONSULT IN

U.S.: Yes
Canada: No
Overseas: No

DYNAMIC PERFORMANCE SYSTEMS, INC.

478 Valermo Dr.
Etobicoke, ON M8W 2M7 CANADA
Tel: (800) 719-9993 (416) 201-0202
Fax: (416) 201-0808
Web Site: www.franchise-profiles.com
E-mail: fred@franchise-profiles.com
Contact: Mr. Fred Berni, President

BUSINESS FOCUS

Looking for a way to select and train great franchisees? The FranchiZe Profile can help you do it with unparalleled accuracy. Unlike other selection tools and profiles, the FranchiZe Profile is concerned solely with predicting performance of your franchise candidate. Rather than describing a personality, it measures the 7 common core values all successful franchisees have in common. Then it compares your candidate to successful franchisees. It gives you pointers on what to watch out for during the selection process. Plus, to help ensure a candidate's success, it gives training recommendations. Also included in every report is an Interviewing Workbook.

Major Areas of Concentration:

1) Franchisee selection
2) Pre-employment testing and training for retail staff and managers

BACKGROUND

Business Established In: 1988
Franchise Consulting Since: 1989
% of Billable Hrs. to Franchise Clients: 100
Full-Time Employees: 1
Full-Time Professionals: NR
Major Franchising Clients in Past 3 Yrs.: U.S. - H&R Block, Maui Wowi Fresh Hawaiian Blends, Yum Brands. Canada - Canadian Tire, M&M Meat Shops. U.K. - Horwath Franchising, Dollond & Aitchison Ltd. New Zealand - Video Ezy NZ, Stirling Sports. Australia - Cookie Man

AREAS CONSULT IN

U.S.: Yes
Canada: Yes
Overseas: Yes - U.K., New Zealand, Australia

ENTREPRENEUR AUTHORITY, THE

5800 Granite Pkwy, Suite 300
Plano, TX 75024
Tel: (866) 246-2884 (972) 731-6766
Fax: (214) 585-0084
Web Site: www.eAuth.com
E-mail: info@eAuth.com
Contact: Mr. David Omholt, President
Other Offices In: North America

BUSINESS FOCUS

The Entrepreneur Authority is an international network of franchise advisors. Through our Franchise Center of Excellence (FCOE), our advisors are trained to create win-win business relationships between franchisors and franchisees. No other network combines the integrity, the dedication to client service and strong franchise acumen as T.E.A.

Major Areas of Concentration:

1) Franchise and self-employment counseling to prospective franchisees
2) Matching qualified franchisees with pre-screened franchisors
3) Helping franchisors create franchisee-friendly franchise systems by adhering to fair franchising standards

BACKGROUND

Business Established In:	2002
Franchise Consulting Since:	2002
% of Billable Hrs. to Franchise Clients:	100
Full-Time Employees:	3
Full-Time Professionals:	15

Major Franchising Clients in Past 3 Yrs.: AAMCO, D.O.T.I., Foot Solutions, Gotcha Covered, Honey Baked Ham Company, Interface Financial Group, Mega Wraps, One-Hour Martinizing, Speed Pro and Sport Clips

AREAS CONSULT IN

U.S.:	Yes
Canada:	Yes
Overseas:	Yes - Mexico, Canada, Great Britain, Germany, Asia

ENTREPRENEUR MEDIA, INC.

2445 McCabe Way, Suite 400
Irvine, CA 92614
Tel: (800) 864-6864 (949) 261-2325
Fax: (949) 752-1180
Web Site: www.entrepreneur.com
E-mail: jreichman@entrepreneur.com
Contact: Ms. Judy Reichman, Director of Franchise Advertising

BUSINESS FOCUS

Entrepreneur Media Inc. is your #1 source for qualified leads. Advertise with Entrepreneur and reach millions of business buyers ready to invest in their futures now. To advertise in Entrepreneur magazine, Entrepreneur's Be Your Own Boss Newsstand Guides and Entrepreneur.com's FranchiseZone and Opportunity Finder, contact Judy Reichman at jreichman@entrepreneur.com.

BACKGROUND

Business Established In:	1973

AREAS CONSULT IN

U.S.:	NR
Canada:	NR
Overseas:	NR

FIRSTDATA DIRECT BUSINESS GROUP

8027 Canyon Lake Circle
Orlando, FL 32835
Tel: (866) 420-4613 (407) 402-6951
Fax: (407) 290-6632
Web Site: www.firstdatadirect.com
E-mail: thomas.epstein@firstdata.com
Contact: Mr. Tom Epstein, Business Development Director
Other Offices In: Atlanta, Denver, Coral Spring, Melville NY

BUSINESS FOCUS

First Data's Direct Business Group (DBG) provides franchisors and franchisees with the highest quality, world class electronic payment acceptance program. We offer the scale, experience, resources, and technology required to help franchisors and franchisees grow and increase profitability. With more than a million merchant locations established, the DBG understands merchants and their needs. With more than 30 years of processing experience, we deliver the reliability and stability that are essential to growing your business.

Major Areas of Concentration:

1) Credit card processing
2) Gift and loyalty cards
3) Debit and check card processing
4) Electronic check conversion and check guarantee

BACKGROUND

Business Established In:	1867
Franchise Consulting Since:	1995
% of Billable Hrs. to Franchise Clients:	20
Full-Time Employees:	5 (Company has 30,000)
Full-Time Professionals:	5

Major Franchising Clients in Past 3 Yrs.: Smoothie King, Gloria Jeans Coffee, Jimmy John's, Charleys Subs, Sbarro, Carvel, Discount Auto Parts, H&R Block, Advance Auto Parts, Athlete's Foot, Brown Shoes, Budget Rent-A-Car, Coast Dental, Saturn Dealers, Subaru Dealers, and many more.

AREAS CONSULT IN

U.S.: Yes
Canada: My group does not, but I can refer to another department in my company.
Overseas: Yes - 87 countries worldwide

FRANCHISE BUSINESS SYSTEMS, INC.

2319 N. Andrews Ave.
Fort Lauderdale, FL 33311
Tel: (800) 382-1040 (954) 563-1269
Fax: (954) 563-2153
Web Site: www.franchiseaccounting.com
E-mail: steve@franchiseaccounting.com
Contact: Mr. Steve Weil, President

BUSINESS FOCUS

Complete franchisor and franchisee accounting and accounting system design firm, from monthly accounting and bookkeeping to outsourcing your entire accounting function including royalty reporting and royalty collection. We are a complete financial management solution.

Major Areas of Concentration:

1) Accounting and Bookkeeping Services
2) Business Consulting and Fianancial Management Seminars
3) Royalty Reporting and Collection
4) Intranet Services

BACKGROUND

Business Established In:	1984
Franchise Consulting Since:	1987
% of Billable Hrs. to Franchise Clients:	95
Full-Time Employees:	25
Full-Time Professionals:	10

Major Franchising Clients in Past 3 Yrs.: Planet Smoothie, Alpha Graphics, PJs Coffee and Tea, ServiceMaster, Amoco, HouseMaster, DOTI

AREAS CONSULT IN

U.S.:	Yes
Canada:	Yes
Overseas:	No

FRANCHISE CONSULTANTS, INC.

4496 35th St.
Orlando, FL 32811
Tel: (800) 933-7351 (407) 245-7776
Fax: (407) 245-7533
Web Site: www.foliagedesign.com
E-mail: john@foliagedesign.com
Contact: Mr. John S. Hagood, President

BUSINESS FOCUS

We are a boutique national franchise consulting company with a unique methodology of validating our customers' business models in anticipation of franchising. Services include business development, document preparation and legal services, marketing or collateral package, operations manual and support manuals, franchise sales, and related start-up services.

Major Areas of Concentration:

1) Business Development - We discuss your business and goals, research your industry, concept and competition, then recommend whether franchising is right for your business. If so, we can help develop or fine tune your concept into a successful prototype.
2) Document Preparation and Legal Services - Our experienced team will walk you through formation, trademark protection, state and federal registration and the preparation of a franchise agreement and UFOC.
3) Operations Manual - Our writers will work closely with you to learn your business and then record this information in a concise format that allows your franchisees to replicate your franchise system and methods of operation.
4) Franchise Sales - We can direct your initial franchise development including handling inquiries, distributing information, meeting with prospects and closing sales.

BACKGROUND

Business Established In:	1989
Franchise Consulting Since:	1980
% of Billable Hrs. to Franchise Clients:	90
Full-Time Employees:	4
Full-Time Professionals:	4

Major Franchising Clients in Past 3 Yrs.: U.S. Lawns, The Perfect Wedding Guide, Foliage Design Systems, Supervision, Ice Magic, FleetBoss, National Home Craft, Money Jingle.com, Daughter On Call, The Mad Matter, Rustic Ranch, Catering Corp. of America

AREAS CONSULT IN

U.S.:	Yes
Canada:	Yes
Overseas:	Yes

FRANCHISE INSIGHTS

442 Route 202/206 North, #224
Bedminster, NJ 07921
Tel: (888) 846-7444 (973) 252-2415
Fax: (973) 252-2416
Web Site: www.franchise-insights.com
E-mail: director@franchise-insights.com
Contact: Mr. Russ Moserowitz, Managing Director

BUSINESS FOCUS

Franchise Insights is an experienced franchise consulting firm, providing clients with innovative, proven and affordable franchise advice and solutions to achieve greater franchise success. Established franchisors and franchisees benefit from our direct experience building greater franchise value, creating stronger franchise relations, and resolving and avoiding franchise conflicts. The advice we offer our clients is based upon the expertise and insights gained as senior executives on the team that created, developed and produced the largest franchise company in the world. That unique experience enables us to recognize what works--and what doesn't. Additionally, Franchise Insights specializes in strategic franchise business planning, motivational speaking, franchise seminars and expert witness services. What makes Franchise Insights different? Experience, Integrity and Satisfaction-- they're not just part of our business, they are our business.

Major Areas of Concentration:
With a combined 40 years of experience as franchisors, our professional careers have been dedicated to achieving franchise success. And this tradition continues as we support our franchising clients in reaching their goals. Whether you are well-established or new to the marketplace and maintain national or regional distribu-

tion, Franchise Insights can provide you with the proven tools to take your business to the next level.
1) Franchisor Operational Support - From assisting in the development of the company's overall growth strategy, to structuring a franchise sales function, to maximizing the effectiveness of your franchisee support program, to managing the compliance with and adherence to your franchise agreements, Franchise Insights will improve the effectiveness and profitability of your franchise organization.
2) Franchisee Support - Put Franchise Insights experience to work for you in selecting the franchise that best suits your needs. We'll also review and negotiate your franchise agreement, not only addressing the standard contract, but also ensuring the often overlooked provisions necessary to best protect your franchise investment are included.
3) Alternative Dispute Resolution - Caught in a dispute between franchisor and franchisee? Understanding the most important factors to both parties, uniquely positions Franchise Insights to assist the parties in finding the most advantageous resolutions.

BACKGROUND

Business Established In:	2003
Franchise Consulting Since:	2003
% of Billable Hrs. to Franchise Clients:	100
Full-Time Employees:	3
Full-Time Professionals:	2

Major Franchising Clients in Past 3 Yrs.: Hospitality International, Sotel Industries, Restaurant Systems International, Salerno's Restaurants, numerous franchisees and attorneys.

AREAS CONSULT IN

U.S.:	Yes
Canada:	Yes
Overseas:	No

FRANCHISE NETWORK GROUP (FRANNET)

4901 Morena Blvd., # 122
San Diego, CA 92117
Tel: (888) 322-FRAN (858) 490-1188
Web Site: www.frannet.com
E-mail: frannet@frannet.com
Contact: Ms. Sarah Bassuk, Group Coordinator
Other Offices In: 50+ office in North America, Africa, Asia, etc.

BUSINESS FOCUS

Franchise Network is the nation's largest group of franchise consultants. We have successfully helped hundreds of franchisors find and add thousands of franchises and franchisees. We also consult on various phases of franchising and have developed proprietary research screening and interpretive tools to enable clients to improve their sales ratios.

Major Areas of Concentration:

1) Matching franchisors and prospective franchisees;
2) Helping existing franchisors expand and improve systems, techniques and methodologies needed to grow their businesses;
3) Doing developmental consulting to enable companies to become franchisors;
4) Creation of marketing and sales materials for franchisors.

BACKGROUND

Business Established In:	1987
Franchise Consulting Since:	1987
% of Billable Hrs. to Franchise Clients:	100
Full-Time Employees:	55
Full-Time Professionals:	58

Major Franchising Clients in Past 3 Yrs.: Great Clips, One Hour Martinizing, Cottman Transmissions, 7-Eleven, Sir Speedy, The Maids International, Speedpro, Signs Plus and Mad Science.

AREAS CONSULT IN

U.S.:	Yes
Canada:	Yes
Overseas:	Yes - Mexico, Chile, South Korea and South Africa

FRANCHISEKNOWHOW, LLC

P.O. Box 714
Stony Brook, NY 11790
Tel: (631) 246-5782
Fax: (631) 689-6905
Web Site: www.franchiseknowhow.com
E-mail: ed@franchiseknowhow.com
Contact: Mr. Ed Teixeira, President
Other Offices In: Beijing and Guanpong, China; Contact: Ms. Fay Deng

BUSINESS FOCUS

FranchiseKnowHow is headed by Ed Teixeira, who has over 25 years of franchise industry experience. FKH provides a full range of services to companies who desire to begin a franchise operation. Other areas of expertise include international franchising, with offices in NY and China. FKH has established strong relationships in the Chinese market. Contact information for China office: Tel: 86-135-1079-2899; 86-10-86671155; 86-10-82783466; Fax: 86-10-82898040; Address: 1104 Chuang Ye Building; Cinxi Road, Shangdi Information Industry Baseaidian District, Beijing, China 100085

Major Areas of Concentration:
FranchiseKnowHow can service any franchisor needs. We have the knowledge and expertise.
1) New Franchise Start-ups
2) International Franchising
3) Franchisee Satisfaction Audits
4) Franchisor Dispute Resolution

BACKGROUND
Business Established In: 2003
Franchise Consulting Since: 2003
% of Billable Hrs. to Franchise Clients: 100
Full-Time Employees: 3
Full-Time Professionals: 3
Major Franchising Clients in Past 3 Yrs.: Netspace, FranchiseMagazine China, Reading Transformations, Aqua200, NobleKnits, Wall Street Deli, Arthur Treachers Fish & Chips

AREAS CONSULT IN
U.S.: Yes
Canada: Yes
Overseas: Yes - Japan, Spain, Thailand, Indonesia, Brazil, Canada, UK, China

FRANCHOICE

6385 Old Shady Oak Rd., # 290
Eden Prairie, MN 55344
Tel: (952) 942-5561
Fax: (952) 942-5793
Web Site: www.franchisechoices.com
E-mail: jbernloehr@franchoice.com
Contact: Mr. Jason Bernloehr, Marketing Manager

BUSINESS FOCUS
FranChoice provides consumers with free guidance and advice to help them select a franchise opportunity that matches their individual interests and financial qualifications. We'll help you build your business and personal model and define exactly where you want your business to take you and how you want to get there. Our goal is to find the "perfect fit" for you. FranChoice works with a number of pre-screened franchisors in a variety of industries. Register for our free service at www.franchisechoices.com.

Major Areas of Concentration:

1) Providing a valuable free service to consumers.
2) Matching prospective franchisees with franchisors.
3) Assisting franchisors with their nationwide expansion. Strengthening public perception of franchising.
4) Assisting franchisors with their nationwide expansion. Strengthening public perception of franchising.

BACKGROUND
Business Established In: 1999
Franchise Consulting Since: 1999
% of Billable Hrs. to Franchise Clients: 100
Full-Time Employees: 8
Full-Time Professionals: 70
Major Franchising Clients in Past 3 Yrs.: Maui Wowi, Cottman Transmission, Great Clips, Fast Frame, Bear Rock Café, Mr. Handyman, Aussie Pet Mobile

AREAS CONSULT IN
U.S.: Yes
Canada: No
Overseas: No

GRAPHIC BUSINESS SOLUTIONS

1912 John Towers Ave.
El Cajon, CA 92020
Tel: (800) 747-9529 (619) 258-4081
Fax: (619) 449-6248
Web Site: www.gogbs.com
E-mail: rita@gogbs.com
Contact: Ms. Rita Cannon, Director of Corporate Marketing

BUSINESS FOCUS
GBS is the leading manufacturer of full-color, custom designed and die-cut refrigerator magnets. Tailored to meet your franchise needs with a specific emphasis on custom imprinting for each franchise location, our magnets are of the highest quality at the most affordable pricing in the industry. From the implementation of your magnetic marketing plan to easy online ordering on a website designed specifically for you, our offering options are diverse. Call for a free marketing consultation.

Major Areas of Concentration:
Did you know the average American opens their refrigerator door 20 times a day? Magnetic marketing works by increasing your brand exposure and your revenue. At no cost to you, GBS will provide the following services:
1) Perform an in-depth consultation of your needs and offer magnetic marketing suggestions
2) Design a quality magnet specific to your franchise
3) Customize a website for your franchise featuring your -magnet, various marketing tips and an EASY one-click ordering process
4) Take and process all orders either directly with your franchisees, or through your corporate office

BACKGROUND
Business Established In: 1994
Franchise Consulting Since: 1994
% of Billable Hrs. to Franchise Clients: N/A
Full-Time Employees: 42
Full-Time Professionals: 12
Major Franchising Clients in Past 3 Yrs.: Available Upon Request.

AREAS CONSULT IN
U.S.: Yes
Canada: Yes
Overseas: Yes

IFRANCHISE GROUP

1820 Ridge Rd., # 300

Homewood, IL 60430
Tel: (708) 957-2300
Fax: (708) 957-2395
Web Site: www.ifranchise.net
E-mail: info@ifranchise.net
Contact: Mr. Mark Siebert, Chief Executive Officer

BUSINESS FOCUS
Franchise consulting for new and established franchisors. The iFranchise Group is comprised of the nation's leading professionals in the field of franchising. Senior consultants for the iFranchise Group bring over 250 years of experience to their clients. Services include franchise feasibility, franchise structure, legal documentation, operations and training materials and assistance with franchise sales and franchise feasibility. Franchise development for start-up franchisors. Franchise marketing and sales. Franchise implementation assistance.

BACKGROUND

Business Established In:	1998
Franchise Consulting Since:	1985
% of Billable Hrs. to Franchise Clients:	100
Full-Time Employees:	20
Full-Time Professionals:	14

Major Franchising Clients in Past 3 Yrs.: Ace Hardware, Bridgestone/Firestone, Crafter's Marketplace, Dippin' Dots, Hallmark, Harris Teeter, Horizon Pharmacy, Line-X, Van Heusen and Successories.

AREAS CONSULT IN

U.S.:	Yes
Canada:	Yes
Overseas:	Yes - Japan, U.K.,

Argentina, Chile, Philippines, Spain

IMPACT MARKETING SERVICES

16845 N. 29th Ave., #301
Phoenix, AZ 85053
Tel: (800) 836-6625 (623) 876-1304
Fax: (623) 876-1329
Web Site: www.impactmarketingservices.com
E-mail: jlee@impactmarketingservices.com
Contact: Mr. John Lee, Principal
Other Offices In: Dallas, TX

BUSINESS FOCUS
IFA Member. Established in 1991. Full-service national marketing and advertising firm. Specialize in development and implementation of strategic marketing plans, local store marketing plans, grand opening and grand re-opening plans, marketing workshops, and store consultation services. Clients: Mail Boxes Etc/The UPS Store since 1991, The Great Frame Up, Pizza Hut. National franchise consumer and business-to-business and multi-regional franchise organizations.

Major Areas of Concentration:

1) Development of annual marketing plans and implementation - corporate and local store planning and consultation.
2) Grand opening/Grand re-opening programs - new stores achieve and exceed break-even faster.
3) Media planning and placement - complete services. Free standing newspaper inserts as low as $26 per thousand.
4) Marketing workshops, training and coaching - motivating field marketing training

BACKGROUND

Business Established In:	1991
Franchise Consulting Since:	1991
% of Billable Hrs. to Franchise Clients:	100
Full-Time Employees:	4
Full-Time Professionals:	4

Major Franchising Clients in Past 3 Yrs.: Mail Boxes Etc/The UPS Store, The Great Frame Up, Audio-Visual Headquarters, MotoPhoto, Winfree Marketing & Sales Institute, Taco Casa

AREAS CONSULT IN

U.S.:	Yes
Canada:	Yes
Overseas:	Yes

KUSHELL ASSOCIATES, INC.

235 Fearrington Post
Pittsboro, NC 27312
Tel: (919) 542-3500
Fax: (919) 542-1156
Web Site: www.kushellassociates.com
E-mail: kushellassociates@msn.com
Contact: Mr. Robert Kushell,
Other Offices In: Partners in South America, Far East and Europe

BUSINESS FOCUS
Our Consulting Group advises multinational, entrepreneurial and Minority companies on how to develop well constructed Franchise Systems. There are 14 distinct modules that we create to convert an existing business into a market ready Franchise Program. We assist established Franchisors with domestic and international growth, marketing and sales strategies. We are very skilled in assisting Franchisors that have strained relations with their Franchisees to create a healthy and harmonious business climate for all parties. We have also focused our extensive Franchise and business knowledge and resources in assisting Minority business owners to convert their existing business into a Franchise Model.

Major Areas of Concentration:

1) Developing Franchise Programs for multi-national and entrepreneurial companies.
2) Assisting Minority owned businesses to become Franchisors.

3) Assisting Franchise Systems to create and maintain healthy relationships with their Franchisees as they focus increasingly on opening more new units.
4) Assisting Franchisors develop and implement a sound international sales and marketing program.

BACKGROUND

Business Established In: 1984
Franchise Consulting Since: 1984
% of Billable Hrs. to Franchise Clients: 100
Full-Time Professionals: 4
Major Franchising Clients in Past 3 Yrs.: Volvo, Money Mailer, Smart House, Amorix, Sandler Sales Institute, Dynamark, Tuffy Muffler, USIC, Restaurant System Intl. And Saudi Fisheries Inc.

AREAS CONSULT IN

U.S.: Yes
Canada: Yes
Overseas: Yes - Saudi Arabia, UAR, Egypt, Taiwan, Hong Kong, Philipines, Brazil, Argentina, Chile, England, Spain, Denmark, Mexico, and Canada

MANAGEMENT 2000

P.O. Box 941419
Houston, TX 77094-8419
Tel: (800) 847-5763 (713) 952-3177
Fax: (713) 952-3830
Web Site: www.mgmt2000.com
E-mail: m2000@mgmt2000.com
Contact: Mr. Bob Gappa, President

BUSINESS FOCUS

What is your company slogan or motto? To be the premier franchise consulting company by giving people what they expect, and more. What makes your services unique to franchises? Management 2000 has been part of the franchise community for over 20 years. Over that time we have seen dramatic changes that affect our business. One of our goals has always been to identify changing conditions that affect the relationships between franchisors and franchisees. Once these have been identified, we structure our programs to specifically address these areas. What services do you provide for franchisors? Our services are designed to help our clients get, keep and create very satisfied customers. We do this by helping clients think through and define solutions to their strategic and operational problems and opportunities. We have designed training programs for all levels of corporate and franchisee personnel. Management 2000 conducts convention speeches and prepares Expert Witness reports for franchisors. Our primary focuses are in helping senior management understand the franchising business and how to enhance the customer experience. What services do you provide to franchisees? We provide franchisees with training programs as they come on board with a new company and subsequent programs with Leaders, Guides, and Participant Workbooks. Where is your company headed in the future? We continually strive to enhance what our customers want and need to successfully grow their businesses. Why do you think franchising is such a popular choice for entrepreneurs? Franchising gives entrepreneurs a way to create wealth. Becoming a franchisee provides the average and above-average worker an opportunity to enhance their lifestyle and secure their financial future.

Major Areas of Concentration:

1) Training/Education: Management 2000 develops & conducts training programs specifically for franchising. We conduct a regular schedule of seminars for franchise recruiters, field personnel arid franchise executives. We customize & conduct these programs for our clients. We write training programs for initial franchisee training, convention workshops and other training to meet clients' specific needs. Our training leads participants to understand the power of franchising & their role in the strategic-partnership between franchisor and franchisee. Programs for field personnel include how to use the consultative approach as well as how to implement business planning & local store marketing with franchisees.
2) Manuals: Management 2000 writes manuals to document a variety of operating systems. Manuals are not boiler plated but are the result of on-site visits with unit and operations personnel. Manuals include pre-opening procedures; field operation guides, conducting audits and visitations, local store marketing, prospecting and sales, creating a customer-driven culture, and managing for profitability. For use throughout the organization by franchise development staff to recruit and select better franchisees, by field personnel for effective franchise consulting; and by franchisees, to insure faithful adherence to the operating system.
3) Consulting: Management 2000 products & services include: complete program for start-up companies, how to Close More Franchise Sales; how to get your franchisees to use business plans; convention speeches: strategic planning; customer acquisition/retention strategies; strategies to build average unit volumes; how to improve the effectiveness of your field consultants; customer service strategies; prospect profiling; franchise attitude survey; improving the effectiveness of your area developers; development of effective growth strategies; research, write & re-write operations manuals; design & write leader's guides and training manuals; customer tracking systems for improved profitability; and improving franchisor/franchisee relations.

BACKGROUND

Business Established In: 1981
Franchise Consulting Since: 1981
% of Billable Hrs. to Franchise Clients: 100
Major Franchising Clients in Past 3 Yrs.: GMAC Real Estate, GNC, H&R Block, Petland, Smoothie King, Pro Source, Link Staffing, Brinker Int'l, Epmark, Applebee's, Allied Domecq, Medicine Shoppe Int'l

AREAS CONSULT IN

U.S.: Yes
Canada: Yes
Overseas: Yes

MICHAEL H. SEID & ASSOCIATES, LLC

94 Mohegan Drive
West Hartford, CT 06117
Tel: (860) 523-4257
Fax: (860) 523-4530
Web Site: www.msaworldwide.com
E-mail: mseid@msaworldwide.com
Contact: Mr. Michael H. Seid, Managing Director
Other Offices In: Atlanta, GA and San Rafael, CA

BUSINESS FOCUS

MSA provides domestic and international franchise advisory services. Our clients typically include: Companies looking to become franchisors; Established franchise systems; Manufacturers for the development of dedicated down stream distribution channels; Companies seeking to enter the United States through a franchising; US franchisors developing internationally; Mergers and acquisition advisory services; Lawyers and their clients requiring litigation support and expert witnesses Our services include feasibility and diagnostic assessments of franchising potential; Start up franchisor design development; Tactical strategic planning; Operating Manuals; Training Programs; Field and headquarters support - review, development and training; Franchisee relationship improvement strategies; Advertising and other cooperatives; Encroachment avoidance programs; Litigation support and expert witness; Due diligence Interim executive services; Crisis management

Major Areas of Concentration:
Established franchisors recognize MSA background as both franchisors and franchisees and our experience in branding, retailing, marketing and finance provide them with a team of advisors who have the practical experience necessary to implement leading edge strategies to improve their systems performance. We have been fortunate in the recognition that the franchising community has bestowed on us. Michael Seid, co-author with the late Dave Thomas, founder of Wendy's of Franchising for Dummies is the first and only professional service provider ever directly elected to the Board of the International Franchise Association.
1) Franchise System Design and Development
2) Strategic and tactical services for established franchisors
3) International Expansion and Development Services
4) Training and Operations Manuals

BACKGROUND

Business Established In:	1987
Franchise Consulting Since:	1987

Major Franchising Clients in Past 3 Yrs.: See website at www.msaworldwide.com

AREAS CONSULT IN

U.S.:	Yes
Canada:	Yes

Overseas: Yes - Kay Ainsley, Managing Director of MSA is the former Director of International for Dominos and Zeibarts and is one of only 12 industry professionals invited to participate on GLOMAK, the IFA's international marketing committee.

NORTHERN LIGHTS FRANCHISE CONSULTANTS CORP.

2000 Argentia Road, Plaza IV, Suite 330
Mississauga, ON L5N 1W1 CANADA
Tel: (877) 667-8449 (905) 812-1219
Fax: (905) 812-5594
Web Site: www.franchiseservices.ca
E-mail: northernlights@interhop.net
Contact: Mr. J. Perry Maisonneuve, Principal

BUSINESS FOCUS

Northern Lights Franchise Consultants Corp. is a management consulting firm specializing in developing and expanding small and medium sized businesses with an expertise in franchising principles and practices. The firm's services include feasibility studies, strategic and business planning, management information systems, compliance audit programs, operating systems reviews, franchise marketing and sales systems, franchise advisory councils and co-operatives, operations manuals, training manuals, financing strategies including private placements and franchise system import/export transactions. The firm also assists franchisees in searching, investigating and financing their initial investment in a suitable franchised business opportunity or to market and re-sell an existing franchised business in a divestment strategy.

Major Areas of Concentration:

1) The development of strategies, systems and infrastructure to support the sustainable development of Emerging Franchisors;
2) Review and evaluation of Mezzanine and Mature Franchise Systems with respect to sector "best practices" and organizational reengineering;
3) Franchise System marketing, advertising and business brokerage - including international expansion; and
4) Franchisee consulting including franchise system search and evaluation, due diligence, business planning, financing and divestment strategies including franchised business resales.

BACKGROUND

Business Established In:	1998
Franchise Consulting Since:	1994
% of Billable Hrs. to Franchise Clients:	90
Full-Time Employees:	5
Full-Time Professionals:	3

Major Franchising Clients in Past 3 Yrs.: African Development Bank; The Beat Goes On; IMAX; Oxford Learning Centres, North American Auctioneers, We Care Health Services Inc., Bio-Lab, Fenice Cosmetics; The Arrow Neighborhood Pubs Group

AREAS CONSULT IN

U.S.:	Yes
Canada:	Yes

Overseas: Yes - South Africa, Nigeria, Egypt, Cote D'Ivoire, Tunisia, Morocco, U.S.A.

<< >>

PECO DISPLAYS

1618 Loch Lomond Dr.
Murray, KY 42071
Tel: (866) 477-0600 (270) 767-0085
Fax: (270) 767-0094
Web Site: www.pecoproducts.com
E-mail: presentationsite@bellsouth.net
Contact: Mr. Dan Van Waes, President

BUSINESS FOCUS
PECO Displays manufactures a line of custom trade show displays at lower than retail prices. We also print custom graphics, banners, posters, and other styles of trade show graphics. Our mission is to provide trade show exhibits and displays at affordable prices for small businesses.

Major Areas of Concentration:

1) 10' trade show displays
2) Exhibit graphics
3) Graphic design
4) Affordable trade show solutions for small businesses

BACKGROUND

Business Established In:	2002
Franchise Consulting Since:	NR
% of Billable Hrs. to Franchise Clients:	NR
Full-Time Employees:	5
Full-Time Professionals:	5

AREAS CONSULT IN

U.S.:	Yes
Canada:	Yes
Overseas:	No

RESTAURANT VALUES

1625 W. Elizabeth, Suite B-4
Ft. Collins, CO 80521
Tel: (970) 484-6598
Fax: (866) 214-3869
Web Site: www.restaurantvalues.com
E-mail: gary@restaurantvalues.com
Contact: Mr. Gary Vette, Owner/Director

BUSINESS FOCUS
Restaurant Values provides a Restaurant Valuation Report with 3 to 5 nationally recognized income and/or market location approaches to the current business value -- independently (not real estate nor business brokers). We use restaurant market data from nationally recognized independent sources, plus support data from CBI's. Also provide a Market Analysis report to determine if a specific market is viable; plus a Fiscal Analysis to determine if the market makes economic sense. Restaurant Values also provides a Financial Review on an existing restaurant -- identifying the "red flags" in expenses and/or income flow.

Major Areas of Concentration:

1) Restaurant Business Valuations
2) Market Analysis
3) Financial Review of expenses on existing restaurants
4) Fiscal Analysis on a proposed restaurant

BACKGROUND

Business Established In:	1980
Franchise Consulting Since:	1997
% of Billable Hrs. to Franchise Clients:	20

Major Franchising Clients in Past 3 Yrs.: VCM Ltd, IHOP, K&J Mgt, Harwood Int, Pizza Inn, Hooter's, KFC

AREAS CONSULT IN

U.S.:	Yes
Canada:	No
Overseas:	No

SANDERSON & ASSOCIATES, LTD.

1052 W. Fulton Market St., 3-W
Chicago, IL 60607
Tel: (312) 829-4350
Web Site: www.sandersonpr.com
E-mail: rhonda@sandersonpr.com
Contact: Ms. Rhonda Sanderson, President

BUSINESS FOCUS
Premier PR firm specializing in franchised concepts. Have represented hundreds of franchisors and their franchisees since 1985. Leads for franchisors and support publicity for franchisees is specialty of this agency.

Major Areas of Concentration:

1) Publicity
2) Lead Generation
3) Support programs for franchisees
4) Media & Public Relations for franchise systems

BACKGROUND

Business Established In:	1985
Franchise Consulting Since:	1985
% of Billable Hrs. to Franchise Clients:	100
Full-Time Employees:	9
Full-Time Professionals:	9

Major Franchising Clients in Past 3 Yrs.: Meineke Discount Mufflers, Cici's Pizza, FASTFRAME, Jimmy John's Gourmet Subs, Cousins Subs, Molly Maid, Bojangles, Back Yard Burgers

AREAS CONSULT IN

U.S.:	Yes
Canada:	Yes

Overseas: Yes - United Kingdom, United Arab Emirates, France

SOURCE BOOK PUBLICATIONS

1814 Franklin St., # 820
Oakland, CA 94612
Tel: (800) 841-0873 (510) 839-5471
Fax: (510) 839-2104
Web Site: www.worldfranchising.com
E-mail: rob@worldfranchising.com
Contact: Mr. Robert E. Bond, Publisher

BUSINESS FOCUS

Source Book Publications is the pre-eminent provider of reliable, up-to-date information on franchising - books, databases, consulting services and Internet sites. *Bond's Franchise Guide* (16 Editions) includes over 1,000 franchisor profiles. *"How Much Can I Make?"* includes 116 recent earnings claim statements. *Bond's Top 100 Franchises* (food, service, and retail franchises) focuses on today's top franchises. *Tips & Traps When Buying A Franchise* provides an insightful overview for prospective franchisees. Source Book Publications also organizes the National Minority Franchising Initiative, a multi-faceted program for the inclusion of minorities in franchising. Custom databases of 2,400+ N. American franchisors. Rental rate of only $1,200.

Major Areas of Concentration:

1) Lead generation for international franchisors through sophisticated directories and specialized publications promoting the 50 "best" franchises by each of 4 major categories.
2) Maintenance of highly accurate databases for those selling goods or services to the franchising industry.
3) Development of interactive Websites that promote franchisors, franchise attorneys and franchise industry service providers.
4) Organizer of the National Minority Franchising Initiative, which includes a Website (www.minorityfranchising.com), a book (Bond's *Minority Franchising Guide*) and a series of intense 2-day weekend seminars throughout the country.

BACKGROUND

Business Established In:	1985
Franchise Consulting Since:	1992
% of Billable Hrs. to Franchise Clients:	100
Full-Time Employees:	4
Full-Time Professionals:	4

Major Franchising Clients in Past 3 Yrs.: Tricon, 7-Eleven, AAMCO, AlphaGraphics, Coverall, FastSigns, GNC, Meineke, PostNet and RadioShack.

AREAS CONSULT IN

U.S.:	Yes
Canada:	Yes
Overseas:	Yes

SOVEREIGN BANK

446 Main St.
Worcester, MA 01608
Tel: (508) 890-6829
Fax: (508) 890-6889
Web Site: www.sovereignbank.com/franchiselending
E-mail: franchiselending@sovereignbank.com
Contact: Mr. Derek Plourde, Vice President

BUSINESS FOCUS

Sovereign Bank is the 18th largest bank in the country pro-forma for pending acquisitions with $60 billion in assets. We understand the nuances and competitive demands of your multi-unit franchise business-- your branding challenges, your growth goals, and the need to increase some store sales while controlling costs. As such, we offer flexible loan structures, a dedicated team of lending professionals, and 20+ years of franchise lending experience.

Major Areas of Concentration:
Sovereign Bank's Franchise Lending Group provides customized financial solutions to multi-unit franchises. We help businesses finance new store expansion, remodels, acquisitions, and real estate. However, we do not stop there. Sovereign provides businesses and business owners with a full array of cash management, leasing, interest rate protection, merchant services, payroll services and wealth management projects.

BACKGROUND

Business Established In:	2002
Franchise Consulting Since:	1980
% of Billable Hrs. to Franchise Clients:	N/A
Full-Time Employees:	11
Full-Time Professionals:	9

Major Franchising Clients in Past 3 Yrs.: Dunkin' Donuts, Baskin Robbins, Papa John's, Panesa Bread, Qdoba Mexican Grill, Bear Rock Café

AREAS CONSULT IN

U.S.:	Yes
Canada:	No
Overseas:	No

<< >>

STARTUPJOURNAL.COM

P.O. Box 300
Princeton, NJ 08543-0300
Tel: (800) 366-3975
Fax: (214) 640-7900
Web Site: www.startupjournal.com
E-mail: marti.gallardo@dowjones.com
Contact: Ms. Marti Gallardo, Director of Classified Advertising
Other Offices In: 545 E. John Carpenter Freeway, Irving, TX 75062

BUSINESS FOCUS

StartupJournal.com is the Web's center for entrepreneurs from The Wall Street Journal, the world's leading business publication. Content comes from the powerful editorial resources of The Wall Street Journal, as well as WSJ.com, industry experts and StartupJournal.com's editorial team. In addition, this highly focused collection of relevant information, resources and tools showcases businesses and franchises for sale. From food and auto services to retail and staffing, StartupJournal.com is a premier resource of franchise opportunities available. StartupJournal.com presents advertisers with a unique opportunity to reach entrepreneurs.

Major Areas of Concentration:

1) Exclusive news, columnists and features focused on starting or buying a business or franchise, plus "how to" information covering all aspects of business ownership.
2) Tools to help entrepreneurs and small-business owners make smarter decisions and better use of their time. For example, the site helps readers write a business plan and search for venture capital.
3) Extensive listings of business opportunities and franchises for sale.
4) Strong demographics for advertisers. StartupJournal.com provides advertisers a unique opportunity to reach readers who are poised to start their own business, and who have the means to do so.

BACKGROUND

Business Established In:	1999

AREAS CONSULT IN

U.S.:	This site is available world-wide
Canada:	NR
Overseas:	NR

<< >>

TRI~POINTE GROUP, LLC

7777 S. Jones Blvd. #2233
Las Vegas, NV 89139
Tel: (866) 835-4040 (702) 263-7144
Fax: (702) 263-7061
Web Site: www.tripointegroup.com
E-mail: tony@tripointegroup.com
Contact: Mr. Anthony Stelluto, CEO

BUSINESS FOCUS

Tri~Pointe Group is a consulting firm that assists the franchise and food service communities with business valuations; start-up, acquisition, expansion or remodel financing and deal management.

Major Areas of Concentration:

1) Business Valuations to assist buyers or sellers to determine a price range and a financing range for the entity in question.
2) Loan Packaging/Loan Origination to assist current and prospective franchisees to obtain financing for acquisitions, expansions, remodels, new development or to restructure existing debt.
3) Merger & Acquisition Project Management to facilitate and expedite closings for buyers or sellers with deals at the Letter of Intent phase.

BACKGROUND

Business Established In:	2004
Franchise Consulting Since:	1998
% of Billable Hrs. to Franchise Clients:	90
Full-Time Employees:	0
Full-Time Professionals:	1

Major Franchising Clients in Past 3 Yrs.: Franchisors: Carl Karcher Enterprises - franchisor for Hardee's and Carl's Jr.; Checker's Drive-In Restaurants; Captain D's Seafood; Edible Arrangements. Franchisees: Thomas Sottile - multi-unit Dunkin' Donuts operator; Harinder Singh - multi-unit Dunkin' Donuts operator, Michael Yung - multi-unit Ground Round operator

AREAS CONSULT IN

U.S.:	Yes
Canada:	No
Overseas:	No

<< >>

VEGARO VEVSTAD FRANCHISE CONSULTING

24124 Lakeside Trail
Crete, IL 60417
Tel: (708) 828-0152
Fax: (708) 672-4473
Web Site: www.franchiseconsultingfirm.com
E-mail: vvevstad@franchiseconsultingfirm.com
Contact: Mr.Vegard Vevstad, President

BUSINESS FOCUS

Vegard Vevstad Franchise Consulting transforms entrepreneurial ventures into global enterprises through franchising and other dedicated channels of distribution. Our multi-cultural senior consultants with advanced degrees in law, management, finance, marketing, teaching, etc., and more than 15 years of worldwide franchise management, consulting, and teaching experience, spanning Fortune 500 companies and over 200 smaller franchise companies in most every industry, guarantee great value and fast, expert service.

Major Areas of Concentration:
We are a full service franchise consulting and development firm providing:
1) Prototype Development. We assess how to improve the profitability of the core business, plan and implement improvements, and document policies and procedures.
2) Enterprise Development. We develop and implement strategies for the entire enterprise, including channels of distribution, feasibility studies, business plans, due diligence investigations, mergers and acquisitions, etc.
3) Channel Development. We structure and document all channel relationships, using detailed pro forma analysis to test important assumptions.
4) Franchisee Development. We develop and implement a complete program to recruit and train channel partners, using a multi-faceted marketing and sales campaign and multi-media assessment and training programs.

BACKGROUND

Business Established In:	2000
Franchise Consulting Since:	2000
% of Billable Hrs. to Franchise Clients:	95
Full-Time Employees:	1
Full-Time Professionals:	1

Major Franchising Clients in Past 3 Yrs.: Cheeky Wadsworth (WI), The Ground Pat'I (LA), Max's of Manila (CO), The Coffee Cup (FL), Smart Start (TX), Floor Coverings Direct (IL), Cajun Boiler's (AR), Potato Valley Café (MD)

AREAS CONSULT IN

U.S.:	Yes
Canada:	Yes

Overseas: Yes - Scandinavia, Switzerland, Spain, Portugal, Kuwait, Philippines, Argentina, Chile, Guatemala, Dominican Republic

WOMEN IN FRANCHISING, INC. (WIF)

53 West Jackson Blvd, Suite 205
Chicago, IL 60604
Tel: (800) 222-4943 (312) 431-1467
Fax: (312) 431-1469
Web Site: www.womeninfranchising.com
E-mail: info@womeninfranchising.com
Contact: Ms. Eileen Foxman, Executive Assistant

BUSINESS FOCUS

Women In Franchising, Inc. (WIF) founded in Chicago, Illinois in 1987, offers franchise consulting services for women and minorities interested in becoming franchisees or franchisors. WIF's offers a number of consulting services including: presenting workshops and seminars that teach prospective franchisees the skills and knowledge needed to evaluate, finance, and purchase a franchise; providing one-on-one assistance to persons who are considering buying a franchise by conducting a UFOC (Uniform Franchise Offering Circular) Review; assisting entrepreneurs in expanding their business via franchising with a Feasibility Study to assess their readiness to franchise.

Major Areas of Concentration:
1) Education and Training: WIF offers expertise in the development, coordination and implementation of franchise business training seminars on a national basis.
2) Federal Contracts: WIF has been a federal contractor in the U.S.
3) Minority Business Development Agency (MBDA), under a program created to stimulate the growth of minority franchises and also with the U.S. Small Business Administration (SBA) to conduct research entitled, Women and Minorities in Franchising and Financing Practices.
4) Consulting Services: WIF provides a variety of tools and one-on-one assistance to prospective franchisees and franchisors including audio seminars, a detailed Operations Manual and sales guidance, and national public relations contracts for recruiting franchisees.
5) Specialized Service: WIF offers consulting services, workshops, and franchisor trade missons targeted to Native American entrepreneurs and tribal governments.

BACKGROUND

Business Established In:	1987
Franchise Consulting Since:	1987
% of Billable Hrs. to Franchise Clients:	100
Full-Time Employees:	4
Full-Time Professionals:	3

Major Franchising Clients in Past 3 Yrs.: Verlo Mattress Factory Stores, Whitewater, Wisconsin; Shape Up Sisters, Aguas Buenas, Puerto Rico; We The People Forms & Service Centers, USA, Santa Barbara, California; Creative Colors International, Tinley Park, Illinois; United States Hispanic Chamber of Commerce,

Washington, D.C.; Women's Business Development Center, Chicago, Illinois; The American Franchisee Association, Chicago, Illinois

AREAS CONSULT IN

U.S.:	Yes
Canada:	Yes
Overseas:	Yes - China and India

<< >>

XPANSHEN MARKETING COMMUNICATIONS

731 N. Weber, Suite 202
Colorado Springs, CO 80903
Tel: (719) 578-8878
Fax: (719) 578-8838
Web Site: www.xpanshen.com
E-mail: info@xpanshen.com
Contact: Ms. Rhonda Bauer, Founder/CEO

BUSINESS FOCUS

We are business invigorators. Xpanshen was founded with one goal in mind -- to help businesses grow and expand. From consumer research to publicity and prospecting, from local store marketing to national advertising campaigns, we analyze the needs, develop the solutions, execute the programs and measure the results. Throughout our process, we sharpen the focus and clarify the objectives. Time and time again we have produced growth for our clients; in traffic, sales and brand awareness. For those companies who recognize that the rules have changed -- call Xpanshen. We'll work right along side of you to meet your company's growth needs.
Major Areas of Concentration:

1) Marketing -- consumer research, competitive research, secret shopper services, strategic planning, stealth marketing programs, special promotions and consumer loyalty programs.
2) Public Relations -- talk shows, pitch and write articles, community involvement, employee communications, crisis communications, special events.
3) Advertising -- national, regional, local branding and sales advertising in the fields of TV, radio, outdoor, print, direct mail, interactive, coupons and other traditional and non-traditional media.
4) Media -- coop program development and management, planning, buying and analysis.

BACKGROUND

Business Established In:	1992
Franchise Consulting Since:	2000
% of Billable Hrs. to Franchise Clients:	35
Full-Time Employees:	6
Full-Time Professionals:	2

Major Franchising Clients in Past 3 Yrs.: International Franchise Association, Lemar's Donuts, Domino's Pizza, Barkbusters, CinnaMonster

AREAS CONSULT IN

U.S.:	Yes
Canada:	No
Overseas:	No

<< >>

WorldFranchising.Com

The Definitive Guide to the World of Franchising

Franchisor Questionnaire

FRANCHISOR INFORMATION

1. **Franchise Trade Name:** ______________________________
2. **Address:** ______________________________
   City: ____________________, **State/Prov.** ________ **Zip/Postal Code:** ________
   Phone: (800) ____________________ **or** (   ) ____________________
   Fax: (   ) ____________________
   Internet: www.____________________ **General Email:** ____________________
3. **Contact Person:** ____________________ **Position:** ____________________
   Email*: ____________________
4. **President/CEO*:** ____________________ **Title*:** ____________________
   Email*: ____________________ (* Will not be published.)

BUSINESS DESCRIPTION

5. Please describe your business. Use the full space available to set your franchise apart from other franchising opportunities, i.e. sell your system to the potential franchisee.

____

____

____

____

____

____

FRANCHISOR BACKGROUND

6. Year company was founded ________.
7. First year as franchisor ________.
8. Actual number of Franchised Units ________ Units
   Actual number of Company-Owned Units ________ Units
9. Total Operating Units ________ Units
10. Of Total Operating Units listed in # 9,
    ________ are in the U.S. ________ are in Canada. ________ are Overseas.
11. A) How many U.S. States have operating units? ________
    B) How many Canadian Provinces have operating units? ________
    C) How many Foreign Countries have operating units? ________
    D) What 3 States/Provinces have the largest number of operating units?
    How many operating units are located in these States/Provinces?

	States/Provinces	# of Units
1.	________	________
2.	________	________
3.	________	________

12. How many new units do you plan to open in the next 12 months? ________ Units

FRANCHISOR QUESTIONNAIRE (cont.)

13. In qualifying a potential franchisee, please rank the following criteria from Unimportant to Very Important. (Please circle.)

	Unimportant				Very Important
Financial Net Worth	1	2	3	4	5
General Business Experience	1	2	3	4	5
Specific Industry Experience	1	2	3	4	5
Formal Education	1	2	3	4	5
Psychological Profile	1	2	3	4	5
Personal Interview(s)	1	2	3	4	5

14. The following States/Province require a separate registration (or disclosure, indicated by an *) document. In which are you currently registered to franchise?

❑ All Below or	❑ IN	❑ ND	❑ WA
❑ CA	❑ MD	❑ OR*	❑ WI
❑ FL*	❑ MI*	❑ RI	❑ DC
❑ HI	❑ MN	❑ SD	
❑ IL	❑ NY	❑ VA	❑Alberta

15. Including the owner/operator, how many employees are recommended to staff the average franchised unit? ________ Full-Time ________ Part-Time

16. What square footage and type(s) of sites do most of your franchise units require? ________ sq. ft.
❑ Free-Standing Building (FS) ❑ Storefront (SF) ❑ Strip Center(SC) ❑ Regional Mall(RM)
❑ Home-Based (HB) ❑ Other ____________________ ❑ Not Applicable

17. Do you encourage conversions? ❑ Yes ❑ No ❑ Not Applicable

FINANCIAL REQUIREMENTS

18. Even though the cash investment may vary substantially by individual unit, what is the range of equity capital (up-front cash) required? $ ____________________

19. What is the range of total investment required? $ ____________________

20. What is the minimum net worth required of the franchisee? $ ____________________

21. How much is the initial franchise fee for a new franchisee? $ ____________________

22. How much is the on-going royalty fee? ____________ % or ____________________

23. How much is the on-going advertising fee? ____________ % or ____________________

24. Do you provide potential franchisees with an Earnings Claim Statement? ❑ Yes ❑ No

TERMS OF CONTRACT

25. What is the term of the original franchise agreement? ____________ Years

26. What is the term of the renewal period? ____________ Years

27. Passive ownership of the initial unit is ❑ Allowed ❑ Allowed, But Discouraged ❑ Not Allowed

28. Do you have Area Development Agreements? ❑ Yes ❑ No
If Yes, for what period? ____________ Years

29. Do you have Sub-Franchisor Contracts covering specified territories? ❑ Yes ❑ No

30. Can the franchisee establish additional outlets within his/her area? ❑ Yes ❑ No

FRANCHISOR QUESTIONNAIRE (cont.)

FRANCHISOR SUPPORT AND TRAINING PROVIDED

31. Do you assist the franchisee in site selection? ❑ Yes ❑ No ❑ Not Applicable

32. Do you assist the franchisee in lease negotiations? ❑ Yes ❑ No ❑ Not Applicable

33. Is financial assistance available? ❑ Yes ❑ No ❑ N.A.; If Yes, ❑ Direct or ❑ Indirect

34. Do you participate in co-operative advertising? ❑ Yes ❑ No ❑ Not Applicable

35. Does your system have a franchisee association? ❑ Yes ❑ No
If Yes, are you a member? ❑ Yes ❑ No

36. How many full-time, paid personnel are currently on your corporate staff? ________________

37. Which of the following on-going services do you provide to the franchisee?

Service	Included in Fees	At Additional Cost	N.A.
A. Central Data Processing	❑	❑	❑
B. Central Purchasing	❑	❑	❑
C. Field Operations Evaluation	❑	❑	❑
D. Field Training	❑	❑	❑
E. Initial Store Opening	❑	❑	❑
F. Inventory Control	❑	❑	❑
G. Franchisee Newsletter	❑	❑	❑
H. Regional Or National Meetings	❑	❑	❑
I. 800 Telephone Hotline	❑	❑	❑

38. Please note the location and duration of any initial training sessions included in the franchise fee?

	Location	Duration
A.	______________________	______________________
B.	______________________	______________________
C.	______________________	______________________

SPECIFIC EXPANSION PLANS

39. In which specific regions of the U.S. are you actively seeking new franchisees?
For example: All U.S., or NW & SW, or NJ Only.

____

40. Are you actively seeking franchisees in Canada? ❑ Yes ❑ No
If Yes, in which Provinces? ❑ All or

____

41. Are you actively seeking franchisees Overseas? ❑ Yes ❑ No
If Yes, in which Provinces? ❑ All or

____

Name of Respondent: ______________________ **Phone:** (   ) ____________

SOURCE BOOK PUBLICATIONS
Serving the Franchising Industry
1814 Franklin Street, Suite 820, Oakland, CA 94612
(510) 839-5471 ❖ Fax: (510) 839-2104 ❖ E-Mail: info@worldfranchising.com
www.franchisingconsultant.com ❖ www.worldfranchising.com ❖ www.franchisingattorney.com

WORLDFRANCHISING.COM

The Definitive Guide to the World of Franchising

RESPONSE FORM

❐ **YES, we wish to participate on the www.worldfranchising.com website and in the 2005 (16th) Edition of *Bond's Franchise Guide*. I understand that we will be charged $300.00 and that the benefits include:**

- An immediate 12-month listing of company profile on www.worldfranchising.com, including 4-color logo and a hot link to company home page
- Website profile updates throughout the year at no charge
- Access to prospective franchisees via the Franchise Expediter™
- Detailed company profile in the 2005 (16th) Edition of *Bond's Franchise Guide*, including black-and-white logo
- Complimentary copy of *Bond's Franchise Guide* upon publication
- Consideration for inclusion in the 2005 (2nd) Edition of *Bond's Top 100 Franchises*

To participate, please do the following:

1. SUBMIT MATERIALS

❐ Page 1-3	Franchisor Questionnaire
❐ Page 4	Response Form
❐ Company Logo	Enclose color and black-and-white company logos on a floppy disk/CDROM or email to logos@worldfranchising.com

❐ Letterhead/Business Card (optional)

Mail or fax materials to Source Book Publications at (510) 839-2104.

2. ENCLOSE PAYMENT

❐ Payment Included

❐ Charge My ❐ Visa ❐ MasterCard

Card #: ______________________ Expiration Date: ____________

Name on Card: ______________________________________

❐ Invoice Us

______________________________ ____________________

Approved By **Date**

____

Company Name

SOURCE BOOK PUBLICATIONS
Serving the Franchising Industry
1814 Franklin Street, Suite 820, Oakland, CA 94612
(510) 839-5471 ❖ Fax: (510) 839-2104 ❖ E-Mail: info@worldfranchising.com
www.franchisingconsultant.com ❖ www.worldfranchising.com ❖ www.franchisingattorney.com

Alphabetical Listing of Franchisors

* Indicates Top 100 Franchise

B

C

D

E

F

G

H

I

J

K

L

O

P

Q

R

S

T

U

V

W

X

Y

Z

Alphabetical Listing of Franchise Attorneys, Consultants and Service Providers

Franchise Attorneys

By Firm

Franchise Consultants and Service Providers